JAVA™ HOW TO PROGRAM

THIRD EDITION

H. M. Deitel
Deitel & Associates, Inc.

P. J. Deitel
Deitel & Associates, Inc.

PRENTICE HALL, Upper Saddle River, New Jersey 07458

Library of Congress Cataloging-in-Publication Data

Deitel, Harvey M.
  Java : how to program / H.M. Deitel, P.J. Deitel. -- 3rd ed.
    p.   cm. -- (How to program series)
  Includes bibliographical references.
  ISBN 0-13-012507-5
    1. Java (Computer program language) I. Deitel, Paul J.
II. Title. III. Series.
QA76.73.J38D45 1999   99-37546
005.13'3--dc21   CIP

Acquisitions Editor: *Petra J. Recter*
Production Editor: *Camille Trentacoste*
Chapter Opener and Cover Designer: *Tamara Newnam Cavallo*
Buyer: *Pat Brown*
Editorial Assistant: *Sarah Burrows*

The authors and publisher of this book have used their best efforts in preparing this book. These efforts include the development, research, and testing of the theories and programs to determine their effectiveness. The authors and publisher make no warranty of any kind, expressed or implied, with regard to these programs or to the documentation contained in this book. The authors and publisher shall not be liable in any event for incidental or consequential damages in connection with, or arising out of, the furnishing, performance, or use of these programs.

Many of the designations used by manufacturers and sellers to distinguish their products are claimed as trademarks and registered trademarks. Where those designations appear in this book, and Prentice Hall and the authors were aware of a trademark claim, the designations have been printed in initial caps or all caps. All product names mentioned remain trademarks or registered trademarks of their respective owners.

Printed in the United States of America

10 9 8 7 6 5 4 3 2 1

ISBN 0-13-012507-5

Prentice-Hall International (UK) Limited, London
Prentice-Hall of Australia Pty. Limited, Sydney
Prentice-Hall Canada Inc., Toronto
Prentice-Hall Hispanoamericana, S.A., Mexico
Prentice-Hall of India Private Limited, New Delhi
Prentice-Hall of Japan, Inc., Tokyo
Prentice-Hall Singapore Pte. Ltd., Singapore
Editora Prentice-Hall do Brasil, Ltda., Rio de Janeiro

JAVA™
HOW TO PROGRAM

THIRD EDITION

Deitel & Deitel
Books and Cyber Classrooms
published by
Prentice Hall

Visual Studio® Series
Getting Started with Microsoft® Visual C++™ *6
    with an Introduction to MFC*
Visual Basic® *6 How to Program*
Getting Started with Microsoft® Visual J++® *1.1*

How to Program Series
Java™ *How to Program, 3/E*
C How to Program, 2/E
C++ How to Program, 2/E
Visual Basic® *6 How to Program*

Multimedia Cyber Classroom Series
Java™ *Multimedia Cyber Classroom, 3/E*
C & C++ Multimedia Cyber Classroom, 2/E
Visual Basic® *6 Multimedia Cyber Classroom*

The Complete Training Course Series
The Complete Java™ *Training Course, 3/E*
The Complete C++ Training Course, 2/E
The Complete Visual Basic® *6 Training Course*

For continuing updates on Prentice Hall and Deitel & Associates, Inc. publications
visit the Prentice Hall web site

   `http//www.prenhall.com/deitel`

To communicate with the authors, send email to:

   `deitel@deitel.com`

For information on corporate on-site seminars and public seminars offered by
Deitel & Associates, Inc. worldwide, visit:

   `http://www.deitel.com`

TO

Dolores Mars

Known affectionately by family, friends and the Prentice Hall publishing world as "Deen:"

You are truly the dean of gracious people. It is a privilege to work with you.

Thank you for being our friend.

Love,

Barbara, Harvey, Paul and Abbey Deitel

Contents

Summary • Terminology • Common Programming Errors • Good Programming Practice • Performance Tips • Software Engineering Observations • Testing and Debugging Tips • Self-Review Exercises • Answers to Self-Review Exercises • Exercises

Summary • Terminology • Common Programming Errors • Good Programming Practices • Performance Tips • Software Engineering Observations • Testing and Debugging Tips • Self-Review Exercises • Answers to Self-Review Exercises • Exercises

Summary • Terminology • Common Programming Errors • Good Programming Practice • Performance Tip • Portability Tips • Software Engineering Observations • Self-Review Exercises • Answers to Self-Review Exercises • Exercises • Bibliography

Illustrations

Preface

Live in fragments no longer. Only connect.
Edward Morgan Forster

Welcome to Java and the exciting world of Internet and World Wide Web programming with the new Java 2 platform. This book is by an old guy and a young guy. The old guy (HMD; Massachusetts Institute of Technology 1967) has been programming and/or teaching programming for 38 years. The young guy (PJD; MIT 1991) has been programming and/or teaching programming for 18 years, and is both a Sun Certified Java Programmer and a Sun Certified Java Developer. The old guy programs and teaches from experience; the young guy does so from an inexhaustible reserve of energy. The old guy wants clarity; the young guy wants performance. The old guy seeks elegance and beauty; the young guy wants results. We got together to produce a book we hope you will find informative, challenging and entertaining.

In November 1995 we attended an Internet/World Wide Web conference in Boston to hear about Java. A Sun Microsystems representative spoke on Java in a packed convention ballroom. We were lucky to get seats. During that presentation, we saw the future of programming unfold. The first edition of *Java How to Program* was born at that moment and was published as the world's first computer science Java textbook.

The world of Java is evolving so rapidly that *Java How to Program: Third Edition* is being published less than three years after the first edition. This creates tremendous challenges for us as authors, for our publisher—Prentice Hall, for instructors, and for students and professional people.

Before Java appeared, we were convinced that C++ would replace C as the dominant application development language and systems programming language for the next decade. But the combination of the World Wide Web and Java now increases the prominence of the Internet in information systems strategic planning and implementation. Organizations want to integrate the Internet "seamlessly" into their information systems. Java is more appropriate than C++ for this purpose.

New Features in Java How to Program: Third Edition

This edition contains many new features and enhancements including:

- Updated to the new **Java 2 platform**.
- Uses **Swing GUI components** in all programs with graphical user interfaces.
- **Simplified early chapters** to make learning Java easier for nonprogrammers.
- **Introduced GUI event handling later** (Chapter 6, "Methods") so nonprogrammers have a foundation of basic programming concepts before seeing this complex topic.
- **Switched the emphasis from applets to applications** to demonstrate Java the way it is typically used in industry.
- Enhanced the coverage of **interfaces**.
- Enhanced the coverage of **GUI event handling**.
- Introduced **inner classes** and their use with GUI event handling.
- Added coverage of Java's new **Java2D graphics** capabilities.
- Added coverage of the **Java Media Framework (JMF)**.
- Added chapters on **Java Database Connectivity (JDBC)**, **Servlets** and **Remote Method Invocation (RMI)**—crucial in building **multitier client/server systems**.
- Added a chapter on **Collections**—Java's reusable data structures and the prepackaged algorithms for manipulating these data structures.
- Added a chapter on **JavaBeans**—Java's reusable software component technology.
- Updated appendices on **Java demos** and **Java Internet and Web resources**.
- Added an appendix on `javadoc` (part of Sun's Java 2 Software Development Kit)—the utility that creates HTML documentation from comments in a program.
- Added an appendix of Internet and Web resources for **Enterprise JavaBeans**.
- Added an appendix of Internet and Web resources for **Jini**.

Why We Wrote *Java How to Program*

Dr. Harvey M. Deitel taught introductory programming courses in universities for 20 years with an emphasis on developing clearly written, well-structured programs. Much of what is taught in these courses is the basic principles of programming with an emphasis on the effective use of control structures and functionalization. We present these topics in *Java How to Program* exactly the way HMD has done in his university courses. Our experience has been that students handle the material in the early chapters on control structures and methods (Java's term for functions) in about the same manner as they handle introductory Pascal or C courses. There is one noticeable difference though: students are highly motivated by the fact that they are learning a leading-edge language (Java) and a leading-edge programming paradigm (object-oriented programming) that will be immediately useful to them as they leave the university environment and head into a world in which the Internet and the World Wide Web have a massive new prominence. This increases their enthusiasm for the material—a big help when you consider that there is much more to learn in a Java course given that students must now master both the base language and substantial class libraries as well. But students quickly discover that they can do great things with Java, so they are willing to put in the extra effort.

Our goal was clear: produce a Java textbook for introductory university-level courses in computer programming for students with little or no programming experience, yet offer the depth and the rigorous treatment of theory and practice demanded by traditional, upper-level C and C++ courses and that satisfies professionals' needs. To meet these goals, we produced a comprehensive book because our text also patiently teaches the principles of control structures, object-oriented programming, the Java language and Java class libraries.

Java How to Program (first edition) was the world's first university computer science textbook on Java. We wrote it fresh on the heels of *C How to Program: Second Edition* and *C++ How to Program*. Hundreds of thousands of university students and professional people worldwide have learned C, C++ and Java from these texts. Upon publication in August, 1999 *Java How to Program: Third Edition* will be used in hundreds of universities and thousands of corporate and government organizations worldwide. Deitel & Associates, Inc. has taught Java courses internationally to thousands of students as we were writing *Java How to Program: Third Edition*. We carefully monitored student reaction to Java and to our materials and tuned these materials accordingly.

We believe in Java. Its conceptualization by Sun Microsystems, the creators of Java, is brilliant: base a new language on two of the world's most widely used implementation languages, C and C++. This immediately gives Java a huge pool of highly skilled programmers who are currently responsible for implementing most of the world's new operating systems, communications systems, database systems, personal computer applications and systems software. Remove the messier, more complex and error-prone C/C++ features (such as pointers, templates, operator overloading and multiple inheritance, among others). Keep the language concise by removing special-purpose features that are used by only small segments of the programming community. Make the language truly portable so it is appropriate for implementing Internet-based and World-Wide-Web-based applications, and build in the features people really need such as strings, graphics, graphical user interface components, exception handling, multithreading, multimedia (audio, images, animation and video), file processing, database processing, Internet and World Wide Web-based client/server networking and distributed computing, and prepackaged data structures. Then make the language available *at no charge* to millions of potential programmers worldwide.

Java was promoted in 1995 as a means of adding "dynamic content" to World-Wide-Web pages. Instead of Web pages with only text and static graphics, people's Web pages "come alive" with audios, videos, animations, interactivity—and soon, three-dimensional imaging. But we saw much more than this. Java's features are precisely what businesses and organizations need to meet today's information processing requirements. So we immediately viewed Java as having the potential to become one of the world's key general-purpose programming languages.

There are a number of for-sale Java products available. However, you do not need them to get started with Java. We intentionally wrote *Java How to Program: Third Edition* using only the *Java 2 Software Development Kit (J2SDK)* that can be downloaded from Sun Microsystems over the Internet. For your convenience, Sun's J2SDK version 1.2.1 is included on the CD-ROM at the end of this book. Through our relationships with Inprise (formerly Borland) and NetBeans, we were also able to include on the CD-ROM two powerful Java integrated development environments (IDEs)—Borland *JBuilder 3 University*

Edition and NetBeans *DeveloperX2*. If you need help getting started, please check the doc-umentation on the CD-ROM first. We will be putting additional information on our Web site: `http://www.deitel.com`.

Java is helping people and organizations unleash their creativity. We see this in the Java courses Deitel & Associates, Inc. teaches. Once our students enter lab, we can't hold them back. They eagerly experiment and explore portions of the Java class libraries that we haven't as yet covered in class. They produce applications that go well beyond anything we've ever tried in our introductory C and C++ courses. And they tell us about projects they "can't wait" to try after the course.

The computer field has never seen anything like the Internet/World Wide Web/Java "explosion" occurring today. People want to communicate. People need to communicate. Sure they have been doing that since the dawn of civilization, but computer communica-tions have been mostly limited to digits, alphabetic characters and special characters passing back and forth. The next major wave is surely multimedia. People want to transmit pictures and they want those pictures to be in color. They want to transmit voices, sounds and audio clips. They want to transmit full-motion color video. And at some point, they will insist on three-dimensional, moving-image transmission. Our current flat, two-dimensional televisions will eventually be replaced with three-dimensional versions that turn our living rooms into "theaters-in-the-round." Actors will perform their roles as if we were watching live theater. Our living rooms will be turned into miniature sports stadiums. Our business offices will enable video conferencing among colleagues half a world apart as if they were sitting around one conference table. The possibilities are intriguing and Java is sure to play a key role in making many of these possibilities become reality.

There have been predictions that the Internet will eventually replace the telephone system. Well, why stop there? It could also replace radio and television as we know them today. It's not hard to imagine the Internet replacing the newspaper with completely elec-tronic news media. This textbook you are reading may someday appear in a museum along-side radios, TVs and newspapers in an "early media of ancient civilization" exhibit.

Teaching Approach

Java How to Program: Third Edition contains a rich collection of examples, exercises, and projects drawn from many fields to provide the student with a chance to solve interesting real-world problems. The book concentrates on the principles of good software engineering and stresses program clarity. We avoid arcane terminology and syntax specifications in fa-vor of teaching by example. Our code examples have been tested on popular Java plat-forms. The book is written by educators who spend most of their time teaching edge-of-the-practice topics in industry classrooms worldwide. The text emphasizes good pedagogy.

Live-Code Teaching Approach
The book is loaded with live-code examples. This is the focus of the way we teach and write about programming, and the focus of each of our multimedia *Cyber Classrooms* as well. Each new concept is presented in the context of a complete, working Java program (applet or application) immediately followed by one or more windows showing the program's out-put. We call this style of teaching and writing our ***live-code approach***. *We use the language to teach the language.* Reading these programs is much like entering and running them on a computer.

Java 2 and Swing from Chapter Two!

Java How to Program: Third Edition "jumps right in" with object-oriented programming, applications and the new Swing-style GUI components from Chapter 2! People tell us this is a "gutsy" move. But Java students really want to "cut to the chase." There is great stuff to be done in Java 2 so let's get right to it! Java is not trivial by any means, but it's fun and students can see immediate results. Students can get graphical, animated, multimedia-based, audio-intensive, multithreaded, database-intensive, network-based programs running quickly through Java 2's extensive class libraries of "reusable components." They can implement impressive projects. They can be much more creative and productive in a one- or two-semester course than is possible in C and C++ introductory courses.

World Wide Web Access

All of the code for *Java How to Program* (and our other publications) is on the Internet at the Deitel & Associates, Inc. Web site **http://www.deitel.com**. Please download all the code then run each program as you read the text. Make changes to the code examples and see what happens. See how the Java compiler "complains" when you make various kinds of errors. Immediately see the effects of making changes to the code. It's a great way to learn programming by doing programming. [You must respect the fact that this is copyrighted material. Feel free to use it as you study Java, but you may not republish any portion of it without explicit permission from the authors and Prentice Hall.]

Objectives

Each chapter begins with a statement of *Objectives*. This tells the student what to expect and gives the student an opportunity, after reading the chapter, to determine if he or she has met these objectives. It is a confidence builder and a source of positive reinforcement.

Quotations

The learning objectives are followed by quotations. Some are humorous, some are philosophical, and some offer interesting insights. Our students enjoy relating the quotations to the chapter material. The quotations are worth a "second look" after you read each chapter.

Outline

The chapter *Outline* helps the student approach the material in top-down fashion. This, too, helps students anticipate what is to come and set a comfortable and effective learning pace.

16,485 Lines of Code in 220 Example Programs (with Program Outputs)

We present Java features in the context of complete, working Java programs. This is the focus of our teaching and our writing. We call it our "live-code" approach. Each program is followed by the outputs produced when the program runs. This enables the student to confirm that the programs run as expected. Reading the book carefully is much like entering and running these programs on a computer. The programs range from just a few lines of code to substantial examples with several hundred lines of code. Students should download all the code for the book from our Web site and run each program while studying that program in the text. The programs are available at **http://www.deitel.com**.

456 Illustrations/Figures

An abundance of charts, line drawings and program outputs is included. The discussion of control structures, for example, features carefully drawn flowcharts. [Note: We do not teach flowcharting as a program development tool, but we do use a brief, flowchart-oriented presentation to specify the precise operation of each of Java's control structures.]

588 Programming Tips

We have included programming tips to help students focus on important aspects of program development. We highlight hundreds of these tips in the form of *Good Programming Practices*, *Common Programming Errors*, *Testing and Debugging Tips*, *Performance Tips*, *Portability Tips*, *Software Engineering Observations* and *Look-and-Feel Observations*. These tips and practices represent the best we have gleaned from a combined five and a half decades of programming and teaching experience. One of our students—a mathematics major—told us that she feels this approach is like the highlighting of axioms, theorems, and corollaries in mathematics books; it provides a basis on which to build good software.

93 Good Programming Practices

When we teach introductory courses, we state that the "buzzword" of each course is "clarity," and we highlight as *Good Programming Practices* techniques for writing programs that are clearer, more understandable, more debuggable, and more maintainable.

150 Common Programming Errors

Students learning a language tend to make certain errors frequently. Focusing the students' attention on these *Common Programming Errors* helps students avoid making the same errors. It also helps reduce the long lines outside instructors' offices during office hours!

43 Testing and Debugging Tips

When we first designed this "tip type," we thought we would use it strictly to tell people how to test and debug Java programs. In fact, many of the tips describe aspects of Java that reduce the likelihood of "bugs" and thus simplify the testing and debugging process for Java programs compared to that for C and C++ programs.

61 Performance Tips

In our experience, teaching students to write clear and understandable programs is by far the most important goal for a first programming course. But students want to write the programs that run the fastest, use the least memory, require the smallest number of keystrokes, or dazzle in other nifty ways. Students really care about performance. They want to know what they can do to "turbo charge" their programs. So we have included 61 *Performance Tips* that highlight opportunities for improving program performance.

19 Portability Tips

Some programmers assume that if they implement an application in Java, the application will automatically be "perfectly" portable across all Java platforms. Unfortunately, this is not always the case. We include *Portability Tips* to help students write portable code, and also to provide insights on how Java achieves its high degree of portability. We had many more portability tips in *C How to Program* and *C++ How to Program*. We needed fewer *Portability Tips* in *Java How to Program* because Java is designed to be portable top-to-bottom (for the most part), so much less conspicuous effort is required on the Java programmer's part to achieve portability than with C or C++.

184 Software Engineering Observations

The object-oriented programming paradigm requires a complete rethinking about the way we build software systems. Java is an effective language for performing good software engineering. The *Software Engineering Observations* highlight architectural and design issues that affect the construction of software systems, especially large-scale systems. Much of what the student learns here will be useful in upper-level courses and in industry as the student begins to work with large, complex real-world systems.

38 Look-and-Feel Observations

We provide *Look-and-Feel Observations* to highlight graphical user interface conventions. These observations help students design their own graphical user interfaces to in conformance with industry norms.

Summary (1016 Summary bullets)

Each chapter ends with additional pedagogical devices. We present a thorough, bullet-list-style *Summary* of the chapter. On average, there are 40 summary bullets per chapter. This helps the students review and reinforce key concepts.

Terminology (2295 Terms)

We include in a *Terminology* section an alphabetized list of the important terms defined in the chapter—again, further reinforcement. On average, there are 90 terms per chapter.

Summary of Tips, Practices and Errors

For ease of reference, we collect at the back of each chapter the *Good Programming Practices*, *Common Programming Errors*, *Testing and Debugging Tips*, *Performance Tips*, *Portability Tips*, *Software Engineering Observations* and *Look-and-Feel Observations*.

444 Self-Review Exercises and Answers (Count Includes Separate Parts)

Extensive self-review exercises and answers are included for self-study. This gives the student a chance to build confidence with the material and prepare for the regular exercises. Students should be encouraged to do all the self-review exercises and check their answers.

959 Exercises (Solutions in Instructor's Manual; Count Includes Separate Parts)

Each chapter concludes with a substantial set of exercises including simple recall of important terminology and concepts; writing individual Java statements; writing small portions of Java methods and classes; writing complete Java methods, classes, applets and applications; and writing major term projects. The large number of exercises across a wide variety of areas enables instructors to tailor their courses to the unique needs of their audiences and to vary course assignments each semester. Instructors can use these exercises to form homework assignments, short quizzes and major examinations. The solutions for the exercises are included in the *Instructor's Manual* and on the disks *available only to instructors* through their Prentice-Hall representatives. [**NOTE: Please do not write to us requesting the instructor's manual. Distribution of this publication is strictly limited to college professors teaching from the book. Instructors may obtain the solutions manual only from their regular Prentice Hall representatives. We regret that we cannot provide the solutions to professionals**.] Solutions to approximately half of the exercises are included on the *Java Multimedia Cyber Classroom: Third Edition* CD (available September 1999 in bookstores and computer stores; please see the last few pages of this book or visit our Web site at **http://www.deitel.com** for ordering instructions).

Approximately 5700 Index Entries (with approximately 9300 Page References)
We have included an extensive *Index* at the back of the book. This helps the student find any term or concept by keyword. The *Index* is useful to people reading the book for the first time and is especially useful to practicing programmers who use the book as a reference. Each of the 2295 terms in the *Terminology* sections appears in the *Index* (along with many more index items from each chapter). Students can use the *Index* in conjunction with the *Terminology* sections to be sure they have covered the key material of each chapter.

"Double Indexing" of All Java Live-Code Examples and Exercises
Java How to Program has 220 live-code examples and 1403 exercises (including parts). Many of the exercises are challenging problems or projects requiring substantial effort. We have "double indexed" each of the live-code examples and most of the more challenging projects. For every Java source-code program in the book, we took the file name with the **.java** extension, such as **LoadAudioAndPlay.java** and indexed it both alphabetically (in this case under "L") and as a subindex item under "Examples." This makes it easier to find examples using particular features. The more substantial exercises, such as "Maze Generator and Walker," are indexed both alphabetically (in this case under "M") and as subindex items under "Exercises."

Bibliography
An extensive bibliography of books, articles and Sun Microsystems Java 2 documentation is included to encourage further reading.

A Tour of the Book

Chapter 1—Introduction to Computers, the Internet and the Web—discusses what computers are, how they work and how they are programmed. The chapter gives a brief history of the development of programming languages from machine languages, to assembly languages, to high-level languages. The origin of the Java programming language is discussed. The chapter includes an introduction to a typical Java programming environment.

Chapter 2—Introduction to Java Applications—provides a lightweight introduction to programming *applications* in the Java programming language. The chapter introduces nonprogrammers to basic programming concepts and constructs. The programs in this chapter illustrate how to display (also called *outputting*) data on the screen to the user and how to obtain (also called *inputting*) data from the user at the keyboard. Some of the input and output is performed using a new *graphical user interface (GUI)* element called **JOptionPane** that provides predefined windows (called dialog boxes) for input and output. This is a change in approach from the previous editions of this book in which we introduced several GUI components and GUI event handling in Chapter 1. **JOptionPane** handles ouputting data to windows and inputting data from windows. This allows a nonprogrammer to concentrate on fundamental programming concepts and constructs rather than the more complex GUI event handling. Using **JOptionPane** here enables us to delay our introduction of GUI event handling to Chapter 6, "Methods." Chapter 2 also provides detailed treatments of *decision making* and *arithmetic operations*. After studying this chapter, the student will understand how to write simple, but complete, Java applications.

Chapter 3—Introduction to Java Applets—introduces another type of Java program called an *applet*. Applets are Java programs designed to be transported over the Internet and executed in World Wide Web browsers (like Netscape Communicator, Sun HotJava and Microsoft Internet Explorer). The chapter begins with an introduction to object technology in which we present basic concepts and terminology of object-based programming and object-oriented programming that are used throughout the text. The chapter introduces applets using several of the sample demonstration applets supplied with the Java 2 Software Development Kit (J2SDK). We use **appletviewer** (a utility supplied with the J2SDK) or a Web browser to execute several sample applets. We then write Java applets that perform tasks similar to the programs of Chapter 2, and we explain the similarities and differences between applets and applications. After studying this chapter, the student will understand how to write simple, but complete, Java applets. The next several chapters use both applets and applications to demonstrate additional key programming concepts.

Chapter 4—Control Structures: Part 1—focuses on the program development process. The chapter discusses how to take a *problem statement* (i.e., a *requirements document*) and from it develop a working Java program, including performing intermediate steps in pseudocode. The chapter introduces some fundamental data types and simple control structures used for decision making (**if** and **if/else**) and repetition (**while**). We examine counter-controlled repetition, sentinel-controlled repetition, and introduce Java's increment, decrement and assignment operators. The chapter uses simple flowcharts to show the flow of control through each of the control structures. The techniques discussed in Chapters 2 through 7 constitute a large part of what has been traditionally taught in the universities under the topic of structured programming. With Java we do object-oriented programming. In doing so, we discover that the insides of the objects we build make abundant use of control structures. We have had a positive experience assigning problems 4.11 through 4.14 in our introductory courses. Since these four problems have similar structure, doing all four is a nice way for students to "get the hang of" the program development process. This chapter helps the student develop good programming habits in preparation for dealing with the more substantial programming tasks in the remainder of the text.

Chapter 5—Control Structures: Part 2—continues the discussions of Java control structures (**for**, the **switch** selection structure and the **do/while** repetition structure). The chapter explains the labeled **break** and **continue** statements with live-code examples. The chapter also contains a discussion of logical operators—**&&** (logical AND), **&** (boolean logical AND), **||** (logical OR), **|** (boolean logical inclusive OR), **^** (boolean logical exclusive OR) and **!** (NOT). There is a substantial exercise set including mathematical, graphical and business applications. Students will enjoy Exercise 5.26 that asks them to write a program with repetition and decision structures that prints the iterative song, "The Twelve Days of Christmas." The more mathematically inclined students will enjoy problems on binary, octal, decimal and hexadecimal number systems, calculating the mathematical constant π with an infinite series, Pythagorean triples and De Morgan's Laws. Our students particularly enjoy the challenges of triangle-printing and diamond-printing in Exercises 5.10 and 5.19; these problems help students learn to deal with nested repetition structures—a complex topic to master in introductory courses.

Chapter 6—Methods—takes a deeper look inside objects. Objects contain data called *instance variables* and executable units called *methods* (these are often called *functions* in non-object-oriented procedural programming languages like C). We explore methods in depth and include a discussion of methods that "call themselves," so-called *recursive* methods. We discuss class-library methods, programmer-defined methods and recursion. The techniques presented in Chapter 6 are essential to the production of properly structured programs, especially the kinds of larger programs and software that system programmers and application programmers are likely to develop in real-world applications. The "divide and conquer" strategy is presented as an effective means for solving complex problems by dividing them into simpler interacting components. Students enjoy the treatment of random numbers and simulation, and they appreciate the discussion of the dice game of craps that makes elegant use of control structures (this is one of our most successful lectures in our introductory courses). The chapter offers a solid introduction to recursion and includes a table summarizing the dozens of recursion examples and exercises distributed throughout the remainder of the book. Some texts leave recursion for a chapter late in the book; we feel this topic is best covered gradually throughout the text. The topic of method overloading (i.e., allowing multiple methods to have the same name as long as they have different "signatures") is motivated and explained clearly.

In this chapter, we also introduce *events* and *event handling*—elements required for programming graphical user interfaces. Events are notifications of state change such as button clicks, mouse clicks, pressing a keyboard key, etc. Java allows programmers to respond to various events with by coding methods called event handlers.

The extensive collection of exercises at the end of the chapter includes several classical recursion problems such as the Towers of Hanoi; we revisit this problem later in the text where we employ graphics, animation and sound to make the problem "come alive." There are many mathematical and graphical examples. Our students particularly enjoy the development of a "Computer-Assisted Instruction" system in Exercises 6.32 and 6.33; we ask students to develop a multimedia version of this system later in the book.

Students will enjoy the challenges of the "mystery programs." The more mathematically inclined students will enjoy problems on perfect numbers, greatest common divisors, prime numbers, and factorials.

Chapter 7—Arrays—explores the processing of data in lists and tables of values. Arrays in Java are processed as objects, further evidence of Java's commitment to almost 100% object-orientation. We discuss the structuring of data into arrays, or groups, of related data items of the same type. The chapter presents numerous examples of both single-subscripted arrays and double-subscripted arrays. It is widely recognized that structuring data properly is just as important as using control structures effectively in the development of properly structured programs. Examples in the chapter investigate various common array manipulations, printing histograms, sorting data, passing arrays to methods and an introduction to the field of survey data analysis (with simple statistics). A feature of this chapter is the discussion of elementary sorting and searching techniques and the presentation of binary searching as a dramatic improvement over linear searching. The end-of-chapter exercises include a variety of interesting and challenging problems such as improved sorting techniques, the design of an airline reservations system, an introduction to the concept of turtle graphics (made famous in the LOGO programming language) and the Knight's Tour and Eight Queens problems that introduce the notions of heuristic programming so widely employed in the field of artificial intelligence. The exercises conclude with a series of recursion problems including the selection sort, palindromes, linear search, binary search, the eight queens, printing an array, printing a string backwards and finding the minimum value in an array. The chapter exercises include a delightful simulation of the classic race between the tortoise and the hare, card shuffling and dealing algorithms, recursive quicksort and recursive maze traversals. A special section entitled "Building Your Own Computer" explains machine language programming and proceeds with the design and implementation of a computer simulator that allows the reader to write and run machine language programs. This unique feature of the text will be especially useful to the reader who wants to understand how computers really work. Our students enjoy this project and often implement substantial enhancements; many enhancements are suggested in the exercises. In Chapter 22, another special section guides the reader through building a compiler; the machine language produced by the compiler is then executed on the machine language simulator produced in Chapter 7. Information is communicated from the compiler to the simulator in sequential files (which the students will master in Chapter 17).

Chapter 8—Object-Based Programming—begins our deeper discussion of classes. The chapter represents a wonderful opportunity for teaching data abstraction the "right way"—through a language (Java) expressly devoted to implementing abstract data types (ADTs). The chapter focuses on the essence and terminology of classes and objects. What is an object? What is a class of objects? What does the inside of an object look like? How are objects created? How are they destroyed? How do objects communicate with one another? Why are classes such a natural mechanism for packaging software as reusable componentry? The chapter discusses implementing ADTs as Java-style classes, accessing class members, enforcing information hiding with **private** instance variables, separating interface from implementation, using access methods and utility methods, and initializing objects with constructors (and using overloaded constructors). The chapter discusses declaring and using constant references, *composition*—the process of building classes that have as members references to objects, the **this** reference that enables an object to "know itself," dynamic memory allocation, **static** class members for containing and manipulating class-wide data, and examples of popular abstract data types such as stacks and queues. The chapter also introduces the **package** statement and discusses how to create reusable packages. The chapter exercises challenge the student to develop classes for complex numbers, rational numbers, times, dates, rectangles, huge integers, a class for playing Tic-Tac-Toe, a savings account class and a class for holding sets of integers.

Chapter 9—Object-Oriented Programming—discusses the relationships among classes of objects and programming with related classes. How can we exploit commonality between classes of objects to minimize the amount of work it takes to build large software systems? What is polymorphism? What does it mean to "program in the general" rather than "programming in the specific?" How does programming in the general make it easy to modify systems and add new features with minimal effort? How can we program for a whole category of objects rather than programming individually for each type of object? The chapter deals with one of the most fundamental capabilities of object-oriented programming languages, inheritance, which is a form of software reusability in which new classes are developed quickly and easily by absorbing the capabilities of existing classes and adding appropriate new capabilities. The chapter discusses the notions of superclasses and subclasses, **protected** members, direct superclasses, indirect superclasses, use of constructors in superclasses and subclasses, and software engineering with inheritance. This chapter introduces *inner classes* that help hide implementation details. Inner classes are most frequently used to create GUI event handlers. Named inner classes can be declared inside other classes and are useful in defining common event handlers for several GUI components. Anonymous inner classes are declared inside methods and are used to create one object—typically an event handler for a specific GUI component. The chapter compares inheritance ("is a" relationships) with composition ("has a" relationships). A feature of the chapter is it's several substantial case studies. In particular, a lengthy case study implements a point, circle and cylinder class hierarchy. The exercises ask the student to compare the creation of new classes by inheritance vs. composition; to extend the inheritance hierarchies discussed in the chapter; to write an inheritance hierarchy for quadrilaterals, trapezoids, parallelograms, rectangles and squares; and to create a more general shape hierarchy with two-dimensional shapes and three-dimensional shapes. The chapter explains polymorphic behavior. When many classes are related through inheritance to a common superclass, each subclass object may be treated as a superclass object. This enables programs to be written in a general manner independent of the specific types of the subclass objects. New kinds of objects can be handled by the same program, thus making systems more extensible. Polymorphism enables programs to eliminate complex **switch** logic in favor of simpler "straight-line" logic. A video game screen manager, for example, can send a "draw" message to every object in a linked list of objects to be drawn. Each object knows how to draw itself. A new type of object can be added to the program without modifying that program as long as that new object also knows how to draw itself. This style of programming is typically used to implement today's popular graphical user interfaces. The chapter distinguishes between **abstract** classes (from which objects cannot be instantiated) and concrete classes (from which objects can be instantiated). The chapter also introduces interfaces—sets of methods that must be defined by any class that **implements** the interface. Interfaces are Java's replacement for the dangerous (albeit powerful) feature of C++ called multiple inheritance

Abstract classes are useful for providing a basic set of methods and default implementation to classes throughout the hierarchy. Interfaces are useful in many situations similar to **abstract** classes, however, interfaces do not include any implementation—no method bodies and no instance variables. A feature of the chapter is its three major polymorphism case studies—a payroll system, a shape hierarchy headed up by an **abstract** class and a shape hierarchy headed up by an interface. The chapter exercises ask the student to discuss a number of conceptual issues and approaches, work with **abstract** classes, develop a basic graphics package, modify the chapter's employee class—and pursue all these projects with polymorphic programming.

Chapter 10—Strings and Characters—deals with processing words, sentences, characters and groups of characters. The key difference between Java and C here is that Java strings are objects. This makes string manipulation more convenient and much safer than in C where string and array manipulations are based on dangerous pointers. We present classes **String**, **StringBuffer**, **Character** and **StringTokenizer**. For each we provide extensive live-code examples demonstrating most of their methods "in action." In all cases we show output windows so the reader can see the precise effects of each of the string and character manipulations. Students will enjoy the card shuffling and dealing example (which they will enhance in the exercises to the later chapters on graphics and multimedia). A key feature of the chapter is an extensive collection of challenging string manipulation exercises related to limericks, pig Latin, text analysis, word processing, printing dates in various formats, check protection, writing the word equivalent of a check amount, Morse Code and metric-to-English conversions. Students will enjoy the challenges of developing their own spell checker and crossword puzzle generator.

Advanced Topics

Chapters 11, 12 and 13 were co-authored with our colleague, Mr. Tem Nieto of Deitel & Associates, Inc. Tem's infinite patience, attention to detail, illustration skills and creativity are apparent throughout these chapters. [Take a fast peek at Figure 12.19 to see what happens when we turn Tem loose!]

Chapter 11—Graphics and Java2D—begins a run of chapters that present the multimedia "sizzle" of Java. We consider Chapters 11 through 25 to be the book's advanced material. This is "fun stuff." Traditional C and C++ programming are pretty much confined to character-mode input/output. Some versions of C++ are supported by platform-dependent class libraries that can do graphics, but using these libraries makes your applications nonportable. Java's graphics capabilities are platform independent and hence, portable—and we mean portable in a worldwide sense. You can develop graphics-intensive Java applets and distribute them over the World Wide Web to colleagues everywhere and they will run nicely on the local Java platforms. We discuss graphics contexts and graphics objects; drawing strings, characters and bytes; color and font control; screen manipulation and paint modes; and drawing lines, rectangles, rounded rectangles, 3-dimensional rectangles, ovals, arcs and polygons. We introduce the Java2D API, new in Java 2, which provides powerful graphical manipulation tools. Fig. 11.22 is an example of how easy it is to use the Java2D API to create complex graphics effects such as textures and gradients. The chapter has 23 figures that painstakingly illustrate each of these graphics capabilities with live-code examples, appealing screen outputs, detailed features tables and detailed line art. Some of the 40 exercises challenge students to develop graphical versions of their solutions to previous exercises on Turtle Graphics, the Knight's Tour, the Tortoise and the Hare simulation, Maze Traversal and the Bucket Sort.

Chapter 12—Basic Graphical User Interface Components—introduces the creation of applets and applications with user-friendly graphical user interfaces (GUIs). This chapter focuses on Java's new *Swing GUI components*. These *platform-independent* GUI components are written entirely in Java. This provides Swing GUI components with great flexibility—the GUI components can be customized to look like the computer platform on which the program executes, or they can use the standard Java look-and-feel that provides an identical user interface across all computer platforms. GUI development is a huge topic, so we divided it into two chapters. These chapters cover the material in sufficient depth to enable you to build "industrial-strength" GUI interfaces. We discuss the new **javax.swing** package, which provides much more powerful GUI components than the Java 1.1 **java.awt** components. Through its 16 programs and many tables and line drawings, the chapter illustrates GUI design principles, the **javax.swing** hierarchy, labels, push buttons, lists, text fields, combo boxes, check boxes, radio buttons, panels, handling mouse events, handling keyboard events and using three of Java's simpler GUI layout managers, namely **FlowLayout**, **BorderLayout** and **GridLayout**. The chapter concentrates on the delegation event model for GUI processing. The 46 exercises challenge the student to create specific GUIs, exercise various GUI features, develop drawing programs that let the user draw with the mouse and control fonts.

Chapter 13—Advanced Graphical User Interface Components—continues the detailed Swing discussion started in Chapter 12. Through its 13 programs, tables and line drawings, the chapter illustrates GUI design principles, the **javax.swing** hierarchy, text areas, subclassing Swing components, sliders, windows, menus, pop-up menus, changing the look-and-feel, and using three of Java's advanced GUI layout managers, namely **Box-Layout**, **CardLayout** and **GridBagLayout**. Two of the most important examples introduced in this chapter are a program that can run as either an applet or application and a program that demonstrates how to create a *multiple document interface* (*MDI*) graphical user interface. MDI is a complex graphical user interface in which one window—called the *parent*—acts as the controlling window for the application. This parent window contains one or more child windows—which are always graphically displayed within the parent window. Most word processors use MDI graphical user interfaces. The chapter concludes with a series of exercises that encourage the reader to develop substantial GUIs with the techniques and components presented in the chapter. One of the key exercises in this chapter is a complete drawing application that asks the reader to create an object oriented-program that keeps track of the shapes the user has drawn. This exercise is likely to challenge the most advanced student. Other exercises use inheritance to subclass Swing components and reinforce layout manager concepts.

Chapter 14—Exception Handling—is one of the most important chapters in the book from the standpoint of building so-called "mission-critical" or "business-critical" applications that require high degrees of robustness and fault tolerance. Things do go wrong, and at today's computer speeds—commonly hundreds of millions operations per second—if they can go wrong they will, and rather quickly at that. Programmers are often a bit naive about using components. They ask, "How do I request that a component do something for me?" They also ask "What value(s) does that component return to me to indicate it has performed the job I asked it to do?" But programmers also need to be concerned with, "What happens when the component I call on to do a job experiences difficulty? How will that component signal that it had a problem?" In Java, when a component (i.e., a class object) encounters difficulty, it can "throw an exception." The environment of that component is programmed to "catch" that exception and deal with it. Java's exception handling capabilities are geared to an object-oriented world in which programmers construct systems largely from reusable, prefabricated components built by other programmers. To use a Java component, you need to know not only how that component behaves when "things go well," but also what exceptions that component throws when "things go poorly." The chapter distinguishes between rather serious system **Error**s (normally beyond the control of most programs) and **Exception**s that programs generally want to deal with to ensure robust operation. The chapter discusses the vocabulary of exception handling. The **try** block executes program code that may execute properly or may **throw** an exception if something goes wrong. Associated with each **try** block are one or more **catch** blocks that handle thrown exceptions attempting to restore order and keep systems "up and running" rather than letting them "crash." Even if order can not be fully restored, the **catch** blocks may perform operations that enable a system to continue executing, albeit at reduced levels of performance—such activity is often referred to as "graceful degradation." Regardless of whether exceptions are thrown or not, a **finally** block accompanying a **try** block will always execute; the **finally** block normally performs cleanup operations like closing files and releasing resources acquired in the **try** block. The material in this chapter is crucial to many of the live-code examples in the remainder of the book. The chapter enumerates many of the **Error**s and **Exception**s of the Java packages. The chapter has some of the most appropriate quotes in the book thanks to Barbara Deitel's painstaking research. The vast majority of the book's *Testing and Debugging Tips* fell naturally out of the material in Chapter 14.

Chapter 15—Multithreading—deals with programming applets and applications that can perform multiple activities in parallel. Although our bodies are quite good at this (breathing, eating, blood circulation, vision, hearing, etc. can all occur in parallel), our conscious minds have trouble with this. Computers used to be built with a single rather expensive processor. Today processors are becoming so inexpensive that it is possible to build computers with many processors that work in parallel—such computers are called *multiprocessors*. The trend is clearly towards computers that can perform many tasks in parallel. Most of today's programming languages, including C and C++, do not include features for expressing parallel operations. These languages are often referred to as "sequential" programming languages or "single-thread-of-control" languages. Java includes capabilities to enable multithreaded applications, i.e., applications that can specify that multiple activities are to occur in parallel. This makes Java better prepared to deal with the more sophisticated multimedia, network-based multiprocessor-based applications programmers will develop in the new millennium. As we will see, multithreading is even effective on single-processor systems. For years, the "old guy" taught operating systems courses and wrote operating systems textbooks, but he never had a multithreaded language like Java available to demonstrate the concepts. In this chapter, we thoroughly enjoyed presenting multithreaded programs that demonstrate clearly the kinds of problems that can occur in parallel programming. There are all kinds of subtleties that develop in parallel programs that you simply never think about when writing sequential programs. A feature of the chapter is the extensive set of examples that show these problems and how to solve them. Another feature is the implementation of the "circular buffer," a popular means of coordinating control between asynchronous, concurrent "producer" and "consumer" processes that, if left to run without synchronization, would cause data to be lost and/or duplicated incorrectly, often with devastating results. We discuss the monitor construct developed by C. A. R. Hoare and implemented in Java; this is a standard topic in operating systems courses. The chapter discusses threads and thread methods. It walks through the various thread states and state transitions with a detailed line drawing showing the life-cycle of a thread. We discuss thread priorities and thread scheduling and use a line drawing to show Java's fixed-priority scheduling mechanism. We examine a producer/consumer relationship without synchronization, observe the problems that occur and then solve the problem with thread synchronization. We implement a producer/consumer relationship with a circular buffer and proper synchronization with a monitor. We discuss daemon threads that "hang around" and perform tasks (e.g., "garbage collection") when processor time is available. We discuss interface **Runnable** that enables objects to run as threads without having to subclass class **Thread**. We close with a discussion of thread groups which, for example, enable separation to be enforced between system threads like the garbage collector and user threads. The chapter has a nice complement of exercises. The featured exercise is the classic readers and writers problem, a favorite in upper-level operating systems courses; citations appear in the exercises for students who wish to research this topic. This is an important problem in database-oriented transaction-processing systems. It raises subtle issues of solving problems in concurrency control while ensuring that every separate activity that needs to receive service does so without the possibility of "indefinite postponement" which could cause some activities never to receive service—a condition also referred to as "starvation." Operating systems professors will enjoy the projects implemented by Java-literate students. We can expect substantial progress in the field of parallel programming as Java's multithreading capabilities enable large numbers of computing students to pursue parallel-programming class projects. When these students enter industry over the next several years, we expect a surge in parallel systems programming and parallel applications programming. We have been predicting this for decades—Java will make it a reality.

If this is your first Java book and you are an experienced computing professional, you may well be thinking, "Hey, this just keeps getting better and better. I can't wait to get started programming in this language. It will let me do all kinds of stuff I'd like to do, but that was never easy for me to do with the other languages I've used." You've got it right. Java is an enabler. So if you liked the multithreading discussion, hold onto your hat, because Java will let you program multimedia applications and make them available instantaneously over the World Wide Web.

Chapter 16—Multimedia: Images, Animation, Audio and Video—deals with Java's capabilities for making computer applications come alive. It is remarkable that students in first programming courses will be writing applications with all these capabilities. The possibilities are intriguing. Imagine having access (over the Internet and through CD-ROM technology) to vast libraries of graphics images, audios and videos and being able to weave your own together with those in the libraries to form creative applications. Already more than half the new computers sold come "multimedia equipped." Within just a few years, new machines equipped for multimedia will be as common as machines with floppy disks are today. We can't wait to see the kinds of term papers and classroom presentations students will be making when they have access to vast public domain libraries of images, drawings, voices, pictures, videos, animations and the like. A "paper" when most of us were in the earlier grades was a collection of characters, possibly handwritten, possibly typewritten. A "paper" in just a few short years will become a multimedia "extravaganza" that makes the subject matter come alive. It will hold your interest, pique your curiosity, make you feel what the subjects of the paper felt when they were making history. Multimedia will make your science labs much more exciting. Textbooks will come alive. Instead of looking at a static picture of some phenomenon, you will watch that phenomenon occur in a colorful, animated, presentation with sounds, videos and various other effects. It will leverage the learning process. People will be able to learn more, learn it in more depth and experience more viewpoints.

The chapter discusses images and image manipulation, audios and animation. The Chapter presents the Java Media Framework (JMF) API which provides Java media **Player**s that "know" how to present a particular multimedia file, saving Java programmers from the implementation details. Presently, the JMF Player API supports several dozen common audio and video media formats. A feature of the chapter is the image maps discussion that enable a program to sense the presence of the mouse pointer over a region of an image, without clicking the mouse. We present a live-code image map application with the icons Prentice Hall artists created for our *Java Multimedia Cyber Classroom* programming tips. As the user moves the mouse pointer across the six icon images, the type of tip is displayed, either "Good Programming Practice" for the thumbs-up icon, "Portability Tip" for the bug with the suitcase icon, and so on. Once you have read the chapter, you will be eager to try out all these techniques, so we have included 68 (!) problems to challenge and entertain you. Here are the exercises that you may want to turn into term projects:

Analog Clock	*Flight Simulator*	*Physics Demo: Bouncing Ball*
Animation	*Floor Planner*	*Physics Demo: Kinetics*
Arithmetic Tutor	*Game of Pool*	*Player Piano*
Artist	*Horse Race*	*Random Inter-Image Transition*
Automated Teller Machine	*Image Flasher*	*Randomly Erasing an Image*
Background Audio	*Image Zooming*	*Reaction Time Tester*
Bubble Help	*Jigsaw Puzzle Generator*	*Rotating Image*
Calendar/Tickler File	*Juggling Teacher*	*Roulette*
Calling Attention to an Image	*Karaoke*	*Screensaver*
Coloring B/W Photographs	*Knight's Tour Walker*	*Scrolling Image Marquee*
Craps	*Limericks*	*Scrolling Test Marquee*
Crossword	*Maze Generator and Walker*	*Sheet Music Generator/Player*
Digital Clock	*Multimedia Aerobics*	*Shuffleboard*
Dynamic Kaleidoscope	*Multimedia Authoring System*	*Story Teller*
Dynamic Customized Newsletter	*Multimedia Simpletron Simulator*	*Synthesizer*
Dynamic Stock Evaluator	*Music Teacher*	*Text Flasher*
Fashion Designer	*One-Armed Bandit*	*Tortoise and the Hare*
15 Puzzle	*Pendulum*	*Towers of Hanoi*
Fireworks Designer	*Pinball Machine*	*Video Games*

You are going to have a great time attacking some of these problems! Some will take a few hours, some are great term projects and some will probably seem unconquerable. We see all kinds of opportunities for multimedia electives starting to appear in the university computing curriculum. We hope you will have contests with your classmates to develop the best solutions to several of these problems.

Chapter 17—Files and Streams—deals with input/output that is accomplished through streams of data directed to and from files. This is one of the most important chapters for programmers who will be developing commercial applications. Modern business is centered around data. In this chapter we translate data (objects) into a persistent format usable by other applications. Being able to store data in files or in databases (Chapter 18) or move it across networks (Chapters 19 through 21) makes it possible for programs to save data and to communicate with each other. This is the real strength of software today. The chapter begins with an introduction to the data hierarchy from bits, to bytes, to fields, to records, to files. Next, Java's simple view of files and streams is presented. We then present a walkthrough of the dozens of classes in Java's extensive input/output files and streams class hierarchy. We put many of these classes to work in live-code examples in this chapter and in Chapters 19 through 21. We show how programs pass data to secondary storage devices like disks and how programs retrieve data already stored on those devices. Sequential-access files are discussed using a series of three programs that show how to open and close files, how to store data sequentially in a file and how to read data sequentially from a file. Random-access files are discussed using a series of four programs that show how to sequentially create a file for random access, how to read and write data to a file with random access, and how to read data sequentially from a randomly accessed file. The fourth random-access program combines many of the techniques of accessing files both sequentially and randomly into a complete transaction-processing program. We discuss buffering and how it helps programs that do significant amounts of input/output perform better. We discuss class **File** that programs use to obtain a variety of information about files and directories. We explain how objects can be output to, and input from, secondary storage devices. Students in our industry seminars have told us that after studying the material on file processing, they were able to produce substantial file-processing programs that were immediately useful to their organizations. The exercises ask the student to implement a variety of programs that build and process sequential-access files and random-access files.

Chapter 18—Java Database Connectivity (JDBC)—introduces the Java technology that enables Java programs to access databases (e.g., Oracle, SQL Server, Sybase, Informix, Access, etc.). The chapter begins with a discussion of database systems and the advantages of combining all of a company's databases into one database system. The chapter explains the importance of *data independence*—separating data from applications. It describes *relational databases*—the most popular type of database used today. We show how to register a database as a *Microsoft ODBC data source*. ODBC is a technology that delivers generic access to different types of databases on a Windows platform. Once a database is registered, we use the *JDBC-to-ODBC bridge database driver* to connect our Java programs to the database. We overview how *Structured Query Language (SQL)* queries are used to create, modify and retrieve records and information from a database. The examples in this chapter use a sample Microsoft Access database named **Books.mdb** containing information about our publications. Enhancing the database topics are illustrations of the **Books.mdb**'s tables and SQL query results. Chapter examples focus on connecting to a database, querying a database and displaying query results. The first example queries **Books.mdb** for a list of all the authors in the **Authors** table and displays the results in a Swing **JTable** component. This example outlines the steps necessary to use JDBC. The second example adds user-defined queries. This is an excellent example that reinforces the student's SQL knowledge. The last example, an address book, is the most substantial of the chapter. Key features of this example include inserting new records, updating existing records and searching for records. The chapter concludes with four substantial exercises including a complete query application and a complete database manipulation application.

Chapters 19, 20 and 21 explain how to write programs that can communicate over computer networks. Our discussion of networking in these chapters focuses on both sides of the *client-server* relationship. The *client* requests that an action be performed and the *server* performs the action and responds to the client. This request-response communication model is the foundation for the highest-level networking in Java—*servlets*.

Chapter 19—Servlets—explores the server-side of Java. This chapter discusses networking with the commonly used *request-response networking model* in which World Wide Web browsers communicate with World Wide Web servers as users browse the Internet. When a user selects a Web site to browse through a Web browser (i.e., the client application), a request is sent to the appropriate Web server (i.e., the server application) which normally responds to the client by sending the appropriate HTML Web page to be displayed by the client's browser. In this networking model, the communication between the client and the server is handled automatically. This chapter begins our discussions of *multitier distributed applications* in which parts of the applications operate on separate computers distributed over a network. This chapter uses Chapter 17's stream technologies and Chapter 18's database technologies. We explore the popular three-tier application model. The three tiers are the *user interface*, the *business logic* (servers and servlets), and *database access* (often JDBC). With this distributed computing model, each tier can be redesigned without affecting the others (provided the communication protocol remains the same). We use the Web's *HyperText Transfer Protocol (HTTP)*. We introduce Sun's Java Servlet Development Kit (JSDK) for creating and testing servlets. We present the steps for downloading, installing and using the JSDK. The chapter examples include handling a *HTTP GET request* when the client wants a page, handling an *HTTP POST request* when the client submits data to the server and *session tracking* (that allows Web site application developers to maintain client-specific information such as items in a Web shopping cart or personal Web site preferences). The capstone of the chapter is a multitier example of a guestbook that uses a servlet to access a database through JDBC. This example clearly illustrates how a servlet is used as the middle tier of a typical three-tier distributed system. The chapter exercises include enhancing the servlet examples with multithreading, enhancing the multitier guestbook example and a project—creating an auction servlet.

Chapter 20—Remote Method Invocation (RMI)—takes a lower-level approach to writing programs that can communicate over networks and continues our discussion of multitier applications. RMI enables Java programs to communicate with each other via method calls that are sent across the network. RMI is a more complex view of networking than servlets in that RMI requires more work on the part of the programmer to set up the initial interactions between applications. Once the mechanism is in place, the communication over the network is transparent to the application. This chapter makes use of the object-based streams technology (object serialization) discussed in Chapter 17.

This chapter contains one RMI example that allows a client to connect to a server and get a list of weather forecasts. The server downloads the weather forecast information from the Web and stores it locally. The client—through RMI—gets the list of weather items from the server and graphically displays the information. Because RMI is a complex topic, we show and discuss each class in this example one at a time as we build up our complete, object-oriented, multi-tier solution. This program is also an excellent object-oriented example! The chapter concludes with seven substantial exercises that include modifying the chapter example to enhance performance, modifying the chapter example to obtain and process the next day's forecast, and creating a project that uses RMI to get a state's weather information.

Chapter 21—Networking—deals with applets and applications that can communicate over computer networks. This chapter presents Java's lowest-level networking capabilities. We write programs that "walk the Web." The chapter examples illustrate an applet interacting with the browser in which it executes, creating a mini Web browser, communicating between two Java programs using streams-based sockets and communicating between two Java programs using packets of data. A key feature of the chapter is the live-code implementation of a collaborative client/server Tic-Tac-Toe game in which two clients play Tic-Tac-Toe with one another arbitrated by a multithreaded server—great stuff! The multithreaded server architecture is exactly what is used today in popular UNIX and Windows NT network servers. The chapter has a nice collection of exercises including several suggested modifications to the multithreaded server example.

Chapter 22—Data Structures—is particularly valuable in second- and third-level university courses. The chapter discusses the techniques used to create and manipulate dynamic data structures such as linked lists, stacks, queues (i.e., waiting lines) and trees. The chapter begins with discussions of self-referential classes and dynamic memory allocation. We proceed with a discussion of how to create and maintain various dynamic data structures. For each type of data structure, we present live-code programs and show sample outputs. Although it is valuable to know how these classes are implemented, Java programmers will quickly discover that many of the data structures they need are already available in class libraries such as Java's own **java.util** that we discuss in Chapter 23 and Java **Collection**s that we discuss in Chapter 24. The chapter helps the student master Java-style references (i.e., Java's replacement for the more dangerous pointers of C and C++). One problem when working with references is that students may have trouble visualizing the data structures and how their nodes are linked together. So we present illustrations that show the links and the sequence in which they are created. The binary tree example is a nice capstone for the study of references and dynamic data structures. This example creates a binary tree; enforces duplicate elimination; and introduces recursive preorder, inorder and postorder tree traversals. Students have a genuine sense of accomplishment when they study and implement this example. They particularly appreciate seeing that the inorder traversal prints the node values in sorted order. The chapter includes a substantial collection of exercises. A highlight of the exercises is the special section "Building Your Own Compiler." This exercise is based on earlier exercises that walk the student through the development of an infix-to-postfix-conversion program and a postfix-expression-evaluation program. We then modify the postfix evaluation algorithm to generate machine-language code. The compiler places this code in a file (using techniques the student mastered in Chapter 17). Students then run the machine language produced by their compilers on the software simulators they built in the exercises of Chapter 7! The many exercises include a supermarket simulation using queueing, recursively searching a list, recursively printing a list backwards, binary tree node deletion, level-order traversal of a binary tree, printing trees, writing a portion of an optimizing compiler, writing an interpreter, inserting/deleting anywhere in a linked list, analyzing the performance of binary tree searching and sorting, and implementing an indexed list class.

Chapter 23—Java Utilities Package and Bit Manipulation—walks through the classes of the **java.util** package and discuss each of Java's bitwise operators. This is a nice chapter for reinforcing the notion of reuse. When classes already exist, it is much faster to develop software by simply reusing these classes than by "reinventing the wheel." Classes are included in class libraries because the classes are generally useful, correct, performance tuned, portability certified and/or for a variety of other reasons. Someone has invested considerable work in preparing these classes so why should you write your own? The world's class libraries are growing at a phenomenal rate. Given this, your skill and value as a programmer will depend on your familiarity with what classes exist and how you can reuse them cleverly to develop high-quality software rapidly. University data structures courses will be changing drastically over the next several years because most important data structures are already implemented in widely available class libraries. This chapter discusses many classes. Two of the most useful are **Vector** (a dynamic array that can grow and shrink as necessary) and **Stack** (a dynamic data structure that allows insertions and deletions from only one end—called the top—thus ensuring last-in-first-out behavior). The beauty of studying these two classes is that they are related through inheritance as discussed in Chapter 9, so the `java.util` package itself implements some classes in terms of others thus avoiding reinventing the wheel and taking advantage of reuse. We also discuss classes **Dictionary**, **Hashtable**, **Properties** (for creating and manipulating persistent **Hashtable**s), **Random** and **BitSet**. The discussion of **BitSet** includes live code for one of the classic applications of **BitSet**s, namely the *Sieve of Eratosthenes* used for determining prime numbers. The chapter discusses in detail Java's powerful bit manipulation capabilities that enable programmers to exercise lower-level hardware capabilities. This helps programs process bit strings, set individual bits on or off and store information more compactly. Such capabilities—inherited from C—are characteristic of low-level assembly languages and are valued by programmers writing system software such as operating systems and networking software.

Chapter 24—Collections—discusses many of the new Java 2 classes (of the `java.util` package) that provide pre-defined implementations of many of the data structures discussed in Chapter 22. This chapter, too, reinforces the notion of reuse. These classes are modeled after a similar class library in C++—the Standard Template Library. Collections provide Java programmers with a standard set of data structures for storing and retrieving data, and a standard set of algorithms (i.e., procedures) that allow programmers to manipulate the data (such as searching for particular data items and sorting data into ascending or descending order). The chapter examples demonstrate collections such as linked-lists, trees, maps, sets, etc., and algorithms for searching, sorting, finding the maximum value, finding the minimum value, etc. Each example clearly shows how powerful and easy to use collections are. The exercises suggest modifications to the chapter examples and ask the reader to reimplement data structures presented in Chapter 22 using collections.

Chapter 25—JavaBeans—discusses wrapping the classes you define as reusable software components called *JavaBeans*. JavaBeans can be graphically manipulated and customized in various Java integrated development environments. We discuss the *JavaBeans Development Kit (BDK)* and the **BeanBox** that can be used to test JavaBeans. The **BeanBox** illustrates the key concepts of manipulating a JavaBean in a typical graphical development environment. The chapter discusses design issues surrounding JavaBean development. In addition, we illustrate how to wrap an application as a *Java Archive (JAR)* file so you can execute the application simply by double-clicking the name of the file in your system's file manager (a typical way to execute an application on many platforms). The chapter examples include an introduction to the **BeanBox**, wrapping a class as a JavaBean, creating a JAR file, loading JavaBeans into the **BeanBox**, adding properties (i.e., characteristics such as color, font, size, etc.) to a JavaBean and creating a JavaBean with a bound property (so that another object is automatically notified when the property's state changes). The chapter also provides a nice section containing JavaBean Web resources. The chapter concludes with seven exercises which include using the JavaBeans provided with the BeanBox, creating an RGB color selector JavaBean and creating a substantial JavaBean for a drawing application.

Appendix A—Java Demos—presents a huge collection of the best Java demos Abbey Deitel was able to track down on the Web. Many of these sites make their source code available to you, so you can download the code and add your own features—a truly great way to learn Java! We encourage our students to do this and we're amazed at the results! You should start your search by checking out Gamelan at **http://www.gamelan.com**.

You can save time finding the best demos by checking out JARS (the Java Applet Rating Service) at **http://www.jars.com**. Here's a list of some of the demos mentioned in Appendix A (the URLs and descriptions of each are in Appendix A):

Animated SDSU Logo	*Java Game Park*	*SabBowl bowling game*
Blitz game	*Java4fun games*	*Sevilla RDM 168*
Bumpy Lens 3D	*Missile Commando*	*Stereoscopic 3D Hypercube*
Centipedo	*Panoramania*	*Teamball demos*
Crazy Counter	*PhotoAlbum II*	*Tube*
Famous Curves Applet Index	*Play A Piano*	*Urbanoids*
Goldmine	*Pyramids*	*Warp 1.5*
Iceblox game	*Sab's Game Arcade*	*Web Billiard*

Appendix B—Java Resources—presents some of the best Java resources available on the Web. This is a great way for you to get into the "world of Java." The appendix lists various Java resources (such as consortia, journals and companies that make various key Java-related products). Here are some of the resources mentioned in Appendix B.

animated applets	Intelligence.com	Object Management Group
applets	IONA Technologies	products
applications	Java Applet Rating Service	Programmers Source
arts and entertainment	Java Developer Connection	projects
audio sites	Java Developer's Journal	publications
books	Java Media Framework	Purple Servlet FAQ
Borland JBuilder IDE	Java Media Player	puzzles
conferences	Java Report	reference materials
consultants	Java Servlet Programming	resources
contests	Java tools	seminars
CORBA homepage	Java Toys	Servlet Central
current information	Java Users Group (JUGs)	Servlet, Inc.
databases	Java Woman	**Servletforum.com**
demos (many with source code)	**java.sun.com**	**ServletSource.com**
Developer.com	JavaBeans Home Page	sites
developer's kit	JavaWorld on-line magazine	software
Development Exchange	learning Java	Sun JDBC FAQ
development tools	links to Java sites	Sun Microsystems
discussion groups	lists of resources	SunWorld on-line magazine
documentation	lists of what is new and cool	Symantec Visual Café IDE
downloadable applets	live chat sessions on Java	Team Java
Enhydra	Locomotive Project	The Java Tutorial
events	Metrowerks CodeWarrior IDE	trade shows
FAQs (frequently asked ?s)	multimedia collections	training (please call us!)
Gamelan	NASA multimedia gallery	tutorials for learning java
games	NetBeans IDE	URLs for Java applets
graphics	news	**www.gamelan.com**
HotJava HTML Component	**news:comp.lang.java**	**www.javaworld.com**
www.servlets.com	newsgroups	Yahoo (Web search engine)
IBM Developers Java Zone	newsletters	

Appendix C—Operator Precedence Chart—lists each of the Java operators and indicates their relative precedence and associativity. We list each operator on a separate line and include the full name of the operator.

Appendix D—ASCII Character Set—lists the characters of the ASCII (American Standard Code for Information Interchange) character set and indicates the character code value for each. Java uses the Unicode character set with 16-bit characters for representing all of the characters in the world's "commercially significant" languages. Unicode includes ASCII as a subset. Currently, most English-speaking countries are using ASCII and just beginning to experiment with Unicode.

Appendix E—Number Systems—discusses the binary (base 2), decimal (base 10), octal (base 8) and hexadecimal (base 16) number systems. This material is valuable for introductory courses in computer science and computer engineering. The appendix is presented with the same pedagogic learnings aids as the chapters of the book. A nice feature of the appendix is its 31 exercises, 19 of which are self-review exercises with answers.

Appendix F—Object-Oriented Elevator Simulator—walks the student through a carefully paced and substantial term project. The appendix begins with a simple introduction to object-oriented thinking so the instructor can assign the elevator case study in parallel with the early chapters of the book. These sections introduce the concepts and terminology of object orientation to help students become familiar with what objects are and how they behave. Next we present a requirements specification for a substantial object-oriented system project, namely building the elevator simulator, and we carefully guide the student through the typical phases of the object-oriented design process. By the time the student has finished the early assignments, he or she has completed a precise object-oriented design of the elevator simulator and is ready—if not eager—to begin programming the elevator in Java.

This appendix is intended as an optional term project for intense first programming courses and for second-level programming courses. We have divided the appendix into 12 carefully paced assignments that enable the student to develop the elevator in parallel with reading the appropriate chapters of the textbook. Section F.1 begins with an introduction to object orientation. We will see that object orientation is a natural way of thinking about the world and writing computer programs. Section F.2 presents the elevator "requirements document" that describes the elevator in sufficient detail for the student to begin the design process. In **Elevator Assignment 1** (Prerequisites: Chapters 2–4) the student begins the object-oriented design process by identifying the classes in the requirements document.

Classes have attributes and behaviors. Class attributes are represented in Java programs by data. In **Elevator Assignment 2** (Prerequisite: Chapter 6) the student concentrates on determining the attributes of the classes needed to implement the elevator simulator. In **Elevator Assignment 3** (Prerequisite: Chapter 8) we concentrate on determining the behaviors of the classes needed to implement the elevator simulator. Behaviors are implemented in Java as methods—Java's term for the member functions with which C++ programmers are familiar. **Elevator Assignment 4** (Prerequisite: Chapter 8) concentrates on the interactions between class objects.

In **Elevator Assignment 5** (Prerequisite: Chapter 8) you begin programming the elevator simulator. For each of the classes you identified in the previous assignments, you write an appropriate class definition. Each class definition is written in a separate file with the `.java` extension. You then write a "driver" applet that tests each of these classes and attempts to run the complete elevator simulation. For this first version of the simulator, you design only a simple, text-oriented output that displays a message for each significant event that occurs. **Elevator Assignment 6** (Prerequisite: Chapter 8) discusses composition, a capability that allows you to create classes that have as members references to objects. Composition enables you to create a building class that contains references to the elevator and to the floors, and, in turn, create an elevator class that contains references to buttons.

Elevator Assignment 7 (Prerequisites: Chapters 11-13) focuses on enhancing the elevator's graphical user interface. **Elevator Assignment 8** (Prerequisites: Chapters 11-13) builds on the GUI you developed in Assignment 7; you will add to the GUI and begin graphically representing the events occurring in your simulation. **Elevator Assignment 9** (Prerequisite: Chapter 15) covers the steps necessary to provide interaction between the GUI and events generated by your simulator. The interaction in many cases will be done with multithreading. **Elevator Assignment 10** (Prerequisite: Chapter 15) covers the steps necessary to provide animation for your simulator. **Elevator Assignment 11** (Prerequisite: Chapter 16) covers the steps necessary to provide additional animation as well some audio for your simulator. **Elevator Assignment 12** (Prerequisite: Chapter 16) enhances the animation of the previous assignment. In **Section F.15** we list several design review questions that address some of the problems that could be encountered in a more elaborate elevator simulator. In **Section F.16** we list 12 significant modifications that can be made to your elevator simulator; some of these require the data structures of Chapters 22, 23 and 24.

Appendix G—Creating `javadoc` Documentation—introduces the `javadoc` documentation generation tool. Sun Microsystems uses `javadoc` to document the Java APIs. The example in this appendix takes the reader through the `javadoc` documentation process. First, we introduce the comment style and tags that `javadoc` recognizes and uses to create documentation. Next, we discuss the commands and options used to run the utility. Finally, we examine the source files `javadoc` uses and the HTML files `javadoc` creates.

Appendix H—Enterprise JavaBeans (EJB) Web Resources and **Appendix I—Jini Web Resources**—provide extensive lists of Web resources for two of the hottest Java topics—Enterprise JavaBeans (EJB) and Jini. Enterprise JavaBeans is a technology designed to be the standard for building distributed applications in Java. Jini is a technology that allows different digital devices to communicate. Jini technology simplifies network interactions. Each of these topics is relatively new in Java and each was a topic of intense discussion at the JavaOne conference in San Francisco (June 1999). We would have liked to provide the same chapter-length treatment of these topics that we provided for other advanced topics, but we regret that we were out of time. So, we did the next best thing— we searched the Web for tutorials, demos and the like to help you get started studying these important technologies.

Software Included with *Java How to Program: Third Edition*

The CD-ROM at the end of this book contains Sun Microsystem's *J2SDK 1.2.1* (i.e., Java 2) software development kit and two powerful Java integrated development environments (IDEs)—NetBeans *DeveloperX2* and Borland *JBuilder 3 University Edition*. The CD also contains the book's examples and an HTML Web page with links to the Deitel & Associates, Inc. Web site, the Prentice Hall Web site and the many Web sites listed in the Appendices. If you have access to the Internet, this Web page can be loaded into your World Wide Web browser to give you quick access to all the resources.

NetBeans *DeveloperX2* is a professional IDE written in Java that includes a graphical user interface designer, code editor, compiler, visual debugger and more. J2SDK 1.2.1 must be installed before installing DeveloperX2.

Borland *JBuilder 3 University Edition* is a customized version of JBuilder designed to meet the unique needs of the education market. The JBuilder 3 University Edition IDE includes an application browser, project manager, code editor, HTML viewer, graphical debugger and compiler. JBuilder 3 supports the latest Java standards, including Java 2, JavaBeans, JAR files, inner classes, internationalization, security and more.

If you have any questions about using this software, please read the introductory documentation on the CD-ROM. We will be putting additional information on our Web site: **http://www.deitel.com**.

Java 2 Multimedia Cyber Classroom: Third Edition and *The Complete Java 2 Training Course: Third Edition*

We have prepared an interactive, CD-ROM-based, software version of *Java How to Program: Third Edition* called the *Java 2 Multimedia Cyber Classroom: Third Edition*. It is loaded with features for learning and reference. The *Cyber Classroom* is wrapped with the textbook at a discount in *The Complete Java 2 Training Course: Third Edition*. If you already have the book and would like to purchase the *Java 2 Multimedia Cyber Classroom: Third Edition* separately, please call 1-800-811-0912 and ask for ISBN# 0-13-014494-0.

The CD has an introduction with the authors overviewing the *Cyber Classroom*'s features. The 220 live-code example Java programs in the textbook truly "come alive" in the *Cyber Classroom*. If you are viewing a program and want to execute it, you simply click on the lightning bolt icon and the program will run. You will immediately see—and hear for the audio-based multimedia programs—the program's outputs. If you want to modify a program and see and hear the effects of your changes, simply click the floppy-disk icon that causes the source code to be "lifted off" the CD and "dropped into" one of your own directories so you can edit the text, recompile the program and try out your new version. Click the audio icon and Paul Deitel will talk about the program and "walk you through" the code.

The *Cyber Classroom* also provides navigational aids including extensive hyperlinking. The *Cyber Classroom* remembers in a "history list" recent sections you have visited and allows you to move forward or backward in that history list. The thousands of index entries are hyperlinked to their text occurrences. You can key in a term using the "find" feature and the *Cyber Classroom* will locate its occurrences throughout the text. The Table of Contents entries are "hot," so clicking a chapter name takes you to that chapter.

Students tell us that they particularly like the hundreds of solved problems from the textbook that are included with the *Cyber Classroom*. Studying and running these extra programs is a great way for students to enhance their learning experience.

Students and professional users of our *Cyber Classrooms* tell us they like the interactivity and that the *Cyber Classroom* is an effective reference because of the extensive hyperlinking and other navigational features. We recently had an email from a person who said that he lives "in the boonies" and cannot take a live course at a university, so the *Cyber Classroom* was the solution to his educational needs.

Professors tell us that their students enjoy using the *Cyber Classroom*, spend more time on the course and master more of the material than in textbook-only courses. Also, the *Cyber Classroom* helps shrink lines outside professors' offices during office hours. We have also published the *C & C++ Multimedia Cyber Classroom* and the *Visual Basic 6 Multimedia Cyber Classroom*. We will publish *Cyber Classroom* editions of our forthcoming books *Internet and World Wide Web How to Program* and *Advanced Java How to Program*.

Advanced Java How to Program

We are preparing *Advanced Java How to Program* for publication in the Fall of 2000. This book is intended for developers and upper-level university students in advanced courses who already know Java and want a deeper treatment and understanding of the language. The book will feature our signature "live-code" approach of complete working programs. The programs will be more substantial than those presented in *Java How to Program: Third Edition*. The book will expand the coverage of Java Database Connectivity (JDBC), remote method invocation (RMI), servlets, JavaBeans and inner classes from *Java How to Program: Third Edition*. The book will also cover emerging and more advanced Java technologies of concern to enterprise application developers including: CORBA/IDL, Enterprise JavaBeans (EJB), XML, Jini, advanced Swing concepts, security, electronic commerce, internationalization, accessibility and Java Native Interface (JNI), among others.

Acknowledgments

One of the great pleasures of writing a textbook is acknowledging the efforts of many people whose names may not appear on the cover, but whose hard work, cooperation, friendship, and understanding were crucial to the production of the book.

Three other people at Deitel & Associates, Inc. devoted long hours to this project. We would like to acknowledge the efforts of Tem Nieto, Barbara Deitel and Abbey Deitel.

Tem Nieto, a graduate of the Massachusetts Institute of Technology, is one of our full-time colleagues at Deitel & Associates, Inc. Tem teaches C, C++, Visual Basic and Java seminars and works with us on textbook writing, course development and multimedia authoring efforts. He is co-author with us of *Visual Basic 6 How to Program*. In *Java How to Program: Third Edition* Tem co-authored Chapters 11, 12, 13, 19 and 24; Appendix F on the object-oriented, multimedia-based elevator simulator project and the Special Section entitled "Building Your Own Compiler" in Chapter 22.

Barbara Deitel managed the preparation of the manuscript and coordinated with Prentice Hall the production of the book. Barbara's efforts are by far the most painstaking of what we do to develop books. She has infinite patience. She handled the endless details involved in publishing the two-color text book, a 600-page instructor's manual and the 650-megabyte CD *Cyber Classroom*. She used FrameMaker page-layout software to prepare the book. Barbara mastered this complex software package and did a marvelous job giving the book its clean style. She spent long hours researching the quotes at the beginning of each chapter. Barbara prepared the *Table of Contents*, the *List of Illustrations* and every one of the 9300 page references in the index. She did all this in parallel with handling her extensive financial and administrative responsibilities at Deitel & Associates, Inc.

Abbey Deitel, a graduate of Carnegie Mellon University's industrial management program, and now Chief Operating Officer of Deitel & Associates, Inc., wrote Appendix A, "Java Demos," Appendix B, "Java Resources," Appendix H, "Enterprise Java Beans Resources," Appendix I, "Jini Resources" and suggested the title for the book. We asked

Abbey to surf the World Wide Web and track down the best Java sites. She didn't have to go far. She immediately discovered Gamelan, a wonderful site listing thousands of significant Java resources and demos. She used various Web search engines and collected this information for you in Appendices A, B, H and I. For each resource and demo, Abbey has provided a brief explanation. Abbey will be maintaining up-to-the-minute versions of these resources and demo listings on our Web site **http://www.deitel.com**.

We would also like to thank David Blumstein, Paul Brandano and Chris Poirier—participants in our Deitel & Associates, Inc. *College Internship Program*. Dave, a senior at Boston University, contributed to Chapters 16, 17, 19 and 21. Dave also assisted with the preparation of the Instructor's manual, the Cyber classroom and the index, and co-authored Appendix G.

Paul Brandano, a senior at Boston College, co-authored Appendices A, B, H and I. Paul also prepared the bibliography.

Chris Poirier, a senior at the University of Rhode Island, helped convert the GUI-based examples from AWT to Swing, wrote initial versions of several of the examples in the servlets and RMI chapters, and contributed to the JDBC chapter.

[*Note:* The Deitel & Associates, Inc. *College Internship Program* offers a limited number of salaried positions to Boston-area college students majoring in Computer Science, Information Technology or Marketing. Students work at our corporate headquarters in Sudbury, Massachusetts full-time in the summers and part-time during the academic year. Full-time positions are available to college graduates. For more information about this competitive program, please contact Abbey Deitel at **deitel@deitel.com** and check our Web site, **http://www.deitel.com**.]

We are fortunate to have been able to work on this project with the talented and dedicated team of publishing professionals at Prentice Hall. We especially appreciate the extraordinary efforts of our computer science editor, Petra Recter, her assistant Sarah Burrows and their boss—our mentor in publishing—Marcia Horton, Editor-in-Chief of Prentice-Hall's Engineering and Computer Science Division. Camille Trentacoste did a marvelous job as production manager.

The *Java 2 Multimedia Cyber Classroom: Third Edition* was developed in parallel with *Java How to Program: Third Edition*. We sincerely appreciate the "new media" insight, savvy and technical expertise of our editor Mark Taub. He did a remarkable job bringing the *Java 2 Multimedia Cyber Classroom: Third Edition* to publication under a tight schedule.

We owe special thanks to the creativity of Tamara Newnam Cavallo (**smart_art@earthlink.net**) who did the art work for our programming tips icons and the cover. She created the delightful creature who shares with you the book's programming tips.

We sincerely appreciate the efforts of our reviewers:

Third Edition Reviewers:
Jeff Boleng (United States Air Force Academy)
Columbus Brown (IBM Retail Store Solutions)
Tim Burke (Sun Certified Java Developer)
Jonathan R. Earl (Technical Training and Consulting)
Richard Enbody (Michigan State University)
Ian Formanek (NetBeans Inc.)

Jim Gips (Boston College)
Jesse Glick (NetBeans Inc.)
Todd Greanier (Frontier Corporation)
Rex Jaeschke (ANSI Java Committee Chairman)
Peter Jones (Sun Microsystems)
Don Kostuch (You Can C Clearly Now)
Marc Loy (Galileo Systems, LLC)
Jim Roberts (Carnegie Mellon University)
Rama Roberts (Sun Microsystems)
Michael Rozlong (Inprise)
Marjan Trutschl (University of Massachusetts at Lowell)
Jaroslav Tulach (NetBeans Inc.)
Willie Walker (Sun Microsystems)
Michael Warres (Sun Microsystems)

First and/or Second Edition Reviewers:
Kate Baumgartner Lowrie (Kronos)
Gordon Bradley (Naval Postgraduate School)
Andrew M. Brown (Bell Laboratories)
Mark Ellis (Reuters)
Richard Enbody (Michigan State University)
Jerry Gulla (Sun Microsystems)
Peter Jones (Sun Microsystems)
Robert Herrmann (Sun Microsystems)
Ken Merson (Borland)
Jim Roberts (Carnegie-Mellon University)
Ian Smith (Georgia Institute of Technology)

Under an impossibly tight time schedule, they scrutinized every aspect of the text and made countless suggestions for improving the accuracy and completeness of the presentation.

We would sincerely appreciate your comments, criticisms, corrections, and suggestions for improving the text. Please address all correspondence to our email address:

`deitel@deitel.com`

We will respond immediately. Well, that's it for now. Welcome to the exciting world of Java programming. We hope you enjoy this look at leading-edge computer applications development. Good luck!

Dr. Harvey M. Deitel
Paul J. Deitel

About the Authors

Dr. Harvey M. Deitel, CEO of Deitel & Associates, Inc., has 38 years experience in the computing field including extensive industry and academic experience. He is one of the world's leading computer science instructors and seminar presenters. Dr. Deitel earned B.S. and M.S. degrees from the Massachusetts Institute of Technology and a Ph.D. from Boston University. He worked on the pioneering virtual memory operating systems projects at IBM and MIT that developed techniques widely implemented today in systems like UNIX, Windows NT and OS/2. He has 20 years of college teaching experience including earning tenure and serving as the Chairman of the Computer Science Department at Boston College before founding Deitel & Associates, Inc. with Paul J. Deitel. He is author or co-author of several dozen books and multimedia packages and is currently writing many more. With translations published in Japanese, Russian, Spanish, Basic Chinese, Advanced Chinese, Korean, French, Polish and Portuguese, Dr. Deitel's texts have earned international recognition. Dr. Deitel has delivered professional seminars internationally to major corporations, government organizations and various branches of the military.

Paul J. Deitel, Executive Vice President of Deitel & Associates, Inc., is a graduate of the Massachusetts Institute of Technology's Sloan School of Management where he studied Information Technology. Through Deitel & Associates, Inc. he has delivered Java, C and C++ courses for industry clients including Compaq, Digital Equipment Corporation, Sun Microsystems, Rogue Wave Software, Computervision, Stratus, Fidelity, Cambridge Technology Partners, Open Environment Corporation, One Wave, Hyperion Software, Lucent Technologies, Adra Systems, Entergy, CableData Systems, NASA at the Kennedy Space Center, the National Severe Storm Laboratory, White Sands Missle Range, IBM and many others. He has lectured on C++ and Java for the Boston Chapter of the Association for Computing Machinery. He has taught satellite-based Java courses through a cooperative venture of Deitel & Associates, Inc., Prentice Hall and the Technology Education Network. He is the co-author of fifteen books and multimedia packages with Harvey Deitel and is currently writing five more.

The Deitels are co-authors of the best-selling introductory college computer-science programming language textbooks, *C How to Program: Second Edition*, *C++ How to Program: Second Edition*, *Java How to Program: Third Edition* and *Visual Basic 6 How to Program*. The Deitels are also co-authors of the *C & C++ Multimedia Cyber Classroom: Second Edition*—Prentice Hall's first multimedia-based textbook, the *Java 2 Multimedia Cyber Classroom: Third Edition* and the *Visual Basic 6 Multimedia Cyber Classroom* co-authored with their colleague Tem R. Nieto. The Deitels are also co-authors of *The Complete C++ Training Course: Second Edition*, The *Complete Visual Basic 6 Training Course* and *The Complete Java 2 Training Course: Third Edition*—these products each contain both the appropriate *How to Program Series* textbook and the appropriate *Multimedia Cyber Classroom*.

About Deitel & Associates, Inc.

Deitel & Associates, Inc. is an internationally recognized corporate training and publishing organization specializing in programming languages, Internet/World Wide Web technology and object technology education. The company provides courses on Java, Visual Basic, C++, Visual C++, Visual J++, C, Internet and World Wide Web programming, and Object-Oriented Analysis and Design. The principals of Deitel & Associates, Inc. are Dr. Harvey M. Deitel and Paul J. Deitel. The company's clients include some of the world's largest computer companies, government agencies, branches of the military and business organizations. Through its publishing partnership with Prentice Hall, Deitel & Associates, Inc. publishes leading-edge programming textbooks, professional books, interactive CD-ROM-based multimedia *Cyber Classrooms*, satellite courses and World Wide Web courses. Deitel & Associates, Inc. and the authors can be reached via email at

> `deitel@deitel.com`

To learn more about Deitel & Associates, Inc., its publications, public seminar schedule and worldwide corporate on-site curriculum, visit:

> `http://www.deitel.com`

Deitel & Associates, Inc. has a limited number of competitive opportunities in its College Internship Program for students in the Boston area. For information, please contact Abbey Deitel at **`deitel@deitel.com`**.

Individuals wishing to purchase Deitel books and multimedia packages can do so through

> `http://www.deitel.com`

Bulk orders by corporations and academic institutions should be placed directly with Prentice Hall—see last few pages of this book for worldwide ordering details.

1

Introduction to Computers, the Internet and the Web

Objectives

- To understand basic computer science concepts.
- To become familiar with different types of programming languages.
- To understand the Java program development environment.
- To understand the role Java plays in developing distributed client/server applications for the Internet and the World Wide Web.
- To preview the remaining chapters of the book.

Our life is frittered away by detail ... Simplify, simplify.
Henry Thoreau

High thoughts must have high language.
Aristophanes

The chief merit of language is clearness.
Galen

My object all sublime
I shall achieve in time.
W. S. Gilbert

He had a wonderful talent for packing thought close, and rendering it portable.
Thomas Babington Macaulay

Egad, I think the interpreter is the hardest to be understood of the two!
Richard Brinsley Sheridan

Outline

Summary • Terminology • Common Programming Error • Good Programming Practices • Performance Tips • Portability Tips • Software Engineering Observations • Testing and De- bugging Tip • Self-Review Exercises • Answers to Self-Review Exercises • Exercises

1.1 Introduction

Welcome to Java! We have worked hard to create what we hope will be an informative, entertaining and challenging learning experience for you. Java is a powerful computer pro- gramming language that is fun to use for novices while simultaneously being appropriate for experienced programmers building substantial information systems. *Java How to Pro- gram: Third Edition* is designed to be an effective learning tool for each of these audiences.

How can one book appeal to both groups? The answer is that the common core of the book emphasizes achieving program *clarity* through the proven techniques of *structured programming* and *object-oriented programming*. Nonprogrammers will learn program- ming the right way from the beginning. We have attempted to write in a clear and straight- forward manner. The book is abundantly illustrated. Perhaps most important, the book presents hundreds of working Java programs and shows the outputs produced when those programs are run on a computer. We teach all Java features in the context of complete working Java programs. We call this the *live-code approach*. These examples are available from three locations—they are on the CD-ROM inside the back cover of this book, they may be downloaded from our Web site **http://www.deitel.com** and they are avail- able on our interactive CD-ROM product, the *Java Multimedia Cyber Classroom: Third Edition*. The Cyber Classroom's features and ordering information appear at the back of this book. The Cyber Classroom also contains answers to approximately half the exercises in this book, including short answers, small programs and many full projects. If you pur- chased *The Complete Java Training Course: Third Edition*, you already have the Cyber Classroom.

The early chapters introduce the fundamentals of computers, computer programming and the Java computer programming language. Novices who have taken our courses tell us that the material in those chapters presents a solid foundation for the deeper treatment of Java in the later chapters. Experienced programmers typically read the early chapters quickly and find that the treatment of Java in the later chapters is rigorous and challenging.

Many experienced programmers have told us that they appreciate our treatment of structured programming. Often they have been programming in structured languages like C or Pascal, but because they were never formally introduced to structured programming, they are not writing the best possible code in these languages. As they review structured programming in the chapters "Control Structures: Part 1" and "Control Structures: Part 2," they are able to improve their C and Pascal programming styles as well. So whether you are a novice or an experienced programmer, there is much here to inform, entertain and challenge you.

Most people are familiar with the exciting things computers do. Using this textbook, you will learn how to command computers to do those things. It is *software* (i.e., the instructions you write to command the computer to perform *actions* and make *decisions*) that controls computers (often referred to as *hardware*), and Java is one of today's most popular software development languages. Java was developed by Sun Microsystems and an implementation of it is available free over the Internet from the Sun Web site

`http://java.sun.com`

This book is based on Sun's most recent Java release—the *Java 2 Platform*. The *Java 2 Platform* describes the Java language, libraries and tools such that others can implement *Java development kits*. Sun provides an implementation of the *Java 2 Platform* called the *Java 2 Software Development Kit (J2SDK), version 1.2* that includes the minimum set of tools you need to write software in Java. The J2SDK is included on the CD-ROM at the back of this book. At the time of this publication, the most recent version was J2SDK 1.2.1. However, the programs in this book should work correctly with any version of J2SDK 1.2.

Computer use is increasing in almost every field of endeavor. In an era of steadily rising costs, computing costs have been decreasing dramatically because of the rapid developments in both hardware and software technology. Computers that might have filled large rooms and cost millions of dollars two decades ago can now be inscribed on the surfaces of silicon chips smaller than a fingernail, costing perhaps a few dollars each. Ironically, silicon is one of the most abundant materials on earth—it is an ingredient in common sand. Silicon chip technology has made computing so economical that approximately 200 million general-purpose computers are in use worldwide helping people in business, industry, government, and their personal lives. That number could easily double in a few years.

This book will challenge you for several reasons. Your peers over the last few years probably learned C or Pascal as their first programming language. They probably learned the programming methodology called *structured programming*. You will learn both structured programming and the exciting newer methodology, *object-oriented programming*. Why do we teach both? We believe that object orientation is the key programming methodology as we begin the new millennium. You will build and work with many *objects* in this course. But you will discover that the internal structure of those objects is often best built using structured programming techniques. Also, the logic of manipulating objects is occasionally best expressed with structured programming.

Another reason we present both methodologies is that there is currently a massive migration from C-based systems (built primarily with structured programming techniques) to C++ and Java-based systems (built primarily with object-oriented programming techniques). There is a huge amount of so-called "legacy C code" in place because C has been in use for three decades. Once people learn C++ and/or Java, they find these languages to be more powerful than C and these people often choose to move their programming projects to C++ and/or Java. They begin converting their legacy systems. Then they begin employing the object-oriented programming capabilities of C++ and/or Java to realize the full benefits of these languages. Often the choice between C++ and Java is made based on the simplicity of Java compared to C++.

Java is certain to become the language of choice in the new millennium for implementing Internet-based and Intranet-based applications and any other software for devices that communicate over a network (such as cellular phones, pagers and personal digital assistants). Do not be surprised when your new stereo and other devices in your home will be networked together using Java technology!

Why is Java an attractive first programming language? There are many reasons. Each of them individually may seem attractive, but perhaps not attractive enough to justify switching from "mainline," industry-proven languages like C and C++. But taken as a whole, Java provides an attractive package for advancing the state of programming language education, especially at the introductory and intermediate levels. Over the near term C, and especially C++, are secure as the "heavy-duty" implementation languages programmers need to build complex, large-scale systems. Java has evolved rapidly into the large-scale applications arena, with many companies dedicated to pure Java development. Java is no longer a language that is simply used to make World Wide Web pages "come alive." As Java continues to evolve, people will start to see it as a perfectly viable, if not preferred language, for meeting most of an organization's programming needs.

For many years languages like C and C++ appealed to universities because of their portability. Introductory courses could be offered in these languages on any hardware/operating system combination as long as a C/C++ compiler was available. But the programming world has become more complex and more demanding. Today users want applications with graphical user interfaces (GUIs). They want applications that use the multimedia capabilities of graphics, images, animation, audio and video. They want applications that can run on the Internet and the World Wide Web, and communicate with other applications. They want applications that can take advantage of the flexibility and performance improvements of multithreading (multithreading enables programmers to specify that several activities should occur in parallel). They want applications with richer file processing than is provided by C or C++. They want applications that are not limited to the desktop or even to some local computer network, but that can integrate Internet components and remote databases as well. They want applications that can be written quickly and correctly in a manner that takes advantage of a world of reuse of prebuilt software components. They want easy access to a growing universe of reusable software components. And programmers want all these benefits in a truly portable manner so that applications will run without modification on a variety of *platforms* (i.e., different types of computers running different operating systems). Java offers all these benefits to the programming community.

Another reason Java is attractive for university courses is that it is fully object oriented. One reason that C++ use has grown so quickly is that it extends C programming into the arena of object orientation. For the huge community of C programmers this has been a powerful advantage. C++ includes ANSI/ISO C and offers the ability to do object-oriented programming as well (ANSI is the American National Standards Institute and ISO is the International Standards Organization). An enormous amount of C code has been written in industry over the last several decades. Because C++ is a superset of C, many organizations find it to be an ideal next step. Programmers can take their C code, compile it, often with nominal changes, in a C++ compiler and continue writing C-like code while mastering the object paradigm. Then the programmers can gradually migrate portions of the legacy C code into C++ as time permits. New systems can be entirely written in object-oriented C++. Such strategies have been appealing to many organizations. The downside is that even after adopting this strategy, companies tend to continue producing C-like code for many years. This, of course, means that they do not quickly realize the full benefits of object-oriented programming and they produce programs that are confusing and hard to maintain due to their hybrid design. Many organizations wish they could plunge 100% into object-oriented development, but the realities of mountains of legacy code and the temptation to take a C-programming approach often prevent this.

Java is a fully object-oriented language with strong support for proper software engineering techniques. It is difficult to write C-like, so-called procedural programs in Java. You must create and manipulate objects. Error processing is built into the language. Many of the complex details of C and C++ programming that prevent programmers from "looking at the big picture" are not included in Java. For universities, these features are powerfully appealing. Students will learn object-oriented programming from the start. They will simply think in an object-oriented manner.

Here, too, there is a trade-off. Organizations turning to Java for new applications development do not want to convert all their legacy code to Java. So Java allows for so-called *native code*. This means that existing C code and C++ code can be integrated with Java code. Although this may seem a bit awkward (and it certainly can be), it presents a pragmatic solution to a problem most organizations face.

The fact that Java is free for download at the Sun Web site, **http://java.sun.com**, is appealing to universities facing tight budgets and lengthy budget planning cycles. Also, as bug fixes and new versions of Java become available, these become available immediately over the Internet, so universities can keep their Java software current.

Can Java be taught in a first programming course—the intended audience for this book? We think so. Prior to writing this book, Deitel & Associates, Inc. instructors taught over 150 Java courses to more than 2000 people at all levels of expertise, including many nonprogrammers. We found that nonprogrammers become productive faster with Java than with C or C++. They are anxious to experiment with Java's powerful features for graphics, graphical user interfaces, multimedia, animation, multithreading, networking and the like—and they are successful at building substantial Java programs even in their first courses.

For many years, the Pascal programming language was the preferred vehicle for use in introductory and intermediate programming courses. Many people said that C was too difficult a language for these courses. In 1992, we published the first edition of *C How to Program,* to encourage universities to try C instead of Pascal in these courses. We used the same pedagogic approach we had used in our university courses for a dozen years, but wrapped the concepts in C rather than Pascal. We found that students were able to handle C at about the same level as Pascal. But there was one noticeable difference. Students appreciated that they were learning a language (C) likely to be valuable to them in industry. Our industry clients appreciated the availability of C-literate graduates who could work immediately on substantial projects rather than first having to go through costly and time-consuming training programs.

The first edition of *C How to Program* included a 60-page introduction to C++ and object-oriented programming. We saw C++ coming on strong, but we felt it would be at least a few more years before the universities would be ready to teach C++ and object-oriented programming (OOP) in introductory courses.

During 1993 we saw a surge in interest in C++ and OOP among our industry clients. But we still did not sense that the universities were ready to switch to C++ and OOP en masse. So in January 1994 we published the Second Edition of *C How to Program* with a 300-page section on C++ and OOP. In May 1994 we published the first edition of *C++ How to Program,* a 950-page book devoted to the premise that C++ and OOP were now ready for prime time in introductory university courses for many schools that wanted to be at the leading edge of programming languages education.

In 1995, we were following the introduction of Java carefully. In November 1995 we attended an Internet conference in Boston. A representative from Sun Microsystems gave a presentation on Java that filled one of the large ballrooms at the Hynes Convention Center. As the presentation proceeded, it became clear to us that Java would play a significant part in the development of interactive, multimedia Web pages. But we immediately saw a much greater potential for the language. We saw Java as the proper language for universities to teach first-year programming language students in this modern world of graphics, images, animation, audio, video, database, networking, multithreading and collaborative computing. At the time, we were busy writing the second edition of *C++ How to Program.* We discussed with our publisher, Prentice Hall, our vision of Java making a strong impact in the university curriculum. We all agreed to delay the second edition of *C++ How to Program* a bit so that we could get the first edition of *Java How to Program* (based on Java 1.0.2) to the market in time for fall 1996 courses.

As Java rapidly evolved to Java 1.1, we wrote *Java How to Program: Second Edition* in 1997, less than a year after the first edition reached bookstores worldwide. Hundreds of universities and corporate training programs worldwide used the second edition.

Java continues to evolve rapidly, so we wrote this third edition of *Java How to Program* updated to the latest *Java 2 platform* (also called *Java 1.2*). In this edition, we simplified the first several chapters to make Java easier to learn for nonprogrammers and we added five new high-end chapters that introduce key enterprise development features. These high-end chapters will form the foundation of our forthcoming text *Advanced Java How to Program.*

So there you have it! You are about to start on a challenging and rewarding path. As you proceed, please share your thoughts on Java and *Java How to Program: Third Edition* with us via email at **deitel@deitel.com**. We respond promptly.

Prentice Hall maintains **http://www.prenhall.com/deitel**—a World Wide Web site dedicated to our Prentice Hall textbooks and multimedia products, including *Java How to Program, The Complete Java Training Course, C++ How to Program, The Complete C++ Training Course, Visual Basic® 6 How to Program, The Complete Visual*

Basic® 6 Training Course, C How to Program and our latest book—*Internet and World Wide Web How to Program.* The site contains companion Web sites for each of our books that include frequently asked questions (FAQs), example downloads, errata, updates, additional text and examples, additional self-test questions, and new developments in programming languages and object-oriented programming technologies. If you would like to learn more about the authors or Deitel & Associates, Inc. please visit our World Wide Web site at **http://www.deitel.com**. Good luck!

1.2 What Is a Computer?

A *computer* is a device capable of performing computations and making logical decisions at speeds millions, and even billions, of times faster than human beings can. For example, many of today's personal computers can perform hundreds of millions of additions per second. A person operating a desk calculator might require decades to complete the same number of calculations a powerful personal computer can perform in one second. (Points to ponder: How would you know whether the person added the numbers correctly? How would you know whether the computer added the numbers correctly?) Today's fastest *supercomputers* can perform hundreds of billions of additions per second—about as many calculations as hundreds of thousands of people could perform in one year! And trillion-instruction-per-second computers are already functioning in research laboratories!

Computers process *data* under the control of sets of instructions called *computer programs.* These computer programs guide the computer through orderly sets of actions specified by people called *computer programmers.*

The various devices (such as the keyboard, screen, disks, memory and processing units) that comprise a computer system are referred to as *hardware.* The computer programs that run on a computer are referred to as *software.* Hardware costs have been declining dramatically in recent years, to the point that personal computers have become a commodity. Unfortunately, software development costs have been rising steadily as programmers develop ever more powerful and complex applications, without being able to significantly improve the technology of software development. In this book you will learn proven software development methods that can reduce software development costs—top-down stepwise refinement, functionalization and object-oriented programming. Object-oriented programming is widely believed to be the significant breakthrough that can greatly enhance programmer productivity.

1.3 Computer Organization

Regardless of differences in physical appearance, virtually every computer may be envisioned as being divided into six *logical units* or sections. These are:

1. *Input unit.* This is the "receiving" section of the computer. It obtains information (data and computer programs) from various *input devices* and places this information at the disposal of the other units so that the information may be processed. Most information is entered into computers today through typewriter-like keyboards, "mouse" devices and disks. In the future, most information will be entered by speaking to computers, by electronically scanning images, and by video recording.

2. *Output unit.* This is the "shipping" section of the computer. It takes information processed by the computer and places it on various *output devices* to make the information available for use outside the computer. Information output from computers is displayed on screens, printed on paper, played through audio speakers, magnetically recorded on disks and tapes, or used to control other devices.

3. *Memory unit.* This is the rapid access, relatively low-capacity "warehouse" section of the computer. It retains information that has been entered through the input unit so that the information may be made immediately available for processing when it is needed. The memory unit also retains information that has already been processed until that information can be placed on output devices by the output unit. The memory unit is often called either *memory, primary memory* or *random access memory (RAM)*.

4. *Arithmetic and logic unit (ALU).* This is the "manufacturing" section of the computer. It is responsible for performing calculations such as addition, subtraction, multiplication and division. It contains the decision mechanisms that allow the computer, for example, to compare two items from the memory unit to determine whether or not they are equal.

5. *Central processing unit (CPU).* This is the "administrative" section of the computer. It is the computer's coordinator and is responsible for supervising the operation of the other sections. The CPU tells the input unit when information should be read into the memory unit, tells the ALU when information from the memory unit should be utilized in calculations and tells the output unit when to send information from the memory unit to certain output devices.

6. *Secondary storage unit.* This is the long-term, high-capacity "warehousing" section of the computer. Programs or data not being used by the other units are normally placed on secondary storage devices (such as disks) until they are needed, possibly hours, days, months or even years later. Information in secondary storage takes longer to access than information in primary memory. The cost per unit of secondary storage is much less than the cost per unit of primary memory.

1.4 Evolution of Operating Systems

Early computers were capable of performing only one *job* or *task* at a time. This form of computer operation is often called single-user *batch processing.* The computer runs a single program at a time while processing data in groups or *batches.* In these early systems, users generally submitted their jobs to the computer center on decks of punched cards. Users often had to wait hours or even days before printouts were returned to their desks.

Software systems called *operating systems* were developed to help make it more convenient to use computers. Early operating systems managed the smooth transition between jobs. This minimized the time it took for computer operators to switch between jobs, and hence increased the amount of work, or *throughput,* computers could process.

As computers became more powerful, it became evident that single-user batch processing rarely utilized the computer's resources efficiently. Instead, it was thought that many jobs or tasks could be made to *share* the resources of the computer to achieve better utilization. This is called *multiprogramming.* Multiprogramming involves the "simultaneous" operation of many jobs on the computer—the computer shares its resources among the jobs competing for its attention. With early multiprogramming operating systems, users still submitted jobs on decks of punched cards and waited hours or days for results.

In the 1960s, several groups in industry and the universities pioneered *timesharing* operating systems. Timesharing is a special case of multiprogramming in which users access the computer through *terminals*, typically devices with keyboards and screens. In a typical timesharing computer system, there may be dozens or even hundreds of users sharing the computer at once. The computer does not actually run all the users' jobs simultaneously. Rather, it runs a small portion of one user's job and then moves on to service the next user. The computer does this so quickly that it may provide service to each user several times per second. Thus the users' programs *appear* to be running simultaneously. An advantage of timesharing is that the user receives almost immediate responses to requests rather than having to wait long periods for results as with previous modes of computing. Also, if a particular user is currently idle, the computer can continue to service other users rather than wait for one user.

1.5 Personal, Distributed and Client/Server Computing

In 1977, Apple Computer popularized the phenomenon of *personal computing.* Initially, it was a hobbyist's dream. Computers became economical enough for people to buy them for their own personal use. In 1981, IBM, the world's largest computer vendor, introduced the IBM Personal Computer. Almost overnight, personal computing became legitimate in business, industry and government organizations.

But these computers were "stand-alone" units—people did their work on their own machines and then transported disks back and forth to share information. Although early personal computers were not powerful enough to timeshare several users, these machines could be linked together in computer networks, sometimes over telephone lines and sometimes in *local area networks (LANs)* within an organization. This led to the phenomenon of *distributed computing,* in which an organization's computing, instead of being performed strictly at some central computer installation, is distributed over networks to the sites at which the real work of the organization is performed. Personal computers were powerful enough to handle the computing requirements of individual users, and to handle the basic communications tasks of passing information back and forth electronically.

Today's most powerful personal computers are as powerful as the million dollar machines of just a decade ago. The most powerful desktop machines—called *workstations*—provide individual users with enormous capabilities. Information is easily shared across computer networks where some computers called *file servers* offer a common store of programs and data that may be used by *client* computers distributed throughout the network, hence the term *client/server computing.* C and C++ have become the programming languages of choice for writing software for operating systems, for computer networking and for distributed client/server applications. Java is rapidly becoming the language of choice for developing Internet-based applications; many programmers have discovered that programming in Java helps them be more productive than programming in C or C++. Today's popular operating systems such as UNIX, Linux, OS/2, MacOS, Windows and Windows NT provide the kinds of capabilities discussed in this section.

1.6 Machine Languages, Assembly Languages and High-Level Languages

Programmers write instructions in various programming languages, some directly understandable by the computer and others that require intermediate *translation* steps. Hundreds of computer languages are in use today. These may be divided into three general types:

1. Machine languages

2. Assembly languages

3. High-level languages

Any computer can directly understand only its own *machine language.* Machine language is the "natural language" of a particular computer. It is defined by the hardware design of that computer. Machine languages generally consist of strings of numbers (ultimately reduced to 1s and 0s) that instruct computers to perform their most elementary operations one at a time. Machine languages are *machine dependent* (i.e., a particular machine language can be used on only one type of computer). Machine languages are cumbersome for humans, as can be seen by the following section of a machine-language program that adds overtime pay to base pay and stores the result in gross pay.

```
+1300042774
+1400593419
+1200274027
```

As computers became more popular, it became apparent that machine-language programming was simply too slow and tedious for most programmers. Instead of using the strings of numbers that computers could directly understand, programmers began using English-like abbreviations to represent the elementary operations of the computer. These English-like abbreviations formed the basis of *assembly languages. Translator programs* called *assemblers* were developed to convert assembly-language programs to machine language at computer speeds. The following section of an assembly-language program also adds overtime pay to base pay and stores the result in gross pay, but more clearly than its machine-language equivalent.

```
LOAD  BASEPAY
ADD   OVERPAY
STORE GROSSPAY
```

Although such code is clearer to humans, it is incomprehensible to computers until translated to machine language.

Computer usage increased rapidly with the advent of assembly languages, but programming in these still required many instructions to accomplish even the simplest tasks. To speed the programming process, *high-level languages* were developed in which single statements could be written to accomplish substantial tasks. The translator programs that convert high-level language programs into machine language are called *compilers.* High-level languages allow programmers to write instructions that look almost like everyday English and contain commonly used mathematical notations. A payroll program written in a high-level language might contain a statement such as:

```
grossPay = basePay + overTimePay
```

Obviously, high-level languages are much more desirable from the programmer's standpoint than either machine languages or assembly languages. C, C++ and Java are among the most powerful and most widely used high-level programming languages.

The process of compiling a high-level language program into machine language can take a considerable amount of computer time. *Interpreter* programs were developed to directly execute high-level language programs without the need for compiling those programs into machine language. Although compiled programs execute much faster than interpreted programs, interpreters are popular in program development environments in which programs are recompiled frequently as new features are added and errors are corrected. Once a program is developed, a compiled version can be produced to run most efficiently. As we study Java, you will see that interpreters have played an especially important part in helping Java achieve its goal of portability across a great variety of platforms.

1.7 History of C++

C++ evolved from C which evolved from two previous languages, BCPL and B. BCPL was developed in 1967 by Martin Richards as a language for writing operating systems software and compilers. Ken Thompson modeled many features in his language B after their counterparts in BCPL and used B to create early versions of the UNIX operating system at Bell Laboratories in 1970 on a Digital Equipment Corporation PDP-7 computer. Both BCPL and B were "typeless" languages—every data item occupied one "word" in memory. For example, it was the programmer's responsibility to treat a data item as a whole number or a real number.

The C language was evolved from B by Dennis Ritchie at Bell Laboratories and was originally implemented on a DEC PDP-11 computer in 1972. C uses many important concepts of BCPL and B while adding data typing and other features. C initially became widely known as the development language of the UNIX operating system. Today, virtually all new major operating systems are written in C and/or C++. Over the past two decades, C has become available for most computers. C is hardware independent. With careful design, it is possible to write C programs that are *portable* to most computers.

By the late 1970s, C had evolved into what is now referred to as "traditional C," or "Kernighan and Ritchie C." The publication by Prentice Hall in 1978 of Kernighan and Ritchie's book, *The C Programming Language,* brought wide attention to the language. This publication became one of the most successful computer science books ever.

The widespread use of C with various types of computers (sometimes called *hardware platforms*) led to many variations. These were similar, but often incompatible. This was a serious problem for programmers who needed to write portable programs that would run on several platforms. It became clear that a standard version of C was needed. In 1983, the X3J11 technical committee was created under the American National Standards Committee on Computers and Information Processing (X3) to "provide an unambiguous and machine-independent definition of the language." In 1989, the standard was approved. ANSI cooperated with the International Standards Organization (ISO) to standardize C worldwide; the joint standard document was published in 1990 and is referred to as ANSI/ISO 9899: 1990. The second edition of Kernighan and Ritchie, published in 1988, reflects this version called ANSI C, a version of the language now used worldwide (Ke88).

C++, an extension of C, was developed by Bjarne Stroustrup in the early 1980s at Bell Laboratories. C++ provides a number of features that "spruce up" the C language, but more important, it provides capabilities for *object-oriented programming*. C++ was recently standardized by the ANSI and ISO committees.

There is a revolution brewing in the software community. Building software quickly, correctly and economically remains an elusive goal, and this at a time when demands for new and more powerful software are soaring. *Objects* are essentially reusable software *components* that model items in the real world. Software developers are discovering that using a modular, object-oriented design and implementation approach can make software development groups much more productive than is possible with previous popular programming techniques such as structured programming. Object-oriented programs are often easier to understand, correct and modify.

Many other object-oriented languages have been developed, including Smalltalk, developed at Xerox's Palo Alto Research Center (PARC). Smalltalk is a pure object-oriented language—literally everything is an object. C++ is a hybrid language—it is possible to program in either a C-like style, an object-oriented style or both.

1.8 History of Java

Perhaps the microprocessor revolution's most important contribution to date is that it made possible the development of personal computers which may soon number 300 million worldwide. Personal computers have had a profound impact on people and the way organizations conduct and manage their business.

Many people believe that the next major area in which microprocessors will have a profound impact is in intelligent consumer electronic devices. Recognizing this, Sun Microsystems funded an internal corporate research project code-named Green in 1991. The project resulted in the development of a C and C++ based language which its creator, James Gosling, called Oak after an oak tree outside his window at Sun. It was later discovered that there already was a computer language called Oak. When a group of Sun people visited a local coffee place, the name Java was suggested and it stuck.

But the Green project ran into some difficulties. The marketplace for intelligent consumer electronic devices was not developing as quickly as Sun had anticipated. Worse yet, a major contract for which Sun competed was awarded to another company. So the project was in danger of being canceled. By sheer good fortune, the World Wide Web exploded in popularity in 1993 and Sun people saw the immediate potential of using Java to create Web pages with so-called *dynamic content*. This breathed new life into the project.

Sun formally announced Java at a major conference in May 1995. Ordinarily, an event like this would not have generated much attention. However, Java generated immediate interest in the business community because of the phenomenal interest in the World Wide Web. Java is now used to create Web pages with dynamic and interactive content, to develop large-scale enterprise applications, to enhance the functionality of World Wide Web servers (the computers that provide the content we see in our Web browsers), to provide applications for consumer devices (such as cell phones, pagers and personal digital assistants), and so on.

1.9 Java Class Libraries

Java programs consist of pieces called *classes*. Classes consist of pieces called *methods* that perform tasks and return information when they complete their tasks. You can program each piece you may need to form a Java program. But most Java programmers take advantage of rich collections of existing classes in *Java class libraries*. The class libraries are also known as the *Java APIs (Applications Programming Interfaces)*. Thus, there are really two pieces to learning the Java "world." The first is learning the Java language itself so that you can program your own classes and the second is learning how to use the classes in the extensive Java class libraries. Throughout the book we discuss many library classes. Class libraries are provided primarily by compiler vendors, but many class libraries are supplied by independent software vendors. Also, many class libraries are available from the Internet and World Wide Web as *shareware* (products you can download for a small fee) and *freeware* (products you can download for free).

Software Engineering Observation 1.1

Use a building block approach to creating programs. Avoid reinventing the wheel. Use existing pieces—this is called software reuse *and it is central to object-oriented programming.*

[Note: We will include many of these observations throughout the text to explain concepts that affect and improve the overall architecture and quality of a software system, and particularly, of large software systems. We will also highlight *Good Programming Practices* (practices that can help you write programs that are clearer, more understandable, more maintainable, and easier to test and debug), *Common Programming Errors* (problems to watch out for so you do not make these same errors in your programs), *Performance Tips* (techniques that will help you write programs that run faster and use less memory), *Portability Tips* (techniques that will help you write programs that can run, with little or no modifications, on a variety of computers; these tips also include general observations about how Java achieves its high degree of portability), *Testing and Debugging Tips* (techniques that will help you remove bugs from your programs, and more important, techniques that will help you write bug-free programs to begin with) and *Look and Feel Observations* (techniques that will help you design the "look" and "feel" of your graphical user interfaces for appearance and ease of use). Many of these techniques and practices are only guidelines; you will, no doubt, develop your own preferred programming style.]

Software Engineering Observation 1.2

When programming in Java you will typically use the following building blocks: classes from class libraries, classes and methods you create yourself, and classes and methods other people create and make available to you.

The advantage of creating your own classes and methods is that you will know exactly how they work. You will be able to examine the Java code. The disadvantage is the time-consuming and complex effort that goes into designing and developing new classes and methods.

Performance Tip 1.1

Using library classes and methods instead of writing your own versions can improve program performance because these classes and methods are carefully written to perform efficiently.

Portability Tip 1.1

Using library classes and methods instead of writing your own versions can improve program portability because these classes and methods are included in virtually all Java implementations.

Software Engineering Observation 1.3

Extensive class libraries of reusable software components are available over the Internet and the World Wide Web. Many of these libraries are available at no charge.

1.10 Other High-Level Languages

Hundreds of high-level languages have been developed, but only a few have achieved broad acceptance. *Fortran* (FORmula TRANslator) was developed by IBM Corporation between 1954 and 1957 to be used for scientific and engineering applications that require complex mathematical computations. Fortran is still widely used.

COBOL (COmmon Business Oriented Language) was developed in 1959 by a group of computer manufacturers and government and industrial computer users. COBOL is used primarily for commercial applications that require precise and efficient manipulation of large amounts of data. Today, about half of all business software is still programmed in COBOL. Approximately one million people are actively writing COBOL programs.

Pascal was designed at about the same time as C. It was created by Professor Nicklaus Wirth and was intended for academic use. We say more about Pascal in the next section.

Basic was developed in 1965 at Dartmouth University as a simple language to help novices become comfortable with programming. *Bill Gates* implemented Basic on several early personal computers. Today, *Microsoft*—the company Bill Gates created—is the world's leading software development organization.

1.11 Structured Programming

During the 1960s, many large software development efforts encountered severe difficulties. Software schedules were typically late, costs greatly exceeded budgets, and the finished products were unreliable. People began to realize that software development was a far more complex activity than they had imagined. Research activity in the 1960s resulted in the evolution of *structured programming*—a disciplined approach to writing programs that are clearer than unstructured programs, easier to test and debug, and easier to modify. Chapter 4 and 5 discuss the principles of structured programming.

One of the more tangible results of this research was the development of the Pascal programming language by Nicklaus Wirth in 1971. Pascal, named after the seventeenth-century mathematician and philosopher Blaise Pascal, was designed for teaching structured programming in academic environments and rapidly became the preferred programming language in most universities. Unfortunately, the language lacks many features needed to make it useful in commercial, industrial and government applications, so it has not been widely accepted in these environments.

The Ada programming language was developed under the sponsorship of the United States Department of Defense (DOD) during the 1970s and early 1980s. Hundreds of separate languages were being used to produce DOD's massive command-and-control software systems. DOD wanted a single language that would fulfill most of its needs. Pascal was chosen as a base, but the final Ada language is quite different from Pascal. The language was named after Lady Ada Lovelace, daughter of the poet Lord Byron. Lady Lovelace is generally credited with writing the world's first computer program in the early 1800s (for the Analytical Engine mechanical computing device designed by Charles Babbage).

One important capability of Ada is called *multitasking;* this allows programmers to specify that many activities are to occur in parallel. The other widely used high-level languages we have discussed—including C and C++—generally allow the programmer to write programs that perform only one activity at a time. Java, through a technique we will explain called *multithreading*, also enables programmers to write programs with parallel activities.

1.12 The Internet and the World Wide Web

The *Internet* was developed more than three decades ago with funding supplied by the Department of Defense. Originally designed to connect the main computer systems of about a dozen universities and research organizations, the Internet today is accessible by hundreds of millions of computers worldwide.

With the introduction of the *World Wide Web*—that allows computer users to locate and view multimedia-based documents on almost any subject—the Internet has literally exploded into what seems certain to become the world's premier communication mechanism.

As we enter the next millennium, the Internet and the World Wide Web will surely be listed among the most important and profound creations of humankind. In the past, most computer applications ran on computers that were not connected to one another. Today's applications can be written to communicate among the world's hundreds of millions of computers. The Internet mixes computing and communications technologies. It makes our work easier. It makes information instantly and conveniently accessible worldwide. It makes it possible for individuals and local small businesses to get worldwide exposure. It is changing the nature of the way business is done. People can search for the best prices on virtually any product or service. Special-interest communities can stay in touch with one another. Researchers can be made instantly aware of the latest breakthroughs worldwide.

Java How to Program: Third Edition presents several chapters of programming techniques that allow Java applications to use the Internet and World Wide Web to interact with other applications and with databases. These capabilities allow Java programmers to develop the enterprise-level distributed applications used in industry today. Java applications can be written to execute on any computer platform, yielding major savings in systems development time and cost for corporations. If you have been hearing a great deal about the Internet and World Wide Web lately, and if you are interested in developing applications to run over the Internet and the Web, learning Java may be the key to challenging and rewarding career opportunities for you.

1.13 Basics of a Typical Java Environment

Java systems generally consist of several parts: an environment, the language, the Java Applications Programming Interface (API), and various class libraries. The following discussion explains a typical Java program development environment as shown in Fig. 1.1.

Java programs normally go through five phases to be executed (Fig. 1.1). These are: *edit, compile, load, verify* and *execute.* If you are not using UNIX, Windows 95/98 or Windows NT, refer to the manuals for your system's Java environment, or ask your instructor how to accomplish these tasks in your environment (that will probably be similar to the environment in Fig. 1.1).

Phase 1 consists of editing a file. This is accomplished with an *editor program.* The programmer types a Java program using the editor and makes corrections if necessary. When the programmer specifies that the file in the editor should be saved, the program is stored on a secondary storage device such as a disk. Java program file names end with the **.java** *extension.* Two editors widely used on UNIX systems are **vi** and **emacs**. On Windows 95/98 and Windows NT simple edit programs like the DOS Edit command and the Windows Notepad will suffice. Java integrated development environments (IDEs) such as NetBeans, Borland's JBuilder, Symantec's Visual Cafe and Microsoft's Visual J++ have built-in editors that are smoothly integrated into the programming environment. We assume the reader knows how to edit a file.

[Note that the NetBeans IDE is written in Java and is free for non-commercial use. It is included on the CD-ROM accompanying this book and can also be downloaded from

http://www.netbeans.com

NetBeans executes on most major platforms. This book is written for any generic Java 2 development environment. It is not dependent on NetBeans. Our example programs should operate properly on most Java integrated development environments.]

In Phase 2 (discussed again in Chapters 2 and 3), the programmer gives the command **javac** to *compile* the program. The Java compiler translates the Java program into *byte-codes*—the language understood by the Java interpreter. To compile a program called **Welcome.java**, type

javac Welcome.java

at the command window of your system (i.e., the MS-DOS prompt in Windows 95/98 and Windows NT or the shell prompt in UNIX). If the program compiles correctly, a file called **Welcome.class** is produced. This is the file containing the bytecodes that will be interpreted during the execution phase.

Phase 3 is called *loading.* The program must first be placed in memory before it can be executed. This is done by the *class loader,* which takes the **.class** file (or files) containing the bytecodes and transfers it to memory. The **.class** file can be loaded from a disk on your system or over a network (such as your local university or company network or even the Internet). There are two types of programs for which the class loader loads **.class** files—*applications* and *applets.* An application is a program such as a word processor program, a spreadsheet program, a drawing program, an email program, etc. that is normally stored and executed from the user's local computer. An applet is a small program that is normally stored on a remote computer that users connect to via a World Wide Web browser. Applets are loaded from a remote computer into the browser, executed in the browser and discarded when execution completes. To execute an applet again, the user must point their browser at the appropriate location on the World Wide Web and reload the program into the browser.

Applications are loaded into memory and executed using the *Java interpreter* via the command **java**. When executing a Java application called **Welcome**, the command

java Welcome

invokes the interpreter for the **Welcome** application and causes the class loader to load information used in the **Welcome** program.

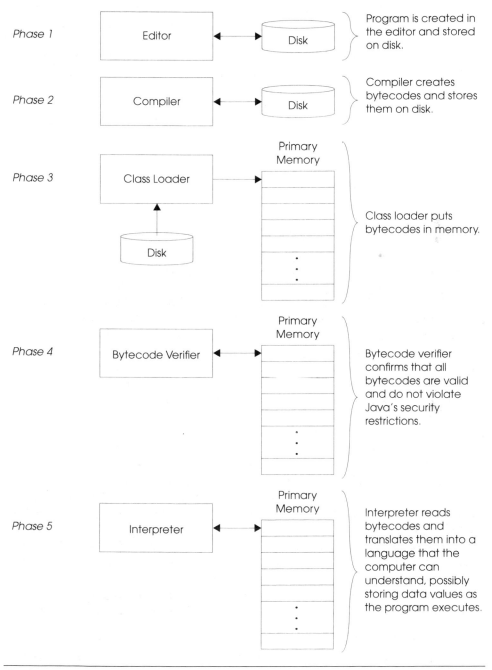

Fig. 1.1   A typical Java environment.

The class loader also is executed when a Java applet is loaded into a World Wide Web browser such as *Netscape's Communicator*, *Microsoft's Internet Explorer* or *Sun's Hot-Java*. Browsers are used to view documents on the World Wide Web called *HTML* (*Hypertext Markup Language*) documents. HTML is used to format a document in a manner that is easily understood by the browser application (we will introduce HTML in Section 3.4; for a detailed treatment of HTML and other Internet programming technologies, please see our text *Internet and World Wide Web How to Program*). An HTML document may refer to a Java applet. When the browser sees an applet referenced in an HTML document, the browser launches the Java class loader to load the applet (normally from the location where the HTML document is stored). Browsers that support Java each have a built-in Java interpreter. Once the applet is loaded, the browser's Java interpreter executes the applet. Applets can also be executed from the command line using the **appletviewer** *command* provided with the J2SDK—the set of tools including the compiler (**javac**), interpreter (**java**), **appletviewer** and other tools used by Java programmers. Like Netscape Communicator, Internet Explorer and HotJava, the **appletviewer** requires an HTML document to invoke an applet. For example, if the **Welcome.html** file refers to the **Welcome** applet, the **appletviewer** command is used as follows:

```
appletviewer Welcome.html
```

This causes the class loader to load the information used in the **Welcome** applet. The **appletviewer** is commonly referred to as the minimum browser—it only knows how to interpret applets.

Before the bytecodes in an applet are executed by the Java interpreter built into a browser or the **appletviewer**, they are verified by the *bytecode verifier* in Phase 4 (this also happens in applications that download bytecodes from a network). This ensures that the bytecodes for classes that are loaded from the Internet (referred to as *downloaded classes*) are valid and that they do not violate Java's security restrictions. Java enforces strong security because Java programs arriving over the network should not be able to cause damage to your files and your system (as computer viruses might).

Finally, in Phase 5, the computer, under the control of its CPU, interprets the program one bytecode at a time, thus performing the actions specified by the program.

Programs may not work on the first try. Each of the preceding phases can fail because of various errors that we will discuss in this text. For example, an executing program might attempt to divide by zero (an illegal operation in Java just as it is in arithmetic). This would cause the Java program to print an error message. The programmer would return to the edit phase, make the necessary corrections and proceed through the remaining phases again to determine if the corrections work properly.

Common Programming Error 1.1

Errors like division-by-zero errors occur as a program runs, so these errors are called run-time errors *or* execution-time errors. *Fatal run-time errors* cause programs to terminate immediately without having successfully performed their jobs. *Nonfatal run-time errors* allow programs to run to completion, often producing incorrect results.

Most programs in Java input and/or output data. When we say that a program prints a result, we normally mean that the result is displayed on a screen. Data may be output to other devices such as disks and hardcopy printers.

1.14 General Notes about Java and This Book

Java is a powerful language. Experienced programmers sometimes take pride in being able to create some weird, contorted, convoluted usage of a language. This is a poor programming practice. It makes programs more difficult to read, more likely to behave strangely, more difficult to test and debug, and more difficult to adapt to changing requirements. This book is also geared for novice programmers, so we stress *clarity*. The following is our first "good programming practice."

Good Programming Practice 1.1

Write your Java programs in a simple and straightforward manner. This is sometimes referred to as KIS *("keep it simple"). Do not "stretch" the language by trying bizarre usages.*

You have heard that Java is a portable language, and that programs written in Java can run on many different computers. *Portability is an elusive goal.* The ANSI C standard document (An90) contains a lengthy list of portability issues, and complete books have been written that discuss portability (Ja89) (Ra90).

Portability Tip 1.2

Although it is easier to write portable programs in Java than in most other programming languages, there are differences among compilers, interpreters and computers that can make portability difficult to achieve. Simply writing programs in Java does not guarantee portability. The programmer will occasionally need to deal directly with compiler and computer variations.

Testing and Debugging Tip 1.1

Always test your Java programs on all systems on which you intend to run those programs.

We have done a careful walkthrough of Sun's Java documentation and audited our presentation against it for completeness and accuracy. However, Java is a rich language, and there are some subtleties in the language and some topics we have not covered. If you need additional technical details on Java, we suggest that you read the most current Java documentation available over the Internet at **http://java.sun.com**. Our book contains an extensive bibliography of books and papers on the Java language in particular and on object-oriented programming in general.

Good Programming Practice 1.2

Read the documentation for the version of Java you are using. Refer to this documentation frequently to be sure you are aware of the rich collection of Java features and that you are using these features correctly.

Good Programming Practice 1.3

Your computer and compiler are good teachers. If after carefully reading your Java documentation manual you are not sure how a feature of Java works, experiment and see what happens. Study each error or warning message you get when you compile your programs and correct the programs to eliminate these messages.

In this book we explain how Java works in its current implementations. Perhaps the most striking problem with the early versions of Java is that Java programs execute interpretively on the client's machine. Interpreters execute slowly compared to fully compiled machine code.

Performance Tip 1.2

Interpreters have an advantage over compilers for the Java world, namely that an interpreted program can begin execution immediately as soon as it is downloaded to the client's machine, whereas a source program to be compiled must first suffer a potentially long delay as the program is compiled before it can be executed.

Although only Java interpreters were available to execute bytecodes at the client's site on early Java systems, Java compilers have been written for most popular platforms. These compilers take the Java bytecodes (or in some cases the Java source code) and compile them into the native machine code of the client's machine. These compiled programs perform comparably to compiled C or C++ code. Because there are not compilers for every Java platform, Java programs will not perform at the same level on all platforms.

Applets present some more interesting issues. Remember, an applet could be coming from virtually any *Web server* in the world. So the applet will have to be able to run on any possible Java platform. Short, fast-executing Java applets can certainly still be interpreted. But what about more substantial, compute-intensive applets. Here the user may be willing to suffer the compilation delay to get better execution performance. For some especially performance-intensive applets the user may have no choice; interpreted code would run too slowly for the applet to perform properly, so the applet would have to be compiled.

An intermediate step between interpreters and compilers is a *just-in-time (JIT) compiler* that, as the interpreter runs, produces compiled code for the programs and executes the programs in machine language rather than reinterpreting them. JIT compilers do not produce machine language that is as efficient as a full compiler. Full compilers for Java are under development now. For the latest information on high-speed Java program translation you may want to read about Sun's *HotSpot* compiler, visit

http://java.sun.com/products/hotspot/

For organizations wanting to do heavy-duty information systems development, Integrated Development Environments (IDEs) are available from the major software suppliers. The IDEs provide many tools for supporting the software development process. Several Java IDEs on the market today are just as powerful as those available for C and C++ systems development. This is a strong signal that Java has been accepted as a viable language for developing substantial software systems.

Sun's Java Database Connectivity (JDBC) standard is intended for people developing industrial-strength database applications. JDBC makes Java effective for developing enterprise information systems.

1.15 A Tour of the Book

You are about to study one of today's most exciting and rapidly developing computer programming languages. Mastering Java will help you develop powerful business and personal computer applications software. In this section we take a tour of the many capabilities of Java you will study in *Java How to Program: Third Edition*.

Chapter 1: Introduction to Computers, the Internet and the World Wide Web
In Chapter 1, we present some historical information about computers and computer programming, and introductory information about Java, the Internet and World Wide Web. We

overview the several tools provided with Sun's Java 2 Software Development Kit (J2SDK). We also present an overview of the remaining chapters in the book.

Chapter 2: Introduction to Java Applications

In Chapter 2, we present our first Java programs. The book uses a technique we call the *live-code approach*. Every concept is presented in the context of a complete working Java program which is immediately followed by the screen output produced when that program is executed on a computer. With Java you can write two kinds of programs: namely, *applets,* designed to be transported over the Internet and executed in World Wide Web browsers like Netscape Communicator, Microsoft's Internet Explorer and Sun's HotJava, and stand-alone *applications,* which are stored on your own computer and are designed to execute independent of a World Wide Web browser. This chapter concentrates on several basic applications. By the end of this chapter you will be writing Java applications that can display information on the screen for the user and input information from the user at the keyboard.

Chapter 3: Introduction to Java Applets

In Chapter 3, we present *applets,* which are designed to be transported over the Internet and executed in World Wide Web browsers. This chapter introduces applets by mimicking several examples from Chapter 2 so you can compare and contrast the two approaches. Because of the flexibility of working with applets as you learn Java, we use many applets in the early chapters. However, the book focuses on Java application development once the fundamental concepts are presented. In Chapters 2 and 3 (and throughout the book), we introduce various graphical user interface (GUI) components. These and other GUI components are discussed in detail in Chapters 12 and 13.

Chapter 4: Control Structures: Part 1

In Chapter 4, we focus on the program development process. The chapter discusses how to take a *problem statement* (i.e., a *requirements document*) and from it develop a working Java program. The chapter introduces some fundamental data types and some simple control structures used for decision making.

Chapter 5: Control Structures: Part 2

Chapter 5 discusses much of the material Java has in common with C, especially the sequence, selection and repetition control structures. The chapter uses flowcharts to show the flow of control through each of the control structures. The chapter concludes with a structured programming summary that enumerates each of the control structures. The techniques discussed in Chapters 4 and 5 constitute a large part of what has been traditionally taught in the universities under the topic of structured programming. With Java we seek to do object-oriented programming. We will discover that the insides of objects can make abundant use of control structures.

Chapter 6: Methods

In Chapter 6, we take a deeper look inside objects. Objects contain data that we will generally refer to as *instance variables*, and executable units called *methods* (often called *functions* in non-object-oriented, procedural programming languages like C). We explore methods in depth and include a discussion of *recursive methods*, i.e., methods that (strangely) call themselves. We enhance our graphical user interface (GUI) discussions to illustrate how to create *buttons* and *text fields* and attach them to applets. We also begin our discussions of *event-driven programming*—causing a program to perform a task in response to user interactions with GUI components. The GUI techniques introduced here are used in applications starting in Chapter 9.

Chapter 7: Arrays

Chapter 7 explores the processing of data in lists and tables of values called *arrays*. Arrays in Java are processed as objects, further evidence of Java's commitment to almost 100% object orientation.

Chapter 8: Object-Based Programming

Chapter 8 focuses on the essence and terminology of objects. What is an object? What is a class of objects? What does the inside of an object look like? How are objects created? How are they destroyed? How do objects communicate with one another? Why are classes such a natural mechanism for packaging software as reusable componentry? We begin defining applications that execute in their own windows that have a variety of GUI components attached to them.

Chapter 9: Object-Oriented Programming

Chapter 9 discusses the relationships among classes of objects and programming with related classes. How can we exploit commonality between classes of objects to minimize the amount of work it takes to build large software systems? What does it mean to "program in the general" rather than "programming in the specific"? How does programming in the general make it easy to modify software systems and add new features with minimal effort? How can we program for a whole category of objects rather than programming individually for each type of object? This chapter introduces applications that execute in their own window (**JFrame**). Such an application can have its own graphical user interface (as designed by the programmer). In this context, the chapter demonstrates *inner classes* and continues our discussion of event handling.

Chapter 10: Strings and Characters

Chapter 10 deals with the processing of words, sentences, characters and groups of characters. The key difference between Java and C here is that Java strings are objects, thus making string manipulation more convenient than in C, but more important, safer than in C, where string manipulation, like array manipulation, is based on dangerous pointers.

Chapter 11: Graphics and Java2D

Chapter 11 begins to introduce the multimedia "sizzle" of Java. Traditional C and C++ programming are pretty much confined to character mode input/output. Some versions of C++ are supported by platform-dependent class libraries that can do graphics, but using one of these libraries makes your applications nonportable. The beauty of Java's graphics capabilities is that they are platform independent and hence, portable.

Chapter 12: Basic Graphical User Interface Components
Chapter 13: Advanced Graphical User Interface Components

Chapter 12 introduces the creation of applets and applications with user-friendly graphical user interfaces (GUIs). Chapter 13 continues the discussion started in Chapter 12. Once again, the key to Java's treatment of these subjects is platform independence. A GUI-based applet or application developed once will run on all Java platforms. This text focuses on

Swing GUI components. These *platform-independent GUI components* are written completely in Java. This provides the Swing GUI components with unparalleled flexibility—the GUI components can be customized to look like the user interface components of the computer platform on which the program executes, or they can use the standard *Java look-and-feel* that provides an identical user interface across all computer platforms.

Chapter 14: Exception Handling
Chapter 14 is one of the most important chapters in the book from the standpoint of building so-called mission-critical or business-critical applications. Things do go wrong, and in fact at today's computer speeds—commonly hundreds of millions of operations per second—if something can go wrong it probably will, and rather quickly at that. Programmers are often a bit naive about using prebuilt components. They ask, "How do I ask a component to do something for me?" They also ask "What value(s) does that component return to me to indicate it has performed the job I asked it to do?" But programmers also need to be concerned with, "What happens when the component I call upon to do a job for me experiences difficulty? How will that component signal to me that it had a problem?" In Java, when a component (i.e., a class object) encounters difficulty, it can "throw" an exception. The environment of that component is programmed to "catch" that exception and deal with it. Java's exception-handling capabilities are especially geared to an object-oriented world in which programmers construct software systems largely from reusable components built by other programmers. To use a Java component, you need to know not only how that component behaves when "things go well," but what exceptions that component throws when "things go poorly."

Chapter 15: Multithreading
Chapter 15 deals with how to program applets and applications that can perform multiple activities in parallel. Although our bodies are quite good at this (breathing, eating, blood circulation, vision, hearing, etc. can all occur in parallel), our conscious minds have trouble with this. Computers used to be built with a single rather expensive processor. Today, processors are becoming so inexpensive that it is possible to build computers with many processors that work in parallel—such computers are called *multiprocessors*. The trend is clearly toward computers that can perform many tasks in parallel. Most of today's programming languages, including C and C++, do not include features for expressing parallel operations. These languages are often referred to as *sequential programming languages* or *single-thread-of-control languages*. Java includes capabilities to enable multithreaded applications (i.e., applications that can specify that multiple activities are to occur in parallel). This makes Java better prepared to deal with the more sophisticated multimedia, network-based multiprocessor-based applications that programmers will be introducing in the new millennium. As we will see, multithreading is even effective on single-processor systems.

Chapter 16: Multimedia: Images, Animation, Audio and Video
Chapter 16 deals with Java's capabilities for images, animation, audio and video, and introduces the *Java Media Player*. It is remarkable that students in first programming courses will be writing applications with all these capabilities. The possibilities are intriguing and endless. Imagine having access (over the Internet and through CD-ROM technology) to vast libraries of graphics images, audios and videos and being able to weave your own together with those in the libraries to form applications. Already more than half the new computers sold come multimedia equipped with CD readers and sound cards.

Chapter 17: Files and Streams
Chapter 18: Java Database Connectivity (JDBC)

The next two chapters introduce data processing in Java. Chapter 17 deals with input/output that is accomplished through streams of data directed from and to files. This is one of the most important chapters for programmers who will be developing commercial applications. How does a program pass data to a secondary storage device like a disk? How does a program retrieve data already stored on disk? What are sequential files? What are random access files? What is buffering and how does it help programs that do significant amounts of input/output perform better?

Chapter 18 discusses how Java can be used to access *relational databases*. Businesses today are driven by data and Java provides a variety of classes for manipulating database data. In this chapter we focus primarily on Java's ability to use JDBC (Java Database Connectivity) to connect to a Microsoft ODBC (Open Database Connectivity) data source through the *JDBC-to-ODBC bridge*. The examples in the chapter use a sample Microsoft Access database, **Books.mdb**, that contains information about several of our textbooks. For accessing the database, we provide an overview of *Structured Query Language (SQL)*.

Chapter 19: Servlets
Chapter 20: Remote Method Invocation (RMI)
Chapter 21: Networking

The next three chapters explain how to write programs that can communicate over computer networks. What is a client? What is a server? How do clients ask servers to perform their services? How do servers give results back to clients? What is a URL (uniform resource locator)? How can a program load World Wide Web pages? How can Java be used to develop collaborative applications? Our discussion of networking over these chapters focuses on both sides of a *client-server relationship*. The *client* requests that an action be performed and the *server* performs the action and responds to the client. This request-response model of communication is the foundation for the highest-level networking in Java—*servlets*.

Chapter 19 discusses networking with the commonly used *request-response networking model* in which World Wide Web browsers communicate with World Wide Web servers as users browse the Internet. When a user selects a Web site to browse through a Web browser (the client application), a request is sent to the appropriate Web server (the server application) which normally responds to the client by sending the appropriate HTML Web page to be displayed by the client's browser. In this networking model, the communication between the client and the server is handled automatically. The chapter begins our discussions of *multi-tier distributed applications* in which parts of the applications operate on separate computers distributed over a network. This chapter makes use of the streams technology of Chapter 17 and the database technology of Chapter 18 as we begin to build real-world applications in Java.

Chapter 20 takes a lower-level approach to writing programs that can communicate over computer networks and continues our discussion of multi-tier applications. RMI enables Java programs to communicate with each other via method calls that are automatically sent across the network. RMI is a more complex view of networking than servlets in that RMI requires more work on the part of the programmer to set up the initial interactions between applications. Once the mechanism is in place, the communication over the network is transparent to the application. Once again, this chapter makes use of the streams technology discussed in Chapter 17.

Chapter 21 introduces the lowest-level Java networking—streams-based sockets and datagram packets. We illustrate how to create simple clients and servers that deal with lower-level networking details. Here, too, Java still performs most of the complex networking tasks for you. Once again we rely on the streams technology of Chapter 17. The examples in this chapter illustrate an applet interacting with the browser in which it executes, creating a mini Web browser, communicating between two Java programs using streams-based sockets, communicating between two Java programs using packets of data and how to write a multithreaded server that can interact with more than one client at a time.

Chapter 22: Data Structures
Chapter 22 deals with arranging data elements into aggregations such as linked lists, stacks, queues and trees. Each data structure has important properties that are useful in a wide variety of applications. We discuss the details of building each of these data structures. This is a valuable experience in crafting useful classes, a crucial skill for Java programmers. Much of the value of this chapter is in general principles that are useful in implementing a wide variety of classes. Although it is useful to know how these classes work, Java programmers will quickly discover that most of the data structures they need are already available in class libraries such as Java's own **java.util** that we discuss in Chapters 23 and 24. Chapter 22 reinforces much of the class crafting technology discussed in Chapters 8 and 9 on object-based programming and object-oriented programming.

Chapter 23: Java Utilities Package and Bit Manipulation
Chapter 23 walks through several classes of the **java.util** package. This chapter reinforces the notion of reuse. Classes are included in class libraries because the classes are generally useful, correct, performance tuned, portability certified and/or for a variety of other reasons. Someone has invested considerable work in preparing these classes, so why not use them? Our belief is that the world's class libraries will grow exponentially over the next many years. If this is the case, then your skill and value as a programmer will depend on your familiarity with what classes already exist and how to reuse them cleverly to develop high-quality software rapidly. This chapter discusses many classes. Two of the most useful are **Vector** (a dynamic array that can grow and shrink as necessary) and **Stack** (a dynamic data structure that allows insertions and deletions from only one end—the *top*—thus ensuring last-in-first-out behavior). The beauty of studying these two classes is that they are related through inheritance as discussed in Chapter 9, so the **java.util** package itself implements some classes in terms of others, taking advantage of reuse.

Chapter 24: Collections
Chapter 24 discusses many of the new classes of the **java.util** package that provide pre-defined implementations of many of the data structures discussed in Chapter 22. This chapter, too, reinforces the notion of reuse. These classes are modeled after a similar class library in C++—the Standard Template Library. *Collections* provide Java programmers with a standard set of data structures for storing and retrieving data, and a standard set of algorithms (i.e., procedures) that allow programmers to manipulate the data (such as searching for particular data items and arranging data in order).

Chapter 25: JavaBeans
Chapter 25 discusses wrapping the Java classes you define as reusable software components. JavaBeans can be graphically manipulated and customized in Java program devel-

opment environments. The chapter introduces the *JavaBeans Development Kit (BDK)* and the *BeanBox* that can be used to test your *beans*. The BeanBox illustrates the key concepts of manipulating a bean in a typical graphical development environment. The chapter discusses design issues surrounding bean development. In addition, we illustrate how to wrap an application as a *Java Archive (JAR)* file so you can execute the application by double-clicking the name of the file in your system's file manager (a typical way to execute an application on many platforms).

Many readers will already have our interactive multimedia CD software version of *Java How to Program: Third Edition*. This Windows 95/98/NT-based software product is called the *Java Multimedia Cyber Classroom: Third Edition* and it accompanies this textbook in our Prentice Hall publication called *The Complete Java Training Course: Third Edition*. The *Java Multimedia Cyber Classroom* contains extensive interactivity features, including hyperlinking, text searching and audio walkthroughs of most of the code examples in *Java How to Program*. It also contains solutions to many of the exercises in the book. Ordering instructions for this CD product are given in the last few pages of this book.

Well, there you have it! We have worked hard to create this book and its optional Cyber Classroom version. The book is loaded with live-code examples, programming tips, self-review exercises and answers, challenging exercises and projects, and numerous study aids to help you master the material. Java is a powerful programming language that will help you write programs quickly and effectively. And Java is a language that scales nicely into the realm of enterprise systems development to help organizations build their key information systems. As you read the book, if something is not clear, or if you find an error, please write to us at **deitel@deitel.com**. We will respond promptly, and we will post corrections and clarifications on our Web site,

        http://www.deitel.com

We hope you enjoy learning with *Java How to Program: Third Edition* as much as we enjoyed writing it!

Summary

- Software controls computers (often referred to as hardware).

- Java is one of today's most popular software development languages.

- Java was developed by Sun Microsystems. Sun provides an implementation of the Java 2 Platform called the Java 2 Software Development Kit (J2SDK), version 1.2 that includes the minimum set of tools you need to write software in Java.

- Java is a fully object-oriented language with strong support for proper software engineering techniques.

- A computer is a device capable of performing computations and making logical decisions at speeds millions, and even billions, of times faster than human beings can.

- Computers process data under the control of sets of instructions called computer programs. These computer programs guide the computer through orderly sets of actions specified by people called computer programmers.

- The various devices (such as the keyboard, screen, disks, memory and processing units) that comprise a computer system are referred to as hardware.

- The computer programs that run on a computer are referred to as software.

- The input unit is the "receiving" section of the computer. It obtains information (data and computer programs) from various input devices and places this information at the disposal of the other units so that the information may be processed.

- The output unit is the "shipping" section of the computer. It takes information processed by the computer and places it on output devices to make it available for use outside the computer.

- The memory unit is the rapid access, relatively low-capacity "warehouse" section of the computer. It retains information that has been entered through the input unit so that the information may be made immediately available for processing when it is needed and retains information that has already been processed until that information can be placed on output devices by the output unit.

- The arithmetic and logic unit (ALU) is the "manufacturing" section of the computer. It is responsible for performing calculations such as addition, subtraction, multiplication and division, and making decisions.

- The central processing unit (CPU) is the "administrative" section of the computer. It is the computer's coordinator and is responsible for supervising the operation of the other sections.

- The secondary storage unit is the long-term, high-capacity "warehousing" section of the computer. Programs or data not being used by the other units are normally placed on secondary storage devices (such as disks) until they are needed, possibly hours, days, months or even years later.

- Early computers were capable of performing only one job or task at a time. This form of computer operation is often called single-user batch processing.

- Software systems called operating systems were developed to help make it more convenient to use computers. Early operating systems managed the smooth transition between jobs and minimized the time it took for computer operators to switch between jobs.

- Multiprogramming involves the "simultaneous" operation of many jobs on the computer—the computer shares its resources among the jobs competing for its attention.

- Timesharing is a special case of multiprogramming in which dozens or even hundreds of users share the computer through terminals. The computer runs a small portion of one user's job and then moves on to service the next user. The computer does this so quickly that it may provide service to each user several times per second, so users' programs appear to run simultaneously.

- An advantage of timesharing is that the user receives almost immediate responses to requests rather than having to wait long periods for results as with previous modes of computing.

- In 1977, Apple Computer popularized the phenomenon of personal computing.

- In 1981, IBM introduced the IBM Personal Computer. Almost overnight, personal computing became legitimate in business, industry and government organizations.

- Although early personal computers were not powerful enough to timeshare several users, these machines could be linked together in computer networks, sometimes over telephone lines and sometimes in local area networks (LANs) within an organization. This led to the phenomenon of distributed computing, in which an organization's computing is distributed over networks to the sites at which the real work of the organization is performed.

- Today, information is easily shared across computer networks where some computers called file servers offer a common store of programs and data that may be used by client computers distributed throughout the network, hence the term client/server computing.

- C and C++ have become the programming languages of choice for writing software for operating systems, for computer networking and for distributed client/server applications.

- Java is rapidly becoming the language of choice for developing Internet-based applications.

- Computer languages may be divided into three general types: machine languages, assembly languages and high-level languages.

- Any computer can directly understand only its own machine language. Machine languages generally consist of strings of numbers (ultimately reduced to 1s and 0s) that instruct computers to perform their most elementary operations one at a time. Machine languages are machine dependent.

- English-like abbreviations formed the basis of assembly languages. Translator programs called assemblers convert assembly-language programs to machine language at computer speeds.

- Compilers translate high-level language programs into machine language programs. High-level languages (like Java) contain English words and conventional mathematical notations.

- Interpreter programs directly execute high-level language programs without the need for compiling those programs into machine language.

- Although compiled programs execute much faster than interpreted programs, interpreters are popular in program development environments in which programs are recompiled frequently as new features are added and errors are corrected.

- Objects are essentially reusable software components that model items in the real world. Modular, object-oriented design and implementation approaches make software development groups more productive than is possible with previous popular programming techniques such as structured programming. Object-oriented programs are often easier to understand, correct and modify.

- Java originated at Sun Microsystems as a project for intelligent consumer electronic devices.

- When the World Wide Web exploded in popularity in 1993, Sun people saw the immediate potential of using Java to create Web pages with so-called dynamic content.

- Java is now used to create Web pages with dynamic and interactive content, to develop large-scale enterprise applications, to enhance the functionality of World Wide Web servers, to provide applications for consumer devices, and so on.

- Java programs consist of pieces called classes. Classes consist of pieces called methods that perform tasks and return information when they complete their tasks.

- Most Java programmers use rich collections of existing classes in Java class libraries.

- FORTRAN (FORmula TRANslator) was developed by IBM Corporation between 1954 and 1957 for scientific and engineering applications that require complex mathematical computations.

- COBOL (COmmon Business Oriented Language) was developed in 1959 by a group of computer manufacturers and government and industrial computer users. COBOL is used primarily for commercial applications that require precise and efficient manipulation of large amounts of data.

- Pascal was designed at about the same time as C. It was created by Professor Nicklaus Wirth and was intended for academic use.

- Basic was developed in 1965 at Dartmouth University as a simple language to help novices become comfortable with programming.

- Structured programming is a disciplined approach to writing programs that are clearer than unstructured programs, easier to test and debug, and easier to modify.

- The Ada language was developed under the sponsorship of the United States Department of Defense (DOD) during the 1970s and early 1980s. One important capability of Ada is called multitasking; this allows programmers to specify that many activities are to occur in parallel.

- Most high-level languages—including C and C++—generally allow the programmer to write programs that perform only one activity at a time. Java, through a technique called multithreading, enables programmers to write programs with parallel activities.

- The Internet was developed more than three decades ago with funding supplied by the Department of Defense. Originally designed to connect the main computer systems of about a dozen universities and research organizations, the Internet today is accessible by hundreds of millions of computers worldwide.

- The World Wide Web allows computer users to locate and view documents over the Internet.

- Java systems generally consist of several parts: an environment, the language, the Java Applications Programming Interface (API), and various class libraries.

- Java programs normally go through five phases to be executed—edit, compile, load, verify and execute.

- Java program file names end with the **.java** extension.

- The Java compiler (**javac**) translates a Java program into bytecodes—the language understood by the Java interpreter. If a program compiles correctly, a file with the **.class** extension is produced. This is the file containing the bytecodes that are interpreted during the execution phase.

- A Java program must first be placed in memory before it can be executed. This is done by the class loader, which takes the **.class** file (or files) containing the bytecodes and transfers it to memory. The **.class** file can be loaded from a disk on your system or over a network.

- An application is a program that is normally stored and executed from the user's local computer.

- An applet is a small program that is normally stored on a remote computer that users connect to via a World Wide Web browser. Applets are loaded from a remote computer into the browser, executed in the browser and discarded when execution completes.

- Applications are loaded into memory and executed using the **java** interpreter.

- Browsers are used to view documents on the World Wide Web called HTML (Hypertext Markup Language) documents.

- When the browser sees an applet in an HTML document, the browser launches the Java class loader to load the applet. The browsers that support Java each have a built-in Java interpreter. Once the applet is loaded, the Java interpreter in the browser begins executing the applet.

- Applets can also be executed from the command line using the **appletviewer** command provided with the Java 2 Software Development Kit (J2SDK). The **appletviewer** is commonly referred to as the minimum browser—it only knows how to interpret applets.

- Before the bytecodes in an applet are executed by the Java interpreter built into a browser or the **appletviewer**, they are verified by the bytecode verifier to ensure that the bytecodes for downloaded classes are valid and that they do not violate Java's security restrictions.

- An intermediate step between interpreters and compilers is a just-in-time (JIT) compiler that, as the interpreter runs, produces compiled code for the programs and executes the programs in machine language rather than reinterpreting them. JIT compilers do not produce machine language that is as efficient as a full compiler.

- For organizations wanting to do heavy-duty information systems development, Integrated Development Environments (IDEs) are available from the major software suppliers. The IDEs provide many tools for supporting the software development process.

Terminology

Ada	Basic
ALU (arithmetic and logic unit)	bytecodes
ANSI C	bytecode verifier
applet	C
appletviewer command	C standard library
application	C++
arithmetic and logic unit (ALU)	**.class** file
array	central processing unit (CPU)
assembly language	class

class libraries
class loader
client
client/server computing
collections
COBOL
compile phase
compile-time error
compiler
computer
computer program
computer programmer
condition
CPU (central processing unit)
disk
distributed computing
dynamic content
editor
edit phase
event-driven programming
execute phase
execution-time error
fatal run-time error
file server
Fortran
freeware
hardware
high-level language
HotSpot compiler
HTML (Hypertext Markup Language)
IDE (Integrated Development Environment)
input device
input/output (I/O)
input unit
instance variable
Internet
interpreter
Java
JavaBeans
javac compiler
.java extension
java interpreter
Java 2 Software Development Kit (J2SDK)
Java Virtual Machine
JDBC (Java Database Connectivity)
JIT (just-in-time) compiler
KIS (keep it simple)
legacy systems
live-code approach
load phase

logic error
machine dependent
machine independent
machine language
memory unit
method
Microsoft
Microsoft's Internet Explorer Web browser
multiprocessor
multitasking
multithreading
Netscape's Communicator Web browser
nonfatal run-time error
object
object-oriented design (OOD)
object-oriented programming (OOP)
output device
output unit
Pascal
personal computing
platforms
portability
primary memory
problem statement
procedural programming
programming language
reference
requirements document
reusable componentry
RMI (Remote Method Invocation)
run-time error
secondary storage unit
server
servlets
shareware
software
software reuse
structured programming
Sun Microsystems
Sun's HotJava Web browser
Swing GUI components
syntax error
throughput
throw an exception
timesharing
translator programs
verify phase
video
Web server
World Wide Web

Common Programming Error

1.1   Errors like division-by-zero errors occur as a program runs, so these errors are called run-time errors or execution-time errors. Fatal run-time errors cause programs to terminate immediately without having successfully performed their jobs. Nonfatal run-time errors allow programs to run to completion, often producing incorrect results.

Good Programming Practices

1.1   Write your Java programs in a simple and straightforward manner. This is sometimes referred to as *KIS* (*"keep it simple"*). Do not "stretch" the language by trying bizarre usages.

1.2   Read the documentation for the version of Java you are using. Refer to this documentation frequently to be sure you are aware of the rich collection of Java features and that you are using these features correctly.

1.3   Your computer and compiler are good teachers. If after carefully reading your Java documentation manual you are not sure how a feature of Java works, experiment and see what happens. Study each error or warning message you get when you compile your programs and correct these programs to eliminate the messages.

Performance Tips

1.1   Using library classes and methods instead of writing your own versions can improve program performance because these classes and methods are carefully written to perform efficiently.

1.2   Interpreters have an advantage over compilers for the Java world, namely that an interpreted program can begin execution immediately as soon as it is downloaded to the client's machine, whereas a source program to be compiled must first suffer a potentially long delay as the program is compiled before it can be executed.

Portability Tips

1.1   Using library classes and methods instead of writing your own versions can improve program portability because these classes and methods are included in virtually all Java implementations.

1.2   Although it is easier to write portable programs in Java than in most other programming languages, there are differences among compilers, interpreters and computers that can make portability difficult to achieve. Simply writing programs in Java does not guarantee portability. The programmer will occasionally need to deal directly with compiler and computer variations.

Software Engineering Observations

1.1   Use a building block approach to creating programs. Avoid reinventing the wheel. Use existing pieces—this is called *software reuse* and it is central to object-oriented programming.

1.2   When programming in Java you will typically use the following building blocks: classes from class libraries, classes and methods you create yourself, and classes and methods other people create and make available to you.

1.3   Extensive class libraries of reusable software components are available over the Internet and the World Wide Web. Many of these libraries are available at no charge.

Testing and Debugging Tip

1.1   Always test your Java programs on all systems on which you intend to run those programs.

Self-Review Exercises

1.1   Fill in the blanks in each of the following:

a) The company that popularized personal computing was _____.
b) The computer that made personal computing legitimate in business and industry was the _____.
c) Computers process data under the control of sets of instructions called _____.
d) The six key logical units of the computer are the _____, _____, _____, _____, _____ and _____.
e) The three classes of languages discussed in the chapter are _____, _____ and _____.
f) The programs that translate high-level language programs into machine language are called _____.
g) The _____ language was developed by Wirth for teaching structured programming in universities.
h) The Department of Defense developed the Ada language with a capability called _____, which allows programmers to specify that many activities can proceed in parallel.

1.2   Fill in the blanks in each of the following sentences about the Java environment.

a) The _____ command from the Java 2 Software Development Kit executes a Java applet.
b) The _____ command from the Java 2 Software Development Kit executes a Java application
c) The _____ command from the Java 2 Software Development Kit compiles a Java program.
d) An _____ file is required to invoke a Java applet.
e) A Java program file must end with the _____ file extension.
f) When a Java program is compiled, the file produced by the compiler ends with the file extension.
g) The file produced by the Java compiler contains _____ that are interpreted to execute a Java applet or application.

1.3   Fill in the blanks in each of the following statements (based on Sections 1.12 and 1.15):

a) The _____ allows computer users to locate and view multimedia-based documents on almost any subject over the Internet.
b) Java _____ are typically stored on your computer and are designed to execute independent of a World Wide Web browsers.
c) Lists and tables of values are called _____.
d) The _____ GUI components are written completely in Java.
e) _____ allows an applet or application to perform multiple activities in parallel.
f) _____ provides access to relational databases in Java.
g) The _____ networking model is used by World Wide Web browsers and World Wide Web servers to communicate.
h) _____ provide Java programmers with a standard set of data structures for storing and retrieving data, and a standard set of algorithms that allow programmers to manipulate the data.
i) In a client/server relationship, the _____ requests that some action be performed and the _____ performs the action and responds.

Answers to Self-Review Exercises

1.1   a) Apple. b) IBM Personal Computer. c) programs. d) input unit, output unit, memory unit, arithmetic and logic unit, central processing unit, secondary storage unit. e) machine languages, assembly languages, high-level languages. f) compilers. g) Pascal. h) multitasking.

1.2   a) **appletviewer**. b) **java**. c) **javac**. d) HTML. e) **.java**. f) **.class**. g) bytecodes.

1.3   a) World Wide Web. b) applications. c) arrays. d) Swing. e) Multithreading. f) JDBC. g) request-response. h) collections. i) client, server.

Exercises

1.4   Categorize each of the following items as either hardware or software:
   a) CPU
   b) Java compiler
   c) ALU
   d) Java interpreter
   e) input unit
   f) an editor program

1.5   Why might you want to write a program in a machine-independent language instead of a machine-dependent language? Why might a machine-dependent language be more appropriate for writing certain types of programs?

1.6   Fill in the blanks in each of the following statements:
   a) Which logical unit of the computer receives information from outside the computer for use by the computer? _____.
   b) The process of instructing the computer to solve specific problems is called _____.
   c) What type of computer language uses English-like abbreviations for machine language instructions? _____.
   d) Which logical unit of the computer sends information that has already been processed by the computer to various devices so that the information may be used outside the computer? _____.
   e) Which logical unit of the computer retains information? _____.
   f) Which logical unit of the computer performs calculations? _____.
   g) Which logical unit of the computer makes logical decisions? _____.
   h) The level of computer language most convenient to the programmer for writing programs quickly and easily is _____.
   i) The only language that a computer can directly understand is called that computer's _____.
   j) Which logical unit of the computer coordinates the activities of all the other logical units? _____.

1.7   Distinguish between the terms *fatal error* and *nonfatal error*. Why might you prefer to experience a fatal error rather than a nonfatal error?

1.8   Fill in the blanks in each of the following statements (based on Sections 1.12 and 1.15):
   a) Java _____ are designed to be transported over the Internet and executed in World Wide Web browsers.
   b) _____ programming causes a program to perform a task in response to user interactions with graphical user interface (GUI) components.
   c) Java's graphics capabilities are _____ and hence, portable.

  d) The standard _____ can be used to provide identical user interfaces across all computer platforms.
  e) Languages that cannot perform multiple activities in parallel are called _____ languages or _____ languages.
  f) Aggregations of data such as linked lists, stacks, queues and trees are called _____.

Introduction to Java Applications

Objectives

- To be able to write simple Java applications.
- To be able to use input and output statements.
- To become familiar with primitive data types.
- To understand basic memory concepts.
- To be able to use arithmetic operators.
- To understand the precedence of arithmetic operators.
- To be able to write decision-making statements.
- To be able to use relational and equality operators.

Comment is free, but facts are sacred.
C. P. Scott

The creditor hath a better memory than the debtor.
James Howell

When faced with a decision, I always ask, "What would be the most fun?"
Peggy Walker

He has left his body to science—
and science is contesting the will.
David Frost

Classes struggle, some classes triumph, others are eliminated.
Mao Zedong

Equality, in a social sense, may be divided into that of condition and that of rights.
James Fenimore Cooper

Outline

2.1 Introduction

The Java language facilitates a disciplined approach to computer program design. We now introduce Java programming and present several examples that illustrate several important features of Java. Each example is analyzed one line at a time. In this chapter and Chapter 3 we present two program styles in Java—*applications* and *applets*. In Chapter 4 and Chapter 5 we present a detailed treatment of *program development* and *program control* in Java.

2.2 A Simple Program: Printing a Line of Text

Java uses notations that may appear strange to nonprogrammers. We begin by considering a simple *application* that displays a line of text. An application is a program that executes using the **java** interpreter (discussed later in this section). The program and its output are shown in Fig. 2.1.

This program illustrates several important features of the Java language. We consider each line of the program in detail. Each program has line numbers for the reader's convenience; those line numbers are not part of Java programs. Line 7 does the "real work" of the program, namely displaying the phrase **Welcome to Java Programming!** on the screen. But let us consider each line in order. Line 1

```
1   // Fig. 2.1: Welcome1.java
2   // A first program in Java
3
4   public class Welcome1 {
5      public static void main( String args[] )
6      {
7         System.out.println( "Welcome to Java Programming!" );
8      }
9   }
```

```
Welcome to Java Programming!
```

Fig. 2.1   A first program in Java.

```
// Fig. 2.1: Welcome1.java
```

begins with **//**, indicating that the remainder of the line is a *comment*. Programmers insert comments to *document* programs and improve program readability. Comments also help other people read and understand your program. Comments do not cause the computer to perform any action when the program is run. Comments are ignored by the Java compiler. The preceding comment simply indicates the figure number and file name for the program of Fig. 2.1. We begin every program with a comment indicating figure number and file name. A comment that begins with **//** is called a *single-line comment* because the comment terminates at the end of the current line. Note that a **//** comment can begin in the middle of a line and continue until the end of that line.

Two other comment notations facilitate writing multiple-line comments. For example,

```
/* This is a multiple
   line comment. It can be
   split over many lines */
```

is a comment that can spread over several lines—sometimes called a *multiple-line comment*—that begins with delimiter **/*** and ends with delimiter ***/**. All text between the delimiters of the comment is ignored by the compiler. A similar form of comment called a *documentation comment* is delimited with **/**** and ***/**.

Common Programming Error 2.1

Forgetting one of the delimiters of a multiple-line comment is a syntax error.

Note: Java absorbed comments delimited with **/*** and ***/** from the C programming language and single-line comments delimited with **//** from the C++ programming language. Java programmers generally use C++-style single-line comments in preference to C-style comments. Throughout this book, we use C++-style single-line comments. Java introduced the documentation comment syntax to enable programmers to highlight portions of programs that the **javadoc** utility program (provided by Sun Microsystems with the Java 2 Software Development Kit) can read and use to prepare documentation for your program automatically. There are subtle issues to using **javadoc**-style comments properly in a program. We do not use **javadoc**-style comments in-line in the book. However, **javadoc**-style comments are explained thoroughly in Appendix G.

Line 2

```
// A first program in Java
```

is a comment that describes the purpose of the program.

Good Programming Practice 2.1

Every program should begin with a comment describing the purpose of the program.

Line 3 is simply a blank line. Blank lines and space characters are often used throughout a program to make the program easier to read. Together, blank lines, space characters and tab characters are known as *white-space* (space characters and tabs are known specifically as *white-space characters*). Such characters are ignored by the compiler. Several conventions for using white-space characters are discussed in this chapter and the next several chapters as these spacing conventions are needed.

Good Programming Practice 2.2

Use blank lines, space characters and tab characters in a program to enhance program readability.

Line 4

```
public class Welcome1 {
```

begins a *class definition* for class **Welcome1**. Every program in Java consists of at least one class definition that is defined by you—the programmer. These classes are known as *programmer-defined classes* or *user-defined classes*. In Chapter 8, "Object-Based Programming," we discuss programs that contain several programmer-defined classes. The **class** *keyword* introduces a class definition in Java and is immediately followed by the *class name* (**Welcome1** in this program). Keywords (or *reserved words*) are reserved for use by Java (we discuss the keywords throughout the text) and are always spelled with all lowercase letters. By convention, all class names in Java begin with a capital first letter and have a capital first letter for every word in the class name (e.g., **SampleClassName**). The name of the class is called an *identifier*. An identifier is a series of characters consisting of letters, digits, underscores (**_**) and dollar signs (**$**) that does not begin with a digit and does not contain any spaces. Some valid identifiers are **Welcome1**, **$value**, **_value**, **m_inputField1** and **button7**. The name **7button** is not a valid identifier because it begins with a digit, and the name **input field** is not a valid identifier because it contains a space. Java is *case sensitive*—uppercase and lowercase letters are different, so **a1** and **A1** are different identifiers.

Common Programming Error 2.2

Java is case sensitive. Not using the proper uppercase and lowercase letters for an identifier is normally a syntax error.

Good Programming Practice 2.3

By convention, you should always begin a class name with a capital first letter.

Good Programming Practice 2.4

When reading a Java program, look for identifiers that start with capital first letters. These normally represent Java classes.

Software Engineering Observation 2.1

*Avoid using identifiers containing dollar signs (**$**) as these are often used by the compiler to create indentifier names.*

In Chapters 2 through 7, every class we define begins with the **public** *keyword*. For now, we will simply require this keyword. The **public** keyword is discussed in detail in Chapter 8, where we also discuss classes that do not begin with keyword **public**. [*Note:* Several times early in this text, we ask you to simply mimic certain Java features we introduce as you write your own Java programs. We specifically do this when it is not yet important to know all the details of a feature to use that feature in Java. All programmers initially learn how to program by mimicking what other programmers have done before them. For each detail we ask you to mimic, we indicate where the full discussion will be presented later in the text.]

When you save your class definition in a file, the class name must be used as part of the file name. For our application, the file name is **Welcome1.java**. All Java class definitions are stored in files ending with the "**.java**" file name extension.

Common Programming Error 2.3

For a **public** *class, it is an error if the file name is not identical to the class name in both spelling and capitalization. Therefore, it is also an error for a file to contain two or more* **public** *classes.*

Common Programming Error 2.4

It is an error not to end a file name with the **.java** *extension for a file containing an application's class definition. The Java compiler will not be able to compile the class definition.*

A *left brace* (at the end of line 4 in this program), **{**, begins the *body* of every class definition. A corresponding *right brace* (at line 9 in this program), **}**, must end each class definition. Notice that lines 5 through 8 are indented. This is one of the spacing conventions mentioned earlier. We define each spacing convention as a *Good Programming Practice.*

Common Programming Error 2.5

If braces do not occur in matching pairs, the compiler indicates an error.

Good Programming Practice 2.5

Whenever you type an opening left brace, **{**, *in your program, immediately type the closing right brace,* **}**, *then reposition the cursor between the braces to begin typing the body. This helps prevent missing braces.*

Good Programming Practice 2.6

Indent the entire body of each class definition one "level" of indentation between the left brace, **{**, *and the right brace,* **}**, *that define the body of the class. This emphasizes the structure of the class definition and helps make the class definition easier to read.*

Good Programming Practice 2.7

Set a convention for the indent size you prefer and then uniformly apply that convention. The Tab key may be used to create indents, but tab stops may vary between editors. We recommend using either 1/4-inch tab stops or (preferably) three spaces to form a level of indent.

Line 5

```
public static void main( String args[] )
```

is a part of every Java application. Java applications automatically begin executing at **main**. The parentheses after **main** indicate that **main** is a program building block called a *method.* Java class definitions normally contain one or more methods. For a Java application class, exactly one of those methods must be called **main** and must be defined as shown on line 5; otherwise, the **java** interpreter will not execute the application. Methods are able to perform tasks and return information when they complete their tasks. The **void** keyword indicates that this method will perform a task (displaying a line of text in this program), but will not return any information when it completes its task. We will see that many methods return information when they complete their task. Methods are explained in detail in Chapter 6. For now, simply mimic **main**'s first line in each of your Java applications.

The left brace, **{**, on line 6 begins the *body of the method definition*. A corresponding right brace, **}**, must end the method definition's body (line 8 of the program). Notice that the line in the body of the method is indented between these braces.

Good Programming Practice 2.8

*Indent the entire body of each method definition one "level" of indentation between the left brace, **{**, and the right brace, **}**, that define the body of the method. This makes the structure of the method stand out and helps make the method definition easier to read.*

Line 7

```
System.out.println( "Welcome to Java Programming!" );
```

instructs the computer to perform an *action*, namely to print the *string* of characters contained between the double quotation marks. A string is sometimes called a *character string*, a *message* or a *string literal*. We refer to characters between double quotation marks generically as strings. White-space characters in strings are not ignored by the compiler.

System.out is known as the *standard output object*. **System.out** allows Java applications to display strings and other types of information in the *command window* from which the Java application is executed. On Microsoft Windows 95/98, the command window is the *MS-DOS prompt*. On Microsoft Windows NT, the command window is the *Command Prompt*. On UNIX, the command window is normally called a *command window*, a *command tool*, a *shell tool* or a *shell*. On computers running an operating system that does not have a command window (such as a Macintosh), the **java** interpreter normally displays a window containing the information displayed by the program.

Method **System.out.println** *displays (or prints) a line* of text in the command window. When **System.out.println** completes its task, it automatically positions the *output cursor* (the location where the next character will be displayed) to the beginning of the next line in the command window (this is similar to you pressing the *Enter* key when typing in a text editor—the cursor is repositioned at the beginning of the next line in your file).

The entire line, including **System.out.println**, its *argument* in the parentheses (the string) and the *semicolon* (**;**), is called a *statement*. Every statement must end with a semicolon (also known as the *statement terminator*). When this statement executes, it displays the message **Welcome to Java Programming!** in the command window.

Common Programming Error 2.6

Omitting the semicolon at the end of a statement is a syntax error. A syntax error is caused when the compiler cannot recognize a statement. The compiler normally issues an error message to help the programmer locate and fix the incorrect statement. Syntax errors are violations of the language rules. Syntax errors are also called compile errors, compile-time errors or compilation errors because they are detected during the compilation phase. You will be unable to execute your program until all the syntax errors are corrected.

Testing and Debugging Tip 2.1

When the compiler reports a syntax error, the error may not be on the line indicated by the error messages. First, check the line where the error was reported. If that line does not contain syntax errors, check the preceding several lines in the program.

Some programmers find it difficult when reading and/or writing a program to match the left and right braces (**{** and **}**) that delimit the body of a class definition or a method definition. For this reason, some programmers prefer to include a single-line comment after a closing right brace (**}**) that ends a method definition and after a closing right brace that ends a class definition. For example, line 8 in our program could include a comment such as

```
} // end of method main()
```

and line 9 in our program could include a comment such as

```
} // end of class Welcome1
```

Each comment indicates the method or class that the right brace terminates.

Good Programming Practice 2.9

*Some programmers prefer to follow the closing right brace (**}**) of the body of a method or class definition with a single-line comment indicating the method or class definition for which the right brace terminates the definition's body.*

We are now ready to compile and execute our program. To compile the program, we open a command window, change to the directory where the program is stored and type

```
javac Welcome1.java
```

If the program contains no syntax errors, the preceding command creates a new file called **Welcome1.class** containing the Java bytecodes that represent our application. These bytecodes will be interpreted by the **java** interpreter when we tell it to execute the program by typing the command

```
java Welcome1
```

which launches the java interpreter and indicates that it should load the "**.class**" file for class **Welcome1**. Note that the "**.class**" file name extension is omitted from the preceding command; otherwise the interpreter will not execute the program. The interpreter automatically calls method **main**. Next, the statement at line 7 of **main** displays "**Welcome to Java Programming!**" Figure 2.2 shows the execution of the application in a Microsoft Windows 95/98 **MS-DOS Prompt**.

Welcome to Java Programming! can be displayed several ways. Class **Welcome2** of Fig. 2.3 uses two statements to produce the same output shown in Fig. 2.1.

Fig. 2.2   Executing the **Welcome1** application in a Microsoft Windows **MS-DOS Prompt**.

```
1   // Fig. 2.3: Welcome2.java
2   // Printing a line with multiple statements
3
4   public class Welcome2 {
5      public static void main( String args[] )
6      {
7         System.out.print( "Welcome to " );
8         System.out.println( "Java Programming!" );
9      }
10  }
```

```
Welcome to Java Programming!
```

Fig. 2.3   Printing on one line with separate statements.

Lines 7 and 8 of Fig. 2.3

```
System.out.print( "Welcome to " );
System.out.println( "Java Programming!" );
```

display one line in the command window. The first statement uses **System.out**'s method **print** to display a string. Unlike **println**, **print** does not position the output cursor at the beginning of the next line in the command window after displaying its argument. The next character displayed in the command window appears immediately after the last character displayed with **print**. Thus, when line 8 executes, the first character displayed, "**J**," appears immediately after the last character displayed with **print** (i.e., the space character inside the right double quote on line 7). Each **print** or **println** statement resumes displaying characters from where the last **print** or **println** stopped displaying characters.

A single statement can display multiple lines by using *newline characters*. Newline characters are "special characters" that indicate to **System.out**'s **print** and **println** methods when they should begin displaying characters from the beginning of the next line in the command window. Figure 2.4 demonstrates using newline characters.

```
1   // Fig. 2.4: Welcome3.java
2   // Printing multiple lines with a single statement
3
4   public class Welcome3 {
5      public static void main( String args[] )
6      {
7         System.out.println( "Welcome\nto\nJava\nProgramming!" );
8      }
9   }
```

```
Welcome
to
Java
Programming!
```

Fig. 2.4   Printing on multiple lines with a single statement.

Line 7

```
System.out.println( "Welcome\nto\nJava\nProgramming!" );
```

produces four separate lines of text in the command window. Normally the characters in a string are displayed exactly as they appear between the double quotes. Notice, however, that the two characters "****" and "**n**" are not printed on the screen. The *backslash* (****) is called an *escape character*. It indicates that a "special" character is to be output. When a backslash is encountered in a string of characters, the next character is combined with the backslash to form an *escape sequence*. The escape sequence **\n** is the *newline character*. It causes the *cursor* (i.e., the current screen position indicator) to move to the beginning of the next line in the command window. Some other common escape sequences are listed in Fig. 2.5.

Although the first several programs display output in the command window, most Java applications that display output use windows or *dialog boxes* to display output. For example, World Wide Web browsers such as Netscape Communicator or Microsoft Internet Explorer display Web pages in their own windows. Email programs typically allow you to type messages in a window provided by the email program or read messages you receive in a window provided by the email program. Dialog boxes are windows that typically are used to display important messages to the user of an application. Java 2 already includes class **JOptionPane** that allows you to easily display a dialog box containing information. The program of Fig. 2.6 displays the same string as Fig. 2.4 in a predefined dialog box called a *message dialog*.

One of the great strengths of Java is its rich set of predefined classes that programmers can reuse rather than "reinventing the wheel." We use a large number of these classes in this book. Java's many predefined classes are grouped into categories of related classes called *packages*. The packages are referred to collectively as the *Java class library* or the *Java applications programming interface (Java API)*. Class **JOptionPane** is defined for us in a package called ***javax.swing***.

Escape sequence	Description
\n	Newline. Position the screen cursor to the beginning of the next line.
\t	Horizontal tab. Move the screen cursor to the next tab stop.
\r	Carriage return. Position the screen cursor to the beginning of the current line; do not advance to the next line. Any characters output after the carriage return overwrite the previous characters output on that line.
\\	Backslash. Used to print a backslash character.
\"	Double quote. Used to print a double quote character. For example,

```
System.out.println( "\"in quotes\"" );
```
displays
```
"in quotes"
```

Fig. 2.5   Some common escape sequences.

```
1   // Fig. 2.6: Welcome4.java
2   // Printing multiple lines in a dialog box
3   import javax.swing.JOptionPane;  // import class JOptionPane
4
5   public class Welcome4 {
6      public static void main( String args[] )
7      {
8         JOptionPane.showMessageDialog(
9            null, "Welcome\nto\nJava\nProgramming!" );
10
11         System.exit( 0 );  // terminate the program
12      }
13   }
```

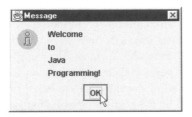

Fig. 2.6   Displaying multiple lines in a dialog box.

Line 3

        `import javax.swing.JOptionPane;`

is an *import* statement. The compiler uses **import** statements to identify and load classes required to compile a Java program. When you use classes from the Java API, the compiler attempts to ensure that you use them correctly. The **import** statements help the
compiler locate the classes you intend to use. Each piece of the package name is a directory
(or folder) on disk. All the packages in the Java API are stored in the directory **java** or
javax that contain many subdirectories including **swing** (a subdirectory of **javax**).
Packages are discussed in detail in Chapter 8, Object-Oriented Programming.

   The preceding line tells the compiler to load the **JOptionPane** class from the
javax.swing package. This package contains many classes that help Java programmers
define *graphical user interfaces (GUIs)* for their application. *GUI components* facilitate
data entry by the user of your program and formatting or presenting data outputs to the user
of your program. For example, Fig. 2.7 contains a Netscape Communicator window. In the
window, there is a bar containing *menus* (**File**, **Edit**, **View**, etc.). Below the menu bar there
is a set of *buttons* that each have a defined task in Netscape Communicator. Below the buttons there is a *text field* in which the user can type the name of the World Wide Web site to
visit. To the left of the text field is a *label* that indicates the purpose of the text field. The
menus, buttons, text fields and labels are part of Netscape Communicator's GUI. They
enable you to interact with the Communicator program. Java contains classes that implement the GUI components described here and others that will be described in Chapters 12
and 13, "Basic Graphical User Interface Components" and "Advanced Graphical User
Interface Components."

button   label   menu   menu bar   text field

Fig. 2.7   A sample Netscape Navigator window with GUI components.

In **main**, lines 8 and 9

```
JOptionPane.showMessageDialog(
    null, "Welcome\nto\nJava\nProgramming!" );
```

indicate a call to method *showMessageDialog* of class **JOptionPane**. The method requires two arguments. When a method requires multiple arguments, the arguments are separated with *commas* (*,*). Until we discuss **JOptionPane** in detail in Chapter 13, the first argument will always be the keyword *null*. The second argument is the string to display.

Method **JOptionPane.showMessageDialog** is a special method of class **JOptionPane** called a *static* method. Such methods are always called using their class name followed by a dot operator (**.**) and the method name. We discuss **static** methods in Chapter 8, "Object-Based Programming."

Executing the preceding statement displays the dialog box shown below. The *title bar* of the dialog contains the string **Message** to indicate that the dialog is presenting a message to the user. The dialog box automatically includes an **OK** button that allows the user to *dismiss (hide) the dialog* by pressing the button. This is accomplished by positioning the *mouse cursor* (also called the *mouse pointer*) over the **OK** button and clicking the mouse.

Title bar

The **OK** button allows the user to dismiss the dialog box.

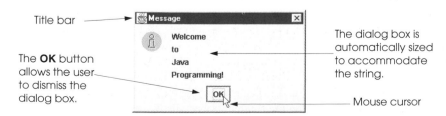

The dialog box is automatically sized to accommodate the string.

Mouse cursor

Good Programming Practice 2.10

Place a space after each comma in an argument list (,) to make programs more readable.

Remember that all statements in Java end with a semicolon (**;**). Therefore, lines 8 and 9 represent one statement. Java allows large statements to be split over many lines. However, you cannot split a statement in the middle of an identifier or in the middle of a string.

Common Programming Error 2.7

Splitting a statement in the middle of an identifier or a string is a syntax error.

Line 11

```
System.exit( 0 );   // terminate the program
```

uses **static** method **exit** of class **System** to terminate the application. This line is required in any application that displays a graphical user interface to terminate the application. Notice once again the syntax used to call the method—the class name (**System**), a dot (**.**) and the method name (**exit**). Remember that identifiers starting with capital first letters normally represent class names. So, you can assume that **System** is a class. The argument **0** to method **exit** indicates that the application terminated successfully (a non-zero value normally indicates that an error occurred). This value is passed to the command window that executed the program. This is useful if the program is executed from a batch file (on Windows 95/98/NT systems) or a shell script (on UNIX systems). Batch files and shell scripts are typically used to execute several programs in sequence such that when the first program ends, the next program begins execution automatically. For more information on batch files or shell scripts, see your operating system's documentation.

Class **System** is part of the package *java.lang*. Notice that class **System** is not imported with an **import** statement at the beginning of the program. Package **java.lang** is automatically imported in every Java program.

Common Programming Error 2.8

*Forgetting to call **System.exit** in an application that displays a graphical user interface prevents the program from terminating properly. This normally results in the command window preventing you from typing any other commands.*

2.3 Another Java Application: Adding Integers

Our next application inputs two integers (whole numbers) typed by a user at the keyboard, computes the sum of these values and displays the result. As the user types each integer and presses the *Enter* key, the integer is read into the program and added to the total.

This program uses another predefined dialog box from class **JOptionPane** called an *input dialog* that allows the user to input a value for use in the program. The program also uses a message dialog to display the results of the addition. Figure 2.8 shows the application and sample screen captures.

Lines 1 and 2

```
// Fig. 2.8: Addition.java
// An addition program
```

are single-line comments stating the figure number, file name and purpose of the program.

```
1   // Fig. 2.8: Addition.java
2   // An addition program
3
4   import javax.swing.JOptionPane;  // import class JOptionPane
5
6   public class Addition {
7      public static void main( String args[] )
8      {
9         String firstNumber,    // first string entered by user
10                secondNumber;   // second string entered by user
11        int number1,           // first number to add
12            number2,           // second number to add
13            sum;               // sum of number1 and number2
14
15        // read in first number from user as a string
16        firstNumber =
17           JOptionPane.showInputDialog( "Enter first integer" );
18
19        // read in second number from user as a string
20        secondNumber =
21           JOptionPane.showInputDialog( "Enter second integer" );
22
23        // convert numbers from type String to type int
24        number1 = Integer.parseInt( firstNumber );
25        number2 = Integer.parseInt( secondNumber );
26
27        // add the numbers
28        sum = number1 + number2;
29
30        // display the results
31        JOptionPane.showMessageDialog(
32           null, "The sum is " + sum, "Results",
33           JOptionPane.PLAIN_MESSAGE );
34
35        System.exit( 0 );   // terminate the program
36     }
37  }
```

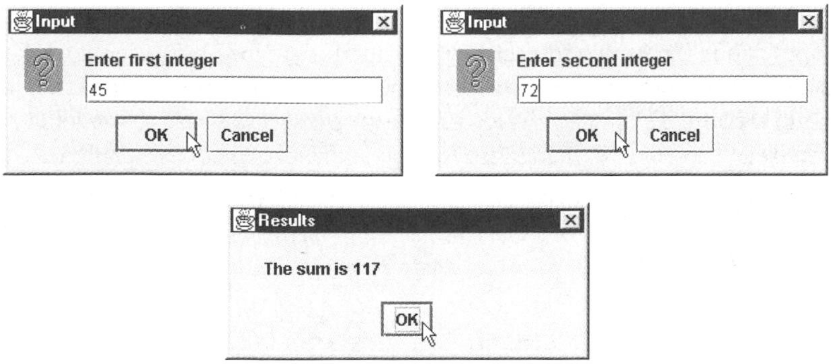

Fig. 2.8   An addition program "in action."

Line 4

```
import javax.swing.JOptionPane;  // import class JOptionPane
```

specifies to the compiler where to locate class **JOptionPane** for use in this application.

As stated earlier, every Java program consists of at least one class definition. Line 6

```
public class Addition {
```

begins the definitions of class **Addition**. The file name for this **public** class must be **Addition.java**.

Remember that all class definitions start with an opening left brace (end of line 6), **{**, and end with a closing right brace, **}** (line 37).

As stated earlier, every application begins execution with method **main** (line 7). The left brace (line 8) marks the beginning of **main**'s body and the corresponding right brace (line 36) marks the end of **main**.

Lines 9 and 10

```
String firstNumber,    // first string entered by user
       secondNumber;   // second string entered by user
```

are a *declaration*. The words **firstNumber** and **secondNumber** are the names of *variables*. A variable is a location in the computer's memory where a value can be stored for use by a program. All variables must be declared with a name and a data type before they can be used in a program. This declaration specifies that the variables **firstNumber** and **secondNumber** are data of type *String* (from package **java.lang**), which means that these variables will hold strings. A variable name can be any valid identifier. Declarations end with a semicolon (**;**) and can be split over several lines with each variable in the declaration separated by a comma (i.e., a *comma-separated list* of variable names). Several variables of the same type may be declared in one declaration or in multiple declarations. We could have written two declarations, one for each variable, but the preceding declaration is more concise. Notice the single-line comments at the end of each line. This is a common syntax used by programmers to indicate the purpose of each variable in the program.

Good Programming Practice 2.11

Choosing meaningful variable names helps a program to be "self-documenting" (i.e., it becomes easier to understand a program simply by reading it rather than having to read manuals or use excessive comments).

Good Programming Practice 2.12

By convention, variable name identifiers begin with a lowercase first letter. As with class names every word in the name after the first word should begin with a capital first letter. For example, identifier **firstNumber** *has a capital* **N** *in its second word* **Number**.

Good Programming Practice 2.13

Some programmers prefer to declare each variable on a separate line. This format allows for easy insertion of a descriptive comment next to each declaration.

Lines 11 through 13

```
int number1,         // first number to add
    number2,         // second number to add
    sum;             // sum of number1 and number2
```

declare that variables **number1**, **number2** and **sum** are data of type *int*, which means that these variables will hold *integer* values (i.e., whole numbers such as 7, –11, 0, 31914).

We will soon discuss the data types **float** and **double** for specifying real numbers (i.e., numbers with decimal points like 3.4, 0.0, –11.19) and variables of type **char** for specifying character data. A **char** variable may hold only a single lowercase letter, a single uppercase letter, a single digit, or a single special character such as **x**, **$**, **7**, ***** and escape sequences (such as the newline character **\n**). Java is also capable of representing characters from many other languages.

Types such as **int**, **double** and **char** are often called *primitive data types* or *built-in data types*. Primitive type names are keywords. The eight primitive types (**boolean**, **char**, **byte**, **short**, **int**, **long**, **float** and **double**) are summarized in Chapter 4.

Lines 15 through 17

```
// read in first number from user as a string
firstNumber =
    JOptionPane.showInputDialog( "Enter first integer" );
```

reads from the user a **String** representing the first of the two integers that will be added. Method **JOptionPane.showInputDialog** displays the following input dialog:

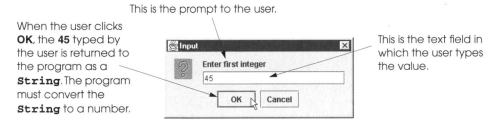

This is the prompt to the user.

When the user clicks **OK**, the **45** typed by the user is returned to the program as a **String**. The program must convert the **String** to a number.

This is the text field in which the user types the value.

The argument to **showInputDialog** indicates to the user what to do in the text field. This message is called a *prompt* because it directs the user to take a specific action. The user types characters in the text field, then clicks the **OK** button to return the string to the program. [If you type and nothing appears in the text field, position the mouse pointer in the text field and click the mouse to activate the text field.] Unfortunately, Java does not provide a simple form of input that is analogous to displaying output in the command window with **System.out.print** and **System.out.println**. For this reason, we normally receive input from a user through a GUI component (an input dialog in this program).

Technically, the user can type anything in the text field of the input. For this program, if the user either types a noninteger value or clicks the **Cancel** button, a run-time logic error will occur. Chapter 14, "Exception Handling," discusses how to make your programs more robust by handling such errors.

The result of the call to **JOptionPane.showInputDialog** (a **String** containing the characters typed by the user) is given to variable **firstNumber** with the *assignment operator* **=**. The statement is read as, "**firstNumber** *gets* the value of **JOptionPane.showInputDialog("Enter first integer")**." The **=** operator is called a *binary operator* because it has two *operands*—**firstNumber** and the result of the expression **JOptionPane.showInputDialog("Enter first integer")**. This whole statement is called an *assignment statement* because it assigns a value to a variable. The expression to the right side of the assignment operator **=** is always evaluated first.

Lines 19 through 21

```
// read in second number from user as a string
secondNumber =
   JOptionPane.showInputDialog( "Enter second integer" );
```

displays an input dialog in which the user types a **String** representing the second of the two integers that will be added.

Lines 23 through 25

```
// convert numbers from type String to type int
number1 = Integer.parseInt( firstNumber );
number2 = Integer.parseInt( secondNumber );
```

convert the two strings input by the user to **int** values that can be used in a calculation. Method *Integer.parseInt* (a **static** method of class **Integer**) converts its **String** argument to an integer. Class **Integer** is part of the package **java.lang**. The integer returned by **Integer.parseInt** in line 24 is assigned to variable **number1**. Any subsequent references to **number1** in the program use this same integer value. The integer returned by **Integer.parseInt** in line 25 is assigned to variable **number2**. Any subsequent references to **number2** in the program use this same integer value.

The assignment statement at line 28

```
sum = number1 + number2;
```

calculates the sum of the variables **number1** and **number2**, and assigns the result to variable **sum** using the assignment operator **=**. The statement is read as, "**sum** *gets* the value of **number1 + number2**." Most calculations are performed in assignment statements.

Good Programming Practice 2.14

Place spaces on either side of a binary operator. This makes the operator stand out and makes the program more readable.

After performing the calculation, lines 31 through 33

```
JOptionPane.showMessageDialog(
   null, "The sum is " + sum, "Results",
   JOptionPane.PLAIN_MESSAGE );
```

use method **JOptionPane.showMessageDialog** to display the result of the addition. The expression

```
"The sum is " + sum
```

from the preceding statement uses the operator **+** to "add" a string (the literal **"The sum is "**) and **sum** (the **int** variable containing the result of the addition on line 28). Java has a version of the **+** operator for *string concatenation* that enables a string and a value of another data type (including another string) to be concatenated—the result of this operation is a new (and normally longer) string. If we assume **sum** contains the value **117**, the expression evaluates as follows: Java determines that the two operands of the **+** operator (the string **"The sum is "** and the integer **sum**) are different types and one of them is a string. Next, **sum** is automatically converted to a string and concatenated with **"The sum is "**, which results in the string **"The sum is 117"**. This string is displayed in the dialog box. Note that the automatic conversion of integer **sum** only occurs because it is concatenated with the string literal **"The sum is "**. Also note that the space between **is** an **117** is part of the string **"The sum is "**. String concatenation is discussed in detail in Chapter 10, "Strings and Characters."

> ### Common Programming Error 2.9
>
> *Confusing the **+** operator used for string concatenation with the **+** operator used for addition can lead to strange results. For example, assuming integer variable **y** has the value **5**, the expression **"y + 2 = " + y + 2** results in the string **"y + 2 = 52"**, not **"y + 2 = 7"**, because first the value of **y** is concatenated with the string **"y + 2 = "**, then the value **2** is concatenated with the new larger string **"y + 2 = 5"**. The expression **"y + 2 = " + (y + 2)** produces the desired result.*

The version of method **showMessageDialog** used in Fig. 2.8 is different from the one discussed in Fig. 2.6 in that it requires four arguments. The following dialog box illustrates the two of the four arguments. As with the first version, the first argument will always be **null** until we discuss class **JOptionPane** in detail in Chapter 12. The second argument is the message to display. The third argument is the string to display in the title bar of the dialog. The fourth argument (**JOptionPane.PLAIN_MESSAGE**) is a value indicating the type of message dialog to display—this type of message dialog does not display an icon to the left of the message.

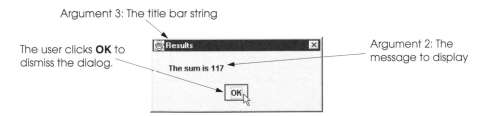

The message dialog types are shown in Fig. 2.9. All message dialog types except **PLAIN_MESSAGE** dialogs display an icon to the user indicating the type of message.

Message dialog type	Icon	Description
JOptionPane.ERROR_MESSAGE		Displays a dialog that indicates an error to the application user.
JOptionPane.INFORMATION_MESSAGE		Displays a dialog with an informational message to the application user—the user can simply dismiss the dialog.
JOptionPane.WARNING_MESSAGE		Displays a dialog that warns the application user of a potential problem.

Fig. 2.9   JOptionPane constants for message dialogs (part 1 of 2).

Message dialog type	Icon	Description
JOptionPane.QUESTION_MESSAGE		Displays a dialog that poses a question to the application user. This normally requires a response such as clicking a **Yes** or **No** button.
JOptionPane.PLAIN_MESSAGE	no icon	Displays a dialog that simply contains a message with no icon.

Fig. 2.9   **JOptionPane** constants for message dialogs (part 2 of 2).

2.4 Memory Concepts

Variable names such as **number1**, **number2** and **sum** actually correspond to *locations* in the computer's memory. Every variable has a *name,* a *type,* a *size* and a *value*.

In the addition program of Fig. 2.8, when the statement

```
number1 = Integer.parseInt( firstNumber );
```

executes, the string previously typed by the user in the input dialog and stored in **first-Number** is converted to an **int** and placed into a memory location to which the name **number1** has been assigned by the compiler. Suppose the user enters the string **45** as the value for **firstNumber**. The program converts **firstNumber** to an **int** and the computer places that integer value **45** into location **number1** as shown in Fig. 2.10.

Whenever a value is placed in a memory location, this value replaces the previous value in that location. The previous value is destroyed (lost).

When the statement

```
number2 = Integer.parseInt( secondNumber );
```

executes, suppose the user enters the string **72** as the value for **secondNumber**. The program converts **secondNumber** to an **int** and the computer places that integer value **72** into location **number2** and memory appears as shown in Fig. 2.11.

Once the program has obtained values for **number1** and **number2**, it adds these values and places the sum into variable **sum**. The statement

```
sum = number1 + number2;
```

performs the addition also replaces (i.e., destroys) **sum**'s previous value. After **sum** is calculated, memory appears as shown in Fig. 2.12. Note that the values of **number1** and **number2** appear exactly as they did before they were used in the calculation of **sum**. These values were used, but not destroyed, as the computer performed the calculation. Thus, when a value is read from a memory location, the process is nondestructive.

number1	45

Fig. 2.10   Memory location showing the name and value of variable **number1**.

| number1 | 45 |
| number2 | 72 |

Fig. 2.11 Memory locations after values for variables **number1** and **number2** have been input.

number1	45
number2	72
sum	117

Fig. 2.12 Memory locations after a calculation.

2.5 Arithmetic

Most programs perform arithmetic calculations. The *arithmetic operators* are summarized in Fig. 2.13. Note the use of various special symbols not used in algebra. The *asterisk (*)* indicates multiplication and the *percent sign (%)* is the *modulus operator*, which is discussed shortly. The arithmetic operators in Fig. 2.13 are binary operators because they each operate on two operands. For example, the expression **sum + value** contains the binary operator **+** and the two operands **sum** and **value**.

Integer division yields an integer quotient; for example, the expression **7 / 4** evaluates to **1** and the expression **17 / 5** evaluates to **3**. Note that any fractional part in integer division is simply discarded (i.e., truncated)—no rounding occurs. Java provides the modulus operator, **%**, that yields the remainder after integer division. The expression **x % y** yields the remainder after **x** is divided by **y**. Thus, **7 % 4** yields **3** and **17 % 5** yields **2**. This operator is most commonly used with integer operands, but also can be used with other arithmetic types. In later chapters, we consider many interesting applications of the modulus operator such as determining if one number is a multiple of another. There is no arithmetic operator for exponentiation in Java (Chapter 5 shows how to perform exponentiation in Java).

Java operation	Arithmetic operator	Algebraic expression	Java expression
Addition	+	$f + 7$	**f + 7**
Subtraction	–	$p - c$	**p - c**
Multiplication	*	bm	**b * m**
Division	/	$x/y \ or \ \dfrac{x}{y} \ or \ x \div y$	**x / y**
Modulus	%	$r \ mod \ s$	**r % s**

Fig. 2.13 Arithmetic operators.

Arithmetic expressions in Java must be written in *straight-line form* to facilitate entering programs into the computer. Thus, expressions such as "**a** divided by **b**" must be written as **a / b** so that all constants, variables and operators appear in a straight line. The following algebraic notation is generally not acceptable to compilers:

$$\frac{a}{b}$$

Parentheses are used in Java expressions in the same manner as in algebraic expressions. For example, to multiply **a** times the quantity **b + c** we write:

```
a * ( b + c )
```

Java applies the operators in arithmetic expressions in a precise sequence determined by the following *rules of operator precedence,* which are generally the same as those followed in algebra:

1. Operators in expressions contained within pairs of parentheses are evaluated first. Thus, *parentheses may be used to force the order of evaluation to occur in any sequence desired by the programmer.* Parentheses are said to be at the "highest level of precedence." In cases of *nested* or *embedded* parentheses, the operators in the innermost pair of parentheses are applied first.

2. Multiplication, division and modulus operations are applied next. If an expression contains several multiplication, division and modulus operations, operators are applied from left to right. Multiplication, division and modulus are said to have the same level of precedence.

3. Addition and subtraction operations are applied last. If an expression contains several addition and subtraction operations, operators are applied from left to right. Addition and subtraction have the same level of precedence.

The rules of operator precedence enable Java to apply operators in the correct order. When we say operators are applied from left to right, we are referring to the *associativity* of the operators. We will see that some operators associate from right to left. Figure 2.14 summarizes these rules of operator precedence. This table will be expanded as additional Java operators are introduced. A complete precedence chart is included in Appendix C.

Operator(s)	Operation(s)	Order of evaluation (precedence)
( )	Parentheses	Evaluated first. If the parentheses are nested, the expression in the innermost pair is evaluated first. If there are several pairs of parentheses "on the same level" (i.e., not nested), they are evaluated left to right.
*, / or %	Multiplication Division Modulus	Evaluated second. If there are several, they are evaluated left to right.
+ or −	Addition Subtraction	Evaluated last. If there are several, they are evaluated left to right.

Fig. 2.14 Precedence of arithmetic operators.

Now let us consider several expressions in light of the rules of operator precedence. Each example lists an algebraic expression and its Java equivalent.

The following is an example of an arithmetic mean (average) of five terms:

Algebra: $m = \dfrac{a + b + c + d + e}{5}$

Java:　　$m = (a + b + c + d + e) / 5;$

The parentheses are required because division has higher precedence than addition. The entire quantity **(a + b + c + d + e)** is to be divided by **5**. If the parentheses are erroneously omitted, we obtain **a + b + c + d + e / 5**, which evaluates as

$$a + b + c + d + \frac{e}{5}$$

The following is an example of the equation of a straight line:

Algebra: $y = mx + b$

Java:　　$y = m * x + b;$

No parentheses are required. The multiplication is applied first because multiplication has a higher precedence than addition. The assignment occurs last because it has a lower precedence than multiplication and division.

The following example contains modulus (**%**), multiplication, division, addition and subtraction operations:

Algebra: $z = pr\%q + w/x - y$

Java: z　=　p　*　r　%　q　+　w　/　x　-　y;
　　　　　　　⑥　　①　　②　　④　　③　　⑤

The circled numbers under the statement indicate the order in which Java applies the operators. The multiplication, modulus and division are evaluated first in left-to-right order (i.e., they associate from left to right) since they have higher precedence than addition and subtraction. The addition and subtraction are applied next. These are also applied left to right.

Not all expressions with several pairs of parentheses contain nested parentheses. For example, the expression

　　　a * (b + c) + c * (d + e)

does not contain nested parentheses. Rather, the parentheses are said to be "on the same level."

To develop a better understanding of the rules of operator precedence, consider how a second-degree polynomial ($y = ax^2 + bx + c$) is evaluated.

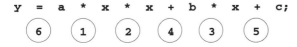

y　=　a　*　x　*　x　+　b　*　x　+　c;
　　　　⑥　　①　　②　　④　　③　　⑤

The circled numbers under the statement indicate the order in which Java applies the operators. There is no arithmetic operator for exponentiation in Java, x^2 is represented as **x * x**.

Suppose **a**, **b**, **c** and **x** are initialized as follows: **a = 2**, **b = 3**, **c = 7** and **x = 5**. Figure 2.15 illustrates the order in which the operators are applied in the preceding second-degree polynomial.

As in algebra, it is acceptable to place unnecessary parentheses in an expression to make the expression clearer. These unnecessary parentheses are also called *redundant parentheses*. For example, the preceding assignment statement might be parenthesized as

```
y = (a * x * x) + (b * x) + c;
```

Good Programming Practice 2.15

Using parentheses for more complex arithmetic expressions even when the parentheses are not necessary can make the arithmetic expressions easier to read.

2.6 Decision Making: Equality and Relational Operators

This section introduces a simple version of Java's **if** *structure* that allows a program to make a decision based on the truth or falsity of some *condition*. If the condition is met (i.e., the condition is *true*), the statement in the body of the **if** structure is executed. If the condition is not met (i.e., the condition is *false*), the body statement is not executed. We will see an example shortly.

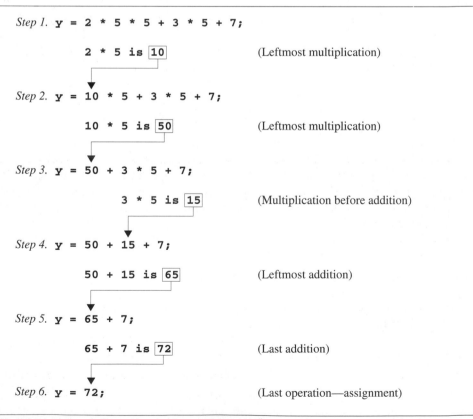

Fig. 2.15 Order in which a second-degree polynomial is evaluated.

Conditions in **if** structures can be formed by using the *equality operators* and *relational operators* summarized in Fig. 2.16. The relational operators all have the same level of precedence and associate left to right. The equality operators both have the same level of precedence, which is lower than the precedence of the relational operators. The equality operators also associate left to right.

Common Programming Error 2.10

It is a syntax error if the operators ==, !=, >= and <= contain spaces between their symbols as in = =, ! =, > = and < =, respectively.

Common Programming Error 2.11

Reversing the operators !=, >= and <= as in =!, => and =<, are each syntax errors.

Common Programming Error 2.12

Confusing the equality operator == with the assignment operator =. The equality operator should be read "is equal to" and the assignment operator should be read "gets" or "gets the value of." Some people prefer to read the equality operator as "double equals" or "equals equals."

The following example uses six **if** statements to compare two numbers input into text fields by the user. If the condition in any of these **if** statements is satisfied, the assignment statement associated with that **if** is executed. The user inputs two values through input dialogs. Next, the values are converted to integers and stored in variables **number1** and **number2**. Then, the comparisons are performed and the results of the comparison are displayed in an information dialog. The program and sample outputs are shown in Fig. 2.17.

The definition of application class **Comparison** begins at line 7

```
public class Comparison {
```

As discussed in the preceding programs, method **main** begins the execution of every Java application.

Standard algebraic equality operator or relational operator	Java equality or relational operator	Example of Java condition	Meaning of Java condition
Equality operators			
=	==	x == y	**x** is equal to **y**
≠	!=	x != y	**x** is not equal to **y**
Relational operators			
>	>	x > y	**x** is greater than **y**
<	<	x < y	**x** is less than **y**
≥	>=	x >= y	**x** is greater than or equal to **y**
≤	<=	x <= y	**x** is less than or equal to **y**

Fig. 2.16 Equality and relational operators.

```
1   // Fig. 2.17: Comparison.java
2   // Using if statements, relational operators
3   // and equality operators
4
5   import javax.swing.JOptionPane;
6
7   public class Comparison {
8      public static void main( String args[] )
9      {
10        String firstNumber,    // first string entered by user
11               secondNumber,   // second string entered by user
12               result;         // a string containing the output
13        int number1,           // first number to compare
14            number2;           // second number to compare
15
16        // read first number from user as a string
17        firstNumber =
18          JOptionPane.showInputDialog( "Enter first integer:" );
19
20        // read second number from user as a string
21        secondNumber =
22          JOptionPane.showInputDialog( "Enter second integer:" );
23
24        // convert numbers from type String to type int
25        number1 = Integer.parseInt( firstNumber );
26        number2 = Integer.parseInt( secondNumber );
27
28        // initialize result to the empty string
29        result = "";
30
31        if ( number1 == number2 )
32           result = result + number1 + " == " + number2;
33
34        if ( number1 != number2 )
35           result = result + number1 + " != " + number2;
36
37        if ( number1 < number2 )
38           result = result + "\n" + number1 + " < " + number2;
39
40        if ( number1 > number2 )
41           result = result + "\n" + number1 + " > " + number2;
42
43        if ( number1 <= number2 )
44           result = result + "\n" + number1 + " <= " + number2;
45
46        if ( number1 >= number2 )
47           result = result + "\n" + number1 + " >= " + number2;
48
```

Fig. 2.17 Using equality and relational operators (part 1 of 2).

```
49          // Display results
50          JOptionPane.showMessageDialog(
51             null, result, "Comparison Results",
52             JOptionPane.INFORMATION_MESSAGE );
53
54          System.exit( 0 );
55       }
56    }
```

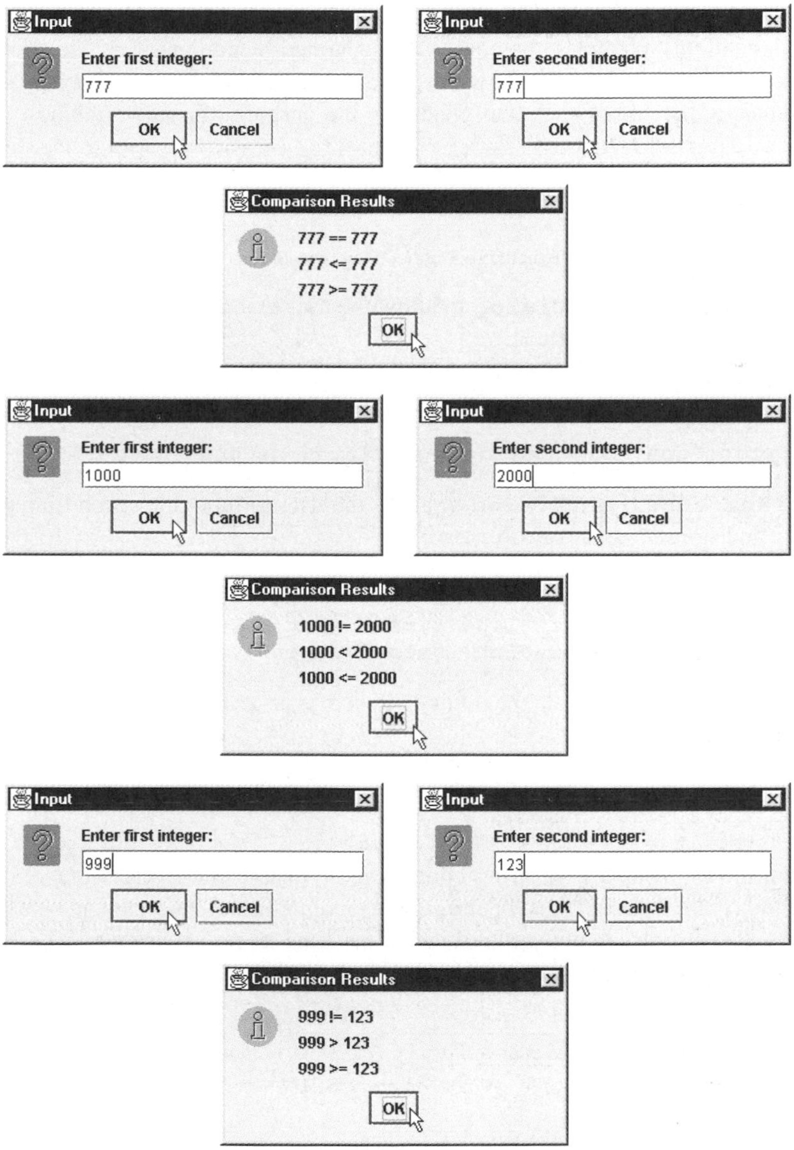

Fig. 2.17   Using equality and relational operators (part 2 of 2).

Lines 10 through 14

```
String firstNumber,     // first string entered by user
       secondNumber,    // second string entered by user
       result;          // a string containing the output
int number1,            // first number to compare
    number2;            // second number to compare
```

declare the variables used in method **main**. Note that there are three variables of type **String** and two variables of type **int**. Remember that variables of the same type may be declared in one declaration or in multiple declarations. If more than one name is declared in a declaration (as in this example), the names are separated by commas (**,**). This is referred to as a comma-separated list (as shown in the **int** declaration above). Once again, notice the comment at the end of each line indicating the purpose of each variable in the program.

Lines 17 and 18

```
firstNumber =
    JOptionPane.showInputDialog( "Enter first integer:" );
```

use **JOptionPane.showInputDialog** to allow the user to input the first integer value as a string and store it in **firstNumber**.

Lines 21 and 22

```
secondNumber =
    JOptionPane.showInputDialog( "Enter second integer:" );
```

use **JOptionPane.showInputDialog** to allow the user to input the second integer value as a string and store it in **secondNumber**.

Lines 25 and 26

```
number1 = Integer.parseInt( firstNumber );
number2 = Integer.parseInt( secondNumber );
```

convert each string input by the user in the input dialogs to type **int** and assign the values to **number1** and **number2**.

Line 29

```
result = "";
```

assigns **result** the *empty string*—a string containing no characters. Every variable declared in a method (such as **main**) must be *initialized* (given a value) before it can be used in an expression. Because we do not yet know what the final **result** string will be, we assigned **result** the empty string as a temporary initial value.

Common Programming Error 2.13

Not initializing a variable defined in a method before that variable is used in the method body is a syntax error.

The **if** structure from lines 31 and 32

```
if ( number1 == number2 )
    result = result + number1 + " == " + number2;
```

compares the values of the variables **number1** and **number2** for equality. If the values are equal, **result** is assigned the value of **result + number1 + " == " + number2**. As discussed in Fig. 2.8, the **+** operator is used in this expression to perform string concatenation. For this discussion, we assume **number1** and **number2** each has the value **123**. First, **number1**'s value is converted to a string and concatenated with **result** (which currently contains the empty string) to produce a string **"123"**. Next, **" == "** is concatenated with **"123"** to produce the string **"123 == "**. Finally, **number2** is concatenated with **"123 == "** to produce the string **"123 == 123"**. The **result** will grow in size due to further string concatenations as the program proceeds through the **if** structures. For example, given the value **123** for **number1** and **number2** in this discussion, the **if** conditions at lines 43 (**<=**) and 46 (**>=**) will also be true. So, the **result** string displayed will be

```
123 == 123
123 <= 123
123 >= 123
```

Common Programming Error 2.14

*Replacing operator **==** in the condition of an **if** structure such as **if (x == 1)** with operator = as in **if (x = 1)** is a syntax error.*

Notice the indentation in the **if** statements throughout the program. Such indentation enhances program readability.

Good Programming Practice 2.16

*Indent the statement in the body of an **if** structure to make the body of the structure stand out and to enhance program readability.*

Good Programming Practice 2.17

Place only one statement per line in a program. This enhances program readability

Common Programming Error 2.15

*Forgetting the left and right parentheses for the condition in an **if** structure is a syntax error. The parentheses are required.*

Notice that there is no semicolon (**;**) at the end of the first line of each **if** structure. Such a semicolon would result in a logic error at execution time. For example,

```
if ( number1 == number2 );
    result = result + number1 + " == " + number2;
```

would actually be interpreted by Java as

```
if ( number1 == number2 )
    ;

result = result + number1 + " == " + number2;
```

where the semicolon on the line by itself—called the *empty statement*—is the statement to execute if the condition in the **if** structure is true. When the empty statement executes, no task is performed in the program. The program then continues with the assignment statement which executes regardless of whether the condition is true or false.

Common Programming Error 2.16

*Placing a semicolon immediately after the right parenthesis of the condition in an **if** structure is normally a logic error. The semicolon would cause the body of the **if** structure to be
empty, so the **if** structure itself would perform no action regardless of whether or not its
condition is true. Worse yet, the intended body statement of the **if** structure would now become a statement in sequence with the **if** structure and would always be executed.*

Notice the use of spacing in Fig. 2.17. Remember that white-space characters such as
tabs, newlines and spaces are normally ignored by the compiler. So, statements may be split
over several lines and may be spaced according to the programmer's preferences without
affecting the meaning of a program. It is incorrect to split identifiers and string literals. Ideally, statements should be kept small, but it is not always possible to do so.

Good Programming Practice 2.18

*A lengthy statement may be spread over several lines. If a single statement must be split
across lines, choose breaking points that make sense such as after a comma in a comma-
separated list, or after an operator in a lengthy expression. If a statement is split across two
or more lines, indent all subsequent lines.*

The chart in Fig. 2.18 shows the precedence of the operators introduced in this chapter.
The operators are shown top to bottom in decreasing order of precedence. Notice that all
these operators, with the exception of the assignment operator **=**, associate from left to
right. Addition is left associative, so an expression like **x + y + z** is evaluated as if it had
been written **(x + y) + z**. The assignment operator **=** associates from right to left, so an
expression like **x = y = 0** is evaluated as if it had been written **x = (y = 0)**, which, as we
will soon see, first assigns the value **0** to variable **y** and then assigns the result of that
assignment, **0**, to **x**.

Good Programming Practice 2.19

*Refer to the operator precedence chart when writing expressions containing many operators.
Confirm that the operators in the expression are performed in the order you expect. If you
are uncertain about the order of evaluation in a complex expression, use parentheses to force
the order, exactly as you would do in algebraic expressions. Be sure to observe that some
operators, such as assignment (**=**), associate right to left rather than left to right.*

Operators	Associativity	Type
( )	left to right	parentheses
* / %	left to right	multiplicative
+ -	left to right	additive
< <= > >=	left to right	relational
== !=	left to right	equality
=	right to left	assignment

Fig. 2.18   Precedence and associativity of the operators discussed so far.

We have introduced many important features of Java including displaying data on the screen, inputting data from the keyboard, performing calculations and making decisions. In Chapter 3, we demonstrate many similar techniques as we introduce Java applet programming. In Chapter 4, we build on the techniques of Chapters 2 and 3 as we introduce *structured programming.* You will become more familiar with indentation techniques. We will study how to specify and vary the order in which statements are executed—this order is called *flow of control.*

Summary

- An application is a program that executes using the **java** interpreter.
- A comment that begins with **//** is called a single-line comment. Programmers insert comments to document programs and improve program readability.
- A string of characters contained between double quotation marks is called a string, a character string, a message or a string literal.
- Blank lines, space characters, newline characters and tab characters are known as white-space characters. White-space characters outside strings are ignored by the compiler.
- Keyword **class** introduces a class definition and is immediately followed by the class name.
- Keywords (or reserved words) are reserved for use by Java.
- By convention, all class names in Java begin with a capital first letter. If a class name has more than one word, each word should be capitalized.
- An identifier is a series of characters consisting of letters, digits, underscores (_) and dollar signs (**$**) that does not begin with a digit, does not contain any spaces and is not a keyword.
- Java is case sensitive—uppercase and lowercase letters are different.
- A left brace, **{**, begins the body of every class definition. A corresponding right brace, **}**, ends each class definition.
- Java applications begin executing at method **main**.
- Methods are able to perform tasks and return information when they complete their tasks.
- The first line of method **main** must be defined as

  ```
  public static void main( String args[] )
  ```

- A left brace, **{**, begins the body of a method definition. A corresponding right brace, **}**, ends the method definition's body.
- **System.out** is known as the standard output object. **System.out** allows Java applications to display strings and other types of information in the command window from which the Java application is executed.
- The escape sequence **\n** means newline. Other escape sequences include **\t** (tab), **\r** (carriage return), **** (backslash) and **\"** (double quote).
- Method **println** of the **System.out** object displays (or prints) a line of information in the command window. When **println** completes its task, it automatically positions to the beginning of the next line in the command window.
- Every statement must end with a semicolon (also known as the statement terminator).
- The difference between **System.out.print** and **System.out.println** is that **System.out.print** does not position to the beginning of the next line in the command window when it finishes displaying its argument. The next character that is displayed in the command window will appear immediately after the last character displayed with **System.out.print**.

- Java contains many predefined classes that are grouped by directories on disk into categories of related classes called packages. The packages are referred to collectively as the Java class library or the Java applications programming interface (Java API).

- Class **JOptionPane** is defined for us in a package called **javax.swing**. Class **JOption-Pane** contains methods that display a dialog box containing information.

- The compiler uses **import** statements to locate classes required to compile a Java program.

- The **javax.swing** package contains many classes that help define a graphical user interface (GUI) for an application. GUI components facilitate data entry by the user of a program and data outputs by a program.

- Method **showMessageDialog** of class **JOptionPane** requires two arguments. Until we discuss **JOptionPane** in detail in Chapter 12, the first argument will always be the keyword **null**. The second argument is the string to display.

- A **static** method is called by following its class name by a dot (**.**) and the method name.

- Method **exit** of class **System** terminates an application. Class **System** is part of the package **java.lang**. Package **java.lang** is automatically imported in every Java program.

- A variable is a location in the computer's memory where a value can be stored for use by a program. A variable name is any valid identifier.

- All variables must be declared with a name and a data type before they can be used in a program.

- Declarations end with a semicolon (**;**) and can be split over several lines with each variable in the declaration separated by a comma (i.e., a comma-separated list of variable names).

- Variables of type **int** hold integer values (i.e., whole numbers such as 7, –11, 0, 31914).

- Types such as **int**, **float**, **double** and **char** are often called primitive data types. Primitive type names are keywords of the Java programming language.

- A prompt directs the user to take a specific action.

- A variable is assigned a value with an assignment statement using the assignment operator **=**. The **=** operator is called a binary operator because it has two operands.

- Method **Integer.parseInt** (a **static** method of class **Integer**) converts its **String** argument to an integer.

- Java has a version of the **+** operator for string concatenation that enables a string and a value of another data type (including another string) to be concatenated.

- Variable names correspond to locations in the computer's memory. Every variable has a name, a type, a size and a value.

- When a value is placed in a memory location, this value replaces the previous value in that location. When a value is read out of a memory location, the process is nondestructive.

- The arithmetic operators are binary operators because they each operate on two operands.

- Integer division yields an integer quotient.

- Arithmetic expressions in Java must be written in straight-line form to facilitate entering programs into the computer.

- Operators in arithmetic expressions are applied in a precise sequence determined by the rules of operator precedence.

- Parentheses may be used to force the order of evaluation of operators to occur in any sequence desired by the programmer.

- When we say operators are applied from left to right, we are referring to the associativity of the operators. Some operators associate from right to left.

- Java's **if** structure allows a program to make a decision based on the truth or falsity of a condition. If the condition is met (the condition is true), the statement in the body of the **if** structure is executed. If the condition is not met (the condition is false), the body statement is not executed.

- Conditions in **if** structures can be formed by using the equality operators and relational operators.

- The empty string is a string containing no characters.

- Every variable declared in a method must be initialized before it can be used in an expression.

Terminology

addition operator (**+**)
applet
application
argument to a method
arithmetic operators
assignment operator (**=**)
assignment statement
associativity of operators
backslash (****) escape character
binary operator
body of a class definition
body of a method definition
braces (**{** and **}**)
case sensitive
character string
class
class definition
.class file extension
class keyword
class name
comma-separated list
command tool
command window
comment (**//**)
compilation error
compile error
compiler
compile-time error
condition
decision
declaration
dialog box
division operator (**/**)
document a program
empty string (**""**)
equality operators
    == "is equal to"
    != "is not equal to"
escape sequence
false
graphical user interface (GUI)

identifier
if structure
import statement
input dialog
int primitive type
integer (**int**)
Integer class
integer division
interpreter
Java
Java applications programming interface (API)
Java class library
Java documentation comment
.java file extension
java interpreter
java.lang package
Java 2 Software Development Kit (J2SDK)
javax.swing package
JOptionPane class
JOptionPane.ERROR_MESSAGE
JOptionPane.INFORMATION_MESSAGE
JOptionPane.PLAIN_MESSAGE
JOptionPane.QUESTION_MESSAGE
JOptionPane.showInputDialog
JOptionPane.showMessageDialog
JOptionPane.WARNING_MESSAGE
left brace **{** begins the body of a class
left brace **{** begins the body of a method
literal
main method
memory
memory location
message
message dialog
method
Microsoft Internet Explorer browser
modulus operator (**%**)
mouse cursor
mouse pointer
MS-DOS Prompt
multiple-line comment

multiplication operator (*****)
nested parentheses
Netscape Communicator browser
newline character (**\n**)
object
operand
operator
package
parentheses (**)**
parseInt method of class **Integer**
precedence
primitive data type
programmer-defined class
prompt
public keyword
relational operators
    > "is greater than"
    < "is less than"
    >= "is greater than or equal to"
    <= "is less than or equal to"
reserved words
right brace **}** ends the body of a class
right brace **}** ends the body of a method
right-to-left associativity
rules of operator precedence
semicolon (**;**) statement terminator

shell tool
single-line comment
standard output object
statement
statement terminator (**;**)
static method
straight-line form
string
String class
string concatenation
string concatenation operator (**+**)
subtraction operator (**-**)
syntax error
System class
System.exit method
System.out
System.out.print method
System.out.println method
title bar of a dialog
true
user-defined class
variable
variable name
variable value
void keyword
white-space characters

Common Programming Errors

2.1   Forgetting one of the delimiters of a multiple-line comment is a syntax error.

2.2   Java is case sensitive. Not using the proper uppercase and lowercase letters for an identifier is normally a syntax error.

2.3   For a **public** class, it is an error if the file name is not identical to the class name in both spelling and capitalization. Therefore, it is also an error for a file to contain two or more **public** classes.

2.4   It is an error not to end a file name with the **.java** extension for a file containing an application's class definition. The Java compiler will not be able to compile the class definition.

2.5   If braces do not occur in matching pairs, the compiler indicates an error.

2.6   Omitting the semicolon at the end of a statement is a syntax error. A syntax error is caused when the compiler cannot recognize a statement. The compiler normally issues an error message to help the programmer locate and fix the incorrect statement. Syntax errors are violations of the language rules. Syntax errors are also called compile errors, compile-time errors or compilation errors because they are detected during the compilation phase. You will be unable to execute your program until all the syntax errors are corrected.

2.7   Splitting a statement in the middle of an identifier or a string is a syntax error.

2.8   Forgetting to call **System.exit** in an application that displays a graphical user interface prevents the program from terminating properly. This normally results in the command window preventing you from typing any other commands.

2.9   Confusing the **+** operator used for string concatenation with the **+** operator used for addition can lead to strange results. For example, assuming integer variable **y** has the value **5**, the expression **"y + 2 = " + y + 2** results in the string **"y + 2 = 52"**, not **"y + 2 = 7"**, because first the value of **y** is concatenated with the string **"y + 2 = "**, then the value **2** is concatenated with the new larger string **"y + 2 = 5"**. The expression **"y + 2 = " + (y + 2)** produces the desired result.

2.10   It is a syntax error if the operators **==**, **!=**, **>=** and **<=** contain spaces between their symbols as in **= =**, **! =**, **> =** and **< =**, respectively.

2.11   Reversing the operators **!=**, **>=** and **<=** as in **=!**, **=>** and **=<**, are each syntax errors.

2.12   Confusing the equality operator **==** with the assignment operator **=**. The equality operator should be read "is equal to" and the assignment operator should be read "gets" or "gets the value of." Some people prefer to read the equality operator as "double equals" or "equals equals."

2.13   Not initializing a variable defined in a method before that variable is used in the method body is a syntax error.

2.14   Replacing operator **==** in the condition of an **if** structure such as **if (x == 1)** with operator **=** as in **if (x = 1)** is a syntax error.

2.15   Forgetting the left and right parentheses for the condition in an **if** structure is a syntax error. The parentheses are required.

2.16   Placing a semicolon immediately after the right parenthesis of the condition in an **if** structure is normally a logic error. The semicolon would cause the body of the **if** structure to be empty, so the **if** structure itself would perform no action regardless of whether or not its condition is true. Worse yet, the intended body statement of the **if** structure would now become a statement in sequence with the **if** structure and would always be executed.

Good Programming Practices

2.1   Every program should begin with a comment describing the purpose of the program.

2.2   Use blank lines, space characters and tab characters in a program to enhance program readability.

2.3   By convention, you should always begin a class name with a capital first letter.

2.4   When reading a Java program, look for identifiers that start with capital first letters. These normally represent Java classes.

2.5   Whenever you type an opening left brace, **{**, in your program, immediately type the closing right brace, **}**, then reposition the cursor between the braces to begin typing the body. This helps prevent missing braces.

2.6   Indent the entire body of each class definition one "level" of indentation between the left brace, **{**, and the right brace, **}**, that define the body of the class. This emphasizes the structure of the class definition and helps make the class definition easier to read.

2.7   Set a convention for the indent size you prefer and then uniformly apply that convention. The *Tab* key may be used to create indents, but tab stops may vary between editors. We recommend using either 1/4-inch tab stops or (preferably) three spaces to form a level of indent.

2.8   Indent the entire body of each method definition one "level" of indentation between the left brace, **{**, and the right brace, **}**, that define the body of the method. This makes the structure of the method stand out and helps make the method definition easier to read.

2.9   Some programmers prefer to follow the closing right brace (**}**) of the body of a method or class definition with a single-line comment indicating the method or class definition for which the right brace terminates the definition's body.

2.10   Place a space after each comma in an argument list (**,**) to make programs more readable.

2.11   Choosing meaningful variable names helps a program to be "self-documenting" (i.e., it becomes easier to understand a program simply by reading it rather than having to read manuals or use excessive comments).

2.12   By convention, variable name identifiers begin with a lowercase first letter. As with class names every word in the name after the first word should begin with a capital first letter. For example, identifier **firstNumber** has a capital **N** in its second word **Number**.

2.13   Some programmers prefer to declare each variable on a separate line. This format allows for easy insertion of a descriptive comment next to each declaration.

2.14   Place spaces on either side of a binary operator. This makes the operator stand out and makes the program more readable.

2.15   Using parentheses for more complex arithmetic expressions even when the parentheses are not necessary can make the arithmetic expressions easier to read.

2.16   Indent the statement in the body of an **if** structure to make the body of the structure stand out and to enhance program readability.

2.17   Place only one statement per line in a program. This enhances program readability

2.18   A lengthy statement may be spread over several lines. If a single statement must be split across lines, choose breaking points that make sense such as after a comma in a comma-separated list, or after an operator in a lengthy expression. If a statement is split across two or more lines, indent all subsequent lines.

2.19   Refer to the operator precedence chart when writing expressions containing many operators. Confirm that the operators in the expression are performed in the order you expect. If you are uncertain about the order of evaluation in a complex expression, use parentheses to force the order, exactly as you would do in algebraic expressions. Be sure to observe that some operators, such as assignment (**=**), associate right to left rather than left to right.

Software Engineering Observation

2.1   Avoid using identifiers containing dollar signs (**$**) as these are often used by the compiler to create indentifier names.

Testing and Debugging Tip

2.1   When the compiler reports a syntax error, the error may not be on the line indicated by the error messages. First, check the line where the error was reported. If that line does not contain syntax errors, check the preceding several lines in the program.

Self-Review Exercises

2.1   Fill in the blanks in each of the following.
   a) The _____ begins the body of every method and the _____ ends the body of every method.
   b) Every statement ends with a _____.
   c) The _____ structure is used to make decisions.
   d) _____ begins a single-line comment.
   e) _____, _____, _____ and _____ are known as white-space.
   f) Class _____ displays message dialogs and input dialogs.
   g) _____ are reserved for use by Java.
   h) Java applications begin execution at method _____.
   i) Methods _____ and _____ display information in the command window.
   j) A _____ method is always called using its class name followed by a dot (**.**) and its method name.

2.2   State whether each of the following is *true* or *false*. If *false*, explain why.
   a) Comments cause the computer to print the text after the **//** on the screen when the program is executed.
   b) All variables must be given a type when they are declared.
   c) Java considers the variables **number** and **NuMbEr** to be identical.
   d) The modulus operator (**%**) can be used only with integer operands.
   e) The arithmetic operators *****, **/**, **%**, **+** and **–** all have the same level of precedence.
   f) Method **Integer.parseInt** converts an integer to a **String**.

2.3   Write Java statements to accomplish each of the following:
   a) Declare variables **c**, **thisIsAVariable**, **q76354** and **number** to be of type **int**.
   b) Display a dialog asking the user to enter an integer.
   c) Convert a **String** to an integer and store the converted value in integer variable **age**. Assume that the **String** is stored in **stringValue**.
   d) If the variable **number** is not equal to **7**, display **"The variable number is not equal to 7"** in a message dialog. (*Hint:* Use the version of the message dialog that requires two arguments.)
   e) Print the message **"This is a Java program"** on one line in the command window.
   f) Print the message **"This is a Java program"** on two lines in the command window where the first line ends with **Java**. Use only one statement.

2.4   Identify and correct the errors in each of the following statements:
   a) ```
if (c < 7);
    JOptionPane.showMessageDialog(null,
        "c is less than 7");
```
   b) ```
if ( c => 7 )
    JOptionPane.showMessageDialog( null,
        "c is equal to or greater than 7" );
```

2.5   Write a statement (or comment) to accomplish each of the following:
   a) State that a program will calculate the product of three integers.
   b) Declare the variables **x**, **y**, **z** and **result** to be of type **int**.
   c) Declare the variables **xVal**, **yVal** and **zVal** to be of type **String**.
   d) Prompt the user to enter the first value, read the value from the user and store it in the variable **xVal**.
   e) Prompt the user to enter the second value, read the value from the user and store it in the variable **yVal**.
   f) Prompt the user to enter the third value, read the value from the user and store it in the variable **zVal**.
   g) Convert **xVal** to an **int** and store the result in the variable **x**.
   h) Convert **yVal** to an **int** and store the result in the variable **y**.
   i) Convert **zVal** to an **int** and store the result in the variable **z**.
   j) Compute the product of the three integers contained in variables **x**, **y** and **z**, and assign the result to the variable **result**.
   k) Display a dialog **"The product is "** followed by the value of the variable **result**.
   l) Return a value from **main** indicating that the program terminated successfully.

2.6   Using the statements you wrote in Exercise 2.5, write a complete program that calculates and prints the product of three integers.

Answers to Self-Review Exercises

2.1   a) Left brace (**{**), right brace (**}**). b) Semicolon (**;**). c) **if**. d) **//**. e) Blank lines, space characters, newline characters and tab characters. f) **JOptionPane**. g) Keywords. h) **main**. i) **System.out.print** and **System.out.println**. j) **static**.

2.2   a) False. Comments do not cause any action to be performed when the program is executed. They are used to document programs and improve their readability.
   b) True.
   c) False. Java is case sensitive, so these variables are distinct.
   d) False. The modulus operator can also be used with noninteger operands in Java.
   e) False. The operators *****, **/** and **%** are on the same level of precedence and the operators **+** and **−** are on a lower level of precedence.
   f) False. **Integer.parseInt** method converts a **String** to an integer (**int**) value.

2.3   a) `int c, thisIsAVariable, q76354, number;`
   b) `value = JOptionPane.showInputDialog( "Enter an integer" );`
   c) `age = Integer.parseInt( stringValue );`
   d) `if ( number != 7 )`
      `    JOptionPane.showMessageDialog( null,`
      `        "The variable number is not equal to 7" );`
   e) `System.out.println( "This is a Java program" );`
   f) `System.out.println( "This is a Java\nprogram" );`

2.4   a) Error: Semicolon after the right parenthesis of the condition in the **if** statement. Correction: Remove the semicolon after the right parenthesis. [*Note:* The result of this error is that the output statement will be executed whether or not the condition in the **if** statement is true. The semicolon after the right parenthesis is considered an empty statement—a statement that does nothing. We will learn more about the empty statement in the next chapter.]
   b) Error: The relational operator **=>** is incorrect.
      Correction: Change **=>** to **>=**.

2.5   a) `// Calculate the product of three integers`
   b) `int x, y, z, result;`
   c) `String xVal, yVal, zVal;`
   d) `xVal = JOptionPane.showInputDialog(`
      `            "Enter first integer:" );`
   e) `yVal = JOptionPane.showInputDialog(`
      `            "Enter second integer:" );`
   f) `zVal = JOptionPane.showInputDialog(`
      `            "Enter third integer:" );`
   g) `x = Integer.parseInt( xVal );`
   h) `y = Integer.parseInt( yVal );`
   i) `z = Integer.parseInt( zVal );`
   j) `result = x * y * z;`
   k) `JOptionPane.showMessageDialog( null,`
      `       "The product is " + result );`
   l) `System.exit( 0 );`

2.6   The program is:

```
1  // Calculate the product of three integers
2  import javax.swing.JOptionPane;
3
4  public class Product {
5     public static void main( String args[] )
6     {
7        int x, y, z, result;
8        String xVal, yVal, zVal;
9
10       xVal = JOptionPane.showInputDialog(
11               "Enter first integer:" );
12       yVal = JOptionPane.showInputDialog(
13               "Enter second integer:" );
14       zVal = JOptionPane.showInputDialog(
15               "Enter third integer:" );
16
17       x = Integer.parseInt( xVal );
18       y = Integer.parseInt( yVal );
19       z = Integer.parseInt( zVal );
20
21       result = x * y * z;
22       JOptionPane.showMessageDialog( null,
23          "The product is " + result );
24
25       System.exit( 0 );
26    }
27  }
```

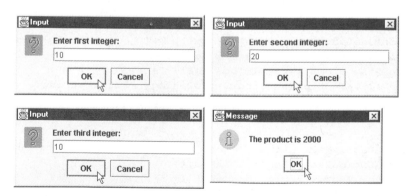

Exercises

2.7   Fill in the blanks in each of the following:

a) _____ are used to document a program and improve its readability.

b) An input dialog capable of receiving input from the user is displayed with method _____ of class _____.

c) A Java statement that makes a decision is _____.

d) Calculations are normally performed by _____ statements.

e) An input dialog capable of receiving input from the user is displayed with method _____ of class _____.

2.8   Write Java statements that accomplish each of the following:
   a) Display the message **"Enter two numbers"** using class **JOptionPane**.
   b) Assign the product of variables **b** and **c** to variable **a**.
   c) State that a program performs a sample payroll calculation (i.e., use text that helps to doc-
       ument a program).

2.9   State whether each of the following is *true* or *false*. If *false*, explain why.
   a) Java operators are evaluated from left to right.
   b) The following are all valid variable names: **_under_bar_**, **m928134**, **t5**, **j7**,
       her_sales$**, **his_$account_total, **a**, **b$**, **c**, **z**, **z2**.
   c) A valid Java arithmetic expression with no parentheses is evaluated from left to right.
   d) The following are all invalid variable names: **3g**, **87**, **67h2**, **h22**, **2h.**

2.10   Fill in the blanks in each of the following:
   a) What arithmetic operations have the same precedence as multiplication? _____.
   b) When parentheses are nested, which set of parentheses is evaluated first in an arithmetic
       expression? _____.
   c) A location in the computer's memory that may contain different values at various times
       throughout the execution of a program is called a _____.

2.11   What displays in the message dialog when each of the following Java statements is performed? Assume **x = 2** and **y = 3**.
   a) **JOptionPane.showMessageDialog(null, "x = " + x);**
   b) **JOptionPane.showMessageDialog(null,**
       "The value of x + x is " + (x + x));
   c) **JOptionPane.showMessageDialog(null, "x =");**
   d) **JOptionPane.showMessageDialog(null,**
       (x + y) + " = " + (y + x));

2.12   Which of the following Java statements contain variables whose values are destroyed (i.e.,
changed or replaced)?
   a) **p = i + j + k + 7;**
   b) **JOptionPane.showMessageDialog(null,**
       "variables whose values are destroyed");
   c) **JOptionPane.showMessageDialog(null, "a = 5");**
   d) **stringVal = JOptionPane.showInputDialog("Enter string:);**

2.13   Given $y = ax^3 + 7$, which of the following are correct statements for this equation?
   a) **y = a * x * x * x + 7;**
   b) **y = a * x * x * (x + 7);**
   c) **y = (a * x) * x * (x + 7);**
   d) **y = (a * x) * x * x + 7;**
   e) **y = a * (x * x * x) + 7;**
   f) **y = a * x * (x * x + 7);**

2.14   State the order of evaluation of the operators in each of the following Java statements and
show the value of **x** after each statement is performed.
   a) **x = 7 + 3 * 6 / 2 - 1;**
   b) **x = 2 % 2 + 2 * 2 - 2 / 2;**
   c) **x = (3 * 9 * (3 + (9 * 3 / (3))));**

2.15   Write an application that displays the numbers 1 to 4 on the same line with each pair of adjacent numbers separated by one space. Write the program using the following methods.
   a) Using one **System.out** statement.
   b) Using four **System.out** statements.

2.16 Write an application that asks the user to enter two numbers, obtains the two numbers from the user and prints the sum, product, difference and quotient of the two numbers. Use the techniques shown in Fig. 2.8.

2.17 Write an application that asks the user to enter two integers, obtains the numbers from the user and displays the larger number followed by the words "**is larger**" in an information message dialog. If the numbers are equal, print the message "**These numbers are equal**." Use the techniques shown in Fig. 2.17.

2.18 Write an application that inputs three integers from the user and displays the sum, average, product, smallest and largest of these numbers in an information message dialog. Use the GUI techniques shown in Fig. 2.17. Note: The average calculation in this exercise should result in an integer representation of the average. So, if the sum of the values is 7, the average will be 2 not 2.3333...

2.19 Write an application that inputs from the user the radius of a circle and prints the circle's diameter, circumference and area. Use the constant value 3.14159 for π. Use the GUI techniques shown in Fig. 2.8. [*Note:* You may also use the predefined constant **Math.PI** for the value of π. This constant is more precise than the value 3.14159. Class **Math** is defined in the **java.lang** package, so you do not need to **import** it.] Use the following formulas (*r* is the radius): *diameter = 2r, circumference = 2πr, area = πr²*.

2.20 Write an application that displays in the command window a box, an oval, an arrow and a diamond using asterisks (*****) as follows:

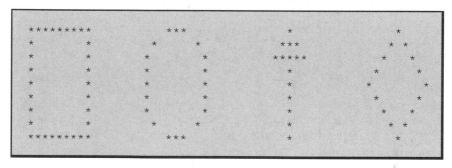

2.21 Modify the program you created in Exercise 2.20 to display the shapes in a **JOption-Pane.PLAIN_MESSAGE** dialog. Does the program display the shapes exactly as in Exercise 2.20?

2.22 What does the following code print?

```
System.out.println( "*\n**\n***\n****\n*****" );
```

2.23 What does the following code print?

```
System.out.println( "*" );
System.out.println( "***" );
System.out.println( "*****" );
System.out.println( "****" );
System.out.println( "**" );
```

2.24 What does the following code print?

```
System.out.print( "*" );
System.out.print( "***" );
System.out.print( "*****" );
System.out.print( "****" );
System.out.println( "**" );
```

2.25   What does the following code print?

```
System.out.print( "*" );
System.out.println( "***" );
System.out.println( "*****" );
System.out.print( "****" );
System.out.println( "**" );
```

2.26   Write an application that reads five integers and determines and prints the largest and the smallest integers in the group. Use only the programming techniques you learned in this chapter.

2.27   Write an application that reads an integer and determines and prints whether it is odd or even. (*Hint:* Use the modulus operator. An even number is a multiple of 2. Any multiple of 2 leaves a remainder of zero when divided by 2.)

2.28   Write an application that reads in two integers and determines and prints if the first is a multiple of the second. (*Hint:* Use the modulus operator.)

2.29   Write an application that displays in the command window a checkerboard pattern as follows:

```
* * * * * * * *
 * * * * * * * *
* * * * * * * *
 * * * * * * * *
* * * * * * * *
 * * * * * * * *
* * * * * * * *
 * * * * * * * *
```

2.30   Modify the program you wrote in Exercise 2.29 to display the checkerboard pattern in a **JOptionPane.PLAIN_MESSAGE** dialog. Does the program display the shapes exactly as in Exercise 2.29?

2.31   Here's a peek ahead. In this chapter you learned about integers and the data type **int**. Java can also represent uppercase letters, lowercase letters and a considerable variety of special symbols. Every character has a corresponding integer representation. The set of characters a computer uses and the corresponding integer representations for those characters is called that computer's character set. You can indicate a character value in a program simply by enclosing that character in single quotes, as with **'A'**.

You can determine the integer equivalent of a character by preceding that character with **(int)**—this is called a cast (we will say more about casts in Chapter 4).

```
(int) 'A'
```

The following statement would output a character and its integer equivalent:

```
System.out.println(
   "The character " + 'A' + " has the value " + (int) 'A' );
```

When the preceding statement executes, it displays the character **A** and the value **65** (from the so-called Unicode character set) as part of the string.

Write an application that displays the integer equivalents of some uppercase letters, lowercase letters, digits and special symbols. At a minimum, display the integer equivalents of the following: **A B C a b c 0 1 2 $ * + /** and the blank character.

2.32   Write an application that inputs one number consisting of five digits from the user, separates the number into its individual digits and prints the digits separated from one another by three spaces each. For example, if the user types in the number **42339**, the program should print

```
4   2   3   3   9
```

(*Hint*: This exercise is possible with the techniques you learned in this chapter. You will need to use both division and modulus operations to "pick off" each digit.)

For the purpose of this exercise assume that the user enters the correct number of digits. What happens when you execute the program and type a number with more than five digits? What happens when you execute the program and type a number with fewer than five digits?

2.33   Using only the programming techniques you learned in this chapter, write an application that calculates the squares and cubes of the numbers from 0 to 10 and prints the resulting values in table format as follows:

```
number   square   cube
0        0        0
1        1        1
2        4        8
3        9        27
4        16       64
5        25       125
6        36       216
7        49       343
8        64       512
9        81       729
10       100      1000
```

[*Note:* This program does not require any input from the user.]

2.34   Write a program that reads a first name and a last name from the user as two separate inputs and concatenates the first name and last name separated by a space. Display in a message dialog the concatenated name.

2.35   Write a program that inputs five numbers and determines and prints the number of negative numbers input, the number of positive numbers input and the number of zeros input.

3

Introduction to Java Applets

Objectives

- To understand the terminology of object-oriented programming.
- To observe some of Java's exciting capabilities through several demonstration applets provided with the Java 2 Software Development Kit.
- To understand the difference between an applet and an application.
- To be able to write simple Java applets.
- To be able to write simple Hypertext Markup Language (HTML) files to load an applet into the **appletviewer** or a World Wide Web browser.
- To understand the difference between variables and references.

He would answer to "Hi!" or to any loud cry
Such as "Fry me!" or "Fritter my wig!"
To "What-you-may-call-um!" or "What-was-his-name!"
But especially "Thing-um-a-jig!"
Lewis Carroll

Painting is only a bridge linking the painter's mind with that of the viewer.
Eugéne Delacroix

My method is to take the utmost trouble to find the right thing to say, and then to say it with the utmost levity.
George Bernard Shaw

Though this be madness, yet there is method in 't.
William Shakespeare

Outline

3.1 Introduction

In Chapter 2, we introduced Java application programming and several important aspects of Java applications. This chapter introduces another type of Java program called a Java *applet*. Unlike a Java application that executes from a command window, an applet is a Java program that runs in the **appletviewer** (a test utility for applets that is included with the J2SDK) or a World Wide Web browser such as Netscape Communicator or Microsoft Internet Explorer. The **appletviewer** (or browser) executes an applet when a *Hypertext Markup Language (HTML) document* containing the applet is opened in the **appletviewer** (or browser).

One of our goals in this chapter is to mimic several features presented in Chapter 2. This provides positive reinforcement of concepts covered previously. Another goal of this chapter is to formally introduce terminology used with object-oriented programming.

As in Chapter 2, there are a few cases where we do not as yet provide all the details necessary to create complex applications and applets in Java. It is important to build your knowledge of fundamental programming concepts first. In Chapters 4 and 5, we present a detailed treatment of *program development* and *program control* in Java. As we proceed through the text, many substantial applications and applets will be presented.

3.2 Thinking About Objects

Now we begin our early introduction to object orientation. We will see that object orientation is a natural way of thinking about the world and of writing computer programs. Why, then, did we not begin with object orientation on page one? Why are we deferring our detailed discussion of object-oriented programming in Java until Chapter 8? The answer is that the objects we will build will be composed in part of structured program pieces, so we need to establish a basis in structured programming first.

In Chapters 2 though 7, we use many object-oriented Java features because Java is an object-oriented programming language—there is simply no way to ignore object-oriented programming in Java! However, Java also contains many constructs from the "conventional" methodology of structured programming supported by many other programming languages. In the first seven chapters, we concentrate on these "conventional" parts of Java as they are important components of all Java programs.

Our strategy in this section is to introduce basic concepts (i.e., "object think") and terminology (i.e., "object speak") of object-oriented programming so we can properly refer to the object-oriented concepts as we encounter them in Chapters 2 through 7. At the end of this book is an appendix containing a substantial object-oriented programming exercise. The appendix considers more substantial object-oriented issues, then attacks a challenging problem with the techniques of *object-oriented design (OOD)*. In the appendix, we analyze a typical problem statement that requires a system to be built, determine which objects are needed to implement the system, determine what attributes the objects will need to have, determine what behaviors these objects will need to exhibit and specify how the objects will need to interact with one another to meet the system requirements. We do all this for a real-world problem rather than an artificial classroom example.

Let us start by introducing some of the key terminology of object orientation. Look around you in the real world. Everywhere you look you see them—*objects*! People, animals, plants, cars, planes, buildings, computers and the like. Humans think in terms of objects. We have the marvelous ability of *abstraction,* which enables us to view screen images as objects such as people, planes, trees and mountains rather than as individual dots of color (called *pixels* for "picture elements"). We can, if we wish, think in terms of beaches rather than grains of sand, forests rather than trees and houses rather than bricks.

We might be inclined to divide objects into two categories—animate objects and inanimate objects. Animate objects are "alive" in some sense. They move around and do things. Inanimate objects, like towels, seem not to do much at all. They just kind of "sit around." All these objects, however, do have some things in common. They all have *attributes* like size, shape, color, weight and the like. And they all exhibit *behaviors;* for example, a ball rolls, bounces, inflates and deflates; a baby cries, sleeps, crawls, walks and blinks; a car accelerates, brakes and turns; a towel absorbs water.

Humans learn about objects by studying their attributes and observing their behaviors. Different objects can have similar attributes and can exhibit similar behaviors. Comparisons can be made, for example, between babies and adults and between humans and chimpanzees. Cars, trucks, little red wagons and skateboards have much in common.

Object-oriented programming (OOP) models real-world objects with software counterparts. It takes advantage of *class* relationships where objects of a certain class—such as a class of vehicles—have the same characteristics. It takes advantage of *inheritance* relationships where newly created classes of objects inherit characteristics of existing classes, yet contain unique characteristics of their own. An object of class convertible certainly has the characteristics of class automobile, but a convertible's roof goes up and down.

Object-oriented programming gives us a more natural and intuitive way to view the programming process—namely by *modeling* real-world objects, their attributes and their behaviors. OOP also models communication between objects. Just as people send *messages* to one another (e.g., a sergeant commanding troops to stand at attention), objects also communicate via messages.

OOP *encapsulates* data (attributes) and methods (behavior) into packages called *objects;* the data and methods of an object are intimately tied together. Objects have the property of *information hiding.* This means that although objects may know how to communicate with one another across well-defined *interfaces,* objects normally are not allowed to know how other objects are implemented—implementation details are hidden within the objects themselves. Surely it is possible to drive a car effectively without knowing the details of how engines, transmissions and exhaust systems work internally. We will see why information hiding is so crucial to good software engineering.

In C and other *procedural programming languages,* programming tends to be *action-oriented,* whereas in Java programming tends to be *object-oriented.* In C, the unit of programming is the *function.* In Java, the unit of programming is the *class* from which objects are eventually *instantiated* (a fancy term for "created"). Java classes contain *methods* (the corresponding concept to functions in C).

C programmers concentrate on writing functions. Groups of actions that perform some common task are formed into functions, and functions are grouped to form programs. Data is certainly important in C, but the view is that data exists primarily in support of the actions that functions perform. The *verbs* in a system specification help the C programmer determine the set of functions that work together to implement the system.

Java programmers concentrate on creating their own *user-defined types* called *classes.* Each class contains data and a set of functions that manipulate the data. The data components of a class are called *instance variables* (or *data members*). The function components of a class are called *methods* (some object-oriented programming languages call them *member functions*). Just as an instance of a built-in (*primitive*) type such as **int** is called a *variable,* an instance of a user-defined type (i.e., a class) is called an *object* (or *instance*). The programmer uses built-in types and other classes as the building blocks for constructing new user-defined types. The focus of attention in Java is on classes (out of which we make objects) rather than functions. The *nouns* in a system specification help the Java programmer determine the set of classes from which objects will be created that will work together to implement the system. Blueprints are to houses as classes are to objects. We can build many houses from one blueprint and we can instantiate many objects from one class.

We will see that when software is packaged as classes, these classes become components that can be reused in future software systems. Just as real estate brokers tell their clients that the three most important factors affecting the price of real estate are "location, location and location," the three most important factors that may most affect the future of software development are "reuse, reuse and reuse."

Indeed, with object technology, we will build most future software by combining "standardized, interchangeable parts" called classes. These parts allow programmers to create new classes without having to "reinvent the wheel." This book will teach you how to "craft valuable classes" for reuse. Each new class you create will have the potential to become a valuable "software asset" that you and other programmers can use to speed and enhance the quality of future software development efforts. This is an exciting possibility.

3.3 Sample Applets from the Java 2 Software Development Kit

We begin by considering several sample applets provided with the Java 2 Software Development Kit (J2SDK) version 1.2.1. The applets we demonstrate give you a sense of Java's capabilities. Each of the sample programs provided with the J2SDK also comes with *source code* (the **.java** files containing the Java applet programs). This source code will be useful to you as you enhance your Java knowledge—you will be able to read the source code provided to learn new and exciting features of the language. Remember, all programmers initially learn new features by mimicking their use in existing programs. The J2SDK comes with many such programs and there are a tremendous number of Java resources on the Internet and World Wide Web that also include Java source code.

The demonstration programs provided with the J2SDK are located in your J2SDK install directory in a subdirectory called **demo**. For Java 2 version 1.2.1, the default location of the **demo** directory on Windows is

        c:\jdk1.2.1\demo

On UNIX it is a directory that you choose followed by **jdk1.2.1/demo**—for example

        /usr/local/jdk1.2.1/demo

For other platforms, there will be a similar directory (or folder) structure. For the purpose of this chapter, we assume on Windows that the J2SDK is installed in **c:\jdk1.2.1** and on UNIX that the J2SDK is installed in your home directory in **~/jdk1.2.1**. [*Note:* You may need to update these locations to reflect your chosen install directory and/or disk drive, or a newer version of the J2SDK.]

If you are using a Java Development tool that does not come with the Sun Java demos, you can download the J2SDK (with the demos) from the Sun Microsystems Java Web site

        http://java.sun.com/products/jdk/1.2/

3.3.1 The TicTacToe Applet

The first applet we demonstrate from the J2SDK demos is the **TicTacToe** applet, which allows you to play Tic-Tac-Toe against the computer. To execute this applet, open a command window (MS-DOS prompt on Windows or a command tool on UNIX) and change directories to the J2SDK's **demo** directory. Both Windows and UNIX use command *cd* to *change directories*. For example, the command

        cd c:\jdk1.2.1\demo

changes to the **demo** directory on Windows and the command

        cd ~/jdk1.2.1/demo

changes to the **demo** directory on UNIX.

The **demo** directory contains two subdirectories—*applets* and *jfc* (you can see these directories by issuing in the command window the **dir** command on Windows or the **ls** command on UNIX). The **applets** directory contains many demonstration applets. The **jfc** (Java Foundation Classes) directory contains many examples of Java's newest graphics and GUI features (some of these examples are also applets). For the demonstrations in this section, change directories to the **applets** directory by issuing the command

        cd applets

on either Windows or UNIX.

Listing the contents of the **applets** directory (with the **dir** command on Windows or the **ls** command on UNIX) indicates that there are many examples. Figure 3.1 shows the subdirectories and provides a brief description of the examples in each subdirectory.

Example	Description
Animator	This applet performs one of four separate animations.
ArcTest	This applet demonstrates drawing arcs. You can interact with the applet to change attributes of the arc that is displayed.
BarChart	This applet draws a simple bar chart.
Blink	This applet displays blinking text in different colors.
CardTest	This applet demonstrates several GUI components and a variety of ways in which GUI components can be arranged on the screen (the arrangement of GUI components is also known as the *layout* of the GUI components).
Clock	This applet draws a clock with rotating "hands," the current date and the current time. The clock is updated once per second.
DitherTest	This applet demonstrates drawing with a graphics technique known as dithering that allows gradual transformation from one color to another.
DrawTest	This applet allows the user to drag the mouse to draw lines and points on the applet in different colors.
Fractal	This applet draws a fractal. Fractals typically require complex calculations to determine how they are displayed.
GraphicsTest	This applet draws a variety of shapes to illustrate graphics capabilities.
GraphLayout	This applet draws a graph consisting of many nodes (represented as rectangles) connected by lines. Drag a node to see the other nodes in the graph adjust on the screen and demonstrate complex graphical interactions.
ImageMap	This applet demonstrates an image with *hot spots*. Positioning the mouse pointer over certain areas of the image highligts the area and a message is displayed in the lower-left corner of the **appletviewer** window. Position over the mouth in the image to hear the applet say "hi."
JumpingBox	This applet moves a rectangle randomly around the screen. Try to catch it by clicking it with the mouse!
MoleculeViewer	This applet present a three-dimensional view of several different chemical molecules. Drag the mouse to view the molecule from different angles.
NervousText	This applet draws text that jumps around the screen.
SimpleGraph	This applet draws a complex curve.
SortDemo	This applet compares three sorting techniques. Sorting (described in Chapter 7) arranges information in order—like alphabetizing words. When you execute the applet, three **appletviewer** windows appear. Click in each one to start the sort. Notice that the sorts all operate at different speeds.
SpreadSheet	This applet demonstrates a simple spreadsheet of rows and columns.
SymbolTest	This applet draws characters from the Java character set.
TicTacToe	This applet allows the user to play Tic-Tac-Toe against the computer.
WireFrame	This applet draws a three-dimensional shape as a wire frame. Drag the mouse to view the shape from different angles.

Fig. 3.1   The examples from the **applets** directory.

Change directories to subdirectory **TicTacToe**. In that directory is an HTML file (**example1.html**) that is used to execute the applet. In the command window, type

```
appletviewer example1.html
```

and press the *Enter* key. This executes the **appletviewer**. The **appletviewer** loads the HTML file specified as its *command-line argument* (**example1.html**), determines from the file which applet to load (we discuss the details of HTML files in Section 3.4) and begins execution of the applet. Figure 3.2 shows several screen captures of playing Tic-Tac-Toe with this applet.

Testing and Debugging Tip 3.1

*If the **appletviewer** command does not work and/or the system indicates that the **appletviewer** command cannot be found, the **PATH** environment variable may not be defined properly on your computer. Review the installation directions for the Java 2 Software Development Kit to ensure that the **PATH** environment variable is correctly defined for your system (on some computers, you may need to restart your computer after defining the **PATH** environment variable).*

You are player **X**. To interact with the applet, point the mouse at the square where you want to place an **X** and click the mouse button (normally, the left mouse button). The applet plays a sound (assuming your computer supports audio playback) and places an **X** in the square if the square is open. If the square is occupied, this is an invalid move and the applet plays a different sound indicating that you cannot make the specified move. After you make a valid move, the applet responds by making its own move (this happens very quickly).

To play again, re-execute the applet by clicking the **appletviewer**'s *Applet* menu and selecting the *Reload* menu item from the menu. To terminate the **appletviewer**, click the **appletviewer**'s **Applet** menu and select the *Quit* menu item.

3.3.2 The DrawTest Applet

The next applet we demonstrate from the demos allows you to draw lines and points in different colors. To draw, you simply drag the mouse on the applet by pressing a mouse button and holding it while you drag the mouse. For this example, change directories to directory **applets**, then to subdirectory **DrawTest**. In that directory is the **example1.html** file that is used to execute the applet. In the command window, type the command

```
appletviewer example1.html
```

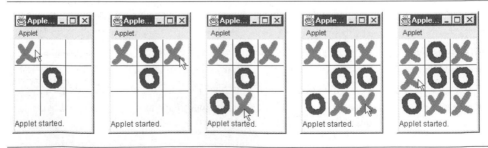

Fig. 3.2   Sample execution of the **TicTacToe** applet.

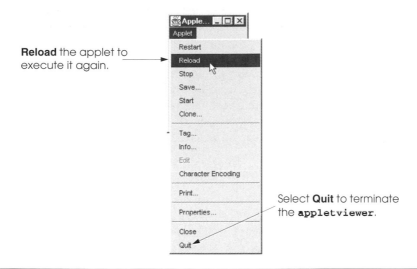

Reload the applet to
execute it again.

Select **Quit** to terminate
the **appletviewer**.

Fig. 3.3 Selecting **Reload** from the **appletviewer**'s **Applet** menu.

and press the *Enter* key. This executes the **appletviewer**. The **appletviewer** loads the HTML file specified as its command-line argument (**example1.html** again), determines from the file which applet to load and begins execution of the applet. Figure 3.4 shows a screen capture of this applet after drawing some lines and points.

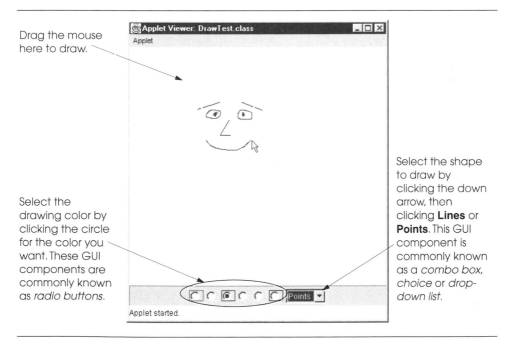

Drag the mouse
here to draw.

Select the shape
to draw by
clicking the down
arrow, then
clicking **Lines** or
Points. This GUI
component is
commonly known
as a *combo box,
choice* or *drop-
down list*.

Select the
drawing color by
clicking the circle
for the color you
want. These GUI
components are
commonly known
as *radio buttons*.

Fig. 3.4 Sample execution of the **DrawTest** applet.

The default shape to draw is a line and the default color is black, so you can immediately draw black lines by dragging the mouse across the applet. To drag the mouse, press and hold the mouse button and move the mouse. Notice that the line follows the mouse pointer around the applet. The line is not permanent until you let go of the mouse button. You can then start a new line by repeating the process.

Select a color by clicking the circle inside one of the colored rectangles at the bottom of the applet. You can select from red, green, blue, pink, orange and black. The GUI components used to present these options are commonly known as *radio buttons*. If you think of a car radio, only one radio station can be selected at a time. Similarly, only one drawing color can be selected at a time.

Try changing the shape from **Lines** to **Points** by clicking the down arrow to the right of the word **Lines** at the bottom of the applet. A list drops down from the GUI component containing the two choices—**Lines** and **Points**. To select **Points**, click the word **Points** in the list. The GUI component closes the list and **Points** are now the current shape. This GUI component is commonly known as a *choice*, *combo box* or *drop-down list*.

To start a new drawing, select **Reload** from the `appletviewer`'s **Applet** menu. To terminate the applet, select **Quit** from the `appletviewer`'s **Applet** menu.

3.3.3 The Java2D Applet

The last applet we demonstrate before defining applets of our own shows many of the complex new two-dimensional drawing capabilities built into Java 2—known as the *Java2D API*. For this example, change directories to the `jfc` directory in the J2SDK's `demo` directory, then change to the `Java2D` directory (you can move up the directory tree toward `demo` using the command "`cd ..`" in both Windows and UNIX). In that directory is an HTML file (`Java2DemoApplet.html`) that is used to execute the applet. In the command window, type the command

```
appletviewer Java2DemoApplet.html
```

and press the *Enter* key. This executes the `appletviewer`. The `appletviewer` loads the HTML file specified as its command-line argument (`Java2DemoApplet.html`), determines from the file which applet to load and begins execution of the applet. This particular demo takes some time to load as it is quite large. Figure 3.5 shows a screen capture of one of this applet's many demonstrations of Java's new two-dimensional graphics capabilities.

At the top of this demo you see tabs that look like file folders in a filing cabinet. This demo provides 11 different tabs with several different features on each tab. To change to a different part of the demo, simply click one of the tabs. Also, try changing the options in the upper-right corner of the applet. Some of these affect the speed with which the applet draws the graphics. For example, click the small box with a check in it (a GUI component known as a *checkbox*) to the left of the word **Anti-Aliasing** to turn off anti-aliasing (a graphics technique for producing smoother on-screen graphics in which the edges of the graphic are blurred). When this feature is turned off (i.e., its *checkbox* is unchecked), the animation speed increases for the animated shapes at the bottom of the demo shown in Fig. 3.5. This is because an animated shape displayed with anti-aliasing takes longer to draw than an animated shape without anti-aliasing.

Click a tab to select a
two-dimensional graphics demo.

Try changing the options to see their
effect on the demonstration.

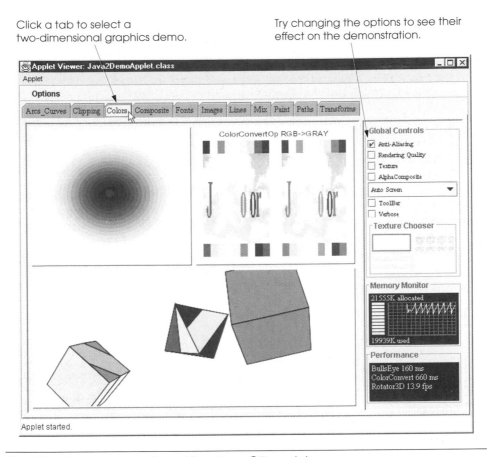

Fig. 3.5   Sample execution of the **Java2D** applet.

3.4 A Simple Java Applet: Drawing a String

Now, let's get started with some applets of our own. Remember, we are just getting start-ed—we have many more topics to learn before we can write applets similar to those dem-onstrated in Section 3.3. However, we will cover many of the same techniques in this book.

We begin by considering a simple applet that mimics the program of Fig. 2.1 by dis-playing the string **"Welcome to Java Programming!"**. The applet and its screen output are shown in Fig. 3.6. The HTML document to load the applet into the **applet-viewer** is shown and discussed in Fig. 3.7.

This program illustrates several important Java features. We consider each line of the program in detail. Line 9 does the "real work" of the program, namely drawing the string **Welcome to Java Programming!** on the screen. But let us consider each line of the program in order. Lines 1 and 2

```
// Fig. 3.6: WelcomeApplet.java
// A first applet in Java
```

```
1  // Fig. 3.6: WelcomeApplet.java
2  // A first applet in Java
3  import javax.swing.JApplet;  // import class JApplet
4  import java.awt.Graphics;    // import class Graphics
5
6  public class WelcomeApplet extends JApplet {
7     public void paint( Graphics g )
8     {
9        g.drawString( "Welcome to Java Programming!", 25, 25 );
10    }
11 }
```

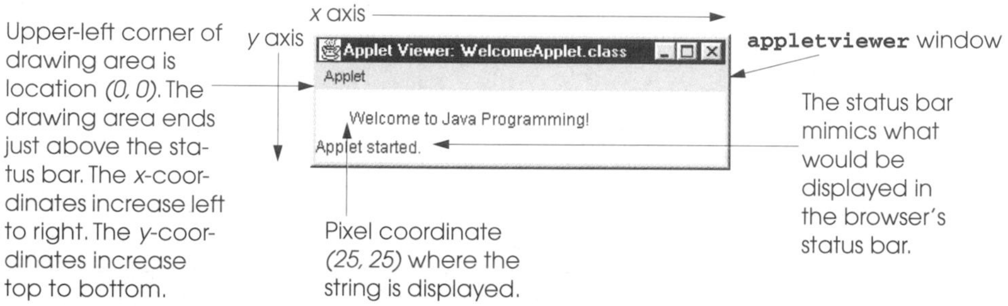
x axis
y axis
Upper-left corner of drawing area is location (0, 0). The drawing area ends just above the status bar. The x-coordinates increase left to right. The y-coordinates increase top to bottom.
Applet Viewer: WelcomeApplet.class
Applet
Welcome to Java Programming!
Applet started.
appletviewer window
The status bar mimics what would be displayed in the browser's status bar.
Pixel coordinate (25, 25) where the string is displayed.

Fig. 3.6 A first program in Java and the program's screen output.

begin with `//`, indicating that the remainder of each line is a comment. The comment on line 1 indicates the figure number and file name for the applet source code. The comment `A first applet in Java` on line 2 simply describes the purpose of the program.

As stated in Chapter 2, Java contains many predefined pieces called classes (or data types) that are grouped into packages in the Java API. Lines 3 and 4

```
import javax.swing.JApplet;  // import class JApplet
import java.awt.Graphics;    // import class Graphics
```

are **`import`** statements that tell the compiler where to locate the classes required to compile this Java applet. These specific lines tell the compiler that class ***`JApplet`*** is located in package **`javax.swing`** and class ***`Graphics`*** is located in package ***`java.awt`***. When you create an applet in Java, you normally import the **`JApplet`** class. You import the **`Graphics`** class so the program can draw graphics (such as lines, rectangles, ovals and strings of characters) on a Java applet (or application later in the book). [*Note:* There is an older class called ***`Applet`*** from package ***`java.applet`*** that is not used with Java's newest GUI components from the **`javax.swing`** package. In this book, we use only class **`JApplet`** with applets.]

Each piece of the package name is a directory (or folder) on disk. All the packages in the Java API are stored in the directory **`java`** or **`javax`** that contain many subdirectories, including **`awt`** and **`swing`**. [*Note:* If you look for these directories on disk, you will not find them because they are stored in a special compressed file called a *Java archive file (JAR file)*. In the J2SDK installation directory structure is a file called ***`rt.jar`*** that contains the **`.class`** files for the entire Java API.]

As with applications, every Java applet is composed of at least one class definition. One key feature of class definitions that was not mentioned in Chapter 2 is that you rarely create a class definition "from scratch." In fact, when you create a class definition, you normally use pieces of an existing class definition. Java uses *inheritance* (mentioned in Section 3.2) to create new classes from existing class definitions. Line 6

```
public class WelcomeApplet extends JApplet {
```

begins a **class** definition for class **WelcomeApplet**. Once again, keyword **class** introduces a class definition and is immediately followed by the class name (**WelcomeApplet** in this class). The *extends keyword* followed by a class name indicates the class (in this case **JApplet**) from which our new class inherits existing pieces. In this inheritance relationship, **JApplet** is called the *superclass* or *base class* and **WelcomeApplet** is called the *subclass* or *derived class*. We discuss inheritance in detail in Chapter 9, "Object-Oriented Programming." Using inheritance here results in a new class definition that has the *attributes* (data) and *behaviors* (methods) of the **JApplet** class as well as the new features we are adding in our **WelcomeApplet** class definition (specifically, the ability to display **Welcome to Java Programming!** on the screen).

A key benefit of extending class **JApplet** is that someone else has already defined "what it means to be an applet." The **appletviewer** and World Wide Web browsers that support applets expect every Java applet to have certain capabilities (attributes and behaviors) and class **JApplet** already provides all those capabilities—programmers do not need to define all these capabilities on their own (again programmers do not need to "reinvent the wheel"). In fact, an applet requires well over 200 different methods to be defined. In our programs to this point, we have defined one method in every program. If we had to define over 200 methods just to display **Welcome to Java Programming!**, we would probably never create an applet! By simply using **extends** to inherit from class **JApplet**, all the methods of **JApplet** are now part of our **WelcomeApplet**.

The inheritance mechanism is easy to use; the programmer does not need to know every detail of class **JApplet** or any other class from which new classes are inherited. The programmer needs to know only that class **JApplet** has already defined the capabilities required to create the minimum applet. To make the best use of any class, however, the programmer should study all the capabilities of the class that is extended.

Good Programming Practice 3.1

Investigate the capabilities of any class in the Java API documentation carefully before inheriting a subclass from it. This helps ensure that the programmer does not unintentionally redefine a capability that is already provided.

Classes are used as "templates" or "blueprints" to *instantiate* (or *create*) *objects* for use in a program. An object (or *instance*) resides in the computer's memory and contains information used by the program. The term *object* normally implies that attributes (data) and behaviors (methods) are associated with the object. The object's methods use the attributes to provide useful services to the *client of the object* (i.e., the code that calls the methods).

Our **WelcomeApplet** class is used to create an object that implements the applet's attributes and behaviors. The default behavior of method **paint** in class **JApplet** is to do nothing. Class **WelcomeApplet** *overrides* (*replaces* or *redefines*) that behavior such that **paint** draws a message on the screen. When the **appletviewer** or browser tells the applet to "draw itself" on the screen by calling method paint, our message **Welcome to Java Programming!** appears rather than a blank screen.

The **appletviewer** or browser in which the applet executes is responsible for creating an object (instance) of class **WelcomeApplet**. [*Note:* The terms *instance* and *object* are often used interchangeably.] The keyword *public* on line 6 is required to enable the browser to create an object of class **WelcomeApplet** and execute the applet. The class that inherits from **JApplet** to create an applet must be a **public** class. The **public** keyword and related keywords (such as **private** and **protected**) are discussed in detail in Chapter 8, "Object-Based Programming." For now, we ask you simply to start all class definitions with the **public** keyword until the discussion of **public** in Chapter 8.

When you save a **public** class in a file, the class's name is used as part of the file name. For our applet, the file name must be **WelcomeApplet.java**. Please note that the file name must be spelled exactly the same as the class name and have the **.java** file name extension.

Common Programming Error 3.1

*It is an error if the file name is not identical in both spelling and capitalization to the **public** class name with the **.java** file name extension.*

Common Programming Error 3.2

*It is an error if a **.java** file contains more than one **public** class.*

Common Programming Error 3.3

*It is an error not to end a Java file name with the **.java** extension.*

Testing and Debugging Tip 3.2

The compiler error message "Public class ClassName *must be defined in a file called* Class-Name.java*" indicates either 1) that the file name does not exactly match the name of the **public** class in the file (including all uppercase and lowercase letters), or 2) that you typed the class name incorrectly when compiling the class (the name must be spelled with the proper uppercase and lowercase letters).*

At the end of line 6, the left brace, **{**, begins the body of the class definition. The corresponding right brace, **}**, on line 11 ends the class definition. Line 7

```
public void paint( Graphics g )
```

begins the definition of the applet's *paint method*. Method **paint** is one of three methods (behaviors) that are guaranteed to be called automatically for you when any applet begins execution. These three methods are **init** (discussed later in this chapter), **start** (discussed later in the book) and **paint**, and they are guaranteed to be called in that order. These methods are called from the **appletviewer** or browser in which the applet is executing. Your applet class gets a "free" version of each of these methods from class **JApplet** when you specify **extends JApplet** in the first line of your applet's class definition. There are several other methods that are also guaranteed to be called during an applet's execution—these methods are discussed in Chapter 6, "Methods."

The free version of each of these methods is defined with an empty body (i.e., by default each of these methods does not perform a task). One of the reasons we inherit all applets from class **JApplet** is to get our free copies of the methods that get called automatically during execution of an applet (and many other methods too).

Why would you want a free copy of a method that does nothing? The predefined start-up sequence of method calls made by the **appletviewer** or browser for every applet is always **init**, **start** and **paint**—this provides an applet programmer a guaranteed start-up sequence of method calls as every applet begins execution. Every applet does not need all three of these methods. However, the **appletviewer** or browser expects each of these methods to be defined so it can provide a consistent start-up sequence for an applet. [*Note:* This is similar to applications always starting execution with **main**.] Inheriting the default versions of these methods guarantees the browser that it can treat each applet uniformly by calling **init**, **start** and **paint** as applet execution begins. Also, the programmer can concentrate on defining only the methods required for a particular applet.

Lines 7 through 10 are the definition of **paint**. The task of method **paint** is to draw graphics (such as lines, ovals and strings of characters) on the screen. Keyword **void** indicates that this method does not return any results when it completes its task. The set of parentheses after **paint** defines the method's *parameter list*. Recall that the parameter list is where methods receive data required to perform their tasks. Normally, this data is passed by the programmer to the method through a *method call* (also known as *invoking a method* or *sending a message*). For example, in Chapter 2 we passed data to **JOption-Pane.showMessageDialog** including the message to display and the type of message dialog. However, method **paint**—which is called for us to draw in the applet's viewable area on the screen—receives the information it needs automatically when the method is called. Method **paint**'s parameter list indicates that it requires a **Graphics** object (named **g**) to perform its task. The **Graphics** object is used by **paint** to draw graphics on the applet. The **public** keyword at the beginning of line 7 is required so the **appletviewer** or browser can call your **paint** method. For now, all method definitions should begin with the **public** keyword. Other alternatives are introduced in Chapter 8.

The left brace, **{**, on line 8 begins the method definition's body. The corresponding right brace, **}**, on line 10 ends the method definition's body. Line 9

```
g.drawString( "Welcome to Java Programming!", 25, 25 );
```

is a statement that instructs the computer to perform an action (or task), namely to display the characters of the character string **Welcome to Java Programming!** on the applet. This statement uses method **drawString** defined by class **Graphics** (this class defines all the graphical drawing capabilities of a Java program, such as drawing strings of characters and drawing shapes such as rectangles, ovals and lines). Method **drawString** is called using the **Graphics** object **g** (in **paint**'s parameter list) followed by a dot operator (**.**) followed by the method name **drawString**. The method name is followed by a set of parentheses containing the argument list **drawString** needs to perform its task.

The first argument to **drawString** is the **String** to draw. The last two arguments in the list—25 and 25—are the *coordinates* (or *position*) at which the bottom-left corner of the string should be drawn in the applet's on-screen area. Coordinates are measured from the upper-left corner of the applet in *pixels* (the upper-left corner of the white area in the screen capture of Fig. 3.6). A pixel ("picture element") is the unit of display for your computer's screen. On a color screen, a pixel appears as one colored dot on the screen. Many personal computers have 640 pixels for the width of the screen and 480 pixels for the height of the screen, for a total of 640 times 480 or 307,200 displayable pixels. Many computer screens have higher screen resolutions, i.e., they have more pixels for the width and height of the screen. The higher the screen resolution, the smaller the applet appears on the screen. Drawing methods from class **Graphics** require coordinates to specify where to draw on the applet (later in the text we demonstrate drawing in applications). The first coordinate is the *x-coordinate* (the number of pixels from the left side of the applet), and the second coordinate is the *y-coordinate* (representing the number of pixels from the top of the applet).

When the preceding statement is executed, it draws the message **Welcome to Java Programming!** on the applet at the coordinates **25** and **25**. Note that the quotation marks enclosing the character string are *not* displayed on the screen.

After class **WelcomeApplet** is defined and saved in file **WelcomeApplet.java**, the class must be compiled using the Java compiler **javac**. In the command window, type the command

```
javac WelcomeApplet.java
```

to compile class **WelcomeApplet**. If there are no syntax errors, the resulting bytecodes are stored in the file **WelcomeApplet.class**.

After compiling the program of Fig. 3.6, we must create an *HTML (Hypertext Markup Language)* file to load the applet into the **appletviewer** (or a browser) to execute. Typically, an HTML file ends with the "**.html**" or "**.htm**" file name extension. Browsers display the contents of documents that contain text (also known as *text files*). To execute a Java applet, you must provide an HTML text file that indicates which applet the **appletviewer** (or browser) should load and execute. Figure 3.7 contains a simple HTML file— **WelcomeApplet.html**—that is used to load into the **appletviewer** (or a browser) the applet defined in Fig. 3.6. [*Note:* For the early part of this book, we always demonstrate applets with the **appletviewer**.]

Good Programming Practice 3.2

*Always test a Java applet in the **appletviewer** and ensure that it is executing correctly before loading the applet into a World Wide Web browser. Browsers often save a copy of an applet in memory until the current browsing session terminates (i.e., all browser windows are closed). Thus, if you change an applet, recompile the applet, then reload the applet in the browser, you may not see the changes because the browser may still be executing the original version of the applet. Close all your browser windows to remove the old version of the applet from memory. Open a new browser window and load the applet to see your changes.*

Software Engineering Observation 3.1

If your World Wide Web browser does not support Java 2, most of the applets in this book will not execute in your browser. This is because most of the applets in this book use features that are new to Java 2 or are not provided by browsers that support Java 1.1. [Note: Later in the book we discuss the Java Plug-In *and how it can be used to provide Java 2 support in today's browsers.]*

```
1   <html>
2   <applet code="WelcomeApplet.class" width=300 height=30>
3   </applet>
4   </html>
```

Fig. 3.7   The **WelcomeApplet.html** file, which loads the **WelcomeApplet** class of Fig. 3.6 into the **appletviewer**.

Many HTML codes (or *tags*) come in pairs. For example, lines 1 and 4 of Fig. 3.7 indicate the beginning and the end, respectively, of the HTML tags in the file. All HTML tags begin with a *left angle bracket,* **<**, and end with a *right angle bracket,* **>**. Lines 2 and 3 are special HTML tags for Java applets. They tell the **appletviewer** (or browser) to load a specific applet and define the size of the applet's display area (its *width* and *height* in pixels) in the **appletviewer** (or browser). Normally, the applet and its corresponding HTML file are stored in the same directory on disk. Typically, an HTML file is loaded into your browser from a computer other than your own that is connected to the Internet. However, HTML files also can reside on your computer (as we demonstrated in Section 3.3). When an HTML file that specifies an applet to execute is loaded into the **appletviewer** (or a browser), the **appletviewer** (or browser) automatically loads the applet's **.class** file (or files) from the same directory on the computer from which the HTML file was loaded.

The **<applet>** *tag* has several components. The first component of the **<applet>** tag on line 2 (**code="WelcomeApplet.class"**) indicates that the file **WelcomeApplet.class** contains the compiled applet class. Remember, when you compile your Java programs, every class is compiled into a separate file that has the same name as the class and ends with the **.class** extension. The second and third components of the **<applet>** tag indicate the *width* and the *height* of the applet in pixels. The upper-left corner of the applet's display area is always at *x*-coordinate 0 and *y*-coordinate 0. The width of this applet is 300 pixels and its height is 30 pixels. You may want (or need) to use larger width and height values to define a larger drawing area for your applets. On line 3, the **</applet>** tag terminates the **<applet>** tag that began on line 2. On line 4, the **</html>** tag specifies the end of the HTML tags that began on line 1 with **<html>**.

Software Engineering Observation 3.2

Generally, each applet should be less than 640 pixels wide and 480 pixels tall (most computer screens support these dimensions as the minimum width and height).

Common Programming Error 3.4

Placing additional characters such as commas (,) between the components in the **<applet>** *tag may cause the* **appletviewer** *or browser to produce an error message indicating a* **MissingResourceException** *when loading the applet.*

Common Programming Error 3.5

Forgetting the ending **</applet>** *tag prevents the applet from loading into the appletviewer or browser properly.*

Testing and Debugging Tip 3.3

If you receive a **MissingResourceException** *error message when loading an applet into the* **appletviewer** *or a browser, check the* **<applet>** *tag in the HTML file carefully for syntax errors. Compare your HTML file to the file in Fig. 3.7 to confirm proper syntax.*

The **appletviewer** only understands the **<applet>** and **</applet>** HTML tags, so it is sometimes referred to as the "minimal browser" (it ignores all other HTML tags). The **appletviewer** is an ideal place to test an applet's execution and ensure that the applet executes properly. Once the applet's execution is verified, you can add **<applet>** and **</applet>** tags to an HTML file that will be viewed by people browsing the Internet. The **appletviewer** is invoked for the **WelcomeApplet** from your computer's command window as follows:

```
appletviewer WelcomeApplet.html
```

Note that the `appletviewer` *requires* an HTML file to load an applet. This is different
from the `java` interpreter for applications which required the class name of the application
class. Also, the preceding command must be issued from the directory in which the HTML
file and the applet's `.class` file are located.

Common Programming Error 3.6

*Running the `appletviewer` with a file name that does not end with `.html` or `.htm` is an
error that prevents the `appletviewer` from loading your applet for execution.*

Portability Tip 3.1

*Test your applets in every browser used by people who view your applet. This will help en-
sure that people who view your applet experience the functionality you expect. [Note: A goal
of the Java Plug-In (discussed later in the book) is to provide consistent applet execution
across many different browsers.]*

3.5 Two More Simple Applets: Drawing Strings and Lines

Let us consider another applet. **Welcome to Java Programming!** can be displayed
several ways. Two **drawString** statements in the **paint** method can print multiple lines
as in Fig. 3.8 (the corresponding HTML file is in Fig. 3.9).

```
1   // Fig. 3.8: WelcomeApplet2.java
2   // Displaying multiple strings
3   import javax.swing.JApplet;   // import class JApplet
4   import java.awt.Graphics;     // import class Graphics
5
6   public class WelcomeApplet2 extends JApplet {
7      public void paint( Graphics g )
8      {
9         g.drawString( "Welcome to", 25, 25 );
10        g.drawString( "Java Programming!", 25, 40 );
11     }
12  }
```

Pixel coordinate *(25, 25)*, where
Welcome to is displayed

Pixel coordinate *(25, 40)*, where
Java Programming! is displayed

Applet Viewer: WelcomeApplet2.class
Applet
Welcome to
Java Programming!
Applet started.

Fig. 3.8   Displaying multiple strings.

```
1   <html>
2   <applet code="WelcomeApplet2.class" width=300 height=45>
3   </applet>
4   </html>
```

Fig. 3.9   The **WelcomeApplet2.html** file, which loads the
           WelcomeApplet2 class of Fig. 3.8 into the **appletviewer**.

Note that each **drawString** can draw at any pixel location on the applet. The reason the two output lines appear as shown in the output window is that we specified the same *x* coordinate (**25**) for each **drawString** so the strings appear aligned at their left sides, and we specified different *y* coordinates (**25** on line 9 and **40** on line 10) so the strings appear at different vertical locations on the applet. If we reverse lines 9 and 10 in the program, the output window will still appear as shown because the pixel coordinates specified in each **drawString** statement are completely independent of the coordinates specified in all other **drawString** statements (and all other drawing operations). The concept of lines of text as shown with methods **System.out.println** and **JOptionPane.showMessageDialog** in Chapter 2 does not exist when drawing graphics. In fact, if you try to output a string containing a newline character (**\n**), you will simply see a small black box at that position in the string.

To make drawing more interesting, the applet of Fig. 3.10 draws two lines and a string. The HTML file to load the applet into the **appletviewer** is shown in Fig. 3.11.

Lines 9 and 10 of method **paint**

```
g.drawLine( 15, 10, 210, 10 );
g.drawLine( 15, 30, 210, 30 );
```

```
1   // Fig. 3.10: WelcomeLines.java
2   // Displaying text and lines
3   import javax.swing.JApplet;   // import class JApplet
4   import java.awt.Graphics;     // import class Graphics
5
6   public class WelcomeLines extends JApplet {
7      public void paint( Graphics g )
8      {
9         g.drawLine( 15, 10, 210, 10 );
10        g.drawLine( 15, 30, 210, 30 );
11        g.drawString( "Welcome to Java Programming!", 25, 25 );
12     }
13  }
```

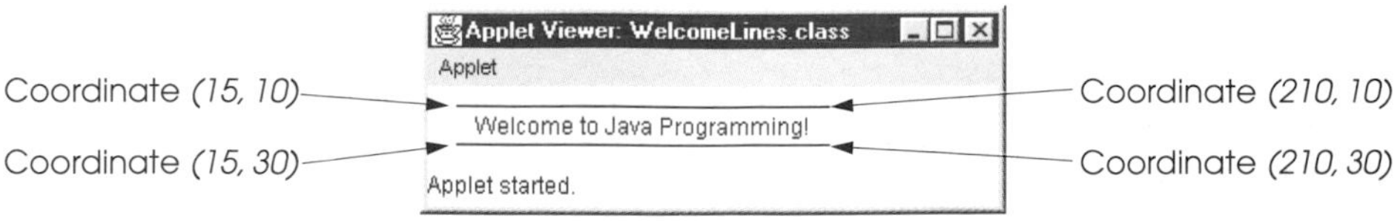

Fig. 3.10 Drawing strings and lines.

```
1   <html>
2   <applet code="WelcomeLines.class" width=300 height=40>
3   </applet>
4   </html>
```

Fig. 3.11 The **WelcomeLines.html** file, which loads the **WelcomeLines** class of Fig. 3.10 into the **appletviewer**.

use *method* ***drawLine*** of class **Graphics** to indicate that the **Graphics** object that **g** refers to should draw lines. Method **drawLine** requires four arguments that represent the two end points of the line on the applet—the *x*-coordinate and *y*-coordinate of the first end point in the line and the *x*-coordinate and *y*-coordinate of the second end point in the line. All coordinate values are specified with respect to the upper-left corner *(0, 0)* coordinate of the applet. When method **drawLine** is called, it simply draws a line between the two specified end points.

3.6 Another Java Applet: Adding Integers

Our next applet (Fig. 3.12) mimics the application of Fig. 2.8 for adding two integers. However, this applet requests that the user enter two *floating-point numbers* (i.e., numbers with a decimal point such as 7.33, 0.0975 and 1000.12345). To store floating-point numbers in memory we introduce primitive data type ***double***, which is used to represent *double-precision floating-point* numbers. There is also primitive data type ***float*** for storing *single-precision floating-point* numbers. A **double** requires more memory to store a floating-point value, but stores it with approximately twice the precision of a **float** (15 significant digits for **double** vs. seven significant digits for **float**).

Once again, we use **JOptionPane.showInputDialog** to request input from the user. The applet then computes the sum of the input values and displays the result by drawing a string inside a rectangle on the applet. The HTML file to load this applet into the **appletviewer** is shown in Fig. 3.13.

```
1   // Fig. 3.12: AdditionApplet.java
2   // Adding two floating-point numbers
3   import java.awt.Graphics;   // import class Graphics
4   import javax.swing.*;       // import package javax.swing
5
6   public class AdditionApplet extends JApplet {
7      double sum;  // sum of the values entered by the user
8
9      public void init()
10     {
11        String firstNumber,    // first string entered by user
12               secondNumber;  // second string entered by user
13        double number1,        // first number to add
14               number2;        // second number to add
15
16        // read in first number from user
17        firstNumber =
18          JOptionPane.showInputDialog(
19            "Enter first floating-point value" );
20
21        // read in second number from user
22        secondNumber =
23          JOptionPane.showInputDialog(
24            "Enter second floating-point value" );
25
```

Fig. 3.12 An addition program "in action" (part 1 of 2).

```
26          // convert numbers from type String to type double
27          number1 = Double.parseDouble( firstNumber );
28          number2 = Double.parseDouble( secondNumber );
29
30          // add the numbers
31          sum = number1 + number2;
32       }
33
34       public void paint( Graphics g )
35       {
36          // draw the results with g.drawString
37          g.drawRect( 15, 10, 270, 20 );
38          g.drawString( "The sum is " + sum, 25, 25 );
39       }
40    }
```

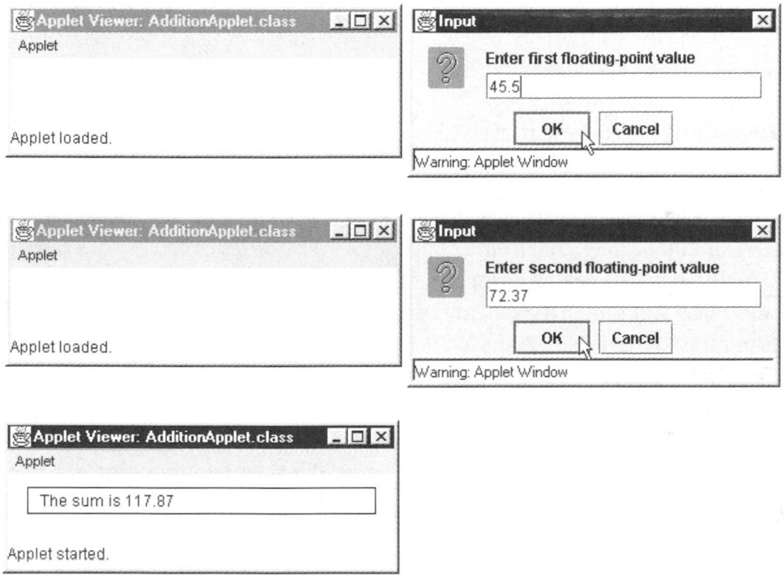

Fig. 3.12   An addition program "in action" (part 1 of 2).

```
1    <html>
2    <applet code="AdditionApplet.class" width=300 height=50>
3    </applet>
4    </html>
```

Fig. 3.13   The **AdditionApplet.html** file, which loads the **AdditionApplet** class of Fig. 3.12 into the **appletviewer**.

Lines 1 and 2

```
// Fig. 3.12: AdditionApplet.java
// Adding two floating-point numbers
```

are single-line comments stating the figure number, file name and purpose of the program.

Line 3

```
import java.awt.Graphics;    // import class Graphics
```

specifies to the compiler where to locate class **Graphics** (package **java.awt**) for use in this application. Actually, the **import** statement at line 3 is not required if we always use the complete name of class **Graphics**—*java.awt.Graphics*—which includes the full package name and class name. For example, the first line of method **paint** can be defined as

```
public void paint( java.awt.Graphics g )
```

Software Engineering Observation 3.3

*The Java compiler does not need **import** statements in a Java source code file if the complete class name—the full package name and class name (e.g., **java.awt.Graphics**)—is specified every time a class name is used in the source code.*

Line 4

```
import javax.swing.*;       // import package javax.swing
```

specifies to the compiler where to locate the entire **javax.swing** package. The asterisk (*****) indicates that all classes in the **javax.swing** package (such as **JApplet** and **JOptionPane**) should be available to the compiler so the compiler can ensure that we use the classes correctly. This allows programmers to use the *shorthand name* (the class name by itself) of any class from the **javax.swing** package in the program. Remember that our last two programs only imported class **JApplet** from the **javax.swing** package. In this program, we use classes **JApplet** and **JOptionPane** from the **javax.swing** package. Importing an entire package into a program is also a shorthand notation so the programmer does not have to provide a separate **import** statement for every class used from that package. Remember that you can always use the complete name of every class, i.e., **javax.swing.JApplet** and **javax.swing.JOptionPane** rather than **import** statements.

Software Engineering Observation 3.4

*The compiler does not load every class in a package when it encounters an **import** statement that uses the ***** (e.g., **javax.swing.***) notation to indicate that multiple classes from the package are used in the program. The compiler searches the package only for those classes used in the program.*

Software Engineering Observation 3.5

*Many package directories have subdirectories. For example, the **java.awt** package directory contains subdirectory **event** for the package **java.awt.event**. When the compiler encounters an **import** statement that uses the ***** (e.g., **java.awt.***) notation to indicate that multiple classes from the package are used in the program, the compiler does not search the subdirectory **event**. This means that you cannot define an **import** of **java.*** to search for classes from all packages.*

Software Engineering Observation 3.6

*When using **import** statements, separate **import** statements must be specified for each package used in a program.*

Common Programming Error 3.7

Assuming that an **import** *statement for an entire package (e.g.,* **java.awt.***) *also im-* **port***s classes from subdirectories in that package (e.g.,* **java.awt.event.***) *results in syntax errors for the classes from the subdirectories. There must be separate import state- ments for every package from which classes are used.*

Remember that applets inherit from the **JApplet** class, so they have all the methods required by the **appletviewer** or a browser to execute the applet. Line 6

```
public class AdditionApplet extends JApplet {
```

begins class **AdditionApplet**'s definition and indicates that it inherits from **JApplet**.

All class definitions start with an opening left brace (end of line 6), **{**, and end with a closing right brace, **}** (line 40).

Common Programming Error 3.8

If braces do not occur in matching pairs, the compiler indicates a syntax error.

Good Programming Practice 3.3

Whenever you type an opening left brace, **{**, *in your program, immediately type the closing right brace,* **}**, *then reposition the cursor between the braces to begin typing the body. This helps prevent missing braces.*

Line 7

```
double sum;   // sum of the values entered by the user
```

is an *instance variable declaration*—every instance (object) of the class contains one copy of each instance variable. For example, if there are 10 instances of this applet executing, each instance has its own copy of **sum**. Thus, there would be 10 separate copies of **sum** (one for each applet). Instance variables are declared in the body of the class definition, but not in the body of any method of the class definition. The preceding declaration states that **sum** is a variable of primitive type **double**.

An important benefit of instance variables is that their identifiers can be used throughout the class definition (i.e., in all methods of the class). Until now, we declared all variables in an application's **main** method. Variables defined in the body of a method are known as *local variables* and can only be used in the body of the method in which they are defined. Another distinction between instance variables and local variables is that instance variables are always assigned a default value and local variables are not. The variable **sum** is initialized to 0.0 automatically because it is an instance variable.

Common Programming Error 3.9

Using a local variable that is not initialized before it is used is a syntax error. Each local variable must be assigned a value before an attempt is made to use that variable's value.

Good Programming Practice 3.4

Initializing instance variables rather than relying on automatic initialization improves pro- gram readability.

This applet contains two methods—**init** (definition on lines 9 through 32) and **paint** (definition on lines 34 through 39). Method **init** is a special applet method that is normally the first method defined by the programmer in an applet and is guaranteed to be the first method called in every applet. Method **init** is called once during an applet's execution. The method normally *initializes* the applet's instance variables (if they need to be initialized to a value other than their default value) and performs any tasks that need to be performed once at the beginning of an applet's execution.

Software Engineering Observation 3.7

The order in which methods are defined in a class definition has no effect on when those methods are called at execution time.

The first line of the **init** method always appears as

```
public void init()
```

indicating that **init** is a **public** method that returns no information (**void**) when it completes and receives no arguments (empty parentheses after **init**) to perform its task.

The left brace (line 10) marks the beginning of **init**'s body, and the corresponding right brace (line 32) marks the end of **init**. Lines 11 and 12

```
String firstNumber,    // first string entered by user
       secondNumber;   // second string entered by user
```

are a declaration for the local **String** variables **firstNumber** and **secondNumber**.

Lines 13 and 14

```
double number1,    // first number to add
       number2;    // second number to add
```

declare that variables **number1** and **number2** are of primitive data type **double**, which means that these variables hold floating-point values. Because these are instance variables, they are automatically initialized to 0.0 (the default for **double** instance variables).

As an important aside, there are actually two types of variables in Java—*primitive data type variables* (normally called *variables*) and *reference variables* (normally called *references*). The identifiers **firstNumber** and **secondNumber** are actually references— names that are used to *refer to objects* in the program. Such references actually contain the location in the computer's memory of an object. In our preceding applets, method **paint** actually receives a reference called **g** that refers to a **Graphics** object. That reference is used to send messages to (i.e., call methods on) the **Graphics** object in memory that allows us to draw on the applet. For example, the statement

```
g.drawString( "Welcome to Java Programming!", 25, 25 );
```

sends the **drawString** message to (calls the **drawString** method on) the **Graphics** object to which **g** refers. As part of the message (method call), we provide the data that **drawString** requires to do its task. The **Graphics** object then draws the **String** at the specified location.

The identifiers **number1**, **number2** and **sum** are the names of *variables*. A variable is similar to an object. The main difference between a variable and an object is that an object is defined by a class definition that can contain both data (instance variables) and methods, whereas a variable is defined by a *primitive (or built-in) data type* (one of **char**, **byte**, **short**, **int**, **long**, **float**, **double** or **boolean**) that can contain only data. A variable can store exactly one value at a time, whereas one object can contain many individual pieces of data. The distinction between a variable and a reference is based on the data type of the identifier (as stated in a declaration). If the data type is a class name, the identifier is a reference to an object and that reference can be used to send messages to (call methods on) that object. If the data type is one of the primitive data types, the identifier is a variable that can be used to store in memory or retrieve from memory a single value of the declared primitive type.

Software Engineering Observation 3.8

A hint to help you determine if an identifier is a variable or a reference is the variable's data type. By convention all class names in Java start with a capitalized first letter. Therefore, if the data type starts with a capitalized first letter, you can normally assume that the identifier is a reference to an object of the declared type (e.g., **Graphics g** *indicates that* **g** *is a reference to a* **Graphics** *object).*

Lines 16 through 19

```
// read in first number from user
firstNumber =
    JOptionPane.showInputDialog(
        "Enter first floating-point value" );
```

read the first floating-point number from the user. Method **JOptionPane.showInputDialog** displays an input dialog that prompts the user to enter a value. The user types a value in the input dialog's text field, then clicks the **OK** button to return the string the user typed to the program. [If you type and nothing appears in the text field, position the mouse pointer in the text field and click the mouse to make the text field active.]

Technically, the user can type anything he or she wants here. For this program if the user either types a non-numeric value or clicks the **Cancel** button, a run-time error will occur and a message will be displayed in the command window from which the appletviewer was executed. Chapter 14, "Exception Handling," discusses how to make your programs more robust by handling such errors.

Variable **firstNumber** is given the result of the call to **JOptionPane.showInputDialog** operation with an assignment statement. The statement is read as "**firstNumber** *gets* the value of **JOptionPane.showInputDialog("Enter first floating-point value")**."

Lines 21 through 24

```
// read in second number from user
secondNumber =
    JOptionPane.showInputDialog(
        "Enter second floating-point value" );
```

read the second floating-point value from the user by displaying an input dialog.

Lines 26 through 28

```
// convert numbers from type String to type int
number1 = Double.parseDouble( firstNumber );
number2 = Double.parseDouble( secondNumber );
```

convert the two strings input by the user to **double** values that can be used in a calculation. Method **Double.parseDouble** (a **static** method of class **Double**) converts its **String** argument to a **double** floating-point value. Class **Double** is part of the package

java.lang. The floating-point value returned by **Double.parseDouble** in line 27 is assigned to variable **number1**. Any subsequent references to **number1** in the method use this same floating-point value. The floating-point value returned by **Double.parse-Double** in line 28 is assigned to variable **number2**. Any subsequent references to **number2** in the method use this same floating-point value.

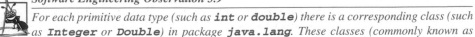

Software Engineering Observation 3.9

*For each primitive data type (such as **int** or **double**) there is a corresponding class (such as **Integer** or **Double**) in package **java.lang**. These classes (commonly known as type-wrappers) provide methods for processing primitive data type values (such as converting a **String** to a primitive data type value or converting a primitive data type value to a **String**). Primitive data types do not have methods. Therefore, methods related to a primitive data type are located in the corresponding type-wrapper class (i.e., method **parse-Double** that converts a **String** to a **double** value is located in class **Double**).*

The assignment statement at line 31

```
sum = number1 + number2;
```

calculates the sum of the variables **number1** and **number2** and assigns the result to variable **sum** using the assignment operator **=**. The statement is read as "**sum** *gets* the value of **number1 + number2**." Most calculations are performed in assignment statements. Notice that instance variable **sum** is used in the preceding statement in method **init** even though **sum** was not defined in method **init**. Because we defined **sum** as an instance variable, we can use it in **init** and all other methods of the class.

At this point the applet's **init** method returns and the **appletviewer** or browser calls the applet's **start** method. We did not define method **start** in this applet so the one provided by class **JApplet** is used here. The **start** method is primarily used with an advanced concept called multithreading (for this reason, we will not see a definition of method **start** for an applet until Chapter 15).

Next, the browser calls the applet's **paint** method. In this example, method **paint** draws a rectangle containing the string with the result of the addition. Line 37

```
g.drawRect( 15, 10, 270, 20 );
```

sends the **drawRect** message to the **Graphics** object to which **g** refers (calls the **Graphics** object's **drawRect** method). Method **drawRect** draws a rectangle based on its four arguments. The first two integer values represent the *upper-left x-coordinate* and *upper-left y-coordinate* where the **Graphics** object begins drawing the rectangle. The third and fourth arguments are non-negative integers that represent the *width* of the rectangle in pixels and the *height* of the rectangle in pixels, respectively. This particular statement draws a rectangle starting at coordinate *(15, 10)* that is **270** pixels wide and **20** pixels high.

Common Programming Error 3.10

*It is a logic error to supply a negative width or negative height as an argument to **Graphics** method **drawRect**. The rectangle will not be displayed and no error will be indicated.*

Common Programming Error 3.11

*It is a logic error to supply two points (i.e., pairs of x- and y-coordinates) as the arguments to **Graphics** method **drawRect**. The third argument must be the width in pixels and the fourth argument must be the height in pixels of the rectangle to draw.*

Common Programming Error 3.12

It is normally a logic error to supply arguments to **Graphics** *method* **drawRect** *that cause the rectangle to draw outside the applet's viewable area (i.e., the width and height of the applet as specified in the HTML document that references the applet). Either increase the applet's width and height in the HTML document or pass arguments to method* **drawRect** *that cause the rectangle to draw inside the applet's viewable area.*

Line 38

```
g.drawString( "The sum is " + sum, 25, 25 );
```

sends the **drawString** message to the **Graphics** object to which **g** refers (calls the **Graphics** object's **drawString** method). The expression

```
"The sum is " + sum
```

from the preceding statement uses the string concatenation operator **+** to concatenate the string **"The sum is "** and **sum** (converted to a string) to create the string displayed by **drawString**. Notice again that instance variable **sum** is used in the preceding statement even though it was not defined in method **paint**.

The benefit of defining **sum** as an instance variable is that we were able to assign **sum** a value in **init** and use **sum**'s value in the **paint** method later in the program. All methods of a class are capable of using the instance variables in the class definition.

Software Engineering Observation 3.10

The only statements that should be placed in an applet's **init** *method are those that are directly related to the one-time initialization of an applet's instance variables. The applet's results should be displayed from other methods of the applet class. Results that involve drawing should be displayed from the applet's* **paint** *method.*

Software Engineering Observation 3.11

The only statements that should be placed in an applet's **paint** *method are those that are directly related to drawing (i.e., calls to methods of class* **Graphics***) and the logic of drawing. Generally, dialog boxes should not be displayed from an applet's* **paint** *method.*

In this chapter and Chapter 2, we have introduced many important features of Java, including applications, applets, displaying data on the screen, inputting data from the keyboard, performing calculations and making decisions. In Chapter 4, we build on these techniques as we introduce *structured programming*. Here, you will become more familiar with indentation techniques. We also study how to specify and vary the order in which statements are executed—this order is called *flow of control*.

3.7 Java Applet Internet and World Wide Web Resources

If you have access to the Internet and the World Wide Web, there are a large number of Java applet resources available to you. The best place to start is at the source—the Sun Microsystems, Inc. Java Web site **http://java.sun.com**. In the upper-left corner of the Web page is an ***Applets*** *hyperlink* that takes you to the Web page

```
http://java.sun.com/applets/index.html
```

This page contains a variety of Java applet resources, including free applets you can use on your own World Wide Web site, the demonstration applets from the J2SDK and a variety of other applets (many of which can be downloaded and used on your own computer). There is also a section entitled "Applets at Work" where you can read about uses of applets in industry.

On the Sun Microsystems Java Web site, visit the *Java Developer Connection*

```
http://java.sun.com/jdc/
```

This free site has close to one million members. The site includes technical support, discussion forums, on-line training courses, technical articles, resources, announcements of new Java features, early access to new Java technologies, and links to other important Java Web sites. Even though the site is free, you must register to use it.

Visit the *Developer.com Web site* at ***http://www.developer.com*** for a wide variety of information on Java and Internet-related topics. The *Java directory page*

```
http://www.developer.com/directories/pages/dir.java.html
```

contains links to thousands of Java applets and other Java resources.

Developer.com includes another Web site that has been a wonderful Java resource since the early days of Java—*Gamelan*. The Gamelan site

```
http://www.gamelan.com
```

calls itself the "Official Directory for Java." This site originally was a large Java repository where individuals traded ideas on Java and examples of Java programming. One of its early benefits was the volume of Java source code that was available to the many people learning Java. It is now an all-around Java resource with Java references, free Java downloads, areas where you can ask questions to Java experts, discussion groups on Java, a glossary of Java-related terminology, upcoming Java-related events, directories for specialized industry topics and hundreds of other Java resources.

Another Developer.com Web site is *JARS*—originally called the *Java Applet Rating Service*. The JARS site

```
http://www.jars.com
```

calls itself the "#1 Java Review Service." This site originally was a large Java repository for applets. Its benefit was that it rated every applet registered at the site as top 1%, top 5% and top 25%, so you could immediately view the best applets on the Web. Early in the development of the Java language, having your applet rated here was a great way to demonstrate your Java programming abilities. JARS is now another all-around resource for Java programmers. Many of the resources for this site, Gamelan and Developer.com, are now shared as these sites are all owned by EarthWeb.

All the resources listed in this section provide hyperlinks to hundreds of other Web sites on the World Wide Web. If you have Internet access, spend some time browsing these sites, executing applets and reading the source code for the applets when it is available. This will help you rapidly expand your Java expertise. See our Appendix B for more Web sites that are of interest to Java programmers.

Summary

- An applet is a Java program that runs in the **appletviewer** (a test utility for applets that is included with the J2SDK) or a World Wide Web browser such as Netscape Communicator or Microsoft Internet Explorer. The **appletviewer** (or browser) executes an applet when a Hypertext Markup Language (HTML) document containing the applet is opened in the **appletviewer** (or browser).

- Object orientation is a natural way of thinking about the world and of writing computer programs.

- Objects have attributes (like size, shape, color, weight and the like) and they exhibit behaviors.

- Humans learn about objects by studying their attributes and observing their behaviors.

- Different objects can have many of the same attributes and exhibit similar behaviors.

- Object-oriented programming (OOP) models real-world objects with software counterparts. It takes advantage of class relationships where objects of a certain class have the same characteristics. It takes advantage of inheritance relationships where newly created classes are derived by inheriting characteristics of existing classes, yet contain unique characteristics of their own.

- Object-oriented programming provides an intuitive way to view the programming process, namely by modeling real-world objects, their attributes and their behaviors.

- OOP also models communication between objects via messages.

- OOP encapsulates data (attributes) and methods (behavior) into objects.

- Objects have the property of information hiding. Although objects may know how to communicate with one another across well-defined interfaces, objects normally are not allowed to know implementation details of other objects.

- Information hiding is crucial to good software engineering.

- In C and other procedural programming languages, programming tends to be action-oriented. Data is certainly important in C, but the view is that data exists primarily in support of the actions that functions perform.

- Java programmers concentrate on creating their own user-defined types called classes. Each class contains data as well as the set of methods that manipulate the data. The data components of a class are called instance variables. The behavior components of a class are called methods.

- In the **appletviewer**, you can execute an applet again by clicking the appletviewer's **Applet** menu and selecting the **Reload** option from the menu. To terminate an applet, click the **appletviewer**'s **Applet** menu and select the **Quit** option.

- Class **Graphics** is located in package **java.awt**. Import the **Graphics** class so the program can draw graphics.

- Class **JApplet** is located in package **javax.swing**. When you create an applet in Java, you normally import the **JApplet** class.

- Each piece of the package name is a directory (or folder) on disk. All the packages in the Java API are stored in the directory **java** or **javax**, which contain many subdirectories.

- Java uses inheritance to create new classes from existing class definitions. Keyword **extends** followed by a class name indicates the class from which a new class inherits.

- In the inheritance relationship, the class following **extends** is called the superclass or base class and the new class is called the subclass or derived class. Using inheritance results in a new class definition that has the attributes (data) and behaviors (methods) of the superclass as well as the new features added in the subclass definition.

- A benefit of extending class **JApplet** is that someone else has already defined "what it means to be an applet." The **appletviewer** and World Wide Web browsers that support applets expect every Java applet to have certain capabilities (attributes and behaviors), and class **JApplet** already provides all those capabilities.

- Classes are used as "templates" or "blueprints" to instantiate (or create) objects in memory for use in a program. An object (or instance) is a region in the computer's memory in which information is stored for use by the program. The term object normally implies that attributes (data) and behaviors (methods) are associated with the object and that those behaviors perform operations on the attributes of the object.

- Method **paint** is one of three methods (behaviors) that are guaranteed to be called automatically for you when any applet begins execution. These three methods are **init**, **start** and **paint**, and they are guaranteed to be called in that order. These methods are called from the **appletviewer** or browser in which the applet is executing.

- The parameter list is where methods receive data required to complete their tasks. Normally, this data is passed by the programmer to the method through a method call (also known as invoking a method).

- Method **drawString** of class **Graphics** draws a string at the specified location on the applet. The first argument to **drawString** is the **String** to draw. The last two arguments in the list are the coordinates (or position) at which the string should be drawn. Coordinates are measured from the upper-left corner of the applet in pixels.

- You must create an HTML (Hypertext Markup Language) file to load an applet into the **appletviewer** (or a browser) to execute.

- Many HTML codes (referred to as tags) come in pairs. HTML tags begin with a left angle bracket **<** and end with a right angle bracket **>**.

- Normally, the applet and its corresponding HTML file are stored in the same directory on disk.

- The first component of the **<applet>** tag indicates the file containing the compiled applet class. The second and third components of the **<applet>** tag indicate the **width** and the **height** of the applet in pixels. Generally, each applet should be less than 640 pixels wide and 480 pixels tall (most computer screens support these dimensions as the minimum width and height).

- The **appletviewer** only understands the **<applet>** and **</applet>** HTML tags, so it is sometimes referred to as the "minimal browser" (it ignores all other HTML tags).

- Method **drawLine** of class **Graphics** draws lines. The method requires four arguments representing the two end points of the line on the applet—the x-coordinate and y-coordinate of the first end point in the line and the x-coordinate and y-coordinate of the second end point in the line. All coordinate values are specified with respect to the upper-left corner (0, 0) coordinate of the applet.

- Primitive data type **double** stores double-precision floating-point numbers. Primitive data type **float** stores single-precision floating-point numbers. A **double** requires more memory to store a floating-point value, but stores it with approximately twice the precision of a **float** (15 significant digits for **double** vs. seven significant digits for **float**).

- The **import** statements are not required if you always use the complete name of a class, including the full package name and class name.

- The asterisk (*****) notation after a package name in an **import** indicates that all classes in the package should be available to the compiler so the compiler can ensure that the classes are used correctly. This allows programmers to use the shorthand name (the class name by itself) of any class from the package in the program.

- Every instance (object) of the class contains one copy of each instance variable. Instance variables are declared in the body of the class definition, but not in the body of any method of the class definition. An important benefit of instance variables is that their identifiers can be used throughout the class definition (i.e., in all methods of the class).

- Variables defined in the body of a method are known as local variables and can only be used in the body of the method in which they are defined.

- Instance variables are always assigned a default value, and local variables are not.

- Method **init** is called once during an applet's execution. The method normally initializes the applet's instance variables and performs any tasks that need to be performed once at the beginning of an applet's execution.

- There are actually two types of variables in Java—primitive data type variables and references.

- References are used to refer to objects in a program. Such variables actually contain the location in the computer's memory of an object. A reference is used to send messages to (i.e., call methods on) the object in memory. As part of the message (method call), we provide the data that the method requires to do its task.

- A variable is similar to an object. The main difference between a variable and an object is that an object is defined by a class definition that can contain both data (instance variables) and methods, whereas a variable is defined by a primitive (or built-in) data type (one of **char**, **byte**, **short**, **int**, **long**, **float**, **double** or **boolean**) that can contain only data.

- A variable can store exactly one value at a time, whereas one object can contain many individual data members.

- If the data type is a class name, the identifier is a reference to an object and that reference can be used to send messages to (call methods on) that object. If the data type is one of the primitive data types, the identifier is a variable that can be used to store in memory or retrieve from memory a single value of the declared primitive type.

- Method **Double.parseDouble** (a **static** method of class **Double**) converts its **String** argument to a **double** floating-point value. Class **Double** is part of the package **java.lang**.

- Method **drawRect** draws a rectangle based on its four arguments. The first two integer values represent the upper-left *x*-coordinate and upper-left *y*-coordinate where the **Graphics** object begins drawing the rectangle. The third and fourth arguments are non-negative integers that represent the width of the rectangle in pixels and the height of the rectangle in pixels, respectively.

Terminology

abstraction
applet
Applet menu
<applet> tag
appletviewer
attribute
base class
behavior
boolean primitive type
browser
built-in data type
byte primitive type
char primitive type
command-line argument
coordinate
create an object
derived class
Double.parseDouble method
double-precision floating-point number

double primitive data type
drawLine method of class **Graphics**
drawRect method of class **Graphics**
drawString method of class **Graphics**
encapsulate
extends keyword
floating-point number
float primitive type
Graphics class
height of an applet
HTML tag
Hypertext Markup Language (HTML)
import statement
information hiding
init method of class **JApplet**
instance variable
instantiate an object
int primitive type
interface

invoke a method
JApplet class
java.awt package
javax.swing package
local variable
logic error
long primitive type
message
method call
Microsoft Internet Explorer
Netscape Communicator
object
object-oriented design
object-oriented programming
paint method of class **JApplet**

parameter list
pixel (picture element)
primitive data type
Quit menu item
references
Reload menu item
short primitive type
single-precision floating-point number
source code
start method of class **JApplet**
subclass
superclass
text file
width of an applet
World Wide Web

Common Programming Errors

3.1 It is an error if the file name is not identical in both spelling and capitalization to the **public** class name with the **.java** file name extension.

3.2 It is an error if a **.java** file contains more than one **public** class.

3.3 It is an error not to end a Java file name with the **.java** extension.

3.4 Placing additional characters such as commas (**,**) between the components in the **<applet>** tag may cause the **appletviewer** or browser to produce an error message indicating a **MissingResourceException** when loading the applet.

3.5 Forgetting the ending **</applet>** tag prevents the applet from loading into the appletviewer or browser properly.

3.6 Running the **appletviewer** with a file name that does not end with **.html** or **.htm** is an error that prevents the **appletviewer** from loading your applet for execution.

3.7 Assuming that an **import** statement for an entire package (e.g., **java.awt.***) also **import**s classes from subdirectories in that package (e.g., **java.awt.event.***) results in syntax errors for the classes from the subdirectories. There must be separate import statements for every package from which classes are used.

3.8 If braces do not occur in matching pairs, the compiler indicates a syntax error.

3.9 Using a local variable that is not initialized before it is used is a syntax error. Each local variable must be assigned a value before an attempt is made to use that variable's value.

3.10 It is a logic error to supply a negative width or negative height as an argument to **Graphics** method **drawRect**. The rectangle will not be displayed and no error will be indicated.

3.11 It is a logic error to supply two points (i.e., pairs of x- and y-coordinates) as the arguments to **Graphics** method **drawRect**. The third argument must be the width in pixels and the fourth argument must be the height in pixels of the rectangle to draw.

3.12 It is normally a logic error to supply arguments to **Graphics** method **drawRect** that cause the rectangle to draw outside the applet's viewable area (i.e., the width and height of the applet as specified in the HTML document that references the applet). Either increase the applet's width and height in the HTML document or pass arguments to method **drawRect** that cause the rectangle to draw inside the applet's viewable area.

Good Programming Practices

3.1 Investigate the capabilities of any class in the Java API documentation carefully before inheriting a subclass from it. This helps ensure that the programmer does not unintentionally redefine a capability that is already provided.

3.2   Always test a Java applet in the **appletviewer** and ensure that it is executing correctly before loading the applet into a World Wide Web browser. Browsers often save a copy of an applet in memory until the current browsing session terminates (i.e., all browser windows are closed). Thus, if you change an applet, recompile the applet, then reload the applet in the browser, you may not see the changes because the browser may still be executing the original version of the applet. Close all your browser windows to remove the old version of the applet from memory. Open a new browser window and load the applet to see your changes.

3.3   Whenever you type an opening left brace, **{**, in your program, immediately type the closing right brace, **}**, then reposition the cursor between the braces to begin typing the body. This helps prevent missing braces.

3.4   Initializing instance variables rather than relying on automatic initialization improves program readability.

Portability Tip

3.1   Test your applets in every browser used by people who view your applet. This will help ensure that people who view your applet experience the functionality you expect. [Note: A goal of the Java Plug-In (discussed later in the book) is to provide consistent applet execution across many different browsers.]

Software Engineering Observations

3.1   If your World Wide Web browser does not support Java 2, most of the applets in this book will not execute in your browser. This is because most of the applets in this book use features that are new to Java 2 or are not provided by browsers that support Java 1.1. [Note: Later in the book we discuss the Java Plug-In and how it can be used to provide Java 2 support in today's browsers.]

3.2   Generally, each applet should be less than 640 pixels wide and 480 pixels tall (most computer screens support these dimensions as the minimum width and height).

3.3   The Java compiler does not need **import** statements in a Java source code file if the complete class name—the full package name and class name (e.g., **java.awt.Graphics**)—is specified every time a class name is used in the source code.

3.4   The compiler does not load every class in a package when it encounters an **import** statement that uses the ***** (e.g., **javax.swing.***) notation to indicate that multiple classes from the package are used in the program. The compiler searches the package only for those classes used in the program.

3.5   Many package directories have subdirectories. For example, the **java.awt** package directory contains subdirectory **event** for the package **java.awt.event**. When the compiler encounters an **import** statement that uses the ***** (e.g., **java.awt.***) notation to indicate that multiple classes from the package are used in the program, the compiler does not search the subdirectory **event**. This means that you cannot define an **import** of **java.*** to search for classes from all packages.

3.6   When using **import** statements, separate **import** statements must be specified for each package used in a program.

3.7   The order in which methods are defined in a class definition has no effect on when those methods are called at execution time.

3.8   A hint to help you determine if an identifier is a variable or a reference is the variable's data type. By convention all class names in Java start with a capitalized first letter. Therefore, if the data type starts with a capitalized first letter, you can normally assume that the identifier is a reference to an object of the declared type (e.g., **Graphics g** indicates that **g** is a reference to a **Graphics** object).

3.9   For each primitive data type (such as **int** or **double**) there is a corresponding class (such as **Integer** or **Double**) in package **java.lang**. These classes (commonly known as type-wrappers) provide methods for processing primitive data type values (such as converting a **String** to a primitive data type value or converting a primitive data type value to a **String**). Primitive data types do not have methods. Therefore, methods related to a primitive data type are located in the corresponding type-wrapper class (i.e., method **parseDouble** that converts a **String** to a **double** value is located in class **Double**).

3.10   The only statements that should be placed in an applet's **init** method are those that are directly related to the one-time initialization of an applet's instance variables. The applet's results should be displayed from other methods of the applet class. Results that involve drawing should be displayed from the applet's **paint** method.

3.11   The only statements that should be placed in an applet's **paint** method are those that are directly related to drawing (i.e., calls to methods of class **Graphics**) and the logic of drawing. Generally, dialog boxes should not be displayed from an applet's **paint** method.

Testing and Debugging Tips

3.1   If the **appletviewer** command does not work and/or the system indicates that the **appletviewer** command cannot be found, the **PATH** environment variable may not be defined properly on your computer. Review the installation directions for the Java 2 Software Development Kit to ensure that the **PATH** environment variable is correctly defined for your system (on some computers, you may need to restart your computer after defining the **PATH** environment variable).

3.2   The compiler error message "Public class ClassName must be defined in a file called ClassName.java" indicates either 1) that the file name does not exactly match the name of the **public** class in the file (including all uppercase and lowercase letters), or 2) that you typed the class name incorrectly when compiling the class (the name must be spelled with the proper uppercase and lowercase letters).

3.3   If you receive a **MissingResourceException** error message when loading an applet into the **appletviewer** or a browser, check the **<applet>** tag in the HTML file carefully for syntax errors. Compare your HTML file to the file in Fig. 3.7 to confirm proper syntax.

Self-Review Exercises

3.1   Fill in the blanks in each of the following.
   c) Class _____ provides methods for drawing.
   d) Java applets begin execution with a series of three method calls: _____, _____ and _____.
   e) Methods _____ and _____ display lines and rectangles.
   f) Keyword _____ is used to indicate that a new class is a subclass of an existing class.
   g) Every Java applet should extend either class _____ or class _____.
   h) A class definition describes the _____ and _____ of an object.
   i) Java's eight primitive data types are _____, _____, _____, _____, _____, _____, _____ and _____.

3.2   State whether each of the following is *true* or *false*. If *false*, explain why.
   a) Method **drawRect** requires four arguments that specify two points on the applet to draw a rectangle.
   b) Method **drawLine** requires four arguments that specify two points on the applet to draw a line.
   c) Type **Double** is a primitive data type.
   d) Data type **int** is used to declare a floating-point number.
   e) Method **Double.parseDouble** converts a **String** to a primitive **double** value.

3.3   Write Java statements to accomplish each of the following:
- a) Display a dialog asking the user to enter a floating-point number.
- b) Convert a **String** to a floating-point number and store the converted value in **double** variable **age**. Assume that the **String** is stored in **stringValue**.
- c) Draw the message **"This is a Java program"** on one line on an applet (assume you are defining this statement in the applet's **paint** method) at position *(10, 10)*.
- d) Draw the message **"This is a Java program"** on two lines on an applet (assume these statements are defined in applet method **paint**) starting at position *(10, 10)* and where the first line ends with **Java**. Make the two lines start at the same *x* coordinate.

Answers to Self-Review Exercises

3.1   a) **Graphics**. b) **init**, **start** and **paint**.   c) **drawLine** and **drawRect**. d) **extends**.   e) **JApplet**, **Applet**.   f) attributes and behaviors. g) **byte**, **short**, **int**, **long**, **float**, **double**, **char** and **boolean**.

3.2
- a) False. Method **drawRect** requires four arguments—two that specify the upper-left corner of the rectangle and two that specify the width and height of the rectangle.
- b) True.
- c) False. Type **Double** is a class in the **java.lang** package. Remember that names that start with a capital first letter are normally class names.
- d) False. Data type **double** or data type **float** can be used to declare a floating-point number. Data type **int** is used to declare integers.
- e) True.

3.3
- a) ```
value = JOptionPane.showInputDialog(
           "Enter a floating-point number");
```
- b) `age = Double.parseDouble( stringValue );`
- c) `g.drawString( "This is a Java program", 10, 10 );`
- d) ```
g.drawString( "This is a Java", 10, 10 );
g.drawString( "program", 10, 25 );
```

Exercises

3.4   Fill in the blanks in each of the following:
- a) Data type _____ declares a single-precision floating-point variable.
- b) If class **Double** provides method **parseDouble** to convert a **String** to a **double** and class **Integer** provides method **parseInt** to convert a **String** to an **int**, then class **Float** probably provides method _____ to convert a **String** to a **float**.
- c) Data type _____ declares a double-precision floating-point variable.
- d) The _____ or a browser can be used to execute a Java applet.
- e) To load an applet into a browser you must first define an _____ file.
- f) The _____ and _____ tags specify that an applet should be loaded and executed.

3.5   State whether each of the following is *true* or *false*. If *false*, explain why.
- a) All browsers support Java 2.
- b) When using an **import** of the form **javax.swing.***, all classes in the package are imported.
- c) You do not need import statements if the full package name and class name are specified each time you refer to a class in a program.

3.6   Write an applet that asks the user to enter two floating-point numbers, obtains the two numbers from the user and draws the sum, product, difference and quotient of the two numbers. Use the techniques shown in Fig. 3.12.

3.7   Write an applet that asks the user to enter two floating-point numbers, obtains the numbers from the user and displays the larger number followed by the words "**is larger**" as a string on the applet. If the numbers are equal, print the message "**These numbers are equal**." Use the techniques shown in Fig. 3.12.

3.8   Write an applet that inputs three floating-point numbers from the user and displays the sum, average, product, smallest and largest of these numbers as strings on the applet. Use the techniques shown in Fig. 3.12.

3.9   Write an applet that inputs from the user the radius of a circle as a floating-point number and draws the circle's diameter, circumference and area. Use the constant value 3.14159 for π. Use the techniques shown in Fig. 3.12. [*Note:* You may also use the predefined constant **Math.PI** for the value of π. This constant is more precise than the value 3.14159. Class **Math** is defined in the **java.lang** package, so you do not need to **import** it.] Use the following formulas (*r* is the radius): *diameter = 2r, circumference = 2πr, area = πr^2*.

3.10   Write an applet that draws a box, an oval, an arrow and a diamond using asterisks (*****) as follows:

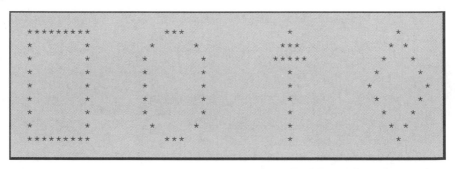

3.11   Write an applet that reads five integers and determines and prints the largest and smallest integers in the group. Use only the programming techniques you learned in this chapter and Chapter 2. Draw the results on the applet.

3.12   Write an applet that reads in two floating-point numbers and determines and prints if the first is a multiple of the second. (*Hint:* Use the modulus operator.) Use only the programming techniques you learned in this chapter and Chapter 2. Draw the results on the applet.

3.13   Write an applet that draws a checkerboard pattern as follows:

3.14   Write an applet that draws a variety of rectangles of different sizes and locations.

3.15   Write an applet that allows the user to input the four arguments required by method **drawRect**, then draws a rectangle using the four input values.

3.16   The **Graphics** class contains a **drawOval** method that takes the exact same four arguments as the **drawRect** method. However, the arguments for the **drawOval** method specify the "bounding box" for the oval. The sides of the bounding box are the boundaries of the oval. Write a Java applet that draws an oval and a rectangle with the same four arguments. You will see that the oval touches the rectangle at the center of each side.

3.17   Modify the solution to Exercise 3.16 to output a variety of ovals of different shapes and sizes.

3.18   Write an applet that allows the user to input the four arguments required by method **drawOval**, then draws an oval using the four input values.

3.19   What does the following code print?

```
g.drawString( "*", 25, 25 );
g.drawString( "***", 25, 55 );
g.drawString( "*****", 25, 85 );
g.drawString( "****", 25, 70 );
g.drawString( "**", 25, 40 );
```

3.20   Using only the programming techniques you learned in Chapters 2 and 3, write an applet that calculates the squares and cubes of the numbers from 0 to 10 and draws the resulting values in table format as follows:

```
number  square  cube
0       0       0
1       1       1
2       4       8
3       9       27
4       16      64
5       25      125
6       36      216
7       49      343
8       64      512
9       81      729
10      100     1000
```

[*Note:* This program does not require any input from the user.]

3.21   Write an applet that reads a first name and a last name from the user as two separate inputs and concatenates the first name and last name separated by a space. Draw a string with the concatenated name.

3.22   Write an applet that inputs five floating-point numbers and determines and prints the number of negative numbers input, number of positive numbers input and the number of zeros input. Use only the programming techniques you learned in this chapter and Chapter 2. Draw the results on the applet.

Control Structures: Part 1

Objectives

- To understand basic problem-solving techniques.
- To be able to develop algorithms through the process of top-down, stepwise refinement.
- To be able to use the **if** and **if/else** selection structures to choose among alternative actions.
- To be able to use the **while** repetition structure to execute statements in a program repeatedly.
- To understand counter-controlled repetition and sentinel-controlled repetition.
- To be able to use the increment, decrement, and assignment operators.

Let's all move one place on.
Lewis Carroll

The wheel is come full circle.
William Shakespeare, *King Lear*

How many apples fell on Newton's head before he took the hint!
Robert Frost, Comment

Outline

4.1 Introduction

Before writing a program to solve a problem, it is essential to have a thorough understanding of the problem and a carefully planned approach to solving the problem. When writing a program, it is equally essential to understand the types of building blocks that are available and to employ proven program construction principles. In this chapter and in Chapter 5 we discuss these issues in our presentation of the theory and principles of structured programming. The techniques you learn here are applicable to most high-level languages, including Java. When we study object-based programming in more depth in Chapter 8, we will see that control structures are helpful in building and manipulating objects.

4.2 Algorithms

Any computing problem can be solved by executing a series of actions in a specific order. A *procedure* for solving a problem in terms of

1. the *actions* to be executed, and

2. the *order* in which these actions are to be executed

is called an *algorithm*. The following example demonstrates that correctly specifying the order in which the actions are to be executed is important.

Consider the "rise-and-shine algorithm" followed by one junior executive for getting out of bed and going to work: (1) get out of bed, (2) take off pajamas, (3) take a shower, (4) get dressed, (5) eat breakfast, (6) carpool to work.

This routine gets the executive to work well-prepared to make critical decisions. Suppose, however, that the same steps are performed in a slightly different order: (1) get out of bed, (2) take off pajamas, (3) get dressed, (4) take a shower, (5) eat breakfast, (6) carpool to work.

In this case, our junior executive shows up for work soaking wet. Specifying the order in which statements are to be executed in a computer program is called *program control*. In this chapter and Chapter 5, we investigate the program control capabilities of Java.

4.3 Pseudocode

Pseudocode is an artificial and informal language that helps programmers develop algorithms. The pseudocode we present here is particularly useful for developing algorithms that will be converted to structured portions of Java programs. Pseudocode is similar to everyday English; it is convenient and user-friendly although it is not an actual computer programming language.

Pseudocode programs are not actually executed on computers. Rather, they help the programmer "think out" a program before attempting to write it in a programming language such as Java. In this chapter, we give several examples of pseudocode programs.

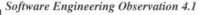

Software Engineering Observation 4.1

Pseudocode is often used to "think out" a program during the program design process. Then the pseudocode program is converted to Java.

The style of pseudocode we present consists purely of characters, so programmers may conveniently type pseudocode programs using an editor program. The computer can produce a fresh printed copy of a pseudocode program on demand. A carefully prepared pseudocode program may be converted easily to a corresponding Java program. This is done in many cases simply by replacing pseudocode statements with their Java equivalents.

Pseudocode normally describes only executable statements—the actions that are performed when the program is converted from pseudocode to Java and is run. Declarations are not executable statements. For example, the declaration

```
int i;
```

tells the compiler the type of variable **i** and instructs the compiler to reserve space in memory for the variable. This declaration does not cause any action—such as input, output or a calculation—to occur when the program is executed. Some programmers choose to list variables and mention the purpose of each at the beginning of a pseudocode program.

4.4 Control Structures

Normally, statements in a program are executed one after the other in the order in which they are written. This is called *sequential execution*. Various Java statements we will soon discuss enable the programmer to specify that the next statement to be executed may be other than the next one in sequence. This is called *transfer of control*.

During the 1960s, it became clear that the indiscriminate use of transfers of control was the root of much difficulty experienced by software development groups. The finger of blame was pointed at the *goto* statement, which allows the programmer to specify a transfer of control to one of a very wide range of possible destinations in a program. The notion of so-called *structured programming* became almost synonymous with *"goto elimination."* Java does not have a **goto** statement.

The research of Bohm and Jacopini[1] had demonstrated that programs could be written without any **goto** statements. The challenge of the era for programmers was to shift their styles to "**goto**-less programming." It was not until the 1970s that programmers started taking structured programming seriously. The results have been impressive as software development groups have reported reduced development times, more frequent on-time delivery of systems and more frequent within-budget completion of software projects. The key to these successes is that structured programs are clearer, easier to debug and modify, and more likely to be bug-free in the first place.

Bohm and Jacopini's work demonstrated that all programs could be written in terms of only three *control structures*, namely the *sequence structure*, the *selection structure* and the *repetition structure*. The sequence structure is built into Java. Unless directed otherwise, the computer executes Java statements one after the other in the order in which they are written. The *flowchart* segment of Fig. 4.1 illustrates a typical sequence structure in which two calculations are performed in order.

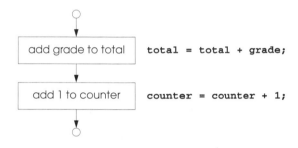

Fig. 4.1   Flowcharting Java's sequence structure.

A flowchart is a graphical representation of an algorithm or of a portion of an algorithm. Flowcharts are drawn using certain special-purpose symbols such as rectangles, diamonds, ovals and small circles; these symbols are connected by arrows called *flowlines*, which indicate the order in which the actions of the algorithm execute.

Like pseudocode, flowcharts are often useful for developing and representing algorithms, although pseudocode is strongly preferred by many programmers. Flowcharts show clearly how control structures operate; that is all we use them for in this text. The reader should carefully compare the pseudocode and flowchart representations of each control structure.

Consider the flowchart segment for the sequence structure in Fig. 4.1. We use the *rectangle symbol*, also called the *action symbol,* to indicate any type of action, including a calculation or an input/output operation. The flowlines in the figure indicate the order in which the actions are to be performed—first, **grade** is to be added to **total**, then **1** is to be added to **counter**. Java allows us to have as many actions as we want in a sequence structure. As we will soon see, anywhere a single action may be placed, we may place several actions in sequence.

When drawing a flowchart that represents a *complete* algorithm, an *oval symbol* containing the word "Begin" is the first symbol used in the flowchart; an oval symbol con-

1. Bohm, C., and G. Jacopini, "Flow Diagrams, Turing Machines, and Languages with Only Two Formation Rules," Communications of the ACM, Vol. 9, No. 5, May 1966, pp. 336–371.

taining the word "End" indicates where the algorithm ends. When drawing only a portion of an algorithm as in Fig. 4.1, the oval symbols are omitted in favor of using *small circle symbols,* also called *connector symbols.*

Perhaps the most important flowcharting symbol is the *diamond symbol,* also called the *decision symbol,* which indicates that a decision is to be made. We will discuss the diamond symbol in the next section.

Java provides three types of selection structures; we discuss each of these in this chapter and in Chapter 5. The **if** selection structure either performs (selects) an action if a condition is true or skips the action if the condition is false. The **if/else** selection structure performs an action if a condition is true and performs a different action if the condition is false. The **switch** selection structure (Chapter 5) performs one of many different actions, depending on the value of an expression.

The **if** structure is called a *single-selection structure* because it selects or ignores a single action (or as we will soon see, a single group of actions). The **if/else** structure is called a *double-selection structure* because it selects between two different actions (or groups of actions). The **switch** structure is called a *multiple-selection structure* because it selects among many different actions (or groups of actions).

Java provides three types of repetition structures, namely **while**, **do/while** and **for** (**do/while** and **for** are covered in Chapter 5). Each of the words **if**, **else**, **switch**, **while**, **do** and **for** are Java *keywords*. These words are reserved by the language to implement various features, such as Java's control structures. Keywords cannot be used as identifiers such as for variable names. A complete list of Java keywords is shown in Fig. 4.2.

Common Programming Error 4.1

Using a keyword as an identifier is a syntax error.

Java Keywords				
abstract	boolean	break	byte	case
catch	char	class	continue	default
do	double	else	extends	false
final	finally	float	for	if
implements	import	instanceof	int	interface
long	native	new	null	package
private	protected	public	return	short
static	super	switch	synchronized	this
throw	throws	transient	true	try
void	volatile	while		

Keywords that are reserved but not used by Java

const	goto

Fig. 4.2   Java keywords.

Well, that is all there is. Java has only seven control structures: sequence, three types of selection and three types of repetition. Each program is formed by combining as many of each type of control structure as is appropriate for the algorithm the program implements. As with the sequence structure of Fig. 4.1, we will see that each control structure is flowcharted with two small circle symbols, one at the entry point to the control structure and one at the exit point.

Single-entry/single-exit control structures make it easy to build programs—the control structures are attached to one another by connecting the exit point of one control structure to the entry point of the next. This is similar to the way a child stacks building blocks, so we call this *control-structure stacking*. We will learn that there is only one other way control structures may be connected—*control-structure nesting*. Thus, algorithms in Java programs are constructed from only seven different types of control structures combined in only two ways.

4.5 The `if` Selection Structure

A selection structure is used to choose among alternative courses of action in a program. For example, suppose that the passing grade on an examination is 60 (out of 100). Then the pseudocode statement

> *If student's grade is greater than or equal to 60*
> > *Print "Passed"*

determines if the condition "student's grade is greater than or equal to 60" is true or false. If the condition is true, then "Passed" is printed, and the next pseudocode statement in order is "performed" (remember that pseudocode is not a real programming language). If the condition is false, the print statement is ignored, and the next pseudocode statement in order is performed. Note that the second line of this selection structure is indented. Such indentation is optional, but it is highly recommended because it emphasizes the inherent structure of structured programs. The Java compiler ignores white-space characters like blanks, tabs and newlines used for indentation and vertical spacing. Programmers insert these white-space characters to enhance program clarity.

Good Programming Practice 4.1

Consistently applying reasonable indentation conventions throughout your programs improves program readability. We suggest a fixed-size tab of about 1/4 inch or three spaces per indent.

The preceding pseudocode *If* statement may be written in Java as

```
if ( studentGrade >= 60 )
    System.out.println( "Passed" );
```

Notice that the Java code corresponds closely to the pseudocode. This is a property of pseudocode that makes it a useful program development tool. The statement in the body of the `if` structure outputs the character string **"Passed"** in the command window.

The flowchart of Fig. 4.3 illustrates the single-selection `if` structure. This flowchart contains what is perhaps the most important flowcharting symbol—the *diamond symbol*, also called the *decision symbol,* which indicates that a decision is to be made. The decision symbol contains an expression, such as a condition, that can be either **true** or **false**. The decision symbol has two flowlines emerging from it. One indicates the direction to be taken when the expression in the symbol is true; the other indicates the direction to be taken when the expression is false. A decision can be made on any expression that evaluates to a value of Java's **boolean** type (i.e., any expression that evaluates to **true** or **false**).

Note that the **if** structure, too, is a single-entry/single-exit structure. We will soon learn that the flowcharts for the remaining control structures also contain (besides small circle symbols and flowlines) only rectangle symbols to indicate the actions to be performed and diamond symbols to indicate decisions to be made. This is the *action/decision model of programming* we have been emphasizing.

We can envision seven bins, each containing only control structures of one of the seven types. These control structures are empty. Nothing is written in the rectangles or in the diamonds. The programmer's task, then, is assembling a program from as many of each type of control structure as the algorithm demands, combining those control structures in only two possible ways (stacking or nesting), and then filling in the actions and decisions in a manner appropriate for the algorithm. We will discuss the variety of ways in which actions and decisions may be written.

4.6 The **if/else** Selection Structure

The **if** selection structure performs an indicated action only when the condition evaluates to **true**; otherwise, the action is skipped. The **if/else** selection structure allows the programmer to specify that a different action is to be performed when the condition is true than when the condition is false. For example, the pseudocode statement

If student's grade is greater than or equal to 60
    Print "Passed"
else
        Print "Failed"

prints *Passed* if the student's grade is greater than or equal to 60 and prints *Failed* if the student's grade is less than 60. In either case, after printing occurs, the next pseudocode statement in sequence is "performed." Note that the body of the *else* is also indented.

Good Programming Practice 4.2

*Indent both body statements of an **if/else** structure.*

The indentation convention you choose should be carefully applied throughout your programs. It is difficult to read programs that do not use uniform spacing conventions.

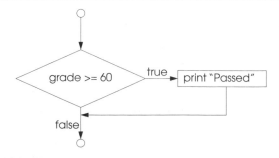

Fig. 4.3   Flowcharting the single-selection **if** structure.

The preceding pseudocode *if/else* structure may be written in Java as

```
if ( studentGrade >= 60 )
    System.out.println( "Passed" );
else
    System.out.println( "Failed" );
```

The flowchart of Fig. 4.4 nicely illustrates the flow of control in the **if/else** structure. Once again, note that (besides small circles and arrows) the only symbols in the flowchart are rectangles (for actions) and a diamond (for a decision). We continue to emphasize this action/decision model of computing. Imagine again a deep bin containing as many empty double-selection structures as might be needed to build a Java algorithm. The programmer's job is to assemble the selection structures (by stacking and nesting) with other control structures required by the algorithm, and to fill in the empty rectangles and empty diamonds with actions and decisions appropriate to the algorithm being implemented.

The *conditional operator (? :)* is closely related to the **if/else** structure. The **? :** is Java's only *ternary operator*—it takes three operands. The operands together with the **? :** form a *conditional expression*. The first operand is a **boolean** expression, the second is the value for the conditional expression if the condition evaluates to **true**, and the third is the value for the conditional expression if the condition evaluates to **false**. For example, the output statement

```
System.out.println(
    studentGrade >= 60 ? "Passed" : "Failed" );
```

contains a conditional expression that evaluates to the string **"Passed"** if the condition **studentGrade >= 60** is true and evaluates to the string **"Failed"** if the condition is false. Thus, this statement with the conditional operator performs essentially the same as the preceding **if/else** statement. The precedence of the conditional operator is low, so the entire conditional expression is normally placed in parentheses. We will see that conditional operators can be used in some situations where **if/else** statements cannot.

*Nested **if/else** structures* test for multiple cases by placing **if/else** structures inside **if/else** structures. For example, the following pseudocode statement will print **A** for exam grades greater than or equal to 90, **B** for grades in the range 80 to 89, **C** for grades in the range 70 to 79, **D** for grades in the range 60 to 69, and **F** for all other grades.

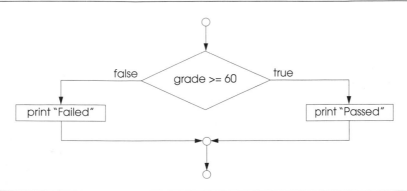

Fig. 4.4   Flowcharting the double-selection **if/else** structure.

If student's grade is greater than or equal to 90
>   *Print "A"*

else
>   *If student's grade is greater than or equal to 80*
>   >   *Print "B"*
>
>   *else*
>   >   *If student's grade is greater than or equal to 70*
>   >   >   *Print "C"*
>   >
>   >   *else*
>   >   >   *If student's grade is greater than or equal to 60*
>   >   >   >   *Print "D"*
>   >   >
>   >   >   *else*
>   >   >   >   *Print "F"*

This pseudocode may be written in Java as

```
if ( studentGrade >= 90 )
   System.out.println( "A" );
else
   if ( studentGrade >= 80 )
      System.out.println( "B" );
   else
      if ( studentGrade >= 70 )
         System.out.println( "C" );
      else
         if ( studentGrade >= 60 )
            System.out.println( "D" );
         else
            System.out.println( "F" );
```

If **studentGrade** is greater than or equal to 90, the first four conditions will be true, but only the **System.out.println** statement after the first test will be executed. After that particular **System.out.println** is executed, the **else** part of the "outer" **if/else** statement is skipped.

Good Programming Practice 4.3

If there are several levels of indentation, each level should be indented the same additional amount of space.

Most Java programmers prefer to write the preceding **if** structure as

```
if ( grade >= 90 )
   System.out.println( "A" );
else if ( grade >= 80 )
   System.out.println( "B" );
else if ( grade >= 70 )
   System.out.println( "C" );
else if ( grade >= 60 )
   System.out.println( "D" );
else
   System.out.println( "F" );
```

Both forms are equivalent. The latter form is popular because it avoids the deep indentation of the code to the right. Such deep indentation often leaves little room on a line, forcing lines to be split and decreasing program readability.

It is important to note that the Java compiler always associates an **else** with the previous **if** unless told to do otherwise by the placement of braces (**{}**). This is referred to as the *dangling-else problem*. For example,

```
if ( x > 5 )
    if ( y > 5 )
        System.out.println( "x and y are > 5" );
    else
        System.out.println( "x is <= 5" );
```

appears to indicate that if **x** is greater than **5**, the **if** structure in its body determines if **y** is also greater than **5**. If so, the string **"x and y are > 5"** is output. Otherwise, it *appears* that if **x** is not greater than **5**, the **else** part of the **if/else** structure outputs the string **"x is <= 5"**.

Beware! The preceding nested **if** structure does not execute as it appears. The compiler actually interprets the preceding structure as

```
if ( x > 5 )
    if ( y > 5 )
        System.out.println( "x and y are > 5" );
    else
        System.out.println( "x is <= 5" );
```

in which the body of the first **if** structure is an **if/else** structure. This structure tests if **x** is greater than **5**. If so, execution continues by testing if **y** is also greater than **5**. If the second condition is true, the proper string—**"x and y are > 5"**—is displayed. However, if the second condition is false, the string **"x is <= 5"** is displayed even though we know **x** is greater than **5**.

To force the preceding nested **if** structure to execute as it was originally intended, the structure must be written as follows:

```
if ( x > 5 ) {
    if ( y > 5 )
        System.out.println( "x and y are > 5" );
}
else
    System.out.println( "x is <= 5" );
```

The braces (**{}**) indicate to the compiler that the second **if** structure is in the body of the first **if** structure and that the **else** is matched with the first **if** structure. In Exercises 4.21 and 4.22 you will investigate the dangling-else problem further.

The **if** selection structure normally expects only one statement in its body. To include several statements in the body of an **if**, enclose the statements in braces (**{** and **}**). A set of statements contained within a pair of braces is called a *compound statement*.

Software Engineering Observation 4.2

A compound statement can be placed anywhere in a program that a single statement can be placed.

The following example includes a compound statement in the **else** part of an **if/else** structure.

```
if (grade >= 60)
   System.out.println( "Passed" );
else {
   System.out.println( "Failed" );
   System.out.println( "You must take this course again." );
}
```

In this case, if **grade** is less than 60, the program executes both statements in the body of the **else** and prints

```
Failed.
You must take this course again.
```

Notice the braces surrounding the two statements in the **else** clause. These braces are important. Without the braces, the statement

```
System.out.println( "You must take this course again." );
```

would be outside the body of the **else** part of the **if** and would execute regardless of whether the grade is less than 60.

Common Programming Error 4.2

Forgetting one or both of the braces that delimit a compound statement can lead to syntax errors or logic errors.

Syntax errors (such as when one brace in a compound statement is left out of the program) are caught by the compiler. A *logic error* (such as the one caused when both braces in a compound statement are left out of the program) has its effect at execution time. A *fatal logic error* causes a program to fail and terminate prematurely. A *nonfatal logic error* allows a program to continue executing, but the program produces incorrect results.

Software Engineering Observation 4.3

Just as a compound statement can be placed anywhere a single statement can be placed, it is also possible to have no statement at all (i.e., the empty statement). The empty statement is represented by placing a semicolon (;) where a statement would normally be.

Common Programming Error 4.3

*Placing a semicolon after the condition in an **if** structure leads to a logic error in single-selection **if** structures and a syntax error in double-selection **if** structures (if the **if** part contains a nonempty body statement).*

Good Programming Practice 4.4

Some programmers prefer to type the beginning and ending braces of compound statements before typing the individual statements within the braces. This helps avoid omitting one or both of the braces.

In this section, we introduced the notion of a compound statement. A compound statement may contain declarations (as does the body of **main**, for example). If so, the compound statement is called a *block*. The declarations in a block are commonly placed first in the block before any action statements, but declarations may be intermixed with action statements. We will discuss the use of blocks in Chapter 6. The reader should avoid using blocks until that time.

4.7 The `while` Repetition Structure

A *repetition structure* allows the programmer to specify that an action is to be repeated while some condition remains true. The pseudocode statement

> *While there are more items on my shopping list*
>   *Purchase next item and cross it off my list*

describes the repetition that occurs during a shopping trip. The condition, "there are more items on my shopping list" may be true or false. If it is true, then the action, "Purchase next item and cross it off my list" is performed. This action will be performed repeatedly while the condition remains true. The statement(s) contained in the *while* repetition structure constitute the body of the *while*. The *while* structure body may be a single statement or a compound statement. Eventually, the condition will become false (when the last item on the shopping list has been purchased and crossed off the list). At this point, the repetition terminates, and the first pseudocode statement after the repetition structure is executed.

Common Programming Error 4.4

*Not providing in the body of a **while** structure an action that eventually causes the condition in the **while** to become false is a logic error. Normally, such a repetition structure will never terminate—an error called an "infinite loop."*

Common Programming Error 4.5

*Spelling the keyword **while** with an uppercase **W** as in **While** (remember that Java is a case-sensitive language) is a syntax error. All of Java's reserved keywords, such as **while**, **if** and **else**, contain only lowercase letters.*

As an example of a **while** structure, consider a program segment designed to find the first power of 2 larger than 1000. Suppose **int** variable **product** has been initialized to 2. When the following **while** structure finishes executing, **product** contains the result:

```
int product = 2;

while ( product <= 1000 )
    product = 2 * product;
```

The flowchart of Fig. 4.5 illustrates the flow of control of the preceding **while** repetition structure. Once again, note that (besides small circles and arrows) the flowchart contains only a rectangle symbol and a diamond symbol.

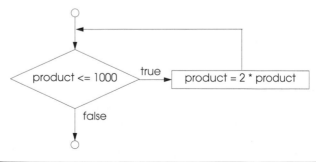

Fig. 4.5   Flowcharting the **while** repetition structure.

Imagine, again, a deep bin of empty **while** structures that may be stacked and nested with other control structures to form a structured implementation of an algorithm's flow of control. The empty rectangles and diamonds are then filled in with appropriate actions and decisions. The flowchart clearly shows the repetition. The flowline emerging from the rectangle wraps back to the decision, which is tested each time through the loop until the decision eventually becomes false. At this point, the **while** structure is exited and control passes to the next statement in the program.

When the **while** structure is entered, **product** is 2. Variable **product** is repeatedly multiplied by 2, taking on the values 4, 8, 16, 32, 64, 128, 256, 512 and 1024 successively. When **product** becomes 1024, the condition **product <= 1000** in the **while** structure becomes **false**. This terminates the repetition with 1024 as **product**'s final value. Execution continues with the next statement after the **while**. [*Note:* If a **while** structure's condition is initially **false** the body statement(s) will never be performed.]

4.8 Formulating Algorithms: Case Study 1 (Counter-Controlled Repetition)

To illustrate how algorithms are developed, we solve several variations of a class-averaging problem. Consider the following problem statement:

> *A class of ten students took a quiz. The grades (integers in the range 0 to 100) for this quiz are available to you. Determine the class average on the quiz.*

The class average is equal to the sum of the grades divided by the number of students. The algorithm for solving this problem on a computer must input each of the grades, perform the averaging calculation, and print the result.

Let us use pseudocode to list the actions to be executed and specify the order in which these actions should be executed. We use *counter-controlled repetition* to input the grades one at a time. This technique uses a variable called a *counter* to control the number of times a set of statements will execute. In this example, repetition terminates when the counter exceeds 10. In this section, we present a pseudocode algorithm (Fig. 4.6) and the corresponding program (Fig. 4.7). In the next section, we show how pseudocode algorithms are developed. Counter-controlled repetition is often called *definite repetition* because the number of repetitions is known before the loop begins executing.

Set total to zero
Set grade counter to one

While grade counter is less than or equal to ten
    Input the next grade
    Add the grade into the total
    Add one to the grade counter

Set the class average to the total divided by ten
Print the class average

Fig. 4.6   Pseudocode algorithm that uses counter-controlled repetition to solve the class-average problem.

Note the references in the algorithm to a total and a counter. A *total* is a variable used to accumulate the sum of a series of values. A counter is a variable used to count—in this case, to count the number of grades entered. Variables used to store totals should normally be initialized to zero before being used in a program; otherwise, the sum would include the previous value stored in the total's memory location.

```java
1   // Fig. 4.7: Average1.java
2   // Class average program with counter-controlled repetition
3   import javax.swing.JOptionPane;
4
5   public class Average1 {
6      public static void main( String args[] )
7      {
8         int total,             // sum of grades
9             gradeCounter,      // number of grades entered
10            gradeValue,        // grade value
11            average;           // average of all grades
12         String grade;         // grade typed by user
13
14         // Initialization Phase
15         total = 0;            // clear total
16         gradeCounter = 1;     // prepare to loop
17
18         // Processing Phase
19         while ( gradeCounter <= 10 ) {  // loop 10 times
20
21            // prompt for input and read grade from user
22            grade = JOptionPane.showInputDialog(
23                     "Enter integer grade: " );
24
25            // convert grade from a String to an integer
26            gradeValue = Integer.parseInt( grade );
27
28            // add gradeValue to total
29            total = total + gradeValue;
30
31            // add 1 to gradeCounter
32            gradeCounter = gradeCounter + 1;
33         }
34
35         // Termination Phase
36         average = total / 10;   // perform integer division
37
38         // display average of exam grades
39         JOptionPane.showMessageDialog(
40            null, "Class average is " + average, "Class Average",
41            JOptionPane.INFORMATION_MESSAGE );
42
43          System.exit( 0 );       // terminate the program
44      }
45   }
```

Fig. 4.7   Class-average program with counter-controlled repetition (part 1 of 2).

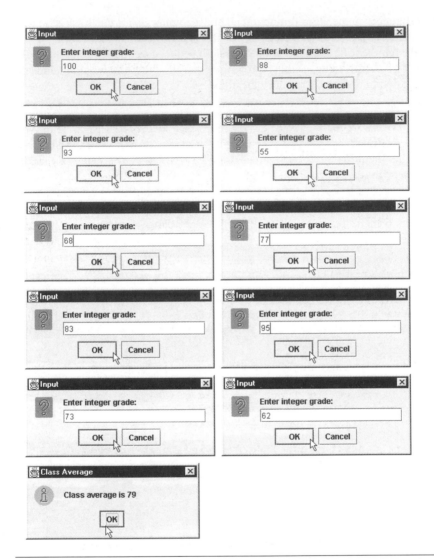

Fig. 4.7   Class-average program with counter-controlled repetition (part 2 of 2).

Good Programming Practice 4.5

Initialize counters and totals.

Line 3

```
import javax.swing.JOptionPane;
```

imports class **JOptionPane** to enable the program to read data from the keyboard and output data to the screen using the input dialog and message dialog shown in Chapter 2.

Line 5 begins the definition of class **Average1**. Remember that an application class definition must contain a **main** method (lines 6–44) to begin execution of the application.

Lines 8 through 12

```
int total,           // sum of grades
    gradeCounter,    // number of grades entered
    gradeValue,      // grade value
    average;         // average of all grades
String grade;        // grade typed by user
```

declare variables **total**, **gradeCounter**, **gradeValue** and **average** to be of type **int** and variable **grade** to be of type **String**. Variable **grade** will store the **String** the user types in the input dialog. Variable **gradeValue** will store the value of **grade** when it is converted from a **String** to an **int**.

Notice that the preceding declarations appear in the body of method **main**. Remember that variables declared in a method definition's body are *local variables* and can only be used from the line of their declaration in the method to the closing right brace (**}**) of the method definition. The declaration of a local variable in a method must appear before the variable is used in that method. A variable declared in one method of a class cannot be accessed directly by other methods of a class.

Good Programming Practice 4.6

Always place a blank line before a declaration that appears between executable statements. This makes the declarations stand out in the program and contributes to program clarity.

Good Programming Practice 4.7

If you prefer to place declarations at the beginning of a method, separate those declarations from the executable statements in that method with one blank line to highlight where the declarations end and the executable statements begin.

Common Programming Error 4.6

Using a local variable before it is initialized (normally with an assignment statement) results in a compile error.

Lines 15 and 16

```
total = 0;            // clear total
gradeCounter = 1;     // prepare to loop
```

are assignment statements that initialize **total** to **0** and **gradeCounter** to **1**.

Note that variables **total** and **gradeCounter** are initialized before they are used in a calculation. Uninitialized local variables used in calculations result in error messages from the compiler stating that the variables may not have been initialized.

Common Programming Error 4.7

Not initializing a local variable results in an error message from the compiler stating that the variable may not have been initialized. You must initialize the local variable to allow the compiler to complete compilation of your program.

Line 19

```
while ( gradeCounter <= 10 ) {  // loop 10 times
```

indicates that the **while** structure should continue as long as the value of **grade-Counter** is less than or equal to 10.

Lines 22 and 23

```
grade = JOptionPane.showInputDialog(
                "Enter integer grade: " );
```

correspond to the pseudocode statement *"Input the next grade."* The statement displays an input dialog with the prompt "**Enter integer grade:**" on the screen.

After the user enters the **grade**, it is converted from a **String** to an **int** (line 26)

```
gradeValue = Integer.parseInt( grade );
```

Remember that class **Integer** is from the **java.lang** package (that is imported automatically by the compiler). Therefore, class **Integer** is not required to be imported.

Next, the program updates the **total** with the new **gradeValue** entered by the user. Line 29

```
total = total + gradeValue;
```

adds **gradeValue** to the previous value of **total** and assigns the result to **total**.

The program is now ready to increment the variable **gradeCounter** to indicate that a grade has been processed and read the next grade from the user. Line 32

```
gradeCounter = gradeCounter + 1;
```

adds **1** to **gradeCounter**, so the condition in the **while** structure will eventually become **false** and terminate the loop.

Line 36

```
average = total / 10;  // perform integer division
```

assigns the results of the average calculation to variable **average**. Lines 39 through 41

```
JOptionPane.showMessageDialog(
    null, "Class average is " + average, "Class Average",
    JOptionPane.INFORMATION_MESSAGE );
```

display an information message dialog containing the string **"Class average is "** followed by the value of variable **average**. The string "**Class Average**" (the third argument) is the title of the message dialog.

Line 43

```
System.exit( 0 );      // terminate the program
```

terminates the application.

After compiling the class definition with **javac**, execute the application from the command window with the command

```
java Average1
```

This executes the Java interpreter and tells it that the **main** method that begins execution of this application is defined in class **Average1**.

Note that the averaging calculation in the program produced an integer result. Actually, the sum of the grade-point values in this example is 794, which when divided by 6 should yield 79.4 (i.e., a number with a decimal point). We will see how to deal with such numbers (called floating-point numbers) again in the next section.

4.9 Formulating Algorithms with Top-Down, Stepwise Refinement: Case Study 2 (Sentinel-Controlled Repetition)

Let us generalize the class-average problem. Consider the following problem:

> *Develop a class-averaging program that will process an arbitrary number of grades each time the program is run.*

In the first class-average example, the number of grades (10) was known in advance. In this example, no indication is given of how many grades are to be entered. The program must process an arbitrary number of grades. How can the program determine when to stop the input of grades? How will it know when to calculate and print the class average?

One way to solve this problem is to use a special value called a *sentinel value* (also called a *signal value*, a *dummy value* or a *flag value*) to indicate "end of data entry." The user types grades in until all legitimate grades have been entered. The user then types the sentinel value to indicate that the last grade has been entered. Sentinel-controlled repetition is often called *indefinite repetition* because the number of repetitions is not known before the loop begins executing.

Clearly, the sentinel value must be chosen so that it cannot be confused with an acceptable input value. Because grades on a quiz are normally nonnegative integers, –1 is an acceptable sentinel value for this problem. Thus, a run of the class-average program might process a stream of inputs such as 95, 96, 75, 74, 89 and –1. The program would then compute and print the class average for the grades 95, 96, 75, 74 and 89 (–1 is the sentinel value, so it should not enter into the averaging calculation).

Common Programming Error 4.8

Choosing a sentinel value that is also a legitimate data value results in a logic error and may prevent a sentinel-controlled loop from terminating properly.

We approach the class-average program with a technique called *top-down, stepwise refinement*, a technique that is essential to the development of well-structured algorithms. We begin with a pseudocode representation of the *top:*

> *Determine the class average for the quiz*

The top is a single statement that conveys the overall function of the program. As such, the top is, in effect, a complete representation of a program. Unfortunately, the top rarely conveys a sufficient amount of detail from which to write the Java algorithm. So we now begin the refinement process. We divide the top into a series of smaller tasks and list these in the order in which they need to be performed. This results in the following *first refinement.*

> *Initialize variables*
> *Input, sum up and count the quiz grades*
> *Calculate and print the class average*

Here, only the sequence structure has been used—the steps listed are to be executed in order, one after the other.

Software Engineering Observation 4.4

Each refinement, as well as the top itself, is a complete specification of the algorithm; only the level of detail varies.

To proceed to the next level of refinement (i.e., the *second refinement*), we commit to specific variables. We need a running total of the numbers, a count of how many numbers have been processed, a variable to receive the value of each grade as it is input and a variable to hold the calculated average. The pseudocode statement

Initialize variables

may be refined as follows:

Initialize total to zero
Initialize counter to zero

Notice that only the variables *total* and *counter* are initialized before they are used; the variables *average* and *grade* (for the calculated average and the user input, respectively) need not be initialized because their values are written over as they are calculated or input.

The pseudocode statement

Input, sum up and count the quiz grades

requires a repetition structure (i.e., a loop) that successively inputs each grade. Because we do not know how many grades are to be processed, we will use sentinel-controlled repetition. The user at the keyboard will type legitimate grades in one at a time. After the last legitimate grade is typed, the user will type the sentinel value. The program will test for the sentinel value after each grade is input and will terminate the loop when the sentinel value is entered by the user. The second refinement of the preceding pseudocode statement is then

Input the first grade (possibly the sentinel)
While the user has not as yet entered the sentinel
    Add this grade into the running total
    Add one to the grade counter
    Input the next grade (possibly the sentinel)

Notice that in pseudocode, we do not use braces around the pseudocode that forms the body of the *while* structure. We simply indent the pseudocode under the *while* to show that it belongs to the *while*. Again, pseudocode is only an informal program development aid.

The pseudocode statement

Calculate and print the class average

may be refined as follows:

If the counter is not equal to zero
    Set the average to the total divided by the counter
    Print the average
else
    Print "No grades were entered"

Notice that we are testing for the possibility of division by zero—a *logic error* that if undetected would cause the program to produce invalid output. The complete second refinement of the pseudocode algorithm for the class-average problem is shown in Fig. 4.8.

Testing and Debugging Tip 4.1

When performing division by an expression whose value could be zero, explicitly test for this case and handle it appropriately in your program (such as printing an error message) rather than allowing the division by zero to occur.

Good Programming Practice 4.8

Include completely blank lines in pseudocode programs to make the pseudocode more readable. The blank lines separate pseudocode control structures and separate the phases of the programs.

Initialize total to zero
Initialize counter to zero

Input the first grade (possibly the sentinel)
While the user has not as yet entered the sentinel
　　Add this grade into the running total
　　Add one to the grade counter
　　Input the next grade (possibly the sentinel)

If the counter is not equal to zero
　　Set the average to the total divided by the counter
　　Print the average
else
　　Print "No grades were entered"

Fig. 4.8　　Pseudocode algorithm that uses sentinel-controlled repetition to solve the class-average problem.

Software Engineering Observation 4.5

Many algorithms can be divided logically into three phases: an initialization phase that initializes the program variables; a processing phase that inputs data values and adjusts program variables accordingly; and a termination phase that calculates and prints the results.

The pseudocode algorithm in Fig. 4.8 solves the more general class-averaging problem. This algorithm was developed after only two levels of refinement. Sometimes more levels are necessary.

Software Engineering Observation 4.6

The programmer terminates the top-down, stepwise refinement process when the pseudocode algorithm is specified in sufficient detail for the programmer to be able to convert the pseudocode to a Java applet or application. Implementing the Java applet or application is then normally straightforward.

The Java application and a sample execution are shown in Fig. 4.9. Although each grade is an integer, the averaging calculation is likely to produce a number with a decimal point (i.e., a real number). The type **int** cannot represent real numbers (i.e., numbers with decimal points), so this program uses data type **double** to handle floating-point numbers. The program also introduces a special operator called a *cast operator* to handle the type conversion we will need for the averaging calculation. These features are explained in detail after the application is presented.

In this example, we see that control structures may be stacked on top of one another (in sequence) just as a child stacks building blocks. The **while** structure (lines 27 through 40) is immediately followed by an **if/else** structure (lines 45 through 57) in sequence. Much of the code in this program is identical to the code in Fig. 4.7, so we concentrate in this example on the new features and issues.

Line 12 declares **double** variable **average**. This change allows us to store the class-average calculation's result as a floating-point number. Line 17 initializes **grade-Counter** to **0** because no grades have been entered yet. Remember that this program uses sentinel-controlled repetition. To keep an accurate record of the number of grades entered, variable **gradeCounter** is only incremented when a valid grade value is entered.

```
1   // Fig. 4.9: Average2.java
2   // Class average program with sentinel-controlled repetition
3   import javax.swing.JOptionPane;
4   import java.text.DecimalFormat;
5
6   public class Average2 {
7      public static void main( String args[] )
8      {
9         int gradeCounter,   // number of grades entered
10            gradeValue,      // grade value
11            total;           // sum of grades
12         double average;     // average of all grades
13         String input;       // grade typed by user
14
15         // Initialization phase
16         total = 0;          // clear total
17         gradeCounter = 0;   // prepare to loop
18
19         // Processing phase
20         // prompt for input and read grade from user
21         input = JOptionPane.showInputDialog(
22                    "Enter Integer Grade, -1 to Quit:" );
23
24         // convert grade from a String to an integer
25         gradeValue = Integer.parseInt( input );
26
27         while ( gradeValue != -1 ) {
28            // add gradeValue to total
29            total = total + gradeValue;
30
31            // add 1 to gradeCounter
32            gradeCounter = gradeCounter + 1;
33
34            // prompt for input and read grade from user
35            input = JOptionPane.showInputDialog(
36                       "Enter Integer Grade, -1 to Quit:" );
37
38            // convert grade from a String to an integer
39            gradeValue = Integer.parseInt( input );
40         }
41
42         // Termination phase
43         DecimalFormat twoDigits = new DecimalFormat( "0.00" );
44
45         if ( gradeCounter != 0 ) {
46            average = (double) total / gradeCounter;
47
48            // display average of exam grades
49            JOptionPane.showMessageDialog( null,
50               "Class average is " + twoDigits.format( average ),
51               "Class Average",
52               JOptionPane.INFORMATION_MESSAGE );
53         }
```

Fig. 4.9   Class-average program with sentinel-controlled repetition (part 1 of 2).

```
54              else
55                 JOptionPane.showMessageDialog( null,
56                    "No grades were entered", "Class Average",
57                    JOptionPane.INFORMATION_MESSAGE );
58
59              System.exit( 0 );      // terminate the program
60           }
61     }
```

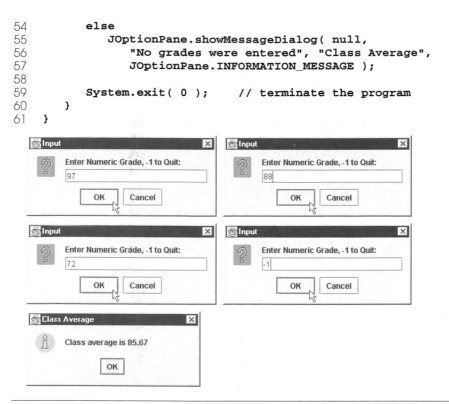

Fig. 4.9   Class-average program with sentinel-controlled repetition (part 2 of 2).

Notice the difference in program logic for sentinel-controlled repetition compared with the counter-controlled repetition in Fig. 4.7. In counter-controlled repetition, we read a value from the user during each pass of the **while** structure for the specified number of passes. In sentinel-controlled repetition, we read one value (line 21) before the program reaches the **while** structure. This value is used to determine if the program's flow of control should enter the body of the **while** structure. If the **while** structure condition is **false** (i.e., the user already typed the sentinel), the body of the **while** structure does not execute (no grades were entered). If, on the other hand, the condition is **true**, the body begins execution and the value entered by the user is processed (added to the **total** in this example). After the value is processed, the next value is input from the user before the end of the **while** structure's body. As the closing right brace (**}**) of the body is reached at line 40, execution continues with the next test of the **while** structure condition using the new value just entered by the user to determine if the **while** structure's body should execute again. Notice that the next value is always input from the user immediately before the **while** structure condition is evaluated. This allows us to determine if the value just entered by the user is the sentinel value *before* that value is processed (i.e., added to the **total**). If the value entered is the sentinel value, the **while** structure terminates and the value is not added to the **total**

Notice the compound statement in the **while** loop in Fig 4.9. Without the braces, the last four statements in the body of the loop would fall outside the loop, causing the computer to interpret this code incorrectly as follows:

```
while ( gradeValue != -1 )
   // add gradeValue to total
   total = total + gradeValue;

// add 1 to gradeCounter
gradeCounter = gradeCounter + 1;

// prompt for input and read grade from user
input = JOptionPane.showInputDialog(
            "Enter Integer Grade, -1 to Quit:" );

// convert grade from a String to an integer
gradeValue = Integer.parseInt( input );
```

This would cause an infinite loop in the program if the user does not input the sentinel **-1** as the input value at line 21 (before the **while** structure) in the program.

Common Programming Error 4.9

Omitting the curly braces that are needed to delineate a compound statement can lead to logic errors such as infinite loops.

Good Programming Practice 4.9

In a sentinel-controlled loop, the prompts requesting data entry should explicitly remind the user what the sentinel value is.

Line 43

```
DecimalFormat twoDigits = new DecimalFormat( "0.00" );
```

declares **twoDigits** as a reference to an object of class ***DecimalFormat***. **Decimal-Format** objects are used to format numbers. In this example, we want to output the class average with two digits to the right of the decimal point (i.e., rounded to the nearest hundredth). The preceding line creates a **DecimalFormat** object that is initialized with the string **"0.00"**. Each **0** is a *format flag* that specifies a required digit position in the formatted floating-point number. This particular format indicates that every number formatted with **twoDigits** will have at least one digit to the left of the decimal point and exactly two digits to the right of the decimal point. If the number does not meet the formatting requirements, **0**s are automatically inserted in the formatted number at the required positions. The ***new*** *operator* creates an object as the program executes by obtaining enough memory to store an object of the type specified to the right of **new**. The process of creating new objects is also known as *creating an instance* or *instantiating an object,* and operator **new** is known as the *dynamic memory allocation operator*. The value in parentheses after the type in a **new** operation is used to *initialize* (give a value to) the new object. Reference **two-Digits** is given the result of the **new** operation with *assignment operator* **=**. The statement is read as "**twoDigits** *gets* the value of **new DecimalFormat("0.00")**."

Software Engineering Observation 4.7

*Objects are always created with operator **new**. An exception to this rule is a string literal such as* **"hello"** *that is contained in quotes. String literals are treated as objects of class* ***String*** *and are instantiated automatically.*

Averages do not always evaluate to integer values. Often, an average is a value such as 3.333 or 2.7 that contains a fractional part. These values are referred to as floating-point numbers and are represented by the data type **double**. The variable **average** is declared to be of type **double** to capture the fractional result of our calculation. However, the result of the calculation **total / gradeCounter** is an integer because **total** and **grade-Counter** are both integer variables. Dividing two integers results in *integer division* in which any fractional part of the calculation is lost (i.e., *truncated*). Because the calculation is performed first, the fractional part is lost before the result is assigned to **average**. To produce a floating-point calculation with integer values, we must create temporary values that are floating-point numbers for the calculation. Java provides the *unary cast operator* to accomplish this task. Line 46

```
average = (double) total / gradeCounter;
```

uses the cast operator **(double)** to create a temporary floating-point copy of its operand—**total**. Using a cast operator in this manner is called *explicit conversion*. The value stored in **total** is still an integer. The calculation now consists of a floating-point value (the temporary **double** version of **total**) divided by the integer **gradeCounter**.

Java only knows how to evaluate arithmetic expressions in which the data types of the operands are identical. To ensure that the operands are of the same type, Java performs an operation called *promotion* (or *implicit conversion*) on selected operands. For example, in an expression containing the data types **int** and **double**, **int** operands are *promoted* to **double**. In our example, we have the temporary **double** version of **total** divided by the **int gradeCounter**. Therefore, **gradeCounter** is promoted to **double**, the calculation is performed and the result of the floating-point division is assigned to **average**. Later in this chapter we discuss all the standard data types and their order of promotion.

Cast operators are available for any data type. The cast operator is formed by placing parentheses around a data type name. The cast operator is a *unary operator* (i.e., an operator that takes only one operand). In Chapter 2, we studied the binary arithmetic operators. Java also supports unary versions of the plus (**+**) and minus (**-**) operators, so the programmer can write expressions like **-7** or **+5**. Cast operators associate from right to left and have the same precedence as other unary operators such as unary **+** and unary **-**. This precedence is one level higher than that of the *multiplicative operators* *****, **/** and **%**, and one level lower than that of parentheses (see the operator precedence chart in Appendix C). We indicate the cast operator with the notation **(type)** in our precedence charts to indicate that any type name can be used to form a cast operator.

Common Programming Error 4.10

Using floating-point numbers in a manner that assumes they are precisely represented real numbers can lead to incorrect results. Real numbers are represented only approximately by computers.

Common Programming Error 4.11

Assuming that integer division rounds (rather than truncates) can lead to incorrect results.

Good Programming Practice 4.10

Do not compare floating-point values for equality or inequality. Rather, test that the absolute value of the difference is less than a specified small value.

Despite the fact that floating-point numbers are not always "100% precise," they have numerous applications. For example, when we speak of a "normal" body temperature of

98.6 we do not need to be precise to a large number of digits. When we view the tempera-ture on a thermometer and read it as 98.6, it may actually be 98.5999473210643. The point here is that calling this number simply 98.6 is fine for most applications.

Another way floating-point numbers develop is through division. When we divide 10 by 3, the result is 3.3333333…, with the sequence of 3s repeating infinitely. The computer allocates only a fixed amount of space to hold such a value, so clearly the stored floating-point value can only be an approximation.

4.10 Formulating Algorithms with Top-Down, Stepwise Refinement: Case Study 3 (Nested Control Structures)

Let us work through another complete problem. We will once again formulate the algo-rithm using pseudocode and top-down, stepwise refinement, and we will write a corres-ponding Java program.

Consider the following problem statement:

A college offers a course that prepares students for the state licensing exam for real estate brokers. Last year, several of the students who completed this course took the licensing ex-amination. Naturally, the college wants to know how well its students did on the exam. You have been asked to write a program to summarize the results. You have been given a list of these 10 students. Next to each name is written a 1 if the student passed the exam and a 2 if the student failed.

Your program should analyze the results of the exam as follows:

1. *Input each test result (i.e., a 1 or a 2). Display the message "Enter result" on the screen each time the program requests another test result.*

2. *Count the number of test results of each type.*

3. *Display a summary of the test results indicating the number of students who passed and the number of students who failed.*

4. *If more than 8 students passed the exam, print the message "Raise tuition."*

After reading the problem statement carefully, we make the following observations about the problem:

1. The program must process test results for 10 students. A counter-controlled loop will be used.

2. Each test result is a number—either a 1 or a 2. Each time the program reads a test result, the program must determine if the number is a 1 or 2. We test for a 1 in our algorithm. If the number is not a 1, we assume that it is a 2. (An exercise at the end of the chapter considers the consequences of this assumption.)

3. Two counters are used to keep track of the exam results—one to count the number of students who passed the exam and one to count the number of students who failed the exam.

4. After the program has processed all the results, it must decide if more than eight students passed the exam.

Let us proceed with top-down, stepwise refinement. We begin with a pseudocode rep-resentation of the top:

Analyze exam results and decide if tuition should be raised

Once again, it is important to emphasize that the top is a complete representation of the program, but several refinements are likely to be needed before the pseudocode can be naturally evolved into a Java program. Our first refinement is

Initialize variables
Input the ten exam grades and count passes and failures
Print a summary of the exam results and decide if tuition should be raised

Here, too, even though we have a complete representation of the entire program, further refinement is necessary. We now commit to specific variables. Counters are needed to record the passes and failures, a counter will be used to control the looping process, and a variable is needed to store the user input. The pseudocode statement

Initialize variables

may be refined as follows:

Initialize passes to zero
Initialize failures to zero
Initialize student to one

Notice that only the counters for the number of passes, number of failures and number of students are initialized. The pseudocode statement

Input the ten quiz grades and count passes and failures

requires a loop that successively inputs the result of each exam. Here it is known in advance that there are precisely ten exam results, so counter-controlled looping is appropriate. Inside the loop (i.e., *nested* within the loop) a double-selection structure will determine whether each exam result is a pass or a failure and will increment the appropriate counter accordingly. The refinement of the preceding pseudocode statement is then

While student counter is less than or equal to ten
*   Input the next exam result*

*   If the student passed*
*   Add one to passes*
*   else*
*   Add one to failures*

*   Add one to student counter*

Notice the use of blank lines to set off the *if/else* control structure to improve program readability. The pseudocode statement

Print a summary of the exam results and decide if tuition should be raised

may be refined as follows:

Print the number of passes
Print the number of failures
If more than eight students passed
*   Print "Raise tuition"*

The complete second refinement appears in Fig. 4.10. Notice that blank lines are also used to set off the *while* structure for program readability.

This pseudocode is now sufficiently refined for conversion to Java. The Java program and two sample executions are shown in Fig. 4.11.

Initialize passes to zero
Initialize failures to zero
Initialize student to one

While student counter is less than or equal to ten
    Input the next exam result

    If the student passed
        Add one to passes
    else
        Add one to failures

    Add one to student counter

Print the number of passes
Print the number of failures
If more than eight students passed
    Print "Raise tuition"

Fig. 4.10 Pseudocode for examination-results problem.

```
1   // Fig. 4.11: Analysis.java
2   // Analysis of examination results.
3   import javax.swing.JOptionPane;
4
5   public class Analysis {
6      public static void main( String args[] )
7      {
8         // initializing variables in declarations
9         int passes = 0,            // number of passes
10            failures = 0,           // number of failures
11            student = 1,            // student counter
12            result;                 // one exam result
13        String input,               // user-entered value
14               output;              // output string
15
16        // process 10 students; counter-controlled loop
17        while ( student <= 10 ) {
18           input = JOptionPane.showInputDialog(
19                      "Enter result (1=pass,2=fail)" );
20           result = Integer.parseInt( input );
21
22           if ( result == 1 )
23              passes = passes + 1;
24           else
25              failures = failures + 1;
26
27           student = student + 1;
28        }
29
30        // termination phase
31        output = "Passed: " + passes +
32                 "\nFailed: " + failures;
```

Fig. 4.11 Java program for examination-results problem (part 1 of 2).

```
33
34          if( passes > 8 )
35             output = output + "\nRaise Tuition";
36
37          JOptionPane.showMessageDialog( null, output,
38             "Analysis of Examination Results",
39             JOptionPane.INFORMATION_MESSAGE );
40
41          System.exit( 0 );
42       }
43    }
```

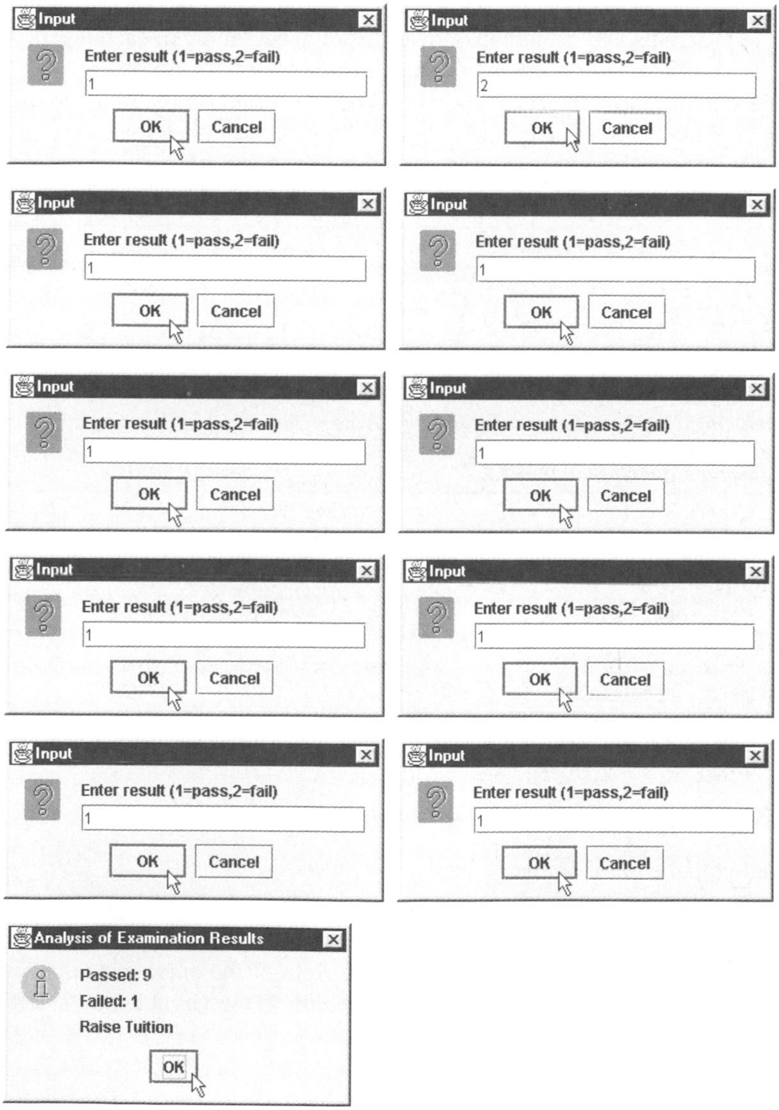

Fig. 4.11   Java program for examination-results problem (part 2 of 2).

Lines 9 through 14

```
int passes = 0,          // number of passes
    failures = 0,        // number of failures
    student = 1,         // student counter
    result;              // one exam result
String input,            // user-entered value
       output;           // output string
```

declare the variables used in **main** to process the examination results. Note that we have taken advantage of a feature of Java that allows variable initialization to be incorporated into declarations (**passes** is assigned **0**, **failures** is assigned **0** and **student** is assigned **1**). Looping programs may require initialization at the beginning of each repetition; such initialization would normally occur in assignment statements.

Notice the use of **String** reference **output** in lines 31, 32 and 35 to build the string that will be displayed in the message dialog at lines 37 through 39. String concatenation operator **+** assembles the components of the final string to be displayed.

Good Programming Practice 4.11

Initializing local variables when they are declared in methods helps the programmer avoid compiler messages warning of uninitialized data.

Software Engineering Observation 4.8

Experience has shown that the most difficult part of solving a problem on a computer is developing the algorithm for the solution. Once a correct algorithm has been specified, the process of producing a working Java program from the algorithm is normally straightforward.

Software Engineering Observation 4.9

Many experienced programmers write programs without ever using program development tools like pseudocode. These programmers feel that their ultimate goal is to solve the problem on a computer, and that writing pseudocode merely delays the production of final outputs. Although this may work for simple and familiar problems, it can lead to serious errors on large, complex projects.

4.11 Assignment Operators

Java provides several assignment operators for abbreviating assignment expressions. For example, the statement

```
c = c + 3;
```

can be abbreviated with the *addition assignment operator* **+=** as

```
c += 3;
```

The **+=** operator adds the value of the expression on the right of the operator to the value of the variable on the left of the operator and stores the result in the variable on the left of the operator. Any statement of the form

    variable **=** *variable operator expression;*

where *operator* is one of the binary operators **+**, **-**, *****, **/** or **%** (or others we will discuss later in the text), can be written in the form *variable operator= expression;*

Thus the assignment **c += 3** adds **3** to **c**. Figure 4.12 shows the arithmetic assignment operators, sample expressions using these operators and explanations.

Performance Tip 4.1

Programmers can write programs a bit faster and compilers can compile programs a bit faster when the "abbreviated" assignment operators are used. Some compilers generate code that runs faster when "abbreviated" assignment operators are used.

Performance Tip 4.2

Many of the performance tips we mention in this text result in nominal improvements, so the reader may be tempted to ignore them. Significant performance improvement is often realized when a supposedly nominal improvement is placed in a loop that may repeat a large number of times.

4.12 Increment and Decrement Operators

Java provides the unary *increment operator*, **++**, and the unary *decrement operator*, **−−**, which are summarized in Fig. 4.13. If a variable **c** is incremented by 1, the increment operator **++** can be used rather than the expressions **c = c + 1** or **c += 1**. If an increment or decrement operator is placed before a variable, it is referred to as the *preincrement* or *predecrement operator,* respectively. If an increment or decrement operator is placed after a variable, it is referred to as the *postincrement* or *postdecrement operator,* respectively.

Preincrementing (predecrementing) a variable causes the variable to be incremented (decremented) by 1, then the new value of the variable is used in the expression in which it appears. Postincrementing (postdecrementing) the variable causes the current value of the variable to be used in the expression in which it appears, then the variable value is incremented (decremented) by 1.

The application of Fig. 4.14 demonstrates the difference between the preincrementing version and the postincrementing version of the **++** increment operator. Postincrementing the variable **c** causes it to be incremented after it is used in the **System.out.println** method call (line 11). Preincrementing the variable **c** causes it to be incremented before it is used in the **System.out.println** method call (line 18).

Assignment operator	Sample expression	Explanation	Assigns
Assume: **int c = 3, d = 5, e = 4, f = 6, g = 12;**			
+=	c += 7	c = c + 7	10 to **c**
-=	d -= 4	d = d - 4	1 to **d**
*=	e *= 5	e = e * 5	20 to **e**
/=	f /= 3	f = f / 3	2 to **f**
%=	g %= 9	g = g % 9	3 to **g**

Fig. 4.12   Arithmetic assignment operators.

Operator	Called	Sample expression	Explanation
++	preincrement	++a	Increment **a** by 1, then use the new value of **a** in the expression in which **a** resides.
++	postincrement	a++	Use the current value of **a** in the expression in which **a** resides, then increment **a** by 1.
--	predecrement	--b	Decrement **b** by 1, then use the new value of **b** in the expression in which **b** resides.
--	postdecrement	b--	Use the current value of **b** in the expression in which **b** resides, then decrement **b** by 1.

Fig. 4.13   The increment and decrement operators.

```
1   // Fig. 4.14: Increment.java
2   // Preincrementing and postincrementing
3
4   public class Increment {
5      public static void main( String args[] )
6      {
7         int c;
8
9         c = 5;
10        System.out.println( c );    // print 5
11        System.out.println( c++ ); // print 5 then postincrement
12        System.out.println( c );    // print 6
13
14        System.out.println();       // skip a line
15
16        c = 5;
17        System.out.println( c );    // print 5
18        System.out.println( ++c ); // preincrement then print 6
19        System.out.println( c );    // print 6
20     }
21   }
```

```
5
5
6

5
6
6
```

Fig. 4.14   The difference between preincrementing and postincrementing.

The program displays the value of **c** before and after the **++** operator is used. The decrement operator (**--**) works similarly.

Good Programming Practice 4.12

Unary operators should be placed next to their operands with no intervening spaces.

Line 14

```
System.out.println();       // skip a line
```

uses **System.out.println** to output a blank line. If **println** receives no arguments, it simply outputs a newline character.

The three assignment statements in Fig 4.11 (lines 23, 25 and 27, respectively)

```
passes = passes + 1;
failures = failures + 1;
student = student + 1;
```

can be written more concisely with assignment operators as

```
passes += 1;
failures += 1;
student += 1;
```

with preincrement operators as

```
++passes;
++failures;
++student;
```

or with postincrement operators as

```
passes++;
failures++;
student++;
```

It is important to note here that when incrementing or decrementing a variable in a statement by itself, the preincrement and postincrement forms have the same effect, and the predecrement and postdecrement forms have the same effect. It is only when a variable appears in the context of a larger expression that preincrementing the variable and post-incrementing the variable have different effects (and similarly for predecrementing and postdecrementing).

Common Programming Error 4.12

Attempting to use the increment or decrement operator on an expression other than an lvalue is a syntax error. An lvalue is a variable or expression that can appear on the left side of an assignment operation. For example, writing ++(x + 1) is a syntax error because (x + 1) is not an lvalue.

The chart in Fig. 4.15 shows the precedence and associativity of the operators introduced to this point. The operators are shown top to bottom in decreasing order of precedence. The second column describes the associativity of the operators at each level of precedence. Notice that the conditional operator (**?:**), the unary operators increment (**++**), decrement (**--**), plus (**+**), minus (**-**) and casts, and the assignment operators **=**, **+=**, **-=**, ***=**, **/=** and **%=** associate from right to left. All other operators in the operator precedence chart of Fig. 4.15 associate from left to right. The third column names the groups of operators.

Operators					Associativity	Type
( )					left to right	parentheses
++	--				right to left	unary postfix
++	--	+	-	(*type*)	right to left	unary
*	/	%			left to right	multiplicative
+	-				left to right	additive
<	<=	>	>=		left to right	relational
==	!=				left to right	equality
? :					right to left	conditional
=	+=	-=	*=	/= %=	right to left	assignment

Fig. 4.15   Precedence and associativity of the operators discussed so far.

4.13 Primitive Data Types

The table in Fig. 4.16 lists the primitive data types in Java. The primitive types are the building blocks for more complicated types. Like its predecessor languages C and C++, Java requires all variables to have a type before they can be used in a program. For this reason, Java is referred to as a *strongly typed language*.

Unlike C and C++, the primitive types in Java are portable across all computer platforms that support Java. This and many other portability features of Java enable programmers to write programs once without knowing which computer platform will execute the program. This is sometimes referred to as "WORA" (Write Once Run Anywhere).

Type	Size in bits	Values	Standard
boolean	8	**true** or **false**	
char	16	'\u0000' to '\uFFFF'	(ISO Unicode character set)
byte	8	−128 to +127	
short	16	−32,768 to +32,767	
int	32	−2,147,483,648 to +2,147,483,647	
long	64	−9,223,372,036,854,775,808 to +9,223,372,036,854,775,807	
float	32	−3.40292347E+38 to +3.40292347E+38	(IEEE 754 floating point)
double	64	−1.79769313486231570E+308 to +1.79769313486231570E+308	(IEEE 754 floating point)

Fig. 4.16   The Java primitive data types.

In C and C++ programs, programmers frequently had to write separate versions of programs to support different computer platforms because the primitive data types were not guaranteed to be identical from computer to computer. For example, an **int** value on one machine might be represented by 16 bits (2 bytes) of memory and an **int** value on another machine might be represented by 32 bits (4 bytes) of memory. In Java, **int** values are always 32 bits (4 bytes).

Portability Tip 4.1

All primitive data types in Java are portable across all platforms that support Java.

Each data type in the table is listed with its size in bits (there are 8 bits to a byte) and its range of values. Because the designers of Java want it to be maximally portable, they chose to use internationally recognized standards for both character formats (Unicode) and for floating-point numbers (IEEE 754).

When instance variables of the primitive data types are declared in a class, they are automatically assigned default values unless specified otherwise by the programmer. Variables of types **char**, **byte**, **short**, **int**, **long**, **float** and **double** are all given the value **0** by default. Variables of type **boolean** are given **false** by default.

Summary

- A procedure for solving a problem in terms of the actions to be executed and the order in which these actions should be executed is called an algorithm.
- Specifying the order in which statements are to be executed in a computer program is called program control.
- Pseudocode helps the programmer "think out" a program before attempting to write it in a programming language such as Java.
- Declarations are messages to the compiler telling it the names and attributes of variables and telling it to reserve space for variables.
- A selection structure is used to choose among alternative courses of action.
- The **if** selection structure executes an indicated action only when the condition is true.
- The **if/else** selection structure specifies separate actions to be executed when the condition is true and when the condition is false.
- Whenever more than one statement is to be executed where normally only a single statement is expected, these statements must be enclosed in braces forming a compound statement. A compound statement can be placed anywhere a single statement can be placed.
- An empty statement indicating that no action is to be taken is indicated by placing a semicolon (**;**) where a statement would normally be.
- A repetition structure specifies that an action is to be repeated while some condition remains true.
- The format for the **while** repetition structure is

      while (*condition*)
          statement

- The Java interpreter executes applications written in Java. To run the Java interpreter for an application, at the command line, type **java** followed by the name of the class in which method **main** is defined and press *Enter*.
- A value that contains a fractional part is referred to as a floating-point number and is represented by the data type **float** or **double**.

- Unary cast operator **(double)** creates a temporary floating-point copy of its operand.
- Java provides the arithmetic assignment operators **+=, -=, *=, /=** and **%=** that help abbreviate certain common types of expressions.
- The increment operator, **++**, and the decrement operator, **--**, increment or decrement a variable by 1. If the operator is prefixed to the variable, the variable is incremented or decremented by 1 first, then used in its expression. If the operator is postfixed to the variable, the variable is used in its expression, then incremented or decremented by 1.
- The primitive types (**boolean**, **char**, **byte**, **short**, **int**, **long**, **float** and **double**) are the building blocks for more complicated types in Java.
- Java requires all variables to have a type before they can be used in a program. For this reason, Java is referred to as a strongly typed language.
- Primitive types in Java are portable across all computer platforms that support Java.
- Java uses internationally recognized standards for both character formats (Unicode) and for floating-point numbers (IEEE 754).
- Variables of types **char**, **byte**, **short**, **int**, **long**, **float** and **double** are all given the value **0** by default. Variables of type **boolean** are given **false** by default.

Terminology

-- operator	initialization
++ operator	integer division
?: operator	ISO Unicode character set
action	logic error
action/decision model	loop-continuation condition
algorithm	loop counter
arithmetic assignment operators:	nested control structures
+=, -=, *=, /= and **%=**	postdecrement operator
block	postincrement operator
body of a loop	predecrement operator
cast operator	preincrement operator
compound statement	promotion
conditional operator (**?:**)	pseudocode
control structure	repetition
counter-controlled repetition	repetition structures
decision	selection
decrement operator (**--**)	sentinel value
definite repetition	sequential execution
double	single-entry/single-exit control structures
double-selection structure	single-selection structure
empty statement (**;**)	stacked control structures
if selection structure	structured programming
if/else selection structure	syntax error
implicit conversion	top-down, stepwise refinement
increment operator (**++**)	unary operator
indefinite repetition	**while** repetition structure
infinite loop	white-space characters

Common Programming Errors

4.1   Using a keyword as an identifier is a syntax error.

4.2   Forgetting one or both of the braces that delimit a compound statement can lead to syntax errors or logic errors.

4.3   Placing a semicolon after the condition in an **if** structure leads to a logic error in single-selection **if** structures and a syntax error in double-selection **if** structures (if the **if** part contains a nonempty body statement).

4.4   Not providing in the body of a **while** structure an action that eventually causes the condition in the **while** to become false is a logic error. Normally, such a repetition structure will never terminate—an error called an "infinite loop."

4.5   Spelling the keyword **while** with an uppercase **W** as in **While** (remember that Java is a case-sensitive language) is a syntax error. All of Java's reserved keywords, such as **while**, **if** and **else**, contain only lowercase letters.

4.6   Using a local variable before it is initialized (normally with an assignment statement) results in a compile error.

4.7   Not initializing a local variable results in an error message from the compiler stating that the variable may not have been initialized. You must initialize the local variable to allow the compiler to complete compilation of your program.

4.8   Choosing a sentinel value that is also a legitimate data value results in a logic error and may prevent a sentinel-controlled loop from terminating properly.

4.9   Omitting the curly braces that are needed to delineate a compound statement can lead to logic errors such as infinite loops.

4.10   Using floating-point numbers in a manner that assumes they are precisely represented real numbers can lead to incorrect results. Real numbers are represented only approximately by computers.

4.11   Assuming that integer division rounds (rather than truncates) can lead to incorrect results.

4.12   Attempting to use the increment or decrement operator on an expression other than an lvalue is a syntax error. An lvalue is a variable or expression that can appear on the left side of an assignment operation. For example, writing **++(x + 1)** is a syntax error because **(x + 1)** is not an lvalue.

Good Programming Practices

4.1   Consistently applying reasonable indentation conventions throughout your programs improves program readability. We suggest a fixed-size tab of about 1/4 inch or three spaces per indent.

4.2   Indent both body statements of an **if/else** structure.

4.3   If there are several levels of indentation, each level should be indented the same additional amount of space.

4.4   Some programmers prefer to type the beginning and ending braces of compound statements before typing the individual statements within the braces. This helps avoid omitting one or both of the braces.

4.5   Initialize counters and totals.

4.6   Always place a blank line before a declaration that appears between executable statements. This makes the declarations stand out in the program and contributes to program clarity.

4.7   If you prefer to place declarations at the beginning of a method, separate those declarations from the executable statements in that method with one blank line to highlight where the declarations end and the executable statements begin.

4.8   Include completely blank lines in pseudocode programs to make the pseudocode more readable. The blank lines separate pseudocode control structures and separate the phases of the programs.

4.9   In a sentinel-controlled loop, the prompts requesting data entry should explicitly remind the user what the sentinel value is.

4.10   Do not compare floating-point values for equality or inequality. Rather, test that the absolute value of the difference is less than a specified small value.

4.11   Initializing local variables when they are declared in methods helps the programmer avoid compiler messages warning of uninitialized data.

4.12   Unary operators should be placed next to their operands with no intervening spaces.

Performance Tips

4.1   Programmers can write programs a bit faster and compilers can compile programs a bit faster when the "abbreviated" assignment operators are used. Some compilers generate code that runs faster when "abbreviated" assignment operators are used.

4.2   Many of the performance tips we mention in this text result in nominal improvements, so the reader may be tempted to ignore them. Significant performance improvement is often realized when a supposedly nominal improvement is placed in a loop that may repeat a large number of times.

Portability Tip

4.1   All primitive data types in Java are portable across all platforms that support Java.

Software Engineering Observations

4.1   Pseudocode is often used to "think out" a program during the program design process. Then the pseudocode program is converted to Java.

4.2   A compound statement can be placed anywhere in a program that a single statement can be placed.

4.3   Just as a compound statement can be placed anywhere a single statement can be placed, it is also possible to have no statement at all (i.e., the empty statement). The empty statement is represented by placing a semicolon (**;**) where a statement would normally be.

4.4   Each refinement, as well as the top itself, is a complete specification of the algorithm; only the level of detail varies.

4.5   Many algorithms can be divided logically into three phases: an initialization phase that initializes the program variables; a processing phase that inputs data values and adjusts program variables accordingly; and a termination phase that calculates and prints the results.

4.6   The programmer terminates the top-down, stepwise refinement process when the pseudocode algorithm is specified in sufficient detail for the programmer to be able to convert the pseudocode to a Java applet or application. Implementing the Java applet or application is then normally straightforward.

4.7   Objects are always created with operator **new**. An exception to this rule is a string literal such as **"hello"** that is contained in quotes. String literals are treated as objects of class **String** and are instantiated automatically.

4.8   Experience has shown that the most difficult part of solving a problem on a computer is developing the algorithm for the solution. Once a correct algorithm has been specified, the process of producing a working Java program from the algorithm is normally straightforward.

4.9   Many experienced programmers write programs without ever using program development tools like pseudocode. These programmers feel that their ultimate goal is to solve the problem on a computer, and that writing pseudocode merely delays the production of final outputs. Although this may work for simple and familiar problems, it can lead to serious errors on large, complex projects.

Testing and Debugging Tip

4.1   When performing division by an expression whose value could be zero, explicitly test for this case and handle it appropriately in your program (such as printing an error message) rather than allowing the division by zero to occur.

Self-Review Exercises

4.1   Answer each of the following questions.
     a) All programs can be written in terms of three types of control structures: _____, _____ and _____.
     b) The _____selection structure is used to execute one action when a condition is true and another action when that condition is false.
     c) Repetition of a set of instructions a specific number of times is called _____ repetition.
     d) When it is not known in advance how many times a set of statements will be repeated, a _____ value can be used to terminate the repetition.

4.2   Write four different Java statements that each add 1 to integer variable **x**.

4.3   Write Java statements to accomplish each of the following:
     a) Assign the sum of **x** and **y** to **z** and increment the value of **x** by 1 after the calculation. Use only one statement.
     b) Test if the value of the variable **count** is greater than 10. If it is, print **"Count is greater than 10"**.
     c) Decrement the variable **x** by 1, then subtract it from the variable **total**. Use only one statement.
     d) Calculate the remainder after **q** is divided by **divisor** and assign the result to **q**. Write this statement two different ways.

4.4   Write a Java statement to accomplish each of the following tasks.
     a) Declare variables **sum** and **x** to be of type **int**.
     b) Assign **1** to variable **x**.
     c) Assign **0** to variable **sum**.
     d) Add variable **x** to variable **sum** and assign the result to variable **sum**.
     e) Print **"The sum is: "** followed by the value of variable **sum**.

4.5   Combine the statements that you wrote in Exercise 4.4 into a Java application that calculates and prints the sum of the integers from 1 to 10. Use the **while** structure to loop through the calculation and increment statements. The loop should terminate when the value of **x** becomes 11.

4.6   Determine the values of each variable after the calculation is performed. Assume that when each statement begins executing, all variables have the integer value 5.
     a) **product *= x++;**
     b) **quotient /= ++x;**

4.7   Identify and correct the errors in each of the following:
     a)
```
while ( c <= 5 ) {
    product *= c;
    ++c;
```
     b)
```
if ( gender == 1 )
    System.out.println( "Woman" );
else;
    System.out.println( "Man" );
```

4.8   What is wrong with the following **while** repetition structure?
```
while ( z >= 0 )
    sum += z;
```

Answers to Self-Review Exercises

4.1   a) Sequence, selection and repetition. b) **if/else**. c) Counter-controlled or definite. d) Sentinel, signal, flag or dummy.

4.2
```
x = x + 1;
x += 1;
++x;
x++;
```

4.3   a) `z = x++ + y;`
b) `if ( count > 10 )`
   `    System.out.println( "Count is greater than 10" );`
c) `total -= --x;`
d) `q %= divisor;`
   `q = q % divisor;`

4.4   a) `int sum, x;`
b) `x = 1;`
c) `sum = 0;`
d) `sum += x;` or `sum = sum + x;`
e) `System.out.println( "The sum is: " + sum );`

4.5
```
// Calculate the sum of the integers from 1 to 10
public class Calculate {
    public static void main( String args[] )
    {
        int sum, x;
        x = 1;
        sum = 0;
        while ( x <= 10 ) {
            sum += x;
            ++x;
        }
        System.out.println( "The sum is: " + sum );
    }
}
```

4.6   a) `product = 25, x = 6;`
b) `quotient = 0, x = 6;`

4.7   a) Error: Missing the closing right brace of the **while** body.
   Correction: Add closing right brace after the statement **++c;**.
b) Error: Semicolon after **else** results in a logic error. The second output statement will always be executed.
   Correction: Remove the semicolon after **else**.

4.8   The value of the variable **z** is never changed in the **while** structure. Therefore, if the loop-continuation condition (**z >= 0**) is true, an infinite loop is created. To prevent the infinite loop, **z** must be decremented so that it eventually becomes less than 0.

Exercises

4.9   Identify and correct the errors in each of the following. [*Note:* There may be more than one error in each piece of code.]
   a) `if ( age >= 65 );`
   `    System.out.println( "Age greater than or equal to 65" );`

```
      else
          System.out.println( "Age is less than 65 )";
   b) int x = 1, total;
      while ( x <= 10 ) {
         total += x;
         ++x;
      }
   c) While ( x <= 100 )
         total += x;
         ++x;
   d) while ( y > 0 ) {
         System.out.println( y );
         ++y;
```

4.10   What does the following program print?

```
   public class Mystery {
      public static void main( String args[] )
      {
         int y, x = 1, total = 0;
         while ( x <= 10 ) {
            y = x * x;
            System.out.println( y );
            total += y;
            ++x;
         }
         System.out.println( "Total is " + total );
      }
   }
```

For Exercises 4.11 through 4.14, perform each of these steps:
   a) Read the problem statement.
   b) Formulate the algorithm using pseudocode and top-down, stepwise refinement.
   c) Write a Java program.
   d) Test, debug and execute the Java program.
   e) Process three complete sets of data.

4.11   Drivers are concerned with the mileage obtained by their automobiles. One driver has kept track of several tankfuls of gasoline by recording miles driven and gallons used for each tankful. Develop a Java application that will input the miles driven and gallons used (both as integers) for each tankful. The program should calculate and display the miles per gallon obtained for each tankful and print the combined miles per gallon obtained for all tankfuls up to this point. All average calculations should produce floating-point results. Use input dialogs to obtain the data from the user.

4.12   Develop a Java application that will determine if a department store customer has exceeded the credit limit on a charge account. For each customer, the following facts are available:
   a) Account number
   b) Balance at the beginning of the month
   c) Total of all items charged by this customer this month
   d) Total of all credits applied to this customer's account this month
   e) Allowed credit limit

The program should input each of these facts from input dialogs as integers, calculate the new balance (= *beginning balance + charges – credits*), display the new balance and determine if the new balance exceeds the customer's credit limit. For those customers whose credit limit is exceeded, the program should display the message, "Credit limit exceeded."

4.13   A large company pays its salespeople on a commission basis. The salespeople receive $200 per week plus 9% of their gross sales for that week. For example, a salesperson who sells $5000 worth of merchandise in a week receives $200 plus 9% of $5000, or a total of $650. You have been supplied with a list of items sold by each salesperson. The values of these items are as follows:

Item	Value
1	239.99
2	129.75
3	99.95
4	350.89

Develop a Java application that inputs one salesperson's items sold for last week and calculates and displays that salesperson's earnings. There is no limit to the number of items sold by a salesperson.

4.14   Develop a Java application that will determine the gross pay for each of three employees. The company pays "straight-time" for the first 40 hours worked by each employee and pays "time-and-a-half" for all hours worked in excess of 40 hours. You are given a list of the employees of the company, the number of hours each employee worked last week and the hourly rate of each employee. Your program should input this information for each employee, and should determine and display the employee's gross pay. Use input dialogs to input the data.

4.15   The process of finding the largest value (i.e., the maximum of a group of values) is used frequently in computer applications. For example, a program that determines the winner of a sales contest would input the number of units sold by each salesperson. The salesperson who sells the most units wins the contest. Write a pseudocode program and then a Java application that inputs a series of 10 single-digit numbers as characters, and determines and prints the largest of the numbers. [*Hint:* Your program should use three variables as follows:

counter:	A counter to count to 10 (i.e., to keep track of how many numbers have been input, and to determine when all 10 numbers have been processed)
number:	The current digit input to the program
largest:	The largest number found so far.]

4.16   Write a Java application that utilizes looping to print the following table of values:

N	10*N	100*N	1000*N
1	10	100	1000
2	20	200	2000
3	30	300	3000
4	40	400	4000
5	50	500	5000

4.17   Using an approach similar to Exercise 4.15, find the *two* largest values of the 10 digits entered. (*Note:* You may input each number only once.)

4.18   Modify the program in Fig. 4.11 to validate its inputs. On any input, if the value entered is other than 1 or 2, keep looping until the user enters a correct value.

4.19   What does the following program print?

```
public class Mystery2 {
   public static void main( String args[] )
   {
      int count = 1;
      while ( count <= 10 ) {
         System.out.println( count % 2 == 1 ?
                                   "****" : "++++++++" );
         ++count;
      }
   }
}
```

4.20   What does the following program print?

```
public class Mystery3 {
   public static void main( String args[] )
   {
      int row = 10, column;
      while ( row >= 1 ) {
         column = 1;
         while ( column <= 10 ) {
            System.out.print( row % 2 == 1 ? "<" : ">" );
            ++column;
         }
         --row;
         System.out.println();
      }
   }
}
```

4.21   *(Dangling-Else Problem)* Determine the output for each of the following when **x** is **9** and **y** is **11** and when **x** is **11** and **y** is **9**. Note that the compiler ignores the indentation in a Java program. Also, the Java compiler always associates an **else** with the previous **if** unless told to do otherwise by the placement of braces (**{}**). Because, on first glance, the programmer may not be sure which **if** an **else** matches, this is referred to as the "dangling-else" problem. We have eliminated the indentation from the following code to make the problem more challenging. (*Hint:* Apply indentation conventions you have learned.)

a)
```
if ( x < 10 )
if ( y > 10 )
System.out.println( "*****" );
else
System.out.println( "#####" );
System.out.println( "$$$$$" );
```

b)
```
if ( x < 10 ) {
if ( y > 10 )
System.out.println( "*****" );
}
else {
System.out.println( "#####" );
System.out.println( "$$$$$" );
}
```

4.22   *(Another Dangling-Else Problem)* Modify the following code to produce the output shown. Use proper indentation techniques. You may not make any changes other than inserting braces and changing the indentation of the code. The compiler ignores indentation in a Java program. We have eliminated the indentation from the following code to make the problem more challenging. [*Note:* It is possible that no modification is necessary.]

```
if ( y == 8 )
if ( x == 5 )
System.out.println( "@@@@@" );
else
System.out.println( "#####" );
System.out.println( "$$$$$" );
System.out.println( "&&&&&" );
```

a) Assuming **x** = **5** and **y** = **8**, the following output is produced.

```
@@@@@
$$$$$
&&&&&
```

b) Assuming **x** = **5** and **y** = **8**, the following output is produced.

```
@@@@@
```

c) Assuming **x** = **5** and **y** = **8**, the following output is produced.

```
@@@@@
&&&&&
```

d) Assuming **x** = **5** and **y** = **7**, the following output is produced. [*Note:* The last three output statements after the **else** are all part of a compound statement.]

```
#####
$$$$$
&&&&&
```

4.23   Write an applet that reads in the size of the side of a square and displays a hollow square of that size out of asterisks using the **drawString** method inside your applet's **paint** method. Use an input dialog to read the size from the user. Your program should work for squares of all side sizes between 1 and 20.

4.24   A palindrome is a number or a text phrase that reads the same backward as forward. For example, each of the following five-digit integers are palindromes: 12321, 55555, 45554 and 11611. Write an application that reads in a five-digit integer and determines whether or not it is a palindrome. If the number is not five digits, display an error message dialog indicating the problem to the user. When the user dismisses the error dialog, allow the user to enter a new value.

4.25   Write an application that inputs an integer containing only 0s and 1s (i.e., a "binary" integer) and print its decimal equivalent. (*Hint:* Use the modulus and division operators to pick off the "binary" number's digits one at a time from right to left. Just as in the decimal number system where the rightmost digit has a positional value of 1 and the next digit left has a positional value of 10, then 100, then 1000, etc., in the binary number system the rightmost digit has a positional value of 1, the next digit left has a positional value of 2, then 4, then 8, etc. Thus the decimal number 234 can be interpreted as 4 * 1 + 3 * 10 + 2 * 100. The decimal equivalent of binary 1101 is 1 * 1 + 0 * 2 + 1 * 4 + 1 * 8 or 1 + 0 + 4 + 8 or 13.)

4.26   Write an application that displays the following checkerboard pattern:

```
 *  *  *  *  *  *  *  *
  *  *  *  *  *  *  *  *
 *  *  *  *  *  *  *  *
  *  *  *  *  *  *  *  *
 *  *  *  *  *  *  *  *
  *  *  *  *  *  *  *  *
 *  *  *  *  *  *  *  *
  *  *  *  *  *  *  *  *
```

Your program may use only three output statements, one of the form

```
System.out.print( "* " );
```

one of the form

```
System.out.print( " " );
```

and one of the form

```
System.out.println();
```

Note that the preceding statement indicates that the program should output a single newline character to drop to the next line on the output. (*Hint:* Repetition structures are required in this exercise.)

4.27   Write an application that keeps displaying in the command window the multiples of the integer 2, namely 2, 4, 8, 16, 32, 64, etc. Your loop should not terminate (i.e., you should create an infinite loop). What happens when you run this program?

4.28   What's wrong with the following statement? Provide the correct statement to add one to the sum of **x** and **y**.

```
System.out.println( ++(x + y) );
```

4.29   Write an application that reads three nonzero values entered by the user in input dialogs and determines and prints if they could represent the sides of a triangle.

4.30   Write an application that reads three nonzero integers and determines and prints if they could be the sides of a right triangle.

4.31   A company wants to transmit data over the telephone, but they are concerned that their phones may be tapped. All of their data is transmitted as four-digit integers. They have asked you to write a program that will encrypt their data so that it may be transmitted more securely. Your application should read a four-digit integer entered by the user in an input dialog and encrypt it as follows: Replace each digit by *(the sum of that digit plus 7) modulus 10*. Then swap the first digit with the third, and swap the second digit with the fourth. Then print the encrypted integer. Write a separate application that inputs an encrypted four-digit integer and decrypts it to form the original number.

4.32 The factorial of a nonnegative integer n is written $n!$ (pronounced "n factorial") and is defined as follows:

$n! = n \cdot (n - 1) \cdot (n - 2) \cdot \ldots \cdot 1$ (for values of n greater than or equal to 1)

and

$n! = 1$ (for $n = 0$).

For example, $5! = 5 \cdot 4 \cdot 3 \cdot 2 \cdot 1$, which is 120.

a) Write an application that reads a nonnegative integer from an input dialog and computes and prints its factorial.

b) Write an application that estimates the value of the mathematical constant e by using the formula

$$e = 1 + \frac{1}{1!} + \frac{1}{2!} + \frac{1}{3!} + \ldots$$

c) Write an application that computes the value of e^x by using the formula:

$$e^x = 1 + \frac{x}{1!} + \frac{x^2}{2!} + \frac{x^3}{3!} + \ldots$$

5

Control Structures: Part 2

Objectives

- To be able to use the **for** and **do/while** repetition structures to execute statements in a program repeatedly.
- To understand multiple selection using the **switch** selection structure.
- To be able to use the **break** and **continue** program control statements.
- To be able to use the logical operators.

Who can control his fate?
William Shakespeare, *Othello*

The used key is always bright.
Benjamin Franklin

Man is a tool-making animal.
Benjamin Franklin

Intelligence . . . is the faculty of making artificial objects, especially tools to make tools.
Henri Bergson

Outline

5.1 Introduction

Before writing a program to solve a particular problem, it is essential to have a thorough
understanding of the problem and a carefully planned approach to solving the problem.
When writing a program, it is equally essential to understand the types of building blocks
that are available and to employ proven program construction principles. In this chapter we
discuss all of these issues in our presentation of the theory and principles of structured programming. The techniques that you will learn here are applicable to most high-level languages, including Java. When we begin our formal treatment of object-based programming
in Java in Chapter 8, we will see that the control structures we study here in Chapter 5 are
helpful in building and manipulating objects.

5.2 Essentials of Counter-Controlled Repetition

Counter-controlled repetition requires:

1. The *name* of a control variable (or loop counter).

2. The *initial value* of the control variable.

3. The *increment* (or *decrement*) by which the control variable is modified each time
   through the loop (also known as *each iteration of the loop*).

4. The condition that tests for the *final value* of the control variable (i.e., whether
   looping should continue).

To see the four elements of counter-controlled repetition, consider the simple applet
shown in Fig. 5.1, which draws 10 lines from the applet's **paint** method. Remember that
an applet requires a separate HTML document to load the applet into the **appletviewer**
or a browser. For the purpose of this applet, the **<applet>** tag specifies a width of **275**
pixels and a height of **105** pixels.

The declaration at line 9

```
int counter = 1;
```

```
1   // Fig. 5.1: WhileCounter.java
2   // Counter-controlled repetition
3   import java.awt.Graphics;
4   import javax.swing.JApplet;
5
6   public class WhileCounter extends JApplet {
7      public void paint( Graphics g )
8      {
9         int counter = 1;              // initialization
10
11        while ( counter <= 10 ) {     // repetition condition
12           g.drawLine( 10, 10, 250, counter * 10 );
13           ++counter;                 // increment
14        }
15     }
16  }
```

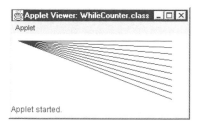

Fig. 5.1   Counter-controlled repetition.

names the control variable (**counter**), declares it to be an integer, reserves space for it in memory and sets it to an *initial value* of **1**. Declarations that include initialization are, in effect, executable statements.

The declaration and initialization of **counter** could also have been accomplished with the declaration and statement

```
int counter;    // declare counter
counter = 1;    // initialize counter to 1
```

The declaration is not executable, but the assignment statement is. We use both methods of initializing variables throughout the book.

Line 12 in the **while** structure uses **Graphics** reference **g**, which refers to the applet's **Graphics** object, to send the **drawLine** message to the **Graphics** object asking it to draw a line. Remember that "sending a message to an object" actually means calling a method to perform a task. One of the **Graphics** object's many services is to draw lines. In previous chapters, we also saw that the **Graphics** object's other services include drawing rectangles, strings and ovals. **Graphics** method **drawLine** requires four arguments that represent the line's first *x* coordinate, first *y* coordinate, second *x* coordinate and second *y* coordinate. In this example, the second *y* coordinate changes value during each iteration of the loop with the calculation **counter * 10**. This causes the second point in each call to **drawLine** to move 10 pixels down the applet's display area.

Line 13 in the **while** structure

```
++counter;
```

increments the control variable by 1 each iteration of the loop (i.e., each time the body of the loop is performed). The loop-continuation condition in the **while** structure tests if the value of the control variable is less than or equal to **10** (the *final value* for which the condition is **true**). Note that the body of this **while** is performed even when the control variable is **10**. The loop terminates when the control variable exceeds **10** (i.e., **counter** becomes **11**).

The program in Fig. 5.1 can be made more concise by initializing **counter** to **0** and by replacing the **while** structure with

```
while ( ++counter <= 10 )     // repetition condition
    g.drawLine( 10, 10, 250, counter * 10 );
```

This code saves a statement (and eliminates the need for braces around the loop's body) because the incrementing is done directly in the **while** condition before the condition is tested (remember that the precedence of **++** is higher than **<=**). Coding in such a condensed fashion takes practice.

Good Programming Practice 5.1

Control counting loops with integer values.

Common Programming Error 5.1

Because floating-point values may be approximate, controlling counting loops with floating-point variables may result in imprecise counter values and inaccurate tests for termination.

Good Programming Practice 5.2

Indent the statements in the body of each control structure.

Good Programming Practice 5.3

Put a blank line before and after each major control structure to make it stand out in the program.

Good Programming Practice 5.4

Too many levels of nesting can make a program difficult to understand. As a general rule, try to avoid using more than three levels of nesting.

Good Programming Practice 5.5

Vertical spacing above and below control structures, and indentation of the bodies of control structures within the control structure headers gives programs a two-dimensional appearance that enhances readability.

5.3 The **for** Repetition Structure

The **for** repetition structure handles all the details of counter-controlled repetition. To illustrate the power of **for**, let us rewrite the applet of Fig. 5.1. The result is shown in Fig. 5.2. Remember that this program requires a separate HTML document to load the applet into the **appletviewer**. For the purpose of this applet, the **<applet>** tag specifies a width of **275** pixels and a height of **105** pixels.

```
17   // Fig. 5.2: ForCounter.java
18   // Counter-controlled repetition with the for structure
19   import java.awt.Graphics;
20   import javax.swing.JApplet;
21
22   public class ForCounter extends JApplet {
23      public void paint( Graphics g )
24      {
25         // Initialization, repetition condition and incrementing
26         // are all included in the for structure header.
27         for ( int counter = 1; counter <= 10; counter++ )
28            g.drawLine( 10, 10, 250, counter * 10 );
29      }
30   }
```

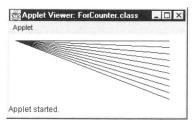

Fig. 5.2   Counter-controlled repetition with the **for** structure.

The applet's **paint** method (that is automatically called by the browser when the applet begins execution) operates as follows. When the **for** structure (line 11) begins executing, the control variable **counter** is initialized to **1** (the first two elements of counter-controlled repetition—control variable *name* and *initial value*). Note that **counter** is declared inside the **for** and thus is known only in the **for** structure's body. Next, the loop-continuation condition **counter <= 10** is checked. The condition contains the *final value* (**10**) of the control variable. Because the initial value of **counter** is **1**, the condition is satisfied (i.e., **true**), so the body statement (line 12) draws a line. Variable **counter** is then incremented in the expression **counter++**, and the loop begins again with the loop-continuation test. Because the control variable is now equal to 2, the final value is not exceeded, so the program performs the body statement again (i.e., performs the next iteration of the loop). This process continues until the control variable **counter** is incremented to 11—this causes the loop-continuation test to fail and repetition terminates. The program continues by performing the first statement after the **for** structure (in this case, method **paint** terminates because the end of its body is reached).

Figure 5.3 takes a closer look at the **for** structure of Fig. 5.2. The **for** structure's first line (including the keyword **for** and everything in parentheses after **for**) is sometimes called the ***for** structure header*. Notice that the **for** structure "does it all"—it specifies each of the items needed for counter-controlled repetition with a control variable. If there is more than one statement in the body of the **for**, braces (**{** and **}**) are required to define the body of the loop.

Notice that Fig. 5.2 uses the loop-continuation condition **counter <= 10**. If the programmer incorrectly wrote **counter < 10**, the loop would be only executed nine times. This is a common logic error called an *off-by-one error*.

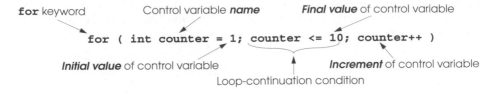

Fig. 5.3   Components of a typical **for** header.

Common Programming Error 5.2

*Using an incorrect relational operator or using an incorrect final value of a loop counter in the condition of a **while**, **for** or **do/while** structure can cause an off-by-one error.*

Good Programming Practice 5.6

*Using the final value in the condition of a **while** or **for** structure and using the **<=** relational operator will help avoid off-by-one errors. For a loop used to print the values 1 to 10, for example, the loop-continuation condition should be **counter <= 10** rather than **counter < 10** (which is an off-by-one error) or **counter < 11** (which is correct). Many programmers prefer so-called zero-based counting, in which to count 10 times through the loop, **counter** would be initialized to zero and the loop-continuation test would be **counter < 10**.*

The general format of the **for** structure is

    for (*expression1*; *expression2*; *expression3*)
      statement

where *expression1* names the loop's control variable and provides its initial value, *expression2* is the loop-continuation condition (containing the control variable's final value) and *expression3* increments the control variable. In most cases the **for** structure can be represented with an equivalent **while** structure with *expression1*, *expression2* and *expression3* placed as follows:

    expression1;

    while (*expression2*) {
      statement
      expression3;
    }

There is an exception to this rule that we will discuss in Section 5.7.

If *expression1* (the initialization section) in the **for** structure header defines the control variable (i.e., the control variable's type is specified before the variable name), the control variable can only be used in the body of the **for** structure (i.e., the value of the control variable will be unknown outside the **for** structure). This restricted use of the control variable name is known as the variable's *scope*. The scope of a variable defines where it can be used in a program. Scope is discussed in detail in Chapter 6, "Methods."

Common Programming Error 5.3

*When the control variable of a **for** structure is initially defined in the initialization section of the **for** structure header, using the control variable after the body of the structure is a syntax error.*

Sometimes, *expression1* and *expression3* in a **for** structure are comma-separated lists of expressions that enable the programmer to use multiple initialization expressions and/or multiple increment expressions. For example, there may be several control variables in a single **for** structure that must be initialized and incremented.

Good Programming Practice 5.7

*Place only expressions involving the control variables in the initialization and increment sections of a **for** structure. Manipulations of other variables should appear either before the loop (if they execute only once, like initialization statements) or in the loop body (if they execute once per iteration of the loop, like incrementing or decrementing statements).*

The three expressions in the **for** structure are optional. If *expression2* is omitted, Java assumes that the loop-continuation condition is **true**, thus creating an infinite loop. One might omit *expression1* if the control variable is initialized elsewhere in the program before the loop. One might omit *expression3* if the increment is calculated by statements in the body of the **for** or if no increment is needed. The increment expression in the **for** structure acts like a stand-alone statement at the end of the body of the **for**. Therefore, the expressions

```
counter = counter + 1
counter += 1
++counter
counter++
```

are equivalent in the increment portion of the **for** structure. Many programmers prefer the form **counter++** because the the control variable increment occurs after the loop body is executed. The postincrementing form therefore seems more natural. Because the variable being incremented here does not appear in an expression, preincrementing and postincrementing have the same effect. The two semicolons in the **for** structure are required.

Common Programming Error 5.4

*Using commas instead of the two required semicolons in a **for** header is a syntax error.*

Common Programming Error 5.5

*Placing a semicolon immediately to the right of the right parenthesis of a **for** header makes the body of that **for** structure an empty statement. This is normally a logic error.*

Software Engineering Observation 5.1

*Placing a semicolon immediately after a **for** header is sometimes used to create a so-called delay loop. Such a **for** loop with an empty body still loops the indicated number of times doing nothing other than the counting. You might use a delay loop, for example, to slow down a program that is producing outputs on the screen too quickly for you to read them. [In Chapter 15, "Multithreading," we introduce a much better technique for introducing delays into programs, so you should never use delay loops.]*

The initialization, loop-continuation condition and increment portions of a **for** structure can contain arithmetic expressions. For example, assume that **x = 2** and **y = 10**. If **x** and **y** are not modified in the loop body, the statement

```
for ( int j = x; j <= 4 * x * y; j += y / x )
```

is equivalent to the statement

```
for ( int j = 2; j <= 80; j += 5 )
```

The "increment" of a **for** structure may be negative, in which case it is really a decrement and the loop actually counts downward.

If the loop-continuation condition is initially **false**, the body of the **for** structure is not performed. Instead, execution proceeds with the statement following the **for** structure.

The control variable is frequently printed or used in calculations in the body of a **for** structure, but it does not have to be. It is common to use the control variable for controlling repetition while never mentioning it in the body of the **for** structure.

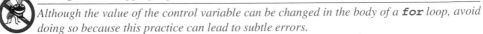 **Testing and Debugging Tip 5.1**

*Although the value of the control variable can be changed in the body of a **for** loop, avoid doing so because this practice can lead to subtle errors.*

The **for** structure is flowcharted much like the **while** structure. For example, the flowchart of the **for** statement

```
for ( int counter = 1; counter <= 10; counter++ )
    g.drawLine( 10, 10, 250, counter * 10 );
```

is shown in Fig. 5.4. This flowchart makes it clear that the initialization occurs only once and that incrementing occurs each time *after* the body statement is performed. Note that (besides small circles and arrows) the flowchart contains only rectangle symbols and a diamond symbol. Imagine, again, that the programmer has access to a deep bin of empty **for** structures—as many as the programmer might need to stack and nest with other control structures to form a structured implementation of an algorithm's flow of control. The rectangles and diamonds are then filled with actions and decisions appropriate to the algorithm.

5.4 Examples Using the **for** Structure

The following examples show methods of varying the control variable in a **for** structure. In each case, we write the appropriate **for** header. Note the change in the relational operator for loops that decrement the control variable.

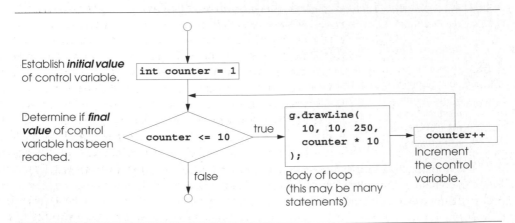

Fig. 5.4   Flowcharting a typical **for** repetition structure.

a) Vary the control variable from **1** to **100** in increments of **1**.

```
for ( int i = 1; i <= 100; i++ )
```

b) Vary the control variable from **100** to **1** in increments of **-1** (decrements of **1**).

```
for ( int i = 100; i >= 1; i-- )
```

Common Programming Error 5.6

*Not using the proper relational operator in the loop-continuation condition of a loop that counts downward (such as using **i <= 1** in a loop counting down to 1) is usually a logic error that will yield incorrect results when the program runs.*

c) Vary the control variable from **7** to **77** in steps of **7**.

```
for ( int i = 7; i <= 77; i += 7 )
```

d) Vary the control variable from **20** to **2** in steps of **-2**.

```
for ( int i = 20; i >= 2; i -= 2 )
```

e) Vary the control variable over the following sequence of values: **2, 5, 8, 11, 14, 17, 20**.

```
for ( int j = 2; j <= 20; j += 3 )
```

f) Vary the control variable over the following sequence of values: **99, 88, 77, 66, 55, 44, 33, 22, 11, 0**.

```
for ( int j = 99; j >= 0; j -= 11 )
```

The next two sample programs demonstrate simple applications of the **for** repetition structure. The application of Fig. 5.5 uses the **for** structure to sum all the even integers from **2** to **100**. Remember that the **java** interpreter is used to execute an application from the command window.

Note that the body of the **for** structure in Fig. 5.5 could actually be merged into the rightmost portion of the **for** header by using a *comma* as follows:

```
for ( int number = 2; number <= 100;
      sum += number, number += 2)
    ;
```

Similarly, the initialization **sum = 0** could be merged into the initialization section of the **for** structure.

Good Programming Practice 5.8

*Although statements preceding a **for** and statements in the body of a **for** can often be merged into the **for** header, avoid doing so because it makes the program more difficult to read.*

Good Programming Practice 5.9

Limit the size of control structure headers to a single line if possible.

```
1   // Fig. 5.5: Sum.java
2   // Counter-controlled repetition with the for structure
3   import javax.swing.JOptionPane;
4
5   public class Sum {
6      public static void main( String args[] )
7      {
8         int sum = 0;
9
10        for ( int number = 2; number <= 100; number += 2 )
11           sum += number;
12
13        JOptionPane.showMessageDialog( null,
14           "The sum is " + sum,
15           "Sum Even Integers from 2 to 100",
16           JOptionPane.INFORMATION_MESSAGE );
17
18        System.exit( 0 );    // terminate the application
19     }
20  }
```

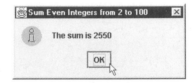

Fig. 5.5   Summation with **for**.

The next example computes compound interest using the **for** structure. Consider the following problem statement:

A person invests $1000.00 in a savings account yielding 5% interest. Assuming that all interest is left on deposit, calculate and print the amount of money in the account at the end of each year for 10 years. Use the following formula for determining these amounts:

$$a = p\,(1 + r)^{\,n}$$

where

> p is the original amount invested (i.e., the principal)
> r is the annual interest rate
> n is the number of years
> a is the amount on deposit at the end of the nth year.

This problem involves a loop that performs the indicated calculation for each of the 10 years the money remains on deposit. The solution is the application shown in Fig. 5.6.

Line 10 in method main

```
double amount, principal = 1000.0, rate = .05;
```

declares three **double** variables and initializes **principal** to **1000.0** and **rate** to **.05**. Line 12

```
DecimalFormat precisionTwo = new DecimalFormat( "0.00" );
```

```java
1   // Fig. 5.6: Interest.java
2   // Calculating compound interest
3   import java.text.DecimalFormat;
4   import javax.swing.JOptionPane;
5   import javax.swing.JTextArea;
6
7   public class Interest {
8      public static void main( String args[] )
9      {
10         double amount, principal = 1000.0, rate = .05;
11
12         DecimalFormat precisionTwo = new DecimalFormat( "0.00" );
13         JTextArea outputTextArea = new JTextArea( 11, 20 );
14
15         outputTextArea.append( "Year\tAmount on deposit\n" );
16
17         for ( int year = 1; year <= 10; year++ ) {
18            amount = principal * Math.pow( 1.0 + rate, year );
19            outputTextArea.append( year + "\t" +
20               precisionTwo.format( amount ) + "\n" );
21         }
22
23         JOptionPane.showMessageDialog(
24            null, outputTextArea, "Compound Interest",
25            JOptionPane.INFORMATION_MESSAGE );
26
27         System.exit( 0 );  // terminate the application
28      }
29   }
```

Compound Interest	
Year	Amount on deposit
1	1050.00
2	1102.50
3	1157.62
4	1215.51
5	1276.28
6	1340.10
7	1407.10
8	1477.46
9	1551.33
10	1628.89

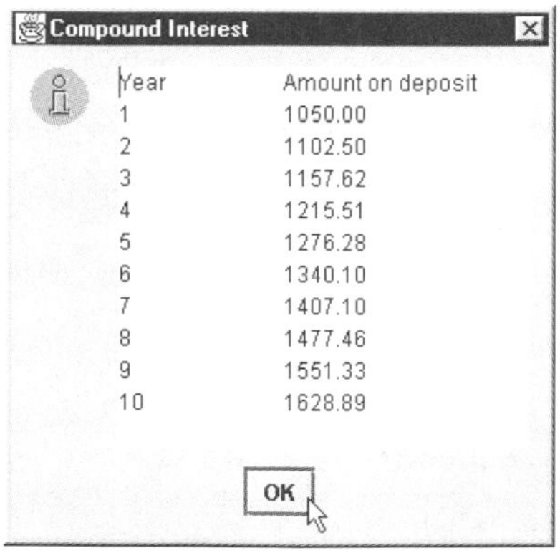

Fig. 5.6   Calculating compound interest with **for**.

declares **DecimalFormat** reference **precisionTwo** and initializes it with a new object of class **DecimalFormat** (from package **java.text**). The format control string **"0.00"** indicates that floating-point numbers formatted with **precisionTwo** will have at least one digit to the left of the decimal point and exactly two digits to the right of the decimal point.

Line 13

```
JTextArea outputTextArea = new JTextArea( 11, 20 );
```

declares **JTextArea** reference **outputTextArea** and initializes it with a new object of class **JTextArea** (from package **javax.swing**). A **JTextArea** is a GUI component that is capable of displaying many lines of text. The arguments in parentheses indicate that the **JTextArea** should contain **11** *rows* and **20** *columns* of text. This determines the size of the **JTextArea** when it is displayed on the screen. We are introducing this GUI component now because we will see many examples throughout the text in which the program outputs will contain too many lines to display on the screen. This GUI component will allow us to scroll through the lines of text so we can see all the program output. One of the many methods for placing text in a **JTextArea** is *append*. Line 15

```
outputTextArea.append( "Year\tAmount on deposit\n" );
```

uses **JTextArea** method **append** to add more text to the end of the **String** that is already in the **JTextArea** to which **outputTextArea** refers. Initially, a **JTextArea** contains an empty **String** (a **String** with no characters in it). The preceding statement appends the column heads for our two columns of output—"**Year**" and "**Amount on Deposit**." The column heads are separated with the escape sequence **\t** (the tab character). Also, the string contains the newline escape sequence **\n**, indicating that any additional text appended to the **JTextArea** should begin on the next line in the **JTextArea**.

The **for** structure executes its body 10 times, varying control variable **year** from 1 to 10 in increments of 1 (note that **year** represents *n* in the problem statement). Java does not include an exponentiation operator. Instead, we use **Math** class **static** method **pow** for this purpose. **Math.pow(x, y)** calculates the value of **x** raised to the **y**th power. Method **Math.pow** takes two arguments of type **double** and returns a **double** value. Constants like **1000.0** and **.05** in Fig. 5.6 are treated as type **double** by Java. Line 18

```
amount = principal * Math.pow( 1.0 + rate, year );
```

performs the calculation from the problem statement

$$a = p \, (1 + r)^n$$

where *a* is **amount**, *p* is **principal**, *r* is **rate** and *n* is **year** in line 18.

Lines 19 and 20

```
outputTextArea.append( year + "\t" +
    precisionTwo.format( amount ) + "\n" );
```

append more text to the end of the **outputTextArea**. The text includes the current **year** value, a tab character (to position to the second column), the result of the method call **precisionTwo.format(amount)**, which formats the **amount** with two digits to the right of the decimal point, and a newline character (to position the cursor in the **JTextArea** at the beginning of the next line).

Lines 23 through 25

```
JOptionPane.showMessageDialog(
    null, outputTextArea, "Compound Interest",
    JOptionPane.INFORMATION_MESSAGE );
```

use **static** method **JOptionPane.showMessageDialog** to display the results in a message dialog. Until now the message displayed has always been a **String**. In this example, the second argument is the **JTextArea** to which **outputTextArea** refers. An interesting feature of class **JOptionPane** is that the message it displays with **showMessageDialog** can be a **String** or a GUI component such as a **JTextArea**. In this example, the message dialog is automatically sized to accommodate the **JTextArea**. We will use this technique several times early in the book to display large text-based outputs. Later we will demonstrate how to add scrolling capability to the **JTextArea** so the user can view a program's output that is too large to display in full on the screen.

Notice that the variables **amount, principal** and **rate** are of type **double**. We did this for simplicity because we are dealing with fractional parts of dollars and we need a type that allows decimal points in its values. Unfortunately, this can cause trouble. Here is a simple explanation of what can go wrong when using **float** or **double** to represent dollar amounts (assuming that dollar amounts are displayed with two digits to the right of the decimal point): Two **double** dollar amounts stored in the machine could be 14.234 (which would normally be rounded to 14.23 for display purposes) and 18.673 (which would normally be rounded to 18.67 for display purposes). When these amounts are added, they produce the internal sum 32.907, which would normally be rounded to 32.91 for display purposes. Thus your printout could appear as

```
   14.23
 + 18.67
 -------
   32.91
```

but a person adding the individual numbers as printed would expect the sum 32.90! You have been warned!

Good Programming Practice 5.10

*Do not use variables of type **float** or **double** to perform precise monetary calculations. The imprecision of floating-point numbers can cause errors that will result in incorrect monetary values. In the exercises, we explore the use of integers to perform monetary calculations. [Note: Class libraries are available for properly performing monetary calculations.]*

Note that the calculation **1.0 + rate** that appears as an argument to the **Math.pow** method is contained in the body of the **for** statement. In fact, this calculation produces the same result each time through the loop, so repeating the calculation is wasteful.

Performance Tip 5.1

Avoid placing expressions whose values do not change inside loops. But even if you do, many of today's sophisticated optimizing compilers will automatically place such expressions outside loops in the generated machine-language code.

Performance Tip 5.2

Many compilers contain optimization features that improve the code you write, but it is still better to write good code from the start.

5.5 The **switch** Multiple-Selection Structure

We have discussed the **if** single-selection structure and the **if/else** double-selection structure. Occasionally, an algorithm will contain a series of decisions in which a variable or expression is tested separately for each of the constant integral values (i.e., values of types **byte**, **short**, **int**, **long** and **char**) it may assume, and different actions are taken. Java provides the **switch** multiple-selection structure to handle such decision making. The applet of Fig. 5.7 demonstrates drawing lines, rectangles or ovals based on the number the user types in an input dialog.

Line 7 in applet **SwitchTest** defines instance variable **choice** of type **int**. This variable will store the user's input that determines which type of shape to draw in **paint**.

```
1    // Fig. 5.7: SwitchTest.java
2    // Counting letter grades
3    import java.awt.Graphics;
4    import javax.swing.*;
5
6    public class SwitchTest extends JApplet {
7       int choice;
8
9       public void init()
10      {
11         String input;
12
13         input = JOptionPane.showInputDialog(
14                    "Enter 1 to draw lines\n" +
15                    "Enter 2 to draw rectangles\n" +
16                    "Enter 3 to draw ovals\n" );
17
18         choice = Integer.parseInt( input );
19      }
20
21      public void paint( Graphics g )
22      {
23         for ( int i = 0; i < 10; i++ ) {
24            switch( choice ) {
25               case 1:
26                  g.drawLine( 10, 10, 250, 10 + i * 10 );
27                  break;
28               case 2:
29                  g.drawRect( 10 + i * 10, 10 + i * 10,
30                              50 + i * 10, 50 + i * 10 );
31                  break;
32               case 3:
33                  g.drawOval( 10 + i * 10, 10 + i * 10,
34                              50 + i * 10, 50 + i * 10 );
35                  break;
36               default:
37                  JOptionPane.showMessageDialog(
38                     null, "Invalid value entered" );
39            } // end switch
40         } // end for
41      } // end paint()
42   } // end class SwitchTest
```

Fig. 5.7   An example using **switch** (part 1 of 2).

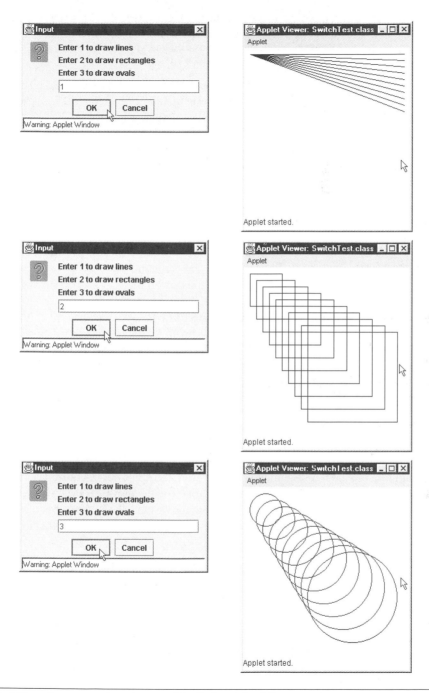

Fig. 5.7   An example using **switch** (part 2 of 2).

Method **init** at line 9 declares local variable **input** of type **String** at line 11. This variable stores the **String** the user types in the input dialog. Lines 13 through 16

```
input = JOptionPane.showInputDialog(
            "Enter 1 to draw lines\n" +
            "Enter 2 to draw rectangles\n" +
            "Enter 3 to draw ovals\n" );
```

display the input dialog with **static** method **JOptionPane.showInputDialog** and prompt the user to enter a 1 to draw lines, a 2 to draw rectangles or a 3 to draw ovals. Line 18 converts input from a **String** to an **int** using **static** method **Integer.parseInt** and assigns the result to **choice**.

Method **paint** (called after methods **init** and **start** and whenever the applet's screen are must be refreshed) at line 21 contains a **for** structure that loops 10 times. Note that the **for** structure header at line 23

```
for ( int i = 0; i < 10; i++ ) {
```

uses zero-based counting in this example. The values of **i** for the 10 iterations of the loop are 0, 1, 2, 3, 4, 5, 6, 7, 8 and 9, and the loop terminates when **i**'s value becomes 10.

Nested in the **for** structure's body is a **switch** structure (lines 24 through 39) that draws shapes based on the integer value input by the user in method **init**. The **switch** structure consists of a series of *case labels* and an optional *default case*.

When the flow of control reaches the **switch** structure, the *controlling expression* (**choice** in this example) in the parentheses following keyword **switch** is evaluated. The value of this expression (which must evaluate to an integral value of type **byte**, **char**, **short** or **int**) is compared with each of *case label*. Assume the user entered the integer **2** as their choice. **2** is compared to each **case** in the **switch**. If a match occurs (**case 2:**), the statements for that **case** are executed. For the integer **2**, lines 29 through 31

```
g.drawRect( 10 + i * 10, 10 + i * 10,
            50 + i * 10, 50 + i * 10 );
break;
```

draw a rectangle using the four arguments that represent the upper-left *x*-coordinate, upper-left *y*-coordinate, and width and height of the rectangle, and the **switch** structure exits immediately with the **break** statement. Then, the counter variable in the **for** structure is incremented and the loop-continuation condition is evaluated to determine if another iteration of the loop should be performed.

The **break** statement causes program control to proceed with the first statement after the **switch** structure (in this case we reach the end of the **for** structure's body, so control flows to the control variable's increment expression in the **for** structure header). The **break** statement is used because the **case**s in a **switch** statement would otherwise run together. If **break** is not used anywhere in a **switch** structure, then each time a match occurs in the structure, the statements for all the remaining **case**s will be executed. (This feature is perfect for programming the iterative song "The Twelve Days of Christmas.") If no match occurs between the controlling expression's value and a **case** label, the **default** case executes and an error message is displayed using a message dialog.

Each **case** can have multiple actions. The **switch** structure is different from other structures in that braces are not required around multiple actions in a **case** of a **switch**. The general **switch** structure (using a **break** in each **case**) is flowcharted in Fig. 5.8. [*Note:* As an exercise, flowchart the general **switch** structure without **break**s.]

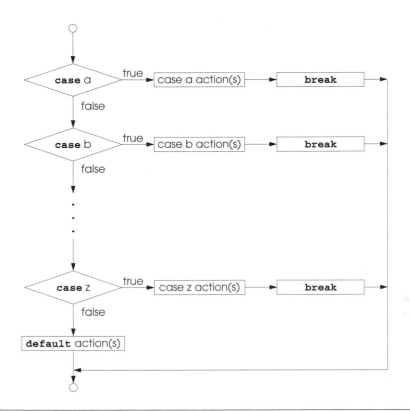

Fig. 5.8   The **switch** multiple-selection structure.

The flowchart makes it clear that each **break** statement at the end of a **case** causes control to immediately exit the **switch** structure. The **break** statement is not required for the last **case** in the **switch** structure (or the **default** case when it appears last) because the program automatically continues with the next statement after the **switch**.

Again, note that (besides small circles and arrows) the flowchart contains only rectangle symbols and diamond symbols. Imagine, again, that the programmer has access to a deep bin of empty **switch** structures—as many as the programmer might need to stack and nest with other control structures to form a structured implementation of an algorithm's flow of control. Again, the rectangles and diamonds are filled with actions and decisions appropriate to the algorithm. Although nested control structures are common, it is rare to find nested **switch** structures in a program.

Common Programming Error 5.7

*Forgetting a **break** statement when one is needed in a **switch** structure is a logic error.*

Good Programming Practice 5.11

*Provide a **default** case in **switch** statements. Cases not explicitly tested in a **switch** statement without a **default** case are ignored. Including a **default** case focuses the programmer on the need to process exceptional conditions. There are situations in which no **default** processing is needed.*

Good Programming Practice 5.12

*Although the **cases** and the **default** case in a **switch** structure can occur in any order, it is considered a good programming practice to place the **default** clause last.*

Good Programming Practice 5.13

*In a **switch** structure, when the **default** clause is listed last, the **break** for that **case** statement is not required. Some programmers include this **break** for clarity and symmetry with other cases.*

Note that listing **case** labels together (such as **case 1: case 2:** with no statements between the cases) performs the same set of actions is to occur for each of the cases.

When using the **switch** structure, remember that the expression after each **case** can only be a *constant integral expression,* (i.e., any combination of character constants and integer constants that evaluates to a constant integer value). A character constant is represented as the specific character in single quotes, such as **'A'**. An integer constant is simply an integer value. The expression after each **case** can also be a *constant variable*—i.e., a variable that contains a value that does not change for the entire program. Such a variable is declared with keyword ***final*** (discussed in Chapter 6, "Methods").

When we discuss object-oriented programming in Chapter 9, we will present a more elegant way to implement **switch** logic. We will use a technique called polymorphism to create programs that are often clearer, easier to maintain and easier to extend than programs using **switch** logic.

5.6 The **do/while** Repetition Structure

The **do/while** repetition structure is similar to the **while** structure. In the **while** structure, the loop-continuation condition is tested at the beginning of the loop before the body of the loop is performed. The **do/while** structure tests the loop-continuation condition *after* the loop body is performed; therefore, *the loop body is always executed at least once.* When a **do/while** terminates, execution continues with the statement after the **while** clause. Note that it is not necessary to use braces in the **do/while** structure if there is only one statement in the body. However, the braces are usually included to avoid confusion between the **while** and **do/while** structures. For example,

```
while ( condition )
```

is normally regarded as the header to a **while** structure. A **do/while** with no braces around the single statement body appears as

```
do
    statement
while ( condition );
```

which can be confusing. The last line—**while(** *condition* **);**—may be misinterpreted by the reader as a **while** structure containing an empty statement (the semicolon by itself). Thus, the **do/while** with one statement is often written as follows to avoid confusion:

```
do {
    statement
} while ( condition );
```

Good Programming Practice 5.14

*Some programmers always include braces in a **do/while** structure even if the braces are not necessary. This helps eliminate ambiguity between the **while** structure and the **do/while** structure containing one statement.*

 Common Programming Error 5.8

*Infinite loops are caused when the loop-continuation condition in a **while**, **for** or **do/while** structure never becomes **false**. To prevent this, make sure there is not a semicolon immediately after the header of a **while** or **for** structure. In a counter-controlled loop, make sure the control variable is incremented (or decremented) in the body of the loop. In a sentinel-controlled loop, make sure the sentinel value is eventually input.*

The applet in Fig. 5.9 uses a **do/while** structure to draw 10 nested circles with **Graphics** method **drawOval**.

```
1   // Fig. 5.9: DoWhileTest.java
2   // Using the do/while repetition structure
3   import java.awt.Graphics;
4   import javax.swing.JApplet;
5
6   public class DoWhileTest extends JApplet {
7      public void paint( Graphics g )
8      {
9         int counter = 1;
10
11        do {
12           g.drawOval( 110 - counter * 10, 110 - counter * 10,
13                       counter * 20, counter * 20 );
14           ++counter;
15        } while ( counter <= 10 );
16     }
17  }
```

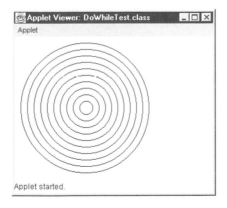

Fig. 5.9   Using the **do/while** repetition structure.

In method **paint**, control variable **counter** is declared and initialized to **1** at line 9. Upon entering the **do/while** structure, lines 12 and 13 send the **drawOval** message to the **Graphics** object to which **g** refers. The four arguments that represent the upper-left *x*-coordinate, upper-left *y*-coordinate, and width and height of the oval's *bounding box* (an imaginary rectangle in which the oval is drawn such that it touches all four sides of the rectangle) are calculated based on the value of control variable **counter**. The innermost oval is drawn first. The bounding box's upper-left corner for each subsequent oval moves closer to the upper-left corner of the applet's screen area. At the same time the width and height of the bounding box are increased to ensure that each new oval contains all the previous ovals. Line 14 increments the **counter** before the loop-continuation test is performed at the bottom of the loop.

The **do/while** flowchart (Fig. 5.10) makes it clear that the loop-continuation condition is not executed until the action is performed at least once. The flowchart contains only a rectangle and a diamond. Imagine, also, that the programmer has access to a bin of empty **do/while** structures—as many as the programmer might need to stack and nest with other control structures to form a structured implementation of an algorithm. The rectangles and diamonds are filled with actions and decisions appropriate to the algorithm.

5.7 The **break** and **continue** Statements

The *break* and *continue* statements alter the flow of control. The **break** statement, when executed in a **while**, **for**, **do/while** or **switch** structure, causes immediate exit from that structure. Execution continues with the first statement after the structure. Common uses of the **break** statement are to escape early from a loop or to skip the remainder of a **switch** structure (as in Fig. 5.7). Figure 5.11 demonstrates the **break** statement in a **for** repetition structure.

When the **if** structure at line 12 in the **for** structure detects that **count** is **5**, **break** is executed. This terminates the **for** structure and the program proceeds to line 18 (immediately after the **for**), where the string concatenation statement produces the final string that is to display in the message dialog at line 20. The loop fully executes its body only four times.

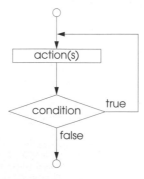

Fig. 5.10   Flowcharting the **do/while** repetition structure.

```
1   // Fig. 5.11: BreakTest.java
2   // Using the break statement in a for structure
3   import javax.swing.JOptionPane;
4
5   public class BreakTest {
6      public static void main( String args[] )
7      {
8         String output = "";
9         int count;
10
11        for ( count = 1; count <= 10; count++ ) {
12           if ( count == 5 )
13              break;   // break loop only if count == 5
14
15           output += count + " ";
16        }
17
18        output += "\nBroke out of loop at count = " + count;
19        JOptionPane.showMessageDialog( null, output );
20        System.exit( 0 );
21     }
22  }
```

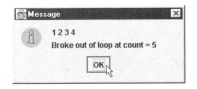

Message

1 2 3 4
Broke out of loop at count = 5

OK

Fig. 5.11   Using the **break** statement in a **for** structure.

The **continue** statement, when executed in a **while**, **for** or **do/while** structure, skips the remaining statements in the body of that structure and proceeds with the next iteration of the loop. In **while** and **do/while** structures, the loop-continuation test is evaluated immediately after the **continue** statement is executed. In the **for** structure, the increment expression is executed, then the loop-continuation test is evaluated. Earlier, we stated that the **while** structure could be used in most cases to represent the **for** structure. The one exception occurs when the increment expression in the **while** structure follows the **continue** statement. In this case, the increment does not execute before the repetition-continuation condition is tested, and the **while** does not execute in the same manner as the **for**. Figure 5.12 uses the **continue** statement in a **for** structure to skip the string concatenation statement at line 15 when the **if** structure at line 12 determines that the value of **count** is **5**. When the **continue** statement executes, program control continues with the increment of the control variable in the **for** structure.

Good Programming Practice 5.15

*Some programmers feel that **break** and **continue** violate structured programming. Because the effects of these statements can be achieved by structured programming techniques, these programmers do not use **break** and **continue**.*

```
1   // Fig. 5.12: ContinueTest.java
2   // Using the continue statement in a for structure
3   import javax.swing.JOptionPane;
4
5   public class ContinueTest {
6      public static void main( String args[] )
7      {
8         String output = "";
9
10        for ( int count = 1; count <= 10; count++ ) {
11           if ( count == 5 )
12              continue;  // skip remaining code in loop
13                         // only if count == 5
14
15           output += count + " ";
16        }
17
18        output += "\nUsed continue to skip printing 5";
19        JOptionPane.showMessageDialog( null, output );
20        System.exit( 0 );
21     }
22  }
```

```
┌─────────────────────────────────────┐
│ 🖼 Message                      [×] │
├─────────────────────────────────────┤
│  ⓘ    1 2 3 4 6 7 8 9 10            │
│        Used continue to skip printing 5 │
│                                     │
│              ┌──────┐               │
│              │  OK  │               │
│              └──────┘               │
└─────────────────────────────────────┘
```

Fig. 5.12   Using the **continue** statement in a **for** structure.

Performance Tip 5.3

*The **break** and **continue** statements, when used properly, perform faster than the corresponding structured techniques.*

Software Engineering Observation 5.2

There is a tension between achieving quality software engineering and achieving the best performing software. Often, one of these goals is achieved at the expense of the other. For all but the most performance-intensive situations apply the following "rule of thumb": First, make your code simple and correct; then make it fast and small, only if necessary.

5.8 The Labeled **break** and **continue** Statements

The **break** statement can only break out of an immediately enclosing **while**, **for**, **do/while** or **switch** structure. To break out of a nested set of structures, you can use the *labeled **break** statement*. This statement, when executed in a **while**, **for**, **do/while** or **switch**, causes immediate exit from that structure and any number of enclosing repetition structures; program execution resumes with the first statement after the enclosing *labeled compound statement* (i.e., a set of statements enclosed in curly braces and preceded by a label). The compound statement can be either a repetition structure (the body would be the compound statement) or it can be a compound statement in which the repetition structure is the first executable code. Labeled **break** statements are commonly used to terminate nested looping structures containing **while**, **for**, **do/while** or **switch** structures. Figure 5.13 demonstrates the labeled **break** statement in a nested **for** structure.

The labeled compound statement (lines 10 through 25) begins with a *label* (an identifier followed by a colon); here we use the label "**stop:**." The compound statement is enclosed in braces at the end of line 10 and line 25 and includes both the nested **for** structure starting at line 11 and the string concatenation statement at line 24. When the **if** structure at line 14 detects that **row** is equal to **5**, the statement

```
break stop;
```

```
1   // Fig. 5.13: BreakLabelTest.java
2   // Using the break statement with a label
3   import javax.swing.JOptionPane;
4
5   public class BreakLabelTest {
6      public static void main( String args[] )
7      {
8         String output = "";
9
10        stop: {   // labeled compound statement
11           for ( int row = 1; row <= 10; row++ ) {
12              for ( int column = 1; column <= 5 ; column++ ) {
13
14                 if ( row == 5 )
15                    break stop; // jump to end of stop block
16
17                 output += "*   ";
18              }
19
20              output += "\n";
21           }
22
23           // the following line is skipped
24           output += "\nLoops terminated normally";
25        }
26
27        JOptionPane.showMessageDialog(
28           null, output,"Testing break with a label",
29           JOptionPane.INFORMATION_MESSAGE );
30        System.exit( 0 );
31     }
32  }
```

Fig. 5.13   Using a labeled **break** statement in a nested **for** structure.

executes. This terminates both the **for** structure at line 12 and its enclosing **for** structure at line 11, and the program proceeds to the statement at line 27 (i.e., the first statement after the labeled compound statement). The inner **for** structure fully executes its body only four times. Notice that the string concatenation statement at line 24 never executes because it is included in the labeled compound statement and the outer **for** structure never completes.

The **continue** statement proceeds with the next iteration (repetition) of the immediately enclosing **while**, **for** or **do/while** structure. The *labeled* **continue** *statement*, when executed in a repetition structure (**while**, **for** or **do/while**), skips the remaining statements in that structure's body and any number of enclosing repetition structures, and proceeds with the next iteration of the enclosing *labeled repetition structure* (i.e., a repetition structure preceded by a label). In labeled **while** and **do/while** structures, the loop-continuation test is evaluated immediately after the **continue** statement is executed. In a labeled **for** structure, the increment expression is executed, then the loop-continuation test is evaluated. Figure 5.14 uses the labeled **continue** statement in a nested **for** structure to cause execution to continue with the next iteration of the outer **for** structure.

The labeled **for** structure (lines 10 through 22) starts at the **nextRow** label. When the **if** structure at line 16 in the inner **for** structure detects that **column** is greater than **row**, the statement

```
continue nextRow;
```

executes and program control continues with the increment of the control variable of the outer **for** loop. Even though the inner **for** structure counts from 1 to 10, the number of ***** characters output on a row never exceeds the value of **row**.

5.9 Logical Operators

So far we have studied only *simple conditions* such as **count <= 10**, **total > 1000** and **number != sentinelValue**. These conditions were expressed in terms of the relational operators **>**, **<**, **>=** and **<=** and the equality operators **==** and **!=**. Each decision tested one condition. To test multiple conditions in the process of making a decision, we performed these tests in separate statements or in nested **if** or **if/else** structures.

Java provides *logical operators* that may be used to form more complex conditions by combining simple conditions. The logical operators are **&&** *(logical AND)*, **&** *(boolean logical AND)*, **||** *(logical OR)*, **|** *(boolean logical inclusive OR)*, **^** *(boolean logical exclusive OR)* and **!** *(logical NOT,* also called *logical negation)*. We will consider examples of each of these.

Suppose we wish to ensure at some point in a program that two conditions are *both* **true** before we choose a certain path of execution. In this case we can use the logical **&&** operator as follows:

```
if ( gender == 1 && age >= 65 )
    ++seniorFemales;
```

This **if** statement contains two simple conditions. The condition **gender == 1** might be evaluated, for example, to determine if a person is a female. The condition **age >= 65** is evaluated to determine if a person is a senior citizen. The two simple conditions are evaluated first because the precedences of **==** and **>=** are both higher than the precedence of **&&**. The **if** statement then considers the combined condition

```
1   // Fig. 5.14: ContinueLabelTest.java
2   // Using the continue statement with a label
3   import javax.swing.JOptionPane;
4
5   public class ContinueLabelTest {
6      public static void main( String args[] )
7      {
8         String output = "";
9
10        nextRow:   // target label of continue statement
11           for ( int row = 1; row <= 5; row++ ) {
12              output += "\n";
13
14              for ( int column = 1; column <= 10; column++ ) {
15
16                 if ( column > row )
17                    continue nextRow; // next iteration of
18                                      // labeled loop
19
20                 output += "*   ";
21              }
22           }
23
24        JOptionPane.showMessageDialog(
25           null, output,"Testing continue with a label",
26           JOptionPane.INFORMATION_MESSAGE );
27        System.exit( 0 );
28     }
29  }
```

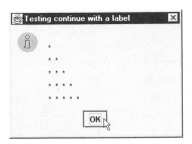

Fig. 5.14 Using a labeled **continue** statement in a nested **for** structure.

```
gender == 1 && age >= 65
```

This condition is **true** *if and only if* both of the simple conditions are **true**. Finally, if this combined condition is indeed **true**, the count of **seniorFemales** is incremented by **1**. If either or both of the simple conditions are **false**, the program skips the incrementing and proceeds to the statement following the **if** structure. The preceding combined condition can be made more readable by adding redundant parentheses:

```
( gender == 1 ) && ( age >= 65 )
```

The table of Fig. 5.15 summarizes the **&&** operator. The table shows all four possible combinations of **false** and **true** values for *expression1* and *expression2*. Such tables are often called *truth tables*. Java evaluates to **false** or **true** all expressions that include relational operators, equality operators and/or logical operators.

Now let us consider the || (logical OR) operator. Suppose we wish to ensure that either *or* both of two conditions are **true** before we choose a certain path of execution. In this case we use the || operator as in the following program segment:

```
if ( semesterAverage >= 90 || finalExam >= 90 )
    System.out.println ( "Student grade is A" );
```

This statement also contains two simple conditions. The condition **semesterAverage >= 90** is evaluated to determine if the student deserves an "A" in the course because of a solid performance throughout the semester. The condition **finalExam >= 90** is evaluated to determine if the student deserves an "A" in the course because of an outstanding performance on the final exam. The **if** statement then considers the combined condition

```
semesterAverage >= 90 || finalExam >= 90
```

and awards the student an "A" if either or both of the simple conditions are **true**. Note that the message "**Student grade is A**" is *not* printed only when both of the simple conditions are **false**. Figure 5.16 is a truth table for the logical OR operator (||).

The **&&** operator has a higher precedence than the || operator. Both operators associate from left to right. An expression containing **&&** or || operators is evaluated only until truth or falsity is known. Thus, evaluation of the expression

```
gender == 1 && age >= 65
```

expression1	expression2	expression1 && expression2
false	false	false
false	true	false
true	false	false
true	true	true

Fig. 5.15   Truth table for the **&&** (logical AND) operator.

expression1	expression2	expression1 || expression2
false	false	false
false	true	true
true	false	true
true	true	true

Fig. 5.16   Truth table for the || (logical OR) operator.

will stop immediately if **gender** is not equal to **1** (i.e., the entire expression is **false**), and continue if **gender** is equal to **1** (i.e., the entire expression could still be **true** if the condition **age >= 65** is **true**). This performance feature for evaluation of logical AND and logical OR expressions is called *short-circuit evaluation.*

Common Programming Error 5.9

*In expressions using operator **&&**, it is possible that a condition—we will call this the dependent condition—may require another condition to be **true** for it to be meaningful to evaluate the dependent condition. In this case, the dependent condition should be placed after the other condition or an error might occur.*

Performance Tip 5.4

*In expressions using operator **&&**, if the separate conditions are independent of one another, make the condition that is most likely to be **false** the leftmost condition. In expressions using operator | |, make the condition that is most likely to be **true** the leftmost condition. This can reduce a program's execution time.*

The *boolean logical AND (**&**)* and *boolean logical inclusive OR (|)* operators, work identically to the regular logical AND and logical OR operators with one exception—the boolean logical operators always evaluate both of their operands (i.e., there is no short-circuit evaluation). Therefore, the expression

```
gender == 1 & age >= 65
```

evaluates **age >= 65** regardless of whether **gender** is equal to **1**. This is useful if the right operand of the boolean logical AND or boolean logical inclusive OR operator has a needed *side effect*—a modification of a variable's value. For example, the expression

```
birthday == true | ++age >= 65
```

guarantees that the condition **++age >= 65** will be evaluated. Thus, the variable **age** will be incremented in the preceding expression regardless of whether the overall expression is **true** or **false**.

Good Programming Practice 5.16

For clarity, avoid expressions with side effects in conditions. The side effects may look clever, but they are often more trouble than they are worth.

A condition containing the *boolean logical exclusive OR (^)* operator is **true** *if and only if one of its operands results in a **true** value and one results in a **false** value.* If both operands are **true** or both are **false**, the result of the entire condition is **false**. Figure 5.17 is a truth table for the boolean logical exclusive OR operator (^). This operator is also guaranteed to evaluate both of its operands (i.e., there is no short-circuit evaluation).

Java provides the **!** (logical negation) operator to enable a programmer to "reverse" the meaning of a condition. Unlike the logical operators **&&**, **&**, | |, | and ^ which combine two conditions (binary operators), the logical negation operator has only a single condition as an operand (unary operator). The logical negation operator is placed before a condition to choose a path of execution if the original condition (without the logical negation operator) is **false**, such as in the following program segment:

```
if ( ! ( grade == sentinelValue ) )
    System.out.println( "The next grade is " + grade );
```

expression1	expression2	expression1 ^ expression2
false	false	false
false	true	true
true	false	true
true	true	false

Fig. 5.17   Truth table for the boolean logical exclusive OR (^) operator.

The parentheses around the condition **grade == sentinelValue** are needed because the logical negation operator has a higher precedence than the equality operator. Figure 5.18 is a truth table for the logical negation operator.

In most cases, the programmer can avoid using logical negation by expressing the condition differently with an appropriate relational or equality operator. For example, the preceding statement may also be written as follows:

```
if ( grade != sentinelValue )
    System.out.println( "The next grade is " + grade );
```

This flexibility can help a programmer express a condition in a more convenient manner.

The application of Fig. 5.19 demonstrates all the logical operators and boolean logical operators by producing their truth tables. The program uses string concatenation to create the string that is displayed in a **JTextArea**.

In the output of Fig. 5.19, the strings "false" and "true" indicate **false** and **true** for the operands in each condition. The result of the condition is shown as **true** or **false**. Note that when you add a **boolean** value to a **String**, Java automatically adds the string "false" or "true" based on the **boolean** value.

Line 8 in method **main**

```
JTextArea outputArea = new JTextArea( 17, 20 );
```

creates a **JTextArea** with 17 rows and 20 columns. Line 9

```
JScrollPane scroller = new JScrollPane( outputArea );
```

declares **JScrollPane** reference **scroller** and initializes it with a new **JScroll-Pane** object. Class **JScrollPane** (from package **javax.swing**) provides a GUI component with scrolling functionality.

expression	!expression
false	true
true	false

Fig. 5.18   Truth table for operator **!** (logical NOT).

```
1   // Fig. 5.19: LogicalOperators.java
2   // Demonstrating the logical operators
3   import javax.swing.*;
4
5   public class LogicalOperators {
6      public static void main( String args[] )
7      {
8         JTextArea outputArea = new JTextArea( 17, 20 );
9         JScrollPane scroller = new JScrollPane( outputArea );
10        String output = "";
11
12        output += "Logical AND (&&)" +
13                  "\nfalse && false: " + ( false && false ) +
14                  "\nfalse && true: " + ( false && true ) +
15                  "\ntrue && false: " + ( true && false ) +
16                  "\ntrue && true: " + ( true && true );
17
18        output += "\n\nLogical OR (||)" +
19                  "\nfalse || false: " + ( false || false ) +
20                  "\nfalse || true: " + ( false || true ) +
21                  "\ntrue || false: " + ( true || false ) +
22                  "\ntrue || true: " + ( true || true );
23
24        output += "\n\nBoolean logical AND (&)" +
25                  "\nfalse & false: " + ( false & false ) +
26                  "\nfalse & true: " + ( false & true ) +
27                  "\ntrue & false: " + ( true & false ) +
28                  "\ntrue & true: " + ( true & true );
29
30        output += "\n\nBoolean logical inclusive OR (|)" +
31                  "\nfalse | false: " + ( false | false ) +
32                  "\nfalse | true: " + ( false | true ) +
33                  "\ntrue | false: " + ( true | false ) +
34                  "\ntrue | true: " + ( true | true );
35
36        output += "\n\nBoolean logical exclusive OR (^)" +
37                  "\nfalse ^ false: " + ( false ^ false ) +
38                  "\nfalse ^ true: " + ( false ^ true ) +
39                  "\ntrue ^ false: " + ( true ^ false ) +
40                  "\ntrue ^ true: " + ( true ^ true );
41
42        output += "\n\nLogical NOT (!)" +
43                  "\n!false: " + ( !false ) +
44                  "\n!true: " + ( !true );
45
46        outputArea.setText( output );
47        JOptionPane.showMessageDialog( null, scroller,
48           "Truth Tables", JOptionPane.INFORMATION_MESSAGE );
49        System.exit( 0 );
50     }
51  }
```

Fig. 5.19   Demonstrating the logical operators (part 1 of 2).

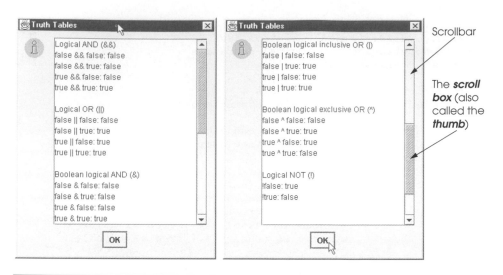

Fig. 5.19 Demonstrating the logical operators (part 2 of 2).

When you execute this application, notice the *scrollbar* on the right side of the **JTextArea**. You can click the *arrows* at the top or bottom of the scrollbar to scroll up or down through the text in the **JTextArea** one line at a time. You can also drag the *scroll box* (also called the *thumb*) up or down to rapidly scroll through the text. A **JScrollPane** object is initialized with the GUI component for which it will provide scrolling functionality (**outputArea** here). This attaches the GUI component to the **JScrollPane**.

Lines 12 through 44 build the **output** string that is to be displayed in the **outputArea**. Line 46 uses method **setText** to replace the text in **outputArea** with the **output** string. Lines 47 and 48 display a message dialog. The second argument, **scroller**, indicates that the **scroller** and the **outputArea** attached to it should be displayed as the message in the message dialog.

The chart in Fig. 5.20 shows the precedence and associativity of the Java operators introduced to this point. The operators are shown from top to bottom in decreasing order of precedence.

5.10 Structured Programming Summary

Just as architects design buildings by employing the collective wisdom of their profession, so should programmers design programs. Our field is younger than architecture is, and our collective wisdom is considerably sparser. We have learned that structured programming produces programs that are easier than unstructured programs to understand and hence are easier to test, debug, modify and even prove correct in a mathematical sense.

Figure 5.21 summarizes Java's control structures. Small circles are used in the figure to indicate the single entry point and the single exit point of each structure. Connecting individual flowchart symbols arbitrarily can lead to unstructured programs. Therefore, the programming profession has chosen to combine flowchart symbols to form a limited set of control structures, and to build structured programs by properly combining control structures in two simple ways.

Operators	Associativity	Type
( )	left to right	parentheses
++ --	right to left	unary postfix
++ -- + - ! (*type*)	right to left	unary
* / %	left to right	multiplicative
+ -	left to right	additive
< <= > >=	left to right	relational
== !=	left to right	equality
&	left to right	boolean logical AND
^	left to right	boolean logical exclusive OR
|	left to right	boolean logical inclusive OR
&&	left to right	logical AND
||	left to right	logical OR
? :	right to left	conditional
= += -= *= /= %=	right to left	assignment

Fig. 5.20   Precedence and associativity of the operators discussed so far.

For simplicity, only single-entry/single-exit control structures are used—there is only one way to enter and only one way to exit each control structure. Connecting control structures in sequence to form structured programs is simple—the exit point of one control structure is connected to the entry point of the next control structure (i.e., the control structures are simply placed one after another in a program); we have called this "control structure stacking." The rules for forming structured programs also allow for control structures to be nested.

Figure 5.22 shows the rules for forming properly structured programs. The rules assume that the rectangle flowchart symbol may be used to indicate any action, including input/output.

Applying the rules of Fig. 5.22 always results in a structured flowchart with a neat, building-block appearance (Fig. 5.23). For example, repeatedly applying rule 2 to the simplest flowchart results in a structured flowchart containing many rectangles in sequence (Fig. 5.24). Notice that rule 2 generates a stack of control structures; so let us call rule 2 the *stacking rule*.

Rule 3 is called the *nesting rule*. Repeatedly applying rule 3 to the simplest flowchart results in a flowchart with neatly nested control structures. For example, in Fig. 5.25, the rectangle in the simplest flowchart is first replaced with a double-selection (**if/else**) structure. Then rule 3 is applied again to both of the rectangles in the double-selection structure, replacing each of these rectangles with double-selection structures. The dashed boxes around each of the double-selection structures represent the rectangle that was replaced in the original simplest flowchart.

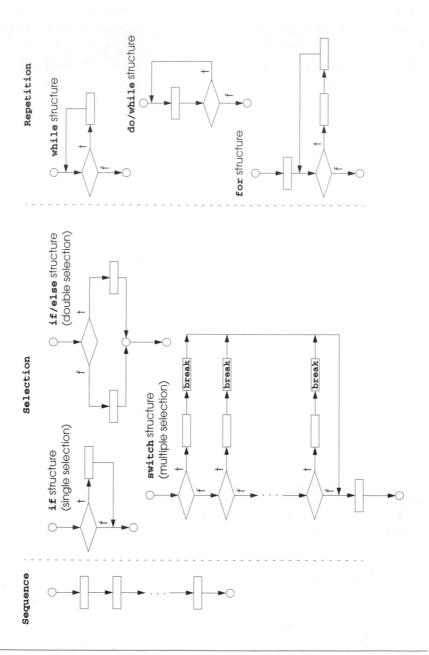

Fig. 5.21   Java's single-entry/single-exit sequence, selection and repetition
structures.

Rule 4 generates larger, more involved and more deeply nested structures. The flow-charts that emerge from applying the rules in Fig. 5.22 constitute the set of all possible structured flowcharts and hence the set of all possible structured programs.

Rules for Forming Structured Programs

1) Begin with the "simplest flowchart" (Fig. 5.23).

2) Any rectangle (action) can be replaced by two rectangles (actions) in sequence.

3) Any rectangle (action) can be replaced by any control structure (sequence, **if**, **if/else**, **switch**, **while**, **do/while** or **for**).

4) Rules 2 and 3 may be applied as often as you like and in any order.

Fig. 5.22   Rules for forming structured programs.

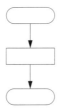

Fig. 5.23   The simplest flowchart.

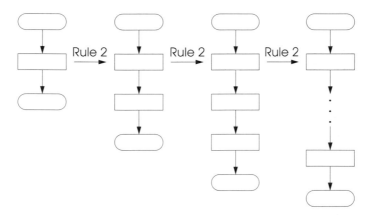

Fig. 5.24   Repeatedly applying rule 2 of Fig. 5.22 to the simplest flowchart.

The beauty of the structured approach is that we use only seven simple single-entry/single-exit pieces, and we assemble them in only two simple ways. Figure 5.26 shows the kinds of stacked building blocks that emerge from applying rule 2 and the kinds of nested building blocks that emerge from applying rule 3. The figure also shows the kind of overlapped building blocks that cannot appear in structured flowcharts (because of the elimination of the **goto** statement).

If the rules in Fig. 5.22 are followed, an unstructured flowchart (such as that in Fig. 5.27) cannot be created. If you are uncertain if a particular flowchart is structured, apply the rules of Fig. 5.22 in reverse to try to reduce the flowchart to the simplest flowchart. If the flowchart is reducible to the simplest flowchart, the original flowchart is structured; otherwise, it is not.

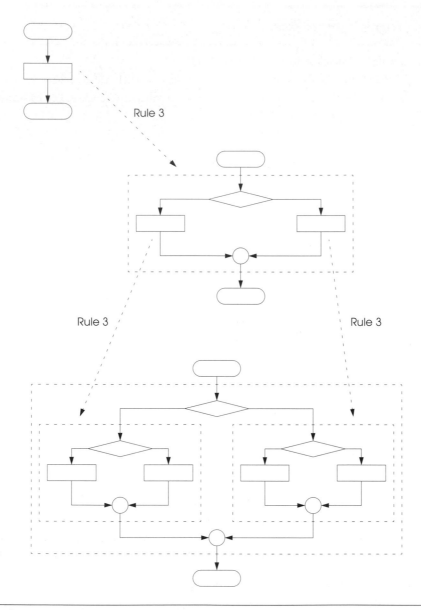

Fig. 5.25 Applying rule 3 of Fig. 5.22 to the simplest flowchart.

Structured programming promotes simplicity. Bohm and Jacopini have given us the result that only three forms of control are needed:

- Sequence
- Selection
- Repetition

Stacked building blocks   Nested building blocks

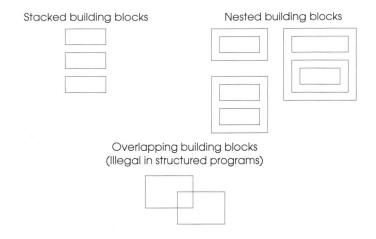

Overlapping building blocks
(Illegal in structured programs)

Fig. 5.26   Stacked, nested and overlapped building blocks.

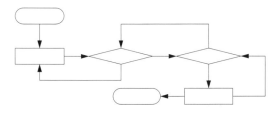

Fig. 5.27   An unstructured flowchart.

Sequence is trivial. Selection is implemented in one of three ways:

- **if** structure (single selection)
- **if/else** structure (double selection)
- **switch** structure (multiple selection)

In fact, it is straightforward to prove that the simple **if** structure is sufficient to provide any form of selection—everything that can be done with the **if/else** structure and the **switch** structure can be implemented by combining **if** structures (although perhaps not as smoothly).

Repetition is implemented in one of three ways:

- **while** structure
- **do/while** structure
- **for** structure

It is straightforward to prove that the **while** structure is sufficient to provide any form of repetition. Everything that can be done with the **do/while** structure and the **for** structure can be done with the **while** structure (although perhaps not as elegantly).

Combining these results illustrates that any form of control ever needed in a Java program can be expressed in terms of:

- sequence
- **if** structure (selection)
- **while** structure (repetition)

And these control structures can be combined in only two ways—stacking and nesting. Indeed, structured programming promotes simplicity.

In this chapter, we discussed how to compose programs from control structures containing actions and decisions. In Chapter 6, we introduce another program structuring unit called the *method*. We will learn to compose large programs by combining methods that, in turn, are composed of control structures. We will also discuss how methods promote software reusability. In Chapter 8, we discuss in more detail Java's other program structuring unit called the *class*. We will then create objects from classes and proceed with our treatment of object-oriented programming.

Summary

- The **for** repetition structure handles all the details of counter-controlled repetition. The general format of the **for** structure is

      for (*expression1*; *expression2*; *expression3*)
          statement

  where *expression1* initializes the loop's control variable, *expression2* is the loop-continuation condition and *expression3* increments the control variable.

- A **JTextArea** is a GUI component that is capable of displaying many lines of text.

- Method **append** adds text to the end of the text in a **JTextArea**.

- An interesting feature of class **JOptionPane** is that the message it displays with **showMessageDialog** can be a **String** or a GUI component such as a **JTextArea**.

- The **do/while** repetition structure tests the loop-continuation condition at the end of the loop, so the body of the loop will be executed at least once. The format for the **do/while** structure is

      do
          statement
      while (*condition*);

- The **break** statement, when executed in one of the repetition structures (**for**, **while** and **do/while**), causes immediate exit from the structure.

- The **continue** statement, when executed in one of the repetition structures (**for**, **while** and **do/while**), skips any remaining statements in the body of the structure and proceeds with the test for the next iteration of the loop.

- The **switch** statement handles a series of decisions in which a particular variable or expression is tested for values it may assume, and different actions are taken. In most programs, it is necessary to include a **break** statement after the statements for each **case**. Several **case**s can execute the same statements by listing the **case** labels together before the statements. The **switch** structure can only test for constant integral expressions.

- Logical operators may be used to form complex conditions by combining conditions. The logical operators are **&&**, **&**, **||**, **|**, **^** and **!**, meaning logical AND, boolean logical AND, logical OR, boolean logical inclusive OR, boolean logical exclusive OR and logical NOT (negation), respectively.

- Class **JScrollPane** (from package **javax.swing**) provides a GUI component with scrolling functionality.

- **JTextArea** method **setText** uses the **String** argument it receives to replace the text in a **JTextArea**.

Terminology

&& operator	labeled **continue** statement
|| operator	labeled repetition structure
! operator	logical AND (**&&**)
append method of class **JTextArea**	logical negation (**!**)
boolean logical AND (**&**)	logical operators
boolean logical exclusive OR (**^**)	logical OR (**||**)
boolean logical inclusive OR (**|**)	**long**
break	loop-continuation condition
case label	multiple selection
continue	nested control structures
counter-controlled repetition	off-by-one error
default case in **switch**	repetition structures
definite repetition	scrollbar
do/while repetition structure	scroll box
for repetition structure	short-circuit evaluation
infinite loop	single-entry/single-exit control structures
JScrollPane class	stacked control structures
JTextArea class	**switch** selection structure
labeled **break** statement	thumb of a scrollbar
labeled compound statement	**while** repetition structure

Common Programming Errors

5.1   Because floating-point values may be approximate, controlling counting loops with floating-point variables may result in imprecise counter values and inaccurate tests for termination.

5.2   Using an incorrect relational operator or using an incorrect final value of a loop counter in the condition of a **while**, **for** or **do/while** structure can cause an off-by-one error.

5.3   When the control variable of a **for** structure is initially defined in the initialization section of the **for** structure header, using the control variable after the body of the structure is a syntax error.

5.4   Using commas instead of the two required semicolons in a **for** header is a syntax error.

5.5   Placing a semicolon immediately to the right of the right parenthesis of a **for** header makes the body of that **for** structure an empty statement. This is normally a logic error.

5.6   Not using the proper relational operator in the loop-continuation condition of a loop that counts downward (such as using **i <= 1** in a loop counting down to 1) is usually a logic error that will yield incorrect results when the program runs.

5.7   Forgetting a **break** statement when one is needed in a **switch** structure is a logic error.

5.8   Infinite loops are caused when the loop-continuation condition in a **while**, **for** or **do/while** structure never becomes **false**. To prevent this, make sure there is not a semicolon immediately after the header of a **while** or **for** structure. In a counter-controlled loop, make sure the control variable is incremented (or decremented) in the body of the loop. In a sentinel-controlled loop, make sure the sentinel value is eventually input.

5.9   In expressions using operator **&&**, it is possible that a condition—we will call this the dependent condition—may require another condition to be **true** for it to be meaningful to evaluate the dependent condition. In this case, the dependent condition should be placed after the other condition or an error might occur.

Good Programming Practices

5.1   Control counting loops with integer values.

5.2   Indent the statements in the body of each control structure.

5.3   Put a blank line before and after each major control structure to make it stand out in the program.

5.4   Too many levels of nesting can make a program difficult to understand. As a general rule, try to avoid using more than three levels of nesting.

5.5   Vertical spacing above and below control structures, and indentation of the bodies of control structures within the control structure headers gives programs a two-dimensional appearance that enhances readability.

5.6   Using the final value in the condition of a **while** or **for** structure and using the **<=** relational operator will help avoid off-by-one errors. For a loop used to print the values 1 to 10, for example, the loop-continuation condition should be **counter <= 10** rather than **counter < 10** (which is an off-by-one error) or **counter < 11** (which is correct). Many programmers prefer so-called zero-based counting, in which to count 10 times through the loop, **counter** would be initialized to zero and the loop-continuation test would be **counter < 10**.

5.7   Place only expressions involving the control variables in the initialization and increment sections of a **for** structure. Manipulations of other variables should appear either before the loop (if they execute only once, like initialization statements) or in the loop body (if they execute once per iteration of the loop, like incrementing or decrementing statements).

5.8   Although statements preceding a **for** and statements in the body of a **for** can be merged into the **for** header, avoid doing so because it makes the program more difficult to read.

5.9   Limit the size of control structure headers to a single line if possible.

5.10   Do not use variables of type **float** or **double** to perform precise monetary calculations. The imprecision of floating-point numbers can cause errors that will result in incorrect monetary values. In the exercises, we explore the use of integers to perform monetary calculations. [*Note:* Class libraries are available for properly performing monetary calculations.]

5.11   Provide a **default** case in **switch** statements. Cases not explicitly tested in a **switch** statement without a **default** case are ignored. Including a **default** case focuses the programmer on the need to process exceptional conditions. There are situations in which no **default** processing is needed.

5.12   Although the **case**s and the **default** case in a **switch** structure can occur in any order, it is considered a good programming practice to place the **default** clause last.

5.13   In a **switch** structure, when the **default** clause is listed last, the **break** statement for that **case** is not required. Some programmers include this **break** for clarity and symmetry with other cases.

5.14   Some programmers always include braces in a **do/while** structure even if the braces are not necessary. This helps eliminate ambiguity between the **while** structure and the **do/while** structure containing one statement.

5.15   Some programmers feel that **break** and **continue** violate structured programming. Because the effects of these statements can be achieved by structured programming techniques, these programmers do not use **break** and **continue**.

5.16   For clarity, avoid expressions with side effects in conditions. The side effects may look clever, but they are often more trouble than they are worth.

Performance Tips

5.1   Avoid placing expressions whose values do not change inside loops. But even if you do, many of today's sophisticated optimizing compilers will automatically place such expressions outside loops in the generated machine-language code.

5.2   Many compilers contain optimization features that improve the code you write, but it is still better to write good code from the start.

5.3   The **break** and **continue** statements, when used properly, perform faster than the corresponding structured techniques.

5.4   In expressions using operator **&&**, if the separate conditions are independent of one another, make the condition that is most likely to be false the leftmost condition. In expressions using operator **||**, make the condition that is most likely to be true the leftmost condition. This can reduce a program's execution time.

Software Engineering Observations

5.1   Placing a semicolon immediately after a **for** header is sometimes used to create a so-called delay loop. Such a **for** loop with an empty body still loops the indicated number of times doing nothing other than the counting. You might use a delay loop, for example, to slow down a program that is producing outputs on the screen too quickly for you to read them. [In Chapter 15, "Multithreading," we introduce a much better technique for introducing delays into programs, so you should never use delay loops.]

5.2   There is a tension between achieving quality software engineering and achieving the best performing software. Often, one of these goals is achieved at the expense of the other. For all but the most performance-intensive situations apply the following "rule of thumb": First, make your code simple and correct; then make it fast and small, only if necessary.

Testing and Debugging Tip

5.1   Although the value of the control variable can be changed in the body of a **for** loop, avoid doing so because this practice can lead to subtle errors.

Self-Review Exercises

5.1   State whether each of the following is *true* or *false*. If *false*, explain why.
    a) The **default** case is required in the **switch** selection structure.
    b) The **break** statement is required in the default case of a **switch** selection structure.
    c) The expression (**x > y && a < b**) is true if either **x > y** is true or **a < b** is true.
    d) An expression containing the **||** operator is true if either or both of its operands is true.

5.2   Write a Java statement or a set of Java statements to accomplish each of the following:
    a) Sum the odd integers between 1 and 99 using a **for** structure. Assume the integer variables **sum** and **count** have been declared.
    b) Calculate the value of **2.5** raised to the power of **3** using the **pow** method.
    c) Print the integers from 1 to 20 using a **while** loop and the counter variable **x**. Assume that the variable **x** has been declared but not initialized. Print only five integers per line. [*Hint:* Use the calculation **x % 5**. When the value of this is 0, print a newline character; otherwise, print a tab character. Assume this is an application—use the **System.out.println()** method to output the newline character and use the **System.out.print('\t')** method to output the tab character.]
    d) Repeat Exercise 5.2 c) using a **for** structure.

5.3   Find the error in each of the following code segments and explain how to correct it.
    a) **x = 1;**

```
while ( x <= 10 );
   x++;
}
```

b)
```
for ( y = .1; y != 1.0; y += .1 )
    System.out.println( y );
```
c)
```
switch ( n ) {
    case 1:
        System.out.println( "The number is 1" );
    case 2:
        System.out.println( "The number is 2" );
        break;
    default:
        System.out.println( "The number is not 1 or 2" );
        break;
}
```
d) The following code should print the values 1 to 10.
```
n = 1;

while ( n < 10 )
    System.out.println( n++ );
```

Answers to Self-Review Exercises

5.1 a) False. The **default** case is optional. If no default action is needed, then there is no need for a **default** case.

b) False. The **break** statement is used to exit the **switch** structure. The **break** statement is not required for the last case in a **switch** structure.

c) False. Both of the relational expressions must be true in order for the entire expression to be true when using the **&&** operator.

d) True.

5.2 a)
```
sum = 0;
for ( count = 1; count <= 99; count += 2 )
    sum += count;
```
b) `Math.pow( 2.5, 3 )`
c)
```
x = 1;

while ( x <= 20 ) {
    System.out.print( x );

    if ( x % 5 == 0 )
        System.out.println();
    else
        System.out.print( '\t' );

    ++x;
}
```
d)
```
for ( x = 1; x <= 20; x++ ) {
    System.out.print( x );

    if ( x % 5 == 0 )
        System.out.println();
    else
        System.out.print( '\t' );
}
```

or

```
for ( x = 1; x <= 20; x++ )

    if ( x % 5 == 0 )
        System.out.println( x );
    else
        System.out.print( x + "\t" );
```

5.3   a)   Error: The semicolon after the **while** header causes an infinite loop and there is a missing left brace.
Correction: Replace the semicolon by a **{** or remove both the **;** and the **}**.

     b)   Error: Using a floating-point number to control a **for** repetition structure may not work because floating-point numbers are represented approximately by most computers.
Correction: Use an integer, and perform the proper calculation in order to get the values you desire.
```
        for ( y = 1; y != 10; y++ )
            System.out.println( (float) y / 10 );
```

     c)   Error: Missing **break** statement in the statements for the first **case**.
Correction: Add a **break** statement at the end of the statements for the first **case**. Note that this is not necessarily an error if the programmer wants the statement of **case 2:** to execute every time the **case 1:** statement executes.

     d)   Error: Improper relational operator used in the **while** repetition-continuation condition.
Correction: Use **<=** rather than **<** or change **10** to **11**.

Exercises

5.4   Find the error in each of the following. [*Note:* There may be more than one error.]

     a)   **For (x = 100, x >= 1, x++)**
```
        System.out.println( x );
```

     b)   The following code should print whether integer **value** is odd or even:
```
    switch ( value % 2 ) {
        case 0:
            System.out.println( "Even integer" );
        case 1:
            System.out.println( "Odd integer" );
    }
```

     c)   The following code should output the odd integers from 19 to 1:
```
    for ( x = 19; x >= 1; x += 2 )
        System.out.println( x );
```

     d)   The following code should output the even integers from 2 to 100:
```
    counter = 2;
    do {
        System.out.println( counter );
        counter += 2;
    } While ( counter < 100 );
```

5.5   What does the following program do?

```
public class Printing {
   public static void main( String args[] )
   {
      for ( int i = 1; i <= 10; i++ ) {

         for ( int j = 1; j <= 5; j++ )
            System.out.print( '@' );

         System.out.println();
      }
   }
}
```

5.6   Write an application that finds the smallest of several integers. Assume that the first value read specifies the number of values to input from the user.

5.7   Write an application that calculates the product of the odd integers from 1 to 15, then displays the results in a message dialog.

5.8   The *factorial* method is used frequently in probability problems. The factorial of a positive integer *n* (written *n!* and pronounced "n factorial") is equal to the product of the positive integers from 1 to *n*. Write an application that evaluates the factorials of the integers from 1 to 5. Display the results in tabular format in a **JTextArea** that is displayed on a message dialog. What difficulty might prevent you from calculating the factorial of 20?

5.9   Modify the compound interest program of Fig. 5.6 to repeat its steps for interest rates of 5, 6, 7, 8, 9 and 10%. Use a **for** loop to vary the interest rate. Add scrolling functionality to the **JTextArea** so you can scroll through all the output.

5.10   Write an application that displays the following patterns separately one below the other. Use **for** loops to generate the patterns. All asterisks (*****) should be printed by a single statement of the form **System.out.print('*');** (this causes the asterisks to print side by side). A statement of the form **System.out.println();** can be used to position to the next line. A statement of the form **System.out.print(' ');** can be used display a space for the last two patterns. There should be no other output statements in the program. (*Hint:* The last two patterns require that each line begin with an appropriate number of blanks.)

```
(A)             (B)              (C)              (D)
*               **********       **********                *
**              *********         *********               **
***             ********           ********              ***
****            *******             *******             ****
*****           ******               ******            *****
******          *****                 *****           ******
*******         ****                   ****          *******
********        ***                     ***         ********
*********       **                       **        *********
**********      *                         *       **********
```

5.11   One interesting application of computers is drawing graphs and bar charts (sometimes called "histograms"). Write an applet that reads five numbers (each between 1 and 30). For each number read, your program should draw a line containing that number of adjacent asterisks. For example, if your program reads the number seven, it should print ***********.

5.12 Modify the applet of Fig. 5.11 to draw filled rectangles instead of lines of asterisks. Method **fillRect** of class **Graphics** requires the same arguments as method **drawRect**. Multiply each number entered by the user by 10 to determine the width of the rectangle.

5.13 A mail order house sells five different products whose retail prices are: product 1 — $2.98, product 2—$4.50, product 3—$9.98, product 4—$4.49, and product 5—$6.87. Write an application that reads a series of pairs of numbers as follows:

   a) Product number
   b) Quantity sold for one day

Your program should use a **switch** structure to help determine the retail price for each product. Your program should calculate and display the total retail value of all products sold last week. Use a **TextField** to obtain the product number from the user. Use a sentinel-controlled loop to determine when the program should stop looping and display the final results.

5.14 Modify the program in Fig. 5.6 to use only integers to calculate the compound interest. (*Hint:* Treat all monetary amounts as integral numbers of pennies. Then "break" the result into its dollar portion and cents portion by using the division and modulus operations, respectively. Insert a period.)

5.15 Assume **i = 1, j = 2, k = 3** and **m = 2**. What does each of the following statements print? Are the parentheses necessary in each case?

   a) **System.out.println(i == 1);**
   b) **System.out.println(j == 3);**
   c) **System.out.println(i >= 1 && j < 4);**
   d) **System.out.println(m <= 99 & k < m);**
   e) **System.out.println(j >= i || k == m);**
   f) **System.out.println(k + m < j | 3 - j >= k);**
   g) **System.out.println(!(k > m));**

5.16 Write an application that prints a table of the binary, octal, and hexadecimal equivalents of the decimal numbers in the range 1 through 256. If you are not familiar with these number systems, read Appendix E, first. Place the results in a **JTextArea** with scrolling functionality. Display the **JTextArea** in a message dialog.

5.17 Calculate the value of π from the infinite series

$$\pi = 4 - \frac{4}{3} + \frac{4}{5} - \frac{4}{7} + \frac{4}{9} - \frac{4}{11} + \cdots$$

Print a table that shows the value of π approximated by one term of this series, by two terms, by three terms, etc. How many terms of this series do you have to use before you first get 3.14? 3.141? 3.1415? 3.14159?

5.18 (*Pythagorean Triples*) A right triangle can have sides that are all integers. The set of three integer values for the sides of a right triangle is called a Pythagorean triple. These three sides must satisfy the relationship that the sum of the squares of two of the sides is equal to the square of the hypotenuse. Write an application to find all Pythagorean triples for **side1, side2** and the **hypotenuse** all no larger than 500. Use a triple-nested **for** loop that tries all possibilities. This is an example of "brute force" computing. You will learn in more advanced computer science courses that there are large numbers of interesting problems for which there is no known algorithmic approach other than using sheer brute force.

5.19 Modify Exercise 5.10 to combine your code from the four separate triangles of asterisks into a single application that prints all four patterns side by side making clever use of nested **for** loops.

```
   *              * * * * * * * * *   * * * * * * * * *              *
   * *            * * * * * * * *       * * * * * * * *            * *
   * * *          * * * * * * *           * * * * * * *          * * *
   * * * *        * * * * * * *           * * * * * *          * * * *
   * * * * *      * * * * * *               * * * * *        * * * * *
   * * * * * *    * * * * *                   * * * * *      * * * * * *
   * * * * * * *  * * * *                       * * * *    * * * * * * *
   * * * * * * * *  * * *                         * * *  * * * * * * * *
   * * * * * * * * *  * *                           * *  * * * * * * * * *
   * * * * * * * * * *  *                             *  * * * * * * * * * *
```

5.20   *(De Morgan's Laws)* In this chapter, we discussed the logical operators **&&**, **&**, **||**, **|**, **^** and **!**. De Morgan's Laws can sometimes make it more convenient for us to express a logical expression. These laws state that the expression **!** (*condition1* **&&** *condition2*) is logically equivalent to the expression (**!** *condition1* **||** **!** *condition2*). Also, the expression **!** (*condition1* **||** *condition2*) is logically equivalent to the expression (**!** *condition1* **&&** **!** *condition2*). Use De Morgan's Laws to write equivalent expressions for each of the following, and then write a program to show that both the original expression and the new expression in each case are equivalent:

a) **!(x < 5) && !(y >= 7)**
b) **!(a == b) || !(g != 5)**
c) **!((x <= 8) && (y > 4))**
d) **!((i > 4) || (j <= 6))**

5.21   Write an application that prints the following diamond shape. You may use output statements that print a single asterisk (*****), a single space or a single newline character. Maximize your use of repetition (with nested **for** structures) and minimize the number of output statements.

5.22   Modify the program you wrote in Exercise 5.21 to read an odd number in the range 1 to 19 to specify the number of rows in the diamond. Your program should then display a diamond of the appropriate size.

5.23   A criticism of the **break** statement and the **continue** statement is that each is unstructured. Actually, **break** statements and **continue** statements can always be replaced by structured statements, although doing so can be awkward. Describe in general how you would remove any **break** statement from a loop in a program and replace that statement with some structured equivalent. (*Hint:* The **break** statement leaves a loop from within the body of the loop. The other way to leave is by failing the loop-continuation test. Consider using in the loop-continuation test a second test that indicates "early exit because of a 'break' condition.") Use the technique you developed here to remove the break statement from the program of Fig. 5.11.

5.24   What does the following program segment do?

```
for ( i = 1; i <= 5; i++ ) {

   for ( j = 1; j <= 3; j++ ) {

      for ( k = 1; k <= 4; k++ )
         System.out.print( '*' );

      System.out.println();
   }

   System.out.println();
}
```

5.25   Describe in general how you would remove any **continue** statement from a loop in a program and replace that statement with some structured equivalent. Use the technique you developed here to remove the **continue** statement from the program of Fig. 5.12.

5.26   *("The Twelve Days of Christmas" Song)* Write an application that uses repetition and **switch** structures to print the song "The Twelve Days of Christmas." One **switch** structure should be used to print the day (i.e., "First," "Second," etc.). A separate **switch** structure should be used to print the remainder of each verse.

6

Methods

Objectives

- To understand how to construct programs modularly from small pieces called methods.
- To introduce the common math methods available in the Java API.
- To be able to create new methods.
- To understand the mechanisms used to pass information between methods.
- To introduce simulation techniques using random number generation.
- To understand how the visibility of identifiers is limited to specific regions of programs.
- To understand how to write and use methods that call themselves.

Form ever follows function.
Louis Henri Sullivan

E pluribus unum.
(One composed of many.)
Virgil

O! call back yesterday, bid time return.
William Shakespeare, *Richard II*

Call me Ishmael.
Herman Melville, *Moby Dick*

When you call me that, smile.
Owen Wister

Outline

Summary • Terminology • Common Programming Errors • Good Programming Practices • Performance Tips • Portability Tip • Software Engineering Observations • Testing and Debugging Tips • Self-Review Exercises • Answers to Self-Review Exercises • Exercises

6.1 Introduction

Most computer programs that solve real-world problems are much larger than the programs presented in the first few chapters. Experience has shown that the best way to develop and maintain a large program is to construct it from small, simple pieces or *modules*. This technique is called *divide and conquer.* This chapter describes many key features of the Java language that facilitate the design, implementation, operation and maintenance of large programs.

6.2 Program Modules in Java

Modules in Java are called *methods* and *classes.* Java programs are written by combining new methods and classes the programmer writes with "prepackaged" methods and classes available in the *Java API* (also referred to as the *Java class library*) and in various other method and class libraries. In this chapter, we concentrate on methods; we will discuss classes in detail beginning with Chapter 8.

The Java API provides a rich collection of classes and methods for performing common mathematical calculations, string manipulations, character manipulations, input/output, error checking and many other useful operations. This makes the programmer's job easier because these methods provide many of the capabilities programmers need. The Java API methods are provided as part of the Java Developer's Kit (JDK).

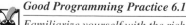

Good Programming Practice 6.1

Familiarize yourself with the rich collection of classes and methods in the Java API and with the rich collections of classes available in various class libraries.

Software Engineering Observation 6.1

Avoid reinventing the wheel. When possible, use Java API classes and methods instead of writing new classes and methods. This reduces program development time and avoids introducing new errors.

Portability Tip 6.1

Using the methods in the Java API helps make programs more portable.

Performance Tip 6.1

Do not try to rewrite existing Java API classes and methods to make them more efficient. You usually will not be able to increase the performance of these classes and methods.

The programmer can write methods to define specific tasks that may be used at many points in a program. These are sometimes referred to as *programmer-defined methods*. The actual statements defining the method are written only once and these statements are hidden from other methods.

A method is *invoked* (i.e., made to perform its designated task) by a *method call*. The method call specifies the method name and provides information (as *arguments*) that the called method needs to do its task. A common analogy for this is the hierarchical form of management. A boss (the *calling method* or *caller*) asks a worker (the *called method*) to perform a task and *return* (i.e., report back) the results when the task is done. The boss method does not know *how* the worker method performs its designated tasks. The worker may call other worker methods and the boss will be unaware of this. We will soon see how this "hiding" of implementation details promotes good software engineering. Figure 6.1 shows the **boss** method communicating with several worker methods in a hierarchical manner. Note that **worker1** acts as a "boss" method to **worker4** and **worker5**. Relationships among methods may be other than the hierarchical structure shown in this figure.

6.3 **Math** Class Methods

Math class methods allow the programmer to perform certain common mathematical calculations. We use various **Math** class methods here to introduce the concept of methods. Throughout the book, we discuss many other methods from the classes of the Java API.

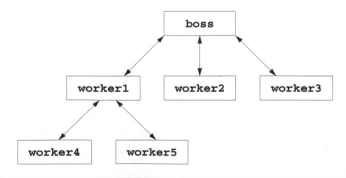

Fig. 6.1   Hierarchical boss method/worker method relationship.

Methods are called by writing the name of the method followed by a left parenthesis followed by the *argument* (or a comma-separated list of arguments) of the method followed by a right parenthesis. For example, a programmer desiring to calculate and print the square root of **900.0** might write

```
System.out.println( Math.sqrt( 900.0 ) );
```

When this statement is executed, the method **Math.sqrt** is called to calculate the square root of the number contained in the parentheses (**900.0**). The number **900.0** is the *argument* of the **Math.sqrt** method. The preceding statement would print **30.0**. The **Math.sqrt** method takes an argument of type **double** and returns a result of type **double**. Note that all **Math** class methods must be invoked by preceding the method name with the class name **Math** and a dot (**.**) operator. Many of the methods defined in previous examples have been called automatically (e.g., **main** in applications, and **init** and **paint** in applets) or have been called using the syntax class name followed by a dot (**.**) operator followed by a method name like the **Math** methods (e.g., **Integer.parseInt**, **Double.parseDouble**, **JOptionPane.showMessageDialog** and **JOption-Pane.showInputDialog**). Normally, most methods in Java are invoked through a reference to an object as in the following line of code from an applet:

```
g.drawString( "Welcome to Java programming!", 25, 25 );
```

This statement might appear in your applet's **paint** method. The statement invokes the **drawString** method of the **Graphics** object to which **g** refers (also referred to as *sending the **drawString** message to object to which **g** refers*). In Chapter 8, we discuss in detail the different types of methods associated with classes and how they are invoked.

Software Engineering Observation 6.2

*It is not necessary to import the **Math** class into a program to use **Math** class methods. The **Math** class is part of the **java.lang** package which is automatically imported by the compiler.*

Common Programming Error 6.1

*Forgetting to invoke a **Math** class method by preceding the method name with the class name **Math** and a dot operator (**.**) results in a syntax error.*

Method arguments may be constants, variables or expressions. If **c1 = 13.0, d = 3.0** and **f = 4.0**, then the statement

```
System.out.println( Math.sqrt( c1 + d * f ) );
```

calculates and prints the square root of **13.0 + 3.0 * 4.0 = 25.0**, namely **5.0**.

Some **Math** class methods are summarized in Fig. 6.2. In the figure, the variables **x** and **y** are of type **double**. The **Math** class also defines two commonly used mathematical constants—**Math.PI** and **Math.E**. The constant **Math.PI** (3.14159265358979323846) of class **Math** is the ratio of a circle's circumference to its diameter. The constant **Math.E** (2.7182818284590452354) is the base value for natural logarithms (calculated with the **Math.log** method).

Method	Description	Example
abs(x)	absolute value of x (this method also has versions for **float**, **int** and **long** values)	if $x > 0$ then abs(x) is x if $x = 0$ then abs(x) is 0 if $x < 0$ then abs(x) is -x
ceil(x)	rounds x to the smallest integer not less than x	ceil(9.2) is 10.0 ceil(-9.8) is -9.0
cos(x)	trigonometric cosine of x (x in radians)	cos(0.0) is 1.0
exp(x)	exponential method e^x	exp(1.0) is 2.71828 exp(2.0) is 7.38906
floor(x)	rounds x to the largest integer not greater than x	floor(9.2) is 9.0 floor(-9.8) is -10.0
log(x)	natural logarithm of x (base e)	log(2.718282) is 1.0 log(7.389056) is 2.0
max(x, y)	larger value of x and y (this method also has versions for **float**, **int** and **long** values)	max(2.3, 12.7) is 12.7 max(-2.3, -12.7) is -2.3
min(x, y)	smaller value of x and y (this method also has versions for **float**, **int** and **long** values)	min(2.3, 12.7) is 2.3 min(-2.3, -12.7) is -12.7
pow(x, y)	x raised to power y (x^y)	pow(2.0, 7.0) is 128.0 pow(9.0, .5) is 3.0
sin(x)	trigonometric sine of x (x in radians)	sin(0.0) is 0.0
sqrt(x)	square root of x	sqrt(900.0) is 30.0 sqrt(9.0) is 3.0
tan(x)	trigonometric tangent of x (x in radians)	tan(0.0) is 0.0

Fig. 6.2   Commonly used **Math** class methods.

6.4 Methods

Methods allow the programmer to modularize a program. All variables declared in method definitions are *local variables*—they are known only in the method in which they are defined. Most methods have a list of *parameters* that provide the means for communicating information between methods via method calls. A method's parameters are also local variables.

There are several motivations for modularizing a program with methods. The divide-and-conquer approach makes program development more manageable. Another motivation is *software reusability*—using existing methods as building blocks to create new programs. With good method naming and definition, programs can be created from standardized methods rather than being built by using customized code. For example, we did not have to define how to convert **String**s to integers and floating-point numbers—such methods are already defined for us in class **Integer** (**parseInt**) and class **Double** (**parse-Double**). A third motivation is to avoid repeating code in a program. Packaging code as a method allows that code to be executed from several locations in a program by calling the method.

Software Engineering Observation 6.3

Each method should be limited to performing a single, well-defined task, and the method name should effectively express that task. This promotes software reusability.

Software Engineering Observation 6.4

If you cannot choose a concise name that expresses what the method does, it is possible that your method is attempting to perform too many diverse tasks. It is usually best to break such a method into several smaller methods.

6.5 Method Definitions

Each program we have presented has consisted of a class definition that contained at least one method definition that called Java API methods to accomplish its tasks. We now consider how programmers write their own customized methods.

Consider an applet (Fig. 6.3) that uses a method **square** (invoked from the applet's **init** method) to calculate the squares of the integers from 1 to 10.

```
1   // Fig. 6.3: SquareInt.java
2   // A programmer-defined square method
3   import java.awt.Container;
4   import javax.swing.*;
5
6   public class SquareInt extends JApplet {
7      public void init()
8      {
9         String output = "";
10
11        JTextArea outputArea = new JTextArea( 10, 20 );
12
13        // get the applet's GUI component display area
14        Container c = getContentPane();
15
16        // attach outputArea to Container c
17        c.add( outputArea );
18
19        int result;
20
21        for ( int x = 1; x <= 10; x++ ) {
22           result = square( x );
23           output += "The square of " + x +
24                     " is " + result + "\n";
25        }
26
27        outputArea.setText( output );
28     }
```

Fig. 6.3   Using programmer-defined method **square** (part 1 of 2).

```
29
30      // square method definition
31      public int square( int y )
32      {
33          return y * y;
34      }
35   }
```

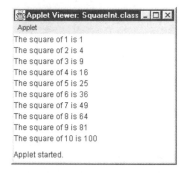

Fig. 6.3   Using programmer-defined method **square** (part 2 of 2).

When the applet begins execution, its **init** method is called first. Line 9 declares **String** reference **output** and initializes it with the empty string. This **String** will contain the results of squaring the values from 1 to 10. Line 11 declares **JTextArea** reference **outputArea** and initializes it with a new **JTextArea** object of 10 rows and 20 columns. The **output** string will be displayed in **outputArea**.

This program is the first in which we display a GUI component on an applet. The on-screen display area for a **JApplet** has a *content pane* to which the GUI components must be attached so they can be displayed at execution time. The content pane is an object of class **Container** from the **java.awt** *package*. This class was **import**ed on line 3 for use in the applet. Line 14

```
Container c = getContentPane();
```

declares **Container** reference **c** and assigns it the result of a call to method **getContentPane**—one of the many methods that our class **SquareInt** inherits from class **JApplet**. Method **getContentPane** returns a reference to the applet's content pane that can be used to attach GUI components like a **JTextArea** to the user interface of the applet.

Line 17

```
c.add( outputArea );
```

places the **JTextArea** GUI component object to which **outputArea** refers on the applet so it can be displayed when the applet is executed. **Container** method **add** attaches a GUI component to a container. For the moment, we can attach only one GUI component to the applet's content pane and that GUI component will automatically occupy the applet's entire drawing area on the screen (as defined by the **width** and **height** of the applet in pixels in the applet's HTML document). Later, we will discuss how to lay out many GUI components on an applet.

Line 19 declares **int** variable **result**, in which the result of each square calculation is stored. Lines 21 through 25 are a **for** repetition structure in which each iteration of the loop calculates the **square** of the current value of control variable **x**, stores the value in **result** and concatenates the **result** to the end of **output**.

Method **square** is *invoked* or *called* on line 22 with the statement

```
result = square( x );
```

When program control reaches this statement, method **square** (defined at line 31) is called. In fact, the **()** represent the *method call operator* which has high precedence. At this point, a copy of the value of **x** (the *argument* to the method call) is made automatically by the program and program control transfers to the first line of method **square**. Method **square** receives the copy of the value of **x** in the *parameter* **y**. Then **square** calculates **y * y**. The result is passed back to the point in **init** where **square** was invoked. The value returned is then assigned to variable **result**. Lines 23 and 24

```
output += "The square of " + x +
          " is " + result + "\n";
```

concatenate **"The square of "**, the value of **x**, **" is "**, the value of **result** and a newline character to the end of **output**. This process is repeated ten times using the **for** repetition structure. Line 27

```
outputArea.setText( output );
```

uses method **setText** to set **outputArea**'s text to the **String output**. Note that references **output**, **outputArea** and **c**, and variable **result** are declared as local variables in **init** because they are used only in **init**. Variables should be declared as instance variables only if they are required for use in more than one method of the class or if their values must be saved between calls to the methods of the class.

The definition of method **square** (line 31) shows that **square** expects an integer parameter **y**—this will be the name used to manipulate the value passed to **square** in the body of method **square**. Keyword **int** preceding the method name indicates that **square** returns an integer result. The ***return*** *statement* in **square** passes the result of the calculation **y * y** back to the calling method. Note that the entire method definition is contained between the braces of the class **SquareInt**. All methods must be defined inside a class definition.

Good Programming Practice 6.2

Place a blank line between method definitions to separate the methods and enhance program readability.

Common Programming Error 6.2

Defining a method outside the braces of a class definition is a syntax error.

The format of a method definition is

return-value-type   method-name (*parameter-list*)
{
    declarations and statements
}

The *method-name* is any valid identifier. The *return-value-type* is the data type of the result returned from the method to the caller. The return-value-type **void** indicates that a method does not return a value. Methods can return at most one value.

Common Programming Error 6.3

Omitting the return-value-type *in a method definition is a syntax error.*

Common Programming Error 6.4

Forgetting to return a value from a method that is supposed to return a value is a syntax error. If a return-value-type *other than* **void** *is specified, the method must contain a* **return** *statement.*

Common Programming Error 6.5

Returning a value from a method whose return type has been declared **void** *is a syntax error.*

The *parameter-list* is a comma-separated list containing the declarations of the parameters received by the method when it is called. There must be one argument in the method call for each parameter in the method definition. The arguments must also be compatible with the type of the parameter. For example, a parameter of type **double** could receive values of 7.35, 22 or –.03546, but not **"hello"** (because a **double** variable cannot contain a **String**). If a method does not receive any values, the *parameter-list* is empty (i.e., the method name is followed by an empty set of parentheses). A type must be listed explicitly for each parameter in the parameter list of a method or a syntax error occurs.

Common Programming Error 6.6

Declaring method parameters of the same type as **float x, y** *instead of* **float x, float y** *is a syntax error because types are required for each parameter in the parameter list.*

Common Programming Error 6.7

Placing a semicolon after the right parenthesis enclosing the parameter list of a method definition is a syntax error.

Common Programming Error 6.8

Redefining a method parameter as a local variable in the method is a syntax error.

Common Programming Error 6.9

Passing to a method an argument that is not compatible with the corresponding parameter's type is a syntax error.

Good Programming Practice 6.3

Although it is not incorrect to do so, do not use the same names for the arguments passed to a method and the corresponding parameters in the method definition. This helps avoid ambiguity.

The *declarations* and *statements* within braces form the *method body*. The method body is also referred to as a *block*. A block is a compound statement that includes declarations. Variables can be declared in any block and blocks can be nested. A method cannot be defined inside another method.

Common Programming Error 6.10

Defining a method inside another method is a syntax error.

Good Programming Practice 6.4

Choosing meaningful method names and meaningful parameter names makes programs more readable and helps avoid excessive use of comments.

Software Engineering Observation 6.5

A method should usually be no longer than one page. Better yet, a method should usually be no longer than half a page. Regardless of how long a method is, it should perform one task well. Small methods promote software reusability.

Testing and Debugging Tip 6.1

Small methods are easier to test, debug and understand than large ones.

Software Engineering Observation 6.6

Programs should be written as collections of small methods. This makes programs easier to write, debug, maintain and modify.

Software Engineering Observation 6.7

A method requiring a large number of parameters may be performing too many tasks. Consider dividing the method into smaller methods that perform the separate tasks. The method header should fit on one line if possible.

Software Engineering Observation 6.8

The method header and method calls must all agree in the number, type and order of parameters and arguments.

There are three ways to return control to the point at which a method was invoked. If the method does not return a result, control is returned when the method-ending right brace is reached or by executing the statement

```
return;
```

If the method does return a result, the statement

```
return expression;
```

returns the value of *expression* to the caller. When a **return** statement is executed, control returns immediately to the point at which a method was invoked.

Note that the example of Fig. 6.3 actually contains two method definitions—**init** (line 7) and **square** (line 31). Remember that the **init** method is automatically called to initialize the applet. In this example, method **init** repeatedly invokes the **square** method to perform a calculation, then displays the results in the **JTextArea** that is attached to the applet's content pane.

Notice the syntax used to invoke method **square**—we use just the method name followed by the arguments to the method in parentheses. Methods in a class definition are allowed to invoke all other methods in the same class definition using this syntax (there is an exception to this discussed in Chapter 8). Methods in the same class definition are both the methods defined in that class and the inherited methods (the methods from the class that the current class **extends—JApplet** in the last example). We have now seen three ways to call a method—a method name by itself (as shown with **square(x)** in this example), a reference to an object followed by the dot (**.**) operator and the method name (such as **g.drawLine(x1, y1, x2, y2)**) and a class name followed by a method name (such as **Integer.parseInt(stringToConvert)**). The last syntax is only for **static** methods of a class (discussed in detail in Chapter 8).

The applet in our next example (Fig. 6.4) uses a programmer-defined method called **maximum** to determine and return the largest of three floating-point values.

```
1   // Fig. 6.4: Maximum.java
2   // Finding the maximum of three doubles
3   import java.awt.Container;
4   import javax.swing.*;
5
6   public class Maximum extends JApplet {
7      public void init()
8      {
9         JTextArea outputArea = new JTextArea();
10
11        String s1 = JOptionPane.showInputDialog(
12                     "Enter first floating-point value" );
13        String s2 = JOptionPane.showInputDialog(
14                     "Enter second floating-point value" );
15        String s3 = JOptionPane.showInputDialog(
16                     "Enter third floating-point value" );
17
18        double number1 = Double.parseDouble( s1 );
19        double number2 = Double.parseDouble( s2 );
20        double number3 = Double.parseDouble( s3 );
21
22        double max = maximum( number1, number2, number3 );
23
24        outputArea.setText( "number1: " + number1 +
25                            "\nnumber2: " + number2 +
26                            "\nnumber3: " + number3 +
27                            "\nmaximum is: " + max );
28
29        // get the applet's GUI component display area
30        Container c = getContentPane();
31
32        // attach outputArea to Container c
33        c.add( outputArea );
34     }
35
36     // maximum method definition
37     public double maximum( double x, double y, double z )
38     {
39        return Math.max( x, Math.max( y, z ) );
40     }
41  }
```

Fig. 6.4   Programmer-defined **maximum** method (part 1 of 2).

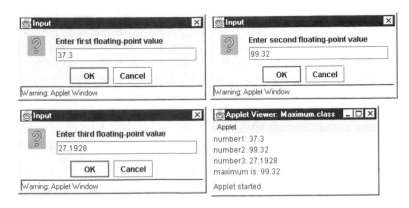

Fig. 6.4   Programmer-defined **maximum** method (part 2 of 2).

The three floating-point values are input by the user via input dialogs (lines 11 through 16 of **init**). Lines 18 through 20 use method **Double.parseDouble** to convert the **String**s input by the user to **double** values. Line 22 passes the three **double** values to method **maximum**, which determines the largest **double** value. This value is returned to method **init** by the **return** statement in method **maximum**. The value returned is assigned to the variable **max**. The three **double** values input by the user and the **max** value are concatenated and displayed in the **JTextArea** with lines 24 through 27.

Notice the implementation of the method **maximum** (line 37). The first line indicates that the method returns a **double** floating-point value, that the method's name is **maximum** and that the method takes three **double** parameters (**x**, **y** and **z**) to accomplish its task. Also, the body of the method contains the statement

```
return Math.max( x, Math.max( y, z ) );
```

which returns the largest of the three floating-point values using two calls to the **Math.max** method. First, method **Math.max** is invoked with the values of variables **y** and **z** to determine the larger of these two values. Next, the value of variable **x** and the result of the first call to **Math.max** are passed to method **Math.max**. Finally, the result of the second call to **Math.max** is returned to the point at which **maximum** was invoked (i.e., the **init** method in this program).

Another important feature of method definitions is the *coercion of arguments* (i.e., the forcing of arguments to the appropriate type to pass to a method). For example, the **Math** class method **sqrt** can be called with an integer argument even though the method is defined in the **Math** class to receive a **double** argument and the method will still work correctly. The statement

```
System.out.println( Math.sqrt( 4 ) );
```

correctly evaluates **Math.sqrt(4)** and prints the value **2**. The method definition's parameter list causes the integer value **4** to be converted to the **double** value **4.0** before the value is passed to **Math.sqrt**. In many cases, argument values that do not correspond precisely to the parameter types in the method definition are converted to the proper type before the method is called. In some cases, attempting these conversions leads to compiler errors if Java's *promotion rules* are not satisfied. The promotion rules specify how types can be converted to other types without losing data. In our **Math.sqrt** example above, an **int** is automatically converted to a **double** without changing its value. However, a **double** converted to an **int** truncates the fractional part of the **double** value. Converting large integer types to small integer types (e.g., **long** to **int**) may also result in changed values.

The promotion rules apply to expressions containing values of two or more data types (also referred to as *mixed-type expressions*) and to primitive data type values passed as arguments to methods. The type of each value in a mixed-type expression is promoted to the "highest" type in the expression (actually, a temporary version of each value is created and used for the expression—the original values remain unchanged). The type of a method argument can be promoted to any "higher" type. Figure 6.5 lists the primitive data types and the types to which each is allowed to be promoted automatically.

Converting values to lower types can result in different values. Therefore, in cases where information may be lost due to conversion, the Java compiler requires the programmer to use a cast operator to force the conversion to occur. To invoke our **square** method, which uses an integer parameter (Fig. 6.3) with the **double** variable **y**, the method call is written as **square((int) y)**. This explicitly casts (converts) the value of **y** to an integer for use in method **square**. Thus, if **y**'s value is **4.5**, method **square** returns **16**, not **20.25**.

Common Programming Error 6.11

*Converting a primitive-data-type value to another primitive data type may change the value if the new data type is not an allowed promotion (e.g., **double** to **int**). Also, converting any integral value to a floating-point value and back to an integral value may introduce rounding errors into the result.*

6.6 Java API Packages

As we have seen, Java contains many predefined classes that are grouped by directories on disk into categories of related classes called packages. Together, these packages are referred to as the Java applications programming interface (Java API).

Type	Allowed promotions
double	None
float	double
long	float or double
int	long, float or double
char	int, long, float or double
short	int, long, float or double
byte	short, int, long, float or double
boolean	None (boolean values are not considered to be numbers in Java)

Fig. 6.5   Allowed promotions for primitive data types.

Throughout the text, **import** statements are used to specify the location of classes required to compile a Java program. For example, to tell the compiler to load the **JApplet** class from the **javax.swing** package, the statement

```
import javax.swing.JApplet;
```

is used. One of the great strengths of Java is the large number of classes in the packages of the Java API that programmers can reuse rather than "reinventing the wheel." We exercise a large number of these classes in this book. Figure 6.6 lists alphabetically the packages of the Java API and provides a brief description of each package. Other packages are available for download from **http://java.sun.com**. Note that most of these packages have not been discussed. This table is provided to give you a sense of the variety of reusable components available in the Java API. When learning Java, you should spend time reading the descriptions of the packages and classes in the Java API documentation.

Package	Description
java.applet	*The Java Applet Package.* This package contains the **Applet** class and several interfaces that enable the creation of applets, interaction of applets with the browser and playing audio clips. In Java 2, class **javax.swing.JApplet** is used to define an applet that uses the *Swing GUI components.*
java.awt	*The Java Abstract Windowing Toolkit Package.* This package contains the classes and interfaces required to create and manipulate graphical user interfaces in Java 1.0 and 1.1. In Java 2, these classes can still be used, but the *Swing GUI components* of the **javax.swing** packages are often used instead.
java.awt.color	*The Java Color Space Package.* This package contains classes that support color spaces.
java.awt.datatransfer	*The Java Data Transfer Package.* This package contains classes and interfaces that enable transfer of data between a Java program and the computer's clipboard (a temporary storage area for data).
java.awt.dnd	*The Java Drag-and-Drop Package.* This package contains classes and interfaces that provide drag-and-drop support between programs.
java.awt.event	*The Java Abstract Windowing Toolkit Event Package.* This package contains classes and interfaces that enable event handling for GUI components in both the **java.awt** and **javax.swing** packages.
java.awt.font	*The Java Font Manipulation Package.* This package contains classes and interfaces for manipulating many different fonts.

Fig. 6.6   Packages of the Java API (part 1 of 4).

Package	Description
`java.awt.geom`	*The Java Two-Dimensional Objects Package.* This package contains classes for manipulating objects that represent two-dimensional graphics.
`java.awt.im`	*The Java Input Method Framework Package.* This package contains classes and an interface that support Japanese, Chinese and Korean language input into a Java program.
`java.awt.image` `java.awt.image.` `   renderable`	*The Java Image Packages.* These packages contain classes and interfaces that enable storing and manipulation of images in a program.
`java.awt.print`	*The Java Printing Package.* This package contains classes and interfaces that support printing from Java programs.
`java.beans` `java.beans.beancontext`	*The Java Beans Packages.* These packages contain classes and interfaces that enable the programmer to create reusable software components (see Chapter 25, "JavaBeans").
`java.io`	*The Java Input/Output Package.* This package contains classes that enable programs to input and output data (see Chapter 17, "Files and Streams").
`java.lang`	*The Java Language Package.* This package contains classes and interfaces required by many Java programs (many are discussed throughout the text) and is automatically imported by the compiler into all programs.
`java.lang.ref`	*The Reference Objects Package.* This package contains classes that enable interaction between a Java program and the garbage collector.
`java.lang.reflect`	*The Java Core Reflection Package.* This package contains classes and interfaces that enable a program to discover the accessible variables and methods of a class dynamically during the execution of a program.
`java.math`	*The Java Arbitrary Precision Math Package.* This package contains classes for performing arbitrary-precision arithmetic.
`java.net`	*The Java Networking Package.* This package contains classes that enable programs to communicate via networks (see Chapter 21, "Networking").
`java.rmi` `java.rmi.activation` `java.rmi.dgc` `java.rmi.registry` `java.rmi.server`	*The Java Remote Method Invocation Packages.* These packages contain classes and interfaces that enable the programmer to create distributed Java programs. Using remote method invocation, a program can call a method of a separate program on the same computer or on a computer anywhere on the Internet (see Chapter 20, "Remote Method Invocation").

Fig. 6.6   Packages of the Java API (part 2 of 4).

Package	Description

`java.security`
`java.security.acl`
`java.security.cert`
`java.security.interfaces`
`java.security.spec`
	The Java Security Packages.
	These packages contains classes and interfaces that enable a Java program to encrypt data and control the access privileges provided to a Java program for security purposes.

`java.sql`	*The Java Database Connectivity Package.* This package contain classes and interfaces that enable a Java program to interact with a database (see Chapter 18, "JDBC").
`java.text`	*The Java Text Package.* This package contains classes and interfaces that enable a Java program to manipulate numbers, dates, characters and strings. This package provides many of Java's internationalization capabilities—features that enable a program to be customized to a specific locale (e.g., an applet may display strings in different languages based on the browser in which it is executing).
`java.util`	*The Java Utilities Package.* This package contains utility classes and interfaces such as: date and time manipulations, random number processing capabilities (**Random**), storing and processing large amounts of data, breaking strings into smaller pieces called tokens (**StringTokenizer**) and other capabilities (see Chapter 22, "Data Structures", Chapter 23, "Java Utilities Package and Bit Manipulation", and Chapter 24, "The Collections API").
`java.util.jar` `java.util.zip`	*The Java Utilities JAR and ZIP Packages.* These packages contain utility classes and interfaces that enable a Java program to combine Java **.class** files and other resource files (such as images and audio) into compressed file called *Java archive (JAR) files* or *ZIP files*.
`javax.accessibility`	*The Java Accessibility Package.* This package contains classes and interfaces that allow a Java program to support technologies for people with disabilities; examples are screen readers and screen magnifiers.
`javax.swing`	*The Java Swing GUI Components Package.* This package contains classes and interfaces for Java's Swing GUI components that provide support for portable GUIs.
`javax.swing.border`	*The Java Swing Borders Package.* This package contains classes and an interface for drawing borders around areas in a GUI.
`javax.swing.colorchooser`	*The Java Swing Color Chooser Package.* This package contains classes and interfaces for the **JColorChooser** predefined dialog for choosing colors.

Fig. 6.6   Packages of the Java API (part 3 of 4).

Package	Description
`javax.swing.event`	*The Java Swing Event Package.* This package contains classes and interfaces that enable event handling for GUI components in the `javax.swing` package.
`javax.swing.` `filechooser`	*The Java Swing File Chooser Package.* This package contains classes and interfaces for the `JFile-Chooser` predefined dialog for locating files on disk.
`javax.swing.plaf` `javax.swing.plaf.basic` `javax.swing.plaf.metal` `javax.swing.plaf.multi`	*The Java Swing Pluggable-Look-and-Feel Packages.* These packages contain classes and an interface used to change the look-and-feel of a Swing-based GUI between the Java look-and-feel, Microsoft Windows look-and-feel and the UNIX Motif look-and-feel. The package also supports development of a customized look-and-feel for a Java program.
`javax.swing.table`	*The Java Swing Table Package.* This package contains classes and interfaces for creating and manipulating spreadsheet-like tables.
`javax.swing.text`	*The Java Swing Text Package.* This package contains classes and interfaces to manipulate text-based GUI components in Swing.
`javax.swing.text.html` `javax.swing.text.html.` `parser`	*The Java Swing HTML Text Packages.* These packages contain classes that provide support for building HTML text editors.
`javax.swing.text.rtf`	*The Java Swing RTF Text Package.* This package contains a class that provides support for building editors that support rich-text formatting.
`javax.swing.tree`	*The Java Swing Tree Package.* This package contains classes and interfaces for creating and manipulating expanding tree GUI components.
`javax.swing.undo`	*The Java Swing Undo Package.* This package contains classes and interfaces that support providing undo and redo capabilities in a Java program.
`org.omg.CORBA` `org.omg.CORBA.` `DynAnyPackage` `org.omg.CORBA.` `ORBPackage` `org.omg.CORBA.` `portable` `org.omg.CORBA.` `TypeCodePackage` `org.omg.CosNaming` `org.omg.CosNaming.` `NamingContextPackage`	*The Object Management Group (OMG) CORBA Packages.* These packages contain classes and interfaces that implement OMG's CORBA APIs that allow a Java program to communicate with programs written in other programming languages in a similar fashion to using Java's RMI packages to communicate between Java programs.

Fig. 6.6   Packages of the Java API (part 4 of 4).

6.7 Random Number Generation

We now take a brief and, it is hoped, entertaining diversion into a popular programming application, namely simulation and game playing. In this section and the next section, we will develop a nicely structured game-playing program that includes multiple methods. The program uses most of the control structures we have studied.

There is something in the air of a gambling casino that invigorates people, from the high-rollers at the plush mahogany-and-felt craps tables to the quarter-poppers at the one-armed bandits. It is the *element of chance,* the possibility that luck will convert a pocketful of money into a mountain of wealth. The element of chance can be introduced through the *random* method from the **Math** class.

Consider the following statement:

```
double randomValue = Math.random();
```

The **random** method generates a **double** value from 0.0 up to (but not including) 1.0. If **random** truly produces values at random, every value from 0.0 up to (but not including) 1.0 has an equal *chance* (or *probability*) of being chosen each time **random** is called.

The range of values produced directly by **random** is often different than what is needed in a specific application. For example, a program that simulates coin tossing might require only 0 for "heads" and 1 for "tails." A program that simulates rolling a six-sided die would require random integers in the range 1 to 6. A program that randomly predicts the next type of spaceship (out of four possibilities) that will fly across the horizon in a video game would require random integers in the range 1 through 4.

To demonstrate **random**, let us develop a program that simulates 20 rolls of a six-sided die and print the value of each roll. We use the multiplication operator (*****) in conjunction with **random** as follows:

```
(int) ( Math.random() * 6 )
```

to produce integers in the range 0 to 5. This is called *scaling.* The number 6 is called the *scaling factor.* The integer cast operator is used to truncate the floating-point part (the part after the decimal point) of each value produced by the preceding expression. We then *shift* the range of numbers produced by adding 1 to our previous result, as in

```
1 + (int) ( Math.random() * 6 )
```

Figure 6.7 confirms that the results are in the range 1 to 6.

```
1   // Fig. 6.7: RandomInt.java
2   // Shifted, scaled random integers
3   import javax.swing.JOptionPane;
4
5   public class RandomInt {
6      public static void main( String args[] )
7      {
8         int value;
9         String output = "";
```

Fig. 6.7 Shifted and scaled random integers (part 1 of 2).

```
10
11          for ( int i = 1; i <= 20; i++ ) {
12             value = 1 + (int) ( Math.random() * 6 );
13             output += value + "  ";
14
15             if ( i % 5 == 0 )
16                output += "\n";
17          }
18
19          JOptionPane.showMessageDialog( null, output,
20             "20 Random Numbers from 1 to 6",
21             JOptionPane.INFORMATION_MESSAGE );
22
23          System.exit( 0 );
24       }
25    }
```

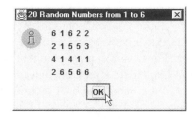

Fig. 6.7   Shifted and scaled random integers (part 2 of 2).

To show that these numbers occur approximately with equal likelihood, let us simulate 6000 rolls of a die with the program of Fig. 6.8. Each integer from 1 to 6 should appear approximately 1000 times.

```
1    // Fig. 6.8: RollDie.java
2    // Roll a six-sided die 6000 times
3    import javax.swing.*;
4
5    public class RollDie {
6       public static void main( String args[] )
7       {
8          int frequency1 = 0, frequency2 = 0,
9              frequency3 = 0, frequency4 = 0,
10             frequency5 = 0, frequency6 = 0, face;
11
12          // summarize results
13          for ( int roll = 1; roll <= 6000; roll++ ) {
14             face = 1 + (int) ( Math.random() * 6 );
15
16             switch ( face ) {
17                case 1:
18                   ++frequency1;
19                   break;
```

Fig. 6.8   Rolling a six-sided die 6000 times (part 1 of 2).

```
20                 case 2:
21                     ++frequency2;
22                     break;
23                 case 3:
24                     ++frequency3;
25                     break;
26                 case 4:
27                     ++frequency4;
28                     break;
29                 case 5:
30                     ++frequency5;
31                     break;
32                 case 6:
33                     ++frequency6;
34                     break;
35             }
36         }
37
38         JTextArea outputArea = new JTextArea( 7, 10 );
39
40         outputArea.setText(
41             "Face\tFrequency" +
42             "\n1\t" + frequency1 +
43             "\n2\t" + frequency2 +
44             "\n3\t" + frequency3 +
45             "\n4\t" + frequency4 +
46             "\n5\t" + frequency5 +
47             "\n6\t" + frequency6 );
48
49         JOptionPane.showMessageDialog( null, outputArea,
50             "Rolling a Die 6000 Times",
51             JOptionPane.INFORMATION_MESSAGE );
52         System.exit( 0 );
53     }
54 }
```

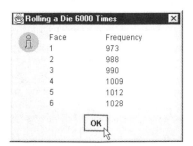

Fig. 6.8   Rolling a six-sided die 6000 times (part 2 of 2).

As the program output shows, by scaling and shifting we have utilized the **random** method to realistically simulate the rolling of a six-sided die. Note that we used nested control structures to determine the number of times each side of the six-sided die occurred. The **for** loop at line 13 iterates 6000 times. During each iteration of the loop, line 14 produces a value from 1 to 6. The nested **switch** structure at line 16 uses the **face** value that was randomly chosen as its controlling expression. Based on the value of **face**, one of the six counter variables is incremented during each iteration of the loop. Note that *no* **default** case is provided in the **switch** structure. After we study arrays in Chapter 7, we will show how to replace the entire **switch** structure in this program with a single-line statement. Run the program several times and observe the results. Notice that a *different* sequence of random numbers is obtained each time the program is executed, so the program results should vary.

The values produced directly by **random** are always in the range

```
0.0 ≤ Math.random() < 1.0
```

Previously we demonstrated how to write a single statement to simulate the rolling of a six-sided die with the statement

```
face = 1 + (int) ( Math.random() * 6 );
```

which always assigns an integer (at random) to variable **face** in the range $1 \leq$ **face** ≤ 6. Note that the width of this range (i.e., the number of consecutive integers in the range) is 6 and the starting number in the range is 1. Referring to the preceding statement, we see that the width of the range is determined by the number used to scale **random** with the multiplication operator (i.e., 6) and the starting number of the range is equal to the number (i.e., 1) added to **(int) (Math.random() * 6)**. We can generalize this result as follows:

```
n = a + (int) ( Math.random() * b );
```

where **a** is the *shifting value* (which is equal to the first number in the desired range of consecutive integers) and **b** is the *scaling factor* (which is equal to the width of the desired range of consecutive integers). In the exercises, we will see that it is possible to choose integers at random from sets of values other than ranges of consecutive integers.

6.8 Example: A Game of Chance

One of the most popular games of chance is a dice game known as "craps," which is played in casinos and back alleys throughout the world. The rules of the game are straightforward:

A player rolls two dice. Each die has six faces. These faces contain 1, 2, 3, 4, 5 and 6 spots, respectively. After the dice have come to rest, the sum of the spots on the two upward faces is calculated. If the sum is 7 or 11 on the first throw, the player wins. If the sum is 2, 3 or 12 on the first throw (called "craps"), the player loses (i.e., the "house" wins). If the sum is 4, 5, 6, 8, 9 or 10 on the first throw, that sum becomes the player's "point." To win, you must continue rolling the dice until you "make your point" (i.e., roll your point value). The player loses by rolling a 7 before making the point.

The applet in Fig. 6.9 simulates the game of craps.

Notice that the player must roll two dice on the first and all subsequent rolls. When you execute the applet, click the **Roll Dice** button to play the game. The lower-left corner of the **appletviewer** window displays the results of each roll. The screen captures show four separate executions of the applet (a win and a loss on the first roll, and a win and a loss after the first roll).

```
1    // Fig. 6.9: Craps.java
2    // Craps
3    import java.awt.*;
4    import java.awt.event.*;
5    import javax.swing.*;
6
7    public class Craps extends JApplet implements ActionListener {
8       // constant variables for status of game
9       final int WON = 0, LOST = 1, CONTINUE = 2;
10
11      // other variables used in program
12      boolean firstRoll = true;    // true if first roll
13      int sumOfDice = 0;           // sum of the dice
14      int myPoint = 0;    // point if no win/loss on first roll
15      int gameStatus = CONTINUE;   // game not over yet
16
17      // graphical user interface components
18      JLabel die1Label, die2Label, sumLabel, pointLabel;
19      JTextField firstDie, secondDie, sum, point;
20      JButton roll;
21
22      // setup graphical user interface components
23      public void init()
24      {
25         Container c = getContentPane();
26         c.setLayout( new FlowLayout() );
27
28         die1Label = new JLabel( "Die 1" );
29         c.add( die1Label );
30         firstDie = new JTextField( 10 );
31         firstDie.setEditable( false );
32         c.add( firstDie );
33
34         die2Label = new JLabel( "Die 2" );
35         c.add( die2Label );
36         secondDie = new JTextField( 10 );
37         secondDie.setEditable( false );
38         c.add( secondDie );
39
40         sumLabel = new JLabel( "Sum is" );
41         c.add( sumLabel );
42         sum = new JTextField( 10 );
43         sum.setEditable( false );
44         c.add( sum );
45
46         pointLabel = new JLabel( "Point is" );
47         c.add( pointLabel );
48         point = new JTextField( 10 );
49         point.setEditable( false );
50         c.add( point );
51
52         roll = new JButton( "Roll Dice" );
53         roll.addActionListener( this );
```

Fig. 6.9   Program to simulate the game of craps (part 1 of 3).

```
54          c.add( roll );
55      }
56
57      // call method play when button is pressed
58      public void actionPerformed( ActionEvent e )
59      {
60          play();
61      }
62
63      // process one roll of the dice
64      public void play()
65      {
66          if ( firstRoll ) {               // first roll of the dice
67              sumOfDice = rollDice();
68
69              switch ( sumOfDice ) {
70                  case 7: case 11:         // win on first roll
71                      gameStatus = WON;
72                      point.setText( "" );  // clear point text field
73                      break;
74                  case 2: case 3: case 12: // lose on first roll
75                      gameStatus = LOST;
76                      point.setText( "" );  // clear point text field
77                      break;
78                  default:                  // remember point
79                      gameStatus = CONTINUE;
80                      myPoint = sumOfDice;
81                      point.setText( Integer.toString( myPoint ) );
82                      firstRoll = false;
83                      break;
84              }
85          }
86          else {
87              sumOfDice = rollDice();
88
89              if ( sumOfDice == myPoint )    // win by making point
90                  gameStatus = WON;
91              else
92                  if ( sumOfDice == 7 )       // lose by rolling 7
93                      gameStatus = LOST;
94          }
95
96          if ( gameStatus == CONTINUE )
97              showStatus( "Roll again." );
98          else {
99              if ( gameStatus == WON )
100                 showStatus( "Player wins. " +
101                     "Click Roll Dice to play again." );
102             else
103                 showStatus( "Player loses. " +
104                     "Click Roll Dice to play again." );
105
```

Fig. 6.9   Program to simulate the game of craps (part 2 of 3).

```
106              firstRoll = true;
107          }
108      }
109
110      // roll the dice
111      public int rollDice()
112      {
113          int die1, die2, workSum;
114
115          die1 = 1 + ( int ) ( Math.random() * 6 );
116          die2 = 1 + ( int ) ( Math.random() * 6 );
117          workSum = die1 + die2;
118
119          firstDie.setText( Integer.toString( die1 ) );
120          secondDie.setText( Integer.toString( die2 ) );
121          sum.setText( Integer.toString( workSum ) );
122
123          return workSum;
124      }
125  }
```

A **JLabel** object   A **JTextField**   A **JButton** object

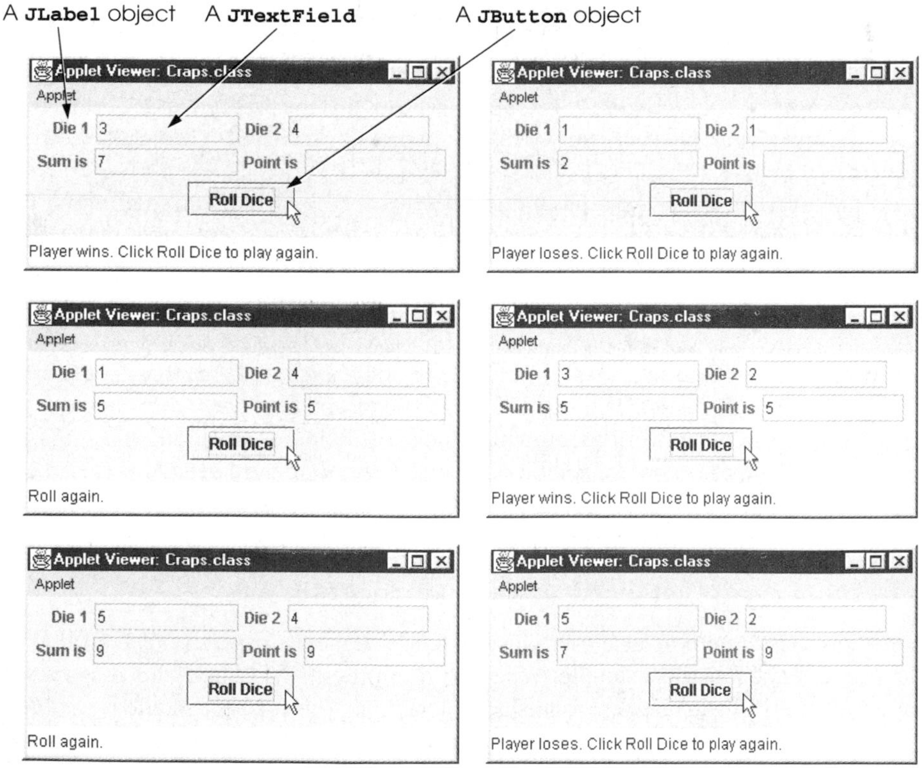

Fig. 6.9   Program to simulate the game of craps (part 3 of 3).

Until now, all user interactions with applications and applets have been through either an input dialog (in which the user could type an input value for the program) or a message dialog (in which a message was displayed to the user and the user could click **OK** to dismiss the dialog). Although these are valid ways to receive input from a user and display output in a Java program, they are fairly limited in their capabilities—an input dialog can obtain only one value at a time from the user and a message dialog can display only one message. It is much more common to receive multiple inputs from the user at once (such as the user entering name and address information) or display many pieces of data at once (such as the values of the dice, the sum of the dice and the point in this example). To begin our introduction to more elaborate user interfaces, this program illustrates two new graphical user interface concepts—attaching several GUI components to an applet and graphical user interface *event handling*.

Lines 3 through 5

```
import java.awt.*;
import java.awt.event.*;
import javax.swing.*;
```

specify to the compiler where to locate the classes used in this applet. The first **import** specifies that the program uses classes from package **java.awt** (specifically, classes **Container** and **FlowLayout**). The second **import** specifies that the program uses classes from package **java.awt.event**. This package contains many data types that enable a program to process a user's interactions with a program's GUI. In this program, we use the **ActionListener** and **ActionEvent** data types from package **java.awt.event**. The last **import** statement specifies that the program uses classes from package **javax.swing** (specifically, classes **JApplet**, **JLabel**, **JTextField** and **JButton**).

As stated earlier, every Java program is based on at least one class definition that extends and enhances an existing class definition via inheritance. Remember that applets inherit from class **JApplet**. Line 7

public class Craps extends JApplet implements ActionListener

indicates that class **Craps** inherits from **JApplet** and *implements* ***ActionListener***. A class can inherit existing attributes and behaviors (data and methods) from another class specified to the right of keyword **extends** in the class definition. In addition, a class can implement one or more *interfaces*. An interface specifies one or more behaviors (i.e., methods) *that you must define* in your class definition. The interface **ActionListener** specifies that this class *must define a method* with the first line

public void actionPerformed(ActionEvent e)

This method's task is to process a user's interaction with the **JButton** (called **Roll Dice** on the user interface) in this example. When the user presses the button, this method will be called automatically in response to the user interaction. This process is called *event handling*. The *event* is the user interaction (pressing the button). The *event handler* is the **actionPerformed** method, which is called automatically in response to the event. We discuss the details of this interaction and method **actionPerformed** shortly. Chapter 9, "Object-Oriented Programming," discusses interfaces in detail. For now, mimic the features we illustrate that support event handling of the GUI components we present.

The game is reasonably involved. The player may win or lose on the first roll, or may win or lose on any roll. Line 9 of the program

```
final int WON = 0, LOST = 1, CONTINUE = 2;
```

creates variables that define the three states of a game of craps—game won, game lost or continue rolling the dice. Keyword ***final*** at the beginning of the declaration indicates that these are *constant variables*. Constant variables must be initialized once only before they are used and cannot be modified thereafter. Constant variables are often called *named constants* or *read-only variables*. Keyword **final** is discussed in detail in Chapters 7 and 8.

Common Programming Error 6.12

*After a **final** variable has been initialized, attempting to assign another value to that variable is a syntax error.*

Good Programming Practice 6.5

*Use only uppercase letters (with underscores between words) in the names of **final** variables. This makes these constants stand out in a program.*

Good Programming Practice 6.6

*Using meaningfully named **final** variables rather than integer constants (such as 2) makes programs more readable.*

Lines 12 through 15

```
boolean firstRoll = true;   // true if first roll
int sumOfDice = 0;          // sum of the dice
int myPoint = 0;    // point if no win/loss on first roll
int gameStatus = CONTINUE;  // game not over yet
```

declare several instance variables that are used throughout the **Craps** applet. Variable **firstRoll** indicates if the next roll of the dice is the first roll in the current game. Variable **sumOfDice** maintains the sum of the dice for the last roll. Variable **myPoint** stores the "point" if the player does not win or lose on the first roll. Variable **gameStatus** keeps track of the current state of the game (**WON**, **LOST** or **CONTINUE**).

Lines 18 through 20

```
JLabel die1Label, die2Label, sumLabel, pointLabel;
JTextField firstDie, secondDie, sum, point;
JButton roll;
```

declare references to the GUI components used in this applet's graphical user interface. References **die1Label**, **die2Label**, **sumLabel** and **pointLabel** all refer to *JLabel* objects. A **JLabel** contains a string of characters to display on the screen. Normally, a **JLabel** indicates the purpose of another graphical user interface element on the screen. In the screen captures of Fig. 6.9, the **JLabel** objects are the text to the left of each rectangle in the first two rows of the user interface. References **firstDie**, **secondDie**, **sum** and **point** all refer to *JTextField* objects. **JTextField**s are used to get a single line of information from the user at the keyboard or to display information on the screen. In the screen captures of Fig. 6.9, the **JTextField** objects are the rectangles to the right of each **JLabel** in the first two rows of the user interface. Reference **roll** refers to a *JButton* object. When the user presses a **JButton**, normally the program responds by performing a task (rolling the dice in this example). The **JButton** object is the rectangle containing the words **Roll Dice** at the bottom of the user interface in Fig. 6.9. We have already used **JTextField**s and **JButton**s in prior examples. Every message dialog and every input dialog contained an **OK** button to dismiss the message dialog or send the user's input to the program. Every input dialog also contained a **JTextField** in which the user typed an input value.

Method **init** (line 23) creates the GUI component objects and attaches them to the user interface. Line 25

```
Container c = getContentPane();
```

declares **Container** reference **c** and assigns it the result of a call to method **getContentPane**. Remember, method **getContentPane** returns a reference to the applet's content pane that can be used to attach GUI components to the user interface of the applet.

Line 26

```
c.setLayout( new FlowLayout() );
```

uses **Container** method **setLayout** to define the *layout manager* for the applet's user interface. Layout managers are provided to arrange GUI components on a **Container** for presentation purposes. The layout managers determine the position and size of every GUI component attached to the container. This enables the programmer to concentrate on the basic "look and feel" and lets the layout managers process most of the layout details.

FlowLayout is the most basic layout manager. GUI components are placed on a **Container** from left to right in the order in which they are attached to the **Container** with method **add**. When the edge of the container is reached, components are continued on the next line. The preceding statement creates a new object of class **FlowLayout** and passes it immediately to method **setLayout**. Normally, the layout is set before any GUI components are added to a **Container**.

[*Note:* Each **Container** can have only one layout manager at a time (separate **Container**s in the same program can have different layout managers). Most Java programming environments provide GUI design tools that help a programmer graphically design a GUI, then automatically write Java code to create the GUI. Some of these GUI designers also allow the programmer to use the layout managers. Chapters 12 and 13 discuss several layout managers that allow more precise control over the layout of the GUI components.]

Lines 28 through 32, 34 through 38, 40 through 44 and 46 through 50 each create a **JLabel** and **JTextField** pair and attach them to the user interface. Because these lines are all quite similar, we concentrate on lines 28 through 32.

```
die1Label = new JLabel( "Die 1" );
c.add( die1Label );
firstDie = new JTextField( 10 );
firstDie.setEditable( false );
c.add( firstDie );
```

Line 28 creates a new **JLabel** object, initializes it with the string **"Die 1"** and assigns the object to reference **die1Label**. This labels the corresponding **JTextField** **firstDie** in the user interface so the user can determine the purpose of the value displayed in **firstDie**. Line 29 attaches the **JLabel** to which **die1Label** refers to the applet's content pane. Line 30 creates a new **JTextField** object, initializes it to be **10** characters wide and assigns the object to reference **firstDie**. This **JTextField** will display the value of the first die after each roll of the dice. Line 31 uses **JTextField** method **setEditable** with the argument **false** to indicate that the user should not be able to type in the **JTextField** (i.e., make the **JTextField** *uneditable*). An uneditable **JTextField** has a gray background by default. An editable **JTextField** has a white background by default (as seen in input dialogs). Line 32 attaches the **JTextField** to which **firstDie** refers to the applet's content pane.

Line 52

```
roll = new JButton( "Roll Dice" );
```

creates a new **JButton** object, initializes it with the string **"Roll Dice"** (this string will appear on the button) and assigns the object to reference **roll**.

Line 53

```
roll.addActionListener( this );
```

specifies that ***this*** applet should *listen* for events from the **JButton roll**. The **this** keyword enables the applet to refer to itself (we discuss **this** in detail in Chapter 8). When the user interacts with a GUI component an *event* is sent to the applet. GUI events are messages indicating that the user of the program interacted with one of the program's GUI components. For example, when you press **JButton roll** in this program, an event is sent to the applet indicating that the user pressed the button. This indicates to the applet that *an action was performed* by the user on the **JButton** and automatically calls method **actionPerformed** to process the user's interaction.

This style of programming is known as *event-driven programming*—the user interacts with a GUI component, the program is notified of the event and the program processes the event. The user's interaction with the GUI "drives" the program. The methods that are called when an event occurs are also known as *event handling methods*. When a GUI event occurs in a program, Java creates an object containing information about the event that occurred and *automatically calls* an appropriate event handling method. Before any event can be processed, each GUI component must know which object in the program defines the event handling method that will be called when an event occurs. In line 53, **JButton** method ***addActionListener*** is used to tell **roll** that the applet (**this**) can *listen* for *action events* and defines method **actionPerformed**. This is called *registering the event handler* with the GUI component (we also like to call it the *start listening* line because the applet is now listening for events from the button). To respond to an action event, we must define a class that **implements ActionListener** (this requires that the class also define method **actionPerformed**) and we must register the event handler with the GUI component. Finally, the last line in **init** attaches the **JButton** to which **roll** refers to the applet's content pane, thus completing the user interface.

Method **actionPerformed** (line 58) is one of several methods that process interactions between the user and GUI components. The first line of the method

```
public void actionPerformed( ActionEvent e )
```

indicates that **actionPerformed** is a **public** method that returns nothing (**void**) when it completes its task. Method **actionPerformed** receives one argument—an **ActionEvent**—when it is called automatically in response to an action performed on a GUI component by the user (in this case pressing the **JButton**). The **ActionEvent** argument contains information about the action that occurred.

We define a method **rollDice** (line 111) to roll the dice and compute and display their sum. Method **rollDice** is defined once, but it is called from two places in the program (lines 67 and 87). Method **rollDice** takes no arguments, so it has an empty parameter list. Method **rollDice** returns the sum of the two dice, so a return type of **int** is indicated in the method header.

The user clicks the "**Roll Dice**" button to roll the dice. This invokes method **actionPerformed** (line 58) of the applet, which then invokes method **play** (defined at line 64). Method **play** checks the **boolean** variable **firstRoll** (line 66) to determine if it is **true** or **false**. If it is **true**, this is the first roll of the game. Line 67 calls **rollDice** (defined at line 111), which picks two random values from 1 to 6, displays the value of the first die, second die and the sum of the dice in the first three **JTextField**s, and returns the sum of the dice. Note that the integer values are converted to **String**s with **static** method **Integer.toString** because **JTextField**s can only display **String**s. After the first roll, the nested **switch** structure at line 69 determines if the game is won or lost, or if the game should continue with another roll. After the first roll, if the game is not over, **sum** is saved in **myPoint** and displayed in **JTextField point**.

The program proceeds to the nested **if/else** structure at line 96, which uses applet method *showStatus* to display in the **appletviewer** status bar

        Roll again.

if **gameStatus** is equal to **CONTINUE** and

        Player wins. Click Roll Dice to play again.

if **gameStatus** is equal to **WON** and

        Player loses. Click Roll Dice to play again.

if **gameStatus** is equal to **LOST**. Method **showStatus** receives a **String** argument and displays it in the status bar of the **appletviewer** or browser. If the game was won or lost, line 106 sets **firstRoll** to **true** to indicate that the next roll of the dice is the first roll of the next game.

The program then waits for the user to click button "**Roll Dice**" again. Each time the user presses **Roll Dice**, method **actionPerformed** invokes method **play** and method **rollDice** is called to produce a new **sum**. If **sum** matches **myPoint**, **gameStatus** is set to **WON**, the **if/else** structure at line 96 executes and the game is complete. If **sum** is equal to **7**, **gameStatus** is set to **LOST**, **if/else** structure at line 96 executes and the game is complete. Clicking the "**Roll Dice**" button starts a new game. Throughout the program, the four **JTextField**s are updated with the new values of the dice and the sum on each roll, and the **JTextField point** is updated each time a new game is started.

Note the interesting use of the various program control mechanisms we have discussed. The craps program uses four methods—**init**, **actionPerformed**, **play** and **rollDice**—and the **switch**, **if/else** and nested **if** structures. Note also the use of multiple **case** labels in the **switch** structure to execute the same statements (lines 70 and 74). In the exercises, we investigate various interesting characteristics of the game of craps.

6.9 Duration of Identifiers

Chapters 2 through 5 used identifiers for variable names and reference names. The attributes of variables and references include name, type, size and value. We also use identifiers as names for user-defined methods and classes. Actually, each identifier in a program has other attributes, including *duration* and *scope*.

An identifier's *duration* (also called its *lifetime*) is the period during which that identifier exists in memory. Some identifiers exist briefly, some are repeatedly created and destroyed and others exist for the entire execution of a program.

An identifier's *scope* is where the identifier can be referenced in a program. Some identifiers can be referenced throughout a program, while others can be referenced from only limited portions of a program. This section discusses duration of identifiers. Section 6.10 discusses the scope of identifiers.

Identifiers that represent local variables in a method (i.e., parameters and variables declared in the method body) have *automatic duration*. Automatic duration variables are created when program control reaches their declaration, they exist while the block in which they are declared is active and they are destroyed when the block in which they are declared is exited. For the remainder of the text, we will refer to variables of automatic duration as automatic variables or local variables.

Software Engineering Observation 6.9

Automatic duration is a means of conserving memory because automatic duration variables are created when program control reaches their declaration and are destroyed when the block in which they are declared is exited.

The instance variables of a class are automatically initialized by the compiler if the programmer does not provide initial values. Variables of the primitive data types are initialized to zero, except boolean variables, which are initialized to **false**. References are initialized to **null**. Unlike instance variables of a class, automatic variables must be initialized by the programmer before they can be used.

Testing and Debugging Tip 6.2

Automatic variables must be initialized before they are used in a method; otherwise, the compiler issues an error message.

Java also has identifiers of *static duration*. Variables and references of static duration exist from the point at which the class that defines them is loaded into memory for execution until the program terminates. Their storage is allocated and initialized when their classes are loaded into memory. Even though the static duration variable and reference names exist when their classes are loaded into memory, this does not mean that these identifiers can be used throughout the program. Duration and scope (where a name can be used) are separate issues, as shown in Section 6.10.

6.10 Scope Rules

The *scope* of an identifier for a variable, reference or method is the portion of the program in which the identifier can be referenced. A local variable or reference declared in a block can be used only in that block or in blocks nested within that block. The scopes for an identifier are *class scope* and *block scope*. There is also a special scope—*method scope*—for labels used with the **break** and **continue** statements (introduced in Chapter 5, "Control Structures: Part 2"). A label is visible only in the method in which it is used.

Methods and instance variables of a class have *class scope*. Class scope begins at the opening left brace, **{**, of the class definition and terminates at the closing right brace, **}**, of the class definition. Class scope enables methods of a class to directly invoke all methods defined in that same class or inherited into that class (such as the methods inherited into our applets from class **JApplet**) and to directly access all instance variables defined in the class. In Chapter 8, we will see that **static** methods are an exception to this rule. In a sense, all instance variables and methods of a class are *global* to the methods of the class in which they are defined (i.e., the methods can modify the instance variables directly and invoke other methods of the class). [*Note:* One of the reasons we use mainly applets in this chapter is to simplify our discussions. We have not as yet introduced a true windowed application in which the methods of our application class will have access to all the other methods of the class and the instance variables of the class.]

Identifiers declared inside a block have *block scope*. Block scope begins at the identifier's declaration and ends at the terminating right brace (**}**) of the block. Local variables of a method have block scope as do method parameters, which are also local variables of the method. Any block may contain variable or reference declarations. When blocks are nested in a method's body and an identifier declared in an outer block has the same name as an identifier declared in an inner block, the compiler generates a syntax error stating that the variable is already defined. If a local variable in a method has the same name as an instance variable, the instance variable is "hidden" until the block terminates execution. In Chapter 8, we discuss how to access such "hidden" instance variables.

Common Programming Error 6.13

Accidentally using the same name for an identifier in an inner block of a method as is used for an identifier in an outer block of the same method results in a syntax error from the compiler.

Good Programming Practice 6.7

Avoid local variable names that hide instance variable names. This can be accomplished by avoiding the use of duplicate identifiers in a class.

Software Engineering Observation 6.10

Automatic duration is an example of the principle of least privilege. *This principle states that each component of a system should have sufficient rights and privileges to accomplish its designated task, but no additional rights or privileges. This helps prevent accidental and/or malicious errors from occurring in systems. Why have variables stored in memory and accessible when they are not needed?*

The applet of Fig. 6.10 demonstrates scoping issues with instance variables and local variables. This example uses the applet's **start** method (line 17) for the first time. Remember, when the **appletviewer** loads an applet, first it creates an instance of the applet, then it calls the applet's **init**, **start** and **paint** methods. Method **start** is always defined with the first line

```
public void start()
```

```java
1    // Fig. 6.10: Scoping.java
2    // A scoping example
3    import java.awt.Container;
4    import javax.swing.*;
5
6    public class Scoping extends JApplet {
7       JTextArea outputArea;
8       int x = 1;        // instance variable
9
10      public void init()
11      {
12         outputArea = new JTextArea();
13         Container c = getContentPane();
14         c.add( outputArea );
15      }
16
17      public void start()
18      {
19         int x = 5;    // variable local to method start
20
21         outputArea.append( "local x in start is " + x );
22
23         methodA();    // methodA has automatic local x
24         methodB();    // methodB uses instance variable x
25         methodA();    // methodA reinitializes automatic local x
26         methodB();    // instance variable x retains its value
27
28         outputArea.append( "\n\nlocal x in start is " + x );
29      }
30
31      public void methodA()
32      {
33         int x = 25;   // initialized each time a is called
34
35         outputArea.append( "\n\nlocal x in methodA is " + x +
36                            " after entering methodA" );
37         ++x;
38         outputArea.append( "\nlocal x in methodA is " + x +
39                            " before exiting methodA" );
40      }
41
42      public void methodB()
43      {
44         outputArea.append( "\n\ninstance variable x is " + x +
45                            " on entering methodB" );
46         x *= 10;
47         outputArea.append( "\ninstance variable x is " + x +
48                            " on exiting methodB" );
49      }
50   }
```

Fig. 6.10 A scoping example (part 1 of 2).

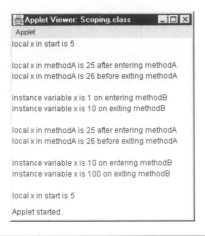

Fig. 6.10   A scoping example (part 2 of 2).

Instance variable **x** (line 8) is declared and initialized to 1. This instance variable is hidden in any block (or method) that declares a variable named **x**. Method **start** declares a local variable **x** (line 19) and initializes it to **5**. This variable is displayed in the **JText-Area outputArea** to show that the instance variable **x** is hidden in **start**. The program defines two other methods—**methodA** and **methodB**—that each take no arguments and return nothing. Each method is called twice from method **start**. Method **methodA** defines automatic variable **x** (line 33) and initializes it to **25**. When **methodA** is called, the variable is displayed in **outputArea**, incremented and displayed again before exiting the method. Each time this method is called, automatic variable **x** is recreated and initialized to **25**. Method **methodB** does not declare any variables. Therefore, when it refers to variable **x**, the instance variable **x** is used. When **methodB** is called, the instance variable is displayed in **outputArea**, multiplied by **10** and displayed again before exiting the method. The next time method **methodB** is called, the instance variable has its modified value, **10**. Finally, the program displays the local variable **x** in **start** again to show that none of the method calls modified the value of **x** because the methods all referred to variables in other scopes.

6.11 Recursion

The programs we have discussed are generally structured as methods that call one another in a disciplined, hierarchical manner. For some problems, it is useful to have methods call themselves. A *recursive method* is a method that calls itself either directly or indirectly through another method. Recursion is an important topic discussed at length in upper-level computer science courses. In this section and the next, simple examples of recursion are presented. This book contains an extensive treatment of recursion. Figure 6.15 (at the end of Section 6.13) summarizes the recursion examples and exercises in the book.

We consider recursion conceptually first, then examine several programs containing recursive methods. Recursive problem-solving approaches have a number of elements in common. A recursive method is called to solve a problem. The method actually knows how to solve only the simplest case(s) or so-called *base case(s)*. If the method is called with a base case, the method returns a result. If the method is called with a more complex problem, the method divides the problem into two conceptual pieces: a piece that the method knows how to do (base case) and a piece that the method does not know how to do. To make recursion feasible, the latter piece must resemble the original problem, but be a slightly simpler or slightly smaller version of the original problem. Because this new problem looks like the original problem, the method invokes (calls) a fresh copy of itself to go to work on the smaller problem—this is referred to as a *recursive call* and is also called the *recursion step*. The recursion step also normally includes the keyword **return** because its result will be combined with the portion of the problem the method knew how to solve to form a result that will be passed back to the original caller.

The recursion step executes while the original call to the method is still open (i.e., it has not finished executing). The recursion step can result in many more recursive calls, as the method divides each new subproblem into two conceptual pieces. For the recursion to eventually terminate, each time the method calls itself with a slightly simpler version of the original problem, the sequence of smaller and smaller problems must converge on the base case. At that point, the method recognizes the base case, returns a result to the previous copy of the method and a sequence of returns ensues up the line until the original method call eventually returns the final result to the caller. This sounds exotic compared to the conventional problem solving we performed to this point. As an example of these concepts at work, let us write a recursive program to perform a popular mathematical calculation.

The factorial of a nonnegative integer *n,* written *n!* (and pronounced "*n* factorial"), is the product

$$n \cdot (n - 1) \cdot (n - 2) \cdot \ldots \cdot 1$$

with 1! equal to 1 and 0! defined to be 1. For example, 5! is the product $5 \cdot 4 \cdot 3 \cdot 2 \cdot 1$, which is equal to 120.

The factorial of an integer, **number**, greater than or equal to 0, can be calculated *iteratively* (nonrecursively) using **for** as follows:

```
factorial = 1;
for ( int counter = number; counter >= 1; counter-- )
    factorial *= counter;
```

A recursive definition of the factorial method is arrived at by observing the following relationship:

$$n! = n \cdot (n - 1)!$$

For example, 5! is clearly equal to 5 * 4!, as is shown by the following:

$$5! = 5 \cdot 4 \cdot 3 \cdot 2 \cdot 1$$
$$5! = 5 \cdot (4 \cdot 3 \cdot 2 \cdot 1)$$
$$5! = 5 \cdot (4!)$$

The evaluation of 5! would proceed as shown in Fig. 6.11. Figure 6.11a shows how the succession of recursive calls proceeds until 1! is evaluated to be 1, which terminates the recursion. Figure 6.11b shows the values returned from each recursive call to its caller until the final value is calculated and returned.

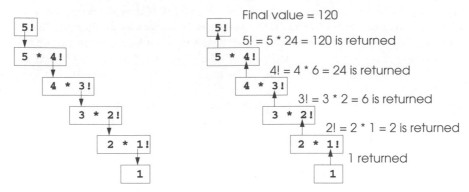

a) Procession of recursive calls.   b) Values returned from each recursive call.

Fig. 6.11   Recursive evaluation of 5!.

Figure 6.12 uses recursion to calculate and print the factorials of the integers 0 to 10 (the choice of the data type **long** will be explained momentarily). The recursive method **factorial** first tests to see if a terminating condition is **true** (i.e., is **number** less than or equal to 1). If **number** is indeed less than or equal to 1, **factorial** returns 1, no further recursion is necessary and the method returns. If **number** is greater than 1, line 28

```
return number * factorial( number - 1 );
```

expresses the problem as the product of **number** and a recursive call to **factorial** evaluating the factorial of **number - 1**. Note that **factorial(number - 1)** is a slightly simpler problem than the original calculation **factorial(number)**.

```
1   // Fig. 6.12: FactorialTest.java
2   // Recursive factorial method
3   import java.awt.*;
4   import javax.swing.*;
5
6   public class FactorialTest extends JApplet {
7      JTextArea outputArea;
8
9      public void init()
10     {
11        outputArea = new JTextArea();
12
13        Container c = getContentPane();
14        c.add( outputArea );
15
16        // calculate the factorials of 0 through 10
17        for ( long i = 0; i <= 10; i++ )
18           outputArea.append(
19              i + "! = " + factorial( i ) + "\n" );
20     }
```

Fig. 6.12   Calculating factorials with a recursive method (part 1 of 2).

```
21
22      // Recursive definition of method factorial
23      public long factorial( long number )
24      {
25         if ( number <= 1 )   // base case
26            return 1;
27         else
28            return number * factorial( number - 1 );
29      }
30   }
```

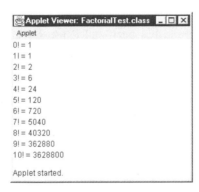

Fig. 6.12   Calculating factorials with a recursive method (part 2 of 2).

Method **factorial** (line 23) receives a parameter of type **long** and returns a result of type **long**. As can be seen in Fig. 6.12, factorial values become large quickly. We chose data type **long** so the program can calculate factorials greater than 20!. Unfortunately, the **factorial** method produces large values so quickly that even **long** does not help us print many factorial values before the size of a **long** variable is exceeded.

We explore in the exercises that **float** and **double** may ultimately be needed by the user desiring to calculate factorials of larger numbers. This points to a weakness in most programming languages, namely that the languages are not easily extended to handle the unique requirements of various applications. As we will see in Chapter 9, "Object-Oriented Programming," Java is an extensible language that allows us to create arbitrarily large integers if we wish. In fact, package **java.math** provides two classes—**BigInteger** and **BigDecimal**—explicitly for arbitrary precision mathematical calculations that cannot be represented with Java's primitive data types.

Common Programming Error 6.14

Forgetting to return a value from a recursive method when one is needed results in a syntax error.

Common Programming Error 6.15

Either omitting the base case or writing the recursion step incorrectly so that it does not converge on the base case will cause infinite recursion, eventually exhausting memory. This is analogous to the problem of an infinite loop in an iterative (nonrecursive) solution.

6.12 Example Using Recursion: The Fibonacci Series

The Fibonacci series

0, 1, 1, 2, 3, 5, 8, 13, 21, ...

begins with 0 and 1 and has the property that each subsequent Fibonacci number is the sum of the previous two Fibonacci numbers.

The series occurs in nature and, in particular, describes a form of spiral. The ratio of successive Fibonacci numbers converges on a constant value of 1.618.... This number, too, repeatedly occurs in nature and has been called the *golden ratio* or the *golden mean.* Humans tend to find the golden mean aesthetically pleasing. Architects often design windows, rooms and buildings whose length and width are in the ratio of the golden mean. Postcards are often designed with a golden mean length/width ratio.

The Fibonacci series may be defined recursively as follows:

fibonacci(0) = 0
fibonacci(1) = 1
fibonacci(n) = fibonacci(n – 1) + fibonacci(n – 2)

Note that there are two base cases for the Fibonacci calculation—*fibonacci(0)* is defined to be 0 and *fibonacci(1)* is defined to be 1. The applet of Fig. 6.13 calculates the ith Fibonacci number recursively using method **fibonacci**. The user enters an integer in the first **JTextField** indicating the ith Fibonacci number to calculate and presses the *Enter* key. Method **actionPerformed** executes automatically in response to the user interface event and calls recursive method **fibonacci** to calculate the specified Fibonacci number. Notice that Fibonacci numbers tend to become large quickly. Therefore, we use data type **long** for the parameter type and the return type in method **fibonacci**. In Fig. 6.13, the screen captures show the results of calculating several Fibonacci numbers.

Once again, method **init** of this applet creates the GUI components and attaches them to the applet's content pane. The layout manager for the content pane is set to **FlowLayout** at line 15.

The event handling in this example is similar to the event handling of the **Craps** applet in Fig. 6.9. Line 22

```
num.addActionListener( this );
```

specifies that **this** applet should listen for events from the **JTextField num**. Remember, the **this** keyword enables the applet to refer to itself. So the preceding statement is the applet telling the **JTextField num** that the applet should be notified (with a call to the applet's **actionPerformed** method) when an action event occurs in the **JTextField**. In this example, the user presses the *Enter* key while typing in the **JTextField num** to generate the action event. Automatically, a message is sent to the applet (i.e., a method—**actionPerformed**—is called on the applet) indicating that the user of the program interacted with one of the program's GUI components (**num**). Remember that the preceding statement to register the applet as the **JTextField num**'s listener will only compile if the applet class also implements **ActionListener** (line 8).

```
1   // Fig. 6.13: FibonacciTest.java
2   // Recursive fibonacci method
3   import java.awt.*;
4   import java.awt.event.*;
5   import javax.swing.*;
6
7   public class FibonacciTest extends JApplet
8                  implements ActionListener {
9      JLabel numLabel, resultLabel;
10     JTextField num, result;
11
12     public void init()
13     {
14        Container c = getContentPane();
15        c.setLayout( new FlowLayout() );
16
17        numLabel =
18           new JLabel( "Enter an integer and press Enter" );
19        c.add( numLabel );
20
21        num = new JTextField( 10 );
22        num.addActionListener( this );
23        c.add( num );
24
25        resultLabel = new JLabel( "Fibonacci value is" );
26        c.add( resultLabel );
27
28        result = new JTextField( 15 );
29        result.setEditable( false );
30        c.add( result );
31     }
32
33     public void actionPerformed( ActionEvent e )
34     {
35        long number, fibonacciValue;
36
37        number = Long.parseLong( num.getText() );
38        showStatus( "Calculating ..." );
39        fibonacciValue = fibonacci( number );
40        showStatus( "Done." );
41        result.setText( Long.toString( fibonacciValue ) );
42     }
43
44     // Recursive definition of method fibonacci
45     public long fibonacci( long n )
46     {
47        if ( n == 0 || n == 1 )  // base case
48           return n;
49        else
50           return fibonacci( n - 1 ) + fibonacci( n - 2 );
51     }
52  }
```

Fig. 6.13   Recursively generating Fibonacci numbers (part 1 of 2).

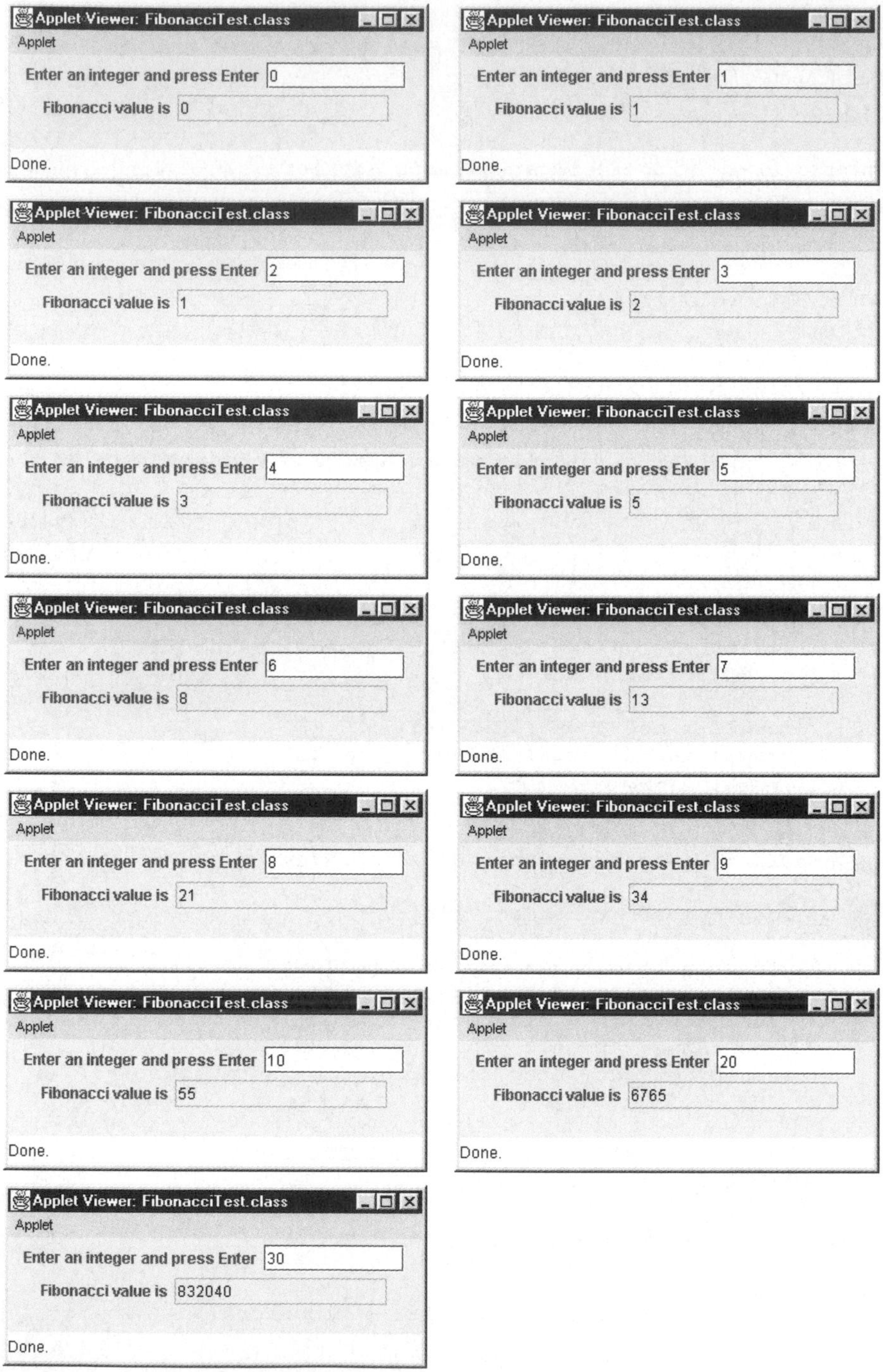

Fig. 6.13   Recursively generating Fibonacci numbers (part 2 of 2).

The call to **fibonacci** (line 39) from **actionPerformed** is not a recursive call, but all subsequent calls to **fibonacci** are recursive. Each time **fibonacci** is invoked, it immediately tests for the base case—**n** equal to 0 or 1. If this is true, **n** is returned (*fibonacci(0)* is 0 and *fibonacci(1)* is 1). Interestingly, if **n** is greater than 1, the recursion step generates *two* recursive calls, each of which is for a slightly simpler problem than the original call to **fibonacci**. Figure 6.14 shows how method **fibonacci** would evaluate **fibonacci(3)**—we abbreviate **fibonacci** as **f** to make the figure more readable.

This figure raises some interesting issues about the order in which Java compilers will evaluate the operands of operators. This is a different issue from the order in which operators are applied to their operands, namely the order dictated by the rules of operator precedence. From Fig. 6.14 it appears that while evaluating **f(3)**, two recursive calls will be made, namely **f(2)** and **f(1)**. But in what order will these calls be made? Most programmers assume the operands will be evaluated left to right. In Java this is true.

The C and C++ languages (on which many of Java's features are based) do not specify the order in which the operands of most operators (including **+**) are evaluated. Therefore, the programmer can make no assumption in those languages about the order in which these calls execute. The calls could in fact execute **f(2)** first, then **f(1)**, or the calls could execute in the reverse order: **f(1)**, then **f(2)**. In this program and in most other programs, it turns out the final result would be the same. But in some programs the evaluation of an operand may have *side effects* that could affect the final result of the expression.

The Java language specifies that the order of evaluation of the operands is left to right. Thus, the method calls are in fact **f(2)** first, then **f(1)**.

Good Programming Practice 6.8

Do not write expressions that depend on the order of evaluation of the operands of an operator. This often results in programs that are difficult to read, debug, modify and maintain.

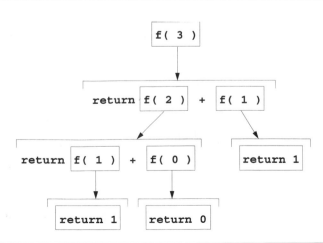

Fig. 6.14   Set of recursive calls to method **fibonacci**.

A word of caution is in order about recursive programs like the one we use here to generate Fibonacci numbers. Each invocation of the **fibonacci** method that does not match one of the base cases (i.e., 0 or 1) results in two more recursive calls to the **fibonacci** method. This rapidly gets out of hand. Calculating the Fibonacci value of 20 using the program in Fig. 6.13 requires 21,891 calls to the **fibonacci** method; calculating the Fibonacci value of 30 requires 2,692,537 calls to the **fibonacci** method.

As you try larger values, you will notice that each consecutive Fibonacci number you ask the applet to calculate results in a substantial increase in calculation time and number of calls to the **fibonacci** method. For example, the Fibonacci value of 31 requires 4,356,617 calls and the Fibonacci value of 32 requires 7,049,155 calls. As you can see, the number of calls to Fibonacci is increasing quickly—1,664,080 additional calls between Fibonacci of 30 and 31 and 2,692,538 additional calls between Fibonacci of 31 and 32. This difference in number of calls made between Fibonacci of 31 and 32 is more than 1.5 times the difference for Fibonacci of 30 and 31. Problems of this nature humble even the world's most powerful computers! Computer scientists study in the field of complexity theory how hard algorithms have to work to do their jobs. Complexity issues are discussed in detail in the upper-level computer science curriculum course generally called "Algorithms."

Performance Tip 6.2

Avoid Fibonacci-style recursive programs, which result in an exponential "explosion" of calls.

6.13 Recursion vs. Iteration

In the previous sections, we studied two methods that can easily be implemented either recursively or iteratively. In this section we compare the two approaches and discuss why the programmer might choose one approach over the other in a particular situation.

Both iteration and recursion are based on a control structure: Iteration uses a repetition structure (such as **for**, **while** or **do/while**); recursion uses a selection structure (such as **if**, **if/else** or **switch**). Both iteration and recursion involve repetition: Iteration explicitly uses a repetition structure; recursion achieves repetition through repeated method calls. Iteration and recursion each involve a termination test: Iteration terminates when the loop-continuation condition fails; recursion terminates when a base case is recognized. Iteration with counter-controlled repetition and recursion each gradually approach termination: Iteration keeps modifying a counter until the counter assumes a value that makes the loop-continuation condition fail; recursion keeps producing simpler versions of the original problem until the base case is reached. Both iteration and recursion can occur infinitely: An infinite loop occurs with iteration if the loop-continuation test never becomes false; infinite recursion occurs if the recursion step does not reduce the problem each time in a manner that converges on the base case.

Recursion has many negatives. It repeatedly invokes the mechanism, and consequently the overhead, of method calls. This can be expensive in both processor time and memory space. Each recursive call causes another copy of the method (actually, only the method's variables) to be created; this can consume considerable memory. Iteration normally occurs within a method, so the overhead of repeated method calls and extra memory assignment is omitted. So why choose recursion?

Software Engineering Observation 6.11

Any problem that can be solved recursively can also be solved iteratively (nonrecursively). A recursive approach is normally chosen in preference to an iterative approach when the recursive approach more naturally mirrors the problem and results in a program that is easier to understand and debug. Another reason to choose a recursive solution is that an iterative solution may not be apparent.

Performance Tip 6.3

Avoid using recursion in performance situations. Recursive calls take time and consume additional memory.

Common Programming Error 6.16

Accidentally having a nonrecursive method call itself either directly or indirectly through another method can cause infinite recursion.

Most programming textbooks introduce recursion much later than we have done here. We feel that recursion is a sufficiently rich and complex topic that it is better to introduce it earlier and spread the examples over the remainder of the text. Figure 6.15 summarizes the recursion examples and exercises in the text.

Let us reconsider some observations we make repeatedly throughout the book. Good software engineering is important. High performance is often important. Unfortunately, these goals are often at odds with one another. Good software engineering is key to making more manageable the task of developing larger and more complex software systems. High performance in these systems is key to realizing the systems of the future, which will place ever greater computing demands on hardware. Where do methods fit in here?

Software Engineering Observation 6.12

Modularizing programs in a neat, hierarchical manner promotes good software engineering. But it has a price.

Performance Tip 6.4

A heavily modularized program—as compared to a monolithic (i.e., one-piece) program without methods—makes potentially large numbers of method calls and these consume execution time and space on a computer's processor(s). But monolithic programs are difficult to program, test, debug, maintain and evolve.

So modularize your programs judiciously, always keeping in mind the delicate balance between performance and good software engineering.

6.14 Method Overloading

Java enables several methods of the same name to be defined as long as these methods have different sets of parameters (based on the number of parameters, the types of the parameters and the order of the parameters). This is called *method overloading*. When an overloaded method is called, the Java compiler selects the proper method by examining the number, types and order of the arguments in the call. Method overloading is commonly used to create several methods with the same name that perform similar tasks, but on different data types.

Chapter	Recursion examples and exercises
6	Factorial method
	Fibonacci method
	Greatest common divisor
	Sum of two integers
	Multiply two integers
	Raising an integer to an integer power
	Towers of Hanoi
	Visualizing recursion
7	Sum the elements of an array
	Print an array
	Print an array backward
	Check if a string is a palindrome
	Minimum value in an array
	Selection sort
	Eight Queens
	Linear search
	Binary search
	Quicksort
	Maze traversal
10	Printing a string input at the keyboard backward
22	Linked list insert
	Linked list delete
	Search a linked list
	Print a linked list backward
	Binary tree insert
	Preorder traversal of a binary tree
	Inorder traversal of a binary tree
	Postorder traversal of a binary tree

Fig. 6.15   Summary of recursion examples and exercises in the text.

Good Programming Practice 6.9

Overloading methods that perform closely related tasks can make programs more readable and understandable.

Figure 6.16 uses overloaded method **square** to calculate the square of an **int** and the square of a **double**.

Overloaded methods are distinguished by their *signature*—a combination of the method's name and its parameter types. If the Java compiler only looked at method names during compilation, the code in Fig. 6.16 would be ambiguous—the compiler would not know how to distinguish the two **square** methods. Logically, the compiler uses longer "mangled" or "decorated" names that include the original method name, the types of each parameter and the exact order of the parameters to determine if the methods in a class are unique in that class.

```
1   // Fig. 6.16: MethodOverload.java
2   // Using overloaded methods
3   import java.awt.Container;
4   import javax.swing.*;
5
6   public class MethodOverload extends JApplet {
7      JTextArea outputArea;
8
9      public void init()
10     {
11        outputArea = new JTextArea( 2, 20 );
12        Container c = getContentPane();
13        c.add( outputArea );
14
15        outputArea.setText(
16           "The square of integer 7 is " + square( 7 ) +
17           "\nThe square of double 7.5 is " + square( 7.5 ) );
18     }
19
20     public int square( int x )
21     {
22        return x * x;
23     }
24
25     public double square( double y )
26     {
27        return y * y;
28     }
29  }
```

```
Applet Viewer: MethodOverload....  _ □ ✕
Applet
The square of integer 7 is 49
The square of double 7.5 is 56.25

Applet started.
```

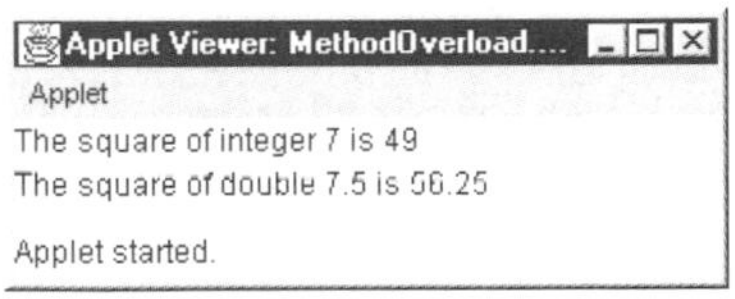

Fig. 6.16 Using overloaded methods.

For example, in Fig. 6.16, the compiler might use the logical name "*square of int*" for the **square** method that specifies an **int** parameter and "*square of double*" for the **square** method that specifies a **double** parameter. If a method **foo**'s definition begins as follows:

```
void foo( int a, float b )
```

the compiler might use the logical name "*foo of int and float.*" If the parameters are specified as follows:

```
void foo( float a, int b )
```

the compiler might use the logical name "*foo of float and int.*" Note that the order of the parameters is important to the compiler. The preceding two **foo** methods are considered to be distinct by the compiler.

So far, the logical names of methods used by the compiler did not mention the return types of the methods. This is because methods cannot be distinguished by return type. The program of Fig. 6.17 illustrates the compiler errors generated when two methods have the same signature and different return types. Overloaded methods can have different return types, but must have different parameter lists. Also, overloaded methods need not have the same number of parameters.

Common Programming Error 6.17

Creating overloaded methods with identical parameter lists and different return types is a syntax error.

6.15 Methods of Class JApplet

We have written many applets to this point in the text, but we have not yet discussed the key methods of class **JApplet** class that are called automatically during the execution of an applet. Figure 6.18 lists the key methods of class **JApplet**, when they get called and the purpose of each method.

These **JApplet** methods are defined by the Java API to do nothing unless you provide a definition in your applet's class definition. If you would like to use one of these methods in an applet you are defining, you *must* define the first line of the method as shown in Fig. 6.18. Otherwise, the method will not get called automatically during the applet's execution.

```
1   // Fig. 6.17: MethodOverload.java
2   // Overloaded methods with identical signatures and
3   // different return types.
4   import javax.swing.JApplet;
5
6   public class MethodOverload extends JApplet {
7      public int square( double x )
8      {
9         return x * x;
10     }
11
12     public double square( double y )
13     {
14        return y * y;
15     }
16  }
```

```
MethodOverload.java:12: Methods can't be redefined with a
        different return type: double square(double) was
        int square(double)
    double square( double y )
                   ^
  1 error
```

Fig. 6.17 Compiler error messages generated from overloaded methods with identical parameter lists and different return types.

Method	When the method is called and its purpose
`public void init()`	This method is called once by the **appletviewer** or browser when an applet is loaded for execution. It performs initialization of an applet. Typical actions performed here are initialization of instance variables and GUI components of the applet, loading of sounds to play or images to display (Chapter 16, "Multimedia") and creation of threads (Chapter 15, "Multithreading").
`public void start()`	This method is called after the **init** method completes execution and every time the user of the browser returns to the HTML page on which the applet resides (after browsing another HTML page). This method performs any tasks that must be completed when the applet is loaded for the first time into the browser and that must be performed every time the HTML page on which the applet resides is revisited. Typical actions performed here include starting an animation (Chapter 16, "Multimedia") and starting other threads of execution (Chapter 15, "Multithreading").
`public void paint( Graphics g )`	This method is called after the **init** method completes execution and the **start** method has started executing to draw on the applet. It is also called automatically every time the applet needs to be repainted. For example, if the user of the browser covers the applet with another open window on the screen, then uncovers the applet, the **paint** method is called. Typical actions performed here involve drawing with the **Graphics** object **g** that is automatically passed to the **paint** method for you.
`public void stop()`	This method is called when the applet should stop executing—normally when the user of the browser leaves the HTML page on which the applet resides. This method performs any tasks that are required to suspend the applet's execution. Typical actions performed here are to stop execution of animations and threads.
`public void destroy()`	This method is called when the applet is being removed from memory—normally when the user of the browser exits the browsing session. This method performs any tasks that are required to destroy resources allocated to the applet.

Fig. 6.18 **JApplet** methods called automatically during an applet's execution.

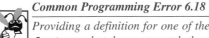

Common Programming Error 6.18

*Providing a definition for one of the **JApplet** methods **init**, **start**, **paint**, **stop** or **destroy** that does not match the method headers shown in Fig. 6.18 results in a method that will not be called automatically during execution of the applet.*

Method **repaint** is also of interest to many applet programmers. The applet's **paint** method is normally called automatically. What if you would like to change the appearance of the applet in response to the user's interactions with the applet? In such situations, you may want to call **paint** directly. However, to call **paint**, we must pass it the **Graphics** parameter it expects. This poses a problem for us. We do not have a **Graphics** object at our disposal to pass to **paint** (we discuss this issue in Chapter 16, "Multimedia"). For this reason, the **repaint** method is provided for you. The statement

```
repaint();
```

invokes another method called *update* and passes it the **Graphics** object for you. The **update** method erases any drawing that was previously done on the applet, then invokes the **paint** method and passes it the **Graphics** object for you. The **repaint** and **update** methods are discussed in detail in Chapter 16, "Multimedia."

Summary

- The best way to develop and maintain a large program is to divide it into several smaller program modules each of which is more manageable than the original program. Modules are written in Java as classes and methods.

- A method is invoked by a method call. The method call mentions the method by name and provides information (as arguments) that the called method needs to perform its task.

- Methods are invoked in a program by writing the name of the method followed by the arguments of the method in parentheses.

- Each argument of a method may be a constant, a variable or an expression.

- A local variable is known only in a method definition. Methods are not allowed to know the implementation details of any other method (including local variables).

- The on-screen display area for a **JApplet** has a content pane to which the GUI components must be attached so they can be displayed at execution time. The content pane is an object of class **Container** from the **java.awt** package.

- Method **getContentPane** returns a reference to the applet's content pane.

- The general format for a method definition is

  > *return-value-type method-name* (*parameter-list*)
  > {
  >   *declarations and statements*
  > }

  The *return-value-type* states the type of the value returned to the calling method. If a method does not return a value, the *return-value-type* is **void**. The *method-name* is any valid identifier. The *parameter-list* is a comma-separated list containing the declarations of the variables that will be passed to the method. If a method does not receive any values, *parameter-list* is empty. The method body is the set of *declarations and statements* that constitute the method.

- An empty parameter list is specified with empty parentheses.

- The arguments passed to a method should match in number, type and order with the parameters in the method definition.

- When a program encounters a method, control is transferred from the point of invocation to the called method, the method is executed and control returns to the caller.

- A called method can return control to the caller in one of three ways. If the method does not return a value, control is returned when the method-ending right brace is reached or by executing the statement

  ```
  return;
  ```

If the method does return a value, the statement

return *expression***;**

returns the value of *expression*.

- There are three ways to call a method—the method name by itself, a reference to an object followed by the dot (**.**) operator and the method name, and a class name followed by a method name. The last syntax is only for **static** methods of a class.

- An important feature of method definitions is the coercion of arguments (i.e., the forcing of arguments to the appropriate type to pass to a method). In many cases, argument values that do not correspond precisely to the parameter types in the method definition are converted to the proper type before the method is called. In some cases, these conversions can lead to compiler errors if Java's promotion rules are not followed.

- The promotion rules specify how types can be converted to other types without losing data. The promotion rules apply to mixed-type expressions. The type of each value in a mixed-type expression is promoted to the "highest" type in the expression.

- Method **Math.random** generates a double value from 0.0 up to (but not including) 1.0.

- Values produced by **Math.random** can be scaled and shifted to produce values in a range.

- The general equation for scaling and shifting a random number is

n = a + (int) (Math.random() * b);

where **a** is the shifting value (the first number in the desired range of consecutive integers) and **b** is the scaling factor (the width of the desired range of consecutive integers).

- A class can inherit existing attributes and behaviors (data and methods) from another class specified to the right of keyword **extends** in the class definition. In addition, a class can implement one or more interfaces. An interface specifies one or more behaviors (i.e., methods) that you must define in your class definition.

- The interface **ActionListener** specifies that this class must define a method with the first line

public void actionPerformed(ActionEvent e)

- The task of method **actionPerformed** is to process a user's interaction with a GUI component that generates an action event. This method is called automatically in response to the user interaction. This process is called event handling. The event is the user interaction (pressing the button). The event handler is the **actionPerformed** method, which is called automatically in response to the event. This style of programming is known as event-driven programming.

- Keyword **final** is used to declare constant variables. Constant variables must be initialized once before they are used and cannot be modified thereafter. Constant variables are often called named constants or read-only variables.

- A **JLabel** contains a string of characters to display on the screen. Normally, a **JLabel** indicates the purpose of another graphical user interface element on the screen.

- **JTextField**s are used to get information from the user at the keyboard or to display information on the screen.

- When the user presses a **JButton**, normally the program responds by performing a task (rolling the dice in this example).

- **Container** method **setLayout** defines the layout manager for the applet's user interface. Layout managers are provided to arrange GUI components on a **Container** for presentation purposes. The layout managers provide basic layout capabilities that determine the position and size of every GUI component attached to the container. This enables the programmer to concentrate on the basic "look and feel" and lets the layout managers process most of the layout details.

- **FlowLayout** is the most basic layout manager. GUI components are placed on a **Container** from left to right in the order in which they are attached to the **Container** with method **add**. When the edge of the container is reached, components are continued on the next line.

- Before any event can be processed, each GUI component must know which object in the program defines the event handling method that will be called when an event occurs. Method **addActionListener** is used to tell a **JButton** that another object is listening for action events and defines method **actionPerformed**. This is called registering the event handler with the GUI component (we also like to call it the start listening line because the applet is now listening for events from the button). To respond to an action event, we must define a class that **implements ActionListener** (this requires that the class also define method **actionPerformed**) and we must register the event handler with the GUI component.

- Method **showStatus** receives a **String** argument and displays it in the status bar of the **appletviewer** or browser.

- Each variable identifier has the attributes duration (lifetime) and scope. An identifier's duration determines when that identifier exists in memory. An identifier's scope is where the identifier can be referenced in a program.

- Identifiers that represent local variables in a method (i.e., parameters and variables declared in the method body) have automatic duration. Automatic duration variables are created when program control reaches their declaration, they exist while the block in which they are declared is active and they are destroyed when the block in which they are declared is exited.

- Java also has identifiers of *static duration*. Variables and references of static duration exist from the point at which the class in which they are defined is loaded into memory for execution until the program terminates. Their storage is allocated and initialized once when their class is loaded into memory. For static duration methods, the name of the method exists when their class is loaded into memory.

- The scopes for an identifier are class scope and block scope. An instance variable declared outside any method has class scope. Such an identifier is "known" in all methods of the class. Identifiers declared inside a block have block scope. Block scope ends at the terminating right brace (**}**) of the block.

- Local variables declared at the beginning of a method have block scope, as do method parameters, which are considered local variables of the method.

- Any block may contain variable declarations.

- A recursive method is a method that calls itself either directly or indirectly.

- If a recursive method is called with a base case, the method returns a result. If the method is called with a more complex problem, the method divides the problem into two or more conceptual pieces: a piece that the method knows how to do and a slightly smaller version of the original problem. Because this new problem looks like the original problem, the method launches a recursive call to work on the smaller problem.

- For recursion to terminate, each time the recursive method calls itself with a slightly simpler version of the original problem, the sequence of smaller and smaller problems must converge on the base case. When the method recognizes the base case, the result is returned to the previous method call and a sequence of returns ensues all the way up the line until the original call of the method eventually returns the final result.

- Both iteration and recursion are based on a control structure: Iteration uses a repetition structure; recursion uses a selection structure.

- Both iteration and recursion involve repetition: Iteration explicitly uses a repetition structure; recursion achieves repetition through repeated method calls.

- Iteration and recursion each involve a termination test: Iteration terminates when the loop-continuation condition fails; recursion terminates when a base case is recognized.

- Iteration and recursion can occur infinitely: An infinite loop occurs with iteration if the loop-continuation test never becomes false; infinite recursion occurs if the recursion step does not reduce the problem in a manner that converges on the base case.

- Recursion repeatedly invokes the mechanism, and consequently the overhead, of method calls. This can be expensive in both processor time and memory space.

- The user presses the *Enter* key while typing in a **JTextField** to generate the action event. The event handling for this GUI component is set up like a **JButton**—a class must be defined that implements **ActionListener** and defines method **actionPerformed**. Also, the **JTextField**'s **addActionListener** method must be called to register the event.

- It is possible to define methods with the same name but with different parameter lists (based on the types of the parameters, the number of parameters and the order of the parameters). This is called method overloading. When an overloaded method is called, the compiler selects the proper method by examining the arguments in the call.

- Overloaded methods can have different return values and must have different parameter lists. Two methods differing only by return type will result in a syntax error.

- The applet's **init** method is called once by the **appletviewer** or browser when an applet is loaded for execution. It performs initialization of an applet. The applet's **start** method is called after the **init** method completes execution and every time the user of the browser returns to the HTML page on which the applet resides (after browsing another HTML page).

- The applet's **paint** method is called after the **init** method completes execution and the **start** method has started executing to draw on the applet. It is also called automatically every time the applet needs to be repainted.

- The applet's **stop** method is called when the applet should suspend execution—normally when the user of the browser leaves the HTML page on which the applet resides.

- The applet's **destroy** method is called when the applet is being removed from memory—normally when the user of the browser exits the browsing session.

- Method **repaint** can be called in an applet to cause a fresh call to **paint**. Method **repaint** invokes another method called **update** and passes it the **Graphics** object. The **update** method erases any drawing that was previously done on the applet, then invokes the **paint** method and passes it the **Graphics** object.

Terminology

ActionEvent class	class
ActionListener interface	class scope
actionPerformed method	coercion of arguments
argument in a method call	constant variable
automatic duration	copy of a value
automatic variable	**destroy** method of **JApplet**
base case in recursion	divide and conquer
block	duration
block scope	element of chance
call a method	factorial method
called method	**final**
caller	FlowLayout class
calling method	**init** method of **JApplet**

invoke a method
iteration
Java API (Java class library)
JButton class of package **javax.swing**
JLabel class of package **javax.swing**
JTextField class of package **javax.swing**
local variable
Math class methods
Math.E
Math.PI
Math.random method
method
method call
method call operator, **()**
method declaration
method definition
method overloading
mixed-type expression
modular program
named constant
overloading
paint method of **JApplet**
parameter in a method definition
programmer-defined method
promotion rules
random number generation

read-only variable
recursion
recursion step
recursive call
recursive method
reference parameter
reference types
repaint method of **JApplet**
return
return value type
scaling
scope
setLayout method of **JApplet**
shifting
showStatus method of **JApplet**
side effects
signature
simulation
software engineering
software reusability
start method of **JApplet**
static storage duration
stop method of **JApplet**
update method of **JApplet**
void

Common Programming Errors

6.1   Forgetting to invoke a **Math** class method by preceding the method name with the class name **Math** and a dot operator (**.**) results in a syntax error.

6.2   Defining a method outside the braces of a class definition is a syntax error.

6.3   Omitting the return-value-type in a method definition is a syntax error.

6.4   Forgetting to return a value from a method that is supposed to return a value is a syntax error. If a return-value-type other than **void** is specified, the method must contain a **return** statement.

6.5   Returning a value from a method whose return type has been declared **void** is a syntax error.

6.6   Declaring method parameters of the same type as **float x, y** instead of **float x, float y** is a syntax error because types are required for each parameter in the parameter list.

6.7   Placing a semicolon after the right parenthesis enclosing the parameter list of a method definition is a syntax error.

6.8   Redefining a method parameter as a local variable in the method is a syntax error.

6.9   Passing to a method an argument that is not compatible with the corresponding parameter's type is a syntax error.

6.10   Defining a method inside another method is a syntax error.

6.11   Converting a primitive-data-type value to another primitive data type may change the value if the new data type is not an allowed promotion (e.g., **double** to **int**). Also, converting any integral value to a floating-point value and back to an integral value may introduce rounding errors into the result.

6.12   After a **final** variable has been initialized, attempting to assign another value to that variable is a syntax error.

6.13 Accidentally using the same name for an identifier in an inner block of a method as is used for an identifier in an outer block of the same method results in a syntax error from the compiler.

6.14 Forgetting to return a value from a recursive method when one is needed results in a syntax error.

6.15 Either omitting the base case or writing the recursion step incorrectly so that it does not converge on the base case will cause infinite recursion, eventually exhausting memory. This is analogous to the problem of an infinite loop in an iterative (nonrecursive) solution. Infinite recursion can also be caused by providing an unexpected input.

6.16 Accidentally having a nonrecursive method call itself either directly or indirectly through another method can cause infinite recursion.

6.17 Creating overloaded methods with identical parameter lists and different return types is a syntax error.

6.18 Providing a definition for one of the **JApplet** methods **init**, **start**, **paint**, **stop** or **destroy** that does not match the method headers shown in Fig. 6.18 results in a method that will not be called automatically during execution of the applet.

Good Programming Practices

6.1 Familiarize yourself with the rich collection of classes and methods in the Java API and with the rich collections of classes available in various class libraries.

6.2 Place a blank line between method definitions to separate the methods and enhance program readability.

6.3 Although it is not incorrect to do so, do not use the same names for the arguments passed to a method and the corresponding parameters in the method definition. This helps avoid ambiguity.

6.4 Choosing meaningful method names and meaningful parameter names makes programs more readable and helps avoid excessive use of comments.

6.5 Use only uppercase letters (with underscores between words) in the names of **final** variables. This makes these constants stand out in a program.

6.6 Using meaningfully named **final** variables rather than integer constants (such as 2) makes programs more readable.

6.7 Avoid local variable names that hide instance variable names. This can be accomplished by avoiding the use of duplicate identifiers in a class.

6.8 Do not write expressions that depend on the order of evaluation of the operands of an operator. This often results in programs that are difficult to read, debug, modify and maintain.

6.9 Overloading methods that perform closely related tasks can make programs more readable and understandable.

Performance Tips

6.1 Do not try to rewrite existing Java API classes and methods to make them more efficient. You usually will not be able to increase the performance of these classes and methods.

6.2 Avoid fibonacci-style recursive programs, which result in an exponential "explosion" of calls.

6.3 Avoid using recursion in performance situations. Recursive calls take time and consume additional memory.

6.4 A heavily modularized program—as compared to a monolithic (i.e., one-piece) program without methods—makes potentially large numbers of method calls and these consume execution time and space on a computer's processor(s). But monolithic programs are difficult to program, test, debug, maintain and evolve.

Portability Tip

6.1   Using the methods in the Java API helps make programs more portable.

Software Engineering Observations

6.1   Avoid reinventing the wheel. When possible, use Java API classes and methods instead of writing new classes and methods. This reduces program development time and avoids introducing new errors.

6.2   It is not necessary to import the **Math** class into a program to use **Math** class methods. The **Math** class is part of the **java.lang** package which is automatically imported by the compiler.

6.3   Each method should be limited to performing a single, well-defined task, and the method name should effectively express that task. This promotes software reusability.

6.4   If you cannot choose a concise name that expresses what the method does, it is possible that your method is attempting to perform too many diverse tasks. It is usually best to break such a method into several smaller methods.

6.5   A method should usually be no longer than one page. Better yet, a method should usually be no longer than half a page. Regardless of how long a method is, it should perform one task well. Small methods promote software reusability.

6.6   Programs should be written as collections of small methods. This makes programs easier to write, debug, maintain and modify.

6.7   A method requiring a large number of parameters may be performing too many tasks. Consider dividing the method into smaller methods that perform the separate tasks. The method header should fit on one line if possible.

6.8   The method header and method calls must all agree in the number, type and order of parameters and arguments.

6.9   Automatic duration is a means of conserving memory because automatic duration variables are created when program control reaches their declaration and are destroyed when the block in which they are declared is exited.

6.10   Automatic duration is an example of the principle of least privilege. This principle states that each component of a system should have sufficient rights and privileges to accomplish its designated task, but no additional rights or privileges. This helps prevent accidental and/or malicious errors from occurring in systems. Why have variables stored in memory and accessible when they are not needed?

6.11   Any problem that can be solved recursively can also be solved iteratively (nonrecursively). A recursive approach is normally chosen in preference to an iterative approach when the recursive approach more naturally mirrors the problem and results in a program that is easier to understand and debug. Another reason to choose a recursive solution is that an iterative solution may not be apparent.

6.12   Modularizing programs in a neat, hierarchical manner promotes good software engineering. But it has a price.

Testing and Debugging Tips

6.1   Small methods are easier to test, debug and understand than large ones.

6.2   Automatic variables must be initialized before they are used in a method; otherwise, the compiler issues an error message.

Self-Review Exercises

6.1   Answer each of the following:
  a) Program modules in Java are called _____ and _____.

b) A method is invoked with a _____.

c) A variable known only within the method in which it is defined is called a _____.

d) The _____ statement in a called method can be used to pass the value of an expression back to the calling method.

e) The keyword _____ is used in a method header to indicate that a method does not return a value.

f) The _____ of an identifier is the portion of the program in which the identifier can be used.

g) The three ways to return control from a called method to a caller are _____, _____ and _____.

h) The _____ method is invoked once when an applet begins execution.

i) The _____ method is used to produce random numbers.

j) The _____ method is invoked each time the user of a browser revisits the HTML page on which an applet resides.

k) The _____ method is invoked to draw on an applet.

l) Variables declared in a block or in a method's parameter list are of _____ duration.

m) The _____ method invokes the applet's **update** method, which in turn invokes the applet's **paint** method.

n) The _____ method is invoked for an applet each time the user of a browser leaves an HTML page on which the applet resides.

o) A method that calls itself either directly or indirectly is a _____ method.

p) A recursive method typically has two components: one that provides a means for the recursion to terminate by testing for a _____ case and one that expresses the problem as a recursive call for a slightly simpler problem than the original call.

q) In Java, it is possible to have various methods with the same name that each operate on different types and/or numbers of arguments. This is called method _____.

r) The _____ qualifier is used to declare read-only variables.

6.2 For the following program, state the scope (either class scope or block scope) of each of the following elements.

a) The variable **x**.

b) The variable **y**.

c) The method **cube**.

d) The method **paint**.

e) The variable **yPos**.

```java
public class CubeTest extends JApplet {
   int x;

   public void paint( Graphics g )
   {
      int yPos = 25;

      for ( x = 1; x <= 10; x++ ) {
         g.drawString( cube( x ), 25, yPos );
         yPos += 15;
      }
   }

   public int cube( int y )
   {
      return y * y * y;
   }
}
```

6.3   Write an application that tests if the examples of the math library method calls shown in Fig. 6.2 actually produce the indicated results.

6.4   Give the method header for each of the following methods.
   a) Method **hypotenuse**, which takes two double-precision, floating-point arguments **side1** and **side2** and returns a double-precision, floating-point result.
   b) Method **smallest**, which takes three integers, **x**, **y**, **z** and returns an integer.
   c) Method **instructions**, which does not take any arguments and does not return a value. [*Note:* Such methods are commonly used to display instructions to a user.]
   d) Method **intToFloat**, which takes an integer argument, **number** and returns a floating-point result.

6.5   Find the error in each of the following program segments and explain how the error can be corrected:
   a)
```
int g() {
    System.out.println( "Inside method g" );
    int h() {
        System.out.println( "Inside method h" );
    }
}
```
   b)
```
int sum( int x, int y ) {
    int result;
    result = x + y;
}
```
   c)
```
int sum( int n ) {
    if ( n == 0 )
        return 0;
    else
        n + sum( n - 1 );
}
```
   d)
```
void f( float a ); {
    float a;
    System.out.println( a );
}
```
   e)
```
void product() {
    int a = 6, b = 5, c = 4, result;
    result = a * b * c;
    System.out.println( "Result is " + result );
    return result;
}
```

6.6   Write a complete Java applet to prompt the user for the **double** radius of a sphere and call method **sphereVolume** to calculate and display the volume of that sphere using the assignment

```
volume = ( 4.0 / 3.0 ) * Math.PI * Math.pow( radius, 3 )
```

The user should input the radius through a **JTextField**. A string can be converted to a **double** value as follows (assume **e** is the **ActionEvent** object passed to the **actionPerformed** method when the user presses the *Enter* key in the **JTextField**):

```
// Create a Double object using the text field value.
Double val = Double.parseDouble( e.getActionCommand() );
```

Note that **e.getActionCommand()** (when executed in **actionPerformed**) returns the string the user typed in the **JTextField** before pressing the *Enter* key in that **JTextField**.

Answers to Self-Review Exercises

6.1   a) Methods and classes. b) Method call. c) Local variable. d) **return**. e) **void**. f) Scope.
g) **return;** or **return** *expression;* or encountering the closing right brace of a method.
h) **init**. i) **Math.random** j) **start**. k) **paint**. l) Automatic. m) **repaint**. n) **stop**.
o) Recursive. p) Base. q) Overloading. r) **final**.

6.2   a) Class scope. b) Block scope. c) Class scope. d) Class scope. e) Block scope.

6.3   The following solution demonstrates the **Math** class methods in Fig. 6.2.

```
1  // Exercise 6.3: MathTest.java
2  // Testing the Math class methods
3
4  public class MathTest {
5     public static void main( String args[] )
6     {
7        System.out.println( "Math.abs( 23.7 ) = " +
8                              Math.abs( 23.7 ) );
9        System.out.println( "Math.abs( 0.0 ) = " +
10                             Math.abs( 0.0 ) );
11        System.out.println( "Math.abs( -23.7 ) = " +
12                             Math.abs( -23.7 ) );
13        System.out.println( "Math.ceil( 9.2 ) = " +
14                             Math.ceil( 9.2 ) );
15        System.out.println( "Math.ceil( -9.8 ) = " +
16                             Math.ceil( -9.8 ) );
17        System.out.println( "Math.cos( 0.0 ) = " +
18                             Math.cos( 0.0 ) );
19        System.out.println( "Math.exp( 1.0 ) = " +
20                             Math.exp( 1.0 ) );
21        System.out.println( "Math.exp( 2.0 ) = " +
22                             Math.exp( 2.0 ) );
23        System.out.println( "Math.floor( 9.2 ) = " +
24                             Math.floor( 9.2 ) );
25        System.out.println( "Math.floor( -9.8 ) = " +
26                             Math.floor( -9.8 ) );
27        System.out.println( "Math.log( 2.718282 ) = " +
28                             Math.log( 2.718282 ) );
29        System.out.println( "Math.log( 7.389056 ) = " +
30                             Math.log( 7.389056 ) );
31        System.out.println( "Math.max( 2.3, 12.7 ) = v +
32                             Math.max( 2.3, 12.7 ) );
33        System.out.println( "Math.max( -2.3, -12.7 ) = " +
34                             Math.max( -2.3, -12.7 ) );
35        System.out.println( "Math.min( 2.3, 12.7 ) = " +
36                             Math.min( 2.3, 12.7 ) );
37        System.out.println( "Math.min( -2.3, -12.7 ) = " +
38                             Math.min( -2.3, -12.7 ) );
39        System.out.println( "Math.pow( 2, 7 ) = " +
40                             Math.pow( 2, 7 ) );
41        System.out.println( "Math.pow( 9, .5 ) = " +
42                             Math.pow( 9, .5 ) );
43        System.out.println( "Math.sin( 0.0 ) = " +
44                             Math.sin( 0.0 ) );
```

```
45          System.out.println( "Math.sqrt( 25.0 ) = " +
46                                 Math.sqrt( 25.0 ) );
47          System.out.println( "Math.tan( 0.0 ) = " +
48                                 Math.tan( 0.0 ) );
49      }
50  }
```

```
Math.abs( 23.7 ) = 23.7
Math.abs( 0.0 ) = 0
Math.abs( -23.7 ) = 23.7
Math.ceil( 9.2 ) = 10
Math.ceil( -9.8 ) = -9
Math.cos( 0.0 ) = 1
Math.exp( 1.0 ) = 2.71828
Math.exp( 2.0 ) = 7.38906
Math.floor( 9.2 ) = 9
Math.floor( -9.8 ) = -10
Math.log( 2.718282 ) = 1
Math.log( 7.389056 ) = 2
Math.max( 2.3, 12.7 ) = 12.7
Math.max( -2.3, -12.7 ) = -2.3
Math.min( 2.3, 12.7 ) = 2.3
Math.min( -2.3, -12.7 ) = -12.7
Math.pow( 2, 7 ) = 128
Math.pow( 9, .5 ) = 3
Math.sin( 0.0 ) = 0
Math.sqrt( 25.0 ) = 5
Math.tan( 0.0 ) = 0
```

6.4   a) **double hypotenuse(double side1, double side2)**
          b) **int smallest(int x, int y, int z)**
          c) **void instructions()**
          d) **float intToFloat(int number)**

6.5   a) Error: Method **h** is defined in method **g**.
          Correction: Move the definition of **h** out of the definition of **g**.
          b) Error: The method is supposed to return an integer, but does not.
          Correction: Delete variable **result** and place the following statement in the method:
              return x + y;
          or add the following statement at the end of the method body:
              return result;
          c) Error: The result of **n + sum(n - 1)** is not returned by this recursive method, resulting in a syntax error.
          Correction: Rewrite the statement in the **else** clause as
              return n + sum(n - 1);
          d) Error: The semicolon after the right parenthesis that encloses the parameter list and redefining the parameter **a** in the method definition are each incorrect.
          Correction: Delete the semicolon after the right parenthesis of the parameter list and delete the declaration **float a;**.
          e) Error: The method returns a value when it is not supposed to.
          Correction: Change the return type to **int**.

6.6   The following solution calculates the volume of a sphere using the radius entered by the user.

```
1   // Exercise 6.6: SphereTest.java
2   import java.awt.*;
3   import java.awt.event.*;
4   import javax.swing.*;
5
6   public class SphereTest extends JApplet
7                implements ActionListener {
8      JLabel prompt;
9      JTextField input;
10
11     public void init()
12     {
13        Container c = getContentPane();
14        c.setLayout( new FlowLayout() );
15
16        prompt = new JLabel( "Enter sphere radius: " );
17        input = new JTextField( 10 );
18        input.addActionListener( this );
19        c.add( prompt );
20        c.add( input );
21     }
22
23     public void actionPerformed( ActionEvent e )
24     {
25        double radius =
26           Double.parseDouble( e.getActionCommand() );
27        showStatus( "Volume is " + sphereVolume( radius ) );
28     }
29
30     public double sphereVolume( double radius )
31     {
32        double volume =
33           ( 4.0 / 3.0 ) * Math.PI * Math.pow( radius, 3 );
34
35        return volume;
36     }
37  }
```

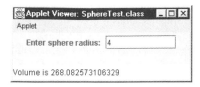

Exercises

6.7   What is the value of **x** after each of the following statements is performed?
a) **x = Math.abs(7.5);**
b) **x = Math.floor(7.5);**
c) **x = Math.abs(0.0);**

d) `x = Math.ceil( 0.0 );`
e) `x = Math.abs( -6.4 );`
f) `x = Math.ceil( -6.4 );`
g) `x = Math.ceil( -Math.abs( -8 + Math.floor( -5.5 ) ) );`

6.8   A parking garage charges a $2.00 minimum fee to park for up to three hours. The garage charges an additional $0.50 per hour for each hour *or part thereof* in excess of three hours. The maximum charge for any given 24-hour period is $10.00. Assume that no car parks for longer than 24 hours at a time. Write an applet that calculates and displays the parking charges for each customer who parked a car in this garage yesterday. You should enter in a **JTextField** the hours parked for each customer. The program should display the charge for the current customer and should calculate and display the running total of yesterday's receipts. The program should use the method **calcu-lateCharges** to determine the charge for each customer. Use the techniques described in Self-Review Exercise 6.6 to read the double value from a **JTextField**.

6.9   An application of method **Math.floor** is rounding a value to the nearest integer. The statement

```
y = Math.floor( x + .5 );
```

will round the number **x** to the nearest integer and assign the result to **y**. Write an applet that reads double values and uses the preceding statement to round each of these numbers to the nearest integer. For each number processed, display both the original number and the rounded number. Use the techniques described in Self-Review Exercise 6.6 to read the double value from a **JTextField**.

6.10   **Math.floor** may be used to round a number to a specific decimal place. The statement

```
y = Math.floor( x * 10 + .5 ) / 10;
```

rounds **x** to the tenths position (the first position to the right of the decimal point). The statement

```
y = Math.floor( x * 100 + .5 ) / 100;
```

rounds **x** to the hundredths position (i.e., the second position to the right of the decimal point). Write an applet that defines four methods to round a number **x** in various ways:
   a) **roundToInteger(number)**
   b) **roundToTenths(number)**
   c) **roundToHundredths(number)**
   d) **roundToThousandths(number)**

For each value read, your program should display the original value, the number rounded to the nearest integer, the number rounded to the nearest tenth, the number rounded to the nearest hundredth and the number rounded to the nearest thousandth.

6.11   Answer each of the following questions.
   a) What does it mean to choose numbers "at random?"
   b) Why is the **Math.random** method useful for simulating games of chance?
   c) Why is it often necessary to scale and/or shift the values produced by **Math.random**?
   d) Why is computerized simulation of real-world situations a useful technique?

6.12   Write statements that assign random integers to the variable n in the following ranges:
   a) $1 \leq n \leq 2$
   b) $1 \leq n \leq 100$
   c) $0 \leq n \leq 9$
   d) $1000 \leq n \leq 1112$
   e) $-1 \leq n \leq 1$
   f) $-3 \leq n \leq 11$

6.13   For each of the following sets of integers, write a single statement that will print a number at random from the set.

      a)   2, 4, 6, 8, 10.
      b)   3, 5, 7, 9, 11.
      c)   6, 10, 14, 18, 22.

6.14   Write a method **integerPower(base, exponent)** that returns the value of

    $base^{\,exponent}$

For example, **integerPower(3, 4) = 3 * 3 * 3 * 3**. Assume that **exponent** is a positive, nonzero integer and **base** is an integer. Method **integerPower** should use **for** or **while** to control the calculation. Do not use any math library methods. Incorporate this method into an applet that reads integer values from **JTextField**s for **base** and **exponent** from the user and performs the calculation with the **integerPower** method. [*Note:* Register for event handling on only the second **JTextField**. The user should interact with the program by typing numbers in both **JTextField**s and pressing *Enter* in the second **JTextField**.]

6.15   Define a method **hypotenuse** that calculates the length of the hypotenuse of a right triangle when the other two sides are given. The method should take two arguments of type **double** and return the hypotenuse as a **double**. Incorporate this method into an applet that reads integer values for **side1** and **side2** from **JTextField**s and performs the calculation with the **hypotenuse** method. Determine the length of the hypotenuse for each of the following triangles. [*Note:* Register for event handling on only the second **JTextField**. The user should interact with the program by typing numbers in both **JTextField**s and pressing *Enter* in the second **JTextField**.]

Triangle	Side 1	Side 2
1	3.0	4.0
2	5.0	12.0
3	8.0	15.0

6.16   Write a method **multiple** that determines for a pair of integers whether the second integer is a multiple of the first. The method should take two integer arguments and return **true** if the second is a multiple of the first and **false** otherwise. Incorporate this method into an applet that inputs a series of pairs of integers (one pair at a time using **JTextField**s). [*Note:* Register for event handling on only the second **JTextField**. The user should interact with the program by typing numbers in both **JTextField**s and pressing *Enter* in the second **JTextField**.]

6.17   Write an applet that inputs integers (one at a time) and passes them one at a time to method **isEven**, which uses the modulus operator to determine if an integer is even. The method should take an integer argument and return **true** if the integer is even and **false** otherwise. Use an input dialog to obtain the data from the user.

6.18   Write a method **squareOfAsterisks** that displays a solid square of asterisks whose side is specified in integer parameter **side**. For example, if **side** is **4**, the method displays

      ****
      ****
      ****
      ****

Incorporate this method into an applet that reads an integer value for **side** from the user at the keyboard and performs the drawing with the **squareOfAsterisks** method. Note that this method should be called from the applet's **paint** method and should be passed the **Graphics** object from **paint**.

6.19   Modify the method created in Exercise 6.18 to form the square out of whatever character is contained in character parameter **fillCharacter**. Thus if **side** is **5** and **fillCharacter** is "**#**", this method should print

```
#####
#####
#####
#####
#####
```

6.20   Use techniques similar to those developed in Exercises 6.18 and 6.19 to produce a program that graphs a wide range of shapes.

6.21   Modify the program of Exercise 6.18 to draw a solid square with the **fillRect** method of the **Graphics** class. Method **fillRect** receives four arguments—*x*-coordinate, *y*-coordinate, width and height. Allow the user to enter the coordinates at which the square should appear.

6.22   Write program segments that accomplish each of the following:
   a) Calculate the integer part of the quotient when integer **a** is divided by integer **b**.
   b) Calculate the integer remainder when integer **a** is divided by integer **b**.
   c) Use the program pieces developed in a) and b) to write a method **displayDigits** that receives an integer between **1** and **99999** and prints it as a series of digits, each pair of which is separated by two spaces. For example, the integer **4562** should be printed as
       4   5   6   2.
   d) Incorporate the method developed in c) into an applet that inputs an integer from an input dialog and invokes **displayDigits** by passing the method the integer entered. Display the results in a message dialog.

6.23   Implement the following integer methods:
   a) Method **celsius** returns the Celsius equivalent of a Fahrenheit temperature using the calculation

```
C = 5.0 / 9.0 * ( F - 32 );
```

   b) Method **fahrenheit** returns the Fahrenheit equivalent of a Celsius temperature.

```
F = 9.0 / 5.0 * C + 32;
```

   c) Use these methods to write an applet that enables the user to enter either a Fahrenheit temperature and display the Celsius equivalent or enter a Celsius temperature and display the Fahrenheit equivalent.

[*Note:* This applet will require that two **JTextField** objects that have registered action events. When **actionPerformed** is invoked, the **ActionEvent** parameter has method **getSource()** to determine the GUI component with which the user interacted. Your **actionPerformed** method should contain an **if/else** structure of the following form:

```
if ( e.getSource() == input1 ) {
   // process input1 interaction here
}
else {  // e.getSource() == input2
   // process input2 interaction here
}
```

where **input1** and **input2** are **JTextField** references.]

6.24   Write a method **minimum3** that returns the smallest of three floating-point numbers. Use the **Math.min** method to implement **minimum3**. Incorporate the method into an applet that reads three values from the user and determines the smallest value. Display the result in the status bar.

6.25   An integer number is said to be a *perfect number* if its factors, including 1 (but not the number itself), sum to the number. For example, 6 is a perfect number because 6 = 1 + 2 + 3. Write a method **perfect** that determines if parameter **number** is a perfect number. Use this method in an applet that determines and displays all the perfect numbers between 1 and 1000. Print the factors of each perfect number to confirm that the number is indeed perfect. Challenge the computing power of your computer by testing numbers much larger than 1000. Display the results in a **JTextArea** that has scrolling functionality.

6.26   An integer is said to be *prime* if it is divisible only by 1 and itself. For example, 2, 3, 5 and 7 are prime, but 4, 6, 8 and 9 are not.
    a) Write a method that determines if a number is prime.
    b) Use this method in an applet that determines and prints all the prime numbers between 1 and 10,000. How many of these 10,000 numbers do you really have to test before being sure that you have found all the primes? Display the results in a **JTextArea** that has scrolling functionality.
    c) Initially you might think that $n/2$ is the upper limit for which you must test to see if a number is prime, but you need only go as high as the square root of n. Why? Rewrite the program and run it both ways. Estimate the performance improvement.

6.27   Write a method that takes an integer value and returns the number with its digits reversed. For example, given the number 7631, the method should return 1367. Incorporate the method into an applet that reads a value from the user. Display the result of the method in the status bar.

6.28   The *greatest common divisor (GCD)* of two integers is the largest integer that evenly divides each of the two numbers. Write a method **gcd** that returns the greatest common divisor of two integers. Incorporate the method into an applet that reads two values from the user. Display the result of the method in the status bar.

6.29   Write a method **qualityPoints** that inputs a student's average and returns 4 if a student's average is 90–100, 3 if the average is 80–89, 2 if the average is 70–79, 1 if the average is 60–69 and 0 if the average is lower than 60. Incorporate the method into an applet that reads a value from the user. Display the result of the method in the status bar.

6.30   Write an applet that simulates coin tossing. Let the program toss the coin each time the user presses the "**Toss**" button. Count the number of times each side of the coin appears. Display the results. The program should call a separate method **flip** that takes no arguments and returns **false** for tails and **true** for heads. [*Note:* If the program realistically simulates the coin tossing, each side of the coin should appear approximately half the time.]

6.31   Computers are playing an increasing role in education. Write a program that will help an elementary school student learn multiplication. Use **Math.random** to produce two positive one-digit integers. It should then display a question in the status bar such as

        `How much is 6 times 7?`

The student then types the answer into a **JTextField**. Your program checks the student's answer. If it is correct, draw the string **"Very good!"** on the applet, then ask another multiplication question. If the answer is wrong, draw the string **"No. Please try again."** on the applet, then let the student try the same question again repeatedly until the student finally gets it right. A separate method should be used to generate each new question. This method should be called once when the applet begins execution and each time the user answers the question correctly. All drawing on the applet should be performed by the **paint** method.

6.32   The use of computers in education is referred to as *computer-assisted instruction* (CAI). One problem that develops in CAI environments is student fatigue. This can be eliminated by varying the computer's dialogue to hold the student's attention. Modify the program of Exercise 6.31 so the various comments are printed for each correct answer and each incorrect answer as follows:

Responses to a correct answer

```
Very good!
Excellent!
Nice work!
Keep up the good work!
```

Responses to an incorrect answer

```
No. Please try again.
Wrong. Try once more.
Don't give up!
No. Keep trying.
```

Use random number generation to choose a number from 1 to 4 that will be used to select an appropriate response to each answer. Use a **switch** structure in the **paint** method to issue the responses.

6.33   More sophisticated computer-aided instructions systems monitor the student's performance over a period of time. The decision to begin a new topic is often based on the student's success with previous topics. Modify the program of Exercise 6.32 to count the number of correct and incorrect responses typed by the student. After the student types 10 answers, your program should calculate the percentage of correct responses. If the percentage is lower than 75%, print **Please ask your instructor for extra help** and reset the program so another student can try the program.

6.34   Write an applet that plays the "guess the number" game as follows: Your program chooses the number to be guessed by selecting a random integer in the range 1 to 1000. The applet displays the prompt **Guess a number between 1 and 1000** next to a **JTextField**. The player types a first guess into the **JTextField** and presses the *Enter* key. If the player's guess is incorrect, your program should display **Too high. Try again.** or **Too low. Try again.** in the status bar to help the player "zero in" on the correct answer and should clear the **JTextField** so the user can enter the next guess. When the user enters the correct answer, display **Congratulations. You guessed the number!** in the status bar and clear the **JTextField** so the user can play again. [*Note:* The guessing technique employed in this problem is similar to a *binary search.*]

6.35   Modify the program of Exercise 6.34 to count the number of guesses the player makes. If the number is 10 or fewer, print **Either you know the secret or you got lucky!** If the player guesses the number in 10 tries, print **Ahah! You know the secret!** If the player makes more than 10 guesses, print **You should be able to do better!** Why should it take no more than 10 guesses? Well with each "good guess" the player should be able to eliminate half of the numbers. Now show why any number 1 to 1000 can be guessed in 10 or fewer tries.

6.36   Write a recursive method **power (base, exponent)** that when invoked returns

$$base^{\ exponent}$$

for example, **power(3, 4) = 3 * 3 * 3 * 3**. Assume that **exponent** is an integer greater than or equal to 1. (*Hint:* The recursion step would use the relationship

$$base^{\ exponent} = base \cdot base^{\ exponent\ -\ 1}$$

and the terminating condition occurs when **exponent** is equal to **1** because

$$base^1 = base$$

Incorporate this method into an applet that enables the user to enter the **base** and **exponent**.)

6.37   *(Towers of Hanoi)* Every budding computer scientist must grapple with certain classic problems and the Towers of Hanoi (see Fig. 6.19) is one of the most famous of these. Legend has it that in a temple in the Far East, priests are attempting to move a stack of disks from one peg to another. The initial stack had 64 disks threaded onto one peg and arranged from bottom to top by decreasing size. The priests are attempting to move the stack from this peg to a second peg under the constraints that exactly one disk is moved at a time and at no time may a larger disk be placed above a smaller disk. A third peg is available for temporarily holding disks. Supposedly, the world will end when the priests complete their task, so there is little incentive for us to facilitate their efforts.

Let us assume that the priests are attempting to move the disks from peg 1 to peg 3. We wish to develop an algorithm that will print the precise sequence of peg-to-peg disk transfers.

If we were to approach this problem with conventional methods, we would rapidly find ourselves hopelessly knotted up in managing the disks. Instead, if we attack the problem with recursion in mind, it immediately becomes tractable. Moving n disks can be viewed in terms of moving only $n - 1$ disks (and hence the recursion) as follows:

a) Move $n - 1$ disks from peg 1 to peg 2, using peg 3 as a temporary holding area.
b) Move the last disk (the largest) from peg 1 to peg 3.
c) Move the $n - 1$ disks from peg 2 to peg 3, using peg 1 as a temporary holding area.

The process ends when the last task involves moving $n = 1$ disk (i.e., the base case). This is accomplished by trivially moving the disk without the need for a temporary holding area.

Write an applet to solve the Towers of Hanoi problem. Allow the user to enter the number of disks in a **JTextField**. Use a recursive **tower** method with four parameters:

a) The number of disks to be moved
b) The peg on which these disks are initially threaded
c) The peg to which this stack of disks is to be moved
d) The peg to be used as a temporary holding area

Your program should display in a **JTextArea** with scrolling functionality the precise instructions it will take to move the disks from the starting peg to the destination peg. For example, to move a stack of three disks from peg 1 to peg 3, your program should print the following series of moves:

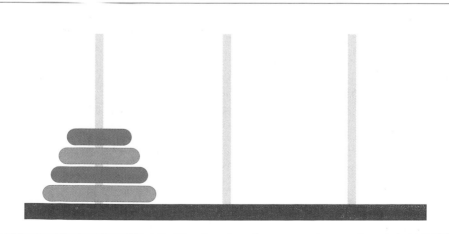

Fig. 6.19   The Towers of Hanoi for the case with four disks.

1 → 3 (This means move one disk from peg 1 to peg 3.)
1 → 2
3 → 2
1 → 3
2 → 1
2 → 3
1 → 3

6.38   Any program that can be implemented recursively can be implemented iteratively, although sometimes with more difficulty and less clarity. Try writing an iterative version of the Towers of Hanoi. If you succeed, compare your iterative version with the recursive version you developed in Exercise 6.37. Investigate issues of performance, clarity and your ability to demonstrate the correctness of the programs.

6.39   *(Visualizing Recursion)* It is interesting to watch recursion "in action." Modify the factorial method of Fig. 6.12 to print its local variable and recursive call parameter. For each recursive call, display the outputs on a separate line and add a level of indentation. Do your utmost to make the outputs clear, interesting and meaningful. Your goal here is to design and implement an output format that helps a person understand recursion better. You may want to add such display capabilities to the many other recursion examples and exercises throughout the text.

6.40   The greatest common divisor of integers **x** and **y** is the largest integer that evenly divides both **x** and **y**. Write a recursive method **gcd** that returns the greatest common divisor of **x** and **y**. The **gcd** of **x** and **y** is defined recursively as follows: If **y** is equal to **0**, then **gcd(x, y)** is **x**; otherwise, **gcd(x, y)** is **gcd(y, x % y)**, where **%** is the modulus operator. Use this method to replace the one you wrote in the applet of Exercise 6.28.

6.41   Exercises 6.31 through 6.33 developed a computer-assisted instruction program to teach an elementary school student multiplication. This exercise suggests enhancements to that program.
   a) Modify the program to allow the user to enter a grade-level capability. A grade level of 1 means to use only single-digit numbers in the problems, a grade level of 2 means to use numbers as large as two digits, etc.
   b) Modify the program to allow the user to pick the type of arithmetic problems he or she wishes to study. An option of 1 means addition problems only, 2 means subtraction problems only, 3 means multiplication problems only, 4 means division problems only and 5 means to randomly intermix problems of all these types.

6.42   Write method **distance**, which calculates the distance between two points (x1, y1) and (x2, y2). All numbers and return values should be of type **double**. Incorporate this method into an applet that enables the user to enter the coordinates of the points.

6.43   What does the following method do?

```
// Parameter b must be a positive
// integer to prevent infinite recursion
public int mystery( int a, int b )
{
   if ( b == 1 )
      return a;
   else
      return a + mystery( a, b - 1 );
}
```

6.44   After you determine what the program of Exercise 6.43 does, modify the method to operate properly after removing the restriction of the second argument being nonnegative. Also, incorporate the method into an applet that enables the user to enter two integers and test the method.

6.45   Write an application that tests as many of the math library methods in Fig. 6.2 as you can. Exercise each of these methods by having your program print out tables of return values for a diversity of argument values.

6.46   Find the error in the following recursive method and explain how to correct it:

```
public int sum( int n )
{
   if ( n == 0 )
      return 0;
   else
      return n + sum(n);
}
```

6.47   Modify the craps program of Fig. 6.9 to allow wagering. Initialize variable **bankBalance** to 1000 dollars. Prompt the player to enter a **wager**. Check that **wager** is less than or equal to **bankBalance**, and if not, have the user reenter **wager** until a valid **wager** is entered. After a correct **wager** is entered, run one game of craps. If the player wins, increase **bankBalance** by **wager** and print the new **bankBalance**. If the player loses, decrease **bankBalance** by **wager**, print the new **bankBalance**, check if **bankBalance** has become zero, and if so, print the message **"Sorry. You busted!"** As the game progresses, print various messages to create some "chatter," such as **"Oh, you're going for broke, huh?"** or **"Aw c'mon, take a chance!"** or **"You're up big. Now's the time to cash in your chips!"**. Implement the "chatter" as a separate method that randomly chooses the string to display.

6.48   Write an applet that uses a method **circleArea** to prompt the user for the radius of a circle and to calculate and print the area of that circle.

7

Arrays

Objectives

- To introduce the array data structure.
- To understand the use of arrays to store, sort and search lists and tables of values.
- To understand how to declare an array, initialize an array and refer to individual elements of an array.
- To be able to pass arrays to methods.
- To understand basic sorting techniques.
- To be able to declare and manipulate multiple-subscript arrays.

With sobs and tears he sorted out
Those of the largest size …
Lewis Carroll

Attempt the end, and never stand to doubt;
Nothing's so hard, but search will find it out.
Robert Herrick

Now go, write it before them in a table,
and note it in a book.
Isaiah 30:8

'Tis in my memory lock'd,
And you yourself shall keep the key of it.
William Shakespeare

Outline

7.1 Introduction

This chapter serves as an introduction to the important topic of data structures. *Arrays* are data structures consisting of related data items of the same type. Arrays are "static" entities in that they remain the same size once they are created, although an array reference may be reassigned to a new array of a different size. Chapter 22, "Data Structures," introduces dynamic data structures such as lists, queues, stacks and trees that may grow and shrink as programs execute. Chapter 23, "Java Utilities Package and Bit Manipulation," discusses class **Vector**, which is an array-like class whose objects can grow and shrink in response to a Java program's changing storage requirements. Chapter 24, "The Collections API," introduces Java's new predefined data structures that enable the programmer to use existing data structures for lists, queues, stacks and trees rather than "reinventing the wheel."

7.2 Arrays

An array is a group of contiguous memory locations that all have the same name and the same type. To refer to a particular location or element in the array, we specify the name of the array and the *position number* of the particular element in the array.

Figure 7.1 shows an integer array called **c**. This array contains 12 *elements.* Any one of these elements may be referred to by giving the name of the array followed by the position number of the particular element in square brackets (**[]**). The first element in every array is the *zeroth element.* Thus, the first element of array **c** is referred to as **c[0]**, the second element of array **c** is referred to as **c[1]**, the seventh element of array **c** is referred to as **c[6]**, and, in general, the *i*th element of array **c** is referred to as **c[i-1]**. Array names follow the same conventions as other variable names.

The position number in square brackets is more formally called a *subscript* (or an index). A subscript must be an integer or an integer expression. If a program uses an expression as a subscript, the expression is evaluated first to determine the subscript. For example, if we assume that variable **a** is equal to **5** and that variable **b** is equal to **6**, then the statement

Name of array (Note that all
elements of this array have the
same name, **c**)

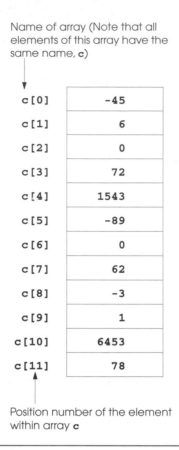

Position number of the element
within array **c**

Fig. 7.1   A 12-element array.

```
c[ a + b ] += 2;
```

adds 2 to array element **c[11]**. Note that a subscripted array name is an *lvalue*—it can be used on the left side of an assignment to place a new value into an array element.

Let us examine array **c** in Fig. 7.1 more closely. The *name* of the array is **c**. The *length* of the array is determined by the following expression:

```
c.length
```

Every array in Java *knows* its own length. The array's 12 elements are referred to as **c[0]**, **c[1]**, **c[2]**, ..., **c[11]**. The *value* of **c[0]** is **-45**, the value of **c[1]** is **6**, the value of **c[2]** is **0**, the value of **c[7]** is **62** and the value of **c[11]** is **78**. To calculate the sum of the values contained in the first three elements of array **c** and store the result in variable **sum**, we would write

```
sum = c[ 0 ] + c[ 1 ] + c[ 2 ];
```

To divide the value of the seventh element of array **c** by **2** and assign the result to the variable **x**, we would write

```
x = c[ 6 ] / 2;
```

Common Programming Error 7.1

It is important to note the difference between the "seventh element of the array" and "array element seven." Because array subscripts begin at 0, the "seventh element of the array" has a subscript of 6, while "array element seven" has a subscript of 7 and is actually the eighth element of the array. This confusion is a source of "off-by-one" errors.

The brackets used to enclose the subscript of an array are an operator in Java. Brackets have the same level of precedence as parentheses. The chart in Fig. 7.2 shows the precedence and associativity of the operators introduced to this point in the text. They are shown top to bottom in decreasing order of precedence with their associativity and type.

7.3 Declaring and Allocating Arrays

Arrays occupy space in memory. The programmer specifies the type of the elements and uses operator **new** to dynamically allocate the number of elements required by each array. Arrays are allocated with **new** because arrays are considered to be objects and all objects must be created with **new**. To allocate 12 elements for integer array **c**, the declaration

```
int c[] = new int[ 12 ];
```

is used. The preceding statement can also be performed in two steps as follows:

```
int c[];              // declares the array
c = new int[ 12 ];    // allocates the array
```

When arrays are allocated, the elements are automatically initialized to zero for the numeric primitive-data-type variables, to **false** for **boolean** variables or to **null** for references (any nonprimitive type).

Operators	Associativity	Type
( ) [ ] .	left to right	highest
++ --	right to left	unary postfix
++ -- + - ! (*type*)	right to left	unary
* / %	left to right	multiplicative
+ -	left to right	additive
< <= > >=	left to right	relational
== !=	left to right	equality
&	left to right	boolean logical AND
^	left to right	boolean logical exclusive OR
|	left to right	boolean logical inclusive OR
&&	left to right	logical AND
||	left to right	logical OR
? :	right to left	conditional
= += -= *= /= %=	right to left	assignment

Fig. 7.2   Precedence and associativity of the operators discussed so far.

Common Programming Error 7.2

Unlike C or C++ the number of elements in the array is never specified in the square brackets after the array name in a declaration. The declaration **int c[12];** *causes a syntax error.*

Memory may be reserved for several arrays with a single declaration. The following declaration reserves 100 elements for **String** array **b** and 27 elements for **String** array **x**:

```
String b[] = new String[ 100 ], x[] = new String[ 27 ];
```

When declaring an array, the type of the array and the square brackets can be combined at the beginning of the declaration to indicate that all identifiers in the declaration represent arrays, as in

```
double[] array1, array2;
```

which declares both **array1** and **array2** as arrays of **double** values. As shown previously, the declaration and initialization of the array can be combined in the declaration. The following declaration reserves 10 elements for **array1** and 20 elements for **array2**:

```
double[] array1 = new double[ 10 ], array2 = new double[ 20 ];
```

Arrays may be declared to contain any data type. It is important to remember that in an array of primitive data type, every element of the array contains one value of the declared data type of the array. For example, every element of an **int** array is an **int** value. However, in an array of a nonprimitive type, every element of the array is a reference to an object of the data type of the array. For example, every element of a **String** array is a reference to a **String** that has the value **null** by default.

7.4 Examples Using Arrays

The application of Fig. 7.3 uses the **new** operator to dynamically allocate an array of 10 elements which are initially zero, then it prints the array in tabular format.

Line 9 declares **n** as a reference capable of referring to array of integers. Line 11 allocates the 10 elements of the array with **new** an initializes the reference. Line 13 appends to **String output** the headings for the columns of output displayed by the program.

Lines 15 and 16

```
for ( int i = 0; i < n.length; i++ )
    output += i + "\t" + n[ i ] + "\n";
```

use a **for** structure to build the **output String** that will be displayed in a **JTextArea** on a message dialog. Note the use of zero-based counting (remember, subscripts start at 0) so the loop can access every element of the array. Also, note the expression **n.length** in the **for** structure condition to determine the length of the array. In this example, the length of the array is 10, so the loop continues executing as long as the value of control variable **i** is less than 10. For a 10-element array, the subscript values are 0 through 9, so using the less than operator **<** guarantees that the loop does not attempt to access an element beyond the end of the array.

```
1    // Fig. 7.3: InitArray.java
2    // initializing an array
3    import javax.swing.*;
4
5    public class InitArray {
6       public static void main( String args[] )
7       {
8          String output = "";
9          int n[];                // declare reference to an array
10
11         n = new int[ 10 ];   // dynamically allocate array
12
13         output += "Subscript\tValue\n";
14
15         for ( int i = 0; i < n.length; i++ )
16            output += i + "\t" + n[ i ] + "\n";
17
18         JTextArea outputArea = new JTextArea( 11, 10 );
19         outputArea.setText( output );
20
21         JOptionPane.showMessageDialog( null, outputArea,
22            "Initializing an Array of int Values",
23            JOptionPane.INFORMATION_MESSAGE );
24
25         System.exit( 0 );
26      }
27   }
```

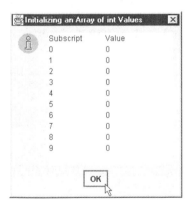

Fig. 7.3   Initializing the elements of an array to zeros.

The elements of an array can be allocated and initialized in the array declaration by following the declaration with an equal sign and a comma-separated *initializer list enclosed in braces* ({ and }). In this case, the array size is determined by the number of elements in the initializer list. For example, the statement

```
int n[] = { 10, 20, 30, 40, 50 };
```

creates a five-element array with subscripts of **0**, **1**, **2**, **3** and **4**. Note that the preceding declaration does not require the new operator to create the array object—this is provided automatically by the compiler when it encounters an array declaration that includes an initializer list.

The application of Fig. 7.4 initializes an integer array with 10 values (line 12) and displays the array in tabular format in a **JTextArea** on a message dialog.

The application of Fig. 7.5 initializes the elements of a 10-element array **s** to the even integers **2, 4, 6, …, 20** and prints the array in tabular format. These numbers are generated by multiplying each successive value of the loop counter by **2** and adding **2**.

```
1   // Fig. 7.4: InitArray.java
2   // initializing an array with a declaration
3   import javax.swing.*;
4
5   public class InitArray {
6      public static void main( String args[] )
7      {
8         String output = "";
9
10        // Initializer list specifies number of elements and
11        // value for each element.
12        int n[] = { 32, 27, 64, 18, 95, 14, 90, 70, 60, 37 };
13
14        output += "Subscript\tValue\n";
15
16        for ( int i = 0; i < n.length; i++ )
17           output += i + "\t" + n[ i ] + "\n";
18
19        JTextArea outputArea = new JTextArea( 11, 10 );
20        outputArea.setText( output );
21
22        JOptionPane.showMessageDialog( null, outputArea,
23           "Initializing an Array with a Declaration",
24           JOptionPane.INFORMATION_MESSAGE );
25
26        System.exit( 0 );
27     }
28  }
```

Fig. 7.4   Initializing the elements of an array with a declaration.

```
1    // Fig. 7.5: InitArray.java
2    // initialize array n to the even integers from 2 to 20
3    import javax.swing.*;
4
5    public class InitArray {
6       public static void main( String args[] )
7       {
8          final int ARRAY_SIZE = 10;
9          int n[];                        // reference to int array
10         String output = "";
11
12         n = new int[ ARRAY_SIZE ];   // allocate array
13
14         // Set the values in the array
15         for ( int i = 0; i < n.length; i++ )
16            n[ i ] = 2 + 2 * i;
17
18         output += "Subscript\tValue\n";
19
20         for ( int i = 0; i < n.length; i++ )
21            output += i + "\t" + n[ i ] + "\n";
22
23         JTextArea outputArea = new JTextArea( 11, 10 );
24         outputArea.setText( output );
25
26         JOptionPane.showMessageDialog( null, outputArea,
27            "Initializing to Even Numbers from 2 to 20",
28            JOptionPane.INFORMATION_MESSAGE );
29
30         System.exit( 0 );
31      }
32   }
```

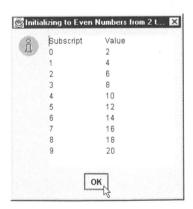

Fig. 7.5   Generating values to be placed into elements of an array.

Line 8

```
final int ARRAY_SIZE = 10;
```

uses the **final** qualifier to declare a so-called constant variable **ARRAY_SIZE** whose value is **10**. Constant variables must be initialized before they are used and cannot be modified thereafter. If an attempt is made to modify a **final** variable after it is declared as shown in the preceding statement, the compiler issues a message like

```
Can't assign a value to a final variable
```

If an attempt is made to modify a **final** variable after it is declared, then initialized in a separate statement, the compiler issues the error message

```
Can't assign a second value to a blank final variable
```

If an attempt is made to use a **final** local variable before it is initialized, the compiler issues the error message

```
Variable variableName may not have been initialized
```

If an attempt is made to use a **final** instance variable before it is initialized, the compiler issues the error message

```
Blank final variable 'variableName' may not have been
initialized. It must be assigned a value in an initializer,
or in every constructor.
```

Constant variables are also called *named constants* or *read-only variables*. They are often used to make a program more readable. Note that the term "constant variable" is an oxymoron—a contradiction in terms—like "jumbo shrimp" or "freezer burn."

Common Programming Error 7.3

Assigning a value to a constant variable after the variable has been initialized is a syntax error.

The application of Fig. 7.6 sums the values contained in the 10-element integer array **a** (declared, allocated and initialized at line 8). The statement (line 12) in the body of the **for** loop does the totaling. It is important to remember that the values being supplied as initializers for array **a** normally would be read into the program. For example, in an applet the user could enter the values through a **JTextField**, or in an application the values could be read from a file on disk (see Chapter 17).

```
1   // Fig. 7.6: SumArray.java
2   // Compute the sum of the elements of the array
3   import javax.swing.*;
4
5   public class SumArray {
6      public static void main( String args[] )
7      {
8         int a[] = { 1, 2, 3, 4, 5, 6, 7, 8, 9, 10 };
9         int total = 0;
10
11        for ( int i = 0; i < a.length; i++ )
12           total += a[ i ];
13
```

Fig. 7.6　Computing the sum of the elements of an array (part 1 of 2).

```
14          JOptionPane.showMessageDialog( null,
15              "Total of array elements: " + total,
16              "Sum the Elements of an Array",
17              JOptionPane.INFORMATION_MESSAGE );
18
19          System.exit( 0 );
20      }
21  }
```

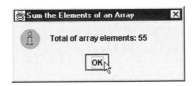

Fig. 7.6   Computing the sum of the elements of an array (part 2 of 2).

Our next example uses arrays to summarize the results of data collected in a survey. Consider the problem statement:

Forty students were asked to rate the quality of the food in the student cafeteria on a scale of 1 to 10 (1 means awful and 10 means excellent). Place the 40 responses in an integer array and summarize the results of the poll.

This is a typical array processing application (see Fig. 7.7). We wish to summarize the number of responses of each type (i.e., 1 through 10). The array **responses** is a 40-element integer array of the students' responses to the survey. We use an 11-element array **frequency** to count the number of occurrences of each response. We ignore the first element, **frequency[0]**, because it is more logical to have the response 1 increment **frequency[1]** than **frequency[0]**. This allows us to use each response directly as a subscript on the **frequency** array. Each element of the array is used as a counter for one of the survey responses.

Good Programming Practice 7.1

Strive for program clarity. It is sometimes worthwhile to trade off the most efficient use of memory or processor time in favor of writing clearer programs.

Performance Tip 7.1

Sometimes performance considerations far outweigh clarity considerations.

The **for** loop (lines 15 through 18) takes the responses one at a time from the array **response** and increments one of the 10 counters in the **frequency** array (**frequency[1]** to **frequency[10]**). The key statement in the loop is

```
++frequency[ responses[ answer ] ];
```

This statement increments the appropriate **frequency** counter depending on the value of **responses[answer]**.

Let's consider several iterations of the **for** loop. When counter **answer** is **0**, **responses[answer]** is the value of the first element of array **responses** (i.e., **1**), so **++frequency[responses[answer]];** is actually interpreted as

```java
1   // Fig. 7.7: StudentPoll.java
2   // Student poll program
3   import javax.swing.*;
4
5   public class StudentPoll {
6      public static void main( String args[] )
7      {
8         int responses[] = { 1, 2, 6, 4, 8, 5, 9, 7, 8, 10,
9                             1, 6, 3, 8, 6, 10, 3, 8, 2, 7,
10                            6, 5, 7, 6, 8, 6, 7, 5, 6, 6,
11                            5, 6, 7, 5, 6, 4, 8, 6, 8, 10 };
12        int frequency[] = new int[ 11 ];
13        String output = "";
14
15        for ( int answer = 0;                // initialize
16              answer < responses.length;     // condition
17              answer++ )                      // increment
18           ++frequency[ responses[ answer ] ];
19
20        output += "Rating\tFrequency\n";
21
22        for ( int rating = 1;
23              rating < frequency.length;
24              rating++ )
25           output += rating + "\t" + frequency[ rating ] + "\n";
26
27        JTextArea outputArea = new JTextArea( 11, 10 );
28        outputArea.setText( output );
29
30        JOptionPane.showMessageDialog( null, outputArea,
31           "Student Poll Program",
32           JOptionPane.INFORMATION_MESSAGE );
33
34        System.exit( 0 );
35     }
36  }
```

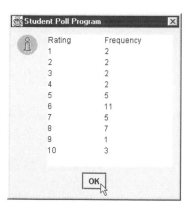

Fig. 7.7   A simple student-poll analysis program.

```
    ++frequency[ 1 ];
```

which increments array element one. In evaluating the expression, start with the value in the innermost set of square brackets (**answer**). Once you know the value of **answer**, plug that value into the expression and evaluate the next outer set of square brackets (**responses[answer]**). Then, use that value as the subscript for the **frequency** array to determine which counter to increment.

When **answer** is **1**, **responses[answer]** is the value of the second element of array **responses** (i.e., **2**), so **++frequency[responses[answer]];** is actually interpreted as

```
    ++frequency[ 2 ];
```

which increments array element two (the third element of the array).

When **answer** is **2**, **responses[answer]** is the value of the third element of array **responses** (i.e., **6**), so **++frequency[responses[answer]];** is actually interpreted as

```
    ++frequency[ 6 ];
```

which increments array element six (the seventh element of the array) and so on. Note that regardless of the number of responses processed in the survey, only an 11-element array is required (ignoring element zero) to summarize the results because all the response values are between 1 and 10 and the subscript values for an 11-element array are 0 through 10. Also note that the results are correct because the elements of the **frequency** array were automatically initialized to zero when the array was allocated with **new**.

If the data contained invalid values such as 13, the program would attempt to add **1** to **frequency[13]**. This is outside the bounds of the array. In the C and C++ programming languages, such a reference would be allowed by the compiler and at execution time. The program would "walk" past the end of the array to where it thought element number 13 was located and add 1 to whatever happened to be at that location in memory. This could potentially modify another variable in the program or even result in premature program termination. Java provides mechanisms to prevent accessing elements outside the bounds of the array.

Testing and Debugging Tip 7.1

When a Java program is executed, the Java interpreter checks array element subscripts to be sure they are valid (i.e., all subscripts must be greater than or equal to 0 and less than the length of the array). If there is an invalid subscript, Java generates an exception.

Testing and Debugging Tip 7.2

Exceptions are used to indicate that an error occurred in a program. They enable the programmer to recover from an error and continue execution of the program instead of abnormally terminating the program. When an invalid array reference is made, an **ArrayIndexOutOfBoundsException** *is generated. Chapter 14 covers exception handling in detail.*

Common Programming Error 7.4

Referring to an element outside the array bounds is a logic error.

Testing and Debugging Tip 7.3

When looping through an array, the array subscript should never go below 0 and should always be less than the total number of elements in the array (one less than the size of the array). Make sure the loop terminating condition prevents accessing elements outside this range.

Testing and Debugging Tip 7.4

Programs should validate the correctness of all input values to prevent erroneous information from affecting a program's calculations.

Our next application (Fig. 7.8) reads numbers from an array and graphs the information in the form of a bar chart (or histogram)—each number is printed, then a bar consisting of that many asterisks is displayed beside the number. The nested **for** loop (lines 13 through 18) actually appends the bars to the **String** that will be displayed in **JTextArea outputArea** on a message dialog. Note the loop continuation condition of the inner **for** structure at line 16 (**j <= n[i]**). Each time the inner **for** structure is reached, it counts from **1** to **n[i]**, thus using a value in array **n** to determine the final value of the control variable **j** and the number of asterisks to display.

```
1   // Fig. 7.8: Histogram.java
2   // Histogram printing program
3   import javax.swing.*;
4
5   public class Histogram {
6      public static void main( String args[] )
7      {
8         int n[] = { 19, 3, 15, 7, 11, 9, 13, 5, 17, 1 };
9         String output = "";
10
11        output += "Element\tValue\tHistogram";
12
13        for ( int i = 0; i < n.length; i++ ) {
14           output += "\n" + i + "\t" + n[ i ] + "\t";
15
16           for ( int j = 1; j <= n[ i ]; j++ ) // print a bar
17              output += "*";
18        }
19
20        JTextArea outputArea = new JTextArea( 11, 30 );
21        outputArea.setText( output );
22
23        JOptionPane.showMessageDialog( null, outputArea,
24           "Histogram Printing Program",
25           JOptionPane.INFORMATION_MESSAGE );
26
27        System.exit( 0 );
28     }
29  }
```

Fig. 7.8   A program that prints histograms (part 1 of 2).

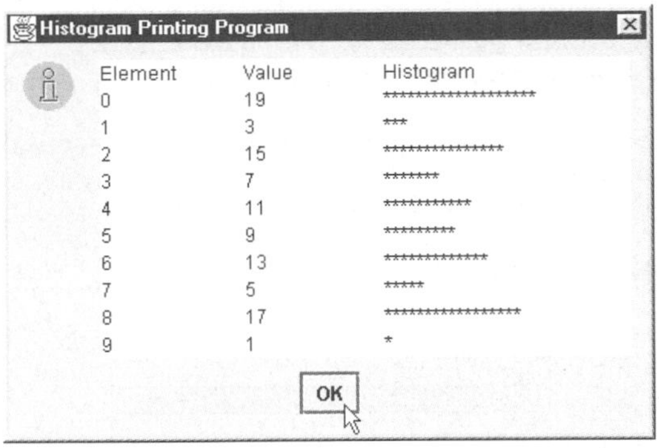

Fig. 7.8   A program that prints histograms (part 2 of 2).

Chapter 6 indicated that there is a more elegant method of writing the dice-rolling program of Fig. 6.8. The program rolled a single six-sided die 6000 times. An array version of this application is shown in Fig. 7.9. Lines 16 through 35 of Fig. 6.8 are replaced by line 13 of this program, which uses the random **face** value as the subscript for array **frequency** to determine which element should be incremented during each iteration of the loop. Because the random number calculation on line 12 produces numbers from 1 to 6 (the values for a six-sided die), the **frequency** array must be large enough to allow subscript values of 1 to 6. The smallest number of elements required for an array to have these subscript values is seven elements (subscript values from 0 to 6). In this program, we ignore element 0 of array **frequency**. Also, lines 18 and 19 of this program replace lines 40 through 47 from Fig. 6.8. Because we can loop through array **frequency**, we do not have to enumerate each line of text to display in the **JTextArea** as we did in Fig. 6.8.

```
1   // Fig. 7.9: RollDie.java
2   // Roll a six-sided die 6000 times
3   import javax.swing.*;
4
5   public class RollDie {
6      public static void main( String args[] )
7      {
8         int face, frequency[] = new int[ 7 ];
9         String output = "";
10
11        for ( int roll = 1; roll <= 6000; roll++ ) {
12           face = 1 + ( int ) ( Math.random() * 6 );
13           ++frequency[ face ];
14        }
15
16        output += "Face\tFrequency";
17
18        for ( face = 1; face < frequency.length; face++ )
19           output += "\n" + face + "\t" + frequency[ face ];
```

Fig. 7.9   Dice-rolling program using arrays instead of **switch** (part 1 of 2).

```
20
21          JTextArea outputArea = new JTextArea( 7, 10 );
22          outputArea.setText( output );
23
24          JOptionPane.showMessageDialog( null, outputArea,
25             "Rolling a Die 6000 Times",
26             JOptionPane.INFORMATION_MESSAGE );
27
28          System.exit( 0 );
29       }
30    }
```

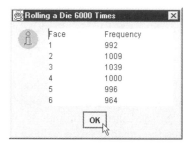

Fig. 7.9   Dice-rolling program using arrays instead of **switch** (part 2 of 2).

7.5 References and Reference Parameters

Two ways to pass arguments to methods (or functions) in many programming languages (like C and C++) are *call-by-value* and *call-by-reference* (also called *pass-by-value* and *pass-by-reference*). When an argument is passed call-by-value, a *copy* of the argument's value is made and passed to the called method.

Testing and Debugging Tip 7.5

With call-by-value, changes to the called method's copy do not affect the original variable's value in the calling method. This prevents the accidental side effects that so greatly hinder the development of correct and reliable software systems.

With call-by-reference, the caller gives the called method the ability to directly access the caller's data and to modify that data if the called method so chooses. Call-by-reference can improve performance because it can eliminate the overhead of copying large amounts of data, but call-by-reference can weaken security because the called method can access the caller's data.

Software Engineering Observation 7.1

Unlike other languages, Java does not allow the programmer to choose whether to pass each argument call-by-value or call-by-reference. Primitive data type variables are always passed call-by-value. Objects are not passed to methods; rather, references to objects are passed to methods. The references themselves are also passed call-by-value. When a method receives a reference to an object, the method can manipulate the object directly.

Software Engineering Observation 7.2

*When returning information from a method via a **return** statement, primitive-data-type variables are always returned by value (i.e., a copy is returned) and objects are always returned by reference (i.e., a reference to the object is returned).*

To pass a reference to an object into a method, simply specify in the method call the reference name. Mentioning the reference by its parameter name in the body of the called method actually refers to the original object in memory, and the original object can be accessed directly by the called method.

Because arrays are treated as objects by Java, arrays are passed to methods call-by-reference—a called method can access the elements of the caller's original arrays. The name of an array is actually a reference to an object that contains the array elements and the **length** instance variable, which indicates the number of elements in the array. In the next section, we demonstrate call-by-value and call-by-reference using arrays.

Performance Tip 7.2

Passing arrays by reference makes sense for performance reasons. If arrays were passed by value, a copy of each element would be passed. For large, frequently passed arrays, this would waste time and would consume considerable storage for the copies of the arrays.

7.6 Passing Arrays to Methods

To pass an array argument to a method, specify the name of the array without any brackets. For example, if array **hourlyTemperatures** has been declared as

```
int hourlyTemperatures[] = new int[ 24 ];
```

the method call

```
modifyArray( hourlyTemperatures );
```

passes array **hourlyTemperatures** to method **modifyArray**. In Java every array object "knows" its own size (via the **length** instance variable). Thus, when we pass an array object into a method we do not separately pass the size of the array as an argument.

Although entire arrays are passed call-by-reference, *individual array elements of primitive data types are passed call-by-value exactly as simple variables are* (the objects referred to by individual elements of a nonprimitive type array are still passed call-by-reference). Such simple single pieces of data are called *scalars* or *scalar quantities.* To pass an array element to a method, use the subscripted name of the array element as an argument in the method call.

For a method to receive an array through a method call, the method's parameter list must specify that an array will be received. For example, the method header for method **modifyArray** might be written as

```
void modifyArray( int b[] )
```

indicating that **modifyArray** expects to receive an integer array in parameter **b**. Because arrays are passed by reference, when the called method uses the array name **b**, it refers to the actual array in the caller (array **hourlyTemperatures** in the preceding call).

The applet of Fig. 7.10 demonstrates the difference between passing an entire array and passing an array element. Once again, we are defining an applet here because we have not yet defined an application that contains methods other than **main**. We are still taking advantage of some of the features provided for free in an applet (such as the automatic creation of an applet object and the automatic calls to **init**, **start** and **paint**). In Chapter 9, "Object-Oriented Programming," we introduce applications that execute in their own windows. At that point we will begin to see applications containing several methods.

```
1   // Fig. 7.10: PassArray.java
2   // Passing arrays and individual array elements to methods
3   import java.awt.Container;
4   import javax.swing.*;
5
6   public class PassArray extends JApplet {
7      JTextArea outputArea;
8      String output;
9
10     public void init()
11     {
12        outputArea = new JTextArea();
13        Container c = getContentPane();
14        c.add( outputArea );
15
16        int a[] = { 1, 2, 3, 4, 5 };
17
18        output = "Effects of passing entire " +
19                    "array call-by-reference:\n" +
20                    "The values of the original array are:\n";
21
22        for ( int i = 0; i < a.length; i++ )
23           output += "   " + a[ i ];
24
25        modifyArray( a );   // array a passed call-by-reference
26
27        output += "\n\nThe values of the modified array are:\n";
28
29        for ( int i = 0; i < a.length; i++ )
30           output += "   " + a[ i ];
31
32        output += "\n\nEffects of passing array " +
33                    "element call-by-value:\n" +
34                    "a[3] before modifyElement: " + a[ 3 ];
35
36        modifyElement( a[ 3 ] );
37
38        output += "\na[3] after modifyElement: " + a[ 3 ];
39        outputArea.setText( output );
40     }
41
42     public void modifyArray( int b[] )
43     {
44        for ( int j = 0; j < b.length; j++ )
45           b[ j ] *= 2;
46     }
47
48     public void modifyElement( int e )
49     {
50        e *= 2;
51     }
52  }
```

Fig. 7.10 Passing arrays and individual array elements to methods (part 1 of 2).

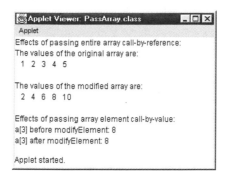

Fig. 7.10   Passing arrays and individual array elements to methods (part 2 of 2).

Lines 12 through 14 in method **init** define the **JTextArea** called **outputArea** and attach it to the applet's content pane. The **for** loop at lines 22 and 23 appends the five elements of integer array **a** to **String output**. Line 25 invokes method **modifyArray** and passes it array **a**. Method **modifyArray** multiplies each element by 2. To illustrate that array **a**'s elements were modified, the **for** loop at lines 29 and 30 appends the five elements of integer array **a** to **String output** again. As the screen capture shows, the elements of **a** are indeed modified by **modifyArray**.

To show the value of **a[3]** before the call to **modifyElement**, lines 32 through 34 append the value of **a[3]** (and other information) to **String output**. Line 36 invokes method **modifyElement** and passes **a[3]**. Remember that **a[3]** is actually one **int** value in the array **a**. Also, remember that values of primitive types are always passed to methods call-by-value. Therefore, a copy of **a[3]** is passed. Method **modifyElement** multiplies its argument by 2 and stores the result in its parameter **e**. The parameter of **modifyElement** is a local variable, so when the method terminates, the local variable is destroyed. Thus, when control is returned to **init**, the unmodified value of **a[3]** is appended to the **String output** at line 38.

7.7 Sorting Arrays

Sorting data (i.e., placing the data into some particular order such as ascending or descending) is one of the most important computing applications. A bank sorts all checks by account number so that it can prepare individual bank statements at the end of each month. Telephone companies sort their lists of accounts by last name and, within that, by first name to make it easy to find phone numbers. Virtually every organization must sort some data and in many cases massive amounts of data. Sorting data is an intriguing problem that has attracted some of the most intense research efforts in the field of computer science. In this chapter we discuss one of the simplest sorting schemes. In the exercises in Chapters 22 and 24 we investigate more complex schemes that yield superior performance.

Performance Tip 7.3

Sometimes, the simplest algorithms perform poorly. Their virtue is that they are easy to write, test and debug. More complex algorithms are sometimes needed to realize maximum performance.

Figure 7.11 sorts the values of the 10-element array **a** into ascending order. The technique we use is called the *bubble sort* or the *sinking sort* because the smaller values gradually "bubble" their way to the top of the array (i.e., toward the first element) like air bubbles rising in water, while the larger values sink to the bottom of the array. The technique makes several passes through the array. On each pass, successive pairs of elements are compared. If a pair is in increasing order (or the values are equal), we leave the values as they are. If a pair is in decreasing order, their values are swapped in the array. The applet contains methods **init**, **bubbleSort** and **swap**. Method **init** (line 8) initializes the applet. Method **bubbleSort** (line 32) is called from **init** to sort array **a**. Method **swap** (line 41) is called from **bubbleSort** to exchange two elements of the array.

```
1   // Fig. 7.11: BubbleSort.java
2   // This program sorts an array's values into
3   // ascending order
4   import java.awt.*;
5   import javax.swing.*;
6
7   public class BubbleSort extends JApplet {
8      public void init()
9      {
10        JTextArea outputArea = new JTextArea();
11        Container c = getContentPane();
12        c.add( outputArea );
13
14        int a[] = { 2, 6, 4, 8, 10, 12, 89, 68, 45, 37 };
15
16        String output = "Data items in original order\n";
17
18        for ( int i = 0; i < a.length; i++ )
19           output += "   " + a[ i ];
20
21        bubbleSort( a );
22
23        output += "\n\nData items in ascending order\n";
24
25        for ( int i = 0; i < a.length; i++ )
26           output += "   " + a[ i ];
27
28        outputArea.setText( output );
29     }
30
31     // sort the elements of an array with bubble sort
32     public void bubbleSort( int b[] )
33     {
34        for ( int pass = 1; pass < b.length; pass++ ) // passes
35           for ( int i = 0; i < b.length - 1; i++ ) // one pass
36              if ( b[ i ] > b[ i + 1 ] )           // one comparison
37                 swap( b, i, i + 1 );              // one swap
38     }
```

Fig. 7.11   Sorting an array with bubble sort (part 1 of 2).

```
39
40      // swap two elements of an array
41      public void swap( int c[], int first, int second )
42      {
43         int hold;  // temporary holding area for swap
44
45         hold = c[ first ];
46         c[ first ] = c[ second ];
47         c[ second ] = hold;
48      }
49   }
```

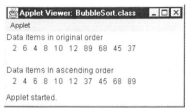

Fig. 7.11   Sorting an array with bubble sort (part 2 of 2).

Lines 16 through 19 append the original values of array **a** to the **String output**.
Line 21 invokes method **bubbleSort** and passes array **a** as the array to sort.

Method **bubbleSort** receives the array as parameter **b**. The nested **for** loop at lines
34 through 37

```
for ( int pass = 1; pass < b.length; pass++ ) // passes
   for ( int i = 0; i < b.length - 1; i++ ) // one pass
      if ( b[ i ] > b[ i + 1 ] )           // one comparison
         swap( b, i, i + 1 );              // one swap
```

performs the sort. The outer loop controls the number of passes of the array. The inner loop
controls the comparisons and swapping (if necessary) of the elements during each pass.

Method **bubbleSort** first compares **b[0]** to **b[1]**, then **b[1]** to **b[2]**, then
b[2] to **b[3]** and so on until it completes the pass by comparing **b[8]** to **b[9]**.
Although there are 10 elements, only nine comparisons are performed. Because of the way
the successive comparisons are made, a large value may move down the array (sink) many
positions on a single pass, but a small value may move up (bubble) only one position. On
the first pass, the largest value is guaranteed to sink to the bottom element of the array,
b[9]. On the second pass, the second largest value is guaranteed to sink to **b[8]**. On the
ninth pass, the ninth largest value sinks to **b[1]**. This leaves the smallest value in **b[0]**,
so only nine passes are needed to sort a 10-element array.

If a comparison reveals that the two elements are in descending order, method **swap**
is invoked to exchange the two elements so they will be in ascending order in the array.
Method **swap** receives a reference to the array (which it calls **c**) and two integers representing the subscripts of the two elements of the array to exchange. The exchange is performed by the three assignments

```
hold = c[ first ];
c[ first ] = c[ second ];
c[ second ] = hold;
```

where the extra variable **hold** temporarily stores one of the two values being swapped. The swap cannot be performed with only the two assignments

```
c[ first ] = c[ second ];
c[ second ] = c[ first ];
```

If **c[first]** is **7** and **c[second]** is **5**, after the first assignment both elements of the array contain **5** and the value **7** is lost. Hence the need for the extra variable **hold**.

The chief virtue of the bubble sort is that it is easy to program. However, the bubble sort runs slowly. This becomes apparent when sorting large arrays. In the exercises, we will develop more efficient versions of the bubble sort and investigate some far more efficient sorts than the bubble sort. More advanced courses (often titled "Data Structures" or "Algorithms" or "Computational Complexity") investigate sorting and searching in greater depth.

7.8 Searching Arrays: Linear Search and Binary Search

Often, a programmer will be working with large amounts of data stored in arrays. It may be necessary to determine whether an array contains a value that matches a certain *key value*. The process of locating a particular element value in an array is called *searching*. In this section we discuss two searching techniques—the simple *linear search* technique and the more efficient *binary search* technique. Exercises 7.31 and 7.32 at the end of this chapter ask you to implement recursive versions of the linear search and the binary search.

In the applet of Fig. 7.12, method **linearSearch** (defined at line 41) uses a **for** structure containing an **if** structure to compare each element of an array with a *search key* (lines 43 through 45). If the search key is found, the method returns the subscript value for the element to indicate the exact position of the search key in the array. If the search key is not found, the method returns **-1** to indicate that the search key was not found (we return **-1** because it is not a valid subscript number). If the array being searched is not in any particular order, it is just as likely that the value will be found in the first element as the last. On average, therefore, the program will have to compare the search key with half the elements of the array. The program contains a 100-element array filled with the even integers from 0 to 198. The user types the search key in a **JTextField** and presses *Enter* to start the search. [*Note:* The array is passed to **linearSearch** even though the array is an instance variable of the class. This is done because an array is normally passed to a method of another class for sorting. For example, class **Arrays** (see Chapter 24) contains a variety of **static** methods for sorting arrays, searching arrays, comparing the contents of arrays and filling arrays of all the primitive types, **Object**s and **String**s.]

The linear search method works well for small arrays or for unsorted arrays. However, for large arrays linear searching is inefficient. If the array is sorted, the high-speed binary search technique can be used.

The binary search algorithm eliminates half of the elements in the array being searched after each comparison. The algorithm locates the middle array element and compares it to the search key. If they are equal, the search key has been found and the subscript of that element is returned. Otherwise, the problem is reduced to searching half of the array. If the search key is less than the middle array element, the first half of the array is searched; otherwise, the second half of the array is searched. If the search key is not the middle element in the specified subarray (piece of the original array), the algorithm is repeated on one quarter of the original array. The search continues until the search key is equal to the middle element of a subarray or until the subarray consists of one element that is not equal to the search key (i.e., the search key is not found).

```java
1   // Fig. 7.12: LinearSearch.java
2   // Linear search of an array
3   import java.awt.*;
4   import java.awt.event.*;
5   import javax.swing.*;
6
7   public class LinearSearch extends JApplet
8                             implements ActionListener {
9      JLabel enterLabel, resultLabel;
10     JTextField enter, result;
11     int a[];
12
13     public void init()
14     {
15        Container c = getContentPane();
16        c.setLayout( new FlowLayout() );
17
18        enterLabel = new JLabel( "Enter integer search key" );
19        c.add( enterLabel );
20
21        enter = new JTextField( 10 );
22        enter.addActionListener( this );
23        c.add( enter );
24
25        resultLabel = new JLabel( "Result" );
26        c.add( resultLabel );
27
28        result = new JTextField( 20 );
29        result.setEditable( false );
30        c.add( result );
31
32        // create array and populate with even integers 0 to 198
33        a = new int[ 100 ];
34
35        for ( int i = 0; i < a.length; i++ )
36           a[ i ] = 2 * i;
37
38     }
39
40     // Search "array" for the specified "key" value
41     public int linearSearch( int array[], int key )
42     {
43        for ( int n = 0; n < a.length; n++ )
44           if ( array[ n ] == key )
45              return n;
46
47        return -1;
48     }
```

Fig. 7.12   Linear search of an array (part 1 of 2).

```
49
50        public void actionPerformed( ActionEvent e )
51        {
52            String searchKey = e.getActionCommand();
53
54            // Array a is passed to linearSearch even though it
55            // is an instance variable. Normally an array will
56            // be passed to a method for searching.
57            int element =
58                linearSearch( a, Integer.parseInt( searchKey ) );
59
60            if ( element != -1 )
61                result.setText( "Found value in element " +
62                                element );
63            else
64                result.setText( "Value not found" );
65        }
66    }
```

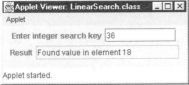
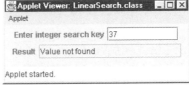

Fig. 7.12   Linear search of an array (part 2 of 2).

In a worst case scenario, searching an array of 1024 elements will take only 10 comparisons using a binary search. Repeatedly dividing 1024 by 2 (because after each comparison we are able to eliminate half of the array) yields the values 512, 256, 128, 64, 32, 16, 8, 4, 2 and 1. The number 1024 (2^{10}) is divided by 2 only ten times to get the value 1. Dividing by 2 is equivalent to one comparison in the binary search algorithm. An array of 1,048,576 (2^{20}) elements takes a maximum of 20 comparisons to find the key. An array of one billion elements takes a maximum of 30 comparisons to find the key. This is a tremendous increase in performance over the linear search that required comparing the search key to an average of half the elements in the array. For a one-billion-element array, this is a difference between an average of 500 million comparisons and a maximum of 30 comparisons! The maximum number of comparisons needed for the binary search of any sorted array is the exponent of the first power of 2 greater than the number of elements in the array.

Figure 7.13 presents the iterative version of method **binarySearch** (line 69). The method receives two arguments—an integer array called **array** (the array to search) and an integer **key** (the search key). The array is passed to **binarySearch** even though the array is an instance variable of the class. Once again, this is done because an array is normally passed to a method of another class for sorting. If **key** matches the **middle** element of a subarray, **middle** (the subscript of the current element) is returned to indicate that the value was found and the search is complete. If **key** does not match the **middle** element of a subarray, the **low** subscript or **high** subscript (both declared in the method) is adjusted so a smaller subarray can be searched. If **key** is less than the middle element, the **high** subscript is set to **middle - 1** and the search is continued on the elements from **low** to **middle - 1**. If **key** is greater than the middle element, the **low** subscript is set to **middle + 1** and the search is continued on the elements from **middle + 1** to **high**. These comparisons are performed by the nested **if/else** structure at lines 83 through 88.

```
1    // Fig. 7.13: BinarySearch.java
2    // Binary search of an array
3    import java.awt.*;
4    import java.awt.event.*;
5    import javax.swing.*;
6    import java.text.*;
7
8    public class BinarySearch extends JApplet
9                             implements ActionListener {
10       JLabel enterLabel, resultLabel;
11       JTextField enter, result;
12       JTextArea output;
13
14       int a[];
15       String display = "";
16
17       public void init()
18       {
19          Container c = getContentPane();
20          c.setLayout( new FlowLayout() );
21
22          enterLabel = new JLabel( "Enter key" );
23          c.add( enterLabel );
24
25          enter = new JTextField( 5 );
26          enter.addActionListener( this );
27          c.add( enter );
28
29          resultLabel = new JLabel( "Result" );
30          c.add( resultLabel );
31
32          result = new JTextField( 22 );
33          result.setEditable( false );
34          c.add( result );
35
36          output = new JTextArea( 6, 60 );
37          output.setFont(
38             new Font( "Courier", Font.PLAIN, 12 ) );
39          c.add( output );
40
41          // create array and fill with even integers 0 to 28
42          a = new int[ 15 ];
43
44          for ( int i = 0; i < a.length; i++ )
45             a[ i ] = 2 * i;
46       }
47
```

Fig. 7.13   Binary search of a sorted array (part 1 of 3).

```
48      public void actionPerformed( ActionEvent e )
49      {
50          String searchKey = e.getActionCommand();
51
52          // initialize display string for the new search
53          display = "Portions of array searched\n";
54
55          // perform the binary search
56          int element =
57              binarySearch( a, Integer.parseInt( searchKey ) );
58
59          output.setText( display );
60
61          if ( element != -1 )
62              result.setText(
63                  "Found value in element " + element );
64          else
65              result.setText( "Value not found" );
66      }
67
68      // Binary search
69      public int binarySearch( int array[], int key )
70      {
71          int low = 0;                     // low subscript
72          int high = array.length - 1;     // high subscript
73          int middle;                      // middle subscript
74
75          while ( low <= high ) {
76              middle = ( low + high ) / 2;
77
78              // The following line is used to display the part
79              // of the array currently being manipulated during
80              // each iteration of the binary search loop.
81              buildOutput( low, middle, high );
82
83              if ( key == array[ middle ] )   // match
84                  return middle;
85              else if ( key < array[ middle ] )
86                  high = middle - 1;   // search low end of array
87              else
88                  low = middle + 1;    // search high end of array
89          }
90
91          return -1;     // searchKey not found
92      }
93
94      // Build one row of output showing the current
95      // part of the array being processed.
96      void buildOutput( int low, int mid, int high )
97      {
98          DecimalFormat twoDigits = new DecimalFormat( "00" );
99
```

Fig. 7.13 Binary search of a sorted array (part 2 of 3).

```
100          for ( int i = 0; i < a.length; i++ ) {
101             if ( i < low || i > high )
102                display += "      ";
103             else if ( i == mid ) // mark middle element in output
104                display += twoDigits.format( a[ i ] ) + "* ";
105             else
106                display += twoDigits.format( a[ i ] ) + "   ";
107          }
108
109          display += "\n";
110       }
111    }
```

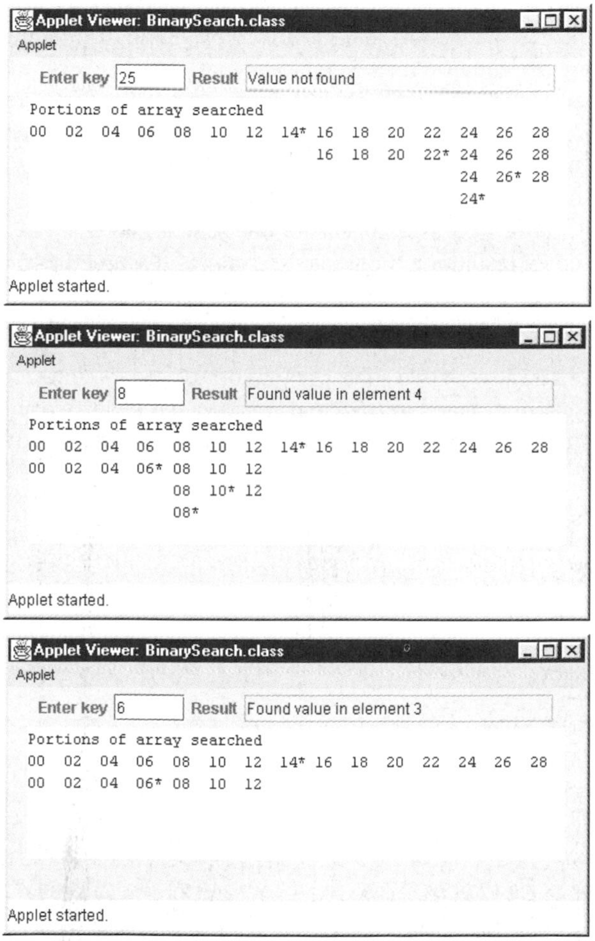

Applet Viewer: BinarySearch.class

Applet

Enter key 25   Result Value not found

```
Portions of array searched
00  02  04  06  08  10  12  14* 16  18  20  22  24  26  28
                            16  18  20  22* 24  26  28
                                            24  26* 28
                                            24*
```

Applet started.

Applet Viewer: BinarySearch.class

Applet

Enter key 8   Result Found value in element 4

```
Portions of array searched
00  02  04  06  08  10  12  14* 16  18  20  22  24  26  28
00  02  04  06* 08  10  12
            08  10* 12
            08*
```

Applet started.

Applet Viewer: BinarySearch.class

Applet

Enter key 6   Result Found value in element 3

```
Portions of array searched
00  02  04  06  08  10  12  14* 16  18  20  22  24  26  28
00  02  04  06* 08  10  12
```

Applet started.

Fig. 7.13   Binary search of a sorted array (part 3 of 3).

The program uses a 15-element array. The first power of 2 greater than the number of array elements is 16 (2^4)—at most four comparisons are required to find the **key**. To illustrate this, method **binarySearch** calls method **buildOutput** (line 81) to output each subarray during the binary search process. The middle element in each subarray is marked with an asterisk (*****) to indicate the element to which the **key** is compared. Each search in this example results in a maximum of four lines of output—one per comparison.

JTextArea output uses *Courier* (a *fixed-width font*—i.e., all characters are the same width) to help align the displayed text in each line of output. Lines 37 and 38

```
output.setFont(
    new Font( "Courier", Font.PLAIN, 12 ) );
```

use method **setFont** to change the font of **output**. Method **setFont** can change the font of text displayed on most GUI components. The method requires a *Font* (package **java.awt**) object as its argument. A **Font** object is initialized with three arguments—the **String** name of the font (**"Courier"**), an **int** representing the style of the font (**Font.PLAIN** indicates plain font) and an **int** representing the point size of the font (**12**). Java provides generic names for several fonts available on every Java platform. *Courier* font is also called *Monospaced*. Other common fonts include *TimesRoman* (also called *Serif*) and *Helvetica* (also called *SansSerif*). Java 2 actually provides access to all fonts on your system. The style can also be **Font.BOLD**, **Font.ITALIC** or **Font.BOLD + Font.ITALIC**. The point size represents the size of the font—there are 72 points to an inch. The actual size of the text as it appears on the screen may vary based on the size of the screen and the screen resolution. Font manipulation is discussed again in Chapter 11.

7.9 Multiple-Subscripted Arrays

Multiple-subscripted arrays with two subscripts are often used to represent *tables* of values consisting of information arranged in *rows* and *columns*. To identify a particular table element, we must specify the two subscripts—by convention, the first identifies the element's row and the second identifies the element's column. Arrays that require two subscripts to identify a particular element are called *double-subscripted arrays*. Note that multiple-subscripted arrays can have more than two subscripts. Java does not support multiple-subscripted arrays directly, but does allow the programmer to specify single-subscripted arrays whose elements are also single-subscripted arrays, thus achieving the same effect. Figure 7.14 illustrates a double-subscripted array, **a**, containing three rows and four columns (i.e., a 3-by-4 array). In general, an array with *m* rows and *n* columns is called an *m-by-n array*.

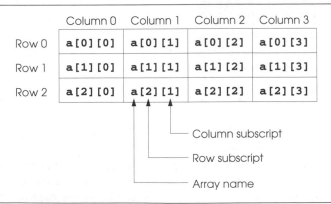

Fig. 7.14   A double-subscripted array with three rows and four columns.

Every element in array **a** is identified in Fig. 7.14 by an element name of the form **a[i][j]**; **a** is the name of the array and **i** and **j** are the subscripts that uniquely identify the row and column of each element in **a**. Notice that the names of the elements in the first row all have a first subscript of **0**; the names of the elements in the fourth column all have a second subscript of **3**.

Multiple-subscripted arrays can be initialized in declarations like a single-subscripted array. A double-subscripted array **b[2][2]** could be declared and initialized with

```
int b[][] = { { 1, 2 }, { 3, 4 } };
```

The values are grouped by row in braces. So, **1** and **2** initialize **b[0][0]** and **b[0][1]**, and **3** and **4** initialize **b[1][0]** and **b[1][1]**. The compiler determines the number of rows by counting the number of sub-initializer lists (represented by sets of braces) in the main initializer list. The compiler determines the number of columns in each row by counting the number of initializer values in the sub-initializer list for that row.

Multiple-subscripted arrays are maintained as arrays of arrays. The declaration

```
int b[][] = { { 1, 2 }, { 3, 4, 5 } };
```

creates integer array **b** with row **0** containing two elements (**1** and **2**) and row **1** containing three elements (**3**, **4** and **5**).

A multiple-subscripted array with the same number of columns in every row can be allocated dynamically. For example, a 3-by-3 array is allocated as follows:

```
int b[][];
b = new int[ 3 ][ 3 ];
```

As with single-subscripted arrays, the elements of a double-subscripted array are automatically initialized when **new** creates the array object.

A multiple-subscripted array in which each row has a different number of columns can be allocated dynamically as follows:

```
int b[][];
b = new int[ 2 ][ ];   // allocate rows
b[ 0 ] = new int[ 5 ]; // allocate columns for row 0
b[ 1 ] = new int[ 3 ]; // allocate columns for row 1
```

The preceding code creates a two-dimensional array with two rows. Row **0** has five columns and row **1** has three columns.

The applet of Fig. 7.15 demonstrates initializing double-subscripted arrays in declarations and using nested **for** loops to traverse the arrays (i.e., manipulate every element of the array).

The program declares two arrays in method **init**. The declaration of **array1** (line 16) provides six initializers in two sublists. The first sublist initializes the first row of the array to the values 1, 2 and 3; and the second sublist initializes the second row of the array to the values 4, 5 and 6. The declaration of **array2** (line 17) provides six initializers in three sublists. The sublist for the first row explicitly initializes the first row to have two elements with values 1 and 2, respectively. The sublist for the second row initializes the second row to have one element with value 3. The sublist for the third row initializes the third row to the values 4, 5 and 6.

```
1   // Fig. 7.15: InitArray.java
2   // Initializing multidimensional arrays
3   import java.awt.Container;
4   import javax.swing.*;
5
6   public class InitArray extends JApplet {
7      JTextArea outputArea;
8
9      // paint the applet
10     public void init()
11     {
12        outputArea = new JTextArea();
13        Container c = getContentPane();
14        c.add( outputArea );
15
16        int array1[][] = { { 1, 2, 3 }, { 4, 5, 6 } };
17        int array2[][] = { { 1, 2 }, { 3 }, { 4, 5, 6 } };
18
19        outputArea.setText( "Values in array1 by row are\n" );
20        buildOutput( array1 );
21
22        outputArea.append( "\nValues in array2 by row are\n" );
23        buildOutput( array2 );
24     }
25
26     public void buildOutput( int a[][] )
27     {
28        for ( int i = 0; i < a.length; i++ ) {
29
30           for ( int j = 0; j < a[ i ].length; j++ )
31              outputArea.append( a[ i ][ j ] + "  " );
32
33           outputArea.append( "\n" );
34        }
35     }
36  }
```

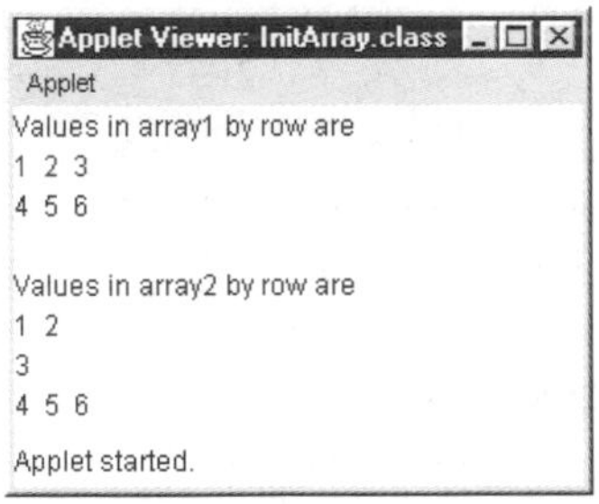

```
Applet Viewer: InitArray.class  _ □ ×
 Applet
Values in array1 by row are
1 2 3
4 5 6

Values in array2 by row are
1 2
3
4 5 6

Applet started.
```

Fig. 7.15 Initializing multidimensional arrays.

Method **init** calls method **buildOutput** from lines 20 and 23 to append each array's elements to **JTextArea outputArea**. The **buildOutput** method definition specifies the array parameter as **int a[][]** to indicate that a double-subscripted array will be received as an argument. Note the use of a nested **for** structure to output the rows of each double-subscripted array. In the outer **for** structure, the expression **a.length** determines the number of rows in the array. In the inner **for** structure, the expression **a[i].length** determines the number of columns in each row of the array. This condition enables the loop to determine for each row the exact number of columns.

Many common array manipulations use **for** repetition structures. For example, the following **for** structure sets all the elements in the third row of array **a** in Fig. 7.14 to zero:

```
for ( int col = 0; col < a[ 2 ].length; col++)
    a[ 2 ][ col ] = 0;
```

We specified the *third* row, therefore we know that the first subscript is always **2** (**0** is the first row and **1** is the second row). The **for** loop varies only the second subscript (i.e., the column subscript). The preceding **for** structure is equivalent to the assignment statements

```
a[ 2 ][ 0 ] = 0;
a[ 2 ][ 1 ] = 0;
a[ 2 ][ 2 ] = 0;
a[ 2 ][ 3 ] = 0;
```

The following nested **for** structure determines the total of all the elements in array **a**.

```
int total = 0;

for ( int row = 0; row < a.length; row++ )
    for ( int col = 0; col < a[ row ].length; col++ )
        total += a[ row ][ col ];
```

The **for** structure totals the elements of the array one row at a time. The outer **for** structure begins by setting the **row** subscript to **0** so the elements of the first row may be totaled by the inner **for** structure. The outer **for** structure then increments **row** to **1**, so the second row can be totaled. Then, the outer **for** structure increments **row** to **2**, so the third row can be totaled. The result can be displayed when the nested **for** structure terminates.

The applet of Fig. 7.16 performs several other common array manipulations on 3-by-4 array **grades**. Each row of the array represents a student and each column represents a grade on one of the four exams the students took during the semester. The array manipulations are performed by four methods. Method **minimum** (line 41) determines the lowest grade of any student for the semester. Method **maximum** (line 54) determines the highest grade of any student for the semester. Method **average** (line 68) determines a particular student's semester average. Method **buildString** (line 79) appends the double-subscripted array to **String output** in a tabular format.

```
1  // Fig. 7.16: DoubleArray.java
2  // Double-subscripted array example
3  import java.awt.*;
4  import javax.swing.*;
5
6  public class DoubleArray extends JApplet {
7     int grades[][] = { { 77, 68, 86, 73 },
8                        { 96, 87, 89, 81 },
9                        { 70, 90, 86, 81 } };
```

Fig. 7.16   Example of using double-subscripted arrays (part 1 of 3).

```
10        int students, exams;
11        String output;
12        JTextArea outputArea;
13
14        // initialize instance variables
15        public void init()
16        {
17           students = grades.length;
18           exams = grades[ 0 ].length;
19
20           outputArea = new JTextArea();
21           Container c = getContentPane();
22           c.add( outputArea );
23
24           // build the output string
25           output = "The array is:\n";
26           buildString();
27
28           output += "\n\nLowest grade: " + minimum() +
29                    "\nHighest grade: " + maximum() + "\n";
30
31           for ( int i = 0; i < students; i++ )
32              output += "\nAverage for student " + i + " is " +
33                      average( grades[ i ] );
34
35           outputArea.setFont(
36              new Font( "Courier", Font.PLAIN, 12 ) );
37           outputArea.setText( output );
38        }
39
40        // find the minimum grade
41        public int minimum()
42        {
43           int lowGrade = 100;
44
45           for ( int i = 0; i < students; i++ )
46              for ( int j = 0; j < exams; j++ )
47                 if ( grades[ i ][ j ] < lowGrade )
48                    lowGrade = grades[ i ][ j ];
49
50           return lowGrade;
51        }
52
53        // find the maximum grade
54        public int maximum()
55        {
56           int highGrade = 0;
57
58           for ( int i = 0; i < students; i++ )
59              for ( int j = 0; j < exams; j++ )
60                 if ( grades[ i ][ j ] > highGrade )
61                    highGrade = grades[ i ][ j ];
62
```

Fig. 7.16   Example of using double-subscripted arrays (part 3 of 3).

```
63          return highGrade;
64       }
65
66    // determine the average grade for a particular
67    // student (or set of grades)
68    public double average( int setOfGrades[] )
69    {
70       int total = 0;
71
72       for ( int i = 0; i < setOfGrades.length; i++ )
73          total += setOfGrades[ i ];
74
75       return ( double ) total / setOfGrades.length;
76    }
77
78    // build output string
79    public void buildString()
80    {
81       output += "                 ";  // used to align column heads
82
83       for ( int i = 0; i < exams; i++ )
84          output += "[" + i + "]   ";
85
86       for ( int i = 0; i < students; i++ ) {
87          output += "\ngrades[" + i + "]   ";
88
89          for ( int j = 0; j < exams; j++ )
90             output += grades[ i ][ j ] + "   ";
91       }
92    }
93 }
```

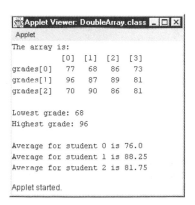

Fig. 7.16　Example of using double-subscripted arrays (part 3 of 3).

Methods **minimum, maximum** and **buildString** each use array **grades** and the variables **students** (number of rows in the array) and **exams** (number of columns in the array). Each method loops through array **grades** using nested **for** structures. The following nested **for** structure is from the method **minimum** definition:

```
int lowGrade = 100;

for ( int i = 0; i < students; i++ )
   for ( int j = 0; j < exams; j++ )
      if ( grades[ i ][ j ] < lowGrade )
         lowGrade = grades[ i ][ j ];
```

The outer **for** structure sets **i** (i.e., the row subscript) to **0** so the elements of the first row can be compared to variable **lowGrade** in the body of the inner **for** structure. The inner **for** structure loops through the four grades of a particular row and compares each grade to **lowGrade**. If a grade is less than **lowGrade**, **lowGrade** is set to that grade. The outer **for** structure then increments the row subscript by **1**. The elements of the second row are compared to variable **lowGrade**. The outer **for** structure then increments the row subscript to **2**. The elements of the third row are compared to variable **lowGrade**. When execution of the nested structure is complete, **lowGrade** contains the smallest grade in the double-subscripted array. Method **maximum** works similarly to method **minimum**.

Method **average** takes one argument—a single-subscripted array of test results for a particular student. When **average** is called, the argument is **grades[i]**, which specifies that a particular row of the double-subscripted array **grades** is to be passed to **average**. For example, the argument **grades[1]** represents the four values (a single-subscripted array of grades) stored in the second row of the double-subscripted array **grades**. Remember that in Java a double-subscripted array is an array with elements that are single-subscripted arrays. Method **average** calculates the sum of the array elements, divides the total by the number of test results and returns the floating-point result as a **double** value.

Summary

- Java stores lists of values in arrays. An array is a contiguous group of related memory locations. These locations are related by the fact that they all have the same name and the same type. To refer to a particular location or element within the array, we specify the name of the array and the subscript of the element.

- A subscript may be an integer or an integer expression. If a program uses an expression as a subscript, the expression is evaluated to determine the particular element of the array.

- Java arrays always begin with element 0; thus it is important to note the difference when referring to the "seventh element of the array" as opposed to "array element seven." The seventh element has a subscript of **6**, while array element seven has a subscript of **7** (actually the eighth element of the array). This is a source of "off-by-one" errors.

- Arrays occupy space in memory and are considered to be objects. Operator **new** must be used to reserve space for an array. For example, the following creates an array of 100 **int** values:

  ```
  int b[] = new int[ 100 ];
  ```

- When declaring an array, the type of the array and the square brackets can be combined at the beginning of the declaration to indicate that all identifiers in the declaration represent arrays, as in

  ```
  double[] array1, array2;
  ```

- The elements of an array can be initialized by declaration (using initializer lists), by assignment and by input.

- Java prevents referencing elements beyond the bounds of an array.

- Constant variables must be initialized with a constant expression before they are used and cannot be modified thereafter.

- To pass an array to a method, the name of the array is passed. To pass a single element of an array to a method, simply pass the name of the array followed by the subscript (contained in square brackets) of the particular element.

- Arrays are passed to methods call-by-reference—therefore, the called methods can modify the element values in the caller's original arrays. Single elements of primitive-data-type arrays are passed to methods call-by-value.

- To receive an array argument, the method's parameter list must specify that an array will be received.

- An array can be sorted using the bubble-sort technique. Several passes of the array are made. On each pass, successive pairs of elements are compared. If a pair is in order (or the values are identical), it is left as is. If a pair is out of order, the values are swapped. For small arrays, the bubble sort is acceptable, but for larger arrays it is inefficient compared to more sophisticated sorting algorithms.

- The linear search compares each element of the array with the search key. If the array is not in any particular order, it is just as likely that the value will be found in the first element as the last. On average, therefore, the program will have to compare the search key with half the elements of the array. Linear search works well for small arrays and is acceptable even for large unsorted arrays.

- For sorted arrays the binary search eliminates from consideration one half of the elements in the array after each comparison. The algorithm locates the middle element of the array and compares it to the search key. If they are equal, the search key is found and the array subscript of that element is returned. Otherwise, the problem is reduced to searching one half of the array that is still under consideration.

- In a worst case scenario, searching a sorted array of 1024 elements will take only 10 comparisons using a binary search.

- Most GUI components have method **setFont** to change the font of the text on the GUI component. The method requires a **Font** (package **java.awt**) object as its argument.

- A **Font** object is initialized with three arguments—a **String** representing the name of the font (**"Courier"**), an **int** representing the style of the font (**Font.PLAIN** indicates plain font) and an **int** representing the point size of the font (**12**). The style can also be **Font.BOLD**, **Font.ITALIC** or **Font.BOLD + Font.ITALIC**. The point size represents the size of the font—there are 72 points to an inch. The actual screen size may vary based on the size of the screen and the screen resolution.

- Arrays may be used to represent tables of values consisting of information arranged in rows and columns. To identify a particular element of a table, two subscripts are specified: The first identifies the row in which the element is contained and the second identifies the column in which the element is contained. Tables or arrays that require two subscripts to identify a particular element are called double-subscripted arrays.

- A double-subscripted array can be initialized with a initializer list of the form

    arrayType arrayName[][] = { { *row1 sub-list* }, { *row2 sub-list* }, ... };

- To dynamically create an array with a fixed number of rows and columns, use

    arrayType arrayName[][] = **new** *arrayType*[*numRows*][*numColumns*];

- To pass one row of a double-subscripted array to a method that receives a single-subscripted array, simply pass the name of the array followed by the row subscript.

Terminology

a[i]	name of an array
a[i][j]	named constant
array	off-by-one error
array initializer list	pass-by-reference
binary search of an array	pass-by-value
bounds checking	pass of a bubble sort
bubble sort	passing arrays to methods
column subscript	position number
constant variable	row subscript
declare an array	search key
double-subscripted array	searching an array
element of an array	**setFont** method
final	single-subscripted array
Font class from **java.awt**	sinking sort
Font.BOLD	sorting
Font.ITALIC	sorting an array
Font.PLAIN	square brackets **[]**
initialize an array	subscript
initializer	table of values
linear search of an array	tabular format
lvalue	temporary area for exchange of values
m-by-n array	value of an element
multiple-subscripted array	zeroth element

Common Programming Errors

7.1   It is important to note the difference between the "seventh element of the array" and "array element seven." Because array subscripts begin at 0, the "seventh element of the array" has a subscript of 6, while "array element seven" has a subscript of 7 and is actually the eighth element of the array. This confusion is a source of "off-by-one" errors.

7.2   Unlike C or C++ the number of elements in the array is never specified in the square brackets after the array name in a declaration. The declaration **int c[12];** causes a syntax error.

7.3   Assigning a value to a constant variable after the variable has been initialized is a syntax error.

7.4   Referring to an element outside the array bounds is a logic error.

Good Programming Practice

7.1   Strive for program clarity. It is sometimes worthwhile to trade off the most efficient use of memory or processor time in favor of writing clearer programs.

Performance Tips

7.1   Sometimes performance considerations far outweigh clarity considerations.

7.2   Passing arrays by reference makes sense for performance reasons. If arrays were passed by value, a copy of each element would be passed. For large, frequently passed arrays, this would waste time and would consume considerable storage for the copies of the arrays.

7.3   Sometimes, the simplest algorithms perform poorly. Their virtue is that they are easy to write, test and debug. More complex algorithms are sometimes needed to realize maximum performance.

Software Engineering Observations

7.1 Unlike other languages, Java does not allow the programmer to choose whether to pass each argument call-by-value or call-by-reference. Primitive data type variables are always passed call-by-value. Objects are not passed to methods; rather, references to objects are passed to methods. The references themselves are also passed call-by-value. When a method receives a reference to an object, the method can manipulate the object directly.

7.2 When returning information from a method via a **return** statement, primitive-data-type variables are always returned by value (i.e., a copy is returned) and objects are always returned by reference (i.e., a reference to the object is returned).

Testing and Debugging Tips

7.1 When a Java program is executed, the Java interpreter checks array element subscripts to be sure they are valid (i.e., all subscripts must be greater than or equal to 0 and less than the length of the array). If there is an invalid subscript, Java generates an exception.

7.2 Exceptions are used to indicate that an error occurred in a program. They enable the programmer to recover from an error and continue the execution of the program instead of abnormally terminating the program. When an invalid array reference is made, an **ArrayIndexOutOfBoundsException** is generated. Chapter 14 covers "Exception Handling" in detail.

7.3 When looping through an array, the array subscript should never go below 0 and should always be less than the total number of elements in the array (one less than the size of the array). Make sure the loop terminating condition prevents accessing elements outside this range.

7.4 Programs should validate the correctness of all input values to prevent erroneous information from affecting a program's calculations.

7.5 With call-by-value, changes to the called method's copy do not affect the original variable's value in the calling method. This prevents the accidental side effects that so greatly hinder the development of correct and reliable software systems.

Self-Review Exercises

7.1 Answer each of the following:
a) Lists and tables of values can be stored in _____.
b) The elements of an array are related by the fact that they have the same _____ and _____.
c) The number used to refer to a particular element of an array is called its _____.
d) The process of placing the elements of an array in order is called _____ the array.
e) Determining if an array contains a certain key value is called _____ the array.
f) An array that uses two subscripts is referred to as a _____ array.

7.2 State whether each of the following is *true* or *false*. If *false*, explain why.
a) An array can store many different types of values.
b) An array subscript should normally be of data type **float**.
c) An individual array element that is passed to a method and modified in that method will contain the modified value when the called method completes execution.

7.3 Answer the following questions regarding an array called **fractions**.
a) Define a constant variable **ARRAY_SIZE** initialized to 10.
b) Declare an array with **ARRAY_SIZE** elements of type **float** and initialize the elements to **0**.
c) Name the fourth element of the array.
d) Refer to array element 4.

e) Assign the value **1.667** to array element 9.

f) Assign the value **3.333** to the seventh element of the array.

g) Sum all the elements of the array using a **for** repetition structure. Define the integer variable **x** as a control variable for the loop.

7.4   Answer the following questions regarding an array called **table**.

a) Declare and create the array as an integer array and with 3 rows and 3 columns. Assume the constant variable **ARRAY_SIZE** has been defined to be 3.

b) How many elements does the array contain?

c) Use a **for** repetition structure to initialize each element of the array to the sum of its subscripts. Assume the integer variables **x** and **y** are declared as control variables.

7.5   Find the error in each of the following program segments and correct the error.

a) ```
final int ARRAY_SIZE = 5;
ARRAY_SIZE = 10;
```

b) Assume ```int b[] = new int[ 10 ];```
```
for (int i = 0; i <= b.length; i++)
    b[i] = 1;
```

c) Assume ```int a[][] = { { 1, 2 }, { 3, 4 } };```
```
a[1, 1] = 5;
```

## Answers to Self-Review Exercises

**7.1**    a) Arrays. b) Name, type. c) Subscript. d) Sorting. e) Searching. f) Double-subscripted.

**7.2**    a) False. An array can store only values of the same type.

b) False. An array subscript must be an integer or an integer expression.

c) False for individual primitive-data-type elements of an array because they are passed call-by-value. If a reference to an array is passed, then modifications to the array elements are reflected in the original. Also, an individual element of a class type passed to a method is passed call-by-reference and changes to the object will be reflected in the original array element.

**7.3**    a) ```final int ARRAY_SIZE = 10;```

b) ```float fractions[] = new float[ ARRAY_SIZE ];```

c) ```fractions[ 3 ]```

d) ```fractions[ 4 ]```

e) ```fractions[ 9 ] = 1.667;```

f) ```fractions[ 6 ] = 3.333;```

g) ```float total = 0;```
```
for (int x = 0; x < fractions.length; x++)
    total += fractions[x];
```

**7.4**    a) ```int table[][] = new int[ ARRAY_SIZE ][ ARRAY_SIZE ];```

b) Nine.

c) ```
for ( int x = 0; x < table.length; x++ )
    for ( int y = 0; y < table[ x ].length; y++ )
        table[ x ][ y ] = x + y;
```

7.5   a) Error: Assigning a value to a constant variable using an assignment statement.
   Correction: Assign the correct value to the constant variable in a **final int** **ARRAY_SIZE** declaration or create another variable.

b) Error: Referencing an array element outside the bounds of the array (**b[10]**).
   Correction: Change the **<=** operator to **<**.

c) Error: Array subscripting done incorrectly.
   Correction: Change the statement to **a[1][1] = 5;**.

Exercises

7.6   Fill in the blanks in each of the following:
   a)   Java stores lists of values in _____.
   b)   The elements of an array are related by the fact that they _____.
   c)   When referring to an array element, the position number contained within brackets is called a _____.
   d)   The names of the four elements of array **p** are _____, _____, _____ and _____.
   e)   Naming an array, stating its type and specifying the number of dimensions in the array is called _____ the array.
   f)   The process of placing the elements of an array into either ascending or descending order is called _____.
   g)   In a double-subscripted array, the first subscript identifies the _____ of an element and the second subscript identifies the _____ of an element.
   h)   An *m*-by-*n* array contains _____ rows, _____ columns and _____ elements.
   i)   The name of the element in row 3 and column 5 of array **d** is _____.

7.7   State whether each of the following is *true* or *false*. If *false*, explain why.
   a)   To refer to a particular location or element within an array, we specify the name of the array and the value of the particular element.
   b)   An array declaration reserves space for the array.
   c)   To indicate that 100 locations should be reserved for integer array **p**, the programmer writes the declaration

        p[100];

   d)   A Java program that initializes the elements of a 15-element array to zero must contain at least one **for** statement.
   e)   A Java program that totals the elements of a double-subscripted array must contain nested **for** statements.

7.8   Write Java statements to accomplish each of the following:
   a)   Display the value of the seventh element of character array **f**.
   b)   Initialize each of the five elements of single-subscripted integer array **g** to **8**.
   c)   Total the elements of floating-point array **c** of 100 elements.
   d)   Copy 11- element array **a** into the first portion of array **b**, containing 34 elements.
   e)   Determine and print the smallest and largest values contained in 99-element floating-point array **w**.

7.9   Consider a 2-by-3 integer array **t**.
   a)   Write a declaration for **t**.
   b)   How many rows does **t** have?
   c)   How many columns does **t** have?
   d)   How many elements does **t** have?
   e)   Write the names of all the elements in the second row of **t**.
   f)   Write the names of all the elements in the third column of **t**.
   g)   Write a single statement that sets the element of **t** in row 1 and column 2 to zero.
   h)   Write a series of statements that initializes each element of **t** to zero. Do not use a repetition structure.
   i)   Write a nested **for** structure that initializes each element of **t** to zero.
   j)   Write a statement that inputs the values for the elements of **t** from the keyboard.
   k)   Write a series of statements that determines and prints the smallest value in array **t**.
   l)   Write a statement that displays the elements of the first row of **t**.
   m)   Write a statement that totals the elements of the fourth column of **t**.

n) Write a series of statements that prints the array **t** in neat, tabular format. List the column subscripts as headings across the top and list the row subscripts at the left of each row.

7.10   Use a single-subscripted array to solve the following problem. A company pays its salespeople on a commission basis. The salespeople receive $200 per week plus 9% of their gross sales for that week. For example, a salesperson who grosses $5000 in sales in a week receives $200 plus 9% of $5000 or a total of $650. Write a program (using an array of counters) that determines how many of the salespeople earned salaries in each of the following ranges (assume that each salesperson's salary is truncated to an integer amount):

a) $200-$299
b) $300-$399
c) $400-$499
d) $500-$599
e) $600-$699
f) $700-$799
g) $800-$899
h) $900-$999
i) $1000 and over

7.11   The bubble sort presented in Fig. 7.11 is inefficient for large arrays. Make the following simple modifications to improve the performance of the bubble sort.

a) After the first pass, the largest number is guaranteed to be in the highest-numbered element of the array; after the second pass, the two highest numbers are "in place"; and so on. Instead of making nine comparisons on every pass, modify the bubble sort to make eight comparisons on the second pass, seven on the third pass and so on.
b) The data in the array may already be in the proper order or near-proper order, so why make nine passes if fewer will suffice? Modify the sort to check at the end of each pass if any swaps have been made. If none has been made, the data must already be in the proper order, so the program should terminate. If swaps have been made, at least one more pass is needed.

7.12   Write statements that perform the following single-subscripted array operations:

a) Set the 10 elements of integer array **counts** to zeros.
b) Add 1 to each of the 15 elements of integer array **bonus**.
c) Print the five values of integer array **bestScores** in column format.

7.13   Use a single-subscripted array to solve the following problem. Read in 20 numbers, each of which is between 10 and 100, inclusive. As each number is read, print it only if it is not a duplicate of a number already read. Provide for the "worst case" in which all 20 numbers are different. Use the smallest possible array to solve this problem.

7.14   Label the elements of 3-by-5 double-subscripted array **sales** to indicate the order in which they are set to zero by the following program segment:

```
for ( int row = 0; row < sales.length; row++ )
   for ( int col = 0; col < sales[ row ].length; col++ )
      sales[ row ][ col ] = 0;
```

7.15   Write a program to simulate the rolling of two dice. The program should use **Math.random** to roll the first die and should use **Math.random** again to roll the second die. The sum of the two values should then be calculated. [*Note:* Since each die can show an integer value from 1 to 6, the sum of the values will vary from 2 to 12, with 7 being the most frequent sum and 2 and 12 being the least frequent sums. Figure 7.17 shows the 36 possible combinations of the two dice. Your program should roll the dice 36,000 times. Use a single-subscripted array to tally the numbers of times each possible sum appears. Print the results in a tabular format. Also, determine if the totals are reasonable (i.e., there are six ways to roll a 7, so approximately one sixth of all the rolls should be 7).]

	1	2	3	4	5	6
1	2	3	4	5	6	7
2	3	4	5	6	7	8
3	4	5	6	7	8	9
4	5	6	7	8	9	10
5	6	7	8	9	10	11
6	7	8	9	10	11	12

Fig. 7.17   The 36 possible outcomes of rolling two dice.

7.16   What does the following program do?

```
1   // Exercise 7.16: WhatDoesThisDo.java
2   import java.awt.*;
3   import javax.swing.*;
4
5   public class WhatDoesThisDo extends JApplet {
6      int result;
7
8      public void init()
9      {
10         int a[] = { 1, 2, 3, 4, 5, 6, 7, 8, 9, 10 };
11
12         result = whatIsThis( a, a.length );
13
14         Container c = getContentPane();
15         JTextArea output = new JTextArea();
16         output.setText( "Result is: " + result );
17         c.add( output );
18      }
19
20      public int whatIsThis( int b[], int size )
21      {
22         if ( size == 1 )
23            return b[ 0 ];
24         else
25            return b[ size - 1 ] + whatIsThis( b, size - 1 );
26      }
27   }
```

7.17   Write a program that runs 1000 games of craps and answers the following questions:
   a) How many games are won on the first roll, second roll, ..., twentieth roll and after the twentieth roll?
   b) How many games are lost on the first roll, second roll, ..., twentieth roll and after the twentieth roll?
   c) What are the chances of winning at craps? [*Note:* You should discover that craps is one of the fairest casino games. What do you suppose this means?]
   d) What is the average length of a game of craps?
   e) Do the chances of winning improve with the length of the game?

7.18 (*Airline Reservations System*) A small airline has just purchased a computer for its new automated reservations system. You have been asked to program the new system. You are to write a program to assign seats on each flight of the airline's only plane (capacity: 10 seats).

Your program should display the following menu of alternatives:

```
Please type 1 for "smoking"
Please type 2 for "nonsmoking"
```

If the person types 1, your program should assign a seat in the smoking section (seats 1-5). If the person types 2, your program should assign a seat in the nonsmoking section (seats 6-10). Your program should then print a boarding pass indicating the person's seat number and whether it is in the smoking or nonsmoking section of the plane.

Use a single-subscripted array to represent the seating chart of the plane. Initialize all the elements of the array to 0 to indicate that all seats are empty. As each seat is assigned, set the corresponding elements of the array to 1 to indicate that the seat is no longer available.

Your program should, of course, never assign a seat that has already been assigned. When the smoking section is full, your program should ask the person if it is acceptable to be placed in the nonsmoking section (and vice versa). If yes, make the appropriate seat assignment. If no, print the message **"Next flight leaves in 3 hours."**

7.19 What does the following program do?

```java
// Exercise 7.19: WhatDoesThisDo2.java
import java.awt.*;
import javax.swing.*;

public class WhatDoesThisDo2 extends JApplet {
   public void init()
   {
      int a[] = { 1, 2, 3, 4, 5, 6, 7, 8, 9, 10 };
      JTextArea outputArea = new JTextArea();

      someFunction( a, 0, outputArea );

      Container c = getContentPane();
      c.add( outputArea );
   }

   public void someFunction( int b[], int x, JTextArea out )
   {
      if ( x < b.length ) {
         someFunction( b, x + 1, out );
         out.append( b[ x ] + "   " );
      }
   }
}
```

7.20 Use a double-subscripted array to solve the following problem. A company has four salespeople (1 to 4) who sell five different products (1 to 5). Once a day, each salesperson passes in a slip for each different type of product sold. Each slip contains:

1. The salesperson number

2. The product number

3. The total dollar value of that product sold that day

Thus, each salesperson passes in between 0 and 5 sales slips per day. Assume that the information from all of the slips for last month is available. Write a program that will read all this information for last month's sales and summarize the total sales by salesperson by product. All totals should be stored in the double-subscripted array **sales**. After processing all the information for last month, display the results in tabular format with each of the columns representing a particular salesperson and each of the rows representing a particular product. Cross total each row to get the total sales of each product for last month; cross total each column to get the total sales by salesperson for last month. Your tabular printout should include these cross totals to the right of the totaled rows and to the bottom of the totaled columns.

7.21   (*Turtle Graphics*) The Logo language, which is popular among young computer users, made the concept of *turtle graphics* famous. Imagine a mechanical turtle that walks around the room under the control of a Java program. The turtle holds a pen in one of two positions, up or down. While the pen is down, the turtle traces out shapes as it moves; while the pen is up, the turtle moves about freely without writing anything. In this problem you will simulate the operation of the turtle and create a computerized sketchpad as well.

Use a 20-by-20 array **floor** which is initialized to zeros. Read commands from an array that contains them. Keep track of the current position of the turtle at all times and whether the pen is currently up or down. Assume that the turtle always starts at position 0,0 of the floor with its pen up. The set of turtle commands your program must process are as follows:

Command	Meaning
1	Pen up
2	Pen down
3	Turn right
4	Turn left
5,10	Move forward 10 spaces (or a number other than 10)
6	Print the 20-by-20 array
9	End of data (sentinel)

Suppose that the turtle is somewhere near the center of the floor. The following "program" would draw and print a 12-by 12 square leaving the pen in the up position:

```
2
5,12
3
5,12
3
5,12
3
5,12
1
6
9
```

As the turtle moves with the pen down, set the appropriate elements of array **floor** to **1**s. When the **6** command (print) is given, wherever there is a **1** in the array, display an asterisk or some other character you choose. Wherever there is a zero, display a blank. Write a program to implement the turtle graphics capabilities discussed here. Write several turtle graphics programs to draw interesting shapes. Add other commands to increase the power of your turtle graphics language.

7.22   (*Knight's Tour*) One of the more interesting puzzlers for chess buffs is the Knight's Tour problem, originally proposed by the mathematician Euler. The question is this: Can the chess piece called the knight move around an empty chessboard and touch each of the 64 squares once and only once? We study this intriguing problem in depth here.

The knight makes L-shaped moves (over two in one direction and then over one in a perpendicular direction). Thus, from a square in the middle of an empty chessboard, the knight can make eight different moves (numbered 0 through 7) as shown in Fig. 7.18.

a) Draw an 8-by-8 chessboard on a sheet of paper and attempt a Knight's Tour by hand. Put a **1** in the first square you move to, a **2** in the second square, a **3** in the third, etc. Before starting the tour, estimate how far you think you will get, remembering that a full tour consists of 64 moves. How far did you get? Was this close to your estimate?

b) Now let us develop a program that will move the knight around a chessboard. The board is represented by an 8-by-8 double-subscripted array **board**. Each of the squares is initialized to zero. We describe each of the eight possible moves in terms of both their horizontal and vertical components. For example, a move of type 0 as shown in Fig. 7.18 consists of moving two squares horizontally to the right and one square vertically upward. Move 2 consists of moving one square horizontally to the left and two squares vertically upward. Horizontal moves to the left and vertical moves upward are indicated with negative numbers. The eight moves may be described by two single-subscripted arrays, **horizontal** and **vertical**, as follows:

```
horizontal[ 0 ] = 2
horizontal[ 1 ] = 1
horizontal[ 2 ] = -1
horizontal[ 3 ] = -2
horizontal[ 4 ] = -2
horizontal[ 5 ] = -1
horizontal[ 6 ] = 1
horizontal[ 7 ] = 2
```

Fig. 7.18   The eight possible moves of the knight.

```
vertical[ 0 ] = -1
vertical[ 1 ] = -2
vertical[ 2 ] = -2
vertical[ 3 ] = -1
vertical[ 4 ] = 1
vertical[ 5 ] = 2
vertical[ 6 ] = 2
vertical[ 7 ] = 1
```

Let the variables **currentRow** and **currentColumn** indicate the row and column of the knight's current position. To make a move of type **moveNumber**, where **moveNumber** is between 0 and 7, your program uses the statements

```
currentRow += vertical[ moveNumber ];
currentColumn += horizontal[ moveNumber ];
```

Keep a counter that varies from **1** to **64**. Record the latest count in each square the knight moves to. Test each potential move to see if the knight already visited that square. Test every potential move to ensure that the knight does not land off the chessboard. Write a program to move the knight around the chessboard. Run the program. How many moves did the knight make?

c) After attempting to write and run a Knight's Tour program, you have probably developed some valuable insights. We will use these to develop a *heuristic* (or strategy) for moving the knight. Heuristics do not guarantee success, but a carefully developed heuristic greatly improves the chance of success. You may have observed that the outer squares are more troublesome than the squares nearer the center of the board. In fact, the most troublesome or inaccessible squares are the four corners.

Intuition may suggest that you should attempt to move the knight to the most troublesome squares first and leave open those that are easiest to get to so when the board gets congested near the end of the tour there will be a greater chance of success.

We may develop an "accessibility heuristic" by classifying each of the squares according to how accessible they are, then always moving the knight (using the knight's L-shaped moves) to the most inaccessible square. We label a double-subscripted array **accessibility** with numbers indicating from how many squares each particular square is accessible. On a blank chessboard, each center square is rated as **8**, each corner square is rated as **2** and the other squares have accessibility numbers of **3**, **4** or **6** as follows:

```
2   3   4   4   4   4   3   2
3   4   6   6   6   6   4   3
4   6   8   8   8   8   6   4
4   6   8   8   8   8   6   4
4   6   8   8   8   8   6   4
4   6   8   8   8   8   6   4
3   4   6   6   6   6   4   3
2   3   4   4   4   4   3   2
```

Write a version of the Knight's Tour using the accessibility heuristic. The knight should always move to the square with the lowest accessibility number. In case of a tie, the knight may move to any of the tied squares. Therefore, the tour may begin in any of the four corners. [*Note:* As the knight moves around the chessboard, your program should reduce the accessibility numbers as more squares become occupied. In this way, at any given time during the tour, each available square's accessibility number will remain equal to precisely the number of squares from which that square may be reached.] Run this version of your program. Did you get a full tour? Modify the program to run 64 tours, one starting from each square of the chessboard. How many full tours did you get?

   d) Write a version of the Knight's Tour program which, when encountering a tie between two or more squares, decides what square to choose by looking ahead to those squares reachable from the "tied" squares. Your program should move to the square for which the next move would arrive at a square with the lowest accessibility number.

7.23   (*Knight's Tour: Brute Force Approaches*) In Exercise 7.22 we developed a solution to the Knight's Tour problem. The approach used, called the "accessibility heuristic," generates many solutions and executes efficiently.

    As computers continue increasing in power, we will be able to solve more problems with sheer computer power and relatively unsophisticated algorithms. Let us call this approach "brute force" problem solving.

   a) Use random number generation to enable the knight to walk around the chessboard (in its legitimate L-shaped moves, of course) at random. Your program should run one tour and print the final chessboard. How far did the knight get?

   b) Most likely, the preceding program produced a relatively short tour. Now modify your program to attempt 1000 tours. Use a single-subscripted array to keep track of the number of tours of each length. When your program finishes attempting the 1000 tours, it should print this information in neat tabular format. What was the best result?

   c) Most likely, the preceding program gave you some "respectable" tours but no full tours. Now "pull all the stops out" and simply let your program run until it produces a full tour. (*Caution:* This version of the program could run for hours on a powerful computer.) Once again, keep a table of the number of tours of each length and print this table when the first full tour is found. How many tours did your program attempt before producing a full tour? How much time did it take?

   d) Compare the brute force version of the Knight's Tour with the accessibility-heuristic version. Which required a more careful study of the problem? Which algorithm was more difficult to develop? Which required more computer power? Could we be certain (in advance) of obtaining a full tour with the accessibility-heuristic approach? Could we be certain (in advance) of obtaining a full tour with the brute force approach? Argue the pros and cons of brute force problem solving in general.

7.24   (*Eight Queens*) Another puzzler for chess buffs is the Eight Queens problem. Simply stated: Is it possible to place eight queens on an empty chessboard so that no queen is "attacking" any other, i.e., no two queens are in the same row, the same column or along the same diagonal? Use the thinking developed in Exercise 7.22 to formulate a heuristic for solving the Eight Queens problem. Run your program. (*Hint:* It is possible to assign a value to each square of the chessboard indicating how many squares of an empty chessboard are "eliminated" if a queen is placed in that square. Each of the corners would be assigned the value 22, as in Fig. 7.19.) Once these "elimination numbers" are placed in all 64 squares, an appropriate heuristic might be: Place the next queen in the square with the smallest elimination number. Why is this strategy intuitively appealing?

Fig. 7.19   The 22 squares eliminated by placing a queen in the upper left corner.

7.25   (*Eight Queens: Brute Force Approaches*) In this exercise you will develop several brute force approaches to solving the Eight Queens problem introduced in Exercise 7.24.

> a) Solve the Eight Queens exercise, using the random brute force technique developed in Exercise 7.23.
>
> b) Use an exhaustive technique (i.e., try all possible combinations of eight queens on the chessboard).
>
> c) Why do you suppose the exhaustive brute force approach may not be appropriate for solving the Knight's Tour problem?
>
> d) Compare and contrast the random brute force and exhaustive brute force approaches.

7.26   (*Knight's Tour: Closed Tour Test*) In the Knight's Tour, a full tour occurs when the knight makes 64 moves touching each square of the chessboard once and only once. A closed tour occurs when the 64th move is one move away from the square in which the knight started the tour. Modify the program you wrote in Exercise 7.22 to test for a closed tour if a full tour has occurred.

7.27   (*The Sieve of Eratosthenes*) A prime integer is any integer that is evenly divisible only by itself and 1. The Sieve of Eratosthenes is a method of finding prime numbers. It operates as follows:

> a) Create an array with all elements initialized to 1 (true). Array elements with prime subscripts will remain 1. All other array elements will eventually be set to zero.
>
> b) Starting with array subscript 2 (subscript 1 must be prime), every time an array element is found whose value is 1, loop through the remainder of the array and set to zero every element whose subscript is a multiple of the subscript for the element with value 1. For array subscript 2, all elements beyond 2 in the array that are multiples of 2 will be set to zero (subscripts 4, 6, 8, 10, etc.); for array subscript 3, all elements beyond 3 in the array that are multiples of 3 will be set to zero (subscripts 6, 9, 12, 15, etc.); and so on.

When this process is complete, the array elements that are still set to one indicate that the subscript is a prime number. These subscripts can then be printed. Write a program that uses an array of 1000 elements to determine and print the prime numbers between 1 and 999. Ignore element 0 of the array.

7.28   (*Bucket Sort*) A bucket sort begins with a single-subscripted array of positive integers to be sorted and a double-subscripted array of integers with rows subscripted from 0 to 9 and columns subscripted from 0 to $n - 1$, where n is the number of values in the array to be sorted. Each row of the double-subscripted array is referred to as a bucket. Write a method **bucketSort** that takes an integer array as an argument and performs as follows:

> a) Place each value of the single-subscripted array into a row of the bucket array based on the value's ones digit. For example, 97 is placed in row 7, 3 is placed in row 3 and 100 is placed in row 0. This is called a "distribution pass."
>
> b) Loop through the bucket array row by row and copy the values back to the original array. This is called a "gathering pass." The new order of the preceding values in the single-subscripted array is 100, 3 and 97.
>
> c) Repeat this process for each subsequent digit position (tens, hundreds, thousands, etc.).

On the second pass, 100 is placed in row 0, 3 is placed in row 0 (because 3 has no tens digit) and 97 is placed in row 9. After the gathering pass, the order of the values in the single-subscripted array is 100, 3 and 97. On the third pass, 100 is placed in row 1, 3 is placed in row 0 and 97 is placed in row 0 (after the 3). After the last gathering pass, the original array is now in sorted order.

Note that the double-subscripted array of buckets is ten times the size of the integer array being sorted. This sorting technique provides better performance than a bubble sort, but requires much more memory. The bubble sort requires space for only one additional element of data. This is an example of the space-time trade-off: The bucket sort uses more memory than the bubble sort, but performs better. This version of the bucket sort requires copying all the data back to the original array on each pass. Another possibility is to create a second double-subscripted bucket array and repeatedly swap the data between the two bucket arrays.

Recursion Exercises

7.29   (*Selection Sort*) A selection sort searches an array looking for the smallest element in the array, then swaps that element with the first element of the array. The process is repeated for the subarray beginning with the second element. Each pass of the array places one element in its proper location. For an array of *n* elements, *n* - 1 passes must be made, and for each subarray, *n* - 1 comparisons must be made to find the smallest value. When the subarray being processed contains one element, the array is sorted. Write recursive method **selectionSort** to perform this algorithm.

7.30   (*Palindromes*) A palindrome is a string that is spelled the same way forward and backward. Some examples of palindromes are: "radar," "able was i ere i saw elba" and (if blanks are ignored) "a man a plan a canal panama." Write a recursive method **testPalindrome** that returns 1 if the string stored in the array is a palindrome and 0 otherwise. The method should ignore spaces and punctuation in the string.

7.31   (*Linear Search*) Modify Fig. 7.12 to use recursive method **linearSearch** to perform a linear search of the array. The method should receive an integer array and the size of the array as arguments. If the search key is found, return the array subscript; otherwise, return –1.

7.32   (*Binary Search*) Modify the program of Fig. 7.13 to use a recursive method **binarySearch** to perform the binary search of the array. The method should receive an integer array and the starting subscript and ending subscript as arguments. If the search key is found, return the array subscript; otherwise, return –1.

7.33   (*Eight Queens*) Modify the Eight Queens program you created in Exercise 7.24 to solve the problem recursively.

7.34   (*Print an array*) Write a recursive method **printArray** that takes an array and the size of the array as arguments and returns nothing. The method should stop processing and return when it receives an array of size zero.

7.35   (*Print a string backward*) Write a recursive method **stringReverse** that takes a character array containing a string as an argument, prints the string backward and returns nothing.

7.36   (*Find the minimum value in an array*) Write a recursive method **recursiveMinimum** that takes an integer array and the array size as arguments and returns the smallest element of the array. The method should stop processing and return when it receives an array of one element.

7.37   (*Quicksort*) In the examples and exercises of this chapter, we discussed the sorting techniques of bubble sort, bucket sort and selection sort. We now present the recursive sorting technique called Quicksort. The basic algorithm for a single-subscripted array of values is as follows:

   a) *Partitioning Step:* Take the first element of the unsorted array and determine its final location in the sorted array (i.e., all values to the left of the element in the array are less than the element and all values to the right of the element in the array are greater than the element). We now have one element in its proper location and two unsorted subarrays.
   b) *Recursive Step:* Perform step 1 on each unsorted subarray.

Each time step 1 is performed on a subarray, another element is placed in its final location of the sorted array and two unsorted subarrays are created. When a subarray consists of one element, it must be sorted, therefore that element is in its final location.

The basic algorithm seems simple enough, but how do we determine the final position of the first element of each subarray? As an example, consider the following set of values (the element in bold is the partitioning element—it will be placed in its final location in the sorted array):

   37 2 6 4 89 8 10 12 68 45

   a) Starting from the rightmost element of the array, compare each element to **37** until an element less than **37** is found, then swap **37** and that element. The first element less than **37** is 12, so **37** and 12 are swapped. The new array is

12 2 6 4 89 8 10 **37** 68 45

Element 12 is in italic to indicate that it was just swapped with **37**.

b) Starting from the left of the array, but beginning with the element after 12, compare each element to **37** until an element greater than **37** is found, then swap **37** and that element. The first element greater than **37** is 89, so **37** and 89 are swapped. The new array is

12 2 6 4 **37** 8 10 *89* 68 45

c) Starting from the right, but beginning with the element before 89, compare each element to **37** until an element less than **37** is found, then swap **37** and that element. The first element less than **37** is 10, so **37** and 10 are swapped. The new array is

12 2 6 4 *10* 8 **37** 89 68 45

d) Starting from the left, but beginning with the element after 10, compare each element to **37** until an element greater than **37** is found, then swap **37** and that element. There are no more elements greater than **37**, so when we compare **37** to itself we know that **37** has been placed in its final location of the sorted array.

Once the partition has been applied on the above array, there are two unsorted subarrays. The subarray with values less than 37 contains 12, 2, 6, 4, 10 and 8. The subarray with values greater than 37 contains 89, 68 and 45. The sort continues with both subarrays being partitioned in the same manner as the original array.

Based on the preceding discussion, write recursive method **quickSort** to sort a single-subscripted integer array. The method should receive as arguments an integer array, a starting subscript and an ending subscript. Method **partition** should be called by **quickSort** to perform the partitioning step.

7.38   (*Maze Traversal*) The following grid of **#**s and dots (**.**) is a double-subscripted array representation of a maze.

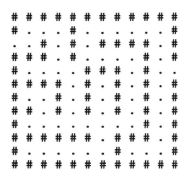

In the preceding double-subscripted array, the **#**s represent the walls of the maze and the dots represent squares in the possible paths through the maze. Moves can only be made to a location in the array that contains a dot.

There is a simple algorithm for walking through a maze that guarantees finding the exit (assuming there is an exit). If there is not an exit, you will arrive at the starting location again. Place your right hand on the wall to your right and begin walking forward. Never remove your hand from the wall. If the maze turns to the right, you follow the wall to the right. As long as you do not remove your hand from the wall, eventually you will arrive at the exit of the maze. There may be a shorter path than the one you have taken, but you are guaranteed to get out of the maze if you follow the algorithm.

Write recursive method **mazeTraverse** to walk through the maze. The method should receive as arguments a 12-by-12 character array representing the maze and the starting location of the maze. As `mazeTraverse` attempts to locate the exit from the maze, it should place the character **X** in each square in the path. The method should display the maze after each move so the user can watch as the maze is solved.

7.39 (*Generating Mazes Randomly*) Write a method `mazeGenerator` that takes as an argument a double-subscripted 12-by-12 character array and randomly produces a maze. The method should also provide the starting and ending locations of the maze. Try your method `mazeTraverse` from Exercise 7.38 using several randomly generated mazes.

7.40 (*Mazes of Any Size*) Generalize methods `mazeTraverse` and `mazeGenerator` of Exercises 7.38 and 7.39 to process mazes of any width and height.

7.41 (*Simulation: The Tortoise and the Hare*) In this problem you will recreate one of the truly great moments in history, namely the classic race of the tortoise and the hare. You will use random number generation to develop a simulation of this memorable event.

Our contenders begin the race at "square 1" of 70 squares. Each square represents a possible position along the race course. The finish line is at square 70. The first contender to reach or pass square 70 is rewarded with a pail of fresh carrots and lettuce. The course weaves its way up the side of a slippery mountain, so occasionally the contenders lose ground.

There is a clock that ticks once per second. With each tick of the clock, your program should adjust the position of the animals according to the following rules:

Animal	Move type	Percentage of the time	Actual move
Tortoise	Fast plod	50%	3 squares to the right
	Slip	20%	6 squares to the left
	Slow plod	30%	1 square to the right
Hare	Sleep	20%	No move at all
	Big hop	20%	9 squares to the right
	Big slip	10%	12 squares to the left
	Small hop	30%	1 square to the right
	Small slip	20%	2 squares to the left

Use variables to keep track of the positions of the animals (i.e., position numbers are 1–70). Start each animal at position 1 (i.e., the "starting gate"). If an animal slips left before square 1, move the animal back to square 1.

Generate the percentages in the preceding table by producing a random integer, i, in the range $1 \leq i \leq 10$. For the tortoise, perform a "fast plod" when $1 \leq i \leq 5$, a "slip" when $6 \leq i \leq 7$ or a "slow plod" when $8 \leq i \leq 10$. Use a similar technique to move the hare.

Begin the race by printing

```
BANG !!!!!
AND THEY'RE OFF !!!!!
```

Then, for each tick of the clock (i.e., each repetition of a loop), print a 70-position line showing the letter **T** in the position of the tortoise and the letter **H** in the position of the hare. Occasionally, the contenders will land on the same square. In this case, the tortoise bites the hare and your program should print **OUCH!!!** beginning at that position. All print positions other than the **T**, the **H** or the **OUCH!!!** (in case of a tie) should be blank.

After each line is printed, test if either animal has reached or passed square 70. If so, print the winner and terminate the simulation. If the tortoise wins, print **TORTOISE WINS!!! YAY!!!** If the hare wins, print **Hare wins. Yuch.** If both animals win on the same tick of the clock, you may want to favor the turtle (the "underdog") or you may want to print **It's a tie**. If neither animal wins, perform the loop again to simulate the next tick of the clock. When you are ready to run your program, assemble a group of fans to watch the race. You'll be amazed at how involved your audience gets!

Later in the book we introduce a number of Java capabilities, such as graphics, images, animation, sound and multithreading. As you study those features, you might enjoy enhancing your tortoise and hare contest simulation.

Special Section: Building Your Own Computer

In the next several problems, we take a temporary diversion away from the world of high-level language programming. We "peel open" a computer and look at its internal structure. We introduce machine-language programming and write several machine-language programs. To make this an especially valuable experience, we then build a computer (through the technique of software-based *simulation*) on which you can execute your machine-language programs!

7.42 (*Machine-Language Programming*) Let us create a computer we will call the Simpletron. As its name implies, it is a simple machine, but as we will soon see, a powerful one as well. The Simpletron runs programs written in the only language it directly understands, that is, Simpletron Machine Language or SML for short.

The Simpletron contains an *accumulator*—a "special register" in which information is put before the Simpletron uses that information in calculations or examines it in various ways. All information in the Simpletron is handled in terms of *words*. A word is a signed four-digit decimal number such as **+3364**, **-1293**, **+0007**, **-0001**, etc. The Simpletron is equipped with a 100-word memory and these words are referenced by their location numbers **00**, **01**, ..., **99**.

Before running an SML program, we must *load* or place the program into memory. The first instruction (or statement) of every SML program is always placed in location **00**. The simulator will start executing at this location.

Each instruction written in SML occupies one word of the Simpletron's memory (and hence instructions are signed four-digit decimal numbers). We shall assume that the sign of an SML instruction is always plus, but the sign of a data word may be either plus or minus. Each location in the Simpletron's memory may contain either an instruction, a data value used by a program or an unused (and hence undefined) area of memory. The first two digits of each SML instruction are the *operation code* specifying the operation to be performed. SML operation codes are summarized in Fig. 7.20.

Operation code	Meaning
Input/output operations:	
`final int READ = 10;`	Read a word from the keyboard into a specific location in memory.
`final int WRITE = 11;`	Write a word from a specific location in memory to the screen.

Fig. 7.20 Simpletron Machine Language (SML) operation codes (part 1 of 2).

Operation code	Meaning
Load/store operations:	
`final int LOAD = 20;`	Load a word from a specific location in memory into the accumulator.
`final int STORE = 21;`	Store a word from the accumulator into a specific location in memory.
Arithmetic operations:	
`final int ADD = 30;`	Add a word from a specific location in memory to the word in the accumulator (leave result in the accumulator).
`final int SUBTRACT = 31;`	Subtract a word from a specific location in memory from the word in the accumulator (leave result in the accumulator).
`final int DIVIDE = 32;`	Divide a word from a specific location in memory into the word in the accumulator (leave result in the accumulator).
`final int MULTIPLY = 33;`	Multiply a word from a specific location in memory by the word in the accumulator (leave result in the accumulator).
Transfer of control operations:	
`final int BRANCH = 40;`	Branch to a specific location in memory.
`final int BRANCHNEG = 41;`	Branch to a specific location in memory if the accumulator is negative.
`final int BRANCHZERO = 42;`	Branch to a specific location in memory if the accumulator is zero.
`final int HALT = 43;`	Halt—the program has completed its task.

Fig. 7.20   Simpletron Machine Language (SML) operation codes (part 2 of 2).

The last two digits of an SML instruction are the *operand*—the address of the memory location containing the word to which the operation applies. Let's consider several simple SML programs.

The first SML program (Example 1) reads two numbers from the keyboard and computes and prints their sum. The instruction **+1007** reads the first number from the keyboard and places it into location **07** (which has been initialized to zero). Then instruction **+1008** reads the next number into location **08**. The *load* instruction, **+2007**, puts the first number into the accumulator and the *add* instruction, **+3008**, adds the second number to the number in the accumulator. *All SML arithmetic instructions leave their results in the accumulator.* The *store* instruction, **+2109**, places the result back into memory location **09** from which the *write* instruction, **+1109**, takes the number and prints it (as a signed four-digit decimal number). The *halt* instruction, **+4300**, terminates execution.

The second SML program (Example 2) reads two numbers from the keyboard and determines and prints the larger value. Note the use of the instruction **+4107** as a conditional transfer of control, much the same as Java's **if** statement.

Example 1 Location	Number	Instruction
00	+1007	(Read A)
01	+1008	(Read B)
02	+2007	(Load A)
03	+3008	(Add B)
04	+2109	(Store C)
05	+1109	(Write C)
06	+4300	(Halt)
07	+0000	(Variable A)
08	+0000	(Variable B)
09	+0000	(Result C)

Example 2 Location	Number	Instruction
00	+1009	(Read A)
01	+1010	(Read B)
02	+2009	(Load A)
03	+3110	(Subtract B)
04	+4107	(Branch negative to 07)
05	+1109	(Write A)
06	+4300	(Halt)
07	+1110	(Write B)
08	+4300	(Halt)
09	+0000	(Variable A)
10	+0000	(Variable B)

Now write SML programs to accomplish each of the following tasks.

a) Use a sentinel-controlled loop to read ten positive numbers. Compute and print their sum.

b) Use a counter-controlled loop to read seven numbers, some positive and some negative, and compute and print their average.

c) Read a series of numbers and determine and print the largest number. The first number read indicates how many numbers should be processed.

7.43   (*A Computer Simulator*) It may at first seem outrageous, but in this problem you are going to build your own computer. No, you will not be soldering components together. Rather, you will use the powerful technique of *software-based simulation* to create an object-oriented *software model* of the Simpletron. You will not be disappointed. Your Simpletron simulator will turn the computer you are using into a Simpletron, and you will actually be able to run, test and debug the SML programs you wrote in Exercise 7.42. Your Simpletron will be an event-driven applet—you will click a button to execute each SML instruction and you will be able to see the instruction "in action."

When you run your Simpletron simulator, it should begin by displaying:

```
*** Welcome to Simpletron! ***
*** Please enter your program one instruction ***
*** (or data word) at a time into the input   ***
*** text field. I will display the location   ***
*** number and a question mark (?). You then   ***
*** type the word for that location. Press the ***
*** Done button to stop entering your program. ***
```

The program should display an **input JTextField** in which the user will type each instruction one at a time and a **Done** button for the user to click when the complete SML program has been entered. Simulate the memory of the Simpletron with a single-subscripted array **memory** that has 100 elements. Now assume that the simulator is running and let us examine the dialog as we enter the program of Example 2 of Exercise 7.42:

```
00 ? +1009
01 ? +1010
02 ? +2009
03 ? +3110
04 ? +4107
05 ? +1109
06 ? +4300
07 ? +1110
08 ? +4300
09 ? +0000
10 ? +0000
```

Your program should use a **JTextField** to display the memory location followed by a question mark. Each of the values to the right of a question mark is typed by the user into the **input JTextField**. When the **Done** button is clicked, the program should display:

```
*** Program loading completed ***
*** Program execution begins   ***
```

The SML program has now been placed (or loaded) in array **memory**. The Simpletron should provide an "**Execute next instruction**" button the user can click to execute each instruction in your SML program. Execution begins with the instruction in location **00** and, like Java, continues sequentially, unless directed to some other part of the program by a transfer of control.

Use the variable **accumulator** to represent the accumulator register. Use the variable **instructionCounter** to keep track of the location in memory that contains the instruction being performed. Use the variable **operationCode** to indicate the operation currently being performed (i.e., the left two digits of the instruction word). Use the variable **operand** to indicate the memory location on which the current instruction operates. Thus, **operand** is the rightmost two digits of the instruction currently being performed. Do not execute instructions directly from memory. Rather, transfer the next instruction to be performed from memory to a variable called **instructionRegister**. Then "pick off" the left two digits and place them in **operationCode** and "pick off" the right two digits and place them in **operand**. Each of the preceding registers should have a corresponding **JTextField** in which its current value can be displayed at all times. When Simpletron begins execution, the special registers are all initialized to 0.

Now let us "walk through" execution of the first SML instruction, **+1009** in memory location **00**. This is called an *instruction execution cycle*.

The **instructionCounter** tells us the location of the next instruction to be performed. We *fetch* the contents of that location from **memory** by using the Java statement

```
instructionRegister = memory[ instructionCounter ];
```

The operation code and the operand are extracted from the instruction register by the statements

```
operationCode = instructionRegister / 100;
operand = instructionRegister % 100;
```

Now the Simpletron must determine that the operation code is actually a *read* (versus a *write*, a *load*, etc.). A **switch** differentiates among the twelve operations of SML.

In the **switch** structure, the behavior of various SML instructions is simulated as follows (we leave the others to the reader):

read:	Display an input dialog with the prompt "**Enter an integer**." Read the value entered, convert it to an integer and store it in location **memory[operand]**.
load:	**accumulator = memory[operand];**
add:	**accumulator += memory[operand];**
branch:	We will discuss the branch instructions shortly.
halt:	This instruction prints the message ***** Simpletron execution terminated *****

When the SML program completes execution, the name and contents of each register as well as the complete contents of memory should be displayed. Such a printout is often called a *computer dump* (and, no, a computer dump is not a place where old computers go). To help you program your dump method, a sample dump format is shown in Fig. 7.23. Note that a dump after executing a Simpletron program would show the actual values of instructions and data values at the moment execution terminated. The sample dump assumes the output will be sent to the display screen with a series of **System.out.print** and **System.out.println** method calls. However, we encourage you to experiment with a version that can be displayed on the applet using a **JTextArea** or an array of **JTextField** objects.

```
REGISTERS:
accumulator              +0000
instructionCounter          00
instructionRegister      +0000
operationCode               00
operand                     00

MEMORY:
        0      1      2      3      4      5      6      7      8      9
 0  +0000  +0000  +0000  +0000  +0000  +0000  +0000  +0000  +0000  +0000
10  +0000  +0000  +0000  +0000  +0000  +0000  +0000  +0000  +0000  +0000
20  +0000  +0000  +0000  +0000  +0000  +0000  +0000  +0000  +0000  +0000
30  +0000  +0000  +0000  +0000  +0000  +0000  +0000  +0000  +0000  +0000
40  +0000  +0000  +0000  +0000  +0000  +0000  +0000  +0000  +0000  +0000
50  +0000  +0000  +0000  +0000  +0000  +0000  +0000  +0000  +0000  +0000
60  +0000  +0000  +0000  +0000  +0000  +0000  +0000  +0000  +0000  +0000
70  +0000  +0000  +0000  +0000  +0000  +0000  +0000  +0000  +0000  +0000
80  +0000  +0000  +0000  +0000  +0000  +0000  +0000  +0000  +0000  +0000
90  +0000  +0000  +0000  +0000  +0000  +0000  +0000  +0000  +0000  +0000
```

Fig. 7.21   A sample dump.

Let us proceed with the execution of our program's first instruction, namely the **+1009** in location **00**. As we have indicated, the **switch** statement simulates this by prompting the user to enter a value into the input dialog, reading the value, converting the value to an integer and storing it in memory location **memory[operand]**. Because your Simpletron is event driven, it waits for the user to type a value into the **input JTextField** and press the *Enter key*. The value is then read into location **09**.

At this point, simulation of the first instruction is completed. All that remains is to prepare the Simpletron to execute the next instruction. Since the instruction just performed was not a transfer of control, we need merely increment the instruction counter register as follows:

```
++instructionCounter;
```

This completes the simulated execution of the first instruction. When the user clicks the **Execute next instruction** button, the entire process (i.e., the instruction execution cycle) begins again with the fetch of the next instruction to be executed.

Now let us consider how the branching instructions—the transfers of control—are simulated. All we need to do is adjust the value in the instruction counter appropriately. Therefore, the unconditional branch instruction (**40**) is simulated within the **switch** as

```
instructionCounter = operand;
```

The conditional "branch if accumulator is zero" instruction is simulated as

```
if ( accumulator == 0 )
   instructionCounter = operand;
```

At this point you should implement your Simpletron simulator and run each of the SML programs you wrote in Exercise 7.42. You may embellish SML with additional features and provide for these in your simulator.

Your simulator should check for various types of errors. During the program loading phase, for example, each number the user types into the Simpletron's **memory** must be in the range **−9999** to **+9999**. Your simulator should test that each number entered is in this range, and, if not, keep prompting the user to reenter the number until the user enters a correct number.

During the execution phase, your simulator should check for various serious errors, such as attempts to divide by zero, attempts to execute invalid operation codes, accumulator overflows (i.e., arithmetic operations resulting in values larger than **+9999** or smaller than **−9999**) and the like. Such serious errors are called *fatal errors*. When a fatal error is detected, your simulator should print an error message such as:

```
*** Attempt to divide by zero ***
*** Simpletron execution abnormally terminated ***
```

and should print a full computer dump in the format we have discussed previously. This will help the user locate the error in the program.

7.44   (*Modifications to the Simpletron Simulator*) In Exercise 7.43, you wrote a software simulation of a computer that executes programs written in Simpletron Machine Language (SML). In this exercise, we propose several modifications and enhancements to the Simpletron Simulator. In Exercises 22.26 and 22.27, we propose building a compiler that converts programs written in a high-level programming language (a variation of Basic) to Simpletron Machine Language. Some of the following modifications and enhancements may be required to execute the programs produced by the compiler.

   a) Extend the Simpletron Simulator's memory to contain 1000 memory locations to enable the Simpletron to handle larger programs.
   b) Allow the simulator to perform modulus calculations. This requires an additional Simpletron Machine Language instruction.

   c) Allow the simulator to perform exponentiation calculations. This requires an additional Simpletron Machine Language instruction.
   d) Modify the simulator to use hexadecimal values rather than integer values to represent Simpletron Machine Language instructions.
   e) Modify the simulator to allow output of a newline. This requires an additional Simpletron Machine Language instruction.
   f) Modify the simulator to process floating-point values in addition to integer values.
   g) Modify the simulator to handle string input. [*Hint:* Each Simpletron word can be divided into two groups, each holding a two-digit integer. Each two-digit integer represents the ASCII decimal equivalent of a character. Add a machine-language instruction that will input a string and store the string beginning at a specific Simpletron memory location. The first half of the word at that location will be a count of the number of characters in the string (i.e., the length of the string). Each succeeding half-word contains one ASCII character expressed as two decimal digits. The machine-language instruction converts each character into its ASCII equivalent and assigns it to a "half-word."]
   h) Modify the simulator to handle output of strings stored in the format of part g). [*Hint:* Add a machine-language instruction that will print a string beginning at a certain Simpletron memory location. The first half of the word at that location is a count of the number of characters in the string (i.e., the length of the string). Each succeeding half-word contains one ASCII character expressed as two decimal digits. The machine-language instruction checks the length and prints the string by translating each two-digit number into its equivalent character.]

7.45 The Fibonacci series

   0, 1, 1, 2, 3, 5, 8, 13, 21, ...

begins with the terms 0 and 1 and has the property that each succeeding term is the sum of the two preceding terms.
   a) Write a *nonrecursive* method **fibonacci(n)** that calculates the nth Fibonacci number. Incorporate this method into an applet that enables the user to enter the value of **n**.
   b) Determine the largest Fibonacci number that can be printed on your system.
   c) Modify the program of part a) to use **double** instead of **int** to calculate and return Fibonacci numbers and use this modified program to repeat part b).

8

Object-Based Programming

Objectives

- To understand encapsulation and data hiding.
- To understand the notions of data abstraction and abstract data types (ADTs).
- To create Java ADTs, namely classes.
- To be able to create, use and destroy objects.
- To be able to control access to object instance variables and methods.
- To appreciate the value of object orientation.
- To understand the use of the **this** reference.
- To understand class variables and class methods.

My object all sublime
I shall achieve in time.
W. S. Gilbert

Is it a world to hide virtues in?
William Shakespeare, *Twelfth Night*

Your public servants serve you right.
Adlai Stevenson

But what, to serve our private ends,
Forbids the cheating of our friends?
Charles Churchill

This above all: to thine own self be true.
William Shakespeare, *Hamlet*

Have no friends not equal to yourself.
Confucius

Outline

8.1 Introduction

Now we investigate object orientation in Java in greater depth. Why did we defer this until now? First, the objects we will build will be composed in part of structured program pieces, so we needed to establish a basis in structured programming with control structures. Second, we wanted to study methods in depth. Third, we wanted to familiarize the reader with arrays which are Java objects.

Through our discussions of object-oriented Java programs in Chapters 2 through 7, we introduced many basic concepts (i.e., "object think") and terminology (i.e., "object speak") of object-oriented programming in Java. We also discussed our program-development methodology: We analyzed many typical problems that required a program—either a Java applet or a Java application—to be built, determined what classes from the Java API were needed to implement the program, determined what instance variables were needed, determined what methods were needed and specified how an object of our class collaborated with objects of Java API classes to accomplish the overall goals of the program.

Let us briefly review some key concepts and terminology of object orientation. OOP *encapsulates* data (*attributes*) and methods (*behaviors*) into *objects;* the data and methods of an object are intimately tied together. Objects have the property of *information hiding.* This means that although objects may know how to communicate with one another across well-defined *interfaces,* objects normally are not allowed to know how other objects are implemented—implementation details are hidden within the objects themselves. Surely it is possible to drive a car effectively without knowing the details of how engines, transmissions and exhaust systems work internally. We will see why information hiding is so crucial to good software engineering.

In C and other *procedural programming languages,* programming tends to be *action-oriented.* In Java, programming is *object-oriented.* In C, the unit of programming is the *function* (called *methods* in Java). In Java, the unit of programming is the *class* from which objects are eventually *instantiated* (i.e., created). Functions do not disappear in Java; rather they are encapsulated as methods with the data they process within the "walls" of classes.

C programmers concentrate on writing functions. Groups of actions that perform some task are formed into functions and functions are grouped to form programs. Data is certainly important in C, but the view is that data exists primarily in support of the actions that functions perform. The *verbs* in a system-requirements document help the C programmer determine the set of functions that will work together to implement the system.

Java programmers concentrate on creating their own *user-defined types* called *classes.* Classes are also referred to as *programmer-defined types.* Each class contains data as well as the set of methods that manipulate the data. The data components of a class are called *instance variables* (these are called *data members* in C++). Just as an instance of a built-in type such as **int** is called a *variable,* an instance of a user-defined type (i.e., a class) is called an *object.* The focus of attention in Java is on objects rather than methods. The *nouns* in a system-requirements document help the Java programmer determine an initial set of classes with which to begin the design process. These classes are then used to instantiate objects that will work together to implement the system.

This chapter explains how to create and use objects, a subject we like to call *object-based programming (OBP).* Chapter 9 introduces *inheritance* and *polymorphism*—two key technologies that enable true *object-oriented programming (OOP).* Although inheritance is not discussed in detail until Chapter 9, inheritance is part of every Java class definition.

Performance Tip 8.1

All Java objects are passed by reference. Only a memory address is passed, not a copy of a possibly large object (as would be the case in a pass by value).

Software Engineering Observation 8.1

It is important to write programs that are understandable and easy to maintain. Change is the rule rather than the exception. Programmers should anticipate that their code will be modified. As we will see, classes facilitate program modifiability.

8.2 Implementing a Time Abstract Data Type with a Class

The application of Fig. 8.1 consists of two classes—**Time1** and **TimeTest**. Class **Time1** is defined in file **Time1.java** (specified in the comment at line 1). Class **TimeTest** is defined in file **TimeTest.java** (specified in the comment at line 49). [Every program in this book that contains more than one file begins the file with a comment indicating the figure number and file name.] Although these two classes are defined in separate files, we number the lines in the program consecutively across both files for discussion purposes in the text. It is important to note that these classes *must* be defined in separate files.

Software Engineering Observation 8.2

Class definitions that begin with keyword **public** *must be stored in a file that has exactly the same name as the class and ends with the* **.java** *file name extension.*

```
1    // Fig. 8.1: Time1.java
2    // Time1 class definition
3    import java.text.DecimalFormat;  // used for number formatting
4
5    // This class maintains the time in 24-hour format
6    public class Time1 extends Object {
7       private int hour;      // 0 - 23
8       private int minute;    // 0 - 59
9       private int second;    // 0 - 59
10
11      // Time1 constructor initializes each instance variable
12      // to zero. Ensures that each Time1 object starts in a
13      // consistent state.
14      public Time1()
15      {
16         setTime( 0, 0, 0 );
17      }
18
19      // Set a new time value using universal time. Perform
20      // validity checks on the data. Set invalid values to zero.
21      public void setTime( int h, int m, int s )
22      {
23         hour = ( ( h >= 0 && h < 24 ) ? h : 0 );
24         minute = ( ( m >= 0 && m < 60 ) ? m : 0 );
25         second = ( ( s >= 0 && s < 60 ) ? s : 0 );
26      }
27
28      // Convert to String in universal-time format
29      public String toUniversalString()
30      {
31         DecimalFormat twoDigits = new DecimalFormat( "00" );
32
33         return twoDigits.format( hour ) + ":" +
34                twoDigits.format( minute ) + ":" +
35                twoDigits.format( second );
36      }
37
38      // Convert to String in standard-time format
39      public String toString()
40      {
41         DecimalFormat twoDigits = new DecimalFormat( "00" );
42
43         return ( (hour == 12 || hour == 0) ? 12 : hour % 12 ) +
44                ":" + twoDigits.format( minute ) +
45                ":" + twoDigits.format( second ) +
46                ( hour < 12 ? " AM" : " PM" );
47      }
48   }
```

Fig. 8.1   Abstract data type **Time1** implementation as a class (part 1 of 2).

Common Programming Error 8.1

*Defining more than one **public** class in the same file is a syntax error.*

```
49   // Fig. 8.1: TimeTest.java
50   // Class TimeTest to exercise class Time1
51   import javax.swing.JOptionPane;
52
53   public class TimeTest {
54      public static void main( String args[] )
55      {
56         Time1 t = new Time1();   // calls Time1 constructor
57         String output;
58
59         output = "The initial universal time is: " +
60                    t.toUniversalString() +
61                    "\nThe initial standard time is: " +
62                    t.toString() +
63                    "\nImplicit toString() call: " + t;
64
65         t.setTime( 13, 27, 6 );
66         output += "\n\nUniversal time after setTime is: " +
67                    t.toUniversalString() +
68                    "\nStandard time after setTime is: " +
69                    t.toString();
70
71         t.setTime( 99, 99, 99 );   // all invalid values
72         output += "\n\nAfter attempting invalid settings: " +
73                    "\nUniversal time: " + t.toUniversalString() +
74                    "\nStandard time: " + t.toString();
75
76         JOptionPane.showMessageDialog( null, output,
77            "Testing Class Time1",
78            JOptionPane.INFORMATION_MESSAGE );
79
80         System.exit( 0 );
81      }
82   }
```

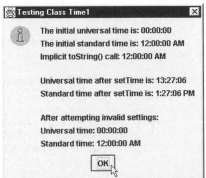

Fig. 8.1   Abstract data type **Time1** implementation as a class (part 2 of 2).

Figure 8.1 (part 1) contains a simple definition for class **Time1**. Our **Time1** class definition begins with line 6

```
public class Time1 extends Object {
```

indicating that class **Time1 extends** class *Object* (from package **java.lang**). Remember that you never really create a class definition "from scratch." In fact, when you create a class definition, you always use pieces of an existing class definition. Java uses *inheritance* to create new classes from existing class definitions. Keyword **extends** followed by class name **Object** indicates the class (in this case **Time1**) from which our new class inherits existing pieces. In this inheritance relationship, **Object** is called the *superclass* or *base class* and **Time1** is called the *subclass* or *derived class*. Using inheritance results in a new class definition that has the *attributes* (data) and *behaviors* (methods) of class **Object** as well as new features we add in our **Time1** class definition. Every class in Java is a subclass of **Object**. Therefore, every class inherits the 11 methods defined by class **Object**. One key **Object** method is *toString*, discussed later in this section. Other methods of class **Object** are discussed as they are needed throughout the text.

Software Engineering Observation 8.3

Every class defined in Java must extend another class. If a class does not explicitly use keyword **extends** *in its definition, the class implicitly* **extends Object**.

The *body* of the class definition is delineated with left and right braces (**{** and **}**) on lines 6 and 48. Class **Time1** contains three integer instance variables—**hour**, **minute** and **second**—that represent the time in *universal-time* format (*24-hour clock* format).

Keywords *public* and *private* are *member access modifiers*. Instance variables or methods declared with member access modifier **public** are accessible wherever the program has a reference to a **Time1** object. Instance variables or methods declared with member access modifier **private** are accessible *only* to methods of the class. Every instance variable or method definition should be preceded by a member access modifier. Member access modifiers can appear multiple times and in any order in a class definition.

Good Programming Practice 8.1

Group members by member access modifier in a class definition for clarity and readability.

The three integer instance variables **hour**, **minute** and **second** are each declared (lines 7 through 9) with member access modifier **private**. This indicates that these instance variables of the class are only accessible to methods of the class. When an object of the class is instantiated (created), such instance variables are encapsulated in the object and can be accessed only through methods of that object's class (normally through the class's **public** methods). Instance variables are normally declared **private** and methods are normally declared **public**. It is possible to have **private** methods and **public** data, as we will see later. The **private** methods are often called *utility methods* or *helper methods* because they can only be called by other methods of that class and are used to support the operation of those methods. Using **public** data is uncommon and is a dangerous programming practice.

Software Engineering Observation 8.4

Methods tend to fall into a number of different categories: methods that get the values of *private* *instance variables; methods that set the values of* *private* *instance variables; methods that implement the services of the class; and methods that perform various mechanical chores for the class, such as initializing class objects, assigning class objects, and converting between classes and built-in types or between classes and other classes.*

Access methods can read or display data. Another common use for access methods is to test the truth or falsity of conditions—such methods are often called *predicate methods.* An example of a predicate method would be an **isEmpty** method for any container class—a class capable of holding many objects—such as a linked list, a stack or a queue (these data structures are discussed in depth in Chapters 22, 23 and 24). A program might test **isEmpty** before attempting to read another item from the container object. A program might test **isFull** before attempting to insert another item into a container object.

Class **Time1** contains the following **public** methods—**Time1** (line 14), **setTime** (line 21), **toUniversalString** (line 29) and **toString** (line 39). These are the *public* methods, *public* services or *public* interface of the class. These methods are used by *clients* (i.e., portions of a program that are users of a class) of the class to manipulate the data stored in objects of the class.

The clients of a class use references to interact with an object of the class. For example, method **paint** in an applet is a client of class **Graphics**—**paint** uses a reference to a **Graphics** object (such as **g**) that it receives as an argument to draw on the applet by calling methods that are **public** services of class **Graphics** (such as **drawString**, **drawLine**, **drawOval** and **drawRect**).

Notice the method with the same name as the class (line 14); it is the *constructor* method of that class. A constructor is a special method that initializes the instance variables of a class object. A class's constructor method is called automatically when an object of that class is instantiated. This constructor simply calls the class's **setTime** method (discussed shortly) with hour, minute and second values specified as 0.

It is common to have several constructors for a class; this is accomplished through *method overloading* (as we will see Fig. 8.4). Constructors can take arguments but cannot return a value. An important difference between constructors and other methods is that constructors *are not allowed to specify a return data type* (not event **void**). Normally, constructors are **public** methods of a class. Non-**public** methods are discussed later.

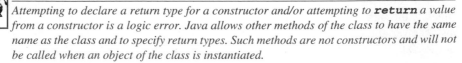

Common Programming Error 8.2

*Attempting to declare a return type for a constructor and/or attempting to **return** a value from a constructor is a logic error. Java allows other methods of the class to have the same name as the class and to specify return types. Such methods are not constructors and will not be called when an object of the class is instantiated.*

Method **setTime** (line 21) is a **public** method that receives three integer arguments and uses them to set the time. Each argument is tested in a conditional expression that determines if the value is in range. For example, the **hour** value must be greater than or equal to 0 and less than 24 because we represent the time in universal time format (0–23 for the hour, 0–59 for the minute and 0–59 for the second). Any value outside this range is an invalid value and is set to zero—ensuring that a **Time1** object always contains valid data. This is also known as *keeping the object in a consistent state.* In cases where invalid data is supplied to **setTime**, the program may want to indicate that an invalid time setting was attempted. We explore this possibility in the exercises.

Good Programming Practice 8.2

Always define a class so its instance variables are maintained in a consistent state.

Method **toUniversalString** (line 29) takes no arguments and returns a **String**. This method produces a universal-time-format string consisting of six digits—two for the hour, two for the minute and two for the second. For example, 13:30:07 represents 1:30:07 PM. Line 31

```
DecimalFormat twoDigits = new DecimalFormat( "00" );
```

creates an instance of class **DecimalFormat** (from package **java.text** imported at line 3) to help format the universal time. Object **twoDigits** is initialized with the *format control string* **"00"**, which indicates that the number format should consist of two digits— each **0** is a placeholder for a digit. If the number being formatted is a single digit, it is automatically preceded by a leading **0** (i.e., **8** is formatted as **08**). The **return** statement at lines 33 through 35

```
return twoDigits.format( hour ) + ":" +
       twoDigits.format( minute ) + ":" +
       twoDigits.format( second );
```

uses method **format** (that returns a formatted **String** containing the number) from object **twoDigits** to format the **hour**, **minute** and **second** values into two-digit strings. Those strings are concatenated with the **+** operator (separated by colons) and returned from method **toUniversalString**.

Method **toString** (line 39) takes no arguments and returns a **String**. This method produces a standard-time-format string consisting of the **hour**, **minute** and **second** values separated by colons and an AM or PM indicator as in **1:27:06 PM**. This method uses the same **DecimalFormat** techniques as method **toUniversalString** to guarantee that the **minute** and **second** values each appear with two digits. Method **toString** is special in that we inherited from class **Object** a **toString** method with exactly the same first line as our **toString** on line 39. The original **toString** method of class **Object** is a generic version that is used mainly as a placeholder that can be redefined by a subclass (similar to methods **init**, **start** and **paint** from class **JApplet**). Our version replaces the version we inherited to provide a **toString** method that is more appropriate for our class. This is known as *overriding* the original method definition (discussed in detail in Chapter 9).

Once the class has been defined, it can be used as a type in declarations such as

```
Time1 sunset,       // reference to object of type Time1
      timeArray[];  // reference to array of Time1 objects
```

The class name is a new type specifier. There may be many objects of a class, just as there may be many variables of a primitive data type such as **int**. The programmer can create new class types as needed; this is one of the reasons why Java is known as an *extensible language*.

The application of Fig. 8.1 (part 2) uses class **Time1**. Method **main** of class **Time-Test** declares and initializes an instance of class **Time1** called **t** with line 56

```
Time1 t = new Time1();  // calls Time1 constructor
```

When the object is instantiated, operator **new** allocates the memory in which the **Time1** object will be stored, then **new** calls the **Time1** constructor to initialize the instance variables of the new **Time1** object. The constructor invokes method **setTime** to explicitly initialize each private instance variable to **0**. Operator **new** then returns a reference to the new object, and that reference is assigned to **t**. Similarly, line 31 in class **Time1**

```
DecimalFormat twoDigits = new DecimalFormat( "00" );
```

uses **new** to allocate the memory for a **DecimalFormat** object, then calls the **Deci-malFormat** constructor with the argument **"00"** to indicate the number format control string.

Software Engineering Observation 8.5

*Every time **new** creates an object of a class, that class's constructor is called to initialize the instance variables of the new object.*

Note that class **Time1** was not **import**ed into the **TimeTest.java** file. Actually, every class in Java is part of a *package* (like the classes from the Java API). If the programmer does not specify the package for a class, the class is automatically placed in the *default package* which includes the compiled classes in the current directory. If a class is in the same package as the class that uses it, an **import** statement is not required. We import classes from the Java API because their **.class** files are not in the same package with each program we write. Section 8.5 illustrates how to define your own packages of classes for reuse.

Line 57 declares a **String** reference **output** that will store the string containing the results to be displayed in a message box. Lines 59 through 63 append to **output** the time in universal-time format (by sending message **toUniversalString** to the object to which **t** refers) and standard-time format (by sending message **toString** to the object to which **t** refers) to confirm that the data were initialized properly. Notice line 63

```
"\nImplicit toString() call: " + t;
```

This line uses a special feature of Java—concatenating a **String** with any object results in an implicit call to the object's **toString** method to convert the object to a **String**, then the **String**s are concatenated. Lines 62 and 63 illustrate that you can call **toString** both explicitly and implicitly in a **String** concatenation operation.

Line 65

```
t.setTime( 13, 27, 6 );
```

sends the **setTime** message to the object to which **t** refers to change the time. Then lines 66 through 69 append the time to **output** again in both formats to confirm that the time was set correctly.

To illustrate that method **setTime** validates the values passed to it, line 71

```
t.setTime( 99, 99, 99 );   // all invalid values
```

calls method **setTime** and attempts to set the instance variables to invalid values. Then lines 72 through 74 append the time to **output** again in both formats to confirm that **set-Time** validated the data. Lines 76 through 78 display a message box with the results of our program. Notice in the last two lines of the output window that the time is set to midnight— the default value of a **Time1** object.

Now that we have seen our first nonapplet, nonapplication class, let us consider several issues of class design.

Again, note that the instance variables **hour**, **minute** and **second** are each declared **private**. Instance variables declared **private** are not accessible outside the class in which they are defined. The philosophy here is that the actual data representation used within the class is of no concern to the class's clients. For example, it would be perfectly reasonable for the class to represent the time internally as the number of seconds since midnight. Clients could use the same **public** methods and get the same results without being aware of this. In this sense, implementation of a class is said to be *hidden* from its clients. Exercise 8.18 asks you to make precisely this modification to the **Time1** class of Fig. 8.1 and show that there is no visible change to the clients of the class.

Software Engineering Observation 8.6

Information hiding promotes program modifiability and simplifies the client's perception of a class.

Software Engineering Observation 8.7

Clients of a class can (and should) use the class without knowing the internal details of how the class is implemented. If the class implementation is changed (to improve performance, for example), provided the class's interface remains constant, the class clients' source code need not change. This makes it much easier to modify systems.

In this program, the **Time1** constructor simply initializes the instance variables to 0 (i.e., the military time equivalent of 12 AM). This ensures that the object is created in a *consistent state* (i.e., all instance variable values are valid). Invalid values cannot be stored in the instance variables of a **Time1** object because the constructor is automatically called when the **Time1** object is created, and subsequent attempts by a client to modify the instance variables are scrutinized by the method **setTime**.

Instance variables can be initialized where they are declared in the class body, by the class's constructor, or they can be assigned values by "set" methods. Instance variables that are not explicitly initialized by the programmer are initialized by the compiler (primitive numeric variables are set to 0, **boolean**s are set to **false** and references are set to **null**).

Good Programming Practice 8.3

Initialize instance variables of a class in that class's constructor.

Every class may include a *finalizer* method called **finalize** that does "termination housekeeping" on each class object before the memory for the object is garbage collected by the system. We will discuss garbage collection and finalizers in detail in Sections 8.14 and 8.15.

It is interesting that the **toUniversalString** and **toString** methods take no arguments. This is because these methods implicitly know that they are to manipulate the instance variables of the particular **Time1** object for which they are invoked. This makes method calls more concise than conventional function calls in procedural programming. It also reduces the likelihood of passing the wrong arguments, the wrong types of arguments and/or the wrong number of arguments as often happens in C function calls.

Software Engineering Observation 8.8

Using an object-oriented programming approach can often simplify method calls by reducing the number of parameters to be passed. This benefit of object-oriented programming derives from the fact that encapsulation of instance variables and methods within an object gives the methods the right to access the instance variables.

Classes simplify programming because the client (or user of the class object) need only be concerned with the **public** operations encapsulated in the object. Such operations are usually designed to be client oriented rather than implementation oriented. Clients need not be concerned with a class's implementation. Interfaces do change, but less frequently than implementations. When an implementation changes, implementation-dependent code must change accordingly. By hiding the implementation we eliminate the possibility of other program parts becoming dependent on the details of the class implementation.

Often, classes do not have to be created "from scratch." Rather, they may be *derived* from other classes that provide operations the new classes can use, or classes can include objects of other classes as members. Such *software reuse* can greatly enhance programmer productivity. Deriving new classes from existing classes is called *inheritance* and is discussed in detail in Chapter 9. Including class objects as members of other classes is called *composition* or *aggregation* and is discussed later in this chapter.

8.3 Class Scope

A class's instance variables and methods belong to that *class's scope*. Within a class's scope, class members are immediately accessible to all of that class's methods and can be referenced simply by name. Outside a class's scope, class members cannot be referenced directly by name. Those class members (such as **public** members) that are visible can only be accessed off a "handle" (i.e., primitive data type members can be referred to by **objectReferenceName.primitiveVariableName** and object members can be referenced by **objectReferenceName.objectMemberName**).

Variables defined in a method are known only to that method (i.e., they are local variables to that method). Such variables are said to have block scope. If a method defines a variable with the same name as a variable with class scope (i.e., an instance variable), the class-scope variable is hidden by the method-scope variable in the method scope. A hidden instance variable can be accessed in the method by preceding its name with the keyword **this** and the dot operator, as in **this.x**. Keyword **this** is discussed later in the chapter.

8.4 Controlling Access to Members

The member access modifiers **public** and **private** are used to control access to a class's instance variables and methods. (In Chapter 9, we will introduce the additional access modifier **protected**.)

As we stated previously, the primary purpose of **public** methods is to present to the class's clients a view of the *services* the class provides (i.e., the public interface of the class). Clients of the class need not be concerned with how the class accomplishes its tasks. For this reason, the **private** members of a class as well as the definitions of its **public** methods (i.e., the class's implementation) are not accessible to the clients of a class.

Common Programming Error 8.3

*An attempt by a method which is not a member of a particular class to access a **private** member of that class is a syntax error.*

Figure 8.2 demonstrates that **private** class members are not accessible by name outside the class. Line 9 attempts to directly access the **private** instance variable **hour** of the **Time1** object to which **t** refers. When this program is compiled, the compiler generates an error stating that the **private** member **hour** is not accessible. [*Note:* This program assumes that the **Time1** class from Fig. 8.1 is used.]

Good Programming Practice 8.4

*Our preference is to list the **private** instance variables of a class first so as you read the code, you see the names and types of the instance variables before they are used in the methods of the class.*

Good Programming Practice 8.5

*Despite the fact that **private** and **public** members may be repeated and intermixed, list all the **private** members of a class first in one group and then list all the **public** members in another group.*

Software Engineering Observation 8.9

*Keep all the instance variables of a class **private**. When necessary provide **public** methods to set the values of **private** instance variables and to get the values of **private** instance variables. This architecture helps hide the implementation of a class from its clients, which reduces bugs and improves program modifiability.*

```
1   // Fig. 8.2: TimeTest.java
2   // Demonstrate errors resulting from attempts
3   // to access private class members.
4   public class TimeTest {
5      public static void main( String args[] )
6      {
7         Time1 t = new Time1();
8
9         t.hour = 7;
10     }
11  }
```

```
TimeTest.java:9: Variable hour in class Time1 not
                accessible from class TimeTest.
        t.hour = 7;
           ^
1 error
```

Fig. 8.2   Erroneous attempt to access private members of a class.

Access to **private** data should be carefully controlled by the class's methods. For example, to allow clients to read the value of **private** data, the class can provide a *"get" method* (also called an *accessor method*). To enable clients to modify **private** data, the class can provide a *"set" method* (also called a *mutator method*). Such modification would seem to violate the notion of **private** data. But a *set* method can provide data validation capabilities (such as range checking) to ensure that the value is set properly. A *set* method can also translate between the form of the data used in the interface and the form used in the implementation. A *get* method need not expose the data in "raw" format; rather, the *get* method can edit the data and limit the view of the data the client will see.

Software Engineering Observation 8.10

*Class designers use **private** data and **public** methods to enforce the notion of information hiding and the principle of least privilege. If the client of a class needs access to data in the class, provide that access through **public** methods of the class. By doing so, the programmer of the class controls how the class's data is manipulated (e.g., data validity checking can prevent invalid data from being stored in an object).*

Software Engineering Observation 8.11

The class designer need not provide set *and/or* get *methods for each **private** data member; these capabilities should be provided only when it makes sense and after careful thought by the class designer.*

Testing and Debugging Tip 8.1

*Making the instance variables of a class **private** and the methods of the class **public** facilitates debugging because problems with data manipulations are localized to the class's methods.*

8.5 Creating Packages

As we have seen in almost every example in the text, classes and *interfaces* (discussed in Chapter 9) from preexisting libraries such as the Java API can be imported into a Java program. Each class and interface in the Java API belongs to a specific package that contains a group of related classes and interfaces. Packages are actually directory structures used to organize classes and interfaces. Packages provide a mechanism for *software reuse*. One of our goals as programmers is to create reusable software components so we are not required to repeatedly redefine code in separate programs. Another benefit of packages is that they provide a convention for *unique class names*. With hundreds of thousands of Java programmers around the world, there is a good chance that the names you choose for classes will conflict with the names that other programmers choose for their classes.

The application of Fig. 8.3 illustrates how to create your own package and use a class from that package in a program.

The steps for creating a reusable class are:

1. Define a **public** class. If the class is not **public**, it can be used only by other classes in the same package.

2. Choose a package name and add a ***package*** statement to the source code file for the reusable class definition.

```
1   // Fig. 8.3: Time1.java
2   // Time1 class definition
3   package com.deitel.jhtp3.ch08;
4   import java.text.DecimalFormat;   // used for number formatting
5
6   // This class maintains the time in 24-hour format
7   public class Time1 extends Object {
8      private int hour;      // 0 - 23
9      private int minute;    // 0 - 59
10     private int second;    // 0 - 59
11
12     // Time1 constructor initializes each instance variable
13     // to zero. Ensures that each Time1 object starts in a
14     // consistent state.
15     public Time1()
16     {
17        setTime( 0, 0, 0 );
18     }
19
20     // Set a new time value using military time. Perform
21     // validity checks on the data. Set invalid values
22     // to zero.
23     public void setTime( int h, int m, int s )
24     {
25        hour = ( ( h >= 0 && h < 24 ) ? h : 0 );
26        minute = ( ( m >= 0 && m < 60 ) ? m : 0 );
27        second = ( ( s >= 0 && s < 60 ) ? s : 0 );
28     }
29
30     // Convert to String in universal-time format
31     public String toUniversalString()
32     {
33        DecimalFormat twoDigits = new DecimalFormat( "00" );
34
35        return twoDigits.format( hour ) + ":" +
36               twoDigits.format( minute ) + ":" +
37               twoDigits.format( second );
38     }
39
40     // Convert to String in standard-time format
41     public String toString()
42     {
43        DecimalFormat twoDigits = new DecimalFormat( "00" );
44
45        return ( (hour == 12 || hour == 0) ? 12 : hour % 12 ) +
46               ":" + twoDigits.format( minute ) +
47               ":" + twoDigits.format( second ) +
48               ( hour < 12 ? " AM" : " PM" );
49     }
50  }
```

Fig. 8.3   Creating a package for software reuse (part 1 of 2).

```
51   // Fig. 8.3: TimeTest.java
52   // Class TimeTest to use imported class Time1
53   import javax.swing.JOptionPane;
54   import com.deitel.jhtp3.ch08.Time1;  // import Time1 class
55
56   public class TimeTest {
57      public static void main( String args[] )
58      {
59         Time1 t = new Time1();
60
61         t.setTime( 13, 27, 06 );
62         String output =
63            "Universal time is: " + t.toUniversalString() +
64            "\nStandard time is: " + t.toString();
65
66         JOptionPane.showMessageDialog( null, output,
67            "Packaging Class Time1 for Reuse",
68            JOptionPane.INFORMATION_MESSAGE );
69
70         System.exit( 0 );
71      }
72   }
```

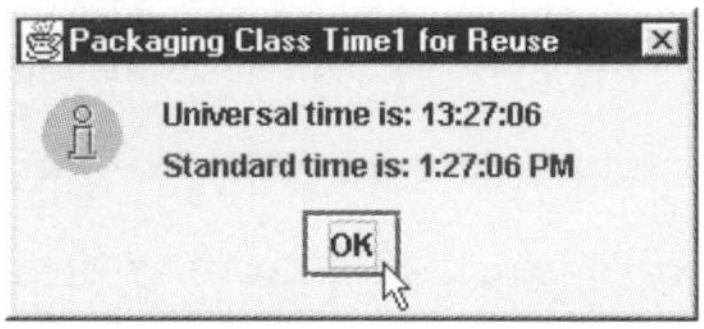

```
Packaging Class Time1 for Reuse      [X]

   i    Universal time is: 13:27:06
        Standard time is: 1:27:06 PM

              [ OK ]
```

Fig. 8.3   Creating a package for software reuse (part 2 of 2).

3. Compile the class so it is placed in the appropriate package directory structure and make the new class available to the compiler and the interpreter.

4. Import the reusable class into a program and use the class.

For *Step 1*, we chose to use the **public** class **Time1** defined in Fig. 8.1. No modifications have been made to the implementation of the class, so we will not discuss the implementation details of the class again here.

To satisfy *Step 2*, we added a **package** statement at the beginning of the file. Line 3

```
package com.deitel.jhtp3.ch08;   // place Time1 in a package
```

uses a **package** statement to define a **package** named **com.deitel.jhtp3.ch08**. Placing a **package** statement at the beginning of a Java source file indicates that the class defined in the file is part of the specified package. The only two statements in Java that can appear outside the braces of a class definition are **package** statements and **import** statements.

Software Engineering Observation 8.12

*A Java source code file has the following order: a **package** statement (if any), **import** statements (if any), then class definitions. Only one of the class definitions can be **public**. Other classes in the file are also placed in the package, but are not reusable. They are in the package to support the reusable class in the file.*

In an effort to provide unique names for every package, Sun Microsystems specifies a convention for package naming. Every package name should start with your Internet domain name in reverse order. For example, our Internet domain name is **deitel.com** so we began our package name with **com.deitel**. If your domain name is *yourcollege*.**edu**, the package name you would use is **edu.***yourcollege*. After the domain name is reversed, you can choose any other names you want for your package. If you are part of a company with many divisions or a university with many schools, you may want to use the name of your division or school as the next name in the package. We chose to use **jhtp3** as the next name in our package name to indicate that this class is from *Java How to Program: Third Edition*. The last name in our package name specifies that this package is for Chapter 8 (**ch08**). [*Note:* We use our own packages several times throughout the book. You can determine the chapter in which one of our reusable classes is defined by looking at the last name in the **import** statement.]

Step 3 is to compile the class so it is stored in the appropriate package and is made available to both the compiler and interpreter. In Java 2, this process is simplified because there is a directory called **classes** where the compiled version of new reusable classes are placed that is well known to both the compiler and the interpreter. This directory is part of the new *Java extension mechanism* that allows programmers to enhance the functionality of Java with their own packages of classes (we discuss the extensions mechanism in more detail in Chapter 25, "JavaBeans"). On Windows, the location of the **classes** directory is

```
c:\jdk1.2.1\jre\classes
```

and on UNIX it is the directory in which you installed the JDK followed by **jdk1.2.1/jre/classes**—for example, the directory

```
/usr/local/jdk1.2.1/jre/classes
```

For other platforms, there will be a similar directory (or folder) structure. The **classes** directory does not exist by default—you must create it before compiling your first class that is to be placed in a package. For the purpose of this chapter, we assume on Windows that the JDK is installed in **c:\jdk1.2.1** and on UNIX that the JDK is installed in your home directory in **~/jdk1.2.1**. [*Note:* You may need to adjust the preceding directory structures to indicate where the JDK is installed on your system and to reflect the version of the JDK that is installed on your system (ours was JDK 1.2.1 at the time of this writing).]

When a Java file containing a **package** statement is compiled, the resulting **.class** file is placed in the directory specified by the **package** statement. The preceding **package** statement indicates that class **Time1** should be placed in the directory **ch08**. The other names—**com**, **deitel** and **jhtp3**—are also directories. The directory names in the **package** statement specify the exact location of the classes in the package. If these directories do not exist before the class is compiled, the compiler creates them.

When compiling a class in a package, there is an extra option (**-d**) that must be passed to the compiler that specifies where to create (or locate) all the directories in the **package** statement. For example, we used the compilation command

```
javac -d c:\jdk1.2.1\jre\classes Time1.java
```

to specify that the first directory specified in our package name should be placed in the directory **c:\jdk1.2.1\jre\classes** (on our Windows 98 computer). After executing the compilation command, the directory **c:\jdk1.2.1\jre\classes** contains a directory called **com**, **com** contains a directory called **deitel**, **deitel** contains a directory called **jhtp3** and **jhtp3** contains a directory called **ch08**. In the **ch08** directory, you can find the file **Time1.class**. If you are operating on a UNIX computer, a typical compilation command would be

```
javac -d $HOME/jdk1.2.1/jre/classes Time1.java
```

This results in the same directory structure discussed above with the **jdk1.2.1/jre/classes** directory appearing in the home directory for your UNIX account. [*Note:* If the J2SDK is installed in a location that is available to many users in your UNIX environment, you may not be able to modify the contents of any directories in the J2SDK directory structure. In this case, you should investigate the **-classpath** option to the Java compiler and the Java interpreter in the on-line Java documentation. This option allows you to specify alternate locations for your packages.]

The **package** directory names become part of the class name when the class is compiled. The class name in this example is actually **com.deitel.jhtp3.ch08.Time1** after the class is compiled. You can use this *fully qualified* name in your programs or you can **import** the class and use its short name (**Time1**) in the program. If there is a naming conflict (i.e., another package also contains a **Time1** class), the fully qualified class names can be used to distinguish between the classes in the program.

Once the class is compiled and stored in its package, the class can be imported into programs (*Step 4*). Line 54

```
import com.deitel.jhtp3.ch08.Time1;   // import Time1 class
```

specifies that class **Time1** should be **import**ed for use in class **TimeTest**. To locate the classes in the package from this example, the compiler or interpreter first locates the directory **c:\jdk1.2.1\jre\classes** (or the appropriate directory for non-Windows systems), then the compiler or interpreter looks in the directory for the first name in the package—**com**. Next, they navigate the directory structure. Directory **com** contains the subdirectory **deitel**. Directory **deitel** contains the subdirectory **jhtp3**. Finally, directory **jhtp3** contains subdirectory **ch08**. In the **ch08** directory is the file **Time1.class**, which is loaded by the compiler to ensure that the class is used properly in a program, or is loaded by the interpreter to execute the program.

8.6 Initializing Class Objects: Constructors

When an object is created, its members can be initialized by a *constructor* method. A constructor is a method with the same name as the class (including case sensitivity). The programmer provides the constructor which is invoked automatically each time an object of that class is instantiated. Instance variables can be initialized implicitly to their default values (**0** for primitive numeric types, **false** for **boolean**s and **null** for references), can be initialized in a constructor of the class, or their values may be set later after the object is created. Constructors cannot specify return types or return values. A class may contain overloaded constructors to provide a variety of means for initializing objects of that class.

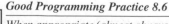

Good Programming Practice 8.6

When appropriate (almost always), provide a constructor to ensure that every object is properly initialized with meaningful values.

When an object of a class is created, *initializers* can be provided in parentheses to the right of the class name. These initializers are passed as arguments to the class's constructor. This technique is demonstrated in the next example. We have also seen this technique several times previously as we created new objects of classes like **DecimalFormat**, **JLabel**, **JTextField**, **JTextArea** and **JButton**. For each of these classes we have seen statements of the form

> **ref** = **new** *ClassName*(*arguments*);

where **ref** is a reference of the appropriate data type, **new** indicates that a new object is being created, *ClassName* indicates the type of the new object and *arguments* specifies the values used by the class's constructor to initialize the object.

If no constructors are defined for a class, the compiler creates a *default constructor* that takes no arguments (also called a *no-argument constructor*). The default constructor for a class calls the default constructor for the class that this class **extends**, then proceeds to initialize the instance variables in the manner we discussed previously (i.e., primitive numeric data type variables to **0**, **boolean**s to **false** and references to **null**). If the class that this class extends does not have a default constructor, the compiler issues an error message. It is also possible for the programmer to provide a no-argument constructor as we showed in class **Time1** and will see in the next example. If any constructors are defined for a class by the programmer, Java will not create a default constructor for the class.

Common Programming Error 8.4

*If constructors are provided for a class, but none of the **public** constructors are no-argument constructors, and an attempt is made to call a no-argument constructor to initialize an object of the class, a syntax error occurs. A constructor may be called with no arguments only if there are no constructors for the class (the default constructor is called) or if there is a no-argument constructor.*

8.7 Using Overloaded Constructors

Methods of a class can be *overloaded* [i.e., several methods in a class can have exactly the same name (as defined in Chapter 6, "Methods")]. To overload a method of a class, simply provide a separate method definition with the same name for each version of the method. Remember that overloaded methods *must* have different parameter lists.

Common Programming Error 8.5

Attempting to overload a method of a class with another method that has the exact same signature (name and parameters) is a syntax error.

The **Time1** constructor in Fig. 8.1 initialized **hour**, **minute** and **second** to **0** (i.e., 12 midnight in military time) with a call to the class's **setTime** method. Figure 8.4 overloads the constructor method to provide a convenient variety of ways to initialize objects of the new class **Time2**. The constructors guarantee that every object begins its existence in a consistent state. In this program, each constructor calls method **setTime** with the values passed to the constructor to ensure that the value supplied for **hour** is in the range 0 to 23 and that the values for **minute** and **second** are each in the range 0 to 59. If a value is out of range, it is set to zero by **setTime** (once again ensuring that each instance variable remains in a consistent state). The appropriate constructor is invoked by matching the number, types and order of the arguments specified in the constructor call with the number, types and order of the parameters specified in each method definition. The matching constructor is called automatically.

```
1   // Fig. 8.4: Time2.java
2   // Time2 class definition
3   package com.deitel.jhtp3.ch08;    // place Time2 in a package
4   import java.text.DecimalFormat;  // used for number formatting
5
6   // This class maintains the time in 24-hour format
7   public class Time2 extends Object {
8      private int hour;      // 0 - 23
9      private int minute;    // 0 - 59
10     private int second;    // 0 - 59
11
12     // Time2 constructor initializes each instance variable
13     // to zero. Ensures that Time object starts in a
14     // consistent state.
15     public Time2() { setTime( 0, 0, 0 ); }
16
17     // Time2 constructor: hour supplied, minute and second
18     // defaulted to 0.
19     public Time2( int h ) { setTime( h, 0, 0 ); }
20
21     // Time2 constructor: hour and minute supplied, second
22     // defaulted to 0.
23     public Time2( int h, int m ) { setTime( h, m, 0 ); }
24
25     // Time2 constructor: hour, minute and second supplied.
26     public Time2( int h, int m, int s ) { setTime( h, m, s ); }
27
28     // Time2 constructor: another Time2 object supplied.
29     public Time2( Time2 time )
30     {
31        setTime( time.hour, time.minute, time.second );
32     }
33
34     // Set a new time value using universal time. Perform
35     // validity checks on the data. Set invalid values to zero.
36     public void setTime( int h, int m, int s )
37     {
38        hour = ( ( h >= 0 && h < 24 ) ? h : 0 );
39        minute = ( ( m >= 0 && m < 60 ) ? m : 0 );
40        second = ( ( s >= 0 && s < 60 ) ? s : 0 );
41     }
42
43     // Convert to String in universal-time format
44     public String toUniversalString()
45     {
46        DecimalFormat twoDigits = new DecimalFormat( "00" );
47
```

Fig. 8.4   Using overloaded constructors (part 1 of 4).

```
48              return twoDigits.format( hour ) + ":" +
49                      twoDigits.format( minute ) + ":" +
50                      twoDigits.format( second );
51      }
52
53      // Convert to String in standard-time format
54      public String toString()
55      {
56          DecimalFormat twoDigits = new DecimalFormat( "00" );
57
58          return ( (hour == 12 || hour == 0) ? 12 : hour % 12 ) +
59                  ":" + twoDigits.format( minute ) +
60                  ":" + twoDigits.format( second ) +
61                  ( hour < 12 ? " AM" : " PM" );
62      }
63  }
```

Fig. 8.4   Using overloaded constructors (part 2 of 4).

```
64  // Fig. 8.4: TimeTest.java
65  // Using overloaded constructors
66  import javax.swing.*;
67  import com.deitel.jhtp3.ch08.Time2;
68
69  public class TimeTest {
70     public static void main( String args[] )
71     {
72        Time2 t1, t2, t3, t4, t5, t6;
73        String output;
74
75        t1 = new Time2();
76        t2 = new Time2( 2 );
77        t3 = new Time2( 21, 34 );
78        t4 = new Time2( 12, 25, 42 );
79        t5 = new Time2( 27, 74, 99 );
80        t6 = new Time2( t4 );    // use t4 as initial value
81
82        output = "Constructed with: " +
83                    "\nt1: all arguments defaulted" +
84                    "\n      " + t1.toUniversalString() +
85                    "\n      " + t1.toString();
86
87        output += "\nt2: hour specified; minute and " +
88                    "second defaulted" +
89                    "\n      " + t2.toUniversalString() +
90                    "\n      " + t2.toString();
91
92        output += "\nt3: hour and minute specified; " +
93                    "second defaulted" +
94                    "\n      " + t3.toUniversalString() +
95                    "\n      " + t3.toString();
96
```

Fig. 8.4   Using overloaded constructors (part 3 of 4).

```
 97          output += "\nt4: hour, minute, and second specified" +
 98                       "\n        " + t4.toUniversalString() +
 99                       "\n        " + t4.toString();
100
101          output += "\nt5: all invalid values specified" +
102                       "\n        " + t5.toUniversalString() +
103                       "\n        " + t5.toString();
104
105          output += "\nt6: Time2 object t4 specified" +
106                       "\n        " + t6.toUniversalString() +
107                       "\n        " + t6.toString();
108
109          JOptionPane.showMessageDialog( null, output,
110             "Demonstrating Overloaded Constructors",
111             JOptionPane.INFORMATION_MESSAGE );
112
113          System.exit( 0 );
114       }
115    }
```

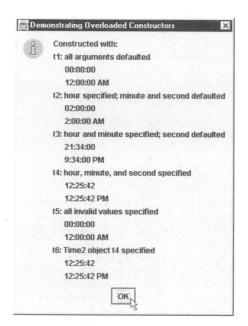

Fig. 8.4   Using overloaded constructors (part 4 of 4).

Most of the code in class **Time2** is identical to class **Time1**, so we concentrate on only the new features here (i.e., the constructors). Line 15 defines the no-argument (default) constructor. Line 19 defines a **Time2** constructor that receives a single **int** argument representing the **hour**. Line 23 defines a **Time2** constructor that receives two **int** arguments representing the **hour** and **minute**. Line 26 defines a **Time2** constructor that receives three **int** arguments representing the **hour**, **minute** and **second**. Line 29 defines a

Time2 constructor that receives a **Time2** reference to another **Time2** object. In this case, the values from the **Time2** argument are used to initialize the **hour**, **minute** and **second**. Notice that none of the constructors specify a return data type (remember, this is not allowed for constructors). Also, notice that all the constructors receive different numbers of arguments and/or different types of arguments. Even though only two of the constructors receive values for the **hour**, **minute** and **second**, all the constructors call **setTime** with values for **hour**, **minute** and **second** and substitute zeros for the missing values to satisfy **setTime**'s requirement of three arguments.

Notice in particular the constructor at lines 29 through 32

```
public Time2( Time2 time )
{
    setTime( time.hour, time.minute, time.second );
}
```

that uses the **hour**, **minute** and **second** values of its argument time to initialize the new **Time2** object. Even though we know that **hour**, **minute** and **second** are declared as **private** variables of class **Time2**, we are able to directly access these values from the object to which **time** refers using the expressions **time.hour**, **time.minute** and **time.second**. This is due to a special relationship between objects of the same class. When one object of a class has a reference to another object of the same class, the first object can access *all* the second object's data and methods.

Lines 75 through 80 create six **Time2** objects to demonstrate how to invoke the different constructors of the class. Line 75 shows that the no-argument constructor is invoked by placing an empty set of parentheses after the class name when allocating a **Time2** object with **new**. Lines 76 through 80 of the program demonstrate passing arguments to the **Time2** constructors. Remember that the appropriate constructor is invoked by matching the number, types and order of the arguments specified in the constructor call with the number, types and order of the parameters specified in each method definition. So, line 76 invokes the constructor at line 19. Line 77 invokes the constructor at line 23. Lines 78 and 79 invoke the constructor at line 26. Line 80 invokes the constructor at line 29.

Note that each **Time2** constructor could be written to include a copy of the appropriate statements from method **setTime**. This may be slightly more efficient because the extra call to **setTime** is eliminated. However, consider changing the representation of the time from three **int** values (requiring 12 bytes of memory) to a single **int** value representing the total number of seconds that have elapsed in the day (requiring 4 bytes of memory). Coding the **Time2** constructors and method **setTime** identically makes such a change in this class definition more difficult. If the implementation of method **setTime** changes, the implementation of the **Time2** constructors would need to change accordingly. Having the **Time2** constructors call **setTime** directly requires any changes to the implementation of **setTime** to be made only once. This reduces the likelihood of a programming error when altering the implementation.

Software Engineering Observation 8.13

If a method of a class already provides all or part of the functionality required by a constructor (or other method) of the class, call that method from the constructor (or other method). This simplifies the maintenance of the code and reduces the likelihood of an error if the implementation of the code is modified. It is also an effective example of reuse.

8.8 Using *Set* and *Get* Methods

Private instance variables can be manipulated only by methods of the class. A typical manipulation might be the adjustment of a customer's bank balance (e.g., a **private** instance variable of a class **BankAccount**) by a method **computeInterest**.

Classes often provide **public** methods to allow clients of the class to *set* (i.e., assign values to) or *get* (i.e., obtain the values of) **private** instance variables. These methods need not be called *set* and *get*, but they often are. As we will see in Chapter 25, "Java-Beans," this naming convention is important for creating reusable software components.

As a naming example, a method that sets instance variable **interestRate** would typically be named **setInterestRate** and a method that gets the **interestRate** would typically be called **getInterestRate**. *Get* methods are also commonly called *accessor methods* or *query methods*. *Set* methods are also commonly called *mutator methods* (because they typically change a value).

It would seem that providing *set* and *get* capabilities is essentially the same as making the instance variables **public**. This is another subtlety of Java that makes the language so desirable for software engineering. If an instance variable is **public**, the instance variable may be read or written at will by any method in the program. If an instance variable is **private**, a **public** *get* method certainly seems to allow other methods to read the data at will but the *get* method controls the formatting and display of the data. A **public** *set* method can—and most likely will—carefully scrutinize attempts to modify the instance variable's value. This ensures that the new value is appropriate for that data item. For example, an attempt to *set* the day of the month for a date to 37 would be rejected, an attempt to *set* a person's weight to a negative value would be rejected, and so on. So, although *set* and *get* methods may provide access to **private** data, the access is restricted by the programmer's implementation of the methods.

The benefits of data integrity are not automatic simply because instance variables are made **private**—the programmer must provide validity checking. Java provides the framework in which programmers can design better programs in a convenient manner.

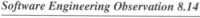

Software Engineering Observation 8.14

Methods that set the values of **private** *data should verify that the intended new values are proper; if they are not, the* set *methods should place the* **private** *instance variables into an appropriate consistent state.*

A class's *set* methods can return values indicating that attempts were made to assign invalid data to objects of the class. This enables clients of the class to test the return values of *set* methods to determine if the objects they are manipulating are valid and to take appropriate action if the objects are not valid. In Chapter 14, "Exception Handling," we illustrate a more robust way in which clients of a class can be notified if an object is not valid.

Good Programming Practice 8.7

Every method that modifies the private instance variables of an object should ensure that the data remains in a consistent state.

The applet of Fig. 8.5 enhances our **Time** class (now called **Time3**) to include *get* and *set* methods for the **hour**, **minute** and **second private** instance variables. The *set* methods strictly control the setting of the instance variables to valid values. Attempts to set any instance variable to an incorrect value cause the instance variable to be set to zero (thus leaving the instance variable in a consistent state). Each *get* method simply returns the

appropriate instance variable's value. This applet also introduces enhanced GUI event handling techniques as we move toward defining our first full-fledged windowed application.

```
1   // Fig. 8.5: Time3.java
2   // Time3 class definition
3   package com.deitel.jhtp3.ch08;    // place Time3 in a package
4   import java.text.DecimalFormat;   // used for number formatting
5
6   // This class maintains the time in 24-hour format
7   public class Time3 extends Object {
8       private int hour;       // 0 - 23
9       private int minute;     // 0 - 59
10      private int second;     // 0 - 59
11
12      // Time3 constructor initializes each instance variable
13      // to zero. Ensures that Time object starts in a
14      // consistent state.
15      public Time3() { setTime( 0, 0, 0 ); }
16
17      // Time3 constructor: hour supplied, minute and second
18      // defaulted to 0.
19      public Time3( int h ) { setTime( h, 0, 0 ); }
20
21      // Time3 constructor: hour and minute supplied, second
22      // defaulted to 0.
23      public Time3( int h, int m ) { setTime( h, m, 0 ); }
24
25      // Time3 constructor: hour, minute and second supplied.
26      public Time3( int h, int m, int s ) { setTime( h, m, s ); }
27
28      // Time3 constructor: another Time3 object supplied.
29      public Time3( Time3 time )
30      {
31          setTime( time.getHour(),
32                   time.getMinute(),
33                   time.getSecond() );
34      }
35
36      // Set Methods
37      // Set a new time value using universal time. Perform
38      // validity checks on the data. Set invalid values to zero.
39      public void setTime( int h, int m, int s )
40      {
41          setHour( h );    // set the hour
42          setMinute( m );  // set the minute
43          setSecond( s );  // set the second
44      }
45
46      // set the hour
47      public void setHour( int h )
48          { hour = ( ( h >= 0 && h < 24 ) ? h : 0 ); }
```

Fig. 8.5 Using *set* and *get* methods (part 1 of 6).

```
49
50      // set the minute
51      public void setMinute( int m )
52         { minute = ( ( m >= 0 && m < 60 ) ? m : 0 ); }
53
54      // set the second
55      public void setSecond( int s )
56         { second = ( ( s >= 0 && s < 60 ) ? s : 0 ); }
57
58      // Get Methods
59      // get the hour
60      public int getHour() { return hour; }
61
62      // get the minute
63      public int getMinute() { return minute; }
64
65      // get the second
66      public int getSecond() { return second; }
67
68      // Convert to String in universal-time format
69      public String toUniversalString()
70      {
71         DecimalFormat twoDigits = new DecimalFormat( "00" );
72
73         return twoDigits.format( getHour() ) + ":" +
74                twoDigits.format( getMinute() ) + ":" +
75                twoDigits.format( getSecond() );
76      }
77
78      // Convert to String in standard-time format
79      public String toString()
80      {
81         DecimalFormat twoDigits = new DecimalFormat( "00" );
82
83         return ( ( getHour() == 12 || getHour() == 0 ) ?
84                12 : getHour() % 12 ) + ":" +
85                twoDigits.format( getMinute() ) + ":" +
86                twoDigits.format( getSecond() ) +
87                ( getHour() < 12 ? " AM" : " PM" );
88      }
89   }
```

Fig. 8.5   Using *set* and *get* methods (part 2 of 6).

The new *set* methods of the class are defined at lines 47, 51 and 55, respectively. Notice that each method performs the same conditional statement that was previously in method **setTime** for setting the **hour**, **minute** or **second**. The addition of these methods caused us to redefine the body of method **setTime** to follow *Software Engineering Observation 8.13*—if a method of a class already provides all or part of the functionality required by another method of the class, call that method from the other method. Notice that **setTime** (line 39) now calls methods **setHour**, **setMinute** and **setSecond**—each of which performs part of **setTime**'s task.

```
90   // Fig. 8.5: TimeTest.java
91   // Demonstrating the Time3 class set and get methods
92   import java.awt.*;
93   import java.awt.event.*;
94   import javax.swing.*;
95   import com.deitel.jhtp3.ch08.Time3;
96
97   public class TimeTest extends JApplet
98                         implements ActionListener {
99      private Time3 t;
100     private JLabel hourLabel, minuteLabel, secondLabel;
101     private JTextField hourField, minuteField,
102                        secondField, display;
103     private JButton tickButton;
104
105     public void init()
106     {
107        t = new Time3();
108
109        Container c = getContentPane();
110
111        c.setLayout( new FlowLayout() );
112        hourLabel = new JLabel( "Set Hour" );
113        hourField = new JTextField( 10 );
114        hourField.addActionListener( this );
115        c.add( hourLabel );
116        c.add( hourField );
117
118        minuteLabel = new JLabel( "Set minute" );
119        minuteField = new JTextField( 10 );
120        minuteField.addActionListener( this );
121        c.add( minuteLabel );
122        c.add( minuteField );
123
124        secondLabel = new JLabel( "Set Second" );
125        secondField = new JTextField( 10 );
126        secondField.addActionListener( this );
127        c.add( secondLabel );
128        c.add( secondField );
129
130        display = new JTextField( 30 );
131        display.setEditable( false );
132        c.add( display );
133
134        tickButton = new JButton( "Add 1 to Second" );
135        tickButton.addActionListener( this );
136        c.add( tickButton );
137
138        updateDisplay();
139     }
140
```

Fig. 8.5   Using *set* and *get* methods (part 3 of 6).

```
141    public void actionPerformed( ActionEvent e )
142    {
143       if ( e.getSource() == tickButton )
144          tick();
145       else if ( e.getSource() == hourField ) {
146          t.setHour(
147             Integer.parseInt( e.getActionCommand() ) );
148          hourField.setText( "" );
149       }
150       else if ( e.getSource() == minuteField ) {
151          t.setMinute(
152             Integer.parseInt( e.getActionCommand() ) );
153          minuteField.setText( "" );
154       }
155       else if ( e.getSource() == secondField ) {
156          t.setSecond(
157             Integer.parseInt( e.getActionCommand() ) );
158          secondField.setText( "" );
159       }
160
161       updateDisplay();
162    }
163
164    public void updateDisplay()
165    {
166       display.setText( "Hour: " + t.getHour() +
167          "; Minute: " + t.getMinute() +
168          "; Second: " + t.getSecond() );
169       showStatus( "Standard time is: " + t.toString() +
170          "; Universal time is: " + t.toUniversalString() );
171    }
172
173    public void tick()
174    {
175       t.setSecond( ( t.getSecond() + 1 ) % 60 );
176
177       if ( t.getSecond() == 0 ) {
178          t.setMinute( ( t.getMinute() + 1 ) % 60 );
179
180          if ( t.getMinute() == 0 )
181             t.setHour( ( t.getHour() + 1 ) % 24 );
182       }
183    }
184 }
```

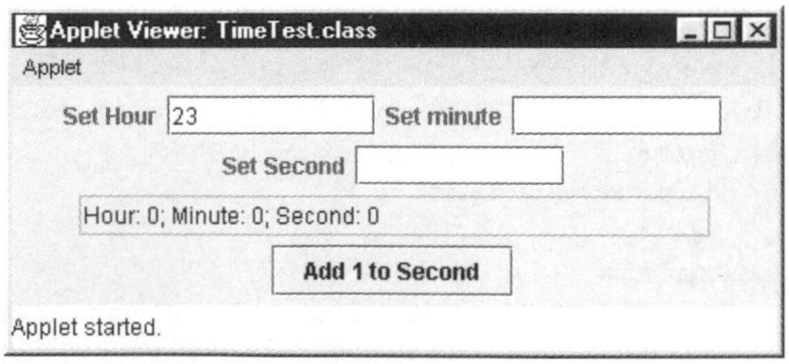

Fig. 8.5   Using *set* and *get* methods (part 4 of 6).

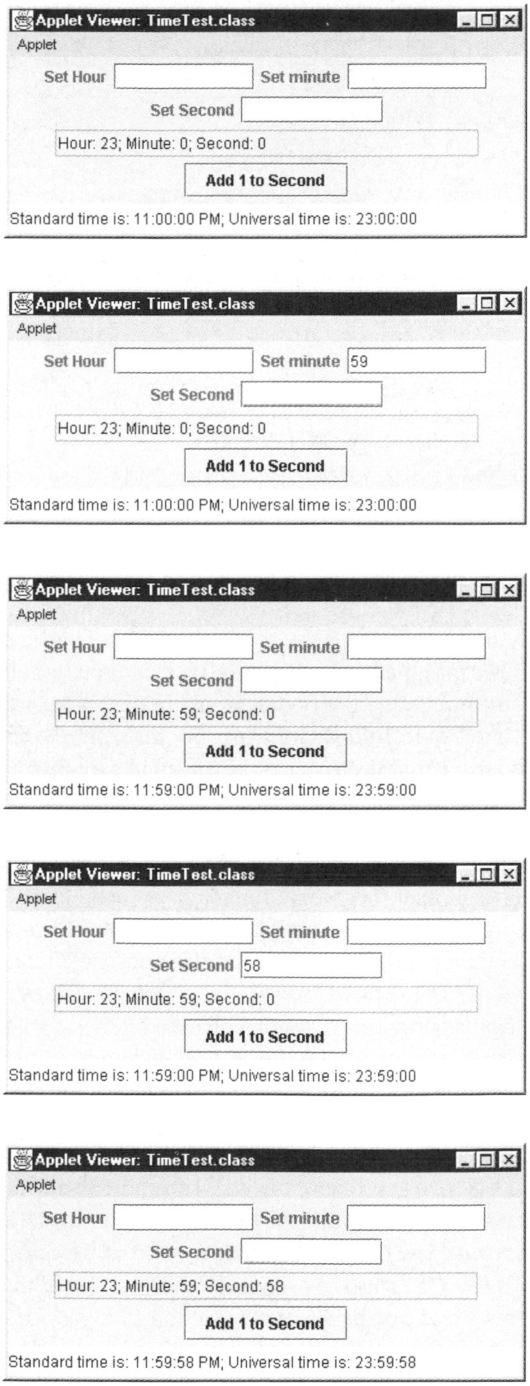

Fig. 8.5   Using *set* and *get* methods (part 5 of 6).

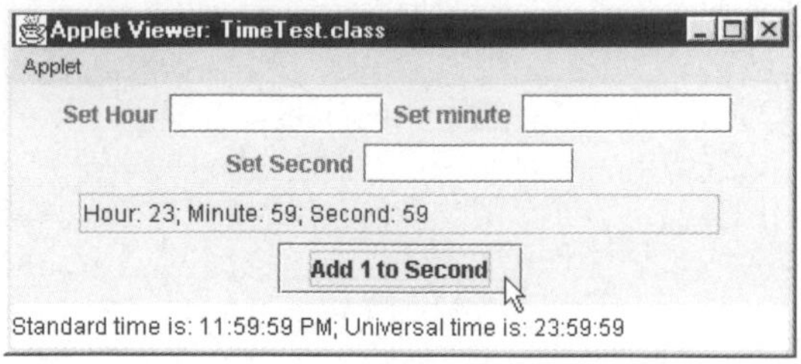

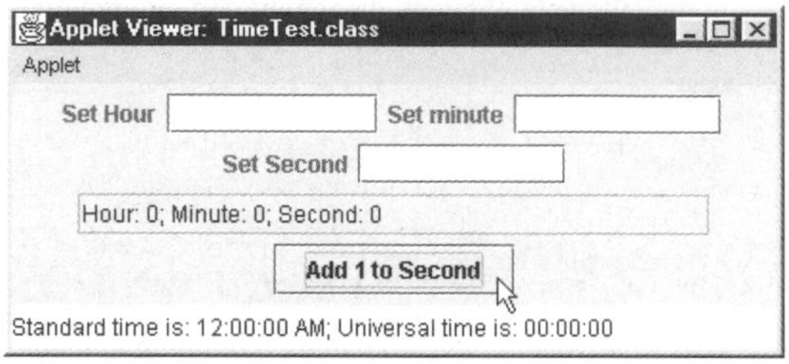

Fig. 8.5   Using *set* and *get* methods (part 6 of 6).

The new *get* methods of the class are defined at lines 60, 63 and 66, respectively. Notice that each method simply returns the **hour**, **minute** or **second** value (a copy of each value is returned because these are all primitive data type variables). The addition of these methods caused us to redefine the bodies of methods **toUniversalString** (line 69) and **toString** (line 79) to follow *Software Engineering Observation 8.13*. In both cases, every use of instance variables **hour**, **minute** and **second** is replaced with a call to **getHour**, **getMinute** and **getSecond**.

Due to the changes in class **Time3** just described, we have minimized the changes that will have to occur in the class definition if the data representation is changed from **hour**, **minute** and **second** to another representation (such as total elapsed seconds in the day). Only the new *set* and *get* method bodies will have to change. This allows the programmer to change the implementation of the class without affecting the clients of the class (as long as all the **public** methods of the class are still called the same way).

The **TimeTest** applet provides a graphical user interface that enables the user to exercise the methods of class **Time3**. The user can set the hour, minute or second value by typing a value in the appropriate **JTextField** and pressing the *Enter* key. The user can also click the "**Add 1 to second**" button to increment the time by one second. The **JTextField** and **JButton** events in this applet are all processed in method **action-Performed** (line 141). Notice that lines 114, 120, 126 and 135 all call **addActionListener** to indicate that the applet should start listening to **JTextField**s **hourField**, **minuteField**, **secondField** and **JButton tickButton**, respectively. Also, notice that all four calls use **this** as the argument, indicating that the object of our applet class **TimeTest** has its **actionPerformed** method invoked for each user interaction with these four GUI components. This poses an interesting question—how do we determine the GUI component with which the user interacted?

In **actionPerformed**, notice the use of **e.getSource()** to determine which GUI component generated the event. For example, line 143

```
if ( e.getSource() == tickButton )
```

determines if **tickButton** was clicked by the user. If so, the body of the **if** structure is executed. Otherwise, the condition in the **if** structure at line 145 is tested, etc. Every event has a *source*—the GUI component with which the user interacted to signal the program to do a task. The **ActionEvent** parameter that is supplied automatically to **actionPerformed** when the event occurs contains a reference to the source. The preceding condition simply asks, "Is the *source* of the event the **tickButton**?"

After each operation, the resulting time is displayed as a string in the status bar of the applet. The output windows illustrate the applet before and after the following operations: setting the hour to 23, setting the minute to 59, setting the second to 58 and incrementing the second twice with the "**Add 1 to second**" button.

Note that when the "**Add 1 to second**" button is clicked, the applet's **tick** method (line 173) is called by method **actionPerformed**. Method **tick** uses all the new *set* and *get* methods to increment the second properly. Although this works, it incurs the performance burden of issuing multiple method calls. In Section 8.12, we discuss the notion of package access as a means of eliminating this performance burden.

Common Programming Error 8.6

A constructor can call other methods of the class, such as set *or* get *methods, but because the constructor is initializing the object, the instance variables may not yet be in a consistent state. Using instance variables before they have been properly initialized is an error.*

Set methods are certainly important from a software engineering standpoint because they can perform validity checking. *Set* and *get* methods have another important software engineering advantage as discussed in the following *Software Engineering Observation*.

Software Engineering Observation 8.15

Accessing private data through set *and* get *methods not only protects the instance variables from receiving invalid values, but also insulates clients of the class from representation of the instance variables. Thus, if representation of the data changes (typically, to reduce the amount of storage required or to improve performance), only the method implementations need to change—the clients need not change as long as the interface provided by the methods remains the same.*

8.9 Software Reusability

Java programmers concentrate on crafting new classes and reusing existing classes. Many *class libraries* exist and others are being developed worldwide. Software is then constructed from existing, well-defined, carefully tested, well-documented, portable, widely available components. This kind of software reusability speeds the development of powerful, high-quality software. *Rapid applications development (RAD)* is of great interest today.

To realize the full potential of software reusability we need to improve cataloging schemes, licensing schemes, protection mechanisms that ensure master copies of classes are not corrupted, description schemes that system designers use to determine if existing objects meet their needs, browsing mechanisms that determine what classes are available and how closely they meet software developer requirements, and the like. Many interesting research and development problems have been solved and many more need to be solved; these problems will be solved because the potential value of software reuse is enormous.

8.10 Final Instance Variables

We have repeatedly emphasized the *principle of least privilege* as one of the most fundamental principles of good software engineering. Let us see one way in which this principle applies to instance variables.

Some instance variables need to be modifiable and some do not. The programmer may use the keyword **final** to specify that a variable is not modifiable and that any attempt to modify the variable is an error. For example,

```
private final int increment = 5;
```

declares a constant instance variable **increment** of type **int** and initializes it to 5.

Software Engineering Observation 8.16

*Declaring an instance variable as **final** helps enforce the principle of least privilege. If an instance variable should not be modified, declare it to be **final** to expressly forbid modification.*

Testing and Debugging Tip 8.2

*Accidental attempts to modify a **final** instance variable are caught at compile time rather than causing execution-time errors. It is always preferable to get bugs out at compile time, if possible, rather than allowing them to slip through to execution time (where studies have found that the cost of repair is often as much as ten times more expensive).*

Common Programming Error 8.7

*Attempting to modify a **final** instance variable after it is initialized is a syntax error.*

The applet of Fig. 8.6 creates a **final** instance variable **INCREMENT** of type **int** and initializes it to 5 in its declaration (line 10). A **final** variable cannot be modified by assignment after it is initialized. Such a variable can be initialized in its declaration or in every constructor of the class.

Common Programming Error 8.8

*Not initializing a **final** instance variable in its declaration or in every constructor of the class is a syntax error.*

```
1   // Fig. 8.6: Increment.java
2   // Initializing a final variable
3   import java.awt.*;
4   import java.awt.event.*;
5   import javax.swing.*;
6
7   public class Increment extends JApplet
8              implements ActionListener {
9      private int count = 0, total = 0;
10     private final int INCREMENT = 5; // constant variable
11
12     private JButton incr;
```

Fig. 8.6   Initializing a **final** variable (part 1 of 2).

```
13
14      public void init()
15      {
16         Container c = getContentPane();
17
18         incr = new JButton( "Click to increment" );
19         incr.addActionListener( this );
20         c.add( incr );
21      }
22
23      public void actionPerformed( ActionEvent e )
24      {
25         total += INCREMENT;
26         count++;
27         showStatus( "After increment " + count +
28                     ": total = " + total );
29      }
30   }
```

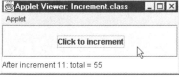

Fig. 8.6   Initializing a **final** variable (part 2 of 2).

Figure 8.7 illustrates compiler errors produced for the program of Fig. 8.6 if instance variable **increment** is declared **final**, but is not initialized in the declaration.

8.11 Composition: Objects as Instance Variables of Other Classes

An **AlarmClock** class object needs to know when it is supposed to sound its alarm, so why not include a reference to a **Time** object as a member of the **AlarmClock** object? Such a capability is called *composition*. A class can have references to objects of other classes as members.

Software Engineering Observation 8.17

One form of software reuse is composition in which a class has references to objects of other classes as members.

```
Increment.java:10: Blank final variable 'increment' may
not have been initialized. It must be assigned a value in
an initializer, or in every constructor.
   private final int increment; // constant variable
                     ^

1 error
```

Fig. 8.7   Compiler error message as a result of not initializing **increment**.

Figure 8.8 uses classes **Employee** and **Date** to demonstrate object references as members of other objects. Class **Employee** contains instance variables **firstName**, **lastName**, **birthDate** and **hireDate**. Members **birthDate** and **hireDate** are references to **Date**s that contain instance variables **month**, **day** and **year**. The program instantiates an **Employee** and initializes and displays its instance variables. The constructor takes eight arguments (**fName**, **lName**, **bMonth**, **bDay**, **bYear**, **hMonth**, **hDay** and **hYear**). Arguments **bMonth**, **bDay** and **bYear** are passed to the **birthDate** constructor and **hMonth**, **hDay** and **hYear** are passed to the **hireDate** constructor.

```
1   // Fig. 8.8: Date.java
2   // Declaration of the Date class.
3   package com.deitel.jhtp3.ch08;
4
5   public class Date extends Object {
6      private int month;   // 1-12
7      private int day;     // 1-31 based on month
8      private int year;    // any year
9
10     // Constructor: Confirm proper value for month;
11     // call method checkDay to confirm proper
12     // value for day.
13     public Date( int mn, int dy, int yr )
14     {
15        if ( mn > 0 && mn <= 12 )          // validate the month
16           month = mn;
17        else {
18           month = 1;
19           System.out.println( "Month " + mn +
20                                " invalid. Set to month 1." );
21        }
22
23        year = yr;                         // could also check
24        day = checkDay( dy );              // validate the day
25
26        System.out.println(
27           "Date object constructor for date " + toString() );
28     }
29
30     // Utility method to confirm proper day value
31     // based on month and year.
32     private int checkDay( int testDay )
33     {
34        int daysPerMonth[] = { 0, 31, 28, 31, 30,
35                               31, 30, 31, 31, 30,
36                               31, 30, 31 };
37
38        if ( testDay > 0 && testDay <= daysPerMonth[ month ] )
39           return testDay;
40
```

Fig. 8.8   Demonstrating an object with a member object reference (part 1 of 4).

```
41          if ( month == 2 &&    // February: Check for leap year
42               testDay == 29 &&
43               ( year % 400 == 0 ||
44                 ( year % 4 == 0 && year % 100 != 0 ) ) )
45            return testDay;
46
47          System.out.println( "Day " + testDay +
48                              " invalid. Set to day 1." );
49
50          return 1;  // leave object in consistent state
51       }
52
53       // Create a String of the form month/day/year
54       public String toString()
55          { return month + "/" + day + "/" + year; }
56    }
```

Fig. 8.8   Demonstrating an object with a member object reference (part 2 of 4).

```
57    // Fig. 8.8: Employee.java
58    // Declaration of the Employee class.
59    package com.deitel.jhtp3.ch08;
60
61    public class Employee extends Object {
62       private String firstName;
63       private String lastName;
64       private Date birthDate;
65       private Date hireDate;
66
67       public Employee( String fName, String lName,
68                        int bMonth, int bDay, int bYear,
69                        int hMonth, int hDay, int hYear)
70       {
71          firstName = fName;
72          lastName = lName;
73          birthDate = new Date( bMonth, bDay, bYear );
74          hireDate = new Date( hMonth, hDay, hYear );
75       }
76
77       public String toString()
78       {
79          return lastName + ", " + firstName +
80                 "   Hired: " + hireDate.toString() +
81                 "   Birthday: " + birthDate.toString();
82       }
83    }
```

Fig. 8.8   Demonstrating an object with a member object reference (part 3 of 4).

```
84   // Fig. 8.8: EmployeeTest.java
85   // Demonstrating an object with a member object.
86   import javax.swing.JOptionPane;
87   import com.deitel.jhtp3.ch08.Employee;
88
89   public class EmployeeTest {
90      public static void main( String args[] )
91      {
92         Employee e = new Employee( "Bob", "Jones", 7, 24, 49,
93                                    3, 12, 88 );
94         JOptionPane.showMessageDialog( null, e.toString(),
95            "Testing Class Employee",
96            JOptionPane.INFORMATION_MESSAGE );
97
98         System.exit( 0 );
99      }
100  }
```

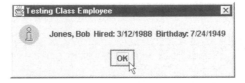

```
Date object constructor for date 7/24/1949
Date object constructor for date 3/12/1988
```

Fig. 8.8   Demonstrating an object with a member object reference (part 4 of 4).

A member object does not need to be initialized immediately with constructor arguments. If an empty argument list is provided when a member object is created, the object's default constructor (or no-argument constructor if one is available) will be called automatically. Values, if any, established by the default constructor (or no-argument constructor) can then be replaced by *set* methods.

Performance Tip 8.2

Initialize member objects explicitly at constructor time. This eliminates the overhead of doubly initializing member objects—once when the member object's default constructor is called and again when set *methods are used to provide initial values for the member object.*

Note that both class **Date** and class **Employee** in Fig. 8.8 are defined as part of the package **com.deitel.jhtp3.ch08** as specified on lines 3 and 59, respectively. Because they are in the same package (i.e., the same directory), class **Employee** does not need to import class **Date** to use it. When the compiler searches for the file **Date.class**, the compiler knows to search the directory where **Employee.class** is located. Classes in a package never need to import other classes from the same package.

8.12 Package Access

When no member access modifier is provided for a method or variable when it is defined in a class, the method or variable is considered to have *package access*. If your program consists of one class definition, this has no specific effects on the program. However, if your program uses multiple classes from the same package (i.e., a group of related classes), these classes can access each other's package-access methods and data directly through a reference to an object.

Performance Tip 8.3

Package access enables objects of different classes to interact without the need for set *and* get *methods that provide access to data, thus eliminating some of the method call overhead.*

Let us consider a mechanical example of package access. The application of Fig. 8.9 contains two classes—the **PackageDataTest** applet class and the **PackageData** class. In the **PackageData** class definition, lines 28 and 29

```
int x;      // package access instance variable
String s;   // package access instance variable
```

declare the instance variables **x** and **s** with no member access modifiers; therefore, these are package access instance variables. The **PackageDataTest** application's **main** method creates an instance of the **PackageData** class (line 10) to demonstrate the ability to modify the **PackageData** instance variables directly (as shown on lines 15 and 16). The results of the modification can be seen in the output window.

```
1   // Fig. 8.9: PackageDataTest.java
2   // Classes in the same package (i.e., the same directory)
3   // can use package access data of other classes in the
4   // same package.
5   import javax.swing.JOptionPane;
6
7   public class PackageDataTest {
8      public static void main( String args[] )
9      {
10         PackageData d = new PackageData();
11         String output;
12
13         output = "After instantiation:\n" + d.toString();
14
15         d.x = 77;          // changing package access data
16         d.s = "Good bye";  // changing package access data
17
18         output += "\nAfter changing values:\n" + d.toString();
19         JOptionPane.showMessageDialog( null, output,
20            "Demonstrating Package Access",
21            JOptionPane.INFORMATION_MESSAGE );
22
23         System.exit( 0 );
24      }
25  }
26
```

Fig. 8.9   Package access to members of a class (part 1 of 2).

```
27  class PackageData {
28      int x;      // package access instance variable
29      String s;   // package access instance variable
30
31      // constructor
32      public PackageData()
33      {
34          x = 0;
35          s = "Hello";
36      }
37
38      public String toString()
39      {
40          return "x: " + x + "     s: " + s;
41      }
42  }
```

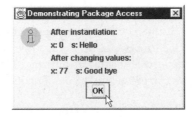

Fig. 8.9 Package access to members of a class (part 2 of 2).

Note that when this program is compiled, two separate files are produced—a **.class** file for class **PackageData** and a **.class** file for class **PackageDataTest**. Every Java class has its own **.class** file. These two **.class** files are placed in the same directory by the compiler automatically and are considered to be part of the same package (they are certainly related by the fact that they are in the same file). Because they are part of the same package, class **PackageDataTest** is allowed to modify the package access data of objects of class **PackageData**.

Software Engineering Observation 8.18

Some people in the OOP community feel that package access corrupts information hiding and weakens the value of the object-oriented design approach.

8.13 Using the `this` Reference

When a method of a class references another member of that class for a specific object of that class, how does Java ensure that the proper object is referenced? The answer is that each object has access to a reference to itself—called the ***this*** *reference*.

The **this** reference is implicitly used to refer to both the instance variables and methods of an object. For now, we show a simple example of using the **this** reference explicitly; later, we show some substantial and subtle examples of using **this**.

Performance Tip 8.4

Java conserves storage by maintaining only one copy of each method per class; this method is invoked by every object of that class. Each object, on the other hand, has its own copy of the class's instance variables.

The application of Fig. 8.10 demonstrates implicit and explicit use of the **this** refer-ence to enable the **main** method of class **ThisTest** to display the private data of a **Sim-pleTime** object.

```
1   // Fig. 8.10: ThisTest.java
2   // Using the this reference to refer to
3   // instance variables and methods.
4   import javax.swing.*;
5   import java.text.DecimalFormat;
6
7   public class ThisTest {
8      public static void main( String args[] )
9      {
10         SimpleTime t = new SimpleTime( 12, 30, 19 );
11
12         JOptionPane.showMessageDialog( null, t.buildString(),
13            "Demonstrating the \"this\" Reference",
14            JOptionPane.INFORMATION_MESSAGE );
15
16         System.exit( 0 );
17      }
18   }
19
20   class SimpleTime {
21      private int hour, minute, second;
22
23      public SimpleTime( int hour, int minute, int second )
24      {
25         this.hour = hour;
26         this.minute = minute;
27         this.second = second;
28      }
29
30      public String buildString()
31      {
32         return "this.toString(): " + this.toString() +
33                "\ntoString(): " + toString() +
34                "\nthis (with implicit toString() call): " +
35                this;
36      }
37
38      public String toString()
39      {
40         DecimalFormat twoDigits = new DecimalFormat( "00" );
41
42         return twoDigits.format( this.hour ) + ":" +
43                twoDigits.format( this.minute ) + ":" +
44                twoDigits.format( this.second );
45      }
46   }
```

Fig. 8.10   Using the **this** reference (part 1 of 2).

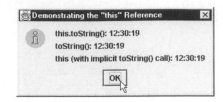

Fig. 8.10   Using the **this** reference (part 2 of 2).

Class **SimpleTime** (lines 20 through 46) defines three **private** instance variables—**hour**, **minute** and **second**. The constructor (line 23) receives three **int** arguments to initialize a **SimpleTime** object. Notice that the parameter names for the constructor are the same as the instance variable names. Remember that a local variable of a method with the same name as an instance variable of a class hides the instance variable in the scope of the method. For this reason, we use the **this** reference to explicitly refer to the instance variables on lines 25 through 27.

Common Programming Error 8.9

In a method in which a method parameter has the same name as one of the class members, use **this** *explicitly if you want to access the class member; otherwise, you will incorrectly reference the method parameter.*

Good Programming Practice 8.8

Avoid using method parameter names that conflict with class member names.

Method **buildString** (lines 30 through 36) returns a **String** created with the statement

```
return "this.toString(): " + this.toString() +
       "\ntoString(): " + toString() +
       "\nthis (with implicit toString() call): " +
       this;
```

that uses the **this** reference three ways. The first line explicitly invokes the class's **toString** method via **this.toString()**. The second line implicitly uses the **this** reference to perform the same task. The third line appends **this** to the string that will be returned. Remember that the **this** reference is a reference to an object—the current **SimpleTime** object being manipulated. As before, any reference added to a **String** results in a call to the **toString** method for the referenced object. Method **buildString** is invoked at line 12 to display the results of the three calls to **toString**. Note that the same time is displayed on all three lines of the output because all three calls to **toString** are for the same object.

Another use of the **this** reference is in enabling *concatenated method calls* (also called *cascaded method calls*). Figure 8.11 illustrates returning a reference to a **Time4** object to enable method calls of class **Time4** to be concatenated. Methods **setTime** (line 40), **setHour** (line 50), **setMinute** (line 58) and **setSecond** (line 66) each have a return type of **Time4** and each has as its last statement

```
return this;
```

to indicate that a reference to the **Time4** object being manipulated should be returned to the caller of the method.

The example again demonstrates the explicit use of the **this** reference inside the body of a class. In class **Time4**, every use of an instance variable of the class and every call to another method in class **Time4** uses the **this** reference explicitly. Most programmers prefer not to use the **this** reference unless it is required or helps clarify a piece of code.

Good Programming Practice 8.9

*Explicitly using **this** can increase program clarity in some contexts in which **this** is optional.*

```
1   // Fig. 8.11: Time4.java
2   // Time4 class definition
3   package com.deitel.jhtp3.ch08;    // place Time4 in a package
4   import java.text.DecimalFormat;   // used for number formatting
5
6   // This class maintains the time in 24-hour format
7   public class Time4 extends Object {
8      private int hour;        // 0 - 23
9      private int minute;      // 0 - 59
10     private int second;      // 0 - 59
11
12     // Time4 constructor initializes each instance variable
13     // to zero. Ensures that Time object starts in a
14     // consistent state.
15     public Time4() { this.setTime( 0, 0, 0 ); }
16
17     // Time4 constructor: hour supplied, minute and second
18     // defaulted to 0.
19     public Time4( int h ) { this.setTime( h, 0, 0 ); }
20
21     // Time4 constructor: hour and minute supplied, second
22     // defaulted to 0.
23     public Time4( int h, int m ) { this.setTime( h, m, 0 ); }
24
25     // Time4 constructor: hour, minute and second supplied.
26     public Time4( int h, int m, int s )
27        { this.setTime( h, m, s ); }
28
29     // Time4 constructor: another Time4 object supplied.
30     public Time4( Time4 time )
31     {
32        this.setTime( time.getHour(),
33                      time.getMinute(),
34                      time.getSecond() );
35     }
36
```

Fig. 8.11   Chaining method calls (part 1 of 5).

```
37      // Set Methods
38      // Set a new Time value using military time. Perform
39      // validity checks on the data. Set invalid values to zero.
40      public Time4 setTime( int h, int m, int s )
41      {
42         this.setHour( h );     // set the hour
43         this.setMinute( m );   // set the minute
44         this.setSecond( s );   // set the second
45
46         return this;      // enables chaining
47      }
48
49      // set the hour
50      public Time4 setHour( int h )
51      {
52         this.hour = ( ( h >= 0 && h < 24 ) ? h : 0 );
53
54         return this;       // enables chaining
55      }
56
57      // set the minute
58      public Time4 setMinute( int m )
59      {
60         this.minute = ( ( m >= 0 && m < 60 ) ? m : 0 );
61
62         return this;       // enables chaining
63      }
64
65      // set the second
66      public Time4 setSecond( int s )
67      {
68         this.second = ( ( s >= 0 && s < 60 ) ? s : 0 );
69
70         return this;       // enables chaining
71      }
72
73      // Get Methods
74      // get the hour
75      public int getHour() { return this.hour; }
76
77      // get the minute
78      public int getMinute() { return this.minute; }
79
80      // get the second
81      public int getSecond() { return this.second; }
82
83      // Convert to String in universal-time format
84      public String toUniversalString()
85      {
86         DecimalFormat twoDigits = new DecimalFormat( "00" );
87
```

Fig. 8.11   Chaining method calls (part 2 of 5).

```
88          return twoDigits.format( this.getHour() ) + ":" +
89                 twoDigits.format( this.getMinute() ) + ":" +
90                 twoDigits.format( this.getSecond() );
91       }
92
93       // Convert to String in standard-time format
94       public String toString()
95       {
96          DecimalFormat twoDigits = new DecimalFormat( "00" );
97
98          return ( ( this.getHour() == 12 ||
99                    this.getHour() == 0 ) ?
100                   12 : this.getHour() % 12 ) + ":" +
101                twoDigits.format( this.getMinute() ) + ":" +
102                twoDigits.format( this.getSecond() ) +
103                ( this.getHour() < 12 ? " AM" : " PM" );
104      }
105 }
```

Fig. 8.11   Chaining method calls (part 3 of 5).

```
106 // Fig. 8.11: TimeTest.java
107 // Chaining method calls together with the this reference
108 import javax.swing.*;
109 import com.deitel.jhtp3.ch08.Time4;
110
111 public class TimeTest {
112    public static void main( String args[] )
113    {
114       Time4 t = new Time4();
115       String output;
116
117       t.setHour( 18 ).setMinute( 30 ).setSecond( 22 );
118
119       output = "Universal time: " + t.toUniversalString() +
120                "\nStandard time: " + t.toString() +
121                "\n\nNew standard time: " +
122                t.setTime( 20, 20, 20 ).toString();
123
124       JOptionPane.showMessageDialog( null, output,
125          "Chaining Method Calls",
126          JOptionPane.INFORMATION_MESSAGE );
127
128       System.exit( 0 );
129    }
130 }
```

Fig. 8.11   Chaining method calls (part 4 of 5).

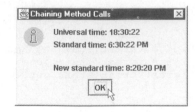

Fig. 8.11   Chaining method calls (part 5 of 5).

Line 117

```
t.setHour( 18 ).setMinute( 30 ).setSecond( 22 );
```

and line 122

```
t.setTime( 20, 20, 20 ).toString();
```

both demonstrate method call chaining.

Why does the technique of returning the **this** reference work? Let us discuss line 117. The dot operator (**.**) associates from left to right, so the expression

```
t.setHour( 18 ).setMinute( 30 ).setSecond( 22 );
```

first evaluates **t.setHour(18)**, then returns a reference to object **t** as the result of this method call. Any time you have a reference in a program (even as the result of a method call), the reference can be followed by a dot operator and a call to one of the methods of the reference type. Thus, the remaining expression is interpreted as

```
t.setMinute( 30 ).setSecond( 22 );
```

The **t.setMinute(30)** call executes and returns a reference to **t**. The remaining expression is interpreted as

```
t.setSecond( 22 );
```

When the statement is complete, the time is **18** for the **hour**, **30** for the **minute** and **22** from the **second**. Note that the calls on line 122

```
t.setTime( 20, 20, 20 ).toString();
```

also use the concatenation feature. These method calls must appear in this order in this expression because **toString** as defined in the class does not return a reference to a **Time4** object. Placing the call to **toString** before the call to **setTime** causes a syntax error. Note that **toString** returns a reference to a **String** object. Therefore, a method of class **String** could be concatenated to the end of line 122.

8.14 Finalizers

We have seen that constructor methods are capable of initializing data in an object of a class when the class is created. Often, constructors acquire various system resources such as memory (when the **new** operator is used). We need a disciplined way to give resources back to the system when they are no longer needed to avoid resource leaks. The most common resource acquired by constructors is memory. Java performs automatic *garbage collection* of memory to help return memory back to the system. When an object is no longer used in the program (i.e., there are no references to the object), the object is *marked for garbage collection*. The memory for such an object can be reclaimed when the *garbage collector* executes. Therefore, memory leaks that are common in other languages like C and C++ (because memory is not automatically reclaimed in those languages) are less likely to happen in Java. However, other resource leaks can occur.

Every class in Java can have a *finalizer method* that returns resources to the system. The finalizer method for an object is guaranteed to be called to perform *termination housekeeping* on the object just before the garbage collector reclaims the memory for the object. A class's finalizer method always has the name **finalize**, receives no parameters and returns no value (i.e., its return type is **void**). A class should have only one **finalize** method that takes no arguments. Method **finalize** is originally defined in class **Object** as a placeholder that does nothing. This guarantees that every class has a **finalize** method for the garbage collector to call.

Finalizers have not been provided for the classes presented so far. Actually, finalizers are rarely used with simple classes. We will see a sample **finalize** method and discuss the garbage collector further in Fig. 8.12.

8.15 Static Class Members

Each object of a class has its own copy of all the instance variables of the class. In certain cases only one copy of a particular variable should be shared by all objects of a class. A *static class variable* is used for these and other reasons. A **static** class variable represents *class-wide information*—all objects of the class share the same piece of data. The declaration of a **static** member begins with the keyword **static**.

Let us motivate the need for **static** class-wide data with a video game example. Suppose we have a video game in with **Martian**s and other space creatures. Each **Martian** tends to be brave and willing to attack other space creatures when the **Martian** is aware that there are at least five **Martian**s present. If there are fewer than five **Martian**s present, each **Martian** becomes cowardly. So each **Martian** needs to know the **martianCount**. We could endow class **Martian** with **martianCount** as instance data. If we do this, then every **Martian** will have a separate copy of the instance data and every time we create a new **Martian** we will have to update the instance variable **martianCount** in every **Martian**. This wastes space with the redundant copies and wastes time in updating the separate copies. Instead, we declare **martianCount** to be **static**. This makes **martianCount** class-wide data. Every **Martian** can see the **martianCount** as if it were instance data of the **Martian**, but only one copy of the static **martianCount** is maintained by Java. This saves space. We save time by having the **Martian** constructor increment the static **martianCount**. Because there is only one copy, we do not have to increment separate copies of **martianCount** for each **Martian** object.

Performance Tip 8.5

*Use **static** class variables to save storage when a single copy of the data will suffice.*

Although **static** class variables may seem like global variables, **static** class variables have class scope. A class's **public static** class members can be accessed through a reference to any object of that class, or they can be accessed through the class name using the dot operator (e.g., **Math.random()**). A class's **private static** class members can be accessed only through methods of the class. Actually, **static** class members exist even when no objects of that class exist—they are available as soon as the class is loaded into memory at execution time. To access a **public static** class member when no objects of the class exist, simply prefix the class name and the dot operator to the class member. To access a **private static** class member when no objects of the class exist, a **public static** method must be provided and the method must be called by prefixing its name with the class name and dot operator.

The program of Fig. 8.12 demonstrates the use of a **private static** class variable and a **public static** method. The class variable **count** is initialized to zero by default. Class variable **count** maintains a count of the number of objects of class **Employee** that have been instantiated and currently reside in memory. This includes objects that have already been marked for garbage collection but have not yet been reclaimed.

```java
1   // Fig. 8.12: Employee.java
2   // Declaration of the Employee class.
3   public class Employee extends Object {
4      private String firstName;
5      private String lastName;
6      private static int count;   // # of objects in memory
7
8      public Employee( String fName, String lName )
9      {
10         firstName = fName;
11         lastName = lName;
12
13         ++count;  // increment static count of employees
14         System.out.println( "Employee object constructor: " +
15                             firstName + " " + lastName );
16      }
17
18      protected void finalize()
19      {
20         --count;  // decrement static count of employees
21         System.out.println( "Employee object finalizer: " +
22                             firstName + " " + lastName +
23                             "; count = " + count );
24      }
25
26      public String getFirstName() { return firstName; }
27
28      public String getLastName() { return lastName; }
29
30      public static int getCount() { return count; }
31   }
```

Fig. 8.12   Using a **static** class variable to maintain a count of the number of objects of a class (part 1 of 3).

```
32    // Fig. 8.12: EmployeeTest.java
33    // Test Employee class with static class variable,
34    // static class method, and dynamic memory.
35    import javax.swing.*;
36
37    public class EmployeeTest {
38       public static void main( String args[] )
39       {
40          String output;
41
42          output = "Employees before instantiation: " +
43                   Employee.getCount();
44
45          Employee e1 = new Employee( "Susan", "Baker" );
46          Employee e2 = new Employee( "Bob", "Jones" );
47
48          output += "\n\nEmployees after instantiation: " +
49                   "\nvia e1.getCount(): " + e1.getCount() +
50                   "\nvia e2.getCount(): " + e2.getCount() +
51                   "\nvia Employee.getCount(): " +
52                   Employee.getCount();
53
54          output += "\n\nEmployee 1: " + e1.getFirstName() +
55                   " " + e1.getLastName() +
56                   "\nEmployee 2: " + e2.getFirstName() +
57                   " " + e2.getLastName();
58
59          // mark objects referred to by e1 and e2
60          // for garbage collection
61          e1 = null;
62          e2 = null;
63
64          System.gc(); // suggest that garbage collector be called
65
66          output += "\n\nEmployees after System.gc(): " +
67                   Employee.getCount();
68
69          JOptionPane.showMessageDialog( null, output,
70             "Static Members and Garbage Collection",
71             JOptionPane.INFORMATION_MESSAGE );
72          System.exit( 0 );
73       }
74    }
```

Fig. 8.12 Using a **static** class variable to maintain a count of the number of objects of a class (part 2 of 3).

When objects of class **Employee** exist, member **count** can be used in any method of an **Employee** object—in this example, **count** is incremented (line 13) by the constructor and decremented (line 20) by the finalizer. When no objects of class **Employee** exist, member **count** can still be referenced, but only through a call to **public static** method **getCount** as follows:

```
Employee.getCount()
```

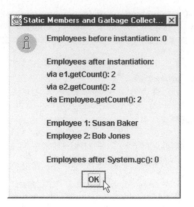

```
Employee object constructor: Susan Baker
Employee object constructor: Bob Jones
Employee object finalizer: Susan Baker; count = 1
Employee object finalizer: Bob Jones; count = 0
```

Fig. 8.12   Using a **static** class variable to maintain a count of the number of objects of a class (part 3 of 3).

In this example, method **getCount** determines the number of **Employee** objects currently in memory. Note that when there are no objects instantiated in the program, the **Employee.getCount()** method call is issued. However, when there are objects instantiated, method **getCount** can also be called through a reference to one of the objects, as in

    e1.getCount()

Good Programming Practice 8.10

*Always invoke **static** methods using the class name and the dot operator (.). This emphasizes to other programmers reading your code that the method being called is a **static** method.*

Notice that the **Employee** class has a **finalize** method (line 18). This method is included to show when it is called by the garbage collector in a program. Method **finalize** is normally declared **protected** so it is not part of the **public** services of a class. We will discuss the **protected** access modifier in detail in Chapter 9.

Method **main** of the **EmployeeTest** application instantiates two **Employee** objects (lines 45 and 46). When each **Employee** object's constructor is invoked, lines 10 and 11 store references to that **Employee**'s first name and last name **String** objects. Note that these two statements *do not* make copies of the original **String**s arguments. Actually, **String** objects in Java are *immutable*—they cannot be modified after they are created (class **String** does not provide any *set* methods). Because a reference cannot be used to modify a **String**, it is safe to have many references to one **String** object in a Java program. This is not normally the case for most other classes in Java.

When **main** is done with the two **Employee** objects, the references **e1** and **e2** are set to **null** at lines 61 and 62. At this point references **e1** and **e2** no longer refer to the objects that were instantiated on lines 45 and 46. This *marks the objects for garbage col-*

lection because there are no more references to the objects in the program.

Eventually, the garbage collector reclaims the memory for these objects (or the memory is reclaimed by the operating system when the program terminates). Because it is not guaranteed when the garbage collector will execute, we make an explicit call to the garbage collector with the line 64

```
System.gc();  // explicit call to garbage collector
```

that uses **public static** method **gc** from class **System** (**java.lang** package) to suggest that the garbage collector execute immediately. However, this is just a suggestion to the Java Virtual Machine (the interpreter)—the suggestion can be ignored. In our example, the garbage collector did execute before lines 69 through 71 displayed the results of the program. The last line of the output indicates that the number of **Employee** objects in memory is 0 after the call to **System.gc()**. Also, the last two lines of the command window output show that the **Employee** object for **Susan Baker** was finalized before the **Employee** object for **Bob Jones**. Because the garbage collector is not guaranteed to execute when **System.gc()** is invoked and because the garbage collector is not guaranteed to collect objects in a specific order, it is possible that the output of this program on your system may differ.

[*Note:* A method declared **static** cannot access non-**static** class members. Unlike non-**static** methods, a **static** method has no **this** reference because **static** class variables and **static** class methods exist independent of any objects of a class and before any objects of the class have been instantiated.]

Common Programming Error 8.10

*Referring to the **this** reference in a **static** method is a syntax error.*

Common Programming Error 8.11

*It is a syntax error for a **static** method to call an instance method or to access an instance variable.*

Software Engineering Observation 8.19

*Any **static** class variables and **static** class methods exist and can be used even if no objects of that class have been instantiated.*

8.16 Data Abstraction and Information Hiding

Classes normally hide their implementation details from the clients of the classes. This is called *information hiding*. As an example of information hiding, let us consider a data structure called a *stack*.

Think of a stack in terms of a pile of dishes. When a dish is placed on the pile, it is always placed at the top (referred to as *pushing* the dish onto the stack), and when a dish is removed from the pile, it is always removed from the top (referred to as *popping* the dish off the stack). Stacks are known as *last-in, first-out (LIFO) data structures*—the last item pushed (inserted) on the stack is the first item popped (removed) from the stack.

The programmer may create a stack class and hide from its clients implementation of the stack. Stacks can easily be implemented with arrays and other methods (such as linked lists; see Chapter 17, "Data Structures," and Chapter 18, "Java Utilities Packages and Bit

Manipulation"). A client of a stack class need not know how the stack is implemented. The client simply requires that when data items are placed in the stack, they will be recalled in last-in, first-out order. This concept is referred to as *data abstraction,* and Java classes define abstract data types (ADTs). Although users may happen to know the details of how a class is implemented, users may not write code that depends on these details. This means that a particular class (such as one that implements a stack and its operations of *push* and *pop*) can be replaced with another version without affecting the rest of the system, as long as the public services of that class does not change (i.e., every method still has the same name, return type and parameter list in the new class definition).

The job of a high-level language is to create a view convenient for programmers to use. There is no single accepted standard view—that is one reason why there are so many programming languages. Object-oriented programming in Java presents yet another view.

Most programming languages emphasize actions. In these languages, data exists in support of the actions programs need to take. Data is "less interesting" than actions, anyway. Data is "crude." There are only a few built-in data types, and it is difficult for programmers to create their own new data types.

This view changes with Java and the object-oriented style of programming. Java elevates the importance of data. The primary activity in Java is creating new data types (i.e., classes) and expressing the interactions among objects of those data types.

To move in this direction, the programming-languages community needed to formalize some notions about data. The formalization we consider is the notion of *abstract data types (ADTs).* ADTs receive as much attention today as structured programming did over the last two decades. ADTs do not replace structured programming. Rather, they provide an additional formalization to further improve the program development process.

What is an abstract data type? Consider the built-in type `int`. What comes to mind is the notion of an integer in mathematics, but `int` on a computer is not precisely what an integer is in mathematics. In particular, computer `int`s are normally quite limited in size. For example, `int` on a 32-bit machine is limited approximately to the range –2 billion to +2 billion. If the result of a calculation falls outside this range, an error occurs and the machine responds in some machine-dependent manner, including the possibility of "quietly" producing an incorrect result. Mathematical integers do not have this problem. So the notion of a computer `int` is really only an approximation to the notion of a real-world integer. The same is true with `float`.

The point is that even the built-in data types provided with programming languages like Java are really only approximations or models of real-world concepts and behaviors. We have taken `int` for granted until this point, but now you have a new perspective to consider. Types like `int`, `float`, `char` and others are all examples of abstract data types. They are essentially ways of representing real-world notions to some satisfactory level of precision within a computer system.

An abstract data type actually captures two notions, namely a *data representation* and the *operations* that are allowed on that data. For example, the notion of `int` defines addition, subtraction, multiplication, division and modulus operations in Java, but division by zero is undefined. Another example is the notion of negative integers whose operations and data representation are clear, but the operation of taking the square root of a negative integer is undefined. In Java, the programmer uses classes to implement abstract data types.

Java has a small set of primitive types. ADTs extend the base programming language.

Software Engineering Observation 8.20

The programmer is able to create new types through the use of the class mechanism. These new types may be designed to be used as conveniently as the built-in types. Thus, Java is an extensible language. Although the language is easy to extend with these new types, the base language itself is not changeable.

New Java classes can be proprietary to an individual, to small groups, to companies, and so on. Many classes are placed in standard *class libraries* intended for wide distribution. This does not necessarily promote standards, although de facto standards are emerging. The full value of Java will be realized only when substantial, standardized class libraries become more widely available than they are today. In the United States, such standardization often happens through *ANSI*, the *American National Standards Institute*. Worldwide standardization often happens through *ISO, the International Standards Organization*. Regardless of how these libraries ultimately appear, the reader who learns Java and object-oriented programming will be ready to take advantage of the new kinds of rapid, component-oriented software development made possible with class libraries.

8.16.1 Example: Queue Abstract Data Type

Each of us stands in line from time to time. A waiting line is also called a *queue*. We wait in line at the supermarket checkout counter, we wait in line to get gasoline, we wait in line to board a bus, we wait in line to pay a toll on the highway, and students know all too well about waiting in line during registration to get the courses they want. Computer systems use many waiting lines internally, so we write programs that simulate what queues are and do.

A queue is a good example of an abstract data type. A queue offers well-understood behavior to its clients. Clients put things in a queue one at a time—using an *enqueue* operation, and the clients get those things back one at a time on demand—using a *dequeue* operation. Conceptually, a queue can become infinitely long. A real queue, of course, is finite. Items are returned from a queue in *first-in, first-out (FIFO)* order—the first item inserted in the queue is the first item removed from the queue.

The queue hides an internal data representation that keeps track of the items currently waiting in line, and it offers a set of operations to its clients, namely *enqueue* and *dequeue*. The clients are not concerned about implementation of the queue. Clients merely want the queue to operate "as advertised." When a client enqueues a new item, the queue should accept that item and place it internally in some kind of first-in, first-out data structure. When the client wants the next item from the front of the queue, the queue should remove the item from its internal representation and should deliver the item to the outside world in FIFO order (i.e., the item that has been in the queue the longest should be the next one returned by the next *dequeue* operation).

The queue ADT guarantees the integrity of its internal data structure. Clients may not manipulate this data structure directly. Only the queue ADT has access to its internal data. Clients may cause only allowable operations to be performed on the data representation; operations not provided in the ADT's public interface are rejected by the ADT in some appropriate manner. This could mean issuing an error message, terminating execution, or simply ignoring the operation request.

Summary

- OOP encapsulates data (attributes) and methods (behaviors) into objects; the data and methods of an object are intimately tied together.

- Objects have the property of information hiding. Objects may know how to communicate with one another across well-defined interfaces, but they normally are not allowed to know how other objects are implemented.

- Java programmers concentrate on creating their own user-defined types called classes. The data components of a class are called instance variables.

- Java uses inheritance to create new classes from existing class definitions.

- Every class in Java is a subclass of **Object**. Thus, every new class definition has the attributes (data) and behaviors (methods) of class **Object**.

- Keywords **public** and **private** are member access modifiers.

- Instance variables and methods declared with member access modifier **public** are accessible wherever the program has a reference to an object of the class in which the they are defined.

- Instance variables and methods declared with member access modifier **private** are accessible only to methods of the class in which they are defined.

- Instance variables are normally declared **private** and methods are normally declared **public**.

- The **public** methods (or **public** services) of a class are used by clients of the class to manipulate the data stored in objects of the class.

- A constructor is a method with the exact same name as the class that initializes the instance variables of an object of the class when the object is instantiated. Constructor methods can be overloaded for a class. Constructors can take arguments but cannot return a value.

- Constructors and other methods that change instance variable values should always maintain objects in a consistent state.

- Method **toString** takes no arguments and returns a **String**. The original **toString** method of class **Object** is a placeholder that is normally redefined by a subclass.

- When an object is instantiated, operator **new** allocates the memory for the object, then **new** calls the constructor for the class to initialize the instance variables of the object.

- If the **.class** files for the classes used in a program are in the same directory as the class that uses them, **import** statements are not required.

- Concatenating a **String** and any object results in an implicit call to the object's **toString** method to convert the object to a **String**, then the **String**s are concatenated.

- Within a class's scope, class members are immediately accessible to all of that class's methods and can be referenced simply by name. Outside a class's scope, class members can only be accessed off a "handle" (i.e., a reference to an object of the class).

- If a method defines a variable with the same name as a variable with class scope, the class-scope variable is hidden by the method-scope variable in the method. A hidden instance variable can be accessed in the method by preceding its name with the keyword **this** and the dot operator.

- Each class and interface in the Java API belongs to a specific package that contains a group of related classes and interfaces.

- Packages are actually directory structures used to organize classes and interfaces. Packages provide a mechanism for software reuse and a convention for unique class names.

- Creating a reusable class requires: defining a **public** class, adding a **package** statement to the class definition file, compiling the class into the appropriate package directory structure to make the new class available to the compiler and the interpreter, and importing the class into a program.

- Java 2 has a directory called **classes** where the compiled version of new reusable classes are placed that is well known to both the compiler and the interpreter.
- When compiling a class in a package, the option **-d** must be passed to the compiler to specify where to create (or locate) all the directories in the **package** statement.
- The **package** directory names become part of the class name when the class is compiled. Use this fully qualified name in programs or **import** the class and use its short name (the name of the class by itself) in the program.
- If no constructors are defined for a class, the compiler creates a default constructor that takes no arguments.
- When one object of a class has a reference to another object of the same class, the first object can access all the second object's data and methods.
- Classes often provide **public** methods to allow clients of the class to *set* (i.e., assign values to) or *get* (i.e., obtain the values of) **private** instance variables. *Get* methods are also commonly called accessor methods or query methods. *Set* methods are also commonly called mutator methods (because they typically change a value).
- Every event has a source—the GUI component with which the user interacted to signal the program to do a task.
- Use the keyword **final** to specify that a variable is not modifiable and that any attempt to modify the variable is an error. A **final** variable cannot be modified by assignment after it is initialized. Such a variable must be initialized in its declaration or in every constructor of the class.
- With composition, a class has references to objects of other classes as members.
- When no member access modifier is provided for a method or variable when it is defined in a class, the method or variable is considered to have package access.
- If a program uses multiple classes from the same package, these classes can access each other's package-access methods and data directly through a reference to an object.
- Each object has access to a reference to itself called the **this** reference that can be used inside the methods of the class to refer to the object's data and other methods explicitly.
- Any time you have a reference in a program (even as the result of a method call), the reference can be followed by a dot operator and a call to one of the methods for the reference type.
- Java performs automatic garbage collection of memory. When an object is no longer used in the program (i.e., there are no references to the object), the object is marked for garbage collection.
- Every class in Java can have a finalizer method that returns resources to the system. A class's finalizer method always has the name **finalize**, receives no parameters and returns no value. Method **finalize** is originally defined in class **Object** as a placeholder that does nothing. This guarantees that every class has a **finalize** method for the garbage collector to call.
- A **static** class variable represents class-wide information—all objects of the class share the same piece of data. A class's **public static** members can be accessed through a reference to any object of that class, or they can be accessed through the class name using the dot operator.
- **public static** method **gc** from class **System** suggests that the garbage collector execute immediately. This suggestion can be ignored. The garbage collector is not guaranteed to collect objects in a specific order.
- A method declared **static** cannot access non-**static** class members. Unlike non-**static** methods, a **static** method has no **this** reference because **static** class variables and **static** class methods exist independent of any objects of a class.
- **static** class members exist even when no objects of that class exist—they are available as soon as the class is loaded into memory at execution time.

Terminology

-d compiler option	instantiate an object of a class
abstract data type (ADT)	interface to a class
access method	member access control
aggregation	member access modifiers
attribute	member access operator (**.**)
behavior	message
cascaded method calls	method
class	method calls
class definition	mutator method
class library	**new** operator
class method (**static**)	no-argument constructor
class scope	object
class variable	object-based programming (OBP)
client of a class	object-oriented programming (OOP)
composition	package access
concatenated method calls	**package** statement
consistent state for an instance variable	predicate method
constructor	principle of least privilege
container class	**private**
data type	programmer-defined type
default constructor	**public**
dot operator (**.**)	public interface of a class
encapsulation	query method
extends	rapid applications development (RAD)
extensibility	reusable code
finalizer	services of a class
get method	set method
helper method	software reusability
implementation of a class	static class variable
information hiding	static method
initialize a class object	**this** reference
instance method	user-defined type
instance of a class	utility method
instance variable	

Common Programming Errors

8.1   Defining more than one **public** class in the same file is a syntax error.

8.2   Attempting to declare a return type for a constructor and/or attempting to **return** a value from a constructor is a logic error. Java allows other methods of the class to have the same name as the class and to specify return types. Such methods are not constructors and will not be called when an object of the class is instantiated.

8.3   An attempt by a method which is not a member of a particular class to access a **private** member of that class is a syntax error.

8.4   If constructors are provided for a class, but none of the **public** constructors are no-argument constructors, and an attempt is made to call a no-argument constructor to initialize an object of the class, a syntax error occurs. A constructor may be called with no arguments only if there are no constructors for the class (the default constructor is called) or if there is a no-argument constructor.

8.5   Attempting to overload a method of a class with another method that has the exact same signature (name and parameters) is a syntax error.

8.6   A constructor can call other methods of the class, such as *set* or *get* methods, but because the constructor is initializing the object, the instance variables may not yet be in a consistent state. Using instance variables before they have been properly initialized is an error.

8.7   Attempting to modify a **final** instance variable after it is initialized is a syntax error.

8.8   Not initializing a **final** instance variable in its declaration or in every constructor of the class is a syntax error.

8.9   In a method in which a method parameter has the same name as one of the class members, use **this** explicitly if you want to access the class member; otherwise, you will incorrectly reference the method parameter.

8.10   Referring to the **this** reference in a **static** method is a syntax error.

8.11   It is a syntax error for a **static** method to call an instance method or to access an instance variable.

Good Programming Practices

8.1   Group members by member access modifier in a class definition for clarity and readability.

8.2   Always define a class so its instance variables are maintained in a consistent state.

8.3   Initialize instance variables of a class in that class's constructor.

8.4   Our preference is to list the **private** instance variables of a class first so as you read the code, you see the names and types of the instance variables before they are used in the methods of the class.

8.5   Despite the fact that **private** and **public** members may be repeated and intermixed, list all the **private** members of a class first in one group and then list all the **public** members in another group.

8.6   When appropriate (almost always), provide a constructor to ensure that every object is properly initialized with meaningful values.

8.7   Every method that modifies the private instance variables of an object should ensure that the data remains in a consistent state.

8.8   Avoid using method parameter names that conflict with class member names.

8.9   Explicitly using **this** can increase program clarity in some contexts in which **this** is optional.

8.10   Always invoke *static* methods using the class name and the dot operator (.). This emphasizes to other programmers reading your code that the method being called is a *static* method.

Performance Tips

8.1   All Java objects are passed by reference. Only a memory address is passed, not a copy of a possibly large object (as would be the case in a pass by value).

8.2   Initialize member objects explicitly at constructor time. This eliminates the overhead of doubly initializing member objects—once when the member object's default constructor is called and again when *set* methods are used to provide initial values for the member object.

8.3   Package access enables objects of different classes to interact without the need for *set* and *get* methods that provide access to data, thus eliminating some of the method call overhead.

8.4   Java conserves storage by maintaining only one copy of each method per class; this method is invoked by every object of that class. Each object, on the other hand, has its own copy of the class's instance variables.

8.5   Use **static** class variables to save storage when a single copy of the data will suffice.

Software Engineering Observations

8.1   It is important to write programs that are understandable and easy to maintain. Change is the rule rather than the exception. Programmers should anticipate that their code will be modified. As we will see, classes facilitate program modifiability.

8.2   Class definitions that begin with keyword **public** must be stored in a file that has exactly the same name as the class and ends with the **.java** file name extension.

8.3   Every class defined in Java must extend another class. If a class does not explicitly use keyword **extends** in its definition, the class implicitly **extends Object**.

8.4   Methods tend to fall into a number of different categories: methods that get the values of **private** instance variables; methods that set the values of **private** instance variables; methods that implement the services of the class; and methods that perform various mechanical chores for the class, such as initializing class objects, assigning class objects, and converting between classes and built-in types or between classes and other classes.

8.5   Every time **new** creates an object of a class, that class's constructor is called to initialize the instance variables of the new object.

8.6   Information hiding promotes program modifiability and simplifies the client's perception of a class.

8.7   Clients of a class can (and should) use the class without knowing the internal details of how the class is implemented. If the class implementation is changed (to improve performance, for example), provided the class's interface remains constant, the class clients' source code need not change. This makes it much easier to modify systems.

8.8   Using an object-oriented programming approach can often simplify method calls by reducing the number of parameters to be passed. This benefit of object-oriented programming derives from the fact that encapsulation of instance variables and methods within an object gives the methods the right to access the instance variables.

8.9   Keep all the instance variables of a class **private**. When necessary provide **public** methods to set the values of **private** instance variables and to get the values of **private** instance variables. This architecture helps hide the implementation of a class from its clients, which reduces bugs and improves program modifiability.

8.10   Class designers use **private** data and **public** methods to enforce the notion of information hiding and the principle of least privilege. If the client of a class needs access to data in the class, provide that access through **public** methods of the class. By doing so, the programmer of the class controls how the class's data is manipulated (e.g., data validity checking can prevent invalid data from being stored in an object).

8.11   The class designer need not provide *set* and/or *get* methods for each **private** data *member*; these capabilities should be provided only when it makes sense and after careful thought by the class designer.

8.12   A Java source code file has the following order: a **package** statement (if any), **import** statements (if any), then class definitions. Only one of the class definitions can be **public**. Other classes in the file are also placed in the package, but are not reusable. They are in the package to support the reusable class in the file.

8.13   If a method of a class already provides all or part of the functionality required by a constructor (or other method) of the class, call that method from the constructor (or other method). This simplifies the maintenance of the code and reduces the likelihood of an error if the implementation of the code is modified. It is also an effective example of reuse.

8.14   Methods that set the values of **private** data should verify that the intended new values are proper; if they are not, the *set* methods should place the **private** instance variables into an appropriate consistent state.

8.15   Accessing private data through *set* and *get* methods not only protects the instance variables from receiving invalid values, but also insulates clients of the class from representation of the instance variables. Thus, if representation of the data changes (typically, to reduce the amount of storage required or to improve performance), only the method implementations need to change—the clients need not change as long as the interface provided by the methods remains the same.

8.16 Declaring an instance variable as **final** helps enforce the principle of least privilege. If an instance variable should not be modified, declare it **final** to expressly forbid modification.

8.17 One form of software reuse is composition in which a class has references to objects of other classes as members.

8.18 Some people in the OOP community feel that package access corrupts information hiding and weakens the value of the object-oriented design approach.

8.19 Any **static** class variables and **static** class methods exist and can be used even if no objects of that class have been instantiated.

8.20 The programmer is able to create new types through the use of the class mechanism. These new types may be designed to be used as conveniently as the built-in types. Thus, Java is an extensible language. Although the language is easy to extend with these new types, the base language itself is not changeable.

Testing and Debugging Tips

8.1 Making the instance variables of a class *private* and the methods of the class *public* facilitates debugging because problems with data manipulations are localized to the class's methods.

8.2 Accidental attempts to modify a **final** instance variable are caught at compile time rather than causing execution-time errors. It is always preferable to get bugs out at compile time, if possible, rather than allowing them to slip through to execution time (where studies have found that the cost of repair is often as much as ten times more expensive).

Self-Review Exercises

8.1 Fill in the blanks in each of the following:
   d) Class members are accessed via the _____ operator in conjunction with a reference to an object of the class.
   e) Members of a class specified as _____ are accessible only to methods of the class.
   f) A _____ is a special method used to initialize the instance variables of a class.
   g) A _____ method is used to assign values to **private** instance variables of a class.
   h) Methods of a class are normally made _____ and instance variables of a class are normally made _____.
   i) A _____ method is used to retrieve values of **private** data of a class.
   j) The keyword _____ introduces a class definition.
   k) Members of a class specified as _____ are accessible anywhere an object of the class is in scope.
   l) The _____ operator dynamically allocates memory for an object of a specified type and returns a _____ to that type.
   m) A _____ instance variable represents class-wide information.
   n) The keyword _____ specifies that an object or variable is not modifiable after it is initialized.
   o) A method declared **static** cannot access _____ class members.

Answers to Self-Review Exercises

8.1   a) dot (**.**). b) **private**. c) constructor. d) set. e) **public**, **private**. f) get. g) **class**. h) **public**. i) **new**, reference. j) **static**. k) **final**. l) non-**static**.

Exercises

8.2   Create a class called **Complex** for performing arithmetic with complex numbers. Write a driver program to test your class.

Complex numbers have the form

```
realPart + imaginaryPart * i
```

where *i* is

$$\sqrt{-1}$$

Use floating-point variables to represent the **private** data of the class. Provide a constructor method that enables an object of this class to be initialized when it is declared. Provide a no-argument constructor with default values in case no initializers are provided. Provide **public** methods for each of the following:

a) Addition of two **Complex** numbers: The real parts are added together and the imaginary parts are added together.

b) Subtraction of two **Complex** numbers: The real part of the right operand is subtracted from the real part of the left operand and the imaginary part of the right operand is subtracted from the imaginary part of the left operand.

c) Printing **Complex** numbers in the form **(a, b)**, where **a** is the real part and **b** is the imaginary part.

8.3   Create a class called **Rational** for performing arithmetic with fractions. Write a driver program to test your class.

Use integer variables to represent the **private** instance variables of the class—the **numerator** and the **denominator**. Provide a constructor method that enables an object of this class to be initialized when it is declared. The constructor should store the fraction in reduced form (i.e., the fraction

2/4

would be stored in the object as 1 in the **numerator** and 2 in the **denominator**). Provide a no-argument constructor with default values in case no initializers are provided. Provide **public** methods for each of the following:

a) Addition of two **Rational** numbers. The result of the addition should be stored in reduced form.

b) Subtraction of two **Rational** numbers. The result of the subtraction should be stored in reduced form.

c) Multiplication of two **Rational** numbers. The result of the multiplication should be stored in reduced form.

d) Division of two **Rational** numbers. The result of the division should be stored in reduced form.

e) Printing **Rational** numbers in the form **a/b**, where **a** is the **numerator** and **b** is the **denominator**.

f) Printing **Rational** numbers in floating-point format. (Consider providing formatting capabilities that enable the user of the class to specify the number of digits of precision to the right of the decimal point.)

8.4   Modify the **Time3** class of Fig. 8.5 to include the **tick** method that increments the time stored in a **Time3** object by one second. Also provide method **incrementMinute** to increment the minute and method **incrementHour** to increment the hour. The **Time3** object should always remain in a consistent state. Write a driver program that tests the **tick** method, the **increment-Minute** method and the **incrementHour** method to ensure that they work correctly. Be sure to test the following cases:

      a) Incrementing into the next minute.
      b) Incrementing into the next hour.
      c) Incrementing into the next day (i.e., 11:59:59 PM to 12:00:00 AM).

8.5   Modify the **Date** class of Fig. 8.8 to perform error checking on the initializer values for instance variables **month**, **day** and **year**. Also, provide a method **nextDay** to increment the day by one. The **Date** object should always remain in a consistent state. Write a driver program that tests the **nextDay** method in a loop that prints the date during each iteration of the loop to illustrate that the **nextDay** method works correctly. Be sure to test the following cases:
      a) Incrementing into the next month.
      b) Incrementing into the next year.

8.6   Combine the modified **Time3** class of Exercise 8.4 and the modified **Date** class of Exercise 8.5 into one class called **DateAndTime**. Modify the **tick** method to call the **nextDay** method if the time is incremented into the next day. Modify methods **toString** and **toUniversalString()** to output the date in addition to the time. Write a driver program to test the new class **DateAndTime**. Specifically test incrementing the time to the next day.

8.7   Modify the set methods in the program of Fig. 8.5 to return appropriate error values if an attempt is made to set one of the instance variables **hour**, **minute** or **second** of an object of class **Time** to an invalid value. (*Hint:* Use **boolean** return types on each method.)

8.8   Create a class **Rectangle**. The class has attributes **length** and **width**, each of which defaults to 1. It has methods that calculate the **perimeter** and the **area** of the rectangle. It has *set* and *get* methods for both **length** and **width**. The *set* methods should verify that **length** and **width** are each floating-point numbers larger than 0.0 and less than 20.0.

8.9   Create a more sophisticated **Rectangle** class than the one you created in Exercise 8.8. This class stores only the Cartesian coordinates of the four corners of the rectangle. The constructor calls a *set* method that accepts four sets of coordinates and verifies that each of these is in the first quadrant with no single *x*- or *y*-coordinate larger than 20.0. The *set* method also verifies that the supplied coordinates do, in fact, specify a rectangle. Provide methods to calculate the **length**, **width**, **perimeter** and **area**. The length is the larger of the two dimensions. Include a predicate method **isSquare** which determines if the rectangle is a square.

8.10   Modify the **Rectangle** class of Exercise 8.9 to include a **draw** method that displays the rectangle inside a 25-by-25 box enclosing the portion of the first quadrant in which the rectangle resides. Use the methods of the **Graphics** class to help output the **Rectangle**. If you feel ambitious, you might include methods to scale the size of the rectangle, rotate it and move it around within the designated portion of the first quadrant.

8.11   Create a class **HugeInteger** which uses a 40-element array of digits to store integers as large as 40 digits each. Provide methods **inputHugeInteger**, **outputHugeInteger**, **addHugeIntegers** and **substractHugeIntegers**. For comparing **HugeInteger** objects, provide methods **isEqualTo**, **isNotEqualTo**, **isGreaterThan**, **isLessThan**, **IsGreaterThanOrEqualTo** and **isLessThanOrEqualTo**—each of these is a "predicate" method that simply returns **true** if the relationship holds between the two **HugeInteger**s and returns **false** if the relationship does not hold. Provide a predicate method **isZero**. If you feel ambitious, also provide the method **multiplyHugeIntegers**, the method **divideHugeIntegers** and the method **modulusHugeIntegers.**

8.12   Create a class **TicTacToe** that will enable you to write a complete program to play the game of Tic-Tac-Toe. The class contains as private data a 3-by-3 double array of integers. The constructor should initialize the empty board to all zeros. Allow two human players. Wherever the first player moves, place a 1 in the specified square; place a 2 wherever the second player moves. Each move must be to an empty square. After each move determine if the game has been won, or if the game is a draw. If you feel ambitious, modify your program so that the computer makes the moves for one of the players automatically. Also, allow the player to specify whether he or she wants to go first or second. If you feel exceptionally ambitious, develop a program that will play three-dimensional Tic-Tac-Toe on a 4-by-4-by-4 board [*Note:* This is a challenging project that could take many weeks of effort!].

8.13   Explain the notion of package access in Java. Explain the negative aspects of package access as described in the text.

8.14   What happens when a return type, even **void**, is specified for a constructor?

8.15   Create a **Date** class with the following capabilities:
  a) Output the date in multiple formats such as

```
MM/DD/YYYY
June 14, 1992
DDD YYYY
```

  b) Use overloaded constructors to create **Date** objects initialized with dates of the formats in part a).

8.16   Create class **SavingsAccount**. Use a **static** class variable to store the **annualInterestRate** for all account holders. Each object of the class contains a **private** instance variable **savingsBalance** indicating the amount the saver currently has on deposit. Provide method **calculateMonthlyInterest** to calculate the monthly interest by multiplying the **savingsBalance** by **annualInterestRate** divided by 12; this interest should be added to **savingsBalance**. Provide a **static** method **modifyInterestRate** that sets the **annualInterestRate** to a new value. Write a driver program to test class **SavingsAccount**. Instantiate two **savingsAccount** objects, **saver1** and **saver2**, with balances of $2000.00 and $3000.00, respectively. Set **annualInterestRate** to 4%, then calculate the monthly interest and print the new balances for each of the savers. Then set the **annualInterestRate** to 5% and calculate the next month's interest and print the new balances for each of the savers.

8.17   Create class **IntegerSet**. Each object of the class can hold integers in the range 0 through 100. A set is represented internally as an array of **boolean**s. Array element **a[i]** is **true** if integer *i* is in the set. Array element **a[j]** is **false** if integer *j* is not in the set. The no-argument constructor initializes a set to the so-called "empty set" (i.e., a set whose array representation contains all **false** values).

Provide the following methods: Method **unionOfIntegerSets** creates a third set which is the set-theoretic union of two existing sets (i.e., an element of the third set's array is set to **true** if that element is **true** in either or both of the existing sets; otherwise, the element of the third set is set to **false**). Method **intersectionOfIntegerSets** creates a third set which is the set-theoretic intersection of two existing sets i.e., an element of the third set's array is set to **false** if that element is **false** in either or both of the existing sets; otherwise, the element of the third set is set to **true**). Method **insertElement** inserts a new integer *k* into a set (by setting **a[k]** to **true**). Method **deleteElement** deletes integer *m* (by setting **a[m]** to **false**). Method **setPrint** prints a set as a list of numbers separated by spaces. Print only those elements that are present in the set. Print --- for an empty set. Method **isEqualTo** determines if two sets are equal. Write a program to test your **IntegerSet** class. Instantiate several **IntegerSet** objects. Test that all your methods work properly.

8.18   It would be perfectly reasonable for the **Time1** class of Fig. 8.1 to represent the time internally as the number of seconds since midnight rather than the three integer values **hour**, **minute** and **second**. Clients could use the same **public** methods and get the same results. Modify the **Time1** class of Fig. 8.1 to implement the **Time1** as the number of seconds since midnight and show that there is no visible change to the clients of the class.

8.19   *(Drawing Program)* Create a drawing applet that randomly draws lines, rectangles and ovals. For this purpose, create a set of "smart" shape classes where objects of these classes know how to draw themselves if provided with a **Graphics** object that tells them where to draw (i.e., the applet's **Graphics** object allows a shape to draw on the applet's background). The class names should be **MyLine**, **MyRect** and **MyOval**.

The data for class **MyLine** should include *x1*, *y1*, *x2* and *y2* coordinates. Method **drawLine** method of class **Graphics** will connect the two points supplied with a line. The data for classes **MyRect** and **MyOval** should include an upper-left *x*-coordinate value, an upper-left *y*-coordinate value, a *width* (must be nonnegative) and a *height* (must be nonnegative). All data in each class must be **private**.

In addition to the data, each class should define at least the following **public** methods:
a) A constructor with no arguments that sets the coordinates to 0.
b) A constructor with arguments that sets the coordinates to the supplied values.
c) Set methods for each individual piece of data that allow the programmer to independently set any piece of data in a shape (e.g., if you have an instance variable **x1**, you should have a method **setX1**).
d) Get methods for each individual piece of data that allow the programmer to independently retrieve any piece of data in a shape (e.g., if you have an instance variable **x1**, you should have a method **getX1**).
e) A **draw** method with the first line

```
public void draw( Graphics g )
```

will be called from the applet's **paint** method to draw a shape onto the screen.

The preceding methods are required. If you would like to provide more methods for flexibility, please do so.

Begin by defining class **MyLine** and an applet to test your classes. The applet should have a **MyLine** instance variable **line** that can refer to one **MyLine** object (created in the applet's **init** method with random coordinates). The applet's **paint** method should draw the shape with a statement like

```
line.draw( g );
```

where **line** is the **MyLine** reference and **g** is the **Graphics** object that the shape will use to draw itself on the applet.

Next, change the single **MyLine** reference into an array of **MyLine** references and hard code several **MyLine** objects into the program for drawing. The applet's **paint** method should walk through the array of **MyLine** objects and draw every one.

After the preceding part is working, you should define the **MyOval** and **MyRect** classes and add objects of these classes into the **MyRect** and **MyOval** arrays. The applet's **paint** method should walk through each array and draw every shape. Create five shapes of each type.

Once the applet is running, select **Reload** from the **appletviewer**'s **Applet** menu to reload the applet. This will cause the applet to choose new random numbers for the shapes and draw the shapes again.

In Chapter 9, we will modify this exercise to take advantage of the similarities between the classes and to avoid reinventing the wheel.

Object-Oriented Programming

Objectives

- To understand inheritance and software reusability.
- To understand superclasses and subclasses.
- To appreciate how polymorphism makes systems extensible and maintainable.
- To understand the distinction between abstract classes and concrete classes.
- To learn how to create abstract classes and interfaces.

Say not you know another entirely, till you have divided an inheritance with him.
Johann Kasper Lavater

This method is to define as the number of a class the class of all classes similar to the given class.
Bertrand Russell

Good as it is to inherit a library, it is better to collect one.
Augustine Birrell

General propositions do not decide concrete cases.
Oliver Wendell Holmes

A philosopher of imposing stature doesn't think in a vacuum. Even his most abstract ideas are, to some extent, conditioned by what is or is not known in the time when he lives.
Alfred North Whitehead

Outline

9.1　Introduction

In this chapter we discuss *object-oriented programming (OOP)* and its key component technologies—*inheritance* and *polymorphism.* Inheritance is a form of software reusability in which new classes are created from existing classes by absorbing their attributes and behaviors and embellishing these with capabilities the new classes require. Software reusability saves time in program development. It encourages reuse of proven and debugged high-quality software, thus reducing problems after a system becomes operational. These are exciting possibilities. Polymorphism enables us to write programs in a general fashion to handle a wide variety of existing and yet-to-be-specified related classes. Polymorphism makes it easy to add new capabilities to a system. Inheritance and polymorphism are effective techniques for dealing with software complexity.

When creating a new class, instead of writing completely new instance variables and instance methods, the programmer can designate that the new class is to *inherit* the instance variables and instance methods of a previously defined *superclass.* The new class is referred to as a *subclass*. Each subclass itself becomes a candidate to be a superclass for some future subclass.

The *direct superclass* of a subclass is the superclass from which the subclass explicitly inherits (via the keyword **extends**). An indirect superclass is inherited from two or more levels up the class hierarchy.

With *single inheritance,* a class is derived from one superclass. Java does not support *multiple inheritance* (as C++ does) but it does support the notion of *interfaces*. Interfaces help Java achieve many of the advantages of multiple inheritance without the associated problems. We will discuss the details of interfaces in this chapter where we consider both general principles as well as a detailed specific example of creating and using interfaces.

A subclass normally adds instance variables and instance methods of its own, so a subclass is generally larger than its superclass. A subclass is more specific than its superclass and represents a smaller group of objects. With single inheritance, the subclass starts out essentially the same as the superclass. The real strength of inheritance comes from the ability to define in the subclass additions to, or replacements for, the features inherited from the superclass.

Every object of a subclass is also an object of that subclass's superclass. However, the converse is not true—superclass objects are not objects of that superclass's subclasses. We will take advantage of this "subclass-object-is-a-superclass-object" relationship to perform some powerful manipulations. For example, we can link a wide variety of different objects related to a common superclass through inheritance into a linked list of superclass objects. This allows a variety of objects to be processed in a general way. As we will see in this chapter, this is a key thrust of object-oriented programming.

We add a new form of member access control in this chapter, namely **protected** access. Subclass methods and methods of other classes in the same package as the superclass can access **protected** superclass members.

Experience in building software systems indicates that significant portions of the code deal with closely related special cases. It becomes difficult in such systems to see the "big picture" because the designer and the programmer become preoccupied with the special cases. Object-oriented programming provides several ways of "seeing the forest through the trees"—a process called *abstraction*.

If a procedural program has many closely related special cases, then it is common to see **switch** structures or nested **if/else** structures that distinguish among the special cases and provide the processing logic to deal with each case individually. We will show how to use inheritance and polymorphism to replace such **switch** logic with much simpler logic.

We distinguish between the *"is a" relationship* and the *"has a" relationship*. "Is a" is inheritance. In an "is a" relationship, an object of a subclass type may also be treated as an object of its superclass type. "Has a" is composition (as we discussed in Chapter 8). In a "has a" relationship, a class object has one or more objects of other classes as members. For example, a car *has a* steering wheel.

A subclass's methods may need to access certain of its superclass's instance variables and methods.

Software Engineering Observation 9.1

*A subclass cannot directly access **private** members of its superclass.*

This is a crucial aspect of software engineering in Java. If a subclass could access the superclass's **private** members, this would violate information hiding in the superclass.

Testing and Debugging Tip 9.1

Hiding **private** *members is a huge help in testing, debugging and correctly modifying systems. If a subclass could access its superclass's* **private** *members, it would then be possible for classes derived from that subclass to access that data as well, and so on. This would propagate access to what is supposed to be* **private** *data, and the benefits of information hiding would be lost throughout the class hierarchy.*

A subclass can, however, access the **public**, **protected** and package access members of its superclass if it is in the same package as the superclass. Superclass members that should not be accessible to a subclass via inheritance are declared **private** in the superclass. A subclass can effect state changes in superclass **private** members only through **public**, **protected** and package access methods provided in the superclass and inherited into the subclass.

A problem with inheritance is that a subclass can inherit methods that it does not need or should not have. When a superclass member is inappropriate for a subclass, that member can be *overridden* (redefined) in the subclass with an appropriate implementation.

Perhaps most exciting is the notion that new classes can inherit from abundant *class libraries*. Organizations develop their own class libraries and can take advantage of other libraries available worldwide. Someday, most software may be constructed from *standardized reusable components* just as hardware is often constructed today. This will help meet the challenges of developing the ever more powerful software we will need in the future.

9.2 Superclasses and Subclasses

Often an object of one class "is an" object of another class as well. A rectangle certainly *is a* quadrilateral (as are squares, parallelograms and trapezoids). Thus, class **Rectangle** can be said to *inherit* from class **Quadrilateral**. In this context, class **Quadrilateral** is a superclass and class **Rectangle** is a subclass. A rectangle *is a* specific type of quadrilateral, but it is incorrect to claim that a quadrilateral *is a* rectangle (the quadrilateral could be a parallelogram). Figure 9.1 shows several simple inheritance examples of superclasses and potential subclasses.

Superclass	Subclasses
Student	GraduateStudent
	UndergraduateStudent
Shape	Circle
	Triangle
	Rectangle
Loan	CarLoan
	HomeImprovementLoan
	MortgageLoan

Fig. 9.1   Some simple inheritance examples (part 1 of 2).

Superclass	Subclasses
Employee	FacultyMember
	StaffMember
Account	CheckingAccount
	SavingsAccount

Fig. 9.1   Some simple inheritance examples (part 2 of 2).

Because inheritance normally produces subclasses with *more* features than their superclasses, the terms *superclass* and *subclass* can be confusing. There is another way, however, to view these terms that makes perfectly good sense. Because every subclass object "is an" object of its superclass, and because one superclass can have many subclasses, the set of objects represented by a superclass is normally larger than the set of objects represented by any of that superclass's subclasses. For example, the superclass **Vehicle** represents in a generic manner all vehicles, such as cars, trucks, boats, bicycles, etc. However, subclass **Car** represents only a small subset of all the **Vehicle**s in the world.

Inheritance relationships form tree-like hierarchical structures. A superclass exists in a hierarchical relationship with its subclasses. A class can certainly exist by itself, but it is when a class is used with the mechanism of inheritance that the class becomes either a superclass that supplies attributes and behaviors to other classes, or the class becomes a subclass that inherits those attributes and behaviors.

Let us develop a simple inheritance hierarchy. A typical university community has thousands of people who are community members. These people consist of employees, students and alumni. Employees are either faculty members or staff members. Faculty members are either administrators (such as deans and department chairpersons) or teaching faculty. This yields the inheritance hierarchy shown in Fig. 9.2. Note that the inheritance hierarchy could contain many other classes. For example, students can be graduate students or undergraduate students. Undergraduate students can be freshman, sophomores, juniors, and seniors. And so on. The arrows in the hierarchy represent the "is a" relationship. For example, based on this class hierarchy that we can state, "an **Employee** *is a* **CommunityMember**," or "a **Teacher** *is a* **Faculty** member." **CommunityMember** is the *direct superclass* of **Employee**, **Student** and **Alumni**. **CommunityMember** is an *indirect superclass* of all the other classes in the hierarchy diagram.

Also, starting from the bottom of the diagram, you can follow the arrows and apply the *is a* relationship all the way up to the topmost superclass in the hierarchy. For example, an **Administrator** *is a* **Faculty** member, *is an* **Employee** and *is a* **CommunityMember**. And in Java, an **Administrator** also *is an* **Object** because all classes in Java have **Object** as one of their direct or indirect superclasses. Thus, all classes in Java are related in a hierarchical relationship in which they share the 11 methods defined by class **Object** that include the **toString** and **finalize** methods discussed previously. Other methods of class **Object** are discussed as they are needed in the text.

Another substantial inheritance hierarchy is the **Shape** hierarchy of Fig. 9.3. There are abundant examples of hierarchies in the real world but students are not accustomed to categorizing the real world in this manner, so it takes some adjustment in their thinking. Actually, biology students have had some practice with hierarchies. Everything we study in biology is grouped into a hierarchy headed by living things and these can be plants or animals and so on.

To specify that class **TwoDimensionalShape** is derived from (or inherits from) class **Shape**, class **TwoDimensionalShape** could be defined in Java as follows:

```
class TwoDimensionalShape extends Shape { ... }
```

With inheritance, **private** members of a superclass are not directly accessible from that class's subclasses. Package access members of the superclass are only accessible in a subclass if both the superclass and its subclass are in the same package. All other superclass members become members of the subclass using their original member access (i.e., **public** members of the superclass become **public** members of the subclass and **protected** members of the superclass become **protected** members of the subclass).

 Software Engineering Observation 9.2

Constructors are never inherited—they are specific to the class in which they are defined.

It is possible to treat superclass objects and subclass objects similarly; that commonality is expressed in the attributes and behaviors of the superclass. Objects of all classes derived from a common superclass can all be treated as objects of that superclass.

We will consider many examples in which we can take advantage of this relationship with an ease of programming not available in non-object-oriented languages such as C.

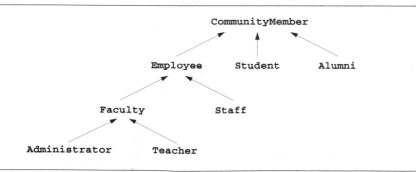

Fig. 9.2   An inheritance hierarchy for university **CommunityMember**s.

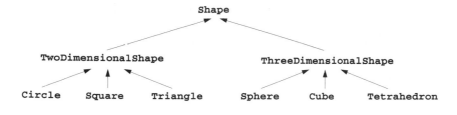

Fig. 9.3   A portion of a **Shape** class hierarchy.

9.3 `protected` Members

A superclass's **public** members are accessible anywhere the program has a reference to that superclass type or one of its subclass types. A superclass's **private** members are accessible only in methods of that superclass.

A superclass's **protected** access members serve as an intermediate level of protection between **public** and **private** access. A superclass's **protected** members may be accessed only by methods of the superclass, by methods of subclasses and by methods of other classes in the same package (**protected** members have package access).

Subclass methods can normally refer to **public** and **protected** members of the superclass simply by using the member names. When a subclass method overrides a superclass method, the superclass method may be accessed from the subclass by preceding the superclass method name with keyword **super** followed by the dot operator (**.**). This technique is illustrated several times throughout the chapter.

9.4 Relationship between Superclass Objects and Subclass Objects

An object of a subclass can be treated as an object of its superclass. This makes possible some interesting manipulations. For example, despite the fact that objects of a variety of classes derived from a particular superclass may be quite different from one another, we can create an array of references to them—as long as we treat them as superclass objects. But the reverse is not true: A superclass object is not also automatically a subclass object.

Common Programming Error 9.1

Treating a superclass object as a subclass object can cause errors.

However an explicit cast can be used to convert a superclass reference to a subclass reference. This can only be done when the superclass reference is actually referencing a subclass object; otherwise, Java will indicate a ***ClassCastException***—an indication that the cast operation is not allowed. Exceptions are discussed in detail in Chapter 14.

Common Programming Error 9.2

Assigning an object of a superclass to a subclass reference (without a cast) is a syntax error.

Software Engineering Observation 9.3

If an object has been assigned to a reference of one of its superclasses, it is acceptable to cast that object back to its own type. In fact, this must be done in order to send that object any of its messages that do not appear in that superclass.

Our first example of inheritance is shown in Fig. 9.4. Every applet we defined has used some of the techniques presented here. We now formalize the inheritance concept.

In Chapter 3, we stated that every class definition in Java must extend another class. However, notice that class **Point** (line 4) does not explicitly use the **extends** keyword. If a new class definition does not explicitly extend an existing class definition, Java implicitly uses class **Object** (package **java.lang**) as the superclass for the new class definition. Class **Object** provides a set of methods that can be used with any object of any class.

Software Engineering Observation 9.4

*Every class in Java extends **Object** unless specified otherwise in the first line of the class definition. Thus, class **Object** is the superclass of the entire Java class hierarchy.*

```
1   // Fig. 9.4: Point.java
2   // Definition of class Point
3
4   public class Point {
5      protected int x, y; // coordinates of the Point
6
7      // No-argument constructor
8      public Point()
9      {
10        // implicit call to superclass constructor occurs here
11        setPoint( 0, 0 );
12     }
13
14     // Constructor
15     public Point( int a, int b )
16     {
17        // implicit call to superclass constructor occurs here
18        setPoint( a, b );
19     }
20
21     // Set x and y coordinates of Point
22     public void setPoint( int a, int b )
23     {
24        x = a;
25        y = b;
26     }
27
28     // get x coordinate
29     public int getX() { return x; }
30
31     // get y coordinate
32     public int getY() { return y; }
33
34     // convert the point into a String representation
35     public String toString()
36        { return "[" + x + ", " + y + "]"; }
37  }
```

Fig. 9.4   Assigning subclass references to superclass references (part 1 of 5).

```
38  // Fig. 9.4: Circle.java
39  // Definition of class Circle
40
41  public class Circle extends Point {  // inherits from Point
42     protected double radius;
43
44     // No-argument constructor
45     public Circle()
46     {
47        // implicit call to superclass constructor occurs here
48        setRadius( 0 );
49     }
```

Fig. 9.4   Assigning subclass references to superclass references (part 2 of 5).

```
50
51      // Constructor
52      public Circle( double r, int a, int b )
53      {
54         super( a, b );  // call to superclass constructor
55         setRadius( r );
56      }
57
58      // Set radius of Circle
59      public void setRadius( double r )
60         { radius = ( r >= 0.0 ? r : 0.0 ); }
61
62      // Get radius of Circle
63      public double getRadius() { return radius; }
64
65      // Calculate area of Circle
66      public double area() { return Math.PI * radius * radius; }
67
68      // convert the Circle to a String
69      public String toString()
70      {
71         return "Center = " + "[" + x + ", " + y + "]" +
72                 "; Radius = " + radius;
73      }
74   }
```

Fig. 9.4 Assigning subclass references to superclass references (part 3 of 5).

```
75   // Fig. 9.4: Test.java
76   // Demonstrating the "is a" relationship
77   import java.text.DecimalFormat;
78   import javax.swing.JOptionPane;
79
80   public class InheritanceTest {
81      public static void main( String args[] )
82      {
83         Point pointRef, p;
84         Circle circleRef, c;
85         String output;
86
87         p = new Point( 30, 50 );
88         c = new Circle( 2.7, 120, 89 );
89
90         output = "Point p: " + p.toString() +
91                 "\nCircle c: " + c.toString();
92
93         // use the "is a" relationship to refer to a Circle
94         // with a Point reference
95         pointRef = c;    // assign Circle to pointRef
96
97         output += "\n\nCircle c (via pointRef): " +
98                 pointRef.toString();
```

Fig. 9.4 Assigning subclass references to superclass references (part 4 of 5).

```
 99
100        // Use downcasting (casting a superclass reference to a
101        // subclass data type) to assign pointRef to circleRef
102        circleRef = (Circle) pointRef;
103
104        output += "\n\nCircle c (via circleRef): " +
105                    circleRef.toString();
106
107        DecimalFormat precision2 = new DecimalFormat( "0.00" );
108        output += "\nArea of c (via circleRef): " +
109                    precision2.format( circleRef.area() );
110
111        // Attempt to refer to Point object
112        // with Circle reference
113        if ( p instanceof Circle ) {
114           circleRef = (Circle) p;  // line 40 in Test.java
115           output += "\n\ncast successful";
116        }
117        else
118           output += "\n\np does not refer to a Circle";
119
120        JOptionPane.showMessageDialog( null, output,
121           "Demonstrating the \"is a\" relationship",
122           JOptionPane.INFORMATION_MESSAGE );
123
124        System.exit( 0 );
125     }
126 }
```

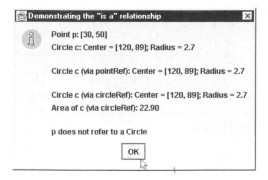

Fig. 9.4   Assigning subclass references to superclass references (part 5 of 5).

Lines 1–37 show a **Point** class definition. Lines 38–74 show a **Circle** class definition; we will see that class **Circle** inherits from class **Point**. Lines 75–126 show an application that demonstrates assigning subclass references to superclass references and casting superclass references to subclass references.

Let us first examine the **Point** class definition in lines 1–37. The **public** services of class **Point** include methods **setPoint**, **getX**, **getY**, **toString** and two **Point** constructors. The instance variables **x** and **y** of **Point** are specified as **protected**. This prevents clients of **Point** objects from directly accessing the data (unless they are classes in the same package), but enables classes derived from **Point** to access the inherited instance variables directly. If the data were specified as **private**, the non-**private** methods of **Point** would have to be used to access the data, even by subclasses. Note that class **Point**'s **toString** method overrides the original **toString** from class **Object**.

Class **Point**'s constructors (lines 8 and 15) must call class **Object**'s constructor. In fact, every subclass constructor is required to call its direct superclass's constructor as its first task either implicitly or explicitly (the syntax for this call is discussed with class **Circle** momentarily). If there is no explicit call to the superclass constructor, Java automatically attempts to call the superclass's default constructor. Note that lines 10 and 17 are comments indicating where the call to the superclass **Object**'s default constructor occurs.

Class **Circle** (lines 38–74) inherits from class **Point**. This is specified in the first line of the class definition

```
public class Circle extends Point {  // inherits from Point
```

Keyword **extends** in the class definition indicates inheritance. All the (non–**private**) members of class **Point** (except the constructors) are inherited into class **Circle**. Thus, the **public** interface to **Circle** includes the **Point public** methods as well as the two overloaded **Circle** constructors and **Circle** methods **setRadius**, **getRadius**, **area** and **toString**. Notice that method **area** (line 66) uses predefined constant **Math.PI** from class **Math** (package **java.lang**) to calculate the area of a circle.

The **Circle** constructors (lines 45 and 52) must invoke a **Point** constructor to initialize the superclass portion (variables **x** and **y** inherited from **Point**) of a **Circle** object. The default constructor at line 45 does not explicitly call a **Point** constructor, so Java automatically calls class **Point**'s default constructor (defined at line 8) that initializes superclass members **x** and **y** to zeros. If the **Point** class contained only the constructor of line 15 (i.e., did not provide a default constructor), a compiler error would occur.

Line 54 in the body of the second **Circle** constructor

```
super( a, b );  // explicit call to superclass constructor
```

explicitly invokes the **Point** constructor (defined at line 11) using the *superclass constructor call syntax* [i.e., keyword **super** followed by a set of parentheses containing the arguments to the superclass constructor (in this case the values **a** and **b** are passed to initialize the superclass members **x** and **y**)]. The call to the superclass constructor must be the first line in the body of the subclass constructor. To explicitly call the superclass default constructor use the statement

```
super();  // explicit call to superclass default constructor
```

Common Programming Error 9.3

*It is a syntax error if a **super** call by a subclass to its superclass constructor is not the first statement in the subclass constructor.*

Common Programming Error 9.4

*It is a syntax error if the arguments to a **super** call by a subclass to its superclass constructor do not match the parameters specified in one of the superclass constructor definitions.*

A subclass can redefine a superclass method using the same signature; this is called *overriding* a superclass method. When that method is mentioned by name in the subclass, the subclass version is automatically called. We have actually been overriding methods in every applet in the book. When we extend **JApplet** to create a new applet class, the new class inherits versions of **init** and **paint** (and many other methods). Each time we defined **init** or **paint**, we were overriding the original version that was inherited. Also, when we provided method **toString** for many of the classes in Chapter 8, we were overriding the original version of **toString** provided by class **Object**. As we will soon see, the **super** reference followed by the dot operator may be used to access the original superclass version of that method from the subclass.

Note that class **Circle**'s **toString** method (line 69) overrides the **Point** class **toString** method (line 35). Class **Point**'s **toString** method overrides the original **toString** method provided by class **Object**. Because class **Object** provides the original **toString** method, every class inherits a **toString** method. This method is used to convert any object of any class into a **String** representation and is sometimes called implicitly by the program (e.g., when an object is added to a **String**). **Circle** method **toString** directly accesses the **protected** instance variables **x** and **y** that were inherited from class **Point**. The values of **x** and **y** are used as part of the **Circle**'s **String** representation. Actually, if you study class **Point**'s **toString** method and class **Circle**'s **toString** method, you will notice that **Circle**'s **toString** uses exactly the same formatting as **Point**'s **toString** for the **Point** parts of the **Circle**. Also, recall our *Software Engineering Observation* indicating that if a method exists that performs part of another method's task, call the method. **Point**'s **toString** performs part of the task of **Circle**'s **toString**. To call **Point**'s **toString** from class **Circle** use the expression

```
super.toString()
```

Software Engineering Observation 9.5

A redefinition of a superclass method in a subclass need not have the same signature as the superclass method. Such a redefinition is not method overriding but is simply an example of method overloading.

Software Engineering Observation 9.6

*Any object can be converted to a **String** with an explicit or implicit call to the object's **toString** method.*

Software Engineering Observation 9.7

*Each class should override method **toString** to return useful information about objects of that class.*

Common Programming Error 9.5

It is a syntax error if a method in a superclass and a method in its subclass have the same signature but a different return type.

The application (lines 75–126) instantiates **Point** object **p** and **Circle** object **c** at lines 87 and 88 in **main**. The **String** representations of each object are appended to **String output** to show that they were initialized correctly (lines 90 and 91). See the first two lines in the output screen capture to confirm this.

Line 95

```
pointRef = c;    // assign Circle to pointRef
```

assigns **Circle c** (a reference to a subclass object) to **pointRef** (a superclass reference). It is always acceptable in Java to assign a subclass reference to a superclass reference (because of the "is a" relationship of inheritance). A **Circle** *is a* **Point** because class **Circle** extends class **Point**. Assigning a superclass reference to a subclass reference is dangerous, as we will see.

Lines 97 and 98 append the result of **pointRef.toString()** to the **String output**. Interestingly, when this **pointRef** is sent the **toString** message, Java knows that the object really is a **Circle**, so it chooses the **Circle toString** method instead of using the **Point toString** method as you might have expected. This is an example of *polymorphism* and *dynamic binding*, concepts we treat in depth later in this chapter. The compiler looks at the preceding expression and asks the question, "Does the data type of the reference **pointRef** (i.e., **Point**) have a **toString** method with no arguments?" The answer to this question is yes (see **Point**'s **toString** definition on line 35). The compiler is simply checking the syntax of the expression and ensuring that the method exists. At execution time, the interpreter asks the question, "What type is the object to which **pointRef** refers?" Every object in Java knows its own data type, so the answer to the question is **pointRef** refers to a **Circle** object. Based on this answer, the interpreter calls the **toString** method of the actual object's data type (i.e., class **Circle**'s **toString** method). See the third line of the screen capture to confirm this. The two key programming techniques we used to achieve this effect are 1) extending class **Point** to create class **Circle** and 2) overriding method **toString** with the exact same signature in class **Point** and class **Circle**.

Line 102

```
circleRef = (Circle) pointRef;
```

casts **pointRef** (which admittedly is referencing a **Circle** at this time in the program's execution) to a **Circle** and assigns the result to **circleRef** (this cast would be dangerous if **pointRef** were really referencing a **Point**, as we will soon discuss). Then we use **circleRef** to append to **String output** the various facts about **Circle circleRef**. Lines 104 and 105 invoke method **toString** to append the **String** representation of the **Circle**. Lines 107 through 109 append the **area** of the **Circle** formatted with an instance of class **DecimalFormat** (package **java.text**) called **precision2** that formats a number with two digits to the right of the decimal point. The format **"0.00"** (specified at line 107) uses **0** twice to indicate the proper number of digits after the decimal point. Each **0** is a required decimal place. The **0** to the left of the decimal point indicates a minimum of one digit to the left of the decimal point.

Next, the **if/else** structure at lines 113 through 118 attempts a dangerous cast in line 114. We cast **Point p** to a **Circle**. At execution time if this is attempted, Java would determine that **p** really references a **Point**, recognize the cast to **Circle** as being dangerous and indicate an improper cast with **ClassCastException** message. However, we prevent this statement from executing with the **if** condition

```
if ( p instanceof Circle ) {
```

that uses operator **instanceof** to determine if the object to which **p** refers *is a* **Circle**. This condition evaluates to **true** only if the object to which **p** refers *is a* **Circle**; otherwise, the condition evaluates to **false**. Because **p** does not refer to a **Circle**, the condition fails and a **String** indicating that **p** does not refer to a **Circle** is appended to **output**.

If we remove the **if** test from the program and execute the program, the following message is generated at execution time:

```
Exception in thread "main"
java.lang.ClassCastException: Point
    at InheritanceTest.main(InheritanceTest.java:40)
```

Such error messages normally include the file name (**InheritanceTest.java**) and line number at which the error occurred (**40**) so you can go to that specific line in the program for debugging. Note that the line number specified—**InheritanceTest.java:40**—is different from the line numbers for file **InheritanceTest.java** shown in the text. This is because the examples in the text are numbered with consecutive line numbers for all files in the same program for discussion purposes. If you open the file **InheritanceTest.java** in an editor, you will find that the error did indeed occur at line 40 (which is line 114 in the whole program).

9.5 Constructors and Finalizers in Subclasses

When an object of a subclass is instantiated, the superclass's constructor should be called to do any necessary initialization of the superclass instance variables of the subclass object. An explicit call to the superclass constructor (via the **super** reference) can be provided as the first statement in the subclass constructor. Otherwise, the subclass constructor will call the superclass default constructor (or no-argument constructor) implicitly.

Superclass constructors are not inherited by subclasses. Subclass constructors, however, can call superclass constructors via the **super** reference.

Software Engineering Observation 9.8

When an object of a subclass is created, first the subclass constructor calls the superclass constructor, the superclass constructor executes, then the remainder of the subclass constructor's body executes.

If the classes in your class hierarchy define **finalize** methods, the subclass **finalize** method should (if overriding **finalize**) invoke the superclass **finalize** method (as its last action) to ensure that all parts of an object are finalized properly when the garbage collector reclaims the memory for the object.

Figure 9.5 shows the order in which superclass and subclass constructors and finalizers are called. For the purpose of this example, class **Point** and class **Circle** are simplified.

Class **Point** (lines 1–31) contains two constructors, a finalizer, a **toString** method and **protected** instance variables **x** and **y**. The constructor and finalizer each print that they are executing then display the **Point** for which they are invoked. Note the use of **this** in the **System.out.println** calls to cause an implicit call to method **toString**. Notice the first line of the **finalize** method (line 23)

```
protected void finalize()
```

Method **finalize** should always be defined as **protected** so subclasses have access to the method but classes that simply use **Point** objects do not.

```
1   // Fig. 9.5: Point.java
2   // Definition of class Point
3   public class Point extends Object {
4      protected int x, y; // coordinates of the Point
5
6      // no-argument constructor
7      public Point()
8      {
9         x = 0;
10        y = 0;
11        System.out.println( "Point constructor: " + this );
12     }
13
14     // constructor
15     public Point( int a, int b )
16     {
17        x = a;
18        y = b;
19        System.out.println( "Point constructor: " + this );
20     }
21
22     // finalizer
23     protected void finalize()
24     {
25        System.out.println( "Point finalizer: " + this );
26     }
27
28     // convert the point into a String representation
29     public String toString()
30        { return "[" + x + ", " + y + "]"; }
31  }
```

Fig. 9.5   Order in which constructors and finalizers are called (part 1 of 4).

```
32  // Fig. 9.5: Circle.java
33  // Definition of class Circle
34  public class Circle extends Point {  // inherits from Point
35     protected double radius;
36
37     // no-argument constructor
38     public Circle()
39     {
40        // implicit call to superclass constructor here
41        radius = 0;
42        System.out.println( "Circle constructor: " + this );
43     }
44
45     // Constructor
46     public Circle( double r, int a, int b )
47     {
48        super( a, b );  // call the superclass constructor
49        radius = r;
```

Fig. 9.5   Order in which constructors and finalizers are called (part 2 of 4).

```
50              System.out.println( "Circle constructor: " + this );
51           }
52
53           // finalizer
54           protected void finalize()
55           {
56              System.out.println( "Circle finalizer: " + this );
57              super.finalize();  // call superclass finalize method
58           }
59
60           // convert the Circle to a String
61           public String toString()
62           {
63              return "Center = " + super.toString() +
64                     "; Radius = " + radius;
65           }
66        }
```

Fig. 9.5   Order in which constructors and finalizers are called (part 3 of 4).

```
67        // Fig. 9.5: Test.java
68        // Demonstrate when superclass and subclass
69        // constructors and finalizers are called.
70        public class Test {
71           public static void main( String args[] )
72           {
73              Circle circle1, circle2;
74
75              circle1 = new Circle( 4.5, 72, 29 );
76              circle2 = new Circle( 10, 5, 5 );
77
78              circle1 = null;  // mark for garbage collection
79              circle2 = null;  // mark for garbage collection
80
81              System.gc();     // call the garbage collector
82           }
83        }
```

```
Point constructor: Center = [72, 29]; Radius = 0.0
Circle constructor: Center = [72, 29]; Radius = 4.5
Point constructor: Center = [5, 5]; Radius = 0.0
Circle constructor: Center = [5, 5]; Radius = 10.0
Circle finalizer: Center = [72, 29]; Radius = 4.5
Point finalizer: Center = [72, 29]; Radius = 4.5
Circle finalizer: Center = [5, 5]; Radius = 10.0
Point finalizer: Center = [5, 5]; Radius = 10.0
```

Fig. 9.5   Order in which constructors and finalizers are called (part 4 of 4).

Class **Circle** (lines 32–66) derives from **Point** and contains two constructors, a finalizer, a **toString** method and protected instance variable **radius**. The constructor and finalizer each print that they are executing, then display the **Circle** for which they are invoked. Note that the **Circle** method **toString** invokes **Point**'s **toString** via **super** (line 63).

Common Programming Error 9.6

*When a superclass method is overridden in a subclass, it is common to have the subclass version call the superclass version and do some additional work. Not using the **super** reference to reference the superclass's method causes infinite recursion because the subclass method actually calls itself.*

Common Programming Error 9.7

*Cascading **super** references to refer to a member (method or variable) several levels up the hierarchy (as in **super.super.x**) is a syntax error.*

Good Programming Practice 9.1

*The last statement in a **finalize** method should always be **super.finalize();** to ensure that the superclass's **finalize** method is called.*

Lines 67–83 show an application that tests this **Point/Circle** inheritance hierarchy. The application begins in method **main** by instantiating **Circle** object **circle1** (line 75). This invokes the **Circle** constructor at line 46, which immediately invokes the **Point** constructor at line 15. The **Point** constructor outputs the values received from the **Circle** constructor by implicitly calling method **toString** and returns program control to the **Circle** constructor. Then the **Circle** constructor outputs the complete **Circle** by calling method **toString**. Notice that the first two lines of the output from this program both show values for **x**, **y** and **radius**. Polymorphism is once again causing the **Circle**'s **toString** method to execute because it is a **Circle** object that is being created. When **toString** is invoked from the **Point** constructor, **0.0** is displayed for the **radius** because the **radius** has not yet been initialized in the **Circle** constructor.

Circle object **circle2** is instantiated next. Again, the **Point** and **Circle** constructors both execute. Notice in the command-line output window that the body of the **Point** constructor is performed before the body of the **Circle** constructor, showing that objects are constructed "inside out."

Lines 78 and 79 set **circle1** to **null** then set **circle2** to **null**. Since each of these objects is no longer needed, Java marks the memory occupied by **circle1** and **circle2** for *garbage collection*. Java guarantees that before the garbage collector runs to reclaim the space for each of these objects, the **finalize** methods for each object will be called. The garbage collector is a low-priority thread that runs automatically whenever processor time is available. We choose here to ask the garbage collector to run with the call **System.gc()** in line 81. Java does not guarantee the order in which objects will be garbage collected; therefore, it cannot guarantee which object's finalizer will execute first. Notice in the command-line output window that both the **Circle** and **Point** **finalize** methods are called when each **Circle** object is garbage collected.

9.6 Implicit Subclass-Object-to-Superclass-Object Conversion

Despite the fact that a subclass object also "is a" superclass object, the subclass type and the superclass type are different. Subclass objects can be treated as superclass objects. This makes sense because the subclass has members corresponding to each of the superclass members—remember that the subclass normally has more members than the superclass has. Assignment in the other direction is not allowed because assigning a superclass object to a subclass reference would leave the additional subclass members undefined.

A reference to a subclass object may be implicitly converted into a reference to a superclass object because a subclass object *is a* superclass object through inheritance.

There are four possible ways to mix and match superclass references and subclass references with superclass objects and subclass objects:

1. Referring to a superclass object with a superclass reference is straightforward.

2. Referring to a subclass object with a subclass reference is straightforward.

3. Referring to a subclass object with a superclass reference is safe because the subclass object *is an* object of its superclass as well. Such code can only refer to superclass members. If this code refers to subclass-only members through the superclass reference, the compiler will report a syntax error.

4. Referring to a superclass object with a subclass reference is a syntax error. The subclass reference must first be cast to a superclass reference.

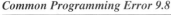

Common Programming Error 9.8

Assigning a subclass object to a superclass reference, and then attempting to reference subclass-only members with the superclass reference, is a syntax error.

As convenient as it may be to treat subclass objects as superclass objects, and to do this by manipulating all these objects with superclass references, there appears to be a problem. In a payroll system, for example, we would like to be able to walk through an array of employees and calculate the weekly pay for each person. But intuition suggests that using superclass references would enable the program to call only the superclass payroll calculation routine (if indeed there is such a routine in the superclass). We need a way to invoke the proper payroll calculation routine for each object, whether it is a superclass object or a subclass object, and to do this simply by using the superclass reference. Actually, this is precisely how Java behaves and is discussed in this chapter when we consider polymorphism and dynamic binding.

9.7 Software Engineering with Inheritance

We can use inheritance to customize existing software. When we use inheritance to create a new class from an existing class, the new class inherits the attributes and behaviors of an existing class, then we can add attributes and behaviors or override superclass behaviors to customize the class to meet our needs.

It can be difficult for students to appreciate the problems faced by designers and implementers on large-scale software projects in industry. People experienced on such projects will invariably state that a key to improving the software development process is encouraging software reuse. Object-oriented programming in general, and Java in particular, certainly does this.

It is the availability of substantial and useful class libraries that delivers the maximum benefits of software reuse through inheritance. As interest in Java grows, interest in Java class libraries will increase. Just as shrink-wrapped software produced by independent software vendors became an explosive growth industry with the arrival of the personal computer, so, too, will the creation and sale of Java class libraries. Application designers will build their applications with these libraries, and library designers will be rewarded by having their libraries wrapped with the applications. What we see coming is a massive worldwide commitment to the development of Java class libraries for a huge variety of applications arenas.

Software Engineering Observation 9.9

Creating a subclass does not affect its superclass's source code or the superclass's Java byte-codes; the integrity of a superclass is preserved by inheritance.

A superclass specifies commonality. All classes derived from a superclass inherit the capabilities of that superclass. In the object-oriented design process, the designer looks for commonality among a set of classes and factors it out to form desirable superclasses. Subclasses are then customized beyond the capabilities inherited from the superclass.

Software Engineering Observation 9.10

Just as the designer of non-object-oriented systems should avoid unnecessary proliferation of functions, the designer of object-oriented systems should avoid unnecessary proliferation of classes. Proliferating classes creates management problems and can hinder software reusability simply because it is more difficult for a potential user of a class to locate that class in a huge collection. The trade-off is to create fewer classes, each providing substantial additional functionality, but such classes might be too rich for certain users.

Performance Tip 9.1

If classes produced through inheritance are larger than they need to be, memory and processing resources may be wasted. Inherit from the class "closest" to what you need.

Note that reading a set of subclass declarations can be confusing because inherited members are not shown, but inherited members are nevertheless present in the subclasses. A similar problem can exist in the documentation of subclasses.

Software Engineering Observation 9.11

In an object-oriented system, classes are often closely related. "Factor out" common attributes and behaviors and place these in a superclass. Then use inheritance to form subclasses without having to repeat common attributes and behaviors.

Software Engineering Observation 9.12

Modifications to a superclass do not require subclasses to change as long as the public interface to the superclass remains unchanged.

9.8 Composition vs. Inheritance

We have discussed *is a* relationships that are implemented by inheritance. We have also discussed *has a* relationships (and seen examples in preceding chapters) in which a class may have objects of other classes as members—such relationships create new classes by *composition* of existing classes. For example, given the classes **Employee**, **BirthDate** and **TelephoneNumber**, it is improper to say that an **Employee** *is a* **BirthDate** or that an **Employee** *is a* **TelephoneNumber**. But it is certainly appropriate to say that an **Employee** *has a* **BirthDate** and that an **Employee** *has a* **TelephoneNumber**.

9.9 Case Study: Point, Circle, Cylinder

Now let us consider a substantial inheritance example. We consider a point, circle, cylinder hierarchy. First we develop and use class **Point** (Fig. 9.6). Then we present an example in which we derive class **Circle** from class **Point** (Fig. 9.7). Finally, we present an example in which we derive class **Cylinder** from class **Circle** (Fig. 9.8).

Figure 9.6 shows class **Point**. Part 1 is the class **Point** definition. Class **Point** is defined as part of package **com.deitel.jhtp3.ch09** (line 3). Note that **Point**'s instance variables are **protected**. Thus, when class **Circle** is derived from class **Point**, the methods of class **Circle** will be able to directly reference coordinates **x** and **y** rather than using access methods. This may result in better performance.

```
1   // Fig. 9.6: Point.java
2   // Definition of class Point
3   package com.deitel.jhtp3.ch09;
4
5   public class Point {
6      protected int x, y; // coordinates of the Point
7
8      // no-argument constructor
9      public Point() { setPoint( 0, 0 ); }
10
11     // constructor
12     public Point( int a, int b ) { setPoint( a, b ); }
13
14     // Set x and y coordinates of Point
15     public void setPoint( int a, int b )
16     {
17        x = a;
18        y = b;
19     }
20
21     // get x coordinate
22     public int getX() { return x; }
23
24     // get y coordinate
25     public int getY() { return y; }
26
27     // convert the point into a String representation
28     public String toString()
29        { return "[" + x + ", " + y + "]"; }
30  }
```

Fig. 9.6   Testing class **Point** (part 1 of 3).

```
31  // Fig. 9.6: Test.java
32  // Applet to test class Point
33  import javax.swing.JOptionPane;
34  import com.deitel.jhtp3.ch09.Point;
35
36  public class Test {
37     public static void main( String args[] )
38     {
39        Point p = new Point( 72, 115 );
```

Fig. 9.6   Testing class **Point** (part 2 of 3).

```
40          String output;
41
42          output = "X coordinate is " + p.getX() +
43                      "\nY coordinate is " + p.getY();
44
45          p.setPoint( 10, 10 );
46
47          // use implicit call to p.toString()
48          output += "\n\nThe new location of p is " + p;
49
50          JOptionPane.showMessageDialog( null, output,
51             "Demonstrating Class Point",
52             JOptionPane.INFORMATION_MESSAGE );
53          System.exit( 0 );
54       }
55    }
```

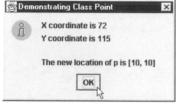

Fig. 9.6   Testing class **Point** (part 3 of 3).

Figure 9.6, part 2 shows a **Test** application for testing class **Point**. The **main** method must use **getX** and **getY** to read the values of **protected** instance variables **x** and **y**. Remember that **protected** instance variables are accessible only to methods of their class, their subclasses and other classes in the same package. Also, note the implicit call to **toString** when **p** is added to a **String** at line 48.

In our next example, the **Point** class definition from Fig. 9.6 is imported, so the class definition is not shown again. Part 1 of Fig. 9.7 shows the **Circle** class definition with the **Circle** method definitions. Part 2 shows a **Test** application.

```
1   // Fig. 9.7: Circle.java
2   // Definition of class Circle
3   package com.deitel.jhtp3.ch09;
4
5   public class Circle extends Point {   // inherits from Point
6      protected double radius;
7
8      // no-argument constructor
9      public Circle()
10     {
11        // implicit call to superclass constructor
12        setRadius( 0 );
13     }
14
```

Fig. 9.7   Testing class **Circle** (part 1 of 4).

```
15        // Constructor
16        public Circle( double r, int a, int b )
17        {
18            super( a, b );  // call the superclass constructor
19            setRadius( r );
20        }
21
22        // Set radius of Circle
23        public void setRadius( double r )
24            { radius = ( r >= 0.0 ? r : 0.0 ); }
25
26        // Get radius of Circle
27        public double getRadius() { return radius; }
28
29        // Calculate area of Circle
30        public double area()
31            { return Math.PI * radius * radius; }
32
33        // convert the Circle to a String
34        public String toString()
35        {
36            return "Center = " + super.toString() +
37                    "; Radius = " + radius;
38        }
39    }
```

Fig. 9.7   Testing class **Circle** (part 2 of 4).

```
40    // Fig. 9.7: Test.java
41    // Applet to test class Circle
42    import javax.swing.JOptionPane;
43    import java.text.DecimalFormat;
44    import com.deitel.jhtp3.ch09.Circle;
45
46    public class Test {
47        public static void main( String args[] )
48        {
49            Circle c = new Circle( 2.5, 37, 43 );
50            DecimalFormat precision2 = new DecimalFormat( "0.00" );
51            String output;
52
53            output = "X coordinate is " + c.getX() +
54                    "\nY coordinate is " + c.getY() +
55                    "\nRadius is " + c.getRadius();
56
57            c.setRadius( 4.25 );
58            c.setPoint( 2, 2 );
59            output +=
60                "\n\nThe new location and radius of c are\n" + c +
61                "\nArea is " + precision2.format( c.area() );
62
```

Fig. 9.7   Testing class **Circle** (part 3 of 4).

```
63              JOptionPane.showMessageDialog( null, output,
64                  "Demonstrating Class Circle",
65                  JOptionPane.INFORMATION_MESSAGE );
66          System.exit( 0 );
67      }
68  }
```

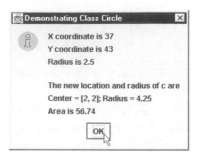

Fig. 9.7   Testing class **Circle** (part 4 of 4).

Note that class **Circle extends** class **Point**. This means that the **public** interface to **Circle** includes the **Point** methods as well as the **Circle** methods **setRadius**, **getRadius**, **area**, **toString** and the **Circle** constructors. Application **Test** instantiates an object of class **Circle** (line 49), then uses *get* methods to obtain the information about the **Circle** object. Method **main** indirectly references the **protected** data of class **Circle** through method calls. Method **main** then uses *set* methods **setRadius** and **setPoint** to reset the radius and coordinates of the center of the circle. Finally, **main** displays the **Circle** object **c** and calculates and displays its area.

Our last example is shown in Fig. 9.8. The **Circle** class definition of Fig. 9.7 is imported here. Part 1 shows the **Cylinder** class definition with the **Cylinder** method definitions. Part 2 is a **Test** application to test the **Cylinder** class.

Note that class **Cylinder extends** class **Circle**. This means that the **public** interface to **Cylinder** includes the **Circle** methods and **Point** methods as well as the **Cylinder** constructor and **Cylinder** methods **setHeight**, **getHeight**, **area** (which overrides the **Circle area** method), **volume** and **toString**. The **Test** application's **main** method instantiates an object of class **Cylinder** (line 54), then uses *get* methods (lines 58–61) to obtain information about the **Cylinder** object. Again, the **Test** applications's **main** method cannot directly reference the **protected** data of class **Cylinder**. Method **main** uses *set* methods **setHeight**, **setRadius** and **setPoint** to reset the **height**, **radius** and coordinates of the **Cylinder**. Then **main** uses **toString**, **area** and **volume** to print the attributes and some facts about the **Cylinder**.

This example nicely demonstrates inheritance and defining and referencing **protected** instance variables. The reader should now be confident with the basics of inheritance. In the next several sections, we show how to program with inheritance hierarchies in a general manner using polymorphism. Data abstraction, inheritance and polymorphism are the crux of object-oriented programming.

```
1   // Fig. 9.8: Cylinder.java
2   // Definition of class Cylinder
3   package com.deitel.jhtp3.ch09;
4
5   public class Cylinder extends Circle {
6      protected double height;   // height of Cylinder
7
8      // No-argument constructor
9      public Cylinder()
10     {
11        // implicit call to superclass constructor here
12        setHeight( 0 );
13     }
14
15     // constructor
16     public Cylinder( double h, double r, int a, int b )
17     {
18        super( r, a, b );
19        setHeight( h );
20     }
21
22     // Set height of Cylinder
23     public void setHeight( double h )
24        { height = ( h >= 0 ? h : 0 ); }
25
26     // Get height of Cylinder
27     public double getHeight() { return height; }
28
29     // Calculate area of Cylinder (i.e., surface area)
30     public double area()
31     {
32        return 2 * super.area() +
33               2 * Math.PI * radius * height;
34     }
35
36     // Calculate volume of Cylinder
37     public double volume() { return super.area() * height; }
38
39     // Convert the Cylinder to a String
40     public String toString()
41     {
42        return super.toString() + "; Height = " + height;
43     }
44  }
```

Fig. 9.8   Testing class **Cylinder** (part 1 of 3).

```
45   // Fig. 9.8: Test.java
46   // Application to test class Cylinder
47   import javax.swing.JOptionPane;
48   import java.text.DecimalFormat;
49   import com.deitel.jhtp3.ch09.Cylinder;
```

Fig. 9.8   Testing class **Cylinder** (part 2 of 3).

```
50
51   public class Test {
52      public static void main( String args[] )
53      {
54          Cylinder c = new Cylinder( 5.7, 2.5, 12, 23 );
55          DecimalFormat precision2 = new DecimalFormat( "0.00" );
56          String output;
57
58          output = "X coordinate is " + c.getX() +
59                      "\nY coordinate is " + c.getY() +
60                      "\nRadius is " + c.getRadius() +
61                      "\nHeight is " + c.getHeight();
62
63          c.setHeight( 10 );
64          c.setRadius( 4.25 );
65          c.setPoint( 2, 2 );
66
67          output +=
68              "\n\nThe new location, radius " +
69              "and height of c are\n" + c +
70              "\nArea is " + precision2.format( c.area() ) +
71              "\nVolume is " + precision2.format( c.volume() );
72
73          JOptionPane.showMessageDialog( null, output,
74              "Demonstrating Class Cylinder",
75              JOptionPane.INFORMATION_MESSAGE );
76          System.exit( 0 );
77      }
78   }
```

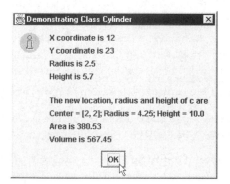

Fig. 9.8   Testing class **Cylinder** (part 3 of 3).

9.10 Introduction to Polymorphism

With *polymorphism*, it is possible to design and implement systems that are more easily *extensible*. Programs can be written to process generically—as superclass objects—objects of all existing classes in a hierarchy. Classes that do not exist during program development can be added with little or no modifications to the generic part of the program—as long as those classes are part of the hierarchy that is being processed generically. The only parts of a program that need modification are those parts that require direct knowledge of the particular class that is added to the hierarchy. We will study two substantial class hierarchies and will show how objects throughout those hierarchies are manipulated polymorphically.

9.11 Type Fields and `switch` Statements

One means of dealing with objects of many different types is to use a **switch** statement to take an appropriate action on each object based on that object's type. For example, in a hierarchy of shapes in which each shape has a **shapeType** instance variable, a **switch** structure could determine which **print** method to call based on the object's **shapeType**.

There are many problems with using **switch** logic. The programmer might forget to make such a type test when one is warranted. The programmer may forget to test all possible cases in a **switch**. If a **switch**-based system is modified by adding new types, the programmer might forget to insert the new cases in existing **switch** statements. Every addition or deletion of a class demands that every **switch** statement in the system be modified; tracking these down can be time consuming and error prone.

As we will see, polymorphic programming can eliminate the need for **switch** logic. The programmer can use Java's polymorphism mechanism to perform the equivalent logic automatically, thus avoiding the kinds of errors typically associated with **switch** logic.

Testing and Debugging Tip 9.2

An interesting consequence of using polymorphism is that programs take on a simplified appearance. They contain less branching logic in favor of simpler sequential code. This simplification facilitates testing, debugging, and program maintenance.

9.12 Dynamic Method Binding

Suppose a set of shape classes such as **Circle**, **Triangle**, **Rectangle**, **Square**, etc. are all derived from superclass **Shape**. In object-oriented programming, each of these classes might be endowed with the ability to draw itself. Each class has its own **draw** method, and the **draw** method implementation for each shape is quite different. When drawing a shape, whatever that shape may be, it would be nice to be able to treat all these shapes generically as objects of the superclass **Shape**. Then to draw any shape, we could simply call method **draw** of superclass **Shape** and let the program determine dynamically (i.e., at execution time) which subclass **draw** method to use based on the actual object's type.

To enable this kind of behavior, we declare **draw** in the superclass, and then we override **draw** in each of the subclasses to draw the appropriate shape.

Software Engineering Observation 9.13

When a subclass chooses not to redefine a method, the subclass simply inherits its immediate superclass's method definition.

If we use a superclass reference to refer to a subclass object and invoke the **draw** method, the program will choose the correct subclass's **draw** method dynamically (i.e., at execution time). This is called *dynamic method binding* and will be illustrated in the case studies later in this chapter.

9.13 `final` Methods and Classes

We saw in Chapter 7 that variables can be declared **final** to indicate that they cannot be modified after they are declared and that they must be initialized when they are declared. It is also possible to define methods and classes with the **final** modifier.

A method that is declared **final** cannot be overridden in a subclass. Methods that are declared **static** and methods that are declared **private** are implicitly **final**. Because a **final** method's definition can never change, the compiler can optimize the program by removing calls to **final** methods and replacing them with the expanded code of their definitions at each method call location—a technique known as *inlining the code.*

A class that is declared **final** cannot be a superclass (i.e., a class cannot inherit from a **final** class). All methods in a **final** class are implicitly **final**.

Performance Tip 9.2

*The compiler can decide to inline a **final** method call and will do so for small, simple **final** methods. Inlining does not violate encapsulation or information hiding (but does improve performance because it eliminates the overhead of making a method call).*

Performance Tip 9.3

*Pipelined processors can improve performance by executing portions of the next several instructions simultaneously, but not if those instructions follow a method call. Inlining (which the compiler can perform on a **final** method) can improve performance in these processors because it eliminates the out-of-line transfer of control associated with a method call.*

Software Engineering Observation 9.14

*A class declared **final** cannot be extended and every method is implicitly **final**.*

9.14 Abstract Superclasses and Concrete Classes

When we think of a class as a type, we assume that objects of that type will be instantiated. However, there are cases in which it is useful to define classes for which the programmer never intends to instantiate any objects. Such classes are called *abstract classes.* Because these are used as superclasses in inheritance situations, we will normally refer to them as *abstract superclasses.* No objects of abstract superclasses can be instantiated.

The sole purpose of an abstract class is to provide an appropriate superclass from which other classes may inherit interface and/or implementation (we will see examples of each shortly). Classes from which objects can be instantiated are called *concrete classes.*

We could have an abstract superclass **TwoDimensionalObject** and derive concrete classes such as **Square**, **Circle**, **Triangle**, etc. We could also have an abstract superclass **ThreeDimensionalObject** and derive concrete classes such as **Cube**, **Sphere**, **Cylinder**, etc. Abstract superclasses are too generic to define real objects; we need to be more specific before we can think of instantiating objects. For example, if someone tells you to "draw the shape," what shape would you draw? Concrete classes provide the specifics that make it reasonable to instantiate objects.

A class is made abstract by declaring it with keyword **abstract**. A hierarchy does not need to contain any **abstract** classes, but as we will see, many good object-oriented systems have class hierarchies headed by **abstract** superclasses. In some cases, **abstract** classes constitute the top few levels of the hierarchy. A good example of this is the shape hierarchy in Fig. 9.2. The hierarchy begins with **abstract** superclass **Shape**. On the next level down we have two more **abstract** superclasses, namely **TwoDimensionalShape** and **ThreeDimensionalShape**. The next level down would start defining concrete classes for two-dimensional shapes such as **Circle** and **Square**, and concrete classes for three-dimensional shapes such as **Sphere** and **Cube**.

9.15 Polymorphism Examples

Here is an example of polymorphism. If class **Rectangle** is derived from class **Quadrilateral**, then a **Rectangle** object *is a* more specific version of a **Quadrilateral** object. An operation (such as calculating the perimeter or the area) that can be performed on an object of class **Quadrilateral** can also be performed on an object of class **Rectangle**. Such operations can also be performed on other "kinds of" **Quadrilateral**s, such as **Square**s, **Parallelogram**s and **Trapezoid**s. When a request is made through a superclass reference to use a method, Java chooses the correct overridden method polymorphically in the appropriate subclass associated with the object.

Here is another example of polymorphism. Suppose we have a video game that manipulates objects of many varieties, including objects of class **Martian, Venutian, Plutonian, SpaceShip, LaserBeam** and the like. Each of these classes extends a common superclass like **GamePiece** that contains a method called **drawYourself**. This method is defined by each subclass. A Java screen manager program would simply maintain some kind of container (such as a **GamePiece** array) of references to objects of these various classes. To refresh the screen periodically the screen manager would simply send each object the same message, namely **drawYourself**. Each object would respond in its own unique way. A **Martian** object would draw itself with the appropriate number of antennae. A **SpaceShip** object would draw itself bright and silvery. A **LaserBeam** object would draw itself as a bright red beam across the screen. Thus, the same message sent to a variety of objects would take on "many forms"—hence the term *polymorphism*.

Such a polymorphic screen manager makes it especially easy to add new types of objects to a system with minimal impact. Suppose we want to add **Mercurian**s to our video game. We certainly have to build a new class **Mercurian** that extends **GamePiece** and provides its own definition of the **drawYourself** method. Then when objects of class **Mercurian** appear in the container, the screen manager need not be modified. It simply sends the message **drawYourself** to every object in the container regardless of the object's type, so the new **Mercurian** objects just "fit right in." Thus, with polymorphism, new types of objects not even envisioned when a system is created may be added without modifications to the system (other than the new class itself, of course).

Through the use of polymorphism, one method call can cause different actions to occur depending on the type of the object receiving the call. This gives the programmer tremendous expressive capability. We will see examples of the power of polymorphism in the next several sections.

Software Engineering Observation 9.15

With polymorphism, the programmer can deal in generalities and let the execution-time environment concern itself with the specifics. The programmer can command a wide variety of objects to behave in manners appropriate to those objects without even knowing the types of those objects.

Software Engineering Observation 9.16

Polymorphism promotes extensibility: Software written to invoke polymorphic behavior is written independent of the types of the objects to which messages (i.e., method calls) are sent. Thus, new types of objects that can respond to existing messages can be added into such a system without modifying the base system.

Software Engineering Observation 9.17

*If a method is declared **final** it cannot be overridden in subclasses, so that method calls may not be sent polymorphically to objects of those subclasses. The method call may still be sent to subclasses but they will all respond identically rather than polymorphically.*

Software Engineering Observation 9.18

*An **abstract** class defines a common interface for the various members of a class hierarchy. The **abstract** class contains methods that will be defined in the subclasses. All classes in the hierarchy can use this same interface through polymorphism.*

Although we cannot instantiate objects of **abstract** superclasses, we *can* declare references to **abstract** superclasses. Such references can be used to enable polymorphic manipulations of subclass objects when such objects are instantiated from concrete classes.

Let us consider more applications of polymorphism. A screen manager needs to display a variety of objects, including new types of objects that will be added to the system even after the screen manager is written. The system may need to display various shapes (i.e., the superclass is **Shape**) such as **Circle**, **Triangle**, **Rectangle**, etc. (each shape class is derived from superclass **Shape**). The screen manager uses superclass references (to **Shape**) to manage the objects to be displayed. To draw any object (regardless of the level at which that object appears in the inheritance hierarchy), the screen manager uses a superclass reference to the object and simply sends a **draw** message to the object. Method **draw** has been declared **abstract** in superclass **Shape** and has been overridden in each of the subclasses. Each **Shape** object knows how to draw itself. The screen manager does not have to worry about what type each object is or whether the screen manager has seen objects of that type before—the screen manager simply tells each object to **draw** itself.

Polymorphism is particularly effective for implementing layered software systems. In operating systems, for example, each type of physical device may operate quite differently from the others. Even so, commands to *read* or *write* data from and to devices can have a certain uniformity. The *write* message sent to a device-driver object needs to be interpreted specifically in the context of that device driver and how that device driver manipulates devices of a specific type. However, the *write* call itself is really no different from the *write* to any other device in the system—simply place some number of bytes from memory onto that device. An object-oriented operating system might use an **abstract** superclass to provide an interface appropriate for all device drivers. Then, through inheritance from that **abstract** superclass, subclasses are formed that all operate similarly. The capabilities (i.e., the **public** interface) offered by the device drivers are provided as **abstract** methods in the **abstract** superclass. The implementations of these **abstract** methods are provided in the subclasses that correspond to the specific types of device drivers.

It is common in object-oriented programming to define an *iterator class* that can walk through all the objects in a container (such as an array). If you want to print a list of objects in a linked list, for example, an iterator object can be instantiated that will return the next element of the linked list each time the iterator is called. Iterators are commonly used in polymorphic programming to walk through an array or a linked list of objects from various levels of a hierarchy. The references in such a list would all be superclass references (see Chapter 22, "Data Structures," for more on linked lists). A list of objects of superclass class **TwoDimensionalShape** could contain objects from the classes **Square**, **Circle**, **Triangle**, etc. Sending a **draw** message to each object in the list would, using polymorphism, draw the correct picture on the screen.

9.16 Case Study: A Payroll System Using Polymorphism

Let us use **abstract** classes, **abstract** methods and polymorphism to perform payroll calculations based on the type of employee (Fig. 9.9). We use an **abstract** superclass **Employee**. The subclasses of **Employee** are **Boss** (paid a fixed weekly salary regardless of the number of hours worked), **CommissionWorker** (paid a flat base salary plus a percentage of sales), **PieceWorker** (paid by the number of items produced) and **HourlyWorker** (paid by the hour and receives overtime pay). Each subclass of **Employee** has been declared **final** because we do not intend to inherit from them again.

An **earnings** method call certainly applies generically to all employees. But the way each person's earnings are calculated depends on the class of the employee, and these classes are all derived from the superclass **Employee**. So **earnings** is declared **abstract** in superclass **Employee** and appropriate implementations of **earnings** are provided for each of the subclasses. Then, to calculate any employee's earnings, the program simply uses a superclass reference to that employee's object and invokes the **earnings** method. In a real payroll system, the various **Employee** objects might be referenced by individual elements in an array of **Employee** references. The program would simply walk through the array one element at a time using the **Employee** references to invoke the **earnings** method of each object.

Software Engineering Observation 9.19

*If a subclass is derived from a superclass with an **abstract** method, and if no definition is supplied in the subclass for that **abstract** method (i.e., if that method is not overridden in the subclass), that method remains **abstract** in the subclass. Consequently, the subclass is also an **abstract** class and must be explicitly declared as an **abstract** class.*

Software Engineering Observation 9.20

*The ability to declare an **abstract** method gives the class designer considerable power over how subclasses will be implemented in a class hierarchy. Any new class that wants to inherit from this class is forced to override the **abstract** method (either directly or by inheriting from a class that has overridden the method). Otherwise, that new class will contain an **abstract** method and thus be an **abstract** class unable to instantiate objects.*

Software Engineering Observation 9.21

*An **abstract** can still have instance data and non-**abstract** methods subject to the normal rules of inheritance by subclasses. An **abstract** class can also have constructors.*

Common Programming Error 9.9

*Attempting to instantiate an object of an **abstract** class (i.e., a class that contains one or more **abstract** methods) is a syntax error.*

Common Programming Error 9.10

*It is a syntax error if a class with one or more **abstract** methods is not explicitly declared **abstract**.*

Let us consider the **Employee** class (Fig. 9.9, lines 1–28). The **public** methods include a constructor that takes the first name and last name as arguments; a **getFirstName** method that returns the first name; a **getLastName** method that returns the last name; a **toString** method that returns the first name and last name separated by a space; and an **abstract** method—**earnings**. Why is this method **abstract**? The answer is that it does not make sense to provide an implementation of this method in the **Employee** class. We cannot calculate the earnings for a generic employee—we must first know *what kind of* employee it is. By making this method **abstract** we are indicating that we will provide an implementation in each concrete subclass, but not in the superclass itself.

Class **Boss** (Fig. 9.9, lines 29–54) is derived from **Employee**. The **public** methods include a constructor that takes a first name, a last name and a weekly salary as arguments, and passes the first name and last name to the **Employee** constructor to initialize the **firstName** and **lastName** members of the superclass part of the subclass object. Other **public** methods include a **setWeeklySalary** method to assign a new value to **private** instance variable **weeklySalary**; an **earnings** method defining how to calculate a **Boss**'s earnings; and a **toString** method that forms a **String** containing the type of the employee (i.e., **"Boss: "**) followed by the boss's name.

Class **CommissionWorker** (Fig. 9.9, lines 55–94) is derived from **Employee**. The **public** methods include a constructor that takes a first name, a last name, a salary, a commission and a quantity of items sold as arguments, and passes the first name and last name to the **Employee** constructor; *set* methods to assign new values to instance variables **salary**, **commission** and **quantity**; an **earnings** method to calculate a **CommissionWorker**'s earnings; and a **toString** method that forms a **String** containing the employee type (i.e., **"Commission worker: "**) followed by the worker's name.

```
1   // Fig. 9.9: Employee.java
2   // Abstract base class Employee
3
4   public abstract class Employee {
5      private String firstName;
6      private String lastName;
7
8      // Constructor
9      public Employee( String first, String last )
10     {
11        firstName = first;
12        lastName = last;
13     }
14
15     // Return the first name
16     public String getFirstName() { return firstName; }
17
18     // Return the last name
19     public String getLastName() { return lastName; }
20
21     public String toString()
22        { return firstName + ' ' + lastName; }
23
24     // Abstract method that must be implemented for each
25     // derived class of Employee from which objects
26     // are instantiated.
27     public abstract double earnings();
28  }
```

Fig. 9.9   **Employee** class hierarchy using an **abstract** superclass (part 1 of 10).

```
29   // Fig. 9.9: Boss.java
30   // Boss class derived from Employee
31
32   public final class Boss extends Employee {
33      private double weeklySalary;
34
35      // Constructor for class Boss
36      public Boss( String first, String last, double s)
37      {
38         super( first, last );   // call superclass constructor
39         setWeeklySalary( s );
40      }
41
42      // Set the Boss's salary
43      public void setWeeklySalary( double s )
44         { weeklySalary = ( s > 0 ? s : 0 ); }
45
46      // Get the Boss's pay
47      public double earnings() { return weeklySalary; }
48
49      // Print the Boss's name
50      public String toString()
51      {
52         return "Boss: " + super.toString();
53      }
54   }
```

Fig. 9.9   **Employee** class hierarchy using an **abstract** superclass (part 2 of 10).

```
55   // Fig. 9.9: CommissionWorker.java
56   // CommissionWorker class derived from Employee
57
58   public final class CommissionWorker extends Employee {
59      private double salary;       // base salary per week
60      private double commission;   // amount per item sold
61      private int quantity;        // total items sold for week
62
63      // Constructor for class CommissionWorker
64      public CommissionWorker( String first, String last,
65                               double s, double c, int q)
66      {
67         super( first, last );   // call superclass constructor
68         setSalary( s );
69         setCommission( c );
70         setQuantity( q );
71      }
72
73      // Set CommissionWorker's weekly base salary
74      public void setSalary( double s )
75         { salary = ( s > 0 ? s : 0 ); }
76
```

Fig. 9.9   **Employee** class hierarchy using an **abstract** superclass (part 3 of 10).

```
77      // Set CommissionWorker's commission
78      public void setCommission( double c )
79          { commission = ( c > 0 ? c : 0 ); }
80
81      // Set CommissionWorker's quantity sold
82      public void setQuantity( int q )
83          { quantity = ( q > 0 ? q : 0 ); }
84
85      // Determine CommissionWorker's earnings
86      public double earnings()
87          { return salary + commission * quantity; }
88
89      // Print the CommissionWorker's name
90      public String toString()
91      {
92          return "Commission worker: " + super.toString();
93      }
94  }
```

Fig. 9.9   **Employee** class hierarchy using an **abstract** superclass (part 4 of 10).

Class **PieceWorker** (Fig. 9.9, lines 95–127) is derived from **Employee**. The **public** methods include a constructor that takes a first name, a last name, a wage per piece and a quantity of items produced as arguments, and passes the first name and last name to the **Employee** constructor; *set* methods to assign new values to instance variables **wagePerPiece** and **quantity**; an **earnings** method defining how to calculate a **PieceWorker**'s earnings; and a **toString** method that forms a **String** containing the type of the employee (i.e., **"Piece worker: "**) followed by the pieceworker's name.

```
95   // Fig. 9.9: PieceWorker.java
96   // PieceWorker class derived from Employee
97
98   public final class PieceWorker extends Employee {
99      private double wagePerPiece; // wage per piece output
100     private int quantity;         // output for week
101
102     // Constructor for class PieceWorker
103     public PieceWorker( String first, String last,
104                         double w, int q )
105     {
106         super( first, last );  // call superclass constructor
107         setWage( w );
108         setQuantity( q );
109     }
110
111     // Set the wage
112     public void setWage( double w )
113         { wagePerPiece = ( w > 0 ? w : 0 ); }
114
```

Fig. 9.9   **Employee** class hierarchy using an **abstract** superclass (part 5 of 10).

```
115     // Set the number of items output
116     public void setQuantity( int q )
117        { quantity = ( q > 0 ? q : 0 ); }
118
119     // Determine the PieceWorker's earnings
120     public double earnings()
121        { return quantity * wagePerPiece; }
122
123     public String toString()
124     {
125        return "Piece worker: " + super.toString();
126     }
127  }
```

Fig. 9.9   **Employee** class hierarchy using an **abstract** superclass (part 6 of 10).

Class **HourlyWorker** (Fig. 9.9, lines 128–159) is derived from **Employee**. The **public** methods include a constructor that takes a first name, a last name, a wage and the number of hours worked as arguments, and passes the first name and last name to the **Employee** constructor; *set* methods to assign new values to instance variables **wage** and **hours**; an **earnings** method defining how to calculate an **HourlyWorker**'s earnings; and a **toString** method that forms a **String** containing the type of the employee (i.e., **"Hourly worker: "**) followed by the hourly worker's name.

```
128  // Fig. 9.9: HourlyWorker.java
129  // Definition of class HourlyWorker
130
131  public final class HourlyWorker extends Employee {
132     private double wage;    // wage per hour
133     private double hours;   // hours worked for week
134
135     // Constructor for class HourlyWorker
136     public HourlyWorker( String first, String last,
137                           double w, double h )
138     {
139        super( first, last );   // call superclass constructor
140        setWage( w );
141        setHours( h );
142     }
143
144     // Set the wage
145     public void setWage( double w )
146        { wage = ( w > 0 ? w : 0 ); }
147
148     // Set the hours worked
149     public void setHours( double h )
150        { hours = ( h >= 0 && h < 168 ? h : 0 ); }
151
152     // Get the HourlyWorker's pay
153     public double earnings() { return wage * hours; }
```

Fig. 9.9   **Employee** class hierarchy using an **abstract** superclass (part 7 of 10).

```
154
155     public String toString()
156     {
157        return "Hourly worker: " + super.toString();
158     }
159  }
```

Fig. 9.9   **Employee** class hierarchy using an **abstract** superclass (part 8 of 10).

Method **main** of the **Test** application (Fig. 9.9, lines 160–211) begins by declaring **Employee** reference, **ref**. Each of the types of **Employee**s is handled similarly in **main**, so we will discuss only the case in which **main** deals with a **Boss** object.

```
160  // Fig. 9.9: Test.java
161  // Driver for Employee hierarchy
162  import javax.swing.JOptionPane;
163  import java.text.DecimalFormat;
164
165  public class Test {
166     public static void main( String args[] )
167     {
168        Employee ref;  // superclass reference
169        String output = "";
170
171        Boss b = new Boss( "John", "Smith", 800.00 );
172        CommissionWorker c =
173           new CommissionWorker( "Sue", "Jones",
174                                    400.0, 3.0, 150);
175        PieceWorker p =
176           new PieceWorker( "Bob", "Lewis", 2.5, 200 );
177        HourlyWorker h =
178           new HourlyWorker( "Karen", "Price", 13.75, 40 );
179
180        DecimalFormat precision2 = new DecimalFormat( "0.00" );
181
182        ref = b;  // Employee reference to a Boss
183        output += ref.toString() + " earned $" +
184                    precision2.format( ref.earnings() ) + "\n" +
185                    b.toString() + " earned $" +
186                    precision2.format( b.earnings() ) + "\n";
187
188        ref = c;  // Employee reference to a CommissionWorker
189        output += ref.toString() + " earned $" +
190                    precision2.format( ref.earnings() ) + "\n" +
191                    c.toString() + " earned $" +
192                    precision2.format( c.earnings() ) + "\n";
193
194        ref = p;  // Employee reference to a PieceWorker
```

Fig. 9.9   **Employee** class hierarchy using an **abstract** superclass (part 9 of 10).

```
195          output += ref.toString() + " earned $" +
196                   precision2.format( ref.earnings() ) + "\n" +
197                   p.toString() + " earned $" +
198                   precision2.format( p.earnings() ) + "\n";
199
200          ref = h;  // Employee reference to an HourlyWorker
201          output += ref.toString() + " earned $" +
202                   precision2.format( ref.earnings() ) + "\n" +
203                   h.toString() + " earned $" +
204                   precision2.format( h.earnings() ) + "\n";
205
206          JOptionPane.showMessageDialog( null, output,
207             "Demonstrating Polymorphism",
208             JOptionPane.INFORMATION_MESSAGE );
209          System.exit( 0 );
210       }
211    }
```

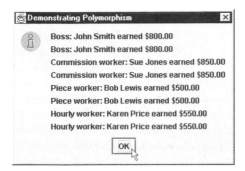

Fig. 9.9   **Employee** class hierarchy using an **abstract** superclass (part 10 of 10).

Line 171

```
Boss b = new Boss ("John", "Smith", 800.00);
```

instantiates subclass object class **Boss** and provides various constructor arguments, including a first name, a last name and a fixed weekly salary. The new object is assigned to **Boss** reference **b**.

Line 182

```
ref = b;  // Employee reference to a Boss
```

assigns to superclass **Employee** reference **ref** a reference to the subclass **Boss** object to which **b** refers. This is precisely what we must do to effect polymorphic behavior.

The method call in line 183

```
ref.toString()
```

invokes the **toString** method of the object referenced by **ref**. The system determines that the referenced object is a **Boss** and invokes subclass **Boss**'s **toString** method—precisely what we call polymorphic behavior. This method call is an example of dynamic method binding—the decision as to what method to invoke is deferred until execution time.

The method call in line 184

```
ref.earnings()
```

invokes the **earnings** method of the object to which **ref** refers. The system determines that the object is a **Boss** and invokes the subclass **Boss**'s **earnings** method rather than the superclass's **earnings** method. This is also an example of dynamic method binding.

The method call in line 185

```
b.toString()
```

explicitly invokes the **Boss** version of method **toString** by using the dot member selection operator off the specific **Boss** reference **b**. This call is included for comparison purposes to ensure that the dynamically bound method invoked with **ref.toString()** was indeed the proper method.

The method call in line 186

```
b.earnings()
```

explicitly invokes the **Boss** version of method **earnings** by using the dot member selection operator with the specific **Boss** reference **b**. This call is also included for comparison purposes to ensure that the dynamically bound method invoked with **ref.earnings()** was indeed the proper method.

To prove that the superclass reference **ref** can be used to invoke **toString** and **earnings** for the other types of employees, lines 188, 194 and 200 each assign a different type of employee object (**CommissionWorker**, **PieceWorker** and **HourlyWorker**, respectively) to the superclass reference **ref**, then the two methods are called after each assignment to show that Java is always capable of determining the type of the referenced object before invoking a method.

9.17 New Classes and Dynamic Binding

Polymorphism certainly works nicely when all possible classes are known in advance. But it also works when new kinds of classes are added to systems.

New classes are accommodated by dynamic method binding (also called *late binding*). An object's type need not be known at compile time for a polymorphic call to be compiled. At execution time, the call is matched with the method of the called object.

A screen manager program can now handle (without recompilation) new types of display objects as they are added to the system. The **draw** method call remains the same. The new objects themselves each contain a **draw** method implementing the actual drawing capabilities. This makes it easy to add new capabilities to systems with minimal impact. It also promotes software reuse.

Performance Tip 9.4

Polymorphism as implemented with dynamic method binding is efficient.

Performance Tip 9.5

*The kinds of polymorphic manipulations made possible with dynamic binding can also be accomplished by using hand-coded **switch** logic based on type fields in objects. The polymorphic code generated by the Java compiler runs with comparable performance to efficiently coded **switch** logic.*

9.18 Case Study: Inheriting Interface and Implementation

Our next example (Fig. 9.10) reexamines the **Point**, **Circle**, **Cylinder** hierarchy except that we now head the hierarchy with **abstract** superclass **Shape**. This hierarchy mechanically demonstrates the power of polymorphism. In the exercises, we explore a more realistic hierarchy of shapes.

Shape contains **abstract** method **getName** so **Shape** must be declared an **abstract** superclass. **Shape** contains two other methods, **area** and **volume**, each of which has an implementation that returns zero by default. **Point** inherits these implementations from **Shape**. This makes sense because both the area and volume of a point are zero. **Circle** inherits the **volume** method from **Point**, but **Circle** provides its own implementation for the **area** method. **Cylinder** provides its own implementations for both the **area** (interpreted as the surface area of the cylinder) and **volume** methods.

In this example, class **Shape** is used to define a set of methods that all **Shape**s in our hierarchy have in common. Defining these methods in class **Shape** enables us to generically call these methods through a **Shape** reference. Remember, the only methods that can be called through any reference are those **public** methods defined in the reference's declared class type and any **public** methods inherited into that class. Thus, we can call **Object** and **Shape** methods through a **Shape** reference.

Note that although **Shape** is an **abstract** superclass, it still contains implementations of methods **area** and **volume**, and these implementations are inheritable. The **Shape** class provides an inheritable interface (set of services) in the form of three methods that all classes of the hierarchy will contain. The **Shape** class also provides some implementations that subclasses in the first few levels of the hierarchy will use.

This case study emphasizes that a subclass can inherit interface and/or implementation from a superclass.

Software Engineering Observation 9.22

Hierarchies designed for implementation inheritance tend to have their functionality high in the hierarchy—each new subclass inherits one or more methods that were defined in a superclass and uses the superclass definitions.

Software Engineering Observation 9.23

Hierarchies designed for interface inheritance tend to have their functionality lower in the hierarchy—a superclass specifies one or more methods that should be called identically for each object in the hierarchy (i.e., they have the same signature), but the individual subclasses provide their own implementations of the method(s).

```
1   // Fig. 9.10: Shape.java
2   // Definition of abstract base class Shape
3
4   public abstract class Shape extends Object {
5       public double area() { return 0.0; }
6       public double volume() { return 0.0; }
7       public abstract String getName();
8   }
```

Fig. 9.10 Shape, point, circle, cylinder hierarchy (part 1 of 8).

```
9   // Fig. 9.10: Point.java
10  // Definition of class Point
11
12  public class Point extends Shape {
13     protected int x, y; // coordinates of the Point
14
15     // no-argument constructor
16     public Point() { setPoint( 0, 0 ); }
17
18     // constructor
19     public Point( int a, int b ) { setPoint( a, b ); }
20
21     // Set x and y coordinates of Point
22     public void setPoint( int a, int b )
23     {
24        x = a;
25        y = b;
26     }
27
28     // get x coordinate
29     public int getX() { return x; }
30
31     // get y coordinate
32     public int getY() { return y; }
33
34     // convert the point into a String representation
35     public String toString()
36        { return "[" + x + ", " + y + "]"; }
37
38     // return the class name
39     public String getName() { return "Point"; }
40  }
```

Fig. 9.10 Shape, point, circle, cylinder hierarchy (part 2 of 8).

```
41  // Fig. 9.10: Circle.java
42  // Definition of class Circle
43
44  public class Circle extends Point {  // inherits from Point
45     protected double radius;
46
47     // no-argument constructor
48     public Circle()
49     {
50        // implicit call to superclass constructor here
51        setRadius( 0 );
52     }
53
54     // Constructor
55     public Circle( double r, int a, int b )
56     {
57        super( a, b );  // call the superclass constructor
```

Fig. 9.10 Shape, point, circle, cylinder hierarchy (part 3 of 8).

```
58              setRadius( r );
59           }
60
61           // Set radius of Circle
62           public void setRadius( double r )
63              { radius = ( r >= 0 ? r : 0 ); }
64
65           // Get radius of Circle
66           public double getRadius() { return radius; }
67
68           // Calculate area of Circle
69           public double area() { return Math.PI * radius * radius; }
70
71           // convert the Circle to a String
72           public String toString()
73              { return "Center = " + super.toString() +
74                      "; Radius = " + radius; }
75
76           // return the class name
77           public String getName() { return "Circle"; }
78        }
```

Fig. 9.10   Shape, point, circle, cylinder hierarchy (part 4 of 8).

```
79     // Fig. 9.10: Cylinder.java
80     // Definition of class Cylinder
81
82     public class Cylinder extends Circle {
83        protected double height;   // height of Cylinder
84
85        // no-argument constructor
86        public Cylinder()
87        {
88           // implicit call to superclass constructor here
89           setHeight( 0 );
90        }
91
92        // constructor
93        public Cylinder( double h, double r, int a, int b )
94        {
95           super( r, a, b );    // call superclass constructor
96           setHeight( h );
97        }
98
99        // Set height of Cylinder
100       public void setHeight( double h )
101          { height = ( h >= 0 ? h : 0 ); }
102
103       // Get height of Cylinder
104       public double getHeight() { return height; }
105
```

Fig. 9.10   Shape, point, circle, cylinder hierarchy (part 5 of 8).

```
106        // Calculate area of Cylinder (i.e., surface area)
107        public double area()
108        {
109           return 2 * super.area() +
110                  2 * Math.PI * radius * height;
111        }
112
113        // Calculate volume of Cylinder
114        public double volume() { return super.area() * height; }
115
116        // Convert a Cylinder to a String
117        public String toString()
118           { return super.toString() + "; Height = " + height; }
119
120        // Return the class name
121        public String getName() { return "Cylinder"; }
122     }
```

Fig. 9.10   Shape, point, circle, cylinder hierarchy (part 6 of 8).

```
123    // Fig. 9.10: Test.java
124    // Driver for point, circle, cylinder hierarchy
125    import javax.swing.JOptionPane;
126    import java.text.DecimalFormat;
127
128    public class Test {
129       public static void main( String args[] )
130       {
131          Point point = new Point( 7, 11 );
132          Circle circle = new Circle( 3.5, 22, 8 );
133          Cylinder cylinder = new Cylinder( 10, 3.3, 10, 10 );
134
135          Shape arrayOfShapes[];
136
137          arrayOfShapes = new Shape[ 3 ];
138
139          // aim arrayOfShapes[0] at subclass Point object
140          arrayOfShapes[ 0 ] = point;
141
142          // aim arrayOfShapes[1] at subclass Circle object
143          arrayOfShapes[ 1 ] = circle;
144
145          // aim arrayOfShapes[2] at subclass Cylinder object
146          arrayOfShapes[ 2 ] = cylinder;
147
148          String output =
149             point.getName() + ": " + point.toString() + "\n" +
150             circle.getName() + ": " + circle.toString() + "\n" +
151             cylinder.getName() + ": " + cylinder.toString();
152
153          DecimalFormat precision2 = new DecimalFormat( "0.00" );
154
```

Fig. 9.10   Shape, point, circle, cylinder hierarchy (part 7 of 8).

```
155        // Loop through arrayOfShapes and print the name,
156        // area, and volume of each object.
157        for ( int i = 0; i < arrayOfShapes.length; i++ ) {
158           output += "\n\n" +
159              arrayOfShapes[ i ].getName() + ": " +
160              arrayOfShapes[ i ].toString() +
161              "\nArea = " +
162              precision2.format( arrayOfShapes[ i ].area() ) +
163              "\nVolume = " +
164              precision2.format( arrayOfShapes[ i ].volume() );
165        }
166
167        JOptionPane.showMessageDialog( null, output,
168           "Demonstrating Polymorphism",
169           JOptionPane.INFORMATION_MESSAGE );
170
171        System.exit( 0 );
172     }
173 }
```

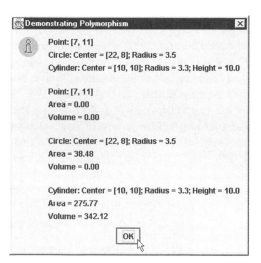

Fig. 9.10   Shape, point, circle, cylinder hierarchy (part 8 of 8).

Superclass **Shape** (Fig. 9.10, lines 1–8) extends **Object**, consists of three **public** methods and does not contain any data (although it could). Method **getName** is **abstract**, so it is overridden in each of the subclasses. Methods **area** and **volume** are defined to return **0.0**. These methods are overridden in subclasses when it is appropriate for those classes to have a different **area** calculation (classes **Circle** and **Cylinder**) and/or a different **volume** calculation (class **Cylinder**).

Class **Point** (Fig. 9.10, lines 9–40) is derived from **Shape**. A **Point** has an area of 0.0 and a volume of 0.0, so the superclass methods **area** and **volume** are not overridden here—they are inherited as defined in **Shape**. Other methods include **setPoint** to assign new **x** and **y** coordinates to a **Point** and **getX** and **getY** to return the **x** and **y** coordinates of a **Point**. Method **getName** is an implementation of the **abstract** method in the superclass. If this method were not defined, class **Point** would be an abstract class.

Class **Circle** (Fig. 9.10, lines 41–78) is derived from **Point**. A **Circle** has a volume of 0.0, so superclass method **volume** is not overridden—it is inherited from class **Point**, which inherited it from **Shape**. A **Circle** has an area different from that of a **Point**, so the **area** method is overridden. Method **getName** is an implementation of the **abstract** method in the superclass. If this method is not overridden here, the **Point** version of **getName** would be inherited. Other methods include **setRadius** to assign a new **radius** to a **Circle** and **getRadius** to return the **radius** of a **Circle**.

Software Engineering Observation 9.24

*A subclass always inherits the most recently defined version of each **public** and **protected** method from its direct and indirect superclasses.*

Class **Cylinder** (Fig. 9.10, lines 79–122) is derived from **Circle**. A **Cylinder** has area and volume different from those of class **Circle**, so the **area** and **volume** methods are both overridden. Method **getName** is an implementation of the **abstract** method in the superclass. If this method had not been overridden here, the **Circle** version of **getName** would be inherited. Other methods include **setHeight** to assign a new **height** to a **Cylinder** and **getHeight** to return the **height** of a **Cylinder**.

Method **main** of class **Test** (Fig. 9.10, lines 123–173) instantiates **Point** object **point**, **Circle** object **circle** and **Cylinder** object **cylinder** (lines 131–133). Next, array **arrayOfShapes** is instantiated (line 137). This array of superclass **Shape** references will refer to each subclass object instantiated. At line 140, the reference **point** is assigned to array element **arrayOfShapes[0]**. At line 143, the reference **circle** is assigned to array element **arrayOfShapes[1]**. At line 146, the reference **cylinder** is assigned to array element **arrayOfShapes[2]**. Now, each superclass **Shape** reference in the array refers to a subclass object of type **Point**, **Circle** or **Cylinder**.

Lines 148 through 151 invoke methods **getName** and **toString** to illustrate that the objects are initialized correctly (see the first three lines of the screen capture).

Next, the **for** structure at lines 157 through 165 walks through **arrayOfShapes** and the following calls are made during each iteration of the loop:

```
arrayOfShapes[ i ].getName()
arrayOfShapes[ i ].toString()
arrayOfShapes[ i ].area()
arrayOfShapes[ i ].volume()
```

Each of these method calls is invoked on the object to which **arrayOfShapes[i]** currently refers. When the compiler looks at each of these calls, it is simply trying to determine if a **Shape** reference (**arrayOfShapes[i]**) can be used to call these methods. For methods **getName**, **area** and **volume** the answer is yes because each of these methods is defined in class **Shape**. For method **toString**, the compiler first looks at class **Shape** to determine that **toString** is not defined there, then the compiler proceeds to **Shape**'s superclass (**Object**) to determine if **Shape** inherited a **toString** method that takes no arguments (which it did, because all **Object**s have a **toString** method).

The screen capture illustrates that all four methods are invoked properly based on the type of the referenced object. First, the string **"Point: "** and the coordinates of the object **point** (**arrayOfShapes[0]**) are output; the area and volume are both **0**. Next, the string **"Circle: "**, the coordinates of object **circle**, and the radius of object **circle** (**arrayOfShapes[1]**) are output; the area of **circle** is calculated and the volume is

0. Finally, the string **"Cylinder: "**, the coordinates of object **cylinder**, the radius of object **cylinder** and the height of object **cylinder** (**arrayOfShapes[2]**) are output; the area of **cylinder** is calculated and the volume of **cylinder** is calculated. All the method calls to **getName**, **toString**, **area** and **volume** are resolved at run-time with dynamic binding.

9.19 Case Study: Creating and Using Interfaces

Our next example (Fig. 9.11) reexamines the **Point**, **Circle**, **Cylinder** hierarchy one last time, replacing **abstract** superclass **Shape** with the interface **Shape**. An interface definition begins with the keyword **_interface_** and contains a set of **public abstract** methods. Interfaces may also contain **public final static** data. To use an interface, a class must specify that it **implements** the interface and the class must define every method in the interface with the number of arguments and the return type specified in the interface definition. If the class leaves one method in the interface undefined, the class becomes an **abstract** class and must be declared **abstract** in the first line of its class definition. Implementing a interface is like signing a contract with the compiler that states, "I will define all the methods specified by the interface."

**Common Programming Error 9.11**

Leaving a method of an **interface** undefined in a class that **implements** the interface results in a compile error indicating that the class must be declared **abstract**.

**Software Engineering Observation 9.25**

Declaring a **final** reference does not affect the object to which the reference refers. Rather, it indicates that the reference always refers to the same object.

We started using the concept of an interface when we introduced GUI event handling in Chapter 6, "Methods." Recall that our applet class included **implements Action-Listener** (an interface in package **java.awt.event**). The reason we were required to define **actionPerformed** in the applets with event handling is because **Action-Listener** is an interface that specifies that **actionPerformed** must be defined. Interfaces are an important part of GUI event handling, as we will discuss in the next section.

An interface is typically used in place of an **abstract** class when there is no default implementation to inherit—i.e., no instance variables and no default method implementations. Like **public abstract** classes, **interface**s are typically **public** data types, so they are normally defined in files by themselves with the same name as the interface and the **.java** extension.

```
1   // Fig. 9.11: Shape.java
2   // Definition of interface Shape
3
4   public interface Shape {
5      public abstract double area();
6      public abstract double volume();
7      public abstract String getName();
8   }
```

Fig. 9.11   Point, circle, cylinder hierarchy with a **Shape** interface (part 1 of 6).

```
46      // Convert to String in standard-time format
47      public String toString()
48      {
49         DecimalFormat twoDigits = new DecimalFormat( "00" );
50
51         return ( ( getHour() == 12 || getHour() == 0 ) ?
52                    12 : getHour() % 12 ) + ":" +
53               twoDigits.format( getMinute() ) + ":" +
54               twoDigits.format( getSecond() ) +
55               ( getHour() < 12 ? " AM" : " PM" );
56      }
57   }
```

Fig. 9.12   Demonstrating an inner class in a windowed application (part 2 of 5).

```
58   // Fig. 9.12: TimeTestWindow.java
59   // Demonstrating the Time class set and get methods
60   import java.awt.*;
61   import java.awt.event.*;
62   import javax.swing.*;
63
64   public class TimeTestWindow extends JFrame {
65      private Time t;
66      private JLabel hourLabel, minuteLabel, secondLabel;
67      private JTextField hourField, minuteField,
68                         secondField, display;
69      private JButton exitButton;
70
71      public TimeTestWindow()
72      {
73         super( "Inner Class Demonstration" );
74
75         t = new Time();
76
77         Container c = getContentPane();
78
79         // create an instance of the inner class
80         ActionEventHandler handler = new ActionEventHandler();
81
82         c.setLayout( new FlowLayout() );
83         hourLabel = new JLabel( "Set Hour" );
84         hourField = new JTextField( 10 );
85         hourField.addActionListener( handler );
86         c.add( hourLabel );
87         c.add( hourField );
88
89         minuteLabel = new JLabel( "Set minute" );
90         minuteField = new JTextField( 10 );
91         minuteField.addActionListener( handler );
92         c.add( minuteLabel );
93         c.add( minuteField );
94
```

Fig. 9.12   Demonstrating an inner class in a windowed application (part 3 of 5).

```
 95            secondLabel = new JLabel( "Set Second" );
 96            secondField = new JTextField( 10 );
 97            secondField.addActionListener( handler );
 98            c.add( secondLabel );
 99            c.add( secondField );
100
101            display = new JTextField( 30 );
102            display.setEditable( false );
103            c.add( display );
104
105            exitButton = new JButton( "Exit" );
106            exitButton.addActionListener( handler );
107            c.add( exitButton );
108        }
109
110        public void displayTime()
111        {
112            display.setText( "The time is: " + t );
113        }
114
115        public static void main( String args[] )
116        {
117            TimeTestWindow window = new TimeTestWindow();
118
119            window.setSize( 400, 140 );
120            window.show();
121        }
122
123        // INNER CLASS DEFINITION FOR EVENT HANDLING
124        private class ActionEventHandler implements ActionListener {
125            public void actionPerformed( ActionEvent e )
126            {
127                if ( e.getSource() == exitButton )
128                    System.exit( 0 );    // terminate the application
129                else if ( e.getSource() == hourField ) {
130                    t.setHour(
131                        Integer.parseInt( e.getActionCommand() ) );
132                    hourField.setText( "" );
133                }
134                else if ( e.getSource() == minuteField ) {
135                    t.setMinute(
136                        Integer.parseInt( e.getActionCommand() ) );
137                    minuteField.setText( "" );
138                }
139                else if ( e.getSource() == secondField ) {
140                    t.setSecond(
141                        Integer.parseInt( e.getActionCommand() ) );
142                    secondField.setText( "" );
143                }
144
```

Fig. 9.12   Demonstrating an inner class in a windowed application (part 4 of 5).

```
145              displayTime();
146          }
147      }
148  }
```

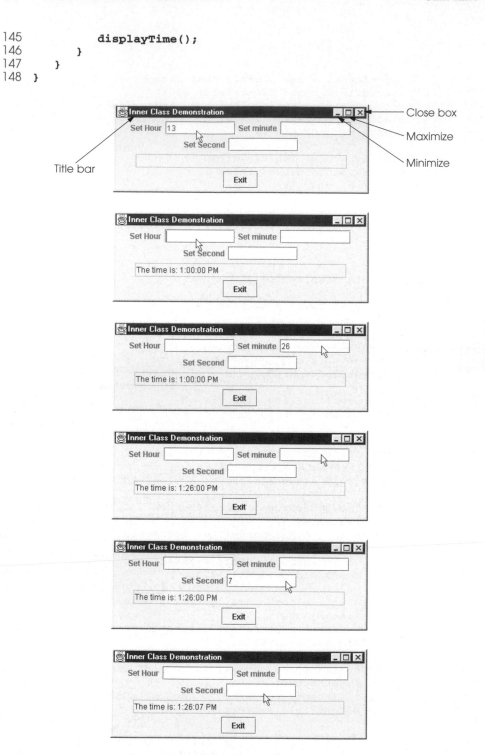

Fig. 9.12 Demonstrating an inner class in a windowed application (part 5 of 5).

Line 64

```
public class TimeTestWindow extends JFrame {
```

indicates that class **TimeTestWindow** extends class *JFrame* (from package **jav-ax.swing**) rather than class **JApplet** (as shown in Fig. 8.5). Superclass **JFrame** provides the basic attributes and behaviors of a window—a *title bar* and buttons to *minimize*, *maximize* and *close* the window (all labeled in the first screen capture). Class **Time-TestWindow** uses the same GUI components as the applet of Fig. 8.5 except that the button (line 69) is now called **exitButton** and is used to terminate the application.

The **init** method of the applet has been replaced by a constructor (line 71) to guarantee that the window's GUI components are created as the application begins executing. Method **main** (line 115) defines a **new** object of class **TimeTestWindow** that results in a call to the constructor. Remember, **init** is a special method that is guaranteed to be called when an applet begins execution. However, this program is not an applet, so the **init** method is not guaranteed to be called.

Several new features appear in the constructor. Line 73 calls the superclass **JFrame** constructor with the string **"Inner Class Demonstration"**. This string is displayed in the title bar of the window by class **JFrame**'s constructor. Line 80

```
ActionEventHandler handler = new ActionEventHandler();
```

defines one instance of our inner class **ActionEventHandler** and assigns it to **handler**. This reference is passed to each of the four calls to **addActionListener** (lines 85, 91, 97 and 106) that register the event handlers for each GUI component that generates events in this example (**hourField, minuteField, secondField** and **exitButton**). Each call to **addActionListener** requires an object of type **ActionListener** to be passed as an argument. Actually, **handler** *is an* **ActionListener**. Line 124 (the first line of the inner class definition)

```
private class ActionEventHandler implements ActionListener {
```

indicates that inner class **ActionEventHandler** implements **ActionListener**. Thus, every object of type **ActionEventHandler** *is an* **ActionListener**. The requirement that **addActionListener** be passed an object of type **ActionListener** is satisfied! The *is a* relationship is used extensively in the GUI event handling mechanism, as you will see over the next several chapters. The inner class is defined as **private** because it will be used only in this class definition. Inner classes can be **private, protected** or **public**.

An inner class object has a special relationship with the outer class object that creates it. The inner class object is allowed to access directly all the instance variables and methods of the outer class object. The **actionPerformed** method (line 125) of class **ActionEventHandler** does just that. Throughout the method, the instance variables **t, exitButton, hourField, minuteField** and **secondField** are used, as is method **displayTime**. Notice that none of these needs a "handle" to the outer class object. This is a free relationship created by the compiler between the outer class and its inner classes.

Software Engineering Observation 9.27

An inner class object is allowed to access directly all the instance variables and methods of the outer class object that defined it.

Software Engineering Observation 9.29

When an anonymous inner class implements an interface, the class must define every method in the interface.

Method **main** creates one instance of class **TimeTestWindow** (line 82), sizes the window (line 93) and displays the window (line 94).

Windows generate a variety of events that are discussed in Chapter 13. For this example we discuss the one event generated when the user clicks the window's close box—a *window closing event*. Lines 84 through 91

```
window.addWindowListener(
    new WindowAdapter() {
        public void windowClosing( WindowEvent e )
        {
            System.exit( 0 );
        }
    }
);
```

enable the user to terminate the application by clicking the window's close box (labeled in the first screen capture. Method ***addWindowListener*** registers a window event listener. The argument to **addWindowListener** must be a reference to an object that *is a* ***WindowListener*** (package **java.awt.event**) (i.e., any object of a class that implements **WindowListener**). However, there are seven different methods that must be defined in every class that implements **WindowListener** and we only need one in this example—***windowClosing***. For event handling interfaces with more than one method, Java provides a corresponding class (called an *adapter class*) that already implements all the methods in the interface for you. All you need to do is extend the adapter class and override the methods you require in your program.

Common Programming Error 9.12

Extending an adapter class and misspelling the name of the method you are overriding is a logic error.

Lines 85 through 90 use special Java syntax to define an anonymous inner class and create one object of that class that is passed as the argument to **addWindowListener**. Line 85

```
new WindowAdapter() {
```

uses operator **new** to create an object. The syntax **WindowAdapter()** begins the definition of an anonymous inner class that extends class **WindowAdapter**. This is similar to beginning a class definition with

```
public class MyHandler extends WindowAdapter {
```

The parentheses after **WindowAdapter** indicate a call to the default constructor of the anonymous inner class. Class **WindowAdapter** implements interface **WindowListener**, so every **WindowAdapter** object *is a* **WindowListener**—the exact type required for the argument to **addWindowListener**.

The opening left brace (**{**) at the end of line 85 and the closing right brace (**}**) at line 90 define the body of the class. Lines 86 through 89 override the one method of **Window-**

Adapter—**windowClosing**—that is called when the user clicks the window's close box. In this example, **windowClosing** terminates the application with a call to **System.exit(0)**.

In the last two examples, we have seen that inner classes can be used to create event handlers and that separate anonymous inner classes can be defined to handle events individually for each GUI component. In Chapters 12 and 13, we revisit this concept as we discuss the event handling mechanism in detail.

9.21 Notes on Inner Class Definitions

This section presents several notes of interest to programmers regarding the definition and use of inner classes.

1. Compiling a class that contains inner classes results in a separate **.class** file for every class. Inner classes with names have the file name *OuterClassName$Inner-ClassName***.class**. Anonymous inner classes have the file name *OuterClass-Name$#***.class**, where # starts at 1 and is incremented for each anonymous inner class encountered during compilation.

2. Inner classes with class names can be defined as **public**, **protected**, package access or **private** and are subject to the same usage restrictions as other members of a class.

3. To access the outer class's **this** reference, use *OuterClassName***.this**.

4. The outer class is responsible for creating objects of its inner classes. To create an object of another class's inner class, first create an object of the outer class and assign it to a reference (we will call it **ref**). Then use a statement of the following form to create an inner class object:

    OuterClassName.*InnerClassName* **innerRef = ref.new** *InnerClassName***();**

5. An inner class can be declared **static**. A **static** inner class does not require an object of its outer class to be defined (whereas a non-**static** inner class does). A **static** inner class does not have access to the outer class's non-**static** members.

9.22 Type-Wrapper Classes for Primitive Types

Each of the primitive types has a *type-wrapper class*. These classes are called **Character**, **Byte**, **Short**, **Integer**, **Long**, **Float**, **Double** and **Boolean**. Each type-wrapper class enables you to manipulate primitive types as objects of class **Object**. Therefore, values of the primitive data types can be processed polymorphically if they are maintained as objects of the type-wrapper classes. Many of the classes we will develop or reuse manipulate and share **Object**s. These classes cannot polymorphically manipulate variables of primitive types, but they can polymorphically manipulate objects of the type-wrapper classes, because every class ultimately is derived from class **Object**.

Each of the numeric classes—**Byte**, **Short**, **Integer**, **Long**, **Float** and **Double**—inherits from class **Number**. Each of the type wrappers is declared **final**, so their methods are implicitly **final** and may not be overridden. Note that many of the methods that process the primitive data types are defined as **static** methods of the type-wrapper classes. If you need to manipulate a primitive value in your program, first refer to the documentation for the type-wrapper classes—the method you need may already be defined. We will use the type-wrapper classes polymorphically in our study of data structures in Chapters 22 and 23.

Summary

- One of the keys to the power of object-oriented programming is achieving software reusability through inheritance.

- Through inheritance, a new class inherits the instance variables and methods of a previously defined superclass. In this case, the new class is referred to as a subclass.

- With single inheritance, a class is derived from one superclass. With multiple inheritance, a subclass inherits from multiple superclasses. Java does not support multiple inheritance, but Java does provide the notion of interfaces (discussed in Chapter 15, "Multithreading"), which offer many of the benefits of multiple inheritance without the associated problems.

- A subclass normally adds instance variables and methods of its own, so a subclass generally is larger than its superclass. A subclass is more specific than its superclass and normally represents fewer objects.

- A subclass cannot access the **private** members of its superclass. A subclass can, however, access the **public**, **protected** and package access members of its superclass; the subclass must be in the superclass's package to use superclass members with package access.

- A subclass constructor always calls the constructor for its superclass first (either explicitly or implicitly) to create and initialize the subclass's superclass members.

- Inheritance enables software reusability, which saves time in development and encourages the use of previously proven and debugged high-quality software.

- Someday most software will be constructed from standardized reusable components exactly as hardware often is today.

- An object of a subclass can be treated as an object of its corresponding superclass, but the reverse is not true.

- A superclass exists in a hierarchical relationship with its subclasses.

- When a class is used with the mechanism of inheritance, it becomes either a superclass that supplies attributes and behaviors to other classes, or the class becomes a subclass that inherits those attributes and behaviors.

- An inheritance hierarchy can be arbitrarily deep within the physical limitations of a particular system, but most inheritance hierarchies have only a few levels.

- Hierarchies are useful for understanding and managing complexity. With software becoming increasingly complex, Java provides mechanisms for supporting hierarchical structures through inheritance and polymorphism.

- **Protected** access serves as an intermediate level of protection between **public** access and **private** access. **Protected** members of a superclass may be accessed by methods of the superclass, by methods of subclasses and by methods of classes in the same package; no other methods can access the **protected** members of a superclass.

- A superclass may be either a direct superclass of a subclass or an indirect superclass of a subclass. A direct superclass is the class that a subclass explicitly **extends**. An indirect superclass is inherited from several levels up the class hierarchy tree.

- When a superclass member is inappropriate for a subclass, the programmer may override that member in the subclass.

- It is important to distinguish between "is a" relationships and "has a" relationships. In a "has a" relationship, a class object has a reference to an object of another class as a member. In an "is a" relationship, an object of a subclass type may also be treated as an object of the superclass type. "Is a" is inheritance. "Has a" is composition.

- A subclass object can be assigned to a superclass reference. This kind of assignment makes sense because the subclass has members corresponding to each of the superclass members.

- A reference to a subclass object may be implicitly converted to a reference for a superclass object.

- It is possible to convert a superclass reference to a subclass reference by using an explicit cast. If the target is not a subclass object, a **ClassCastException** is thrown.

- A superclass specifies commonality. All classes derived from a superclass inherit the capabilities of that superclass. In the object-oriented design process, the designer looks for commonality among classes and factors it out to form superclasses. Subclasses are then customized beyond the capabilities inherited from the superclass.

- Reading a set of subclass declarations can be confusing because inherited superclass members are not listed in the subclass declarations, but these members are indeed present in the subclasses.

- With polymorphism, it becomes possible to design and implement systems that are more easily extensible. Programs can be written to process objects of types that may not exist when the program is under development.

- Polymorphic programming can eliminate the need for **switch** logic, thus avoiding the kinds of errors associated with **switch** logic.

- An abstract method is declared by preceding the method's definition with the keyword **abstract** in the superclass.

- There are many situations in which it is useful to define classes for which the programmer never intends to instantiate any objects. Such classes are called **abstract** classes. Because these are used only as superclasses, we will normally refer to them as **abstract** superclasses. No objects of an **abstract** class may be instantiated.

- Classes from which objects can be instantiated are called concrete classes.

- A class is made abstract by declaring it with the keyword **abstract**.

- If a subclass is derived from a superclass with an **abstract** method without supplying a definition for that **abstract** method in the subclass, that method remains **abstract** in the subclass. Consequently, the subclass is also an **abstract** class (and cannot instantiate any objects).

- When a request is made through a superclass reference to use a method, Java chooses the correct overridden method in the subclass associated with the object.

- Through the use of polymorphism, one method call can cause different actions to occur, depending on the type of the object receiving the call.

- Although we cannot instantiate objects of **abstract** superclasses, we can declare references to **abstract** superclasses. Such references can then be used to enable polymorphic manipulations of subclass objects when such objects are instantiated from concrete classes.

- New classes are regularly added to systems. New classes are accommodated by dynamic method binding (also called late binding). The type of an object need not be known at compile time for a method call to be compiled. At execution time, the appropriate method of the receiving object is selected.

- With dynamic method binding, at execution time the call to a method is routed to the method version appropriate for the class of the object receiving the call.

- When a superclass provides a method, subclasses can override the method, but they do not have to override it. Thus a subclass can use a superclass's version of a method.

- An interface definition begins with the keyword **interface** and contains a set of **public abstract** methods. Interfaces may also contain **public final static** data.

- To use an interface, a class must specify that it **implements** the interface and that class must define every method in the interface with the number of arguments and the return type specified in the interface definition.

- An interface is typically used in place of an abstract class when there is no default implementation to inherit.

- When a class implements an interface, the same "is a" relationship provided by inheritance applies.

- To implement more than one interface, simply provide a comma-separated list of interface names after keyword **implements** in the class definition.

- Inner classes are defined inside the scope of other classes.

- An inner class can also be defined inside a method of a class. Such an inner class has access to its outer class's members and to the **final** local variables for the method in which it is defined.

- Inner class definitions are used mainly in event handling.

- Class **JFrame** provides the basic attributes and behaviors of a window—a title bar and buttons to minimize, maximize and close the window.

- An inner class object has a special relationship with the outer class object that creates it. The inner class object is allowed to access directly all the instance variables and methods of the outer class object.

- Because an anonymous inner class has no name, one object of the anonymous inner class must be created at the point where the class is defined in the program.

- An anonymous inner class can implement an interface or extend a class.

- The event generated when the user clicks the window's close box is a window closing event.

- Method **addWindowListener** registers a window event listener. The argument to **addWindowListener** must be a reference to an object that is a **WindowListener** (package **java.awt.event**).

- For event handling interfaces with more than one method, Java provides a corresponding class (called an adapter class) that already implements all the methods in the interface for you. Class **WindowAdapter** implements interface **WindowListener**, so every **WindowAdapter** object *is a* **WindowListener**.

- Compiling a class that contains inner classes results in a separate **.class** file for every class.

- Inner classes with class names can be defined as **public**, **protected**, package access or **private** and are subject to the same usage restrictions as other members of a class.

- To access the outer class's **this** reference, use *OuterClassName*.**this**.

- The outer class is responsible for creating objects of its non-**static** inner classes.

- An inner class can be declared **static**.

Terminology

abstract class	**Boolean** class
abstract method	**Character** class
abstract superclass	class hierarchy
abstraction	client of a class
anonymous inner class	composition
base class	direct superclass
Double class	**Object** class

dynamic method binding
extends
extensibility
final class
final instance variable
final method
garbage collection
"has a" relationship
hierarchical relationship
implementation inheritance
implicit reference conversion
indirect superclass
infinite recursion error
inheritance
inheritance hierarchy
inner class
Integer class
interface
interface inheritance
"is a" relationship
JFrame class
late binding
Long class
member access control
member object
method overriding
multiple inheritance
Number class

object-oriented programming (OOP)
override a method
override an **abstract** method
overriding vs. overloading
polymorphism
protected member of a class
reference to an **abstract** class
setSize method
show method
single inheritance
software reusability
standardized software components
subclass
subclass constructor
subclass reference
super
superclass
superclass constructor
superclass reference
switch logic
this
type-wrapper class
"uses a" relationship
WindowAdapter class
windowClosing method
WindowEvent class
WindowListener interface

Common Programming Errors

9.1   Treating a superclass object as a subclass object can cause errors.

9.2   Assigning an object of a superclass to a subclass reference (without a cast) is a syntax error.

9.3   It is a syntax error if a **super** call by a subclass to its superclass constructor is not the first statement in the subclass constructor.

9.4   It is a syntax error if the arguments to a **super** call by a subclass to its superclass constructor do not match the parameters specified in one of the superclass constructor definitions.

9.5   It is a syntax error if a method in a superclass and a method in its subclass have the same signature but a different return type.

9.6   When a superclass method is overridden in a subclass, it is common to have the subclass version call the superclass version and do some additional work. Not using the **super** reference to reference the superclass's method causes infinite recursion because the subclass method actually calls itself.

9.7   Cascading **super** references to refer to a member (method or variable) several levels up the hierarchy (as in **super.super.x**) is a syntax error.

9.8   Assigning a subclass object to a superclass reference, and then attempting to reference subclass-only members with the superclass reference, is a syntax error.

9.9   Attempting to instantiate an object of an **abstract** class (i.e., a class that contains one or more **abstract** methods) is a syntax error.

9.10   It is a syntax error if a class with one or more **abstract** methods is not explicitly declared **abstract**.

9.11   Leaving a method of an **interface** undefined in a class that **implements** the interface results in a compile error indicating that the class must be declared **abstract**.

9.12   Extending an adapter class and misspelling the name of the method you are overriding is a logic error.

Good Programming Practice

9.1   The last statement in a **finalize** method should always be **super.finalize();** to ensure that the superclass's **finalize** method is called.

Performance Tips

9.1   If classes produced through inheritance are larger than they need to be, memory and processing resources may be wasted. Inherit from the class "closest" to what you need.

9.2   The compiler can decide to inline a **final** method call and will do so for small, simple **final** methods. Inlining does not violate encapsulation or information hiding (but does improve performance because it eliminates the overhead of making a method call).

9.3   Pipelined processors can improve performance by executing portions of the next several instructions simultaneously, but not if those instructions follow a method call. Inlining (which the compiler can perform on a **final** method) can improve performance in these processors because it eliminates the out-of-line transfer of control associated with a method call.

9.4   Polymorphism as implemented with dynamic method binding is efficient.

9.5   The kinds of polymorphic manipulations made possible with dynamic binding can also be accomplished by using hand-coded **switch** logic based on type fields in objects. The polymorphic code generated by the Java compiler runs with comparable performance to efficiently coded **switch** logic.

Software Engineering Observations

9.1   A subclass cannot directly access **private** members of its superclass.

9.2   Constructors are never inherited—they are specific to the class in which they are defined.

9.3   If an object has been assigned to a reference of one of its superclasses, it is acceptable to cast that object back to its own type. In fact, this must be done in order to send that object any of its messages that do not appear in that superclass.

9.4   Every class in Java extends Object unless specified otherwise in the first line of the class definition. Thus, class **Object** is the superclass of the entire Java class hierarchy.

9.5   A redefinition of a superclass method in a subclass need not have the same signature as the superclass method. Such a redefinition is not method overriding but is simply an example of method overloading.

9.6   Any object can be converted to a **String** with an explicit or implicit call to the object's **toString** method.

9.7   Each class should override method **toString** to return useful information about objects of that class.

9.8   When an object of a subclass is created, first the subclass constructor calls the superclass constructor, the superclass constructor executes, then the remainder of the subclass constructor's body executes.

9.9   Creating a subclass does not affect its superclass's source code or the superclass's Java bytecodes; the integrity of a superclass is preserved by inheritance.

9.10   Just as the designer of non-object-oriented systems should avoid unnecessary proliferation of functions, the designer of object-oriented systems should avoid unnecessary proliferation of classes. Proliferating classes creates management problems and can hinder software reusability simply because it is more difficult for a potential user of a class to locate that class in a huge collection. The trade-off is to create fewer classes, each providing substantial additional functionality, but such classes might be too rich for certain users.

9.11   In an object-oriented system, classes are often closely related. "Factor out" common attributes and behaviors and place these in a superclass. Then use inheritance to form subclasses without having to repeat common attributes and behaviors.

9.12   Modifications to a superclass do not require subclasses to change as long as the public interface to the superclass remains unchanged.

9.13   When a subclass chooses not to redefine a method, the subclass simply inherits its immediate superclass's method definition.

9.14   A class declared **final** cannot be extended and every method is implicitly **final**.

9.15   With polymorphism, the programmer can deal in generalities and let the execution-time environment concern itself with the specifics. The programmer can command a wide variety of objects to behave in manners appropriate to those objects without even knowing the types of those objects.

9.16   Polymorphism promotes extensibility: Software written to invoke polymorphic behavior is written independent of the types of the objects to which messages (i.e., method calls) are sent. Thus, new types of objects that can respond to existing messages can be added into such a system without modifying the base system.

9.17   If a method is declared **final** it cannot be overridden in subclasses, so that method calls may not be sent polymorphically to objects of those subclasses. The method call may still be sent to subclasses but they will all respond identically rather than polymorphically.

9.18   An **abstract** class defines a common interface for the various members of a class hierarchy. The **abstract** class contains methods that will be defined in the subclasses. All classes in the hierarchy can use this same interface through polymorphism.

9.19   If a subclass is derived from a superclass with an **abstract** method, and if no definition is supplied in the subclass for that **abstract** method (i.e., if that method is not overridden in the subclass), that method remains **abstract** in the subclass. Consequently, the subclass is also an **abstract** class and must be explicitly declared as an **abstract** class.

9.20   The ability to declare an **abstract** method gives the class designer considerable power over how subclasses will be implemented in a class hierarchy. Any new class that wants to inherit from this class is forced to override the **abstract** method (either directly or by inheriting from a class that has overridden the method). Otherwise, that new class will contain an **abstract** method and thus be an **abstract** class unable to instantiate objects.

9.21   An **abstract** can still have instance data and non-**abstract** methods subject to the normal rules of inheritance by subclasses. An **abstract** class can also have constructors.

9.22   Hierarchies designed for implementation inheritance tend to have their functionality high in the hierarchy—each new subclass inherits one or more methods that were defined in a superclass and uses the superclass definitions.

9.23   Hierarchies designed for interface inheritance tend to have their functionality lower in the hierarchy—a superclass specifies one or more methods that should be called identically for each object in the hierarchy (i.e., they have the same signature), but the individual subclasses provide their own implementations of the method(s).

9.24   A subclass always inherits the most recently defined version of each **public** and **protected** method from its direct and indirect superclasses.

9.25   Declaring a **final** reference does not affect the object to which the reference refers. Rather, it indicates that the reference always refers to the same object.

9.26   All methods of class **Object** can be called using a reference of an interface data type—a reference refers to an object and all objects have the methods defined by class **Object**.

9.27 An inner class object is allowed to access directly all the instance variables and methods of the outer class object that defined it.

9.28 An inner class defined in a method is allowed to access directly all the instance variables and methods of the outer class object that defined it and any **final** local variables in the method.

9.29 When an anonymous inner class implements an interface, the class must define every method in the interface.

Testing and Debugging Tips

9.1 Hiding **private** members is a huge help in testing, debugging and correctly modifying systems. If a subclass could access its superclass's **private** members, it would then be possible for classes derived from that subclass to access that data as well, and so on. This would propagate access to what is supposed to be **private** data, and the benefits of information hiding would be lost throughout the class hierarchy.

9.2 An interesting consequence of using polymorphism is that programs take on a simplified appearance. They contain less branching logic in favor of simpler sequential code. This simplification facilitates testing, debugging, and program maintenance.

Self-Review Exercises

9.1 Fill in the blanks in each of the following:
   a) If the class **Alpha** inherits from the class **Beta**, class **Alpha** is called the _____ class and class **Beta** is called the _____ class.
   b) Inheritance enables _____, which saves time in development and encourages using previously proven and high-quality software components.
   c) An object of a _____ class can be treated as an object of its corresponding _____ class.
   d) The four member access specifiers are _____, _____, _____ and _____.
   e) A "has a" relationship between classes represents _____ and an "is a" relationship between classes represents _____.
   f) Using polymorphism helps eliminate _____ logic.
   g) If a class contains one or more **abstract** methods, it is an _____ class.
   h) A method call resolved at run-time is referred to as _____ binding.

9.2 a) A subclass may call any non-**private** superclass method by prepending _____ to the method call.
   b) A superclass typically represents a larger number of objects than its subclass represents (*true/false*).
   c) A subclass typically encapsulates less functionality than does its superclass. (*true/false*).

Answers to Self-Review Exercises

9.1 a) sub, super. b) software reusability. c) sub, super. d) **public**, **protected**, **private** and package access. e) composition, inheritance. f) **switch**. g) **abstract**. h) dynamic.

9.2 a) **super**
   b) true
   c) false

Exercises

9.3 Consider the class **Bicycle**. Given your knowledge of some common components of bicycles, show a class hierarchy in which the class **Bicycle** inherits from other classes, which, in turn, inherit from yet other classes. Discuss the instantiation of various objects of class **Bicycle**. Discuss inheritance from class **Bicycle** for other closely related subclasses.

9.4   Define each of the following terms: single inheritance, multiple inheritance, interface, superclass and subclass.

9.5   Discuss why casting a superclass reference to a subclass reference is potentially dangerous.

9.6   Distinguish between single inheritance and multiple inheritance. Why does Java not support multiple inheritance? What feature of Java helps realize the benefits of multiple inheritance?

9.7   (*True/False*) A subclass is generally smaller than its superclass.

9.8   (*True/False*) A subclass object is also an object of that subclass's superclass.

9.9   Some programmers prefer not to use **protected** access because it breaks information hiding in the superclass. Discuss the relative merits of using **protected** access vs. **private** access in superclasses.

9.10   Many programs written with inheritance could be solved with composition instead, and vice versa. Discuss the relative merits of these approaches in the context of the **Point**, **Circle**, **Cylinder** class hierarchy in this chapter. Rewrite the program of Fig. 9.10 (and the supporting classes) to use composition rather than inheritance. After you do this, reassess the relative merits of the two approaches both for the **Point**, **Circle**, **Cylinder** problem and for object-oriented programs in general.

9.11   Rewrite the **Point**, **Circle**, **Cylinder** program of Fig. 9.10 as a **Point**, **Square**, **Cube** program. Do this two ways—once with inheritance and once with composition.

9.12   In the chapter, we stated, "When a superclass method is inappropriate for a subclass, that method can be overridden in the subclass with an appropriate implementation." If this is done, does the subclass-is-a-superclass-object relationship still hold? Explain your answer.

9.13   Study the inheritance hierarchy of Fig. 9.2. For each class, indicate some common attributes and behaviors consistent with the hierarchy. Add some other classes (i.e., **UndergraduateStudent**, **GraduateStudent**, **Freshman**, **Sophomore**, **Junior**, **Senior**, etc.), to enrich the hierarchy.

9.14   Write an inheritance hierarchy for classes **Quadrilateral**, **Trapezoid**, **Parallelogram**, **Rectangle** and **Square**. Use **Quadrilateral** as the superclass of the hierarchy. Make the hierarchy as deep (i.e., as many levels) as possible. The **private** data of **Quadrilateral** should include the *(x, y)* coordinate pairs for the four endpoints of the **Quadrilateral**. Write a driver program that instantiates and displays objects of each of these classes. [In Chapter 11, "Graphics and Java2D," you will learn how to use Java's drawing capabilities.]

9.15   Write down all the shapes you can think of—both two-dimensional and three-dimensional—and form those shapes into a shape hierarchy. Your hierarchy should have superclass **Shape**, from which class **TwoDimensionalShape** and class **ThreeDimensionalShape** are derived. Once you have developed the hierarchy, define each of the classes in the hierarchy. We will use this hierarchy in the exercises to process all shapes as objects of superclass **Shape**.

9.16   How is it that polymorphism enables you to program "in the general" rather than "in the specific"? Discuss the key advantages of programming "in the general."

9.17   Discuss the problems of programming with **switch** logic. Explain why polymorphism is an effective alternative to using **switch** logic.

9.18   Distinguish between inheriting interface and inheriting implementation. How do inheritance hierarchies designed for inheriting interface differ from those designed for inheriting implementation?

9.19   Distinguish between non-**abstract** methods and **abstract** methods.

9.20   (*True/False*) All methods in an **abstract** superclass must be declared **abstract**.

9.21   Suggest one or more levels of **abstract** superclasses for the **Shape** hierarchy discussed in the beginning of this chapter (the first level is **Shape** and the second level consists of the classes **TwoDimensionalShape** and **ThreeDimensionalShape**).

9.22   How does polymorphism promote extensibility?

9.23   You have been asked to develop a flight simulator that will have elaborate graphical outputs. Explain why polymorphic programming would be especially effective for a problem of this nature.

9.24   Develop a basic graphics package. Use the **Shape** class inheritance hierarchy from Fig. 9.3. Limit yourself to two-dimensional shapes such as squares, rectangles, triangles and circles. Interact with the user. Let the user specify the position, size, shape and fill colors to be used in drawing each shape. The user can specify many items of the same shape. As you create each shape, place a **Shape** reference to each new **Shape** object into an array. Each class has its own **draw** method. Write a polymorphic screen manager that walks through the array sending **draw** messages to each object in the array to form a screen image. Redraw the screen image each time the user specifies an additional shape. Investigate the methods of class **Graphics** to help draw each shape.

9.25   Modify the payroll system of Fig. 9.9 to add **private** instance variables **birthDate** (use class **Date** from Fig. 8.8) and **departmentCode** (an **int**) to class **Employee**. Assume this payroll is processed once per month. Then, as your program calculates the payroll for each **Employee** (polymorphically), add a $100.00 bonus to the person's payroll amount if this is the month in which the **Employee**'s birthday occurs.

9.26   In Exercise 9.15, you developed a **Shape** class hierarchy and defined the classes in the hierarchy. Modify the hierarchy so that class **Shape** is an **abstract** superclass containing the interface to the hierarchy. Derive **TwoDimensionalShape** and **ThreeDimensionalShape** from class **Shape**—these classes should also be **abstract**. Use an **abstract print** method to output the type and dimensions of each class. Also include **area** and **volume** methods so these calculations can be performed for objects of each concrete class in the hierarchy. Write a driver program that tests the **Shape** class hierarchy.

9.27   Rewrite your solution to Exercise 9.26 to use a **Shape** interface instead of an abstract **Shape** class.

9.28   *(Drawing Application)* Modify the drawing program of Exercise 8.19 to create a drawing application that draws random lines, rectangles and ovals. [*Note:* Like an applet, a **JFrame** has a **paint** method that you can override to draw on the background of the **JFrame**.]

    For this exercise, modify the **MyLine**, **MyOval** and **MyRect** classes of Exercise 8.19 to create the class hierarchy in Fig. 9.14. The classes of the **MyShape** hierarchy should be "smart" shape classes where objects of these classes know how to draw themselves (if provided with a **Graphics** object that tells them where to draw). The only **switch** or **if/else** logic in this program should be to determine the type of shape object to create (use random numbers to pick the shape type and the coordinates of each shape). Once an object from this hierarchy is created, it will be manipulated for the rest of its lifetime as a superclass **MyShape** reference.

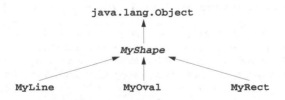

Fig. 9.14   The **MyShape** hierarchy.

Class **MyShape** in Fig. 9.14 *must* be **abstract**. The only data representing the coordinates of the shapes in the hierarchy should be defined in class **MyShape**. Lines, rectangles and ovals can all be drawn if you know two points in space. Lines require $x1$, $y1$, $x2$ and $y2$ coordinates. The **draw-Line** method of the **Graphics** class will connect the two points supplied with a line. If you have the same four coordinate values ($x1$, $y1$, $x2$ and $y2$) for ovals and rectangles, you can calculate the four arguments needed to draw them. Each requires an upper-left x-coordinate value (minimum of the two x-coordinate values), an upper-left y-coordinate value (minimum of the two y coordinate values), a *width* (difference between the two x-coordinate values; must be nonnegative) and a *height* (difference between the two y-coordinate values; must be nonnegative). [*Note:* In Chapter 12, each x,y pair will be captured using mouse events from mouse interactions between the user and the program's background. These coordinates will be stored in an appropriate shape object as selected by the user. As you begin the exercise, you will use random coordinate values as arguments to the constructor.]

In addition to the data for the hierarchy, class **MyShape** should define at least the following methods:

a) A constructor with no arguments that sets the coordinates to 0.

b) A constructor with arguments that sets the coordinates to the supplied values.

c) Set methods for each individual piece of data that allow the programmer to independently set any piece of data for a shape in the hierarchy (e.g., if you have an instance variable **x1**, you should have a method **setX1**).

d) Get methods for each individual piece of data that allow the programmer to independently retrieve any piece of data for a shape in the hierarchy (e.g., if you have an instance variable **x1**, you should have a method **getX1**).

e) The **abstract** method

```
public abstract void draw( Graphics g );
```

This method will be called from the program's **paint** method to draw a shape onto the screen.

The preceding methods are required. If you would like to provide more methods for flexibility, please do so. However, be sure that any method you define in this class is a method that would be used by *all* shapes in the hierarchy.

All data *must* be **private** to class **MyShape** in this exercise (this forces you to use proper encapsulation of the data and provide proper *set/get* methods to manipulate the data). You are not allowed to define new data that can be derived from existing information. As explained previously, the upper-left x, upper-left y, *width* and *height* needed to draw an oval or rectangle can be calculated if you already know two points in space. All subclasses of **MyShape** should provide two constructors that mimic those provided by class **MyShape**.

Objects of the **MyOval** and **MyRect** classes should not calculate their upper-left x-coordinate, upper-left y-coordinate, *width* and *height* until they are about to draw. Never modify the $x1$, $y1$, $x2$ and $y2$ coordinates of a **MyOval** or **MyRect** object to prepare to draw them. Instead, use the temporary results of the calculations described above. This will help us enhance the program in Chapter 12 by allowing the user to select each shape's coordinates with the mouse.

There should be no **MyLine**, **MyOval** or **MyRect** references in the program—only **MyShape** references that refer to **MyLine**, **MyOval** and **MyRect** objects are allowed. The program should keep an array of **MyShape** references containing all shapes. The program's **paint** method should walk through the array of **MyShape** references and draw every shape (i.e., call every shape's **draw** method).

Begin by defining class **MyShape**, class **MyLine** and an application to test your classes. The application should have a **MyShape** instance variable that can refer to one **MyLine** object (created in the application's constructor). The **paint** method (for your subclass of **JFrame**) should draw the shape with a statement like

```
currentShape.draw( g );
```

where **currentShape** is the **MyShape** reference and **g** is the **Graphics** object that the shape will use to draw itself on the background of the window.

Next, change the single **MyShape** reference into an array of **MyShape** references and hard code several **MyLine** objects into the program for drawing. The application's **paint** method should walk through the array of shapes and draw every shape.

After the preceding part is working, you should define the **MyOval** and **MyRect** classes and add objects of these classes into the existing array. For now, all the shape objects should be created in the constructor for your subclass of **JFrame**. In Chapter 12, we will create the objects when the user chooses a shape and begins drawing it with the mouse.

9.29 In Exercise 9.28, you defined a **MyShape** hierarchy in which classes **MyLine**, **MyOval** and **MyRect** subclass **MyShape** directly. If the hierarchy was properly designed, you should be able to see the tremendous similarities between the **MyOval** and **MyRect** classes. Redesign and reimplement the code for the **MyOval** and **MyRect** classes to "factor out" the common features into the **abstract** class **MyBoundedShape** to produce the hierarchy in Fig. 9.15.

Class **MyBoundedShape** should define two constructors that mimic the constructors of class **MyShape** and methods that calculate the upper-left *x*-coordinate, upper-left *y*-coordinate, *width* and *height*. No new data pertaining to the dimensions of the shapes should be defined in this class. Remember, the values needed to draw an oval or rectangle can be calculated from two *(x,y)* coordinates. If designed properly, the new **MyOval** and **MyRect** classes should each have two constructors and a **draw** method.

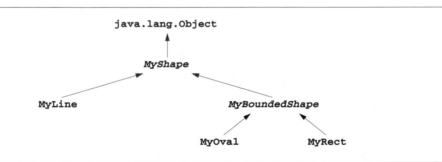

Fig. 9.15   The **MyShape** hierarchy.

Strings and Characters

Objectives

- To be able to create and manipulate nonmodifiable character string objects of class **String**.
- To be able to create and manipulate modifiable character string objects of class **StringBuffer**.
- To be able to create and manipulate objects of class **Character**.
- To be able to use a **StringTokenizer** object to break a **String** object into individual components called tokens.

The chief defect of Henry King
Was chewing little bits of string.
Hilaire Belloc

Vigorous writing is concise. A sentence should contain no
unnecessary words, a paragraph no unnecessary sentences.
William Strunk, Jr.

I have made this letter longer than usual, because I lack the
time to make it short.
Blaise Pascal

The difference between the almost-right word & the right word
is really a large matter—it's the difference between the
lightning bug and the lightning.
Mark Twain

Mum's the word.
Miguel de Cervantes, *Don Quixote de la Mancha*

Outline

10.1 Introduction

In this chapter, we introduce Java's string and character processing capabilities. The techniques discussed here are appropriate for developing text editors, word processors, page layout software, computerized typesetting systems and other kinds of text-processing software. We have already presented several string processing capabilities in the text. In this chapter we discuss in detail the capabilities of class **String**, class **StringBuffer** and class **Character** from the **java.lang** package and class **StringTokenizer** from the **java.util** package.

10.2 Fundamentals of Characters and Strings

Characters are the fundamental building blocks of Java source programs. Every program is composed of a sequence of characters that—when grouped together meaningfully—is interpreted by the computer as a series of instructions used to accomplish a task. A program may contain *character constants*. A character constant is an integer value represented as a character in single quotes. As we stated previously, the value of a character constant is the integer value of the character in the *Unicode character set*. For example, **'z'** represents the integer value of **z**, and **'\n'** represents the integer value of newline. See Appendix D for the integer equivalents of these characters.

A string is a series of characters treated as a single unit. A string may include letters, digits and various *special characters,* such as **+, -, *, /, $** and others. A string is an object of class **String**. *String literals* or *string constants* (often called *anonymous **String** objects*) are written as a sequence of characters in double quotation marks as follows:

"John Q. Doe"	(a name)
"9999 Main Street"	(a street address)
"Waltham, Massachusetts"	(a city and state)
"(201) 555-1212"	(a telephone number)

Performance Tip 10.1

*Java treats all anonymous **String**s with the same contents as one anonymous **String** object that has many references. This conserves memory.*

A **String** may be assigned in a declaration to a **String** reference. The declaration

```
String color = "blue";
```

initializes **String** reference **color** to refer to the anonymous **String** object **"blue"**.

Software Engineering Observation 10.1

*If there are multiple occurrences of the same anonymous **String** object in a single class definition, there will be one copy of the anonymous **String** object referenced from each location in the program that uses the anonymous **String**.*

10.3 **String** Constructors

Class **String** provides nine constructors for initializing **String** objects in a variety of ways. Seven of the constructors arc demonstrated in Fig. 10.1. All the constructors are used in the **StringConstructors** application's **main** method.

```
1   // Fig. 10.1: StringConstructors.java
2   // This program demonstrates the String class constructors.
3   import javax.swing.*;
4
5   public class StringConstructors {
6      public static void main( String args[] )
7      {
8         char charArray[] = { 'b', 'i', 'r', 't', 'h', ' ',
9                              'd', 'a', 'y' };
10        byte byteArray[] = { (byte) 'n', (byte) 'e', (byte) 'w',
11                             (byte) ' ', (byte) 'y', (byte) 'e',
12                             (byte) 'a', (byte) 'r' };
13        StringBuffer buffer;
14        String s, s1, s2, s3, s4, s5, s6, s7, output;
```

Fig. 10.1   Demonstrating the **String** class constructors (part 1 of 2).

```
15
16          s = new String( "hello" );
17          buffer =
18             new StringBuffer( "Welcome to Java Programming!" );
19
20          // use the String constructors
21          s1 = new String();
22          s2 = new String( s );
23          s3 = new String( charArray );
24          s4 = new String( charArray, 6, 3 );
25          s5 = new String( byteArray, 4, 4 );
26          s6 = new String( byteArray );
27          s7 = new String( buffer );
28
29          output = "s1 = " + s1 +
30                      "\ns2 = " + s2 +
31                      "\ns3 = " + s3 +
32                      "\ns4 = " + s4 +
33                      "\ns5 = " + s5 +
34                      "\ns6 = " + s6 +
35                      "\ns7 = " + s7;
36
37          JOptionPane.showMessageDialog( null, output,
38             "Demonstrating String Class Constructors",
39             JOptionPane.INFORMATION_MESSAGE );
40
41          System.exit( 0 );
42       }
43    }
```

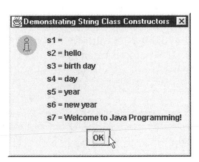

Fig. 10.1   Demonstrating the **String** class constructors (part 2 of 2).

Line 21

```
s1 = new String();
```

instantiates a new **String** object and assigns it to reference **s1** using class **String**'s default constructor. The new **String** object contains no characters (the *empty string*) and has a length of 0.

Line 22

```
s2 = new String( s );
```

instantiates a new **String** object and assigns it to reference **s2** using class **String**'s copy constructor. The new **String** object contains a copy of the characters in the **String** object **s** that is passed as an argument to the constructor.

Software Engineering Observation 10.2

In most cases, it is not necessary to make a copy of an existing **String** *object.* **String** *objects are* immutable—*their character contents cannot be changed after they are created. Also, if there are one or more references to a* **String** *object (or any object for that matter) the object cannot be reclaimed by the garbage collector. Thus, a* **String** *reference cannot be used to modify a* **String** *object or to delete a* **String** *object from memory as in other programming languages such as C or C++.*

Line 23

```
s3 = new String( charArray );
```

instantiates a new **String** object and assigns it to reference **s3** using class **String**'s constructor that takes a character array as an argument. The new **String** object contains a copy of the characters in the array.

Line 24

```
s4 = new String( charArray, 6, 3 );
```

instantiates a new **String** object and assigns it to reference **s4** using class **String**'s constructor that takes a **char** array and two integers as arguments. The second argument specifies the starting position (the **offset**) from which characters in the array are copied. The third argument specifies the number of characters (the **count**) to be copied from the array. The new **String** object contains a copy of the specified characters in the array. If the **offset** or the **count** specified as arguments result in accessing an element outside the bounds of the character array, a **StringIndexOutOfBoundsException** is thrown. We discuss exceptions in detail in Chapter 14.

Line 25

```
s5 = new String( byteArray, 4, 4 );
```

instantiates a new **String** object and assigns it to reference **s5** using class **String**'s constructor that receives a **byte** array and two integers as arguments. The second and third arguments specify the **offset** and **count**, respectively. The new **String** object contains a copy of the specified **byte**s in the array. If the **offset** or the **count** specified as arguments result in accessing an element outside the bounds of the character array, a **StringIndexOutOfBoundsException** is thrown.

Line 26

```
s6 = new String( byteArray );
```

instantiates a new **String** object and assigns it to reference **s6** using class **String**'s constructor that takes a **byte** array as an argument. The new **String** object contains a copy of the bytes in the array.

Line 27

```
s7 = new String( buffer );
```

instantiates a new **String** object and assigns it to reference **s7** using class **String**'s constructor that receives a **StringBuffer** as an argument. A **StringBuffer** is a dynamically resizable and modifiable string. The new **String** object contains a copy of the characters in the **StringBuffer**. Lines 17 and 18

```
buffer =
    new StringBuffer( "Welcome to Java Programming!" );
```

create a new object of class **StringBuffer** using the constructor that receives a **String** argument ("**Welcome to Java Programming**") and assign the new object to reference **buffer**. We discuss **StringBuffer**s in detail later in this chapter. The screen capture for the program displays the contents of each **String**.

10.4 String Methods length, charAt and getChars

The application of Fig. 10.2 presents **String** methods **length**, **charAt** and **get-Chars**, which determine the length of a **String**, get the character at a specific location in a **String** and get the entire set of characters in a **String**, respectively.

```
1   // Fig. 10.2: StringMisc.java
2   // This program demonstrates the length, charAt and getChars
3   // methods of the String class.
4   //
5   // Note: Method getChars requires a starting point
6   // and ending point in the String. The starting point is the
7   // actual subscript from which copying starts. The ending point
8   // is one past the subscript at which the copying ends.
9   import javax.swing.*;
10
11  public class StringMisc {
12     public static void main( String args[] )
13     {
14        String s1, output;
15        char charArray[];
16
17        s1 = new String( "hello there" );
18        charArray = new char[ 5 ];
19
20        // output the string
21        output = "s1: " + s1;
22
23        // test the length method
24        output += "\nLength of s1: " + s1.length();
25
26        // loop through the characters in s1 and display reversed
27        output += "\nThe string reversed is: ";
28
29        for ( int i = s1.length() - 1; i >= 0; i-- )
30           output += s1.charAt( i ) + " ";
31
```

Fig. 10.2   The **String** class character manipulation methods (part 1 of 2).

```
32              // copy characters from string into char array
33              s1.getChars( 0, 5, charArray, 0 );
34              output += "\nThe character array is: ";
35
36              for ( int i = 0; i < charArray.length; i++ )
37                 output += charArray[ i ];
38
39              JOptionPane.showMessageDialog( null, output,
40                 "Demonstrating String Class Constructors",
41                 JOptionPane.INFORMATION_MESSAGE );
42
43              System.exit( 0 );
44          }
45      }
```

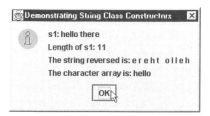

Fig. 10.2   The **String** class character manipulation methods (part 2 of 2).

Line 24

```
output += "\nLength of s1: " + s1.length();
```

uses **String** method **length** to determine the number of characters in **String s1**. Like arrays, **String**s always know their own size. However, unlike arrays, **String**s do not have a **length** instance variable that specifies the number of elements in a **String**.

Common Programming Error 10.1

*Attempting to determine the length of a **String** via an instance variable called **length** (e.g., **s1.length**) is a syntax error. The **String** method **length** must be used. (e.g., **s1.length()**).*

The **for** structure at line 29 appends to **String output** the characters of the **String s1** in reverse order. The **String** method **charAt** returns the character at a specific position in the **String**. Method **charAt** receives an integer argument that is used as the *position number* (or *index*) and returns the character at that position. Like arrays, the first element of a **String** is considered to be at position 0.

Common Programming Error 10.2

*Attempting to access a character that is outside the bounds of a **String** (i.e., an index less than 0 or an index greater than or equal to the **String**'s length) results in a **StringIndexOutOfBoundsException***

Line 33

```
s1.getChars( 0, 5, charArray, 0 );
```

uses **String** method **getChars** to copy the characters of a **String** into a character array. The first argument is the starting index from which characters are copied in the **String**. The second argument is the index that is one past the last character to be copied from the **String**. The third argument is the character array into which the characters are copied. The last argument is the starting index where the copied characters are placed in the character array. The **char** array contents are then appended one character at a time to **String output** with the **for** structure at line 36 for display purposes.

10.5 Comparing **Strings**

Java provides a variety of methods for comparing **String** objects; these are demonstrated in the next two examples. To understand just what it means for one string to be "greater than" or "less than" another string, consider the process of alphabetizing a series of last names. The reader would, no doubt, place "Jones" before "Smith" because the first letter of "Jones" comes before the first letter of "Smith" in the alphabet. But the alphabet is more than just a list of 26 letters—it is an ordered list of characters. Each letter occurs in a specific position within the list. "Z" is more than just a letter of the alphabet; "Z" is specifically the twenty-sixth letter of the alphabet.

How does the computer know that one letter comes before another? All characters are represented inside the computer as numeric codes (see Appendix D). When the computer compares two strings, it actually compares the numeric codes of the characters in the strings.

Figure 10.3 demonstrates the **String** methods **equals**, **equalsIgnoreCase**, **compareTo** and **regionMatches**, and demonstrates using the equality operator **==** to compare **String** objects.

```
1   // Fig. 10.3: StringCompare
2   // This program demonstrates the methods equals,
3   // equalsIgnoreCase, compareTo, and regionMatches
4   // of the String class.
5   import javax.swing.JOptionPane;
6
7   public class StringCompare {
8      public static void main( String args[] )
9      {
10         String s1, s2, s3, s4, output;
11
12         s1 = new String( "hello" );
13         s2 = new String( "good bye" );
14         s3 = new String( "Happy Birthday" );
15         s4 = new String( "happy birthday" );
16
17         output = "s1 = " + s1 + "\ns2 = " + s2 +
18                  "\ns3 = " + s3 + "\ns4 = " + s4 + "\n\n";
19
```

Fig. 10.3   Demonstrating **String** comparisons (part 1 of 3).

```
20          // test for equality
21          if ( s1.equals( "hello" ) )
22             output += "s1 equals \"hello\"\n";
23          else
24             output += "s1 does not equal \"hello\"\n";
25
26          // test for equality with ==
27          if ( s1 == "hello" )
28             output += "s1 equals \"hello\"\n";
29          else
30             output += "s1 does not equal \"hello\"\n";
31
32          // test for equality--ignore case
33          if ( s3.equalsIgnoreCase( s4 ) )
34             output += "s3 equals s4\n";
35          else
36             output += "s3 does not equal s4\n";
37
38          // test compareTo
39          output +=
40             "\ns1.compareTo( s2 ) is " + s1.compareTo( s2 ) +
41             "\ns2.compareTo( s1 ) is " + s2.compareTo( s1 ) +
42             "\ns1.compareTo( s1 ) is " + s1.compareTo( s1 ) +
43             "\ns3.compareTo( s4 ) is " + s3.compareTo( s4 ) +
44             "\ns4.compareTo( s3 ) is " + s4.compareTo( s3 ) +
45             "\n\n";
46
47          // test regionMatches (case sensitive)
48          if ( s3.regionMatches( 0, s4, 0, 5 ) )
49             output += "First 5 characters of s3 and s4 match\n";
50          else
51             output +=
52                "First 5 characters of s3 and s4 do not match\n";
53
54          // test regionMatches (ignore case)
55          if ( s3.regionMatches( true, 0, s4, 0, 5 ) )
56             output += "First 5 characters of s3 and s4 match";
57          else
58             output +=
59                "First 5 characters of s3 and s4 do not match";
60
61          JOptionPane.showMessageDialog( null, output,
62             "Demonstrating String Class Constructors",
63             JOptionPane.INFORMATION_MESSAGE );
64
65          System.exit( 0 );
66       }
67    }
```

Fig. 10.3   Demonstrating **String** comparisons (part 2 of 3).

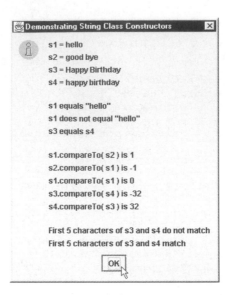

Fig. 10.3   Demonstrating **String** comparisons (part 3 of 3).

The condition in the **if** structure at line 21

```
s1.equals( "hello" )
```

uses method **equals** to compare **String s1** and anonymous **String "hello"** for equality. Method **equals** (inherited into **String** from its superclass **Object**) tests any two objects for equality (i.e., the contents of the two objects are identical). The method returns **true** if the objects are equal and **false** otherwise. The preceding condition is **true** because **String s1** was initialized with a copy of the anonymous **String "hello"**. Method **equals** uses a *lexicographical comparison*—the integer Unicode values that represent each character in each **String** are compared. Thus, if the **String "hello"** is compared to the **String "HELLO"** the result is **false** because the integer representation of a lowercase letter is different from that of the corresponding uppercase letter.

The condition in the **if** structure at line 27

```
s1 == "hello"
```

uses the equality operator **==** to compare **String s1** for equality with the anonymous **String "hello"**. *Operator **==** has different functionality when it is used to compare references and when it is used to compare values of primitive data types.* When primitive data type values are compared with **==**, the result is **true** if both values are identical. When references are compared with **==**, the result is **true** if both references *refer to the same object in memory*. To compare the actual contents (or state information) of objects for equality, methods (such as **equals**) must be invoked. The preceding condition evaluates to **false** in this program because the reference **s1** was initialized with the statement

```
s1 = new String( "hello" );
```

which creates a new **String** object with a copy of anonymous **String "hello"** and assigns the new object to reference **s1**. If **s1** had been initialized with the statement

```
s1 = "hello";
```

which directly assigns the anonymous **String "hello"** to the reference **s1**, the condition would be **true**. This is because, once again, Java treats all anonymous **String** objects with the same contents as one anonymous **String** object that has many references. Thus, lines 12, 21 and 27 all refer to the same anonymous **String** object **"hello"** in memory.

If you are sorting **String**s, you may compare them for equality with method **equalsIgnoreCase**, which ignores the case of the letters in each **String** when performing the comparison. Thus, the **String "hello"** and the **String "HELLO"** compare as equal. The **if** structure at line 33 uses the condition

```
s3.equalsIgnoreCase( s4 )
```

to compare **String s3**—**Happy Birthday**—for equality with **String s4**—**happy birthday**. The result of this comparison is **true**.

Lines 40 through 44 use the **String** method **compareTo** to compare **String** objects. For example, the expression

```
s1.compareTo( s2 )
```

on line 40 compares **String s1** to **String s2**. Method **compareTo** returns 0 if the **String**s are equal, a negative number if the **String** that invokes **compareTo** is less than the **String** that is passed as an argument and a positive number if the **String** that invokes **compareTo** is greater than the **String** that is passed as an argument. Method **compareTo** uses a lexicographical comparison.

The condition in the **if** structure at line 48

```
s3.regionMatches( 0, s4, 0, 5 )
```

uses **String** method **regionMatches** to compare portions of two **String** objects for equality. The first argument is the starting index in the **String** that invokes the method. The second argument is a comparison **String**. The third argument is the starting index in the comparison **String**. The last argument is the number of characters to compare between the two **String**s. The method returns **true** only if the specified number of characters are lexicographically equal.

Finally, the condition in the **if** structure at line 55

```
s3.regionMatches( true, 0, s4, 0, 5 )
```

uses a second version of **String** method **regionMatches** to compare portions of two **String** objects for equality. If the first argument is **true**, the method ignores the case of the characters being compared. The remaining arguments are identical to those described for the **regionMatches** method with four arguments.

The second example of this section (Fig. 10.4) demonstrates the **startsWith** and **endsWith** methods of class **String**. Application **StringStartEnd**'s **main** method defines an array of **String**s called **strings** containing **"started"**, **"starting"**, **"ended"** and **"ending"**. The remainder of method **main** consists of three **for** structures that test the elements of the array to determine if they start with or end with a particular set of characters.

```
1   // Fig. 10.4: StringStartEnd.java
2   // This program demonstrates the methods startsWith and
3   // endsWith of the String class.
4   import javax.swing.*;
5
6   public class StringStartEnd {
7      public static void main( String args[] )
8      {
9         String strings[] = { "started", "starting",
10                              "ended", "ending" };
11        String output = "";
12
13        // Test method startsWith
14        for ( int i = 0; i < strings.length; i++ )
15           if ( strings[ i ].startsWith( "st" ) )
16              output += "\"" + strings[ i ] +
17                         "\" starts with \"st\"\n";
18
19        output += "\n";
20
21        // Test method startsWith starting from position
22        // 2 of the string
23        for ( int i = 0; i < strings.length; i++ )
24           if ( strings[ i ].startsWith( "art", 2 ) )
25              output +=
26                 "\"" + strings[ i ] +
27                 "\" starts with \"art\" at position 2\n";
28
29        output += "\n";
30
31        // Test method endsWith
32        for ( int i = 0; i < strings.length; i++ )
33           if ( strings[ i ].endsWith( "ed" ) )
34              output += "\"" + strings[ i ] +
35                         "\" ends with \"ed\"\n";
36
37        JOptionPane.showMessageDialog( null, output,
38           "Demonstrating String Class Comparisons",
39           JOptionPane.INFORMATION_MESSAGE );
40
41        System.exit( 0 );
42     }
43  }
```

Fig. 10.4   String class **startsWith** and **endsWith** methods (part 1 of 2).

The first **for** structure (line 14) uses the version of method **startsWith** that takes a **String** argument. The condition in the **if** structure (line 15)

```
strings[ i ].startsWith( "st" )
```

determines if the **String** at location **i** of the array starts with the characters **"st"**. If so, the method returns **true** and **strings[i]** is appended to **String output** for display purposes.

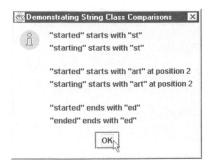

Fig. 10.4   String class **startsWith** and **endsWith** methods (part 2 of 2).

The second **for** structure (line 23) uses the version of method **startsWith** that takes a **String** and an integer as arguments. The integer argument specifies the index at which the comparison should begin in the **String**. The condition in the **if** structure

```
strings[ i ].startsWith( "art", 2 )
```

determines if the **String** at location **i** of the array starts with the characters **"art"** beginning with the character at index **2** in each **String**. If so, the method returns **true** and **strings[i]** is appended to **String output** for display purposes.

The third **for** structure (line 32) uses method **endsWith**, which takes a **String** argument. The condition in the **if** structure

```
strings[ i ].endsWith( "ed" )
```

determines if the **String** at location **i** of the array ends with the characters **"ed"**. If so, the method returns **true** and **strings[i]** is appended to **String output** for display purposes.

10.6 String Method hashCode

Often, it is necessary to store **String**s and other data types in a manner that allows the information to be found quickly. One of the best ways to store information for fast lookup is a hash table. A *hash table* stores information using a special calculation on the object to be stored that produces a *hash code*. The hash code is used to choose the location in the table at which to store the object. When the information needs to be retrieved, the same calculation is performed, the hash code is determined and a lookup of that location in the table results in the value that was stored there previously. Every object has the ability to be stored in a hash table. Class **Object** defines method **hashCode** to perform the hash code calculation. This method is inherited by all subclasses of **Object**. Method **hashCode** is overridden by **String** to provide a good hash code distribution based on the contents of the **String**. We will say more about hashing in Chapter 23.

The example in Fig. 10.5 demonstrates the **hashCode** method for two **String**s containing **"hello"** and **"Hello"**. Note that the hash code value for each **String** is different. That is because the **String**s themselves are lexicographically different.

```
1   // Fig. 10.5: StringHashCode.java1
2   // This program demonstrates the method
3   // hashCode of the String class.
4   import javax.swing.*;
5
6   public class StringHashCode {
7      public static void main( String args[] )
8      {
9         String s1 = "hello",
10               s2 = "Hello";
11
12        String output =
13           "The hash code for \"" + s1 + "\" is " +
14           s1.hashCode() +
15           "\nThe hash code for \"" + s2 + "\" is " +
16           s2.hashCode();
17
18        JOptionPane.showMessageDialog( null, output,
19           "Demonstrating String Method hashCode",
20           JOptionPane.INFORMATION_MESSAGE );
21
22        System.exit( 0 );
23     }
24  }
```

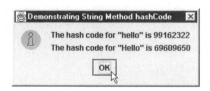

Fig. 10.5   The **String** class **hashCode** method.

10.7 Locating Characters and Substrings in **Strings**

Often it is useful to search for a character or set of characters in a **String**. For example, if you are creating your own word processor, you may want to provide a capability for searching through the document. The application of Fig. 10.6 demonstrates the many versions of **String** methods **indexOf** and **lastIndexOf** that search for a specified character or substring in a **String**. All the searches in this example are performed on the **String letters** (initialized with **"abcdefghijklmabcdefghijklm"**) in method **main** method of class **StringIndexMethods**.

```
1   // Fig. 10.6: StringIndexMethods.java
2   // This program demonstrates the String
3   // class index methods.
4   import javax.swing.*;
5
```

Fig. 10.6   The **String** class searching methods (part 1 of 3).

```
6  public class StringIndexMethods {
7     public static void main( String args[] )
8     {
9        String letters = "abcdefghijklmabcdefghijklm";
10       String output;
11
12       // test indexOf to locate a character in a string
13       output = "'c' is located at index " +
14                   letters.indexOf( 'c' );
15
16       output += "\n'a' is located at index " +
17                   letters.indexOf( 'a', 1 );
18
19       output += "\n'$' is located at index " +
20                   letters.indexOf( '$' );
21
22       // test lastIndexOf to find a character in a string
23       output += "\n\nLast 'c' is located at index " +
24                   letters.lastIndexOf( 'c' );
25
26       output += "\nLast 'a' is located at index " +
27                   letters.lastIndexOf( 'a', 25 );
28
29       output += "\nLast '$' is located at index " +
30                   letters.lastIndexOf( '$' );
31
32       // test indexOf to locate a substring in a string
33       output += "\n\n\"def\" is located at index " +
34                   letters.indexOf( "def" );
35
36       output += "\n\"def\" is located at index " +
37                   letters.indexOf( "def", 7 );
38
39       output += "\n\"hello\" is located at index " +
40                   letters.indexOf( "hello" );
41
42       // test lastIndexOf to find a substring in a string
43       output += "\n\nLast \"def\" is located at index " +
44                   letters.lastIndexOf( "def" );
45
46       output += "\nLast \"def\" is located at index " +
47                   letters.lastIndexOf( "def", 25 );
48
49       output += "\nLast \"hello\" is located at index " +
50                   letters.lastIndexOf( "hello" );
51
52       JOptionPane.showMessageDialog( null, output,
53          "Demonstrating String Class \"index\" Methods",
54          JOptionPane.INFORMATION_MESSAGE );
55
56       System.exit( 0 );
57    }
58 }
```

Fig. 10.6 The **String** class searching methods (part 2 of 3).

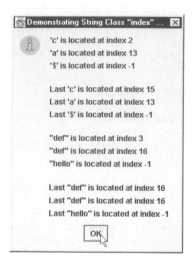

Fig. 10.6   The **String** class searching methods (part 3 of 3).

The statements at lines 13 through 20 use method **indexOf** to locate the first occurrence of a character in a **String**. If the character is found, the index of that character in the **String** is returned; otherwise, –1 is returned. There are two versions of **indexOf** that search for characters in a **String**. The expression on line 14

```
letters.indexOf( 'c' )
```

uses method **indexOf** that takes one integer argument which is the integer representation of a character. Remember that a character constant in single quotes specifies the integer representation of the character in the Unicode character set. The expression at line 17

```
letters.indexOf( 'a', 1 )
```

uses the second version of method **indexOf**, which takes two integer arguments—the integer representation of a character and the starting index at which the search of the **String** should begin.

The statements at lines 23 through 30 use method **lastIndexOf** to locate the last occurrence of a character in a **String**. The search is performed from the end of the **String** toward the beginning of the **String**. If the character is found, the index of that character in the **String** is returned; otherwise, –1 is returned. There are two versions of **lastIndexOf** that search for characters in a **String**. The expression at line 24

```
letters.lastIndexOf( 'c' )
```

uses the version of method **lastIndexOf** that takes one integer argument that is the integer representation of a character. The expression at line 27

```
letters.lastIndexOf( 'a', 25 )
```

uses the version of method **lastIndexOf** that takes two integer arguments—the integer representation of a character and the highest index from which to begin searching backward for the character.

Lines 33 through 50 of the program demonstrate the **indexOf** and **lastIndexOf** methods—each of which takes a **String** as its first argument. These versions of the methods perform identically to those described above except that they search for sequences of characters (or substrings) that are specified by their **String** arguments.

10.8 Extracting Substrings from **Strings**

Class **String** provides two **substring** methods to enable a new **String** object to be created by copying part of an existing **String** object. Each method returns a new **String** object. Both methods are demonstrated in Fig. 10.7. The expression from line 14

```
letters.substring( 20 )
```

uses the **substring** method that takes one integer argument. The argument specifies the starting index from which characters are copied in the original **String**. The substring returned contains a copy of the characters from the starting index to the end of the **String**. If the index specified as an argument is outside the bounds of the **String**, a **StringIndexOutOfBoundsException** is generated.

```
1   // Fig. 10.7: SubString.java
2   // This program demonstrates the
3   // String class substring methods.
4   import javax.swing.*;
5
6   public class SubString {
7      public static void main( String args[] )
8      {
9         String letters = "abcdefghijklmabcdefghijklm";
10        String output;
11
12        // test substring methods
13        output = "Substring from index 20 to end is " +
14                 "\"" + letters.substring( 20 ) + "\"\n";
15
16        output += "Substring from index 0 up to 6 is " +
17                  "\"" + letters.substring( 0, 6 ) + "\"";
18
19        JOptionPane.showMessageDialog( null, output,
20           "Demonstrating String Class Substring Methods",
21           JOptionPane.INFORMATION_MESSAGE );
22
23        System.exit( 0 );
24     }
25  }
```

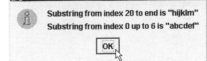

Fig. 10.7   The **String** class **substring** methods.

The expression from line 17

```
letters.substring( 0, 6 )
```

uses the **substring** method that takes two integer arguments. The first argument specifies the starting index from which characters are copied in the original **String**. The second argument specifies the index one beyond the last character to be copied (i.e., copy up to, but not including, that index in the **String**). The substring returned contains copies of the specified characters from the original **String**. If the arguments are outside the bounds of the **String**, a **StringIndexOutOfBoundsException** is generated.

10.9 Concatenating Strings

The **String** method **concat** (Fig. 10.8) concatenates two **String** objects and returns a new **String** object containing the characters from both original **String**s. If the argument **String** has no characters in it, the original **String** is returned. The expression

```
s1.concat( s2 )
```

at line 18 appends the characters from the **String s2** to the end of the **String s1**. The original **String**s **s1** and **s2** are not modified.

```
1   // Fig. 10.8: StringConcat.java
2   // This program demonstrates the String class concat method.
3   // Note that the concat method returns a new String object. It
4   // does not modify the object that invoked the concat method.
5   import javax.swing.*;
6
7   public class StringConcat {
8      public static void main( String args[] )
9      {
10         String s1 = new String( "Happy " ),
11                s2 = new String( "Birthday" ),
12                output;
13
14         output = "s1 = " + s1 +
15                  "\ns2 = " + s2;
16
17         output += "\n\nResult of s1.concat( s2 ) = " +
18                  s1.concat( s2 );
19
20         output += "\ns1 after concatenation = " + s1;
21
22         JOptionPane.showMessageDialog( null, output,
23            "Demonstrating String Method concat",
24            JOptionPane.INFORMATION_MESSAGE );
25
26         System.exit( 0 );
27      }
28   }
```

Fig. 10.8   The **String** method **concat** (part 1 of 2).

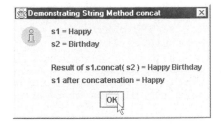

Fig. 10.8   The **String** method **concat** (part 2 of 2).

10.10 Miscellaneous **String** Methods

Class **String** provides several methods that return modified copies of **String**s or that return a character array. These methods are demonstrated in the application of Fig. 10.9.

```
1   // Fig. 10.9: StringMisc2.java
2   // This program demonstrates the String methods replace,
3   // toLowerCase, toUpperCase, trim, toString and toCharArray
4   import javax.swing.*;
5
6   public class StringMisc2 {
7      public static void main( String args[] )
8      {
9         String s1 = new String( "hello" ),
10                s2 = new String( "GOOD BYE" ),
11                s3 = new String( "   spaces   " ),
12                output;
13
14        output = "s1 = " + s1 +
15                 "\ns2 = " + s2 +
16                 "\ns3 = " + s3;
17
18        // test method replace
19        output += "\n\nReplace 'l' with 'L' in s1: " +
20                  s1.replace( 'l', 'L' );
21
22        // test toLowerCase and toUpperCase
23        output +=
24           "\n\ns1.toUpperCase() = " + s1.toUpperCase() +
25           "\ns2.toLowerCase() = " + s2.toLowerCase();
26
27        // test trim method
28        output += "\n\ns3 after trim = \"" + s3.trim() + "\"";
29
30        // test toString method
31        output += "\n\ns1 = " + s1.toString();
32
33        // test toCharArray method
34        char charArray[] = s1.toCharArray();
```

Fig. 10.9   Miscellaneous **String** methods (part 1 of 2).

```
35              output += "\n\ns1 as a character array = ";
36
37              for ( int i = 0; i < charArray.length; ++i )
38                  output += charArray[ i ];
39
40              JOptionPane.showMessageDialog( null, output,
41                  "Demonstrating Miscellaneous String Methods",
42                  JOptionPane.INFORMATION_MESSAGE );
43
44              System.exit( 0 );
45          }
46      }
```

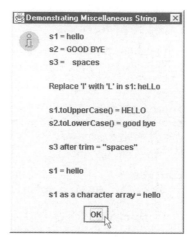

Fig. 10.9   Miscellaneous **String** methods (part 2 of 2).

In line 20, the expression

```
s1.replace( 'l', 'L' )
```

uses **String** method **replace** to return a new **String** object in which every occurrence in **String s1** of character **'l'** is replaced with character **'L'**. The original **String** is unchanged. If there are no occurrences of the first argument in the **String**, the original **String** is returned.

In line 24, the expression

```
s1.toUpperCase()
```

uses **String** method **toUpperCase** to generate a new **String** object with uppercase letters where corresponding lowercase letters reside in **s1**. The method returns a new **String** object containing the converted **String** and the original **String** is unchanged. If there are no characters to convert to uppercase letters, the original **String** is returned.

The expression

```
s2.toLowerCase()
```

from line 25 uses **String** method **toLowerCase** to return a new **String** object with lowercase letters where corresponding uppercase letters reside in **s1**. The original **String** is unchanged. If there are no characters to convert to lowercase letters, the original **String** is returned.

The expression

s3.trim()

from line 28 uses **String** method **trim** to generate a new **String** object that removes all white-space characters that appear at the beginning or end of the **String** to which the **trim** message is sent. The method returns a new **String** object containing the **String** without leading or trailing white-space characters. The original **String** is unchanged.

The expression

s1.toString()

from line 31 returns the **String s1**. Why is the **toString** method provided for class **String**? All objects can be converted to **String**s in Java by using method **toString**, which originates in the **Object** class. If a class that inherits from **Object** (such as **String**) does not override method **toString**, the default version from class **Object** is used. The default version creates a **String** consisting of the object's class name and the hash code for the object. The **toString** method is normally used to express the contents of an object as text. Method **toString** is provided in class **String** to ensure that the proper **String** value is returned.

The statement

char charArray[] = s1.toCharArray();

from line 34 creates a new character array containing a copy of the characters in **String s1** and assigns it to **charArray**.

10.11 Using **String** Method **valueOf**

Class **String** provides a set of **static** class methods that take arguments of various types, convert those arguments to strings and return them as **String** objects. Class **StringValueOf** (Fig. 10.10) demonstrates the **String** class **valueOf** methods.

```
1   // Fig. 10.10: StringValueOf.java
2   // This program demonstrates the String class valueOf methods.
3   import javax.swing.*;
4
5   public class StringValueOf {
6      public static void main( String args[] )
7      {
8         char charArray[] = { 'a', 'b', 'c', 'd', 'e', 'f' };
9         boolean b = true;
10        char c = 'Z';
11        int i = 7;
12        long l = 10000000;
13        float f = 2.5f;
14        double d = 33.333;
```

Fig. 10.10   The **String** class **valueOf** methods (part 1 of 2).

```
15          Object o = "hello";  // Assign to an Object reference
16          String output;
17
18          output = "char array = " + String.valueOf( charArray ) +
19                  "\npart of char array = " +
20                  String.valueOf( charArray, 3, 3 ) +
21                  "\nboolean = " + String.valueOf( b ) +
22                  "\nchar = " + String.valueOf( c ) +
23                  "\nint = " + String.valueOf( i ) +
24                  "\nlong = " + String.valueOf( l ) +
25                  "\nfloat = " + String.valueOf( f ) +
26                  "\ndouble = " + String.valueOf( d ) +
27                  "\nObject = " + String.valueOf( o );
28
29          JOptionPane.showMessageDialog( null, output,
30             "Demonstrating String Class valueOf Methods",
31             JOptionPane.INFORMATION_MESSAGE );
32
33          System.exit( 0 );
34       }
35   }
```

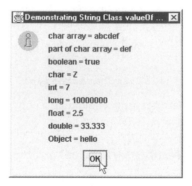

Fig. 10.10 The **String** class **valueOf** methods (part 2 of 2).

The expression

> `String.valueOf( charArray )`

from line 18 copies the contents of the character array **charArray** into a new **String** object and returns the new **String**.

The expression

> `String.valueOf( charArray, 3, 3 )`

from line 20 copies a portion of the contents of the character array **charArray** into a new **String** object and returns the new **String**. The second argument specifies the starting index from which the characters are copied. The third argument specifies the number of characters to copy.

There are seven other versions of method **valueOf**, which take arguments of type **boolean**, **char**, **int**, **long**, **float**, **double** and **Object**, respectively. These are demonstrated in lines 21 through 27 of the program. Note that the version of **valueOf** that takes an **Object** as an argument can do so because all **Object**s can be converted to **String**s with the **toString** method.

10.12 String Method **intern**

Comparing large **String** objects is a relatively slow operation. **String** method **intern** can improve **String** comparison performance. When **String** method **intern** is invoked on a **String** object it returns a reference to a **String** object that is guaranteed to have the same contents. Subsequent invocations of **intern** on different **String** objects that have the same contents as the original **String** object result in multiple references to the same **String** object. This is useful for efficient **String** comparisons of large **String**s. Once **intern** has been performed, the **String** references can be compared with **==** (which simply compares two references—a fast operation) rather than using **String** comparison methods such as **equals** and **equalsIgnoreCase** (which require comparing each pair of corresponding characters in each **String**—a time-consuming iterative operation). The program of Fig. 10.11 demonstrates the **intern** method.

```
1   // Fig. 10.11: StringIntern.java
2   // This program demonstrates the intern method
3   // of the String class.
4   import javax.swing.*;
5
6   public class StringIntern {
7      public static void main( String args[] )
8      {
9         String s1, s2, s3, s4, output;
10
11        s1 = new String( "hello" );
12        s2 = new String( "hello" );
13
14        // Test strings to determine if they are the same
15        // String object in memory.
16        if ( s1 == s2 )
17           output =
18              "s1 and s2 are the same object in memory";
19        else
20           output =
21              "s1 and s2 are not the same object in memory";
22
23        // Test strings for equality of contents
24        if ( s1.equals( s2 ) )
25           output += "\ns1 and s2 are equal";
26        else
27           output += "\ns1 and s2 are not equal";
28
29        // Use String intern method to get a unique copy of
30        // "hello" referred to by both s3 and s4.
31        s3 = s1.intern();
32        s4 = s2.intern();
```

Fig. 10.11   The **String** class **valueOf** methods (part 1 of 2).

```
33
34          // Test strings to determine if they are the same
35          // String object in memory.
36          if ( s3 == s4 )
37             output +=
38                "\ns3 and s4 are the same object in memory";
39          else
40             output +=
41                "\ns3 and s4 are not the same object in memory";
42
43          // Determine if s1 and s3 refer to the same object
44          if ( s1 == s3 )
45             output +=
46                "\ns1 and s3 are the same object in memory";
47          else
48             output +=
49                "\ns1 and s3 are not the same object in memory";
50
51          // Determine if s2 and s4 refer to the same object
52          if ( s2 == s4 )
53             output +=
54                "\ns2 and s4 are the same object in memory";
55          else
56             output +=
57                "\ns2 and s4 are not the same object in memory";
58
59          // Determine if s1 and s4 refer to the same object
60          if ( s1 == s4 )
61             output +=
62                "\ns1 and s4 are the same object in memory";
63          else
64             output +=
65                "\ns1 and s4 are not the same object in memory";
66
67          JOptionPane.showMessageDialog( null, output,
68             "Demonstrating String Method intern",
69             JOptionPane.INFORMATION_MESSAGE );
70
71          System.exit( 0 );
72       }
73    }
```

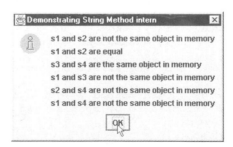

Fig. 10.11   The **String** class **valueOf** methods (part 2 of 2).

The program declares five **String** references—**s1, s2, s3, s4** and **output**. **String**s **s1** and **s2** are initialized with copies of **"hello"**. The first **if** structure (line 16) uses operator **==** to determine that **String**s **s1** and **s2** are the same object. The second **if** structure (line 24) uses method **equals** to determine that the contents of **String**s **s1** and **s2** are equal. Line 31

```
s3 = s1.intern();
```

uses method **intern** to get a reference to a **String** with the same contents as object **s1** and assigns the reference to **s3**. Line 32

```
s4 = s2.intern();
```

also uses method **intern** to get a reference to a **String** object. However, because **String s1** and **String s2** have the same contents, the reference returned by this call to **intern** is a reference to the same **String** object returned by **s1.intern()**.

The third **if** structure (line 36) uses operator **==** to determine that **String**s **s3** and **s4** are the same object. The fourth **if** structure (line 44) uses operator **==** to determine that **String**s **s1** and **s3** are *not* the same object. Technically, they could refer to the same object, but they are not guaranteed to refer to the same object unless the objects they refer to were returned by calls to **intern** on **String**s with the same contents. In this case, **s1** refers to the **String** it was assigned in method **main**. The fifth **if** structure (line 52) uses operator **==** to determine that **String**s **s2** and **s4** are *not* the same object (this is because the second **intern** call results in a reference to the same object returned by **s1.intern()**, not **String s2**). The sixth **if** structure (line 60) uses operator **==** to determine that **String**s **s1** and **s4** are not the same object.

10.13 StringBuffer Class

The **String** class provides many capabilities for processing **String**s. However, once a **String** object is created, its contents can never change. The next several sections discuss the features of class **StringBuffer** for creating and manipulating dynamic string information—i.e., modifiable **String**s. Every **StringBuffer** is capable of storing a number of characters specified by its capacity. If the capacity of a **StringBuffer** is exceeded, the capacity is automatically expanded to accommodate the additional characters. As we will see, class **StringBuffer** is also used to implement operators **+** and **+=** for **String** concatenation.

Performance Tip 10.2

String objects are constant strings and **StringBuffer** *objects are modifiable strings. Java distinguishes constant strings and modifiable strings for optimization purposes; in particular, Java can perform certain optimizations involving* **String** *objects (such as sharing one* **String** *object among multiple references) because it knows these objects will not change.*

Performance Tip 10.3

When given the choice between using a **String** *object to represent a string versus a* **StringBuffer** *object to represent that string, always use a* **String** *object if indeed the object will not change; this improves performance.*

Common Programming Error 10.3

*Invoking **StringBuffer** methods that are not methods of class **String** on **String** objects is a syntax error.*

10.14 StringBuffer Constructors

Class **StringBuffer** provides three constructors (demonstrated in Fig. 10.12). Line 10

```
buf1 = new StringBuffer();
```

uses the default **StringBuffer** constructor to create a **StringBuffer** with no characters in it and an initial capacity of 16 characters. Line 11

```
buf2 = new StringBuffer( 10 );
```

uses **StringBuffer** constructor that takes an integer argument to create a **String-Buffer** with no characters in it and the initial capacity specified in the integer argument (i.e., **10**).

```
1   // Fig. 10.12: StringBufferConstructors.java
2   // This program demonstrates the StringBuffer constructors.
3   import javax.swing.*;
4
5   public class StringBufferConstructors {
6      public static void main( String args[] )
7      {
8         StringBuffer buf1, buf2, buf3;
9
10        buf1 = new StringBuffer();
11        buf2 = new StringBuffer( 10 );
12        buf3 = new StringBuffer( "hello" );
13
14        String output =
15           "buf1 = " + "\"" + buf1.toString() + "\"" +
16           "\nbuf2 = " + "\"" + buf2.toString() + "\"" +
17           "\nbuf3 = " + "\"" + buf3.toString() + "\"";
18
19        JOptionPane.showMessageDialog( null, output,
20           "Demonstrating StringBuffer Class Constructors",
21           JOptionPane.INFORMATION_MESSAGE );
22
23        System.exit( 0 );
24     }
25  }
```

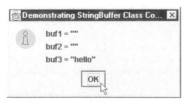

Fig. 10.12　The **StringBuffer** class constructors.

Line 12

```
buf3 = new StringBuffer( "hello" );
```

uses the **StringBuffer** constructor that takes a **String** argument to create a **StringBuffer** containing the characters of the **String** argument. The initial capacity is the number of characters in the **String** argument plus 16.

The statement on lines 14 through 17 uses **StringBuffer** method **toString** to convert the **StringBuffer**s into **String** objects that can be displayed with **draw-String**. Note the use of operator **+** to concatenate **String**s for output. In Section 10.17 we discuss how the **StringBuffer** is used to implement the **+** operator and **+=** operator.

10.15 StringBuffer Methods length, capacity, setLength and ensureCapacity

Class **StringBuffer** provides the **length** and **capacity** methods to return the number of characters currently in a **StringBuffer** and the number of characters that can be stored in a **StringBuffer** without allocating more memory, respectively. Method **ensureCapacity** is provided to allow the programmer to guarantee that a **String-Buffer** has a minimum capacity. Method **setLength** is provided to enable the programmer to increase or decrease the length of a **StringBuffer**. The program of Fig. 10.13 demonstrates these methods.

```
1   // Fig. 10.13: StringBufferCapLen.java
2   // This program demonstrates the length and
3   // capacity methods of the StringBuffer class.
4   import javax.swing.*;
5
6   public class StringBufferCapLen {
7      public static void main( String args[] )
8      {
9         StringBuffer buf =
10           new StringBuffer( "Hello, how are you?" );
11
12        String output = "buf = " + buf.toString() +
13                        "\nlength = " + buf.length() +
14                        "\ncapacity = " + buf.capacity();
15
16        buf.ensureCapacity( 75 );
17        output += "\n\nNew capacity = " + buf.capacity();
18
19        buf.setLength( 10 );
20        output += "\n\nNew length = " + buf.length() +
21                  "\nbuf = " + buf.toString();
22
23        JOptionPane.showMessageDialog( null, output,
24           "StringBuffer length and capacity Methods",
25           JOptionPane.INFORMATION_MESSAGE );
26
```

Fig. 10.13 **StringBuffer length** and **capacity** methods (part 1 of 2).

```
27          System.exit( 0 );
28     }
29  }
```

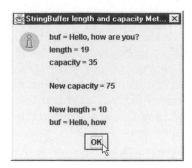

Fig. 10.13 **StringBuffer length** and **capacity** methods (part 2 of 2).

The program contains one **StringBuffer** called **buf**. Line 10 of the program uses the **StringBuffer** constructor that takes a **String** argument to instantiate and initialize the **StringBuffer** with **"Hello, how are you?"**. Lines 12 through 14 append to **output** the contents, the length and the capacity of the **StringBuffer**. Notice in the output window that the capacity of the **StringBuffer** is initially 35. Remember that the **StringBuffer** constructor that takes a **String** argument creates a **StringBuffer** object with an initial capacity that is the length of the **String** passed as an argument plus 16.

Line 16

```
    buf.ensureCapacity( 75 );
```

expands the capacity of the **StringBuffer** to a minimum of 75 characters. Actually, if the original capacity is less than the argument, the method ensures a capacity that is the greater of the number specified as an argument or twice the original capacity plus 2. If the **StringBuffer**'s current capacity is more than the specified capacity, the **String-Buffer**'s capacity remains unchanged.

Line 19

```
    buf.setLength( 10 );
```

uses method **setLength** to set the length of the **StringBuffer** to 10. If the specified length is less than the current number of characters in the **StringBuffer**, the characters are truncated to the specified length (i.e., the characters in the **StringBuffer** after the specified length are discarded). If the specified length is greater than the number of characters currently in the **StringBuffer**, null characters (characters with the numeric representation 0) are appended to the **StringBuffer** until the total number of characters in the **StringBuffer** is equal to the specified length.

10.16 StringBuffer Methods charAt, setCharAt, getChars and reverse

Class **StringBuffer** provides the **charAt**, **setCharAt**, **getChars** and **reverse** methods to manipulate the characters in a **StringBuffer**. Method **charAt** takes an integer argument and returns the character in the **StringBuffer** at that index. Method **setCharAt** takes an integer and a character argument and sets the character at the specified position to the character argument. The index specified in the **charAt** and **setCharAt** methods must be greater than or equal to 0 and less than the **StringBuffer** length; otherwise, a **StringIndexOutOfBoundsException** is generated.

Common Programming Error 10.4

*Attempting to access a character that is outside the bounds of a **StringBuffer** (i.e., an index less than 0 or an index greater than or equal to the **StringBuffer**'s length) results in a **StringIndexOutOfBoundsException***.

Method **getChars** returns a character array containing a copy of the characters in the **StringBuffer**. This method takes four arguments—the starting index from which characters should be copied in the **StringBuffer**, the index one past the last character to be copied from the **StringBuffer**, the character array into which the characters are to be copied and the starting location in the character array where the first character should be placed. Method **reverse** reverses the contents of the **StringBuffer**. Each of these methods is demonstrated in Fig. 10.14.

```
1   // Fig. 10.14: StringBufferChars.java
2   // The charAt, setCharAt, getChars, and reverse methods
3   // of class StringBuffer.
4   import javax.swing.*;
5
6   public class StringBufferChars {
7      public static void main( String args[] )
8      {
9         StringBuffer buf = new StringBuffer( "hello there" );
10
11        String output = "buf = " + buf.toString() +
12                        "\nCharacter at 0: " + buf.charAt( 0 ) +
13                        "\nCharacter at 4: " + buf.charAt( 4 );
14
15        char charArray[] = new char[ buf.length() ];
16        buf.getChars( 0, buf.length(), charArray, 0 );
17        output += "\n\nThe characters are: ";
18
19        for ( int i = 0; i < charArray.length; ++i )
20           output += charArray[ i ];
21
22        buf.setCharAt( 0, 'H' );
23        buf.setCharAt( 6, 'T' );
24        output += "\n\nbuf = " + buf.toString();
25
26        buf.reverse();
27        output += "\n\nbuf = " + buf.toString();
28
29        JOptionPane.showMessageDialog( null, output,
30           "Demonstrating StringBuffer Character Methods",
31           JOptionPane.INFORMATION_MESSAGE );
```

Fig. 10.14   **StringBuffer** class character manipulation methods (part 1 of 2).

```
32
33              System.exit( 0 );
34      }
35 }
```

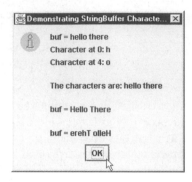

Fig. 10.14 **StringBuffer** class character manipulation methods (part 2 of 2).

10.17 StringBuffer append Methods

Class **StringBuffer** provides 10 overloaded **append** methods to allow various data type values to be added to the end of a **StringBuffer**. Versions are provided for each of the primitive data types and for character arrays, **String**s and **Object**s (remember that method **toString** produces a **String** representation of any **Object**). Each of the methods takes its argument, converts it to a **String** and appends it to the **String-Buffer**. The **append** methods are demonstrated in Fig. 10.15.

```
1  // Fig. 10.15: StringBufferAppend.java
2  // This program demonstrates the append
3  // methods of the StringBuffer class.
4  import javax.swing.*;
5
6  public class StringBufferAppend {
7     public static void main( String args[] )
8     {
9        Object o = "hello";
10       String s = "good bye";
11       char charArray[] = { 'a', 'b', 'c', 'd', 'e', 'f' };
12       boolean b = true;
13       char c = 'Z';
14       int i = 7;
15       long l = 10000000;
16       float f = 2.5f;
17       double d = 33.333;
18       StringBuffer buf = new StringBuffer();
19
20       buf.append( o );
21       buf.append( "   " );
```

Fig. 10.15 The **StringBuffer** class **append** methods (part 1 of 2).

```
22          buf.append( s );
23          buf.append( "   " );
24          buf.append( charArray );
25          buf.append( "   " );
26          buf.append( charArray, 0, 3 );
27          buf.append( "   " );
28          buf.append( b );
29          buf.append( "   " );
30          buf.append( c );
31          buf.append( "   " );
32          buf.append( i );
33          buf.append( "   " );
34          buf.append( l );
35          buf.append( "   " );
36          buf.append( f );
37          buf.append( "   " );
38          buf.append( d );
39
40          JOptionPane.showMessageDialog( null,
41             "buf = " + buf.toString(),
42             "Demonstrating StringBuffer append Methods",
43             JOptionPane.INFORMATION_MESSAGE );
44
45          System.exit( 0 );
46       }
47    }
```

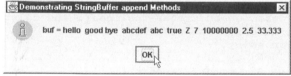

Fig. 10.15 The **StringBuffer** class **append** methods (part 2 of 2).

Actually, **StringBuffer**s and the **append** methods are used by the compiler to implement the **+** and **+=** operators for concatenating **String**s. For example, the statement

```
String s = "BC" + 22;
```

concatenates **String "BC"** and integer **22**. The concatenation is performed as follows:

```
new StringBuffer( "BC" ).append( 22 ).toString();
```

First, a **StringBuffer** is created with the default **String "BC"** as its contents. Next, integer **22** is appended to the end of the **StringBuffer**. Finally, the **StringBuffer** is converted to a **String** with method **toString** and the result is assigned to **String s**. The statement

```
s += "!";
```

is actually performed as follows:

```
s = new StringBuffer( s ).append( "!" ).toString()
```

First, a **StringBuffer** is created containing the default **String s**. Next the **String "!"** is appended to the end of the **StringBuffer**. Finally, the **StringBuffer** is converted to a **String** with method **toString** and the result is assigned to **String s**.

10.18 **StringBuffer** Insertion and Deletion Methods

Class **StringBuffer** provides nine overloaded **insert** methods to allow various data type values to be inserted at any position in a **StringBuffer**. Versions are provided for each of the primitive data types and for character arrays, **String**s and **Object**s (remember that method **toString** produces a **String** representation of any **Object**). Each of the methods takes its second argument, converts it to a **String** and inserts it preceding the index specified by the first argument. The index specified by the first argument must be greater than or equal to **0** and less than the length of the **StringBuffer**; otherwise, a **StringIndexOutOfBoundsException** is generated. Class **StringBuffer** also provides methods *delete* and *deleteCharAt* for deleting characters at any position in a **StringBuffer**. Method **delete** takes two arguments—the starting subscript and the subscript one past the end of the characters to delete. All characters beginning at the starting subscript up to but not including the ending subscript are deleted. Method **deleteCharAt** takes one argument—the subscript of the character to delete. Invalid subscripts cause both methods to throw a **StringIndexOutOfBoundsException**. The **insert** and delete methods are demonstrated in Fig. 10.16.

```
1   // Fig. 10.16: StringBufferInsert.java
2   // This program demonstrates the insert and delete
3   // methods of class StringBuffer.
4   import javax.swing.*;
5
6   public class StringBufferInsert {
7      public static void main( String args[] )
8      {
9         Object o = "hello";
10        String s = "good bye";
11        char charArray[] = { 'a', 'b', 'c', 'd', 'e', 'f' };
12        boolean b = true;
13        char c = 'K';
14        int i = 7;
15        long l = 10000000;
16        float f = 2.5f;
17        double d = 33.333;
18        StringBuffer buf = new StringBuffer();
19
20        buf.insert( 0, o );
21        buf.insert( 0, "   " );
22        buf.insert( 0, s );
23        buf.insert( 0, "   " );
24        buf.insert( 0, charArray );
25        buf.insert( 0, "   " );
26        buf.insert( 0, b );
```

Fig. 10.16   The **StringBuffer** class **insert** methods (part 1 of 2).

```
27          buf.insert( 0, "  " );
28          buf.insert( 0, c );
29          buf.insert( 0, "  " );
30          buf.insert( 0, i );
31          buf.insert( 0, "  " );
32          buf.insert( 0, l );
33          buf.insert( 0, "  " );
34          buf.insert( 0, f );
35          buf.insert( 0, "  " );
36          buf.insert( 0, d );
37
38          String output = "buf after inserts:\n" + buf.toString();
39
40          buf.deleteCharAt( 10 );      // delete 5 in 2.5
41          buf.delete( 2, 6 );          // delete .333 in 33.333
42
43          output += "\n\nbuf after deletes:\n" + buf.toString();
44
45          JOptionPane.showMessageDialog( null, output,
46             "Demonstrating StringBufferer Inserts and Deletes",
47             JOptionPane.INFORMATION_MESSAGE );
48
49          System.exit( 0 );
50       }
51    }
```

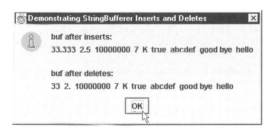

Fig. 10.16   The **StringBuffer** class **insert** methods (part 2 of 2).

10.19 **Character** Class Examples

Java provides a number of classes that enable primitive variables to be treated as objects. The classes are **Boolean, Character, Double, Float, Byte, Short, Integer** and **Long**. These classes (except **Boolean** and **Character**) are derived from **Number**. These eight classes are known as *type wrappers* and they are part of the **java.lang** package. Objects of these classes can be used anywhere in a program that an **Object** or a **Number** is expected. In this section, we present class **Character**—the type-wrapper class for characters.

Most **Character** class methods are **static** and take at least a character argument and perform either a test or a manipulation of the character. These class also contains a constructor that receives a **char** argument to initialize a **Character** object and several non-**static** methods. Most of the methods of class **Character** are presented in the next three examples. For more information on class **Character** (and all the wrapper classes), see the **java.lang** package in the Java API documentation.

Figure 10.17 demonstrates some **static** methods that test characters to determine if they are a specific character type and the **static** methods that perform case conversions on characters. Each method is used in method **buildOutput** of class **StaticCharMethods**. You can enter any character and apply the preceding methods to the character. Note the use of inner classes for the event handling as demonstrated in Chapter 9.

```
1   // Fig. 10.17: StaticCharMethods.java
2   // Demonstrates the static character testing methods
3   // and case conversion methods of class Character
4   // from the java.lang package.
5   import javax.swing.*;
6   import java.awt.*;
7   import java.awt.event.*;
8
9   public class StaticCharMethods extends JFrame {
10      private char c;
11      private JLabel prompt;
12      private JTextField input;
13      private JTextArea outputArea;
14
15      public StaticCharMethods()
16      {
17         super( "Static Character Methods" );
18
19         Container container = getContentPane();
20         container.setLayout( new FlowLayout() );
21
22         prompt =
23            new JLabel( "Enter a character and press Enter" );
24         container.add( prompt );
25
26         input = new JTextField( 5 );
27         input.addActionListener(
28            new ActionListener() {
29               public void actionPerformed( ActionEvent e )
30               {
31                  String s = e.getActionCommand();
32                  c = s.charAt( 0 );
33                  buildOutput();
34               }
35            }
36         );
37         container.add( input );
38
39         outputArea = new JTextArea( 10, 20 );
40         container.add( outputArea );
41
42         setSize( 300, 250 );  // set the window size
43         show();               // show the window
44      }
```

Fig. 10.17   **static** character testing methods and case conversion methods of class **Character** (part 1 of 3).

```
45
46        public void buildOutput()
47        {
48           outputArea.setText(
49              "is defined: " + Character.isDefined( c ) +
50              "\nis digit: " + Character.isDigit( c ) +
51              "\nis Java letter: " +
52              Character.isJavaIdentifierStart( c ) +
53              "\nis Java letter or digit: " +
54              Character.isJavaIdentifierPart( c ) +
55              "\nis letter: " + Character.isLetter( c ) +
56              "\nis letter or digit: " +
57              Character.isLetterOrDigit( c ) +
58              "\nis lower case: " + Character.isLowerCase( c ) +
59              "\nis upper case: " + Character.isUpperCase( c ) +
60              "\nto upper case: " + Character.toUpperCase( c ) +
61              "\nto lower case: " + Character.toLowerCase( c ) );
62        }
63
64        public static void main( String args[] )
65        {
66           StaticCharMethods application = new StaticCharMethods();
67
68           application.addWindowListener(
69              new WindowAdapter() {
70                 public void windowClosing( WindowEvent e )
71                 {
72                    System.exit( 0 );
73                 }
74              }
75           );
76        }
77     }
```

Static Character Methods	_ □ ×		Static Character Methods	_ □ ×
Enter a character and press Enter A			Enter a character and press Enter 8	
is defined: true			is defined: true	
is digit: false			is digit: true	
is Java letter: true			is Java letter: false	
is Java letter or digit: true			is Java letter or digit: true	
is letter: true			is letter: false	
is letter or digit: true			is letter or digit: true	
is lower case: false			is lower case: false	
is upper case: true			is upper case: false	
to upper case: A			to upper case: 8	
to lower case: a			to lower case: 8	

Fig. 10.17   **static** character testing methods and case conversion methods of class **Character** (part 2 of 3).

The expression at line 49

```
Character.isDefined( c )
```

uses method **Character.isDefined** to determine if character **c** is defined in the Unicode character set. If so, the method returns **true**; otherwise, it returns **false**.

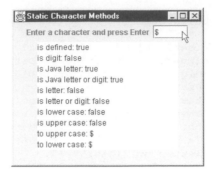

Fig. 10.17   **static** character testing methods and case conversion methods of class **Character** (part 3 of 3).

The expression at line 50

```
Character.isDigit( c )
```

uses method **Character.isDigit** to determine if character **c** is a defined Unicode digit. If so, the method returns **true**; otherwise, it returns **false**.

The expression at line 52

```
Character.isJavaIdentifierStart( c )
```

uses method **Character.isJavaIdentifierStart** to determine if **c** is a character that can be used as the first character of an identifier in Java [i.e., a letter, an underscore (_) or a dollar sign (**$**)]. If so, the method returns **true**; otherwise, it returns **false**.

The expression at line 54

```
Character.isJavaIdentifierPart( c )
```

uses method **Character.isJavaIdentifierPart** to determine if character **c** is a character that can be used in an identifier in Java [i.e., a digit, a letter, an underscore (_) or a dollar sign (**$**)]. If so, the method returns **true**; otherwise, it returns **false**.

The expression at line 55

```
Character.isLetter( c )
```

uses method **Character.isLetter** to determine if character **c** is a letter. If so, the method returns **true**; otherwise, it returns **false**.

The expression at line 57

```
Character.isLetterOrDigit( c )
```

uses method **Character.isLetterOrDigit** to determine if character **c** is a letter or a digit. If so, the method returns **true**; otherwise, it returns **false**.

The expression at line 58

```
Character.isLowerCase( c )
```

uses method **Character.isLowerCase** to determine if character **c** is a lowercase letter. If so, the method returns **true**; otherwise, it returns **false**.

The expression at line 59

```
Character.isUpperCase( c )
```

uses method **Character.isUpperCase** to determine if character **c** is an uppercase letter. If so, the method returns **true**; otherwise, it returns **false**.

The expression at line 60

```
Character.toUpperCase( c )
```

uses method **Character.toUpperCase** to convert the character **c** to its uppercase equivalent. The method returns the converted character if the character has an uppercase equivalent; otherwise, the method returns its original argument. The expression at line 61

```
Character.toLowerCase( c )
```

uses method **Character.toLowerCase** to convert the character **c** to its lowercase equivalent. The method returns the converted character if the character has a lowercase equivalent; otherwise, the method returns its original argument.

Figure 10.18 demonstrates **static Character** methods **digit** and **forDigit**, which perform conversions between characters and digits in different number systems. Common number systems include decimal (base 10), octal (base 8), hexadecimal (base 16) and binary (base 2). The base of a number is also known as its *radix*. For more information on conversions between number systems, see Appendix E.

```
1   // Fig. 10.18: StaticCharMethods2.java
2   // Demonstrates the static character conversion methods
3   // of class Character from the java.lang package.
4   import javax.swing.*;
5   import java.awt.*;
6   import java.awt.event.*;
7
8   public class StaticCharMethods2 extends JFrame {
9      private char c;
10     private int digit, radix;
11     private JLabel prompt1, prompt2;
12     private JTextField input, radixField;
13     private JButton toChar, toInt;
14
15     public StaticCharMethods2()
16     {
17        super( "Character Conversion Methods" );
18
19        Container con = getContentPane();
20        con.setLayout( new FlowLayout() );
21
22        prompt1 = new JLabel( "Enter a digit or character " );
23        input = new JTextField( 5 );
24        con.add( prompt1 );
25        con.add( input );
```

Fig. 10.18   **Character** class **static** conversion methods (part 1 of 3).

```
26
27            prompt2 = new JLabel( "Enter a radix " );
28            radixField = new JTextField( 5 );
29            con.add( prompt2 );
30            con.add( radixField );
31
32            toChar = new JButton( "Convert digit to character" );
33            toChar.addActionListener(
34               new ActionListener() {
35                  public void actionPerformed( ActionEvent e )
36                  {
37                     digit = Integer.parseInt( input.getText() );
38                     radix =
39                        Integer.parseInt( radixField.getText() );
40                     JOptionPane.showMessageDialog( null,
41                        "Convert digit to character: " +
42                        Character.forDigit( digit, radix ) );
43                  }
44               }
45            );
46            con.add( toChar );
47
48            toInt = new JButton( "Convert character to digit" );
49            toInt.addActionListener(
50               new ActionListener() {
51                  public void actionPerformed( ActionEvent e )
52                  {
53                     String s = input.getText();
54                     c = s.charAt( 0 );
55                     radix =
56                        Integer.parseInt( radixField.getText() );
57                     JOptionPane.showMessageDialog( null,
58                        "Convert character to digit: " +
59                        Character.digit( c, radix ) );
60                  }
61               }
62            );
63            con.add( toInt );
64
65            setSize( 275, 150 );  // set the window size
66            show();                // show the window
67         }
68
69         public static void main( String args[] )
70         {
71            StaticCharMethods2 app = new StaticCharMethods2();
72
73            app.addWindowListener(
74               new WindowAdapter() {
75                  public void windowClosing( WindowEvent e )
76                  {
```

Fig. 10.18 Character class static conversion methods (part 2 of 3).

```
77                        System.exit( 0 );
78                     }
79                  }
80              );
81        }
82  }
```

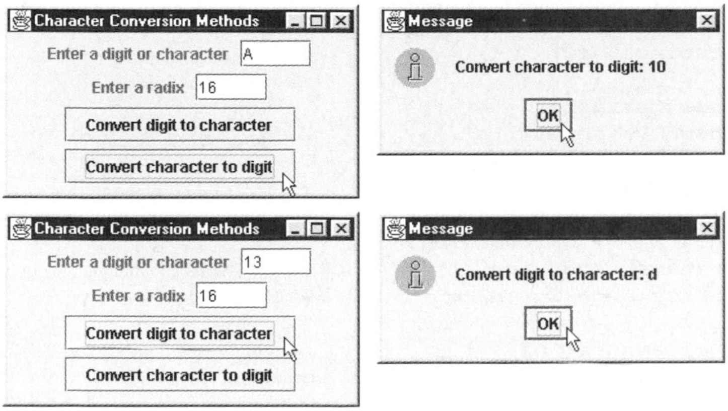

Fig. 10.18 Character class static conversion methods (part 3 of 3).

The expression at line 42

```
Character.forDigit( digit, radix )
```

uses method **forDigit** to convert the integer **digit** into a character in the number system specified by the integer **radix** (also known as the base of the number). For example, the integer **13** in base 16 (the **radix**) has the character value **'d'**. Note that the lowercase and uppercase letters are equivalent in number systems.

The expression at line 59

```
Character.digit( c, radix )
```

uses method **digit** to convert the character **c** into an integer in the number system specified by the integer **radix** (i.e., the base of the number). For example, the character **'A'** in base 16 (the **radix**) has the integer value 10.

The program of Fig. 10.19 demonstrates the non-**static** methods of class **Character**—the constructor, **charValue**, **toString**, **hashCode** and **equals**.

Lines 11 and 12

```
c1 = new Character( 'A' );
c2 = new Character( 'a' );
```

instantiate two **Character** objects and pass character literals to the constructor to initialize those objects.

The expression on line 15

```
c1.charValue()
```

uses **Character** method **charValue** to return the **char** value stored in **Character** object **c1**.

```java
1   // Fig. 10.19: OtherCharMethods.java
2   // Demonstrate the non-static methods of class
3   // Character from the java.lang package.
4   import javax.swing.*;
5
6   public class OtherCharMethods {
7      public static void main( String args[] )
8      {
9         Character c1, c2;
10
11        c1 = new Character( 'A' );
12        c2 = new Character( 'a' );
13
14        String output =
15           "c1 = " + c1.charValue() +
16           "\nc2 = " + c2.toString() +
17           "\n\nhash code for c1 = " + c1.hashCode() +
18           "\nhash code for c2 = " + c2.hashCode();
19
20        if (  c1.equals( c2 ) )
21           output += "\n\nc1 and c2 are equal";
22        else
23           output += "\n\nc1 and c2 are not equal";
24
25        JOptionPane.showMessageDialog( null, output,
26           "Demonstrating Non-Static Character Methods",
27           JOptionPane.INFORMATION_MESSAGE );
28
29        System.exit( 0 );
30     }
31  }
```

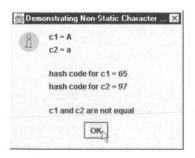

Fig. 10.19 Non-**static** methods of class **Character**.

The expression on line 16

```java
    c2.toString()
```

returns a **String** representation of **Character** object **c2** using method **toString**.
The expressions on lines 17 and 18

```java
    c1.hashCode()
    c2.hashCode()
```

perform **hashCode** calculations on the **Character** objects **c1** and **c2**, respectively. Remember that hash code values are used to store objects in hash tables for fast lookup capabilities (see Chapter 23).

The **if** structure condition on line 20

```
c1.equals( c2 )
```

uses method **equals** to determine if the object **c1** has the same contents as the object **c2** (i.e., the characters inside each object are equal).

10.20 Class **StringTokenizer**

When you read a sentence, your mind breaks the sentence into individual words, or *tokens,* each of which conveys meaning to you. Compilers also perform tokenization. They break up statements into individual pieces like keywords, identifiers, operators and other elements of a programming language. In this section we study Java's **StringTokenizer** class (from package **java.util**) that breaks a string into its component tokens. Tokens are separated from one another by delimiters, typically white-space characters such as blank, tab, newline and carriage return. Other characters may also be used as delimiters to separate tokens. The program of Fig. 10.20 demonstrates class **StringTokenizer**. The window for class **TokenTest** displays a **JTextField** where the user types a sentence to tokenize. Output in this program is displayed in a **JTextArea**.

```
1   // Fig. 10.20: TokenTest.java
2   // Testing the StringTokenizer class of the java.util package
3   import javax.swing.*;
4   import java.util.*;
5   import java.awt.*;
6   import java.awt.event.*;
7
8   public class TokenTest extends JFrame {
9       private JLabel prompt;
10      private JTextField input;
11      private JTextArea output;
12
13      public TokenTest()
14      {
15          super( "Testing Class StringTokenizer" );
16
17          Container c = getContentPane();
18          c.setLayout( new FlowLayout() );
19
20          prompt =
21              new JLabel( "Enter a sentence and press Enter" );
22          c.add( prompt );
23
24          input = new JTextField( 20 );
25          input.addActionListener(
26              new ActionListener() {
```

Fig. 10.20   Tokenizing strings with a **StringTokenizer** object (part 1 of 2).

```
27                    public void actionPerformed( ActionEvent e )
28                    {
29                        String stringToTokenize = e.getActionCommand();
30                        StringTokenizer tokens =
31                            new StringTokenizer( stringToTokenize );
32
33                        output.setText( "Number of elements: " +
34                            tokens.countTokens() +
35                            "\nThe tokens are:\n" );
36
37                        while ( tokens.hasMoreTokens() )
38                            output.append( tokens.nextToken() + "\n" );
39                    }
40                }
41            );
42        c.add( input );
43
44        output = new JTextArea( 10, 20 );
45        output.setEditable( false );
46        c.add( new JScrollPane( output ) );
47
48        setSize( 275, 260 );   // set the window size
49        show();                // show the window
50    }
51
52    public static void main( String args[] )
53    {
54        TokenTest app = new TokenTest();
55
56        app.addWindowListener(
57            new WindowAdapter() {
58                public void windowClosing( WindowEvent e )
59                {
60                    System.exit( 0 );
61                }
62            }
63        );
64    }
65 }
```

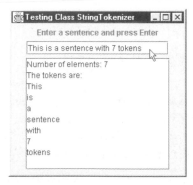

Fig. 10.20 Tokenizing strings with a **StringTokenizer** object (part 2 of 2).

When the user presses the *Enter* key in the **JTextField**, method **actionPer-formed** (at line 27) is invoked. Line 29

```
String stringToTokenize = e.getActionCommand();
```

assigns **String** reference **stringToTokenize** the value in the text in the **JText-Field** returned by **e.getActionCommand()**. Next, lines 30 and 31

```
StringTokenizer tokens =
    new StringTokenizer( stringToTokenize );
```

create an instance of class **StringTokenizer**. This **StringTokenizer** constructor takes a **String** argument and creates a **StringTokenizer** for **stringToTokenize** that will use the default delimiter string **" \n\t\r"** consisting of a space, a newline, a tab and a carriage return for tokenization. There are two other constructors for class **StringTokenizer**. In the version that takes two **String** arguments, the second **String** is the delimiter **String**. In the version that takes three arguments, the second **String** is the delimiter **String** and the third argument (a **boolean**) determines if the delimiters are also returned as tokens (only if the argument is **true**). This is useful if you need to know what the delimiters are.

Lines 33 through 35

```
output.setText( "Number of elements: " +
    tokens.countTokens() +
    "\nThe tokens are:\n" );
```

use the **JTextArea** method **setText** to display the concatenated **String** specified as its argument in the **JTextArea**. In the preceding statement, the expression

```
tokens.countTokens()
```

uses the **StringTokenizer** method **countTokens** to determine the number of tokens in the **String** to be tokenized.

The **while** structure at lines 37 and 38

```
while ( tokens.hasMoreTokens() )
    output.append( tokens.nextToken() + "\n" );
```

uses condition **tokens.hasMoreTokens()** to determine if there are more tokens in the **String** being tokenized. If so, the **append** method is invoked for the **JTextArea** **output** to append the next token to the **String** in the **JTextArea**. The next token is obtained with a call to **tokens.nextToken()** that returns a **String**. The token is output followed by a newline character so subsequent tokens appear on separate lines.

If you would like to change the delimiter **String** while tokenizing a **String**, you may do so by specifying a new delimiter string in a **nextToken** call as follows:

```
tokens.nextToken( newDelimiterString );
```

This feature is not demonstrated in the program.

10.21 A Card Shuffling and Dealing Simulation

In this section, we use random number generation to develop a card shuffling and dealing simulation program. This program can then be used to implement programs that play specific card games.

We develop application **DeckOfCards** (Fig. 10.21), which creates a deck of 52 playing cards using **Card** objects, then enables the user to deal each card by clicking on a "**Deal card**" button. Each card dealt is displayed in a **JTextField**. The user can also shuffle the deck at any time by clicking on a "**Shuffle cards**" button.

```
1   // Fig. 10.21: DeckOfCards.java
2   // Card shuffling and dealing program
3   import javax.swing.*;
4   import java.awt.*;
5   import java.awt.event.*;
6
7   public class DeckOfCards extends JFrame {
8      private Card deck[];
9      private int currentCard;
10     private JButton dealButton, shuffleButton;
11     private JTextField displayCard;
12     private JLabel status;
13
14     public DeckOfCards()
15     {
16        super( "Card Dealing Program" );
17
18        String faces[] = { "Ace", "Deuce", "Three", "Four",
19                           "Five", "Six", "Seven", "Eight",
20                           "Nine", "Ten", "Jack", "Queen",
21                           "King" };
22        String suits[] = { "Hearts", "Diamonds",
23                           "Clubs", "Spades" };
24
25        deck = new Card[ 52 ];
26        currentCard = -1;
27
28        for ( int i = 0; i < deck.length; i++ )
29           deck[ i ] = new Card( faces[ i % 13 ],
30                                 suits[ i / 13 ] );
31
32        Container c = getContentPane();
33        c.setLayout( new FlowLayout() );
34
35        dealButton = new JButton( "Deal card" );
36        dealButton.addActionListener(
37           new ActionListener() {
38              public void actionPerformed( ActionEvent e )
39              {
40                 Card dealt = dealCard();
41
```

Fig. 10.21 Card dealing program (part 1 of 3).

```
42                           if ( dealt != null ) {
43                               displayCard.setText( dealt.toString() );
44                               status.setText( "Card #: " + currentCard );
45                           }
46                           else {
47                               displayCard.setText(
48                                   "NO MORE CARDS TO DEAL" );
49                               status.setText(
50                                   "Shuffle cards to continue" );
51                           }
52                       }
53                   }
54               );
55               c.add( dealButton );
56
57               shuffleButton = new JButton( "Shuffle cards" );
58               shuffleButton.addActionListener(
59                   new ActionListener() {
60                       public void actionPerformed( ActionEvent e )
61                       {
62                           displayCard.setText( "SHUFFLING ..." );
63                           shuffle();
64                           displayCard.setText( "DECK IS SHUFFLED" );
65                       }
66                   }
67               );
68               c.add( shuffleButton );
69
70               displayCard = new JTextField( 20 );
71               displayCard.setEditable( false );
72               c.add( displayCard );
73
74               status = new JLabel();
75               c.add( status );
76
77               setSize( 275, 120 );  // set the window size
78               show();               // show the window
79           }
80
81           public void shuffle()
82           {
83               currentCard = -1;
84
85               for ( int i = 0; i < deck.length; i++ ) {
86                   int j = ( int ) ( Math.random() * 52 );
87                   Card temp = deck[ i ];   // swap
88                   deck[ i ] = deck[ j ];   // the
89                   deck[ j ] = temp;        // cards
90               }
91
92               dealButton.setEnabled( true );
93           }
94
```

Fig. 10.21   Card dealing program (part 2 of 3).

```
95      public Card dealCard()
96      {
97          if ( ++currentCard < deck.length )
98              return deck[ currentCard ];
99          else {
100             dealButton.setEnabled( false );
101             return null;
102         }
103     }
104
105     public static void main( String args[] )
106     {
107         DeckOfCards app = new DeckOfCards();
108
109         app.addWindowListener(
110             new WindowAdapter() {
111                 public void windowClosing( WindowEvent e )
112                 {
113                     System.exit( 0 );
114                 }
115             }
116         );
117     }
118 }
119
120 class Card {
121     private String face;
122     private String suit;
123
124     public Card( String f, String s )
125     {
126         face = f;
127         suit = s;
128     }
129
130     public String toString() { return face + " of " + suit; }
131 }
```

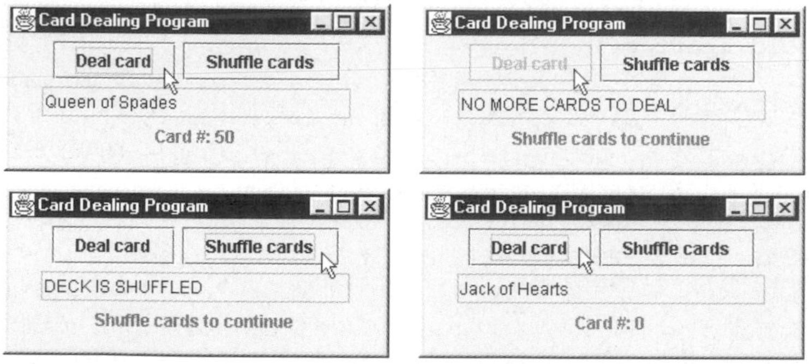

Fig. 10.21   Card dealing program (part 3 of 3).

Class **Card** (lines 120 through 131) contains two **String** instance variables—**face** and **suit**—that are used to store references to the face name and suit name for a specific

Card. The constructor for the class receives two **String**s that it uses to initialize **face** and **suit**. Method **toString** is provided to create a **String** consisting of the **face** of the card, the **String " of "** and the **suit** of the card.

Class **DeckOfCards** (line 7) consists of an array **deck** of 52 **Card**s, an integer **currentCard** representing the most recently dealt card in the deck array (–1 if no cards have been dealt yet) and the GUI components used to manipulate the deck of cards. The constructor method of the application instantiates the **deck** array (line 25) and uses the **for** structure at lines 28 through 30

```
for ( int i = 0; i < deck.length; i++ )
   deck[ i ] = new Card( faces[ i % 13 ],
                         suits[ i / 13 ] );
```

to fill the **deck** array with **Card**s. Note that each **Card** is instantiated and initialized with two **String**s—one from the **faces** array (**String**s **"Ace"** through **"King"**) and one from the **suits** array (**"Hearts"**, **"Diamonds"**, **"Clubs"** and **"Spades"**). The calculation **i % 13** always results in a value from 0 to 12 (the thirteen subscripts of the **faces** array), and the calculation **i / 13** always results in a value from 0 to 3 (the four subscripts in the **suits** array). When the **deck** array is initialized, it contains the cards with faces ace through king in order for each suit.

When the user clicks the **Deal card** button, method **actionPerformed** (line 38) invokes method **dealCard** (defined at line 95) to get the next card in the array. If the **deck** is not empty, a **Card** object reference is returned; otherwise, **null** is returned. If the reference is not **null**, lines 43 and 44

```
displayCard.setText( dealt.toString() );
status.setText( "Card #: " + currentCard );
```

display the **Card** in the **JTextField displayCard** and display the card number in the **JLabel status**.

If the reference returned by **dealCard** was **null**, the **String** "NO MORE CARDS TO DEAL" is displayed in the **JTextField** and the **String** "Shuffle cards to continue" is displayed in the **JLabel**.

When the user clicks the **Shuffle cards** button, its **actionPerformed** method (line 60) invokes method **shuffle** (defined on line 81) to shuffle the cards. The method loops through all 52 cards (array subscripts 0 to 51). For each card, a number between 0 and 51 is picked randomly. Next, the current **Card** object and the randomly selected **Card** object are swapped in the array. A total of only 52 swaps are made in a single pass of the entire array, and the array of **Card** objects is shuffled! When the shuffling is complete, the **String** "DECK IS SHUFFLED" is displayed in the **JTextField**.

Notice the use of method **setEnabled** at lines 92 and 100 to activate and deactivate the **dealButton**. Method **setEnabled** can be used on many GUI components. When it is called with a **false** argument, the GUI component for which it is called is disabled so the user cannot interact with it. To reactivate the button, method **setEnabled** is called with a **true** argument.

Summary

- A character constant's value is its integer value in the Unicode character set. Strings may include letters, digits and special characters such as **+**, **-**, *****, **/** and **$**. A string in Java is an object of class

String. String literals or string constants are often referred to as anonymous **String** objects and are written in double quotes in a program.

- Class **String** provides nine constructors.
- **String** method **length** returns the number of characters in a **String**.
- **String** method **charAt** returns the character at a specific position.
- Method **equals** is used to test any two objects for equality (i.e., the contents of the two objects are identical). The method returns **true** if the objects are equal and **false** otherwise. Method **equals** uses a lexicographical comparison for **String**s.
- When primitive data type values are compared with **==**, the result is **true** if both values are identical. When references are compared with **==**, the result is **true** if both references refer to the same object in memory.
- Java treats all anonymous **String**s with the same contents as one anonymous **String** object.
- **String** method **equalsIgnoreCase** performs a case-insensitive **String** comparison.
- **String** method **compareTo** returns 0 if the **String**s it is comparing are equal, a negative number if the **String** that invokes **compareTo** is less than the **String** that is passed as an argument, and a positive number if the **String** that invokes **compareTo** is greater than the **String** that is passed as an argument. Method **compareTo** uses a lexicographical comparison.
- **String** method **regionMatches** compares portions of two **String**s for equality.
- **String** method **startsWith** determines if a **String** starts with the characters specified as an argument. **String** method **endsWith** determines if a **String** ends with the characters specified as an argument.
- Method **hashCode** performs a hash code calculation that enables a **String** object to be stored in a hash table. This method is inherited from **Object** and overridden by **String**.
- **String** method **indexOf** locates the first occurrence of a character or a substring in a **String**. Method **lastIndexOf** locates the last occurrence of a character or a substring in a **String**.
- **String** method **substring** copies and returns part of an existing **String** object.
- **String** method **concat** concatenates two **String** objects and returns a new **String** object containing the characters from both original **String**s.
- **String** method **replace** returns a new **String** object that replaces every occurrence in a **String** of its first character argument with its second character argument.
- **String** method **toUpperCase** returns a new **String** with uppercase letters in the positions where the original **String** had lowercase letters. Method **toLowerCase** returns a new **String** with lowercase letters in the positions where the original **String** had uppercase letters.
- **String** method **trim** returns a new **String** object in which all white-space characters (such as spaces, newlines and tabs) have been removed from the beginning or end of a **String**.
- **String** method **toCharArray** returns a new character array containing a copy of the characters in a **String**.
- **String** class method **valueOf** returns its argument converted to a string.
- The first time **String** method **intern** is invoked on a **String** it returns a reference to that **String** object. Subsequent invocations of **intern** on different **String** objects that have the same contents as the original **String** result in multiple references to the original **String** object.
- Class **StringBuffer** provides three constructors that enable **StringBuffer**s to be initialized with no characters and an initial capacity of 16 characters; with no characters and an initial capacity specified in the integer argument; or with a copy of the characters of the **String** argument and an initial capacity which is the number of characters in the **String** argument plus 16.

- **StringBuffer** method **length** returns the number of characters currently stored in a **StringBuffer**. Method **capacity** returns the number of characters that can be stored in a **StringBuffer** without allocating more memory.

- Method **ensureCapacity** ensures that a **StringBuffer** has a minimum capacity. Method **setLength** increases or decreases the length of a **StringBuffer**.

- **StringBuffer** method **charAt** returns the character at the specified index. Method **setCharAt** sets the character at the specified position. Method **getChars** returns a character array containing a copy of the characters in the **StringBuffer**.

- Class **StringBuffer** provides overloaded **append** methods to add primitive data type, character array, **String** and **Object** values to the end of a **StringBuffer**.

- **StringBuffer**s and the **append** methods are used by the Java compiler to implement the **+** and **+=** operators for concatenating **String**s.

- Class **StringBuffer** provides overloaded **insert** methods to insert primitive data type, character array, **String** and **Object** values at any position in a **StringBuffer**.

- Class **Character** provides a constructor that takes a character argument.

- **Character** method **isDefined** determines if a character is defined in the Unicode character set. If so, the method returns **true**; otherwise, it returns **false**.

- **Character** method **isDigit** determines if a character is a defined Unicode digit. If so, the method returns **true**; otherwise, it returns **false**.

- **Character** method **isJavaIdentifierStart** determines if a character is a character that can be used as the first character of an identifier in Java [i.e., a letter, an underscore (_) or a dollar sign (**$**)]. If so, the method returns **true**; otherwise, it returns **false**.

- **Character** method **isJavaIdentifierPart** determines if a character is a character that can be used in an identifier in Java [i.e., a digit, a letter, an underscore (_) or a dollar sign (**$**)]. If so, the method returns **true**; otherwise, it returns **false**. Method **isLetter** determines if a character is a letter. If so, the method returns **true**; otherwise, it returns **false**. Method **isLetterOrDigit** determines if a character is a letter or a digit. If so, the method returns **true**; otherwise, it returns **false**.

- **Character** method **isLowerCase** determines if a character is a lowercase letter. If so, the method returns **true**; otherwise, **false**. **Character** method **isUpperCase** determines if a character is an uppercase letter. If so, the method returns **true**; otherwise, **false**.

- **Character** method **toUpperCase** converts a character to its uppercase equivalent. Method **toLowerCase** converts a character to its lowercase equivalent.

- **Character** method **digit** converts its character argument into an integer in the number system specified by its integer argument **radix**. Method **forDigit** converts its integer argument **digit** into a character in the number system specified by its integer argument **radix**.

- **Character** method **charValue** returns the **char** stored in a **Character** object. Method **toString** returns a **String** representation of a **Character**.

- **Character** method **hashCode** performs a hash code calculation on a **Character**.

- **StringTokenizer**'s default constructor creates a **StringTokenizer** for its **String** argument that will use the default delimiter string **" \n\t\r"**, consisting of a space, a newline, a tab and a carriage return for tokenization.

- In the **StringTokenizer** constructor that takes two **String** arguments, the second **String** is the delimiter **String**. In the **StringTokenizer** constructor that takes three arguments, the second **String** is the delimiter **String** and the third argument (a **boolean**) determines if the delimiters are also returned as tokens.

- **StringTokenizer** method **countTokens** returns the number of tokens in the **String** to be tokenized.
- **StringTokenizer** method **hasMoreTokens** determines if there are more tokens in the **String** being tokenized.
- **StringTokenizer** method **nextToken** returns a **String** with the next token.

Terminology

append method of class **StringBuffer**
appending strings to other strings
array of strings
capacity method of class **StringBuffer**
Character class
character code
character constant
character set
charAt method of class **String**
charAt method of class **StringBuffer**
charValue method of class **Character**
compareTo method of class **String**
comparing strings
concat method of class **String**
concatenation
copying strings
countTokens method (**StringTokenizer**)
delimiter
digit method of class **Character**
endsWith method of class **String**
equalsIgnoreCase method of class **String**
equals method of class **String**
forDigit method of class **Character**
getChars method of class **String**
getChars method of class **StringBuffer**
hashCode method of class **Character**
hashCode method of class **String**
hash table
hasMoreTokens method
hexadecimal digits
indexOf method of class **String**
insert method of class **StringBuffer**
intern method of class **String**
isDefined method of class **Character**
isDigit method of class **Character**
isJavaIdentifierPart method
isJavaIdentifierStart method
isLetter method of class **Character**
isLetterOrDigit method of **Character**
isLowerCase method of class **Character**

isUpperCase method of class **Character**
lastIndexOf method of class **String**
length method of class **String**
length method of class **StringBuffer**
length of a string
literal
nextToken method of **StringTokenizer**
numeric code representation of a character
printing character
regionMatches method of class **String**
replace method of class **String**
search string
setCharAt method of class **StringBuffer**
startsWith method of class **String**
string
StringBuffer class
String class
string concatenation
string constant
StringIndexOutOfBoundsException
string literal
string processing
StringTokenizer class
substring method of **String** class
toCharArray method of class **String**
token
tokenizing strings
toLowerCase method of class **Character**
toLowerCase method of class **String**
toString method of class **Character**
toString method of class **String**
toString method of class **StringBuffer**
toUpperCase method of class **Character**
toUpperCase method of class **String**
trim method of class **String**
Unicode
valueOf method of class **String**
white-space characters
word processing

Common Programming Errors

10.1   Attempting to determine the length of a **String** via an instance variable called **length** (e.g., **s1.length**) is a syntax error. The **String** method **length** must be used. (e.g., **s1.length()**).

10.2   Attempting to access a character that is outside the bounds of a **String** (i.e., an index less than 0 or an index greater than or equal to the **String**'s length) results in a **StringIndexOutOfBoundsException**.

10.3   Invoking **StringBuffer** methods that are not methods of class **String** on **String** objects is a syntax error.

10.4   Attempting to access a character that is outside the bounds of a **StringBuffer** (i.e., an index less than 0 or an index greater than or equal to the **StringBuffer**'s length) results in a **StringIndexOutOfBoundsException**.

Performance Tips

10.1   Java treats all anonymous **String**s with the same contents as one anonymous **String** object that has many references. This conserves memory.

10.2   **String** objects are constant strings and **StringBuffer** objects are modifiable strings. Java distinguishes constant strings and modifiable strings for optimization purposes; in particular, Java can perform certain optimizations involving **String** objects (such as sharing one **String** object between multiple references) because it knows these objects will not change.

10.3   When given the choice between using a **String** object to represent a string versus a **StringBuffer** object to represent that string, always use a **String** object if indeed the object will not change; this improves performance.

Software Engineering Observations

10.1   If there are multiple occurrences of the same anonymous **String** object in a single class definition, there will be one copy of the anonymous **String** object referenced from each location in the program that uses the anonymous **String**.

10.2   In most cases, it is not necessary to make a copy of an existing **String** object. **String** objects are immutable—their character contents cannot be changed after they are created. Also, if there are one or more references to a **String** object (or any object for that matter) the object cannot be reclaimed by the garbage collector. Thus, a **String** reference cannot be used to modify a **String** object or to delete a **String** object from memory as in other programming languages such as C or C++.

Self-Review Exercises

10.1   State whether each of the following is *true* or *false*. If *false*, explain why.
   a) When **String** objects are compared with **==**, the result is **true** if the **String**s contain the same values.
   b) A **String** can be modified after it is created.

10.2   For each of the following, write a single statement that performs the indicated task.
   a) Compare the string in **s1** to the string in **s2** for equality of contents.
   b) Append the string **s2** to the string **s1** using **+=**.
   c) Determine the length of the string in **s1**.

Answers to Self-Review Exercises

10.1   a) False. **String** objects that are compared with operator **==** are actually compared to determine if they are the same object in memory.

b) False. **String** objects are constant and cannot be modified after they are created. **StringBuffer** objects can be modified after they are created.

10.2   a) **s1.equals(s2)**

b) **s1 += s2;**

c) **s1.length()**

Exercises

NOTE: Exercises 10.3 through 10.6 are reasonably challenging. Once you have done these problems, you ought to be able to implement most popular card games easily.

10.3   Modify the program in Fig. 10.21 so that the card dealing method deals a five-card poker hand. Then write the following additional methods:

a) Determine if the hand contains a pair.

b) Determine if the hand contains two pairs.

c) Determine if the hand contains three of a kind (e.g., three jacks).

d) Determine if the hand contains four of a kind (e.g., four aces).

e) Determine if the hand contains a flush (i.e., all five cards of the same suit).

f) Determine if the hand contains a straight (i.e., five cards of consecutive face values).

g) Determine if the hand contains a full house (i.e., two cards of one face value and three cards of another face value).

10.4   Use the methods developed in Exercise 10.3 to write a program that deals two five-card poker hands, evaluates each hand, and determines which is the better hand.

10.5   Modify the program developed in Exercise 10.4 so that it can simulate the dealer. The dealer's five-card hand is dealt "face down" so the player cannot see it. The program should then evaluate the dealer's hand and, based on the quality of the hand, the dealer should draw one, two, or three more cards to replace the corresponding number of unneeded cards in the original hand. The program should then reevaluate the dealer's hand. (*Caution:* This is a difficult problem!)

10.6   Modify the program developed in Exercise 10.5 so that it can handle the dealer's hand automatically, but the player is allowed to decide which cards of the player's hand to replace. The program should then evaluate both hands and determine who wins. Now use this new program to play 20 games against the computer. Who wins more games, you or the computer? Have one of your friends play 20 games against the computer. Who wins more games? Based on the results of these games, make appropriate modifications to refine your poker playing program (this, too, is a difficult problem). Play 20 more games. Does your modified program play a better game?

10.7   Write an application that uses **String** method **compareTo** to compare two strings input by the user. Output whether the first string is less than, equal to or greater than the second.

10.8   Write an application that uses **String** method **regionMatches** to compare two strings input by the user. The program should input the number of characters to be compared and the starting index of the comparison. The program should state whether the first string is less than, equal to or greater than the second string. Ignore the case of the characters when performing the comparison.

10.9   Write an application that uses random number generation to create sentences. Use four arrays of strings called **article**, **noun**, **verb** and **preposition**. Create a sentence by selecting a word at random from each array in the following order: **article**, **noun**, **verb**, **preposition**, **article** and **noun**. As each word is picked, concatenate it to the previous words in the sentence. The words should be separated by spaces. When the final sentence is output, it should start with a capital letter and end with a period. The program should generate 20 sentences and output them to a text area.

The arrays should be filled as follows: the **article** array should contain the articles **"the"**, **"a"**, **"one"**, **"some"** and **"any"**; the **noun** array should contain the nouns **"boy"**, **"girl"**, **"dog"**, **"town"** and **"car"**; the **verb** array should contain the verbs **"drove"**, **"jumped"**, **"ran"**, **"walked"** and **"skipped"**; the **preposition** array should contain the prepositions **"to"**, **"from"**, **"over"**, **"under"** and **"on"**.

After the preceding program is written, modify the program to produce a short story consisting of several of these sentences. (How about the possibility of a random term paper writer!)

10.10   *(Limericks)* A limerick is a humorous five-line verse in which the first and second lines rhyme with the fifth, and the third line rhymes with the fourth. Using techniques similar to those developed in Exercise 10.9, write a Java program that produces random limericks. Polishing this program to produce good limericks is a challenging problem, but the result will be worth the effort!

10.11   *(Pig Latin)* Write an application that encodes English language phrases into pig Latin. Pig Latin is a form of coded language often used for amusement. Many variations exist in the methods used to form pig Latin phrases. For simplicity, use the following algorithm:

To form a pig Latin phrase from an English language phrase, tokenize the phrase into words with an object of class **StringTokenizer**. To translate each English word into a pig Latin word, place the first letter of the English word at the end of the word and add the letters "**ay**." Thus the word "**jump**" becomes "**umpjay**," the word "**the**" becomes "**hetay**," and the word "**computer**" becomes "**omputercay**." Blanks between words remain as blanks. Assume the following: The English phrase consists of words separated by blanks, there are no punctuation marks and all words have two or more letters. Method **printLatinWord** should display each word. Each token returned from **nextToken** is passed to method **printLatinWord** to print the pig Latin word. Enable the user to input the sentence. Keep a running display of all the converted sentences in a text area.

10.12   Write an application that inputs a telephone number as a string in the form **(555) 555-5555**. The program should use an object of class **StringTokenizer** to extract the area code as a token, the first three digits of the phone number as a token and the last four digits of the phone number as a token. The seven digits of the phone number should be concatenated into one string. The program should convert the area code string to **int** (remember **parseInt**!) and convert the phone number string to **long**. Both the area code and the phone number should be printed. Remember that you will have to change delimiter characters during the tokenization process.

10.13   Write an application that inputs a line of text, tokenizes the line with an object of class **StringTokenizer** and outputs the tokens in reverse order.

10.14   Use the string comparison methods discussed and the techniques for sorting arrays developed in Chapter 7 to write a program that alphabetizes a list of strings. Allow the user to enter the strings in a text field. Display the results in a text area.

10.15   Write an application that inputs text and outputs the text in uppercase and lowercase letters.

10.16   Write an application that inputs several lines of text and a search character, and uses method **String** method **indexOf** to determine the number of occurrences of the character in the text.

10.17   Write an application based on the program of Exercise 10.16 that inputs several lines of text and uses **String** method **indexOf** to determine the total number of occurrences of each letter of the alphabet in the text. Uppercase and lowercase letters should be counted together. Store the totals for each letter in an array, and print the values in tabular format after the totals have been determined.

10.18   Write an application that reads a series of strings and outputs only those strings beginning with the letter "**b**." The results should be output to a text area.

10.19   Write an application that reads a series of strings and prints only those strings ending with the letters "**ED**." The results should be output to a text area.

10.20   Write an application that inputs an integer code for a character and displays the corresponding character. Modify this program so that it generates all possible three-digit codes in the range 000 to 255 and attempts to print the corresponding characters. Display the results in a text area.

10.21   Write your own versions of the **string** methods for searching strings.

10.22   Write a program that reads a five-letter word from the user and produces all possible three-letter words that can be derived from the letters of the five-letter word. For example, the three-letter words produced from the word "bathe" include the commonly used words "ate", "bat", "bet", "tab", "hat", "the" and "tea."

Special Section: Advanced String Manipulation Exercises

The preceding exercises are keyed to the text and designed to test the reader's understanding of fundamental string manipulation concepts. This section includes a collection of intermediate and advanced string manipulation exercises. The reader should find these problems challenging, yet entertaining. The problems vary considerably in difficulty. Some require an hour or two of program writing and implementation. Others are useful for lab assignments that might require two or three weeks of study and implementation. Some are challenging term projects.

10.23   *(Text Analysis)* The availability of computers with string manipulation capabilities has resulted in some rather interesting approaches to analyzing the writings of great authors. Much attention has been focused on whether William Shakespeare ever lived. Some scholars believe there is substantial evidence indicating that Christopher Marlowe or other authors actually penned the masterpieces attributed to Shakespeare. Researchers have used computers to find similarities in the writings of these two authors. This exercise examines three methods for analyzing texts with a computer.

    a) Write an application that reads several lines of text from the keyboard and prints a table indicating the number of occurrences of each letter of the alphabet in the text. For example, the phrase

        To be, or not to be: that is the question:

    contains one "a," two "b's," no "c's," etc.

    b) Write an application that reads several lines of text and prints a table indicating the number of one-letter words, two-letter words, three-letter words, etc. appearing in the text. For example, the phrase

        Whether 'tis nobler in the mind to suffer

    contains

Word length	Occurrences
1	0
2	2
3	1
4	2 (including 'tis)
5	0
6	2
7	1

c) Write an application that reads several lines of text and prints a table indicating the number of occurrences of each different word in the text. The first version of your program should include the words in the table in the same order in which they appear in the text. For example, the lines

```
To be, or not to be: that is the question:
Whether 'tis nobler in the mind to suffer
```

contain the words "to" three times, the word "be" two times, the word "or" once, etc. A more interesting (and useful) printout should then be attempted in which the words are sorted alphabetically.

10.24   *(Printing Dates in Various Formats)* Dates are printed in several common formats. Two of the more common formats are

```
04/25/1955 and April 25, 1955
```

Write an application that reads a date in the first format and prints that date in the second format.

10.25   *(Check Protection)* Computers are frequently employed in check-writing systems such as payroll and accounts payable applications. Many strange stories circulate regarding weekly paychecks being printed (by mistake) for amounts in excess of $1 million. Incorrect amounts are printed by computerized check-writing systems because of human error and/or machine failure. Systems designers build controls into their systems to prevent such erroneous checks from being issued.

Another serious problem is the intentional alteration of a check amount by someone who intends to cash a check fraudulently. To prevent a dollar amount from being altered, most computerized check-writing systems employ a technique called *check protection.*

Checks designed for imprinting by computer contain a fixed number of spaces in which the computer may print an amount. Suppose a paycheck contains eight blank spaces in which the computer is supposed to print the amount of a weekly paycheck. If the amount is large, then all eight of those spaces will be filled, for example:

```
1,230.60 (check amount)
--------
12345678 (position numbers)
```

On the other hand, if the amount is less than $1000, then several of the spaces would ordinarily be left blank. For example,

```
   99.87
--------
12345678
```

contains three blank spaces. If a check is printed with blank spaces, it is easier for someone to alter the amount of the check. To prevent a check from being altered, many check-writing systems insert *leading asterisks* to protect the amount as follows:

```
***99.87
--------
12345678
```

Write an application that inputs a dollar amount to be printed on a check, and then prints the amount in check-protected format with leading asterisks if necessary. Assume that nine spaces are available for printing the amount.

10.26   *(Writing the Word Equivalent of a Check Amount)* Continuing the discussion of the previous exercise, we reiterate the importance of designing check-writing systems to prevent alteration of check amounts. One common security method requires that the check amount be written both in numbers and "spelled out" in words as well. Even if someone is able to alter the numerical amount of the check, it is extremely difficult to change the amount in words.

Many computerized check-writing systems do not print the amount of the check in words. Perhaps the main reason for this omission is the fact that most high-level languages used in commercial applications do not contain adequate string manipulation features. Another reason is that the logic for writing word equivalents of check amounts is somewhat involved.

Write an application that inputs a numeric check amount and writes the word equivalent of the amount. For example, the amount 112.43 should be written as

ONE HUNDRED TWELVE and 43/100

10.27 *(Morse Code)* Perhaps the most famous of all coding schemes is the Morse code, developed by Samuel Morse in 1832 for use with the telegraph system. The Morse code assigns a series of dots and dashes to each letter of the alphabet, each digit, and a few special characters (such as period, comma, colon, and semicolon). In sound-oriented systems, the dot represents a short sound and the dash represents a long sound. Other representations of dots and dashes are used with light-oriented systems and signal-flag systems.

Separation between words is indicated by a space, or, quite simply, the absence of a dot or dash. In a sound-oriented system, a space is indicated by a short period of time during which no sound is transmitted. The international version of the Morse code appears in Fig. 10.22.

Character	Code	Character	Code
A	.–	T	–
B	–...	U	..–
C	–.–.	V	...–
D	–..	W	.––
E	.	X	–..–
F	..–.	Y	–.––
G	––.	Z	––..
H	....		
I	..	Digits	
J	.–––	1	.––––
K	–.–	2	..–––
L	.–..	3	...––
M	––	4	....–
N	–.	5	.....
O	–––	6	–....
P	.––.	7	––...
Q	––.–	8	–––..
R	.–.	9	––––.
S	...	0	–––––

Fig. 10.22 The letters of the alphabet as expressed in international Morse code.

Write an application that reads an English language phrase and encodes the phrase into Morse code. Also write a program that reads a phrase in Morse code and converts the phrase into the English language equivalent. Use one blank between each Morse-coded letter and three blanks between each Morse-coded word.

10.28   *(A Metric Conversion Program)* Write an application that will assist the user with metric conversions. Your program should allow the user to specify the names of the units as strings (i.e., centimeters, liters, grams, etc. for the metric system and inches, quarts, pounds, etc. for the English system) and should respond to simple questions such as

```
"How many inches are in 2 meters?"
"How many liters are in 10 quarts?"
```

Your program should recognize invalid conversions. For example, the question

```
"How many feet in 5 kilograms?"
```

is not a meaningful question because **"feet"** is a unit of length while **"kilograms"** is a unit of mass.

Special Section: Challenging String Manipulation Projects

10.29   *(Project: A Spelling Checker)* Many popular word processing software packages have built-in spell checkers.

In this project, you are asked to develop your own spell-checker utility. We make suggestions to help get you started. You should then consider adding more capabilities. Use a computerized dictionary (if you have access to one) as a source of words.

Why do we type so many words with incorrect spellings? In some cases, it is because we simply do not know the correct spelling, so we make a "best guess." In some cases, it is because we transpose two letters (e.g., "defualt" instead of "default"). Sometimes we double-type a letter accidentally (e.g., "hanndy" instead of "handy"). Sometimes we type a nearby key instead of the one we intended (e.g., "biryhday" instead of "birthday"). And so on.

Design and implement a spell-checker application in Java. Your program should maintain an array **wordList** of strings. Enable the user to enter these strings. [*Note:* In Chapter 17 we introduce file processing. Once you have this capability, you can obtain the words for the spell checker from a computerized dictionary stored in a file.]

Your program should ask a user to enter a word. The program should then look up that word in the **wordList** array. If the word is present in the array, your program should print "**Word is spelled correctly**."

If the word is not present in the array, your program should print "**word is not spelled correctly**." Then your program should try to locate other words in **wordList** that might be the word the user intended to type. For example, you can try all possible single transpositions of adjacent letters to discover that the word "default" is a direct match to a word in **wordList**. Of course, this implies that your program will check all other single transpositions, such as "edfault," "dfeault," "deafult," "defalut," and "defautl." When you find a new word that matches one in **wordList**, print that word in a message, such as "**Did you mean "default?"**."

Implement other tests, such as replacing each double letter with a single letter and any other tests you can develop to improve the value of your spell checker.

10.30   *(Project: A Crossword Puzzle Generator)* Most people have worked a crossword puzzle, but few have ever attempted to generate one. Generating a crossword puzzle is suggested here as a string manipulation project requiring substantial sophistication and effort.

There are many issues the programmer must resolve to get even the simplest crossword puzzle generator program working. For example, how does one represent the grid of a crossword puzzle inside the computer? Should one use a series of strings, or should double-subscripted arrays be used?

The programmer needs a source of words (i.e., a computerized dictionary) that can be directly referenced by the program. In what form should these words be stored to facilitate the complex manipulations required by the program?

The really ambitious reader will want to generate the "clues" portion of the puzzle, in which the brief hints for each "across" word and each "down" word are printed for the puzzle worker. Merely printing a version of the blank puzzle itself is not a simple problem.

Graphics and Java2D

Objectives

- To understand graphics contexts and graphics objects.
- To understand and be able to manipulate colors.
- To understand and be able to manipulate fonts.
- To understand and be able to use **Graphics** methods for drawing lines, rectangles, rectangles with rounded corners, three-dimensional rectangles, ovals, arcs and polygons.
- To be able to use methods of class **Graphics2D** from the Java2D API to draw lines, rectangles, rectangles with rounded corners, ellipses, arcs and general paths.
- To be able to specify **Paint** and **Stroke** characteristics of shapes displayed with **Graphics2D**.

One picture is worth ten thousand words.
Chinese proverb

Treat nature in terms of the cylinder, the sphere, the cone, all in perspective.
Paul Cezanne

Nothing ever becomes real till it is experienced—even a proverb is no proverb to you till your life has illustrated it.
John Keats

A picture shows me at a glance what it takes dozens of pages of a book to expound.
Ivan Sergeyevich

Outline

11.1 Introduction[1]

In this chapter, we overview several of Java's capabilities for drawing two-dimensional shapes, controlling colors and controlling fonts. One of Java's initial appeals was its support for graphics that enabled Java programmers to visually enhance their applets and applications. Java now contains many more sophisticated drawing capabilities as part of the *Java2D API*. The chapter begins with an introduction to many of the original drawing capabilities of Java. Next, we present several of the new and more powerful Java2D capabilities, such as controlling the style of lines used to draw shapes and controlling how shapes are filled with color and patterns.

Figure 11.1 shows a portion of the Java class hierarchy that includes several of the basic graphics classes and Java2D API classes and interfaces covered in this chapter. Class **Color** contains methods and constants for manipulating colors. Class **Font** contains methods and constants for manipulating fonts. Class **FontMetrics** contains methods for obtaining font information. Class **Polygon** contains methods for creating polygons. Class **Graphics** contains methods for drawing strings, lines, rectangles and other shapes. The bottom half of the figure lists several classes and interfaces from the Java2D API. Class **BasicStroke** helps specify the drawing characteristics of lines. Classes **Gradient-Paint** and **TexturePaint** help specify the characteristics for filling shapes with colors or patterns. Classes **GeneralPath**, **Arc2D**, **Ellipse2D**, **Line2D**, **Rectangle2D** and **RoundRectangle2D** define a variety of Java2D shapes.

To begin drawing in Java, we must first understand Java's *coordinate system* (Fig. 11.2), which is a scheme for identifying every possible point on the screen. By default, the upper-left corner of a GUI component (such as an applet or a window) has the coordinates (0, 0). A coordinate pair is composed of an *x-coordinate* (the *horizontal coordinate*) and a *y-coordinate* (the *vertical coordinate*). The *x*-coordinate is the horizontal distance moving right from the upper-left corner. The *y*-coordinate is the vertical distance moving down from the upper-left corner. The *x-axis* describes every horizontal coordinate, and the *y-axis* describes every vertical coordinate.

---

1. This chapter was coauthored with Mr. Tem Nieto of Deitel & Associates, Inc.

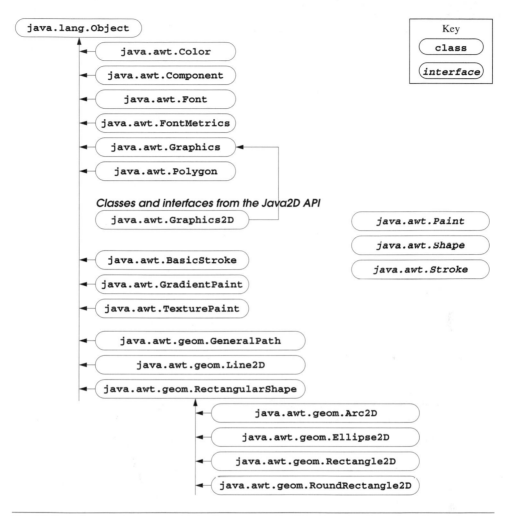

Fig. 11.1   Some classes and interfaces used in this chapter from Java's original graphics capabilities and from the Java2D API.

Software Engineering Observation 11.1

*The upper-left coordinate (0, 0) of a window is actually behind the title bar of the window. For this reason, drawing coordinates should be adjusted to draw inside the borders of the window. Class **Container** (a superclass of all windows in Java) has method **getInsets** that returns an **Insets** object (package **java.awt**) for this purpose. An **Insets** object has four **public** members—**top**, **bottom**, **left** and **right**—that represent the number of pixels from each edge of the window to the drawing area for the window.*

     Text and shapes are displayed on the screen by specifying coordinates. Coordinate units are measured in *pixels*. A pixel is a display monitor's smallest unit of resolution.

Portability Tip 11.1

Different display monitors have different resolutions (i.e., the density of pixels varies). This may cause graphics to appear to be different sizes on different monitors.

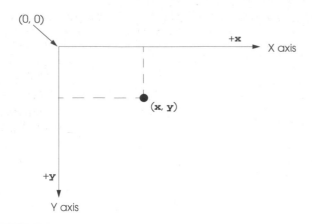

Fig. 11.2   Java coordinate system. Units are measured in pixels.

11.2 Graphics Contexts and Graphics Objects

A Java *graphics context* enables drawing on the screen. A **Graphics** object manages a graphics context by controlling how information is drawn. **Graphics** objects contain methods for drawing, font manipulation, color manipulation and the like. Every applet we have seen in the text that performs drawing on the screen has used the **Graphics** object **g** (the argument to the applet's **paint** method) to manage the applet's graphics context. In this chapter, we demonstrate drawing in applications. However, every technique shown here can be used in applets.

The **Graphics** class is an **abstract** class (i.e., **Graphics** objects cannot be instantiated). This contributes to Java's portability. Because drawing is performed differently on each platform that supports Java, there cannot be one class that implements drawing capabilities on all systems. For example, the graphics capabilities that enable a PC running Microsoft Windows to draw a rectangle are different from the graphics capabilities that enable a UNIX workstation to draw a rectangle—and those are both different from the graphics capabilities that enable a Macintosh to draw a rectangle. When Java is implemented on each platform, a derived class of **Graphics** is created that actually implements all the drawing capabilities. This implementation is hidden from us by the **Graphics** class, which supplies the interface that enables us to write programs that use graphics in a platform-independent manner.

Class **Component** is the superclass for many of the classes in the **java.awt** package (we discuss class **Component** in Chapter 12). **Component** method **paint** takes a **Graphics** object as an argument. This object is passed to the **paint** method by the system when a paint operation is required for a **Component**. The header for the **paint** method is

```
public void paint( Graphics g )
```

The **Graphics** object **g** receives a reference to an object of the system's derived **Graphics** class. The preceding method header should look familiar to you—it is the same one we have been using in our applet classes. Actually, the **Component** class is an indirect base class of class **JApplet**—the superclass of every applet in this book. Many capabilities of class **JApplet** are inherited from class **Component**. The **paint** method defined in class **Component** does nothing by default—it must be overridden by the programmer.

The **paint** method is seldom called directly by the programmer because drawing graphics is an *event-driven process*. When an applet executes, the **paint** method is automatically called (after calls to the **JApplet**'s **init** and **start** methods). For **paint** to be called again, an *event* must occur (such as covering and uncovering the applet). Similarly, when any **Component** is displayed, that **Component**'s **paint** method is called.

If the programmer needs to call **paint**, a call is made to the **Component** class **repaint** method. Method **repaint** requests a call to the **Component** class **update** method as soon as possible to clear the **Component**'s background of any previous drawing, then **update** calls **paint** directly. The **repaint** method is frequently called by the programmer to force a **paint** operation. Method **repaint** should not be overridden because it performs some system-dependent tasks. The **update** method is seldom called directly and sometimes overridden. Overriding the **update** method is useful for "smoothing" animations (i.e., reducing "flicker") as we will discuss in Chapter 16, "Multimedia." The headers for **repaint** and **update** are

```
public void repaint()
public void update( Graphics g )
```

Method **update** takes a **Graphics** object as an argument which is supplied automatically by the system when **update** is called.

In this chapter we focus on the **paint** method. In the next chapter we concentrate more on the event-driven nature of graphics and discuss the **repaint** and **update** methods in more detail. We also discuss class **JComponent**—a superclass of many GUI components in package **javax.swing**. Subclasses of **JComponent** typically paint from their **paintComponent** methods.

11.3 Color Control

Colors enhance the appearance of a program and help convey meaning. For example, a traffic light has three different color lights—red indicates stop, yellow indicates caution and green indicates go.

Class *Color* defines methods and constants for manipulating colors in a Java program. The predefined color constants are summarized in Fig. 11.3, and several color methods and constructors are summarized in Fig. 11.4. Note that two of the methods in Fig. 11.4 are **Graphics** methods that are specific to colors.

Color Constant	Color	RGB value
`public final static Color orange`	orange	255, 200, 0
`public final static Color pink`	pink	255, 175, 175
`public final static Color cyan`	cyan	0, 255, 255
`public final static Color magenta`	magenta	255, 0, 255

Fig. 11.3   **Color** class **static** constants and RGB values (part 1 of 2).

Color Constant	Color	RGB value
`public final static Color yellow`	yellow	255, 255, 0
`public final static Color black`	black	0, 0, 0
`public final static Color white`	white	255, 255, 255
`public final static Color gray`	gray	128, 128, 128
`public final static Color lightGray`	light gray	192, 192, 192
`public final static Color darkGray`	dark gray	64, 64, 64
`public final static Color red`	red	255, 0, 0
`public final static Color green`	green	0, 255, 0
`public final static Color blue`	blue	0, 0, 255

Fig. 11.3   `Color` class `static` constants and RGB values (part 2 of 2).

Method	Description
`public Color( int r, int g, int b )`	Creates a color based on red, green and blue contents expressed as integers from 0 to 255.
`public Color( float r, float g, float b )`	Creates a color based on red, green and blue contents expressed as floating-point values from 0.0 to 1.0.
`public int getRed()        // Color class`	Returns a value between 0 and 255 representing the red content.
`public int getGreen()        // Color class`	Returns a value between 0 and 255 representing the green content.
`public int getBlue()        // Color class`	Returns a value between 0 and 255 representing the blue content.
`public Color getColor()        // Graphics class`	Returns a `Color` object representing the current color for the graphics context.
`public void setColor( Color c ) // Graphics class`	Sets the current color for drawing with the graphics context.

Fig. 11.4   `Color` methods and color-related `Graphics` methods.

Every color is created from a red, a green and a blue component. Together these components are called *RGB values*. All three RGB components can be integers in the range 0 to 255, or all three RGB parts can be floating-point values in the range 0.0 to 1.0. The first RGB part defines the amount of red, the second defines the amount of green and the third defines the amount of blue. The larger the RGB value, the greater the amount of that particular color. Java enables the programmer to choose from $256 \times 256 \times 256$ (or approximately 16.7 million) colors. However, not all computers are capable of displaying all these colors. If this is the case, the computer will display the closest color it can.

Common Programming Error 11.1

Spelling any **static Color** *class constant with an initial capital letter is a syntax error.*

Two **Color** constructors are shown in Fig 11.4—one that takes three **int** arguments and one that takes three **float** arguments, with each argument specifying the amount of red, green and blue, respectively. The **int** values must be between 0 and 255 and the **float** values must be between 0.0 and 1.0. The new **Color** object will have the specified amounts of red, green and blue. **Color** methods **getRed**, **getGreen** and **getBlue** return integer values from 0 to 255 representing the amount of red, green and blue, respectively. **Graphics** method **getColor** returns a **Color** object representing the current drawing color. **Graphics** method **setColor** sets the current drawing color.

The application of Fig. 11.5 demonstrates several methods from Fig. 11.4 by drawing filled rectangles and strings in several different colors.

```
1   // Fig. 11.5: ShowColors.java
2   // Demonstrating Colors
3   import java.awt.*;
4   import javax.swing.*;
5   import java.awt.event.*;
6
7   public class ShowColors extends JFrame {
8      public ShowColors()
9      {
10        super( "Using colors" );
11
12        setSize( 400, 130 );
13        show();
14     }
15
16     public void paint( Graphics g )
17     {
18        // set new drawing color using integers
19        g.setColor( new Color( 255, 0, 0 ) );
20        g.fillRect( 25, 25, 100, 20 );
21        g.drawString( "Current RGB: " + g.getColor(), 130, 40 );
22
23        // set new drawing color using floats
24        g.setColor( new Color( 0.0f, 1.0f, 0.0f ) );
25        g.fillRect( 25, 50, 100, 20 );
26        g.drawString( "Current RGB: " + g.getColor(), 130, 65 );
27
28        // set new drawing color using static Color objects
29        g.setColor( Color.blue );
30        g.fillRect( 25, 75, 100, 20 );
31        g.drawString( "Current RGB: " + g.getColor(), 130, 90 );
```

Fig. 11.5   Demonstrating setting and getting a **Color** (part 1 of 2).

```
32
33              // display individual RGB values
34              Color c = Color.magenta;
35              g.setColor( c );
36              g.fillRect( 25, 100, 100, 20 );
37              g.drawString( "RGB values: " + c.getRed() + ", " +
38                  c.getGreen() + ", " + c.getBlue(), 130, 115 );
39          }
40
41      public static void main( String args[] )
42      {
43          ShowColors app = new ShowColors();
44
45          app.addWindowListener(
46              new WindowAdapter() {
47                  public void windowClosing( WindowEvent e )
48                  {
49                      System.exit( 0 );
50                  }
51              }
52          );
53      }
54  }
```

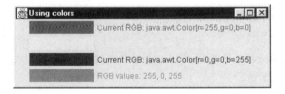

Fig. 11.5   Demonstrating setting and getting a **Color** (part 2 of 2).

When the application begins execution, class **ShowColors'** **paint** method is called to paint the window. Line 19

```
g.setColor( new Color( 255, 0, 0 ) );
```

uses **Graphics** method **setColor** to set the current drawing color. Method **setColor** receives a **Color** object. The expression **new Color(255, 0, 0)** creates a new **Color** object that represents red (red value **255** and **0** for the green and blue values). Line 20

```
g.fillRect( 25, 25, 100, 20 );
```

uses **Graphics** method **fillRect** to draw a filled rectangle in the current color. Method **fillRect** receives the same parameters as method **drawRect** (discussed in Chapter 3). Line 21

```
g.drawString( "Current RGB: " + g.getColor(), 130, 40 );
```

uses **Graphics** method **drawString** to draw a **String** in the current color. The expression **g.getColor()** retrieves the current color from the **Graphics** object. The returned **Color** is concatenated with string **"Current RGB: "** resulting in an implicit call to class **Color**'s **toString** method. Notice that the **String** representation of the **Color** object contains the class name and package (**java.awt.Color**), and the red, green and blue values.

Lines 24 through 26 and lines 29 through 31 perform the same tasks again. Line 24

```
g.setColor( new Color( 0.0f, 1.0f, 0.0f ) );
```

uses the **Color** constructor with three **float** arguments to create the color green (**0.0f** for red, **1.0f** for green and **0.0f** for blue). Note the syntax of the constants. The letter **f** appended to a floating-point constant indicates that the constant should be treated as type **float**. Normally, floating-point constants are treated as type **double**.

Line 29 sets the current drawing color to one of the predefined **Color** constants (**Color.blue**). Note that the new operator is not needed to create the constant. Because the **Color** constants are **static**, they are defined when class **Color** is loaded into memory at execution time.

The statement at lines 37 and 38 demonstrates **Color** methods **getRed**, **getGreen** and **getBlue** on the predefined **Color.magenta** object.

Software Engineering Observation 11.2

*To change the color, you must create a new **Color** object (or use one of the predefined **Color** constants) as there are no set methods in class **Color** to change the characteristics of the current color.*

One of the newer features of Java is the predefined GUI component *JColorChooser* (package **javax.swing**) for selecting colors. The application of Fig. 11.6 enables you to press a button to display a **JColorChooser** dialog. When you select a color and press the dialog's **OK** button, the background color of the application window changes colors.

```
1   // Fig. 11.6: ShowColors2.java
2   // Demonstrating JColorChooser
3   import java.awt.*;
4   import javax.swing.*;
5   import java.awt.event.*;
6
7   public class ShowColors2 extends JFrame {
8       private JButton changeColor;
9       private Color color = Color.lightGray;
10      private Container c;
11
12      public ShowColors2()
13      {
14          super( "Using JColorChooser" );
15
16          c = getContentPane();
17          c.setLayout( new FlowLayout() );
18
19          changeColor = new JButton( "Change Color" );
```

Fig. 11.6   Demonstrating the **JColorChooser** dialog (part 1 of 3).

```
20          changeColor.addActionListener(
21             new ActionListener() {
22                public void actionPerformed( ActionEvent e )
23                {
24                   color =
25                      JColorChooser.showDialog( ShowColors2.this,
26                         "Choose a color", color );
27
28                   if ( color == null )
29                      color = Color.lightGray;
30
31                   c.setBackground( color );
32                   c.repaint();
33                }
34             }
35          );
36          c.add( changeColor );
37
38          setSize( 400, 130 );
39          show();
40       }
41
42       public static void main( String args[] )
43       {
44          ShowColors2 app = new ShowColors2();
45
46          app.addWindowListener(
47             new WindowAdapter() {
48                public void windowClosing( WindowEvent e )
49                {
50                   System.exit( 0 );
51                }
52             }
53          );
54       }
55    }
```

Fig. 11.6   Demonstrating the **JColorChooser** dialog (part 2 of 3).

Lines 24 through 26 (from method **actionPerformed** for **changeColor**)

```
color =
   JColorChooser.showDialog( ShowColors2.this,
      "Choose a color", color );
```

use **static** method *showDialog* of class **JColorChooser** to display the color chooser dialog. This method returns the selected **Color** object (or **null** if the user presses **Cancel** or closes the dialog without pressing **OK**).

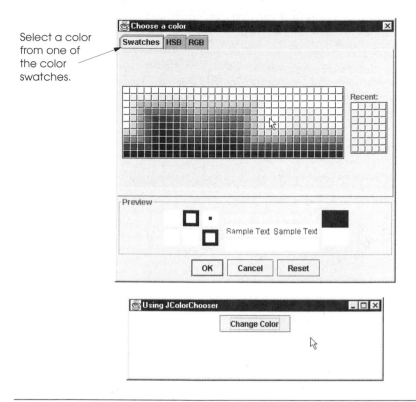

Select a color
from one of
the color
swatches.

Fig. 11.6   Demonstrating the **JColorChooser** dialog (part 3 of 3).

Method **showDialog** takes three arguments—a reference to its parent **Component**, a **String** to display in the title bar of the dialog and the initial selected **Color** for the dialog. The parent component is the window from which the dialog is displayed. While the color chooser dialog is on the screen, the user cannot interact with the parent component. This type of dialog is called a *modal dialog* and is discussed in Chapter 13. Notice the special syntax **ShowColors2.this** used in the preceding statement. When using an inner class, you can access the outer class object's **this** reference by qualifying **this** with the name of the outer class and the dot (**.**) operator.

After the user selects a color, lines 28 and 29 determine if **color** is **null**, and if so, set **color** to the default **Color.lightGray**. Line 31

```
c.setBackground( color );
```

uses method **setBackground** to change the background color of the content pane (represented by **Container c** in this program). Method **setBackground** is one of the many **Component** methods that can be used on most GUI components. Line 32

```
c.repaint();
```

ensures that the background is repainted by calling **repaint** for the content pane. This schedules a call to the content pane's **update** method, which repaints the background of the content pane in the current background color.

The second screen capture of Fig. 11.6 demonstrates the default **JColorChooser** dialog that allows the user to select a color from a variety of *color swatches*. Notice that there are actually three tabs across the top of the dialog—***Swatches***, ***HSB*** and ***RGB***. These represent three different ways to select a color. The **HSB** tab allows you to select a color based on *hue*, *saturation* and *brightness*. The **RGB** tab allows you to select a color using sliders to select the red, green and blue components of the color. The **HSB** and **RGB** tabs are shown in Fig. 11.7.

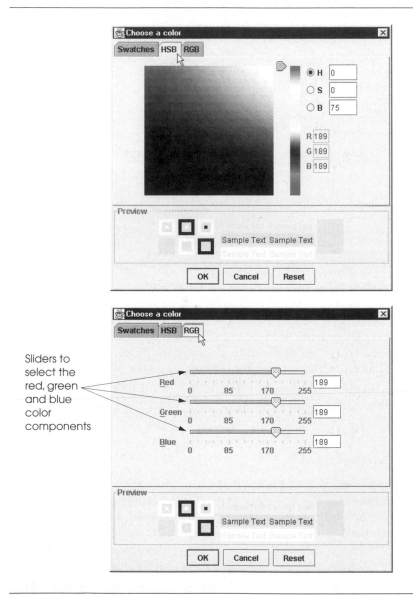

Fig. 11.7   The **HSB** and **RGB** tabs of the **JColorChooser** dialog.

11.4 Font Control

This section introduces methods and constants for font control. Most font methods and font constants are part of class **Font**. Some methods of class **Font** and class **Graphics** are summarized in Fig. 11.8.

Class **Font**'s constructor takes three arguments—the *font name, font style* and *font size*. The font name is any font currently supported by the system where the program is running, such as standard Java fonts **Monospaced**, **SansSerif** and **Serif**. The font style is **Font.PLAIN**, **Font.ITALIC** or **Font.BOLD** (**static** constants of class **Font**). Font styles can be used in combination (e.g., **Font.ITALIC + Font.BOLD**). The font size is measured in points. A *point* is 1/72 of an inch. **Graphics** method **setFont** sets the current drawing font—the font in which text will be displayed—to its **Font** argument.

Method or constant	Description

public final static int PLAIN   // Font class
> A constant representing a plain font style.

public final static int BOLD   // Font class
> A constant representing a plain font style.

public final static int ITALIC   // Font class
> A constant representing an italic font style.

public Font(String name, int style, int size)
> Creates a **Font** object with the specified font, style and size.

public int getStyle()   // Font class
> Returns an integer value indicating the current font style.

public int getSize()   // Font class
> Returns an integer value indicating the current font size.

public String getName()   // Font class
> Returns the current font name as a string.

public String getFamily()   // Font class
> Returns the font's family name as a string.

public boolean isPlain()   // Font class
> Tests a font for a plain font style. Returns **true** if the font is plain.

public boolean isBold()   // Font class
> Tests a font for a bold font style. Returns **true** if the font is bold.

public boolean isItalic()   // Font class
> Tests a font for an italic font style. Returns **true** if the font is italic.

public Font getFont()   // Graphics class
> Returns a **Font** object reference representing the current font.

public void setFont(Font f)   // Graphics class
> Sets the current font to the font, style and size specified by the **Font** object reference **f**.

Fig. 11.8   **Font** methods, constants and font-related **Graphics** methods.

Portability Tip 11.2

*The number of fonts varies greatly across systems. The JDK guarantees that the fonts **Serif**, **Monospaced**, **SansSerif**, **Dialog** and **DialogInput** will be available.*

Common Programming Error 11.2

Specifying a font that is not available on a system is a logic error. Java will substitute that system's default font.

The program of Fig. 11.9 displays text in four different fonts with each font in a different size. The program uses the **Font** constructor to initialize **Font** objects on lines 20, 25, 30 and 37 (each in a call to **Graphics** method **setFont** to change the drawing font). Each call to the **Font** constructor passes a font name (**Serif**, **Monospaced** or **SansSerif**) as a **String**, a font style (**Font.PLAIN**, **Font.ITALIC** or **Font.BOLD**) and a font size. Once **Graphics** method **setFont** is invoked, all text displayed following the call will appear in the new font until the font is changed. Note that line 35 changes the drawing color to red, so the next string displayed appears in red.

Software Engineering Observation 11.3

*To change the font, you must create a new **Font** object as there are no set methods in class **Font** to change the characteristics of the current font.*

```
1   // Fig. 11.9: Fonts.java
2   // Using fonts
3   import java.awt.*;
4   import javax.swing.*;
5   import java.awt.event.*;
6
7   public class Fonts extends JFrame {
8      public Fonts()
9      {
10        super( "Using fonts" );
11
12        setSize( 420, 125 );
13        show();
14     }
15
16     public void paint( Graphics g )
17     {
18        // set current font to Serif (Times), bold, 12pt
19        // and draw a string
20        g.setFont( new Font( "Serif", Font.BOLD, 12 ) );
21        g.drawString( "Serif 12 point bold.", 20, 50 );
22
23        // set current font to Monospaced (Courier),
24        // italic, 24pt and draw a string
25        g.setFont( new Font( "Monospaced", Font.ITALIC, 24 ) );
26        g.drawString( "Monospaced 24 point italic.", 20, 70 );
27
```

Fig. 11.9   Using **Graphics** method **setFont** to change **Font**s (part 1 of 2).

```
28              // set current font to SansSerif (Helvetica),
29              // plain, 14pt and draw a string
30              g.setFont( new Font( "SansSerif", Font.PLAIN, 14 ) );
31              g.drawString( "SansSerif 14 point plain.", 20, 90 );
32
33              // set current font to Serif (times), bold/italic,
34              // 18pt and draw a string
35              g.setColor( Color.red );
36              g.setFont(
37                 new Font( "Serif", Font.BOLD + Font.ITALIC, 18 ) );
38              g.drawString( g.getFont().getName() + " " +
39                            g.getFont().getSize() +
40                            " point bold italic.", 20, 110 );
41           }
42
43        public static void main( String args[] )
44        {
45           Fonts app = new Fonts();
46
47           app.addWindowListener(
48              new WindowAdapter() {
49                 public void windowClosing( WindowEvent e )
50                 {
51                    System.exit( 0 );
52                 }
53              }
54           );
55        }
56     }
```

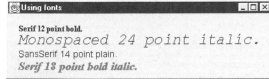

Fig. 11.9   Using **Graphics** method **setFont** to change **Font**s (part 2 of 2).

Often it is necessary to get information about the current font such as the font name, the font style and the font size. Several **Font** methods used to get font information are summarized in Fig. 11.8. Method **getStyle** returns an integer value representing the current style. The integer value returned is either **Font.PLAIN**, **Font.ITALIC**, **Font.BOLD** or any combination of **Font.PLAIN**, **Font.ITALIC** and **Font.BOLD**.

Method **getSize** returns the font size in points. Method **getName** returns the current font name as a **String**. Method **getFamily** returns the name of the font family to which the current font belongs. The name of the font family is platform specific.

  Portability Tip 11.3

Java uses standardized font names and maps these into system-specific font names for portability. This is transparent to the programmer.

Font methods are also available to test the style of the current font and are summarized in Fig. 11.8. The **isPlain** method returns **true** if the current font style is plain.

The **isBold** method returns **true** if the current font style is bold. The **isItalic** method returns **true** if the current font style is italic.

Sometimes precise information about a font's metrics must be known—such as *height*, *descent* (the amount a character dips below the baseline), *ascent* (the amount a character rises above the baseline) and *leading* (the difference between the height and the ascent). Figure 11.10 illustrates some of the common *font metrics*. Note that the coordinate passed to **drawString** corresponds to the lower-left corner of the baseline of the font.

Class **FontMetrics** defines several methods for obtaining font metrics. These methods and **Graphics** method **getFontMetrics** are summarized in Fig. 11.11.

The program of Fig. 11.12 uses the methods of Fig. 11.11 to obtain font metric information for two fonts.

Line 19 creates and sets the current drawing font to a **SansSerif**, bold, 12-point font. Line 20 uses **Graphics** method **getFontMetrics** to obtain the **FontMetrics** object for the current font. Line 21 uses an implicit call to class **Font**'s **toString** method to output the string representation of the font. Lines 22 through 25 use **Font-Metric** methods to obtain the ascent, descent, height and leading for the font.

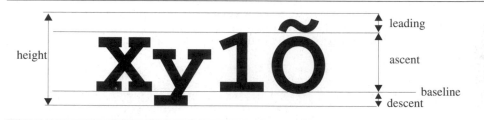

Fig. 11.10   Font metrics.

Method	Description
public int getAscent() *// FontMetrics class*	
Returns a value representing the ascent of a font in points.	
public int getDescent() *// FontMetrics class*	
Returns a value representing the descent of a font in points.	
public int getLeading() *// FontMetrics class*	
Returns a value representing the leading of a font in points.	
public int getHeight() *// FontMetrics class*	
Returns a value representing the height of a font in points.	
public FontMetrics getFontMetrics() *// Graphics class*	
Returns the **FontMetrics** object for the current drawing **Font**.	
public FontMetrics getFontMetrics(Font f) *// Graphics class*	
Returns the **FontMetrics** object for the specified **Font** argument.	

Fig. 11.11   **FontMetrics** and **Graphics** methods for obtaining font metrics.

```
1    // Fig. 11.12: Metrics.java
2    // Demonstrating methods of class FontMetrics and
3    // class Graphics useful for obtaining font metrics
4    import java.awt.*;
5    import java.awt.event.*;
6    import javax.swing.*;
7
8    public class Metrics extends JFrame {
9       public Metrics()
10      {
11         super( "Demonstrating FontMetrics" );
12
13         setSize( 510, 210 );
14         show();
15      }
16
17      public void paint( Graphics g )
18      {
19         g.setFont( new Font( "SansSerif", Font.BOLD, 12 ) );
20         FontMetrics fm = g.getFontMetrics();
21         g.drawString( "Current font: " + g.getFont(), 10, 40 );
22         g.drawString( "Ascent: " + fm.getAscent(), 10, 55 );
23         g.drawString( "Descent: " + fm.getDescent(), 10, 70 );
24         g.drawString( "Height: " + fm.getHeight(), 10, 85 );
25         g.drawString( "Leading: " + fm.getLeading(), 10, 100 );
26
27         Font font = new Font( "Serif", Font.ITALIC, 14 );
28         fm = g.getFontMetrics( font );
29         g.setFont( font );
30         g.drawString( "Current font: " + font, 10, 130 );
31         g.drawString( "Ascent: " + fm.getAscent(), 10, 145 );
32         g.drawString( "Descent: " + fm.getDescent(), 10, 160 );
33         g.drawString( "Height: " + fm.getHeight(), 10, 175 );
34         g.drawString( "Leading: " + fm.getLeading(), 10, 190 );
35      }
36
37      public static void main( String args[] )
38      {
39         Metrics app = new Metrics();
40
41         app.addWindowListener(
42            new WindowAdapter() {
43               public void windowClosing( WindowEvent e )
44               {
45                  System.exit( 0 );
46               }
47            }
48         );
49      }
50   }
```

Fig. 11.12 Obtaining font metric information (part 1 of 2).

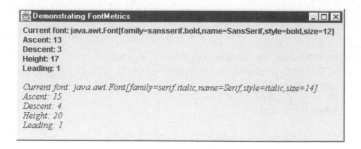

Fig. 11.12 Obtaining font metric information (part 2 of 2).

Line 27 creates a new **Serif**, italic, 14-point font. Line 28 uses a second version of **Graphics** method **getFontMetrics**, which receives a **Font** argument and returns a corresponding **FontMetrics** object. Lines 31 to 34 obtain the ascent, descent, height and leading for the font. Notice that the font metrics are slightly different for the two fonts.

11.5 Drawing Lines, Rectangles and Ovals

This section presents a variety of **Graphics** methods for drawing lines, rectangles and ovals. The methods and their parameters are summarized in Fig. 11.13. For each drawing method that requires a **width** and **height** parameter, the **width** and **height** must be nonnegative values. Otherwise, the shape will not display.

Method	Description
`public void drawLine( int x1, int y1, int x2, int y2 )`	
	Draws a line between the point (**x1**, **y1**) and the point (**x2**, **y2**).
`public void drawRect( int x, int y, int width, int height )`	
	Draws a rectangle of the specified **width** and **height**. The top-left corner of the rectangle has the coordinates (**x**, **y**).
`public void fillRect( int x, int y, int width, int height )`	
	Draws a solid rectangle with the specified **width** and **height**. The top-left corner of the rectangle has the coordinate (**x**, **y**).
`public void clearRect( int x, int y, int width, int height )`	
	Draws a solid rectangle with the specified **width** and **height** in the current background color. The top-left corner of the rectangle has the coordinate (**x**, **y**).
`public void drawRoundRect( int x, int y, int width, int height, int arcWidth, int arcHeight )`	
	Draws a rectangle with rounded corners in the current color with the specified **width** and **height**. The **arcWidth** and **arcHeight** determine the rounding of the corners (see Fig. 11.15).

Fig. 11.13 **Graphics** methods that draw lines, rectangles and ovals (part 1 of 2).

Method	Description

public void fillRoundRect(int x, int y, int width, int height,
**   int arcWidth, int arcHeight)**

> Draws a solid rectangle with rounded corners in the current color with the specified **width** and **height**. The **arcWidth** and **arcHeight** determine the rounding of the corners (see Fig. 11.15).

public void draw3DRect(int x, int y, int width, int height,
**   boolean b)**

> Draws a three-dimensional rectangle in the current color with the specified **width** and **height**. The top-left corner of the rectangle has the coordinates (**x**, **y**). The rectangle appears raised when **b** is **true** and is lowered when **b** is **false**.

public void fill3DRect(int x, int y, int width, int height,
**   boolean b)**

> Draws a filled three-dimensional rectangle in the current color with the specified **width** and **height**. The top-left corner of the rectangle has the coordinates (**x**, **y**). The rectangle appears raised when **b** is **true** and is lowered when **b** is **false**.

public void drawOval(int x, int y, int width, int height)

> Draws an oval in the current color with the specified **width** and **height**. The bounding rectangle's top-left corner is at the coordinates (**x**, **y**). The oval touches all four sides of the bounding rectangle at the center of each side (see Fig. 11.16).

public void fillOval(int x, int y, int width, int height)

> Draws a filled oval in the current color with the specified **width** and **height**. The bounding rectangle's top-left corner is at the coordinates (**x**, **y**). The oval touches all four sides of the bounding rectangle at the center of each side (see Fig. 11.16).

Fig. 11.13 Graphics methods that draw lines, rectangles and ovals (part 2 of 2).

The application of Fig. 11.14 demonstrates drawing a variety of lines, rectangles, 3D rectangles, rounded rectangles and ovals.

```
1   // Fig. 11.14: LinesRectsOvals.java
2   // Drawing lines, rectangles and ovals
3   import java.awt.*;
4   import java.awt.event.*;
5   import javax.swing.*;
6
7   public class LinesRectsOvals extends JFrame {
8      private String s = "Using drawString!";
9
```

Fig. 11.14 Demonstrating **Graphics** method **drawLine** (part 1 of 2).

```
10      public LinesRectsOvals()
11      {
12          super( "Drawing lines, rectangles and ovals" );
13
14          setSize( 400, 165 );
15          show();
16      }
17
18      public void paint( Graphics g )
19      {
20          g.setColor( Color.red );
21          g.drawLine( 5, 30, 350, 30 );
22
23          g.setColor( Color.blue );
24          g.drawRect( 5, 40, 90, 55 );
25          g.fillRect( 100, 40, 90, 55 );
26
27          g.setColor( Color.cyan );
28          g.fillRoundRect( 195, 40, 90, 55, 50, 50 );
29          g.drawRoundRect( 290, 40, 90, 55, 20, 20 );
30
31          g.setColor( Color.yellow );
32          g.draw3DRect( 5, 100, 90, 55, true );
33          g.fill3DRect( 100, 100, 90, 55, false );
34
35          g.setColor( Color.magenta );
36          g.drawOval( 195, 100, 90, 55 );
37          g.fillOval( 290, 100, 90, 55 );
38      }
39
40      public static void main( String args[] )
41      {
42          LinesRectsOvals app = new LinesRectsOvals();
43
44          app.addWindowListener(
45              new WindowAdapter() {
46                  public void windowClosing( WindowEvent e )
47                  {
48                      System.exit( 0 );
49                  }
50              }
51          );
52      }
53  }
```

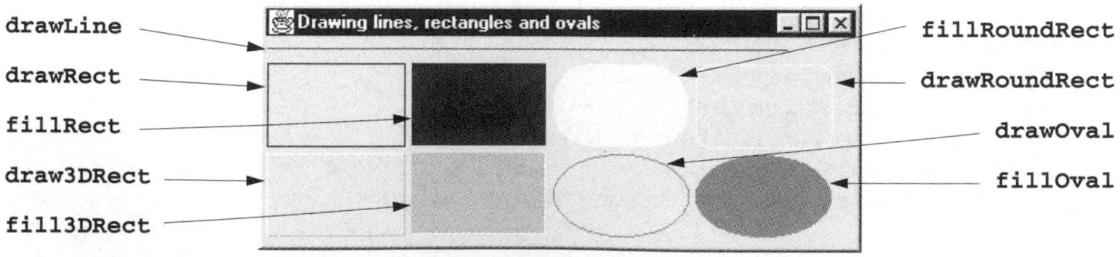

Fig. 11.14 Demonstrating **Graphics** method **drawLine** (part 2 of 2).

dMethods **fillRoundRect** (line 28) and **drawRoundRect** (line 29) draw rectangles with rounded corners. Their first two arguments specify the coordinates of the upper-left corner of the *bounding rectangle*—the area in which the rounded rectangle will be drawn. Note that the upper-left corner coordinates are not the edge of the rounded rectangle but the coordinates where the edge would be if the rectangle had square corners. The third and fourth arguments specify the **width** and **height** of the rectangle. Their last two arguments—**arcWidth** and **arcHeight**—determine the horizontal and vertical diameters of the arcs used to represent the corners.

Methods **draw3DRect** (line 32) and **fill3DRect** (line 33) take the same arguments. The first two arguments specify the top-left corner of the rectangle. The next two arguments specify the **width** and **height** of the rectangle, respectively. The last argument determines if the rectangle is *raised* (**true**) or *lowered* (**false**). The three-dimensional effect of **draw3DRect** appears as two edges of the rectangle in the original color and two edges in a slightly darker color. The three-dimensional effect of **fill3DRect** appears as two edges of the rectangle in the original drawing color and the fill and other two edges in a slightly darker color. Raised rectangles have the original drawing color edges at the top and left of the rectangle. Lowered rectangles have the original drawing color edges at the bottom and right of the rectangle. The three-dimensional effect is difficult to see in some colors.

Figure 11.15 labels the arc width, arc height, width and height of a rounded rectangle. Using the same value for **arcWidth** and **arcHeight** produces a quarter circle at each corner. When **width**, **height**, **arcWidth** and **arcHeight** have the same values, the result is a circle. If the values for **width** and **height** are the same and the values of **arcWidth** and **arcHeight** are 0, the result is a square.

Both the **drawOval** and **fillOval** methods take the same four arguments. The first two arguments specify the top-left coordinate of the bounding rectangle that contains the oval. The last two arguments specify the **width** and **height** of the bounding rectangle, respectively. Figure 11.16 shows an oval bounded by a rectangle. Note that the oval touches the center of all four sides of the bounding rectangle (the bounding rectangle is not displayed on the screen).

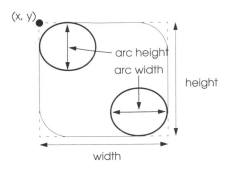

Fig. 11.15 The arc width and arc height for rounded rectangles.

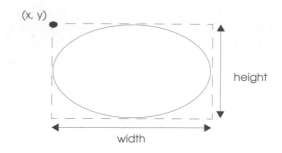

Fig. 11.16   An oval bounded by a rectangle.

11.6 Drawing Arcs

An *arc* is a portion of a oval. Arc angles are measured in degrees. Arcs *sweep* from a *starting angle* the number of degrees specified by their *arc angle*. The starting angle indicates in degrees where the arc begins. The arc angle specifies the total number of degrees through which the arc sweeps. Figure 11.17 illustrates two arcs. The left set of axes shows an arc sweeping from zero degrees to approximately 110 degrees. Arcs that sweep in a counterclockwise direction are measured in *positive degrees*. The right set of axes shows an arc sweeping from zero degrees to approximately –110 degrees. Arcs that sweep in a clockwise direction are measured in *negative degrees*. Notice the dashed boxes around the arcs in Fig. 11.17. When drawing an arc, we specify a bounding rectangle for an oval. The arc will sweep along part of the oval. The **Graphics** methods—*drawArc* and *fillArc*—for drawing arcs are summarized in Fig. 11.18.

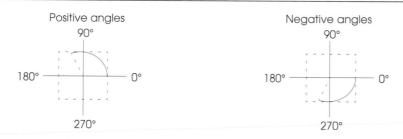

Fig. 11.17   Positive and negative arc angles.

Method	Description

**public void drawArc(int x, int y, int width, int height,
                       int startAngle, int arcAngle)**

Draws an arc relative to the bounding rectangle's top-left coordinates (*x, y*) with the specified **width** and **height**. The arc segment is drawn starting at **startAngle** and sweeps **arcAngle** degrees.

Fig. 11.18   **Graphics** methods for drawing arcs.

Method	Description

```
public void fillArc( int x, int y, int width, int height,
                     int startAngle, int arcAngle )
```

Draws a solid arc (i.e., a sector) relative to the bounding rectangle's top-left coordinates *(x, y)* with the specified **width** and **height**. The arc segment is drawn starting at **startAngle** and sweeps **arcAngle** degrees.

Fig. 11.18 Graphics methods for drawing arcs.

The program of Fig. 11.19 demonstrates the arc methods of Fig. 11.18. The program draws six arcs (three unfilled and three filled). To illustrate the bounding rectangle that helps determine where the arc appears, the first three arcs are displayed inside a yellow rectangle that has the same **x, y, width** and **height** arguments as the arcs.

```
1   // Fig. 11.19: DrawArcs.java
2   // Drawing arcs
3   import java.awt.*;
4   import javax.swing.*;
5   import java.awt.event.*;
6
7   public class DrawArcs extends JFrame {
8      public DrawArcs()
9      {
10        super( "Drawing Arcs" );
11
12        setSize( 300, 170 );
13        show();
14     }
15
16     public void paint( Graphics g )
17     {
18        // start at 0 and sweep 360 degrees
19        g.setColor( Color.yellow );
20        g.drawRect( 15, 35, 80, 80 );
21        g.setColor( Color.black );
22        g.drawArc( 15, 35, 80, 80, 0, 360 );
23
24        // start at 0 and sweep 110 degrees
25        g.setColor( Color.yellow );
26        g.drawRect( 100, 35, 80, 80 );
27        g.setColor( Color.black );
28        g.drawArc( 100, 35, 80, 80, 0, 110 );
29
30        // start at 0 and sweep -270 degrees
31        g.setColor( Color.yellow );
32        g.drawRect( 185, 35, 80, 80 );
```

Fig. 11.19 Demonstrating **drawArc** and **fillArc** (part 1 of 2).

```
33          g.setColor( Color.black );
34          g.drawArc( 185, 35, 80, 80, 0, -270 );
35
36          // start at 0 and sweep 360 degrees
37          g.fillArc( 15, 120, 80, 40, 0, 360 );
38
39          // start at 270 and sweep -90 degrees
40          g.fillArc( 100, 120, 80, 40, 270, -90 );
41
42          // start at 0 and sweep -270 degrees
43          g.fillArc( 185, 120, 80, 40, 0, -270 );
44       }
45
46       public static void main( String args[] )
47       {
48          DrawArcs app = new DrawArcs();
49
50          app.addWindowListener(
51             new WindowAdapter() {
52                public void windowClosing( WindowEvent e )
53                {
54                   System.exit( 0 );
55                }
56             }
57          );
58       }
59    }
```

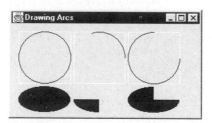

Fig. 11.19   Demonstrating **drawArc** and **fillArc** (part 2 of 2).

11.7 Drawing Polygons and Polylines

Polygons are multisided shapes. *Polylines* are a series of connected points. **Graphics** methods for drawing polygons and polylines are discussed in Fig. 11.20. Note that some methods require a ***Polygon*** object (package **java.awt**). Class **Polygon**'s constructors are also described in Fig. 11.20.

The program of Fig. 11.21 draws polygons and polylines using the methods and constructors in Fig. 11.20.

Lines 18 through 20 create two **int** arrays and use them to specify the points for **Polygon poly1**. The **Polygon** constructor call at line 20 receives array **xValues**, which contains the *x*-coordinate of each point, array **yValues**, which contains the *y*-coordinate of each point, and 6 (the number of points in the polygon). Line 22 displays **poly1** by passing it as an argument to **Graphics** method **drawPolygon**.

Method	Description

```
public void drawPolygon( int xPoints[], int yPoints[],
                         int points )
```

Draws a polygon. The *x*-coordinate of each point is specified in the **xPoints** array and the *y*-coordinate of each point is specified in the **yPoints** array. The last argument specifies the number of **points**. This method draws a closed polygon—even if the last point is different from the first point.

```
public void drawPolyline( int xPoints[], int yPoints[],
                          int points )
```

Draws a series of connected lines. The *x*-coordinate of each point is specified in the **xPoints** array and the *y*-coordinate of each point is specified in the **yPoints** array. The last argument specifies the number of **points**. If the last point is different from the first point, the polyline is not closed.

```
public void drawPolygon( Polygon p )
```

Draws the specified closed polygon.

```
public void fillPolygon( int xPoints[], int yPoints[],
                         int points )
```

Draws a solid polygon. The *x*-coordinate of each point is specified in the **xPoints** array and the *y*-coordinate of each point is specified in the **yPoints** array. The last argument specifies the number of **points**. This method draws a closed polygon—even if the last point is different from the first point.

```
public void fillPolygon( Polygon p )
```

Draws the specified solid polygon. The polygon is closed.

```
public Polygon()                              // Polygon class
```

Constructs a new polygon object. The polygon does not contain any points.

```
public Polygon( int xValues[], int yValues[],     // Polygon class
                int numberOfPoints )
```

Constructs a new polygon object. The polygon has **numberOfPoints** sides, with each point consisting of an *x*-coordinate from **xValues** and a *y*-coordinate from **yValues**.

Fig. 11.20 Graphics methods for drawing polygons and class **Polygon** constructors.

```
1  // Drawing polygons
2  import java.awt.*;
3  import java.awt.event.*;
4  import javax.swing.*;
5
6  public class DrawPolygons extends JFrame {
```

Fig. 11.21 Demonstrating **drawPolygon** and **fillPolygon** (part 1 of 3).

```
 7        public DrawPolygons()
 8        {
 9           super( "Drawing Polygons" );
10
11           setSize( 275, 230 );
12           show();
13        }
14
15        public void paint( Graphics g )
16        {
17           int xValues[] = { 20, 40, 50, 30, 20, 15 };
18           int yValues[] = { 50, 50, 60, 80, 80, 60 };
19           Polygon poly1 = new Polygon( xValues, yValues, 6 );
20
21           g.drawPolygon( poly1 );
22
23           int xValues2[] = { 70, 90, 100, 80, 70, 65, 60 };
24           int yValues2[] = { 100, 100, 110, 110, 130, 110, 90 };
25
26           g.drawPolyline( xValues2, yValues2, 7 );
27
28           int xValues3[] = { 120, 140, 150, 190 };
29           int yValues3[] = { 40, 70, 80, 60 };
30
31           g.fillPolygon( xValues3, yValues3, 4 );
32
33           Polygon poly2 = new Polygon();
34           poly2.addPoint( 165, 135 );
35           poly2.addPoint( 175, 150 );
36           poly2.addPoint( 270, 200 );
37           poly2.addPoint( 200, 220 );
38           poly2.addPoint( 130, 180 );
39
40           g.fillPolygon( poly2 );
41        }
42
43        public static void main( String args[] )
44        {
45           DrawPolygons app = new DrawPolygons();
46
47           app.addWindowListener(
48             new WindowAdapter() {
49                public void windowClosing( WindowEvent e )
50                {
51                   System.exit( 0 );
52                }
53             }
54           );
55        }
56     }
```

Fig. 11.21   Demonstrating **drawPolygon** and **fillPolygon** (part 2 of 3).

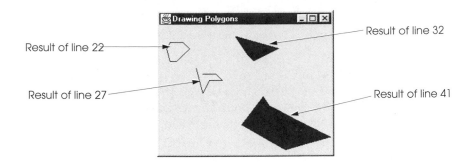

Fig. 11.21   Demonstrating **drawPolygon** and **fillPolygon** (part 3 of 3).

Lines 24 and 25 create two **int** arrays and use them to specify the points for a series of connected lines. Array **xValues2** contains the *x*-coordinate of each point and array **yValues2** contains the *y*-coordinate of each point. Line 27 uses **Graphics** method **drawPolyline** to display the series of connected lines specified with the arguments **xValues2**, **yValues2** and **7** (the number of points).

Lines 29 through 30 create two **int** arrays and use them to specify the points of a polygon. Array **xValues3** contains the *x*-coordinate of each point and array **yValues3** contains the *y*-coordinate of each point. Line 32 displays a polygon by passing to **Graphics** method **fillPolygon** the two arrays (**xValues3** and **yValues3**) and the number of points to draw (**4**).

Common Programming Error 11.3

*An **ArrayIndexOutOfBoundsException** is thrown if the number of points specified in the third argument to method **drawPolygon** or method **fillPolygon** is greater than the number of elements in the arrays of coordinates that define the polygon to display.*

Line 34 creates **Polygon poly2** with no points. Lines 35 through 39 use **Polygon** method **addPoint** to add pairs of *x*- and *y*-coordinates to the **Polygon**. Line 41 displays **Polygon poly2** by passing it to **Graphics** method **fillPolygon**.

11.8 The Java2D API

The new *Java2D API* provides advanced two-dimensional graphics capabilities for programmers who require detailed and complex graphical manipulations. The API includes features for processing line art, text and images in packages **java.awt**, **java.awt.image**, **java.awt.color**, **java.awt.font**, **java.awt.geom**, **java.awt.print** and **java.awt.image.renderable**. The capabilities of the API are far too broad to cover in this textbook. For an overview of the capabilities, see the Java2D demo (demonstrated in Chapter 3). In this section, we present an overview of several Java2D capabilities.

Drawing with the Java2D API is accomplished with an instance of class *Graphics2D* (package **java.awt**). Class **Graphics2D** is a subclass of class **Graphics**, so it has all the graphics capabilities demonstrated earlier in this chapter. In fact, the actual object we have used to draw in every **paint** method is a **Graphics2D** object that is passed to method **paint** and accessed via the superclass **Graphics** reference **g**. To access the **Graphics2D** capabilities, we must downcast the **Graphics** reference passed to **paint** to a **Graphics2D** reference with a statement such as

```
Graphics2D g2d = ( Graphics2D ) g;
```

The programs of the next several sections use this technique.

11.9 Java2D Shapes

Next, we present several Java2D shapes from package **java.awt.geom**, including
Ellipse2D.Double, **Rectangle2D.Double**, **RoundRectangle2D.Double**,
Arc2D.Double and **Line2D.Double**. Note the syntax of each class name. Each of
these classes represents a shape with dimensions specified as double-precision floating-
point values. There is a separate version of each represented with single-precision floating-
point values (such as **Ellipse2D.Float**). In each case, **Double** is a **static** inner
class of the class to the left of the dot operator (e.g., **Ellipse2D**). To use the **static**
inner class, we simply qualify its name with the outer class name.

The program of Fig. 11.22 demonstrates several Java2D shapes and drawing characteristics, such as thick lines, filling shapes with patterns and drawing dashed lines. These
are just a few of the many capabilities provided by Java2D.

```
1   // Fig. 11.22: Shapes.java
2   // Demonstrating some Java2D shapes
3   import javax.swing.*;
4   import java.awt.event.*;
5   import java.awt.*;
6   import java.awt.geom.*;
7   import java.awt.image.*;
8
9   public class Shapes extends JFrame {
10     public Shapes()
11     {
12        super( "Drawing 2D shapes" );
13
14        setSize( 425, 160 );
15        show();
16     }
17
18     public void paint( Graphics g )
19     {
20        // create 2D by casting g to Graphics2D
21        Graphics2D g2d = ( Graphics2D ) g;
22
23        // draw 2D ellipse filled with a blue-yellow gradient
24        g2d.setPaint(
25           new GradientPaint( 5, 30,          // x1, y1
26                              Color.blue,     // initial Color
27                              35, 100,        // x2, y2
28                              Color.yellow,   // end Color
29                              true ) );       // cyclic
30        g2d.fill( new Ellipse2D.Double( 5, 30, 65, 100 ) );
31
```

Fig. 11.22 Demonstrating some Java2D shapes (part 1 of 3).

```
32          // draw 2D rectangle in red
33          g2d.setPaint( Color.red );
34          g2d.setStroke( new BasicStroke( 10.0f ) );
35          g2d.draw(
36             new Rectangle2D.Double( 80, 30, 65, 100 ) );
37
38          // draw 2D rounded rectangle with a buffered background
39          BufferedImage buffImage =
40             new BufferedImage(
41                10, 10, BufferedImage.TYPE_INT_RGB );
42
43          Graphics2D gg = buffImage.createGraphics();
44          gg.setColor( Color.yellow ); // draw in yellow
45          gg.fillRect( 0, 0, 10, 10 ); // draw a filled rectangle
46          gg.setColor( Color.black );  // draw in black
47          gg.drawRect( 1, 1, 6, 6 );   // draw a rectangle
48          gg.setColor( Color.blue );   // draw in blue
49          gg.fillRect( 1, 1, 3, 3 );   // draw a filled rectangle
50          gg.setColor( Color.red );    // draw in red
51          gg.fillRect( 4, 4, 3, 3 );   // draw a filled rectangle
52
53          // paint buffImage onto the JFrame
54          g2d.setPaint(
55             new TexturePaint(
56                buffImage, new Rectangle( 10, 10 ) ) );
57          g2d.fill(
58             new RoundRectangle2D.Double(
59                155, 30, 75, 100, 50, 50 ) );
60
61          // draw 2D pie-shaped arc in white
62          g2d.setPaint( Color.white );
63          g2d.setStroke( new BasicStroke( 6.0f ) );
64          g2d.draw(
65             new Arc2D.Double(
66                240, 30, 75, 100, 0, 270, Arc2D.PIE ) );
67
68          // draw 2D lines in green and yellow
69          g2d.setPaint( Color.green );
70          g2d.draw( new Line2D.Double( 395, 30, 320, 150 ) );
71
72          float dashes[] = { 10 };
73
74          g2d.setPaint( Color.yellow );
75          g2d.setStroke(
76             new BasicStroke( 4,
77                              BasicStroke.CAP_ROUND,
78                              BasicStroke.JOIN_ROUND,
79                              10, dashes, 0 ) );
80          g2d.draw( new Line2D.Double( 320, 30, 395, 150 ) );
81       }
82
```

Fig. 11.22   Demonstrating some Java2D shapes (part 2 of 3).

```
83      public static void main( String args[] )
84      {
85          Shapes app = new Shapes();
86
87          app.addWindowListener(
88             new WindowAdapter() {
89                public void windowClosing( WindowEvent e )
90                {
91                   System.exit( 0 );
92                }
93             }
94          );
95      }
96   }
```

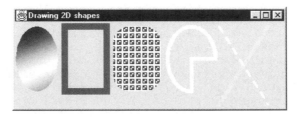

Fig. 11.22   Demonstrating some Java2D shapes (part 3 of 3).

Line 21 casts the **Graphics** reference received by **paint** to a **Graphics2D** reference and assigns it to **g2d** to allow access to the **Java2D** features.

The first shape we draw is an oval filled with gradually changing colors. Lines 24 through 29

```
g2d.setPaint(
   new GradientPaint( 5, 30,        // x1, y1
                      Color.blue,   // initial Color
                      35, 100,      // x2, y2
                      Color.yellow, // end Color
                      true ) );     // cyclic
```

invoke **Graphics2D** method *setPaint* to set the *Paint* object that determines the color for the shape to display. A **Paint** object is an object of any class that implements interface **java.awt.Paint**. The **Paint** object can be something as simple as one of the predefined **Color** objects introduced in Section 11.3 (class **Color** implements **Paint**) or the **Paint** object can be an instance of the Java2D API's *GradientPaint*, *SystemColor* or *TexturePaint* classes. In this case, we use a **GradientPaint** object.

Class **GradientPaint** helps draw a shape in a gradually changing colors—called a *gradient*. The **GradientPaint** constructor used here requires seven arguments. The first two arguments specify the starting coordinate for the gradient. The third argument specifies the starting **Color** for the gradient. The fourth and fifth arguments specify the ending coordinate for the gradient. The sixth argument specifies the ending **Color** for the gradient. The last argument specifies if the gradient is cyclic (**true**) or acyclic (**false**). The two coordinates determine the direction of the gradient. Because the second coordinate *(35, 100)* is down and to the right of the first coordinate *(5, 30)*, the gradient goes down and to the right at an angle. Because this gradient is cyclic (**true**), the color starts with blue, gradually becomes yellow, then gradually returns to blue. If the gradient is acyclic, the color transitions from the first color specified (e.g., blue) to the second color (e.g., yellow). Line 30

```
g2d.fill( new Ellipse2D.Double( 5, 30, 65, 100 ) );
```

uses **Graphics2D** method *fill* to draw a filled *Shape* object. The **Shape** object is an instance of any class that implements interface **Shape** (package **java.awt**)—in this case, an instance of class **Ellipse2D.Double**. The **Ellipse2D.Double** constructor receives four arguments specifying the bounding rectangle for the ellipse to display.

Next we draw a red rectangle with a thick border. Line 33 uses **setPaint** to set the **Paint** object to **Color.red**. Line 34

```
g2d.setStroke( new BasicStroke( 10.0f ) );
```

uses **Graphics2D** method *setStroke* to set the characteristics of the rectangle's border (or the lines for any other shape). Method **setStroke** requires a *Stroke* object as its argument. The **Stroke** object is an instance of any class that implements interface **Stroke** (package **java.awt**)—in this case, an instance of class *BasicStroke*. Class **BasicStroke** provides a variety of constructors to specify the width of the line, how the line ends (called the *end caps*), how lines join together (called *line joins*) and the dash attributes of the line (if it is a dashed line). The constructor here specifies that the line should be 10 pixels wide.

Lines 35 and 36

```
g2d.draw(
    new Rectangle2D.Double( 80, 30, 65, 100 ) );
```

use **Graphics2D** method *draw* to draw a *Shape* object—in this case, an instance of class **Rectangle2D.Double**. The **Rectangle2D.Double** constructor receives four arguments specifying the upper-left *x*-coordinate, upper-left *y*-coordinate, width and height of the rectangle.

Next we draw a rounded rectangle filled with a pattern created in a *BufferedImage* (package **java.awt.image**) object. Lines 39 through 41

```
BufferedImage buffImage =
    new BufferedImage(
        10, 10, BufferedImage.TYPE_INT_RGB );
```

create the **BufferedImage** object. Class **BufferedImage** can be used to produce images in color and gray scale. This particular **BufferedImage** is 10 pixels wide and 10 pixels tall. The third constructor argument **BufferedImage.TYPE_INT_RGB** indicates that the image is stored in color using the RGB color scheme.

To create the fill pattern for the rounded rectangle, we must first draw into the **BufferedImage**. Line 43

```
Graphics2D gg = buffImage.createGraphics();
```

creates a **Graphics2D** object that can be used to draw into the **BufferedImage**. Lines 44 through 51 use methods **setColor**, **fillRect** and **drawRect** (discussed earlier in this chapter) to create the pattern.

Lines 54 through 56

```
g2d.setPaint(
    new TexturePaint(
        buffImage, new Rectangle( 10, 10 ) ) );
```

set the **Paint** object to a new **TexturePaint** (package **java.awt**) object. A **TexturePaint** object uses the image stored in its associated **BufferedImage** as the fill texture for a filled-in shape. The second argument specifies the **Rectangle** area from the **BufferedImage** that will be replicated through the texture. In this case, the **Rectangle** is the same size as the **BufferedImage**. However, a smaller portion of the **BufferedImage** can be used.

Lines 57 through 59

```
g2d.fill(
    new RoundRectangle2D.Double(
        155, 30, 75, 100, 50, 50 ) );
```

use **Graphics2D** method **fill** to draw a filled **Shape** object—in this case, an instance of class *RoundRectangle2D.Double*. The **RoundRectangle2D.Double** constructor receives six arguments specifying the rectangle dimensions and the arc width and arc height used to determine the rounding of the corners.

Next we draw a pie-shaped arc with a thick white line. Line 62 sets the **Paint** object to **Color.white**. Line 63 sets the **Stroke** object to a new **BasicStroke** for a line 6 pixels wide. Lines 64 through 66

```
g2d.draw(
    new Arc2D.Double(
        240, 30, 75, 100, 0, 270, Arc2D.PIE ) );
```

use **Graphics2D** method **draw** to draw a **Shape** object—in this case, an **Arc2D.Double**. The **Arc2D.Double** constructor's first four arguments specifying the upper-left *x*-coordinate, upper-left *y*-coordinate, width and height of the bounding rectangle for the arc. The fifth argument specifies the start angle. The sixth argument specifies the arc angle. The last argument specifies the how the arc is closed. Constant *Arc2D.PIE* indicates that the arc is closed by drawing two lines. One line from the arc's starting point to the center of the bounding rectangle and one line from the center of the bounding rectangle to the ending point. Class **Arc2D** provides two other **static** constants for specifying how the arc is closed. Constant *Arc2D.CHORD* draws a line from the starting point to the ending point. Constant *Arc2D.OPEN* specifies that the arc is not closed.

Finally, we draw two lines using *Line2D* objects—one solid and one dashed. Line 69 sets the **Paint** object to **Color.green**. Line 70

```
g2d.draw( new Line2D.Double( 395, 30, 320, 150 ) );
```

uses **Graphics2D** method **draw** to draw a **Shape** object—in this case, an instance of class **Line2D.Double**. The **Line2D.Double** constructor's arguments specify starting coordinates and ending coordinates of the line.

Line 72 defines a one-element **float** array containing the value 10. This array will be used to describe the dashes in the dashed line. In this case, each dash will be 10 pixels long. To create dashes of different lengths in a pattern, simply provide the lengths of each dash as an element in the array. Line 74 sets the **Paint** object to **Color.yellow**. Lines 75 through 79

```
g2d.setStroke(
   new BasicStroke( 4,
                    BasicStroke.CAP_ROUND,
                    BasicStroke.JOIN_ROUND,
                    10, dashes, 0 ) );
```

set the **Stroke** object to a new **BasicStroke**. The line will be **4** pixels wide and will have rounded ends (**BasicStroke.CAP_ROUND**). If lines join together (as in a rectangle at the corners), the joining of the lines will be rounded (**Basic-Stroke.JOIN_ROUND**). The **dashes** argument specifies the dash lengths for the line. The last argument indicates the starting subscript in the **dashes** array for the first dash in the pattern. Line 80 then draws a line with the current **Stroke**.

A general path is a shape constructed from straight lines and complex curves. A general path is represented with an object of class *GeneralPath* (package **java.awt.geom**). The program of Fig. 11.23 demonstrates drawing a general path in the shape of a five-pointed star.

```
1   // Fig. 11.23: Shapes2.java
2   // Demonstrating a general path
3   import javax.swing.*;
4   import java.awt.event.*;
5   import java.awt.*;
6   import java.awt.geom.*;
7
8   public class Shapes2 extends JFrame {
9      public Shapes2()
10     {
11        super( "Drawing 2D Shapes" );
12
13        setBackground( Color.yellow );
14        setSize( 400, 400 );
15        show();
16     }
17
18     public void paint( Graphics g )
19     {
20        int xPoints[] =
21           { 55, 67, 109, 73, 83, 55, 27, 37, 1, 43 };
22        int yPoints[] =
23           { 0, 36, 36, 54, 96, 72, 96, 54, 36, 36 };
24
25        Graphics2D g2d = ( Graphics2D ) g;
26
27        // create a star from a series of points
28        GeneralPath star = new GeneralPath();
29
```

Fig. 11.23   Demonstrating some Java2D shapes (part 1 of 3).

```
30              // set the initial coordinate of the General Path
31              star.moveTo( xPoints[ 0 ], yPoints[ 0 ] );
32
33              // create the star--this does not draw the star
34              for ( int k = 1; k < xPoints.length; k++ )
35                  star.lineTo( xPoints[ k ], yPoints[ k ] );
36
37              // close the shape
38              star.closePath();
39
40              // translate the origin to (200, 200)
41              g2d.translate( 200, 200 );
42
43              // rotate around origin and draw stars in random colors
44              for ( int j = 1; j <= 20; j++ ) {
45                  g2d.rotate( Math.PI / 10.0 );
46                  g2d.setColor(
47                      new Color( ( int ) ( Math.random() * 256 ),
48                              ( int ) ( Math.random() * 256 ),
49                                  ( int ) ( Math.random() * 256 ) ) );
50                  g2d.fill( star );    // draw a filled star
51              }
52          }
53
54          public static void main( String args[] )
55          {
56              Shapes2 app = new Shapes2();
57
58              app.addWindowListener(
59                  new WindowAdapter() {
60                      public void windowClosing( WindowEvent e )
61                      {
62                          System.exit( 0 );
63                      }
64                  }
65              );
66          }
67  }
```

Fig. 11.23   Demonstrating some Java2D shapes (part 2 of 3).

Lines 20 through 23 define two **int** arrays representing the *x*- and *y*-coordinates of the points in the star. Line 28

```
GeneralPath star = new GeneralPath();
```

defines **GeneralPath** object **star**.
Line 31

```
star.moveTo( xPoints[ 0 ], yPoints[ 0 ] );
```

uses **GeneralPath** method *moveTo* to specify the first point in the **star**. The **for** structure at lines 34 and 35

Fig. 11.23   Demonstrating some Java2D shapes (part 3 of 3).

```
for ( int k = 1; k < xPoints.length; k++ )
    star.lineTo( xPoints[ k ], yPoints[ k ] );
```

use **GeneralPath** method *lineTo* to draw a line to the next point in the **star**. Each new call to **lineTo** draws a line from the previous point to the current point. Line 38

```
star.closePath();
```

uses **GeneralPath** method *closePath* to draw a line from the last point to the point specified in the last call to **moveTo**. This completes the general path.
  Line 41

```
g2d.translate( 200, 200 );
```

uses **Graphics2D** method *translate* to move the drawing origin to location *(200, 200)*. All drawing operations now use location *(200, 200)* as *(0, 0)*.
  The **for** structure at line 44 draws the **star** 20 times by rotating it around the new origin point. Line 45

```
g2d.rotate( Math.PI / 10.0 );
```

uses **Graphics2D** method *rotate* to rotate the next displayed shape. The argument specifies the rotation angle in radians (with $360° = 2\pi$ radians). Line 50 uses **Graphics2D** method **fill** to draw a filled version of the **star**.

Summary

- A coordinate system is a scheme for identifying every possible point on the screen.
- The upper-left corner of a GUI component has the coordinates *(0, 0)*. A coordinate pair is composed of an *x*-coordinate (the horizontal coordinate) and a *y*-coordinate (the vertical coordinate).

- Coordinate units are measured in pixels. A pixel is a display monitor's smallest unit of resolution.

- A graphics context enables drawing on the screen in Java. A **Graphics** object manages a graphics context by controlling how information is drawn.

- **Graphics** objects contain methods for drawing, font manipulation, color manipulation, etc.

- Method **paint** is normally called in response to an *event* such as uncovering a window.

- Method **repaint** requests a call to **Component** method **update** as soon as possible to clear the **Component**'s background of any previous drawing, then **update** calls **paint** directly.

- Class **Color** defines methods and constants for manipulating colors in a Java program.

- Java uses RGB colors in which the red, green and blue color components are integers in the range 0 to 255 or floating-point values in the range 0.0 to 1.0. The larger the RGB value, the greater the amount of that particular color.

- **Color** methods **getRed**, **getGreen** and **getBlue** return integer values from 0 to 255 representing the amount of red, green and blue in a **Color**.

- Class **Color** provides 13 predefined **Color** objects.

- **Graphics** method **getColor** returns a **Color** object representing the current drawing color. **Graphics** method **setColor** sets the current drawing color.

- Java provides class **JColorChooser** to display a dialog for selecting colors.

- **static** method **showDialog** of class **JColorChooser** displays a color chooser dialog. This method returns the selected **Color** object (or **null** if none is selected).

- The default **JColorChooser** dialog allows you to select a color from a variety of color swatches. The **HSB** tab allows you to select a color based on hue, saturation and brightness. The **RGB** tab allows you to select a color using sliders for the red, green and blue components of the color.

- **Component** method **setBackground** (one of the many **Component** methods that can be used on most GUI components) changes the background color of a component.

- Class **Font**'s constructor takes three arguments—the font name, the font style and the font size. The font name is any font currently supported by the system. The font style is **Font.PLAIN**, **Font.ITALIC** or **Font.BOLD**. The font size is measured in points.

- **Graphics** method **setFont** sets the drawing font.

- Class **FontMetrics** defines several methods for obtaining font metrics.

- **Graphics** method **getFontMetrics** with no arguments obtains the **FontMetrics** object for the current font. **Graphics** method **getFontMetrics** that receives a **Font** argument returns a corresponding **FontMetrics** object.

- Methods **draw3DRect** and **fill3DRect** take five arguments specifying the top-left corner of the rectangle, the **width** and **height** of the rectangle, and whether the rectangle is raised (**true**) or lowered (**false**).

- Methods **drawRoundRect** and **fillRoundRect** draw rectangles with rounded corners. Their first two arguments specify the upper-left corner, the third and fourth arguments specify the **width** and **height**, and the last two arguments—**arcWidth** and **arcHeight**—determine the horizontal and vertical diameters of the arcs used to represent the corners.

- Methods **drawOval** and **fillOval** take the same arguments—the top-left coordinate and the **width** and the **height** of the bounding rectangle that contains the oval.

- An arc is a portion of an oval. Arcs sweep from a starting angle the number of degrees specified by their arc angle. The starting angle specifies where the arc begins and the arc angle specifies the total number of degrees through which the arc sweeps. Arcs that sweep counterclockwise are measured in positive degrees and arcs that sweep clockwise are measured in negative degrees.

- Methods **drawArc** and **fillArc** take the same arguments—the top-left coordinate, the **width** and the **height** of the bounding rectangle that contains the arc, and the **startAngle** and **arcAngle** that define the sweep of the arc.

- Polygons are multisided shapes. Polylines are a series of connected points.

- One **Polygon** constructor receives an array containing the x-coordinate of each point, an array containing the y-coordinate of each point and the number of points in the polygon.

- One version of **Graphics** method **drawPolygon** displays a **Polygon** object. Another version receives an array containing the x-coordinate of each point, an array containing the y-coordinate of each point and the number of points in the polygon and displays the corresponding polygon.

- **Graphics** method **drawPolyline** displays a series of connected lines specified by its arguments (an array containing the x-coordinate of each point, an array containing the y-coordinate of each point and the number of points).

- **Polygon** method **addPoint** adds pairs of x- and y-coordinates to a **Polygon**.

- The Java2D API provides advanced two-dimensional graphics capabilities for processing line art, text and images.

- To access the **Graphics2D** capabilities, downcast the **Graphics** reference passed to **paint** to a **Graphics2d** reference as in **(Graphics2D) g**.

- **Graphics2D** method **setPaint** sets the **Paint** object that determines the color and texture for the shape to display. A **Paint** object is an object of any class that implements interface **java.awt.Paint**. The **Paint** object can be a **Color** or an instance of the Java2D API's **GradientPaint**, **SystemColor** or **TexturePaint** classes.

- Class **GradientPaint** draws a shape in a gradually changing color—called a gradient.

- **Graphics2D** method **fill** draws a filled **Shape** object. The **Shape** object is an instance of any class that implements interface **Shape**.

- The **Ellipse2D.Double** constructor receives four arguments specifying the bounding rectangle for the ellipse to display.

- **Graphics2D** method **setStroke** sets the characteristics of the lines used to draw a shape. Method **setStroke** requires a **Stroke** object as its argument. The **Stroke** object is an instance of any class that implements interface **Stroke**, such as a **BasicStroke**.

- **Graphics2D** method **draw** draws a **Shape** object. The **Shape** object is an instance of any class that implements interface **Shape**.

- The **Rectangle2D.Double** constructor receives four arguments specifying the upper-left x-coordinate, upper-left y-coordinate, width and height of the rectangle.

- Class **BufferedImage** can be used to produce images in color and gray scale.

- A **TexturePaint** object uses the image stored in its associated **BufferedImage** as the fill texture for a filled-in shape.

- The **RoundRectangle2D.Double** constructor receives six arguments specifying the rectangle dimensions and the arc width and arc height used to determine the rounding of the corners.

- The **Arc2D.Double** constructor's first four arguments specify the upper-left x-coordinate, upper-left y-coordinate, width and height of the bounding rectangle for the arc. The fifth argument specifies the start angle. The sixth argument specifies the end angle. The last argument specifies the type of arc (**Arc2D.PIE**, **Arc2D.CHORD** or **Arc2D.OPEN**).

- The **Line2D.Double** constructor's arguments specify starting and ending line coordinates.

- A general path is a shape constructed from straight lines and complex curves represented with an object of class **GeneralPath** (package **java.awt.geom**).

- **GeneralPath** method **moveTo** specifies the first point in a general path. **GeneralPath** method **lineTo** draws a line to the next point in the general path. Each new call to **lineTo** draws a line from the previous point to the current point. **GeneralPath** method **closePath** draws a line from the last point to the point specified in the last call to **moveTo**.

- **Graphics2D** method **translate** moves the drawing origin to a new location. All drawing operations now use that location as *(0, 0)*.

Terminology

addPoint method
angle
arc bounded by a rectangle
arc height
arc sweeping through an angle
arc width
Arc2D.Double class
ascent
background color
baseline
bounding rectangle
BufferedImage class
closed polygon
closePath method
Color class
Component class
coordinate
coordinate system
degree
descent
draw method
drawArc method
draw an arc
drawLine method
drawOval method
drawPolygon method
drawPolyline method
drawRect method
drawRoundRect method
draw3DRect method
Ellipse2D.Double class
event
event-driven process
fill method
fillArc method
filled polygon
fillOval method
fillPolygon method
fillRect method
fillRoundRect method
fill3DRect method
font

Font class
font metrics
FontMetrics class
font name
font style
GeneralPath class
getAscent method
getBlue method
getDescent method
getFamily method
getFont method
getFontList method
getFontMetrics method
getGreen method
getHeight method
getLeading method
getName method
getRed method
getSize method
getStyle method
GradientPaint class
Graphics class
graphics context
graphics object
Graphics2D class
isBold method
isItalic method
isPlain method
Java2D API
leading
lineTo method
Line2D.Double class
Monospaced font
moveTo method
negative degrees
Paint interface
paint method
pixel
point
polygon
Polygon class
positive degrees

Rectangle2D.Double class

repaint method

RGB value

RoundRectangle2D.Double class

SansSerif font

Serif font

setColor method

setFont method

setPaint method

setStroke method

Shape interface

Stroke interface

SystemColor class

TexturePaint class

translate method

update method

vertical component

x axis

x coordinate

y axis

y coordinate

Common Programming Errors

11.1 Spelling any **static Color** class constant with an initial capital letter is a syntax error.

11.2 Specifying a font that is not available on a system is a logic error. Java will substitute that system's default font.

11.3 An **ArrayIndexOutOfBoundsException** is thrown if the number of points specified in the third argument to method **drawPolygon** or method **fillPolygon** is greater than the number of elements in the arrays of coordinates that define the polygon to display.

Portability Tips

11.1 Different display monitors have different resolutions (i.e., the density of pixels varies). This may cause graphics to appear to be different sizes on different monitors.

11.2 The number of fonts varies greatly across systems. The JDK guarantees that the fonts **Serif**, **Monospaced**, **SansSerif**, **Dialog** and **DialogInput** will be available.

11.3 Java uses standardized font names and maps these into system-specific font names for portability. This is transparent to the programmer.

Software Engineering Observations

11.1 The upper-left coordinate *(0, 0)* of a window is actually behind the title bar of the window. For this reason, drawing coordinates should be adjusted to draw inside the borders of the window. Class **Container** (a superclass of all windows in Java) has method **getInsets** that returns an **Insets** object (package **java.awt**) for this purpose. An **Insets** object has four **public** members—**top**, **bottom**, **left** and **right**—that represent the number of pixels from each edge of the window to the drawing area for the window.

11.2 To change the color, you must create a new **Color** object (or use one of the predefined **Color** constants) as there are no *set* methods in class **Color** to change the characteristics of the current color.

11.3 To change the font, you must create a new **Font** object as there are no *set* methods in class **Font** to change the characteristics of the current font.

Self-Review Exercises

11.1 Fill in the blanks in each of the following:

    a) In Java2D, method _____ of class _____ sets the characteristics of a line used to draw a shape.

    b) Class _____ helps define the fill for a shape such that the fill gradually changes from one color to another.

    c) The _____ method of class **Graphics** draws a line between two points.

    d) RGB is short for _____, _____ and _____.

   e) Font sizes are measured in units called _____.
   f) Class _____ helps define the fill for a shape using a pattern drawn in a **Buffered-Image**.

11.2   State whether each of the following is *true* or *false*. If *false*, explain why.
   a) The first two arguments of **Graphics** method **drawOval** specify the center coordinate of the oval.
   b) In the Java coordinate system, *x* values increase from left to right.
   c) Method **fillPolygon** draws a solid polygon in the current color.
   d) Method **drawArc** allows negative angles.
   e) Method **getSize** returns the size of the current font in centimeters.
   f) Pixel coordinate *(0, 0)* is located at the exact center of the monitor.

11.3   Find the error(s) in each of the following and explain how to correct the error(s). Assume that **g** is a **Graphics** object.
   a) `g.setFont( "SansSerif" );`
   b) `g.erase( x, y, w, h );    // clear rectangle at (x, y)`
   c) `Font f = new Font( "Serif", Font.BOLDITALIC, 12 );`
   d) `g.setColor( Color.Yellow );  // change color to yellow`

Answers to Self-Review Exercises

11.1   a) **setStroke, Graphics2D**. b) **GradientPaint**. c) **drawLine**. d) red, green, blue. e) points. f) **TexturePaint**.

11.2   a) False. The first two arguments specify the upper-left corner of the bounding rectangle.
   b) True.
   c) True.
   d) True.
   e) False. Font sizes are measured in points.
   f) False. The coordinate *(0,0)* corresponds to the upper-left corner of a GUI component on which drawing occurs.

11.3   a) The **setFont** method takes a **Font** object as an argument—not a **String**.
   b) The **Graphics** class does not have an **erase** method. The **clearRect** method should be used.
   c) **Font.BOLDITALIC** is not a valid font style. To get a bold italic font, use **Font.BOLD + Font.ITALIC**.
   d) **Yellow** should begin with a lowercase letter: `g.setColor( Color.yellow );`.

Exercises

11.4   Fill in the blanks in each of the following:
   a) Class _____ of the Java2D API is used to define ovals.
   b) Methods **draw** and **fill** of class **Graphics2D** require an object of type _____ as their argument.
   c) The three constants that specify font style are _____, _____ and _____.
   d) **Graphics2D** method _____ sets the painting color for Java2D shapes.

11.5   State whether each of the following is *true* or *false*. If *false*, explain why.
   a) The **drawPolygon** method automatically connects the endpoints of the polygon.
   b) The **drawLine** method draws a line between two points.
   c) The **fillArc** method uses degrees to specify the angle.
   d) In the Java coordinate system, *y* values increase from top to bottom.
   e) The **Graphics** class inherits directly from class **Object**.

f) The **Graphics** class is an **abstract** class.

g) The **Font** class inherits directly from class **Graphics**.

11.6 Write a program that draws a series of eight concentric circles. The circles should be separated by 10 pixels. Use the **drawOval** method of class **Graphics**.

11.7 Write a program that draws a series of eight concentric circles. The circles should be separated by 10 pixels. Use the **drawArc** method.

11.8 Modify your solution to Exercise 11.6 to draw the ovals using instances of class **Ellipse2D.Double** and method **draw** of class **Graphics2D**.

11.9 Write a program that draws lines of random lengths in random colors.

11.10 Modify your solution to Exercise 11.9 to draw random lines, in random colors and random line thicknesses. Use class **Line2D.Double** and method **draw** of class **Graphics2D** to draw the lines.

11.11 Write a program that displays randomly generated triangles in different colors. Each triangle should be filled with a different color. Use class **GeneralPath** and method **fill** of class **Graphics2D** to draw the triangles.

11.12 Write a program that randomly draws characters in different font sizes and colors.

11.13 Write a program that draws an 8-by-8 grid. Use the **drawLine** method.

11.14 Modify your solution to Exercise 11.13 to draw the grid using instances of class **Line2D.Double** and method **draw** of class **Graphics2D**.

11.15 Write a program that draws a 10-by-10 grid. Use the **drawRect** method.

11.16 Modify your solution to Exercise 11.15 to draw the grid using instances of class **Rectangle2D.Double** and method **draw** of class **Graphics2D**.

11.17 Write a program that draws a tetrahedron (a pyramid). Use class **GeneralPath** and method **draw** of class **Graphics2D**.

11.18 Write a program that draws a cube. Use class **GeneralPath** and method **draw** of class **Graphics2D**.

11.19 In Exercise 3.9, you wrote an applet that input the radius of a circle from the user and displayed the circle's diameter, circumference and area. Modify your solution to Exercise 3.9 to read a set of coordinates in addition to the radius. Then draw the circle and display the circle's diameter, circumference and area using an **Ellipse2D.Double** object to represent the circle and method **draw** of class **Graphics2D** to display the circle.

11.20 Write an application that simulates a screen saver. The application should randomly draw lines using method **drawLine** of class **Graphics**. After drawing 100 lines, the application should clear itself and start drawing lines again. To allow the program to draw continuously, place a call to **repaint** as the last line in method **paint**. Do you notice any problems with this on your system?

11.21 Here is a peek ahead. Package **javax.swing** contains a class called *Timer* that is capable of calling method **actionPerformed** of interface **ActionListener** at a fixed time interval (specified in milliseconds). Modify your solution to Exercise 11.20 to remove the call to **repaint** from method **paint**. Define your class so it implements **ActionListener** (the **actionPerformed** method should simply call **repaint**). Define an instance variable of type **Timer** called **timer** in your class. In the constructor for your class, write the following statements:

```
timer = new Timer( 1000, this );
timer.start();
```

this creates an instance of class **Timer** that will call **this** object's **actionPerformed** method every **1000** milliseconds (i.e., every second).

11.22   Modify your solution to Exercise 11.21 to enable the user to enter the number of random lines that should be drawn before the application clears itself and starts drawing lines again. Use a **JText-Field** to obtain the value. The user should be able to type a new number into the **JTextField** at any time during the program's execution. *Note:* Combining Swing GUI components and drawing leads to interesting problems for which we present solutions in Chapters 12 and 13. For now, the first line of your **paint** method should be

        super.paint(g);

to ensure that the GUI components are displayed properly. You will notice that some of the randomly drawn lines will obscure the **JTextField**. Use an inner class definition to perform event handling for the **JTextField**.

11.23   Modify your solution to Exercise 11.21 to randomly choose different shapes to display (use methods of class **Graphics**).]

11.24   Modify your solution to Exercise 11.23 to use classes and drawing capabilities of the Java2D API. For shapes such as rectangles and ellipses, draw them with randomly generated gradients (use class **GradientPaint** to generate the gradient).

11.25   Write a graphical version of your solution to Exercise 6.37—the *Towers of Hanoi*. After studying Chapter 16, you will be able to implement a version of this exercise using Java's image, animation and audio capabilities.

11.26   Modify the die-rolling program of Fig. 7.9 so that it updates the counts for each side of the die after each roll. Convert the application into a windowed application (i.e., a subclass of **JFrame**) and use **Graphics** method **drawString** to output the totals.

11.27   Modify your solution to Exercise 7.21—*Turtle Graphics*—to add a graphical user interface using **JTextField**s and **JButton**s. Also, draw lines rather than drawing asterisks (*****). When the turtle graphics program specifies a move, translate the number of positions into a number of pixels on the screen by multiplying the number of positions by 10 (or any value you choose). Implement the drawing with Java2D API features. [*Note:* Combining Swing GUI components and drawing leads to interesting problems for which we present solutions in Chapters 12 and 13. For now, the first line of your **paint** method should be

        super.paint(g);

to ensure that the GUI components are displayed properly.]

11.28   Produce a graphical version of the *Knight's Tour* problem (Exercises 7.22, 7.23 and 7.26). As each move is made, the appropriate cell of the chessboard should be updated with the proper move number. If the result of the program is a *full tour* or a *closed tour*, the program should display an appropriate message. If you would like, use class **Timer** (see Exercise 11.24) to help animate the Knight's Tour. Every second, the next move should be made.

11.29   Produce a graphical version of the *Tortoise and the Hare* simulation (Exercise 7.41). Simulate the mountain by drawing an arc that extends from the bottom-left of the window to the top-right of the window. The tortoise and the hare should race up the mountain. Implement the graphical output so the tortoise and the hare are actually printed on the arc every move. [**Note:** Extend the length of the race from 70 to 300 to allow yourself a larger graphics area.]

11.30   Produce a graphical version of the *Maze Traversal* problem (Exercises 7.38-7.40). Use the mazes you produced as guides for creating the graphical versions. While the maze is being solved, a small circle should be displayed in the maze indicating the current position. If you would like, use class **Timer** (see Exercise 11.24) to help animate the traversal of the maze. Every second, the next move should be made.

11.31   Produce a graphical version of the *Bucket Sort* (Exercise 7.28) that shows each value being placed into the appropriate bucket and eventually being copied back to the original array.

11.32   Write a program that uses method **drawPolyline** to draw a spiral.

11.33   Write a program that inputs four numbers and graphs the numbers as a pie chart. Use class **Arc2D.Double** and method **fill** of class **Graphics2D** to perform the drawing. Draw each piece of the pie in a separate color.

11.34   Write an applet that inputs four numbers and graphs the numbers as a bar graph. Use class **Rectangle2D.Double** and method **fill** of class **Graphics2D** to perform the drawing. Draw each bar in a different color.

12

Basic Graphical User Interface Components

Objectives

- To understand the design principles of graphical user interfaces.
- To be able to build graphical user interfaces.
- To understand the packages containing graphical user interface components and event handling classes and interfaces.
- To be able to create and manipulate buttons, labels, lists, text fields and panels.
- To understand mouse events and keyboard events.
- To understand and be able to use layout managers.

… the wisest prophets make sure of the event first.
Horace Walpole

Do you think I can listen all day to such stuff?
Lewis Carroll

Speak the affirmative; emphasize your choice by utter ignoring of all that you reject.
Ralph Waldo Emerson

You pays your money and you takes your choice.
Punch

Guess if you can, choose if you dare.
Pierre Corneille

All hope abandon, ye who enter here!
Dante Alighieri

Exit, pursued by a bear.
William Shakespeare

Outline

12.1 Introduction[1]

A *graphical user interface* (*GUI*) presents a pictorial interface to a program. A GUI (pronounced "GOO-EE") gives a program a distinctive "look" and "feel." By providing different applications with a consistent set of intuitive user interface components, GUIs allow the user to spend less time trying to remember which keystroke sequences do what and spend more time using the program in a productive manner.

Look-and-Feel Observation 12.1

Consistent user interfaces also enable a user to learn new applications faster.

As an example of a GUI, Fig. 12.1 contains a Netscape Communicator window with some of its GUI components labeled. In the window, there is a *menu bar* containing *menus* (**File**, **Edit**, **View**, etc.). Below the menu bar there is a set of *buttons* that each have a defined task in Netscape Communicator. Below the buttons there is a *text field* in which the user can type the name of the World Wide Web site to visit. To the left of the text field is a *label* that indicates the purpose of the text field. The menus, buttons, text fields and labels

---

1. This chapter was coauthored with Tem Nieto of Deitel & Associates, Inc.

are part of Netscape Communicator's GUI. They enable you to interact with the Communicator program. In this chapter and the next, we will demonstrate these GUI components.

GUIs are built from *GUI components* (sometimes called *controls* or *widgets*—shorthand notation for *window gadgets*). A GUI component is an object with which the user interacts via the mouse or the keyboard. Several common GUI components are listed in Fig 12.2. In the sections that follow, we discuss each of these GUI components in detail. In the next chapter, we discuss more advanced GUI components.

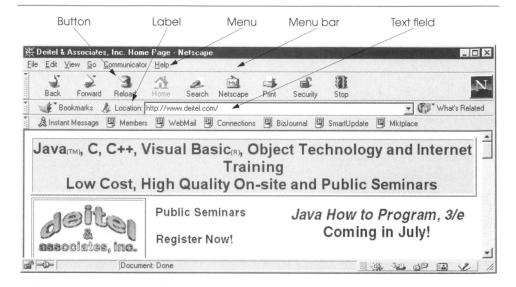

Fig. 12.1   A sample Netscape Communicator window with GUI components.

Component	Description
JLabel	An area where uneditable text or icons can be displayed.
JTextField	An area in which the user inputs data from the keyboard. The area can also display information.
JButton	An area that triggers an event when clicked.
JCheckBox	A GUI component that is either selected or not selected.
JComboBox	A drop-down list of items from which the user can make a selection by clicking an item in the list or by typing into the box, if permitted.
JList	An area where a list of items is displayed from which the user can make a selection by clicking once on any element in the list. Double-clicking an element in the list generates an action event. Multiple elements can be selected.
JPanel	A container in which components can be placed.

Fig. 12.2   Some basic GUI components.

12.2 Swing Overview

The classes that are used to create the GUI components of Fig. 12.2 are part of the *Swing GUI components* from package **javax.swing**. These are the newest GUI components of the Java 2 platform. *Swing components* (as they are commonly called) are written, manipulated and displayed completely in Java (so-called *pure Java* components).

The original GUI components from the *Abstract Windowing Toolkit* package **java.awt** (also called the *AWT*) are tied directly to the local platform's graphical user interface capabilities. So, a Java program executing on different Java platforms has a different appearance and sometimes even different user interactions on each platform. Together, the appearance and how the user interacts with the program are known as that program's *look and feel*. The Swing components allow the programmer to specify a different look and feel for each platform, or a uniform look and feel across all platforms, or even to change the look-and-feel while the program is running.

Look-and-Feel Observation 12.2

Because Swing components are written in Java, they provide a greater level of portability and flexibility than the original Java GUI components from package **java.awt**.

Swing components are often referred to as *lightweight components*—they are written completely in Java so they are not "weighed down" by the complex GUI capabilities of the platform on which they are used. AWT components (many of which parallel the Swing components) that are tied to the local platform are correspondingly called *heavyweight components*—they rely on the local platform's *windowing system* to determine their functionality and their look and feel. Each heavyweight component has a *peer* (from package **java.awt.peer**) that is responsible for the interactions between the component and the local platform to display and manipulate the component. Several Swing components are still heavyweight components. In particular, subclasses of **java.awt.Window** (such as **JFrame** used in several previous chapters) that display windows on the screen still require direct interaction with the local windowing system. As such, heavyweight Swing GUI components are less flexible than many of the lightweight components we will demonstrate.

Portability Tip 12.1

The look of a GUI defined with heavyweight GUI components from package **java.awt** *may vary across platforms. Heavyweight components "tie" into the "local" platform GUI, which varies from platform to platform.*

Figure 12.3 shows an inheritance hierarchy of the classes that define attributes and behaviors that are common to most Swing components. Each class is displayed with its fully qualified package name and class name. Much of each GUI component's functionality is derived from these classes. A class that inherits from the **Component** class *is a component*. For example, class **Container** inherits from class **Component**, and class **Component** inherits from **Object**. Thus, a **Container** *is a* **Component** and *is an* **Object**, and a **Component** *is an* **Object**. A class that inherits from class **Container** *is a* **Container**. Thus, a **JComponent** *is a* **Container**.

Software Engineering Observation 12.1

To effectively use GUI components, the **javax.swing** *and* **java.awt** *inheritance hierarchies must be understood—especially class* **Component***, class* **Container** *and class* **JComponent***, which define features common to most Swing components.*

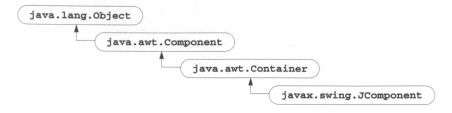

Fig. 12.3   Common superclasses of many of the Swing components.

Class **Component** defines the methods that can be applied to an object of any subclass of **Component**. Two of the methods that originate in class **Component** have been used frequently to this point in the text—**paint** and **repaint**. It is important to understand the methods of class **Component** because much of the functionality inherited by every subclass of **Component** is defined by the **Component** class originally. Operations common to most GUI components (both Swing and AWT) are found in class **Component**.

Good Programming Practice 12.1

*Study the methods of class **Component** in the Java 2 SDK on-line documentation to learn the capabilities common to most GUI components.*

A **Container** is a collection of related components. In applications with **JFrame**s and in applets, we attach components to the content pane—a **Container**. Class **Container** defines the set of methods that can be applied to an object of any subclass of **Container**. One method that originates in class **Container** that has been used frequently to this point in the text is **add** for adding components to a content pane. Another method that originates in class **Container** is **setLayout**, which has been used to specify the layout manager that helps a **Container** position and size its components.

Good Programming Practice 12.2

*Study the methods of class **Container** in the Java 2 SDK on-line documentation to learn the capabilities common to every container for GUI components.*

Class **JComponent** is the superclass to most Swing components. This class defines the set of methods that can be applied to an object of any subclass of **JComponent**.

Good Programming Practice 12.3

*Study the methods of class **JComponent** in the Java 2 SDK on-line documentation to learn the capabilities common to every container for GUI components.*

Swing components that subclass **JComponent** have many features, including:

1. A *pluggable look and feel* that can be used to customize the look and feel when the program executes on different platforms.

2. Shortcut keys (called *mnemonics*) for direct access to GUI components through the keyboard.

3. Common event handling capabilities for cases where several GUI components initiate the same actions in a program.

4. Brief descriptions of a GUI component's purpose (called *tool tips*) that are displayed when the mouse cursor is positioned over the component for a short time.

5. Support for assistive technologies such as braille screen readers for blind people.

6. Support for user interface *localization*—customizing the user interface for display in different languages and cultural conventions.

These are just some of the many features of the Swing components. We discuss several of these features here and in Chapter 13.

12.3 JLabel

Labels provide text instructions or information on a GUI. Labels are defined with class **JLabel**—a subclass of **JComponent**. A label displays a single line of *read-only text*. Once labels are created, programs rarely change a label's contents. The application of Fig. 12.4 demonstrates **JLabel**s.

Good Programming Practice 12.4

*Study the methods of class **javax.swing.JLabel** in the Java 2 SDK on-line documentation to learn the complete capabilities of the class before using it.*

```
1   // Fig. 12.4: LabelTest.java
2   // Demonstrating the JLabel class.
3   import javax.swing.*;
4   import java.awt.*;
5   import java.awt.event.*;
6
7   public class LabelTest extends JFrame {
8      private JLabel label1, label2, label3;
9
10     public LabelTest()
11     {
12        super( "Testing JLabel" );
13
14        Container c = getContentPane();
15        c.setLayout( new FlowLayout() );
16
17        // JLabel constructor with a string argument
18        label1 = new JLabel( "Label with text" );
19        label1.setToolTipText( "This is label1" );
20        c.add( label1 );
21
22        // JLabel constructor with string, Icon and
23        // alignment arguments
24        Icon bug = new ImageIcon( "bug1.gif" );
25        label2 = new JLabel( "Label with text and icon",
26                             bug, SwingConstants.LEFT );
27        label2.setToolTipText( "This is label2" );
28        c.add( label2 );
29
30        // JLabel constructor no arguments
31        label3 = new JLabel();
32        label3.setText( "Label with icon and text at bottom" );
```

Fig. 12.4   Demonstrating class **JLabel** (part 1 of 2).

```
33          label3.setIcon( bug );
34          label3.setHorizontalTextPosition(
35             SwingConstants.CENTER );
36          label3.setVerticalTextPosition(
37             SwingConstants.BOTTOM );
38          label3.setToolTipText( "This is label3" );
39          c.add( label3 );
40
41          setSize( 275, 170 );
42          show();
43       }
44
45       public static void main( String args[] )
46       {
47          LabelTest app = new LabelTest();
48
49          app.addWindowListener(
50             new WindowAdapter() {
51                public void windowClosing( WindowEvent e )
52                {
53                   System.exit( 0 );
54                }
55             }
56          );
57       }
58    }
```

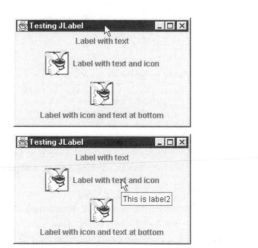

Fig. 12.4   Demonstrating class **JLabel** (part 2 of 2).

The program declares three **JLabel** references with line 8

```
private JLabel label1, label2, label3;
```

The **JLabel** objects are instantiated in the constructor (line 10). The statement

```
label1 = new JLabel( "Label with text" );
```

at line 18 creates a **JLabel** object with the text **"Label with text"**. The text is displayed on the label automatically.

Line 19

```
label1.setToolTipText( "This is label1" );
```

uses method *setToolTipText* (inherited into class **JLabel** from class **JComponent**) to specify the tool tip (see the second screen capture in Fig. 12.4) that is displayed automatically when the user positions the mouse cursor over the label in the GUI. When you execute this program, try positioning the mouse over each label to see its tool tip. Line 20 adds **label1** to the content pane.

Look-and-Feel Observation 12.3

*Use tool tips (set with **JComponent** method **setToolTipText**) to add descriptive text to your GUI components. This text helps the user determine the GUI component's purpose in the user interface.*

Many Swing components can display images by specifying an **Icon** as an argument to their constructor or by using a method that is normally called *setIcon*. An **Icon** is an object of any class that implements interface **Icon** (package **javax.swing**). One such class is *ImageIcon* (package **javax.swing**), which supports two image formats— *Graphics Interchange Format (GIF)* and *Joint Photographic Experts Group (JPEG)*. File names for each of these types typically end with **.gif** or **.jpg** (or **.jpeg**), respectively. We discuss images in more detail in Chapter 16, "Multimedia." Line 24

```
Icon bug = new ImageIcon( "bug1.gif" );
```

defines an **ImageIcon** object. The file **bug1.gif** contains the image to load and store in the **ImageIcon** object. This file is assumed to be in the same directory as the program (we will discuss locating the file elsewhere in Chapter 16). The **ImageIcon** object is assigned to **Icon** reference **bug**. Remember, class **ImageIcon** implements interface **Icon**, therefore an **ImageIcon** *is an* **Icon**.

Class **JLabel** supports the display of **Icon**s. Lines 25 and 26

```
label2 = new JLabel( "Label with text and icon",
                     bug, SwingConstants.LEFT );
```

use another **JLabel** constructor to create a label that displays the text **"Label with text and icon"** and the **Icon** to which **bug** refers, and is *left justified* or *left aligned* (i.e., the icon and text are at the left side of the label's area on the screen). Interface *SwingConstants* (package **javax.swing**) defines a set of common integer constants (such as **SwingConstants.LEFT**) that are used with many Swing components. By default, the text appears to the right of the image when a label contains both text and an image. Both the horizontal and vertical alignments of a label can be set with methods *setHorizontalAlignment* and *setVerticalAlignment*, respectively. Line 27 specifies the tool tip text for **label2**. Line 28 adds **label2** to the content pane.

Common Programming Error 12.1

Forgetting to add a component to a container so it can be displayed is a run-time logic error.

Common Programming Error 12.2

Adding to a container a component that has not been instantiated throws a **NullPointer-Exception***.*

Class **JLabel** provides many methods to configure a label after it has been instantiated. Line 31 creates a **JLabel** and invokes the no-argument (default constructor). Such a label has no text or **Icon**. Line 32

```
label3.setText( "Label with icon and text at bottom" );
```

uses **JLabel** method *setText* to set the text displayed on the label. A corresponding method *getText* retrieves the current text displayed on a label. Line 33

```
label3.setIcon( bug );
```

uses **JLabel** method *setIcon* to set the **Icon** displayed on the label. A corresponding method *getIcon* retrieves the current **Icon** displayed on a label. Lines 34 through 37

```
label3.setHorizontalTextPosition(
    SwingConstants.CENTER );
label3.setVerticalTextPosition(
    SwingConstants.BOTTOM );
```

use **JLabel** methods *setHorizontalTextPosition* and *setVerticalTextPosition* to specify the text position in the label. The preceding statements indicate that the text will be centered horizontally and will appear at the bottom of the label. Thus, the **Icon** will appear above the text. Line 38 sets the tool tip text for the **label3**. Line 39 adds **label3** to the content pane.

12.4 Event Handling Model

In the preceding section, we did not discuss event handling because there are no specific events for **JLabel** objects. GUIs are *event driven* (i.e., they generate *events* when the user of the program interacts with the GUI). Some common interactions are moving the mouse, clicking the mouse, clicking a button, typing in a text field, selecting an item from a menu, closing a window, etc. When a user interaction occurs, an event is automatically sent to the program. GUI event information is stored in an object of a class that extends **AWTEvent**. Figure 12.5 illustrates a hierarchy containing many of the event classes we use from package **java.awt.event**. Many of these event classes are discussed throughout this chapter and Chapter 13. The event types from package *java.awt.event* are still used with the Swing components. Additional event types have also been added that are specific to several types of Swing components. New Swing component event types are defined in package *javax.swing.event*.

To process a graphical user interface event, the programmer must perform two key tasks—register an *event listener* and implement an *event handler*. An event listener for a GUI event is an object of a class that implements one or more of the event-listener interfaces from package **java.awt.event** and package **javax.swing.event**. Many of the event listener types are common to both Swing and AWT components. Such types are defined in package **java.awt.event** and many of these are shown in Fig. 12.6 [*Note:* A shaded background indicates an interface in the diagram.] Additional event listener types that are specific to Swing components are defined in package **javax.swing.event**.

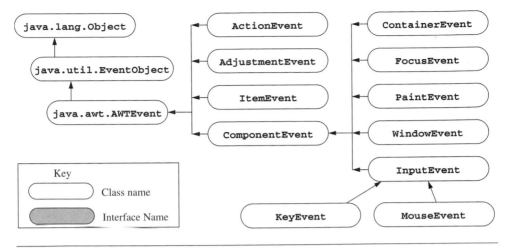

Fig. 12.5   Some event classes of package `java.awt.event`.

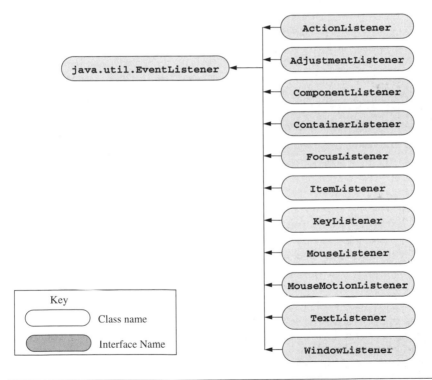

Fig. 12.6   Event-listener interfaces of package `java.awt.event`.

An event listener object "listens" for specific types of events generated in the same object or by other objects (normally GUI components) in a program. An event handler is a method that is automatically called in response to a particular type of event. Each event-listener interface specifies one or more event handling methods that *must* be defined in the class that implements the event-listener interface. Remember that interfaces define

abstract methods. Any class that implements an interface must define all the methods of that interface; otherwise, the class is an **abstract** class and cannot be used to create objects. The use of event listeners in event handling is known as the *delegation event model*—the processing of an event is delegated to a particular object in the program.

When an event occurs, the GUI component with which the user interacted notifies its registered listeners by calling each listener's appropriate event handling method. For example, when the user presses the *Enter* key in a **JTextField**, the registered listener's **actionPerformed** method is called. How did the event handler get registered? How does the GUI component know to call **actionPerformed** as opposed to some other event handling method? We answer these questions and diagram the interaction as part of the next example.

12.5 JTextField and JPasswordField

*JTextField*s and *JPasswordField*s (package **javax.swing**) are single-line areas in which text can be entered by the user from the keyboard or text can simply be displayed. A **JPasswordField** shows that a character was typed as the user enters characters, but hides the characters assuming that they represent a password that should remain known only to the user. When the user types data into a **JTextField** or **JPasswordField** and presses the *Enter* key, an action event occurs. If an event listener is registered, the event is processed and the data in the **JTextField** or **JPasswordField** can be used in the program. Class **JTextField** extends class *JTextComponent* (package **javax.swing.text**), which provides many features common to Swing's text-based components. Class **JPasswordField** extends **JTextField** and adds several methods that are specific to processing passwords.

Common Programming Error 12.3

*Using a lowercase **f** in the class names **JTextField** or **JPasswordField** is a syntax error.*

The application of Fig. 12.7 uses classes **JTextField** and **JPasswordField** to create and manipulate four fields. When the user presses *Enter* in the currently active field (the currently active component "has the *focus*"), a message dialog box containing the text in the field is displayed. When an event occurs in the **JPasswordField**, the password is revealed.

```
1   // Fig. 12.7: TextFieldTest.java
2   // Demonstrating the JTextField class.
3   import java.awt.*;
4   import java.awt.event.*;
5   import javax.swing.*;
6
7   public class TextFieldTest extends JFrame {
8      private JTextField text1, text2, text3;
9      private JPasswordField password;
10
```

Fig. 12.7   Demonstrating **JTextField**s and **JPasswordField**s (part 1 of 3).

```
11      public TextFieldTest()
12      {
13         super( "Testing JTextField and JPasswordField" );
14
15         Container c = getContentPane();
16         c.setLayout( new FlowLayout() );
17
18         // construct textfield with default sizing
19         text1 = new JTextField( 10 );
20         c.add( text1 );
21
22         // construct textfield with default text
23         text2 = new JTextField( "Enter text here" );
24         c.add( text2 );
25
26         // construct textfield with default text and
27         // 20 visible elements and no event handler
28         text3 = new JTextField( "Uneditable text field", 20 );
29         text3.setEditable( false );
30         c.add( text3 );
31
32         // construct textfield with default text
33         password = new JPasswordField( "Hidden text" );
34         c.add( password );
35
36         TextFieldHandler handler = new TextFieldHandler();
37         text1.addActionListener( handler );
38         text2.addActionListener( handler );
39         text3.addActionListener( handler );
40         password.addActionListener( handler );
41
42         setSize( 325, 100 );
43         show();
44      }
45
46      public static void main( String args[] )
47      {
48         TextFieldTest app = new TextFieldTest();
49
50         app.addWindowListener(
51            new WindowAdapter() {
52               public void windowClosing( WindowEvent e )
53               {
54                  System.exit( 0 );
55               }
56            }
57         );
58      }
59
60      // inner class for event handling
61      private class TextFieldHandler implements ActionListener {
62         public void actionPerformed( ActionEvent e )
63         {
```

Fig. 12.7   Demonstrating **JTextField**s and **JPasswordField**s (part 2 of 3).

```
64              String s = "";
65
66              if ( e.getSource() == text1 )
67                  s = "text1: " + e.getActionCommand();
68              else if ( e.getSource() == text2 )
69                  s = "text2: " + e.getActionCommand();
70              else if ( e.getSource() == text3 )
71                  s = "text3: " + e.getActionCommand();
72              else if ( e.getSource() == password ) {
73                  JPasswordField pwd =
74                      (JPasswordField) e.getSource();
75                  s = "password: " +
76                      new String( pwd.getPassword() );
77              }
78
79              JOptionPane.showMessageDialog( null, s );
80          }
81      }
82  }
```

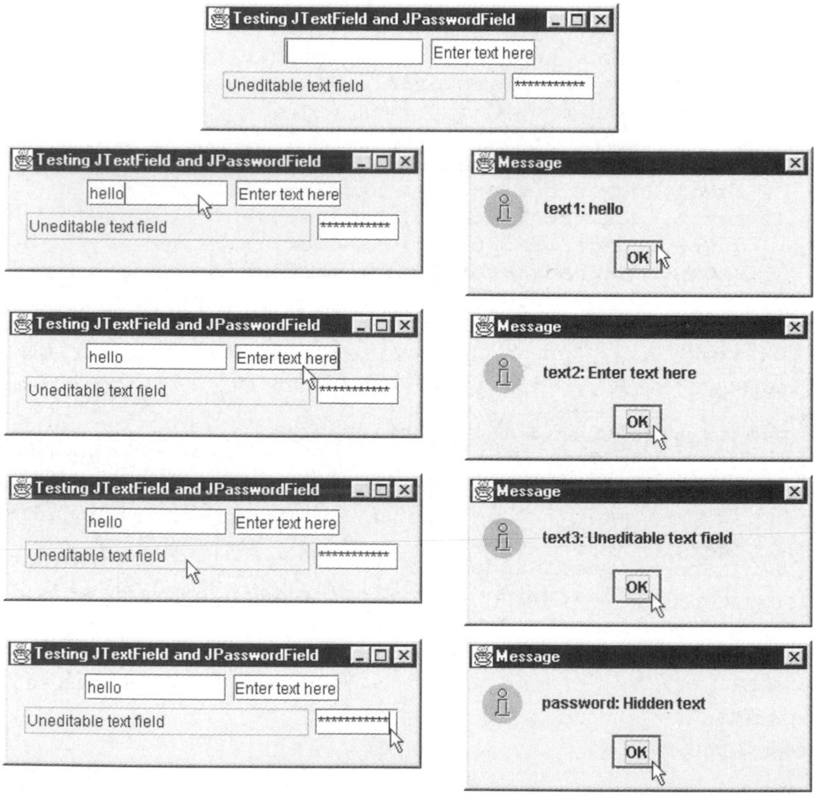

Fig. 12.7   Demonstrating **JTextField**s and **JPasswordField**s (part 3 of 3).

Lines 8 and 9 declare three references for **JTextField**s (**text1**, **text2** and **text3**) and a **JPasswordField** (**password**). Each of these is instantiated in the constructor (line 11). Line 19

```
text1 = new JTextField( 10 );
```

defines **JTextField text1** with **10** columns of text. The width of the text field will be the width in pixels of the average character in the text field's current font multiplied by 10. Line 20 adds **text1** to the content pane.

Line 23

```
text2 = new JTextField( "Enter text here" );
```

defines **JTextField text2** with the initial text **"Enter text here"** to display in the text field. The width of the text field is determined by the text. Line 24 adds **text2** to the content pane.

Line 28

```
text3 = new JTextField( "Uneditable text field", 20 );
```

defines **JTextField text3** and call the **JTextField** constructor with two arguments—the default text **"Uneditable text field"** to display in the text field and the number of columns (**20**). The width of the text field is determined by the number of columns specified. Line 29

```
text3.setEditable( false );
```

uses method *setEditable* (inherited into **JTextField** from class **JTextComponent**) to indicate that the user cannot modify the text in the text field. Line 30 adds **text3** to the content pane.

Line 33

```
password = new JPasswordField( "Hidden text" );
```

defines **JPasswordField password** with the text **"Hidden text"** to display in the text field. The width of the text field is determined by the text. Notice that the text is displayed as a string of asterisks when the program executes. Line 34 adds **password** to the content pane.

For the event handling in this example, we defined inner class **TextFieldHandler** (lines 61 to 81). Class **JTextField** handler (discussed in detail shortly) implements interface **ActionListener**. Thus, every instance of class **TextFieldHandler** *is an* **ActionListener**. Line 36

```
TextFieldHandler handler = new TextFieldHandler();
```

defines an instance of class **TextFieldHandler** and assigns it to reference **handler**. This one instance will be used as the event-listener object for the **JTextField**s and the **JPasswordField** in this example.

Lines 37 through 40

```
text1.addActionListener( handler );
text2.addActionListener( handler );
text3.addActionListener( handler );
password.addActionListener( handler );
```

are the event registration statements that specify the event listener object for each of the three **JTextField**s and for the **JPasswordField**. After these statements execute, the object to which **handler** refers is *listening for events* (i.e., it will be notified when an event occurs) on these four objects. In each case, method **addActionListener** of class **JTextField** is called to register the event. Method **addActionListener** receives as its argument an **ActionListener** object. Thus, any object of a class that implements interface **ActionListener** (i.e., any object that *is an* **ActionListener**) can be supplied as an argument to this method. The object to which **handler** refers *is an* **Action-Listener** because its class implements interface **ActionListener**. Now, when the user presses *Enter* in any of these four fields, method **actionPerformed** (line 62) in class **TextFieldHandler** is called to handle the event.

Software Engineering Observation 12.2

The event listener for an event must implement the appropriate event-listener interface.

Method **actionPerformed** uses its **ActionEvent** argument's method **get-Source** to determine the GUI component with which the user interacted and creates a **String** to display in a message dialog box. **ActionEvent** method **getActionCommand** returns the text in the **JTextField** that generated the event. If the user interacted with the **JPasswordField**, lines 73 and 74

```
JPasswordField pwd =
    (JPasswordField) e.getSource();
```

cast the **Component** reference returned by **e.getSource()** to a **JPasswordField** reference so that lines 75 and 76

```
s = "password: " +
    new String( pwd.getPassword() );
```

can use **JPasswordField** method *getPassword* to obtain the password and create the **String** to be displayed. Method **getPassword** returns the password as an array of type **char** that is used as an argument to a **String** constructor to create a **String**. Line 79 displays a message box indicating the GUI component reference name and the text the user typed in the field.

Note that even an uneditable **JTextField** can generate an event. Also note that the actual text of the password is displayed when you press *Enter* in the **JPasswordField** (of course, you would normally not do this!).

Common Programming Error 12.4

Forgetting to register an event handler object for a particular GUI component's event type results in no events being handled for that component for that event type.

Using a separate class to define an event listener is a common programming practice for separating the GUI interface from the implementation of its event handler. For the remainder of this chapter and Chapter 13, many programs use separate event-listener classes to process GUI events in an attempt to make the code more reusable. Any class that has potential for reuse beyond the example in which the class is introduced has been placed in a package so it can be imported into other programs for reuse.

Good Programming Practice 12.5

Use separate classes to process GUI events.

> ***Software Engineering Observation 12.3***
>
> *Using separate classes to handle GUI events leads to more reusable, reliable and readable software components that can be placed in packages and used in many programs.*

12.5.1 How Event Handling Works

Let us illustrate how the event handling mechanism works using **JTextField text1** from the preceding example. We have two remaining open questions from Section 12.4:

1. How did the event handler get registered?
2. How does the GUI component know to call **actionPerformed** as opposed to some other event handling method?

The first question is answered by the event-registration performed in lines 37 through 40 of the program. Figure 12.8 diagrams **JTextField text1** and its registered event handler.

Every **JComponent** has an object of class ***EventListenerList*** (package **javax.swing.event**) called ***listenerList*** as an instance variable. All registered listeners are stored in the **listenerList** (diagrammed as an array in Fig. 12.8). When the statement

```
text1.addActionListener( handler );
```

executes in Fig. 12.7, a new entry is placed in the **listenerList** for **JTextField text1** indicating both the reference to the listener object and the type of listener (in this case **ActionListener**).

The type is important in answering the second question—how does the GUI component know to call **actionPerformed** rather than another event handling method? Every **JComponent** actually supports several different event types, including *mouse events*, *key events* and others. When an event occurs, the event is *dispatched* only to the event listeners of the appropriate type. The dispatching of an event is simply calling the event handling method for each registered listener for that event type.

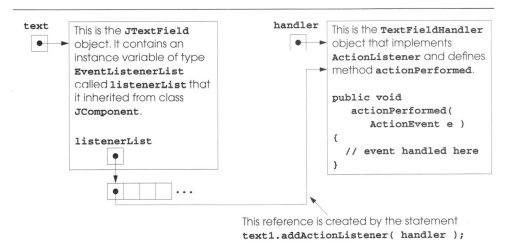

Fig. 12.8   Event registration for **JTextField text1**.

Each event type has a corresponding event-listener interface. For example, **Action-Event**s are handled by **ActionListener**s, *MouseEvent*s are handled by *MouseListener*s (and *MouseMotionListener*s as we will see) and *KeyEvent*s are handled by *KeyListener*s. When an event is generated by a user interaction with a component, the component is handed a unique *event ID* specifying the event type that occurred. The GUI component uses the event ID to decide the type of listener to which the event should be dispatched and the method to call. In the case of an **ActionEvent**, the event is dispatched to every registered **ActionListener**'s **actionPerformed** method (the only method in interface **ActionListener**). In the case of a **Mouse-Event**, the event is dispatched to every registered **MouseListener** (or **Mouse-MotionListener**). The event ID of the **MouseEvent** determines which of the seven different mouse event handling methods are called. All of this decision logic is handled for you by the GUI components. We discuss other event types and event-listener interfaces as they are needed with each new component we cover.

12.6 JButton

A *button* is a component the user clicks to trigger a specific action. A Java program can use several types of buttons, including *command buttons*, *check boxes*, *toggle buttons* and *radio buttons*. Figure 12.9 shows the inheritance hierarchy of the Swing buttons we cover in this chapter. As you can see in the diagram, all the button types are subclasses of **Abstract-Button** (package **javax.swing**), which defines many of the features that are common to Swing buttons. In this section, we concentrate on buttons that are typically used to initiate a command. Other button types are covered in the next several sections.

A command button generates an **ActionEvent** when the user clicks the button with the mouse. Command buttons are created with class **JButton**, which inherits from class **AbstractButton**. The text on the face of a **JButton** is called a *button label*. A GUI can have many **JButton**s, but each button label should typically be unique.

> *Look-and-Feel Observation 12.4*
>
> *Having more than one **JButton** with the same label makes the **JButton**s ambiguous to the user. Be sure to provide a unique label for each button.*

The application of Fig. 12.10 creates two **JButton**s and demonstrates that **JButton**s (like **JLabel**s) support the display of **Icon**s. Event handling for the buttons is performed by a single instance of inner class **ButtonHandler** (line 52).

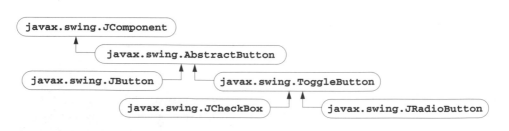

Fig. 12.9   The button hierarchy.

```
1   // Fig. 12.10: ButtonTest.java
2   // Creating JButtons.
3   import java.awt.*;
4   import java.awt.event.*;
5   import javax.swing.*;
6
7   public class ButtonTest extends JFrame {
8      private JButton plainButton, fancyButton;
9
10     public ButtonTest()
11     {
12        super( "Testing Buttons" );
13
14        Container c = getContentPane();
15        c.setLayout( new FlowLayout() );
16
17        // create buttons
18        plainButton = new JButton( "Plain Button" );
19        c.add( plainButton );
20
21        Icon bug1 = new ImageIcon( "bug1.gif" );
22        Icon bug2 = new ImageIcon( "bug2.gif" );
23        fancyButton = new JButton( "Fancy Button", bug1 );
24        fancyButton.setRolloverIcon( bug2 );
25        c.add( fancyButton );
26
27        // create an instance of inner class ButtonHandler
28        // to use for button event handling
29        ButtonHandler handler = new ButtonHandler();
30        fancyButton.addActionListener( handler );
31        plainButton.addActionListener( handler );
32
33        setSize( 275, 100 );
34        show();
35     }
36
37     public static void main( String args[] )
38     {
39        ButtonTest app = new ButtonTest();
40
41        app.addWindowListener(
42           new WindowAdapter() {
43              public void windowClosing( WindowEvent e )
44              {
45                 System.exit( 0 );
46              }
47           }
48        );
49     }
50
```

Fig. 12.10   Demonstrating command buttons and action events (part 1 of 2).

```
51      // inner class for button event handling
52      private class ButtonHandler implements ActionListener {
53         public void actionPerformed( ActionEvent e )
54         {
55            JOptionPane.showMessageDialog( null,
56               "You pressed: " + e.getActionCommand() );
57         }
58      }
59   }
```

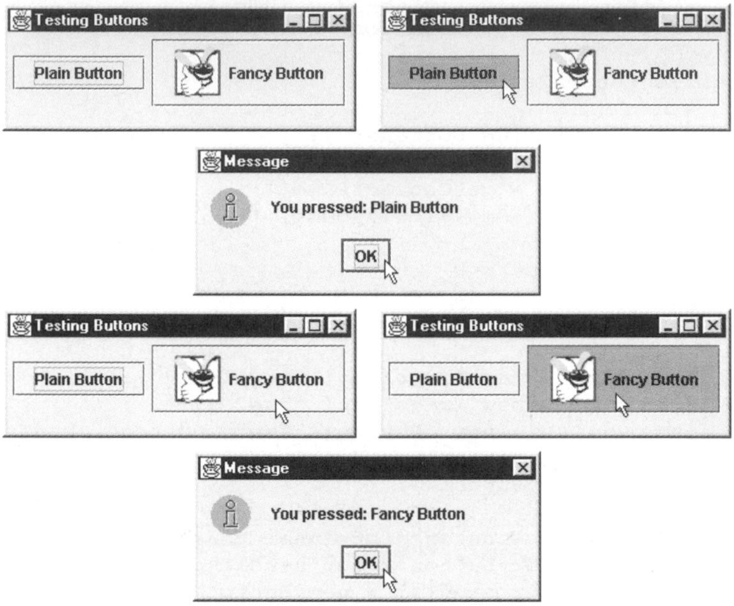

Fig. 12.10   Demonstrating command buttons and action events (part 2 of 2).

Line 8 declares two references to instances of class **JButton**—**plainButton** and **fancyButton**—that are instantiated in the constructor (line 10).

Line 18

```
        plainButton = new JButton( "Plain Button" );
```

creates **plainButton** with the button label **"Plain Button"**. Line 19 adds the button to the content pane.

A **JButton** can display **Icon**s. To provide the user with an extra level of visual inter-activity with the GUI, a **JButton** can also have a *rollover* **Icon**—an **Icon** that is dis-played when the mouse is positioned over the button. The icon on the button changes as the mouse moves in and out of the button's area on the screen. Lines 21 and 22

```
        Icon bug1 = new ImageIcon( "bug1.gif" );
        Icon bug2 = new ImageIcon( "bug2.gif" );
```

create two **ImageIcon** objects that represent the default **Icon** and rollover **Icon** for the **JButton** created at line 23. Both statements assume the image files are stored in the same directory as the program (this is commonly the case for applications that use images).

Line 23

```
fancyButton = new JButton( "Fancy Button", bug1 );
```

creates **fancyButton** with default text **"Fancy Button"** and the **Icon bug1**. By default, the text is displayed to the right of the icon. Line 24

```
fancyButton.setRolloverIcon( bug2 );
```

uses method ***setRolloverIcon*** (inherited from class **AbstractButton** into class **JButton**) to specify the image displayed on the button when the user positions the mouse over the button. Line 25 adds the button to the content pane.

Look-and-Feel Observation 12.5

*Using rollover icons for **JButton**s provides the user with visual feedback indicating that if they click the mouse, the button's action will occur.*

JButtons (like **JTextField**s) generate **ActionEvent**s. As mentioned previously, an **ActionEvent** can be processed by any **ActionListener** object. Lines 29 through 31

```
ButtonHandler handler = new ButtonHandler();
fancyButton.addActionListener( handler );
plainButton.addActionListener( handler );
```

register an **ActionListener** object for each **JButton**. Inner class **ButtonHandler** (lines 52 through 58) defines **actionPerformed** to display a message dialog box containing the label for the button that was pressed by the user. **ActionEvent** method **getActionCommand** returns the label on the button that generated the event.

12.7 JCheckBox and JRadioButton

The Swing GUI components contain three types of *state buttons*—***JToggleButton***, ***JCheckBox*** and ***JRadioButton***—that have on/off or true/false values. **JToggle-Button**s are frequently used with *toolbars* (sets of small buttons typically located on a bar across the top of a window) and are covered in Chapter 13. Classes **JCheckBox** and **JRadioButton** are subclasses of **JToggleButton**. A **JRadioButton** is different from a **JCheckBox** in that there are normally several **JRadioButton**s that are grouped together and only one of the **JRadioButton**s in the group can be selected (true) at any time. We first discuss class **JCheckBox**.

Look-and-Feel Observation 12.6

*Because class **AbstractButton** supports displaying text and images on a button, all subclasses of **AbstractButton** also support displaying text and images.*

The application of Fig. 12.11 uses two **JCheckBox** objects to change the font style of the text displayed in a **JTextField**. One **JCheckBox** applies a bold style when selected and the other applies an italic style when selected. If both are selected, the style of the font is bold and italic. When the program is initially executed, neither **JCheckBox** is checked (true).

```java
1    // Fig. 12.11: CheckBoxTest.java
2    // Creating Checkbox buttons.
3    import java.awt.*;
4    import java.awt.event.*;
5    import javax.swing.*;
6
7    public class CheckBoxTest extends JFrame {
8        private JTextField t;
9        private JCheckBox bold, italic;
10
11       public CheckBoxTest()
12       {
13           super( "JCheckBox Test" );
14
15           Container c = getContentPane();
16           c.setLayout(new FlowLayout());
17
18           t = new JTextField( "Watch the font style change", 20 );
19           t.setFont( new Font( "TimesRoman", Font.PLAIN, 14 ) );
20           c.add( t );
21
22           // create checkbox objects
23           bold = new JCheckBox( "Bold" );
24           c.add( bold );
25
26           italic = new JCheckBox( "Italic" );
27           c.add( italic );
28
29           CheckBoxHandler handler = new CheckBoxHandler();
30           bold.addItemListener( handler );
31           italic.addItemListener( handler );
32
33           addWindowListener(
34              new WindowAdapter() {
35                 public void windowClosing( WindowEvent e )
36                 {
37                    System.exit( 0 );
38                 }
39              }
40           );
41
42           setSize( 275, 100 );
43           show();
44       }
45
46       public static void main( String args[] )
47       {
48           new CheckBoxTest();
49       }
50
51       private class CheckBoxHandler implements ItemListener {
52           private int valBold = Font.PLAIN;
53           private int valItalic = Font.PLAIN;
```

Fig. 12.11   Program that creates two **JCheckBox** buttons (part 1 of 2).

```
54
55          public void itemStateChanged( ItemEvent e )
56          {
57             if ( e.getSource() == bold )
58                if ( e.getStateChange() == ItemEvent.SELECTED )
59                   valBold = Font.BOLD;
60                else
61                   valBold = Font.PLAIN;
62
63             if ( e.getSource() == italic )
64                if ( e.getStateChange() == ItemEvent.SELECTED )
65                   valItalic = Font.ITALIC;
66                else
67                   valItalic = Font.PLAIN;
68
69             t.setFont(
70                new Font( "TimesRoman", valBold + valItalic, 14 ) );
71             t.repaint();
72          }
73       }
74    }
```

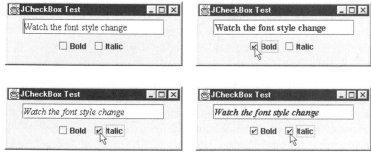

Fig. 12.11   Program that creates two **JCheckBox** buttons (part 2 of 2).

After the **JTextField** is created and initialized, line 19

```
t.setFont( new Font( "TimesRoman", Font.PLAIN, 14 ) );
```

sets the font of the **JTextField** to **TimesRoman**, **PLAIN** style and **14**-point size. Next, the constructor creates two **JCheckBox** objects with lines 23 and 26

```
bold = new JCheckBox( "Bold" );
italic = new JCheckBox( "Italic" );
```

The **String** passed to the constructor is the *check box label* that appears to the right of the **JCheckBox** by default.

When the user clicks a **JCheckBox** an **ItemEvent** is generated that can be handled by an **ItemListener** (any object of a class that implements interface **ItemListener**). An **ItemListener** must define method ***itemStateChanged***. In this example, the event handling is performed by an instance of inner class **CheckBoxHandler** (lines 51 through 73). Lines 29 through 31

```
CheckBoxHandler handler = new CheckBoxHandler();
bold.addItemListener( handler );
italic.addItemListener( handler );
```

create an instance of class **CheckBoxHandler** and register it with method **addItem-Listener** as the **ItemListener** for both the **bold** and **italic JCheckBox**es.

Method **itemStateChanged** (line 55) is called when the uses clicks either the **bold** or **italic JCheckBox**. The method uses **e.getSource()** to determine which **JCheckBox** was clicked. If it was **JCheckBox bold**, the **if/else** structure at lines 58 through 61

```
if ( e.getStateChange() == ItemEvent.SELECTED )
    valBold = Font.BOLD;
else
    valBold = Font.PLAIN;
```

uses **ItemEvent** method *getStateChange* to determine the state of the button (**ItemEvent.SELECTED** or **ItemEvent.DESELECTED**). If the state is selected, integer **valBold** is assigned **Font.BOLD**; otherwise, **valBold** is assigned **Font.PLAIN**. A similar **if/else** structure is executed if **JCheckBox italic** is clicked. If the **italic** state is selected, integer **valItalic** is assigned **Font.ITALIC**; otherwise, **valItalic** is assigned **Font.PLAIN**. The sum of **valBold** and **valItalic** is used at lines 69 and 70 as the style of the new font for the **JTextField**.

Radio buttons (defined with class *JRadioButton*) are similar to check boxes in that they have two states—*selected* and *not selected* (also called *deselected*). However, radio buttons normally appear as a *group* in which only one radio button can be selected at a time. Selecting a different radio button in the group automatically forces all other radio buttons in the group to be deselected. Radio buttons are used to represent a set of *mutually exclusive* options (i.e., multiple options in the group would not be selected at the same time). The logical relationship between radio buttons is maintained by a *ButtonGroup* object (package **javax.swing**). The **ButtonGroup** object itself is not a GUI component. Therefore, a **ButtonGroup** object is not displayed in a user interface. Rather, the individual **JRadioButton** objects from the group are displayed in the GUI.

Common Programming Error 12.5

*Adding a **ButtonGroup** object (or an object of any other class that does not derive from **Component**) to a container is a syntax error.*

The application of Fig. 12.12 is similar to the preceding program. The user can alter the font style of a **JTextField**'s text. The program uses radio buttons that permit only a single font style in the group to be selected at a time.

Lines 25 through 32 in the constructor define each **JRadioButton** object and add it to the application window's content pane. Each **JRadioButton** is initialized with a constructor call like line 25

```
plain = new JRadioButton( "Plain", true );
```

This constructor supplies the label that appears to the right of the **JRadioButton** by default and the initial state of the **JRadioButton**. A **true** second argument indicates that the **JRadioButton** should appear selected when it is displayed.

```
1   // Fig. 12.12: RadioButtonTest.java
2   // Creating radio buttons using ButtonGroup and JRadioButton.
3   import java.awt.*;
4   import java.awt.event.*;
5   import javax.swing.*;
6
7   public class RadioButtonTest extends JFrame {
8      private JTextField t;
9      private Font plainFont, boldFont,
10                     italicFont, boldItalicFont;
11     private JRadioButton plain, bold, italic, boldItalic;
12     private ButtonGroup radioGroup;
13
14     public RadioButtonTest()
15     {
16        super( "RadioButton Test" );
17
18        Container c = getContentPane();
19        c.setLayout( new FlowLayout() );
20
21        t = new JTextField( "Watch the font style change", 25 );
22        c.add( t );
23
24        // Create radio buttons
25        plain = new JRadioButton( "Plain", true );
26        c.add( plain );
27        bold = new JRadioButton( "Bold", false);
28        c.add( bold );
29        italic = new JRadioButton( "Italic", false );
30        c.add( italic );
31        boldItalic = new JRadioButton( "Bold/Italic", false );
32        c.add( boldItalic );
33
34        // register events
35        RadioButtonHandler handler = new RadioButtonHandler();
36        plain.addItemListener( handler );
37        bold.addItemListener( handler );
38        italic.addItemListener( handler );
39        boldItalic.addItemListener( handler );
40
41        // create logical relationship between JRadioButtons
42        radioGroup = new ButtonGroup();
43        radioGroup.add( plain );
44        radioGroup.add( bold );
45        radioGroup.add( italic );
46        radioGroup.add( boldItalic );
47
48        plainFont = new Font( "TimesRoman", Font.PLAIN, 14 );
49        boldFont = new Font( "TimesRoman", Font.BOLD, 14 );
50        italicFont = new Font( "TimesRoman", Font.ITALIC, 14 );
51        boldItalicFont =
52           new Font( "TimesRoman", Font.BOLD + Font.ITALIC, 14 );
53        t.setFont( plainFont );
```

Fig. 12.12   Creating and manipulating radio buttons (part 1 of 2).

```
54
55          setSize( 300, 100 );
56          show();
57       }
58
59       public static void main( String args[] )
60       {
61          RadioButtonTest app = new RadioButtonTest();
62
63          app.addWindowListener(
64             new WindowAdapter() {
65                public void windowClosing( WindowEvent e )
66                {
67                   System.exit( 0 );
68                }
69             }
70          );
71       }
72
73       private class RadioButtonHandler implements ItemListener {
74          public void itemStateChanged( ItemEvent e )
75          {
76             if ( e.getSource() == plain )
77                t.setFont( plainFont );
78             else if ( e.getSource() == bold )
79                t.setFont( boldFont );
80             else if ( e.getSource() == italic )
81                t.setFont( italicFont );
82             else if ( e.getSource() == boldItalic )
83                t.setFont( boldItalicFont );
84
85             t.repaint();
86          }
87       }
88 }
```

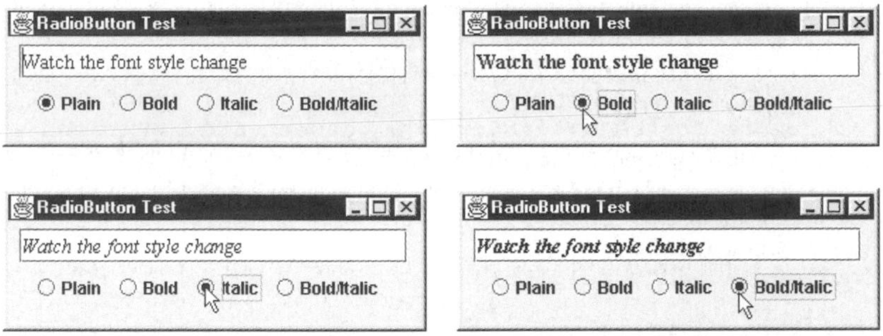

Fig. 12.12   Creating and manipulating radio buttons (part 2 of 2).

JRadioButtons, like JCheckBoxes, generate ItemEvents when they are clicked. Lines 35 through 39 create an instance of inner class RadioButtonHandler (defined at line 73) and register it to handle the ItemEvent generated when the user clicks any one of the JRadioButtons.

Line 42

```
radioGroup = new ButtonGroup();
```

instantiates a **ButtonGroup** object and assigns it to reference **radioGroup**. This object is the "glue" that binds the four **JRadioButton** objects together to form the logical relationship that allows only one of the four buttons to be selected at a time. Lines 43 through 46 use **ButtonGroup** method *add* to associate each of the **JRadioButton**s with **radioGroup**. If more than one selected **JRadioButton** object is added to the group, the last selected **JRadioButton** added will be selected when the GUI is displayed.

Class **RadioButtonHandler** (line 73) implements interface **ItemListener** so it can handle item events generated by the **JRadioButton**s. Each **JRadioButton** in the program has an instance of this class (**handler**) registered as its **ItemListener**. When the user clicks a **JRadioButton**, **ButtonGroup radioGroup** turns off the previously selected **JRadioButton** and method **itemStateChanged** (line 74) executes. The method determines which **JRadioButton** was clicked using method **getSource** (inherited indirectly from **EventObject** into **ItemEvent**), then sets the font in the **JTextField** to one of the **Font** objects created in the constructor.

12.8 JComboBox

A *combo box* (sometimes called a *drop-down list*) provides a list of items from which the user can make a selection. Combo boxes are implemented with class **JComboBox**, which inherits from class **JComponent**. **JComboBox**es generate **ItemEvent**s like **JCheckBox**es and **JRadioButton**s.

The application of Fig. 12.13 uses a **JComboBox** to provide a list of four image file names. When an image file name is selected, the corresponding image is displayed as an **Icon** on a JLabel. The screen captures for this program show the **JComboBox** list after the selection was made to illustrate which image file name was selected.

```
1   // Fig. 12.13: ComboBoxTest.java
2   // Using a JComboBox to select an image to display.
3   import java.awt.*;
4   import java.awt.event.*;
5   import javax.swing.*;
6
7   public class ComboBoxTest extends JFrame {
8      private JComboBox images;
9      private JLabel label;
10     private String names[] =
11        { "bug1.gif", "bug2.gif",
12          "travelbug.gif", "buganim.gif" };
13     private Icon icons[] =
14        { new ImageIcon( names[ 0 ] ),
15          new ImageIcon( names[ 1 ] ),
16          new ImageIcon( names[ 2 ] ),
17          new ImageIcon( names[ 3 ] ) };
18
```

Fig. 12.13   Program that uses a **JComboBox** to select an icon (part 1 of 3).

```
19      public ComboBoxTest()
20      {
21          super( "Testing JComboBox" );
22
23          Container c = getContentPane();
24          c.setLayout( new FlowLayout() );
25
26          images = new JComboBox( names );
27          images.setMaximumRowCount( 3 );
28
29          images.addItemListener(
30              new ItemListener() {
31                  public void itemStateChanged( ItemEvent e )
32                  {
33                      label.setIcon(
34                          icons[ images.getSelectedIndex() ] );
35                  }
36              }
37          );
38
39          c.add( images );
40
41          label = new JLabel( icons[ 0 ] );
42          c.add( label );
43
44          setSize( 350, 100 );
45          show();
46      }
47
48      public static void main( String args[] )
49      {
50          ComboBoxTest app = new ComboBoxTest();
51
52          app.addWindowListener(
53              new WindowAdapter() {
54                  public void windowClosing( WindowEvent e )
55                  {
56                      System.exit( 0 );
57                  }
58              }
59          );
60      }
61  }
```

A **scrollbar** to scroll through   scroll arrows   scroll box
the items in the list.

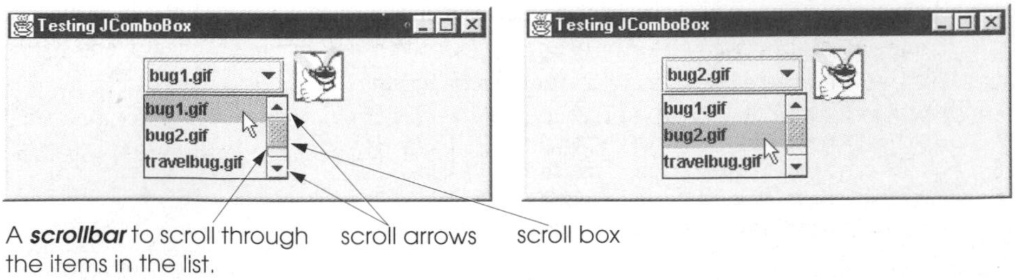

Fig. 12.13   Program that uses a **JComboBox** to select an icon (part 2 of 3).

Fig. 12.13 Program that uses a **JComboBox** to select an icon (part 3 of 3).

Lines 13 through 17

```
private Icon icons[] =
    { new ImageIcon( names[ 0 ] ),
      new ImageIcon( names[ 1 ] ),
      new ImageIcon( names[ 2 ] ),
      new ImageIcon( names[ 3 ] ) };
```

declare and initialize array icons with four new **ImageIcon** objects. **String** array **names** (defined on lines 10 through 12) contains the names of the four image files that are stored in the same directory as the application.

Line 26

```
images = new JComboBox( names );
```

creates a **JComboBox** object using the **String**s in array **names** as the elements in the list. A numeric *index* keeps track of the ordering of items in the **JComboBox**. The first item is added at index 0; the next item is added at index 1, and so forth. The first item added to a **JComboBox** appears as the currently selected item when the **JComboBox** is displayed. Other items are selected by clicking the **JComboBox**. When clicked, the **JComboBox** expands into a list from which the user can make a selection.

Line 27

```
images.setMaximumRowCount( 3 );
```

uses **JComboBox** method ***setMaximumRowCount*** to set the maximum number of elements that are displayed when the user clicks the **JComboBox**. If there are more items in the **JComboBox** than the maximum number of elements that are displayed, the **JComboBox** automatically provides a *scrollbar* (see the first screen capture) that allows the user to view all the elements in the list. The user can click the *scroll arrows* at the top and bottom of the scrollbar to move up and down through the list one element at a time, or the user can drag the *scroll box* in the middle of the scrollbar up and down to move through the list. To drag the scroll box, hold the mouse button down with the mouse cursor on the scroll box and move the mouse.

Look-and-Feel Observation 12.7

Set the maximum row count for a **JComboBox** *to a number of rows that prevents the list from expanding outside the bounds of the window or applet in which it is used. This will ensure that the list displays correctly when it is expanded by the user.*

Lines 29 through 37

```
images.addItemListener(
    new ItemListener() {
        public void itemStateChanged( ItemEvent e )
        {
            label.setIcon(
                icons[ images.getSelectedIndex() ] );
        }
    }
);
```

register an instance of an anonymous inner class that implements **ItemListener** as the listener for **JComboBox images**. When the user makes a selection from **images**, method **itemStateChanged** (line 31) sets the **Icon** for **label**. The **Icon** is selected from array **icons** by determining the index number of the selected item in the **JComboBox** with method *getSelectedIndex* in line 34.

12.9 JList

A *list* displays a series of items from which the user may select one or more items. Lists are created with class **JList**, which inherits from class **JComponent**. Class **JList** supports *single-selection lists* (i.e., lists that allow only one item to be selected at a time) and *multiple-selection lists* (lists that allow any number of items to be selected). In this section, we discuss single-selection lists.

The application of Fig. 12.14 creates a **JList** of 13 colors. When a color name is clicked in the **JList**, a *ListSelectionEvent* occurs and the application window content pane's background color changes.

```
1   // Fig. 12.14: ListTest.java
2   // Selecting colors from a JList.
3   import java.awt.*;
4   import java.awt.event.*;
5   import javax.swing.*;
6   import javax.swing.event.*;
7
8   public class ListTest extends JFrame {
9       private JList colorList;
10      private Container c;
11
12      private String colorNames[] =
13          { "Black", "Blue", "Cyan", "Dark Gray", "Gray", "Green",
14            "Light Gray", "Magenta", "Orange", "Pink", "Red",
15            "White", "Yellow" };
16
17      private Color colors[] =
18          { Color.black, Color.blue, Color.cyan, Color.darkGray,
19            Color.gray, Color.green, Color.lightGray,
20            Color.magenta, Color.orange, Color.pink, Color.red,
21            Color.white, Color.yellow };
```

Fig. 12.14   Selecting colors from a **JList** (part 1 of 3).

```
22
23      public ListTest()
24      {
25         super( "List Test" );
26
27         c = getContentPane();
28         c.setLayout( new FlowLayout() );
29
30         // create a list with the items in the colorNames array
31         colorList = new JList( colorNames );
32         colorList.setVisibleRowCount( 5 );
33
34         // do not allow multiple selections
35         colorList.setSelectionMode(
36            ListSelectionModel.SINGLE_SELECTION );
37
38         // add a JScrollPane containing the JList
39         // to the content pane
40         c.add( new JScrollPane( colorList ) );
41
42         // set up event handler
43         colorList.addListSelectionListener(
44            new ListSelectionListener() {
45               public void valueChanged( ListSelectionEvent e )
46               {
47                  c.setBackground(
48                     colors[ colorList.getSelectedIndex() ] );
49               }
50            }
51         );
52
53         setSize( 350, 150 );
54         show();
55      }
56
57      public static void main( String args[] )
58      {
59         ListTest app = new ListTest();
60
61         app.addWindowListener(
62            new WindowAdapter() {
63               public void windowClosing( WindowEvent e )
64               {
65                  System.exit( 0 );
66               }
67            }
68         );
69      }
70   }
```

Fig. 12.14   Selecting colors from a **JList** (part 2 of 3).

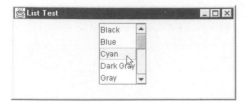

Fig. 12.14   Selecting colors from a **JList** (part 3 of 3).

A **JList** object is instantiated at line 31

```
colorList = new JList( colorNames );
```

and assigned to reference **colorList** in the constructor. The argument to the **JList**
constructor is the array of **Object**s (in this case **String**s) to display in the list. Line 32

```
colorList.setVisibleRowCount( 5 );
```

uses **JList** method *setVisibleRowCount* to determine the number of items that are
visible in the list.

Lines 35 and 36

```
colorList.setSelectionMode(
    ListSelectionModel.SINGLE_SELECTION );
```

use **JList** method *setSelectionMode* to specify the *selection mode* for the list. Class
ListSelectionModel (package **javax.swing**) defines three constants to specify a
JList's selection mode—*SINGLE_SELECTION*, *SINGLE_INTERVAL_SELECTION*
and *MULTIPLE_INTERVAL_SELECTION*. A **SINGLE_SELECTION** list allows only
one item to be selected at a time. A **SINGLE_INTERVAL_SELECTION** list is a multiple-
selection list that allows several items in a contiguous range in the list to be selected. A
MULTIPLE_INTERVAL_SELECTION list is a multiple-selection list that does not restrict the items that can be selected.

Class **JList** *does not* automatically provide a scrollbar if there are more items in the
list than the number of visible rows. In this case, a *JScrollPane* object is used to provide
the automatic scrolling capability for the **JList**. Line 40

```
c.add( new JScrollPane( colorList ) );
```

adds a new instance of class *JScrollPane* to the content pane. The **JScrollPane**
constructor receives as its argument the **JComponent** for which it will provide automatic
scrolling functionality (in this case **JList colorList**). Notice in the screen captures
that a scrollbar created by the **JScrollPane** appears at the right side of the **JList**. The
scrollbar only appears when the number of items in the **JList** exceeds the number of visible items.

Lines 43 through 51

```
colorList.addListSelectionListener(
   new ListSelectionListener() {
      public void valueChanged( ListSelectionEvent e )
      {
         c.setBackground(
            colors[ colorList.getSelectedIndex() ] );
      }
   }
);
```

use **JList** method ***addListSelectionListener*** to register an instance of an anonymous inner class that implements ***ListSelectionListener*** (defined in package **javax.swing.event**) as the listener for **JList colorList**. When the user makes a selection from **colorList**, method ***valueChanged*** (line 45) executes and sets the background color of the content pane with method ***setBackground*** (inherited from class **Component** into class **Container**). The color is selected from the array **colors** with the selected item's index in the list that is returned by **JList** method **getSelectedIndex**.

12.10 Multiple-Selection Lists

A *multiple-selection list* enables the user to select many items from a **JList**. A **SINGLE_INTERVAL_SELECTION** list allows selection of a contiguous range of items in the list by clicking the first item, then holding the *Shift* key while clicking the last item to select in the range. A **MULTIPLE_INTERVAL_SELECTION** list allows continuous range selection as described for a **SINGLE_INTERVAL_SELECTION** list and allows miscellaneous items to be selected by holding the *Ctrl* key while clicking each item to select. To deselect an item, hold the *Ctrl* key while clicking the item a second time.

The application of Fig. 12.15 uses multiple-selection lists to copy items from one **JList** to another. One list is a **MULTIPLE_INTERVAL_SELECTION** list and the other is a **SINGLE_INTERVAL_SELECTION** list. When you execute the program, try using the selection techniques described above to select items in both lists.

```
1   // Fig. 12.15: MultipleSelection.java
2   // Copying items from one List to another.
3   import javax.swing.*;
4   import java.awt.*;
5   import java.awt.event.*;
6
7   public class MultipleSelection extends JFrame {
8      private JList colorList, copyList;
9      private JButton copy;
10     private String colorNames[] =
11        { "Black", "Blue", "Cyan", "Dark Gray", "Gray",
12          "Green", "Light Gray", "Magenta", "Orange", "Pink",
13          "Red", "White", "Yellow" };
14
```

Fig. 12.15   Using a multiple-selection **JList** (part 1 of 3).

```
15        public MultipleSelection()
16        {
17            super( "Multiple Selection Lists" );
18
19            Container c = getContentPane();
20            c.setLayout( new FlowLayout() );
21
22            colorList = new JList( colorNames );
23            colorList.setVisibleRowCount( 5 );
24            colorList.setFixedCellHeight( 15 );
25            colorList.setSelectionMode(
26                ListSelectionModel.MULTIPLE_INTERVAL_SELECTION );
27            c.add( new JScrollPane( colorList ) );
28
29            // create copy button
30            copy = new JButton( "Copy >>>" );
31            copy.addActionListener(
32                new ActionListener() {
33                    public void actionPerformed( ActionEvent e )
34                    {
35                        // place selected values in copyList
36                        copyList.setListData(
37                            colorList.getSelectedValues() );
38                    }
39                }
40            );
41            c.add( copy );
42
43            copyList = new JList();
44            copyList.setVisibleRowCount( 5 );
45            copyList.setFixedCellWidth( 100 );
46            copyList.setFixedCellHeight( 15 );
47            copyList.setSelectionMode(
48                ListSelectionModel.SINGLE_INTERVAL_SELECTION );
49            c.add( new JScrollPane( copyList ) );
50
51            setSize( 300, 120 );
52            show();
53        }
54
```

Fig. 12.15   Using a multiple-selection **JList** (part 2 of 3).

Line 22 creates **JList colorList** and initialize it with the **String**s in the array **colorNames**. Line 23 sets the number of visible rows in **colorList** to **5**. Line 24

```
        colorList.setFixedCellHeight( 15 );
```

uses **JList** method *setFixedCellHeight* to specify the height in pixels of each item in the **JList**. Lines 25 and 26 specify that **colorList** is a **MULTIPLE_INTER-VAL_SELECTION** list. Line 27 adds a new **JScrollPane** containing **colorList** to the content pane. Lines 43 through 49 perform similar tasks for **JList copyList**, which is defined as a **SINGLE_INTERVAL_SELECTION** list. Line 45

```
55      public static void main( String args[] )
56      {
57          MultipleSelection app = new MultipleSelection();
58
59          app.addWindowListener(
60              new WindowAdapter() {
61                  public void windowClosing( WindowEvent e )
62                  {
63                      System.exit( 0 );
64                  }
65              }
66          );
67      }
68  }
```

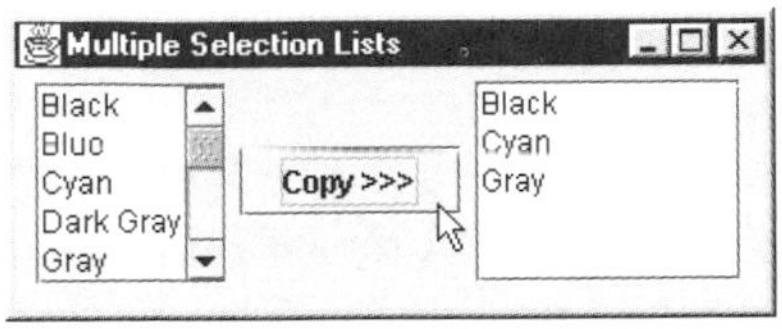

Fig. 12.15   Using a multiple-selection **JList** (part 3 of 3).

```
copyList.setFixedCellWidth( 100 );
```

uses **JList** method ***setFixedCellWidth*** to set **copyList**'s width to 100 pixels.

A multiple-selection list does not have a specific event associated with making multiple selections. Normally, an event generated by another GUI component (known as an *external event*) specifies when the multiple selections in a **JList** should be processed. In this example, the user clicks **JButton copy** to trigger the event that copies the selected items in **colorList** to **copyList**.

When the user clicks **copy** method, **actionPerformed** (line 33) is called. Lines 36 and 37

```
copyList.setListData(
    colorList.getSelectedValues() );
```

use **JList** method ***setListData*** to set the items displayed in **copyList** to the selected values from **colorList** that are returned by **JList** method ***getSelectedValues*** as an array of **Object**s.

12.11 Mouse Event Handling

This section presents the ***MouseListener*** and ***MouseMotionListener*** event-listener interfaces for handling *mouse events*. Mouse events can be trapped for any GUI component that derives from **java.awt.Component**. The methods of interfaces **MouseListener** and **MouseMotionListener** are summarized in Fig. 12.16.

Each of the mouse event handling methods takes a ***MouseEvent*** object as its argument. A **MouseEvent** object contains information about the mouse event that occurred, including the x- and y-coordinates of the location where the event occurred. The **MouseListener** and **MouseMotionListener** methods are called automatically when the mouse interacts with a **Component** if listener objects are registered for a particular **Component**. Method *mousePressed* is called when a mouse button is pressed with the mouse cursor over a component. Using methods and constants of class *InputEvent* (the superclass of **MouseEvent**), a program can determine which mouse button the user clicked. Method *mouseClicked* is called whenever a mouse button is released without moving the mouse after a **mousePressed** operation. Method *mouse-Released* is called whenever a mouse button is released. Method *mouseEntered* is called when the mouse cursor enters the physical boundaries of a **Component**. Method *mouseExited* is called when the mouse cursor leaves the physical boundaries of a **Component**. Method *mouseDragged* is called when the mouse button is pressed and held, and the mouse is moved (a process known as *dragging*). The **mouseDragged** event is preceded by a **mousePressed** event and followed by a **mouseReleased** event. Method *mouseMoved* is called when the mouse is moved with the mouse cursor over a component (and no mouse buttons pressed).

Look-and-Feel Observation 12.8

Method calls to **mouseDragged** *are sent to the* **MouseMotionListener** *for the* **Component** *on which the drag operation started. Similarly, the* **mouseReleased** *method call is sent to the* **MouseListener** *for the* **Component** *on which the drag operation started.*

MouseListener and MouseMotionListener interface methods

public void mousePressed(MouseEvent e)   // MouseListener

Called when a mouse button is pressed with the mouse cursor on a component.

public void mouseClicked(MouseEvent e)   // MouseListener

Called when a mouse button is pressed and released on a component without moving the mouse cursor.

public void mouseReleased(MouseEvent e)   // MouseListener

Called when a mouse button is released after being pressed. This event is always preceded by a **mousePressed** event.

public void mouseEntered(MouseEvent e)   // MouseListener

Called when the mouse cursor enters the bounds of a component.

public void mouseExited(MouseEvent e)   // MouseListener

Called when the mouse cursor leaves the bounds of a component.

public void mouseDragged(MouseEvent e)   // MouseMotionListener

Called when the mouse button is pressed and the mouse is moved. This event is always preceded by a call to **mousePressed**.

public void mouseMoved(MouseEvent e)   // MouseMotionListener

Called when the mouse is moved with the mouse cursor on a component.

Fig. 12.16   MouseListener and **MouseMotionListener** interface methods.

The **MouseTracker** application (Fig. 12.17) demonstrates the **MouseListener** and **MouseMotionListener** methods. The application class implements both interfaces so it can listen for its own mouse events. Note that all seven methods from these two interfaces must be defined by the programmer when a class implements both interfaces.

```java
1  // Fig. 12.17: MouseTracker.java
2  // Demonstrating mouse events.
3
4  import java.awt.*;
5  import java.awt.event.*;
6  import javax.swing.*;
7
8  public class MouseTracker extends JFrame
9              implements MouseListener, MouseMotionListener {
10    private JLabel statusBar;
11
12    public MouseTracker()
13    {
14       super( "Demonstrating Mouse Events" );
15
16       statusBar = new JLabel();
17       getContentPane().add( statusBar, BorderLayout.SOUTH );
18
19       // application listens to its own mouse events
20       addMouseListener( this );
21       addMouseMotionListener( this );
22
23       setSize( 275, 100 );
24       show();
25    }
26
27    // MouseListener event handlers
28    public void mouseClicked( MouseEvent e )
29    {
30       statusBar.setText( "Clicked at [" + e.getX() +
31                          ", " + e.getY() + "]" );
32    }
33
34    public void mousePressed( MouseEvent e )
35    {
36       statusBar.setText( "Pressed at [" + e.getX() +
37                          ", " + e.getY() + "]" );
38    }
39
40    public void mouseReleased( MouseEvent e )
41    {
42       statusBar.setText( "Released at [" + e.getX() +
43                          ", " + e.getY() + "]" );
44    }
45
```

Fig. 12.17 Demonstrating mouse event handling (part 1 of 3).

```
46      public void mouseEntered( MouseEvent e )
47      {
48         statusBar.setText( "Mouse in window" );
49      }
50
51      public void mouseExited( MouseEvent e )
52      {
53         statusBar.setText( "Mouse outside window" );
54      }
55
56      // MouseMotionListener event handlers
57      public void mouseDragged( MouseEvent e )
58      {
59         statusBar.setText( "Dragged at [" + e.getX() +
60                          ", " + e.getY() + "]" );
61      }
62
63      public void mouseMoved( MouseEvent e )
64      {
65         statusBar.setText( "Moved at [" + e.getX() +
66                          ", " + e.getY() + "]" );
67      }
68
69      public static void main( String args[] )
70      {
71         MouseTracker app = new MouseTracker();
72
73         app.addWindowListener(
74            new WindowAdapter() {
75               public void windowClosing( WindowEvent e )
76               {
77                  System.exit( 0 );
78               }
79            }
80         );
81      }
82   }
```

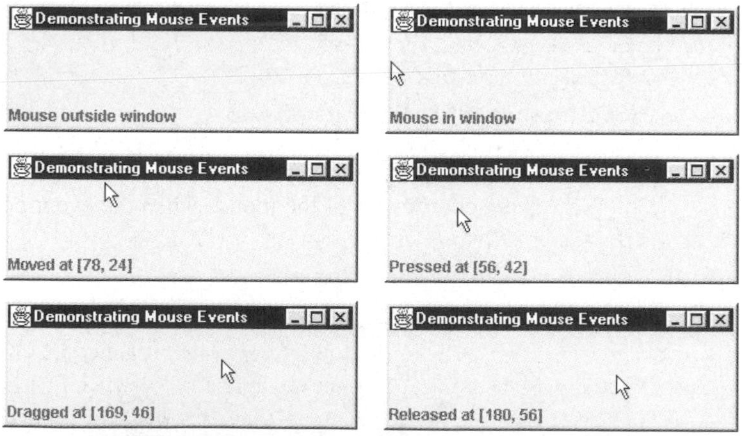

Fig. 12.17 Demonstrating mouse event handling (part 2 of 3).

Fig. 12.17   Demonstrating mouse event handling (part 3 of 3).

Each mouse event results in a **String** displayed in **JLabel statusBar** at the bottom of the window.

Lines 16 and 17 in the constructor

```
statusBar = new JLabel();
getContentPane().add( statusBar, BorderLayout.SOUTH );
```

define **JLabel statusBar** and attach it to the content pane. Until now, each time we used the content pane, method **setLayout** was called to set the content pane's layout manager to a **FlowLayout**. This allowed the content pane to display the GUI components we attached to it from left to right. If the GUI components do not fit on one line, the **Flow-Layout** creates additional lines to continue displaying the GUI components. Actually, the default layout manager is a **BorderLayout** that divides the content pane's area into five regions—north, south, east, west and center. Line 17 uses a new version of **Container** method **add** to attach **statusBar** to the region **BorderLayout.SOUTH**, which extends across the entire bottom of the content pane. We discuss **BorderLayout** and several other layout managers in detail later in this chapter.

Lines 20 and 21 in the constructor

```
addMouseListener( this )
addMouseMotionListener( this );
```

register the **MouseTracker** window object as the listener for its own mouse events. Methods **addMouseListener** and **addMouseMotionListener** are **Component** methods that can be used to register mouse event listeners for an object of any class that extends **Component**.

When the mouse enters or exits the application area, method **mouseEntered** (line 46) and method **mouseExited** (line 51) are called, respectively. Both methods display a message in **statusBar** indicating that the mouse is inside the application or the mouse is outside the application (see the first two screen captures).

When any of the other five events occur, they display a message in **statusBar** that includes a **String** that represents the event that occurred and the coordinates where the mouse event occurred. The *x* and *y* coordinates of the mouse when the event occurred are obtained with **MouseEvent** methods *getX* and *getY*, respectively.

12.12 Adapter Classes

Many of the event-listener interfaces provide multiple methods; **MouseListener** and **MouseMotionListener** are examples. It is not always desirable to define every method in an event-listener interface. For example, a program may only need the **mouse-Clicked** handler from interface **MouseListener** or the **mouseDragged** handler from **MouseMotionListener**. In our windowed applications (subclasses of **JFrame**) terminating the application has been handled with **windowClosing** from interface **Win-dowListener**, which actually specifies seven window-event-handling methods. For many of the listener interfaces that contain multiple methods, package **java.awt.event** and package **javax.swing.event** provide event-listener *adapter classes*. An adapter class implements an interface and provides a default implementation (with an empty method body) of every method in the interface. The **java.awt.event** adapter classes are shown in Fig. 12.18 along with the interfaces they implement.

The programmer can extend the adapter class to inherit the default implementation of every method then override the method(s) needed for event handling. The default implementation of each method in the adapter class has an empty body. This is exactly what we have been doing in each application example that extends **JFrame** and defines method **windowClosing** to handle the closing of the window and termination of the application.

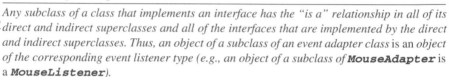

Software Engineering Observation 12.4

*Any subclass of a class that implements an interface has the "is a" relationship in all of its direct and indirect superclasses and all of the interfaces that are implemented by the direct and indirect superclasses. Thus, an object of a subclass of an event adapter class is an object of the corresponding event listener type (e.g., an object of a subclass of **MouseAdapter** is a **MouseListener**).*

The **Painter** application of Fig. 12.19 uses the **mouseDragged** event handler to create a simple drawing program. The user can draw pictures with the mouse by dragging the mouse on the background of the window. Because we do not intend to use method **mouseMoved**, our **MouseMotionListener** is defined as a subclass of **Mouse-MotionAdapter**. This class already defines both **mouseMoved** and **mouseDragged**, so we can simply override **mouseDragged** to provide the drawing functionality.

Event adapter class	Implements interface
ComponentAdapter	ComponentListener
ContainerAdapter	ContainerListener
FocusAdapter	FocusListener
KeyAdapter	KeyListener
MouseAdapter	MouseListener
MouseMotionAdapter	MouseMotionListener
WindowAdapter	WindowListener

Fig. 12.18   Event adapter classes and the interfaces they implement.

```
1   // Fig. 12.19: Painter.java
2   // Using class MouseMotionAdapter.
3   import javax.swing.*;
4   import java.awt.event.*;
5   import java.awt.*;
6
```

Fig. 12.19   Program that demonstrates adapter classes (part 1 of 2).

```
7   public class Painter extends JFrame {
8      private int xValue = -10, yValue = -10;
9
10     public Painter()
11     {
12        super( "A simple paint program" );
13
14        getContentPane().add(
15           new Label( "Drag the mouse to draw" ),
16           BorderLayout.SOUTH );
17
18        addMouseMotionListener(
19           new MouseMotionAdapter() {
20              public void mouseDragged( MouseEvent e )
21              {
22                 xValue = e.getX();
23                 yValue = e.getY();
24                 repaint();
25              }
26           }
27        );
28
29        setSize( 300, 150 );
30        show();
31     }
32
33     public void paint( Graphics g )
34     {
35        g.fillOval( xValue, yValue, 4, 4 );
36     }
37
38     public static void main( String args[] )
39     {
40        Painter app = new Painter();
41
42        app.addWindowListener(
43           new WindowAdapter() {
44              public void windowClosing( WindowEvent e )
45              {
46                 System.exit( 0 );
47              }
48           }
49        );
50     }
51  }
```

Fig. 12.19   Program that demonstrates adapter classes (part 2 of 2).

The instance variables **xValue** and **yValue** store the coordinates of the **mouse-Dragged** event. Initially, the coordinates are set outside the window area to prevent an oval from drawing on the background area in the first call to **paint** when the window is displayed. Lines 18 through 27 register a **MouseMotionListener** to listen for the window's mouse motion events (remember that a call to a method that is not preceded by a reference and a dot operator is really preceded by "**this.**", indicating that the method is called for the current instance of the class at execution time). Lines 19 through 26

```
new MouseMotionAdapter() {
   public void mouseDragged( MouseEvent e )
   {
      xValue = e.getX();
      yValue = e.getY();
      repaint();
   }
}
```

define an anonymous inner class that extends class **MouseMotionAdapter** (which implements **MouseMotionListener**). The anonymous inner class inherits a default implementation of both method **mouseMoved** and method **mouseDragged**. Thus, the anonymous inner class already satisfies the requirement that in all methods an interface must be implemented. However, the default methods do nothing by default when they are called. So, we override method **mouseDragged** at line 20 to capture the *x*- and *y*-coordinates of the mouse-dragged event and store them in instance variables **xValue** and **yValue**, then call **repaint** to initiate drawing the next oval on the background (performed by method **paint** at line 33).

Lines 42 through 49

```
app.addWindowListener(
   new WindowAdapter() {
      public void windowClosing( WindowEvent e )
      {
         System.exit( 0 );
      }
   }
);
```

register a **WindowListener** to listen for the application window's window events (such as closing the window). Lines 43 through 48 define an anonymous inner class that extends class **WindowAdapter** (which implements **WindowListener**). The anonymous inner class inherits a default implementation of seven different window-event-handler methods. Thus, the anonymous inner class already satisfies the requirement that in all methods an interface must be implemented. However, the default methods do nothing when they are called. So, we override method **windowClosing** at line 44 to terminate the application when the user clicks the application window's close box.

Notice that as you drag the mouse all the ovals remain on the window. This is due to a special feature of Swing GUI components called *double buffering* in which all drawing actually occurs in an image stored in memory, then the entire image is displayed on the window (or other GUI component, as we will see). This helps present smooth graphics display in a Swing GUI. We discuss double buffering in Chapter 16, "Multimedia."

The **MouseDetails** application of Fig. 12.20 demonstrates how to determine the number of mouse clicks (i.e., the click count) and how to distinguish between the different mouse buttons. The event listener in this program is an object of inner class **Mouse-ClickHandler** (line 43) that extends **MouseAdapter** so we can define just the **mouseClicked** method we need in this example.

```
1   // Fig. 12.20: MouseDetails.java
2   // Demonstrating mouse clicks and
3   // distinguishing between mouse buttons.
4   import javax.swing.*;
5   import java.awt.*;
6   import java.awt.event.*;
7
8   public class MouseDetails extends JFrame {
9      private String s = "";
10     private int xPos, yPos;
11
12     public MouseDetails()
13     {
14        super( "Mouse clicks and buttons" );
15
16        addMouseListener( new MouseClickHandler() );
17
18        setSize( 350, 150 );
19        show();
20     }
21
22     public void paint( Graphics g )
23     {
24        g.drawString( "Clicked @ [" + xPos + ", " + yPos + "]",
25                      xPos, yPos );
26     }
27
28     public static void main( String args[] )
29     {
30        MouseDetails app = new MouseDetails();
31
32        app.addWindowListener(
33           new WindowAdapter() {
34              public void windowClosing( WindowEvent e )
35              {
36                 System.exit( 0 );
37              }
38           }
39        );
40     }
41
```

Fig. 12.20   Distinguishing among left, center and right mouse button clicks (part 1 of 2).

```
42        // inner class to handle mouse events
43        private class MouseClickHandler extends MouseAdapter {
44           public void mouseClicked( MouseEvent e )
45           {
46              xPos = e.getX();
47              yPos = e.getY();
48
49              String s =
50                 "Clicked " + e.getClickCount() + " time(s)";
51
52              if ( e.isMetaDown() )        // Right mouse button
53                 s += " with right mouse button";
54              else if ( e.isAltDown() )   // Middle mouse button
55                 s += " with center mouse button";
56              else                        // Left mouse button
57                 s += " with left mouse button";
58
59              setTitle( s );  // set the title bar of the window
60              repaint();
61           }
62        }
63     }
```

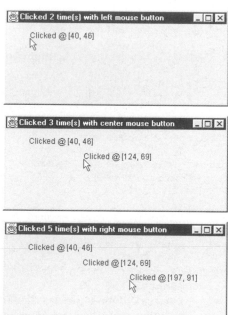

Fig. 12.20   Distinguishing among left, center and right mouse button clicks
(part 2 of 2).

A user of a Java program may be on a system with a one-, two- or three-button mouse. Java provides a mechanism to distinguish among mouse buttons. Class **MouseEvent** inherits several methods from class **InputEvent** that can distinguish between mouse buttons on a multi-button mouse or can mimic a multi-button mouse with a combined keystroke and mouse-button click. Figure 12.21 shows the **InputEvent** methods used to distinguish between mouse-button clicks. Java assumes that every mouse contains a left mouse button. Thus, it is simple to test for a left-mouse-button click. However, users with a one- or two-button mouse must use a combination of pressing keys on the keyboard and clicking the mouse at the same time to simulate the missing buttons on the mouse. In the case of a one- or two-button mouse, this program assumes that the center mouse button is clicked if the user holds the *Alt* key and clicks the left mouse button on a two-button mouse or the only mouse button on a one-button mouse. In the case of a one-button mouse, this program assumes that the right mouse button is clicked if the user holds the *Meta* key and clicks the mouse button.

Method **mouseClicked** (line 44) first captures the coordinates where the event occurred and stores them in instance variables **xPos** and **yPos** of class **MouseDetails**. Lines 49 and 50 create a string containing the number of mouse clicks (as returned by **MouseEvent** method *getClickCount* at line 50). The nested **if** structure at line 52 uses methods **isMetaDown** and **isAltDown** to determine which mouse button the user clicked and appends an appropriate string to **String s** in each case. The resulting string is displayed in the title bar of the window with method *setTitle* (inherited into class **JFrame** from class **Frame**) at line 59. Line 60 calls **repaint** to initiate a call to **paint** to draw a string at the location where the user clicked the mouse.

12.13 Keyboard Event Handling

This section presents the **KeyListener** event-listener interface for handling *key events*. Key events are generated when keys on the keyboard are pressed and released. A class that implements **KeyListener** must provide definitions for methods *keyPressed*, *key-Released* and *keyTyped*, each of which receives a *KeyEvent* as its argument. Class **KeyEvent** is a subclass of **InputEvent**. Method **keyPressed** is called in response to pressing any key. Method **keyTyped** is called in response to pressing any key that is not an *action key* (e.g., an arrow key, *Home*, *End*, *Page Up*, *Page Down*, a function key, *Num Lock*, *Print Screen*, *Scroll Lock*, *Caps Lock* and *Pause*). Method **keyReleased** is called when the key is released after any **keyPressed** or **keyTyped** event.

InputEvent method	Description
isMetaDown()	This method returns **true** when the user clicks the right mouse button on a mouse with two or three buttons. To simulate a right-mouse-button click on a one-button mouse, the user can press the *Meta* key on the keyboard and click the mouse button.
isAltDown()	This method returns **true** when the user clicks the middle mouse button on a mouse with three buttons. To simulate a middle-mouse-button click on a one- or two-button mouse, the user can press the *Alt* key on the keyboard and click the mouse button.

Fig. 12.21   InputEvent methods that help distinguish among left-, center- and right- mouse- button clicks.

Figure 12.22 demonstrates the **KeyListener** methods. Class **KeyDemo** implements the **KeyListener** interface, so all three methods are defined in the application.

```
1   // Fig. 12.22: KeyDemo.java
2   // Demonstrating keystroke events.
3   import javax.swing.*;
4   import java.awt.*;
5   import java.awt.event.*;
6
7   public class KeyDemo extends JFrame implements KeyListener {
8      private String line1 = "", line2 = "";
9      private String line3 = "";
10     private JTextArea textArea;
11
12     public KeyDemo()
13     {
14        super( "Demonstrating Keystroke Events" );
15
16        textArea = new JTextArea( 10, 15 );
17        textArea.setText( "Press any key on the keyboard..." );
18        textArea.setEnabled( false );
19
20        // allow frame to process Key events
21        addKeyListener( this );
22
23        getContentPane().add( textArea );
24
25        setSize( 350, 100 );
26        show();
27     }
28
29     public void keyPressed( KeyEvent e )
30     {
31        line1 = "Key pressed: " +
32                  e.getKeyText( e.getKeyCode() );
33        setLines2and3( e );
34     }
35
36     public void keyReleased( KeyEvent e )
37     {
38        line1 = "Key released: " +
39                  e.getKeyText( e.getKeyCode() );
40        setLines2and3( e );
41     }
42
43     public void keyTyped( KeyEvent e )
44     {
45        line1 = "Key typed: " + e.getKeyChar();
46        setLines2and3( e );
47     }
48
```

Fig. 12.22   Demonstrating key event handling (part 1 of 2).

```
49      private void setLines2and3( KeyEvent e )
50      {
51         line2 = "This key is " +
52                    ( e.isActionKey() ? "" : "not " ) +
53                    "an action key";
54
55         String temp =
56            e.getKeyModifiersText( e.getModifiers() );
57
58         line3 = "Modifier keys pressed: " +
59                    ( temp.equals( "" ) ? "none" : temp );
60
61         textArea.setText(
62            line1 + "\n" + line2 + "\n" + line3 + "\n" );
63      }
64
65      public static void main( String args[] )
66      {
67         KeyDemo app = new KeyDemo();
68
69         app.addWindowListener(
70            new WindowAdapter() {
71               public void windowClosing( WindowEvent e )
72               {
73                  System.exit( 0 );
74               }
75            }
76         );
77      }
78   }
```

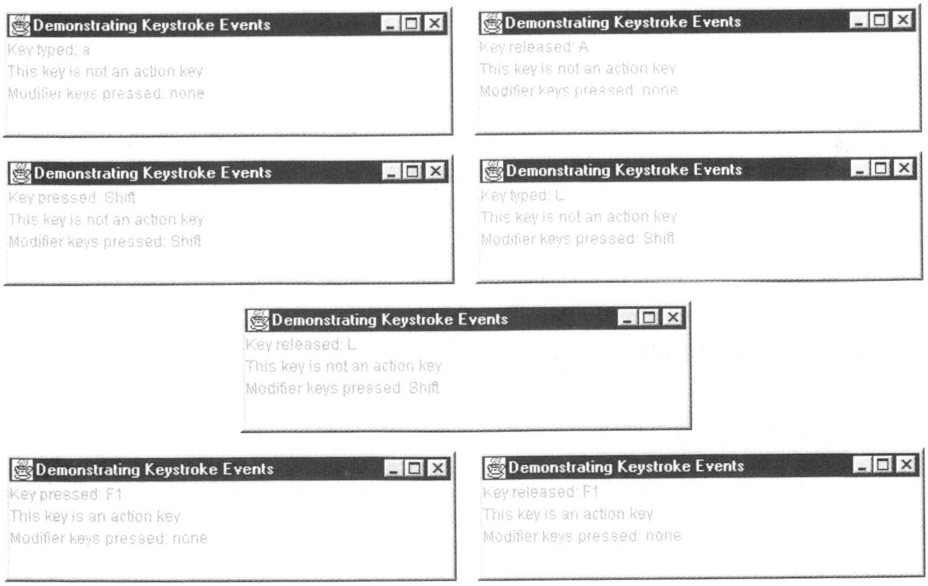

Fig. 12.22   Demonstrating key event handling (part 2 of 2).

The constructor (line 12) registers the application to handle its own key events with method **addKeyListener** at line 21. Method **addKeyListener** is defined in class **Component**, so every subclass of **Component** can notify **KeyListener**s of key events for that **Component**.

Line 23 in the constructor adds **JTextArea textArea** (where the program's output is displayed) to the content pane. Notice in the screen captures that **textArea** occupies the entire window. This is due to the content pane's default **BorderLayout** (discussed in Fig. 12.19 and later in this chapter). When a single **Component** is added to a **Border-Layout**, the **Component** occupies the entire **Container** by default.

Methods **keyPressed** (line 29) and **keyReleased** (line 36) use **KeyEvent** method **getKeyCode** to get the *virtual key code* of the key that was pressed. Class **KeyEvent** maintains a set of constants—the virtual key code constants—that represent every key on the keyboard. These constants can be compared with the return value of **get-KeyCode** to test for individual keys on the keyboard. The value returned by **getKey-Code** is passed to **KeyEvent** method **getKeyText**, which returns a **String** containing the name of the key that was pressed. For a complete list of virtual key constants, see the on-line documentation for class **KeyEvent** (package **java.awt.event**). Method **keyTyped** (line 43) uses **KeyEvent** method **getKeyChar** to get the Unicode value of the character typed.

All three event handling methods finish by calling method **setLines2and3** (line 49) and passing it the **KeyEvent** object. This method uses **KeyEvent** method **isActionKey** to determine if the key in the event was an action key. Also, **InputEvent** method **getModifiers** is called to determine if any modifier keys (such as *Shift*, *Alt* and *Ctrl*) were pressed when the key event occurred. The result of this method is passed to **KeyEvent** method **getKeyModifiersText**, which produces a string containing the names of the pressed modifier keys.

[*Note:* If you need to test for a specific key on the keyboard, class **KeyEvent** provides a *key constant* for every key on the keyboard. These constants can be used from the key event handlers to determine if a particular key was pressed. Also, to determine whether the *Alt*, *Ctrl*, *Meta* and *Shift* keys are pressed individually, **InputEvent** methods **isAlt-Down**, **isControlDown**, **isMetaDown** and **isShiftDown** each return a **boolean** indicating if the particular key was pressed during the key event.]

12.14 Layout Managers

Layout managers are provided to arrange GUI components on a container for presentation purposes. The layout managers provide basic layout capabilities that are easier to use than determining the exact position and size of every GUI component. This enables the programmer to concentrate on the basic "look and feel" and lets the layout managers process most of the layout details.

Look-and-Feel Observation 12.9

Most Java programming environments provide GUI design tools that help a programmer graphically design a GUI, then automatically write Java code to create the GUI.

Some GUI designers also allow the programmer to use the layout managers described here and in Chapter 13. Figure 12.23 summarizes the layout managers presented in this chapter. Other layout managers are discussed in Chapter 13.

Layout manager	Description
FlowLayout	Default for **java.awt.Applet**, **java.awt.Panel** and **javax.swing.JPanel**. Places components sequentially (left to right) in the order they were added. It is also possible to specify the order of the components using the **Container** method **add** that takes a **Component** and an integer index position as arguments.
BorderLayout	Default for the content panes of **JFrame**s (and other windows) and **JApplet**s. Arranges the components into five areas: North, South, East, West and Center.
GridLayout	Arranges the components into rows and columns.

Fig. 12.23   Layout managers.

Most previous applet and application examples in which we created our own GUI used layout manager *FlowLayout*. Class *FlowLayout* inherits from class **Object** and implements interface *LayoutManager*, which defines the methods a layout manager uses to arrange and size GUI components on a container.

12.14.1 FlowLayout

FlowLayout is the most basic layout manager. GUI components are placed on a container from left to right in the order in which they are added to the container. When the edge of the container is reached, components are continued on the next line. Class **FlowLayout** allows GUI components to be *left-aligned*, *centered* (the default) and *right-aligned*.

The application of Fig. 12.24 creates three **JButton** objects and adds them to the application using a **FlowLayout** layout manager. The components are automatically center-aligned. When the user clicks **Left,** the alignment for the layout manager is changed to a left-aligned **FlowLayout**. When the user clicks **Right**, the alignment for the layout manager is changed to a right-aligned **FlowLayout**. When the user clicks **Center**, the alignment for the layout manager is changed to a center-aligned **FlowLayout**. Each button has its own event handler that is defined with an inner class that implements **ActionListener**.

```
1   // Fig. 12.24: FlowLayoutDemo.java
2   // Demonstrating FlowLayout alignments.
3   import java.awt.*;
4   import java.awt.event.*;
5   import javax.swing.*;
6
7   public class FlowLayoutDemo extends JFrame {
8       private JButton left, center, right;
9       private Container c;
10      private FlowLayout layout;
```

Fig. 12.24   Program that demonstrates components in **FlowLayout** (part 1 of 3).

```
11
12    public FlowLayoutDemo()
13    {
14        super( "FlowLayout Demo" );
15
16        layout = new FlowLayout();
17
18        c = getContentPane();
19        c.setLayout( layout );
20
21        left = new JButton( "Left" );
22        left.addActionListener(
23            new ActionListener() {
24                public void actionPerformed( ActionEvent e )
25                {
26                    layout.setAlignment( FlowLayout.LEFT );
27
28                    // re-align attached components
29                    layout.layoutContainer( c );
30                }
31            }
32        );
33        c.add( left );
34
35        center = new JButton( "Center" );
36        center.addActionListener(
37            new ActionListener() {
38                public void actionPerformed( ActionEvent e )
39                {
40                    layout.setAlignment( FlowLayout.CENTER );
41
42                    // re-align attached components
43                    layout.layoutContainer( c );
44                }
45            }
46        );
47        c.add( center );
48
49        right = new JButton( "Right" );
50        right.addActionListener(
51            new ActionListener() {
52                public void actionPerformed( ActionEvent e )
53                {
54                    layout.setAlignment( FlowLayout.RIGHT );
55
56                    // re-align attached components
57                    layout.layoutContainer( c );
58                }
59            }
60        );
61        c.add( right );
62
```

Fig. 12.24   Program that demonstrates components in **FlowLayout** (part 2 of 3).

```
63            setSize( 300, 75 );
64            show();
65        }
66
67        public static void main( String args[] )
68        {
69            FlowLayoutDemo app = new FlowLayoutDemo();
70
71            app.addWindowListener(
72                new WindowAdapter() {
73                    public void windowClosing( WindowEvent e )
74                    {
75                        System.exit( 0 );
76                    }
77                }
78            );
79        }
80    }
```

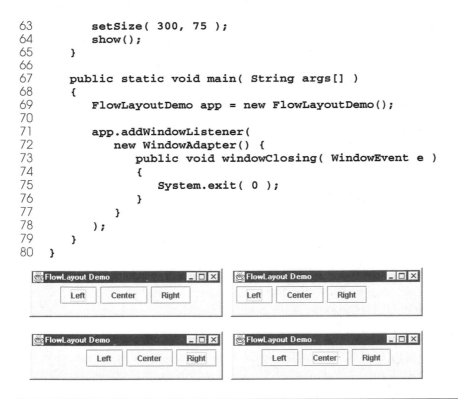

Fig. 12.24   Program that demonstrates components in **FlowLayout** (part 3 of 3).

As seen previously, a container's layout is set with method **setLayout** of class **Container**. Line 19

```
        c.setLayout( layout );
```

sets the content pane's layout manager to the **FlowLayout** defined at line 16. Normally, the layout is set before any GUI components are added to a container.

> **Look-and-Feel Observation 12.10**
>
> *Each container can have only one layout manager at a time (separate containers in the same program can have different layout managers).*

Each button's **actionPerformed** event handler executes two statements. For example, line 26 in method **actionPerformed** for button **left**

```
        layout.setAlignment( FlowLayout.LEFT );
```

uses **FlowLayout** method *setAlignment* to change the alignment for the **FlowLay-out** to a left-aligned (*FlowLayout.LEFT*) **FlowLayout**. Line 29

```
        layout.layoutContainer( c );
```

uses **LayoutManager** interface method *layoutContainer* to specify that the content pane should be rearranged based on the adjusted layout.

According to which button was clicked, the **actionPerformed** method for each button sets the **FlowLayout**'s alignment to **FlowLayout.LEFT**, *FlowLayout.CENTER* or *FlowLayout.RIGHT*.

12.14.2 BorderLayout

The *BorderLayout* layout manager (the default layout manager for the content pane) arranges components into five regions: *North, South, East, West and Center* (North corresponds to the top of the container). Class **BorderLayout** inherits from **Object** and implements interface *LayoutManager2* (a subinterface of **LayoutManager** that adds several methods for enhanced layout processing).

Up to five components can be added directly to a **BorderLayout**—one for each region. The components placed in the North and South regions extend horizontally to the sides of the container and are as tall as the components placed in those regions. The East and West regions expand vertically between the North and South regions and are as wide as the components placed in those regions. The component placed in the Center region expands to take all remaining space in the layout (this is the reason the **JTextArea** in Fig. 12.25 occupies the entire window). If all five regions are occupied, the entire container's space is covered by GUI components. If the North or South region is not occupied, the GUI components in the East, Center and West regions expand vertically to fill the remaining space. If the East or West region is not occupied, the GUI component in the Center region expands horizontally to fill the remaining space. If the Center region is not occupied, the area is left empty—the other GUI components do not expand to fill the remaining space.

The application of Fig. 12.25 demonstrates the **BorderLayout** layout manager using five **JButton**s.

```
1    // Fig. 12.25: BorderLayoutDemo.java
2    // Demonstrating BorderLayout.
3    import java.awt.*;
4    import java.awt.event.*;
5    import javax.swing.*;
6
7    public class BorderLayoutDemo extends JFrame
8                                  implements ActionListener {
9       private JButton b[];
10      private String names[] =
11         { "Hide North", "Hide South", "Hide East",
12           "Hide West", "Hide Center" };
13      private BorderLayout layout;
14
15      public BorderLayoutDemo()
16      {
17         super( "BorderLayout Demo" );
18
19         layout = new BorderLayout( 5, 5 );
20
```

Fig. 12.25   Demonstrating components in **BorderLayout** (part 1 of 3).

```
21          Container c = getContentPane();
22          c.setLayout( layout );
23
24          // instantiate button objects
25          b = new JButton[ names.length ];
26
27          for ( int i = 0; i < names.length; i++ ) {
28             b[ i ] = new JButton( names[ i ] );
29             b[ i ].addActionListener( this );
30          }
31
32          // order not important
33          c.add( b[ 0 ], BorderLayout.NORTH );   // North position
34          c.add( b[ 1 ], BorderLayout.SOUTH );   // South position
35          c.add( b[ 2 ], BorderLayout.EAST );    // East position
36          c.add( b[ 3 ], BorderLayout.WEST );    // West position
37          c.add( b[ 4 ], BorderLayout.CENTER );  // Center position
38
39          setSize( 300, 200 );
40          show();
41       }
42
43       public void actionPerformed( ActionEvent e )
44       {
45          for ( int i = 0; i < b.length; i++ )
46             if ( e.getSource() == b[ i ] )
47                b[ i ].setVisible( false );
48             else
49                b[ i ].setVisible( true );
50
51          // re-layout the content pane
52          layout.layoutContainer( getContentPane() );
53       }
54
55       public static void main( String args[] )
56       {
57          BorderLayoutDemo app = new BorderLayoutDemo();
58
59          app.addWindowListener(
60             new WindowAdapter() {
61                public void windowClosing( WindowEvent e )
62                {
63                   System.exit( 0 );
64                }
65             }
66          );
67       }
68    }
```

Fig. 12.25   Demonstrating components in **BorderLayout** (part 2 of 3).

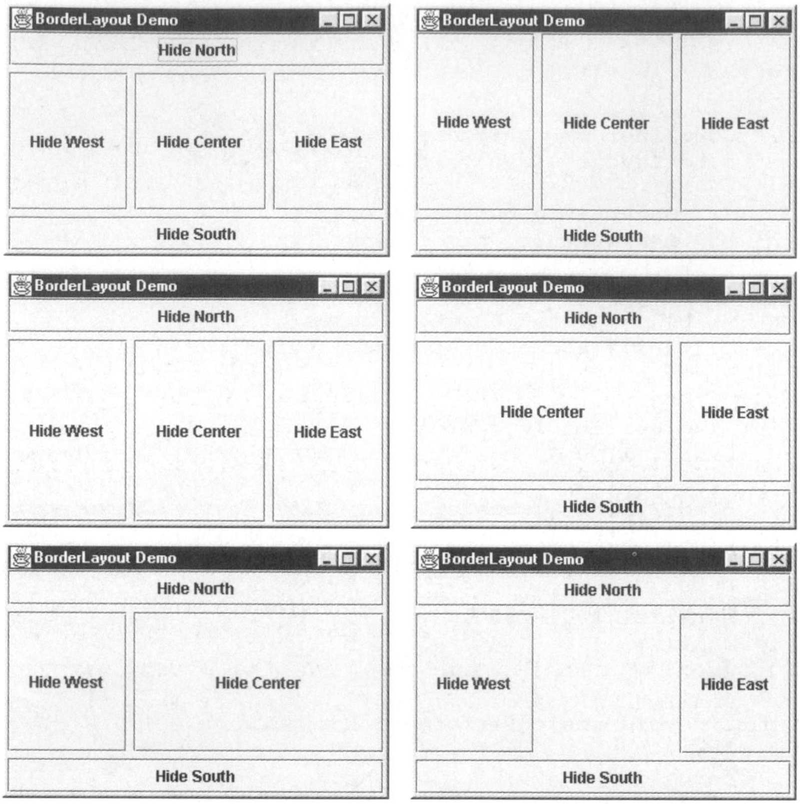

Fig. 12.25   Demonstrating components in **BorderLayout** (part 3 of 3).

Line 19 in the constructor

```
layout = new BorderLayout( 5, 5 );
```

defines a **BorderLayout**. The arguments specify the number of pixels between components that are arranged horizontally (*horizontal gap space*) and the number of pixels between components that are arranged vertically (*vertical gap space*), respectively. The default **BorderLayout** constructor supplies 0 pixels of gap space horizontally and vertically. Line 22 uses method **setLayout** to set the content pane's layout to **layout**.

Adding **Component**s to a **BorderLayout** requires a different **add** method from class **Container**, which takes two arguments—the **Component** to add and the region in which the **Component** will be placed. For example, line 33

```
add( b[ 0 ], BorderLayout.NORTH );   // North position
```

specifies that the **b[0]** is to be placed in the **NORTH** position. The components can be added in any order, but only one component can be added to each region.

Look-and-Feel Observation 12.11

*If no region is specified when adding a **Component** to a **BorderLayout**, it is assumed that the **Component** should be added to region **BorderLayout.CENTER***

Common Programming Error 12.6

*Adding more than one component to a particular region in a **BorderLayout** results in only the last component added being displayed. There is no error message to indicate this problem.*

When the user clicks on a particular **JButton** in the layout, method **actionPer-formed** (line 43) is called. The **for** loop at line 46 uses the following **if/else** structure:

```
if ( e.getSource() == b[ i ] )
   b[ i ].setVisible( false );
else
   b[ i ].setVisible( true );
```

to hide the particular **JButton** that generated the event. Method *setVisible* (inherited into **JButton** from class **Component**) is called with a **false** argument to hide the **JButton**. If the current **JButton** in the array is not the one that generated the event, method **setVisible** is called with a **true** argument to ensure that the **JButton** is displayed on the screen. Line 52

```
layout.layoutContainer( getContentPane() );
```

uses **LayoutManager** method **layoutContainer** to recalculate the layout of the content pane. Notice in the screen captures of Fig. 12.25 that certain regions in the **BorderLayout** change shape as **JButton**s are hidden and displayed in other regions. Try resizing the application window to see how the various regions resize based on the width and height of the window.

12.14.3 GridLayout

The *GridLayout* layout manager divides the container into a grid so that components can be placed in rows and columns. Class **GridLayout** inherits directly from class **Object** and implements interface **LayoutManager**. Every **Component** in a **GridLayout** has the same width and height. Components are added to a **GridLayout** starting at the top-left cell of the grid and proceeding left-to-right until the row is full. Then the process continues lcft-to-right on the next row of the grid, etc.

Figure 12.26 demonstrates the **GridLayout** layout manager using six **JButton**s.

```
1    // Fig. 12.26: GridLayoutDemo.java
2    // Demonstrating GridLayout.
3    import java.awt.*;
4    import java.awt.event.*;
5    import javax.swing.*;
6
7    public class GridLayoutDemo extends JFrame
8                               implements ActionListener {
9       private JButton b[];
10      private String names[] =
11         { "one", "two", "three", "four", "five", "six" };
```

Fig. 12.26   Program that demonstrates components in **GridLayout** (part 1 of 3).

```
12       private boolean toggle = true;
13       private Container c;
14       private GridLayout grid1, grid2;
15
16       public GridLayoutDemo()
17       {
18          super( "GridLayout Demo" );
19
20          grid1 = new GridLayout( 2, 3, 5, 5 );
21          grid2 = new GridLayout( 3, 2 );
22
23          c = getContentPane();
24          c.setLayout( grid1 );
25
26          // create and add buttons
27          b = new JButton[ names.length ];
28
29          for (int i = 0; i < names.length; i++ ) {
30             b[ i ] = new JButton( names[ i ] );
31             b[ i ].addActionListener( this );
32             c.add( b[ i ] );
33          }
34
35          setSize( 300, 150 );
36          show();
37       }
38
39       public void actionPerformed( ActionEvent e )
40       {
41          if ( toggle )
42             c.setLayout( grid2 );
43          else
44             c.setLayout( grid1 );
45
46          toggle = !toggle;
47          c.validate();
48       }
49
50       public static void main( String args[] )
51       {
52          GridLayoutDemo app = new GridLayoutDemo();
53
54          app.addWindowListener(
55             new WindowAdapter() {
56                public void windowClosing( WindowEvent e )
57                {
58                   System.exit( 0 );
59                }
60             }
61          );
62       }
63    }
```

Fig. 12.26   Program that demonstrates components in **GridLayout** (part 2 of 3).

Fig. 12.26   Program that demonstrates components in **GridLayout** (part 3 of 3).

Lines 20 and 21 in the constructor

```
grid1 = new GridLayout( 2, 3, 5, 5 );
grid2 = new GridLayout( 3, 2 );
```

define two **GridLayout** objects. The **GridLayout** constructor used at line 20 specifies a **GridLayout** with **2** rows, **3** columns, **5** pixels of horizontal-gap space between **Component**s in the grid and **5** pixels of vertical-gap space between **Component**s in the grid. The **GridLayout** constructor used at line 21 specifies a **GridLayout** with **3** rows, **2** columns and no gap space.

The **JButton** objects in this example initially are arranged using **grid1** (set for the content pane at line 24 with method **setLayout**). The first component is added to the first column of the first row. The next component is added to the second column of the first row, etc. When a **JButton** is pressed, method **actionPerformed** (line 39) is called. Every call to **actionPerformed** toggles the layout between **grid2** and **grid1**.

Line 47

```
c.validate();
```

illustrates another way to re-layout a container for which the layout has changed. **Container** method *validate* recomputes the container's layout based on the current layout manager for the **Container** and the current set of displayed GUI components.

12.15 Panels

Complex GUIs (like Fig. 12.1) require that each component be placed in an exact location. They often consist of multiple *panels* with each panel's components arranged in a specific layout. Panels are created with class *JPanel*—a subclass of **JComponent**. Class **JComponent** inherits from class **java.awt.Container**, so every **JPanel** is a **Container**. Thus **JPanel**s may have components, including other panels, added to them.

The program of Fig. 12.27 demonstrates how a **JPanel** can be used to create a more complex layout for **Component**s.

After **JPanel buttonPanel** is created at line 16, lines 19 and 20

```
buttonPanel.setLayout(
    new GridLayout( 1, buttons.length ) );
```

set **buttonPanel**'s layout to a **GridLayout** of one row and five columns (there are five **JButton**s in array **buttons**). The five **JButton**s in array **buttons** are added to the **JPanel** in the loop at line 24 with the statement

```
buttonPanel.add( buttons[ i ] );
```

```java
1   // Fig. 12.27: PanelDemo.java
2   // Using a JPanel to help lay out components.
3   import java.awt.*;
4   import java.awt.event.*;
5   import javax.swing.*;
6
7   public class PanelDemo extends JFrame {
8      private JPanel buttonPanel;
9      private JButton buttons[];
10
11     public PanelDemo()
12     {
13        super( "Panel Demo" );
14
15        Container c = getContentPane();
16        buttonPanel = new JPanel();
17        buttons = new JButton[ 5 ];
18
19        buttonPanel.setLayout(
20           new GridLayout( 1, buttons.length ) );
21
22        for ( int i = 0; i < buttons.length; i++ ) {
23           buttons[ i ] = new JButton( "Button " + (i + 1) );
24           buttonPanel.add( buttons[ i ] );
25        }
26
27        c.add( buttonPanel, BorderLayout.SOUTH );
28
29        setSize( 425, 150 );
30        show();
31     }
32
33     public static void main( String args[] )
34     {
35        PanelDemo app = new PanelDemo();
36
37        app.addWindowListener(
38           new WindowAdapter() {
39              public void windowClosing( WindowEvent e )
40              {
41                 System.exit( 0 );
42              }
43           }
44        );
45     }
46  }
```

Fig. 12.27 A **JPanel** with five **JButton**s in a **GridLayout** attached to the **SOUTH** region of a **BorderLayout** (part 1 of 2).

Notice that the buttons are added directly to the **JPanel**—class **JPanel** does not have a content pane like an applet or a **JFrame**. Line 27

```java
c.add( buttonPanel, BorderLayout.SOUTH );
```

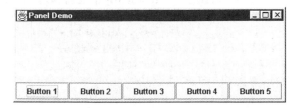

Fig. 12.27   A **JPanel** with five **JButton**s in a **GridLayout** attached to the **SOUTH** region of a **BorderLayout** (part 2 of 2).

uses the content pane's default **BorderLayout** to add **buttonPanel** to the **SOUTH** region. Note that the **SOUTH** region is as tall as the buttons on **buttonPanel**. A **JPanel** is sized to the components it contains. As more components are added, the **JPanel** grows (according to the restrictions of its layout manager) to accommodate the components. Resize the window to see how the layout manager affects the size of the **JButton**s.

Summary

- A graphical user interface (GUI) presents a pictorial interface to a program. A GUI (pronounced "GOO-EE") gives a program a distinctive "look" and "feel."

- By providing different applications with a consistent set of intuitive user interface components, GUIs allow the user to spend more time using the program in a productive manner.

- GUIs are built from GUI components (sometimes called controls or widgets). A GUI component is a visual object with which the user interacts via the mouse or the keyboard.

- Swing GUI components are defined in package **javax.swing**. Swing components are written, manipulated and displayed completely in Java.

- The original GUI components from the Abstract Windowing Toolkit package **java.awt** are tied directly to the local platform's graphical user interface capabilities.

- Swing components are lightweight components. AWT components are tied to the local platform and are called heavyweight components—they must rely on the local platform's windowing system to determine their functionality and their look and feel.

- Several Swing GUI components are heavyweight GUI components: in particular, subclasses of **java.awt.Window** (such as **JFrame**) that display windows on the screen. Heavyweight Swing GUI components are less flexible than lightweight components.

- Much of each Swing GUI component's functionality is inherited from classes **Component**, **Container** and **JComponent** (the superclass to most Swing components).

- A **Container** is an area where components can be placed.

- **JLabel**s provide text instructions or information on a GUI.

- **JComponent** method **setToolTipText** specifies the tool tip that is displayed automatically when the user positions the mouse cursor over a **JComponent** in the GUI.

- Many Swing components can display images by specifying an **Icon** as an argument to their constructor or by using a method **setIcon**.

- Class **ImageIcon** (package **javax.swing**) supports two image formats—Graphics Interchange Format (GIF) and Joint Photographic Experts Group (JPEG).

- Interface **SwingConstants** (package **javax.swing**) defines a set of common integer constants (such as **SwingConstants.LEFT**) that are used with many Swing components.

- By default, the text of a **JComponent** appears to the right of the image when the **JComponent** contains both text and an image.

- The horizontal and vertical alignments of a **JLabel** can be set with methods **setHorizontalAlignment** and **setVerticalAlignment**. Method **setText** sets the text displayed on the label. Method **getText** retrieves the current text displayed on a label. Methods **setHorizontalTextPosition** and **setVerticalTextPosition** specify the text position in a label.

- **JComponent** method **setIcon** sets the **Icon** displayed on a **JComponent**. Method **getIcon** retrieves the current **Icon** displayed on a **JComponent**.

- GUIs generate events when the user interacts with the GUI. Information about a GUI event is stored in an object of a class that extends **AWTEvent**.

- To process an event, the programmer must register an event listener and implement one or more event handlers.

- The use of event listeners in event handling is known as the delegation event model—the processing of an event is delegated to a particular object in the program.

- When an event occurs, the GUI component with which the user interacted notifies its registered listeners by calling each listener's appropriate event handling method.

- **JTextField**s and **JPasswordField**s are single-line areas in which text can be entered by the user from the keyboard or text can simply be displayed. A **JPasswordField** shows that a character was typed as the user enters characters, but automatically hides the characters.

- When the user types data into a **JTextField** or **JPasswordField** and presses the *Enter* key, an **ActionEvent** occurs.

- **JTextComponent** method **setEditable** determines whether the user can modify the text in a **JTextComponent**.

- **JPasswordField** method **getPassword** returns the password as an array of type **char**.

- Every **JComponent** contains an object of class **EventListenerList** (package **javax.swing.event**) called **listenerList** in which all registered listeners are stored.

- Every **JComponent** supports several different event types, including mouse events, key events and others. When an event occurs, the event is dispatched only to the event listeners of the appropriate type. Each event type has a corresponding event-listener interface.

- When an event is generated by a user interaction with a component, the component is handed a unique event ID specifying the event type. The GUI component uses the event ID to decide the type of listener to which the event should be dispatched and the event handler method to call.

- A **JButton** generates an **ActionEvent** when the user clicks the button with the mouse.

- An **AbstractButton** can have a rollover **Icon** that is displayed when the mouse is positioned over the button. The icon changes as the mouse moves in and out of the button's area on the screen. **AbstractButton** method **setRolloverIcon** specifies the image displayed on a button when the user positions the mouse over the button.

- The Swing GUI components contain three state button types—**JToggleButton**, **JCheckBox** and **JRadioButton**—that have on/off or true/false values. Classes **JCheckBox** and **JRadioButton** are subclasses of **JToggleButton**.

- When the user clicks a **JCheckBox**, an **ItemEvent** is generated that can be handled by an **ItemListener**. **ItemListener**s must define method **itemStateChanged**. **ItemEvent** method **getStateChange** determines the state of a **JToggleButton**.

- **JRadioButton**s are similar to **JCheckBox**es in that they have two states—selected and not selected (also called deselected). **JRadioButton**s normally appear as a group in which only one radio button can be selected at a time.

- The logical relationship between radio buttons is maintained by a **ButtonGroup** object.

- The **JRadioButton** constructor supplies the label that appears to the right of the **JRadioButton** by default and the initial state of the **JRadioButton**. A **true** second argument indicates that the **JRadioButton** should appear selected when it is displayed.

- **JRadioButton**s generate **ItemEvent**s when they are clicked.

- **ButtonGroup** method **add** associates a **JRadioButton** with a **ButtonGroup**. If more than one selected **JRadioButton** object is added to the group, the last selected **JRadioButton** added will be selected when the GUI is displayed.

- A **JComboBox** (sometimes called a drop-down list) provides a list of items from which the user can make a selection. **JComboBox**es generate **ItemEvent**s. A numeric index keeps track of the ordering of items in a **JComboBox**. The first item is added at index 0; the next item is added at index 1, and so forth. The first item added to a **JComboBox** appears as the currently selected item when the **JComboBox** is displayed. **JComboBox** method **getSelectedIndex** returns the index number of the selected item.

- A **JList** displays a series of items from which the user may select one or more items. Class **JList** supports single- and multiple-selection lists. When an item is clicked in a **JList**, a **ListSelectionEvent** occurs.

- **JList** method **setVisibleRowCount** determines the number of items that are visible in the list. Method **setSelectionMode** specifies the selection mode for the list.

- Class **JList** does not automatically provide a scrollbar if there are more items in the list than the number of visible rows. A **JScrollPane** object is used to provide the automatic scrolling capability for a **JList**.

- A **SINGLE_INTERVAL_SELECTION** list allows selection of a contiguous range of items by clicking the first item, then holding the Shift key while clicking the last item to select in the range.

- A **MULTIPLE_INTERVAL_SELECTION** list allows continuous range selection as described for a **SINGLE_INTERVAL_SELECTION** list and allows miscellaneous items to be selected by holding the *Ctrl* key while clicking each item to select.

- **JList** method **setFixedCellHeight** specifies the height in pixels of each item in a **JList**. Method **setFixedCellWidth** sets the width in pixels of a **JList**.

- Normally, an event generated by another GUI component (known as an external event) specifies when the multiple selections in a **JList** should be processed.

- **JList** method **setListData** sets the items displayed in a **JList**. Method **getSelected-Values** returns the selected items as an array of **Object**s.

- Mouse events can be trapped for any GUI component that derives from **java.awt.Component** using **MouseListener**s and **MouseMotionListener**s.

- Each mouse event handling method takes as its argument a **MouseEvent** object containing information about the mouse event and the location where the event occurred.

- Methods **addMouseListener** and **addMouseMotionListener** are **Component** methods used to register mouse event listeners for an object of any class that extends **Component**.

- Many of the event-listener interfaces provide multiple methods. For each there is a corresponding event listener adapter class that provides a default implementation of every method in the interface. The programmer can extend the adapter class to inherit the default implementation of every method and simply override the method or methods needed for event handling in the program.

- **MouseEvent** method **getClickCount** returns the number of mouse clicks.

- **InputEvent** methods **isMetaDown** and **isAltDown** are used to determine which mouse button the user clicked.

- **KeyListener**s handle key events that are generated when keys on the keyboard are pressed and released. A **KeyListener** must provide definitions for methods **keyPressed**, **keyReleased** and **keyTyped**, each of which receives a **KeyEvent** as its argument.

- Method **keyPressed** is called in response to pressing any key. Method **keyTyped** is called in response to pressing any key that is not an action key (i.e., an arrow key, *Home*, *End*, *Page Up*, *Page Down*, a function key, *Num Lock*, *Print Screen*, *Scroll Lock*, *Caps Lock* and *Pause*). Method **keyReleased** is called when the key is released after any **keyPressed** or **keyTyped** event.

- **KeyEvent** method **getKeyCode** gets the virtual key code of the key that was pressed. Class **KeyEvent** maintains a set of virtual key code constants that represent every key on the keyboard.

- **KeyEvent** method **getKeyText** returns a **String** containing the name of the key that corresponds to its virtual key code argument. Method **getKeyChar** gets the Unicode value of the character typed. Method **isActionKey** determines if the key in the event was an action key.

- **InputEvent** method **getModifiers** determines if any modifier keys (such as *Shift*, *Alt* and *Ctrl*) were pressed when the key event occurred. **KeyEvent** method **getKeyModifiersText** produces a string containing the names of the pressed modifier keys.

- Layout managers arrange GUI components on a container for presentation purposes.

- **FlowLayout** lays out components from left to right in the order in which they are added to the container. When the edge of the container is reached, components are continued on the next line.

- **FlowLayout** method **setAlignment** changes the alignment for the **FlowLayout** to **FlowLayout.LEFT**, **FlowLayout.CENTER** or **FlowLayout.RIGHT**.

- The **BorderLayout** layout manager arranges components into five regions: North, South, East, West and Center. One component can be added to each region.

- **LayoutManager** method **layoutContainer** recalculates the layout of its **Container** argument.

- The **GridLayout** layout manager divides the container into a grid of rows and columns. Components are added to a **GridLayout** starting at the top-left cell and proceeding left-to-right until the row is full. Then the process continues left-to-right on the next row of the grid, etc.

- **Container** method **validate** recomputes the container's layout based on the current layout manager for the **Container** and the current set of displayed GUI components.

- Panels are created with class **JPanel**, which inherits from class **JComponent**. **JPanel**s may have components, including other panels, added to them.

Terminology

Abstract Windowing Toolkit	assistive technologies
AbstractButton class	**BorderLayout** class
ActionEvent class	**BorderLayout.CENTER**
ActionListener interface	**BorderLayout.EAST**
actionPerformed method	**BorderLayout.NORTH**
adapter class	**BorderLayout.SOUTH**
add method of **ButtonGroup**	**BorderLayout.WEST**
add method of class **Container**	button
addItemListener method	button label
addKeyListener method	**ButtonGroup** class
addListSelectionListener method	centered
addMouseListener method	check box
addMouseMotionListener method	check box label

command button
Component class
ComponentAdapter class
ComponentListener interface
Container class
ContainerAdapter class
ContainerListener interface
control
delegation event model
dispatch an event
dragging
drop-down list
event
event driven
event handler
event ID
event listener
event-listener interface
EventListenerList class
EventObject class
FlowLayout class
FlowLayout.CENTER
FlowLayout.LEFT
FlowLayout.RIGHT
focus
FocusAdapter class
FocusListener interface
Font.BOLD
Font.ITALIC
Font.PLAIN
getActionCommand method
getClickCount method
getIcon method
getKeyChar method of **KeyEvent**
getKeyCode method of **KeyEvent**
getKeyModifiersText method
getKeyText method of **KeyEvent**
getModifiers method of **InputEvent**
getPassword method of **JPasswordField**
getSelectedIndex method of **JComboBox**
getSelectedIndex method of **JList**
getSelectedValues method of **JList**
getSource method of **ActionEvent**
getStateChange method of **ItemEvent**
getText method of **JLabel**
getX method of **MouseEvent**
getY method of **MouseEvent**
.gif file name extension
Graphics Interchange Format (GIF)
GridLayout class

GUI component
heavyweight component
horizontal gap space
Icon interface
ImageIcon class
InputEvent class
isActionKey method of **KeyEvent**
isAltDown method of **InputEvent**
isMetaDown method of **InputEvent**
ItemEvent class
ItemEvent.DESELECTED
ItemEvent.SELECTED
ItemListener interface
itemStateChanged method
java.awt package
java.awt.event package
javax.swing package
javax.swing.event package
JButton class
JCheckBox class
JComboBox class
JComponent class
JLabel class
JList class
Joint Photographic Experts Group (JPEG)
JPanel class
JPasswordField class
.jpg file name extension
JRadioButton class
JScrollPane class
JTextComponent class
JTextField class
JToggleButton class
KeyAdapter class
KeyEvent class
KeyListener interface
keyPressed method of **KeyListener**
keyReleased method of **KeyListener**
keyTyped method of **KeyListener**
label
layout manager
layoutContainer method
LayoutManger interface
left aligned
left justified
lightweight component
"listen" for an event
ListSelectionEvent class
ListSelectionListener interface
ListSelectionModel interface

look-and-feel
menu
menu bar
MouseAdapter class
mouseClicked method
mouseDragged method
mouseEntered method
MouseEvent class
mouseExited method
MouseListener interface
MouseMotionAdapter class
MouseMotionListener interface
mouseMoved method
mousePressed method
mouseReleased method
multiple-selection list
password
pluggable look and feel
radio button
read-only text
register an event listener
right-aligned
rollover icon
scroll arrow
scroll box
scrollbar
selection mode
setAlignment method
setBackground method
setEditable method
setFixedCellHeight method

setFixedCellWidth method
setHorizontalAlignment method
setHorizontalTextPosition method
setIcon method
setLayout method of class **Container**
setListData method of **JList**
setMaximumRowCount method
setRolloverIcon method
setSelectionMode method
setText method
setToolTipText method
setVerticalAlignment method
setVerticalTextPosition method
setVisible method
setVisibleRowCount method
shortcut key (mnemonics)
single-selection list
Swing GUI component
SwingConstants interface
tool tips
toolbar
user interface localization
validate method
valueChanged method
vertical gap space
widget (window gadget)
window
WindowAdapter class
windowClosing method
windowing system
WindowListener interface

Common Programming Errors

12.1   Forgetting to add a component to a container so it can be displayed is a run-time logic error.

12.2   Adding to a container a component that has not been instantiated throws a **NullPointer-Exception**.

12.3   Using a lowercase **f** in the class names **JTextField** or **JPasswordField** is a syntax error.

12.4   Forgetting to register an event handler object for a particular GUI component's event type results in no events being handled for that component for that event type.

12.5   Adding a **ButtonGroup** object (or an object of any other class that does not derive from **Component**) to a container is a syntax error.

12.6   Adding more than one component to a particular region in a **BorderLayout** results in only the last component added being displayed. There is no error message to indicate this problem.

Good Programming Practices

12.1   Study the methods of class **Component** in the Java 2 SDK on-line documentation to learn the capabilities common to most GUI components.

12.2   Study the methods of class **Container** in the Java 2 SDK on-line documentation to learn the capabilities common to every container for GUI components.

12.3   Study the methods of class **JComponent** in the Java 2 SDK on-line documentation to learn the capabilities common to every container for GUI components.

12.4   Study the methods of class **javax.swing.JLabel** in the Java 2 SDK on-line documentation to learn the complete capabilities of the class before using it.

12.5   Use separate classes to process GUI events.

Look-and-Feel Observations

12.1   Consistent user interfaces also enable a user to learn new applications faster.

12.2   Because Swing components are written in Java, they provide a greater level of portability and flexibility than the original Java GUI components from package **java.awt**.

12.3   Use tool tips (set with **JComponent** method **setToolTipText**) to add descriptive text to your GUI components. This text helps the user determine the GUI component's purpose in the user interface.

12.4   Having more than one **JButton** with the same label makes the **JButton**s ambiguous to the user. Be sure to provide a unique label for each button.

12.5   Using rollover icons for **JButton**s provides the user with visual feedback indicating that if they click the mouse the button's action will occur.

12.6   Because class **AbstractButton** supports displaying text and images on a button, all subclasses of **AbstractButton** also support displaying text and images.

12.7   Set the maximum row count for a **JComboBox** to a number of rows that prevents the list from expanding outside the bounds of the window or applet in which it is used. This will ensure that the list displays correctly when it is expanded by the user.

12.8   Method calls to **mouseDragged** are sent to the **MouseMotionListener** for the **Component** on which the drag operation started. Similarly, the **mouseReleased** method call is sent to the **MouseListener** for the **Component** on which the drag operation started.

12.9   Most Java programming environments provide GUI design tools that help a programmer graphically design a GUI, then automatically write Java code to create the GUI.

12.10   Each container can have only one layout manager at a time (separate containers in the same program can have different layout managers).

12.11   If no region is specified when adding a **Component** to a **BorderLayout**, it is assumed that the **Component** should be added to region **BorderLayout.CENTER**.

Portability Tip

12.1   The look of a GUI defined with heavyweight GUI components from package **java.awt** may vary across platforms. Heavyweight components "tie" into the "local" platform GUI, which varies from platform to platform.

Software Engineering Observations

12.1   To effectively use GUI components, the **javax.swing** and **java.awt** inheritance hierarchies must be understood—especially class **Component**, class **Container** and class **JComponent**, which define features common to most Swing components.

12.2   The event listener for an event must implement the appropriate event-listener interface.

12.3   Using separate classes to handle GUI events leads to more reusable, reliable and readable software components that can be placed in packages and used in many programs.

12.4   Any subclass of a class that implements an interface has the "is a" relationship in all of its direct and indirect superclasses and all of the interfaces that are implemented by the direct and indirect superclasses. Thus, an object of a subclass of an event adapter class is an object of the corresponding event listener type (e.g., an object of a subclass of **MouseAdapter** is a **MouseListener**).

Self-Review Exercises

12.1 Fill in the blanks in each of the following:
a) Method _____ is called when the mouse is moved and an event listener is registered to handle the event.
b) Text that cannot be modified by the user is called _____ text.
c) A _____ arranges GUI components on a **Container**.
d) The **add** method for attaching GUI components is a _____ class method.
e) GUI is an acronym for _____.
f) Method _____ is used to set the layout manager for a container.
g) A **mouseDragged** method call is preceded by a _____ method call and followed by a _____ method call.

12.2 State whether each of the following is *true* or *false*. If *false*, explain why.
a) **BorderLayout** is the default layout manager for a content pane.
b) When the mouse cursor is moved into the bounds of a GUI component, method **mouseOver** is called.
c) A **JPanel** cannot be added to another **JPanel**.
d) In a **BorderLayout**, two buttons added to the **NORTH** region will be placed side-by-side.
e) When using **BorderLayout**, a maximum of five components may be used.

12.3 Find the error(s) in each of the following and explain how to correct it (them).
a) `buttonName = JButton( "Caption" );`
b) `JLabel aLabel, JLabel;     // create references`
c) `txtField = new JTextField( 50, "Default Text" );`
d) `Container c = getContentPane();`
   `setLayout( new BorderLayout() );`
   `button1 = new JButton( "North Star" );`
   `button2 = new JButton( "South Pole" );`
   `c.add( button1 );`
   `c.add( button2 );`

Answers to Self-Review Exercises

12.1 a) **mouseMoved**. b) uneditable (read-only). c) layout manager. d) **Container**. e) graphical user interface. f) **setLayout**. g) **mousePressed**, **mouseReleased**.

12.2 a) True.
b) False. Method **mouseEntered** is called.
c) False. A **JPanel** can be added to another **JPanel** because **JPanel** derives indirectly from **Component**. Therefore, a **JPanel** is a **Component**. Any **Component** can be added to a **Container**.
d) False. Only the last button added will be displayed. Remember that only one component can be added to each region in a **BorderLayout**.
e) True.

12.3 a) **new** is needed to instantiate the object.
b) **JLabel** is a class name and cannot be used as a variable name.
c) The arguments passed to the constructor are reversed. The **String** must be passed first.
d) **BorderLayout** has been set and components are being added without specifying the region. Proper **add** statements might be

```
c.add( button1, BorderLayout.NORTH );
c.add( button2, BorderLayout.SOUTH );
```

Exercises

12.4 Fill in the blanks in each of the following:
   a) The **JTextField** class inherits directly from _____.
   b) The layout managers discussed in this chapter are _____, _____ and _____.
   c) **Container** method _____ attaches a GUI component to a container.
   d) Method _____ is called when a mouse button is released (without moving the mouse).
   e) The _____ class is used to create a group of **JRadioButton**s.

12.5 State whether each of the following is *true* or *false*. If *false*, explain why.
   a) Only one layout manager can be used per **Container**.
   b) GUI components can be added to a **Container** in any order in a **BorderLayout**.
   c) **JRadioButton**s provide a series of mutually exclusive options (only one can be **true** at a time).
   d) **Graphics** method **setFont** is used to set the font for text fields.
   e) A **JList** displays a scrollbar if there are more items in the list than can be displayed.
   f) A **Mouse** object contains a method called **mouseDragged**.

12.6 State whether each of the following is *true* or *false*. If *false*, explain why.
   a) A **JApplet** does not have a content pane.
   b) A **JPanel** is a **JComponent**.
   c) A **JPanel** is a **Component**.
   d) A **JLabel** is a **Container**.
   e) A **JList** is a **JPanel**.
   f) An **AbstractButton** is a **JButton**.
   g) A **JTextField** is an **Object**.
   h) **ButtonGroup** inherits from **JComponent**.

12.7 Find any error(s) in each of the following and explain how to correct it (them).
   a) **import javax.swing.***   **// include swing package**
   b) **panelObject.GridLayout(8, 8); // set GridLayout**
   c) **c.setLayout(new FlowLayout(FlowLayout.DEFAULT));**
   d) **c.add(eastButton, EAST);   // BorderLayout**

12.8 Create the following GUI. You do not have to provide any functionality.

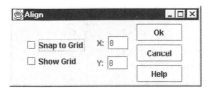

12.9 Create the following GUI. You do not have to provide any functionality.

12.10   Create the following GUI. You do not have to provide any functionality.

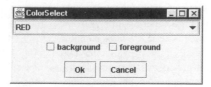

12.11   Create the following GUI. You do not have to provide any functionality.

12.12   Write a temperature conversion program that converts from Fahrenheit to Celsius. The Fahrenheit temperature should be entered from the keyboard (via a **JTextField**). A **JLabel** should be used to display the converted temperature. Use the following formula for the conversion:

$$Celsius = 5/9 \infty (Fahrenheit - 32)$$

12.13   Enhance the temperature conversion program of Exercise 12.12 by adding the Kelvin temperature scale. The program should also allow the user to make conversions between any two scales. Use the following formula for the conversion between Kelvin and Celsius (in addition to the formula in Exercise 12.12):

$$Kelvin = Celsius + 273$$

12.14   Write an application that allows the user to draw a rectangle by dragging the mouse on the application window. The upper-left coordinate should be the location where the user presses the mouse button, and the lower-right coordinate should be the location where the user releases the mouse button. Also display the area of the rectangle in a **JLabel** in the **SOUTH** region of a **BorderLayout**. Use the following formula for the area:

$$area = width \infty height$$

12.15   Modify the program of Exercise. 12.14 to draw different shapes. The user should be allowed to choose from an oval, an arc, a line, a rectangle with rounded corners and a predefined polygon. Also display the mouse coordinates in the status bar.

12.16   Write a program that will allow the user to draw a shape with the mouse. The shape to draw should be determined by a **KeyEvent** using the following keys: *c* draws a circle, *o* draws an oval, *r* draws a rectangle and *l* draws a line. The size and placement of the shape should be determined by the **mousePressed** and **mouseReleased** events. Display the name of the current shape in a **JLabel** in the **SOUTH** region of a **BorderLayout**. The initial shape should default to a circle.

12.17   Create an application that enables the user to paint a picture. The user should be able to choose the shape to draw, the color in which the shape should appear and whether the shape should be filled with color. Use the graphical user interface components we discussed in this chapter, such as **JComboBox**es, **JRadioButton**s and **JCheckBox**es, to allow the user to select various options. The program should provide a **JButton** object that allows the user to erase the window.

12.18   Write a program that uses **System.out.println** statements to print out events as they occur. Provide a **JComboBox** with a minimum of four items. The user should be able to choose an event to "monitor" from the **JComboBox**. When that particular event occurs, display information about the event in a message dialog box. Use method **toString** on the event object to convert it to a string representation.

12.19 Write a program that draws a square. As the mouse moves over the drawing area, repaint the square with the upper-left corner of the square following the exact path of the mouse cursor.

12.20 Modify the program of Fig. 12.19 to incorporate colors. Provide a "toolbar" of **JRadioButton** objects at the bottom of the window that lists the following six colors: red, black, magenta, blue, green and yellow. The toolbar should consist of six buttons, each with the appropriate color name. When a new color is selected, drawing should occur in the new color.

12.21 Write a program that plays "guess the number" as follows: Your program chooses the number to be guessed by selecting an integer at random in the range 1–1000. The program then displays in a label:

> **I have a number between 1 and 1000 can you guess my number?**
> **Please enter your first guess.**

A **JTextField** should be used to input the guess. As each guess is input the background color should change to either red or blue. Red indicates that the user is getting "warmer" and blue indicates that the user is getting "colder." A **JLabel** should display either "**Too High**" or "**Too Low**" to help the user zero in on the correct answer. When the user gets the correct answer, "**Correct!**" should be displayed and the **JTextField** used for input should be changed to uneditable. A **JButton** should be provided to allow the user to play the game again. When the **JButton** is clicked, a new random number should be generated and the input **JTextField** changed to editable.

12.22 It is often useful to display the events that occur during the execution of a program to help understand when the events occur and how they are generated. Write a program that enables the user to generate and process every event discussed in this chapter. The program should provide methods from the **ActionListener**, **ItemListener**, **ListSelectionListener**, **MouseListener**, **MouseMotionListener** and **KeyListener** interfaces to display messages when the events occur. Use method **toString** to convert the event objects received in each event handler into a **String** that can be displayed. Method **toString** creates a **String** containing all the information in the event object.

12.23 Modify your solution to Exercise 12.17 to enable the user to select a font and a font size, then type text into a **JTextField**. When the user presses *Enter,* the text should be displayed on the background in the chosen font and size. Modify the program further to allow the user to specify the exact position at which the text should be displayed.

12.24 Write a program that allows the user to select a shape from a **JComboBox**, then draws that shape 20 times with random locations and dimensions in method **paint**. The first item in the **JComboBox** should be the default shape that is displayed the first time **paint** is called.

12.25 Modify Exercise 12.24 to draw each of the 20 randomly sized shapes in a randomly selected color. Use all 13 predefined **Color** objects in an array of **Color**s.

12.26 Modify Exercise 12.25 to allow the user to select the color in which shapes should be drawn from a **JColorChooser** dialog.

12.27 Write a program using methods from interface **MouseListener** that allows the user to press the mouse button, drag the mouse and release the mouse button. When the mouse is released, draw a rectangle with the appropriate upper-left corner, width and height. (*Hint:* The **mousePressed** method should capture the set of coordinates at which the user presses and holds the mouse button initially, and the **mouseReleased** method should capture the set of coordinates at which the user releases the mouse button. Both methods should store the appropriate coordinate values. All calculations of the width, height and upper-left corner should be performed by the **paint** method before the shape is drawn.)

12.28   Modify Exercise 12.27 to provided a "rubber-banding" effect. As the user drags the mouse, the user should be able to see the current size of the rectangle to know exactly what the rectangle will look like when the mouse button is released. (*Hint:* Method **mouseDragged** should perform the same tasks as **mouseReleased**.)

12.29   Modify Exercise 12.28 to allow the user to select which shape to draw. A **JComboBox** should provide options including at least rectangle, oval, line and rounded rectangle.

12.30   Modify Exercise 12.29 to allow the user to select the drawing color from a **JColor-Chooser** dialog box.

12.31   Modify Exercise 12.30 to allow the user to specify if a shape should be filled or empty when it is drawn. The user should click a **JCheckBox** to indicate filled or empty.

12.32   *(Painting program)* Using the techniques of Exercises 9.28, 9.29, 12.27 through 12.30 and the graphics techniques of Chapter 11, rewrite Exercise 12.31 to allow the user to draw multiple shapes and store each shape in an array of shapes (if you feel ambitious, investigate the capabilities of class **Vector** in Chapter 23). For this program, create your own classes (like those in the class hierarchy described in Exercises 9.28 and 9.29) from which objects will be created to store each shape the user draws. The classes should store the location, dimensions and color of each shape and should indicate if the shape is filled or unfilled. Your classes should all derive from a class called **MyShape** that has all the common features of every shape type. Every subclass of **MyShape** should have its own method **draw**, which returns **void** and receives a **Graphics** object as its argument. When the application window's **paint** method is called, it should walk through the array of shapes and display each shape by polymorphically calling the shape's **draw** method (passing the **Graphics** object as an argument). Each shape's **draw** method should know how to draw the shape. As a minimum, your program should provide the following classes: **MyLine**, **MyOval**, **MyRect**, **MyRoundRect**. Design the class hierarchy for maximum software reuse and place all your classes in the package **shapes**. Import this package into your program.

12.33   Modify Exercise 12.32 to provide an **Undo** button that can be used repeatedly to undo the last painting operation. If there are no shapes in the array of shapes, the Undo button should be disabled.

13

Advanced Graphical User Interface Components

Objectives

- To create and manipulate text areas, sliders, menus, popup menus and windows.
- To be able to create customized **JPanel** objects.
- To be able to create a program that can execute as either an applet or an application.
- To be able to change the look-and-feel of a GUI using Swing's pluggable look-and-feel (PLAF).
- To be able to create a multiple document interface with **JDesktopPane** and **JInternalFrame**.
- To be ablc to use advanced layout managers.

I claim not to have controlled events, but confess plainly that events have controlled me.
Abraham Lincoln

A good symbol is the best argument, and is a missionary to persuade thousands.
Ralph Waldo Emerson

Capture its reality in paint!
Paul Cézanne

Outline

13.1 Introduction[1]

In this chapter, we continue our study of GUIs. We discuss more advanced components and layout managers and lay the groundwork for building complex GUIs.

We begin our discussion with another text-based GUI component—*JTextArea*—which allows multiple lines of text to be displayed or input. We continue with two examples of *customizing class **JPanel*** in which we discuss issues that relate to painting on Swing GUI components. These examples will help resolve several issues you may have encountered in earlier exercises.

Next, we illustrate how to design a Java program that can execute as both an applet and an application. An important aspect of any complete GUI is a system of *menus* that enable the user to effectively perform tasks in the program. The next two examples discuss how to create and use menus.

The look-and-feel of a Swing GUI can be uniform across all platforms on which the Java program is executed, or the GUI can be customized using Swing's *pluggable look-and-feel (PLAF)*. The next example illustrates how to change between Swing's default *metal look-and-feel*, a look-and-feel that simulates *Motif* (a popular UNIX look-and-feel) and one that simulates Microsoft's Windows look-and-feel.

Many of today's applications use a *multiple document interface (MDI),* [i.e., a main window (often called the *parent window*) containing other windows (often called *child win-*

---

1. This chapter was coauthored with Mr. Tem Nieto of Deitel & Associates, Inc.

dows] to manage several open *documents* that are being processed in parallel. For example, many email programs allow you to have several email windows open at the same time so you can compose and/or read multiple email messages. The next example discusses Swing's classes that provide support for creating multiple document interfaces.

Finally, the chapter finishes with a series of examples discussing several advanced layout managers for organizing graphical user interfaces.

Swing is a large and complex topic. There are many more GUI components and capabilities than can be presented here. Several more Swing GUI components are introduced in the remaining chapters of this book as they are needed. Our book *Advanced Java How to Program* will discuss other more advanced Swing components and capabilities.

13.2 JTextArea

*JTextArea*s provide an area for manipulating multiple lines of text. Like class **JTextField**, class **JTextArea** inherits from **JTextComponent**, which defines common methods for **JTextField**s, **JTextArea**s and several other text-based GUI components.

The application of Fig. 13.1 demonstrates **JTextArea**s. One **JTextArea** displays text that the user can select. The other **JTextArea** is uneditable. Its purpose is to display the text the user selected in the first **JTextArea**. **JTextArea**s do not have action events like **JTextField**s. Often, an *external event*, (i.e., an event generated by a different GUI component) indicates when the text in a **JTextArea** should be processed. For example, when typing an email message, you often click a **Send** button to take the text of the message and send it to the recipient. Similarly, when editing a document in a word processor, you normally save the file by selecting a menu item called **Save** or **Save As...**. In this program, the button **Copy >>>** generates the external event that causes the selected text in the left **JTextArea** to be copied and displayed in the right **JTextArea**.

> *Look-and-Feel Observation 13.1*
>
> *Often an external event determines when the text in a **JTextArea** should be processed.*

```
1    // Fig. 13.1: TextAreaDemo.java
2    // Copying selected text from one text area to another.
3    import java.awt.*;
4    import java.awt.event.*;
5    import javax.swing.*;
6
7    public class TextAreaDemo extends JFrame {
8       private JTextArea t1, t2;
9       private JButton copy;
10
11      public TextAreaDemo()
12      {
13         super( "TextArea Demo" );
14
15         Box b = Box.createHorizontalBox();
16
```

Fig. 13.1   Copying selected text from one text area to another (part 1 of 3).

```
17          String s = "This is a demo string to\n" +
18                     "illustrate copying text\n" +
19                     "from one TextArea to \n" +
20                     "another TextArea using an\n"+
21                     "external event\n";
22
23          t1 = new JTextArea( s, 10, 15 );
24          b.add( new JScrollPane( t1 ) );
25
26          copy = new JButton( "Copy >>>" );
27          copy.addActionListener(
28             new ActionListener() {
29                public void actionPerformed( ActionEvent e )
30                {
31                   t2.setText( t1.getSelectedText() );
32                }
33             }
34          );
35          b.add( copy );
36
37          t2 = new JTextArea( 10, 15 );
38          t2.setEditable( false );
39          b.add( new JScrollPane( t2 ) );
40
41          Container c = getContentPane();
42          c.add( b );     // Box placed in BorderLayout.CENTER
43          setSize( 425, 200 );
44          show();
45       }
46
47       public static void main( String args[] )
48       {
49          TextAreaDemo app = new TextAreaDemo();
50
51          app.addWindowListener(
52             new WindowAdapter() {
53                public void windowClosing( WindowEvent e )
54                {
55                   System.exit( 0 );
56                }
57             }
58          );
59       }
60    }
```

Fig. 13.1   Copying selected text from one text area to another (part 2 of 3).

In the constructor method, line 15

```
Box b = Box.createHorizontalBox();
```

creates a *Box container* (package `javax.swing`) to which the GUI components will be attached. Class **Box** is a subclass of `java.awt.Container` that uses a *BoxLayout* layout manager to arrange the GUI components either horizontally or vertically. The **Box-Layout** layout manager is discussed in detail in Section 13.13. Class **Box** provides static

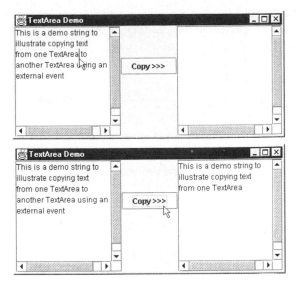

Fig. 13.1   Copying selected text from one text area to another (part 3 of 3).

method ***createHorizontalBox*** to create a **Box** that automatically arranges the components attached to it from left to right in the order that the components are attached.

The application instantiates **JTextArea** objects **t1** (line 23) and **t2** (line 37). Each **JTextArea** has **10** visible rows and **15** visible columns. Line 23

```
t1 = new JTextArea( s, 10, 15 );
```

specifies that the default string **s** should be displayed in the **JTextArea**. A **JTextArea** does not provide scrollbars in the event that there is more text than can be displayed in the **JTextArea**. For this reason, line 24

```
b.add( new JScrollPane( t1 ) );
```

creates a **JScrollPane** object that is initialized with **JTextArea t1** and both horizontal and vertical scrolling as necessary. The **JScrollPane** object is then added directly to the **Box** container **b**.

Lines 26 through 35 instantiate **JButton** object **copy** with the label "**Copy >>>**," create an anonymous inner class to handle **copy**'s **ActionEvent** and add **copy** to the **Box** container **b**. This button provides the external event that determines when the selected text in **t1** should be copied to **t2**. When the user clicks **copy**, line 31

```
t2.setText( t1.getSelectedText() );
```

in **actionPerformed** indicates that method ***getSelectedText*** (inherited into **JTextArea** from **JTextComponent**) should return the *selected text* from **t1**. Text is selected by dragging the mouse over the desired text to highlight it. Method **setText** then changes the text in **t2** to the returned **String**.

Lines 37 through 39 create **JTextArea t2** and add it to the **Box** container **b**. Lines 41 and 42 obtain the content pane for the window and add the **Box** to the content pane.

Remember that the default layout of the content pane is a **BorderLayout** and that the add method attaches its argument to the **CENTER** of the **BorderLayout** by default.

Note: It is sometimes desirable when text reaches the right side of a **JTextArea** to have the text wrap to the next line. This is referred to as *automatic word wrap*.

> **Look-and-Feel Observation 13.2**
>
> *To provide automatic word wrap functionality for a **JTextArea**, invoke **JTextArea** method **setLineWrap** with a true argument.*

Note: You can set the horizontal and vertical *scrollbar policies* for the **JScrollPane** when a **JScrollPane** is constructed or with methods **setHorizontalScrollBar-Policy** and **setVerticalScrollBarPolicy** of class **JScrollPane** at any time. Class **JScrollPane** provides the constants

```
JScrollPane.VERTICAL_SCROLLBAR_ALWAYS
JScrollPane.HORIZONTAL_SCROLLBAR_ALWAYS
```

to indicate that a scrollbar should always appear, constants

```
JScrollPane.VERTICAL_SCROLLBAR_AS_NEEDED
JScrollPane.HORIZONTAL_SCROLLBAR_AS_NEEDED
```

to indicate that a scrollbar should appear only if necessary, and constants

```
JScrollPane.VERTICAL_SCROLLBAR_NEVER
JScrollPane.HORIZONTAL_SCROLLBAR_NEVER
```

to indicate that a scrollbar should never appear. If the horizontal scrollbar policy is set to **JScrollPane.HORIZONTAL_SCROLLBAR_NEVER**, a **JTextArea** attached to the **JScrollPane** will exhibit automatic word wrap behavior.

13.3 Creating a Customized Subclass of **JPanel**

A **JPanel** can be used as a *dedicated drawing area* that can receive mouse events and is often extended to create new components. In earlier exercises you may have noticed that combining Swing GUI components and drawing in one window or applet often leads to improper display of the GUI components or the graphics. This is because Swing GUI components are displayed using the same graphics techniques as the drawings and are displayed in the same area as the drawings. The order in which the GUI components are displayed and the drawing is performed may result in drawing over the GUI components or GUI components obscuring the graphics. To fix this problem, we can separate the GUI and the graphics by creating dedicated drawing areas as subclasses of **JPanel**.

> **Look-and-Feel Observation 13.3**
>
> *Combining graphics and Swing GUI components may lead to incorrect display of the graphics, the GUI components or both. Using **JPanel**s for drawing can eliminate this problem by providing a dedicated area for graphics.*

Swing components that inherit from class **JComponent** contain method *paintComponent* that helps them draw properly in the context of a Swing GUI. When customizing a **JPanel** for use as a dedicated drawing area, method **paintComponent** should be overridden as follows:

```
public void paintComponent( Graphics g )
{
    super.paintComponent( g );

    // your additional drawing code
}
```

Notice the call to the superclass version of **paintComponent** appears as the first statement in the body of the overridden method. This ensures that painting occurs in the proper order and that Swing's painting mechanism remains intact. If the superclass version of **paintComponent** is not called, typically the customized GUI component (the subclass of **JPanel** in this case) will not be displayed properly on the user interface. Also, if the superclass version is called after performing the customized drawing statements, the results will typically be erased.

Look-and-Feel Observation 13.4

*When overriding a **JComponent**'s **paintComponent** method, the first statement in the body should always be a call to the superclass's original version of the method.*

Common Programming Error 13.1

*When overriding a **JComponent**'s **paintComponent** method, not calling the superclass's original version of **paintComponent** prevents the GUI component from displaying properly on the GUI.*

Common Programming Error 13.2

*When overriding a **JComponent**'s **paintComponent** method, calling the superclass's original version of **paintComponent** after other drawing is performed erases the other drawings.*

Classes **JFrame** and **JApplet** are not subclasses of **JComponent**; therefore, they do not contain method **paintComponent**. To draw directly on subclasses of **JFrame** and **JApplet**, override method **paint**.

Look-and-Feel Observation 13.5

*Calling **repaint** for a Swing GUI component indicates that the component should be painted as soon as possible. The background of the GUI component is cleared only if the component is opaque. Most Swing components are transparent by default. **JComponent** method **setOpaque** can be passed a **boolean** argument indicating if the component is opaque (**true**) or transparent (**false**). The GUI components of package **java.awt** are different from Swing components in that **repaint** results in a call to **Component** method **update** (which clears the component's background) and **update** calls method **paint** (rather than **paintComponent**).*

Figure 13.2 demonstrates a customized subclass of **JPanel**. Class **CustomPanel** has its own **paintComponent** method that draws a circle or a square depending on the value passed to its **draw** method. For this purpose, **CustomPanel** line 7

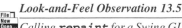

defines constants that are used to specify the shape a **CustomPanel** draws on itself with each call to its **paintComponent** method. The application consists of two classes— **CustomPanel** to draw the chosen shape and **CustomPanelTest** to run the application.

```
1   // Fig. 13.2: CustomPanel.java
2   // A customized JPanel class.
3   import java.awt.*;
4   import javax.swing.*;
5
6   public class CustomPanel extends JPanel {
7      public final static int CIRCLE = 1, SQUARE = 2;
8      private int shape;
9
10     public void paintComponent( Graphics g )
11     {
12        super.paintComponent( g );
13
14        if ( shape == CIRCLE )
15           g.fillOval( 50, 10, 60, 60 );
16        else if ( shape == SQUARE )
17           g.fillRect( 50, 10, 60, 60 );
18     }
19
20     public void draw( int s )
21     {
22        shape = s;
23        repaint();
24     }
25  }
```

Fig. 13.2   Extending class **JPanel** (part 1 of 3).

```
26  // Fig. 13.2: CustomPanelTest.java
27  // Using a customized Panel object.
28  import java.awt.*;
29  import java.awt.event.*;
30  import javax.swing.*;
31
32  public class CustomPanelTest extends JFrame {
33     private JPanel buttonPanel;
34     private CustomPanel myPanel;
35     private JButton circle, square;
36
37     public CustomPanelTest()
38     {
39        super( "CustomPanel Test" );
40
41        myPanel = new CustomPanel();    // instantiate canvas
42        myPanel.setBackground( Color.green );
43
44        square = new JButton( "Square" );
45        square.addActionListener(
46           new ActionListener() {
47              public void actionPerformed( ActionEvent e )
48              {
49                 myPanel.draw( CustomPanel.SQUARE );
```

Fig. 13.2   Extending class **JPanel** (part 2 of 3).

```
50                      }
51                  }
52              );
53
54          circle = new JButton( "Circle" );
55          circle.addActionListener(
56              new ActionListener() {
57                  public void actionPerformed( ActionEvent e )
58                  {
59                      myPanel.draw( CustomPanel.CIRCLE );
60                  }
61              }
62          );
63
64          buttonPanel = new JPanel();
65          buttonPanel.setLayout( new GridLayout( 1, 2 ) );
66          buttonPanel.add( circle );
67          buttonPanel.add( square );
68
69          Container c = getContentPane();
70          c.add( myPanel, BorderLayout.CENTER );
71          c.add( buttonPanel, BorderLayout.SOUTH );
72
73          setSize( 300, 150 );
74          show();
75      }
76
77      public static void main( String args[] )
78      {
79          CustomPanelTest app = new CustomPanelTest();
80
81          app.addWindowListener(
82              new WindowAdapter() {
83                  public void windowClosing( WindowEvent e )
84                  {
85                      System.exit( 0 );
86                  }
87              }
88          );
89      }
90  }
```

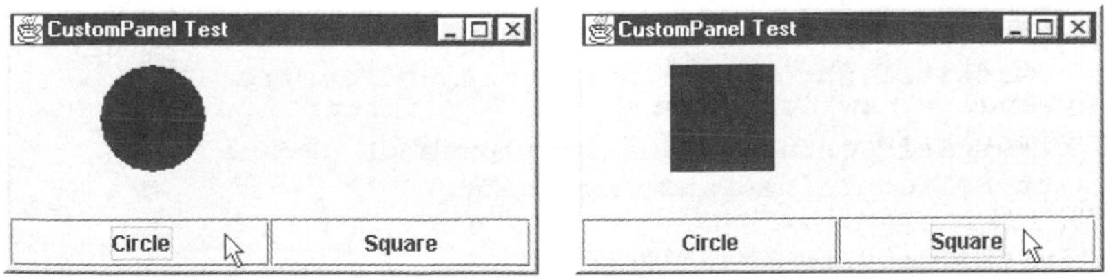

Fig. 13.2   Extending class **JPanel** (part 3 of 3).

Class **CustomPanel** (lines 6 through 25) contains one instance variable **shape** that keeps track of the shape to be drawn. Method **paintComponent** (line 10) is overridden in class **CustomPanel** to draw a shape on the panel. If **shape** is **CIRCLE**, **Graphics** method **fillOval** draws a solid circle. If **shape** is **SQUARE**, **Graphics** method **fillRect** draws a solid square. Method **draw** (line 20) sets instance variable **shape** and calls **repaint** to refresh the **CustomPanel** object. Note that calling **repaint** (which is really **this.repaint()**) for the **CustomPanel** schedules a repaint operation for the **CustomPanel**. Method **paintComponent** will be called to repaint the **Custom-Panel**. When **paintComponent** is called, the appropriate shape is drawn on the panel.

The constructor (line 37) of class **CustomPanelTest** instantiates a **Custom-Panel** object and sets its background color to green so the **CustomPanel** area is visible on the application. Next, **JButton** objects **circle** and **square** are instantiated. Lines 45 through 52 define an anonymous inner class to handle the **square**'s **ActionEvent**. Lines 55 through 62 define an anonymous inner class to handle the **circle**'s **Action-Event**. Lines 49 and 59 each call method **draw** of **CustomPanel myPanel**. In each case, the appropriate constant (**CustomPanel.CIRCLE** or **CustomPanel.SQUARE**) is passed as an argument to indicate which shape to draw.

For layout of the buttons, **JPanel buttonPanel** is created with a **GridLayout** of one row and two columns and the buttons are added to **buttonPanel**. Finally, **myPanel** is added to the Center region and **buttonPanel** is added to the South region of the content pane's **BorderLayout**. Note that the **BorderLayout** automatically expands the **myPanel** to fill the Center region.

13.4 Creating a Self-Contained Subclass of JPanel

JPanels do not generate conventional events like buttons, text fields and windows, but are capable of recognizing lower-level events such as mouse events and key events. Figure 13.3 allows the user to draw an oval on a subclass of **JPanel** with the mouse. Class **SelfContainedPanel** listens for its own mouse events and draws an oval on itself. The location and size of the oval are determined by the user pressing and holding the mouse button, dragging the mouse and releasing the mouse button. Class **SelfContained-Panel** is placed in package **com.deitel.jhtp3.ch13** for future reuse. For this reason, it is imported (line 7) into the **SelfContainedPanelTest** application class.

```
1   // Fig. 13.3: SelfContainedPanelTest.java
2   // Creating a self-contained subclass of JPanel
3   // that processes its own mouse events.
4   import java.awt.*;
5   import java.awt.event.*;
6   import javax.swing.*;
7   import com.deitel.jhtp3.ch13.SelfContainedPanel;
8
9   public class SelfContainedPanelTest extends JFrame {
10      private SelfContainedPanel myPanel;
11
12      public SelfContainedPanelTest()
13      {
14         myPanel = new SelfContainedPanel();
15         myPanel.setBackground( Color.yellow );
16
```

Fig. 13.3   Capturing mouse events with a **JPanel** (part 1 of 5).

```
17            Container c = getContentPane();
18            c.setLayout( new FlowLayout() );
19            c.add( myPanel );
20
21            addMouseMotionListener(
22               new MouseMotionListener() {
23                  public void mouseDragged( MouseEvent e )
24                  {
25                     setTitle( "Dragging: x=" + e.getX() +
26                               "; y=" + e.getY() );
27                  }
28
29                  public void mouseMoved( MouseEvent e )
30                  {
31                     setTitle( "Moving: x=" + e.getX() +
32                               "; y=" + e.getY() );
33                  }
34               }
35            );
36
37            setSize( 300, 200 );
38            show();
39         }
40
41         public static void main( String args[] )
42         {
43            SelfContainedPanelTest app =
44               new SelfContainedPanelTest();
45
46            app.addWindowListener(
47               new WindowAdapter() {
48                  public void windowClosing( WindowEvent e )
49                  {
50                     System.exit( 0 );
51                  }
52               }
53            );
54         }
55   }
```

Fig. 13.3   Capturing mouse events with a **JPanel** (part 2 of 5).

```
56   // Fig. 13.3: SelfConainedPanel.java
57   // A self-contained JPanel class that
58   // handles its own mouse events.
59   package com.deitel.jhtp3.ch13;
60
61   import java.awt.*;
62   import java.awt.event.*;
63   import javax.swing.*;
64
```

Fig. 13.3   Capturing mouse events with a **JPanel** (part 3 of 5).

```
65  public class SelfContainedPanel extends JPanel {
66     private int x1, y1, x2, y2;
67
68     public SelfContainedPanel()
69     {
70        addMouseListener(
71           new MouseAdapter() {
72              public void mousePressed( MouseEvent e )
73              {
74                 x1 = e.getX();
75                 y1 = e.getY();
76              }
77
78              public void mouseReleased( MouseEvent e )
79              {
80                 x2 = e.getX();
81                 y2 = e.getY();
82                 repaint();
83              }
84           }
85        );
86
87        addMouseMotionListener(
88           new MouseMotionAdapter() {
89              public void mouseDragged( MouseEvent e )
90              {
91                 x2 = e.getX();
92                 y2 = e.getY();
93                 repaint();
94              }
95           }
96        );
97     }
98
99     public Dimension getPreferredSize()
100    {
101       return new Dimension( 150, 100 );
102    }
103
104    public void paintComponent( Graphics g )
105    {
106       super.paintComponent( g );
107
108       g.drawOval( Math.min( x1, x2 ), Math.min( y1, y2 ),
109                   Math.abs( x1 - x2 ), Math.abs( y1 - y2 ) );
110    }
111 }
```

Fig. 13.3   Capturing mouse events with a **JPanel** (part 4 of 5).

The constructor method (line 12) of application class **SelfContainedPanelTest** creates an instance of class **SelfContainedPanel** and sets the background color of the **SelfContainedPanel** to yellow so that its area is visible against the background of the application window.

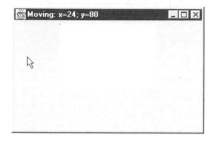

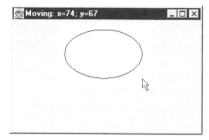
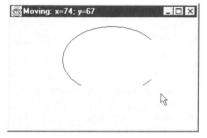

Fig. 13.3   Capturing mouse events with a **JPanel** (part 5 of 5).

So we can demonstrate the difference between mouse motion events on the **Self-ContainedPanel** and mouse motion events on the application window, lines 21 through 35 create an anonymous inner class to handle the application's mouse motion events. Event handlers **mouseDragged** and **mouseMoved** use method **setTitle** (inherited from class **java.awt.Frame**) to display a **String** in the window's title bar indicating the *x* and *y* coordinates where the mouse motion event occurred.

Class **SelfContainedPanel** (lines 65 through 111) extends class **JPanel**. Instance variables **x1** and **y1** store the initial coordinates where the **mousePressed** event occurs on the **SelfContainedPanel**. Instance variables **x2** and **y2** store the coordinates where the user drags the mouse or releases the mouse button. All the coordinates are with respect to the upper-left corner of the **SelfContainedPanel**.

Look-and-Feel Observation 13.6

Drawing on any GUI component is performed with coordinates that are measured from the upper-left corner (0, 0) of that GUI component.

The **SelfContainedPanel** constructor (line 68) uses methods **addMouseListener** and **addMouseMotionListener** to register anonymous inner class objects to handle both the mouse events and the mouse motion events for the **SelfContainedPanel**. Only **mousePressed** (line 72), **mouseReleased** (line 78) and **mouseDragged** (line 89) are actually overridden to perform tasks. The other mouse event handling methods are inherited from class **MouseAdapter** and class **MouseMotionAdapter** when the anonymous inner classes are defined.

By extending class **JPanel**, we are actually creating a new GUI component. Layout managers often use a GUI component's ***getPreferredSize*** method (inherited from class **java.awt.Component**) to determine the preferred width and height of a component when laying out that component as part of a GUI. If a new component has a preferred width and height, it should override method **getPreferredSize** (lines 99 through 102) to return that width and height as an object of class *Dimension* (package **java.awt**).

Look-and-Feel Observation 13.7

*The default size of a **JPanel** object is 0 pixels wide and 0 pixels tall.*

Look-and-Feel Observation 13.8

*When subclassing **JPanel** (or any other **JComponent**), override method **getPreferredSize** if the new component should have a specific preferred width and height.*

Method **paintComponent** (line 104) is overridden in class **SelfContained-Panel** to draw an oval. The width, height and upper-left corner are determined by the user pressing and holding the mouse button, dragging the mouse and releasing the mouse button on the **SelfContainedPanel** drawing area.

The initial coordinates **x1** and **y1** on the **SelfContainedPanel** drawing area are captured in method **mousePressed** (line 72). As the user drags the mouse after the initial **mousePressed** operation, the program generates a series of calls to **mouseDragged** (line 89) while the user continues to hold the mouse button and move the mouse. Each call captures in variables **x2** and **y2** the current location of the mouse with respect to the upper-left corner of the **SelfContainedPanel** and calls **repaint** to draw the current version of the oval. Drawing is strictly confined to the **SelfContainedPanel** even if the user drags outside the **SelfContainedPanel** drawing area. Anything drawn off the **SelfContainedPanel** is *clipped*—pixels are not displayed outside the bounds of the **SelfContainedPanel**.

The calculations provided in method **paintComponent** determine the proper upper-left corner using method **Math.min** twice to find the smaller *x* coordinate and *y* coordinate. The oval's width and height must be positive values or the oval is not displayed. Method **Math.abs** gets the absolute value of the subtractions **x1 - x2** and **y1 - y2** that determine the width and height of the oval's bounding rectangle, respectively. When the calculations are complete, **paintComponent** draws the oval. The call to the superclass version of **paintComponent** at the beginning of the method guarantees that the previous oval displayed on the **SelfContainedPanel** is erased before the new one is displayed.

Look-and-Feel Observation 13.9

*Most Swing GUI components can be transparent or opaque. If a Swing GUI component is opaque, when its **paintComponent** method is called, its background will be cleared. Otherwise, its background will not be cleared.*

Look-and-Feel Observation 13.10

*Class **JComponent** provides method **setOpaque** that takes a **boolean** argument to determine if a **JComponent** is opaque (**true**) or transparent (**false**).*

Look-and-Feel Observation 13.11

***JPanel** objects are opaque by default.*

When the user releases the mouse button, method **mouseReleased** (line 78) captures in variables **x2** and **y2** the final location of the mouse and invokes **repaint** to draw the final version of the oval.

When executing this program try dragging from the background of the application window into the **SelfContainedPanel** area to see that the drag events are sent to the application window rather than the **SelfContainedPanel**. Then, start a new drag operation in the **SelfContainedPanel** area and drag out to the background of the application window to see that the drag events are sent to the **SelfContainedPanel** rather than to the application window.

> **Look-and-Feel Observation 13.12**
>
> *A mouse drag operation begins with a mouse pressed event. All subsequent mouse drag events (for which **mouseDragged** will be called) are sent to the GUI component that received the original mouse pressed event.*

13.5 JSlider

*JSlider*s enable the user to select from a range of integer values. Class **JSlider** inherits from **JComponent**. Figure 13.4 shows a horizontal **JSlider** with *tick marks* and the *thumb* that allows the user to select a value. **JSlider**s are highly customizable in that they can display major tick marks, minor tick marks and labels for the tick marks. They also support *snap-to ticks* where positioning the thumb between two tick marks causes the thumb to *snap* to the closest tick mark.

Most Swing GUI components support user interactions through the mouse and the keyboard. For example, if a **JSlider** has the *focus* (i.e., it is the currently selected GUI component in the user interface), the *left arrow key* and *right arrow key* cause the thumb of the **JSlider** to decrease or increase by 1, respectively. The *down arrow key* and *up arrow key* also cause the thumb of the **JSlider** to decrease or increase by 1, respectively. The *PgDn key* (page down) and *PgUp key* (page up) cause the thumb of the **JSlider** to decrease or increase by *block increments* of one-tenth of the range of values, respectively. The *Home key* moves the thumb to the minimum value of the **JSlider** and the *End key* moves the thumb to the maximum value of the **JSlider**.

> **Look-and-Feel Observation 13.13**
>
> *Most Swing components support user interactions through the mouse and the keyboard.*

JSliders have either a *horizontal orientation* or a *vertical orientation*. For a horizontal **JSlider**, the minimum value is at the extreme left and the maximum value is at the extreme right of the **JSlider**. For a vertical **JSlider**, the minimum value is at the extreme bottom and the maximum value is at the extreme top of the **JSlider**. The relative position of the thumb indicates the current value of the **JSlider**.

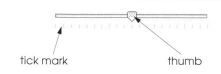

tick mark   thumb

Fig. 13.4   A horizontal **JSlider** component.

Look-and-Feel Observation 13.14

*The minimum and maximum value positions on a **JSlider** can be switched by calling the **JSlider** method **setInverted** with boolean argument **true**.*

The program of Fig. 13.5 allows the user to size a circle drawn on a subclass of **JPanel**. The diameter of the circle is controlled with a horizontal **JSlider**. Application class **SliderDemo** creates the **JSlider** that controls the diameter of the circle. Class **OvalPanel** is a subclass of **JPanel** that knows how to draw a circle on itself using its own instance variable **diameter** to determine the diameter of the circle (the **diameter** is used as the width and height of the bounding box in which the circle is displayed). The **diameter** value is set when the user interacts with the **JSlider**. When the interaction occurs, the event handler calls method **setDiameter** in class **OvalPanel** to set the **diameter** and calls **repaint** to draw the new circle. The **repaint** call results in a call to **OvalPanel**'s **paintComponent** method.

```
1   // Fig. 13.5: SliderDemo.java
2   // Using JSliders to size an oval.
3   import java.awt.*;
4   import java.awt.event.*;
5   import javax.swing.*;
6   import javax.swing.event.*;
7
8   public class SliderDemo extends JFrame {
9       private JSlider diameter;
10      private OvalPanel myPanel;
11
12      public SliderDemo()
13      {
14          super( "Slider Demo" );
15
16          myPanel = new OvalPanel();
17          myPanel.setBackground( Color.yellow );
18
19          diameter = new JSlider( SwingConstants.HORIZONTAL,
20                                  0, 200, 10 );
21          diameter.setMajorTickSpacing( 10 );
22          diameter.setPaintTicks( true );
23          diameter.addChangeListener(
24             new ChangeListener() {
25                public void stateChanged( ChangeEvent e )
26                {
27                   myPanel.setDiameter( diameter.getValue() );
28                }
29             }
30          );
31
32          Container c = getContentPane();
33          c.add( diameter, BorderLayout.SOUTH );
34          c.add( myPanel, BorderLayout.CENTER );
35
```

Fig. 13.5   Using a **JSlider** to determine the diameter of a circle (part 1 of 4).

```
36            setSize( 220, 270 );
37            show();
38        }
39
40        public static void main( String args[] )
41        {
42            SliderDemo app = new SliderDemo();
43
44            app.addWindowListener(
45                new WindowAdapter() {
46                    public void windowClosing( WindowEvent e )
47                    {
48                        System.exit( 0 );
49                    }
50                }
51            );
52        }
53    }
```

Fig. 13.5   Using a **JSlider** to determine the diameter of a circle (part 2 of 4).

```
54    // Fig. 13.5: OvalPanel.java
55    // A customized JPanel class.
56    import java.awt.*;
57    import javax.swing.*;
58
59    public class OvalPanel extends JPanel {
60        private int diameter = 10;
61
62        public void paintComponent( Graphics g )
63        {
64            super.paintComponent( g );
65            g.fillOval( 10, 10, diameter, diameter );
66        }
67
68        public void setDiameter( int d )
69        {
70            diameter = ( d >= 0 ? d : 10 );  // default diameter 10
71            repaint();
72        }
73
74        // the following methods are used by layout managers
75        public Dimension getPreferredSize()
76        {
77            return new Dimension( 200, 200 );
78        }
79
80        public Dimension getMinimumSize()
81        {
82            return getPreferredSize();
83        }
84    }
```

Fig. 13.5   Using a **JSlider** to determine the diameter of a circle (part 3 of 4).

Fig. 13.5   Using a **JSlider** to determine the diameter of a circle (part 4 of 4).

The constructor (line 12) for **SliderDemo** instantiates **OvalPanel** object **myPanel** and sets its background color (lines 16 and 17). Lines 19 and 20

```
diameter = new JSlider( SwingConstants.HORIZONTAL,
                        0, 200, 10 );
```

instantiate **JSlider** object **diameter** to control the diameter of the circle drawn on the **OvalPanel**. The orientation of **diameter** is **HORIZONTAL** (a constant in interface **SwingConstants**). The second and third constructor arguments indicate the minimum and maximum integer values in the range of values for this **JSlider**. The last constructor argument indicates that the initial value of the **JSlider** (i.e., where the thumb is displayed) should be **10**.

Lines 21 and 22

```
diameter.setMajorTickSpacing( 10 );
diameter.setPaintTicks( true );
```

customize the appearance of the **JSlider**. Method *setMajorTickSpacing* indicates that each tick mark represents 10 values in the range of values supported by the **JSlider**. Method *setPaintTicks* with a **true** argument indicates that the tick marks should be displayed (they are not displayed by default). See the **JSlider** on-line documentation for more information on methods that are used to customize a **JSlider**'s appearance.

JSliders generate *ChangeEvents* (package **javax.swing.event**) when the user interacts with a **JSlider**. An object of a class that implements interface *ChangeListener* (package **javax.swing.event**) and defines method *stateChanged* that can respond to **ChangeEvent**s. Lines 23 through 30

```
diameter.addChangeListener(
   new ChangeListener() {
      public void stateChanged( ChangeEvent e )
      {
         myPanel.setDiameter( diameter.getValue() );
      }
   }
);
```

create an anonymous inner class that implements **ChangeListener** and register an object of that class to handle **diameter**'s events. When method **stateChanged** is called in response to a user interaction, it calls **myPanel**'s **setDiameter** method and passes the current value of the **JSlider** as an argument. Method *getValue* of class *JSlider* returns the current thumb position.

Class **OvalPanel** (lines 59 through 84) contains a **paintComponent** method (line 62) that draws a filled oval (a circle in this example), a **setDiameter** method (line 68) that changes the **diameter** of the circle and **repaint**s the **OvalPanel**, a **getPreferredSize** method (line 75) that defines the preferred width and height of an **Oval-Panel**, and a **getMinimumSize** method (line 80) that defines the minimum width and height of an **OvalPanel**.

Look-and-Feel Observation 13.15

*If a new GUI component has a minimum width and height (i.e., smaller dimensions would render the component ineffective on the display), override method **getMinimumSize** to return the minimum width and height as an instance of class **Dimension**.*

Look-and-Feel Observation 13.16

*For many GUI components method **getMinimumSize** is defined to return the result of a call to that component's **getPreferredSize** method.*

13.6 Windows

Most applications from Chapter 9 to this chapter have used an instance of a subclass of **JFrame** as the application window. In this section, we discuss several important issues regarding **JFrame**s.

A *JFrame* is a *window* with a *title bar* and a *border*. Class **JFrame** is a subclass of *java.awt.Frame* (which is a subclass of **java.awt.Window**). As such, **JFrame** is one of the few Swing GUI components that is not considered to be a lightweight GUI component. Unlike most Swing components, **JFrame** is not written completely in Java. In fact, when you display a window from a Java program, the window is part of the local platform's set of GUI components—the window will look like all other windows displayed on that platform. When a Java program executes on a Macintosh and displays a window, the window's title bar and borders will look like other Macintosh applications. When a Java program executes on Microsoft Windows and displays a window, the window's title bar and borders will look like other Microsoft Windows applications. And when a Java program executes on a Unix platform and displays a window, the window's title bar and borders will look like other Unix applications on that platform.

Class **JFrame** supports three operations when the user closes the window. By default, a window is hidden (i.e., removed from the screen) when the user closes a window. This can be controlled with **JFrame** method *setDefaultCloseOperation*. Interface *WindowConstants* (package **javax.swing**) defines three constants for use with this method—**DISPOSE_ON_CLOSE**, **DO_NOTHING_ON_CLOSE** and **HIDE_ON_CLOSE** (the default). Most platforms allow a limited number of total windows to be displayed on the screen. As such, a window is a valuable resource that should be given back to the system when it is no longer needed. Class **Window** (an indirect superclass of **JFrame**) defines method *dispose* for this purpose. When a **Window** is no longer needed in an application you should explicitly **dispose** of the **Window**. This can be done by explicitly calling the

Window's **dispose** method or by calling method **setDefaultCloseOperation** with the argument **WindowConstants.DISPOSE_ON_CLOSE**. Also, terminating an application will return window resources to the system. Setting the default close operation to **DO_NOTHING_ON_CLOSE** indicates that you will determine what to do when the user indicates that the window should be closed.

Software Engineering Observation 13.1

Windows are a valuable system resource that should be returned to the system when they are no longer needed.

By default, a window is not displayed on the screen until its *show* method is called. A window can also be displayed by calling its *setVisible* method (inherited from class **java.awt.Component**) with **true** as an argument. Also, a window's size should be set with a call to method *setSize* (inherited from class **java.awt.Component**). The position of a window when it appears on the screen is specified with method **setLocation** (inherited from class **java.awt.Component**).

Common Programming Error 13.3

*Forgetting to call method **show** or method **setVisible** on a window is a run-time logic error; the window is not displayed.*

Common Programming Error 13.4

*Forgetting to call the **setSize** method on a window is a run-time logic error—only the title bar appears.*

All windows generate *window events* when the user manipulates the window. Event listeners are registered for window events with method *addWindowListener* of class **Window**. The *WindowListener* interface (implemented by window event listeners) provides seven methods for handling window events—*windowActivated* (called when the window is made active by clicking the window), *windowClosed* (called after the window is closed), *windowClosing* (called when the user initiates closing of the window), *windowDeactivated* (called when another window is made active), *windowIconified* (called when the user minimizes a window), *windowDeiconified* (called when a window is restored from being minimized) and *windowOpened* (called when a window is first displayed on the screen).

Most windows have an icon at the top-left or top-right corner that enables a user to close the window and terminate a program. Most windows also have an icon in the upper-left corner of the window that displays a menu when the user clicks the icon. This menu normally contains a **Close** option to close the window and several other options for manipulating the window.

13.7 Designing Programs that Execute as Applets or Applications

It is sometimes desirable to design a Java program that can execute both as a stand-alone application and as an applet in a Web browser. Such a program can be used to provide the same functionality to users worldwide by making the applet available for download via Web and can be installed on a computer as a stand-alone application. The next example discusses how to create a small program that can execute both as an applet and as an application. [*Note:* In Chapters 17 through 21 we discuss a variety of issues that make applets different from applications and prevent certain aspects of applications from working in an applet due to the security restrictions that are often placed on applets.]

JFrames are often used to create *GUI-based applications*. The **JFrame** provides the space in which the application GUI is built. When the **JFrame** is closed, the application terminates. In this section, we demonstrate how to convert an applet into a GUI-based application. The program of Fig. 13.6 presents an applet that can also be executed as an application.

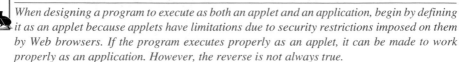

Software Engineering Observation 13.2

When designing a program to execute as both an applet and an application, begin by defining it as an applet because applets have limitations due to security restrictions imposed on them by Web browsers. If the program executes properly as an applet, it can be made to work properly as an application. However, the reverse is not always true.

Our applet class **DrawShapes** presents the user with three buttons which when pressed cause an instance of class **DrawPanel** (line 100) to randomly draw a line, a rectangle or an oval (depending on which button is pressed). The applet does not contain any new features as far as GUI components, layouts or drawing are concerned. The only new feature is that the **DrawShapes** class now also contains a **main** method (line 41) that can be used to execute the program as an application. We discuss this method in detail below.

```
1   // Fig. 13.6: DrawShapes.java
2   // Draw random lines, rectangles and ovals
3   import java.awt.*;
4   import java.awt.event.*;
5   import javax.swing.*;
6
7   public class DrawShapes extends JApplet {
8       private JButton choices[];
9       private String names[] = { "Line", "Rectangle", "Oval" };
10      private JPanel buttonPanel;
11      private DrawPanel drawingArea;
12      private int width = 300, height = 200;
13
14      public void init()
15      {
16          drawingArea = new DrawPanel( width, height );
17
18          choices = new JButton[ names.length ];
19          buttonPanel = new JPanel();
20          buttonPanel.setLayout(
21              new GridLayout( 1, choices.length ) );
22          ButtonHandler handler = new ButtonHandler();
23
24          for ( int i = 0; i < choices.length; i++ ) {
25              choices[ i ] = new JButton( names[ i ] );
26              buttonPanel.add( choices[ i ] );
27              choices[ i ].addActionListener( handler );
28          }
```

Fig. 13.6   Creating a GUI-based application from an applet (part 1 of 4).

```
29
30          Container c = getContentPane();
31          c.add( buttonPanel, BorderLayout.NORTH );
32          c.add( drawingArea, BorderLayout.CENTER );
33       }
34
35       public void setWidth( int w )
36          { width = ( w >= 0 ? w : 300 ); }
37
38       public void setHeight( int h )
39          { height = ( h >= 0 ? h : 200 ); }
40
41       public static void main( String args[] )
42       {
43          int width, height;
44
45          if ( args.length != 2 ) {  // no command-line arguments
46             width = 300;
47             height = 200;
48          }
49          else {
50             width = Integer.parseInt( args[ 0 ] );
51             height = Integer.parseInt( args[ 1 ] );
52          }
53
54          // create window in which applet will execute
55          JFrame applicationWindow =
56             new JFrame( "An applet running as an application" );
57
58          applicationWindow.addWindowListener(
59             new WindowAdapter() {
60                public void windowClosing( WindowEvent e )
61                {
62                   System.exit( 0 );
63                }
64             }
65          );
66
67          // create one applet instance
68          DrawShapes appletObject = new DrawShapes();
69          appletObject.setWidth( width );
70          appletObject.setHeight( height );
71
72          // call applet's init and start methods
73          appletObject.init();
74          appletObject.start();
75
76          // attach applet to center of window
77          applicationWindow.getContentPane().add( appletObject );
78
79          // set the window's size
80          applicationWindow.setSize( width, height );
81
```

Fig. 13.6   Creating a GUI-based application from an applet (part 2 of 4).

```
82            // showing the window causes all GUI components
83            // attached to the window to be painted
84            applicationWindow.show();
85         }
86
87         private class ButtonHandler implements ActionListener {
88            public void actionPerformed( ActionEvent e )
89            {
90               for ( int i = 0; i < choices.length; i++ )
91                  if ( e.getSource() == choices[ i ] ) {
92                     drawingArea.setCurrentChoice( i );
93                     break;
94                  }
95            }
96         }
97      }
98
99      // subclass of JPanel to allow drawing in a separate area
100     class DrawPanel extends JPanel {
101        private int currentChoice = -1;  // don't draw first time
102        private int width = 100, height = 100;
103
104        public DrawPanel( int w, int h )
105        {
106           width = ( w >= 0 ? w : 100 );
107           height = ( h >= 0 ? h : 100 );
108        }
109
110        public void paintComponent( Graphics g )
111        {
112           super.paintComponent( g );
113
114           switch( currentChoice ) {
115              case 0:
116                 g.drawLine( randomX(), randomY(),
117                             randomX(), randomY() );
118                 break;
119              case 1:
120                 g.drawRect( randomX(), randomY(),
121                             randomX(), randomY() );
122                 break;
123              case 2:
124                 g.drawOval( randomX(), randomY(),
125                             randomX(), randomY() );
126                 break;
127           }
128        }
129
130        public void setCurrentChoice( int c )
131        {
132           currentChoice = c;
133           repaint();
134        }
```

Fig. 13.6   Creating a GUI-based application from an applet (part 3 of 4).

```
135
136    private int randomX()
137       { return (int) ( Math.random() * width ); }
138
139    private int randomY()
140       { return (int) ( Math.random() * height ); }
141 }
```

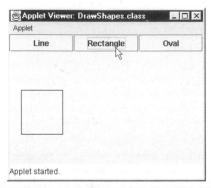

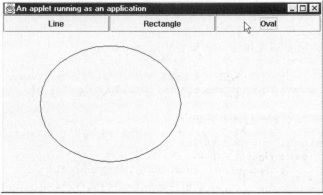

Fig. 13.6   Creating a GUI-based application from an applet (part 4 of 4).

The HTML document that loads the applet into the **appletviewer** or a Web browser specifies the applet's width and height as 300 and 200, respectively. When the program executes as an application with the **java** interpreter, you can supply arguments to the program (called *command-line arguments*) that specify the width and height of the application window. For example, the command

java DrawShapes 600 400

specifies two command-line arguments—600 and 400—that are used as the width and height of the application window. The command-line arguments are automatically passed to **main** as the array of **String**s called **args** that has been declared in every application's **main** method, but not used until this point. The first argument after the application class name is the first **String** in the array **args**, and the length of the array is the total number of command-line arguments. Line 41

```
public static void main( String args[] )
```

begins the definition of **main** and declares array **args** as an array of **String**s that allows the application to access the command-line arguments. Line 43 defines variables **width** and **height** that are used to specify the size of the application window.

Lines 45 through 52

```
if ( args.length != 2 ) {   // no command-line arguments
    width = 300;
    height = 200;
}
else {
    width = Integer.parseInt( args[ 0 ] );
    height = Integer.parseInt( args[ 1 ] );
}
```

determine the initial width and height of the application window. The **if** condition tests **args.length** to determine the number of elements in the array. If the number of elements is not 2, the **width** and **height** are set to 300 and 200 by default. Otherwise, lines 50 and 51 convert the command-line arguments from **String**s to **int** values with **parseInt** and use them as the **width** and **height**. [*Note:* This program assumes that the user inputs whole number values for the command-line arguments; if not, an exception will occur. In Chapter 14, we discuss how to make our programs more robust by dealing with improper values when they occur.]

When an applet executes in the **appletviewer** (or a browser), the window in which it executes is supplied by the **appletviewer** (or browser). When a program executes an application, if a window is needed, it must be created by the application. Lines 55 and 56

```
JFrame applicationWindow =
    new JFrame( "An applet running as an application" );
```

create the **JFrame** to which we will attach the applet. As with any **JFrame** that is used as the application's primary window, you should provide a mechanism to terminate the application. Lines 58 through 65 register an instance of an anonymous inner class that extends **WindowAdapter** to handle the window closing event by terminating the application.

 Software Engineering Observation 13.3

To execute an applet as an application, the application must provide a window in which the applet can be displayed.

When an applet executes in the **appletviewer** or a browser, one object of the applet class is created by the **appletviewer** or browser to execute the applet's tasks. In an application, no objects are created unless the application explicitly creates them. Line 68

```
DrawShapes appletObject = new DrawShapes();
```

defines one instance of applet class **DrawShapes**. Notice the call to the no-argument constructor. We did not define a constructor in class **DrawShapes** (as is normally the case in an applet class). Remember that the compiler provides a default constructor for a class that does not define any constructors. Lines 69 and 70 call **DrawShapes** methods **setWidth** and **setHeight** to validate the values for **width** and **height** (improper values are set to 300 and 200, respectively).

Software Engineering Observation 13.4

To execute an applet as an application, the application must create an instance of the applet class to execute.

When an applet executes in the **appletviewer** (or a browser), three methods are guaranteed to be called by the **appletviewer** (or a browser)—**init**, **start** and **paint**. However, these methods are not special to an application—these methods are not automatically invoked or required by an application. Lines 73 and 74

```
appletObject.init();
appletObject.start();
```

invoke the **appletObject**'s **init** method to initialize the applet and set up its GUI, then invoke method **start**. [*Note:* In our example, we did not override method **start**. It is called here to mimic the start-up sequence normally followed for an applet.]

Software Engineering Observation 13.5

*When executing an applet as an application, the application must call **init** and **start** explicitly to simulate the normal applet start-up sequence of method calls.*

When an applet executes in the **appletviewer** (or a browser), the applet is normally attached to the **appletviewer** (or browser) window by the **appletviewer** (or browser). In an application, the applet object must be explicitly attached to the application window. Line 77

```
applicationWindow.getContentPane().add( appletObject );
```

obtains a reference to the **applicationWindow**'s content pane and adds the **appletObject** to the default **CENTER** of the content pane's **BorderLayout**. The **appletObject** will occupy the entire window.

Software Engineering Observation 13.6

When executing an applet as an application, the application must attach the applet object to its window.

Finally, as with any window, the application window must be sized and displayed on the screen. Line 80 sets the application window's size and line 84 displays the window. When any window is displayed, all the components attached to the window receive calls to their **paint** methods (if they are heavyweight components) or their **paintComponent** methods (if they are lightweight subclasses of **JComponent**). Thus, displaying the application window results in a call to the applet's **paint** method to complete the normal start-up sequence for the applet.

Try executing this program as an applet and as an application to see that it has the same functionality when executed.

13.8 Using Menus with Frames

Menus are an integral part of GUIs. Menus allow the user to perform actions without unnecessarily "cluttering" a graphical user interface with extra GUI components. In Swing GUIs, menus can only be attached to objects of the classes that provide method **setJMenuBar**. Two such classes are **JFrame** and **JApplet**. The classes used to define menus are *JMenuBar*, *JMenuItem*, *JMenu*, *JCheckBoxMenuItem* and class *JRadioButtonMenuItem*.

Look-and-Feel Observation 13.17

Menus simplify GUIs by reducing the number of components the user views.

Class **JMenuBar** (a subclass of **JComponent**) contains the methods necessary to manage a *menu bar*. A menu bar, which is a container for menus.

Class **JMenuItem** (a subclass of **javax.swing.AbstractButton**) contains the methods necessary to manage *menu items*. A menu item is a GUI component inside a menu that when selected causes an action to be performed. A menu item can be used to initiate an action or it can be a *submenu* that provides more menu items from which the user can select. Submenus are useful for grouping related menu items in a menu.

Class **JMenu** (a subclass of **javax.swing.JMenuItem**) contains the methods necessary for managing *menus*. Menus contain menu items and are added to menu bars or to other menus as submenus. When a menu is clicked, the menu expands to show its list of menu items. Clicking a menu item generates an action event.

Class **JCheckBoxMenuItem** (a subclass of **javax.swing.JMenuItem**) contains the methods necessary to manage menu items that can be toggled on or off. When a **JCheckBoxMenuItem** is selected, a check appears to the left of the menu item. When the **JCheckBoxMenuItem** is selected again, the check to the left of the menu item is removed.

Class **JRadioButtonMenuItem** (a subclass of **javax.swing.JMenuItem**) contains the methods necessary to manage menu items that can be toggled on or off like **JCheckBoxMenuItem**s. When multiple **JRadioButtonMenuItem**s are maintained as part of a **ButtonGroup**, only one item in the group can be selected at a given time. When a **JRadioButtonMenuItem** is selected, a filled circle appears to the left of the menu item. When another **JRadioButtonMenuItem** is selected, the filled circle to the left of the previously selected menu item is removed.

The application of Fig. 13.7 demonstrates various types of menu items. The program also demonstrates how to specify special characters called mnemonics that can provide quick access to a menu or menu item from the keyboard. Mnemonics can be used with objects of all classes that have subclass **javax.swing.AbstractButton**.

```
1   // Fig. 13.7: MenuTest.java
2   // Demonstrating menus
3   import javax.swing.*;
4   import java.awt.event.*;
5   import java.awt.*;
6
7   public class MenuTest extends JFrame {
8       private Color colorValues[] =
9           { Color.black, Color.blue, Color.red, Color.green };
10      private JRadioButtonMenuItem colorItems[], fonts[];
11      private JCheckBoxMenuItem styleItems[];
12      private JLabel display;
```

Fig. 13.7   Using **JMenu**s and mnemonics (part 1 of 5).

```
13      private ButtonGroup fontGroup, colorGroup;
14      private int style;
15
16      public MenuTest()
17      {
18          super( "Using JMenus" );
19
20          JMenuBar bar = new JMenuBar();  // create menubar
21          setJMenuBar( bar );  // set the menubar for the JFrame
22
23          // create File menu and Exit menu item
24          JMenu fileMenu = new JMenu( "File" );
25          fileMenu.setMnemonic( 'F' );
26          JMenuItem aboutItem = new JMenuItem( "About..." );
27          aboutItem.setMnemonic( 'A' );
28          aboutItem.addActionListener(
29              new ActionListener() {
30                  public void actionPerformed( ActionEvent e )
31                  {
32                      JOptionPane.showMessageDialog( MenuTest.this,
33                          "This is an example\nof using menus",
34                          "About", JOptionPane.PLAIN_MESSAGE );
35                  }
36              }
37          );
38          fileMenu.add( aboutItem );
39
40          JMenuItem exitItem = new JMenuItem( "Exit" );
41          exitItem.setMnemonic( 'x' );
42          exitItem.addActionListener(
43              new ActionListener() {
44                  public void actionPerformed( ActionEvent e )
45                  {
46                      System.exit( 0 );
47                  }
48              }
49          );
50          fileMenu.add( exitItem );
51          bar.add( fileMenu );     // add File menu
52
53          // create the Format menu, its submenus and menu items
54          JMenu formatMenu = new JMenu( "Format" );
55          formatMenu.setMnemonic( 'r' );
56
57          // create Color submenu
58          String colors[] =
59              { "Black", "Blue", "Red", "Green" };
60          JMenu colorMenu = new JMenu( "Color" );
61          colorMenu.setMnemonic( 'C' );
62          colorItems = new JRadioButtonMenuItem[ colors.length ];
63          colorGroup = new ButtonGroup();
64          ItemHandler itemHandler = new ItemHandler();
65
```

Fig. 13.7   Using **JMenu**s and mnemonics (part 2 of 5).

```
66          for ( int i = 0; i < colors.length; i++ ) {
67              colorItems[ i ] =
68                  new JRadioButtonMenuItem( colors[ i ] );
69              colorMenu.add( colorItems[ i ] );
70              colorGroup.add( colorItems[ i ] );
71              colorItems[ i ].addActionListener( itemHandler );
72          }
73
74          colorItems[ 0 ].setSelected( true );
75          formatMenu.add( colorMenu );
76          formatMenu.addSeparator();
77
78          // create Font submenu
79          String fontNames[] =
80              { "TimesRoman", "Courier", "Helvetica" };
81          JMenu fontMenu = new JMenu( "Font" );
82          fontMenu.setMnemonic( 'n' );
83          fonts = new JRadioButtonMenuItem[ fontNames.length ];
84          fontGroup = new ButtonGroup();
85
86          for ( int i = 0; i < fonts.length; i++ ) {
87              fonts[ i ] =
88                  new JRadioButtonMenuItem( fontNames[ i ] );
89              fontMenu.add( fonts[ i ] );
90              fontGroup.add( fonts[ i ] );
91              fonts[ i ].addActionListener( itemHandler );
92          }
93
94          fonts[ 0 ].setSelected( true );
95          fontMenu.addSeparator();
96
97          String styleNames[] = { "Bold", "Italic" };
98          styleItems = new JCheckBoxMenuItem[ styleNames.length ];
99          StyleHandler styleHandler = new StyleHandler();
100
101          for ( int i = 0; i < styleNames.length; i++ ) {
102              styleItems[ i ] =
103                  new JCheckBoxMenuItem( styleNames[ i ] );
104              fontMenu.add( styleItems[ i ] );
105              styleItems[ i ].addItemListener( styleHandler );
106          }
107
108          formatMenu.add( fontMenu );
109          bar.add( formatMenu );   // add Format menu
110
111          display = new JLabel(
112              "Sample Text", SwingConstants.CENTER );
113          display.setForeground( colorValues[ 0 ] );
114          display.setFont(
115              new Font( "TimesRoman", Font.PLAIN, 72 ) );
116
117          getContentPane().setBackground( Color.cyan );
118          getContentPane().add( display, BorderLayout.CENTER );
```

Fig. 13.7   Using **JMenu**s and mnemonics (part 3 of 5).

```
119
120         setSize( 500, 200 );
121         show();
122      }
123
124      public static void main( String args[] )
125      {
126         MenuTest app = new MenuTest();
127
128         app.addWindowListener(
129            new WindowAdapter() {
130               public void windowClosing( WindowEvent e )
131               {
132                  System.exit( 0 );
133               }
134            }
135         );
136      }
137
138      class ItemHandler implements ActionListener {
139         public void actionPerformed( ActionEvent e )
140         {
141            for ( int i = 0; i < colorItems.length; i++ )
142               if ( colorItems[ i ].isSelected() ) {
143                  display.setForeground( colorValues[ i ] );
144                  break;
145               }
146
147            for ( int i = 0; i < fonts.length; i++ )
148               if ( e.getSource() == fonts[ i ] ) {
149                  display.setFont( new Font(
150                     fonts[ i ].getText(), style, 72 ) );
151                  break;
152               }
153
154            repaint();
155         }
156      }
157
158      class StyleHandler implements ItemListener {
159         public void itemStateChanged( ItemEvent e )
160         {
161            style = 0;
162
163            if ( styleItems[ 0 ].isSelected() )
164               style += Font.BOLD;
165
166            if ( styleItems[ 1 ].isSelected() )
167               style += Font.ITALIC;
168
169            display.setFont( new Font(
170               display.getFont().getName(), style, 72 ) );
171
```

Fig. 13.7   Using **JMenu**s and mnemonics (part 4 of 5).

```
172              repaint();
173         }
174     }
175 }
```

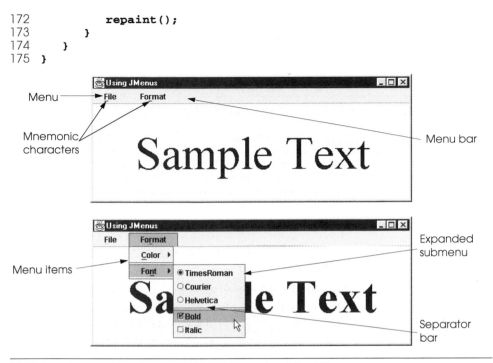

Fig. 13.7   Using **JMenu**s and mnemonics (part 5 of 5).

Class **MenuTest** (line 7) is a completely self-contained class—it defines all the GUI components and event handling for the menu items. Most of the code for this application appears in the class's constructor (line 16).

Lines 20 and 21

```
JMenuBar bar = new JMenuBar();  // create menubar
setJMenuBar( bar );  // set the menubar for the JFrame
```

create the **JMenuBar** and attach it to the application window with **JFrame** method **set-JMenuBar**.

Common Programming Error 13.5

*Forgetting to set the menu bar with **JFrame** method **setJMenuBar** results in the menu bar not being displayed on the **JFrame**.*

Lines 24 through 51 set up the **File** menu and attach it to the menu bar. The **File** menu contains an **About...** menu item that displays a message dialog when the menu item is selected and an **Exit** menu item that can be selected to terminate the application.

Line 24

```
JMenu fileMenu = new JMenu( "File" );
```

creates **fileMenu** and passes to the constructor the string "**File**" as the name of the menu. Line 25

```
fileMenu.setMnemonic( 'F' );
```

uses **AbstractButton** method *setMnemonic* (inherited into class **JMenu**) to indicate that **F** is the *mnemonic* for this menu. Pressing the *Alt* key and the letter *F* opens the menu just as clicking the menu name with the mouse would. In the GUI, the mnemonic character in the menu's name is displayed with an underline (see the screen captures).

Look-and-Feel Observation 13.18

Mnemonics provide quick access to menu commands and button commands through the keyboard.

Look-and-Feel Observation 13.19

*Different mnemonics should be used for each button or menu item. Normally, the first letter in the label on the menu item or button is used as the mnemonic. If multiple buttons or menu items start with the same letter, choose the next most prominent letter in the name (e.g., **x** is commonly chosen for a button or menu item called **Exit**).*

Lines 26 and 27

```
JMenuItem aboutItem = new JMenuItem( "About..." );
aboutItem.setMnemonic( 'A' );
```

define **JMenuItem aboutItem** with the name "**About...**" and set its mnemonic to the letter **A**. This menu item is added to **fileMenu** at line 38. To access the **About...** item through the keyboard, press the *Alt* key and letter *F* to open the **File** menu, then press *A* to select the **About...** menu item. Lines 28 through 37 create an **ActionListener** to listen for selection of **aboutItem**. Lines 32 through 34

```
JOptionPane.showMessageDialog( MenuTest.this,
    "This is an example\nof using menus",
    "About", JOptionPane.PLAIN_MESSAGE );
```

display a message dialog box. In most prior uses of **showMessageDialog**, the first argument has been **null**. The purpose of the first argument is to specify the *parent window* for the dialog box. The parent window helps determine where the dialog box will be displayed. If the parent window is specified as null, the dialog box is normally displayed in the center of the screen. If the parent window is not null, the dialog box is normally displayed centered horizontally over the parent window and just below the top of the window.

Dialog boxes can be either *modal* or *modeless*. A *modal dialog box* does not allow any other window in the application to be accessed until the dialog box is dismissed. A *modeless dialog box* allows other windows to be accessed while the dialog is displayed. By default, the dialogs displayed with class **JOptionPane** are modal dialogs. Class *JDialog* can be used to create your own modeless or modal dialogs.

Line 38

```
fileMenu.add( aboutItem );
```

adds **aboutItem** to **fileMenu** with **JMenu** method *add*.

Lines 40 through 50 define menu item **exitItem**, set its mnemonic to **x** and register an **ActionListener** that terminates the application when **exitItem** is selected.

Line 51

```
bar.add( fileMenu );     // add File menu
```

uses **JMenuBar** method *add* to attach the **fileMenu** to **bar**.

Look-and-Feel Observation 13.20

Menus normally appear left to right in the order that they are added.

Lines 54 and 55 create menu **formatMenu** and set its mnemonic to **r** (**F** is not used because that is the **File** menu's mnemonic).

Lines 60 and 61 create menu **colorMenu** (this will be a submenu in the **Format** menu) and set its mnemonic to **C**. Line 62 creates **JRadioButtonMenuItem** array **colorItems** that will refer to the menu items in **colorMenu**. Line 63 creates the **ButtonGroup colorGroup** that will ensure that only one of the menu items in the **Color** submenu is selected at a time. Line 64 defines an instance of inner class **ItemHandler** (defined at lines 138 to 156) that will be used to respond to selections from the **Color** submenu and the **Font** submenu (discussed shortly). The **for** structure at lines 66 through 72 creates each **JRadioButtonMenuItem** in array **colorItems**, adds each menu item to **colorMenu**, adds each menu item to **colorGroup** and registers the **ActionListener** for each menu item.

Line 74

```
colorItems[ 0 ].setSelected( true );
```

uses **AbstractButton** method **setSelected** to indicate that the first element in the **colorItems** array should be selected. Line 75 adds the **colorMenu** as a submenu of the **formatMenu**.

Look-and-Feel Observation 13.21

Adding a menu as a menu item in another menu automatically makes the added menu a submenu. When the mouse is positioned over a submenu (or the submenu's mnemonic is pressed), the submenu expands to show its menu items.

Line 76

```
formatMenu.addSeparator();
```

adds a *separator* line to the menu. The separator appears as a horizontal line in the menu.

Look-and-Feel Observation 13.22

Separators can be added to a menu to logically group menu items.

Lines 79 through 94 create the **Font** submenu and several **JRadioButtonMenuItem**s and indicate that the first element of **JRadioButtonMenuItem** array **fonts** should be selected. Line 98 creates a **JCheckBoxMenuItem** array to represent the menu items for specifying bold and italic styles for the fonts. Line 99 defines an instance of inner class **StyleHandler** (defined at lines 158 through 174) to respond to the **JCheckBoxMenuItem** events. The **for** structure at lines 101 through 106 creates each **JCheckBoxMenuItem**, adds each menu item to **fontMenu** and registers the **ItemListener** for each menu item. Line 108 adds **fontMenu** as a submenu of **formatMenu**. Line 109 adds the **formatMenu** to **bar**.

Lines 111 through 115 create a **JLabel** for which the font, font color and font style are controlled through the **Format** menu. The initial foreground color is set to the first element of array **colorValues** (**Color.black**) and the initial font is set to **Times-**

Roman with **PLAIN** style and **72**-point size. Line 117 sets the background color of the window's content pane to **Color.cyan**, and line 118 attaches the **JLabel** to the **CENTER** of the content pane's **BorderLayout**.

Method **actionPerformed** of class **ItemHandler** (line 138) uses two **for** structures to determine which font or color menu item generated the event and sets the font or color of the **JLabel display**, respectively. The **if** condition at line 142 uses **AbstractButton** method *isSelected* to determine which **JRadioButtonMenuItem** for selecting colors is selected. The **if** condition at line 148 uses **EventSource** method *getSource* to get a reference to the **JRadioButtonMenuItem** that generated the event. Line 150 uses **AbstractButton** method *getText* to obtain the name of the font from the menu item.

Method **itemStateChanged** of class **StyleHandler** (line 158) is called if the user selects a **JCheckBoxMenuItem** in the **fontMenu**. Lines 163 and 166 determine if either or both of the **JCheckBoxMenuItem**s are selected and use their combined state to determine the new style of the font.

Look-and-Feel Observation 13.23

*Any lightweight GUI component (i.e., a component that subclasses **JComponent**) can be added to a **JMenu** or to a **JMenuBar**.*

13.9 Using **JPopupMenus**

Many of today's computer applications provide so-called *context-sensitive popup menus*. In Swing, such menus are created with class **JPopupMenu** (a subclass of **JComponent**). These menus provide options that are specific to the component for which the *popup trigger event* was generated. On most systems, the popup trigger event occurs when the user presses and releases the right mouse button.

Look-and-Feel Observation 13.24

The popup trigger event is platform specific. On most platforms that use a mouse with multiple mouse buttons, the popup trigger event is generated when the user clicks the right mouse button.

Figure 13.8 creates a **JPopupMenu** that allows the user to select one of three colors and change the background color of the window. When the user clicks the right mouse button on the **PopupTest** window's background, a **JPopupMenu** of colors is displayed. If the user clicks one of the **JRadioButtonMenuItem**s that represents a color, method **actionPerformed** of class **ItemHandler** changes the background color of the window's content pane.

```
1   // Fig. 13.8: PopupTest.java
2   // Demonstrating JPopupMenus
3   import javax.swing.*;
4   import java.awt.event.*;
5   import java.awt.*;
6
```

Fig. 13.8   Using a **PopupMenu** object (part 1 of 3).

```
7    public class PopupTest extends JFrame {
8       private JRadioButtonMenuItem items[];
9       private Color colorValues[] =
10          { Color.blue, Color.yellow, Color.red };
11
12      public PopupTest()
13      {
14         super( "Using JPopupMenus" );
15
16         final JPopupMenu popupMenu = new JPopupMenu();
17         ItemHandler handler = new ItemHandler();
18         String colors[] = { "Blue", "Yellow", "Red" };
19         ButtonGroup colorGroup = new ButtonGroup();
20         items = new JRadioButtonMenuItem[ 3 ];
21
22         // construct each menu item and add to popup menu; also
23         // enable event handling for each menu item
24         for ( int i = 0; i < items.length; i++ ) {
25            items[ i ] = new JRadioButtonMenuItem( colors[ i ] );
26            popupMenu.add( items[ i ] );
27            colorGroup.add( items[ i ] );
28            items[ i ].addActionListener( handler );
29         }
30
31         getContentPane().setBackground( Color.white );
32
33         // define a MouseListener for the window that displays
34         // a JPopupMenu when the popup trigger event occurs
35         addMouseListener(
36            new MouseAdapter() {
37               public void mousePressed( MouseEvent e )
38                  { checkForTriggerEvent( e ); }
39
40               public void mouseReleased( MouseEvent e )
41                  { checkForTriggerEvent( e ); }
42
43               private void checkForTriggerEvent( MouseEvent e )
44               {
45                  if ( e.isPopupTrigger() )
46                     popupMenu.show( e.getComponent(),
47                                     e.getX(), e.getY() );
48               }
49            }
50         );
51
52         setSize( 300, 200 );
53         show();
54      }
55
56      public static void main( String args[] )
57      {
58         PopupTest app = new PopupTest();
59
```

Fig. 13.8   Using a **PopupMenu** object (part 2 of 3).

```
60          app.addWindowListener(
61             new WindowAdapter() {
62                public void windowClosing( WindowEvent e )
63                {
64                   System.exit( 0 );
65                }
66             }
67          );
68       }
69
70       private class ItemHandler implements ActionListener {
71          public void actionPerformed( ActionEvent e )
72          {
73             // determine which menu item was selected
74             for ( int i = 0; i < items.length; i++ )
75                if ( e.getSource() == items[ i ] ) {
76                   getContentPane().setBackground(
77                      colorValues[ i ] );
78                   repaint();
79                   return;
80                }
81          }
82       }
83    }
```

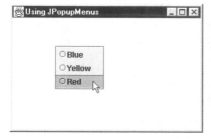

Fig. 13.8   Using a **PopupMenu** object (part 3 of 3).

The constructor for class **PopupTest** (line 12) defines the **JPopupMenu** at line 16

```
final JPopupMenu popupMenu = new JPopupMenu();
```

The reference is declared **final** so it can be used in the anonymous inner class (lines 36 through 49) defined to handle the mouse events of the window.

Software Engineering Observation 13.7

*Local variables must be declared **final** to be used in an anonymous inner class definition.*

The **for** structure at lines 24 through 29 creates **JRadioButtonMenuItem**s to add to the **JPopupMenu**, adds them to the **JPopupMenu** (line 26), adds them to **Button-Group colorGroup** (to maintain one selected **JRadioButtonMenuItem** at a time) and registers an **ActionListener** for each menu item.

Lines 35 through 50 register an instance of an anonymous inner class that extends **MouseAdapter** to handle the mouse events of the application window. Methods

mousePressed (line 37) and **mouseReleased** (line 40) are overridden to check for the popup-trigger event. Each method calls **private** utility method **checkForTriggerEvent** (line 43) to determine if the popup-trigger event occurred. **MouseEvent** method *isPopupTrigger* returns **true** if the popup-trigger event occurred. If so, method *show* of class **JPopupMenu** is invoked to display the **JPopupMenu**. The first argument to method **show** specifies the *origin component,* whose position helps determine where the **JPopupMenu** will appear on the screen. The last two arguments are the *x* and *y* coordinates from the origin component's upper-left corner at which the **JPopupMenu** should appear.

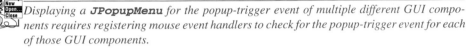

Look-and-Feel Observation 13.25

*Displaying a **JPopupMenu** for the popup-trigger event of multiple different GUI components requires registering mouse event handlers to check for the popup-trigger event for each of those GUI components.*

When a menu item is selected from the popup menu, method **actionPerformed** of **private** inner class **ItemHandler** (line 70) determines which **JRadioButtonMenuItem** was selected by the user, then sets the background color of the window's content pane.

13.10 Pluggable Look-and-Feel

A program that uses Java's Abstract Windowing Toolkit GUI components (package *java.awt*) takes on the look-and-feel of the platform on which the program executes. A Java program running on a Macintosh looks like other programs running on a Macintosh. A Java program running on Microsoft Windows looks like other programs running on Microsoft Windows. A Java program running on a UNIX platform looks like other programs running on that UNIX platform. This may be desirable, because it allows users of the program on each platform to use the GUI components with which they are already familiar. However, this also introduces interesting portability issues.

Portability Tip 13.1

*Programs that use Java's Abstract Windowing Toolkit GUI components (package **java.awt**) take on the look-and-feel of the platform on which they execute.*

Portability Tip 13.2

GUI components on each platform have different looks that may require different amounts of space to display. This may change the layout and alignments of GUI components.

Portability Tip 13.3

GUI components on each platform have different default functionality (e.g., some platforms allow a button with the focus to be "pressed" with the space bar and some do not).

Swing's lightweight GUI components eliminate many of these issues by providing uniform functionality across platforms and by defining a uniform cross-platform look-and-feel (known as the metal look-and-feel). Swing also provides the flexibility to customize the look-and-feel to appear as a Microsoft Windows-style look-and-feel or a Motif-style (UNIX) look-and-feel.

The program of Fig. 13.9 demonstrates how to change the look-and-feel of a Swing GUI. The program creates several GUI components so you can see the change in the look-

and-feel of several GUI components at the same time. The first output window shows the standard metal look-and-feel, the second output window shows the Motif look-and-feel and the third output window shows the Windows look-and-feel.

```
1   // Fig. 13.9: LookAndFeelDemo.java
2   // Changing the look and feel.
3   import javax.swing.*;
4   import java.awt.*;
5   import java.awt.event.*;
6
7   public class LookAndFeelDemo extends JFrame {
8      private String strings[] = { "Metal", "Motif", "Windows" };
9      private UIManager.LookAndFeelInfo looks[];
10     private JRadioButton radio[];
11     private ButtonGroup group;
12     private JButton button;
13     private JLabel label;
14     private JComboBox comboBox;
15
16     public LookAndFeelDemo()
17     {
18        super( "Look and Feel Demo" );
19
20        Container c = getContentPane();
21
22        JPanel northPanel = new JPanel();
23        northPanel.setLayout( new GridLayout( 3, 1, 0, 5 ) );
24        label = new JLabel( "This is a Metal look-and-feel",
25                            SwingConstants.CENTER );
26        northPanel.add( label );
27        button = new JButton( "JButton" );
28        northPanel.add( button );
29        comboBox = new JComboBox( strings );
30        northPanel.add( comboBox );
31
32        c.add( northPanel, BorderLayout.NORTH );
33
34        JPanel southPanel = new JPanel();
35        radio = new JRadioButton[ strings.length ];
36        group = new ButtonGroup();
37        ItemHandler handler = new ItemHandler();
38        southPanel.setLayout(
39           new GridLayout( 1, radio.length ) );
40
41        for ( int i = 0; i < radio.length; i++ ) {
42           radio[ i ] = new JRadioButton( strings[ i ] );
43           radio[ i ].addItemListener( handler );
44           group.add( radio[ i ] );
45           southPanel.add( radio[ i ] );
46        }
47
```

Fig. 13.9   Changing the look-and-feel of a Swing-based GUI (part 1 of 3).

```
48            c.add( southPanel, BorderLayout.SOUTH );
49
50            // get the installed look-and-feel information
51            looks = UIManager.getInstalledLookAndFeels();
52
53            setSize( 300, 200 );
54            show();
55
56            radio[ 0 ].setSelected( true );
57        }
58
59        private void changeTheLookAndFeel( int value )
60        {
61            try {
62                UIManager.setLookAndFeel(
63                    looks[ value ].getClassName() );
64                SwingUtilities.updateComponentTreeUI( this );
65            }
66            catch ( Exception e ) {
67                e.printStackTrace();
68            }
69        }
70
71        public static void main( String args[] )
72        {
73            LookAndFeelDemo dx = new LookAndFeelDemo();
74
75            dx.addWindowListener(
76                new WindowAdapter() {
77                    public void windowClosing( WindowEvent e )
78                    {
79                        System.exit( 0 );
80                    }
81                }
82            );
83        }
84
85        private class ItemHandler implements ItemListener {
86            public void itemStateChanged( ItemEvent e )
87            {
88                for ( int i = 0; i < radio.length; i++ )
89                    if ( radio[ i ].isSelected() ) {
90                        label.setText( "This is a " +
91                            strings[ i ] + " look-and-feel" );
92                        comboBox.setSelectedIndex( i );
93                        changeTheLookAndFeel( i );
94                    }
95            }
96        }
97    }
```

Fig. 13.9   Changing the look-and-feel of a Swing-based GUI (part 2 of 3).

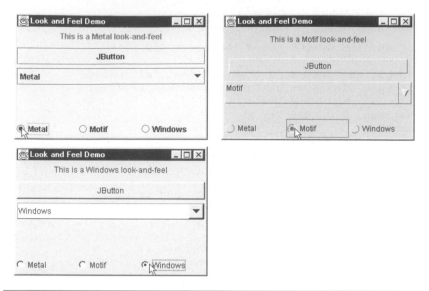

Fig. 13.9   Changing the look-and-feel of a Swing-based GUI (part 3 of 3).

Because all the GUI components and event handling have been covered before, we concentrate on only the mechanism for changing the look-and-feel in this example.

Class **UIManager** (package **javax.swing**) contains **public static** inner class **LookAndFeelInfo** that is used to maintain information about a look-and-feel. Line 9

```
        private UIManager.LookAndFeelInfo looks[];
```

declares an array of type **UIManager.LookAndFeelInfo** (notice the syntax used to access the inner class **LookAndFeelInfo**). Line 51

```
        looks = UIManager.getInstalledLookAndFeels();
```

uses **static** method **getInstalledLookAndFeels** of class **UIManager** to get the array of **UIManager.LookAndFeelInfo** objects that describe the installed look-and-feels.

Performance Tip 13.1

*Each look-and-feel is actually represented by a Java class. **UIManager** method **getInstalledLookAndFeels** does not load each class. Rather, it provides access to the names of the look-and-feels so a choice of look-and-feel can be made (presumably one time at the program's start-up). This reduces the overhead of loading additional classes that are not needed by the program.*

Utility method **changeTheLookAndFeel** (lines 59 through 69) is called by the event handler (defined in **private** inner class **ItemHandler** at lines 85 through 96) for the **JRadioButton**s at the bottom of the user interface. The event handler passes an integer representing the element in **UIManager.LookAndFeelInfo** array **looks** that should be used to change the look-and-feel. Lines 62 and 63

```
        UIManager.setLookAndFeel(
            looks[ value ].getClassName() );
```

use **static** method ***setLookAndFeel*** of class **UIManager** to change the look-and-feel. Method ***getClassName*** of class **UIManager.LookAndFeelInfo** determines the name of the look-and-feel class that corresponds to the **UIManager.LookAndFeelInfo**. If the look-and-feel class is not already loaded, it will be loaded as part of the call to **setLookAndFeel**. Line 64

```
SwingUtilities.updateComponentTreeUI( this );
```

uses **static** method ***updateComponentTreeUI*** of class ***SwingUtilities*** (package **javax.swing**) to change the look-and-feel of every component attached to its argument (this instance of class **LookAndFeelDemo**) to the new look-and-feel.

The preceding two statements appear in a special block of code called a ***try*** block. This code is part of the *exception handling mechanism* discussed in detail in the next chapter. This code is required in case lines 62 and 63 attempt to change the look-and-feel to a look-and-feel that does not exist. Lines 66 through 68 complete the exception handling mechanism with a ***catch*** *handler* that simply processes this problem (if it occurs) by printing an error message at the command line.

13.11 Using JDesktopPane and JInternalFrame

Many of today's applications use a *multiple document interface (MDI)* [i.e., a main window (often called the *parent window*) containing other windows (often called *child windows*)] to manage several open *documents* that are being processed in parallel. For example, many email programs allow you to have several email windows open at the same time so you can compose and/or read multiple email messages. Similarly, many word processors allow the user to open multiple documents in separate windows so the user can switch between the documents without having to close the current document to open another document. The program of Fig. 13.10 demonstrates Swing's ***JDesktopPane*** and ***JInternalFrame*** classes, which provide support for creating multiple document interfaces. The child windows simply display an image of the cover of this book.

```
1   // Fig. 13.10: DesktopTest.java
2   // Demonstrating JDesktopPane.
3   import javax.swing.*;
4   import java.awt.event.*;
5   import java.awt.*;
6
7   public class DesktopTest extends JFrame {
8      public DesktopTest()
9      {
10         super( "Using a JDesktopPane" );
11
12         JMenuBar bar = new JMenuBar();
13         JMenu addMenu = new JMenu( "Add" );
14         JMenuItem newFrame = new JMenuItem( "Internal Frame" );
15         addMenu.add( newFrame );
16         bar.add( addMenu );
17         setJMenuBar( bar );
```

Fig. 13.10 Changing the look-and-feel of a Swing-based GUI (part 1 of 3).

```
18
19          final JDesktopPane theDesktop = new JDesktopPane();
20          getContentPane().add( theDesktop );
21
22          newFrame.addActionListener(
23             new ActionListener() {
24                public void actionPerformed( ActionEvent e ) {
25                   JInternalFrame frame =
26                      new JInternalFrame(
27                         "Internal Frame",
28                         true, true, true, true );
29
30                   Container c = frame.getContentPane();
31                   MyJPanel panel = new MyJPanel();
32
33                   c.add( panel, BorderLayout.CENTER );
34                   frame.setSize(
35                      panel.getImageWidthHeight().width,
36                      panel.getImageWidthHeight().height );
37                   frame.setOpaque( true );
38                   theDesktop.add( frame );
39                }
40             }
41          );
42
43          setSize( 500, 400 );
44          show();
45       }
46
47       public static void main( String args[] )
48       {
49          DesktopTest app = new DesktopTest();
50
51          app.addWindowListener(
52             new WindowAdapter() {
53                public void windowClosing( WindowEvent e )
54                {
55                   System.exit( 0 );
56                }
57             }
58          );
59       }
60    }
61
62    class MyJPanel extends JPanel {
63       private ImageIcon imgIcon;
64
65       public MyJPanel()
66       {
67          imgIcon = new ImageIcon( "jhtp3.gif" );
68       }
69
```

Fig. 13.10   Changing the look-and-feel of a Swing-based GUI (part 2 of 3).

```
70        public void paintComponent( Graphics g )
71        {
72            imgIcon.paintIcon( this, g, 0, 0 );
73        }
74
75        public Dimension getImageWidthHeight()
76        {
77            return new Dimension( imgIcon.getIconWidth(),
78                                  imgIcon.getIconHeight() );
79        }
80    }
```

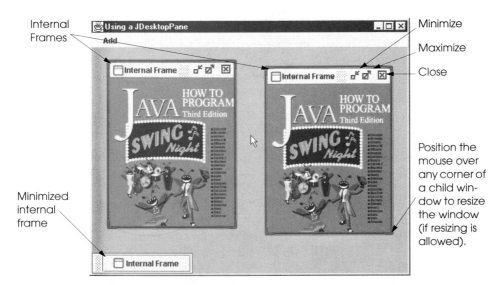

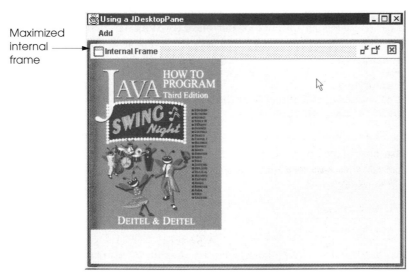

Fig. 13.10   Changing the look-and-feel of a Swing-based GUI (part 3 of 3).

Lines 12 through 17 define a **JMenuBar**, a **JMenu** and a **JMenuItem**, add the **JMenuItem** to the **JMenu**, add the **JMenu** to the **JMenuBar**, and set the **JMenuBar** for the application window. When the user selects the **JMenuItem newFrame**, a new **JInternalFrame** object will be created and displayed.

Line 19

```
final JDesktopPane theDesktop = new JDesktopPane();
```

declares *JDesktopPane* (package **javax.swing**) reference **theDesktop** and assigns it a new **JDesktopPane** object. The **JDesktopPane** object is used to manage the **JInternalFrame** child windows that will be displayed. The reference is declared **final** so it can be used in the anonymous inner class defined at line 23. Line 20 adds the **JDesktopPane** to the application window's content pane.

Lines 22 through 41 register an instance of an anonymous inner class that implements **ActionListener** to handle the event when the user selects the **newFrame** menu item. When the event occurs, method **actionPerformed** (line 24) creates a **JInternalFrame** object with lines 25 through 28

```
JInternalFrame frame =
    new JInternalFrame(
        "Internal Frame",
        true, true, true, true );
```

The **JInternalFrame** constructor used here requires five arguments—a **String** for the title bar of the internal window, a **boolean** indicating if the internal frame should be resizable by the user, a **boolean** indicating if the internal frame should be closable by the user, a **boolean** indicating if the internal frame should be maximizable by the user and a **boolean** indicating if the internal frame should be minimizable by the user. For each of the boolean arguments a **true** value indicates that the operation should be allowed.

As with **JFrame**s and **JApplet**s, a **JInternalFrame** has a content pane to which GUI components can be attached. Line 30 gets a reference to the **JInternalFrame**'s content pane. Line 31 creates an instance of our class **MyJPanel** (defined at lines 62 through 80) that is added to the **JInternalFrame**'s content pane at line 33.

Lines 34 through 36

```
frame.setSize(
    panel.getImageWidthHeight().width,
    panel.getImageWidthHeight().height );
```

set the size of the child window. Class **MyJPanel** defines method **getImageWidthHeight** to return an instance of class **java.awt.Dimension**, which contains two **public** instance variables—**width** and **height**—that are used here as the width and height of the child window.

Line 37

```
frame.setOpaque( true );
```

indicates that the child window should be opaque. By default, **JInternalFrame**s are transparent. When a transparent child window is maximized, other windows and icons on the **JDesktopPane** are visible through the maximized child window's background. The preceding statement prevents this effect.

Line 38

```
theDesktop.add( frame );
```

adds the **JInternalFrame** to the **JDesktopPane**.

Classes **JInternalFrame** and **JDesktopPane** provide many methods for managing child windows. See the on-line documentation for a complete list of these methods.

13.12 Layout Managers

In the preceding chapter, we introduced three layout managers—**FlowLayout**, **BorderLayout** and **GridLayout**. This section presents three additional layout managers (summarized in Fig. 13.11). We discuss these layout managers in the sections that follow.

13.13 BoxLayout Layout Manager

The *BoxLayout layout manager* arranges GUI components horizontally along the *x*-axis or vertically along the *y*-axis of a container. The program of Fig. 13.12 demonstrates **BoxLayout** and the container class **Box** that uses **BoxLayout** as its default layout manager.

Layout manager	Description
BoxLayout	A layout manager that allows GUI components to be arranged left-to-right or top-to-bottom in a container. Class **Box** defines a container with **BoxLayout** as its default layout manager and provides static methods to create a **Box** with a horizontal or vertical **BoxLayout**.
CardLayout	A layout manager that stacks components like a deck of cards. If a component in the deck is a container, it can use any layout manager. Only the component at the "top" of the deck is visible.
GridBagLayout	A layout manager similar to **GridLayout**. Unlike **GridLayout** each component size can vary and components can be added in any order.

Fig. 13.11 Additional layout managers.

```
1   // Fig. 13.12: BoxLayoutDemo.java
2   // Demonstrating BoxLayout.
3   import javax.swing.*;
4   import java.awt.*;
5   import java.awt.event.*;
6
7   public class BoxLayoutDemo extends JFrame {
8      public BoxLayoutDemo()
9      {
10         super( "Demostrating BoxLayout" );
11         final int SIZE = 3;
12
```

Fig. 13.12 Demonstrating the **BoxLayout** layout manager (part 1 of 3).

```
13            Container c = getContentPane();
14            c.setLayout( new BorderLayout( 30, 30 ) );
15
16            Box boxes[] = new Box[ 4 ];
17
18            boxes[ 0 ] = Box.createHorizontalBox();
19            boxes[ 1 ] = Box.createVerticalBox();
20            boxes[ 2 ] = Box.createHorizontalBox();
21            boxes[ 3 ] = Box.createVerticalBox();
22
23            // add buttons to boxes[ 0 ]
24            for ( int i = 0; i < SIZE; i++ )
25               boxes[ 0 ].add( new JButton( "boxes[0]: " + i ) );
26
27            // create strut and add buttons to boxes[ 1 ]
28            for ( int i = 0; i < SIZE; i++ ) {
29               boxes[ 1 ].add( Box.createVerticalStrut( 25 ) );
30               boxes[ 1 ].add( new JButton( "boxes[1]: " + i ) );
31            }
32
33            // create horizontal glue and add buttons to boxes[ 2 ]
34            for ( int i = 0; i < SIZE; i++ ) {
35               boxes[ 2 ].add( Box.createHorizontalGlue() );
36               boxes[ 2 ].add( new JButton( "boxes[2]: " + i ) );
37            }
38
39            // create rigid area and add buttons to boxes[ 3 ]
40            for ( int i = 0; i < SIZE; i++ ) {
41               boxes[ 3 ].add(
42                  Box.createRigidArea( new Dimension( 12, 8 ) ) );
43               boxes[ 3 ].add( new JButton( "boxes[3]: " + i ) );
44            }
45
46            // create horizontal glue and add buttons to panel
47            JPanel panel = new JPanel();
48            panel.setLayout(
49               new BoxLayout( panel, BoxLayout.Y_AXIS ) );
50
51            for ( int i = 0; i < SIZE; i++ ) {
52               panel.add( Box.createGlue() );
53               panel.add( new JButton( "panel: " + i ) );
54            }
55
56            // place panels on frame
57            c.add( boxes[ 0 ], BorderLayout.NORTH );
58            c.add( boxes[ 1 ], BorderLayout.EAST );
59            c.add( boxes[ 2 ], BorderLayout.SOUTH );
60            c.add( boxes[ 3 ], BorderLayout.WEST );
61            c.add( panel, BorderLayout.CENTER );
62
63            setSize( 350, 300 );
64            show();
65         }
```

Fig. 13.12   Demonstrating the **BoxLayout** layout manager (part 2 of 3).

```
66
67      public static void main( String args[] )
68      {
69          BoxLayoutDemo app = new BoxLayoutDemo();
70
71          app.addWindowListener(
72              new WindowAdapter() {
73                  public void windowClosing( WindowEvent e )
74                  {
75                      System.exit( 0 );
76                  }
77              }
78          );
79      }
80  }
```

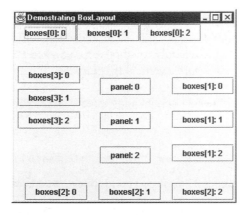

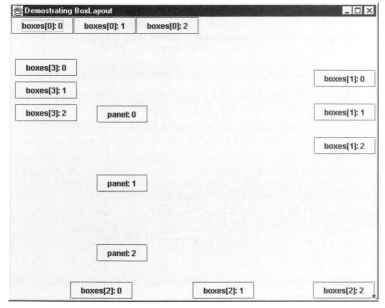

Fig. 13.12   Demonstrating the **BoxLayout** layout manager (part 3 of 3).

In the constructor for class **BoxLayoutDemo**, lines 13 and 14 obtain a reference to the content pane and set its layout to a **BorderLayout** with 30 pixels of horizontal and 30 pixels of vertical gap space between components. The space is to help isolate each of the containers with **BoxLayout** in this example.

Lines 16 through 21

```
Box boxes[] = new Box[ 4 ];

boxes[ 0 ] = Box.createHorizontalBox();
boxes[ 1 ] = Box.createVerticalBox();
boxes[ 2 ] = Box.createHorizontalBox();
boxes[ 3 ] = Box.createVerticalBox();
```

define an array of **Box** container references called **boxes** and initialize each element of the array with **Box** objects. Elements 0 and 2 of the array are initialized with **static** method *createHorizontalBox* of class **Box**, which returns a **Box** container with a horizontal **BoxLayout** (GUI components are arranged left-to-right). Elements 1 and 3 of the array are initialized with **static** method *createVerticalBox* of class **Box**, which returns a **Box** container with a vertical **BoxLayout** (GUI components are arranged top-to-bottom).

The **for** structure at lines 24 and 25 adds three **JButton**s to **boxes[0]** (a horizontal **Box**).

```
for ( int i = 0; i < SIZE; i++ )
   boxes[ 0 ].add( new JButton( "boxes[0]: " + i ) );
```

The **for** structure at lines 28 through 31 adds three **JButton**s to **boxes[1]** (a vertical **Box**).

```
for ( int i = 0; i < SIZE; i++ ) {
   boxes[ 1 ].add( Box.createVerticalStrut( 25 ) );
   boxes[ 1 ].add( new JButton( "boxes[1]: " + i ) );
}
```

Before adding each button, line 29 adds a *vertical strut* to the container with **static** method *createVerticalStrut* of class **Box**. A vertical strut is an invisible GUI component that has a fixed pixel height and is used to guarantee a fixed amount of space between GUI components. The argument to method **createVerticalStrut** determines the height of the strut in pixels. Class **Box** also defines method *createHorizontalStrut* for horizontal **BoxLayout**s.

The **for** structure at lines 34 through 37 adds three **JButton**s to **boxes[2]** (a horizontal **Box**).

```
for ( int i = 0; i < SIZE; i++ ) {
   boxes[ 2 ].add( Box.createHorizontalGlue() );
   boxes[ 2 ].add( new JButton( "boxes[2]: " + i ) );
}
```

Before adding each button, line 35 adds *horizontal glue* to the container with **static** method *createHorizontalGlue* of class **Box**. Horizontal glue is an invisible GUI component that can be used between fixed-size GUI components to occupy additional space. Normally, extra space appears to the right of the last horizontal GUI component or below the last vertical GUI component in a **BoxLayout**. Glue allows the extra space to be placed between GUI components. Class **Box** also defines method ***createVerti-calGlue*** for vertical **BoxLayout**s.

The **for** structure at lines 40 through 44 adds three **JButton**s to **boxes[3]** (a vertical **Box**).

```
for ( int i = 0; i < SIZE; i++ ) {
    boxes[ 3 ].add(
        Box.createRigidArea( new Dimension( 12, 8 ) ) );
    boxes[ 3 ].add( new JButton( "boxes[3]: " + i ) );
}
```

Before adding each button, line 41 adds a *rigid area* to the container with **static** method ***createRigidArea*** of class **Box**. A rigid area is an invisible GUI component that always has a fixed pixel width and height. The argument to method **createRigidArea** is a **Dimension** object that specifies the width and height of the rigid area.

Lines 47 through 49

```
JPanel panel = new JPanel();
panel.setLayout(
    new BoxLayout( panel, BoxLayout.Y_AXIS ) );
```

create a **JPanel** object and set its layout in the conventional manner using **Container** method **setLayout**. The **BoxLayout** constructor receives a reference to the container for which it controls the layout and a constant indicating if the layout is horizontal (***Box-Layout.X_AXIS***) or vertical (***BoxLayout.Y_AXIS***).

The **for** structure at lines 51 through 54 adds three **JButton**s to **panel**.

```
for ( int i = 0; i < SIZE; i++ ) {
    panel.add( Box.createGlue() );
    panel.add( new JButton( "panel: " + i ) );
}
```

Before adding each button, line 52 adds a glue component to the container with **static** method ***createGlue*** of class **Box**.

The **Box** containers and the **JPanel** are attached to the content pane's **Border-Layout** at lines 57 through 61. Try executing the application. When the window appears, resize the window to see how the glue components, strut components and rigid area affect the layout in each container.

13.14 CardLayout Layout Manager

The ***CardLayout*** *layout manager* arranges components into a "deck" of cards where only the top card is visible. Any card in the deck can be placed at the top of the deck at any time using methods of class **CardLayout**. Each card is usually a container such as a panel, and each card can use any layout manager. Class **CardLayout** inherits from **Object** and implements the **LayoutManager2** interface.

The program of Fig. 13.13 creates five panels. **JPanel deck** uses the **CardLayout** layout manager to control the card that is displayed. **JPanel**s **card1**, **card2** and **card3** are used as individual cards in **deck**. **JPanel buttons** contains four buttons (with labels **First card**, **Next card**, **Previous card** and **Last card**) that enable the user to manipulate the deck. When the user clicks the **First card** button, the first card in **deck** (i.e., **card1**) is displayed. When the user clicks the **Last card** button, the last card (i.e., **card3**) in **deck** is displayed. Each time the user clicks the **Previous card** button, the previous card in **deck** is displayed. Each time the user clicks the **Next card** button, the next card in **deck** is displayed. Clicking the **Previous card** button or the **Next card** button repeatedly allows the user to cycle through the **deck** of cards. Application class **CardDeck** implements **ActionListener**, so the action events generated by the **JButton**s on **JPanel buttons** are handled by the application in its **actionPerformed** method.

Class **CardDeck** declares a reference of type **CardLayout** called **cardManager** (line 9). This reference is used to invoke **CardLayout** methods that manipulate the cards in the deck.

```
1   // Fig. 13.13: CardDeck.java
2   // Demonstrating CardLayout.
3   import javax.swing.*;
4   import java.awt.*;
5   import java.awt.event.*;
6
7   public class CardDeck extends JFrame
8                         implements ActionListener {
9      private CardLayout cardManager;
10     private JPanel deck;
11     private JButton controls[];
12     private String names[] = { "First card", "Next card",
13                                "Previous card", "Last card" };
14
15     public CardDeck()
16     {
17        super( "CardLayout " );
18
19        Container c = getContentPane();
20
21        // create the JPanel with CardLayout
22        deck = new JPanel();
23        cardManager = new CardLayout();
24        deck.setLayout( cardManager );
25
26        // set up card1 and add it to JPanel deck
27        JLabel label1 =
28           new JLabel( "card one", SwingConstants.CENTER );
29        JPanel card1 = new JPanel();
30        card1.add( label1 );
31        deck.add( card1, label1.getText() ); // add card to deck
32
33        // set up card2 and add it to JPanel deck
34        JLabel label2 =
35           new JLabel( "card two", SwingConstants.CENTER );
36        JPanel card2 = new JPanel();
```

Fig. 13.13   Demonstrating the **CardLayout** layout manager (part 1 of 3).

```
37            card2.setBackground( Color.yellow );
38            card2.add( label2 );
39            deck.add( card2, label2.getText() ); // add card to deck
40
41            // set up card3 and add it to JPanel deck
42            JLabel label3 = new JLabel( "card three" );
43            JPanel card3 = new JPanel();
44            card3.setLayout( new BorderLayout() );
45            card3.add( new JButton( "North" ), BorderLayout.NORTH );
46            card3.add( new JButton( "West" ), BorderLayout.WEST );
47            card3.add( new JButton( "East" ), BorderLayout.EAST );
48            card3.add( new JButton( "South" ), BorderLayout.SOUTH );
49            card3.add( label3, BorderLayout.CENTER );
50            deck.add( card3, label3.getText() ); // add card to deck
51
52            // create and layout buttons that will control deck
53            JPanel buttons = new JPanel();
54            buttons.setLayout( new GridLayout( 2, 2 ) );
55            controls = new JButton[ names.length ];
56
57            for ( int i = 0; i < controls.length; i++ ) {
58               controls[ i ] = new JButton( names[ i ] );
59               controls[ i ].addActionListener( this );
60               buttons.add( controls[ i ] );
61            }
62
63            // add JPanel deck and JPanel buttons to the applet
64            c.add( buttons, BorderLayout.WEST );
65            c.add( deck, BorderLayout.EAST );
66
67            setSize( 450, 200 );
68            show();
69         }
70
71         public void actionPerformed( ActionEvent e )
72         {
73            if ( e.getSource() == controls[ 0 ] )
74               cardManager.first( deck ); // show first card
75            else if ( e.getSource() == controls[ 1 ] )
76               cardManager.next( deck );   // show next card
77            else if ( e.getSource() == controls[ 2 ] )
78               cardManager.previous( deck );   // show previous card
79            else if ( e.getSource() == controls[ 3 ] )
80               cardManager.last( deck );   // show last card
81         }
82
83         public static void main( String args[] )
84         {
85            CardDeck cardDeckDemo = new CardDeck();
86
87            cardDeckDemo.addWindowListener(
88               new WindowAdapter() {
```

Fig. 13.13   Demonstrating the **CardLayout** layout manager (part 2 of 3).

```
89              public void windowClosing( WindowEvent e )
90              {
91                  System.exit( 0 );
92              }
93          }
94      );
95  }
96 }
```

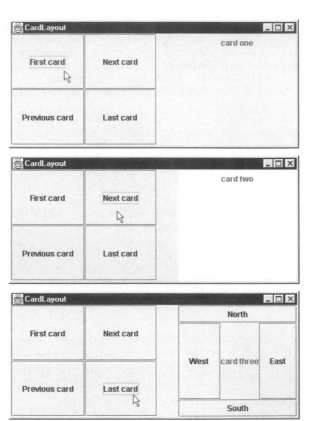

Fig. 13.13   Demonstrating the **CardLayout** layout manager (part 3 of 3).

The constructor method (line 15) builds the GUI. Lines 22 through 24

```
deck = new JPanel();
cardManager = new CardLayout();
deck.setLayout( cardManager );
```

create **JPanel deck**, create **CardLayout** object **cardManager** and set the layout manager for **deck** to **cardManager**. Next, **JPanel**s **card1**, **card2** and **card3** and their GUI components are created. As we set up each card, we add the card to **deck** using **Container** method **add** with two arguments—a **Component** and a **String**. The **Component** is the **JPanel** object that represents the card. The **String** argument identifies the card. For example, line 31

```
deck.add( card1, label1.getText() ); // add card to deck
```

adds **JPanel card1** to deck and uses **JLabel label1**'s label as the **String** identifier for the card. **JPanel**s **card2** and **card3** are added to **deck** at lines 39 and 50, respectively. Next, the **JPanel buttons** and its **JButton** objects are created (lines 53 through 61). Line 59 registers the **ActionListener** for each **JButton**. Finally, **buttons** and **deck** are added to the content pane's West and East regions, respectively.

Method **actionPerformed** (line 71) determines which **JButton** generated the event using **EventObject** method **getSource**. **CardLayout** methods *first*, *previous*, *next* and *last* are used to display a particular card based on which **JButton** the user pressed. Method **first** displays the first card added to the deck. Method **previous** displays the previous card in the deck. Method **next** displays the next card in the deck. Method **last** displays the last card in the deck. Note that **deck** is passed to each of these methods.

13.15 GridBagLayout Layout Manager

The most complex and most powerful of the predefined layout managers is *GridBagLayout*. This layout is similar to **GridLayout** because **GridBagLayout** also arranges components in a grid. However, **GridBagLayout** is more flexible. The components can vary in size (i.e., they can occupy multiple rows and columns) and can be added in any order.

The first step in using **GridBagLayout** is determining the appearance of the GUI. This step does not involve any programming; all that is needed is a piece of paper. First, draw the GUI. Next draw a grid over the GUI dividing the components into rows and columns. The initial row and column numbers should be 0 so the **GridBagLayout** layout manager can properly place the components in the grid. The row and column numbers will be used to place each component in an exact position in the grid. Figure. 13.14 demonstrates drawing the lines for the rows and columns over a GUI.

To use **GridBagLayout**, a *GridBagConstraints* object must be constructed. This object specifies how a component is placed in a **GridBagLayout**. Several **GridBagConstraints** instance variables are summarized in Fig. 13.15.

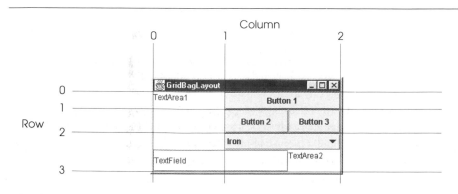

Fig. 13.14   Designing a GUI that will use **GridBagLayout**.

GridBagConstraints instance variable	Description
gridx	The column in which the component will be placed.
gridy	The row in which the component will be placed.
gridwidth	The number of columns the component occupies.
gridheight	The number of rows the component occupies.
weightx	The portion of extra space to allocate horizontally. The components can become wider when extra space is available.
weighty	The portion of extra space to allocate vertically. The components can become taller when extra space is available.

Fig. 13.15   GridBagConstraints instance variables.

Variables *gridx* and *gridy* specify the row and column where the upper-left corner of the component is placed in the grid. Variable **gridx** corresponds to the column and the variable **gridy** corresponds to the row. In Fig. 13.14, the **JComboBox** (displaying "**Iron**") has a **gridx** value of 1 and a **gridy** value of 2.

Variable *gridwidth* specifies the number of columns a component occupies. In Fig. 13.14, the **JComboBox** button occupies two columns. Variable *gridheight* specifies the number of rows a component occupies. In Fig. 13.14, the **JTextArea** on the left side of the window occupies three rows.

Variable *weightx* specifies how to distribute extra horizontal space to components in a **GridBagLayout** when the container is resized. A zero value indicates that the component does not grow horizontally on its own. However, if the component spans a column containing a component with nonzero **weightx** value, the component with zero **weightx** value will grow horizontally in the same proportion as the other component(s) in the same column. This is because each component must be maintained in the same row and column in which it was originally placed.

Variable *weighty* specifies how to distribute extra vertical space to components in a **GridBagLayout** when the container is resized. A zero value indicates that the component does not grow vertically on its own. However, if the component spans a row containing a component with non zero **weighty** value, the component with zero **weighty** value grows vertically in the same proportion as the other component(s) in the same row.

In Fig. 13.14, the effects of **weighty** and **weightx** cannot easily be seen until the container is resized and additional space becomes available. Components with larger weight values occupy more of the additional space than components with smaller weight values. The exercises explore the effects of varying **weightx** and **weighty**.

Components should be given nonzero positive weight values—otherwise the components will "huddle" together in the middle of the container. Figure 13.16 shows the GUI of Fig. 13.14—where all weights have been set to zero.

Common Programming Error 13.6

Using a negative value for either **weightx** *or* **weighty** *is a logic error.*

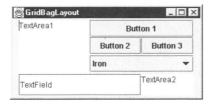

Fig. 13.16   GridBagLayout with the weights set to zero.

GridBagConstraints instance variable *fill* specifies how much of the component's area (the number of rows and columns the component occupies in the grid) is occupied. The variable **fill** is assigned one of the following **GridBagConstraints** constants: *NONE*, *VERTICAL*, *HORIZONTAL* or *BOTH*. The default value is **NONE**, which indicates that the component will not grow in either direction. **VERTICAL** indicates that the component will grow vertically. **HORIZONTAL** indicates that the component will grow horizontally. **BOTH** indicates that the component will grow in both directions.

GridBagConstraints instance variable *anchor* specifies the location of the component in the area when the component does not fill the entire area. The variable **anchor** is assigned one of the following **GridBagConstraints** constants: *NORTH*, *NORTHEAST*, *EAST*, *SOUTHEAST*, *SOUTH*, *SOUTHWEST*, *WEST*, *NORTHWEST* or *CENTER*. The default value is **CENTER**.

The program of Fig. 13.17 uses the **GridBagLayout** layout manager to arrange the components in the GUI of Fig. 13.14. The program does nothing other than demonstrate how to use **GridBagLayout**.

The GUI consists of three **JButton**s, two **JTextArea**s, a **JComboBox** and a **JTextField**. The layout manager for the content pane is **GridBagLayout**. Lines 17 and 18

```
gbLayout = new GridBagLayout();
container.setLayout( gbLayout );
```

instantiate the **GridBagLayout** object and set the layout manager for the content pane to **gbLayout**. The **GridBagConstraints** object used to determine the location and size of each component in the grid is instantiated with line 21

```
gbConstraints = new GridBagConstraints()
```

Lines 23 through 30 instantiate each of the GUI components that will be added to the content pane.

JTextArea ta is the first component added to the **GridBagLayout**. The values for **weightx** and **weighty** values are not specified in **gbConstraints**, so each has the value zero by default. Thus, the **JTextArea** will not resize itself even if space is available. However, the **JTextArea** spans multiple rows, so the vertical size is subject to the **weighty** values of **JButton**s **b2** and **b3**. When either **b2** or **b3** is resized vertically based on its **weighty** value, the **JTextArea** is also resized.

```
1   // Fig. 13.17: GridBagDemo.java
2   // Demonstrating GridBagLayout.
3   import javax.swing.*;
4   import java.awt.*;
5   import java.awt.event.*;
6
7   public class GridBagDemo extends JFrame {
8      private Container container;
9      private GridBagLayout gbLayout;
10     private GridBagConstraints gbConstraints;
11
12     public GridBagDemo()
13     {
14        super( "GridBagLayout" );
15
16        container = getContentPane();
17        gbLayout = new GridBagLayout();
18        container.setLayout( gbLayout );
19
20        // instantiate gridbag constraints
21        gbConstraints = new GridBagConstraints();
22
23        JTextArea ta = new JTextArea( "TextArea1", 5, 10 );
24        JTextArea tx = new JTextArea( "TextArea2", 2, 2 );
25        String names[] = { "Iron", "Steel", "Brass" };
26        JComboBox cb = new JComboBox( names );
27        JTextField tf = new JTextField( "TextField" );
28        JButton b1 = new JButton( "Button 1" );
29        JButton b2 = new JButton( "Button 2" );
30        JButton b3 = new JButton( "Button 3" );
31
32        // text area
33        // weightx and weighty are both 0: the default
34        // anchor for all components is CENTER: the default
35        gbConstraints.fill = GridBagConstraints.BOTH;
36        addComponent( ta, 0, 0, 1, 3 );
37
38        // button b1
39        // weightx and weighty are both 0: the default
40        gbConstraints.fill = GridBagConstraints.HORIZONTAL;
41        addComponent( b1, 0, 1, 2, 1 );
42
43        // combo box
44        // weightx and weighty are both 0: the default
45        // fill is HORIZONTAL
46        addComponent( cb, 2, 1, 2, 1 );
47
48        // button b2
49        gbConstraints.weightx = 1000;  // can grow wider
50        gbConstraints.weighty = 1;      // can grow taller
51        gbConstraints.fill = GridBagConstraints.BOTH;
52        addComponent( b2, 1, 1, 1, 1 );
```

Fig. 13.17 Demonstrating the **GridBagLayout** layout manager (part 1 of 3).

```
53
54            // button b3
55            // fill is BOTH
56            gbConstraints.weightx = 0;
57            gbConstraints.weighty = 0;
58            addComponent( b3, 1, 2, 1, 1 );
59
60            // textfield
61            // weightx and weighty are both 0: fill is BOTH
62            addComponent( tf, 3, 0, 2, 1 );
63
64            // textarea
65            // weightx and weighty are both 0: fill is BOTH
66            addComponent( tx, 3, 2, 1, 1 );
67
68            setSize( 300, 150 );
69            show();
70         }
71
72      // addComponent is programmer defined
73      private void addComponent( Component c,
74         int row, int column, int width, int height )
75      {
76         // set gridx and gridy
77         gbConstraints.gridx = column;
78         gbConstraints.gridy = row;
79
80         // set gridwidth and gridheight
81         gbConstraints.gridwidth = width;
82         gbConstraints.gridheight = height;
83
84         // set constraints
85         gbLayout.setConstraints( c, gbConstraints );
86         container.add( c );        // add component
87      }
88
89      public static void main( String args[] )
90      {
91         GridBagDemo app = new GridBagDemo();
92
93         app.addWindowListener(
94            new WindowAdapter() {
95               public void windowClosing( WindowEvent e )
96               {
97                  System.exit( 0 );
98               }
99            }
100        );
101     }
102 }
```

Fig. 13.17   Demonstrating the **GridBagLayout** layout manager (part 2 of 3).

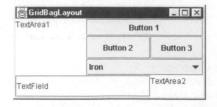

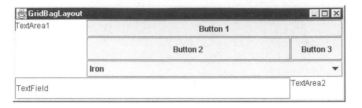

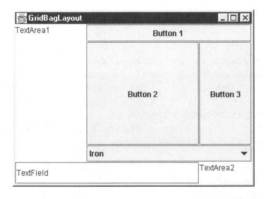

Fig. 13.17   Demonstrating the **GridBagLayout** layout manager (part 3 of 3).

Line 35

```
gbConstraints.fill = GridBagConstraints.BOTH;
```

sets variable **fill** in **gbConstraints** to **GridBagConstraints.BOTH**, causing the **JTextArea** to always fill its entire allocated area in the grid. An **anchor** value is not specified in **gbConstraints**, so the default of **CENTER** is used. We do not use variable **anchor** in this program, so all components will use **CENTER** by default. Line 36

```
addComponent( ta, 0, 0, 1, 3 );
```

calls our utility method ***addComponent*** method (defined at line 73). The **JTextArea** object, the row, the column, the number of columns to span and the number of rows to span are passed as arguments.

Method **addComponent**'s parameters are a **Component** reference **c** and integers **row**, **column**, **width** and **height**. Lines 77 and 78

```
gbConstraints.gridx = column;
gbConstraints.gridy = row;
```

set the **GridBagConstraints** variables **gridx** and **gridy**. The **gridx** variable is assigned the column in which the **Component** will be placed, and the **gridy** value is assigned the row in which the **Component** will be placed. Lines 81 and 82

```
gbContraints.gridwidth = width;
gbContraints.gridheight = height;
```

set the **GridBagConstraints** variables **gridwidth** and **gridheight**. The **gridwidth** variable specifies the number of columns the **Component** will span in the grid and the **gridheight** variable specifies the number of rows the **Component** will span in the grid. Line 85

```
gbLayout.setConstraints( c, gbContraints );
```

sets the **GridBagConstraints** for a component in the **GridBagLayout**. Method *setConstraints* of class **GridBagLayout** takes a **Component** argument and a **GridBagConstraints** argument. Method **add** (line 86) is used to add the component to the content pane.

JButton object **b1** is the next component added (lines 40 and 41). The values of **weightx** and **weighty** are still zero. The **fill** variable is set to **HORIZONTAL**—the component will always fill its area in the horizontal direction. The vertical direction is not filled. Since the **weighty** value is zero, the button will become taller only if another component in the same row has a nonzero **weighty** value. **JButton b1** is located at row 0, column 1. One row and two columns are occupied.

JComboBox cb is the next component added (line 46). The **weightx** and **weighty** values are zero and the **fill** variable is set to **HORIZONTAL**. The **JComboBox** button will grow only in the horizontal direction. Note that the **weightx**, **weighty** and **fill** variables remain set in **gbConstraints** until they are changed. The **JComboBox** button is placed at row 2, column 1. One row and two columns are occupied.

JButton object **b2** is the next component added (lines 49 through 52). **JButton b2** is given a **weightx** value of **1000** and a **weighty** value of **1**. The area occupied by the button is capable of growing in the vertical and horizontal directions. The **fill** variable is set to **BOTH**, which specifies that the button will always fill the entire area. When the window is resized, **b2** will grow. The button is placed at row 1, column 1. One row and one column are occupied.

JButton b3 is added next (lines 56 through 58). Both the **weightx** value and **weighty** value are set to zero and the value of **fill** is **BOTH**. **JButton b3** will grow if the window is resized; it is affected by the weight values of **b2**. Note that the **weightx** value for **b2** is much larger than **b3**. When resizing occurs, **b2** will occupy a larger percentage of the new space. The button is placed at row 1, column 2. One row and one column are occupied.

Both the **JTextField** (line 62) and **JTextArea tx** (line 66) have a **weightx** value of 0 and a **weighty** value of 0. The value of **fill** is **BOTH**. The **JTextField** is placed at row 3, column 0 and the **JTextArea** is placed at row 3, column 2. The **JTextField** occupies one row and two columns. The **JTextArea** occupies one row and one column.

When you execute this application, try resizing the window to see how the constraints for each GUI component affect its position and size in the window.

13.16 GridBagConstraints Constants RELATIVE and REMAINDER

A variation of **GridBagLayout** does not use the **gridx** and **gridy**. Rather, **Grid-bagConstraints** constants *RELATIVE* and *REMAINDER* are used in their place. **RELATIVE** specifies that the next-to-last component in a particular row should be placed to the right of the previous component in that row. **REMAINDER** specifies that a component is the last component in a row. Any component that is not the second-to-last or last component on a row must specify values for **GridbagConstraints** variables **gridwidth** and **gridheight**. Class **GridBagDemo2** in Fig. 13.18 arranges components in **GridBagLayout** using these constants.

```
1   // Fig. 13.18: GridBagDemo2.java
2   // Demonstrating GridBagLayout constants.
3   import javax.swing.*;
4   import java.awt.*;
5   import java.awt.event.*;
6
7   public class GridBagDemo2 extends JFrame {
8       private GridBagLayout gbLayout;
9       private GridBagConstraints gbConstraints;
10      private Container container;
11
12      public GridBagDemo2()
13      {
14          super( "GridBagLayout" );
15
16          container = getContentPane();
17          gbLayout = new GridBagLayout();
18          container.setLayout( gbLayout );
19
20          // instantiate gridbag constraints
21          gbConstraints = new GridBagConstraints();
22
23          // create GUI components
24          String metals[] = { "Copper", "Aluminum", "Silver" };
25          JComboBox comboBox = new JComboBox( metals );
26
27          JTextField textField = new JTextField( "TextField" );
28
29          String fonts[] = { "Serif", "Monospaced" };
30          JList list = new JList( fonts );
31
32          String names[] =
33              { "zero", "one", "two", "three", "four" };
34          JButton buttons[] = new JButton[ names.length ];
35
36          for ( int i = 0; i < buttons.length; i++ )
37              buttons[ i ] = new JButton( names[ i ] );
```

Fig. 13.18   Demonstrating the **GridBagConstraints** constants **RELATIVE** and **REMAINDER** (part 1 of 3).

```
38
39          // define GUI component constraints
40          // textField
41          gbConstraints.weightx = 1;
42          gbConstraints.weighty = 1;
43          gbConstraints.fill = GridBagConstraints.BOTH;
44          gbConstraints.gridwidth = GridBagConstraints.REMAINDER;
45          addComponent( textField );
46
47          // buttons[0] -- weightx and weighty are 1: fill is BOTH
48          gbConstraints.gridwidth = 1;
49          addComponent( buttons[ 0 ] );
50
51          // buttons[1] -- weightx and weighty are 1: fill is BOTH
52          gbConstraints.gridwidth = GridBagConstraints.RELATIVE;
53          addComponent( buttons[ 1 ] );
54
55          // buttons[2] -- weightx and weighty are 1: fill is BOTH
56          gbConstraints.gridwidth = GridBagConstraints.REMAINDER;
57          addComponent( buttons[ 2 ] );
58
59          // comboBox -- weightx is 1: fill is BOTH
60          gbConstraints.weighty = 0;
61          gbConstraints.gridwidth = GridBagConstraints.REMAINDER;
62          addComponent( comboBox );
63
64          // buttons[3] -- weightx is 1: fill is BOTH
65          gbConstraints.weighty = 1;
66          gbConstraints.gridwidth = GridBagConstraints.REMAINDER;
67          addComponent( buttons[ 3 ] );
68
69          // buttons[4] -- weightx and weighty are 1: fill is BOTH
70          gbConstraints.gridwidth = GridBagConstraints.RELATIVE;
71          addComponent( buttons[ 4 ] );
72
73          // list -- weightx and weighty are 1: fill is BOTH
74          gbConstraints.gridwidth = GridBagConstraints.REMAINDER;
75          addComponent( list );
76
77          setSize( 300, 200 );
78          show();
79       }
80
81       // addComponent is programmer-defined
82       private void addComponent( Component c )
83       {
84          gbLayout.setConstraints( c, gbConstraints );
85          container.add( c );          // add component
86       }
87
```

Fig. 13.18 Demonstrating the **GridBagConstraints** constants **RELATIVE** and **REMAINDER** (part 2 of 3).

```
88    public static void main( String args[] )
89    {
90       GridBagDemo2 app = new GridBagDemo2();
91
92       app.addWindowListener(
93          new WindowAdapter() {
94             public void windowClosing( WindowEvent e )
95             {
96                System.exit( 0 );
97             }
98          }
99       );
100   }
101 }
```

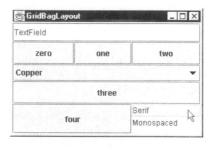

Fig. 13.18   Demonstrating the **GridBagConstraints** constants **RELATIVE** and **REMAINDER** (part 3 of 3).

Lines 17 and 18

```
gbLayout = new GridBagLayout();
container.setLayout( gbLayout );
```

construct a **GridBagLayout** and set the content pane's layout manager to **GridBag-Layout**.

The components that are placed in **GridBagLayout** are each constructed (lines 24 through 37). The components are five **JButtons**, one **JTextField**, one **JList** and one **JComboBox**.

The **JTextField** is added first (lines 41 through 45). The **weightx** and **weighty** values are set to 1. The **fill** variable is set to **BOTH**. Line 44

```
gbConstraints.gridwidth = GridBagConstraints.REMAINDER;
```

specifies that the **JTextField** is the last component on the line. The **JTextField** is added to the content pane with a call to our utility method **addComponent** (defined at line 82). Method **addComponent** takes a **Component** argument and uses **GridBag-Layout** method **setConstraints** to set the constraints for the **Component**. Method **add** attaches the component to the content pane.

JButton buttons[0] (lines 48 and 49) has **weightx** and **weighty** values of 1. The **fill** variable is **BOTH**. Because **buttons[0]** is not one of the last two components on the row, it is given a **gridwidth** of 1 so it occupies one column. The **JButton** is added to the content pane with a call to utility method **addComponent**.

JButton buttons[1] (lines 52 and 53) has **weightx** and **weighty** values of 1. The **fill** variable is **BOTH**. The statement

```
gbConstraints.gridwidth = GridBagConstraints.RELATIVE;
```

specifies that the **JButton** is to be placed relative to the previous component. The **Button** is added to the **JFrame** with a call to **addComponent**.

JButton buttons[2] (lines 56 and 57) has **weightx** and **weighty** values of 1. The **fill** variable is **BOTH**. This **JButton** is the last component on the line, so **REMAINDER** is used. The **JButton** is added to the content pane with a call to utility method **addComponent**.

The **JComboBox** button (lines 60 through 62) has a **weightx** of 1 and a **weighty** of 0. The **JComboBox** will not grow in the vertical direction. The **JComboBox** is the only component on the line, so **REMAINDER** is used. The **JComboBox** is added to the content pane with a call to utility method **addComponent**.

JButton buttons[3] (lines 65 through 67) has **weightx** and **weighty** values of 1. The **fill** variable is **BOTH**. This **JButton** is the only component on the line, so **REMAINDER** is used. The **JButton** is added to the content pane with a call to utility method **addComponent**.

JButton buttons[4] (lines 70 and 71) has **weightx** and **weighty** values of 1. The **fill** variable is **BOTH**. This **JButton** is the next-to-last component on the line, so **RELATIVE** is used. The **JButton** is added to the content pane with a call to utility method **addComponent**.

The **JList** component (lines 74 and 75) has **weightx** and **weighty** values of 1. The **fill** variable is **BOTH**. The **JList** is added to the content pane with a call to utility method **addComponent**.

Summary

- **JTextArea**s provide an area for manipulating multiple lines of text. Like class **JTextField**, class **JTextArea** inherits from **JTextComponent**.

- An external event (i.e., an event generated by a different GUI component) normally indicates when the text in a **JTextArea** should be processed.

- Scrollbars are provided for a **JTextArea** by attaching it to a **JScrollPane** object.

- Method **getSelectedText** returns the selected text from a **JTextArea**. Text is selected by dragging the mouse over the desired text to highlight it.

- Method **setText** sets the text in a **JTextArea**.

- To provide automatic word wrap in a **JTextArea**, attach it to a **JScrollPane** with horizontal scrollbar policy **JScrollPane.HORIZONTAL_SCROLLBAR_NEVER**.

- The horizontal and vertical scrollbar policies for a **JScrollPane** are set when a **JScrollPane** is constructed or with methods **setHorizontalScrollBarPolicy** and **setVerticalScrollBarPolicy** of class **JScrollPane**.

- A **JPanel** can be used as a a dedicated drawing area that can receive mouse events and is often extended to create new GUI components.

- Swing components that inherit from class **JComponent** contain method **paintComponent**, which helps them draw properly in the context of a Swing GUI. **JComponent** method **paintComponent** should be overridden as follows:

```
public void paintComponent( Graphics g )
{
    super.paintComponent( g );

    // your additional drawing code
}
```

The call to the superclass version of **paintComponent** ensures that painting occurs in the proper order and that Swing's painting mechanism remains intact. If the superclass version of **paint-Component** is not called, typically the customized GUI component will not be displayed properly on the user interface. Also, if the superclass version is called after performing the customized drawing statements, the results will typically be erased.

* Classes **JFrame** and **JApplet** are not subclasses of **JComponent**; therefore, they do not contain method **paintComponent** (they have method **paint**).

* Calling **repaint** for a Swing GUI component indicates that the component should be painted as soon as possible. The background of the GUI component is cleared only if the component is opaque. Most Swing components are transparent by default. **JComponent** method **setOpaque** can be passed a **boolean** argument indicating if the component is opaque (**true**) or transparent (**false**). The GUI components of package **java.awt** are different from Swing components in that **repaint** results in a call to **Component** method **update** (which clears the component's background) and **update** calls method **paint** (rather than **paintComponent**).

* Method **setTitle** displays a **String** in a window's title bar.

* Drawing on any GUI component is performed with coordinates that are measured from the upper-left corner (0, 0) of that GUI component.

* Layout managers often use a GUI component's **getPreferredSize** method to determine the preferred width and height of a component when laying out that component as part of a GUI. If a new component has a preferred width and height, it should override method **getPreferred-Size** to return that width and height as an object of class **Dimension** (package **java.awt**).

* The default size of a **JPanel** object is 0 pixels wide and 0 pixels tall.

* A mouse drag operation begins with a mouse pressed event. All subsequent mouse drag events (for which **mouseDragged** will be called) are sent to the GUI component that received the original mouse pressed event.

* **JSlider**s enable the user to select from a range of integer values. **JSlider**s are highly customizable in that they can display major tick marks, minor tick marks and labels for the tick marks. They also support snap-to ticks, where positioning the thumb between two tick marks causes the thumb to snap to the closest tick mark.

* Most Swing GUI components support user interactions through both the mouse and the keyboard.

* If a **JSlider** has the focus, the *left arrow* key and *right arrow* key cause the thumb of the **JS-lider** to decrease or increase by 1. The *down arrow* key and *up arrow* key also cause the thumb of the **JSlider** to decrease or increase by 1, respectively. The *PgDn* key (page down) and *PgUp* key (page up) cause the thumb of the **JSlider** to decrease or increase by block increments of one-tenth of the range of values, respectively. The *Home* key moves the thumb to the minimum value of the **JSlider** and the *End* key moves the thumb to the maximum value of the **JSlider**.

* **JSlider**s have either a horizontal orientation or a vertical orientation. For a horizontal **JSlider**, the minimum value is at the extreme left and the maximum value is at the extreme right of the **JSlider**. For a vertical **JSlider**, the minimum value is at the extreme bottom and the maximum value is at the extreme top of the **JSlider**. The relative position of the thumb indicates the current value of the **JSlider**.

- Method **setMajorTickSpacing** of class **JSlider** sets the spacing for tick marks on a **JSlider**. Method **setPaintTicks** with a **true** argument indicates that the tick marks should be displayed.

- **JSlider**s generate **ChangeEvent**s (package **javax.swing.event**) when the user interacts with a **JSlider**. A **ChangeListener** (package **javax.swing.event**) defines method **stateChanged** that can respond to **ChangeEvent**s.

- Method **getValue** of class **JSlider** returns the current thumb position.

- A **JFrame** is a window with a title bar and a border. Class **JFrame** is a subclass of **java.awt.Frame** (which is a subclass of **java.awt.Window**).

- Class **JFrame** supports three operations when the user closes the window. By default, a window is hidden when the user closes a window. This can be controlled with **JFrame** method **setDefaultCloseOperation**. Interface **WindowConstants** (package **javax.swing**) defines three constants for use with this method—**DISPOSE_ON_CLOSE**, **DO_NOTHING_ON_CLOSE** and **HIDE_ON_CLOSE** (the default).

- By default, a window is not displayed on the screen until its **show** method is called. A window can also be displayed by calling its **setVisible** method with **true** as an argument.

- A window's size should be set with a call to method **setSize**. The position of a window when it appears on the screen is specified with method **setLocation**.

- All windows generate window events when the user manipulates the window. Event listeners are registered for window events with method **addWindowListener** of class **Window**. The **WindowListener** interface provides seven methods for handling window events—**windowActivated** (called when the window is made active by clicking the window), **windowClosed** (called after the window is closed), **windowClosing** (called when the user initiates closing of the window), **windowDeactivated** (called when another window is made active), **windowIconified** (called when the user minimizes a window), **windowDeiconified** (called when a window is restored from being minimized) and **windowOpened** (called when a window is first displayed on the screen).

- The command-line arguments are automatically passed to **main** as the array of **String**s called **args**. The first argument after the application class name is the first **String** in the array **args**, and the length of the array is the total number of command-line arguments.

- Menus are an integral part of GUIs. Menus allow the user to perform actions without unnecessarily "cluttering" a graphical user interface with extra GUI components.

- In Swing GUIs, menus can only be attached to objects of the classes that provide method **setJMenuBar**. Two such classes are **JFrame** and **JApplet**.

- The classes used to define menus are **JMenuBar**, **JMenuItem**, **JMenu**, **JCheckBoxMenuItem** and class **JRadioButtonMenuItem**.

- A **JMenuBar** is a container for menus.

- A **JMenuItem** is a GUI component inside a menu that, when selected, causes an action to be performed. A **JMenuItem** can be used to initiate an action or it can be a submenu that provides more menu items from which the user can select.

- A **JMenu** contains menu items and can be added to a **JMenuBar** or to other **JMenu**s as submenus. When a menu is clicked, the menu expands to show its list of menu items.

- When a **JCheckBoxMenuItem** is selected, a check appears to the left of the menu item. When the **JCheckBoxMenuItem** is selected again, the check to the left of the menu item is removed.

- When multiple **JRadioButtonMenuItem**s are maintained as part of a **ButtonGroup**, only one item in the group can be selected at a given time. When a **JRadioButtonMenuItem** is selected, a filled circle appears to the left of the menu item. When another **JRadioButtonMenu-Item** is selected, the filled circle to the left of the previously selected menu item is removed.

- **JFrame** method **setJMenuBar** attaches a menu bar to a **JFrame**.

- **AbstractButton** method **setMnemonic** (inherited into class **JMenu**) specifies the mnemonic for an **AbstractButton** object. Pressing the *Alt* key and the mnemonic performs the **AbstractButton**'s action (in the case of a menu, it opens the menu).

- Mnemonic characters are normally displayed with an underline.

- Dialog boxes can be either modal or modeless. A modal dialog box does not allow any other window in the application to be accessed until the dialog box is dismissed. A modeless dialog box allows other windows to be accessed while the dialog is displayed. By default, the dialogs displayed with class **JOptionPane** are modal dialogs. Class **JDialog** can be used to create your own modeless or modal dialogs.

- **JMenu** method **addSeparator** adds a separator line to a menu.

- Context-sensitive popup menus are created with class **JPopupMenu**. These menus provide options that are specific to the component for which the popup-trigger event was generated. On most systems, the popup-trigger event occurs when the user presses and releases the right mouse button.

- **MouseEvent** method **isPopupTrigger** returns **true** if the popup-trigger event occurred.

- Method **show** of class **JPopupMenu** displays a **JPopupMenu**. The first argument to method **show** specifies the origin component, whose position helps determine where the **JPopupMenu** will appear on the screen. The last two arguments are the *x* and *y* coordinates from the origin component's upper-left corner at which the **JPopupMenu** should appear.

- Class **UIManager** contains a **public static** inner class called **LookAndFeelInfo** that is used to maintain information about a look-and-feel.

- **UIManager static** method **getInstalledLookAndFeels** gets an array of **UIManager.LookAndFeelInfo** objects that describe the installed look-and-feels.

- **UIManager static** method **setLookAndFeel** changes the look-and-feel.

- **SwingUtilities static** method **updateComponentTreeUI** changes the look-and-feel of every component attached to its **Component** argument to the new look-and-feel.

- Many of today's applications use a multiple document interface (MDI) [i.e., a main window (often called the parent window) containing other windows (often called child windows)] to manage several open documents that are being processed in parallel.

- Swing's **JDesktopPane** and **JInternalFrame** classes provide support for creating multiple document interfaces.

- **BoxLayout** is a layout manager that allows GUI components to be arranged left-to-right or top-to-bottom in a container. Class **Box** defines a container with **BoxLayout** as its default layout manager and provides static methods to create a **Box** with a horizontal or vertical **BoxLayout**.

- **CardLayout** is a layout manager that stacks components like a deck of cards. Each container in the stack can use any layout manager. Only the container at the "top" of the deck is visible.

- **GridBagLayout** is a layout manager similar to **GridLayout**. Unlike **GridLayout**, each component size can vary and components can be added in any order.

- **Box static** method **createHorizontalBox** returns a **Box** container with a horizontal **BoxLayout**. **Box static** method **createVerticalBox** of class **Box** returns a **Box** container with a vertical **BoxLayout**.

- **Box static** method **createVerticalStrut** adds a vertical strut to a container. A vertical strut is an invisible GUI component that has a fixed pixel height and is used to guarantee a fixed amount of space between GUI components. Class **Box** also defines method **createHorizontalStrut** for horizontal **BoxLayout**s.

- **Box static** method **createHorizontalGlue** adds horizontal glue to a container. Horizontal glue is an invisible GUI component that can be used between fixed-size GUI components to occupy additional space. Class **Box** also defines method **createVerticalGlue** for vertical **BoxLayout**s.

- **Box static** method **createRigidArea** adds a rigid area to a container. A rigid area is an invisible GUI component that always has a fixed pixel width and height.

- The **BoxLayout** constructor receives a reference to the container for which it controls the layout and a constant indicating if the layout is horizontal (**BoxLayout.X_AXIS**) or vertical (**BoxLayout.Y_AXIS**).

- **CardLayout** methods **first**, **previous**, **next** and **last** are used to display a particular card. Method **first** displays the first card. Method **previous** displays the previous card. Method **next** displays the next card. Method **last** displays the last card.

- To use **GridBagLayout**, a **GridBagConstraints** object must be used to specify how a component is placed in a **GridBagLayout**.

- Method **setConstraints** of class **GridBagLayout** takes a **Component** argument and a **GridBagConstraints** argument and sets the constraints of the **Component**.

Terminology

addSeparator method of class **JMenu**
addWindowListener method of **Window**
anchor variable of **GridBagConstraints**
automatic word wrap
Box class
BoxLayout layout manager
BoxLayout.X_AXIS
BoxLayout.Y_AXIS
CardLayout layout manager
ChangeEvent class
ChangeListener interface
child window
command-line arguments
context-sensitive popup menu
createHorizontalBox method of **Box**
createHorizontalGlue method of **Box**
createHorizontalStrut method of **Box**
createRigidArea method of **Box**
createVerticalBox method of **Box**
createVerticalGlue method of **Box**
createVerticalStrut method of **Box**
dedicated drawing area
Dimension class
dispose method of class **Window**
external event
fill variable of **GridBagConstraints**
first method of **CardLayout**
getClassName method

getInstalledLookAndFeels method
getMinimumSize method of **Component**
getPreferredSize method of **Component**
getSelectedText method
getValue method of class **JSlider**
GridBagConstraints class
GridBagConstraints.BOTH
GridBagConstraints.CENTER
GridBagConstraints.EAST
GridBagConstraints.HORIZONTAL
GridBagConstraints.NONE
GridBagConstraints.NORTH
GridBagConstraints.NORTHEAST
GridBagConstraints.NORTHWEST
GridBagConstraints.RELATIVE
GridBagConstraints.REMAINDER
GridBagConstraints.SOUTH
GridBagConstraints.SOUTHEAST
GridBagConstraints.SOUTHWEST
GridBagConstraints.VERTICAL
GridBagConstraints.WEST
GridBagLayout layout manager
gridheight variable
gridwidth variable
gridx variable of **GridBagConstraints**
gridy variable of **GridBagConstraints**
isPopupTrigger method of **MouseEvent**
JCheckBoxMenuItem class

Common Programming Errors

13.1   When overriding a **JComponent**'s **paintComponent** method, not calling the super-class's original version of **paintComponent** prevents the GUI component from display-ing properly on the GUI.

13.2   When overriding a **JComponent**'s **paintComponent** method, calling the superclass's original version of **paintComponent** after other drawing is performed erases the other drawings.

13.3   Forgetting to call method **show** or method **setVisible** on a window is a run-time logic error; the window is not displayed.

13.4   Forgetting to call the **setSize** method on a window is a run-time logic error—only the title bar appears.

13.5   Forgetting to set the menu bar with **JFrame** method **setJMenuBar** results in the menu bar not being displayed on the **JFrame**.

13.6   Using a negative value for either **weightx** or **weighty** is a logic error.

Look-and-Feel Observations

13.1 Often an external event determines when the text in a **JTextArea** should be processed.

13.2 To provide automatic word wrap functionality for a **JTextArea**, invoke **JTextArea** method **setLineWrap** with a true argument.

13.3 Combining graphics and Swing GUI components may lead to incorrect display of the graphics, the GUI components or both. Using **JPanel**s for drawing can eliminate this problem by providing a dedicated area for graphics.

13.4 When overriding a **JComponent**'s **paintComponent** method, the first statement in the body should always be a call to the superclass's original version of the method.

13.5 Calling **repaint** for a Swing GUI component indicates that the component should be painted as soon as possible. The background of the GUI component is cleared only if the component is opaque. Most Swing components are transparent by default. **JComponent** method **setOpaque** can be passed a **boolean** argument indicating if the component is opaque (**true**) or transparent (**false**). The GUI components of package **java.awt** are different from Swing components in that **repaint** results in a call to **Component** method **update** (which clears the component's background) and **update** calls method **paint** (rather than **paintComponent**).

13.6 Drawing on any GUI component is performed with coordinates that are measured from the upper-left corner *(0, 0)* of that GUI component.

13.7 The default size of a **JPanel** object is 0 pixels wide and 0 pixels tall.

13.8 When subclassing **JPanel** (or any other **JComponent**), override method **getPreferredSize** if the new component should have a specific preferred width and height.

13.9 Most Swing GUI components can be transparent or opaque. If a Swing GUI component is opaque, when its **paintComponent** method is called, its background will be cleared. Otherwise, its background will not be cleared.

13.10 Class **JComponent** provides method **setOpaque** that takes a **boolean** argument to determine if a **JComponent** is opaque (**true**) or transparent (**false**).

13.11 **JPanel** objects are opaque by default.

13.12 A mouse drag operation begins with a mouse pressed event. All subsequent mouse drag events (for which **mouseDragged** will be called) are sent to the GUI component that received the original mouse pressed event.

13.13 Most Swing components support user interactions through the mouse and the keyboard.

13.14 The minimum and maximum value positions on a **JSlider** can be switched by calling the **JSlider** method **setInverted** with boolean argument **true**.

13.15 If a new GUI component has a minimum width and height (i.e., smaller dimensions would render the component ineffective on the display), override method **getMinimumSize** to return the minimum width and height as an instance of class **Dimension**.

13.16 For many GUI components method **getMinimumSize** is defined to return the result of a call to that component's **getPreferredSize** method.

13.17 Menus simplify GUIs by reducing the number of components the user views.

13.18 Mnemonics provide quick access to menu commands and button commands through the keyboard.

13.19 Different mnemonics should be used for each button or menu item. Normally, the first letter in the label on the menu item or button is used as the mnemonic. If multiple buttons or menu items start with the same letter, choose the next most prominent letter in the name (e.g., **x** is commonly chosen for a button or menu item called **Exit**).

13.20 Menus normally appear left to right in the order that they are added.

13.21 Adding a menu as a menu item in another menu automatically makes the added menu a submenu. When the mouse is positioned over a submenu (or the submenu's mnemonic is pressed), the submenu expands to show its menu items.

13.22   Separators can be added to a menu to logically group menu items.

13.23   Any lightweight GUI component (i.e., a component that subclasses **JComponent**) can be added to a **JMenu** or to a **JMenuBar**.

13.24   The popup trigger event is platform specific. On most platforms that use a mouse with multiple mouse buttons, the popup trigger event is generated when the user clicks the right mouse button.

13.25   Displaying a **JPopupMenu** for the popup-trigger event of multiple different GUI components requires registering mouse event handlers to check for the popup-trigger event for each of those GUI components.

Performance Tip

13.1   Each look-and-feel is actually represented by a Java class. **UIManager** method **getInstalledLookAndFeels** does not load each class. Rather, it provides access to the names of the look-and-feels so a choice of look-and-feel can be made (presumably one time at the program's start-up). This reduces the overhead of loading additional classes that are not needed by the program.

Portability Tips

13.1   Programs that use Java's Abstract Windowing Toolkit GUI components (package **java.awt**) take on the look-and-feel of the platform on which they execute.

13.2   GUI components on each platform have different looks that may require different amounts of space to display. This may change the layout and alignments of GUI components.

13.3   GUI components on each platform have different default functionality (e.g., some platforms allow a button with the focus to be "pressed" with the space bar and some do not).

Software Engineering Observations

13.1   Windows are a valuable system resource that should be returned to the system when they are no longer needed.

13.2   When designing a program to execute as both an applet and an application, begin by defining it as an applet because applets have limitations due to security restrictions imposed on them by Web browsers. If the program executes properly as an applet, it can be made to work properly as an application. However, the reverse is not always true.

13.3   To execute an applet as an application, the application must provide a window in which the applet can be displayed.

13.4   To execute an applet as an application, the application must create an instance of the applet class to execute.

13.5   When executing an applet as an application, the application must call **init** and **start** explicitly to simulate the normal applet start-up sequence of method calls.

13.6   When executing an applet as an application, the application must attach the applet object to its window.

13.7   Local variables must be declared **final** to be used in an anonymous inner class definition.

Self-Review Exercises

13.1   Fill in the blanks in each of the following:

e) The _____ class is used to create a menu object.

f) The _____ method places a separator bar in a menu.

g) Passing **false** to a **TextArea**'s _____ method prevents its text from being modified by the user.

h) **JSlider** events are handled by the _____ method of interface _____.

i) The **GridBagConstraints** instance variable _____ is set to **CENTER** by default.

13.2   State whether each of the following is *true* or *false*. If *false*, explain why.
   a) When the programmer creates a **Frame**, a minimum of one menu must be created and added to the **Frame**.
   b) The variable **fill** belongs to the **GridBagLayout** class.
   c) **JFrame**s and applets cannot be used together in the same program.
   d) The top-left corner of a **JFrame** or applet has a coordinate of (0, 0).
   e) A **JTextArea**'s text is always read-only.
   f) Class **JTextArea** is a direct subclass of class **Component**.
   g) The default layout for a **Box** is **BoxLayout**.

13.3   Find the error(s) in each of the following and explain how to correct the error(s).
   a) `JMenubar b;`
   b) `mySlider = JSlider( 1000, 222, 100, 450 );`
   c) `gbc.fill = GridBagConstraints.NORTHWEST;   // set fill`
   d) `// override to paint on a customized Swing component`
       `public void paintcomponent( Graphics g )`
       `{`
       `    g.drawString( "HELLO", 50, 50 );`
       `}`
   e) `// create a JFrame and display it`
       `JFrame f = new JFrame( "A Window" );`
       `f.show();`

Answers to Self-Review Exercises

13.1   a) **JMenu**. b) **addSeparator**. c) **setEditable**. d) **stateChanged, ChangeListener**. e) **anchor**.

13.2   a) False. A **JFrame** does not require any menus.
   b) False. The variable **fill** belongs to the **GridBagConstraints** class.
   c) False. They can be used together.
   d) True.
   e) False. **JTextArea**s are editable by default.
   f) False. **JTextArea** derives from class **JTextComponent**.
   g) True.

13.3   a) **JMenubar** should be **JMenuBar**.
   b) The first argument to the constructor should be either **SwingConstants.HORIZONTAL** or **SwingConstants.VERTICAL**, and the **new** operator must be used after the = operator.
   c) The constant should be either **BOTH, HORIZONTAL, VERTICAL** or **NONE**.
   d) **paintcomponent** should be **paintComponent** and the method should call **super.paintComponent(g)** as its first statement.
   e) The **JFrame**'s **setSize** method must also be called to determine the size of the window.

Exercises

13.4   Fill in the blanks in each of the following:
   a) A dedicated drawing area can be defined as a subclass of _____.
   b) A **JMenuItem** that is a **JMenu** is called a _____.
   c) Both **JTextField**s and **JTextArea**s inherit directly from class _____.
   d) The _____ method attaches a **JMenuBar** to a **JFrame**.

e) Container class _____ has a default **BoxLayout**.

f) A _____ manages a set of child windows defined with class **JInternalFrame**.

13.5   State whether each of the following is *true* or *false*. If *false*, explain why.

a) Menus require a **JMenuBar** object so they can be attached to a **JFrame**.

b) A **JPanel** object is capable of receiving mouse events.

c) **CardLayout** is the default layout manager for a **JFrame**.

d) Method **setEditable** is a **JTextComponent** method.

e) The **GridBagLayout** layout manager implements **LayoutManager**.

f) **JPanel** objects are containers to which other GUI components can be attached.

g) Class **JFrame** inherits directly from class **Container**.

h) **JApplet**s can contain menus.

13.6   Find the error(s) in each of the following. Explain how to correct the error(s).

a) `x.add( new JMenuItem( "Submenu Color" ) ); // create submenu`

b) `c.setLayout( m = new GridbagLayout() );`

c) `String s = JTextArea.getText();`

13.7   Write a program that displays a circle of random size and calculates and displays the area, radius, diameter and circumference. Use the following equations: *diameter = 2 ∞ radius*, *area = π ∞ radius²*, *circumference = 2 ∞ π ∞ radius*. Use the constant **Math.PI** for pi (π). All drawing should be done on a subclass of **JPanel** and the results of the calculations should be displayed in a read-only **JTextArea**.

13.8   Enhance the program of Exercise 13.7 by allowing the user to alter the radius with a **JSlider**. The program should work for all radii in the range 100 to 200. As the radius changes, the diameter, area and circumference should be updated and displayed. The initial radius should be 150. Use the equations of Exercise 13.7. All drawing should be done on a subclass of **JPanel** and the results of the calculations should be displayed in a read-only **JTextArea**.

13.9   Explore the effects of varying the **weightx** and **weighty** values of the program of Fig. 13.17. What happens when a component has a nonzero weight, but is not allowed to fill the whole area (i.e., the **fill** value is not **BOTH**)?

13.10   Write a program that uses the **paint** method to draw the current value of a **JSlider** on a subclass of **JPanel**. In addition, provide a **JTextField** where a specific value can be entered. The **JTextField** should display the current value of the **JSlider** at all times. A **JLabel** should be used to identify the **JTextField**. The **JSlider** methods **setValue** and **getValue** should be used. [*Note:* The **setValue** method is a **public** method that does not return a value and takes one integer argument—the **JSlider** value, which determines the position of the thumb.]

13.11   Modify the program of Fig. 13.13 to use a single **JComboBox** instead of the four separate **JButton**s. Each "card" should not be modified.

13.12   Modify the program of Fig. 13.13 by adding a minimum of two new "cards" to the deck.

13.13   Define a subclass of **JPanel** called **MyColorChooser** that provides three **JSlider** objects and three **JTextField** objects. Each **JSlider** represents the values from 0 to 255 for the red, green and blue parts of a color. Use the red, green and blue values as the arguments to the **Color** constructor to create a new **Color** object. Display the current value of each **JSlider** in the corresponding **JTextField**. When the user changes the value of the **JSlider**, the **JTextField** should be changed accordingly. Define class **MyColorChooser** so it can be reused in other applications or applets. Use your new GUI component as part of an applet that displays the current **Color** value by drawing a filled rectangle.

13.14   Modify the **MyColorChooser** class of Exercise 13.13 to allow the user to type an integer value into a **JTextField** to set the red, green or blue value. When the user presses *Enter* in the **JTextField**, the corresponding **JSlider** should be set to the appropriate value.

13.15   Modify the applet of Exercise 13.14 to draw the current color as a rectangle on an instance of a subclass of **JPanel** called **DrawPanel**. Class **DrawPanel** should provide its own **paint-Component** method to draw the rectangle and should provide *set* methods to set the red, green, and blue values for the current color. When any *set* method is invoked for the class **DrawPanel**, the object should automatically **repaint** itself.

13.16   Modify the applet of Exercise 13.15 to allow the user to drag the mouse across the **Draw-Panel** to draw a shape in the current color. Enable the user to choose what shape to draw.

13.17   Modify the program of Exercise 13.16 to enable the program to run as an application. The existing applet's code should only be modified by adding a **main** method to launch the application in its own **JFrame**. Provide the user with the ability to terminate the application by clicking the close box on the window that is displayed and by selecting **Exit** from a **File** menu. Use the techniques shown in Fig. 13.6.

13.18   *(Complete Drawing Application)* Using the techniques developed in Exercises 12.27–12.33 and Exercises 13.13–13.17, create a complete drawing program that can execute as both an applet and an application. The program should use the GUI components of Chapters 12 and 13 to enable the user to select the shape, color and fill characteristics. Each shape should be stored in an array of **MyShape** objects, where **MyShape** is the superclass in your hierarchy of shape classes (see Exercises 9.28 and 9.29). Use a **JDesktopPane** and **JInternalFrame**s to allow the user to create multiple separate drawings in separate child windows. Create the user interface as a separate child window containing all the GUI components that allow the user to determine the characteristics of the shape to be drawn. The user can then click in any **JInternalFrame** to draw the shape.

13.19   A company pays its employees as managers (who receive a fixed weekly salary), hourly workers (who receive a fixed hourly wage for up to the first 40 hours they work and "time-and-a-half," i.e., 1.5 times their hourly wage, for overtime hours worked), commission workers (who receive $250 plus 5.7% of their gross weekly sales) or pieceworkers (who receive a fixed amount of money per item for each of the items they produce—each pieceworker in this company works on only one type of item). Write an application to compute the weekly pay for each employee. Each type of employee has its own pay code: Managers have paycode 1, hourly workers have code 2, commission workers have code 3 and pieceworkers have code 4. Use a **switch** to compute each employee's pay based on that employee's paycode. Use a **CardLayout** to display the appropriate GUI components that allow the user to enter the facts your program needs to calculate each employee's pay based on that employee's paycode.

14

Exception Handling

Objectives

- To understand exception and error handling.
- To be able to use **try** blocks to delineate code in which an exception may occur.
- To be able to **throw** exceptions.
- To use **catch** blocks to specify exception handlers.
- To use the **finally** block to release resources.
- To understand the Java exception hierarchy.
- To create programmer-defined exceptions.

It is common sense to take a method and try it. If it fails, admit it frankly and try another. But above all, try something.
Franklin Delano Roosevelt

O! throw away the worser part of it,
And live the purer with the other half.
William Shakespeare

If they're running and they don't look where they're going
I have to come out from somewhere and catch them.
Jerome David Salinger

And oftentimes excusing of a fault
Doth make the fault the worse by the excuse.
William Shakespeare

I never forget a face, but in your case I'll make an exception.
Groucho (Julius Henry) Marx

Outline

14.1 Introduction

In this chapter, we introduce *exception handling*. An *exception* is an indication that a problem occurred during the program's execution. The extensibility of Java can increase the number and types of errors that can occur. Every new class can add its own error possibilities. The features presented here enable programmers to write clearer, more robust, more fault-tolerant programs. We also consider when exception handling should not be used.

The style and details of exception handling in Java as presented in this chapter are based in part on the work of Andrew Koenig and Bjarne Stroustrup as presented in their paper, "Exception Handling for C++ (revised)," published in the *Proceedings of the USENIX C++ Conference* held in San Francisco in April, 1990. Their work forms the basis of C++ exception handling. Java's designers chose to implement an exception handling mechanism similar to that used in C++.

Error handling code varies in nature and quantity among software systems depending on the application and whether the software is a product for release. Products tend to contain far more error handling code than does "casual" software.

There are many popular means for dealing with errors. Most commonly, error handling code is interspersed throughout a system's code. Errors are dealt with at the places in the code where the errors can occur. The advantage to this approach is that a programmer reading code can see the error processing in the immediate vicinity of the code and determine if the proper error checking has been implemented.

The problem with this scheme is that the code in a sense becomes "polluted" with the error processing. It becomes more difficult for a programmer concerned with the application itself to read the code and determine if it is functioning correctly. This can make it difficult to understand and maintain the application.

Some common examples of exceptions are an out-of-bounds array subscript, arithmetic overflow (i.e., a value outside the representable range of values), division by zero, invalid method parameters and memory exhaustion.

Good Programming Practice 14.1

Using Java exception handling enables the programmer to remove the error handling code from the "main line" of the program's execution. This improves program clarity and enhances modifiability.

Separating error handling code from the main line of program code is consistent with the virtues of separability we have discussed in the contexts of both structured programming and object-oriented programming.

Java exception handling enables a program to catch all types of exceptions, or to catch all exceptions of a certain type, or to catch all exceptions of related types. This makes programs more robust by reducing the likelihood that errors will not be caught by a program.

Exception handling is provided to enable programs to catch and handle errors rather than letting them occur and suffering the consequences. Exception handling is designed for dealing with *synchronous errors* such as an attempt to divide by zero (that occurs as the program executes the divide instruction). Exception handling is not designed to deal with *asynchronous* events such as disk I/O completions, network message arrivals, mouse clicks, keystrokes and the like; these are best handled through other means, such as Java event listeners.

Exception handling is used in situations in which the system can recover from the malfunction causing the exception. The recovery procedure is called an *exception handler*.

Exception handling is typically used in situations in which a malfunction will be dealt with in a different scope (i.e., a method that is higher in the execution stack) from that which detected the malfunction. A program that carries on an interactive dialog with a user should not use exceptions to process keyboard input problems.

Software Engineering Observation 14.1

Use exceptions for malfunctions that must be processed in a different method from where they are detected. Use conventional error handling techniques for local error processing in which a method is able to deal with its own exceptions.

Good Programming Practice 14.2

Avoid using exception handling for purposes other than error handling because this can reduce program clarity.

There is another reason to avoid using exception handling techniques for conventional program control. Exception handling is designed for error processing, which is an infrequent activity that is often used because a program is about to terminate. It is not required that Java implement exception handling for the kind of optimal performance that might be expected of production code.

Performance Tip 14.1

Although it is possible to use exception handling for purposes other than error handling, this can reduce program performance.

Performance Tip 14.2

When an exception does not occur, little or no overhead is imposed by the presence of exception handling code. When exceptions happen, they do incur execution-time overhead.

Testing and Debugging Tip 14.1

Exception handling helps improve a program's fault tolerance. It becomes "more pleasant" to write error-processing code, so programmers are more likely to provide it.

Good Programming Practice 14.3

Using Java's standardized exception handling rather than having programmers use a diversity of "home-grown" techniques can improve program clarity on large projects.

Most programs written today support only a single thread of execution. The techniques discussed in this chapter apply even for multithreaded programs. We discuss multi-threading in Chapter 15.

We will see that exceptions are objects of classes derived from superclass **Exception**. We will show how to deal with "uncaught" exceptions. We will consider how unexpected exceptions are handled by Java. We will show how related exception types can be represented by exception subclasses that are derived from a common exception superclass.

Exception handling can be viewed as another means of returning control from a method or exiting a block of code. Normally, when an exception occurs, the exception is handled by a caller of the method generating the exception, by a caller of that caller, or however far back in the call stack it becomes necessary to go to find a handler for that exception.

Software Engineering Observation 14.2

Exception handling is particularly well-suited to systems of separately developed components. Such systems are typical of real-world software systems and products. Exception handling makes it easier to combine the components and have them work together effectively.

Software Engineering Observation 14.3

With other programming languages that do not support exception handling, programmers often delay writing error-processing code, and sometimes programmers simply forget to include it. This often results in less-robust, and thus inferior, software products. Java forces the programmer to deal with exception handling from the inception of a project. Still, the programmer must put considerable effort into incorporating an exception-handling strategy into software projects.

Software Engineering Observation 14.4

It is best to incorporate your exception-handling strategy into a system from the inception of the design process. It is difficult to add effective exception handling after a system has been implemented.

14.2 When Exception Handling Should Be Used

Exception handling should be used

- to process only exceptional situations where a method is unable to complete its task for reasons it cannot control.

- to process exceptions from program components that are not geared to handling those exceptions directly.

- to process exceptions from software components such as methods, libraries and classes that are likely to be widely used, and where those components cannot handle their own exceptions.

- on large projects to handle exceptions in a uniform manner project wide.

Software Engineering Observation 14.5

The client of a library class will likely have unique error processing in mind for an exception generated in the library class. It is unlikely that a library class will perform error processing that would meet the unique needs of all clients. Exceptions are an appropriate means for dealing with errors produced by library classes.

14.3 Other Error Handling Techniques

We have presented various ways of dealing with exceptional situations prior to this chapter. A program can ignore the exceptions. This can be devastating for software products released to the general public, or for special-purpose software needed for mission-critical situations. But for software developed for your own purposes, it is common to ignore many kinds of errors. A program could be directed to abort upon encountering an exceptional situation. This prevents a program from running to completion and producing incorrect results. For many types of errors this is a good strategy. Such a strategy is inappropriate for mission-critical applications. Resource issues are also important here. If a program obtains a resource, the program should normally return that resource before program termination.

Common Programming Error 14.1

Aborting a program could leave a resource in a state in which other programs would not be able to acquire the resource, hence we would have a so-called "resource leak."

Good Programming Practice 14.4

If your method is capable of handling a given type of exception, then handle it rather than passing the exception on to other regions of your program. This makes programs clearer.

Performance Tip 14.3

If an error can be processed locally instead of throwing an exception, do so. This will improve program execution speed. Exception handling is slow compared to local processing.

14.4 The Basics of Java Exception Handling

Java exception handling is geared to situations in which the method that detects an error is unable to deal with it. Such a method will *throw an exception*. There is no guarantee that there will be "anything out there" (i.e., an *exception handler*—code that executes when an exception has been detected) specifically geared to processing that kind of exception. If there is, the exception will be *caught* and *handled*. The following *Testing and Debugging Tip* describes what happens if no appropriate exception handler can be found.

Testing and Debugging Tip 14.2

All Java applets and certain Java applications are GUI-based. Some Java applications are not GUI-based; these are often called command-line applications (or console applications). When an exception is not caught in a command-line application, the program terminates (i.e., Java exits) after the default exception handler runs. When an exception is not caught in an applet or a GUI-based application, the GUI is still displayed and the user can continue using the applet or application even after the default exception handler runs. However, the GUI may be in an inconsistent state.

The programmer encloses in a **try** *block* the code that may generate an exception. The **try** block is immediately followed by zero or more **catch** *blocks*. Each **catch** block specifies the type of exception it can catch and contains an exception handler. After the last

catch block, an optional **finally** block provides code that always executes regardless of whether or not an exception occurs; as we will see, the **finally** block is an ideal place for code that releases resources to prevent "resource leaks." If there are no **catch** blocks following a **try** block, the **finally** block is required.

When an exception is thrown, program control leaves the **try** block and the **catch** blocks are searched in order for an appropriate handler (we will soon discuss what makes a handler "appropriate"). If the type of the thrown exception matches the parameter type in one of the **catch** blocks, the code for that **catch** block is executed. If no exceptions are thrown in the **try** block, the exception handlers for that block are skipped and the program resumes execution after the last **catch** block. If a **finally** block appears after the last **catch** block, it is executed regardless of whether or not an exception is thrown.

We can specify with a **throws** clause the exceptions a method throws. An exception can be thrown from statements in the method, or the exception can be thrown from a method called directly or indirectly from the **try** block. The point at which the **throw** is executed is called the *throw point*.

Once an exception is thrown, the block in which the exception is thrown expires and control cannot return to the throw point. Thus Java uses the *termination model of exception handling* rather than the *resumption model of exception handling*. In the resumption model, control would return to the point at which the exception was thrown and resume execution.

When an exception occurs, it is possible to communicate information to the exception handler from the vicinity in which the exception occurred. That information is the type of the thrown object itself or information harvested from the vicinity in which the exception occurred and placed into the thrown object.

Software Engineering Observation 14.6

A key to Java-style exception handling is that the portion of a program or system that handles the exception can be distant from the portion of the program that generates the exception.

14.5 An Exception Handling Example: Divide by Zero

Now let us consider a simple example of exception handling. The application of Fig. 14.1 uses **try**, **throw** and **catch** to detect, indicate and handle exceptions. The application displays two **JTextField**s in which the user can type integers. When the user presses the *Enter* key in the second **JTextField**, method **actionPerformed** is called to read the two integers from the **JTextField**s and pass the integers to method **quotient** to calculate the quotient of the two values and return a **double** result. If the user types 0 in the second **JTextField**, the program uses an exception to indicate that the user is attempting a division by zero. Also, if the user types a value that is not an integer in either **JTextField**, a **NumberFormatException** occurs.

Consider the sample executions shown in the five output windows. The first window show a successful execution. The user typed the values 100 and 7. The third **JTextField** shows the result of the division performed by method **quotient**. In the second output window, the user entered the string "hello" in the second **JTextField**. When the user presses *Enter* in the second **JTextField**, an error message dialog is displayed indicating that an integer must be entered. In the last two windows, a zero denominator is entered and the program detects the problem, throws an exception and issues an appropriate diagnostic message. Now let's discuss the program.

```
1    // Fig. 14.1: DivideByZeroException.java
2    // Definition of class DivideByZeroException.
3    // Used to throw an exception when a
4    // divide-by-zero is attempted.
5    public class DivideByZeroException
6                  extends ArithmeticException {
7       public DivideByZeroException()
8       {
9          super( "Attempted to divide by zero" );
10      }
11
12      public DivideByZeroException( String message )
13      {
14         super( message );
15      }
16   }
```

Fig. 14.1 A simple exception handling example with divide by zero (part 1 of 4).

```
17   // Fig. 14.1: DivideByZeroTest.java
18   // A simple exception handling example.
19   // Checking for a divide-by-zero-error.
20   import java.text.DecimalFormat;
21   import javax.swing.*;
22   import java.awt.*;
23   import java.awt.event.*;
24
25   public class DivideByZeroTest extends JFrame
26                                 implements ActionListener {
27      private JTextField input1, input2, output;
28      private int number1, number2;
29      private double result;
30
31      // Initialization
32      public DivideByZeroTest()
33      {
34         super( "Demonstrating Exceptions" );
35
36         Container c = getContentPane();
37         c.setLayout( new GridLayout( 3, 2 ) );
38
39         c.add( new JLabel( "Enter numerator ",
40                          SwingConstants.RIGHT ) );
41         input1 = new JTextField( 10 );
42         c.add( input1 );
43
44         c.add(
45            new JLabel( "Enter denominator and press Enter ",
46                      SwingConstants.RIGHT ) );
47         input2 = new JTextField( 10 );
48         c.add( input2 );
49         input2.addActionListener( this );
```

Fig. 14.1 A simple exception handling example with divide by zero (part 2 of 4).

```
50
51         c.add( new JLabel( "RESULT ", SwingConstants.RIGHT ) );
52         output = new JTextField();
53         c.add( output );
54
55         setSize( 425, 100 );
56         show();
57      }
58
59      // Process GUI events
60      public void actionPerformed( ActionEvent e )
61      {
62         DecimalFormat precision3 = new DecimalFormat( "0.000" );
63
64         output.setText( "" ); // empty the output JTextField
65
66         try {
67            number1 = Integer.parseInt( input1.getText() );
68            number2 = Integer.parseInt( input2.getText() );
69
70            result = quotient( number1, number2 );
71            output.setText( precision3.format( result ) );
72         }
73         catch ( NumberFormatException nfe ) {
74            JOptionPane.showMessageDialog( this,
75               "You must enter two integers",
76               "Invalid Number Format",
77               JOptionPane.ERROR_MESSAGE );
78         }                    Arithmetic
79         catch ( DivideByZeroException dbze ) {
80            JOptionPane.showMessageDialog( this, dbze.toString(),
81               "Attempted to Divide by Zero",
82               JOptionPane.ERROR_MESSAGE );
83         }
84      }
85
86      // Definition of method quotient. Used to demonstrate
87      // throwing an exception when a divide-by-zero error
88      // is encountered.
89      public double quotient( int numerator, int denominator )
90         throws DivideByZeroException
91      {
92         if ( denominator == 0 )
93            throw new DivideByZeroException();
94
95         return ( double ) numerator / denominator;
96      }
97
98      public static void main( String args[] )
99      {
100        DivideByZeroTest app = new DivideByZeroTest();
101
```

Fig. 14.1   A simple exception handling example with divide by zero (part 3 of 4).

```
102            app.addWindowListener(
103               new WindowAdapter() {
104                  public void windowClosing( WindowEvent e )
105                  {
106                     e.getWindow().dispose();
107                     System.exit( 0 );
108                  }
109               }
110            );
111     }
112 }
```

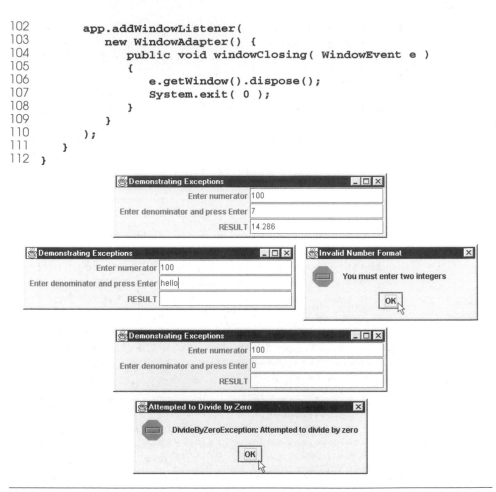

Fig. 14.1 A simple exception handling example with divide by zero (part 4 of 4).

Java can test for a division by zero when the values in the division are both integers. However, our program is going to perform a floating-point division of two integers by casting the first integer to a **double** before the calculation is performed. Floating-point division by zero is allowed by Java and results in a value of positive or negative infinity (constants for these values can be found in class **Float** and class **Double** of the **java.lang** package). We would still like to indicate to the user of our program that they are attempting a division by zero. To do so, we must either find an appropriate **Exception** class for a divide-by-zero situation or we must create one. When we search the **Exception** classes of the **java.lang** package we find a whole set of **RuntimeException** classes. The one that most closely matches our needs is **ArithmeticException**. We could use this class directly, but instead we choose to create our own more specific class **DivideByZeroException** (lines 1–16).

Good Programming Practice 14.5

Associating each type of serious execution-time malfunction with an appropriately named **Exception** *class improves program clarity.*

Class **DivideByZeroException** extends class **ArithmeticException**. We chose to extend class **ArithmeticException** because dividing by zero occurs in arithmetic. A typical exception class has two constructors—one that takes no arguments and specifies a default exception message, and one that receives the exception message as a **String**. The default constructor (lines 7–10) uses **super** to pass the **ArithmeticException** constructor the string **"Attempted to divide by zero"** as the exception message that indicates what went wrong. The other constructor (lines 12–15) uses **super** to pass the **ArithmeticException** constructor the **String** received as an argument.

Now consider the **DivideByZeroTest** application (lines 17–112). The application's constructor (lines 32–57) builds a graphical user interface with three **JLabel**s (all right aligned) and three **JTextField**s and registers the **DivideByZeroTest** object as the **ActionListener** for **JTextField input2**.

After the user enters the denominator and presses the *Enter* key, method **actionPerformed** (lines 60–84) is called. Next, method **actionPerformed** proceeds with a **try** block (lines 66–72) that encloses the code that may **throw** an exception and that must be abandoned if an exception occurs. The statements that read the integers from the **JTextField**s (lines 67 and 68) each use method **Integer.parseInt** to convert **String**s to **int** values. Method **parseInt** throws a **NumberFormatException** if the **String** being converted is not a valid integer. The division that can cause the divide-by-zero error is not explicitly listed in the **try** block. Rather, the call to method **quotient** (line 70) invokes the code that attempts the division. Method **quotient** (lines 89–96) **throw**s the **DivideByZeroException** object, as we will see momentarily. In general, errors may surface through explicitly mentioned code in a **try** block, through calls to a method, or even through deeply nested method calls initiated by code in a **try** block.

The **try** block is immediately followed by two **catch** blocks—lines 73–78 contain the exception handler for the **NumberFormatException** and lines 79–83 contain the exception handler for the **DivideByZeroException**. In general, when an exception is thrown within a **try** block, the exception is caught by a **catch** block that specifies an appropriate type that matches the thrown exception (i.e., has the exact same type as the thrown exception or is a super class of the thrown exception). In Fig. 14.1, the first **catch** block specifies that it will catch exception objects of type **NumberFormatException** (this type matches the type of the object thrown in method **Integer.parseInt**) and the second **catch** block specifies that it will catch exception objects of type **DivideByZeroException** (this type matches the type of the object thrown in method **quotient**). Only the matching **catch** handler executes if an exception is thrown. Both our exception handlers simply display an error message dialog, but exception handlers can be more elaborate than this. After executing an exception handler, control proceeds to the first statement after the last **catch** block.

If the code in the **try** block does not **throw** an exception, then the **catch** handlers are skipped and execution resumes with the first line of code after the **catch** handlers. In Fig. 14.1, method **actionPerformed** simply returns, but the program could continue executing more statements after the **catch** blocks.

 Testing and Debugging Tip 14.3

With exception handling, a program can continue executing after dealing with a problem. This helps ensure robust applications that contribute to what is called mission-critical computing *or* business-critical computing.

Now let us examine method **quotient**. When the **if** statement determines that **denominator** is zero, the body of the **if** executes a **throw** statement that creates and **throw**s a new **DivideByZeroException** object. This object will be caught by the **catch** block specifying type **DivideByZeroException** after the **try** block. The thrown object is received in parameter **dbze** (line 79) specified in the second **catch** handler, and the message is displayed by converting **dbze** to a **String** via **toString** and passing this **String** as the message to display in the error message dialog.

If **denominator** is not zero, no exception is thrown, the division is performed and the result of the division is returned to the point of invocation of method **quotient** in the **try** block (line 70). We then display the result of the calculation in the third **JText-Field**. The **catch** blocks are skipped and the **actionPerformed** method completes execution normally.

Note that when **quotient** throws the **DivideByZeroException**, **quotient**'s block expires. This would cause any of its local variables to be destroyed—objects that were referenced by local variables in the block have their reference counts decremented accordingly (and are possibly marked for garbage collection). If this exception is thrown, the **try** block from which the method was called also expires before line 71 can execute. Here, too, if there were local variables created in the **try** prior to the exception being thrown, these variables would be destroyed.

If a **NumberFormatException** is generated by lines 67 or 68, the **try** block expires and execution continues with the exception handler at line 73. An error message dialog is displayed to tell the user to enter integers, then the **actionPerformed** method continues with the next valid statement after the **catch** blocks (i.e., the method terminates in this example).

14.6 Try Blocks

An exception that occurs in a **try** block is normally caught by a handler specified by a **catch** block immediately following that **try** block.

```
try {
    ...
}
catch( ExceptionType ref ) {
    ...
}
```

A **try** block can be followed by zero or more **catch** blocks.

Common Programming Error 14.2

*It is a syntax error to separate with other code the **catch** handlers that correspond to a particular **try** block.*

If a **try** block executes and no exceptions are thrown, all the exception handlers are skipped and control resumes with the first statement after the last exception handler. If a **finally** block follows the last **catch** block, the code in the **finally** block executes regardless of whether or not an exception is thrown.

Testing and Debugging Tip 14.4

*A **finally** block is where to place code that will release resources acquired in a **try** block. This strategy is an effective way to avoid resource leaks.*

14.7 Throwing an Exception

The ***throw*** statement is executed to indicate that an exception has occurred (i.e., a method could not complete successfully). This is called *throwing an exception*. A **throw** statement specifies an object to be thrown. The operand of a **throw** can be of any class derived from class **Throwable**. The two immediate subclasses of class **Throwable** are **Exception** and **Error**. **Error**s are particularly serious system problems that generally should not be caught. **Exception**s are caused by problems most Java programmers will want to deal with. If the operand is an object of class **Exception**, it is called an *exception object*.

Testing and Debugging Tip 14.5

*When **toString** is invoked on any **Throwable** object, its resulting **String** includes the descriptive **String** that was supplied to the constructor.*

Testing and Debugging Tip 14.6

*If it is necessary to pass information about the malfunction that caused an exception, such information can be placed in the thrown object. That information can then be referenced through the parameter name in the **catch** handler.*

Testing and Debugging Tip 14.7

An object can be thrown without containing information to be passed; in this case, knowledge that an exception of this type has been raised may provide sufficient information for the handler to do its job correctly.

When an exception is thrown, control exits the current **try** block and proceeds to an appropriate **catch** handler (if one exists) after that **try** block. It is possible that the **throw** point could be in a deeply nested scope within a **try** block; control will still proceed to the **catch** handler. It is also possible that the **throw** point could be in a deeply nested method call; still, control will proceed to the **catch** handler.

A **try** block may appear to contain no error checking and include no **throw** statements, but code referenced in the **try** block could certainly cause error-checking code in constructors to execute and possibly throw exceptions. Code in a **try** block may perform array subscripting on an array object. If an invalid array subscript is specified, the array object throws an **ArrayIndexOutOfBoundsException**. Any method call can invoke code that might **throw** an exception or call another method that throws an exception.

Although an exception can terminate program execution, it need not do this. However, an exception does terminate at least the block in which the exception occurred.

14.8 Catching an Exception

Exception handlers are contained in **catch** blocks. Each **catch** block starts with the keyword **catch** followed by parentheses containing a class name (specifying the type of exception to be caught) and a parameter name. The object caught by the handler can be referenced through this parameter. This is followed by a block delineating the exception handling code. When an exception is caught, the code in the **catch** block is executed.

Common Programming Error 14.3

*Assuming that after an exception is processed, control will return to the first statement after the **throw** can lead to errors.*

Common Programming Error 14.4

*Specifying a comma-separated list of **catch** arguments is a syntax error. A **catch** can have only a single argument.*

Common Programming Error 14.5

*It is a syntax error to **catch** the same type in two different **catch** blocks associated with a particular **try** block.*

A **catch** that catches an **Exception** object

```
catch( Exception e )
```

means to catch all exceptions.

Common Programming Error 14.6

*Placing **catch(Exception e)** before other **catch** blocks that catch specific types of exceptions would prevent those blocks from ever being executed; **catch(Exception e)** must always be placed last in the list of exception handlers following a **try** block, or a syntax error occurs.*

Software Engineering Observation 14.7

*If you catch all exceptions with **catch(Exception e)** you can use the **instanceof** operator to probe the type of the exception. For example, the boolean condition **x instanceof Y** evaluates to **true** if object **x** is an instance of class **Y**, and **false** otherwise.*

It is possible that no handler will match a particular thrown object. This causes the search for a match to continue in the next enclosing **try** block. As this process continues, it may eventually be determined that there is no handler on the execution stack that matches the type of the thrown object; in this case a non-GUI-based application terminates—applets and GUI-based applications return to their regular event processing.

It is possible that several exception handlers will provide an acceptable match to the type of the exception. This can happen for several reasons. First, there can be a "catch-all" handler **catch(Exception e)** that will catch any exception. Second, because of inheritance relationships, it is possible that a subclass object can be caught either by a handler specifying the subclass type, or by handlers specifying the types of any superclasses of that subclass. The first exception handler that matches the exception type is executed.

Software Engineering Observation 14.8

If several handlers match the type of an exception, and if each of these handles the exception differently, then the order of the handlers will affect the manner in which the exception is handled.

Common Programming Error 14.7

*It is a syntax error if a **catch** that catches a superclass object is placed before a **catch** that catches an object of a subclass of that superclass.*

Sometimes a program may process many closely related types of exceptions. Instead of providing separate exception classes and **catch** handlers for each, a programmer can provide a single exception class and **catch** handler for a group of exceptions. As each exception occurs, the exception object can be created with different instance data such as a type code. The **catch** handler can examine this data to distinguish the type of the exception. Actually, this style of programming is discouraged in object-oriented languages like Java because inheritance and polymorphism takes care of this situation more elegantly.

By default, if no handler is found for an exception, a non-GUI-based application terminates. Although this may seem like the right thing to do, it is not what programmers using other languages without exception handling features are used to doing. Rather, errors often simply happen and then program execution continues, possibly only "hobbling" along.

A **try** block followed by several exception handlers resembles a **switch** statement, but a **break** statement is not used to exit an exception handler in a manner that skips over the remaining exception handlers. Each **catch** block defines a distinct scope, whereas all the cases in a **switch** statement are contained within the single scope of the **switch**.

An exception cannot access objects defined within its **try** block because the **try** block has expired when the handler begins executing.

What happens when an exception occurs in an exception handler? The **try** block that noticed the exception has expired when the exception handler begins running, so exceptions occurring in an exception handler need to be processed outside the **try** block in which the original exception was thrown. The outer **try** block watches for errors occurring in the original **try** block's **catch** handlers.

Exception handlers can be written a variety of ways. They can rethrow an exception (as we will see in the next section). They can convert one type of exception into another by throwing a different type of exception. They can perform any necessary recovery and resume execution after the last exception handler. They can look at the situation causing the error, remove the cause of the error, and retry by calling the original method that caused an exception. They can simply return a status value to their environment, etc.

It is not possible to return to the **throw** point by issuing a **return** statement in a **catch** handler. Such a **return** simply returns to the method that called the method containing the **catch** block. Again, the **throw** point is in a block that has expired, so returning via a **return** statement would not make sense.

Software Engineering Observation 14.9

Another reason not to use exceptions for conventional flow of control is that these "additional" exceptions can "get in the way" of genuine error-type exceptions. It becomes more difficult for the programmer to keep track of the larger number of exception cases. Exceptional situations should be rare, not commonplace.

Common Programming Error 14.8

*Assuming that an exception thrown from a **catch** handler will be processed by that handler or any other handler associated with the same **try** block can lead to logic errors.*

14.9 Rethrowing an Exception

It is possible that the **catch** handler that catches an exception may decide it cannot process the exception or it may want to let some other **catch** handler handle it. In this case, the handler that received **Exception e** can simply rethrow the exception with the statement

```
throw e;
```

Such a **throw** rethrows the exception to the next enclosing **try** block.

Even if a handler can process an exception, and regardless of whether it does any processing on that exception, the handler can still rethrow the exception for further processing outside the handler. A rethrown exception is detected by the next enclosing **try** block and is handled by an exception handler listed after that enclosing **try** block.

14.10 Throws Clause

A **throws** clause lists the exceptions that can be thrown by a method.

```
int g( float h ) throws a, b, c
{
    // method body
}
```

The types of exceptions that are thrown by a method are specified in the method definition with a **throws** clause. A method can **throw** objects of the indicated classes, or it can **throw** objects of subclasses.

Some exceptions can occur at any point during the execution of the program. Many of these exceptions can be avoided by coding properly. These are *run-time exceptions* and they derive from class **RuntimeException**. For example, if your program attempts to access an out-of-range array subscript, an exception of type **ArrayIndexOutOf-BoundsException** (derived from **RuntimeException**) is thrown. Your program can clearly avoid such a problem; hence, it is a run-time exception.

Another run-time exception occurs when your program creates an object reference but has not yet created an object and attached it to the reference. Attempting to use such a **null** reference causes a **NullPointerException** to be thrown. Clearly, your program could have avoided this circumstance; hence, it is a run-time exception. Another run-time exception is an invalid cast which throws a **ClassCastException**.

There are a variety of exceptions that are not **RuntimeException**s. Two of the most common are **InterruptedException**s (see Chapter 15, "Multithreading") and **IOException**s (see Chapter 17, "Files and Streams").

Not all errors and exceptions that can be thrown from a method are listed in the **throws** clause. **Error**s do not need to be listed, nor do **RuntimeException**s (avoidable exceptions). **Error**s are serious system problems that can occur almost anywhere and most users will not be able to deal with them. You should be dealing with **Runtime-Exception**s directly rather than passing them on to other regions of your program. Non-**RuntimeException**s a method explicitly throws and non-**RuntimeException**s thrown by methods the method calls must be listed in the method's **throws** clause.

Software Engineering Observation 14.10

*If a non-**RuntimeException** is thrown by a method, or if that method calls methods that throw non-**RuntimeException**s, each of those exceptions must be declared in the **throws** clause of that method or caught in a **try/catch** in that method.*

Java distinguishes *checked **Exception**s* versus *unchecked **RuntimeException**s* and **Error**s. A method's checked exceptions need to be listed in that method's **throws** clause. Because **Error**s and **RuntimeException**s can be thrown from almost any method, it would be cumbersome for programmers to be required to list them; these are not required to be listed in a method's **throws** clause, and hence are said to be "unchecked." All non-**RuntimeException**s a method can **throw** must be listed in that method's **throws** clause, and hence are said to be "checked."

Common Programming Error 14.9

It is a syntax error if a method throws a checked exception not in that method's **throws** *clause.*

Common Programming Error 14.10

Attempting to throw a checked exception from a method that has no **throws** *clause is a syntax error.*

Software Engineering Observation 14.11

If your method calls other methods that explicitly **throw** *checked exceptions, those exceptions must be listed in the* **throws** *clause of your method, unless your method catches those exceptions. This is Java's "***catch***-or-declare" requirement.*

Common Programming Error 14.11

If a subclass method overrides a superclass method, it is an error for the subclass method to list more exceptions in its **throws** *list than the overridden superclass method does. A subclass's* **throws** *list can contain a subset of a superclass's* **throws** *list.*

Java's **catch**-or-declare requirement demands that the programmer either **catch** each checked exception or place it in the **throws** clause of a method. Of course, placing a checked exception in the **throws** clause would force other methods to deal with the checked exception as well. If a programmer feels a particular checked exception is unlikely to occur, the programmer might elect to catch that checked exception and do nothing with it to avoid being forced to deal with it later. This can of course come back to haunt you because as a program evolves it may become important to deal with this checked exception.

Testing and Debugging Tip 14.8

Do not try to circumvent Java's **catch***-or-declare requirement by simply catching exceptions and doing nothing with them. Exceptions are generally of a serious enough nature that they need to be dealt with rather than suppressed.*

Testing and Debugging Tip 14.9

The Java compiler, through the **throws** *list used with exception handling, forces programmers to deal with the exceptions that can be thrown from each method a program calls. This helps avoid bugs that arise in programs when programmers ignore the fact that things can go wrong and make no provisions for these problems.*

Software Engineering Observation 14.12

Subclass methods that do not override their corresponding superclass methods exhibit the same exception handling behavior of the inherited superclass methods. The **throws** *list of a subclass method that overrides a superclass method may not have more exceptions than the* **throws** *list of the overridden superclass method.*

Common Programming Error 14.12

The Java compiler requires that a method either catch any checked exceptions thrown in the method (either directly from the method's code itself or indirectly through called methods), or declare checked **Exception***s the method can* **throw** *to other methods; otherwise, the Java compiler issues a syntax error.*

Testing and Debugging Tip 14.10

*Suppose a method **throws** all subclasses of a particular superclass. You may be tempted to list only the superclass in the **throws** clause. Instead, explicitly list all the subclasses. This focuses the programmer's attention on the specific **Exception**s that must be dealt with and will often help avoid bugs caused by processing **Exception**s in too general a manner.*

Figures 14.2 through 14.7 list many of Java's **Error**s and **Exception**s hierarchically for the packages **java.lang**, **java.util**, **java.io**, **java.awt** and **java.net**. The exception and error classes for the other packages of the Java API can be found in the Java on-line documentation. The on-line documentation for each method in the API specifies if that method throws exceptions and what the exceptions are that can be thrown. We show a portion of Java's **Error** hierarchy in Fig. 14.2. Most Java programmers will simply ignore **Error**s. They are serious but rare events.

Figure 14.3 is particularly important because it lists many of Java's **RuntimeException**s. Although Java programmers will not declare these exceptions in **throws** clauses, these are the exceptions that will commonly be caught and handled in Java applications. All but two of these **RuntimeException**s are in the **java.lang** package.

The java.lang package errors

Error (all in **java.lang** except for **AWTError**, which is in **java.awt**)
    LinkageError
       ClassCircularityError
       ClassFormatError
       ExceptionInInitializerError
       IncompatibleClassChangeError
         AbstractMethodError
         IllegalAccessError
         InstantiationError
         NoSuchFieldError
         NoSuchMethodError
       NoClassDefFoundError
       UnsatisfiedLinkError
       VerifyError
    ThreadDeath
    VirtualMachineError (Abstract class)
       InternalError
       OutOfMemoryError
       StackOverflowError
       UnknownError
    AWTError (in **java.awt**)

Fig. 14.2   The **java.lang** package errors .

The `java.lang` package exceptions

```
Exception
    ClassNotFoundException
    CloneNotSupportedException
    IllegalAccessException
    InstantiationException
    InterruptedException
    NoSuchFieldException
    NoSuchMethodException
    RuntimeException
        ArithmeticException
        ArrayStoreException
        ClassCastException
        IllegalArgumentException
            IllegalThreadStateException
            NumberFormatException
        IllegalMonitorStateException
        IllegalStateException
        IndexOutOfBoundsException
            ArrayIndexOutOfBoundsException
            StringIndexOutOfBoundsException
        NegativeArraySizeException
        NullPointerException
        SecurityException
```

Fig. 14.3   The `java.lang` package exceptions.

Figure 14.4 lists Java's other three **RuntimeException**s data types. We will encounter these exceptions in Chapter 23 when we study the **Vector** class. A **Vector** is a dynamic array that can grow and shrink to accommodate a program's varying storage requirements.

Figure 14.5 lists Java's **IOException**s. These are all checked exceptions that can occur during input/output and file processing.

Figure 14.6 lists the **java.awt** package's only checked **Exception**, the **AWTException**. This is a checked exception that is thrown by various abstract windowing toolkit methods.

Figure 14.7 lists the **IOException**s of the **java.net** package. These are all checked **Exception**s that indicate various networking problems.

The `java.util` package exceptions

```
Exception
    RuntimeException
        EmptyStackException
        MissingResourceException
        NoSuchElementException
    TooManyListenersException
```

Fig. 14.4   The `java.util` package exceptions.

The `java.io` package exceptions

```
Exception
    IOException
        CharConversionException
        EOFException
        FileNotFoundException
        InterruptedIOException
        ObjectStreamException
            InvalidClassException
            InvalidObjectException
            NotActiveException
            NotSerializableException
            OptionalDataException
            StreamCorruptedException
            WriteAbortedException
        SyncFailedException
        UnsupportedCodingException
        UTFDataFormatException
```

Fig. 14.5   The `java.io` package exceptions .

The `java.awt` package exceptions

```
Exception
        AWTException
```

Fig. 14.6   The `java.awt` package exceptions (part 1 of 2).

The `java.awt` package exceptions

```
        RuntimeException

            IllegalStateException

                IllegalComponentStateException
```

Fig. 14.6   The **`java.awt`** package exceptions (part 2 of 2).

The `java.net` package exceptions

```
Exception

    IOException

        BindException

        MalformedURLException

        ProtocolException

        SocketException

            ConnectException

            NoRouteToHostException

        UnknownHostException

        UnknownServiceException
```

Fig. 14.7   The **`java.net`** package exceptions.

14.11 Constructors, Finalizers and Exception Handling

First, let us deal with an issue we have mentioned, but that has yet to be satisfactorily resolved. What happens when an error is detected in a constructor? The problem is that a constructor cannot return a value, so how do we let the program know that an object has not been properly constructed? One scheme is simply to return the improperly constructed object and hope that anyone using the object would make appropriate tests to determine that the object is in fact bad. Another scheme is to set some global variable outside the constructor, but this is a poor programming practice. A thrown exception passes to the outside world the information about the failed constructor and the responsibility to deal with the failure.

Exceptions thrown in constructors cause objects built as part of the object being constructed to be marked for eventual garbage collection. Before each object is garbage collected, its **finalize** method will be called. Once again, Java does not guarantee the order in which objects will be garbage collected and therefore it does not guarantee the order in which **finalize** methods will be called.

14.12 Exceptions and Inheritance

Various exception classes can be derived from a common superclass. If a **catch** is written to catch exception objects of a superclass type, it can also catch all objects of subclasses of that superclass. This can allow for polymorphic processing of related errors.

Using inheritance with exceptions enables an exception handler to catch related errors with a concise notation. One could certainly catch each subclass exception object individually, but it is more concise to catch the superclass exception object instead. This only makes sense if the handling behavior would be the same for all subclasses of course. Otherwise, catch each subclass exception individually.

Testing and Debugging Tip 14.11

Catching subclass exception objects individually is subject to error if the programmer forgets to explicitly test for one or more of the subclass types; catching the superclass guarantees that objects of all subclasses will be caught.

14.13 `finally` Block

Programs that obtain certain types of resources must explicitly return those resources to the system to avoid so-called *resource leaks*. In programming languages like C and C++ the most common kind of resource leak is a memory leak. Java performs automatic garbage collection of memory no longer needed by programs, thus avoiding most memory leaks. But other kinds of resource leaks can occur in Java.

Software Engineering Observation 14.13

*A **finally** block typically contains code to release resources acquired in its corresponding **try** block; this is an effective way to eliminate resource leaks. For example, the **finally** block should close any files opened in the **try** block.*

Testing and Debugging Tip 14.12

Actually, Java does not completely eliminate memory leaks. There is a subtle issue here. Java will not garbage collect an object until there are no more references to the object. Thus, memory leaks can occur, but only if programmers erroneously keep references to unwanted objects. Most memory leak problems are solved by Java's garbage collection.

The **finally** block is optional; if it is present it is placed after the last of a **try** block's **catch** blocks as follows:

```
try {
    statements;
    resource-acquisition statements;
}
catch ( AKindOfException ex1 ) {
    exception-handling statements;
}
catch ( AnotherKindOfException ex2 ) {
    exception-handling statements;
}
finally {
    statement;
    resource-release statements;
}
```

Java guarantees that a **finally** block (if one is present) will be executed regardless of whether or not any exception is thrown in a **try** block or any of its corresponding **catch** blocks. Java also guarantees that a **finally** block (if one is present) will be executed if a **try** block is exited via a **return**, **break** or **continue** statement. Resource-release code is placed in a **finally** block. Suppose a resource is allocated in a **try** block.

If no exception occurs, the **catch** handlers are skipped and control proceeds to the **finally** block, which frees the resource and control proceeds to the first statement after the **finally** block.

If an exception occurs, the rest of the **try** block is skipped and if the exception is caught by one of the **catch** handlers, the exception is handled and control still proceeds to the **finally** block, which releases the resource and control proceeds to the first statement after the **finally** block.

If an exception that occurs in the **try** block cannot be caught by one of the **catch** handlers, the rest of the **try** block is skipped (as the **try** block expires) and control proceeds to the **finally** block, which releases the resource and then the exception is passed up the call chain until some calling method chooses to **catch** it. If no method chooses to deal with it, a non-GUI-based application terminates.

If a **catch** handler throws an exception, the **finally** block is still executed and the exception is passed up the call chain for a calling method to **catch** and handle.

The Java application of Fig. 14.8 demonstrates that the **finally** block (if one is present) executes even if an exception is not thrown in the corresponding **try** block. The program contains methods **main**, **throwException** and **doesNotThrowException**. Methods **throwException** and **doesNotThrowException** are declared **static** so they can be called directly from **main** (another **static** method).

Method **main** begins executing, enters its **try** block and immediately calls **throwException**. Method **throwException** throws an **Exception** (line 23), catches it (line 25) and rethrows it (line 29). The rethrown exception will be handled in **main**, but first the **finally** block (lines 33–36) executes. The rethrown exception is detected in the **try** block in **main** (lines 7–9) and handled by the **catch** block (lines 10–13). Next, method **doesNotThrowException** is called. No exception is thrown in its **try** block, so the **catch** block is skipped, but the **finally** block nevertheless executes. Control proceeds past the **finally** block. Because there are no statements following **finally** control returns to **main** and the program terminates.

```
1   // Fig. 14.8: UsingExceptions.java
2   // Demonstration of the try-catch-finally
3   // exception handling mechanism.
4   public class UsingExceptions {
5      public static void main( String args[] )
6      {
7         try {
8            throwException();
9         }
10        catch ( Exception e )
11        {
12           System.err.println( "Exception handled in main" );
13        }
14
15        doesNotThrowException();
16     }
```

Fig. 14.8   Demonstration of the **try-catch-finally** exception handling mechanism (part 1 of 2).

```
17
18   public static void throwException() throws Exception
19   {
20      // Throw an exception and immediately catch it.
21      try {
22         System.out.println( "Method throwException" );
23         throw new Exception();  // generate exception
24      }
25      catch( Exception e )
26      {
27         System.err.println(
28            "Exception handled in method throwException" );
29         throw e;  // rethrow e for further processing
30
31         // any code here would not be reached
32      }
33      finally {
34         System.err.println(
35            "Finally executed in throwException" );
36      }
37
38      // any code here would not be reached
39   }
40
41   public static void doesNotThrowException()
42   {
43      try {
44         System.out.println( "Method doesNotThrowException" );
45      }
46      catch( Exception e )
47      {
48         System.err.println( e.toString() );
49      }
50      finally {
51         System.err.println(
52            "Finally executed in doesNotThrowException" );
53      }
54
55      System.out.println(
56         "End of method doesNotThrowException" );
57   }
58 }
```

```
Method throwException
Exception handled in method throwException
Finally executed in throwException
Exception handled in main
Method doesNotThrowException
Finally executed in doesNotThrowException
End of method doesNotThrowException
```

Fig. 14.8 Demonstration of the **try-catch-finally** exception handling mechanism (part 2 of 2).

The Java application in Fig. 14.9 demonstrates that when an exception thrown in a **try** block is *not* caught in a corresponding **catch** block, the exception will be detected in the next outer **try** block and will be handled by an appropriate **catch** block (if one is present) associated with that outer **try** block.

When method **main** executes, line 7 in the **try** block calls method **throwException**. In the **try** block of method **throwException**, line 19 throws an **Exception**. This terminates the **try** block immediately and control proceeds to the **catch** handler at line 21. Because the type being caught (i.e., **RuntimeException**) is not an exact match with the thrown type (i.e., **Exception**) and is not a superclass of the thrown type, the exception is not caught in method **throwException**. The exception must be handled before normal program execution can continue. Therefore, method **throwException** terminates (but not until its **finally** block executes) and returns control to the point from which it was called in the program (line 7). Because line 7 is in the enclosing **try** block and the exception has not yet been handled, the **try** block terminates and an attempt is made to catch the exception at line 9. Because the type being caught (i.e., **Exception**) matches the thrown type, the exception is processed and the program terminates at the end of **main**.

```
1   // Fig. 14.9: UsingExceptions.java
2   // Demonstration of stack unwinding.
3   public class UsingExceptions {
4      public static void main( String args[] )
5      {
6         try {
7            throwException();
8         }
9         catch ( Exception e ) {
10           System.err.println( "Exception handled in main" );
11        }
12     }
13
14     public static void throwException() throws Exception
15     {
16        // Throw an exception and catch it in main.
17        try {
18           System.out.println( "Method throwException" );
19           throw new Exception();        // generate exception
20        }
21        catch( RuntimeException e ) {  // nothing caught here
22           System.err.println( "Exception handled in " +
23                               "method throwException" );
24        }
25        finally {
26           System.err.println( "Finally is always executed" );
27        }
28     }
29  }
```

Fig. 14.8   Demonstration of stack unwinding (part 1 of 2).

```
Method throwException
Finally is always executed
Exception handled in main
```

Fig. 14.9   Demonstration of stack unwinding (part 2 of 2).

As we have seen, a **finally** block may be entered for a variety of reasons, such as a **try** completing successfully, an exception being thrown and then handled by a local **catch**, an exception being thrown for which no local **catch** is available, or a program control statement like a **return**, **break** or **continue** being executed. Normally, the **finally** block will execute, then behave appropriately (we will call this **finally**'s "continuation action") depending on the reason it was entered. For example, if an exception is thrown in the **finally** block, the continuation action will be for *that* exception to be processed in the next enclosing **try** block. Unfortunately, if there was an exception that had not yet been caught, that exception is lost and the more recent exception is processed. This is dangerous.

Common Programming Error 14.13

If an exception is thrown for which no local **catch** *is available, when control enters the local* **finally** *block, the* **finally** *block could also* **throw** *an exception. If this happens, the first exception will be lost.*

Testing and Debugging Tip 14.13

Avoid placing code that can **throw** *an exception in a* **finally** *block.*

Good Programming Practice 14.6

Java's exception handling mechanism is intended to remove error-processing code from the main line of a program's code to improve program clarity. Do not place **try-catch-finally** *around every statement that may throw an exception. This makes programs difficult to read. Rather, place one* **try** *block around a significant portion of your code, then follow that* **try** *block with* **catch** *blocks that handle each of the things that can go wrong, then follow the* **catch** *blocks with a single* **finally** *block.*

Software Engineering Observation 14.14

As a rule, resources should be released as soon as it is apparent that they are no longer needed. This makes these resources immediately available for reuse and can improve program performance.

Software Engineering Observation 14.15

If a **try** *block has a corresponding* **finally** *block, the* **finally** *block will be executed even if the* **try** *block is exited with* **return**, **break** *or* **continue**; *then the effect of the* **return**, **break** *or* **continue** *will occur.*

14.14 Using **printStackTrace** and **getMessage**

Exceptions derive from class **Throwable**. Class **Throwable** offers a **printStackTrace** method that prints the method call stack. By calling this method for an **Exception** object that has been caught, a program can print the method call stack. This is often helpful in testing and debugging. In this section, we consider an example that exercises the **printStackTrace** method and another useful method, **getMessage**.

Testing and Debugging Tip 14.14

*All **Throwable** objects contain a **printStackTrace** method that prints a stack trace for the object.*

Testing and Debugging Tip 14.15

An exception that is not caught eventually causes Java's default exception handler to run. This displays the name of the exception, the optional character string that was supplied when the exception was constructed, and a complete execution stack trace. The stack trace shows the complete method call stack. This lets the programmer see the path of execution that led to the exception file-by-file (and thus class-by-class) and method-by-method. This information is helpful in debugging a program.

There are two constructors for class **Exception**. The first constructor

```
public Exception()
```

takes no arguments. The second constructor

```
public Exception( String informationString )
```

takes an argument **informationString** which is descriptive information about this kind of **Exception** that will be carried in every object of this class. The **informationString** stored in the **Exception** may be queried with method **getMessage**.

Testing and Debugging Tip 14.16

***Exception** classes have a constructor that accepts a **String**. Using this form of the constructor is helpful in determining the source of the exception via method **getMessage()**.*

Figure 14.10 demonstrates **getMessage** and **printStackTrace**. Method **getMessage** returns the descriptive **String** stored in an exception. Method **printStackTrace** outputs to the standard error stream (normally, the command line or console) an error message with the class name of the exception, the descriptive **String** stored in the exception and a list of the methods that had not completed execution when the exception was thrown (i.e., all methods currently residing on the method call stack).

```
1   // Fig. 14.10: UsingExceptions.java
2   // Demonstrating the getMessage and printStackTrace
3   // methods inherited into all exception classes.
4   public class UsingExceptions {
5      public static void main( String args[] )
6      {
7         try {
8            method1();
9         }
10        catch ( Exception e ) {
11           System.err.println( e.getMessage() + "\n" );
```

Fig. 14.10   Using **getMessage** and **printStackTrace** (part 1 of 2).

```
12              e.printStackTrace();
13          }
14      }
15
16      public static void method1() throws Exception
17      {
18          method2();
19      }
20
21      public static void method2() throws Exception
22      {
23          method3();
24      }
25
26      public static void method3() throws Exception
27      {
28          throw new Exception( "Exception thrown in method3" );
29      }
30  }
```

```
Exception thrown in method3
java.lang.Exception: Exception thrown in method3
        at UsingExceptions.method3(UsingExceptions.java:28)
        at UsingExceptions.method2(UsingExceptions.java:23)
        at UsingExceptions.method1(UsingExceptions.java:18)
        at UsingExceptions.main(UsingExceptions.java:8)
```

Fig. 14.10 Using **getMessage** and **printStackTrace** (part 2 of 2).

In the program, **main** invokes **method1**, **method1** invokes **method2** and **method2** invokes **method3**. At this point, the method call stack for the program is

```
method3
method2
method1
main
```

with the last method called (**method3**) at the top and the first method called (**main**) at the bottom. When **method3** throws an **Exception** (line 28), a stack trace message is generated and stored in the **Exception** object. The stack trace reflects the throw point in the code (i.e., line 28). Then, the stack unwinds to the first method in the method call stack in which the exception can be caught (i.e., **main** because it contains a **catch** handler for **Exception**). The **catch** handler then uses **getMessage** and **printStackTrace** on the **Exception** object **e** to produce the output. Notice that the line numbers in the output window correspond to the line numbers in the program.

Summary

- Some common examples of exceptions are memory exhaustion, an out-of-bounds array subscript, arithmetic overflow, division by zero and invalid method parameters.

- Exception handling is designed for dealing with synchronous malfunctions (i.e., those that occur as the result of a program's execution).

- Exception handling is typically used in situations in which a malfunction will be dealt with in a different scope from that which detected the malfunction.

- Exceptions should not be used as an alternative mechanism for specifying flow of control.

- Exception handling should be used to process exceptions from software components such as methods, libraries, and classes that are likely to be widely used, and where it does not make sense for those components to handle their own exceptions.

- Exception handling should be used on large projects to handle error processing in a standardized manner for the entire project.

- Java exception handling is geared to situations in which the method that detects an error is unable to deal with it. Such a method will **throw** an exception. If the exception matches the type of the parameter in one of the **catch** blocks, the code for that **catch** block is executed.

- The programmer encloses in a **try** block the code that may generate an error that will produce an exception. The **try** block is immediately followed by one or more **catch** blocks. Each **catch** block specifies the type of exception it can catch and handle. Each **catch** block is an exception handler.

- If no exceptions are thrown in the **try** block, the exception handlers for that block are skipped and the program resumes execution after the last **catch** block, after executing a **finally** block if one is provided.

- Exceptions are thrown in a **try** block in a method or from a method called directly or indirectly from the **try** block.

- It is possible to communicate information to the exception handler from the point of the exception. That information is the type of thrown object or it is information harvested from the vicinity and placed into the thrown object.

- The operand of a **throw** can be of any class derived from **Throwable**. The immediate subclasses of **Throwable** are **Error** and **Exception**.

- **RuntimeException**s and **Error**s are said to be "unchecked." Non-**RuntimeException**s are said to be "checked." The checked exceptions thrown by a particular method must be specified in that method's **throws** clause.

- Exceptions are caught by the closest exception handler (for the **try** block from which the exception was thrown) specifying an appropriate type.

- An exception terminates the block in which the exception occurred.

- A handler may rethrow the object to an outer **try** block.

- **catch(Exception e)** catches all **Exception**s.

- **catch(Error err)** catches all **Error**s.

- **catch(Throwable t)** catches all **Exception**s and **Error**s.

- If no handler matches a particular thrown object, the search for a match continues in an enclosing **try** block.

- Exception handlers are searched in order for an appropriate match based on type. The first handler that matches is executed. When that handler finishes executing, control resumes with the first statement after the last **catch** block.

- The order of the exception handlers affects how an exception is handled.

- A subclass object can be caught either by a handler specifying that subclass type or by handlers specifying the types of any direct or indirect superclasses of that subclass.

- If no handler is found for an exception, a non-GUI-based application terminates; an applet or a GUI-based application will return to its regular event handling.

- An exception handler cannot access variables in the scope of its **try** block because by the time the exception handler begins executing, the **try** block has expired. Information the handler needs is normally passed in the thrown object.

- Exception handlers can rethrow an exception. They can convert one type of exception into another by throwing a different exception. They can perform any necessary recovery and resume execution after the last exception handler. They can look at the situation causing the error, remove the cause of the error and retry by calling the original method that caused an exception. They can simply return some status value to their environment.

- A handler that catches a subclass object should be placed before a handler that catches a superclass object. If the superclass handler were first, it would catch superclass objects and the objects of subclasses of that superclass.

- When an exception is caught, it is possible that resources may have been allocated but not yet released in the **try** block. A **finally** block should release these resources.

- It is possible that the handler that catches an exception may decide it cannot process the exception. In this case, the handler can simply rethrow the exception. A **throw** followed by the exception object name rethrows the exception.

- Even if a handler can process an exception, and regardless of whether it does any processing on that exception, the handler can rethrow the exception for further processing outside the handler. A rethrown exception is detected by the next enclosing **try** block (normally in a calling method) and is handled by an appropriate exception handler (if there is one) listed after that enclosing **try** block.

- A **throws** clause lists the checked exceptions that may be thrown from a method. A method may **throw** the indicated exceptions, or it may **throw** subclass types. If a checked exception not listed in the **throws** clause is thrown, a syntax error occurs.

- A powerful reason for using inheritance with exceptions is to **catch** a variety of related errors easily with concise notation. One could certainly **catch** each type of subclass exception object individually, but it is more concise to simply **catch** the superclass exception object.

Terminology

ArithmeticException
array exceptions
ArrayIndexOutOfBoundsException
business-critical computing
catch a group of exceptions
catch all exceptions
catch an exception
catch block
catch(Exception e)
catch-or-declare requirement
checked **Exception**s
ClassCastException
declare exceptions that can be thrown
default exception handler
EmptyStackException
Error class
Error class hierarchy

error handling
exception
Exception class
Exception class hierarchy
exception handler
exception handling
exception object
fault tolerance
FileNotFoundException
finally block
getMessage method of **Throwable** class
handle an exception
IllegalAccessException
IncompatibleClassChangeException
instanceof operator
InstantiationException
InternalException

`InterruptedException`
`IOException`
library exception classes
memory exhaustion
mission-critical computing
`NegativeArraySizeException`
`NoClassDefFoundException`
non-run-time exception
`NullPointerException`
`null` reference
`OutOfMemoryError`
`printStackTrace` method (`Throwable`)
resource leak
resumption model of exception handling

rethrow an exception
`RuntimeException`
stack unwinding
synchronous error
termination model of exception handling
throw an exception
throw point
`throw` statement
`Throwable` class
`throws` clause
`try` block
unchecked `Exception`s
`UnsatisfiedLinkException`

Common Programming Errors

14.1   Aborting a program could leave a resource in a state in which other programs would not be able to acquire the resource, hence we would have a so-called "resource leak."

14.2   It is a syntax error to separate with other code the **catch** handlers that correspond to a particular **try** block.

14.3   Assuming that after an exception is processed, control will return to the first statement after the **throw** can lead to errors.

14.4   Specifying a comma-separated list of **catch** arguments is a syntax error. A **catch** can have only a single argument.

14.5   It is a syntax error to **catch** the same type in two different **catch** blocks associated with a particular **try** block.

14.6   Placing **catch(Exception e)** before other **catch** blocks that catch specific types of exceptions would prevent those blocks from ever being executed; **catch(Exception e)** must always be placed last in the list of exception handlers following a **try** block, or a syntax error occurs.

14.7   It is a syntax error if a **catch** that catches a superclass object is placed before a **catch** that catches an object of a subclass of that superclass.

14.8   Assuming that an exception thrown from a **catch** handler will be processed by that handler or any other handler associated with the same **try** block can lead to logic errors.

14.9   It is a syntax error if a method throws a checked exception not in that method's **throws** clause.

14.10   Attempting to throw a checked exception from a method that has no **throws** clause is a syntax error.

14.11   If a subclass method overrides a superclass method, it is an error for the subclass method to list more exceptions in its **throws** list than the overridden superclass method does. A subclass's **throws** list can contain a subset of a superclass's **throws** list.

14.12   The Java compiler requires that a method either catch any checked exceptions thrown in the method (either directly from the method's code itself or indirectly through called methods), or declare checked **Exception**s the method can **throw** to other methods; otherwise, the Java compiler issues a syntax error.

14.13   If an exception is thrown for which no local **catch** is available, when control enters the local **finally** block, the **finally** block could also **throw** an exception. If this happens, the first exception will be lost.

Good Programming Practices

14.1   Using Java exception handling enables the programmer to remove the error-handling code from the "main line" of the program's execution. This improves program clarity and enhances modifiability.

14.2   Avoid using exception handling for purposes other than error handling because this can reduce program clarity.

14.3   Using Java's standardized exception handling rather than having programmers use a diversity of "home-grown" techniques can improve program clarity on large projects.

14.4   If your method is capable of handling a given type of exception then handle it rather than passing the exception on to other regions of your program. This makes programs clearer.

14.5   Associating each type of serious execution-time malfunction with an appropriately named **Exception** class improves program clarity.

14.6   Java's exception handling mechanism is intended to remove error-processing code from the main line of a program's code to improve program clarity. Do not place **try-catch-finally** around every statement that may throw an exception. This makes programs difficult to read. Rather, place one **try** block around a significant portion of your code, then follow that **try** block with **catch** blocks that handle each of the things that can go wrong, then follow the **catch** blocks with a single **finally** block.

Performance Tips

14.1   Although it is possible to use exception handling for purposes other than error handling, this can reduce program performance.

14.2   When an exception does not occur, little or no overhead is imposed by the presence of exception-handling code. When exceptions happen, they do incur execution-time overhead.

14.3   If an error can be processed locally instead of throwing an exception, do so. This will improve program execution speed. Exception handling is slow compared to local processing.

Software Engineering Observations

14.1   Use exceptions for malfunctions that must be processed in a different method from where they are detected. Use conventional error handling techniques for local error processing in which a method is able to deal with its own exceptions.

14.2   Exception handling is particularly well-suited to systems of separately developed components. Such systems are typical of real-world software systems and products. Exception handling makes it easier to combine the components and have them work together effectively.

14.3   With other programming languages that do not support exception handling, programmers often delay writing error-processing code, and sometimes programmers simply forget to include it. This often results in less-robust, and thus inferior, software products. Java forces the programmer to deal with exception handling from the inception of a project. Still, the programmer must put considerable effort into incorporating an exception-handling strategy into software projects.

14.4   It is best to incorporate your exception-handling strategy into a system from the inception of the design process. It is difficult to add effective exception handling after a system has been implemented.

14.5   The client of a library class will likely have unique error processing in mind for an exception generated in the library class. It is unlikely that a library class will perform error processing that would meet the unique needs of all clients. Exceptions are an appropriate means for dealing with errors produced by library classes.

14.6   A key to Java-style exception handling is that the portion of a program or system that handles the exception can be distant from the portion of the program that generates the exception.

14.7   If you catch all exceptions with **catch(Exception e)** you can use the **instanceof** operator to probe the type of the exception. For example, the boolean condition **x instanceof Y** evaluates to **true** if object **x** is an instance of class **Y**, and **false** otherwise.

14.8   If several handlers match the type of an exception, and if each of these handles the exception differently, the order of the handlers affects the manner in which the exception is handled.

14.9   Another reason not to use exceptions for conventional flow of control is that these "additional" exceptions can "get in the way" of genuine error-type exceptions. It becomes more difficult for the programmer to keep track of the larger number of exception cases. Exceptional situations should be rare, not commonplace.

14.10   If a non-**RuntimeException** is thrown by a method, or if that method calls methods that throw non-**RuntimeExceptions**, each of those exceptions must be declared in the **throws** clause of that method or caught in a **try/catch** in that method.

14.11   If your method calls other methods that explicitly **throw** checked exceptions, those exceptions must be listed in the **throws** clause of your method, unless your method catches those exceptions. This is Java's "**catch**-or-declare" requirement.

14.12   Subclass methods that do not override their corresponding superclass **methods** exhibit the same exception handling behavior of the inherited superclass methods. The **throws** list of a subclass method that overrides a superclass method may not have more exceptions than the **throws** list of the overridden superclass method.

14.13   A **finally** block typically contains code to release resources acquired in its corresponding **try** block; this is an effective way to eliminate resource leaks. For example, the **finally** block should close any files opened in the **try** block.

14.14   As a rule, resources should be released as soon as it is apparent that they are no longer needed. This makes these resources immediately available for reuse and can improve program performance.

14.15   If a **try** block has a corresponding **finally** block, the **finally** block will be executed even if the **try** block is exited with **return**, **break** or **continue**; then the effect of the **return**, **break** or **continue** will occur.

Testing and Debugging Tips

14.1   Exception handling helps improve a program's fault tolerance. It becomes "more pleasant" to write error-processing code, so programmers are more likely to provide it.

14.2   All Java applets and certain Java applications are GUI-based. Some Java applications are not GUI-based; these are often called command-line applications (or console applications). When an exception is not caught in a command-line application, the program terminates (i.e., Java exits) after the default exception handler runs. When an exception is not caught in an applet or a GUI-based application, the GUI is still displayed and the user can continue using the applet or application even after the default exception handler runs. However, the GUI may be in an inconsistent state.

14.3   With exception handling, a program can continue executing after dealing with a problem. This helps ensure robust applications that contribute to what is called mission-critical computing or business-critical computing.

14.4   A **finally** block is where to place code that will release resources acquired in a **try** block. This strategy is an effective way to avoid resource leaks.

14.5   When **toString** is invoked on any **Throwable** object, its resulting **String** includes the descriptive **String** that was supplied to the constructor.

14.6   If it is necessary to pass information about the malfunction that caused an exception, such information can be placed in the thrown object. That information can then be referenced through the parameter name in the **catch** handler.

14.7   An object can be thrown without containing information to be passed; in this case, knowledge that an exception of this type has been raised may provide sufficient information for the handler to do its job correctly.

14.8   Do not try to circumvent Java's **catch**-or-declare requirement by simply catching exceptions and doing nothing with them. Exceptions are generally of a serious enough nature that they need to be dealt with rather than suppressed.

14.9   The Java compiler, through the **throws** list used with exception handling, forces programmers to deal with the exceptions that can be thrown from each method a program calls. This helps avoid bugs that arise in programs when programmers ignore the fact that things can go wrong and make no provisions for these problems.

14.10   Suppose a method **throw**s all subclasses of a particular superclass. You may be tempted to list only the superclass in the **throws** clause. Instead, explicitly list all the subclasses. This focuses the programmer's attention on the specific **Exception**s that must be dealt with and will often help avoid bugs caused by processing **Exception**s in too general a manner.

14.11   Catching subclass exception objects individually is subject to error if the programmer forgets to explicitly test for one or more of the subclass types; catching the superclass guarantees that objects of all subclasses will be caught.

14.12   Actually, Java does not completely eliminate memory leaks. There is a subtle issue here. Java will not garbage collect an object until there are no more references to the object. Thus, memory leaks can occur, but only if programmers erroneously keep references to unwanted objects. Most memory leak problems are solved by Java's garbage collection.

14.13   Avoid placing code that can **throw** an exception in a **finally** block.

14.14   All **Throwable** objects contain a **printStackTrace** method that prints a stack trace for the object.

14.15   An exception that is not caught eventually causes Java's default exception handler to run. This displays the name of the exception, the optional character string that was supplied when the exception was constructed, and a complete execution stack trace. The stack trace shows the complete method call stack. This lets the programmer see the path of execution that led to the exception file-by-file (and thus class-by-class) and method-by-method. This information is helpful in debugging a program.

14.16   **Exception** classes have a constructor that accepts a **String** argument. Using this form of the constructor is helpful in determining the source of the exception via method **getMessage()**.

Self-Review Exercises

14.1   List five common examples of exceptions.

14.2   Why should exception handling techniques not be used for conventional program control?

14.3   Why are exceptions particularly appropriate for dealing with errors produced by library classes and methods?

14.4   What is a "resource leak"?

14.5   If no exceptions are thrown in a **try** block, where does control proceed to when the **try** block completes execution?

14.6   What happens if an exception occurs and an appropriate exception handler cannot be found?

14.7   Give a key advantage of using **catch(Exception e)**.

14.8   Should a conventional applet or application catch **Error** objects?

14.9   What happens if several handlers match the type of the thrown object?

14.10   Why would a programmer specify a superclass type as the type of a **catch** handler and then throw objects of subclass types?

14.11   How might a **catch** handler be written to process related types of errors without using inheritance among exception classes?

14.12   What is the key reason for using **finally** blocks?

14.13   Does throwing an **Exception** have to cause program termination?

14.14   What happens when a **catch** handler throws an **Exception**?

14.15   What happens to a local reference in a **try** block when that block throws an **Exception**?

Answers to Self-Review Exercises

14.1   Memory exhaustion, array subscript out of bounds, arithmetic overflow, division by zero, invalid method parameters.

14.2   (a) **Exception** handling is designed to handle infrequently occurring situations that often result in program termination, so compiler writers are not required to implement exception handling to perform optimally. (b) Flow of control with conventional control structures is generally clearer and more efficient than with exceptions. (c) Problems can occur because the stack is unwound when an exception occurs and resources allocated prior to the exception may not be freed. (d) The "additional" exceptions can get in the way of genuine error-type exceptions. It becomes more difficult for the programmer to keep track of the larger number of exception cases.

14.3   It is unlikely that library classes and methods could perform error processing that would meet the unique needs of all users.

14.4   A resource leak occurs when an executing program does not properly release a resource when the resource is no longer needed. If the program attempts to use the resource again in the future, the program may not be able to access the resource.

14.5   The exception handlers (in the **catch** blocks) for that **try** block are skipped and the program resumes execution after the last **catch** block. If there is a **finally** block, it is executed and the program resumes execution after the **finally** block.

14.6   A non-GUI-based application terminates; an applet or a GUI-based application resumes regular event processing.

14.7   The form **catch(Exception e)** catches any type of exception thrown in a **try** block. An advantage is that no thrown **Exception** can slip by.

14.8   **Error**s are usually serious problems with the underlying Java system; most programs will not want to catch **Error**s.

14.9   The first matching **Exception** handler after the **try** block is executed.

14.10   This is a nice way to catch related types of exceptions, but it should be used carefully.

14.11   Provide a single **Exception** subclass and **catch** handler for a group of exceptions. As each exception occurs, the exception object can be created with different instance data. The **catch** handler can examine this data to distinguish the type of the **Exception**.

14.12   The **finally** block is the preferred means for preventing resource leaks.

14.13   No, but it does terminate the block in which the **Exception** is thrown.

14.14   The exception will be processed by a **catch** handler (if one exists) associated with the **try** block (if one exists) enclosing the **catch** handler that caused the exception.

14.15   The reference is removed from memory and the reference count for the referenced object is decremented. If the reference count is zero, the object is marked for garbage collection.

Exercises

14.16   Under what circumstances would you use the following statement?

```
catch ( Exception e ) { throw e; }
```

14.17   List the benefits of exception handling over conventional means of error processing.

14.18   Describe an object-oriented technique for handling related exceptions.

14.19   Until this chapter, we have found that dealing with errors detected by constructors is a bit awkward. Explain why exception handling is an effective means for dealing with constructor failure.

14.20   Suppose a program throws an exception and the appropriate exception handler begins executing. Now suppose that the exception handler itself throws the same exception. Does this create an infinite recursion? Explain your answer.

14.21   Use inheritance to create an exception superclass and various exception subclasses. Write a program to demonstrate that the **catch** specifying the superclass catches subclass exceptions.

14.22   Write a Java program that shows that all finalizers for objects constructed in a block are not necessarily called after an exception is thrown from that block.

14.23   Write a Java program that demonstrates how various exceptions are caught with

```
catch ( Exception e )
```

14.24   Write a Java program that shows that the order of exception handlers is important. If you try to catch a superclass exception type before a subclass type, the compiler should generate errors. Explain why these errors occur.

14.25   Write a Java program that shows a constructor passing information about constructor failure to an exception handler after a **try** block.

14.26   Write a Java program that illustrates rethrowing an exception.

14.27   Write a Java program which shows that a method with its own **try** block does not have to catch every possible error generated within the **try**. Some exceptions can slip through to, and be handled in, other scopes.

Multithreading

Objectives

- To understand the notion of multithreading.
- To appreciate how multithreading can improve performance.
- To understand how to create, manage and destroy threads.
- To understand the life cycle of a thread.
- To study several examples of thread synchronization.
- To understand thread priorities and scheduling.
- To understand daemon threads and thread groups.

The spider's touch, how exquisitely fine!
Feels at each thread, and lives along the line.
Alexander Pope

A person with one watch knows what time it is; a person with two watches is never sure.
Proverb

Conversation is but carving!
Give no more to every guest,
Then he's able to digest.
Jonathan Swift

Learn to labor and to wait.
Henry Wadsworth Longfellow

The most general definition of beauty…Multeity in Unity.
Samuel Taylor Coleridge

Outline

15.1 Introduction

It would be nice if we could "do one thing at a time" and "do it well," but that is simply not how the world works. The human body performs a great variety of operations *in parallel,* or as we will say throughout this chapter, *concurrently.* Respiration, blood circulation and digestion, for example, can occur concurrently. All of the senses—seeing, touching, smelling, tasting and hearing—can occur concurrently. An automobile can be accelerating, turning, air conditioning and playing music concurrently. Computers, too, perform operations concurrently. It is common today for desktop personal computers to be compiling a program, printing a file and receiving electronic mail messages over a network concurrently.

Concurrency is important in our lives. Ironically, though, most programming languages do not enable programmers to specify concurrent activities. Rather, programming languages generally provide only a simple set of control structures that enable programmers to perform one action at a time and then proceed to the next action after the previous one is finished. The kind of concurrency that computers perform today is normally implemented as operating systems "primitives" available only to highly experienced "systems programmers."

The *Ada* programming language developed by the United States Department of Defense made concurrency primitives widely available to defense contractors building command and control systems. But Ada has not been widely used in universities and commercial industry.

Java is unique among popular general-purpose programming languages in that it makes concurrency primitives available to the applications programmer. The programmer specifies that applications contain *threads of execution,* each thread designating a portion of a program that may execute concurrently with other threads. This capability, called *multithreading,* gives the Java programmer powerful capabilities not available in C and C++, the languages on which Java is based. C and C++ are called *single-threaded* languages.

Software Engineering Observation 15.1

*Unlike many languages that do not have built-in multithreading (such as C and C++) and must therefore make calls to operating system multithreading primitives, Java includes multithreading primitives as part of the language itself (actually in classes **Thread**, **Thread-Group**, **ThreadLocal** and **ThreadDeath** of the **java.lang** package). This encourages the use of multithreading among a larger part of the applications programming community.*

We will discuss many applications of concurrent programming. When programs download large files such as audio clips or video clips from the World Wide Web, we do not want to wait until an entire clip is downloaded before starting the playback. So we can put multiple threads to work: one that downloads a clip, and another that plays the clip so that these activities, or *tasks,* may proceed concurrently. To avoid choppy playback, we will coordinate the threads so that the player thread does not begin until there is a sufficient amount of the clip in memory to keep the player thread busy.

Another example of multithreading is Java's automatic garbage collection. C and C++ place with the programmer the responsibility for reclaiming dynamically allocated memory. Java provides a *garbage collector thread* that automatically reclaims dynamically allocated memory that is no longer needed.

Testing and Debugging Tip 15.1

In C and C++, programmers must explicitly provide statements for reclaiming dynamically allocated memory. When memory is not reclaimed (because a programmer forgets to do so, or because of a logic error or because an exception diverts program control), this results in an all-too-common error called a memory leak *that can eventually exhaust the supply of free memory and may cause program termination. Java's automatic garbage collection eliminates the vast majority of memory leaks, i.e., those that are due to orphaned (unreferenced) objects.*

Java's garbage collector runs as a low-priority thread. When Java determines that there are no longer any references to an object, it marks the object for eventual garbage collection. The garbage collector thread runs when processor time is available and when there are no higher-priority runnable threads. The garbage collector will, however, run immediately when the system is out of memory.

Performance Tip 15.1

Java's garbage collection is not as efficient as the dynamic memory management code the best C and C++ programmers write, but it is relatively efficient and much safer for the programmer.

Performance Tip 15.2

*Setting an object reference to **null** marks that object for eventual garbage collection (if there are no other references to the object). This can help conserve memory in a system in which an automatic object is not going out of scope because the method it is in will execute for a lengthy period.*

Writing multithreaded programs can be tricky. Although the human mind can perform many functions concurrently, humans find it difficult to jump between parallel "trains of thought." To see why multithreading can be difficult to program and understand, try the following experiment: Open three books to page 1. Now try reading the books concurrently. Read a few words from the first book, then read a few words from the second book, then read a few words from the third book, then loop back and read the next few words from the first book, and so on. After a brief time you will rapidly appreciate the challenges of multithreading: switching between books, reading briefly, remembering your place in each book, moving the book you are reading closer so you can see it, pushing books you are not reading aside, and amidst all this chaos, trying to comprehend the content of the books!

Performance Tip 15.3

A problem with single-threaded applications is that possibly lengthy activities must complete before other activities can begin. Users feel they already spend too much time waiting with Internet and World Wide Web applications, so multithreading is immediately appealing.

Although Java is perhaps the world's most portable programming language, certain portions of the language are nevertheless platform dependent. In particular, there are differences among the first three Java platforms implemented, namely the Solaris implementation and the Win32 implementation (i.e., Windows-based implementations for Windows 95 and Windows NT).

The Solaris Java platform runs a thread of a given priority to completion or until a higher-priority thread becomes ready. At that point *preemption* occurs, i.e., the processor is given to the higher-priority thread while the previously running thread must wait.

In the 32-bit Java implementations for Windows 95 and Windows NT, threads are *timesliced*. This means that each thread is given a limited amount of time (called a time *quantum*) to execute on a processor, and when that time expires the thread is made to wait while all other threads of equal priority get their chances to use their quantum in *round-robin* fashion. Then the original thread resumes execution. Thus, on Windows 95 and Windows NT, a running thread can be preempted by a thread of equal priority, whereas on the Solaris implementation, a running Java thread can only be preempted by a higher-priority thread. Future Solaris Java systems are expected to perform timeslicing as well.

Portability Tip 15.1

Java multithreading is platform dependent. Thus, a multithreaded application could behave differently on different Java implementations.

15.2 Class **Thread**: An Overview of the **Thread** Methods

In this section we overview the various thread-related methods in the Java API. We use many of these methods in live-code examples throughout the chapter. The reader should refer to the Java API directly for more details on using each method, especially the exceptions thrown by each method.

Class **Thread** (package **java.lang**) has several constructors. The constructor

```
public Thread( String threadName )
```

constructs a **Thread** object whose name is **threadName**. The constructor

```
public Thread()
```

constructs a **Thread** whose name is **"Thread-"** concatenated with a number, like **Thread-1**, **Thread-2**, and so on.

The code that "does the real work" of a thread is placed in its **run** method. The **run** method can be overridden in a subclass of **Thread** or it may be overridden in a **Runnable** object; **Runnable** is an important Java *interface* that we study in Section 15.10.

A program launches a thread's execution by calling the thread's **start** method, which, in turn, calls the **run** method. After **start** launches the thread, **start** returns to its caller immediately. The caller then executes concurrently with the launched thread. The **start** method throws an **IllegalThreadStateException** if the thread it is trying to start has already been started.

The **static** method **sleep** is called with an argument specifying how long the currently executing thread should sleep (in milliseconds); while a thread sleeps, it does not contend for the processor, so other threads can execute. This can give lower-priority threads a chance to run.

The **interrupt** method is called to interrupt a thread. The **static** method **interrupted** returns **true** if the current thread has been interrupted and **false** otherwise. Method call **isInterrupted** (a non-**static** method) is sent to some other thread to determine if that thread has been interrupted.

Method **isAlive** returns **true** if **start** has been called for a given thread and the thread is not dead (i.e., its controlling **run** method has not completed execution).

We will discuss the **yield** method in detail after we have considered thread priorities and thread scheduling.

Method **setName** sets a **Thread**'s name. Method **getName** returns the name of the **Thread**. Method **toString** returns a **String** consisting of the name of the thread, the priority of the thread and the thread's **ThreadGroup** (discussed in Section 15.11).

The **static** method **currentThread** returns a reference to the currently executing **Thread**.

Method **join** waits for the **Thread** to which the message is sent to die before the calling **Thread** can proceed; no argument or an argument of 0 milliseconds to method **join** indicates that the current **Thread** will wait forever for the target **Thread** to die before the calling **Thread** proceeds. Such waiting can be dangerous; it can lead to two particularly serious problems called *deadlock* and *indefinite postponement*. We will discuss these momentarily.

Testing and Debugging Tip 15.2

Method **dumpStack** *is useful for debugging multithreaded applications. A program calls* **static** *method* **dumpStack** *to print a method-call stack trace for the current* **Thread***.*

15.3 Thread States: Life Cycle of a Thread

At any time, a thread is said to be in one of several *thread states* (illustrated in Fig. 15.1). Let us say that a thread that was just created is in the *born* state. The thread remains in this state until the thread's **start** method is called; this causes the thread to enter the *ready* state (also known as the *runnable* state). The highest-priority *ready* thread enters the *running state* when the system assigns a processor to the thread (i.e., the thread begins executing). A thread enters the *dead* state when its **run** method completes or terminates for any reason—a *dead* thread will eventually be disposed of by the system.

One common way for a *running* thread to enter the *blocked state* is when the thread issues an input/output request. In this case, a *blocked* thread becomes *ready* when the I/O it is waiting for completes. A *blocked* thread cannot use a processor even if one is available.

When a **sleep** method is called in a *running* thread, that thread enters the *sleeping* state. A *sleeping* thread becomes *ready* after the designated sleep time expires. A *sleeping* thread cannot use a processor even if one is available.

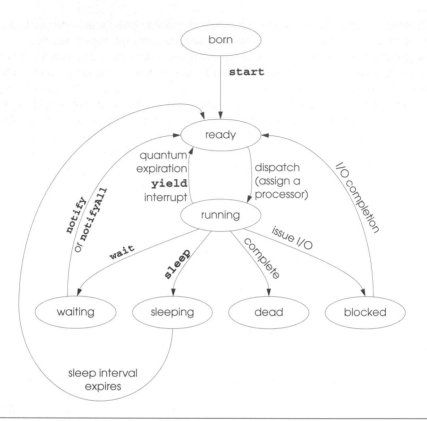

Fig. 15.1   Life cycle of a thread.

When a *running* thread calls **wait** the thread enters a *waiting* state for the particular object on which **wait** was called. One thread in the *waiting* state for a particular object becomes *ready* on a call to **notify** issued by another thread associated with that object. Every thread in the *waiting* state for a given object becomes ready on a call to **notifyAll** by another thread associated with that object. The **wait**, **notify** and **notifyAll** methods will be discussed in more depth shortly when we consider monitors.

A thread enters the *dead state* when its **run** method either completes or throws an uncaught exception.

15.4 Thread Priorities and Thread Scheduling

Every Java applet or application is multithreaded. Every Java thread has a priority in the range **Thread.MIN_PRIORITY** (a constant of 1) and **Thread.MAX_PRIORITY** (a constant of 10). By default, each thread is given priority **Thread.NORM_PRIORITY** (a constant of 5). Each new thread inherits the priority of the thread that creates it.

Some Java platforms support a concept called *timeslicing* and some do not. Without timeslicing, each thread in a set of equal-priority threads runs to completion (unless the thread leaves the running state and enters the waiting, sleeping or blocked state) before that thread's peers get a chance to execute. With timeslicing, each thread receives a brief burst of processor time called a *quantum* during which that thread can execute. At the completion of the quantum, even if that thread has not finished executing, the processor is taken away from that thread and given to the next thread of equal priority if one is available.

The job of the Java *scheduler* is to keep a highest-priority thread running at all times, and if timeslicing is available, to ensure that several equally high-priority threads each execute for a quantum in *round-robin* fashion (i.e., these threads can be timesliced). Figure 15.2 illustrates Java's multilevel priority queue for threads. In the figure, threads A and B each execute for a quantum in round-robin fashion until both threads complete execution. Next, thread C runs to completion. Then, threads D, E and F each execute for a quantum in round-robin fashion until they all complete execution. This process continues until all threads run to completion. Note that new higher-priority threads could postpone—possibly indefinitely—the execution of lower-priority threads. Such *indefinite postponement* is often referred to more colorfully as *starvation*.

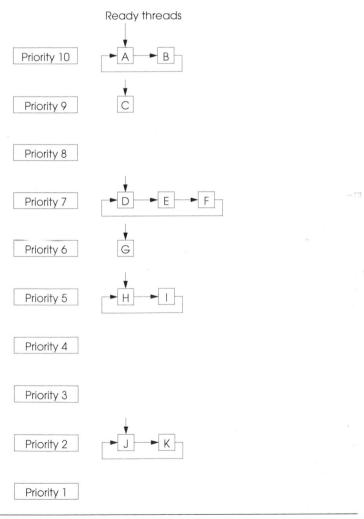

Fig. 15.2   Java thread priority scheduling.

A thread's priority can be adjusted with method *setPriority* which takes an **int** argument. If the argument is not in the range 1 through 10, **setPriority** throws an **IllegalArgumentException**. Method *getPriority* returns the thread's priority.

A thread can call the **yield** method to give other threads a chance to execute. Actually, whenever a higher-priority thread becomes ready, the current thread is preempted, so a thread cannot **yield** to a higher-priority thread because the first thread will have been preempted when the higher-priority thread became ready. Similarly, **yield** always allows the highest-priority *ready* thread to run, so if only lower-priority threads are ready at the time of a **yield** call, the current thread will be the highest-priority thread and will continue executing. Therefore, a thread **yield**s to give threads of an equal priority a chance to run. On a timesliced system this is unnecessary because threads of equal priority will each execute for their quantum (or until they lose the processor for some other reason) and other threads of equal priority will execute in *round-robin* fashion. Thus **yield** is appropriate for non-timesliced systems in which a thread would ordinarily run to completion before another thread of equal priority would have an opportunity to run.

Performance Tip 15.4

On non-timesliced systems, cooperating threads of equal priority should periodically call **yield** *to enable their peers to proceed smoothly.*

Portability Tip 15.2

Applets should be programmed to work on all Java platforms to realize Java's goal of true portability. When designing applets that use threads, you must consider the threading capabilities of all the platforms on which the applet will execute.

A thread executes unless it dies, it becomes blocked for input/output (or some other reason), it calls **sleep**, it calls **wait**, it calls **yield**, it is preempted by a thread of higher priority or its quantum expires. A thread with a higher priority than the running thread can become ready (and hence preempt the running thread) if a *sleeping* thread finishes sleeping, if I/O completes for a thread waiting for that I/O or if either **notify** or **notifyAll** is called on a thread that called **wait**.

The application of Fig. 15.3 demonstrates basic threading techniques, including creation of a class derived from **Thread**, construction of a **Thread** and using the **Thread** class **sleep** method. Each thread of execution we create in the program displays its name after sleeping for a random amount of time between 0 and 5 seconds. The program consists of two classes—**ThreadTester** and **PrintThread**.

Class **PrintThread**—which inherits from **Thread** so each object of the class can execute in parallel—consists of instance variable **sleepTime**, a constructor and a **run** method. Variable **sleepTime** stores a random integer value chosen when a **PrintThread** object is constructed. Each **PrintThread** object sleeps for the amount of time specified by **sleepTime** then outputs its name.

The **PrintThread** constructor (line 30) initializes **sleepTime** to a random integer between 0 and 4999 (0 to 4.999 seconds). Then, the name of the thread and the value of **sleepTime** are output to show the values for the particular **PrintThread** being constructed. The name of each thread is specified as a **String** argument to the **PrintThread** constructor and is passed to the superclass constructor at line 32. *Note:* It is possible to allow class **Thread** to choose a name for your thread by using the **Thread** class's default constructor.

```
1    // Fig. 15.3: ThreadTester.java
2    // Show multiple threads printing at different intervals.
3
4    public class ThreadTester {
5       public static void main( String args[] )
6       {
7          PrintThread thread1, thread2, thread3, thread4;
8
9          thread1 = new PrintThread( "thread1" );
10         thread2 = new PrintThread( "thread2" );
11         thread3 = new PrintThread( "thread3" );
12         thread4 = new PrintThread( "thread4" );
13
14         System.err.println( "\nStarting threads" );
15
16         thread1.start();
17         thread2.start();
18         thread3.start();
19         thread4.start();
20
21         System.err.println( "Threads started\n" );
22      }
23   }
24
25   class PrintThread extends Thread {
26      private int sleepTime;
27
28      // PrintThread constructor assigns name to thread
29      // by calling Thread constructor
30      public PrintThread( String name )
31      {
32         super( name );
33
34         // sleep between 0 and 5 seconds
35         sleepTime = (int) ( Math.random() * 5000 );
36
37         System.err.println( "Name: " + getName() +
38                             ";  sleep: " + sleepTime );
39      }
40
41      // execute the thread
42      public void run()
43      {
44         // put thread to sleep for a random interval
45         try {
46            System.err.println( getName() + " going to sleep" );
47            Thread.sleep( sleepTime );
48         }
49         catch ( InterruptedException exception ) {
50            System.err.println( exception.toString() );
51         }
52
```

Fig. 15.3   Multiple threads printing at random intervals (part 1 of 2).

```
53              // print thread name
54              System.err.println( getName() + " done sleeping" );
55      }
56  }}
```

```
Name: thread1;   sleep: 1653
Name: thread2;   sleep: 2910
Name: thread3;   sleep: 4436
Name: thread4;   sleep: 201

Starting threads
Threads started

thread1 going to sleep
thread2 going to sleep
thread3 going to sleep
thread4 going to sleep
thread4 done sleeping
thread1 done sleeping
thread2 done sleeping
thread3 done sleeping
```

```
Name: thread1;   sleep: 3876
Name: thread2;   sleep: 64
Name: thread3;   sleep: 1752
Name: thread4;   sleep: 3120

Starting threads
Threads started

thread2 going to sleep
thread4 going to sleep
thread1 going to sleep
thread3 going to sleep
thread2 done sleeping
thread3 done sleeping
thread4 done sleeping
thread1 done sleeping
```

Fig. 15.3   Multiple threads printing at random intervals (part 2 of 2).

When a **PrintThread**'s **start** method (inherited from **Thread**) is invoked, the **PrintThread** object enters the *ready* state. When the system assigns a processor to the **PrintThread** object, it enters the *running* state and its **run** method begins execution. Method **run** prints a **String** in the command window indicating that the thread is going to sleep then invokes the **sleep** method (line 47) to immediately put the thread into a *sleeping* state. When the thread awakens, it is placed into a *ready* state again until it is assigned a processor. When the **PrintThread** object enters the *running* state again, it outputs its name (indicating that the thread is done sleeping), its **run** method terminates and the thread object enters the *dead* state. Note that the **sleep** method can throw a checked **InterruptedException** (if another thread invokes the sleeping thread's **interrupt** method), therefore **sleep** must be called in a **try** block (in this example, we simply output the **String** representation of the exception if one occurs).

Class **ThreadTester**'s **main** method (line 5) instantiates four **PrintThread** objects and invokes the **Thread** class **start** method on each one to place all four **PrintThread** objects in a *ready* state. Note that the program terminates execution when the last **PrintThread** awakens and prints its name. Also note that the **main** method terminates after starting the four **PrintThread**s, but the application does not terminate until the last thread dies.

15.5 Thread Synchronization

Java uses *monitors* (as discussed by C.A.R. Hoare in his 1974 paper cited in Exercise 15.24) to perform synchronization. Every object with **synchronized** methods is a monitor. The monitor allows one thread at a time to execute a **synchronized** method on the object. This is accomplished by *locking* the object when the **synchronized** method is invoked—also known as *obtaining the lock*. If there are several **synchronized** methods, only one **synchronized** method may be active on an object at once; all other threads attempting to invoke **synchronized** methods must wait. When a **synchronized** method finishes executing, the lock on the object is released and the monitor lets the highest-priority *ready* thread attempting to invoke a **synchronized** method proceed. *Note:* Java also has **synchronized** *blocks* of code (discussed in the example of Section 15.10).

A thread executing in a **synchronized** method may determine that it cannot proceed, so the thread voluntarily calls **wait**. This removes the thread from contention for the processor and from contention for the monitor object. The thread now waits in the *waiting* state while other threads try to enter the monitor object. When a thread executing a **synchronized** method completes, the thread can **notify** a waiting thread to become *ready* again so it can attempt to obtain the lock on the monitor object again and execute. The **notify** acts as a signal to the waiting thread that the condition the waiting thread has been waiting for is now satisfied, so it is acceptable for that thread to reenter the monitor. If a thread calls **notifyAll**, then all threads waiting for the object become eligible to reenter the monitor (i.e., they are all placed in a *ready* state). Remember that only one of those threads can obtain the lock on the object at a time. Methods **wait**, **notify** and **notifyAll** are inherited by all classes from class **Object**. So any object has the potential to be a monitor.

Common Programming Error 15.1

Threads in the waiting state for a monitor object must eventually be awakened explicitly with a **notify** *(or* **interrupt**) *or the thread will wait forever. This may cause deadlock.*

Testing and Debugging Tip 15.3

Be sure that every call to **wait** *has a corresponding call to* **notify** *that will eventually end the waiting or call* **notifyAll** *as a safeguard.*

Performance Tip 15.5

Synchronization to achieve correctness in multithreaded programs can make programs run slower due to the monitor overhead and frequently moving threads between the running, waiting and ready states. There is not much to say, however, for highly efficient, incorrect multithreaded programs!

Testing and Debugging Tip 15.4

*The locking that occurs with the execution of **synchronized** methods could lead to dead-lock if the locks are never released. When exceptions occur, Java's exception mechanism co-ordinates with Java's synchronization mechanism to release appropriate synchronization locks to avoid these kinds of deadlocks.*

Monitor objects maintain a list of all threads waiting to enter the monitor object to execute **synchronized** methods. A thread is inserted in the list and waits for the object if that thread calls a **synchronized** method of the object while another thread is already executing in a **synchronized** method of that object. A thread also is inserted in the list if the thread calls **wait** while operating inside the object. However, it is important to distinguish waiting threads that blocked because the monitor was busy vs. threads that explicitly called **wait** inside the monitor. Upon completion of a **synchronized** method, outside threads that blocked because the monitor was busy can proceed to enter the object. Threads that explicitly invoked **wait** can only proceed when notified via a call by another thread to **notify** or **notifyAll**. When it is acceptable for waiting thread to proceed, the scheduler selects the thread with the highest priority.

Common Programming Error 15.2

*It is an error if a thread issues a **wait**, a **notify** or a **notifyAll** on an object without having acquired a lock for the object. This causes an **IllegalMonitorStateExcep-tion** to be thrown.*

15.6 Producer/Consumer Relationship without Thread Synchronization

In a *producer/consumer relationship*, a *producer thread* calling a *produce* method may see that the consumer thread has not read the last message from a shared region of memory called a *buffer*, so the producer thread will call **wait**. When a *consumer thread* reads the message, it will call **notify** to allow a waiting producer to proceed. When a consumer thread enters the monitor and finds the buffer empty, it calls **wait**. A producer finding the buffer empty, writes to the buffer, then calls **notify** so a waiting consumer can proceed.

Shared data can get corrupted if we do not synchronize access among multiple threads. Consider a producer/consumer relationship in which a producer thread deposits a sequence of numbers (we use 1, 2, 3, …) into a slot of shared memory. The consumer thread reads this data from the shared memory and prints the data. We print what the producer produces as it produces it and what the consumer consumes as it consumes it. Figure 15.4 demonstrates a producer and a consumer accessing a single shared cell (**int** variable **sharedInt**) of memory without any synchronization. Because the threads are not synchronized, data can be lost if the producer places new data into the slot before the consumer consumes the previous data, and data can be "doubled" if the consumer consumes data again before the producer produces the next item. To show these possibilities, the consumer thread in this example keeps a total of all the values it reads. The producer thread produces values from 1 to 10. If the consumer is able to read each value produced once, the total would be 55. However, if you execute this program several times, you will see that the total is rarely, if ever, 55.

```
1    // Fig. 15.4: SharedCell.java
2    // Show multiple threads modifying shared object.
3    public class SharedCell {
4       public static void main( String args[] )
5       {
6          HoldIntegerUnsynchronized h =
7             new HoldIntegerUnsynchronized();
8          ProduceInteger p = new ProduceInteger( h );
9          ConsumeInteger c = new ConsumeInteger( h );
10
11         p.start();
12         c.start();
13      }
14   }
```

Fig. 15.4   Threads modifying a shared object without synchronization (part 1 of 4).

```
15   // Fig. 15.4: ProduceInteger.java
16   // Definition of threaded class ProduceInteger
17   public class ProduceInteger extends Thread {
18      private HoldIntegerUnsynchronized pHold;
19
20      public ProduceInteger( HoldIntegerUnsynchronized h )
21      {
22         super( "ProduceInteger" );
23         pHold = h;
24      }
25
26      public void run()
27      {
28         for ( int count = 1; count <= 10; count++ ) {
29            // sleep for a random interval
30            try {
31               Thread.sleep( (int) ( Math.random() * 3000 ) );
32            }
33            catch( InterruptedException e ) {
34               System.err.println( e.toString() );
35            }
36
37            pHold.setSharedInt( count );
38         }
39
40         System.err.println( getName() +
41            " finished producing values" +
42            "\nTerminating " + getName() );
43      }
44   }
```

Fig. 15.4   Threads modifying a shared object without synchronization (part 2 of 4).

```
45  // Fig. 15.4: ConsumeInteger.java
46  // Definition of threaded class ConsumeInteger
47  public class ConsumeInteger extends Thread {
48     private HoldIntegerUnsynchronized cHold;
49
50     public ConsumeInteger( HoldIntegerUnsynchronized h )
51     {
52        super( "ConsumeInteger" );
53        cHold = h;
54     }
55
56     public void run()
57     {
58        int val, sum = 0;
59
60        do {
61           // sleep for a random interval
62           try {
63              Thread.sleep( (int) ( Math.random() * 3000 ) );
64           }
65           catch( InterruptedException e ) {
66              System.err.println( e.toString() );
67           }
68
69           val = cHold.getSharedInt();
70           sum += val;
71        } while ( val != 10 );
72
73        System.err.println(
74           getName() + " retrieved values totaling: " + sum +
75           "\nTerminating " + getName() );
76     }
77  }
```

Fig. 15.4 Threads modifying a shared object without synchronization (part 3 of 4).

The program consists of four classes—**SharedCell** (line 3), **ProduceInteger** (line 17), **ConsumeInteger** (line 47) and **HoldIntegerUnsynchronized** (line 80). Class **SharedCell**'s **main** method (line 4) instantiates the shared **HoldIntegerUnsynchronized** object **h** and uses it as the argument to the constructors for the **ProduceInteger** object **p** and the **ConsumeInteger** object **c**. The object **h** contains the data that will be shared between the two threads.

Next, method **main** invokes the **Thread** class **start** method on the **ProduceInteger** object **p** and the **ConsumeInteger** object **c** to place them in the *ready* state. This launches these threads.

Class **ProduceInteger**—a subclass of **Thread**—consists of instance variable **pHold**, a constructor and a **run** method. Instance variable **pHold** is initialized (line 23) in the constructor to refer to the **HoldIntegerUnsynchronized** object **h** that was passed as an argument.

```
78   // Fig. 15.4: HoldIntegerUnsynchronized.java
79   // Definition of class HoldIntegerUnsynchronized
80   public class HoldIntegerUnsynchronized {
81      private int sharedInt = -1;
82
83      public void setSharedInt( int val )
84      {
85         System.err.println( Thread.currentThread().getName() +
86            " setting sharedInt to " + val );
87         sharedInt = val;
88      }
89
90      public int getSharedInt()
91      {
92         System.err.println( Thread.currentThread().getName() +
93            " retrieving sharedInt value " + sharedInt );
94         return sharedInt;
95      }
96   }
```

```
ConsumeInteger retrieving sharedInt value -1
ConsumeInteger retrieving sharedInt value -1
ProduceInteger setting sharedInt to 1
ProduceInteger setting sharedInt to 2
ConsumeInteger retrieving sharedInt value 2
ProduceInteger setting sharedInt to 3
ProduceInteger setting sharedInt to 4
ProduceInteger setting sharedInt to 5
ConsumeInteger retrieving sharedInt value 5
ProduceInteger setting sharedInt to 6
ProduceInteger setting sharedInt to 7
ProduceInteger setting sharedInt to 8
ConsumeInteger retrieving sharedInt value 8
ConsumeInteger retrieving sharedInt value 8
ProduceInteger setting sharedInt to 9
ConsumeInteger retrieving sharedInt value 9
ConsumeInteger retrieving sharedInt value 9
ProduceInteger setting sharedInt to 10
ProduceInteger finished producing values
Terminating ProduceInteger
ConsumeInteger retrieving sharedInt value 10
ConsumeInteger retrieved values totaling: 49
Terminating ConsumeInteger
```

Fig. 15.4   Threads modifying a shared object without synchronization (part 4 of 4).

Class **ProduceInteger**'s **run** method (line 26) consists of a **for** structure that loops 10 times. Each iteration of the loop first invokes method **sleep** to put the **ProduceInteger** object into the *sleeping* state for a random time interval between 0 and 3 seconds. When the thread awakens, class **HoldIntegerUnsynchronized**'s **setSharedInt** method is invoked (line 37) with the value of control variable **count** to set the shared object's instance variable **sharedInt**. When the loop completes, the **Pro-**

duceInteger thread displays a line in the command window indicating that it has finished producing data and terminates (i.e., the thread dies).

Class **ConsumeInteger**—a subclass of **Thread**—consists of instance variable **cHold**, a constructor and a **run** method. Instance variable **cHold** is initialized (line 53) in the constructor to refer to the **HoldIntegerUnsynchronized** object **h** that was passed as an argument. Class **ConsumeInteger**'s **run** method (line 56) consists of a **do/while** structure that loops until the value 10 is read from the **HoldIntegerUnsynchronized** object to which **cHold** refers. Each iteration of the loop invokes method **sleep** to put the **ConsumeInteger** object into the *sleeping* state for a random time interval between 0 and 3 seconds. Next, class **HoldIntegerUnsynchronized**'s **getSharedInt** method is called (line 69) to get the value of the shared object's instance variable **sharedInt**. Then, the value returned by **getSharedInt** is added to the variable sum (line 70). When the loop completes, the **ConsumeInteger** thread displays a line in the command window indicating that it has finished consuming data and terminates (i.e., the thread dies).

Class **HoldIntegerUnsynchronized**'s **setSharedInt** method (line 83) and a **getSharedInt** method (line 90) do not synchronize access to instance variable **sharedInt** (declared at line 81). Ideally, we would like every value produced by the **ProduceInteger** object **p** to be consumed exactly once by the **ConsumeInteger** object **c**. However, when we study the output of Fig. 15.4 we see that the values 1, 3, 4, 6 and 7 are lost (i.e., never seen by the consumer) and the values 8 and 9 are incorrectly retrieved more than once by the consumer. Also, notice that the consumer twice retrieved value –1 (the default value of **sharedInt** set at line 81) before the producer ever assigned 1 to the **sharedInt** variable. This example clearly demonstrates that access to shared data by concurrent threads must be carefully controlled or a program may produce incorrect results.

To solve the problems of lost data and doubled data in the previous example, we will *synchronize* access of the concurrent producer and consumer threads to the shared data. Each method used by a producer or consumer to access the shared data is declared with the **synchronized** keyword. When a method declared **synchronized** is running in an object, the object is *locked* so no other **synchronized** method can run in that object at the same time.

15.7 Producer/Consumer Relationship with Thread Synchronization

The application in Fig. 15.5 demonstrates a producer and a consumer accessing a shared cell of memory with synchronization so that the consumer only consumes after the producer produces a value. Classes **SharedCell** (line 3), **ProduceInteger** (line 17) and **ConsumeInteger** (line 47) are identical to Fig. 15.4 except that they use the new class **HoldIntegerSynchronized** in this example. Class **HoldIntegerSynchronized** (line 82) contains two instance variables—**sharedInt** and **writeable**. Also, method **setSharedInt** and method **getSharedInt** are now **synchronized** methods. Because **HoldIntegerSynchronized** contains **synchronized** methods, objects of class **HoldIntegerSynchronized** are considered to be monitors. Instance variable **writeable**—known as the monitor's *condition variable*—is used by the **setSharedInt** method to determine if the thread that calls it can write to the shared memory

location and is used by the **getSharedInt** method to determine if the thread that calls it
can read from the shared memory location.

```
1   // Fig. 15.5: SharedCell.java
2   // Show multiple threads modifying shared object.
3   public class SharedCell {
4      public static void main( String args[] )
5      {
6         HoldIntegerSynchronized h =
7            new HoldIntegerSynchronized();
8         ProduceInteger p = new ProduceInteger( h );
9         ConsumeInteger c = new ConsumeInteger( h );
10
11        p.start();
12        c.start();
13     }
14  }
```

Fig. 15.5   Threads modifying a shared object with synchronization (part 1 of 5).

```
15  // Fig. 15.5: ProduceInteger.java
16  // Definition of threaded class ProduceInteger
17  public class ProduceInteger extends Thread {
18     private HoldIntegerSynchronized pHold;
19
20     public ProduceInteger( HoldIntegerSynchronized h )
21     {
22        super( "ProduceInteger" );
23        pHold = h;
24     }
25
26     public void run()
27     {
28        for ( int count = 1; count <= 10; count++ ) {
29           // sleep for a random interval
30           try {
31              Thread.sleep( (int) ( Math.random() * 3000 ) );
32           }
33           catch( InterruptedException e ) {
34              System.err.println( e.toString() );
35           }
36
37           pHold.setSharedInt( count );
38        }
39
40        System.err.println( getName() +
41           " finished producing values" +
42           "\nTerminating " + getName() );
43     }
44  }
```

Fig. 15.5   Threads modifying a shared object with synchronization (part 2 of 5).

```
45   // Fig. 15.5: ConsumeInteger.java
46   // Definition of threaded class ConsumeInteger
47   public class ConsumeInteger extends Thread {
48      private HoldIntegerSynchronized cHold;
49
50      public ConsumeInteger( HoldIntegerSynchronized h )
51      {
52         super( "ConsumeInteger" );
53         cHold = h;
54      }
55
56      public void run()
57      {
58         int val, sum = 0;
59
60         do {
61            // sleep for a random interval
62            try {
63               Thread.sleep( (int) ( Math.random() * 3000 ) );
64            }
65            catch( InterruptedException e ) {
66               System.err.println( e.toString() );
67            }
68
69            val = cHold.getSharedInt();
70            sum += val;
71         } while ( val != 10 );
72
73         System.err.println(
74            getName() + " retrieved values totaling: " + sum +
75            "\nTerminating " + getName() );
76      }
77   }
```

Fig. 15.5   Threads modifying a shared object with synchronization (part 3 of 5).

Instance variable **writeable** (defined at line 84) is a **boolean** used by methods **setSharedInt** and **getSharedInt** of class **HoldIntegerSynchronized**. If **writeable** is **true**, **setSharedInt** can place a value into variable **sharedInt** because the variable currently does not contain information. However, this means **get-SharedInt** currently cannot read the value of **sharedInt**. If **writeable** is **false**, **getSharedInt** can read a value from variable **sharedInt** because the variable currently does contain information. However, this means **setSharedInt** currently cannot place a value into **sharedInt**.

When the **ProduceInteger** thread object invokes synchronized method **set-SharedInt**, a lock is acquired on the **HoldIntegerSynchronized** monitor object. The **while** structure at line 88 tests the **writeable** variable with the condition **!writeable**. If this condition is **true**, method **wait** is invoked. This places the **Pro-duceInteger** thread object that called method **setSharedInt** into the *waiting* state for the **HoldIntegerSynchronized** object and *releases the lock* on it so other **syn-chronized** methods can be invoked on the object.

```
78   // Fig. 15.5: HoldIntegerSynchronized.java
79   // Definition of class HoldIntegerSynchronized that
80   // uses thread synchronization to ensure that both
81   // threads access sharedInt at the proper times.
82   public class HoldIntegerSynchronized {
83      private int sharedInt = -1;
84      private boolean writeable = true;  // condition variable
85
86      public synchronized void setSharedInt( int val )
87      {
88         while ( !writeable ) {  // not the producer's turn
89            try {
90               wait();
91            }
92            catch ( InterruptedException e ) {
93               e.printStackTrace();
94            }
95         }
96
97         System.err.println( Thread.currentThread().getName() +
98            " setting sharedInt to " + val );
99         sharedInt = val;
100
101         writeable = false;
102         notify();  // tell a waiting thread to become ready
103      }
104
105      public synchronized int getSharedInt()
106      {
107         while ( writeable ) {    // not the consumer's turn
108            try {
109               wait();
110            }
111            catch ( InterruptedException e ) {
112               e.printStackTrace();
113            }
114         }
115
116         writeable = true;
117         notify();  // tell a waiting thread to become ready
118
119         System.err.println( Thread.currentThread().getName() +
120            " retrieving sharedInt value " + sharedInt );
121         return sharedInt;
122      }
123   }
```

Fig. 15.5   Threads modifying a shared object with synchronization (part 4 of 5).

```
ProduceInteger setting sharedInt to 1
ConsumeInteger retrieving sharedInt value 1
ProduceInteger setting sharedInt to 2
ConsumeInteger retrieving sharedInt value 2
ProduceInteger setting sharedInt to 3
ConsumeInteger retrieving sharedInt value 3
ProduceInteger setting sharedInt to 4
ConsumeInteger retrieving sharedInt value 4
ProduceInteger setting sharedInt to 5
ConsumeInteger retrieving sharedInt value 5
ProduceInteger setting sharedInt to 6
ConsumeInteger retrieving sharedInt value 6
ProduceInteger setting sharedInt to 7
ConsumeInteger retrieving sharedInt value 7
ProduceInteger setting sharedInt to 8
ConsumeInteger retrieving sharedInt value 8
ProduceInteger setting sharedInt to 9
ConsumeInteger retrieving sharedInt value 9
ProduceInteger setting sharedInt to 10
ProduceInteger finished producing values
Terminating ProduceInteger
ConsumeInteger retrieving sharedInt value 10
ConsumeInteger retrieved values totaling: 55
Terminating ConsumeInteger
```

Fig. 15.5   Threads modifying a shared object with synchronization.

The **ProduceInteger** object remains in the *waiting* state until it is *notified* that it may proceed—at which point it enters the *ready* state and waits for a processor to be assigned to it. When the **ProduceInteger** object reenters the *running* state, the lock on the **HoldIntegerSynchronized** object is reacquired implicitly and the **setSharedInt** method continues executing in the **while** structure with the next statement after **wait**. There are no more statements, so the **while** condition is tested again. If the condition is **false**, a line is output to the command window indicating that the producer is setting **sharedInt** to a new value, **sharedInt** is assigned **val** (the argument passed to **setSharedInt**), **writeable** is set to **false** to indicate that the shared memory is now full (i.e., a consumer can read the value and a producer cannot put another value there yet) and method **notify** is invoked. If there are any *waiting* threads, one thread in the *waiting* state is placed into the *ready* state, indicating that the thread can now attempt its task again (as soon as it is assigned a processor). The **notify** method returns immediately and method **setSharedInt** returns to its caller.

Methods **getSharedInt** and **setSharedInt** are implemented similarly. When the **ConsumeInteger** object invokes method **getSharedInt**, a lock is acquired on the **HoldIntegerSynchronized** object. The **while** structure at line 107 tests the **writeable** variable. If **writeable** is **true** (i.e., there is nothing to consume), the **wait** method is invoked. This places the **ConsumeInteger** thread object that called method **getSharedInt** into the *waiting* state for the **HoldIntegerSynchronized** object and releases the lock on it so other **synchronized** methods can be invoked on the object. The **ConsumeInteger** object remains in the *waiting* state until it is *notified* that it may proceed—at which point it enters the *ready* state and waits for a processor to be assigned to it. When the **ConsumeInteger** object reenters the *running* state, the lock on the **HoldIntegerSynchronized** object is reacquired and the **setSharedInt** method continues executing in the **while** structure with the next statement after **wait**. There are no more statements, so the **while** condition is tested again. If the condition is **false**, **writeable** is set to **true** to indicate that the shared memory is now empty and method **notify** is invoked. If there are any *waiting* threads, one thread in the *waiting* state is placed into the *ready* state, indicating that the thread can now attempt its task again (as soon as it is assigned a processor). The **notify** method returns immediately, a line is output to the command window indicating that the consumer is retrieving **sharedInt** and the value of **sharedInt** is returned to **getSharedInt**'s caller.

When we study the output in Fig. 15.5, we observe that every integer produced is consumed once—no values are lost and no values are doubled. Also, the consumer cannot read a value until the producer produces a value.

15.8 Producer/Consumer Relationship: The Circular Buffer

The program of Fig. 15.5 does access the shared data correctly, but it may not perform optimally. Because the threads are running asynchronously, we cannot predict their relative speeds. If the producer wants to produce faster than the consumer can consume, it cannot do so. To enable the producer to continue producing we can use a *circular buffer* which has enough extra cells to handle the "extra" production. The program of Fig. 15.6 demonstrates a producer and a consumer accessing a circular buffer (in this case, a shared array of five cells) with synchronization so that the consumer only consumes a value when there are one or more values in the array and the producer only produces a value when there are one or more available cells in the array. This program is implemented as a windowed application that sends its output to a **JTextArea**. Class **SharedCell**'s constructor creates the **HoldIntegerSynchronized**, **ProduceInteger** and **ConsumeInteger** objects. The **HoldIntegerSynchronized** object **h** is passed a reference to a **JTextArea** object in which the program's output is displayed.

Once again, the main changes in this example are to the definition of class **HoldIntegerSynchronized**. The class now contains six instance variables—**sharedInt** is a five-element integer array that is used as the circular buffer, **writeable** indicates if a producer can write into the circular buffer, **readable** indicates if a consumer can read from the circular buffer, **readLoc** indicates the current position from which the next value can be read by a consumer, **writeLoc** indicates the next location in which a value can be placed by a producer and **output** is the **JTextArea** used for displaying output.

Method **setSharedInt** (line 134) performs the same tasks as it did in Fig. 15.5 with a few modifications. When execution continues at line 146 after the **while** loop, the produced value is placed into the circular buffer at location **writeLoc**. Next, **readable** is set to **true** because there is at least one value in the buffer to be read. The value produced and the cell where the value was placed are appended to the **JTextArea** with method **append**. Then, **writeLoc** is updated for the next call to **setSharedInt**. The output is continued with the current **writeLoc** and **readLoc** values and the values in the circular buffer. If the **writeLoc** is equal to the **readLoc**, the circular buffer is currently full, so **writeable** is set to **false** and the string **BUFFER FULL** is displayed. Finally, method **notify** is invoked to indicate that a waiting thread should move to the ready state.

```
1   // Fig. 15.6: SharedCell.java
2   // Show multiple threads modifying shared object.
3   import java.text.DecimalFormat;
4   import java.awt.*;
5   import java.awt.event.*;
6   import javax.swing.*;
7
8   public class SharedCell extends JFrame {
9      public SharedCell()
10     {
11        super( "Demonstrating Thread Synchronization" );
12        JTextArea output = new JTextArea( 20, 30 );
13
14        getContentPane().add( new JScrollPane( output ) );
15        setSize( 500, 500 );
16        show();
17
18        // set up threads and start threads
19        HoldIntegerSynchronized h =
20           new HoldIntegerSynchronized( output );
21        ProduceInteger p = new ProduceInteger( h, output );
22        ConsumeInteger c = new ConsumeInteger( h, output );
23
24        p.start();
25        c.start();
26     }
27
28     public static void main( String args[] )
29     {
30        SharedCell app = new SharedCell();
31        app.addWindowListener(
32           new WindowAdapter() {
33              public void windowClosing( WindowEvent e )
34              {
35                 System.exit( 0 );
36              }
37           }
38        );
39     }
40  }
```

Fig. 15.6   Threads modifying a shared array of cells (part 1 of 8).

```
41  // Fig. 15.6: ProduceInteger.java
42  // Definition of threaded class ProduceInteger
43  import javax.swing.JTextArea;
44
45  public class ProduceInteger extends Thread {
46     private HoldIntegerSynchronized pHold;
47     private JTextArea output;
48
```

Fig. 15.6   Threads modifying a shared array of cells (part 2 of 8).

```
49        public ProduceInteger( HoldIntegerSynchronized h,
50                               JTextArea o )
51        {
52           super( "ProduceInteger" );
53           pHold = h;
54           output = o;
55        }
56
57        public void run()
58        {
59           for ( int count = 1; count <= 10; count++ ) {
60              // sleep for a random interval
61              // Note: Interval shortened purposely to fill buffer
62              try {
63                 Thread.sleep( (int) ( Math.random() * 500 ) );
64              }
65              catch( InterruptedException e ) {
66                 System.err.println( e.toString() );
67              }
68
69              pHold.setSharedInt( count );
70           }
71
72           output.append( "\n" + getName() +
73              " finished producing values" +
74              "\nTerminating " + getName() + "\n" );
75        }
76     }
```

Fig. 15.6   Threads modifying a shared array of cells (part 3 of 8).

```
77     // Fig. 15.6: ConsumeInteger.java
78     // Definition of threaded class ConsumeInteger
79     import javax.swing.JTextArea;
80
81     public class ConsumeInteger extends Thread {
82        private HoldIntegerSynchronized cHold;
83        private JTextArea output;
84
85        public ConsumeInteger( HoldIntegerSynchronized h,
86                               JTextArea o )
87        {
88           super( "ConsumeInteger" );
89           cHold = h;
90           output = o;
91        }
92
93        public void run()
94        {
95           int val, sum = 0;
96
```

Fig. 15.6   Threads modifying a shared array of cells (part 4 of 8).

```
 97              do {
 98                 // sleep for a random interval
 99                 try {
100                    Thread.sleep( (int) ( Math.random() * 3000 ) );
101                 }
102                 catch( InterruptedException e ) {
103                    System.err.println( e.toString() );
104                 }
105
106                 val = cHold.getSharedInt();
107                 sum += val;
108              } while ( val != 10 );
109
110              output.append( "\n" + getName() +
111                 " retrieved values totaling: " + sum +
112                 "\nTerminating " + getName() + "\n" );
113           }
114   }
```

Fig. 15.6   Threads modifying a shared array of cells (part 5 of 8).

```
115   // Fig. 15.6: HoldIntegerSynchronized.java
116   // Definition of class HoldIntegerSynchronized that
117   // uses thread synchronization to ensure that both
118   // threads access sharedInt at the proper times.
119   import javax.swing.JTextArea;
120   import java.text.DecimalFormat;
121
122   public class HoldIntegerSynchronized {
123      private int sharedInt[] = { -1, -1, -1, -1, -1 };
124      private boolean writeable = true;
125      private boolean readable = false;
126      private int readLoc = 0, writeLoc = 0;
127      private JTextArea output;
128
129      public HoldIntegerSynchronized( JTextArea o )
130      {
131         output = o;
132      }
133
134      public synchronized void setSharedInt( int val )
135      {
136         while ( !writeable ) {
137            try {
138               output.append( " WAITING TO PRODUCE " + val );
139               wait();
140            }
141            catch ( InterruptedException e ) {
142               System.err.println( e.toString() );
143            }
144         }
145
```

Fig. 15.6   Threads modifying a shared array of cells (part 6 of 8).

```
146          sharedInt[ writeLoc ] = val;
147          readable = true;
148
149          output.append( "\nProduced " + val +
150                          " into cell " + writeLoc );
151
152          writeLoc = ( writeLoc + 1 ) % 5;
153
154          output.append( "\twrite " + writeLoc +
155                          "\tread " + readLoc);
156          displayBuffer( output, sharedInt );
157
158          if ( writeLoc == readLoc ) {
159             writeable = false;
160             output.append( "\nBUFFER FULL" );
161          }
162
163          notify();
164       }
165
166       public synchronized int getSharedInt()
167       {
168          int val;
169
170          while ( !readable ) {
171             try {
172                output.append( " WAITING TO CONSUME" );
173                wait();
174             }
175             catch ( InterruptedException e ) {
176                System.err.println( e.toString() );
177             }
178          }
179
180          writeable = true;
181          val = sharedInt[ readLoc ];
182
183          output.append( "\nConsumed " + val +
184                          " from cell " + readLoc );
185
186          readLoc = ( readLoc + 1 ) % 5;
187
188          output.append( "\twrite " + writeLoc +
189                          "\tread " + readLoc );
190          displayBuffer( output, sharedInt );
191
192          if ( readLoc == writeLoc ) {
193             readable = false;
194             output.append( "\nBUFFER EMPTY" );
195          }
196
197          notify();
```

Fig. 15.6   Threads modifying a shared array of cells (part 7 of 8).

```
198        return val;
199      }
200
201      public void displayBuffer( JTextArea out, int buf[] )
202      {
203        DecimalFormat formatNumber = new DecimalFormat( " #;-#" );
204        output.append( "\tbuffer: " );
205
206        for ( int i = 0; i < buf.length; i++ )
207          out.append( " " + formatNumber.format( buf[ i ] ));
208      }
209  }
```

Demonstrating Thread Synchronization			
WAITING TO CONSUME			
Produced 1 into cell 0	write 1	read 0	buffer: 1 -1 -1 -1 -1
Consumed 1 from cell 0	write 1	read 1	buffer: 1 -1 -1 -1 -1
BUFFER EMPTY			
Produced 2 into cell 1	write 2	read 1	buffer: 1 2 -1 -1 -1
Produced 3 into cell 2	write 3	read 1	buffer: 1 2 3 -1 -1
Consumed 2 from cell 1	write 3	read 2	buffer: 1 2 3 -1 -1
Produced 4 into cell 3	write 4	read 2	buffer: 1 2 3 4 -1
Produced 5 into cell 4	write 0	read 2	buffer: 1 2 3 4 5
Produced 6 into cell 0	write 1	read 2	buffer: 6 2 3 4 5
Produced 7 into cell 1	write 2	read 2	buffer: 6 7 3 4 5
BUFFER FULL WAITING TO PRODUCE 8			
Consumed 3 from cell 2	write 2	read 3	buffer: 6 7 3 4 5
Produced 8 into cell 2	write 3	read 3	buffer: 6 7 8 4 5
BUFFER FULL WAITING TO PRODUCE 9			
Consumed 4 from cell 3	write 3	read 4	buffer: 6 7 8 4 5
Produced 9 into cell 3	write 4	read 4	buffer: 6 7 8 9 5
BUFFER FULL WAITING TO PRODUCE 10			
Consumed 5 from cell 4	write 4	read 0	buffer: 6 7 8 9 5
Produced 10 into cell 4	write 0	read 0	buffer: 6 7 8 9 10
BUFFER FULL			
ProduceInteger finished producing values			
Terminating ProduceInteger			
Consumed 6 from cell 0	write 0	read 1	buffer: 6 7 8 9 10
Consumed 7 from cell 1	write 0	read 2	buffer: 6 7 8 9 10
Consumed 8 from cell 2	write 0	read 3	buffer: 6 7 8 9 10
Consumed 9 from cell 3	write 0	read 4	buffer: 6 7 8 9 10
Consumed 10 from cell 4	write 0	read 0	buffer: 6 7 8 9 10
BUFFER EMPTY			
ConsumeInteger retrieved values totaling: 55			
Terminating ConsumeInteger			

Fig. 15.6   Threads modifying a shared array of cells (part 8 of 8).

Method **getSharedInt** (line 166) also performs the same tasks in this example as it did in Fig. 15.5, with a few minor modifications. When execution continues at line 180 after the **while** loop, **writeable** is set to **true** because there is at least one open position in the buffer in which a value can be placed. Next, **val** is assigned the value at location **readLoc** in the circular buffer. The value consumed and the cell from which the value was read are appended to the **JTextArea** with method **append**. Then, **readLoc** is updated for the next call to method **getSharedInt**. The output line in the **JTextArea** is continued with the current **writeLoc** and **readLoc** values and the current values in the circular buffer. If the **readLoc** is equal to the **writeLoc**, the circular buffer is currently empty, so **readable** is set to **false** and the string **BUFFER EMPTY** is displayed. Finally, method **notify** is invoked to place the next waiting thread into the *ready* state and the retrieved value is returned to the calling method.

In the program of Fig. 15.6, the outputs have been augmented to include the current **writeLoc** and **readLoc** values. Also, the current contents of the buffer **sharedInt** are displayed. The elements of the **sharedInt** array were initialized to –1 for output purposes so you can see each value inserted into the buffer. Notice that after the fifth value is placed in the fifth element of the buffer, the sixth value is inserted at the beginning of the array—thus providing the *circular buffer* effect. Method **displayBuffer** (line 201) uses a **DecimalFormat** object to format the contents of the array **buf**. The format control string **" #;-#"** indicates a positive number format and a negative number format— the formats are separated by a semicolon (**;**). The format specifies that positive values should be preceded by a space and negative values should be preceded by a minus sign.

15.9 Daemon Threads

A *daemon thread* is a thread that runs for the benefit of other threads. Daemon threads run in the background (i.e., when processor time is available that would otherwise go to waste). Unlike conventional user threads, daemon threads do not prevent a program from terminating. The garbage collector is a daemon thread. Non-daemon threads are conventional user threads. We designate a thread as a daemon with the method call

```
setDaemon( true );
```

A **false** argument means that the thread is not a daemon thread. A program can include a mixture of daemon threads and non-daemon threads. When only daemon threads remain in a program, the program exits. If a thread is to be a daemon, it must be set as such before its **start** method is called or an **IllegalThreadStateException** is thrown. Method **isDaemon** returns **true** if a thread is a daemon thread and **false** otherwise.

15.10 Runnable Interface

C++ supports multiple inheritance in which a subclass can inherit from multiple superclasses. Multiple inheritance is powerful but it is complex to use and suffers from ambiguity and performance problems. Java does not support multiple inheritance. This choice is consistent with Java's omission of a number of other complex C++ topics. Java does, however, support the notion of *interfaces* (see Chapter 9, "Object-Oriented Programming")—a simpler scheme that delivers some of the key advantages of multiple inheritance.

Until now we extended class **Thread** to create new classes that support multithreading. We overrode the **run** method to specify the tasks to be performed concurrently. However, if we want multithreading supported in a class that is already derived from a class other than **Thread**, we must **implement** the *Runnable interface* in that class. Class **Thread** itself implements the **Runnable** interface (package **java.lang**) as expressed in the class header

```
public class Thread extends Object implements Runnable
```

Implementing the **Runnable** interface gives us the ability to treat our new class as a **Runnable** object (just like inheriting from a class allows us to treat our subclass as an object of its superclass). As with deriving from the **Thread** class, the code that controls the thread is placed in the **run** method.

We create a thread with the new class by passing to the **Thread** class constructor

```
public Thread( Runnable runnableObject )
```

a reference to an object of the class that implements the **Runnable** interface. The **Thread** constructor registers the **run** method of the **runnableObject** as the method to be invoked when the thread begins execution. [*Note:* Class **Thread** actually provides four constructors that receive a **Runnable** argument.]

The constructor

```
public Thread( Runnable runnableObject, String threadName )
```

constructs a **Thread** with the name **threadName** and registers method **run** of its argument **runnableObject** as the method to be invoked when the thread begins execution.

Figure 15.7 demonstrates an applet that implements the **Runnable** interface. The example also demonstrates how to temporarily suspend a thread (i.e., temporarily prevent it from executing), how to resume a suspended thread and how to terminate a thread that executes until a condition becomes false. Each of these techniques is important because Thread methods **suspend**, **resume** and **stop** are now deprecated in the Java 2 API.

The applet class **RandomCharacters** displays three **JLabel**s and three **JCheck-Box**es. A separate thread of execution is associated with each **JLabel** and button pair. Each thread randomly displays letters from the alphabet in its corresponding **JLabel** object. The applet defines the **String alphabet** containing the letters from A to Z. This string is shared among the three threads. The applet's **start** method (line 40) instantiates three **Thread** objects and initializes each with **this** (i.e., the **Runnable** applet object) then invokes the **Thread** class **start** method on each **Thread** placing the threads in the *ready* state.

```java
1   // Fig. 15.7: RandomCharacters.java
2   // Demonstrating the Runnableinterface
3   import java.awt.*;
4   import java.awt.event.*;
5   import javax.swing.*;
6
7   public class RandomCharacters extends JApplet
8                                 implements Runnable,
9                                            ActionListener {
10     private String alphabet = "ABCDEFGHIJKLMNOPQRSTUVWXYZ";
11     private JLabel outputs[];
12     private JCheckBox checkboxes[];
13     private final static int SIZE = 3;
14
15     private Thread threads[];
16     private boolean suspended[];
17
18     public void init()
19     {
20        outputs = new JLabel[ SIZE ];
21        checkboxes = new JCheckBox[ SIZE ];
```

Fig. 15.7 Demonstrating the **Runnable** interface (part 1 of 3).

```
22          threads = new Thread[ SIZE ];
23          suspended = new boolean[ SIZE ];
24
25          Container c = getContentPane();
26          c.setLayout( new GridLayout( SIZE, 2, 5, 5 ) );
27
28          for ( int i = 0; i < SIZE; i++ ) {
29             outputs[ i ] = new JLabel();
30             outputs[ i ].setBackground( Color.green );
31             outputs[ i ].setOpaque( true );
32             c.add( outputs[ i ] );
33
34             checkboxes[ i ] = new JCheckBox( "Suspended" );
35             checkboxes[ i ].addActionListener( this );
36             c.add( checkboxes[ i ] );
37          }
38       }
39
40       public void start()
41       {
42          // create threads and start every time start is called
43          for ( int i = 0; i < threads.length; i++ ) {
44             threads[ i ] =
45                new Thread( this, "Thread " + (i + 1) );
46             threads[ i ].start();
47          }
48       }
49
50       public void run()
51       {
52          Thread currentThread = Thread.currentThread();
53          int index = getIndex( currentThread );
54          char displayChar;
55
56          while ( threads[ index ] == currentThread ) {
57             // sleep from 0 to 1 second
58             try {
59                Thread.sleep( (int) ( Math.random() * 1000 ) );
60
61                synchronized( this ) {
62                   while ( suspended[ index ] &&
63                             threads[ index ] == currentThread )
64                      wait();
65                }
66             }
67             catch ( InterruptedException e ) {
68                System.err.println( "sleep interrupted" );
69             }
70
71             displayChar = alphabet.charAt(
72                                   (int) ( Math.random() * 26 ) );
```

Fig. 15.7   Demonstrating the **Runnable** interface (part 2 of 3).

```
73                    outputs[ index ].setText( currentThread.getName() +
74                       ": " + displayChar );
75              }
76
77           System.err.println(
78              currentThread.getName() + " terminating" );
79        }
80
81        private int getIndex( Thread current )
82        {
83           for ( int i = 0; i < threads.length; i++ )
84              if ( current == threads[ i ] )
85                 return i;
86
87           return -1;
88        }
89
90        public synchronized void stop()
91        {
92           // stop threads every time stop is called
93           // as the user browses another Web page
94           for ( int i = 0; i < threads.length; i++ )
95              threads[ i ] = null;
96
97           notifyAll();
98        }
99
100       public synchronized void actionPerformed( ActionEvent e )
101       {
102          for ( int i = 0; i < checkboxes.length; i++ ) {
103             if ( e.getSource() == checkboxes[ i ] ) {
104                suspended[ i ] = !suspended[ i ];
105
106                outputs[ i ].setBackground(
107                   !suspended[ i ] ? Color.green : Color.red );
108
109                if ( !suspended[ i ] )
110                   notify();
111
112                return;
113             }
114          }
115       }
116    }
```

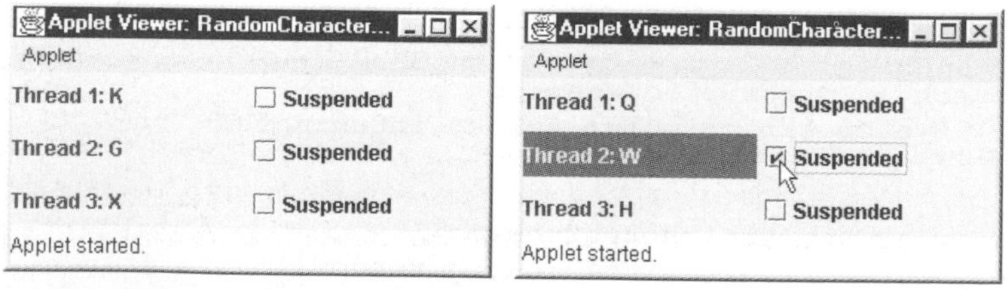

Fig. 15.7   Demonstrating the **Runnable** interface (part 3 of 3).

The **run** method (line 50) defines three local variables. Line 52

```
Thread currentThread = Thread.currentThread();
```

uses **static** method **currentThread** of class **Thread** to determine the currently executing **Thread** object. Line 53

```
int index = getIndex( currentThread );
```

calls utility method **getIndex** (defined at line 81) to determine the index of the currently executing thread in the array **threads**. The **index** is used to determine the **JLabel** object in which the random characters picked by the current thread are displayed.

The **while** loop at line 56 continues to execute as long as the specified **Thread** reference is equal to the currently executing thread (**currentThread**). In each iteration of the loop, the thread sleeps for a random interval from 0 to 1 second.

When the user clicks the **JCheckBox** to the right of a particular **JLabel**, the corresponding **Thread** should be *suspended* (temporarily prevented from executing) or *resumed* (allowed to continue executing). In previous versions of Java, methods **suspend** and **resume** of class **Thread** were provided to suspend and resume a thread's execution. These methods are now deprecated (i.e., they should no longer be used) because they introduce the possibility of deadlock in a program if they are not used correctly. Suspending and resuming a thread can be implemented using thread synchronization and methods **wait** and **notify** of class **Object**. Lines 61 through 65

```
synchronized( this ) {
    while ( suspended[ index ] &&
        threads[ index ] == currentThread )
        wait();
}
```

define a ***synchronized*** *block* of code (also called a ***synchronized*** *statement*) that helps suspend the currently executing **Thread**. When the **Thread** reaches the **synchronized** block, the applet object (**this**) is locked and the **while** structure tests **suspended[index]** to determine if the **Thread** should be suspended (i.e., **true**). If so, line 64 invokes the **wait** method to place the **Thread** in the waiting state. When the **Thread** should resume, the **notify** method (line 110) is called. Line 71 chooses a random character from the **alphabet** string. Line 73 displays the character on the appropriate **JLabel** object.

If the user clicks the **Suspended** check box next to a particular **JLabel**, the **actionPerformed** method (line 100) is invoked. The method determines which check box received the event. Using the index of that check box, line 104 toggles the corresponding **boolean** in array **suspended**. Lines 106 and 107 set the background color of the **JLabel** to red if the thread is being suspended and green if the thread is being resumed. If the appropriate **boolean** variable is **false**, method **notify** is invoked (line 110) to move the waiting thread into the ready state and prepare the thread to resume execution. When the thread is dispatched to the processor to resume execution, the **while** condition at lines 62 and 63 in the **run** method fails and the loop terminates. Execution of the run method then continues from line 71.

The applet's **stop** method (line 90) is provided to stop all three threads if the user leaves the Web page on which this applet resides (you can simulate this by selecting **Stop** from the **appletviewer**'s **Applet** menu). The **for** loop at line 94 sets each **Thread** reference in array **threads** to **null**. Line 97 invokes **Object** method **notifyAll** to ensure that all waiting threads get ready to execute. When the **while** loop condition at line 56 is encountered for each thread, the condition fails and the **run** method terminates. Thus, each thread dies. If the user returns to the Web page, the applet's **start** method is invoked and three new threads are instantiated and started.

Performance Tip 15.6

*Stopping applet threads when leaving a Web page is a polite programming practice because it prevents your applet from using processor time (which can reduce performance) on the browser's machine when the applet is not being viewed. The threads can be restarted from the applet's **start** method, which is invoked by the browser when the Web page is revisited by the user.*

15.11 Thread Groups

Sometimes it is useful to identify various threads as belonging to a *thread group*; class **ThreadGroup** contains methods for creating and manipulating thread groups. At constructor time the group is given a unique name via a **String** argument.

The threads in a thread group can be dealt with as a group. It may, for example, be desirable to **interrupt** all the threads in a group. A thread group can be the *parent thread group* to a *child thread group*. Method calls sent to a parent thread group are also sent to all the threads in that parent's child thread groups.

Class **ThreadGroup** provides two constructors. The constructor

```
public ThreadGroup( String stringName )
```

constructs a **ThreadGroup** with name **stringName**. The constructor

```
public ThreadGroup( ThreadGroup parentThreadGroup,
                    String stringName )
```

constructs a child **ThreadGroup** of **parentThreadGroup** called **stringName**.

Class **Thread** provides three constructors that enable the programmer to instantiate a **Thread** and associate it with a **ThreadGroup**. The constructor

```
public Thread( ThreadGroup threadGroup, String stringName )
```

constructs a **Thread** that belongs to **threadGroup** and has the name **stringName**. This constructor is normally invoked for derived classes of **Thread** whose objects should be associated with a **ThreadGroup**.

The constructor

```
public Thread( ThreadGroup threadGroup,
               Runnable runnableObject )
```

constructs a **Thread** that belongs to **threadGroup** and that invokes the **run** method of **runnableObject** when the thread is assigned a processor to begin execution.

The constructor

```
public Thread( ThreadGroup threadGroup,
               Runnable runnableObject,
               String stringName )
```

constructs a **Thread** that belongs to **threadGroup** and that invokes the **run** method of **runnableObject** when the thread is assigned a processor to begin execution. The name of this **Thread** is indicated by **stringName**.

Class **ThreadGroup** contains many methods for processing groups of threads. Some of these methods are summarized here. For more information on these methods, see the Java API documentation.

1. Method **activeCount** reports the number of active threads in a thread group plus the number of active threads in all its child thread groups.

2. Method **enumerate** has four versions. Two versions copy into an array of **Thread** references the active threads in the **ThreadGroup** (one of these also allows you to recursively get copies of all the active threads in child **Thread-Group**). Two versions copy into an array of **ThreadGroup** references the active child thread groups in the **ThreadGroup** (one of these also allows you to recursively get copies of all the active thread groups in all the child **Thread-Group**s).

3. Method **getMaxPriority** returns the maximum priority of a **ThreadGroup**. Method **setMaxPriority** sets a new maximum priority for a **ThreadGroup**.

4. Method **getName** returns as a **String** the **ThreadGroup**'s name.

5. Method **getParent** determines the parent of a thread group.

6. Method **parentOf** returns **true** if the **ThreadGroup** to which the message is sent is the parent of, or the same as, the **ThreadGroup** supplied as an argument and returns **false** otherwise.

Testing and Debugging Tip 15.5

*Method **list** lists the **ThreadGroup**. This can help in debugging.*

Summary

- Computers perform operations concurrently such as compiling a program, printing a file, and receiving electronic mail messages over a network.

- Programming languages generally provide only a simple set of control structures that enable programmers to perform one action at a time and then proceed to the next action after the previous one is finished.

- The concurrency that computers perform today is normally implemented as operating systems "primitives" available only to highly experienced "systems programmers."

- Java makes concurrency primitives available to the programmer.

- Applications contain threads of execution, each thread designating a portion of a program that may execute concurrently with other threads. This capability is called multithreading.

- Java provides a low-priority garbage collector thread that reclaims dynamically allocated memory that is no longer needed. The garbage collector runs when processor time is available and there are no higher-priority runnable threads. The garbage collector runs immediately when the system is out of memory to try to reclaim memory.

- Method **run** contains the code that controls a thread's execution.

- A program launches a thread's execution by calling the thread's **start** method, which, in turn, calls the **run** method.

- Method **interrupt** is called to interrupt a thread. The **interrupted** method returns **true** if the current thread has been interrupted and **false** otherwise. Method **isInterrupted** determines if a thread has been interrupted.

- Method **isAlive** returns **true** if **start** has been called for a given thread and the thread is not dead (i.e., its stop method has not been called and its controlling run method has not completed execution).

- Method **setName** sets the name of the **Thread**. Method **getName** returns the name of the **Thread**. Method **toString** returns a **String** consisting of the name of the thread, the priority of the thread and the thread's group.

- Method **currentThread** returns a reference to the executing **Thread**.

- Method **join** waits for the **Thread** to which the message is sent to die before the current **Thread** can proceed.

- Waiting can be dangerous; it can lead to two serious problems called deadlock and indefinite postponement; indefinite postponement is also called starvation.

- A thread that was just created is in the born state. The thread remains in this state until the thread's **start** method is called; this causes the thread to enter the ready state.

- A highest-priority ready thread enters the running state when the system assigns a processor to the thread.

- A thread enters the dead state when its **run** method completes or terminates for any reason; a dead thread will eventually be disposed of by the system.

- A running thread enters the blocked state when the thread issues an input/output request. A blocked thread becomes ready when the I/O it is waiting for completes. A blocked thread cannot use a processor even if one is available.

- When a running thread's **sleep** method is called, that thread enters the sleeping state. A sleeping thread becomes ready after the designated sleep time expires. A sleeping thread cannot use a processor even if one is available.

- When a running method calls **wait** the thread enters a waiting state for the particular object in which the thread was running. A thread in the waiting state for a particular object becomes ready on a call to **notify** issued by another thread associated with that object.

- Every thread in the waiting state for a given object becomes ready on a call to **notifyAll** by another thread associated with that object.

- Every Java thread has a priority in the range **Thread.MIN_PRIORITY** (a constant of 1) and **Thread.MAX_PRIORITY** (a constant of 10). By default, each thread is given priority **Thread.NORM_PRIORITY** (a constant of 5).

- Some Java platforms support a concept called timeslicing and some do not. Without timeslicing, threads of equal priority run to completion before their peers get a chance to execute. With timeslicing, each thread receives a brief burst of processor time called a quantum during which that thread can execute. At the completion of the quantum, even if that thread has not finished executing, the processor is taken away from that thread and given to the next thread of equal priority if one is available.

- The job of the Java scheduler is to keep a highest-priority thread running at all times, and if timeslicing is available, to ensure that several equally high-priority threads each execute for a quantum in round-robin fashion.

- A thread's priority can be adjusted with the **setPriority** method. Method **getPriority** returns the thread's priority.

- A thread can call the **yield** method to give other threads a chance to execute.

- Every object that has **synchronized** methods has a monitor. The monitor lets only one thread at a time execute a **synchronized** method on the object.

- A thread executing in a **synchronized** method may determine that it cannot proceed, so the thread voluntarily calls **wait**. This removes the thread from contention for the processor and from contention for the object.

- A thread that has called **wait** is awakened by a thread that calls **notify**. The **notify** acts as a signal to the waiting thread that the condition the waiting thread has been waiting for is now (or could be) satisfied, so it is acceptable for that thread to reenter the monitor.

- A daemon thread serves other threads. When only daemon threads remain in a program, Java will exit. If a thread is to be a daemon, it must be set as such before its **start** method is called.

- To support multithreading in a class derived from some class other than **Thread**, implement the **Runnable** interface in that class.

- Implementing the **Runnable** interface gives us the ability to treat the new class as a **Runnable** object (just like inheriting from a class allows us to treat our subclass as an object of its superclass). As with deriving from the **Thread** class, the code that controls the thread is placed in the **run** method.

- A thread with a **Runnable** class is created by passing to the **Thread** class constructor a reference to an object of the class that implements the **Runnable** interface. The **Thread** constructor registers the **run** method of the **runnableObject** as the method to be invoked when the thread begins execution.

- Class **ThreadGroup** contains the methods for creating and manipulating groups of related threads in a program.

Terminology

asynchronous threads	**getParent** method of **ThreadGroup** class
blocked on I/O	highest-priority runnable thread
blocked (state of a thread)	**IllegalArgumentException**
busy wait	**IllegalMonitorStateException**
child thread group	**IllegalThreadStateException**
circular buffer	indefinite postponement
concurrency	inherit thread priority
concurrent execution of threads	**InterruptedException**
condition variable	**InterruptedException** class
consumer	**interrupt** method
consumer thread	**interrupted** method
context	interthread communication
currentThread method	I/O completion
daemon thread	**isAlive** method
dead (state of a thread)	**isDaemon** method
deadlock	**isInterrupted** method
death of a thread	**join** method
destroy method	kill a thread
dumpStack method	**MAX_PRIORITY**(10)
Error class **ThreadDeath**	memory leak
execution context	**MIN_PRIORITY**(1)
fixed-priority scheduling	monitor
garbage collection by a low-priority thread	multiple inheritance
getName method	multiprocessing

Common Programming Errors

15.1   Threads in the waiting state for a monitor object must eventually be awakened explicitly with a **notify** (or **interrupt**) or the thread will wait forever. This may cause deadlock.

15.2   It is an error if a thread issues a **wait**, a **notify** or a **notifyAll** on an object without having acquired a lock for the object. This causes an **IllegalMonitorStateException** to be thrown.

Performance Tips

15.1   Java's garbage collection is not as efficient as the dynamic memory management code the best C and C++ programmers write, but it is relatively efficient and much safer for the programmer.

15.2   Setting an object reference to **null** marks that object for eventual garbage collection (if there are no other references to the object). This can help conserve memory in a system in which an automatic object is not going out of scope because the method it is in will execute for a lengthy period.

15.3   A problem with single-threaded applications is that possibly lengthy activities must complete before other activities can begin. Users feel they already spend too much time waiting with Internet and World Wide Web applications, so multithreading is immediately appealing.

15.4   On non-timesliced systems, cooperating threads of equal priority should periodically call **yield** to enable their peers to proceed smoothly.

15.5   Synchronization to achieve correctness in multithreaded programs can make programs run slower due to the monitor overhead and frequently moving threads between the running, waiting and ready states. There is not much to say, however, for highly efficient, incorrect multithreaded programs!

15.6   Stopping applet threads when leaving a Web page is a polite programming practice because it prevents your applet from using processor time (which can reduce performance) on the browser's machine when the applet is not being viewed. The threads can be restarted from the applet's **start** method, which is invoked by the browser when the Web page is revisited by the user.

Portability Tips

15.1   Java multithreading is platform dependent. Thus, a multithreaded application could behave differently on different Java implementations.

15.2   Applets should be programmed to work on all Java platforms to realize Java's goal of true portability. When designing applets that use threads, you must consider the threading capabilities of all the platforms on which the applet will execute.

Software Engineering Observation

15.1   Unlike many languages that do not have built-in multithreading (such as C and C++) and must therefore make calls to operating system multithreading primitives, Java includes multithreading primitives as part of the language itself (actually in classes **Thread**, **Thread-Group**, **ThreadLocal** and **ThreadDeath** of the **java.lang** package). This encourages the use of multithreading among a larger part of the applications programming community.

Testing and Debugging Tips

15.1   In C and C++, programmers must explicitly provide statements for reclaiming dynamically allocated memory. When memory is not reclaimed (because a programmer forgets to do so, or because of a logic error or because an exception diverts program control), this results in an all-too-common error called a *memory leak* that can eventually exhaust the supply of free memory and may cause program termination. Java's automatic garbage collection eliminates the vast majority of memory leaks [i.e., those that are due to orphaned (unreferenced) objects].

15.2   Method **dumpStack** is useful for debugging multithreaded applications. A program calls **static** method **dumpStack** to print a method-call stack trace for the current **Thread**.

15.3   Be sure that every call to **wait** has a corresponding call to **notify** that will eventually end the waiting or use **notifyAll** as a safeguard.

15.4   The locking that occurs with the execution of *synchronized* methods could lead to deadlock if the locks are never released. When exceptions occur, Java's exception mechanism coordinates with Java's synchronization mechanism to release appropriate synchronization locks to avoid these kinds of deadlocks.

15.5   Method **list** lists the **ThreadGroup**. This can help in debugging.

Self-Review Exercises

15.1   Fill in the blanks in each of the following:
    a) C and C++ are _____-threaded languages whereas Java is a _____-threaded language.
    b) Java provides a _____ thread that automatically reclaims dynamically allocated memory.
    c) Java eliminates most _____ errors that occur commonly in languages like C and C++ when dynamically allocated memory is not explicitly reclaimed by the program.

d) Three reasons a thread that is alive could be not runnable (i.e., blocked) are _____, _____ and _____.

e) A thread enters the dead state when _____.

f) A thread's priority can be changed with the _____ method.

g) A thread may give up the processor to a thread of the same priority by calling the _____ method.

h) To wait for a designated number of milliseconds and then resume execution, a thread should call the _____ method.

i) The _____ method moves a thread in the object's *waiting* state to the ready state.

15.2 State whether each of the following is *true* or *false*. If *false*, explain why.

a) A thread is not runnable if it is dead.

b) In Java, a higher-priority runnable thread will preempt threads of lower priority.

c) The Windows and Windows NT Java systems use timeslicing. Therefore, they can enable threads to preempt threads of the same priority.

d) Threads may **yield** to threads of lower priority.

Answers to Self-Review Exercises

15.1 a) single, multi. b) garbage collector. c) memory leak. d) waiting, sleeping, blocked for input/output. e) its **run** method terminates. f) **setPriority**. g) **yield**. h) **sleep**. i) **notify**.

15.2 a) True

b) True.

c) False. Timeslicing allows a thread to execute until its timeslice (or quantum) expires. Then other threads of equal priority can execute.

d) False. Threads can only yield to threads of equal priority.

Exercises

15.3 State whether each of the following is *true* or *false*. If *false*, explain why.

a) The **sleep** method does not consume processor time while a thread sleeps.

b) Declaring a method **synchronized** guarantees that deadlock cannot occur.

c) Java provides a powerful capability called multiple inheritance.

d) **Thread** methods **suspend** and **resume** are deprecated.

15.4 Define each of the following terms.

a) thread

b) multithreading

c) ready state

d) blocked state

e) preemptive scheduling

f) **Runnable** interface

g) monitor

h) **notify** method

i) producer/consumer relationship

15.5 a) List each of the reasons stated in this chapter for using multithreading.

b) List additional reasons for using multithreading.

15.6 List each of the three reasons given in the text for entering the blocked state. For each of these, describe how the program will normally leave the blocked state and enter the runnable state.

15.7 Distinguish between preemptive scheduling and nonpreemptive scheduling. Which does Java use?

15.8   What is timeslicing? Give a fundamental difference in how scheduling is performed on Java systems that support timeslicing vs. on Java systems that do not support timeslicing.

15.9   Why would a thread ever want to call **yield**?

15.10   What aspects of developing Java applets for the World Wide Web encourage applet designers to use **yield** and **sleep** abundantly?

15.11   If you choose to write your own **start** method, what must you be sure to do to make sure that your threads start up properly?

15.12   Distinguish among each of the following means of pausing threads:
   a) busy wait.
   b) sleep.
   c) blocking I/O.

15.13   Write a Java statement that tests if a thread is alive.

15.14   a) What is multiple inheritance?
   b) Explain why Java does not offer multiple inheritance.
   c) What feature does Java offer instead of multiple inheritance?
   d) Explain the typical use of this feature.
   e) How does this feature differ from **abstract** classes?

15.15   Distinguish between the notions of **extends** and **implements**.

15.16   Discuss each of the following terms in the context of monitors:
   a) monitor.
   b) producer.
   c) consumer.
   d) **wait**.
   e) **notify**.
   f) **InterruptedException**.
   g) **synchronized**.

15.17   *(Tortoise and the Hare)* In the Chapter 7 exercises you were asked to simulate the legendary race of the tortoise and the hare. Implement a new version of that simulation, this time placing each of the animals in separate threads. At the start of the race call the **start** methods for each of the threads. Use **wait**, **notify** and **notifyAll** to synchronize the animals' activities.

15.18   *(Multithreaded, Networked, Collaborative Applications)* In Chapter 21 we will cover networking in Java. A multithreaded Java application can communicate concurrently with several host computers. This creates the possibility of being able to build some interesting kinds of collaborative applications. In anticipation of studying networking in Chapter 21, develop proposals for several possible multithreaded networked applications. After studying Chapter 21, implement some of those applications.

15.19   Write a Java program to demonstrate that as a high-priority thread executes, it will delay the execution of all lower-priority threads.

15.20   If your system supports timeslicing, write a Java program that demonstrates timeslicing among several equal-priority threads. Show that a lower-priority thread's execution is deferred by the timeslicing of the higher-priority threads.

15.21   Write a Java program that demonstrates a high-priority thread using **sleep** to give lower-priority threads a chance to run.

15.22   If your system does not support timeslicing, write a Java program that demonstrates two threads using **yield** to enable one another to execute.

15.23   Two problems that can occur in systems like Java, that allow threads to wait, are deadlock, in which one or more threads will wait forever for an event that cannot occur, and indefinite postponement, in which one or more threads will be delayed for some unpredictably long time. Give an example of how each of these problems can occur in a multithreaded Java program.

15.24   *(Readers and Writers)* This exercise asks you to develop a Java monitor to solve a famous problem in concurrency control. This problem was first discussed and solved by P. J. Courtois, F. Heymans and D. L. Parnas in their research paper, "Concurrent Control with Readers and Writers," *Communications of the ACM,* Vol. 14, No. 10, October 1971, pp. 667–668. The interested student might also want to read C. A. R. Hoare's seminal research paper on monitors, "Monitors: An Operating System Structuring Concept," *Communications of the ACM,* Vol. 17, No. 10, October 1974, pp. 549–557. Corrigendum, *Communications of the ACM,* Vol. 18, No. 2, February 1975, p. 95. [The readers and writers problem is discussed at length in Chapter 5 of the author's book: Deitel, H. M., *Operating Systems*, Reading, MA: Addison-Wesley, 1990.]

With multithreading, many threads can access shared data; as we have seen, access to shared data needs to be carefully synchronized to avoid corrupting the data.

Consider an airline reservation system in which many clients are attempting to book seats on particular flights between particular cities. All of the information about flights and seats is stored in a common database in memory. The database consists of many entries, each representing a seat on a particular flight for a particular day between particular cities. In a typical airline reservation scenario, the client will probe around in the database looking for the "optimal" flight to meet that client's needs. So a client may probe the database many times before deciding to try and book a particular flight. A seat that was available during this probing phase could easily be booked by someone else before the client has a chance to book it after deciding on it. In that case, when the client attempts to make the reservation, the client will discover that the data has changed and the flight is no longer available.

The client probing around the database is called a *reader*. The client attempting to book the flight is called a *writer*. Clearly, any number of readers can be probing shared data at once, but each writer needs exclusive access to the shared data to prevent the data from being corrupted.

Write a multithreaded Java program that launches multiple reader threads and multiple writer threads, each attempting to access a single reservation record. A writer thread has two possible transactions, **makeReservation** and **cancelReservation**. A reader has one possible transaction, **queryReservation**.

First implement a version of your program that allows unsynchronized access to the reservation record. Show how the integrity of the database can be corrupted. Next implement a version of your program that uses Java monitor synchronization with **wait** and **notify** to enforce a disciplined protocol for readers and writers accessing the shared reservation data. In particular, your program should allow multiple readers to access the shared data simultaneously when no writer is active. But if a writer is active, then no readers should be allowed to access the shared data.

Be careful. This problem has many subtleties. For example, what happens when there are several active readers and a writer wants to write? If we allow a steady stream of readers to arrive and share the data, they could indefinitely postpone the writer (who may become tired of waiting and take his or her business elsewhere). To solve this problem, you might decide to favor writers over readers. But here, too, there is a trap, because a steady stream of writers could then indefinitely postpone the waiting readers, and they, too, might choose to take their business elsewhere! Implement your monitor with the following methods: **startReading**, which is called by any reader who wants to begin accessing a reservation, **stopReading** to be called by any reader who has finished reading a reservation, **startWriting** to be called by any writer who wants to make a reservation and **stopWriting** to be called by any writer who has finished making a reservation.

15.25   Write a program that bounces a blue ball inside an applet. The ball should be initiated with a **mousePressed** event. When the ball hits the edge of the applet, the ball should bounce off the edge and continue in the opposite direction.

15.26   Modify the program of Exercise 15.25 to add a new ball each time the user clicks the mouse. Provide for a minimum of 20 balls. Randomly choose the color for each new ball.

15.27   Modify the program of Exercise 15.26 to add shadows. As a ball moves, draw a solid-black oval at the bottom of the applet. You may consider adding a 3D effect by increasing or decreasing the size of each ball when a ball hits the edge of the applet.

15.28   Modify the program of Exercise 15.25 or 15.26 to bounce the balls off each other when they collide.

16

Multimedia: Images, Animation, Audio and Video

Objectives

- To understand how to get and display images.
- To be able to create animations from sequences of images; to control animation speed and flicker.
- To be able to get, play, loop and stop sounds.
- To be able to monitor the loading of images with class **MediaTracker**; to create image maps.
- To customize applets with the **param** tag.

The wheel that squeaks the loudest … gets the grease.
John Billings (Henry Wheeler Shaw)

Noise proves nothing. Often a hen who has merely laid an egg cackles as if she had laid an asteroid.
Mark Twain, *Following the Equator*

We'll use a signal I have tried and found far-reaching and easy to yell. Waa-hoo!
Zane Grey

A wide screen just makes a bad film twice as bad.
Samuel Goldwyn

There is a natural hootchy-kootchy motion to a goldfish.
Walt Disney

Between the motion and the act falls the shadow.
Thomas Stearns Eliot, *The Hollow Men*

What we experience of nature is in models, and all of nature's models are so beautiful.
Richard Buckminster Fuller

Outline

16.1 Introduction

Welcome to what may be the largest revolution in the history of the computer industry. Those of us who entered the field decades ago were primarily interested in using computers to do arithmetic calculations at high speed. But as the computer field evolves, we are beginning to realize that the data manipulation capabilities of computers are now equally important. The "sizzle" of Java is *multimedia*, the use of *sound*, *images*, *graphics* and *video* to make applications "come alive." Today many people consider two-dimensional color video to be the "ultimate" in multimedia. But within the decade, we expect all kinds of exciting new three-dimensional applications. Multimedia programming offers many new challenges. The field is already enormous and will grow rapidly.

People are rushing to equip their computers for multimedia. Most new computers are sold "multimedia ready" with CD-ROM or DVD drives, audio boards and sometimes with special video capabilities.

Among users who want graphics, two-dimensional graphics no longer suffice. Now many people want three-dimensional, high-resolution, color graphics. True three-dimensional imaging may become available within the next decade. Imagine having ultra-high-resolution, "theater-in-the-round," three-dimensional television. Sporting and entertainment events will take place on your living room floor! Medical students worldwide will see operations being performed thousands of miles away as if they were occurring in the same room. People will be able to learn how to drive with extremely realistic driving simulators in their homes before they get behind the wheel. The possibilities are exciting and endless.

Multimedia demands extraordinary computing power. Until recently, affordable computers with this kind of power were not available. But today's ultra-fast processors like the SPARC Ultra from Sun Microsystems, the Pentium from Intel, the Alpha from Compaq Computer Corporation and the R8000 from MIPS/Silicon Graphics (among others) are making effective multimedia possible. The computer and communications industries will be primary beneficiaries of the multimedia revolution. Users will be willing to pay for the faster processors, larger memories and wider communications bandwidths that will be needed to support multimedia applications. Ironically, users may not have to pay more as fierce competition in these industries forces prices down.

We need programming languages that make creating multimedia applications easy. Most programming languages do not have built-in multimedia capabilities. But Java, through the packages of classes that are an integral part of the Java programming world, provides extensive multimedia facilities that will enable you to start developing powerful multimedia applications immediately.

In this chapter we present a series of "live-code" examples that cover many of the interesting multimedia features you will need to build useful applications. We will cover the basics of manipulating images, creating smooth animations, playing sounds, playing videos, creating image maps that can sense when the cursor is over them even without a mouse click and customizing applets via parameters supplied from the HTML file that invokes an applet. The chapter exercises suggest dozens of challenging and interesting projects and even mention some "million-dollar" ideas that may help you make your fortune! When we were creating these exercises it seemed that the ideas just kept flowing. Multimedia seems to leverage creativity in ways that we have not experienced with "conventional" computer capabilities.

16.2 Downloading the Java Media Framework

Java's multimedia capabilities are rapidly evolving. Originally, Java supported basic image manipulations and playback of audio clips in *Sun Audio file format* (such files end with the *.au file extension*). There is now a standard extension to the Java API called the *Java Media Framework version 1.1 (JMF 1.1)* that provides enhanced processing of images and enhanced audio playback supporting many of today's popular audio formats. The JMF also includes video playback capabilities for several video formats. Future versions of the JMF will include many new features such as the ability to record audio and video.

Some examples in this chapter rely on the JMF 1.1 which is not currently part of the Java 2 Software Development Kit (J2SDK). Therefore, to use several of the examples in this chapter, you will need to download the JMF from the Sun Microsystems Web site

```
http://java.sun.com/products/java-media/jmf/1.1/
```

At this site you will find downloads of the JMF for Microsoft Windows and Solaris. There is also a platform-independent version and a version for Web servers from which a client downloads an applet that uses JMF features. Read the installation instructions carefully before installing the software. [*Note:* At the time of this publication, an early access of the JMF version 2.0 was available via the JMF home page

```
http://java.sun.com/products/java-media/jmf/index.html
```

The examples in this chapter were written and tested only with JMF 1.1.]

16.3 Loading, Displaying and Scaling Images

Java's multimedia capabilities include graphics, images, animations, sounds and video. We begin our multimedia discussion with images.

The applet of Fig. 16.1 demonstrates loading an *Image* (package **java.awt**) and loading an *ImageIcon* (package **javax.swing**). The applet displays the **Image** in its original size and scaled to twice its original width and twice its original height using two versions of **Graphics** method *drawImage*. The applet also draws the **ImageIcon** using its method *paintIcon*. Class **ImageIcon** is particularly useful because it can be used to easily load an image into any applet or application.

Lines 10 and 11 declare an **Image** reference and an **ImageIcon** reference, respectively. Class **Image** is an **abstract** class; therefore, you cannot create an object of class **Image** directly. Rather, you must request that an **Image** be loaded and returned to you. Class **Applet** (the superclass of **JApplet**) provides a method that does just that. Line 16 in the applet's **init** method

```
logo1 = getImage( getDocumentBase(), "logo.gif" );
```

```
1   / Fig. 16.1: LoadImageAndScale.java
2   // Load an image and display it in its original size
3   // and scale it to twice its original width and height.
4   // Load and display the same image as an ImageIcon.
5   import java.applet.Applet;
6   import java.awt.*;
7   import javax.swing.*;
8
9   public class LoadImageAndScale extends JApplet {
10      private Image logo1;
11      private ImageIcon logo2;
12
13      // load the image when the applet is loaded
14      public void init()
15      {
16          logo1 = getImage( getDocumentBase(), "logo.gif" );
17          logo2 = new ImageIcon( "logo.gif" );
18      }
19
20      // display the image
21      public void paint( Graphics g )
22      {
23          // draw the original image
24          g.drawImage( logo1, 0, 0, this );
25
26          // draw the image scaled to fit the width of the applet
27          // and the height of the applet minus 120 pixels
28          g.drawImage( logo1, 0, 120,
29                        getWidth(), getHeight() - 120, this );
30
31          // draw the icon using its paintIcon method
32          logo2.paintIcon( this, g, 180, 0 );
33      }
34  }
```

Fig. 16.1   Loading and displaying an image in an applet (part 1 of 2).

Fig. 16.1   Loading and displaying an image in an applet (part 2 of 2).

uses **Applet** method **getImage** to load an **Image** into the applet. This version of **get-Image** takes two arguments—a location where the image is stored and the file name of the image. In the first argument, **Applet** method **getDocumentBase** is used to determine the location of the image on the Internet (or on your computer if that is where the applet came from). We assume that the image to be loaded is stored in the same directory as the HTML file that invoked the applet. Method **getDocumentBase** returns the location of the HTML file on the Internet as an object of class **URL** (package **java.net**). A **URL** stores a *Uniform (or Universal) Resource Locator*—a standard format for an address of a piece of information on the Internet. We discuss **URL**s in more depth in Chapters 18 through 21. The second argument specifies an image file name. Java currently supports two image formats—*Graphics Interchange Format (GIF)* and *Joint Photographic Experts Group (JPEG)*. File names for each of these types end with **.gif** or **.jpg** (or **.jpeg**) respectively.

 Portability Tip 16.1

*Class **Image** is an **abstract** class, so **Image** objects cannot be created directly. To achieve platform independence, the Java implementation on each platform provides its own subclass of **Image** to store image information.*

When method **getImage** is invoked, it launches a separate thread of execution in which the image is loaded (or downloaded from the Internet). This enables the program to continue execution while the image is being loaded. *Note:* If the requested file is not available, method **getImage** does not indicate an error.

Class **ImageIcon** is not an **abstract** class; therefore, you can create an **Image-Icon** object. Line 17 in the applet's **init** method

```
logo2 = new ImageIcon( "logo.gif" );
```

creates an **ImageIcon** object that loads the same **logo.gif** image. Class **ImageIcon** provides several constructors that allow an **ImageIcon** object to be initialized with an image from the local computer or with an image stored on a Web server on the Internet.

The applet's **paint** method displays the images. Line 24

```
g.drawImage( logo1, 0, 0, this );
```

uses **Graphics** method **drawImage** which receives four arguments (there are actually six overloaded versions of this method). The first argument is a reference to the **Image** object in which the image is stored (**logo1**). The second and third arguments are the x and y coordinates where the image should be displayed on the applet (the coordinates indicate the upper-left corner of the image). The last argument is a reference to an *ImageObserver* object. Normally, the **ImageObserver** is the object on which the image is displayed— we used **this** to indicate the applet. An **ImageObserver** can be any object that implements the **ImageObserver** interface. Interface **ImageObserver** is implemented by class **Component** (one of class **Applet**'s indirect superclasses). Therefore, all **Component**s can be **ImageObserver**s. This argument is important when displaying large images that require a long time to download from the Internet. It is possible that a program will display the image before it is completely downloaded. The **ImageObserver** is automatically notified to update the image that was displayed as the remainder of the image is loaded. When you run this applet, watch carefully as pieces of the image are displayed while the image loads. [*Note:* On faster computers, you may not notice this effect.]

Lines 28 and 29

```
g.drawImage( logo1, 0, 120,
             getWidth(), getHeight() - 120, this );
```

use another version of **Graphics** method **drawImage** to output a *scaled* version of the image. The fourth and fifth arguments specify the *width* and *height* of the image for display purposes. The image is automatically scaled to fit the specified width and height. The fourth argument indicates that the width of the scaled image should be the width of the applet and the fifth argument indicates that the height should be 120 pixels less than the height of the applet. The width and height of the applet are determined with methods **getWidth** and **getHeight** (inherited from class **Component**).

Line 33

```
logo2.paintIcon( this, g, 180, 0 );
```

uses **ImageIcon** method *paintIcon* to display the image. The method requires four arguments—a reference to the **Component** on which the image will be displayed, a reference to the **Graphics** object that will be used to render the image, the x-coordinate of the upper-left corner of the image and the y-coordinate of the upper-left corner of the image.

If you compare the two ways in which we loaded and displayed images in this example, you can see that using **ImageIcon** is simpler. You can create objects of class **ImageIcon** directly and there is no need to use an **ImageObserver** reference when displaying the image. For this reason, we use class **ImageIcon** for the remainder of the chapter. [*Note:* Class **ImageIcon**'s **paintIcon** method does not allow scaling of an image. However, the class provides method **getImage** which returns an **Image** reference that can be used with **Graphics** method **drawImage** to display a scaled image.]

16.4 Loading and Playing Audio Clips

Java programs can manipulate and play *audio clips*. It is easy for users to capture their own audio clips and there is a variety of clips available in software products and over the Internet. Your system needs to be equipped with audio hardware (speakers and a sound board) to be able to play the audio clips.

Java provides two mechanisms for playing sounds in an applet—the **Applet**'s *play* method and the *play* method from the **AudioClip** *interface*. If you would like to play a sound once in a program, the **Applet** method **play** will load the sound and play it for you once; the sound is marked for garbage collection when it is done playing. The **Applet** method **play** method has two forms:

```
public void play( URL location, String soundFileName );
public void play( URL soundURL );
```

The first version loads the audio clip stored in file **soundFileName** from **location** and plays the sound. The first argument is normally a call to the applet's **getDocumentBase** or *getCodeBase method*. Method **getDocumentBase** indicates the location of the HTML file that loaded the applet. Method **getCodeBase** indicates where the **.class** file for the applet is located. The second version of method **play** takes a **URL** that contains the location and the file name of the audio clip. The statement

```
play( getDocumentBase(), "hi.au" );
```

loads the audio clip in file **hi.au** and plays it once.

The *sound engine* that plays the audio clips supports several audio file formats including *Sun Audio file format (**.au** extension), Windows Wave file format (**.wav** extension), Macintosh AIFF file format (**.aif** or **.aiff** extension)* and *Musical Instrument Digital Interface (MIDI) file format (**.mid** or **.rmi** extensions)*. The Java Media Framework (JMF) supports other additional formats.

The program of Fig. 16.2 demonstrates loading and playing an **AudioClip** (package **java.applet**). This technique is more flexible than **Applet** method **play**. It allows the audio to be stored in the program so the audio can be reused throughout the program's execution. **Applet** method *getAudioClip* has two forms that take the same arguments as the **play** method described above. Method **getAudioClip** returns a reference to an **AudioClip**. Once an **AudioClip** is loaded, three methods can be invoked for the object—*play*, *loop* and *stop*. Method **play** plays the audio once. Method **loop** continuously loops the audio clip in the background. Method **stop** terminates an audio clip that is currently playing. In the program, each of these methods is associated with a button on the applet.

```
1   // Fig. 16.2: LoadAudioAndPlay.java
2   // Load an audio clip and play it.
3   import java.applet.*;
4   import java.awt.*;
5   import java.awt.event.*;
6   import javax.swing.*;
```

Fig. 16.2   Loading and playing an **AudioClip** (part 1 of 3).

```
7
8    public class LoadAudioAndPlay extends JApplet {
9       private AudioClip sound1, sound2, currentSound;
10      private JButton playSound, loopSound, stopSound;
11      private JComboBox chooseSound;
12
13      // load the image when the applet begins executing
14      public void init()
15      {
16         Container c = getContentPane();
17         c.setLayout( new FlowLayout() );
18
19         String choices[] = { "Welcome", "Hi" };
20         chooseSound = new JComboBox( choices );
21         chooseSound.addItemListener(
22            new ItemListener() {
23               public void itemStateChanged( ItemEvent e )
24               {
25                  currentSound.stop();
26
27                  currentSound =
28                     chooseSound.getSelectedIndex() == 0 ?
29                        sound1 : sound2;
30               }
31            }
32         );
33         c.add( chooseSound );
34
35         ButtonHandler handler = new ButtonHandler();
36         playSound = new JButton( "Play" );
37         playSound.addActionListener( handler );
38         c.add( playSound );
39         loopSound = new JButton( "Loop" );
40         loopSound.addActionListener( handler );
41         c.add( loopSound );
42         stopSound = new JButton( "Stop" );
43         stopSound.addActionListener( handler );
44         c.add( stopSound );
45
46         sound1 = getAudioClip(
47                    getDocumentBase(), "welcome.wav" );
48         sound2 = getAudioClip(
49                    getDocumentBase(), "hi.au" );
50         currentSound = sound1;
51      }
52
53      // stop the sound when the user switches Web pages
54      // (i.e., be polite to the user)
55      public void stop()
56      {
57         currentSound.stop();
58      }
59
```

Fig. 16.2   Loading and playing an **AudioClip** (part 2 of 3).

```
60      private class ButtonHandler implements ActionListener {
61         public void actionPerformed( ActionEvent e )
62         {
63            if ( e.getSource() == playSound )
64               currentSound.play();
65            else if ( e.getSource() == loopSound )
66               currentSound.loop();
67            else if ( e.getSource() == stopSound )
68               currentSound.stop();
69         }
70      }
71   }
```

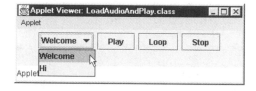

Fig. 16.2   Loading and playing an **AudioClip** (part 3 of 3).

Lines 46 through 49 in the applet's **init** method

```
sound1 = getAudioClip(
            getDocumentBase(), "welcome.wav" );
sound2 = getAudioClip(
            getDocumentBase(), "hi.au" );
```

use **getAudioClip** to load two audio files—a Windows Wave file (**welcome.wav**) and a Sun Audio file (**hi.au**). The user can select which audio clip to play from **JComboBox chooseSound**. Notice that the applet's stop method is overridden at line 55. When the user switches Web pages, the applet's **stop** method is called. This version of **stop** ensures that a playing audio clip is stopped. Otherwise the audio clip will continue to play in the background. This is not really a problem, but can be annoying to the user if the audio clip is looping. The **stop** method is provided here to be polite to the user.

Good Programming Practice 16.1

When playing audio clips in an applet or application, provide a mechanism for the user to disable the audio.

16.5 The Java Media Player

In this section we present the basic *Java Media Player* that comes with the Java Media Framework from Sun Microsystems (see Section 16.2 for information on downloading the JMF). The player is capable of playing all the audio formats mentioned in Section 16.4 and a variety of other audio and video formats such as *AVI* (**.avi** *extension*), *GSM* (**.gsm** *extension*), *MPEG-1* (**.mpg** *or* **.mpeg** *extension*), *Apple QuickTime™* (**.mov** *extension*), *RMF* (**.rmf** *extension*), *RTP* (**.rtp** *extension*) *and* Vivo (**.viv** *extension*).

The application of Fig. 16.3 enables you to choose a media file from a *JFileChooser dialog box*. The program then creates a Java Media Player to play the specified audio or video file. For the purposes of this example we used the sample media files that come with the JMF. If you installed the JMF in its default installation directory, these files can be found in the

       `c:\JMF1.1\samples\media`

directory on Windows or

       `~/JMF1.1/samples/media`

on Solaris.

```
1   // Fig. 16.3: MediaPlayerDemo.java
2   // Uses a Java Media Player to play media files.
3   import java.awt.*;
4   import java.awt.event.*;
5   import java.io.*;
6   import javax.swing.*;
7   import javax.media.*;
8
9   public class MediaPlayerDemo extends JFrame {
10      private Player player;
11      private File file;
12
13      public MediaPlayerDemo()
14      {
15          super( "Demonstrating the Java Media Player" );
16
17          JButton openFile = new JButton( "Open file to play" );
18          openFile.addActionListener(
19              new ActionListener() {
20                  public void actionPerformed( ActionEvent e )
21                  {
22                      openFile();
23                      createPlayer();
24                  }
25              }
26          );
27          getContentPane().add( openFile, BorderLayout.NORTH );
28
29          setSize( 300, 300 );
30          show();
31      }
32
33      private void openFile()
34      {
35          JFileChooser fileChooser = new JFileChooser();
36
37          fileChooser.setFileSelectionMode(
38              JFileChooser.FILES_ONLY );
39          int result = fileChooser.showOpenDialog( this );
40
```

Fig. 16.3   Demonstrating the Java Media Player (part 1 of 4).

```
41            // user clicked Cancel button on dialog
42            if ( result == JFileChooser.CANCEL_OPTION )
43               file = null;
44            else
45               file = fileChooser.getSelectedFile();
46         }
47
48         private void createPlayer()
49         {
50            if ( file == null )
51               return;
52
53            removePreviousPlayer();
54
55            try {
56               // create a new player and add listener
57               player = Manager.createPlayer( file.toURL() );
58               player.addControllerListener( new EventHandler() );
59               player.start();  // start player
60            }
61            catch ( Exception e ){
62               JOptionPane.showMessageDialog( this,
63                  "Invalid file or location", "Error loading file",
64                  JOptionPane.ERROR_MESSAGE );
65            }
66         }
67
68         private void removePreviousPlayer()
69         {
70            if ( player == null )
71               return;
72
73            player.close();
74
75            Component visual = player.getVisualComponent();
76            Component control = player.getControlPanelComponent();
77
78            Container c = getContentPane();
79
80            if ( visual != null )
81               c.remove( visual );
82
83            if ( control != null )
84               c.remove( control );
85         }
86
87         public static void main(String args[])
88         {
89            MediaPlayerDemo app = new MediaPlayerDemo();
90
```

Fig. 16.3   Demonstrating the Java Media Player (part 2 of 4).

```
 91            app.addWindowListener(
 92               new WindowAdapter() {
 93                  public void windowClosing( WindowEvent e )
 94                  {
 95                     System.exit(0);
 96                  }
 97               }
 98            );
 99         }
100
101         // inner class to handler events from media player
102         private class EventHandler implements ControllerListener {
103            public void controllerUpdate( ControllerEvent e ) {
104               if ( e instanceof RealizeCompleteEvent ) {
105                  Container c = getContentPane();
106
107                  // load Visual and Control components if they exist
108                  Component visualComponent =
109                     player.getVisualComponent();
110
111                  if ( visualComponent != null )
112                     c.add( visualComponent, BorderLayout.CENTER );
113
114                  Component controlsComponent =
115                     player.getControlPanelComponent();
116
117                  if ( controlsComponent != null )
118                     c.add( controlsComponent, BorderLayout.SOUTH );
119
120                  c.doLayout();
121               }
122            }
123         }
124   }
```

Initial GUI at execution

Fig. 16.3   Demonstrating the Java Media Player (part 3 of 4).

Selecting a media file to play from a **JFileChooser** dialog box

The **Sample3.mpg** file loaded and playing

Fig. 16.3 Demonstrating the Java Media Player (part 4 of 4).

Initially, the GUI consists only of a button (**openFile**). When the user presses the button, method **actionPerformed** (line 20 in the anonymous inner class) invokes our utility methods **openFile** (defined at line 33) and **createPlayer** (defined at line 48).

Method **openFile** creates a **JFileChooser** dialog box (package **javax.swing**) at line 35. When displayed, a **JFileChooser** (see the second screen in Fig. 16.3) allows the user to select a file from the computer's local file system. Lines 37 and 38

```
fileChooser.setFileSelectionMode(
    JFileChooser.FILES_ONLY );
```

use **JFileChooser** method *setFileSelectionMode* to indicate that the user can select only files (directories are excluded) from the local file system. Line 39

```
int result = fileChooser.showOpenDialog( this );
```

uses **JFileChooser** method *showOpenDialog* to display an **Open** *dialog* for choosing files to open (in Chapter 17, "Files and Streams," we illustrate how to display a **Save** *dialog*). The method returns an integer (assigned to **result**) that indicates the user's action (i.e., whether the user selected a file or cancelled the dialog). The **if** structure at line 42

```
if ( result == JFileChooser.CANCEL_OPTION )
```

tests the result to determine if the user cancelled (*JFileChooser.CANCEL_OPTION*) the dialog—i.e., the user did not select a file. If so, *File* (package *java.io*) reference **file** is set to **null** (line 43) to indicate that no file was selected. If a file was selected, line 45

```
file = fileChooser.getSelectedFile();
```

uses **JFileChooser** method *getSelectedFile* to obtain a **File** object containing the name and location of the selected file. Class **File** is discussed in more detail in Chapter 17, "Files and Streams."

Method **createPlayer** (line 48) first determines if the **file** reference is **null**. If so, the method simply returns without attempting to create a media player. Next, our utility method **removePreviousPlayer** (defined at line 68) is invoked to close a previously opened media player (if there is not such a player, the method returns immediately). The code in the try block (lines 55 through 60) attempts to create a new media player and start playing a media clip. Class *Manager* of the JMF's *javax.media* package is used to create a media player. Line 57

```
player = Manager.createPlayer( file.toURL() );
```

uses **Manager** method *createPlayer* to obtain an object that implements the *Player* interface (package **javax.media**). Method **createPlayer** determines if the specified media clip is a valid and supported format. If so, it returns the correct **Player** for the specified media clip. There are several versions of method **createPlayer**. The one used here expects to receive a **URL** (package **java.net**) indicating the name of the file containing the media clip to load and the location of the file on the Internet (or local file system). Class **File** provides method *toURL* to convert the file name and location represented by the **File** object into a valid **URL** format.

The application can respond to *media events* generated by the **Player** by providing an event handler that implements interface *ControllerListener* (package **javax.media**). Line 58

```
player.addControllerListener( new EventHandler() );
```

registers an instance of **private** inner class **EventHandler** (defined at line 102) the as the listener for **player**'s *ControllerEvents*. Line 59 calls **Player** method *start* method to indicate that the **Player** should begin playing the loaded clip. If any exceptions occur in the **try** block, a message dialog is displayed to indicate that an exception occurred.

When a media event occurs, method *controllerUpdate* (line 103) is invoked. The argument to this method is a *ContollerEvent* (package **javax.media**). This class actually has 21 direct and indirect subclasses that can also be arguments to method **controllerUpdate**. This provides programmers with flexible options for processing media events. In this example, we explicitly test the event object to determine if it is an instance of class *RealizeCompleteEvent*. This is the type of the event object passed to *controllerUpdate* when the **Player** determines the type of media clip and loads the clip. Try adding the following statement

```
System.out.println( e );
```

as the first statement in method **controllerUpdate** to see the many different event types that are passed to this method and to see how frequently the method is called.

Next, we attach the **Player** and its controls to the GUI. Lines 108 through 112

```
Component visualComponent =
   player.getVisualComponent();

if ( visualComponent != null )
   c.add( visualComponent, BorderLayout.CENTER );
```

use **Player** method *getVisualComponent* to obtain a **Component** on which the visual aspect of the media clip can be rendered. This method returns **null** for audio clips. If the return value is not **null**, line 112 adds **visualComponent** to the **CENTER** of the content pane's **BorderLayout**. Lines 114 through 118

```
Component controlsComponent =
   player.getControlPanelComponent();

if ( controlsComponent != null )
   c.add( controlsComponent, BorderLayout.SOUTH );
```

use **Player** method *getControlPanelComponent* to obtain a **Component** on which **Player** controls are displayed. If the return value is not **null**, line 118 adds **controlsComponent** to the **SOUTH** of the content pane's **BorderLayout**. Line 120 uses **Container** method **doLayout** to indicate that the content pane should re-layout its currently displayed set of components.

Method **removePreviousPlayer** (line 68) is called to remove the previous media player each time a new media player is about to be loaded. Line 73 calls method **close** (inherited into interface **Player** from interface *Controller*) to close the current **Player**. Lines 75 and 76 obtain references to the visual and control **Component**s of the **Player**. The **if** structures at lines 80 and 83 determine if the references are not **null**, and, if so, use **Container** method *remove* to remove the **Component**s from the user interface in anticipation of a new **Player**'s **Component**s being displayed.

Figure 16.4 illustrates two common control bars for the Java Media Player. The top control bar is typically displayed while a clip containing audio is playing. The *pause* button temporarily stops the playing clip. When a clip is paused, the bottom control bar is displayed with a *play* button to continue playing the clip from the point at which the clip was paused. In the middle of each control bar is a *position indicator*. The small circle on the position indicator can be dragged to the left to continue playing from an earlier point in the clip, or the small circle can be dragged to the right to continue playing from an later point in the clip. To the right of the position indicator is a *mute* button to toggle the audio on and off. To the right of the mute button are up and down arrows for *volume* control. The last button on the bar is the information button that displays a dialog box containing information about the currently loaded clip.

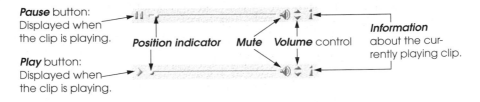

Fig. 16.4   Controls for the Java Media Player when an audio or video is playing.

An excellent Web site for obtaining audio and video files to demonstrate the Java Media Player is the NASA Web site

http://www.nasa.gov

The site contains a Multimedia Gallery full of images, audio and video that can be downloaded and played on your computer. Each image, audio or video file is typically marked with its file format. Try downloading some audio and video files from the site and using them with the application of Fig. 16.3.

16.6 Animating a Series of Images

The next example demonstrates animating a series of images that are stored in an array. The application uses the same techniques to load and display **ImageIcon**s as shown in Fig. 16.1. In previous editions of this text, we used a series of animation examples to demonstrate various techniques for smoothing an animation. One of the key techniques involved a concept called *graphics double buffering*. However, because of new features of Swing GUI components that already implement the smoothing techniques, we can simply concentrate on the animation concept.

The animation presented in Fig. 16.5 is designed as a subclass of **JPanel** (called **LogoAnimator**) so it can be attached to an application window or possibly to a **JApplet**. Class **LogoAnimator** also defines a **main** method (defined at line 71 to execute the animation as an application. Method **main** defines an instance of class **JFrame** and attaches a **LogoAnimator** object to the **JFrame** to display the animation.

```
1  // Fig. 16.5: LogoAnimator.java
2  // Animation a series of images
3  import java.awt.*;
4  import java.awt.event.*;
5  import javax.swing.*;
6
7  public class LogoAnimator extends JPanel
8                            implements ActionListener {
9     protected ImageIcon images[];
10    protected int totalImages = 30,
11                  currentImage = 0,
12                  animationDelay = 50; // 50 millisecond delay
13    protected Timer animationTimer;
```

Fig. 16.5   Animating a series of images (part 1 of 3).

```
14
15     public LogoAnimator()
16     {
17        setSize( getPreferredSize() );
18
19        images = new ImageIcon[ totalImages ];
20
21        for ( int i = 0; i < images.length; ++i )
22           images[ i ] =
23              new ImageIcon( "images/deitel" + i + ".gif" );
24
25        startAnimation();
26     }
27
28     public void paintComponent( Graphics g )
29     {
30        super.paintComponent( g );
31
32        if ( images[ currentImage ].getImageLoadStatus() ==
33             MediaTracker.COMPLETE ) {
34           images[ currentImage ].paintIcon( this, g, 0, 0 );
35           currentImage = ( currentImage + 1 ) % totalImages;
36        }
37     }
38
39     public void actionPerformed( ActionEvent e )
40     {
41        repaint();
42     }
43
44     public void startAnimation()
45     {
46        if ( animationTimer == null ) {
47           currentImage = 0;
48           animationTimer = new Timer( animationDelay, this );
49           animationTimer.start();
50        }
51        else  // continue from last image displayed
52           if ( ! animationTimer.isRunning() )
53              animationTimer.restart();
54     }
55
56     public void stopAnimation()
57     {
58        animationTimer.stop();
59     }
60
61     public Dimension getMinimumSize()
62     {
63        return getPreferredSize();
64     }
65
```

Fig. 16.5   Animating a series of images (part 2 of 3).

```
66      public Dimension getPreferredSize()
67      {
68         return new Dimension( 160, 80 );
69      }
70
71      public static void main( String args[] )
72      {
73         LogoAnimator anim = new LogoAnimator();
74
75         JFrame app = new JFrame( "Animator test" );
76         app.getContentPane().add( anim, BorderLayout.CENTER );
77
78         app.addWindowListener(
79            new WindowAdapter() {
80               public void windowClosing( WindowEvent e )
81               {
82                  System.exit( 0 );
83               }
84            }
85         );
86
87         // The constants 10 and 30 are used below to size the
88         // window 10 pixels wider than the animation and
89         // 30 pixels taller than the animation.
90         app.setSize( anim.getPreferredSize().width + 10,
91                      anim.getPreferredSize().height + 30 );
92         app.show();
93      }
94   }
```

Fig. 16.5   Animating a series of images (part 3 of 3).

Class **LogoAnimator** maintains an array of **ImageIcon**s that are loaded in the constructor. As each **ImageIcon** object is instantiated in the **for** structure at line 21, the **ImageIcon** constructor loads one image for the animation (there are 30 total images) with the statement

```
images[ i ] =
   new ImageIcon( "images/deitel" + i + ".gif" );
```

The argument uses string concatenation to assemble the file name from the pieces **"images/deitel"**, **i**, and **".gif"**. Each of the images in the animation is in one of the files "**deitel0.gif**" through "**deitel29.gif**." The value of the control variable in the **for** structure is used to select one of the 30 images.

Performance Tip 16.1

It is more efficient to load the frames of the animation as one image than to load each image separately (a painting program can be used to combine the frames of the animation into one image). If the images are being loaded from the World Wide Web, every image loaded requires a separate connection to the site where the images are stored.

Performance Tip 16.2

Loading all the frames of an animation as one large image may force your program to wait to begin displaying the animation.

After loading the images, the constructor calls **startAnimation** (defined at line 44) to begin the animation. The animation is driven by an instance of class *Timer* (package **javax.swing**). An object of class **Timer** generates **ActionEvent**s at a fixed interval in milliseconds (normally specified as an argument to the **Timer**'s constructor) and notifies all of its registered **ActionListener**s that the event occurred. Lines 46 through 50

```
if ( animationTimer == null ) {
   currentImage = 0;
   animationTimer = new Timer( animationDelay, this );
   animationTimer.start();
}
```

determine if the **Timer** reference **animationTimer** is **null**. If so, **currentImage** is set to 0 to indicate that the animation should begin with the image in the first element of array **images**. Line 48 assigns a new **Timer** object to **animationTimer**. The **Timer** constructor receives two arguments—the delay in milliseconds (**animationDelay** is 50 in this example) and the **ActionListener** that will respond to the **Timer**'s **Action-Event**s (**this LogoAnimator** implements **ActionListener** at line 8). Line 49 starts the **Timer** object. Once started, **animationTimer** will generate an **Action-Event** every 50 milliseconds in this example. Lines 51 through 53

```
else  // continue from last image displayed
   if ( ! animationTimer.isRunning() )
      animationTimer.restart();
```

are for programs that may stop the animation and restart it. For example, to make an animation "browser friendly" in an applet, the animation should be stopped when the user switches Web pages. If the user returns to the Web page with the animation, method **startAnimation** can be called to restart the animation. The **if** condition at line 52 uses **Timer** method **isRunning** to determine if the **Timer** is currently running (i.e., generating events). If it is not running, line 53 calls **Timer** method **restart** to indicate that the **Timer** should start generating events again.

In response to every **Timer** event in this example, method **actionPerformed** (line 39) calls method **repaint**. This schedules a call to the **LogoAnimator**'s **update** method (inherited from class **JPanel**) which, in turn, results in a call to the **LogoAnimator**'s **paintComponent** method (line 28). Remember that any subclass of **JComponent** that performs drawing should do so in its **paintComponent** method. As mentioned in Chapter 13, the first statement in any **paintComponent** method should be a call to the superclass's **paintComponent** method to ensure that Swing components are displayed correctly. The **if** condition at lines 32 and 33

```
if ( images[ currentImage ].getImageLoadStatus() ==
     MediaTracker.COMPLETE ) {
```

uses **ImageIcon** method ***getImageLoadStatus*** to determine if the image to display is completely loaded into memory. Only complete images should be displayed to make the animation as smooth as possible. When the image is fully loaded, the method returns ***MediaTracker.COMPLETE***. An object of class ***MediaTracker*** (package **java.awt**) is used by class **ImageIcon** to track the loading of an image.

When loading images into a program, the images can be registered with an object of class **MediaTracker** to enable the program to determine when an image is loaded completely. Class **MediaTracker** also provides the ability to wait for an image or several images to load before allowing a program to continue and to determine if an error occurred while loading an image. We do not need to create a **MediaTracker** directly in this example, because class **ImageIcon** does this for us. However, when using class **Image** (as shown in Fig. 16.1), you may want to create your own **MediaTracker**.

Performance Tip 16.3

Some people who are experienced with **MediaTracker** *objects have reported that they can have a detrimental effect on performance. Keep this in mind as an area to scrutinize if you need to tune your multimedia applications.*

Performance Tip 16.4

Using **MediaTracker** *method* **waitForAll** *to wait for all registered images to completely load may result is a long delay between when the program begins execution and when the images are actually displayed. The more images and the larger the images, the more time the user will have to wait. Use* **MediaTracker** *method* **waitForAll** *only to wait for small numbers of images to load completely.*

If the image is fully loaded, lines 34 and 35

```
images[ currentImage ].paintIcon( this, g, 0, 0 );
currentImage = ( currentImage + 1 ) % totalImages;
```

paint the **ImageIcon** at element **currentImage** in the array and prepare for the next image to be displayed by incrementing **currentImage** by 1. Notice the modulus calculation to ensure that the value of **currentImage** is set to 0 when it is incremented past 29 (the last element subscript in the array).

Method **stopAnimation** (line 56), stops the animation with line 58

```
animationTimer.stop();
```

which uses **Timer** method ***stop*** to indicate that the **Timer** should stop generating events. This, in turn, prevents **actionPerformed** from calling **repaint** to initiate the painting of the next image in the array.

Software Engineering Observation 16.1

When creating an animation for use in an applet, provide a mechanism for disabling the animation when the user browses a new Web page separate from the page on which the animation applet resides.

Methods **getMinimumSize** (line 61) and **getPreferredSize** (line 66) are overridden to help a layout manager determine the appropriate size of a **LogoAnimator** in a layout. In this example, the images are 160 pixels wide and 80 pixels tall, so method **getPreferredSize** returns a **Dimension** object containing 160 and 80. Method **getMinimumSize** simply calls **getPreferredSize** (a common programming practice). Notice in **main** (line 71) that the size of the application window is set (lines 90 and 91) to the preferred width of the animation plus 10 pixels and the preferred height of the animation plus 30 pixels. This is because a window's width and height specify the outer bounds of the window, not the window's *client area* (the area in which GUI components can be attached).

In this example, we were able to take advantage of several features that help produce a smooth animation and controllable animation—**ImageIcon** objects loaded the images, an object of a subclass of **JPanel** displayed the images and a **Timer** object controlled the animation.

16.7 Animation Issues

When you execute the application in Fig. 16.5, you may notice that the images take time to load. If an animation is not designed correctly, this often results in partial images being displayed. You may be able to see that each image displays in pieces. This is often the result of the image format that is used. For example, GIF images can be stored in *interlaced* and *non-interlaced* formats. The format indicates the order in which the pixels of the image are stored. The pixels of a non-interlaced image are stored in the same order that the pixels appear on the screen. As a non-interlaced image is displayed, it appears in chunks from top to bottom as the pixel information is read. The pixels of an interlaced image are stored in rows of pixels, but the rows are out of order. For example, the rows of pixels in the image may be stored in the order 1, 5, 9, 13, …, followed by 2, 6, 10, 14, …, and so on. When the image is displayed, it appears to fade in as the first batch of rows presents a rough outline of the picture and the subsequent batches of rows refine the displayed image until the entire image is complete. To help prevent partial images from appearing in previous versions of Java, we tracked the loading of images using a **MediaTracker** object. Only fully loaded images are displayed to produce the smoothest animation. Every image to track must be registered with the **MediaTracker**. This is now performed by class **ImageIcon**'s constructor.

Software Engineering Observation 16.2

*Class **ImageIcon** uses a **MediaTracker** object to determine the status of the image it is loading.*

Good Programming Practice 16.2

In an applet, always display something while images load. The longer a user must wait to see information appear on the screen, the more likely they will leave the Web page before the information appears.

Another common problem with animations is that the animation *flickers* as each image is displayed. This is due to the **update** method being called in response to each **repaint**. In AWT GUI components, when **update** clears the background of the GUI component, it does so by drawing a filled rectangle the size of the component in the current background color. This would cover the image that was just displayed. Thus, the animation would draw an image, sleep for a fraction of a second, clear the background (causing a flicker) and draw the next image. In subclasses of Swing's **JPanel** (or any other Swing component), method **update** is overridden to prevent clearing of the background if the component is transparent (the background will be cleared if the component is opaque). This helps eliminate flicker.

> ### Look-and-Feel Observation 16.1
> *Swing components override method **update** to prevent clearing of the background (for transparent components) in response to **repaint** messages.*

If you want to develop multimedia-based applications, your users will want smooth sound and animations. Choppy presentations are unacceptable. This often happens when you write applications that draw directly to the screen. One other technique used to produce smooth animation (and other graphics) is *graphics double buffering*. While the program renders one image on the screen, it can build the next image in an *off-screen buffer*. Then, when it is time for that next image to be displayed, it can be placed on the screen smoothly. Of course, there is a *space/time trade-off*. The extra memory required can be substantial, but the improved display performance may be well worth it.

Graphics double buffering is also useful in programs that need to use drawing capabilities in methods other than **paint** or **paintComponent** (where we have done all our drawing to this point). The off-screen buffer can be passed between methods or even between objects of different classes to allow other methods or objects to draw on the off-screen buffer. The results of the drawing can then be displayed at a later time.

> ### Performance Tip 16.5
> *Double buffering can reduce or eliminate flicker in an animation, but it can visibly slow the speed at which the animation runs.*

When all the pixels of an image do not display at once, an animation has more flicker. When an image is drawn using graphics double buffering, by the time the image is displayed, it will have already been drawn off the screen and the partial images that the user normally would see are hidden from the user. All the pixels will be displayed for the user in one "blast" so the flicker is substantially reduced or eliminated.

The basic concept of a graphics double buffer is as follows: create a blank **Image**, draw on the blank **Image** (using methods of the **Graphics** class) and display the image. The **Image** stores the pixels that will be copied to the screen. The **Graphics** reference is used to draw the pixels. Every image has an associated graphics context—i.e., an object of class **Graphics** that enables drawing to be performed. The **Image** and **Graphics** references used for graphics double buffering are often referred to as the *off-screen image* and the *off-screen graphics context* because they are not actually manipulating screen pixels.

Swing GUI components are displayed using Java's drawing capabilities. Therefore, Swing GUI components are subject to many of the same drawing problems encountered with a typical animation. By default, Swing uses graphics double buffering to render all Swing GUI components. By designing our **LogoAnimator** as a subclass of **JPanel**, we are able to take advantage of Swing's built-in graphics double-buffering to produce the smoothest possible animation.

> ### Look-and-Feel Observation 16.2
> *Swing GUI components are rendered using graphics double buffering by default.*

16.8 Customizing Applets via the HTML `param` Tag

When browsing the World Wide Web you will often come across applets that are in the public domain—you can use them free of charge on your own Web pages (normally in exchange for crediting the applet's creator). One common feature of such applets is the ability to customize the applet via parameters that are supplied from the HTML file that invokes the applet. For example, the following HTML from file **LogoApplet.html**

```
<html>
<applet code="LogoApplet.class" width=400 height=400>
<param name="totalimages" value="30">
<param name="imagename" value="deitel">
<param name="animationdelay" value="200">
</applet>
</html>
```

invokes the applet **LogoApplet** (Fig. 16.6) and specifies three parameters. The *param tag* lines must appear between the starting and ending **applet** tags. These values can then be used to customize the applet. Any number of **param** tags can appear between the starting and ending **applet** tags. Each parameter has a *name* and a *value*. **Applet** method *getParameter* is used to get the **value** associated with a specific parameter and return the **value** as a **String**. The argument passed to **getParameter** is a **String** containing the name of the parameter in the **param** tag. For example, the statement

```
parameter = getParameter( "animationdelay" );
```

gets the value associated with the **animationdelay** parameter and assigns it to **String** reference **parameter**. If there is not a **param** tag containing the specified parameter, **getParameter** returns **null**.

In Fig. 16.6 we modified class **LogoAnimator** so it can be used from an applet and customized via parameters in the applet's HTML file. Class **LogoApplet** allows Web page designers to customize the animation to use their own images. Three parameters are provided. Parameter **animationdelay** is the number of milliseconds to sleep between images being displayed. This value will be converted to an integer and used as the value for instance variable **sleepTime**. Parameter **imagename** is the base name of the images to be loaded. This **String** will be assigned to instance variable **imageName**. The applet assumes that the images are in a subdirectory named **images** that can be found in the same directory as the applet. The applet also assumes that the image file names are numbered from 0. Parameter **totalimages** represents the total number of images in the animation. Its value will be converted to an integer and assigned to instance variable **totalImages**.

```
1   // Fig. 16.6: LogoAnimator.java
2   // Animating a series of images
3   import java.awt.*;
4   import java.awt.event.*;
5   import javax.swing.*;
6
```

Fig. 16.6   Customizing an applet via the **param** HTML tag (part 1 of 5).

```
7   public class LogoAnimator extends JPanel
8                           implements ActionListener {
9      protected ImageIcon images[];
10     protected int totalImages = 30,
11                     currentImage = 0,
12                     animationDelay = 50; // 50 millisecond delay
13     protected String imageName = "deitel";
14     protected Timer animationTimer;
15
16     public LogoAnimator()
17     {
18        initializeAnim();
19     }
20
21     // new constructor to support customization
22     public LogoAnimator( int num, int delay, String name )
23     {
24        totalImages = num;
25        animationDelay = delay;
26        imageName = name;
27
28        initializeAnim();
29     }
30
31     private void initializeAnim()
32     {
33        images = new ImageIcon[ totalImages ];
34
35        for ( int i = 0; i < images.length; ++i )
36           images[ i ] = new ImageIcon( "images/" +
37                              imageName + i + ".gif" );
38
39        // moved here so getPreferredSize can check the size of
40        // the first loaded image.
41        setSize( getPreferredSize() );
42
43        startAnimation();
44     }
45
46     public void paintComponent( Graphics g )
47     {
48        super.paintComponent( g );
49
50        if ( images[ currentImage ].getImageLoadStatus() ==
51             MediaTracker.COMPLETE ) {
52           images[ currentImage ].paintIcon( this, g, 0, 0 );
53           currentImage = ( currentImage + 1 ) % totalImages;
54        }
55     }
56
57     public void actionPerformed( ActionEvent e )
58     {
```

Fig. 16.6   Customizing an applet via the **param** HTML tag (part 2 of 5).

```
59          repaint();
60       }
61
62    public void startAnimation()
63    {
64       if ( animationTimer == null ) {
65          currentImage = 0;
66          animationTimer = new Timer( animationDelay, this );
67          animationTimer.start();
68       }
69       else  // continue from last image displayed
70          if ( ! animationTimer.isRunning() )
71             animationTimer.restart();
72    }
73
74    public void stopAnimation()
75    {
76       animationTimer.stop();
77    }
78
79    public Dimension getMinimumSize()
80    {
81       return getPreferredSize();
82    }
83
84    public Dimension getPreferredSize()
85    {
86       return new Dimension( images[ 0 ].getIconWidth(),
87                             images[ 0 ].getIconHeight() );
88    }
89
90    public static void main( String args[] )
91    {
92       LogoAnimator anim = new LogoAnimator();
93
94       JFrame app = new JFrame( "Animator test" );
95       app.getContentPane().add( anim, BorderLayout.CENTER );
96
97       app.addWindowListener(
98          new WindowAdapter() {
99             public void windowClosing( WindowEvent e )
100             {
101                System.exit( 0 );
102             }
103          }
104       );
105
106       app.setSize( anim.getPreferredSize().width + 10,
107                    anim.getPreferredSize().height + 30 );
108       app.show();
109    }
110 }
```

Fig. 16.6   Customizing an applet via the **param** HTML tag (part 3 of 5).

```
111   // Fig. 16.6: LogoApplet.java
112   // Customizing an applet via HTML parameters
113   //
114   // HTML parameter "animationdelay" is an int indicating
115   // milliseconds to sleep between images (default 50).
116   //
117   // HTML parameter "imagename" is the base name of the images
118   // that will be displayed (i.e., "deitel" is the base name
119   // for images "deitel0.gif," "deitel1.gif," etc.). The applet
120   // assumes that images are in an "images" subdirectory of
121   // the directory in which the applet resides.
122   //
123   // HTML parameter "totalimages" is an integer representing the
124   // total number of images in the animation. The applet assumes
125   // images are numbered from 0 to totalimages - 1 (default 30).
126
127   import java.awt.*;
128   import javax.swing.*;
129
130   public class LogoApplet extends JApplet{
131      public void init()
132      {
133         String parameter;
134
135         parameter = getParameter( "animationdelay" );
136         int animationDelay = ( parameter == null ? 50 :
137                                Integer.parseInt( parameter ) );
138
139         String imageName = getParameter( "imagename" );
140
141         parameter = getParameter( "totalimages" );
142         int totalImages = ( parameter == null ? 0 :
143                             Integer.parseInt( parameter ) );
144
145         // Create an instance of LogoAnimator
146         LogoAnimator animator;
147
148         if ( imageName == null || totalImages == 0 )
149            animator = new LogoAnimator();
150         else
151            animator = new LogoAnimator( totalImages,
152                          animationDelay, imageName );
153
154         setSize( animator.getPreferredSize().width,
155                  animator.getPreferredSize().height );
156         getContentPane().add( animator, BorderLayout.CENTER );
157
158         animator.startAnimation();
159      }
160   }
```

Fig. 16.6   Customizing an applet via the **param** HTML tag (part 4 of 5).

Fig. 16.6   Customizing an applet via the **param** HTML tag (part 5 of 5).

Class **LogoAnimator** has several new features to enable it to be used in and custom-ized by the **LogoApplet**. At line 13, instance variable **imageName** is defined. This will store either the default base name **"deitel"** that is part of every file name, or it will store the customized name passed to the applet from the HTML document.

There are now two constructors—a default constructor (line 16) and a constructor that takes arguments to customize the animation (line 22). Both constructors call our new utility method **initializeAnim** (line 31) to load the images and start the animation. The state-ments in **initializeAnim** were originally in the default constructor. The **setSize** method call at line 41 (which used to precede the loading of the images) was moved to line 41 so the **LogoAnimator** can be resized based on the width and height of the first image in the animation. To accommodate resizing based on the first image, method **getPre-ferredSize** (line 84) now returns a **Dimension** object containing the width and height of the first image in the animation.

Class **LogoApplet** (line 130) defines an **init** method in which the three HTML parameters are read with **Applet** method **getParameter** (lines 135, 139 and 141). After the parameters are read and the two integer parameters are converted to **int** values, the **if/else** structure at lines 148 through 152 creates a **LogoAnimator**. If the **ima-geName** is **null** or **totalImages** is **0**, the default **LogoAnimator** constructor is called and the default animation will be used. Otherwise, the **totalImages**, **anima-tionDelay** and **imageName** are passed to the three-argument **LogoAnimator** con-structor and the constructor uses those arguments to customize the animation.

16.9 Image Maps

A common technique for creating more interesting Web pages is the use of *image maps*. An image map is an image that has *hot areas* that the user can click to accomplish a task such as loading a different Web page into a browser. When the user positions the mouse pointer over a hot area, normally a descriptive message is displayed in the status area of the browser. This technique can be used to implement a *bubble help* system. When the user po-sitions the mouse pointer over a particular element on the screen, a system with bubble help usually displays a message in a small window that appears over the screen element. In Java, the message can be displayed in the status bar.

Figure 16.7 loads an image containing several icons from the *Java Multimedia Cyber Classroom*—the interactive-CD, multimedia version of this text. These icons may look familiar; they are designed to mimic the icons used in this book. The program allows the user to position the mouse pointer over an icon and display a descriptive message for the icon. Event handler **mouseMoved** (line 24) takes the *x*-coordinate of the mouse and passes it to method **translateLocation** (line 42). The *x*-coordinate is tested to determine the icon over which the mouse was positioned when the **mouseMoved** method was called. Method **translateLocation** then returns a message indicating what the icon represents. This message is displayed in the **appletviewer**'s (or browser's) status bar.

Clicking in this applet will not cause any action. In Chapter 21, "Networking," we discuss the techniques required to load another Web page into a browser. Once we have these networking capabilities, we can modify this applet to enable each icon to be associated with a different URL.

```
1   // Fig. 16.7: ImageMap.java
2   // Demonstrating an image map.
3   import java.awt.*;
4   import java.awt.event.*;
5   import javax.swing.*;
6
7   public class ImageMap extends JApplet {
8      private ImageIcon mapImage;
9      private int width, height;
10
11     public void init()
12     {
13         addMouseListener(
14            new MouseAdapter() {
15               public void mouseExited( MouseEvent e )
16               {
17                  showStatus( "Pointer outside applet" );
18               }
19            }
20         );
21
22         addMouseMotionListener(
23            new MouseMotionAdapter() {
24               public void mouseMoved( MouseEvent e )
25               {
26                  showStatus( translateLocation( e.getX() ) );
27               }
28            }
29         );
30
31         mapImage = new ImageIcon( "icons2.gif" );
32         width = mapImage.getIconWidth();
33         height = mapImage.getIconHeight();
34         setSize( width, height );
35     }
36
37     public void paint( Graphics g )
38     {
39         mapImage.paintIcon( this, g, 0, 0 );
40     }
41
```

Fig. 16.7   Demonstrating an image map (part 1 of 2).

```
42      public String translateLocation( int x )
43      {
44          // determine width of each icon (there are 6)
45          int iconWidth = width / 6;
46
47          if ( x >= 0 && x <= iconWidth )
48              return "Common Programming Error";
49          else if ( x > iconWidth && x <= iconWidth * 2 )
50              return "Good Programming Practice";
51          else if ( x > iconWidth * 2 && x <= iconWidth * 3 )
52              return "Performance Tip";
53          else if ( x > iconWidth * 3 && x <= iconWidth * 4 )
54              return "Portability Tip";
55          else if ( x > iconWidth * 4 && x <= iconWidth * 5 )
56              return "Software Engineering Observation";
57          else if ( x > iconWidth * 5 && x <= iconWidth * 6 )
58              return "Testing and Debugging Tip";
59
60          return "";
61      }
62  }
```

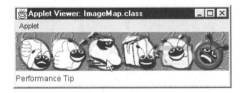

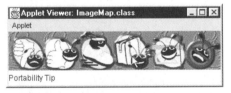

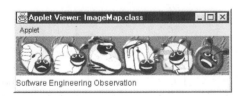

Fig. 16.7 Demonstrating an image map (part 2 of 2).

16.10 Java Plug-In

Throughout the text, we have defined many applets. Applets are supposed to be able to execute either in the **appletviewer** test program supplied with the J2SDK from Sun Microsystems or in a Java-enabled Web browser such as Sun's HotJava, Netscape's Communicator or Microsoft's Internet Explorer. Unfortunately, there are many different browser versions being used worldwide. Some support only Java 1.0 and many support Java 1.1, but few support the Java 2 Platform. Also, even the browsers that support Java 1.1 do so inconsistently.

Portability Tip 16.2

Not all Web browsers support Java. Those that do often support different versions and are not always consistent across all platforms.

If you would like to use the features of the Java 2 platform in an applet, Sun provides the *Java Plug-in* to bypass a browser's Java support and use a complete version of the *Java Runtime Environment (JRE)* that is installed on the user's local computer. If the JRE does not already exist on the client machine, it can be downloaded and installed.

Performance Tip 16.6

Because of the size of the Java Plug-in, it is difficult and inefficient to download the Plug-in for users with slower Internet connections. For this reason, the Plug-in is ideal for corporate intranets where users are connected to a high-speed network. Once the Plug-in is downloaded, it does not need to be downloaded again.

To specify that an applet should use the Java Plug-in rather than the browser's Java support, the applet's **<applet>**, **<param>** and **</applet>** tags in the HTML file must be converted to indicate that the Plug-in should be used to execute the applet. Sun provides a conversion utility called the *Java Plug-in 1.2 HTML Converter* that performs the conversion for you. Complete information on downloading and using the Java Plug-in and the HTML converter are available at the Web site

> **http://java.sun.com/products/plugin/**

Once you have downloaded and installed the Java Plug-in HTML converter, you can execute it by typing the command

> **java HTMLConverter**

in the directory where you installed the converter. The screen captures of Fig. 16.8 illustrate the Java Plug-in HTML Converter. Part 1 shows the GUI for the HTML Converter. We selected the **One File** radio button to indicate that we intend to convert one file. Click the **Browse...** button to the right of this option to choose the file to convert. This displays the dialog box in Part 2 of Fig. 16.8. After selecting the file to convert, the HTML converter appears as in Part 3 of Fig. 16.8. We expanded the **Template File** combo box to show the pre-defined conversion templates. We selected the first template that converts the HTML file so the plug-in is used for the applet when it executes in Microsoft's Internet Explorer or Netscape's Navigator browsers (Note: Navigator is now known as Communicator). After selecting the appropriate template file, click the **Convert...** button at the bottom of the HTML Converter window. The dialog box in Part 4 is displayed to show the status and results of the conversion.

The Java Plug-in HTML Converter. This program allows you to convert all the HTML files in one directory or select a specific file. In this case, **One File** is selected.

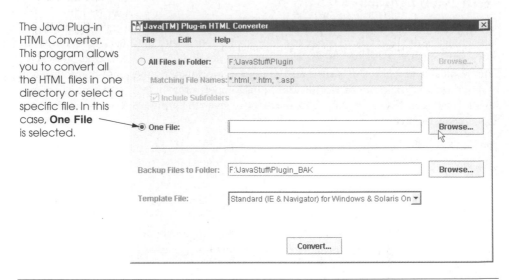

Fig. 16.8   The Java Plug-in HTML Converter (part 1 of 4).

This dialog allows you to select the file that will be converted.

Fig. 16.8   The Java Plug-in HTML Converter (part 2 of 4).

16.11 Internet and World Wide Web Resources

This section presents several Internet and Web resources for the Java Media Framework and other multimedia related sites.

http://java.sun.com/products/java-media/jmf/
> The *Java Media Framework home page* on the Java Web site. Here you can download the latest Sun implementation of the JMF. The site also contains the documentation for the JMF.

http://java.sun.com/products/java-media/jmf/forDevelopers/ playerapi/packages.html
> The on-line site for the **javax.media** API descriptions. These can also be downloaded from the JMF home page.

The HTML Converter window after a file is selected for conversion.

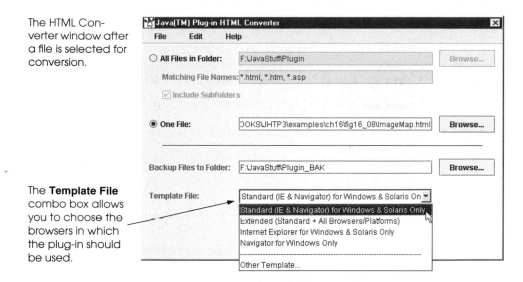

The **Template File** combo box allows you to choose the browsers in which the plug-in should be used.

Fig. 16.8   The Java Plug-in HTML Converter (part 3 of 4).

The confirmation dialog showing that one applet was found in the HTML file and converted.

Fig. 16.8   The Java Plug-in HTML Converter (part 4 of 4).

http://www.nasa.gov/gallery/index.html

The *NASA multimedia gallery* contains a wide variety of images, audio clips and video clips that you can download and use to test your Java multimedia programs.

http://sunsite.sut.ac.jp/multimed/

The *Sunsite Japan Multimedia Collection* also provides a wide variety of images, audio clips and video clips that you can download for educational purposes.

http://www.anbg.gov.au/anbg/index.html

The *Australian National Botanic Gardens* Web site provides links to sounds of many animals. Try the *Common Birds* link.

**http://java.sun.com/products/java-media/jmf/forDevelopers/
playerguide/index.html**

This site provides an HTML-based on-line guide to the Java Media Player.

Summary

- The Java Media Framework version 1.1 (JMF 1.1) is a standard extension to the Java API that provides enhanced processing of images and enhanced audio playback. The JMF also includes video playback capabilities for several video formats.

- **Applet** method **getImage** loads an **Image**. One version of **getImage** takes two arguments—a location where the image is stored and the file name of the image.

- **Applet** method **getDocumentBase** returns the location of the applet's HTML file on the Internet as an object of class **URL** (package **java.net**).

- A **URL** stores a Uniform (or Universal) Resource Locator—a standard format for an address of a piece of information on the Internet.

- Java supports two image formats—Graphics Interchange Format (GIF) and Joint Photographic Experts Group (JPEG). File names for each of these types end with **.gif** or **.jpg** (or **.jpeg**), respectively.

- Class **ImageIcon** provides constructors that allow an **ImageIcon** object to be initialized with an image from the local computer or with an image stored on a Web server on the Internet.

- **Graphics** method **drawImage** receives four arguments—a reference to the **Image** object in which the image is stored, the x and y coordinates where the image should be displayed and a reference to an **ImageObserver** object.

- Another version of **Graphics** method **drawImage** outputs a scaled image. The fourth and fifth arguments specify the width and height of the image for display purposes.

- Interface **ImageObserver** is implemented by class **Component** (an indirect superclass of **Applet**). **ImageObserver**s are notified to update an image that was displayed as the remainder of the image is loaded.

- **ImageIcon** method **paintIcon** displays the **ImageIcon**'s image. The method requires four arguments—a reference to the **Component** on which the image will be displayed, a reference to the **Graphics** object used to render the image, the x-coordinate of the upper-left corner of the image and the y-coordinate of the upper-left corner of the image.

- Class **ImageIcon**'s **paintIcon** method does not allow scaling of an image. The class provides method **getImage** which returns an **Image** reference that can be used with **Graphics** method **drawImage** to display a scaled version of an image.

- **Applet** method **play** has two forms:

```
public void play( URL location, String soundFileName );
public void play( URL soundURL );
```

One version loads the audio clip stored in file **soundFileName** from **location** and plays the sound. The other takes a **URL** that contains the location and the file name of the audio clip.

- **Applet** method **getDocumentBase** indicates the location of the HTML file that loaded the applet. Method **getCodeBase** indicates where the **.class** file for an applet is located.

- The sound engine that plays audio clips supports several audio file formats including Sun Audio file format (**.au** extension), Windows Wave file format (**.wav** extension), Macintosh AIFF file format (**.aif** or **.aiff** extension) and Musical Instrument Digital Interface (MIDI) file format (**.mid** or **.rmi** extensions). The Java Media Framework (JMF) supports other additional formats.

- **Applet** method **getAudioClip** has two forms that take the same arguments as the **play** method. Method **getAudioClip** returns a reference to an **AudioClip**. **AudioClip**s have three methods—**play**, **loop** and **stop**. Method **play** plays the audio once. Method **loop** continuously loops the audio clip. Method **stop** terminates an audio clip that is currently playing.

- The Java Media Player is capable of playing all the audio formats mentioned in Section 16.4 and a variety of other audio and video formats such as AVI (**.avi** extension), GSM (**.gsm** extension), MPEG-1 (**.mpg** extension), Apple QuickTime™ (**.mov** extension), RMF (**.rmf** extension), RTP (**.rtp** extension) and Vivo (**.viv** extension).

- A **JFileChooser** allows the user to select a file from the computer's local file system. **JFileChooser** method **setFileSelectionMode** sets the file selection mode. **JFileChooser** method **showOpenDialog** displays an **Open** dialog for choosing files to open. The method returns an integer that indicates the user's action (i.e., whether the user selected a file or cancelled the dialog). **JFileChooser** method **getSelectedFile** obtains a **File** object containing the name and location of the selected file.

- Class **Manager** (package **javax.media**) creates media players with method **createPlayer** that returns an object that implements the **Player** interface (package **javax.media**). Method **createPlayer** determines if the specified media clip is a valid and supported format. If so, it returns the correct **Player** for the specified media clip.

- Class **File** provides method **toURL** to convert the file name and location represented by the **File** object into a valid **URL** format.

- Programs can respond to media events generated by a **Player** by providing an event handler that implements interface **ControllerListener** (package **javax.media**).

- When a media event occurs, method **controllerUpdate** is invoked on the registered listeners and passed a **ContollerEvent** (package **javax.media**). This class has 21 direct and indirect subclasses that can also be arguments to method **controllerUpdate**. This provides programmers with flexible options for processing media events.

- A **RealizeCompleteEvent** occurs when the **Player** determines the type of media clip and loads the clip.

- **Player** method **getVisualComponent** obtains a **Component** on which the visual aspect of the media clip can be rendered. **Player** method **getControlPanelComponent** obtains a **Component** on which **Player** controls are displayed.

- A typical control bar for the Java Media Player contains a pause button, a position indicator, a mute button, a volume control and an information button. When a clip is paused, the control bar is displayed with a play button rather than a pause button.

- **Timer** objects generate **ActionEvent**s at fixed intervals in milliseconds and notify their registered **ActionListener**s that the events occurred. The **Timer** constructor receives two arguments—the delay in milliseconds and the **ActionListener**. **Timer** method **start** indicates that the **Timer** should start generating events. **Timer** method **stop** indicates that the **Timer** should stop generating events. **Timer** method **restart** indicates that the **Timer** should start generating events again.

- **ImageIcon** method **getImageLoadStatus** determines if an image is completely loaded into memory. The method returns **MediaTracker.COMPLETE** if the image is fully loaded.

- Images can be registered with an object of class **MediaTracker** to enable the program to determine when an image is loaded completely.

- GIF images can be stored in interlaced and non-interlaced formats. The format indicates the order in which the pixels of the image are stored. The pixels of a non-interlaced image are stored in the same order that the pixels appear on the screen. As a non-interlaced image is displayed, it appears in chunks from top to bottom as the pixel information is read. The pixels of an interlaced image are stored in rows of pixels, but the rows are out of order. When the image is displayed, it appears to fade in as the first batch of rows presents a rough outline of the picture and the subsequent batches of rows refine the displayed image until the entire image is complete.

- A common problem with animations is that the animation flickers as each image is displayed. This is normally due to the **update** method being called in response to each **repaint**. In subclasses of Swing's **JPanel** (or any other Swing component), method **update** is overridden to prevent clearing of the background.

- A technique used to produce smooth animation is graphics double buffering. While the program renders one image on the screen, it can build the next image in an off-screen buffer. Then, when it is time for that next image to be displayed, it can be placed on the screen smoothly.

- Swing GUI components are displayed using Java's drawing capabilities. Therefore, Swing GUI components are subject to many of the same drawing problems encountered with a typical animation. By default, Swing uses graphics double buffering to render all Swing GUI components.

- Applets can be customized via parameters (the **<param>** tag) that are supplied from the HTML file that invokes the applet. The **<param>** tag lines must appear between the starting **applet** tag and the ending **applet** tag. Each parameter has a **name** and a **value**.

- **Applet** method **getParameter** gets the **value** associated with a specific parameter and returns the **value** as a **String**. The argument passed to **getParameter** is a **String** containing the name of the parameter in the **param** tag. If there is no **param** tag containing the specified parameter, **getParameter** returns **null**.

- An image map is an image that has hot areas that the user can click to accomplish a task such as loading a different Web page into a browser.

- To use the features of the Java 2 platform in an applet, Sun provides the Java Plug-in to bypass a browser's Java support and use a complete version of the Java Runtime Environment (JRE) that is installed on the user's local computer.

- To specify that an applet should use the Java Plug-in rather than the browser's Java support, the applet's **<applet>**, **<param>** and **</applet>** tags in the HTML file must be converted to indicate that the Plug-in should be used to execute the applet. Sun provides a conversion utility called the Java Plug-in 1.2 HTML Converter that performs the conversion for you.

Terminology

.aif file name extension
.aiff file name extension
animating a series of images
animation
Apple QuickTime™ file (**.mov**)
audio clip
.au file name extension
AVI file (**.avi**)
.avi file name extension
bubble help system
control bar of the Java Media Player
ControllerEvent class
ControllerListener interface
controllerUpdate method
createPlayer method of class **Manager**
customize an applet
drawImage method of class **Graphics**
File class
getAudioClip method of class **Applet**
getCodeBase method of class **Applet**

getControlPanelComponent method
getDocumentBase method of class **Applet**
getHeight method of class **Component**
getIconHeight method of class **ImageIcon**
getIconWidth method of class **ImageIcon**
getImage method of class **Applet**
getImage method of class **ImageIcon**
getImageLoadStatus method
getParameter method of class **Applet**
getSelectedFile method of
getVisualComponent method of **Player**
getWidth method of class **Component**
.gif file name extension
graphics
graphics double buffering
Graphics Interchange Format (GIF)
.gsm file name extension
GSM file (**.gsm**)
height of an image
hot area of an image map

HTML file
Image class
image map
ImageIcon class
ImageObserver interface
images
information button
interlaced GIF image
Java Media Framework
Java Media Framework version 1.1 (JMF 1.1)
Java Media Player
Java Plug-in
Java Plug-in 1.2 HTML Converter
Java Runtime Environment (JRE)
java.net package
javax.media package
JFileChooser class
JFileChooser.CANCEL_OPTION
JFileChooser.FILES_ONLY
Joint Photographic Experts Group (JPEG)
.jpeg file name extension
.jpg file name extension
loop method of interface **AudioClip**
Macintosh AIFF file (**.aif** or **.aiff**)
Manager class
media event
MediaTracker class
MediaTracker.COMPLETE
.mid file name extension
.mov file name extension
MPEG-1 file (**.mpg**)
.mpeg file name extension
.mpg file name extension
multimedia
Musical Instrument Digital Interface (MIDI)
mute button
name attribute of **param** tag
non-interlaced GIF image
off-screen buffer
off-screen graphics context
off-screen image
Open dialog
paintIcon method of class **ImageIcon**

param tag
pause button
play button
play method of class **Applet**
play method of interface **AudioClip**
Player interface
position indicator
RealizeCompleteEvent class
reduce animation flicker
remove method of class **Container**
repaint method of class **Component**
restart method of class **Timer**
RMF file (**.rmf**)
.rmf file name extension
.rmi file name extension
RTP file (**.rtp**)
.rtp file name extension
Save dialog
scaling an image
setFileSelectionMode method
showOpenDialog method
sound
sound engine
space/time trade-off
start method of class **Timer**
start method of interface **Player**
stop method of class **Timer**
stop method of interface **AudioClip**
Sun Audio file (**.au**)
Sun Audio file format (**.au**)
Timer class
toURL method of class **File**
Uniform Resource Locator (URL)
update method of class **Component**
URL class
value attribute of **param** tag
video
Vivo file (**.viv**)
.viv file name extension
volume control
.wav file name extension
width of an image
Windows Wave file (**.wav**)

Good Programming Practice

16.1   When playing audio clips in an applet or application, provide a mechanism for the user to disable the audio.

16.2   In an applet, always display something while images load. The longer a user must wait to see information appear on the screen, the more likely they will leave the Web page before the information appears.

Look-and-Feel Observations

16.1   Swing components override method **update** to prevent clearing of the background (for transparent components) in response to **repaint** messages.

16.2   Swing GUI components are rendered using graphics double buffering by default.

Performance Tips

16.1   It is more efficient to load the frames of the animation as one image than to load each image separately (a painting program can be used to combine the frames of the animation into one image). If the images are being loaded from the World Wide Web, every image loaded requires a separate connection to the site where the images are stored.

16.2   Loading all the frames of an animation as one large image may force your program to wait to begin displaying the animation.

16.3   Some people who are experienced with **MediaTracker** objects have reported that they can have a detrimental effect on performance. Keep this in mind as an area to scrutinize if you need to tune your multimedia applications.

16.4   Using **MediaTracker** method **waitForAll** to wait for all registered images to completely load may result is a long delay between when the program begins execution and when the images are actually displayed. The more images and the larger the images, the more time the user will have to wait. Use **MediaTracker** method **waitForAll** only to wait for small numbers of images to load completely.

16.5   Double buffering can reduce or eliminate flicker in an animation, but it can visibly slow the speed at which the animation runs.

16.6   Because of the size of the Java Plug-in, it is difficult and inefficient to download the Plug-in for users with slower Internet connections. For this reason, the Plug-in is ideal for corporate intranets where users are connected to a high-speed network. Once the Plug-in is downloaded, it does not need to be downloaded again.

Portability Tips

16.1   Class **Image** is an **abstract** class, so **Image** objects cannot be created directly. To achieve platform independence, the Java implementation on each platform provides its own subclass of **Image** to store image information.

16.2   Not all Web browsers support Java. Those that do often support different versions and are not always consistent across all platforms.

Software Engineering Observation

16.1   When creating an animation for use in an applet, provide a mechanism for disabling the animation when the user browses a new Web page separate from the page on which the animation applet resides.

16.2   Class **ImageIcon** uses a **MediaTracker** object to determine the status of the image it is loading.

Self-Review Exercises

16.1   Fill in the blanks in each of the following:
   a) **Applet** method _____ loads an image into an applet.
   b) **Applet** method _____ returns as an object of class **URL** the location on the Internet of the HTML file that invoked the applet.
   c) A _____ is a standard format for an address of a piece of information on the Internet.
   d) **Graphics** method _____ displays an image on an applet.

e) An animation often flickers as each image is displayed. This is due to the applet's _____ method being called. When this method clears the applet, it does so by drawing a filled rectangle the size of the applet in the current background color. This covers the image that was just drawn causing a flicker.

f) With the technique of _____, while the program renders one image on the screen, it can be building the next image in an off-screen buffer. Then, when it is time for that next image to be displayed, it can be placed on the screen smoothly.

g) As an _____ image is displayed, it appears to fade in as the first batch of rows presents a rough outline of the picture and the subsequent batches of rows refine the displayed image until the entire image is complete.

h) There are two key pieces to implementing a graphics double buffer—an _____ reference and a _____ reference. The first is where the actual pixels to be displayed are stored; the second is used to draw the pixels.

i) Images can be registered with a _____ object to enable the program to determine when an image is loaded completely.

j) Java provides two mechanisms for playing sounds in an applet—the **Applet**'s *play* method and the *play* method from the _____ *interface.*

k) An _____ is an image that has *hot areas* that the user can click to accomplish a task such as loading a different Web page.

l) Method _____ of class **ImageIcon** displays the **ImageIcon**'s image.

16.2 State whether each of the following is true or false. If false, explain why.

a) Java currently supports two image formats. File names for each of these types end with **.jif** or **.gpg**, respectively.

b) Overriding the applet's **update** method to call **paint** without clearing the applet will significantly reduce animation flicker.

c) A sound will be garbage collected as soon as it is done playing.

d) Swing GUI components have built-in graphics double buffering.

Answers to Self-Review Exercises

16.1 a) **getImage**. b) **getDocumentBase**. c) **URL**. d) **drawImage**. e) **update**. f) graphics double buffering. g) interlaced. h) **Image, Graphics**. i) **MediaTracker**. j) **AudioClip**. k) image map. l) **paintIcon**.

16.2 a) False; should be **.gif** or **.jpg** b) True. c) False, the sound will be marked for garbage collection (if it is not referenced by an **AudioClip**) and will be garbage collected when the garbage collector is able to run. d) True.

Exercises

16.3 Describe how to make an animation "browser friendly."

16.4 Discuss the various aspects of flicker elimination in Java.

16.5 Explain the technique of graphics double buffering.

16.6 Describe the Java methods for playing and manipulating audio clips.

16.7 How can Java applets be customized with information from an HTML file?

16.8 How is a **MediaTracker** object used? What cautions should you keep in mind when using a **MediaTracker**? Do you need to use class **MediaTracker** when loading images with **ImageIcon**?

16.9 Explain how image maps are used. List ten applications of image maps.

16.10   *(Animation)* Create a a general-purpose Java animation program. Your program should allow the user to specify the sequence of frames to be displayed, the speed at which the images are displayed, audios that should be played while the animation is running and so on.

16.11   *(Story Teller)* Record audio for a large number of nouns, verbs, articles, prepositions, etc. Then use random number generation to forms sentences and have your program speak the sentences.

16.12   *(Limericks)* Modify the limerick writing program you wrote in Exercise 10.10 to sing the limericks your program creates.

16.13   *(Screensaver)* Use animation of a series of your favorite images to create a screensaver program. Create various special effects that explode the images, spin the images, fade them in and out, move them off the edge of the screen, and the like.

16.14   *(Randomly Erasing an Image)* Suppose an image is displayed in a rectangular screen area. One way to erase the image is simply to set every pixel to the same color immediately, but this is a dull visual effect. Write a Java program that displays an image then erases it by using random-number generation to select individual pixels to erase. After most of the image is erased, erase all of the remaining pixels at once. You can refer to individual pixels by having a line that starts and ends at the same point. You might try several variants of this problem. For example, you might display lines randomly or you might display shapes randomly to erase regions of the screen.

16.15   *(Random Inter-Image Transition)* Here is a nice visual effect. If you are displaying one image in a given area on the screen and you would like to transition to another image in the same screen area, store the new screen image in an off-screen buffer and randomly copy pixels from the new image to the display area overlaying the previous pixels at those locations. When the vast majority of the pixels have been copied, copy the entire new image to the display area to be sure you are displaying the complete new image. To implement this program you may need to use the **PixelGrabber** and **MemoryImageSource** classes (see the Java API documentation for descriptions of these classes). You might try several variants of this problem. For example, you might select all the pixels in a randomly selected straight line or shape in the new image and overlay those pixels above the corresponding positions of the old image.

16.16   *(Background Audio)* Add background audio to one of your favorite applications by using the **loop** method of class **AudioClip** to play the sound in the background while you interact with your application in the normal way. Rewrite the program to use the Java Media Player.

16.17   *(Project: Multimedia Aerobics)* Here is a product idea that could help you make your fortune! Millions of people do aerobics exercises every day to help stay fit. Develop a Java aerobics program that displays animated sequences of exercises with appropriate background music, sounds, instructions and words of encouragement. Internationalize your program by offering the instructions in several languages and by playing music appropriate for each region. Allow the users to customize their exercise programs to meet their particular exercise needs. Allow the users to customize their exercise programs for beginner, intermediate and advanced levels. Add other features as appropriate.

16.18   *(Project: Multimedia Authoring System)* Develop a general-purpose multimedia authoring system. Your program should allow the user to form multimedia presentations consisting of text, audios, images, animations and eventually, videos. Your program lets the user weave together a presentation consisting of any of these multimedia elements that are selected from a catalog your program displays. Provide controls to allow the user to customize the presentation dynamically as the presentation is delivered.

16.19   *(Video Games)* Video games have become wildly popular. Develop your own Java video game program. Have a contest with your classmates to develop the best original video game.

16.20   *(Scrolling Marquee Sign)* Create a Java program that scrolls dotted characters right-to-left (or left-to-right if that is appropriate for your language) across a Marquee-like display sign. As an option, display the text in a continuous loop so that after the text goes off the sign at one end it reappears at the other end.

16.21 *(Text Flasher)* Create a Java program that repeatedly flashes text on the screen. Do this by interspersing the text with a plain background color image. Allow the user to control the "blink speed" and the background color or pattern.

16.22 *(Image Flasher)* Create a Java program that repeatedly flashes an image on the screen. Do this by interspersing the image with a plain background color image.

16.23 *(Scrolling Image Marquee)* Create a Java program that scrolls an image across a Marquee screen.

16.24 *(Physics Demo: Bouncing Ball)* Develop an animated program that shows a bouncing ball. Give the ball a constant horizontal velocity. Allow the user to specify the coefficient of restitution, e.g., a coefficient of restitution of 75% means that after the ball bounces it returns to only 75% of its height before it was bounced. Your demo should take gravity into effect—this will cause the bouncing ball to trace a parabolic path. Track down a "boing" sound (like a spring bouncing) and play the sound every time the ball hits the ground.

16.25 *(Pendulum)* Develop an animated program that shows a pendulum swinging. Allow the user to specify a damping factor that gradually slows the pendulum to an eventual stop.

16.26 *(Project: Flight Simulator)* Develop your own flight simulator Java program. This is a very challenging project. It is also an excellent candidate for a contest with your classmates.

16.27 *(Towers of Hanoi)* Write an animated version of the Towers of Hanoi problem we presented in Exercise 6.37. As each disk is lifted off a peg or slid onto a peg play a "whooshing" sound. As each disk lands on the pile play a "clunking" sound. Play some appropriate background music.

16.28 *(Tortoise and the Hare)* Develop a multimedia version of the Tortoise and Hare simulation we presented in Exercise 7.41. You might record an announcer's voice calling the race, "The contenders are at the starting line." "And they're off!" "The Hare pulls out in front." "The Tortoise is coming on strong." etc. As the race proceeds, play the appropriate recorded audios. Play sounds to simulate the animals' running, and don't forget the crowd cheering! Do an animation of the animals racing up the side of the slippery mountain.

16.29 *(Bubble Help)* Use an image map to implement a "bubble help" facility. When the mouse cursor passes over a given image, display some appropriate text to assist your user who may not be sure what a particular image is supposed to designate. You might build in a bit of a delay so that the help messages are only displayed when the mouse cursor lingers over an image.

16.30 *(Digital Clock)* Implement a program that displays a digital clock on the screen. You might add options to scale the clock; display day, month and year; issue an alarm; play certain audios at designated times and the like.

16.31 *(Analog Clock)* Create a Java program that displays an analog clock with hour, minute and second hands that move appropriately as the time changes.

16.32 *(Dynamic Stock Portfolio Evaluator)* Create a Java program that will read a file describing an investor's stock portfolio. For each stock the investor owns, the file contains the stock ticker symbol and the number of shares of that stock the investor owns. The program then accesses some stock quotation service available over the Internet (this requires techniques from Chapter 21, Networking) and filters out only those stock transactions for the stocks in the investor's portfolio. As the program fetches new stock prices, it displays a spreadsheet on the screen and dynamically updates the spreadsheet. The spreadsheet shows each stock symbol, the latest price of that stock, the number of shares and the latest total value of shares of that stock. The spreadsheet also totals the latest value of the investor's entire portfolio. An investor could run your Java program in a small portion of his or her screen while proceeding with other work.

16.33   *(Dynamic Customized Newsletter)* After you complete Chapter 21 you will understand how to develop Internet-based Java applications that access the World Wide Web. Develop a "newspaper of the future" in which your user uses a graphical user interface to design a customized dynamic newspaper which meets that user's unique information needs. Then have your application harvest information from the World Wide Web at the designated intervals, possibly continuously. You'll be amazed to see how many popular publications offer computerized versions at no charge on the Web.

16.34   *(Dynamic Audio and Graphical Kaleidoscope)* Develop a kaleidoscope program that displays reflected graphics to simulate the popular children's toy. Incorporate audio effects that "mirror" your program's dynamically changing graphics.

16.35   *(Automatic Jigsaw Puzzle Generator)* Create a Java jigsaw puzzle generator and manipulator. Your user specifies an image. Your program loads and displays the image. Then your program breaks the image into randomly selected shapes and shuffles the shapes. The user then uses the mouse to move the puzzle pieces around to solve the puzzle. Add appropriate audio sounds as the pieces are being shuffled around and snapped back into place. You might keep tabs on each piece and where it really belongs and then use audio effects to help the user get the pieces into correct positions.

16.36   *(Teaching Juggling)* If you've ever tried juggling, you know how difficult it is. It is especially difficult to learn from a book, because books cannot possibly display the dynamics of juggling. Develop a multimedia-based Java program that helps frustrated juggling students (like the older author) learn how to juggle. In particular, your simulation should show the details of juggling various numbers of items. You should probably read a good book on juggling before you begin this assignment.

16.37   *(Maze Generator and Walker)* Develop a multimedia-based maze generator and traverser program based on the maze programs you wrote in Exercises 7.38, 7.39 and 7.40. Let the user customize the maze by specifying the number of rows and columns and by indicating the level of difficulty. Have an animated mouse walk the maze. Use audio to dramatize the movement of your mouse character.

16.38   *(Knight's Tour Walker)* Develop multimedia-based versions of the Knight's Tour programs you wrote in Exercises 7.22 and 7.23.

16.39   *(Pinball Machine)* Here's another contest problem. Develop a Java program that simulates a pinball machine of your own design. Have a contest with your classmates to develop the best original multimedia pinball machine. Use every possible multimedia trick you can think of to add "pizzazz" to your pinball game. Try to keep the game mechanisms close to those of real pinball games.

16.40   *(Roulette)* Study the rules for the game of roulette and implement a multimedia-based version of the game. Create an animated spinning roulette wheel. Use audio to simulate the sound of the ball jumping the various compartments that correspond to each of the numbers. Use an audio to simulate the sound of the ball falling into its final slot. While the roulette wheel is spinning, allow multiple players to place their bets. When the ball lands in its final slot, you should update the bank accounts of each of the players with the appropriate wins or losses.

16.41   *(Craps)* Simulate the complete game of craps. Use a graphical representation of a craps table. Allow multiple players to place their bets. Use an animation of the player who is rolling the dice and show the animated dice rolling eventually to a stop. Use audio to simulate some of the chatter around the craps table. After each roll, the system should update the bank accounts of each of the players depending on the bets they have made.

16.42   *(One-Armed Bandit)* Develop a multimedia simulation of a one-armed bandit. Have three spinning wheels. Place various fruits and symbols on each wheel. Use true random-number generation to simulate the spinning of each wheel and the stopping of each wheel on a symbol.

16.43   *(Horse Race)* Create a Java simulation of a horse race. Have multiple contenders. Use audios for a race announcer. Play the appropriate audios to indicate the correct status of each of the contenders throughout the race. Use audios to announce the final results. You might try to simulate the kind of horse race games that are often played at carnivals. The players get turns at the mouse and have to perform some skill-oriented manipulation with the mouse to advance their horses.

16.44   *(Shuffleboard)* Develop a multimedia-based simulation of the game of shuffleboard. Use appropriate audio and visual effects.

16.45   *(Game of Pool)* Create a multimedia-based simulation of the game of pool. Each player takes turns using the mouse to position a pool stick and to hit the stick against the ball at the appropriate angle to try to get the pool balls to fall into the pockets. Your program should keep score.

16.46   *(Fashion Designer)* Develop a multimedia-based fashion design tool that will help a fashion designer design high-fashion clothing. Your tool should allow the designer to choose colors, shapes, decorative accents and the like to create clothing designs.

16.47   *(Artist)* Design a Java art program that will give an artist a great variety of capabilities to draw, use images, use animations and the like to create a dynamic multimedia art display.

16.48   *(Fireworks Designer)* Create a Java program that someone might use to create a fireworks display. Create a variety of fireworks demonstrations. Then orchestrate the firing of the fireworks for maximum effect.

16.49   *(Floor Planner)* Develop a Java program that will help someone arrange furniture in his or her home. Add features that help the person achieve the best possible arrangement.

16.50   *(Crossword)* Crossword puzzles are among the most popular pastimes. Develop a crossword puzzle program. Your multimedia-based program should enable the player to place and erase words easily. Tie your program to a large computerized dictionary. Your program should be able to suggest words based on which letters have already been filled in. Provide other features that will make the crossword puzzle enthusiast's job easier.

16.51   *(15 Puzzle)* Write a multimedia-based Java program that enables the user to play the game of 15. There is a 4-by-4 board for a total of 16 slots. One of the slots is empty. The other slots are occupied by 15 tiles numbered 1 through 15. Any tile next to the currently empty slot can be moved into the currently empty slot by clicking on the tile. Your program should create the board with the tiles out of order. The goal is to arrange the tiles into sequential order row by row.

16.52   *(Synthesizer)* Develop a multimedia-based Java program that simulates a musical synthesizer. Your program should display a keyboard along with a variety of sound options. The user plays music by pressing the appropriate keys in sequence and for the proper duration. The user can select from a variety of instrument sounds like piano, clarinet, drums, cymbals and the like.

16.53   *(Player Piano)* Create a Java program that functions as a player piano. Your program receives encoded sheet music in a file indicating what notes or combinations of notes are to be played for what durations. You can prerecord audios for each of the 88 notes on the piano.

16.54   *(Sheet Music Generator/Player)* Write a Java program that displays sheet music for the files you created in the previous exercise.

16.55   *(Music Teacher)* Develop a Java program that will help a student learn to play the piano. Your program should display the keyboard and use a variety of visual and audio techniques.

16.56   *(Arithmetic Tutor)* Develop a multimedia version of the Computer-Assisted Instruction (CAI) systems you developed in Exercises 6.31, 6.32 and 6.33.

16.57   *(Karaoke)* Create a Karaoke system that plays the music for a song and displays the words for your user to sing at the appropriate time.

16.58   *(Calling Attention to an Image)* If you want to emphasize an image, you might place a row of simulated light bulbs around your image. You can let the light bulbs flash in unison or you can let them fire on and off in sequence one after the other.

16.59   *(Physics Demo: Kinetics)* If you have taken physics, implement a Java program that will demo concepts like energy, inertia, momentum, velocity, acceleration, friction, coefficient of restitution, gravity and others. Create visual effects and use audios for emphasis and realism.

16.60   *(On-Line Product Catalog)* Companies are rapidly realizing the potential for doing business on the Web. Develop an on-line multimedia catalog from which your customers may select products to be shipped. After reading Chapter 21, you will be able to handle the networking aspects of this problem. If you have an actual company, you should read the latest articles on secure transmission of credit card IDs over the Internet.

16.61   *(Reaction Time/Reaction Precision Tester)* Create a Java program that moves a randomly created shape around the screen. The user moves the mouse to catch and click on the shape. The shape's speed and size can be varied. Keep statistics on how much time the user typically takes to catch a shape of a given size. The user will probably have more difficulty catching faster moving smaller shapes.

16.62   *(Image Zooming)* Create a program that enables you to zoom in on, or away from, an image.

16.63   *(Calendar/Tickler File)* Create a general purpose calendar and "tickler" file. Use audio and images. For example, the program should sing "Happy Birthday" when you use it on your birthday. Have the program display images and play audios associated with important events. Have the program remind you in advance of important events. It would be nice, for example, to have the program give you a week's warning so you can pick up an appropriate greeting card for that special person.

16.64   *(Rotating Images)* Create a Java program that lets you rotate an image through some number of degrees (out of a maximum of 360 degrees). The program should let you specify that you want to spin the image continuously. The program should let you adjust the spin speed dynamically.

16.65   *(Coloring Black and White Photographs and Images)* Create a Java program that lets you paint a black and white photograph with color. Provide a color palette for selecting colors. Your program should let you apply different colors to different regions of the image.

16.66   *(Project: Automated Teller Machine) [Note: This project will require that you use advanced Java techniques from Chapters 16, 17 and 21. We suggest that you do as much as you can now with the Java graphics, GUI, multithreading and multimedia technologies you studied in Chapters 11 through 16. Then incorporate file processing after you complete Chapter 17 and incorporate client/ server networking after you complete Chapter 21. This is an excellent group project.]* One of the authors had the privilege of teaching at the division of one of the largest banks in the United States that builds the hardware and software for the automated teller machines that the bank deploys worldwide. During this teaching engagement the author got a behind-the-scenes peek at the "automated teller machine of the future." Develop the framework of a Java *application* that implements an automated teller machine and simulates its interaction with a bank's accounts maintained by another computer. The first version of your program should simulate automated teller machines pretty much as they operate today. Then let your creative juices flow and try to design your own version of the "automated teller machine of the future." Use graphics, animation, sound and any other capabilities of Java, the World Wide Web and the Internet that you wish to employ.

16.67   *(Multimedia-Based Simpletron Simulator)* Modify the Simpletron simulator that you developed in the exercises in the previous chapters to include multimedia features. Add computer-like sounds to indicate that the Simpletron is executing instructions. Add a breaking glass sound when a fatal error occurs. Use flashing lights to indicate which cells of memory and/or which registers are currently being manipulated. Use other multimedia techniques as appropriate to make your Simpletron simulator more valuable as an educational tool to its users.

16.68   *(Morse Code)* Modify your solution to Exercise 10.26 to output the morse code using audio clips. Use two different audio clips for the dot and dash characters in Morse code.

17

Files and Streams

Objectives

- To be able to create, read, write and update files.
- To understand the Java streams class hierarchy.
- To be able to use the **FileInputStream** and **FileOutputStream** classes.
- To be able to use the **ObjectInputStream** and **ObjectOutputStream** classes.
- To be able to use class **RandomAccessFile**.
- To be able to use a **JFileChooser** dialog to access files and directories.
- To become familiar with sequential-access and random-access file processing.
- To be able to use the **File** class.

I can only assume that a "Do Not File" document is filed in a "Do Not File" file.
Senator Frank Church
Senate Intelligence Subcommittee Hearing, 1975

Consciousness … does not appear to itself chopped up in bits. … A "river" or a "stream" are the metaphors by which it is most naturally described.
William James

I read part of it all the way through.
Samuel Goldwyn

It is quite a three-pipe problem.
Sir Arthur Conan Doyle

Outline

Summary • Terminology • Common Programming Errors • Good Programming Practices • Performance Tips • Software Engineering Observation • Self-Review Exercises • Answers to Self-Review Exercises • Exercises

17.1 Introduction

Storage of data in variables and arrays is temporary—the data is lost when a local variable "goes out of scope" or when the program terminates. *Files* are used for long-term retention of large amounts of data, even after the program that created the data terminates. Data maintained in files is often called *persistent data*. Computers store files on *secondary storage devices* such as magnetic disks, optical disks and magnetic tapes. In this chapter, we explain how data files are created, updated, and processed by Java programs. We consider both "sequential-access" files and "random-access" files and indicate the kinds of applications for which each is best suited. Stream processing is a large subject. We have two goals in this chapter—to introduce the sequential-access and random-access file processing paradigms and to provide the reader with sufficient stream processing capabilities to support the networking features introduced in Chapter 21.

File processing is one of the most important capabilities a language must have to support commercial applications that typically process massive amounts of persistent data. In this chapter we discuss Java's powerful and abundant file-processing and stream input/output features.

Software Engineering Observation 17.1

It would be dangerous to enable applets arriving from anywhere on the World Wide Web to be able to read and write files on the client system. By default, most web browsers prevent applets from performing file processing on the client system. Therefore, file-processing programs are generally implemented as Java applications.

17.2 Data Hierarchy

Ultimately, all data items processed by a computer are reduced to combinations of zeros and ones. This occurs because it is simple and economical to build electronic devices that can assume two stable states—one state represents **0** and the other state represents **1**. It is remarkable that the impressive functions performed by computers involve only the most fundamental manipulations of **0**s and **1**s.

The smallest data item in a computer can assume the value **0** or the value **1**. Such a data item is called a *bit* (short for "*b*inary dig*it*"—a digit that can assume one of two values). Computer circuitry performs various simple bit manipulations such as examining the value of a bit, setting the value of a bit, and reversing a bit (from **1** to **0** or from **0** to **1**).

It is cumbersome for programmers to work with data in the low-level form of bits. Instead, programmers prefer to work with data in forms such as *decimal digits* (i.e., 0, 1, 2, 3, 4, 5, 6, 7, 8 and 9), *letters* (e.g., A through Z, and a through z), and *special symbols* (i.e., $, @, %, &, *, (,), -, +, ", :, ?, /, and many others). Digits, letters, and special symbols are referred to as *characters*. The set of all characters used to write programs and represent data items on a particular computer is called that computer's *character set*. Since computers can process only **1**s and **0**s, every character in a computer's character set is represented as a pattern of **1**s and **0**s (characters in Java are *Unicode* characters composed of 2 *bytes*). Bytes are most commonly composed of eight bits. Programmers create programs and data items with characters; computers manipulate and process these characters as patterns of bits.

Just as characters are composed of bits, *fields* are composed of characters. A field is a group of characters that conveys meaning. For example, a field consisting of uppercase and lowercase letters can be used to represent a person's name.

Data items processed by computers form a *data hierarchy* in which data items become larger and more complex in structure as we progress from bits, to characters, to fields, etc.

A *record* (i.e., a `class` in Java) is typically composed of several fields (called instance variables in Java). In a payroll system, for example, a record for a particular employee might consist of the following fields:

1. Employee identification number

2. Name

3. Address

4. Hourly pay rate

5. Number of exemptions claimed

6. Year-to-date earnings

7. Amount of taxes withheld

Thus, a record is a group of related fields. In the preceding example, each of the fields belongs to the same employee. Of course, a particular company may have many employees, and will have a payroll record for each employee. A *file* is a group of related records. A company's payroll file normally contains one record for each employee. Thus, a payroll file for a small company might contain only 22 records, whereas a payroll file for a large company might contain 100,000 records. It is not unusual for a company to have many files, some containing millions, or even billions, of characters of information. Figure 17.1 illustrates the *data hierarchy*.

To facilitate the retrieval of specific records from a file, at least one field in each record is chosen as a *record key*. A record key identifies a record as belonging to a particular person or entity that is unique from all other records. In the payroll record described previously, the employee identification number would normally be chosen as the record key.

There are many ways of organizing records in a file. The most common type of organization is called a *sequential file* in which records are typically stored in order by the record-key field. In a payroll file, records are usually placed in order by employee identification number. The first employee record in the file contains the lowest employee identification number, and subsequent records contain increasingly higher employee identification numbers.

Most businesses utilize many different files to store data. For example, companies may have payroll files, accounts receivable files (listing money due from clients), accounts payable files (listing money due to suppliers), inventory files (listing facts about all the items handled by the business), and many other types of files. A group of related files is sometimes called a *database*. A collection of programs designed to create and manage databases is called a *database management system* (DBMS).

17.3 Files and Streams

Java views each file as a sequential *stream* of bytes (Fig. 17.2). Each file ends either with an *end-of-file marker* or at a specific byte number recorded in a system-maintained administrative data structure. When a file is *opened*, an object is created and a stream is associated with the object. Three stream objects are created for us automatically when we begin executing a Java program—**System.in**, **System.out** and **System.err**. The streams associated with these objects provide communication channels between a program and a particular file or device. For example, object **System.in** (*standard input stream object*) enables a program to input bytes from the keyboard, object **System.out** (*standard output stream object*) enables a program to output data to the screen, and object **System.err** (*standard error stream object*) enables a program to output error messages to the screen. Each of these streams can be redirected—e.g., **System.out** can be redirected to send its output to a file on disk.

To perform file processing in Java, the package **java.io** must be imported. This package includes definitions for the stream classes such as **FileInputStream** (for input from a file) and **FileOutputStream** (for output to a file). Files are opened by creating objects of these stream classes that inherit from classes **InputStream** and **OutputStream**, respectively. Thus, the methods of these stream classes can all be applied to file streams as well. To perform input and output of data types, objects of class **ObjectInputStream**, **DataInputStream**, **ObjectOutputStream** and **DataOutputStream** will be used together with the file stream classes. The inheritance relationships of many of the Java I/O classes are summarized in Fig. 17.3. The following discussion overviews the capabilities of each of the classes in Fig. 17.3.

Java offers many classes for performing input/output. In this section we give a brief overview of each and explain how they relate to one another. In the rest of the chapter, we put several key stream classes to work as we implement a variety of file-processing programs that create, manipulate and destroy sequential-access files and random-access files. We also include a detailed example on the **File** class which is useful for obtaining information about files and directories. In Chapter 21, "Networking," we use stream classes extensively to implement networking applications.

InputStream (a subclass of **Object**) and *OutputStream* (a subclass of **Object**) are **abstract** classes that define methods for performing input and output respectively; their derived classes override these methods.

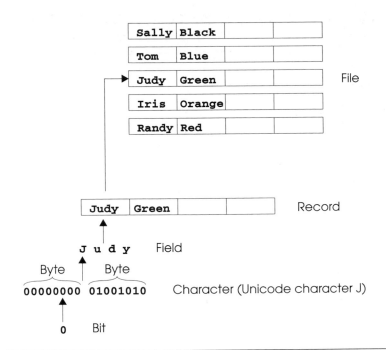

Fig. 17.1   The data hierarchy.

File input/output is done with ***FileInputStream*** (a subclass of **InputStream**) and ***FileOutputStream*** (a subclass of **OutputStream**). We use these classes extensively in the examples in this chapter.

Pipes are synchronized communication channels between threads. A pipe is established between two threads. One thread sends data to another by writing to a ***PipedOutputStream*** (a subclass of **OutputStream**). The target thread reads information from the pipe via a ***PipedInputStream*** (a subclass of **InputStream**).

0	1	2	3	4	5	6	7	8	9	...	n-1	
										...		end-of-file marker

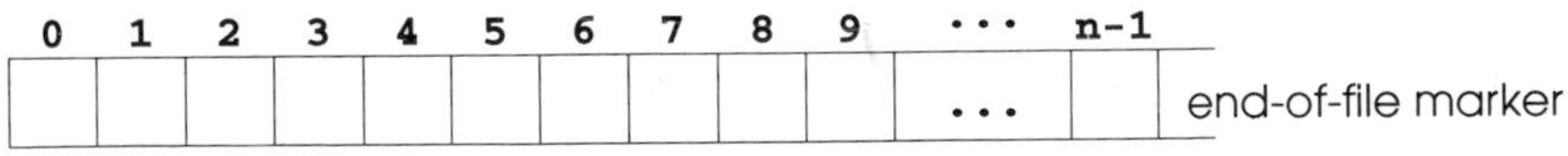

Fig. 17.2   Java's view of a file of *n* bytes.

A portion of the class hierarchy of the `java.io` package

```
java.lang.Object
    File
    FileDescriptor
```

Fig. 17.3   A portion of the class hierarchy of the **java.io** package (part 1 of 3).

A portion of the class hierarchy of the `java.io` package

```
InputStream
    ByteArrayInputStream
    FileInputStream
    FilterInputStream
        BufferedInputStream
        DataInputStream
        PushbackInputStream
    ObjectInputStream
    PipedInputStream
    SequenceInputStream
OutputStream
    ByteArrayOutputStream
    FileOutputStream
    FilterOutputStream
        BufferedOutputStream
        DataOutputStream
        PrintStream
    ObjectOutputStream
    PipedOutputStream
RandomAccessFile
Reader
    BufferedReader
        LineNumberReader
    CharArrayReader
    FilterReader
        PushbackReader
    InputStreamReader
        FileReader
    PipedReader
    StringReader
Writer
    BufferedWriter
    CharArrayWriter
    FilterWriter
```

Fig. 17.3   A portion of the class hierarchy of the **java.io** package (part 2 of 3).

A portion of the class hierarchy of the `java.io` package

```
OutputStreamWriter
    FileWriter
PipedWriter
PrintWriter
StringWriter
```

Fig. 17.3   A portion of the class hierarchy of the **java.io** package (part 3 of 3).

A *PrintStream* (a subclass of **FilterOutputStream**) is used for performing output to the screen (or the "standard output" as defined by your local operating system). Actually, we have been using **PrintStream** output throughout the text to this point; **System.out** is a **PrintStream** (as is **System.err**).

A **FilterInputStream** *filters* an **InputStream** and a **FilterOutStream** filters an **OutputStream**; filtering simply means that the filter stream provides additional functionality such as buffering, monitoring line numbers or aggregating data bytes into meaningful primitive-data-type units.

Reading data as raw bytes is fast but crude. Usually programs read data as aggregates of bytes that form an **int**, a **float**, a **double**, and so on.

A *RandomAccessFile* is useful for *direct-access applications* such as *transaction-processing applications* like airline-reservations systems and point-of-sale systems. With a *sequential-access file* each successive input/output request reads or writes the next consecutive set of data in the file. With a *random-access file*, each successive input/output request may be directed to any part of the file, perhaps widely separated from the part of the file referenced in the previous request. Direct-access applications provide rapid access to specific data items in large files; such applications are often used while people are waiting for answers—these answers must be made available quickly or the people may become impatient and "take their business elsewhere."

The **DataInput** interface is implemented by class **DataInputStream** and class **RandomAccessFile** (discussed later in the chapter) that each need to read primitive data types from a stream. **DataInputStream**s enable a program to read binary data from an **InputStream**. The **DataInput** interface includes methods **read** (for **byte** arrays), **readBoolean**, **readByte**, **readChar**, **readDouble**, **readFloat**, **read-Fully** (for **byte** arrays), **readInt**, **readLong**, **readShort**, **readUnsigned-Byte**, **readUnsignedShort**, **readUTF** (for strings) and **skipBytes**.

The **DataOutput** interface is implemented by class **DataOutputStream** (a subclass of **FilterOutputStream**) and class **RandomAccessFile** that each need to write primitive data types to an **OutputStream**. **DataOutputStream**s enable a program to write binary data to an **OutputStream**. The **DataOutput** interface includes methods **flush**, **size**, **write** (for a **byte**), **write** (for a **byte** array), **write-Boolean**, **writeByte**, **writeBytes**, **writeChar**, **writeChars** (for Unicode **String**s), **writeDouble**, **writeFloat**, **writeInt**, **writeLong**, **writeShort** and **writeUTF**.

Buffering is an I/O-performance-enhancement technique. With a **BufferedOutputStream** (a subclass of class **FilterOutputStream**) each output statement does not necessarily result in an actual physical transfer of data to the output device. Rather, each output operation is directed to a region in memory called a *buffer* that is large enough to hold the data of many output operations. Then actual transfer to the output device is performed in one large *physical output operation* each time the buffer fills. The output operations directed to the output buffer in memory are often called *logical output operations*.

Performance Tip 17.1

Because typical physical output operations are extremely slow compared to typical processor speeds, buffering outputs normally yields significant performance improvements over unbuffered outputs.

With a **BufferedInputStream** (a subclass of class **FilterInputStream**) many "logical" chunks of data from a file are read as one large *physical input operation* into a memory buffer. As a program requests each new chunk of data, it is taken from the buffer (this is sometimes referred to as a *logical input operation*). When the buffer is empty, the next actual physical input operation from the input device is performed to read in the next group of "logical" chunks of data. Thus, the number of actual physical input operations is small compared with the number of read requests issued by the program.·

Performance Tip 17.2

Because typical input operations are extremely slow compared to processor speeds, buffering inputs normally yields significant performance improvements over unbuffered inputs.

With a **BufferedOutputStream** a partially filled buffer can be forced out to the device at any time with an explicit **flush** as follows:

```
testBufferedOutputStream.flush();
```

A **PushBackInputStream** (a subclass of class **FilterInputStream**) is used for more exotic applications than most users will need. Essentially, the application reading a **PushBackInputStream** reads bytes from the stream and forms aggregates consisting of several bytes. Sometimes, to determine that one aggregate is complete, the application must read the first character the "past the end" of the first aggregate. Once the program has determined that the current aggregate is complete, the extra character is "pushed back" onto the stream. **PushBackInputStream**s are used by programs like compilers that *parse* their inputs, i.e., break them into meaningful units (such as the keywords, identifiers and operators that the Java compiler must recognize).

When object instance variables are output to a disk file, in a sense we lose the object's type information. We only have data, not type information, on a disk. If the program that is going to read this data knows what object type it corresponds to, then the data is simply read into objects of that type. Sometimes we would like to read or write an entire object to a file. The **ObjectInputStream** and **ObjectOutputStream** classes which respectively implement the **ObjectInput** and **ObjectOutput** interfaces, are used for this purpose. We often chain **ObjectInputStream**s to **FileInputStream**s. (We also chain **ObjectOutputStream**s to **FileOutputStream**s.) The **ObjectOutput** interface has a **writeObject** which takes an **Object** as an argument and writes its information to the **OutputStream**. Correspondingly, the **ObjectInput** interface requires method **readObject** which reads and returns an **Object** from an **Input-**

Stream. This object can then be cast to the desired type. Additionally, these interfaces include other **Object**-centric methods as well as the same methods as **DataInput** and **DataOutput** for reading and writing primitive data types.

Java stream I/O includes capabilities for inputting from **byte** arrays in memory and outputting to **byte** arrays in memory. A **ByteArrayInputStream** (a subclass of **abstract** class **InputStream**) performs its inputs from a **byte** array in memory. A **ByteArrayOutputStream** (a subclass of **abstract** class **OutputStream**) outputs to a **byte** array in memory. An application of **byte**-array I/O is data validation. A program can input an entire line at a time from the input stream into a **byte** array. Then a validation routine can scrutinize the contents of the **byte** array and correct the data, if necessary. The program can now proceed to input from the **byte** array, knowing that the input data is in the proper format. Outputting to a **byte** array is a nice way to take advantage of the powerful output formatting capabilities of Java streams. Data can be prepared in a **byte** array to mimic the edited screen format. That array could then be written to a disk file to preserve the screen image.

A **SequenceInputStream** (a subclass of **abstract** class **InputStream**) enables several **InputStream**s to be concatenated so that the program sees the group as one continuous **InputStream**. As the end of each input stream is reached, the stream is closed and the next stream in the sequence is opened.

Class *BufferedReader* (a subclass of **abstract** class *Reader*) and class *BufferedWriter* (a subclass of **abstract** class *Writer*) enable efficient buffering for character-based streams. Character-based streams use Unicode characters—such streams can process data in any language that is represented by the Unicode character set.

Class *CharArrayReader* and class *CharArrayWriter* read and write a stream of characters to a character array.

A *PushbackReader* (a subclass of **abstract** class *FilterReader*) enables characters to be placed back on a character stream. A *LineNumberReader* (a subclass of *BufferedReader*) is a buffered character-stream that keeps track of line numbers (i.e., a newline, a return or a carriage-return line-feed combination).

Class *FileReader* (a subclass of *InputStreamReader*) and class *FileWriter* (a subclass of *OutputStreamWriter*) read and write characters to a file. Class *PipedReader* and class *PipedWriter* are piped-character streams. Class *StringReader* and *StringWriter* read and write characters to **String**s. A *PrintWriter* writes characters to a stream.

Class **File** enables programs to obtain information about a file or directory. We discuss class **File** extensively in Section 17.12

17.4 Creating a Sequential-Access File

Java imposes no structure on a file. Thus, notions like "record" do not exist in Java files. Therefore, the programmer must structure files to meet the requirements of applications. In the following example, we see how the programmer can impose a simple record structure on a file. First we present the program, then we analyze it in detail.

Figure 17.4 creates a simple sequential-access file that might be used in an accounts receivable system to help manage the money owed by a company's credit clients. For each client, the program obtains an account number, the client's first name, the client's last name, and the client's balance (i.e., the amount the client still owes the company for goods and services received in the past). The data obtained for each client constitutes a record for that client. The account number is used as the record key in this application; that is, the file will be created and maintained in account number order. This program assumes the user enters the records in account number order. In a comprehensive accounts receivable system, a sorting capability would be provided so the user could enter the records in any order—the records would then be sorted and written to the file.

```java
1    // Fig. 17.4: BankUI.java
2    // A reusable GUI for the examples in this chapter.
3    package com.deitel.jhtp3.ch17;
4    import java.awt.*;
5    import javax.swing.*;
6
7    public class BankUI extends JPanel {
8       protected final static String names[] = { "Account number",
9          "First name", "Last name", "Balance",
10         "Transaction Amount" };
11      protected JLabel labels[];
12      protected JTextField fields[];
13      protected JButton doTask, doTask2;
14      protected JPanel innerPanelCenter, innerPanelSouth;
15      protected int size = 4;
16      public static final int ACCOUNT = 0, FIRST = 1, LAST = 2,
17                              BALANCE = 3, TRANSACTION = 4;
18
19      public BankUI()
20      {
21         this( 4 );
22      }
23
24      public BankUI( int mySize )
25      {
26         size = mySize;
27         labels = new JLabel[ size ];
28         fields = new JTextField[ size ];
29
30         for ( int i = 0; i < labels.length; i++ )
31            labels[ i ] = new JLabel( names[ i ] );
32
33         for ( int i = 0; i < fields.length; i++ )
34            fields[ i ] = new JTextField();
35
36         innerPanelCenter = new JPanel();
37         innerPanelCenter.setLayout( new GridLayout( size, 2 ) );
38
39         for ( int i = 0; i < size; i++ ) {
40            innerPanelCenter.add( labels[ i ] );
41            innerPanelCenter.add( fields[ i ] );
42         }
43
```

Fig. 17.4   Creating a sequential file (part 1 of 7).

Because most of the programs in this chapter have a similar GUI, we created class **BankUI** to encapsulate this GUI (see the second screen in Fig. 17.4). We also created class **BankAccountRecord** to encapsulate the client record information (i.e., account, first name, etc.) used by the examples in this chapter.

```
44           doTask = new JButton();
45           doTask2 = new JButton();
46           innerPanelSouth = new JPanel();
47           innerPanelSouth.add( doTask2 );
48           innerPanelSouth.add( doTask );
49
50           setLayout( new BorderLayout() );
51           add( innerPanelCenter, BorderLayout.CENTER );
52           add( innerPanelSouth, BorderLayout.SOUTH );
53           validate();
54       }
55
56       public JButton getDoTask() { return doTask; }
57
58       public JButton getDoTask2() { return doTask2; }
59
60       public JTextField[] getFields() { return fields; }
61
62       public void clearFields()
63       {
64           for ( int i = 0; i < size; i++ )
65               fields[ i ].setText( "" );
66       }
67
68       public void setFieldValues( String s[] )
69           throws IllegalArgumentException
70       {
71           if ( s.length != size )
72               throw new IllegalArgumentException( "There must be "
73                   + size + " Strings in the array" );
74
75           for ( int i = 0; i < size; i++ )
76               fields[ i ].setText( s[ i ] );
77       }
78
79       public String[] getFieldValues()
80       {
81           String values[] = new String[ size ];
82
83           for ( int i = 0; i < size; i++ )
84               values[ i ] = fields[ i ].getText();
85
86           return values;
87       }
88   }
```

Fig. 17.4   Creating a sequential file (part 2 of 7).

```
89   // Fig. 17.4: BankAccountRecord.java
90   // A class that represents one record of information.
91   package com.deitel.jhtp3.ch17;
92   import java.io.Serializable;
93
94   public class BankAccountRecord implements Serializable {
95      private int account;
96      private String firstName;
97      private String lastName;
98      private double balance;
99
100     public BankAccountRecord()
101     {
102        this( 0, "", "", 0.0 );
103     }
104
105     public BankAccountRecord( int acct, String first,
106                               String last, double bal )
107     {
108        setAccount( acct );
109        setFirstName( first );
110        setLastName( last );
111        setBalance( bal );
112     }
113
114     public void setAccount( int acct )
115     {
116        account = acct;
117     }
118
119     public int getAccount() { return account; }
120
121     public void setFirstName( String first )
122     {
123        firstName = first;
124     }
125
126     public String getFirstName() { return firstName; }
127
128     public void setLastName( String last )
129     {
130        lastName = last;
131     }
132
133     public String getLastName() { return lastName; }
134
135     public void setBalance( double bal )
136     {
137        balance = bal;
138     }
139
140     public double getBalance() { return balance; }
141  }
```

Fig. 17.4   Creating a sequential file (part 3 of 7).

```
142  // Fig. 17.4: CreateSequentialFile.java
143  // Demonstrating object output with class ObjectOutputStream.
144  // The objects are written sequentially to a file.
145  import java.io.*;
146  import java.awt.*;
147  import java.awt.event.*;
148  import javax.swing.*;
149  import com.deitel.jhtp3.ch17.BankUI;
150  import com.deitel.jhtp3.ch17.BankAccountRecord;
151
152  public class CreateSequentialFile extends JFrame {
153     private ObjectOutputStream output;
154     private BankUI userInterface;
155     private JButton enter, open;
156
157     public CreateSequentialFile()
158     {
159        super( "Creating a Sequential File of Objects" );
160
161        getContentPane().setLayout( new BorderLayout() );
162        userInterface = new BankUI();
163
164        enter = userInterface.getDoTask();
165        enter.setText( "Enter" );
166        enter.setEnabled( false );  // disable button to start
167        enter.addActionListener(
168           new ActionListener() {
169              public void actionPerformed( ActionEvent e )
170              {
171                 addRecord();
172              }
173           }
174        );
175
176        addWindowListener(
177           new WindowAdapter() {
178              public void windowClosing( WindowEvent e )
179              {
180                 if ( output != null ) {
181                    addRecord();
182                    closeFile();
183                 }
184                 else
185                    System.exit( 0 );
186              }
187           }
188        );
189        open = userInterface.getDoTask2();
190
191        open.setText( "Save As" );
192        open.addActionListener(
193           new ActionListener() {
```

Fig. 17.4   Creating a sequential file (part 4 of 7).

```
194                     public void actionPerformed( ActionEvent e )
195                     {
196                         openFile();
197                     }
198                }
199            );
200            getContentPane().add( userInterface,
201                                    BorderLayout.CENTER );
202
203            setSize( 300, 200 );
204            show();
205        }
206
207        private void openFile()
208        {
209            JFileChooser fileChooser = new JFileChooser();
210            fileChooser.setFileSelectionMode(
211                JFileChooser.FILES_ONLY );
212
213            int result = fileChooser.showSaveDialog( this );
214
215            // user clicked Cancel button on dialog
216            if ( result == JFileChooser.CANCEL_OPTION )
217                return;
218
219            File fileName = fileChooser.getSelectedFile();
220
221            if ( fileName == null ||
222                    fileName.getName().equals( "" ) )
223                JOptionPane.showMessageDialog( this,
224                    "Invalid File Name",
225                    "Invalid File Name",
226                    JOptionPane.ERROR_MESSAGE );
227            else {
228                // Open the file
229                try {
230                    output = new ObjectOutputStream(
231                            new FileOutputStream( fileName ) );
232                    open.setEnabled( false );
233                    enter.setEnabled( true );
234                }
235                catch ( IOException e ) {
236                    JOptionPane.showMessageDialog( this,
237                        "Error Opening File", "Error",
238                        JOptionPane.ERROR_MESSAGE );
239                }
240            }
241        }
242
243        private void closeFile()
244        {
245            try {
246                output.close();
```

Fig. 17.4   Creating a sequential file (part 5 of 7).

```
247            System.exit( 0 );
248         }
249         catch( IOException ex ) {
250            JOptionPane.showMessageDialog( this,
251               "Error closing file",
252               "Error", JOptionPane.ERROR_MESSAGE );
253            System.exit( 1 );
254         }
255      }
256
257      public void addRecord()
258      {
259         int accountNumber = 0;
260         BankAccountRecord record;
261         String fieldValues[] = userInterface.getFieldValues();
262
263         // If the account field value is not empty
264         if ( ! fieldValues[ 0 ].equals( "" ) ) {
265            // output the values to the file
266            try {
267               accountNumber =
268                  Integer.parseInt( fieldValues[ 0 ] );
269
270               if ( accountNumber > 0 ) {
271                  record = new BankAccountRecord(
272                     accountNumber, fieldValues[ 1 ],
273                     fieldValues[ 2 ],
274                     Double.parseDouble( fieldValues[ 3 ] ) );
275                  output.writeObject( record );
276                  output.flush();
277               }
278
279               // clear the TextFields
280               userInterface.clearFields();
281            }
282            catch ( NumberFormatException nfe ) {
283               JOptionPane.showMessageDialog( this,
284                  "Bad account number or balance",
285                  "Invalid Number Format",
286                  JOptionPane.ERROR_MESSAGE );
287            }
288            catch ( IOException io ) {
289               closeFile();
290            }
291         }
292      }
293
294      public static void main( String args[] )
295      {
296         new CreateSequentialFile();
297      }
298 }
```

Fig. 17.4   Creating a sequential file (part 6 of 7).

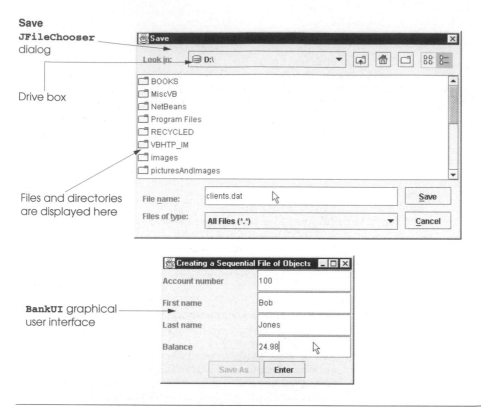

Save
JFileChooser
dialog

Drive box

Files and directories
are displayed here

BankUI graphical
user interface

Fig. 17.4   Creating a sequential file (part 7 of 7).

Class **BankUI** (lines 7 through 88) contains two **JButton**s and arrays of **JLabel**s
and **JTextField**s. The number of **JLabel**s and **JTextField**s is set with the constructor on line 24. A no argument constructor (line 19) is also provided that passes a
default value of four to the constructor of line 24. Methods **getFieldValues**, **set-
FieldValues** and **clearFields** are used to manipulate the text of the **JText-
Field**s. Methods **getFields**, **getDoTask** and **getDoTask2** return individual GUI
components so that a client program can add **ActionListener**s, etc.

Class **BankAccountRecord** (lines 89 through 141) implements interface **Serializable** which allows objects of **BankAccountRecord** to be used with **Object-
InputStream**s and **ObjectOutputStream**s. This class contains **private** data
members **account**, **firstName**, **lastName** and **balance**. This class also provides
public "get" and "set" methods for accessing the **private** data members.

Now let us discuss the code that creates the sequential-access file (line 142). In this
example, we introduce class **JFileChooser** (package **javax.swing**) for selecting
files (see the first screen in Fig. 17.4). Line 209 constructs a **JFileChooser** instance and
assigns it to reference **fileChooser**. Line 210, calls method **setFileSelection-
Mode** to specify whether or not files and/or directories can be selected by the user. For this
program, we use **JFileChooser static** constant **FILES_ONLY** to indicate that only
files can be selected. Other **static** constants include **FILES_AND_DIRECTORIES** and
DIRECTORIES_ONLY.

Line 213,

```
int result = fileChooser.showSaveDialog( this );
```

calls method ***showSaveDialog*** to display the **JFileChooser** dialog titled **Save**. Argument **this** specifies the **JFileChooser** dialog's *parent* which is used to determine the position of the dialog on the screen (if **null** is passed, the dialog is displayed in the center of the window). When displayed, a **JFileChooser** dialog does not allow the user to interact with any other program window until the **JFileChooser** dialog is closed (by clicking **Save** or **Close**). Dialogs that behave in this fashion are called *modal* dialogs. The user selects the drive, directory and file name and clicks **Save**. Method **showSaveDialog** returns an integer specifying which button (**Save** or **Close**) was clicked to close the dialog. Line 216, tests if **Cancel** was clicked by comparing **result** to **static** constant *CANCEL_OPTION*. If so, the method is exited.

The file the user selected is retrieved by calling method ***getSelectedFile*** (line 219). Method **getSelectedFile** returns an object—of type **File**—that encapsulates information about the file (i.e., name, location, etc.). This **File** object does not open the file. We assign this **File** object to the reference **fileName**.

As stated previously, files are opened by creating objects of stream classes **FileInputStream** and **FileOutputStream**. In this example, the file is to be opened for output, so a **FileOutputStream** object is created with the constructor call (line 231)

```
new FileOutputStream( fileName )
```

One argument is passed to the **FileOutputStream**'s constructor—a **File** object. Existing files opened for output are *truncated*—all data in the file is discarded.

Class **FileOutputStream** provides methods for writing **byte** arrays and individual **byte**s to a file. For this program, we need to write objects to a file—a capability not provided by **FileOutputStream**. The solution to this problem is a technique called *chaining of stream objects*—the ability to add the services of one stream to another. To chain an **ObjectOutputStream** to the **FileOutputStream**, we pass the **FileOutputStream** object to the **ObjectOutputStream**'s constructor (line 231)

```
output = new ObjectOutputStream(
         new FileOutputStream( fileName ) );
```

If an ***IOException*** (an exception that is thrown when a file is opened for writing on a drive with insufficient space, a read-only file is opened for writing, a nonexistent file is opened for reading, etc.) occurs, a **JOptionPane** is displayed. If construction of the two streams does not throw an **IOException**, the file is open. Reference **output** can then be used to write objects to the file.

Common Programming Error 17.1

Opening an existing file for output when, in fact, the user wants to preserve the file; the contents of the file are discarded without warning.

Common Programming Error 17.2

Not opening a file before attempting to reference it in a program.

The program assumes data is input correctly and in the proper record number order. The user populates the **JTextField**s and clicks **Enter** to write the data to the file. The **Enter** button's **actionPerformed** method calls our method **addRecord** to perform the write operation. Method *writeObject* is called (line 275) to write the **record** object to file. Method *flush* (line 276) is called to ensure that any data stored in memory is written to the file.

When the user clicks the close box (the **x** in the GUI's top-right corner), **output** is tested against **null** for equality (line 180). If the stream is open, methods **addRecord** and **closeFile** (line 243) are called. Method **closeFile** calls method *close* for **output**.

Performance Tip 17.3

Always release resources explicitly and at the earliest possible moment at which it is determined that the resource is no longer needed. This makes the resource immediately available to be reused by your program or by another program, thus improving resource utilization.

When using chained stream objects, the outermost object (the **ObjectOutputStream** in this example) should be used to close the file.

Performance Tip 17.4

Explicitly close each file as soon as it is known that the program will not reference the file again. This can reduce resource usage in a program that will continue executing long after it no longer needs to be referencing a particular file. This practice also improves program clarity.

In the sample execution for the program of Fig. 17.4, we entered information for five accounts (see Fig. 17.5). The program does not show how the data records actually appear in the file. To verify that the file has been created successfully, in the next section we create a program to read the file.

17.5 Reading Data from a Sequential-Access File

Data are stored in files so that they may be retrieved for processing when needed. The previous section demonstrated how to create a file for sequential access. In this section, we discuss how to read data sequentially from a file

Sample Data			
100	Bob	Jones	24.98
200	Steve	Doe	-345.67
300	Pam	White	0.00
400	Sam	Stone	-42.16
500	Sue	Rich	224.62

Fig. 17.5   Sample data for the program of Fig. 17.4.

The program of Fig. 17.6 reads records from a file created by the program of Fig. 17.4 and displays the contents of the records. Files are opened for input by creating a **FileInputStream** object. The name of the file to open is passed as an argument to the **FileInputStream** constructor. In the last example (Fig. 17.4), we wrote objects to the file using an **ObjectOutputStream** object. Data must be read from the file in the same format in which it was written to the file. Therefore, we use an **ObjectInputStream** chained to a **FileInputStream** in this program.

```java
1   // Fig. 17.6: ReadSequentialFile.java
2   // This program reads a file of objects sequentially
3   // and displays each record.
4   import java.io.*;
5   import java.awt.*;
6   import java.awt.event.*;
7   import javax.swing.*;
8   import com.deitel.jhtp3.ch17.*;
9
10  public class ReadSequentialFile extends JFrame {
11      private ObjectInputStream input;
12      private BankUI userInterface;
13      private JButton nextRecord, open;
14
15      // Constructor -- initialize the Frame
16      public ReadSequentialFile()
17      {
18          super( "Reading a Sequential File of Objects" );
19
20          getContentPane().setLayout( new BorderLayout() );
21          userInterface = new BankUI();
22          nextRecord = userInterface.getDoTask();
23          nextRecord.setText( "Next Record" );
24          nextRecord.setEnabled( false );
25
26          nextRecord.addActionListener(
27              new ActionListener() {
28                  public void actionPerformed( ActionEvent e )
29                  {
30                      readRecord();
31                  }
32              }
33          );
34
35          addWindowListener(
36              new WindowAdapter() {
37                  public void windowClosing( WindowEvent e )
38                  {
39                      if ( input != null )
40                          closeFile();
41
```

Fig. 17.6   Reading a sequential file (part 1 of 4).

```
42                      System.exit( 0 );
43                   }
44               }
45           );
46           open = userInterface.getDoTask2();
47
48           open.setText( "Open File" );
49           open.addActionListener(
50              new ActionListener() {
51                 public void actionPerformed( ActionEvent e )
52                 {
53                    openFile();
54                 }
55              }
56           );
57
58           getContentPane().add( userInterface,
59                                 BorderLayout.CENTER );
60           pack();
61           setSize( 300, 200 );
62           show();
63       }
64
65       private void openFile()
66       {
67           JFileChooser fileChooser = new JFileChooser();
68
69           fileChooser.setFileSelectionMode(
70              JFileChooser.FILES_ONLY );
71           int result = fileChooser.showOpenDialog( this );
72
73           // user clicked Cancel button on dialog
74           if ( result == JFileChooser.CANCEL_OPTION )
75              return;
76
77           File fileName = fileChooser.getSelectedFile();
78
79           if ( fileName == null ||
80               fileName.getName().equals( "" ) )
81              JOptionPane.showMessageDialog( this,
82                 "Invalid File Name",
83                 "Invalid File Name",
84                 JOptionPane.ERROR_MESSAGE );
85           else {
86              // Open the file
87              try {
88                 input = new ObjectInputStream(
89                          new FileInputStream( fileName ) );
90                 open.setEnabled( false );
91                 nextRecord.setEnabled( true );
92              }
```

Fig. 17.6   Reading a sequential file (part 2 of 4).

```
93            catch ( IOException e ) {
94               JOptionPane.showMessageDialog( this,
95                  "Error Opening File", "Error",
96                  JOptionPane.ERROR_MESSAGE );
97            }
98         }
99      }
100
101    public void readRecord()
102    {
103       BankAccountRecord record;
104
105       // input the values from the file
106       try {
107          record = ( BankAccountRecord ) input.readObject();
108          String values[] = {
109             String.valueOf( record.getAccount() ),
110             record.getFirstName(),
111             record.getLastName(),
112             String.valueOf( record.getBalance() ) };
113          userInterface.setFieldValues( values );
114       }
115       catch ( EOFException eofex ) {
116          nextRecord.setEnabled( false );
117          JOptionPane.showMessageDialog( this,
118             "No more records in file",
119             "End of File", JOptionPane.ERROR_MESSAGE );
120       }
121       catch ( ClassNotFoundException cnfex ) {
122          JOptionPane.showMessageDialog( this,
123             "Unable to create object",
124             "Class Not Found", JOptionPane.ERROR_MESSAGE );
125       }
126       catch ( IOException ioex ) {
127          JOptionPane.showMessageDialog( this,
128             "Error during read from file",
129             "Read Error", JOptionPane.ERROR_MESSAGE );
130       }
131    }
132
133    private void closeFile()
134    {
135       try {
136          input.close();
137          System.exit( 0 );
138       }
139       catch ( IOException e ) {
140          JOptionPane.showMessageDialog( this,
141             "Error closing file",
142             "Error", JOptionPane.ERROR_MESSAGE );
143          System.exit( 1 );
144       }
145    }
```

Fig. 17.6   Reading a sequential file (part 3 of 4).

```
146
147    public static void main( String args[] )
148    {
149        new ReadSequentialFile();
150    }
151  }
```

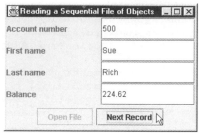

Fig. 17.6   Reading a sequential file (part 4 of 4).

Because much of the code in this example is similar to Fig. 17.4, we discuss only the key lines of code that are different. On line 71, we call **JFileChooser** method *show-OpenDialog* to display the **Open** dialog (first screen in Fig. 17.6). The behavior and GUI are the same (except that **Save** is replaced by **Open**) as the dialog displayed by **showSaveDialog**.

Line 88

```
input = new ObjectInputStream(
            new FileInputStream( fileName ) );
```

creates a **ObjectInputStream** object and assigns it to **input**. The **File fileName** is passed to the **FileInputStream** constructor which opens the file.

The program reads a record from the file each time the user clicks the **Next** button. Method **readRecord** (line 101) is called from **Next**'s **actionPerformed** method to read one record from the file. The statement (line107)

```
record = ( BankAccountRecord ) input.readObject();
```

calls method ***readObject*** to read an **Object** from the **ObjectInputStream**. In order to use **BankAccountRecord** specific methods, we cast the returned **Object** to **BankAccountRecord**. If the end-of-file marker is reached while reading, an ***EndOfFileException*** is thrown.

To retrieve data sequentially from a file, programs normally start reading from the beginning of the file, and read all the data consecutively until the desired data are found. It may be necessary to process the file sequentially several times (from the beginning of the file) during the execution of a program. Class **FileInputStream** does not provide the ability to reposition to the beginning of the file to read the file again. However, **RandomAccessFile** objects can reposition to the beginning of the file. Class **RandomAccessFile** provides all the capabilities of the classes **FileInputStream**, **FileOutputStream**, **DataInputStream** and **DataOutputStream**, and adds several other methods including ***seek*** that repositions the *file-position pointer* (the byte number of the next byte in the file to be read or written) to any position in the file.

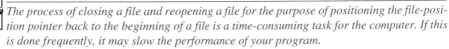

Performance Tip 17.5

The process of closing a file and reopening a file for the purpose of positioning the file-position pointer back to the beginning of a file is a time-consuming task for the computer. If this is done frequently, it may slow the performance of your program.

The program of Fig. 17.7 (with outputs in Fig. 17.8) enables a credit manager to display the account information for those customers with zero balances (i.e., customers who do not owe the company any money), credit balances (i.e., customers to whom the company owes money), and debit balances (i.e., customers who owe the company money for goods and services received in the past).

```
1    // Fig. 17.7: CreditInquiry.java
2    // This program reads a file sequentially and displays the
3    // contents in a text area based on the type of account the
4    // user requests (credit balance, debit balance or
5    // zero balance).
6    import java.io.*;
7    import java.awt.*;
8    import java.awt.event.*;
9    import java.text.DecimalFormat;
10   import javax.swing.*;
11   import com.deitel.jhtp3.ch17.BankAccountRecord;
12
13   public class CreditInquiry extends JFrame {
14      private JTextArea recordDisplay;
15      private JButton open, done, credit, debit, zero;
16      private JPanel buttonPanel;
17      private ObjectInputStream input;
18      private FileInputStream fileInput;
19      private File fileName;
20      private String accountType;
21
```

Fig. 17.7   Credit inquiry program (part 1 of 5).

```
22      public CreditInquiry()
23      {
24         super( "Credit Inquiry Program" );
25
26         Container c = getContentPane();
27         c.setLayout( new BorderLayout() );
28         buttonPanel = new JPanel();
29
30         open = new JButton( "Open File" );
31         open.addActionListener(
32            new ActionListener() {
33               public void actionPerformed( ActionEvent e )
34               {
35                  openFile( true );
36               }
37            }
38         );
39         buttonPanel.add( open );
40
41         credit = new JButton( "Credit balances" );
42         credit.addActionListener(
43            new ActionListener() {
44               public void actionPerformed( ActionEvent e )
45               {
46                  accountType = e.getActionCommand();
47                  readRecords();
48               }
49            }
50         );
51         buttonPanel.add( credit );
52
53         debit = new JButton( "Debit balances" );
54         debit.addActionListener(
55            new ActionListener() {
56               public void actionPerformed( ActionEvent e )
57               {
58                  accountType = e.getActionCommand();
59                  readRecords();
60               }
61            }
62         );
63         buttonPanel.add( debit );
64
65         zero = new JButton( "Zero balances" );
66         zero.addActionListener(
67            new ActionListener() {
68               public void actionPerformed( ActionEvent e )
69               {
70                  accountType = e.getActionCommand();
71                  readRecords();
72               }
73            }
74         );
```

Fig. 17.7   Credit inquiry program (part 2 of 5).

```
75          buttonPanel.add( zero );
76
77          done = new JButton( "Done" );
78          buttonPanel.add( done );
79          done.addActionListener(
80             new ActionListener() {
81                public void actionPerformed( ActionEvent e )
82                {
83                   if ( fileInput != null )
84                      closeFile();
85
86                   System.exit( 0 );
87                }
88             }
89          );
90
91          recordDisplay = new JTextArea();
92       JScrollPane scroller = new JScrollPane( recordDisplay );
93          c.add( scroller, BorderLayout.CENTER );
94          c.add( buttonPanel, BorderLayout.SOUTH );
95
96          credit.setEnabled( false );
97          debit.setEnabled( false );
98          zero.setEnabled( false );
99
100         pack();
101         setSize( 600, 250 );
102         show();
103      }
104
105      private void openFile( boolean firstTime )
106      {
107         if ( firstTime ) {
108            JFileChooser fileChooser = new JFileChooser();
109
110            fileChooser.setFileSelectionMode(
111               JFileChooser.FILES_ONLY );
112            int result = fileChooser.showOpenDialog( this );
113
114            // user clicked Cancel button on dialog
115            if ( result == JFileChooser.CANCEL_OPTION )
116               return;
117
118            fileName = fileChooser.getSelectedFile();
119         }
120
121         if ( fileName == null ||
122            fileName.getName().equals( "" ) )
123            JOptionPane.showMessageDialog( this,
124               "Invalid File Name",
125               "Invalid File Name",
126               JOptionPane.ERROR_MESSAGE );
```

Fig. 17.7   Credit inquiry program (part 3 of 5).

```
127         else {
128             // Open the file
129             try {
130                 // close file from previous operation
131                 if ( input != null )
132                     input.close();
133
134                 fileInput = new FileInputStream( fileName );
135                 input = new ObjectInputStream( fileInput );
136                 open.setEnabled( false );
137                 credit.setEnabled( true );
138                 debit.setEnabled( true );
139                 zero.setEnabled( true );
140             }
141             catch ( IOException e ) {
142                 JOptionPane.showMessageDialog( this,
143                     "File does not exist",
144                     "Invalid File Name",
145                     JOptionPane.ERROR_MESSAGE );
146             }
147         }
148     }
149
150     private void closeFile()
151     {
152         try {
153             input.close();
154         }
155         catch ( IOException ioe ) {
156             JOptionPane.showMessageDialog( this,
157                 "Error closing file",
158                 "Error", JOptionPane.ERROR_MESSAGE );
159             System.exit( 1 );
160         }
161     }
162
163     private void readRecords()
164     {
165         BankAccountRecord record;
166         DecimalFormat twoDigits = new DecimalFormat( "0.00" );
167         openFile( false );
168
169         try {
170             recordDisplay.setText( "The accounts are:\n" );
171
172             // input the values from the file
173             while ( true ) {
174                 record =
175                     ( BankAccountRecord ) input.readObject();
176
```

Fig. 17.7   Credit inquiry program (part 4 of 5).

```
177              if ( shouldDisplay( record.getBalance() ) )
178                 recordDisplay.append( record.getAccount() +
179                    "\t" + record.getFirstName() + "\t" +
180                    record.getLastName() + "\t" +
181                    twoDigits.format( record.getBalance() ) +
182                    "\n" );
183           }
184        }
185        catch ( EOFException eof ) {
186           closeFile();
187        }
188        catch ( ClassNotFoundException cnfex ) {
189           JOptionPane.showMessageDialog( this,
190              "Unable to create object",
191              "Class Not Found", JOptionPane.ERROR_MESSAGE );
192        }
193        catch ( IOException e ) {
194           JOptionPane.showMessageDialog( this,
195              "Error reading from file",
196              "Error", JOptionPane.ERROR_MESSAGE );
197        }
198     }
199
200     private boolean shouldDisplay( double balance )
201     {
202        if ( accountType.equals( "Credit balances" ) &&
203              balance < 0 )
204           return true;
205        else if ( accountType.equals( "Debit balances" ) &&
206                 balance > 0 )
207           return true;
208        else if ( accountType.equals( "Zero balances" ) &&
209                 balance == 0 )
210           return true;
211
212        return false;
213     }
214
215     public static void main( String args[] )
216     {
217        final CreditInquiry app = new CreditInquiry();
218
219        app.addWindowListener(
220           new WindowAdapter() {
221              public void windowClosing( WindowEvent e )
222              {
223                 app.closeFile();
224                 System.exit( 0 );
225              }
226           }
227        );
228     }
229 }
```

Fig. 17.7 Credit inquiry program (part 5 of 5).

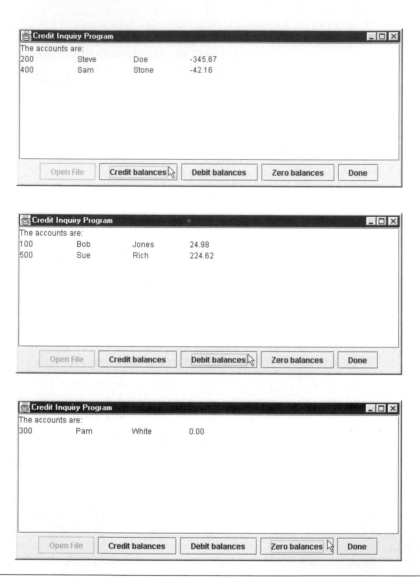

Fig. 17.8   Sample outputs of the credit inquiry program of Fig. 17.7.

The program displays buttons that allow a credit manager to obtain credit information. The **Credit balances** button produces a list of accounts with credit balances. The **Debit balances** button produces a list of accounts with debit balances. The **Zero balances** button produces a list of accounts with zero balances. The **Done** button terminates program execution.

Records are displayed in a **JTextArea** called **recordDisplay**. The record information is collected by reading through the entire file and determining if each record satisfies the criteria for the account type selected by the credit manager. Clicking a button (other than the **Done**) sets variable **accountType** to the clicked button's text (e.g., **Zero balances**, etc.) and invokes method **readRecords** that loops through the file and reads every record. Method **shouldDisplay** is called to determine if the current record satisfies the account type requested. If **shouldDisplay** returns **true**, the account information for the current record is appended to the **JTextArea** named **recordDisplay**. When the end-of-file marker is reached, line 186

```
closeFile();
```

calls **closeFile** to close the file.

17.6 Updating Sequential-Access Files

Data that is formatted and written to a sequential-access file as shown in Section 17.4 cannot be modified without reading and writing all the data in the file. For example, if the name **White** needed to be changed to **Worthington**, the old name cannot simply be overwritten. Such updating can be done, but it is awkward. To make the preceding name change, the records before **White** in a sequential-access file could be copied to a new file, the updated record would then be written to the new file, and the records after **White** would be copied to the new file. This requires processing every record in the file to update one record. If many records are being updated in one pass of the file, this technique can be acceptable.

17.7 Random-Access Files

So far, we have seen how to create sequential-access files and to search through them to locate particular information. Sequential-access files are inappropriate for so-called "*instant-access*" *applications* in which a particular record of information must be located immediately. Some popular instant-access applications are airline reservation systems, banking systems, point-of-sale systems, automated-teller machines and other kinds of *transaction-processing systems* that require rapid access to specific data. The bank at which you have your account may have hundreds of thousands or even millions of other customers, yet when you use an automated teller machine, your account is checked for sufficient funds in seconds. This kind of instant access is possible with *random-access files*. Individual records of a random-access file can be accessed directly (and quickly) without searching through other records. Random-access files are sometimes called *direct-access files*.

As we have said, Java does not impose structure on a file. So the application that wants to use random-access files must literally create them. A variety of techniques can be used to create random-access files. Perhaps the simplest is to require that all records in a file are of the same fixed length.

Using fixed-length records makes it easy for a program to calculate (as a function of the record size and the record key) the exact location of any record relative to the beginning of the file. We will soon see how this facilitates immediate access to specific records, even in large files.

Figure 17.9 illustrates Java's view of a random-access file composed of fixed-length records (each record in this figure is 100 bytes long). A random-access file is like a railroad train with many cars—some empty and some with contents.

Data can be inserted in a random-access file without destroying other data in the file. Data stored previously also can be updated or deleted without rewriting the entire file. In the following sections we explain how to create a random-access file, enter data, read the data both sequentially and randomly, update the data and delete data no longer needed.

17.8 Creating a Random-Access File

RandomAccessFile objects have all the capabilities of **DataInputStream** and **DataOutputStream** objects discussed earlier. When a **RandomAccessFile** stream is associated with a file, data is read or written beginning at the location in the file specified by the file-position pointer, and all data is read or written as primitive data types. When writing an **int** value, 4 bytes are output to the file. When reading a **double** value, 8 bytes are input from the file. The size of the data types is guaranteed because Java has fixed sizes for all primitive data types regardless of the computing platform.

Random-access file-processing programs rarely write a single field to a file. Normally, they write one object at a time, as we show in the following examples.

Consider the following problem statement:

Create a transaction-processing program capable of storing up to 100 fixed-length records for a company that can have up to 100 customers. Each record should consist of an account number that will be used as the record key, a last name, a first name and a balance. The program should be able to update an account, insert a new account and delete an account.

The next several sections introduce the techniques necessary to create this credit-processing program. Figure 17.10 contains the **Record** class that is used by the next four programs for both reading records from, and writing records to, a file.

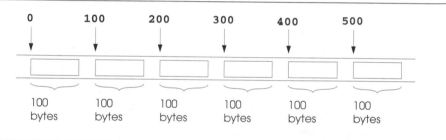

Fig. 17.9   Java's view of a random-access file.

```
1   // Fig. 17.10: Record.java
2   // Record class for the RandomAccessFile programs.
3   package com.deitel.jhtp3.ch17;
4   import java.io.*;
5   import com.deitel.jhtp3.ch17.BankAccountRecord;
6
7   public class Record extends BankAccountRecord {
8
9       public Record()
10      {
11          this( 0, "", "", 0.0 );
12      }
13
14      public Record( int acct, String first,
15                     String last, double bal )
16      {
```

Fig. 17.10   Record class used in the random-access file programs (part 1 of 2).

```
17            super( acct, first, last, bal );
18         }
19
20         // Read a record from the specified RandomAccessFile
21         public void read( RandomAccessFile file ) throws IOException
22         {
23            setAccount( file.readInt() );
24            setFirstName( padName( file ) );
25            setLastName( padName( file ) );
26            setBalance( file.readDouble() );
27         }
28
29         private String padName( RandomAccessFile f )
30            throws IOException
31         {
32            char name[] = new char[ 15 ], temp;
33
34            for ( int i = 0; i < name.length; i++ ) {
35               temp = f.readChar();
36               name[ i ] = temp;
37            }
38
39            return new String( name ).replace( '\0', ' ' );
40         }
41
42         // Write a record to the specified RandomAccessFile
43         public void write( RandomAccessFile file ) throws IOException
44         {
45            file.writeInt( getAccount() );
46            writeName( file, getFirstName() );
47            writeName( file, getLastName() );
48            file.writeDouble( getBalance() );
49         }
50
51         private void writeName( RandomAccessFile f, String name )
52            throws IOException
53         {
54            StringBuffer buf = null;
55
56            if ( name != null )
57               buf = new StringBuffer( name );
58            else
59               buf = new StringBuffer( 15 );
60
61            buf.setLength( 15 );
62            f.writeChars( buf.toString() );
63         }
64
65         // NOTE: This method contains a hard coded value for the
66         // size of a record of information.
67         public static int size() { return 72; }
68      }
```

Fig. 17.10 Record class used in the random-access file programs (part 2 of 2).

Class **Record** inherits **BankAccountRecord**'s implementation (which includes **private** instance variables—**account**, **lastName**, **firstName** and **balance**—as well as their **public** get and set methods).

Method **read** reads one record from the **RandomAccessFile** object passed in as an argument. Methods *readInt* and *readDouble* are used to read the **account** and **balance**, respectively. Method **read** calls **private** method **padName** twice to read (using method *readChar*) fifteen characters from the **RandomAccessFile** for the **firstName** and the **LastName**. If a name is shorter than 15 characters, Java fills each extra character with a null byte ('**\0**'). Swing components, such as **JTextField**s, cannot display null byte characters (they are displayed as rectangles). Line 39

```
return new String( name ).replace( '\0', ' ' );
```

solves this problem by replacing null bytes with spaces.

Method **write** writes one record to the **RandomAccessFile** object passed in as an argument. This method uses method *writeInt* to output the integer **account**, method *writeChars* to output the **firstName** and **lastName** character arrays and method *writeDouble* to output the **double balance**. Note: In order to ensure that all records in the **RandomAccessFile** have the same size, we write exactly 15 characters for the first name and exactly 15 characters for the last name. Method **writeName** performs the write operations for **firstName** and **lastName**.

Figure 17.11 illustrates opening a random-access file and writing data to the disk. This program writes 100 **Record**s using method **write**. Each **Record** object contains **0** for the account number, **null** for the last name, **null** for the first name, and **0.0** for the balance. The file is initialized to create the proper amount of "empty" space in which the account data will be stored and to enable us to determine in subsequent programs if each record is empty or contains data.

Line 40

```
file = new RandomAccessFile( fileName, "rw" );
```

```java
1   // Fig. 17.11: CreateRandFile.java
2   // This program creates a random access file sequentially
3   // by writing 100 empty records to disk.
4   import com.deitel.jhtp3.ch17.Record;
5   import java.io.*;
6   import javax.swing.*;
7
8   public class CreateRandomFile {
9      private Record blank;
10     private RandomAccessFile file;
11
12     public CreateRandomFile()
13     {
14        blank = new Record();
15        openFile();
16     }
```

Fig. 17.11 Creating a random-access file sequentially (part 1 of 2).

attempts to open a **File** for use in this program. Two arguments are passed to the **RandomAccessFile** constructor—the file name and the *file open mode*. The file open mode for a **RandomAccessFile** is either **"r"** to open the file for reading or **"rw"** to open the file for reading and writing.

```
17
18      private void openFile()
19      {
20          JFileChooser fileChooser = new JFileChooser();
21                      fileChooser.setFileSelectionMode(
22                              JFileChooser.FILES_ONLY );
23          int result = fileChooser.showSaveDialog( null );
24
25          // user clicked Cancel button on dialog
26          if ( result == JFileChooser.CANCEL_OPTION )
27              return;
28
29          File fileName = fileChooser.getSelectedFile();
30
31          if ( fileName == null ||
32              fileName.getName().equals( "" ) )
33              JOptionPane.showMessageDialog( null,
34                  "Invalid File Name",
35                  "Invalid File Name",
36                  JOptionPane.ERROR_MESSAGE );
37          else {
38              // Open the file
39              try {
40                  file = new RandomAccessFile( fileName, "rw" );
41
42                  for ( int i = 0; i < 100; i++ )
43                      blank.write( file );
44
45                  System.exit( 0 );
46              }
47              catch ( IOException e ) {
48                  JOptionPane.showMessageDialog( null,
49                      "File does not exist",
50                      "Invalid File Name",
51                      JOptionPane.ERROR_MESSAGE );
52                  System.exit( 1 );
53              }
54          }
55      }
56
57      public static void main( String args[] )
58      {
59          new CreateRandomFile();
60      }
61  }
```

Fig. 17.11 Creating a random-access file sequentially (part 2 of 2).

If an **IOException** occurs during the open process, a message dialog is displayed and the program terminates. If the file is opened properly, the program uses a **for** structure (lines 42) to execute the following line 100 times

```
blank.write( file );
```

This statement causes the data members of object **blank** to be written to the file associated with **RandomAccessFile** object **file**.

17.9 Writing Data Randomly to a Random-Access File

Figure 17.12 writes data to a file which is opened with the **"rw"** mode for reading and writing. It uses the **RandomAccessFile** method *seek* to determine the exact location in the file at which a record of information is stored. Method **seek** sets the file-position pointer to a specific position in the file relative to the beginning of the file, and the **Record** class method **write** outputs the data. This program assumes the user does not enter duplicate account numbers and that the user enters appropriate data in each **JTextField**.

```
1   // Fig. 17.12: WriteRandomFile.java
2   // This program uses TextFields to get information from the
3   // user at the keyboard and writes the information to a
4   // random-access file.
5   import com.deitel.jhtp3.ch17.*;
6   import javax.swing.*;
7   import java.io.*;
8   import java.awt.event.*;
9   import java.awt.*;
10
11  public class WriteRandomFile extends JFrame {
12     private RandomAccessFile output;
13     private BankUI userInterface;
14     private JButton enter, open;
15
16     // Constructor -- intialize the Frame
17     public WriteRandomFile()
18     {
19        super( "Write to random access file" );
20
21        userInterface = new BankUI();
22        enter = userInterface.getDoTask();
23        enter.setText( "Enter" );
24        enter.setEnabled( false );
25        enter.addActionListener(
26           new ActionListener() {
27              public void actionPerformed( ActionEvent e )
28              {
29                 addRecord();
30              }
31           }
32        );
```

Fig. 17.12   Writing data randomly to a random-access file (part 1 of 4).

```
33
34          addWindowListener(
35             new WindowAdapter() {
36                public void windowClosing( WindowEvent e )
37                {
38                   if ( output != null ) {
39                      addRecord();
40                      closeFile();
41                   }
42                   else
43                      System.exit( 0 );
44                }
45             }
46          );
47          open = userInterface.getDoTask2();
48
49          open.setText( "Save As" );
50          open.addActionListener(
51             new ActionListener() {
52                public void actionPerformed( ActionEvent e )
53                {
54                   // Open the file
55                   openFile();
56                }
57             }
58          );
59          getContentPane().add( userInterface,
60                                BorderLayout.CENTER );
61
62          setSize( 300, 150 );
63          show();
64       }
65
66       private void openFile()
67       {
68          JFileChooser fileChooser = new JFileChooser();
69
70          fileChooser.setFileSelectionMode(
71             JFileChooser.FILES_ONLY );
72          int result = fileChooser.showSaveDialog( this );
73
74          // user clicked Cancel button on dialog
75          if ( result == JFileChooser.CANCEL_OPTION )
76             return;
77
78          File fileName = fileChooser.getSelectedFile();
79
80          if ( fileName == null ||
81               fileName.getName().equals( "" ) )
82             JOptionPane.showMessageDialog( this,
83                "Invalid File Name",
84                "Invalid File Name",
85                JOptionPane.ERROR_MESSAGE );
```

Fig. 17.12   Writing data randomly to a random-access file (part 2 of 4).

```
86          else {
87             // Open the file
88             try {
89                output = new RandomAccessFile( fileName, "rw" );
90                enter.setEnabled( true );
91                open.setEnabled( false );
92             }
93             catch ( IOException e ) {
94                JOptionPane.showMessageDialog( this,
95                   "File does not exist",
96                   "Invalid File Name",
97                   JOptionPane.ERROR_MESSAGE );
98             }
99          }
100      }
101
102      private void closeFile()
103      {
104         try {
105            output.close();
106            System.exit( 0 );
107         }
108         catch( IOException ex ) {
109            JOptionPane.showMessageDialog( this,
110               "Error closing file",
111               "Error", JOptionPane.ERROR_MESSAGE );
112            System.exit( 1 );
113         }
114      }
115
116      public void addRecord()
117      {
118         int accountNumber = 0;
119         String fields[] = userInterface.getFieldValues();
120         Record record = new Record();
121
122         if ( !fields[ BankUI.ACCOUNT ].equals( "" ) ) {
123            // output the values to the file
124            try {
125               accountNumber =
126                  Integer.parseInt( fields[ BankUI.ACCOUNT ] );
127
128               if ( accountNumber > 0 && accountNumber <= 100 ) {
129                  record.setAccount( accountNumber );
130
131                  record.setFirstName( fields[ BankUI.FIRST ] );
132                  record.setLastName( fields[ BankUI.LAST ] );
133                  record.setBalance( Double.parseDouble(
134                                    fields[ BankUI.BALANCE ] ) );
135
136                  output.seek( ( accountNumber - 1 ) *
137                               Record.size() );
```

Fig. 17.12   Writing data randomly to a random-access file (part 3 of 4).

```
138                        record.write( output );
139                    }
140
141                    userInterface.clearFields();   // clear TextFields
142                }
143                catch ( NumberFormatException nfe ) {
144                    JOptionPane.showMessageDialog( this,
145                        "Bad account number or balance",
146                        "Invalid Number Format",
147                        JOptionPane.ERROR_MESSAGE );
148                }
149                catch ( IOException io ) {
150                    closeFile();
151                }
152            }
153        }
154
155        // Create a WriteRandomFile object and start the program
156        public static void main( String args[] )
157        {
158            new WriteRandomFile();
159        }
160    }
```

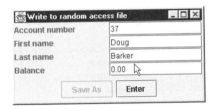

Fig. 17.12   Writing data randomly to a random-access file (part 4 of 4).

The user enters values for the account number, first name, last name and balance. When the user clicks the **Enter** button, method **addRecord** of the **WriteRandomFile** class is invoked to retrieve the data from the **BankAccountUI**'s **JTextField**s, store the data in **Record** class object **data**, and call the **write** method of the **Record** class to output the data.

Line 136

```
output.seek( ( accountNumber - 1 ) *
                 Record.size() );
```

calls method **seek** to position the file-position pointer for object **output** to the byte location calculated by **(accountNumber - 1) * Record.size()**. Because the account number is between 1 and 100, 1 is subtracted from the account number when calculating the byte location of the record. Thus, for record 1, the file-position pointer is set to byte 0 of the file. The calculation result is implicitly promoted from **int** to **long** because method **seek** requires a **long** value as an argument.

When the user closes the window, the program attempts to add the last record to the file (if there is one waiting to be output), closes the file and terminates the program.

17.10 Reading Data Sequentially from a Random-Access File

In the previous sections, we created a random-access file and wrote data to that file. In this section, we develop a program (Fig. 17.13) that opens a **RandomAccessFile** for reading with the **"r"** file open mode, reads through the file sequentially and displays only those records containing data. This program produces an additional benefit. See if you can determine what it is; we will reveal it at the end of this section.

Good Programming Practice 17.1

*Open a file with the **"r"** file open mode for input if the contents of the file should not be modified. This prevents unintentional modification of the file's contents. This is another example of the principle of least privilege.*

```
1   // Fig. 17.13: ReadRandomFile.java
2   // This program reads a random-access file sequentially and
3   // displays the contents one record at a time in text fields.
4   import java.io.*;
5   import java.awt.*;
6   import java.awt.event.*;
7   import java.text.DecimalFormat;
8   import javax.swing.*;
9   import com.deitel.jhtp3.ch17.*;
10
11  public class ReadRandomFile extends JFrame {
12     private BankUI userInterface;
13     private RandomAccessFile input;
14     private JButton next, open;
15
16     public ReadRandomFile()
17     {
18        super( "Read Client File" );
19
20        userInterface = new BankUI();
21        next = userInterface.getDoTask();
22        next.setText( "Next" );
23        next.setEnabled( false );
24        next.addActionListener(
25           new ActionListener() {
26              public void actionPerformed( ActionEvent e )
27              {
28                 readRecord();
29              }
30           }
31        );
32
33        addWindowListener(
34           new WindowAdapter() {
35              public void windowClosing( WindowEvent e )
36              {
```

Fig. 17.13 Reading a random-access file sequentially (part 1 of 4).

```
37                    if ( input != null ) {
38                        closeFile();
39                    }
40                    else
41                        System.exit( 0 );
42                }
43            }
44        );
45        open = userInterface.getDoTask2();
46
47        open.setText( "Read File" );
48        open.addActionListener(
49            new ActionListener() {
50                public void actionPerformed( ActionEvent e )
51                {
52                    openFile();
53                }
54            }
55        );
56        getContentPane().add( userInterface );
57
58        setSize( 300, 150 );
59        show();
60    }
61
62    private void openFile()
63    {
64        JFileChooser fileChooser = new JFileChooser();
65
66        fileChooser.setFileSelectionMode(
67            JFileChooser.FILES_ONLY );
68        int result = fileChooser.showOpenDialog( this );
69
70        // user clicked Cancel button on dialog
71        if ( result == JFileChooser.CANCEL_OPTION )
72            return;
73
74        File fileName = fileChooser.getSelectedFile();
75
76        if ( fileName == null ||
77            fileName.getName().equals( "" ) )
78            JOptionPane.showMessageDialog( this,
79                "Invalid File Name",
80                "Invalid File Name",
81                JOptionPane.ERROR_MESSAGE );
82        else {
83            // Open the file
84            try {
85                input = new RandomAccessFile( fileName, "r" );
86                next.setEnabled( true );
87                open.setEnabled( false );
88            }
```

Fig. 17.13 Reading a random-access file sequentially (part 2 of 4).

```
89              catch ( IOException e ) {
90                 JOptionPane.showMessageDialog( this,
91                    "File does not exist",
92                    "Invalid File Name",
93                    JOptionPane.ERROR_MESSAGE );
94              }
95           }
96        }
97
98        public void readRecord()
99        {
100          DecimalFormat twoDigits = new DecimalFormat( "0.00" );
101          Record record = new Record();
102
103          // read a record and display
104          try {
105             do {
106                record.read( input );
107             } while ( record.getAccount() == 0 );
108
109             String values[] = {
110                String.valueOf( record.getAccount() ),
111                record.getFirstName(),
112                record.getLastName(),
113                String.valueOf( record.getBalance() ) };
114             userInterface.setFieldValues( values );
115          }
116          catch ( EOFException eof ) {
117             closeFile();
118          }
119          catch ( IOException e ) {
120             JOptionPane.showMessageDialog( this,
121                "Error Reading File",
122                "Error",
123                JOptionPane.ERROR_MESSAGE );
124             System.exit( 1 );
125          }
126       }
127
128       private void closeFile()
129       {
130          try {
131             input.close();
132             System.exit( 0 );
133          }
134          catch( IOException ex ) {
135             JOptionPane.showMessageDialog( this,
136                "Error closing file",
137                "Error", JOptionPane.ERROR_MESSAGE );
138             System.exit( 1 );
139          }
140       }
```

Fig. 17.13   Reading a random-access file sequentially (part 3 of 4).

```
141
142     public static void main( String args[] )
143     {
144         new ReadRandomFile();
145     }
146 }
```

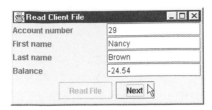

Fig. 17.13   Reading a random-access file sequentially (part 4 of 4).

When the user clicks the **Next** button to read the next record in the file, class **Read-RandomFile**'s **readRecord** method (line 98) is invoked. This method invokes class **Record**'s **read** method to read the data into **Record** class object **data**. Method **readRecord** reads from the file until it reads a record with a non-zero account number (0 is the initial value for the account). When a valid account number (i.e., a non-zero value) is read, the loop terminates and the record data is displayed in the text fields. When the user clicks the **Done** button or when the end-of-file marker is encountered while reading, method **closeFile** is invoked to close the file and terminate the program.

What about that additional benefit we promised? If you examine the GUI as the program executes, you will notice that the records are displayed in sorted order (by account number)! This is a simple consequence of the way we stored these records in the file using direct-access techniques. Compared to the bubble sort we have seen (Chapter 7), sorting with direct-access techniques is blazingly fast. The speed is achieved by making the file large enough to hold every possible record that might be created. This, of course, means that the file could be sparsely occupied most of the time, a waste of storage. So here is yet another example of the space/time trade-off: By using large amounts of space, we are able to develop a much faster sorting algorithm.

17.11 Example: A Transaction-Processing Program

We now present a substantial transaction-processing program (Fig. 17.14) using a random-access file to achieve "instant" access processing. The program maintains a bank's account information. The program updates existing accounts, adds new accounts and deletes accounts. We assume that the program of Fig. 17.11 has been executed to create a file and that the program of Fig. 17.12 has been executed to insert initial data.

This program GUI consists of a window containing internal frames. We do this using the classes **JInternalFrame** and **JDesktopPane** introduced in Chapter 13. The internal frame has four buttons to select various tasks as shown here:

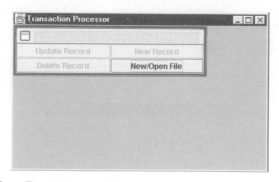

When the **Update Record** button is clicked, the following **Update Record** internal frame allows the user to update an existing account (after entering an account number and pressing *Enter*). The event handler validates the account number, then reads the record with **Record** method **read**. Next, the account number is compared to zero (i.e., no record) to determine if the record contains information. If not, a message is displayed stating that the record does not exist. The **Transaction amount JTextField** initially contains the string **charge (+) or payment (-)**. The user should select this text and type the transaction amount (a positive value for a charge or a negative value for a payment) then press *Enter*. Method **addRecord** takes the transaction amount, adds it to the current balance and calls method **setBalance** to update the display. Clicking **Save Changes** writes the updated record to disk; clicking **Cancel** closes the internal frame without writing the record to disk.

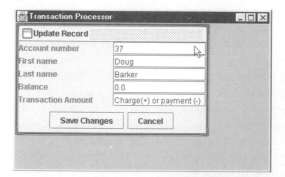

The following window shows a sample of a transaction being input:

When clicked, the **New Record** button displays the following **New Record** internal frame which allows the user to add a new record. The user enters data in the **JText-Field**s and clicks **Save Changes** to write the record to disk. If the account number already exists, an error dialog is displayed and the record is not written to disk. Clicking **Cancel** closes the internal frame without attempting to write the record.

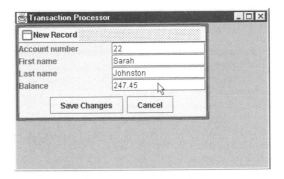

Clicking the **Delete Record** button displays the following **Delete Record** internal frame which allows the user to delete a record from the file. The user enters the account number in the **JTextField** and presses *Enter*. Only an existing record can be deleted, so if the specified account is empty, an error message is displayed. Clicking the **Delete Record** button in the internal frame sets the record's account number to 0 (which this application considers to be an empty record). Clicking **Cancel** closes the internal frame without attempting to delete the record.

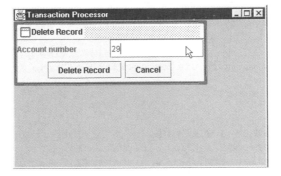

The **Done** button terminates program execution. The program is shown in Fig. 17.14. The file is opened by creating a **RandomAccessFile** object with the **"rw"** (reading and writing) file open mode.

```
1   // Fig. 17.14: TransactionProcessor.java
2   // Transaction processing program using RandomAccessFiles.
3   // This program reads a random-access file sequentially,
4   // updates record already written to the file, creates new
```

Fig. 17.14 Transaction-processing program (part 1 of 12).

```
5    // record to be placed in the file and deletes data
6    // already in the file.
7    import java.awt.*;
8    import java.awt.event.*;
9    import java.io.*;
10   import java.text.DecimalFormat;
11   import com.deitel.jhtp3.ch17.*;
12   import javax.swing.*;
13
14   public class TransactionProcessor extends JFrame  {
15      private JDesktopPane desktop;
16      private JButton open, updateRecord, newRecord, deleteRecord;
17      private JInternalFrame mainDialog;
18      private UpdateDialog updateDialog;
19      private NewDialog newDialog;
20      private DeleteDialog deleteDialog;
21      private RandomAccessFile file;
22      private Record record;
23
24      public TransactionProcessor()
25      {
26         super( "Transaction Processor" );
27
28         desktop = new JDesktopPane();
29
30         mainDialog = new JInternalFrame();
31         updateRecord = new JButton( "Update Record" );
32         updateRecord.setEnabled( false );
33         updateRecord.addActionListener(
34            new ActionListener() {
35               public void actionPerformed( ActionEvent e )
36               {
37                  mainDialog.setVisible( false );
38                  updateDialog.setVisible( true );
39               }
40            }
41         );
42
43         deleteRecord = new JButton( "Delete Record" );
44         deleteRecord.setEnabled( false );
45         deleteRecord.addActionListener(
46            new ActionListener() {
47               public void actionPerformed( ActionEvent e )
48               {
49                  mainDialog.setVisible( false );
50                  deleteDialog.setVisible( true );
51               }
52            }
53         );
54
55         newRecord = new JButton( "New Record" );
56         newRecord.setEnabled( false );
```

Fig. 17.14   Transaction-processing program (part 2 of 12).

```
57        newRecord.addActionListener(
58           new ActionListener() {
59              public void actionPerformed( ActionEvent e )
60              {
61                 mainDialog.setVisible( false );
62                 newDialog.setVisible( true );
63              }
64           }
65        );
66
67        open = new JButton( "New/Open File" );
68        open.addActionListener(
69           new ActionListener() {
70              public void actionPerformed( ActionEvent e )
71              {
72                 open.setEnabled( false );
73                 openFile();
74                 ActionListener l = new ActionListener() {
75                    public void actionPerformed( ActionEvent e )
76
77                    {
78                      mainDialog.setVisible( true );
79                    }
80                 };
81                 updateDialog = new UpdateDialog( file, l );
82                 desktop.add( updateDialog );
83                 updateRecord.setEnabled( true );
84
85                 deleteDialog = new DeleteDialog( file, l );
86                 desktop.add ( deleteDialog );
87                 deleteRecord.setEnabled( true );
88
89                 newDialog = new NewDialog( file, l );
90                 desktop.add( newDialog );
91                 newRecord.setEnabled( true );
92
93              }
94           }
95        );
96
97        Container c = mainDialog.getContentPane();
98        c.setLayout( new GridLayout( 2, 2 ) );
99        c.add( updateRecord );
100       c.add( newRecord );
101       c.add( deleteRecord );
102       c.add( open );
103
104       setSize( 400, 250 );
105       mainDialog.setSize( 300, 80 );
106       desktop.add( mainDialog, BorderLayout.CENTER );
107       getContentPane().add( desktop );
```

Fig. 17.14   Transaction-processing program (part 3 of 12).

```
108          addWindowListener(
109             new WindowAdapter() {
110                public void windowClosing( WindowEvent e )
111                {
112                   if ( file != null )
113                      closeFile();
114
115                   System.exit( 0 );
116                }
117             }
118          );
119          show();
120       }
121
122       private void openFile()
123       {
124          JFileChooser fileChooser = new JFileChooser();
125
126          fileChooser.setFileSelectionMode(
127             JFileChooser.FILES_ONLY );
128
129          int result = fileChooser.showOpenDialog( this );
130
131          // user clicked Cancel button on dialog
132          if ( result == JFileChooser.CANCEL_OPTION )
133             return;
134
135          File fileName = fileChooser.getSelectedFile();
136
137          if ( fileName == null ||
138               fileName.getName().equals( "" ) )
139             JOptionPane.showMessageDialog( this,
140                "Invalid File Name",
141                "Invalid File Name",
142                JOptionPane.ERROR_MESSAGE );
143          else {
144             // Open the file
145             try {
146                file = new RandomAccessFile( fileName, "rw" );
147                updateRecord.setEnabled( true );
148                newRecord.setEnabled( true );
149                deleteRecord.setEnabled( true );
150                open.setEnabled( false );
151             }
152             catch ( IOException e ) {
153                JOptionPane.showMessageDialog( this,
154                   "File does not exist",
155                   "Invalid File Name",
156                   JOptionPane.ERROR_MESSAGE );
157             }
158          }
159       }
```

Fig. 17.14   Transaction-processing program (part 4 of 12).

```
160
161     private void closeFile()
162     {
163        try {
164           file.close();
165           System.exit( 0 );
166        }
167        catch( IOException ex ) {
168           JOptionPane.showMessageDialog( this,
169              "Error closing file",
170              "Error", JOptionPane.ERROR_MESSAGE );
171           System.exit( 1 );
172        }
173     }
174
175     public static void main( String args[] )
176     {
177        new TransactionProcessor();
178     }
179  }
180
181  class UpdateDialog extends JInternalFrame {
182     private RandomAccessFile file;
183     private BankUI userInterface;
184     private JButton cancel, save;
185     private JTextField account;
186
187     public UpdateDialog( RandomAccessFile f, ActionListener l )
188     {
189        super( "Update Record" );
190
191        file = f;
192        userInterface = new BankUI( 5 );
193
194        cancel = userInterface.getDoTask();
195        cancel.setText( "Cancel" );
196        cancel.addActionListener(
197           new ActionListener() {
198              public void actionPerformed( ActionEvent e )
199              {
200                 setVisible( false );
201                 userInterface.clearFields();
202              }
203           }
204        );
205        cancel.addActionListener( l );
206
207        save = userInterface.getDoTask2();
208        save.setText( "Save Changes" );
209        save.addActionListener(
210           new ActionListener() {
211              public void actionPerformed( ActionEvent e )
212              {
```

Fig. 17.14   Transaction-processing program (part 5 of 12).

```
213                         addRecord( getRecord() );
214                         setVisible( false );
215                         userInterface.clearFields();
216                      }
217                   }
218             );
219          save.addActionListener( l );
220
221          JTextField transaction =
222             userInterface.getFields()[ BankUI.TRANSACTION ];
223          transaction.addActionListener(
224                new ActionListener() {
225                   public void actionPerformed( ActionEvent e )
226                   {
227                      try {
228                         Record record = getRecord();
229                         double change = Double.parseDouble(
230                                userInterface.getFieldValues()
231                                [ BankUI.TRANSACTION ] );
232                         String[] values = {
233                            String.valueOf( record.getAccount() ),
234                            record.getFirstName(),
235                            record.getLastName(),
236                            String.valueOf( record.getBalance()
237                                        + change ),
238                            "Charge(+) or payment (-)" };
239
240                         userInterface.setFieldValues( values );
241                      }
242                      catch ( NumberFormatException nfe ) {
243                        JOptionPane.showMessageDialog( new JFrame(),
244                            "Invalid Transaction",
245                            "Invalid Number Format",
246                            JOptionPane.ERROR_MESSAGE );
247                      }
248                   }
249                }
250             );
251
252          account = userInterface.getFields()[ BankUI.ACCOUNT ];
253          account.addActionListener(
254             new ActionListener() {
255                public void actionPerformed( ActionEvent e )
256                {
257                   Record record = getRecord();
258
259                   if ( record.getAccount() != 0 )  {
260                      String values[] = {
261                         String.valueOf( record.getAccount() ),
262                         record.getFirstName(),
263                         record.getLastName(),
264                         String.valueOf( record.getBalance() ),
265                         "Charge(+) or payment (-)" };
```

Fig. 17.14   Transaction-processing program (part 6 of 12).

```
266                             userInterface.setFieldValues( values );
267                         }
268                     }
269                 }
270         );
271         getContentPane().add( userInterface,
272                             BorderLayout.CENTER );
273         setSize( 300, 175 );
274         setVisible( false );
275     }
276
277     private Record getRecord()
278     {
279         Record record = new Record();
280
281         try {
282             int accountNumber = Integer.parseInt(
283                                     account.getText() );
284
285             if ( accountNumber < 1 || accountNumber > 100 ) {
286                 JOptionPane.showMessageDialog( this,
287                     "Account Does Not Exist",
288                     "Error", JOptionPane.ERROR_MESSAGE );
289                 return( record );
290             }
291
292             file.seek( ( accountNumber - 1 ) * Record.size() );
293             record.read( file );
294
295             if ( record.getAccount() == 0 )
296                 JOptionPane.showMessageDialog( this,
297                     "Account Does Not Exist",
298                     "Error", JOptionPane.ERROR_MESSAGE );
299         }
300         catch ( NumberFormatException nfe ) {
301             JOptionPane.showMessageDialog( this,
302                 "Invalid Account",
303                 "Invalid Number Format",
304                 JOptionPane.ERROR_MESSAGE );
305         }
306         catch ( IOException io ) {
307             JOptionPane.showMessageDialog( this,
308                 "Error Reading File",
309                 "Error", JOptionPane.ERROR_MESSAGE );
310         }
311
312         return record;
313     }
314
315     public void addRecord( Record record )
316     {
317         try {
318             int accountNumber = record.getAccount();
```

Fig. 17.14 Transaction-processing program (part 7 of 12).

```
319
320                   file.seek( ( accountNumber - 1 ) * Record.size() );
321                   String[] values = userInterface.getFieldValues();
322                   record.write( file );
323               }
324           catch ( IOException io ) {
325               JOptionPane.showMessageDialog( this,
326                   "Error Writing To File",
327                   "Error", JOptionPane.ERROR_MESSAGE );
328           }
329           catch ( NumberFormatException nfe ) {
330               JOptionPane.showMessageDialog( this,
331               "Bad Balance",
332               "Invalid Number Format",
333               JOptionPane.ERROR_MESSAGE );
334           }
335       }
336 }
337
338 class NewDialog extends JInternalFrame  {
339     private RandomAccessFile file;
340     private BankUI userInterface;
341     private JButton cancel, save;
342     private JTextField account;
343
344     public NewDialog( RandomAccessFile f, ActionListener l )
345     {
346         super( "New Record" );
347
348         file = f;
349         userInterface = new BankUI();
350
351         cancel = userInterface.getDoTask();
352         cancel.setText( "Cancel" );
353         cancel.addActionListener(
354             new ActionListener() {
355                 public void actionPerformed( ActionEvent e )
356                 {
357                     setVisible( false );
358                     userInterface.clearFields();
359                 }
360             }
361         );
362         cancel.addActionListener( l );
363
364         account = userInterface.getFields()[ BankUI.ACCOUNT ];
365         save = userInterface.getDoTask2();
366         save.setText( "Save Changes" );
367         save.addActionListener(
368             new ActionListener() {
369                 public void actionPerformed( ActionEvent e )
370                 {
371                     addRecord( getRecord() );
```

Fig. 17.14   Transaction-processing program (part 8 of 12).

```
372                          setVisible( false );
373                          userInterface.clearFields();
374                       }
375                    }
376              );
377           save.addActionListener( l );
378
379           getContentPane().add( userInterface,
380                                  BorderLayout.CENTER );
381           setSize( 300, 150 );
382           setVisible( false );
383        }
384
385        private Record getRecord()
386        {
387           Record record = new Record();
388
389           try {
390              int accountNumber = Integer.parseInt(
391                                    account.getText() );
392
393              if ( accountNumber < 1 || accountNumber > 100 ) {
394                 JOptionPane.showMessageDialog( this,
395                    "Account Does Not Exist",
396                    "Error", JOptionPane.ERROR_MESSAGE );
397                 return record;
398              }
399
400              file.seek( ( accountNumber - 1 ) * Record.size() );
401              record.read( file );
402           }
403           catch ( NumberFormatException nfe ) {
404              JOptionPane.showMessageDialog( this,
405                 "Account Does Not Exist",
406                 "Invalid Number Format",
407                 JOptionPane.ERROR_MESSAGE );
408           }
409           catch ( IOException io ) {
410              JOptionPane.showMessageDialog( this,
411                 "Error Reading File",
412                 "Error", JOptionPane.ERROR_MESSAGE );
413           }
414
415           return record;
416        }
417
418        public void addRecord( Record record )
419        {
420           int accountNumber = 0;
421           String[] fields = userInterface.getFieldValues();
422
```

Fig. 17.14   Transaction-processing program (part 9 of 12).

```
423          if ( record.getAccount() != 0 ) {
424              JOptionPane.showMessageDialog( this,
425                  "Record Already Exists",
426                  "Error", JOptionPane.ERROR_MESSAGE );
427              return;
428          }
429
430          // output the values to the file
431          try {
432              accountNumber =
433                  Integer.parseInt( fields[ BankUI.ACCOUNT ] );
434              record.setAccount( accountNumber  );
435              record.setFirstName( fields[ BankUI.FIRST ] );
436              record.setLastName( fields[ BankUI.LAST ] );
437              record.setBalance( Double.parseDouble(
438                              fields[ BankUI.BALANCE ] ) );
439              file.seek( ( accountNumber - 1 ) * Record.size() );
440              record.write( file );
441          }
442          catch ( NumberFormatException nfe ) {
443              JOptionPane.showMessageDialog( this,
444                  "Invalid Balance",
445                  "Invalid Number Format",
446                  JOptionPane.ERROR_MESSAGE );
447          }
448          catch ( IOException io ) {
449              JOptionPane.showMessageDialog( this,
450                  "Error Writing To File",
451                  "Error", JOptionPane.ERROR_MESSAGE );
452          }
453      }
454  }
455
456  class DeleteDialog extends JInternalFrame {
457      private RandomAccessFile file;  // file for output
458      private BankUI userInterface;
459      private JButton cancel, delete;
460      private JTextField account;
461
462      public DeleteDialog( RandomAccessFile f, ActionListener 1 )
463      {
464          super( "Delete Record" );
465
466          file = f;
467          userInterface = new BankUI( 1 );
468
469          cancel = userInterface.getDoTask();
470          cancel.setText( "Cancel" );
471          cancel.addActionListener(
472              new ActionListener() {
473                  public void actionPerformed( ActionEvent e )
474                  {
```

Fig. 17.14   Transaction-processing program (part 10 of 12).

```
475                            setVisible( false );
476                       }
477                   }
478               );
479               cancel.addActionListener( l );
480
481               delete = userInterface.getDoTask2();
482               delete.setText( "Delete Record" );
483               delete.addActionListener(
484                   new ActionListener() {
485                       public void actionPerformed( ActionEvent e )
486                       {
487                           addRecord( getRecord() );
488                           setVisible( false );
489                           userInterface.clearFields();
490                       }
491                   }
492               );
493               delete.addActionListener( l );
494
495               account = userInterface.getFields()[ BankUI.ACCOUNT ];
496               account.addActionListener(
497                   new ActionListener() {
498                       public void actionPerformed( ActionEvent e )
499                       {
500                           Record record = getRecord();
501                       }
502                   }
503               );
504               getContentPane().add( userInterface,
505                                     BorderLayout.CENTER );
506
507               setSize( 300, 100 );
508               setVisible( false );
509           }
510
511           private Record getRecord()
512           {
513               Record record = new Record();
514
515               try {
516                   int accountNumber = Integer.parseInt(
517                                           account.getText() );
518                   if ( accountNumber < 1 || accountNumber > 100 ) {
519                       JOptionPane.showMessageDialog( this,
520                           "Account Does Not Exist",
521                           "Error", JOptionPane.ERROR_MESSAGE );
522                       return( record );
523                   }
524
525                   file.seek( ( accountNumber - 1 ) * Record.size() );
526                   record.read( file );
527
```

Fig. 17.14 Transaction-processing program (part 11 of 12).

```
528             if ( record.getAccount() == 0 )
529                JOptionPane.showMessageDialog( this,
530                   "Account Does Not Exist",
531                   "Error", JOptionPane.ERROR_MESSAGE );
532          }
533          catch ( NumberFormatException nfe ) {
534             JOptionPane.showMessageDialog( this,
535                "Account Does Not Exist",
536                "Invalid Number Format",
537                JOptionPane.ERROR_MESSAGE );
538          }
539          catch ( IOException io ) {
540            JOptionPane.showMessageDialog( this,
541               "Error Reading File",
542               "Error", JOptionPane.ERROR_MESSAGE );
543          }
544
545          return record;
546       }
547
548       public void addRecord( Record record )
549       {
550          if ( record.getAccount() == 0 )
551             return;
552
553          try {
554
555             int accountNumber = record.getAccount();
556
557             file.seek( ( accountNumber - 1 ) * Record.size() );
558             record.setAccount( 0 );
559             record.write( file );
560          }
561          catch ( IOException io ) {
562             JOptionPane.showMessageDialog( this,
563                "Error Writing To File",
564                "Error", JOptionPane.ERROR_MESSAGE );
565          }
566       }
567 }
```

Fig. 17.14   Transaction-processing program (part 12 of 12).

17.12 Class `File`

As we stated at the beginning of this chapter, the **java.io** package contains an abundance of classes for processing input and output. We have concentrated on the classes for processing sequential files (**FileInputStream** and **FileOutputStream**), for processing object streams (**ObjectInputStream** and **ObjectOutputStream**) and for processing random-access files (**RandomAccessFile**). In this section we discuss class **File** which is particularly useful for retrieving from disk information about a file or a directory. Objects of class **File** do not actually open a file or provide any file-processing capabilities.

One application of using a **File** object is checking if a file exists. In *Common Programming Error 17.1*, we warned that opening an existing file for output using a **FileOutputStream** object discards the contents of that file *without warning*. A **File** object can be used to determine if the file already exists. If so, you can open it with a **RandomAccessFile** object instead of a **FileOutputStream** object, or you can at least warn the user that they are about to discard the original file's contents.

Good Programming Practice 17.2

*Use a **File** object to determine if a file exists before opening the file with a **FileOutputStream** object.*

A **File** object is initialized using one of three constructors. The constructor

```
public File( String name )
```

stores the **String** argument **name** in the object. The **name** can contain *path information* as well as a file or directory name. A file or directory's path leads you to the file or directory on disk. The path includes some or all of the directories leading to the file or directory. An *absolute path* contains all the directories starting with the *root directory* that lead to a specific file or directory. Every file or directory on a particular disk drive has the same root directory in its path. A *relative path* contains a subset of the directories leading to a specific file or directory. Relative paths start from the directory in which the application was started.

The constructor

```
public File( String pathToName, String name )
```

uses argument **pathToName** (an absolute or relative path) to locate the file or directory specified by **name**.

The constructor

```
public File( File directory, String name )
```

uses the previously created **File** object **directory** (an absolute or relative path) to locate the file or directory specified by **name**.

Some commonly used **public** methods of class **File** are shown in Fig. 17.15. See the Java API for other **File** methods.

Method	Description
boolean canRead()	Returns **true** if a file is readable; **false** otherwise.
boolean canWrite()	Returns **true** if a file is writeable; **false** otherwise.
boolean exists()	Returns **true** if the name specified as the argument to the **File** constructor is a file or directory in the specified path; **false** otherwise.
boolean isFile()	Returns **true** if the name specified as the argument to the **File** constructor is a file; **false** otherwise.

Fig. 17.15 Some commonly used **File** methods (part 1 of 2).

Method	Description
boolean isDirectory()	Returns **true** if the name specified as the argument to the **File** constructor is a directory; **false** otherwise.
boolean isAbsolute()	Returns **true** if the arguments specified to the **File** constructor indicate an absolute path to a file or directory; **false** otherwise.
String getAbsolutePath()	Returns a **String** with the absolute path of the file or directory.
String getName()	Returns a **String** with the name of the file or directory.
String getPath()	Returns a **String** with the path of the file or directory.
String getParent()	Returns a **String** with the parent directory of the file or directory—i.e., the directory in which the file or directory can be found.
long length()	Returns the length of the file in bytes. If the **File** object represents a directory, **0** is returned.
long lastModified()	Returns a platform-dependent representation of the time at which the file or directory was last modified. The value returned is only useful for comparison with other values returned by this method.
String[] list()	Returns an array of **String**s representing the contents of a directory.

Fig. 17.15   Some commonly used **File** methods (part 2 of 2).

Figure 17.16 demonstrates class **File**. Class **FileTest** creates a GUI containing a **JTextField** for entering a file name or directory name and a **JTextArea** for displaying information about the file name or directory name input.

The user types a file name or directory name into the text field and presses the *Enter* key. The **actionPerformed** method (line 31) of class **FileTest** creates a new **File** object and assigns it to name. Next, the condition in the **if** structure at line 35—**name.exists()**—is tested. If name the user typed does not exist, the **actionPerformed** method proceeds to line 79 and displays a message dialog containing the name the user typed followed by "**Does Not Exist**." Otherwise, the body of the **if** structure is executed. The program outputs the name of the file or directory, then outputs the results of testing the **File** object with **isFile**, **isDirectory** and **isAbsolute**. Next, the values returned by **lastModified**, **length**, **getPath**, **getAbsolutePath** and **getParent** are displayed. Finally, if the **File** object represents a file, the contents of the file are read into the program and displayed in the **JTextArea**. A **RandomAccessFile** object is used so we can open the file for reading and read the file one line at a time with method **readLine** (line 59). Note that the **RandomAccessFile** object was initialized with the **File** object **name** (line 53). If the **File** object represents a directory, the contents of the directory are read into the program using **File** method **list**, then the directory contents are displayed in the **JTextArea**.

```
1   // Fig. 17.16: FileTest.java
2   // Demonstrating the File class.
3   import java.awt.*;
4   import java.awt.event.*;
5   import java.io.*;
6   import javax.swing.*;
7
8   public class FileTest extends JFrame
9                         implements ActionListener {
10     private JTextField enter;
11     private JTextArea output;
12
13     public FileTest()
14     {
15        super( "Testing class File" );
16
17        enter = new JTextField(
18           "Enter file or directory name here" );
19        enter.addActionListener( this );
20        output = new JTextArea();
21        Container c = getContentPane();
22        ScrollPane p = new ScrollPane();
23        p.add( output );
24        c.add( enter, BorderLayout.NORTH );
25        c.add( p, BorderLayout.CENTER );
26
27        setSize( 400, 400 );
28        show();
29     }
30
31     public void actionPerformed( ActionEvent e )
32     {
33        File name = new File( e.getActionCommand() );
34
35        if ( name.exists() ) {
36           output.setText(
37              name.getName() + " exists\n" +
38              ( name.isFile() ? "is a file\n" :
39                                "is not a file\n" ) +
40              ( name.isDirectory() ? "is a directory\n" :
41                                     "is not a directory\n" ) +
42              ( name.isAbsolute() ? "is absolute path\n" :
43                                    "is not absolute path\n" ) +
44              "Last modified: " + name.lastModified() +
45              "\nLength: " + name.length() +
46              "\nPath: " + name.getPath() +
47              "\nAbsolute path: " + name.getAbsolutePath() +
48              "\nParent: " + name.getParent() );
49
50           if ( name.isFile() ) {
51              try {
52                 RandomAccessFile r =
53                    new RandomAccessFile( name, "r" );
```

Fig. 17.16   Demonstrating class **File** (part 1 of 3).

```
54
55                        StringBuffer buf = new StringBuffer();
56                        String text;
57                        output.append( "\n\n" );
58
59                        while( ( text = r.readLine() ) != null )
60                           buf.append( text + "\n" );
61
62                        output.append( buf.toString() );
63                     }
64                     catch( IOException e2 ) {
65                        JOptionPane.showMessageDialog( this,
66                           "FILE ERROR",
67                           "FILE ERROR", JOptionPane.ERROR_MESSAGE );
68                     }
69                  }
70               else if ( name.isDirectory() ) {
71                  String directory[] = name.list();
72
73                  output.append( "\n\nDirectory contents:\n");
74
75                  for ( int i = 0; i < directory.length; i++ )
76                     output.append( directory[ i ] + "\n" );
77               }
78            }
79            else {
80               JOptionPane.showMessageDialog( this,
81                  e.getActionCommand() + " Does Not Exist",
82                  "FILE ERROR", JOptionPane.ERROR_MESSAGE );
83            }
84         }
85
86         public static void main( String args[] )
87         {
88            FileTest app = new FileTest();
89
90            app.addWindowListener(
91               new WindowAdapter() {
92                  public void windowClosing( WindowEvent e )
93                  {
94                     System.exit( 0 );
95                  }
96               }
97            );
98         }
99      }
```

Fig. 17.16   Demonstrating class **File** (part 2 of 3).

The first output demonstrates a **File** object associated with the **jfc** directory from the Java Developer's Kit. The second output of this program demonstrates a **File** object associated with the **readme** file from the Java Developer's Kit. In both cases, we specified an absolute path on our personal computer.

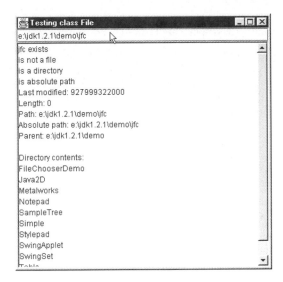

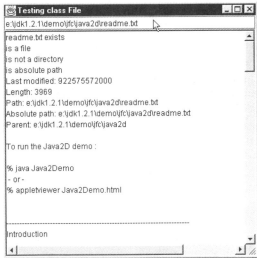

Fig. 17.16 Demonstrating class **File** (part 3 of 3).

Note that the **** *separator character* is used to separate directories and files in the path. On a UNIX workstation, the separator character would be a **/** character. Java actually processes both characters as identical in a path name. So, if we specified the path **c:\java/README** which uses one of each separator character, Java still processes the file properly.

> **Common Programming Error 17.3**
>
> *Using* **** *as a directory separator rather than* **** *in a string literal is a logic error. A single* **** *indicates that the* **** *and the next character represent an escape sequence. To insert a* **** *in a string literal you must use* ****.

Summary

- All data items processed by a computer are reduced to combinations of zeros and ones.

- The smallest data item in a computer (a bit) can assume the value **0** or the value **1**.

- Digits, letters, and special symbols are referred to as characters. The set of all characters used to write programs and represent data items on a particular computer is called that computer's character set. Every character in a computer's character set is represented as a pattern of **1**s and **0**s (characters in Java are Unicode characters composed of 2 bytes).

- A field is a group of characters (or bytes) that conveys meaning.

- A record is a group of related fields.

- At least one field in a record is chosen as a record key to identify a record as belonging to a particular person or entity that is unique from all other records in the file.

- Java imposes no structure on a file. Notions like "record" do not exist in Java. The programmer must structure a file appropriately to meet the requirements of an application.

- A collection of programs designed to create and manage databases is called a database management system (DBMS).

- Java views each file as a sequential stream of bytes.

- Each file ends in some machine-dependent form of end-of-file marker.

- Streams provide communication channels between files and programs.

- The package **java.io** must be imported into a program to perform Java file I/O. This package includes the definitions for the stream classes such as **FileInputStream**, **FileOutputStream**, **DataInputStream** and **DataOutputStream**.

- Files are opened by instantiating objects of stream classes **FileInputStream**, **FileOutputStream** and **RandomAccessFile**.

- **InputStream** (a subclass of **Object**) and **OutputStream** (a subclass of **Object**) are **abstract** classes that define methods for performing input and output respectively; their derived classes override these methods.

- File input/output is done with **FileInputStream** (a subclass of **InputStream**) and **FileOutputStream** (a subclass of **OutputStream**).

- Pipes are synchronized communication channels between threads. A pipe is established between two threads. One thread sends data to another by writing to a **PipedOutputStream** (a subclass of **OutputStream**). The target thread reads information from the pipe via a **PipedInputStream** (a subclass of **InputStream**).

- A **PrintStream** (a subclass of **FilterOutputStream**) is used for performing output to the screen (or the "standard output" as defined by your local operating system). **System.out** is a **PrintStream** (as is **System.err**).

- A **FilterInputStream** filters an **InputStream** and a **FilterOutStream** filters an **OutputStream**; filtering simply means that the filter stream provides additional functionality such as buffering, monitoring line numbers or aggregating data bytes into meaningful primitive-data-type units.

- Reading data as raw bytes is fast but crude. Usually programs read data as aggregates of bytes that form an **int**, a **float**, a **double**, and so on. To accomplish this we use a **DataInputStream** (a subclass of class **FilterInputStream**).

- Interface **DataInput** is implemented by class **DataInputStream** and class **RandomAccessFile** that each need to read primitive data types from a stream.

- **DataInputStream**s enable a program to read binary data from an **InputStream**.

- The **DataInput** interface includes methods **read** (for **byte** arrays), **readBoolean**, **read-Byte**, **readChar**, **readDouble**, **readFloat**, **readFully** (for **byte** arrays) **readInt**, **readLine**, **readLong**, **readShort**, **readUnsignedByte**, **readUnsignedShort**, **readUTF** (for Unicode) and **skipBytes**.

- The **DataOutput** interface is implemented by class **DataOutputStream** (a subclass of class **FilterOutputStream**) and class **RandomAccessFile** that each need to write primitive data types to an **OutputStream**.

- **DataOutputStream**s enable a program to write binary data to an **OutputStream**. The **DataOutput** interface includes methods **flush**, **size**, **write** (for a byte), **write** (for a **byte** array), **writeBoolean**, **writeByte**, **writeBytes**, **writeChar**, **writeChars** (for Unicode **String**s), **writeDouble**, **writeFloat**, **writeInt**, **writeLong**, **write-Short** and **writeUTF**.

- Buffering is an I/O-performance-enhancement technique.

- With a **BufferedOutputStream** (a subclass of class **FilterOutputStream**) each output statement does not necessarily result in an actual physical transfer of data to the output device. Rather, each output operation is directed to a region in memory called a buffer that is large enough to hold the data of many output operations. Then actual output to the output device is performed in one large physical output operation each time the buffer fills. The output operations directed to the output buffer in memory are often called logical output operations.

- With a **BufferedInputStream** many "logical" chunks of data from a file are read as one large physical input operation into a memory buffer. As a program requests each new chunk of data, it is taken from the buffer (this is sometimes referred to as a logical input operation). When the buffer is empty, the next physical input operation from the input device is performed to read in the next group of "logical" chunks of data. Thus, the number of physical input operations is small compared with the number of read requests issued by the program.

- With a **BufferedOutputStream** a partially filled buffer can be forced out to the device at any time with an explicit **flush**

- The **ObjectInput** interface is similar to the **DataInput** interface but includes additional methods to read **Object**s from **InputStream**s.

- The **ObjectOutput** interface is similar to the **DataOutput** interface but includes additional methods to write **Object**s to **OutputStream**s.

- The **ObjectInputStream** and **ObjectOutputStream** classes implement the **Object-Input** and **ObjectOutput** interfaces, respectively.

- A **PushBackInputStream** is a subclass of class **FilterInputStream**. The application reading a **PushBackInputStream** reads bytes from the stream and forms aggregates consisting of several bytes. Sometimes, to determine that one aggregate is complete, the application must read the first character the "past the end" of the first aggregate. Once the program has determined that the current aggregate is complete, the extra character is "pushed back" onto the stream.

- **PushBackInputStream**s are used by programs like compilers that *parse* their inputs, i.e., break them into meaningful units (such as the keywords, identifiers and operators that the Java compiler must recognize).

- A **RandomAccessFile** (a subclass of **Object**) is useful for direct-access applications such as transaction-processing applications like airline-reservations systems and point-of-sale systems.

- With a sequential-access file each successive input/output request reads or writes the next consecutive set of data in the file.

- With a random-access file, each successive input/output request may be directed to any part of the file, perhaps widely separated from the part of the file referenced in the previous request.

- Direct-access applications provide rapid access to specific data items in large files; such applications are often used while people are waiting for answers—these answers must be made available quickly or the people may become impatient and "take their business elsewhere."

- A **ByteArrayInputStream** (a subclass of **abstract** class **InputStream**) performs its inputs from a **byte** array in memory.

- A **ByteArrayOutputStream** (a subclass of **abstract** class **OutputStream**) outputs to a **byte** array in memory.

- An application of **byte**-array input/output is data validation. A program can input an entire line at a time from the input stream into a **byte** array. Then a validation routine can scrutinize the contents of the **byte** array and correct the data, if necessary. The program can now proceed to input from the **byte** array, knowing that the input data is in the proper format.

- A **StringBufferInputStream** (a subclass of **abstract** class **InputStream**) inputs from a **StringBuffer** object.

- A **SequenceInputStream** (a subclass of **abstract** class **InputStream**) enables several **InputStream**s to be concatenated so that the program sees the group as one continuous **InputStream**. As the end of each input stream is reached, the stream is closed and the next stream in the sequence is opened.

- Class **BufferedReader** and class **BufferedWriter** enable efficient buffering for character-based streams.

- Class **CharArrayReader** and class **CharArrayWriter** read and write a stream of characters to a character array.

- A **PushbackReader** (a subclass of **abstract** class **FilterReader**) enables characters to be placed back on a character stream. A **LineNumberReader** (a subclass of **BufferedReader**) is a buffered character-stream that keeps track of line numbers (i.e., a newline, a return or a carriage-return line-feed combination).

- Class **FileReader** (a subclass of **InputStreamReader**) and class **FileWriter** (a subclass of **OutputStreamWriter**) read and write characters to a file. Class **PipedReader** and class **PipedWriter** are piped-character streams. Class **StringReader** and **StringWriter** read and write characters to **String**s. A **PrintWriter** writes characters to a stream.

- Class **File** enables programs to obtain information about a file or directory.

- Files are opened for output by creating a **FileOutputStream** class object. One argument is passed to the constructor—the filename. Existing files are truncated and all data in the file is lost. Nonexistent files are created.

- Programs may process no files, one file, or several files. Each file has a unique name and is associated with an appropriate file stream object. All file-processing methods must refer to a file with the appropriate object.

- A file-position pointer indicates the position in the file from which the next input is to occur or at which the next output is to be placed.

- A convenient way to implement random-access files is by using only fixed-length records. Using this technique, a program can quickly calculate the exact location of a record relative to the beginning of the file.

- Data can be inserted in a random-access file without destroying other data in the file. Data can be updated or deleted without rewriting the entire file.

- The **RandomAccessFile** class has the same capabilities for input and output as the **DataInputStream** and **DataOutputStream** classes and also supports seeking to a specific byte position in the file with method **seek**.

Terminology

absolute path
alphabetic field
binary digit
bit
buffer
BufferedInputStream class
BufferedOutputStream class
BufferedReader class
BufferedWriter class
buffering
byte
ByteArrayInputStream class
ByteArrayOutputStream class
CANCEL_OPTION constant
canRead method of **File** class
canWrite method of **File** class
chaining stream objects
character field
character set
CharArrayReader class
CharArrayWriter class
close a file
close method
data hierarchy
database
database management system (DBMS)
data validation
DataInput interface
DataOutput interface
decimal digit
direct-access applications
DIRECTORIES_ONLY constant
directory
end-of-file
end-of-file marker
EndOfFileException
exists method of **File** class
field
file
File class
FileInputStream class
file name
file-position pointer
FileInputStream class
FileOutputStream class
FileReader class
FILES_AND_DIRECTORIES constant
FILES_ONLY constant
FileWriter class

FilterInputStream class
FilterOutputStream class
FilterReader class
flush
getAbsolutePath method of **File** class
getName method of **File** class
getParent method of **File** class
getPath method of **File** class
getSelectedFile method
input stream
InputStream class
InputStreamReader class
instant-access application
IOException
isAbsolute method of **File** class
isDirectory method of **File** class
isFile method of **File** class
JFileChooser class
lastModified method of **File** class
LineNumberReader class
list method of **File** class
length method of **File** class
logical input operation
logical output operation
memory buffer
modal dialog
numeric field
ObjectInput interface
ObjectInputStream class
ObjectOutput interface
ObjectOutputStream class
open a file
output stream
OutputStream class
OutputStreamWriter class
partially filled buffer
persistent data
physical input operation
physical output operation
pipe
PipedInputStream class
PipedOutputStream class
PipedReader class
PipedWriter class
PrintStream class
PrintWriter class
PushBackInputStream class
PushbackReader class
r file open mode

random-access file
RandomAccessFile class
read method
readBoolean method
readByte method
readChar method
readDouble method
Reader class
readFloat method
readFully method
readInt method
readLong method
readObject method
readShort method
readUnsignedByte method
readUnsignedShort method
record
record key
relative path
root directory
rw file open mode
SequenceInputStream class
sequential-access file
standard output
seek method

setFileSelectionMode method
Serializable interface
showOpenDialog method
showSaveDialog method
StringReader class
StringWriter class
System.err (standard error stream)
System.in (standard input stream)
System.out (standard output stream)
transaction-processing systems
truncate an existing file
Unicode character set
write method
writeBoolean method
writeByte method
writeBytes method
writeChar method
writeChars method
writeDouble method
writeFloat method
writeInt method
writeLong method
Writer class
writeShort method
writeObject method

Common Programming Errors

17.1   Opening an existing file for output when, in fact, the user wants to preserve the file; the contents of the file are discarded without warning.

17.2   Not opening a file before attempting to reference it in a program.

17.3   Using \ as a directory separator rather than \\ in a string literal is a logic error. A single \ indicates that the \ and the next character represent an escape sequence. To insert a \ in a string literal you must use \\.

Good Programming Practices

17.1   Open a file with the **"r"** file open mode for input if the contents of the file should not be modified. This prevents unintentional modification of the file's contents. This is another example of the principle of least privilege.

17.2   Use a **File** object to determine if a file exists before opening the file with a **FileOutputStream** object.

Performance Tips

17.1   Because typical physical output operations are extremely slow compared to typical processor speeds, buffering outputs normally yields significant performance improvements over unbuffered outputs.

17.2   Because typical input operations are extremely slow compared to processor speeds, buffering inputs normally yields significant performance improvements over unbuffered inputs.

17.3   Always release resources explicitly and at the earliest possible moment at which it is determined that the resource is no longer needed. This makes the resource immediately available to be reused by your program or by another program, thus improving resource utilization.

17.4   Explicitly close each file as soon as it is known that the program will not reference the file again. This can reduce resource usage in a program that will continue executing long after it no longer needs to be referencing a particular file. This practice also improves program clarity.

17.5   The process of closing a file and reopening a file for the purpose of positioning the file-position pointer back to the beginning of a file is a time-consuming task for the computer. If this is done frequently, it may slow the performance of your program.

Software Engineering Observation

17.1   It would be dangerous to enable applets arriving from anywhere on the World Wide Web to be able to read and write files on the client system. By default, most web browsers prevent applets from performing file processing on the client system. Therefore, file-processing programs are generally implemented as Java applications.

Self-Review Exercises

17.1   Fill in the blanks in each of the following:
   a) Ultimately, all data items processed by a computer are reduced to combinations of _____and _____.
   b) The smallest data item a computer can process is called a _____.
   c) A _____ is a group of related records.
   d) Digits, letters, and special symbols are referred to as _____.
   e) A group of related files is called a _____.
   f) Method _____ of the file stream classes **FileOutputStream**, **FileInputStream**, and **RandomAccessFile** closes a file.
   g) **RandomAccessFile** method _____ reads an integer from the specified stream.
   h) **RandomAccessFile** method _____ reads a line of text from the specified stream.
   i) **RandomAccessFile** method _____ sets the file-position pointer to a specific location in a file for input or output.

17.2   State which of the following are *true* and which are *false*. If *false*, explain why.
   a) The programmer must explicitly create the **System.in**, **System.out** and **System.err** objects.
   b) If the file-position pointer points to a location in a sequential file other than the beginning of the file, the file must be closed and reopened to read from the beginning of the file.
   c) It is not necessary to search through all the records in a random-access file to find a specific record.
   d) Records in random-access files must be of uniform length.
   e) Method **seek** must seek relative to the beginning of a file.

17.3   Assume that each of the following statements applies to the same program.
   a) Write a statement that opens file **"oldmast.dat"** for input; use **ObjectInputStream** object **inOldMaster** chained to a **FileInputStream** object.
   b) Write a statement that opens file **"trans.dat"** for input; use **ObjectInputStream** object **inTransaction** chained to a **FileInputStream** object.
   c) Write a statement that opens file **"newmast.dat"** for output (and creation); use **ObjectOutputStream** object **outNewMaster** chained to a **FileOutputStream**.
   d) Write a set of statements that read a record from the file **"oldmast.dat"**. The record consists of integer **accountNum**, string **name**, and floating-point **currentBalance**; use **ObjectInputStream** object **inOldMaster**.
   e) Write a set of statements that read a record from the file **"trans.dat"**. The record consists of integer **accountNum** and floating-point **dollarAmount**; use **ObjectInputStream** object **inTransaction**.

f) Write a set of statements that output a record to the file **"newmast.dat"**. The record consists of integer **accountNum**, string **name**, and floating point **currentBalance**; use **DataOutputStream** object **outNewMaster**.

17.4 Find the error and show how to correct it in each of the following.

a) Assume **account**, **company** and **amount** are declared.

```
ObjectOutputStream os;
os.writeInt( account );
os.writeChars( company );
os.writeDouble( amount );
```

b) The following statement should read a record from the file **"payables.dat"**. The **ObjectInputStream** object **inPayable** refers to this file, and **FileInput-Stream** object **inReceivable** refers to the file **"receivables.dat"**.

```
account = inReceivable.readInt();
companyID = inReceivable.readLong();
amount = inReceivable.readDouble();
```

Answers to Self-Review Exercises

17.1 a) 1s, 0s. b) Bit. c) File. d) Characters. e) Database. f) **close**. g) **readInt**. h) **readLine**. i) **seek**.

17.2 a) False. These three streams are created automatically for the programmer.

b) True.

c) True.

d) False. Records in a random-access file are normally of uniform length.

e) True.

17.3 a) **ObjectInputStream inOldMaster;**
inOldMaster = new ObjectInputStream(
                    new FileInputStream("oldmast.dat"));

b) **ObjectInputStream inTransaction;**
inTransaction = new ObjectInputStream(
                         new FileInputStream("trans.dat"));

c) **ObjectOutputStream outNewMaster;**
outNewMaster = new ObjectOutputStream(
                    new FileOutputStream("newmast.dat"));

d) **accountNum = inOldMaster.readInt();**
name = inOldMaster.readUTF();
currentBalance = inOldMaster.readDouble();

e) **accountNum = inTransaction.readInt();**
dollarAmount = inTransaction.readDouble();

f) **outNewMaster.writeInt(accountNum);**
outNewMaster.writeUTF(name);
outNewMaster.writeDouble(currentBalance);

17.4 a) Error: The file has not been opened before the attempt is made to output data to the stream.

Correction: Create a new **ObjectOutputStream** object chained to a **FileOutput-Stream** object to open the file for output.

b) Error: The incorrect **FileInputStream** object is being used to read a record from file **"payables.dat"**.

Correction: Use object **inPayable** to refer to **"payables.dat"**.

Exercises

17.5 Fill in the blanks in each of the following:
   a) Computers store large amounts of data on secondary storage devices as _____.
   b) A _____ is composed of several fields.
   c) A field that may contain only digits, letters, and blanks is called an_____ field.
   d) To facilitate the retrieval of specific records from a file, one field in each record is chosen as a _____.
   e) The vast majority of information stored in computer systems is stored in _____ files.
   f) The standard stream objects are _____ , _____ and_____ .

17.6 State which of the following are *true* and which are *false*. If *false*, explain why.
   a) The impressive functions performed by computers essentially involve the manipulation of zeros and ones.
   b) People specify programs and data items as characters; computers then manipulate and process these characters as groups of zeros and ones.
   c) A person's 5-digit zip code is an example of a numeric field.
   d) A person's street address is generally considered to be an alphabetic field.
   e) Data items represented in computers form a data hierarchy in which data items become larger and more complex as we progress from fields to characters to bits, etc.
   f) A record key identifies a record as belonging to a particular field.
   g) Companies store all their information in a single file to facilitate computer processing.
   h) When a program creates a file, the file is automatically retained by the computer for future reference.

17.7   Exercise 17.3 asked the reader to write a series of single statements. Actually, these statements form the core of an important type of file-processing program, namely, a file-matching program. In commercial data processing, it is common to have several files in each application system. In an accounts receivable system, for example, there is generally a master file containing detailed information about each customer such as the customer's name, address, telephone number, outstanding balance, credit limit, discount terms, contract arrangements, and possibly a condensed history of recent purchases and cash payments.

As transactions occur (i.e., sales are made and cash payments arrive in the mail), they are entered into a file. At the end of each business period (i.e., a month for some companies, a week for others, and a day in some cases) the file of transactions (called **"trans.dat"** in Exercise 17.3) is applied to the master file (called **"oldmast.dat"** in Exercise 17.3), thus updating each account's record of purchases and payments. During an updating run, the master file is rewritten as a new file (**"newmast.dat"**), which is then used at the end of the next business period to begin the updating process again.

File-matching programs must deal with certain problems that do not exist in single-file programs. For example, a match does not always occur. A customer on the master file may not have made any purchases or cash payments in the current business period, and therefore no record for this customer will appear on the transaction file. Similarly, a customer who did make some purchases or cash payments may have just moved to this community, and the company may not have had a chance to create a master record for this customer.

Use the statements in Exercise 17.3 as a basis for writing a complete file-matching accounts receivable program. Use the account number on each file as the record key for matching purposes. Assume that each file is a sequential file with records stored in increasing account number order.

When a match occurs (i.e., records with the same account number appear on both the master file and the transaction file), add the dollar amount on the transaction file to the current balance on the master file, and write the **"newmast.dat"** record. (Assume that purchases are indicated by positive amounts on the transaction file, and that payments are indicated by negative amounts.) When there is a master record for a particular account but no corresponding transaction record, merely write the master record to **"newmast.dat"**. When there is a transaction record but no corresponding master record, print the message **"Unmatched transaction record for account number ..."** (fill in the account number from the transaction record).

17.8   After writing the program of Exercise 17.7, write a simple program to create some test data for checking out the program. Use the following sample account data:

Master file Account number	Name	Balance
100	Alan Jones	348.17
300	Mary Smith	27.19
500	Sam Sharp	0.00
700	Suzy Green	-14.22

Transaction file Account number	Transaction amount
100	27.14
300	62.11
400	100.56
900	82.17

Run the program of Exercise 17.7 using the files of test data created in Exercise 17.8. Print the new master file. Check that the accounts have been updated correctly.

17.9   It is possible (actually common) to have several transaction records with the same record key. This occurs because a particular customer might make several purchases and cash payments during a business period. Rewrite your accounts receivable file-matching program of Exercise 17.7 to provide for the possibility of handling several transaction records with the same record key. Modify the test data of Exercise 17.8 to include the following additional transaction records:

Account number	Dollar amount
300	83.89
700	80.78
700	1.53

17.10   You are the owner of a hardware store and need to keep an inventory that can tell you what different tools you have, how many of each you have on hand, and the cost of each one. Write a program that initializes the random-access file **"hardware.dat"** to one hundred empty records, lets you input the data concerning each tool, enables you to list all your tools, lets you delete a record for a tool that you no longer have, and lets you update *any* information in the file. The tool identification number should be the record number. Use the following information to start your file:

Record #	Tool name	Quantity	Cost
3	Electric sander	18	35.99
19	Hammer	128	10.00
26	Jig saw	16	14.25
39	Lawn mower	10	79.50
56	Power saw	8	89.99
76	Screwdriver	236	4.99
81	Sledge hammer	32	19.75
88	Wrench	65	6.48

17.11 *(Telephone Number Word Generator)* Standard telephone keypads contain the digits 0 through 9. The numbers 2 through 9 each have three letters associated with them (see Fig. 17.17).

Many people find it difficult to memorize phone numbers, so they use the correspondence between digits and letters to develop seven-letter words that correspond to their phone numbers. For example, a person whose telephone number is 686-2377 might use the correspondence indicated in Fig. 17.17 to develop the seven-letter word "NUMBERS." Each seven-letter word corresponds to exactly one seven-digit telephone number. The restaurant wishing to increase its takeout business could surely do so with the number 825-3688 (i.e., "TAKEOUT").

Each seven-letter phone number corresponds to many separate seven-letter words. Unfortunately, most of these represent unrecognizable juxtapositions of letters. It is possible, however, that the owner of a barber shop would be pleased to know that the shop's telephone number, 424-7288, corresponds to "HAIRCUT." The owner of a liquor store would, no doubt, be delighted to find that the store's number, 233-7226, corresponds to "BEERCAN." A veterinarian with the phone number 738-2273 would be pleased to know that the number corresponds to the letters "PETCARE." An automotive dealership would be pleased to know that the dealership number, 639-2277, corresponds to "NEWCARS."

Write a program that, given a seven-digit number, writes to a file every possible seven-letter word combination corresponding to that number. There are 2187 (3^7) such words. Avoid phone numbers with the digits 0 and 1.

Digit	Letters
2	A B C
3	D E F
4	G H I
5	J K L
6	M N O
7	P R S
8	T U V
9	W X Y

Fig. 17.17   Telephone keypad digits and letters.

18

Java Database Connectivity (JDBC)

Objectives

- To understand the relational database model.
- To use the classes and interfaces of the `java.sql` package to query a database, insert data into a database and update data in a database.
- To understand basic database queries using Structured Query Language (SQL).

It is a capital mistake to theorize before one has data.
Arthur Conan Doyle

Now go, write it before them in a table, and note it in a book, that it may be for the time to come for ever and ever.
The Holy Bible: The Old Testament

Let's look at the record.
Alfred Emanuel Smith

True art selects and paraphrases, but seldom gives a verbatim translation.
Thomas Bailey Aldrich

Get your facts first, and then you can distort them as much as you please.
Mark Twain

I like two kinds of men: domestic and foreign.
Mae West

Outline

Summary • Terminology • Common Programming Errors • Good Programming Practice • Performance Tip • Portability Tips • Software Engineering Observations • Self-Review Exercises • Answers to Self-Review Exercises • Exercises • Bibliography

18.1 Introduction[1]

In Chapter 17 we discussed sequential and random-access file processing. Sequential file processing is appropriate for applications in which most or all of the file's information is to be processed. Random access file processing is appropriate for applications—especially transaction processing—in which it is crucial to be able to locate and possibly update an individual piece of data quickly, and in which only a small portion of a file's data is to be processed at once. Java provides solid capabilities for both types of file processing.

One problem with each of these schemes is that they simply provide for accessing data—they do not offer any capabilities for querying the data conveniently. Database systems not only provide file-processing capabilities, they organize data in a manner that facilitates satisfying sophisticated queries. The most popular style of database system on the kinds of computers that use Java is the *relational database*. Object-oriented databases are have also become popular in recent years. A language called *Structured Query Language (SQL)* is almost universally used among relational database systems to make *queries* (i.e., to request information that satisfies given criteria). Java enables programmers to write code

---

1. Portions of Sections 18.1, 18.2, 18.3 and 18.6 based on Deitel, H. M., *Operating Systems, 2/E*, pp. 404–409 (De90). Reading, MA: Addison-Wesley, 1990.

that uses SQL queries to access the information in relational database systems. Some popular relational database software packages include Microsoft Access, Sybase, Oracle, Informix and Microsoft SQL Server. In this chapter, we introduce the *Java Database Connectivity (JDBC) API* and use it to manipulate a Microsoft Access Database.

18.2 Database Systems

The availability of inexpensive massive direct access storage has caused a tremendous amount of research and development activity in the area of *database systems*. A *database* is an integrated collection of data. A database system involves the data itself, the hardware on which the data resides, the software (called a *database management system* or *DBMS*) that controls the storage and retrieval of data, and the users themselves.

18.2.1 Advantages of Database Systems

C. J. Date (Da81) lists several important advantages of database systems.

- Redundancy can be reduced.
- Inconsistency can be avoided.
- The data can be shared.
- Standards can be enforced.
- Security restrictions can be applied.
- Integrity can be maintained.
- Conflicting requirements can be balanced.

In non-database systems, each distinct application maintains its own files, often with considerable redundancy and a variety of physical formats. In database systems, redundancy is reduced by integrating separate files.

Sharing is one of the most important benefits of database systems. Existing applications can reference the same data.

Centralized control makes it possible to enforce standards rigidly. This becomes particularly important in computer networks in which data migration between systems occurs.

Security is an intriguing issue in database systems. The data may actually be more at risk because it is collected and retained in a central location rather than being dispersed throughout physically separate files in many locations. To counter this, database systems must be designed with elaborate access controls.

18.2.2 Data Independence

One of the most important aspects of database systems is *data independence* (i.e., applications need not be concerned with how the data is physically stored or accessed). An application is said to be *data dependent* if the storage structure and accessing strategy cannot be changed without affecting the application significantly.

Data independence makes it convenient for various applications to have different *views* of the same data. From the system's standpoint, data independence makes it possible for the storage structure and accessing strategy to be modified in response to the installation's changing requirements, but without the need to modify functioning applications.

18.2.3 Database Languages

Users access a database via statements in a database language. Application programs may use a conventional high-level language like Java, C, C++, Visual Basic, COBOL, PL/I or Pascal; a user may make requests of the database in a specially designed *query language* that makes it easy to express requests in the context of a particular application.

Such languages are referred to as host languages. Each host language ordinarily includes a *database sublanguage (DSL)* concerned with the specifics of database objects and operations. Generally, each data sublanguage is a combination of two languages, namely a *data definition language (DDL)* that provides facilities for defining database objects, and a *data manipulation language (DML)* that provides features for specifying the processing to be performed on database objects. The popular query language SQL (Structured Query Language) that we discuss in Section 18.6 provides both DDL and DML.

18.2.4 Distributed Database

A distributed database (Wi88) is a database that is spread across the computer systems of a network. Ordinarily in such systems each data item is stored at the location in which it is most frequently used, but it remains accessible to other network users.

Distributed systems provide the control and economics of local processing with the advantages of information accessibility over a geographically dispersed organization. They can be costly to implement and operate, however, and they can suffer from increased vulnerability to security violations.

18.3 Relational Database Model

Three different database models have achieved widespread popularity: hierarchical, network and relational. In this text, we concentrate on the most popular of these models—the relational database model.

The relational model developed by Codd (Co70) (Co72) (Bl88) (Co88) (Re88) is a logical representation of the data that allows the relationships between the data to be considered without concerning oneself with the physical implementation of the data structures.

A relational database is composed of *tables*. Figure 18.1 illustrates a sample table that might be used in a personnel system. The name of the table is EMPLOYEE and its primary purpose is to illustrate the various attributes of an employee and how they are related to a specific employee. Any particular row of the table is called a *record* (or *row*). This table consists of six records. The employee number field of each record in this table is used as the *primary key* for referencing data in the table. The records of Fig. 18.1 are ordered by primary key. Tables in a database normally have primary keys, but primary keys are not required. The primary key can be composed of more than one column (or field) in the database. Primary key fields in a table cannot contain duplicate values.

Each column of the table represents a different *field*. Records are normally unique (by primary key) within a table, but particular field values may be duplicated between records. For example, three different records in table EMPLOYEE contain department number 413.

Different users of a database are often interested in different data items and different relationships between those data items. Some users want only certain subsets of the table columns. Other users of a database wish to combine smaller tables into larger ones to produce more complex tables. Codd calls the subset operation *projection* and the combination operation *join*.

Using the table of Fig. 18.1, for example, we might use the projection operation to create a new table called DEPARTMENT-LOCATOR whose purpose is to show where departments are located. This new table is shown in Fig. 18.2. In Java, a table is manipulated as a **ResultSet** object.

The relational database organization has many advantages over the hierarchical and network schemes.

1. The tabular representation used in the relational scheme is easy for users to comprehend and easy to implement in the physical database system.

2. It is relatively easy to convert virtually any other type of database structure into the relational scheme. Thus, the scheme may be viewed as a universal form of representation.

3. The projection and join operations are easy to implement and make it easy to create the new tables needed for particular applications.

4. Searches in a database can be faster than in schemes that require following a series of pointers.

Table: EMPLOYEE

	Number	Name	Department	Salary	Location
	23603	JONES, A.	413	1100	NEW JERSEY
	24568	KERWIN, R.	413	2000	NEW JERSEY
A record	34589	LARSON, P.	642	1800	LOS ANGELES
	35761	MYERS, B.	611	1400	ORLANDO
	47132	NEUMANN, C.	413	9000	NEW JERSEY
	78321	STEPHENS, T.	611	8500	ORLANDO

Primary key   A column

Fig. 18.1   Relational database structure.

Table: DEPARTMENT-LOCATOR

Department	Location
413	NEW JERSEY
611	ORLANDO
642	LOS ANGELES

Fig. 18.2   A table formed by projection.

5. Relational structures are easier to modify than hierarchical or network structures. In environments where flexibility is important, this becomes critical.

6. The clarity and visibility of the database improve with the relational structure. It is much easier to search tabular data than it is to unwind possibly arbitrarily complex interconnections of data elements in a pointer-based mechanism.

18.4 Relational Database Overview: The Books.mdb Database

In this section we provide an overview of Structured Query Language (SQL) in the context of a sample database we created for this chapter. Before we get into SQL, we overview the tables of the **Books.mdb** database. We will use this database throughout the chapter to introduce various database concepts, including the use of SQL to obtain useful information from the database and to manipulate the database. The database can be found with the examples for this book.

The database consists of four tables—**Authors**, **Publishers**, **AuthorISBN** and **Titles**. The **Authors** table (shown in Fig. 18.3) consists of four fields that maintain each author's unique ID number in the database, first name, last name and the year in which the author was born. Figure 18.4 contains the data from the **Authors** table of the **Books.mdb** database.

The **Publishers** table (shown in Fig. 18.5) consists of two fields representing each publisher's unique ID and name. Figure 18.6 contains the data from the **Publishers** table of the **Books.mdb** database.

Field	Description
AuthorID	The author's ID number in the database. This is the primary key field for this table.
FirstName	The author's first name.
LastName	The author's last name.
YearBorn	The author's year of birth.

Fig. 18.3   **Authors** table from **Books.mdb**.

AuthorID	FirstName	LastName	YearBorn
1	Harvey	Deitel	1946
2	Paul	Deitel	1968
3	Tem	Nieto	1969

Fig. 18.4   Data from the **Authors** table of **Books.mdb**.

The **AuthorISBN** table (Fig. 18.7) consists of two fields that maintain each ISBN number and its corresponding author's ID number. This table will help link the names of the authors with the titles of their books. Figure 18.8 contains the data from the **Author-ISBN** table of the **Biblio.mdb** database. [*Note:* Some of the ISBN numbers are actually placeholders for proper ISBN numbers. We did not have final ISBN numbers for several of our publications at the time of this writing.]

Field	Description
PublisherID	The publisher's ID number in the database. This is the primary key field for this table.
PublisherName	The abbreviated name for the publisher.

Fig. 18.5   **Publishers** table from **Books.mdb**.

PublisherID	PublisherName
1	Prentice Hall
2	Prentice Hall PTR

Fig. 18.6   Data from the **Publishers** table of **Books.mdb**.

Field	Description
ISBN	The ISBN number for a book.
AuthorID	The author's ID number, which allows the database to connect each book to a specific author. The ID number in this field must also appear in the **Authors** table.

Fig. 18.7   **AuthorISBN** table from **Books.mdb**.

ISBN	AuthorID	ISBN	AuthorID
0-13-010671-2	1	0-13-020522-2	3
0-13-010671-2	2	0-13-082714-2	1
0-13-020522-2	1	0-13-082714-2	2
0-13-020522-2	2	0-13-082925-0	1

Fig. 18.8   Data from the **AuthorISBN** table of **Books.mdb** (part 1 of 2).

ISBN	AuthorID	ISBN	AuthorID
0-13-082925-0	2	0-13-565912-4	2
0-13-082927-7	1	0-13-565912-4	3
0-13-082927-7	2	0-13-899394-7	1
0-13-082928-5	1	0-13-899394-7	2
0-13-082928-5	2	0-13-904947-9	1
0-13-082928-5	3	0-13-904947-9	2
0-13-083054-2	1	0-13-904947-9	3
0-13-083054-2	2	0-13-GSVCPP-x	1
0-13-083055-0	1	0-13-GSVCPP-x	2
0-13-083055-0	2	0-13-IWCTC-x	1
0-13-118043-6	1	0-13-IWCTC-x	2
0-13-118043-6	2	0-13-IWCTC-x	3
0-13-226119-7	1	0-13-IWWW-x	1
0-13-226119-7	2	0-13-IWWW-x	2
0-13-271974-6	1	0-13-IWWW-x	3
0-13-271974-6	2	0-13-IWWWIM-x	1
0-13-456955-5	1	0-13-IWWWIM-x	2
0-13-456955-5	2	0-13-IWWWIM-x	3
0-13-456955-5	3	0-13-JAVA3-x	1
0-13-528910-6	1	0-13-JAVA3-x	2
0-13-528910-6	2	0-13-JCTC2-x	1
0-13-565912-4	1	0-13-JCTC2-x	2

Fig. 18.8   Data from the **AuthorISBN** table of **Books.mdb** (part 2 of 2).

The **Titles** table (Fig. 18.9) consists of six fields that maintain general information about each book in the database including the ISBN number, title, edition number, year published, a description of the book and the publisher's ID number. Figure 18.10 contains the data from the **Titles** table. [Note: We did not show the **Description** field of the **Titles** table in Fig. 18.10.]

Field	Description
ISBN	ISBN number of the book.
Title	Title of the book.
EditionNumber	The edition number of the book.

Fig. 18.9   **Titles** table from **Books.mdb** (part 1 of 2).

Field	Description
YearPublished	Year in which the book was published.
Description	A description of the book.
PublisherID	The publisher's ID number. This value must correspond to an ID number in the **Publishers** table.

Fig. 18.9   **Titles** table from **Books.mdb** (part 2 of 2).

ISBN	Title	Edition-Number	Year-Published	PublisherID
0-13-226119-7	C How to Program	2	1994	1
0-13-528910-6	C++ How to Program	2	1997	1
0-13-899394-7	Java How to Program	2	1997	1
0-13-java3-x	Java How to Program	3	1999	1
0-13-456955-5	Visual Basic 6 How to Program	1	1998	1
0-13-iwww-x	Internet and World Wide Web How to Program	1	1999	1
0-13-gsvcpp-x	Getting Started with Visual C++ 6 with an Introduction to MFC	1	1999	1
0-13-565912-4	C++ How to Program Instructor's Manual with Solutions Disk	2	1998	1
0-13-904947-9	Java How to Program Instructor's Manual with Solution Disk	2	1997	1
0-13-020522-2	Visual Basic 6 How to Program Instructor's Manual with Solution Disk	1	1999	1
0-13-iwwwim-x	Internet and World Wide Web How to Program Instructor's Manual with Solutions Disk	1	1999	1
0-13-082925-0	The Complete C++ Training Course	2	1998	2
0-13-082927-7	The Complete Java Training Course	2	1997	2
0-13-082928-5	The Complete Visual Basic 6 Training Course	1	1999	2
0-13-jctc2-x	The Complete Java Training Course	3	1999	2
0-13-iwctc-x	The Internet and World Wide Web How to Program Complete Training Course	1	1999	2
0-13-082714-2	C++ How to Program 2/e and Getting Started with Visual C++ 5.0 Tutorial	2	1998	1

Fig. 18.10   Data from the **Titles** table of **Books.mdb** (part 1 of 2).

ISBN	Title	Edition-Number	Year-Published	PublisherID
0-13-010671-2	Java How to Program 2/e and Getting Started with Visual J++ 1.1 Tutorial	2	1998	1
0-13-083054-2	The Complete C++ Training Course 2/e and Getting Started with Visual C++ 5.0 Tutorial	2	1998	1
0-13-083055-0	The Complete Java Training Course 2/e and Getting Started with Visual J++ 1.1 Tutorial	2	1998	1
0-13-118043-6	C How to Program	1	1992	1
0-13-271974-6	Java Multimedia Cyber Classroom	1	1996	2

Fig. 18.10 Data from the **Titles** table of **Books.mdb** (part 2 of 2).

Figure 18.11 illustrates the relationships between the tables in the **Books.mdb** database. The field name in bold in each table is that table's *primary key*. A table's primary key uniquely identifies each record in the table. Every record must have a value in the primary key field and the value must be unique. This is known as the *Rule of Entity Integrity*.

The lines between the tables represent the relationships. Consider the line between the **Publishers** and **Titles** tables. On the **Publishers** end of the line there is a **1** and on the **Titles** end there is an infinity symbol. This indicates that every publisher in the **Publishers** table can have an arbitrary number of books in the **Titles** table. This relationship is referred to as the *one-to-many relationship*. The **PublisherID** field in the **Titles** table is referred to as a *foreign key*—a field in a table for which every entry has a unique value in another table and where the field in the other table is the primary key for that table (i.e., **PublisherID** in the **Publishers** table). Foreign keys are specified when creating a table. The foreign key helps maintain the *Rule of Referential Integrity*— every foreign key field value must appear in another table's primary key field. Foreign keys enable information from multiple tables to be joined together for analysis purposes. There is a one-to-many relationship between a primary key and its corresponding foreign key.

Common Programming Error 18.1

When a field is specified as the primary key field, not providing a value for that field in every record breaks the Rule of Entity Integrity and is an error.

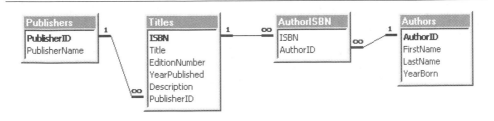

Fig. 18.11 Table relationships in **Books.mdb**.

Common Programming Error 18.2

When a field is specified as the primary key field, providing duplicate values for multiple records is an error.

The line between the **AuthorISBN** and **Authors** tables indicates that for each author in the **Authors** table there can be an infinite number of ISBNs for books that author wrote in the **AuthorISBN** table. The **AuthorID** field in the **AuthorISBN** table is a foreign key of the **AuthorID** field (the primary key) of the **Authors** table. This table is used to link information in the **Titles** and **Authors** tables.

Finally, the line between the **Titles** and **AuthorISBN** tables illustrates a one-to-many relationship—a title can be written by any number of authors.

18.5 Structured Query Language

In this section we provide an overview of Structured Query Language (SQL) in the context of the **Books.mdb** sample database we provided for this chapter. You will be able to use the SQL queries discussed here in the examples later in the chapter.

The SQL query keywords (Fig. 18.12) are discussed in the context of complete SQL queries in the next several sections. Note that there are other SQL keywords that are beyond the scope of this text. [*Note:* For more information on SQL, please refer to the bibliography at the end of this chapter. You can also find information on SQL on the Internet.]

18.5.1 Basic SELECT Query

Now, we will consider several SQL queries that allow us to extract information from the **Books.mdb** database.

A typical SQL query "selects" information from one or more tables in a database. Such selections are performed by **SELECT** *queries*. The simplest format of a **SELECT** query is

        SELECT * FROM *TableName*

In the preceding query, the asterisk (*****) indicates that all row and columns from *TableName* should be selected and *TableName* specifies the table in the database from which the data will be selected. For example, to select the entire contents of the **Authors** table (i.e., all the data in Fig. 18.4, use the query

        SELECT * FROM Authors

To select specific fields from a table, replace the asterisk (*****) with a comma-separated list of the field names to select. For example, to select only the fields **AuthorID** and **LastName** for all rows in the table use the query

        SELECT AuthorID, LastName FROM Authors

The preceding query returns the data in Fig. 18.13.

Software Engineering Observation 18.1

If a field name contains spaces, it must be enclosed in square brackets ([]) in the query.

SQL keyword	Description
SELECT	Select (retrieve) fields from one or more tables.
FROM	Tables from which to get fields. Required in every **SELECT**.
WHERE	Criteria for selection that determine the rows to be retrieved.
GROUP BY	How to group records.
HAVING	Used with the **GROUP BY** clause to specify criteria for grouping records in the query results.
ORDER BY	Criteria for ordering of records.

Fig. 18.12   SQL query keywords.

AuthorID	LastName
1	Deitel
2	Deitel
3	Nieto

Fig. 18.13   **AuthorID** and **LastName** from the **Authors** table.

18.5.2 WHERE Clause

Often it is necessary to locate records in a database that satisfy certain *selection criteria*. Only records that match the selection criteria are actually selected. SQL uses the optional *WHERE clause* in a **SELECT** query to specify the selection criteria for the query. The simplest format of a **SELECT** query with selection criteria is

> **SELECT** * **FROM** *TableName* **WHERE** *criteria*

For example, to select all fields from the **Authors** table where the author's **YearBorn** is greater than or equal to **1950**, use the query

> **SELECT** * **FROM Authors WHERE YearBorn > 1960**

Our database contains only three authors in the **Authors** table. Two of the authors were born after 1960, so the two records in Fig. 18.14 are returned by the preceding query.

AuthorID	FirstName	LastName	YearBorn
2	Paul	Deitel	1968
3	Tem	Nieto	1969

Fig. 18.14   Authors born after 1960 from the **Authors** table.

Performance Tip 18.1

Using selection criteria improves performance by selecting fewer records from the database.

The **WHERE** clause condition can contain operators **<, >, <=, >=, =, <>** and **LIKE**. Operator **LIKE** is used for *pattern matching* with wildcard characters *asterisk (*)* and *question mark (?)*. Pattern matching allows SQL to search for similar strings. An asterisk (*****) in the pattern indicates any number of characters in a row at the asterisk's location in the pattern. For example, the following query locates the records of all the authors whose last names start with the letter **d**:

SELECT * FROM Authors WHERE LastName LIKE 'd*'

Notice that the pattern string is surrounded by single-quote characters. The preceding query produces the two records shown in Fig. 18.15 because two of the three authors in our database have last names starting with the letter **d**.

Portability Tip 18.1

SQL is case sensitive on some database systems.

Portability Tip 18.2

*Not all database systems support the **LIKE** operator.*

Good Programming Practice 18.1

By convention, SQL keywords should use all capital letters on systems that are not case sensitive to make the SQL keywords stand out in an SQL query.

A question mark (**?**) in the pattern string indicates a single character at that position in the pattern. For example, the following query locates the records of all the authors whose last names start with any character (specified with **?**) followed by the letter **i** followed by any number of additional characters (specified with *****):

SELECT * FROM Authors WHERE LastName LIKE '?i*'

The preceding query produces the record in Fig. 18.16 because only one author in our database has a last name that contains the letter **i** as its second letter.

A query can be specialized to allow any character in a range of characters in one position of the pattern string. A range of characters can be specified as follows

[*startValue–endValue***]**

AuthorID	FirstName	LastName	YearBorn
1	Harvey	Deitel	1946
2	Paul	Deitel	1968

Fig. 18.15   Authors whose last names start with **d** from the **Authors** table.

AuthorID	FirstName	LastName	YearBorn
3	Tem	Nieto	1969

Fig. 18.16 Authors from the **Authors** table whose last names contain **i** as the second letter.

where *startValue* indicates the first character in the range and *endValue* represents the last value in the range. For example, the following query locates the records of all the authors whose last names start with any letter (specified with the **?**) followed by any letter in the range **a** to **i** (specified with **[a-i]**) followed by any number of additional characters (specified with *****):

> **SELECT * FROM Authors WHERE LastName LIKE '?[a-i]*'**

The preceding query returns all the records of the **Authors** table (Fig. 18.4) because every author in the table has a last name that contains a second letter in the range **a** to **i**.

18.5.3 ORDER BY Clause

The results of a query can be arranged in ascending or descending order using the optional ***ORDER BY*** *clause*. The simplest form of an **ORDER BY** clause is

> **SELECT * FROM** *TableName* **ORDER BY** *field* **ASC**
> **SELECT * FROM** *TableName* **ORDER BY** *field* **DESC**

where **ASC** specifies ascending (lowest to highest) order, **DESC** specifies descending (highest to lowest) order and *field* represents the field that is used for sorting purposes.

For example, to obtain the list of authors in ascending order by last name (Fig. 18.17), use the query

> **SELECT * FROM Authors ORDER BY LastName ASC**

Note that the default sorting order is ascending, so **ASC** is optional.

To obtain the same list of authors in descending order by last name (Fig. 18.18), use the query

> **SELECT * FROM Authors ORDER BY LastName DESC**

AuthorID	FirstName	LastName	YearBorn
2	Paul	Deitel	1968
1	Harvey	Deitel	1946
3	Tem	Nieto	1969

Fig. 18.17 Authors from the **Authors** table in ascending order by **LastName**.

AuthorID	FirstName	LastName	YearBorn
3	Tem	Nieto	1969
2	Paul	Deitel	1968
1	Harvey	Deitel	1946

Fig. 18.18 Authors from the **Authors** table in descending order by **LastName**.

Multiple fields can be used for ordering purposes with an **ORDER BY** clause of the form

ORDER BY *field1 SortingOrder*, *field2 SortingOrder*, ...

where *SortingOrder* is either **ASC** or **DESC**. Note that the *SortingOrder* does not have to be identical for each field. The query

```
SELECT * FROM Authors ORDER BY LastName, FirstName
```

sorts in ascending order all the authors by last name, then by first name. If any authors have the same last name, their records are returned in sorted order by their first name (Fig. 18.19).

The **WHERE** and **ORDER BY** clauses can be combined in one query. For example, the query

```
SELECT * FROM Titles
WHERE Title LIKE '*How to Program'
ORDER BY Title ASC
```

returns all records from the **Titles** table that have a **Title** ending with "**How to Program**" and orders them in ascending order by **Title**. The results of the query are shown in Fig. 18.20 (to save space we do not show the **Description** field). [*Note:* When we construct a query for use in Java we will simply create one long string containing the entire query. When we display queries in the text, we often use multiple lines and indentation for readability.]

18.5.4 Using INNER JOIN to Merge Data from Multiple Tables

Often it is necessary to merge data from multiple tables into a single view for analysis purposes. This is referred to as *joining* the tables and is accomplished using an **INNER JOIN** operation in the **FROM** clause of a **SELECT** query. An **INNER JOIN** merges records from two or more tables by testing for matching values in a field that is common to both tables. The simplest format of an **INNER JOIN** clause is

SELECT * **FROM** *Table1* **INNER JOIN** *Table2* **ON** *Table1.field* = *Table2.field*

The **ON** part of the **INNER JOIN** clause specifies the fields from each table that should be compared to determine which records will be selected. For example, to merge the **First-Name** and **LastName** fields from the **Authors** table with the **ISBN** field from the **AuthorISBN** table in ascending order by **LastName** and **FirstName** so you can see the ISBN numbers for the books that each author wrote, use the query

AuthorID	FirstName	LastName	YearBorn
1	Harvey	Deitel	1946
2	Paul	Deitel	1968
3	Tem	Nieto	1969

Fig. 18.19   Authors from the **Authors** table in ascending order by **LastName** and by **FirstName**.

ISBN	Title	Edition-Number	Year-Published	PublisherID
0-13-118043-6	C How to Program	1	1992	1
0-13-226119-7	C How to Program	2	1994	1
0-13-528910-6	C++ How to Program	2	1997	1
0-13-iwww-x	Internet and World Wide Web How to Program	1	1999	1
0-13-java3-x	Java How to Program	3	1999	1
0-13-899394-7	Java How to Program	2	1997	1
0-13-456955-5	Visual Basic 6 How to Program	1	1998	1

Fig. 18.20   Books from the **Titles** table whose titles end with **How to Program** in ascending order by **Title**.

```
SELECT FirstName, LastName, ISBN
FROM Authors INNER JOIN AuthorISBN
ON Authors.AuthorID = AuthorISBN.AuthorID
ORDER BY LastName, FirstName
```

Notice the use of the syntax *TableName.FieldName* in the **ON** part of the **INNER JOIN**. This syntax specifies the fields from each table that should be compared to join the tables. The "*TableName.*" syntax is required if the fields have the same name in both tables. The same syntax can be used in a query any time it is necessary to distinguish between fields in different tables that happen to have the same name.

As always, the **FROM** clause (including the **INNER JOIN**) can be followed by **WHERE** and **ORDER BY** clauses. Figure 18.21 shows the results of the preceding query.

FirstName	LastName	ISBN	FirstName	LastName	ISBN
Harvey	Deitel	0-13-gsvcpp-x	Harvey	Deitel	0-13-010671-2
Harvey	Deitel	0-13-271974-6	Harvey	Deitel	0-13-118043-6

Fig. 18.21   Authors and the ISBN numbers for the books they have written in ascending order by **LastName** and **FirstName** (part 1 of 2).

FirstName	LastName	ISBN	FirstName	LastName	ISBN
Harvey	Deitel	0-13-528910-6	Paul	Deitel	0-13-082928-5
Harvey	Deitel	0-13-083055-0	Paul	Deitel	0-13-082925-0
Harvey	Deitel	0-13-565912-4	Paul	Deitel	0-13-020522-2
Harvey	Deitel	0-13-083054-2	Paul	Deitel	0-13-904947-9
Harvey	Deitel	0-13-899394-7	Paul	Deitel	0-13-java3-x
Harvey	Deitel	0-13-904947-9	Paul	Deitel	0-13-iwwwim-x
Harvey	Deitel	0-13-226119-7	Paul	Deitel	0-13-iwww-x
Harvey	Deitel	0-13-082928-5	Paul	Deitel	0-13-iwctc-x
Harvey	Deitel	0-13-456955-5	Paul	Deitel	0-13-gsvcpp-x
Harvey	Deitel	0-13-iwwwim-x	Paul	Deitel	0-13-226119-7
Harvey	Deitel	0-13-iwctc-x	Paul	Deitel	0-13-899394-7
Harvey	Deitel	0-13-jctc2-x	Paul	Deitel	0-13-565912-4
Harvey	Deitel	0-13-082925-0	Paul	Deitel	0-13-528910-6
Harvey	Deitel	0-13-iwww-x	Paul	Deitel	0-13-jctc2-x
Harvey	Deitel	0-13-082714-2	Paul	Deitel	0-13-456955-5
Harvey	Deitel	0-13-082927-7	Paul	Deitel	0-13-271974-6
Harvey	Deitel	0-13-java3-x	Tem	Nieto	0-13-082928-5
Harvey	Deitel	0-13-020522-2	Tem	Nieto	0-13-565912-4
Paul	Deitel	0-13-118043-6	Tem	Nieto	0-13-456955-5
Paul	Deitel	0-13-010671-2	Tem	Nieto	0-13-iwctc-x
Paul	Deitel	0-13-083055-0	Tem	Nieto	0-13-iwww-x
Paul	Deitel	0-13-082927-7	Tem	Nieto	0-13-020522-2
Paul	Deitel	0-13-083054-2	Tem	Nieto	0-13-iwwwim-x
Paul	Deitel	0-13-082714-2	Tem	Nieto	0-13-904947-9

Fig. 18.21   Authors and the ISBN numbers for the books they have written in ascending order by **LastName** and **FirstName** (part 2 of 2).

18.5.5 TitleAuthor Query from Books.mdb

The **Books.mdb** database contains one predefined query (**TitleAuthor**) that produces a table containing the book title, ISBN number, author's first name, author's last name, book's year published and publisher's name for each book in the database. For books with multiple authors, the query produces a separate composite record for each author. The **TitleAuthor** query is shown in Fig. 18.22. A portion of the query results are shown in Fig. 18.23.

```
1   SELECT Titles.Title, Titles.ISBN, Authors.FirstName,
2          Authors.LastName, Titles.YearPublished,
3          Publishers.PublisherName
4   FROM
5       (Publishers INNER JOIN Titles
6           ON Publishers.PublisherID = Titles.PublisherID)
7       INNER JOIN
8       (Authors INNER JOIN AuthorISBN ON
9           Authors.AuthorID = AuthorISBN.AuthorID)
10      ON Titles.ISBN = AuthorISBN.ISBN
11  ORDER BY Titles.Title
```

Fig. 18.22   The **TitleAuthor** query from the **Books.mdb** database.

Title	ISBN	First Name	Last-Name	Year-Published	Publisher-Name
C How to Program	0-13-226119-7	Paul	Deitel	1994	Prentice Hall
C How to Program	0-13-118043-6	Paul	Deitel	1992	Prentice Hall
C How to Program	0-13-118043-6	Harvey	Deitel	1992	Prentice Hall
C How to Program	0-13-226119-7	Harvey	Deitel	1994	Prentice Hall
C++ How to Program	0-13-528910-6	Harvey	Deitel	1997	Prentice Hall
C++ How to Program	0-13-528910-6	Paul	Deitel	1997	Prentice Hall
…					
Internet and World Wide Web How to Program	0-13-IWWW-x	Paul	Deitel	1999	Prentice Hall
Internet and World Wide Web How to Program	0-13-IWWW-x	Harvey	Deitel	1999	Prentice Hall
Internet and World Wide Web How to Program	0-13-IWWW-x	Tem	Nieto	1999	Prentice Hall
…					
Java How to Program	0-13-JAVA3-x	Harvey	Deitel	1999	Prentice Hall
Java How to Program	0-13-899394-7	Paul	Deitel	1997	Prentice Hall
Java How to Program	0-13-899394-7	Harvey	Deitel	1997	Prentice Hall
Java How to Program	0-13-JAVA3-x	Paul	Deitel	1999	Prentice Hall
…					
Visual Basic 6 How to Program	0-13-456955-5	Harvey	Deitel	1998	Prentice Hall
Visual Basic 6 How to Program	0-13-456955-5	Paul	Deitel	1998	Prentice Hall
Visual Basic 6 How to Program	0-13-456955-5	Tem	Nieto	1998	Prentice Hall

Fig. 18.23   A portion of the query results from the **TitleAuthor** query.

The indentation in the preceding query is simply to make the query more readable. Let us now break down the query into its various parts. Lines 1 through 3 indicate the fields that will be returned by the query and their order in the returned table from left to right. This query will select the **Title** and **ISBN** fields from the **Titles** table, the **FirstName** and **LastName** fields from the **Authors** table, the **YearPublished** field from the **Titles** table and the **PublisherName** field from the **Publishers** table. For the purpose of this query, we fully qualified each field name with its table name (e.g., **Titles.ISBN**).

Lines 4 through 11 specify the **INNER JOIN** operations that will combine information from the tables. Notice that there are three **INNER JOIN** operations. Remember that an **INNER JOIN** is performed on two tables. It is important to note that either of those two tables can be the result of another query or another **INNER JOIN**. Parentheses are used to nest the **INNER JOIN** operations and the parentheses are always evaluated from the innermost set of parentheses first. So, we begin with the **INNER JOIN**

```
(Publishers INNER JOIN Titles
      ON Publishers.PublisherID = Titles.PublisherID)
```

that specifies the **Publishers** table and the **Titles** table should be joined **ON** the condition that the **PublisherID** number in each table matches. The resulting temporary table contains all the information about each book and the publisher that published it.

Moving to the other nested set of parentheses, an **INNER JOIN** is performed on the **Authors** table and the **AuthorISBN** table using

```
(Authors INNER JOIN AuthorISBN ON
      Authors.AuthorID = AuthorISBN.AuthorID)
```

This **INNER JOIN** joins the **Authors** table and the **AuthorISBN** table **ON** the condition that the **AuthorID** field in the **Authors** table matches the **AuthorID** field from the **AuthorISBN** table. Remember that the **AuthorISBN** table may have multiple entries for each **ISBN** number if there is more than one author for that book.

Next, the results of the two preceding **INNER JOIN** operation are combined with the **INNER JOIN**

```
(Publishers INNER JOIN Titles
   ON Publishers.PublisherID = Titles.PublisherID)
INNER JOIN
(Authors INNER JOIN AuthorISBN ON
   Authors.AuthorID = AuthorISBN.AuthorID)
ON Titles.ISBN = AuthorISBN.ISBN
```

that combines the two temporary tables **ON** the condition that the **Titles.ISBN** field in the first temporary table matches the **AuthorISBN.ISBN** field in the second temporary table. The result of all these **INNER JOIN** operations is a temporary table from which the appropriate fields are selected for the results of this query.

Finally, line 11 of the query

```
ORDER BY Titles.Title
```

indicates that all the titles should be sorted in ascending order (the default).

18.6 A First Example

In this example, we perform a simple query on the **Books.mdb** database that retrieves all the information about all the authors in the **Authors** table and displays the data in a **JTable** component. The program of Fig. 18.24 illustrates connecting to the database, querying the database and displaying the results. The following discussion presents the key JDBC aspects of the program. Section 18.6.1 discusses registering the database as an ODBC data source on a computer running the Microsoft Windows operating system. *Note:* The steps in Section 18.6.1 must be performed before executing the program of Fig. 18.24.

```
1   // Fig. 18.24: TableDisplay.java
2   // This program displays the contents of the Authors table
3   // in the Books database.
4   import java.sql.*;
5   import javax.swing.*;
6   import java.awt.*;
7   import java.awt.event.*;
8   import java.util.*;
9
10  public class TableDisplay extends JFrame {
11      private Connection connection;
12      private JTable table;
13
14      public TableDisplay()
15      {
16          // The URL specifying the Books database to which
17          // this program connects using JDBC to connect to a
18          // Microsoft ODBC database.
19          String url = "jdbc:odbc:Books";
20          String username = "anonymous";
21          String password = "guest";
22
23          // Load the driver to allow connection to the database
24          try {
25              Class.forName( "sun.jdbc.odbc.JdbcOdbcDriver" );
26
27              connection = DriverManager.getConnection(
28                  url, username, password );
29          }
30          catch ( ClassNotFoundException cnfex ) {
31              System.err.println(
32                  "Failed to load JDBC/ODBC driver." );
33              cnfex.printStackTrace();
34              System.exit( 1 );  // terminate program
35          }
36          catch ( SQLException sqlex ) {
37              System.err.println( "Unable to connect" );
38              sqlex.printStackTrace();
39          }
40
```

Fig. 18.24   Connecting to a database, querying the database and displaying the results (part 1 of 4).

```
41            getTable();
42
43            setSize( 450, 150 );
44            show();
45        }
46
47        private void getTable()
48        {
49            Statement statement;
50            ResultSet resultSet;
51
52            try {
53                String query = "SELECT * FROM Authors";
54
55                statement = connection.createStatement();
56                resultSet = statement.executeQuery( query );
57                displayResultSet( resultSet );
58                statement.close();
59            }
60            catch ( SQLException sqlex ) {
61                sqlex.printStackTrace();
62            }
63        }
64
65        private void displayResultSet( ResultSet rs )
66            throws SQLException
67        {
68            // position to first record
69            boolean moreRecords = rs.next();
70
71            // If there are no records, display a message
72            if ( ! moreRecords ) {
73                JOptionPane.showMessageDialog( this,
74                    "ResultSet contained no records" );
75                setTitle( "No records to display" );
76                return;
77            }
78
79            setTitle( "Authors table from Books" );
80
81            Vector columnHeads = new Vector();
82            Vector rows = new Vector();
83
84            try {
85                // get column heads
86                ResultSetMetaData rsmd = rs.getMetaData();
87
88                for ( int i = 1; i <= rsmd.getColumnCount(); ++i )
89                    columnHeads.addElement( rsmd.getColumnName( i ) );
90
```

Fig. 18.24   Connecting to a database, querying the database and displaying the results (part 2 of 4).

```
91              // get row data
92              do {
93                 rows.addElement( getNextRow( rs, rsmd ) );
94              } while ( rs.next() );
95
96              // display table with ResultSet contents
97              table = new JTable( rows, columnHeads );
98              JScrollPane scroller = new JScrollPane( table );
99              getContentPane().add(
100                 scroller, BorderLayout.CENTER );
101             validate();
102          }
103          catch ( SQLException sqlex ) {
104             sqlex.printStackTrace();
105          }
106       }
107
108       private Vector getNextRow( ResultSet rs,
109                                  ResultSetMetaData rsmd )
110          throws SQLException
111       {
112          Vector currentRow = new Vector();
113
114          for ( int i = 1; i <= rsmd.getColumnCount(); ++i )
115             switch( rsmd.getColumnType( i ) ) {
116                case Types.VARCHAR:
117                      currentRow.addElement( rs.getString( i ) );
118                   break;
119                case Types.INTEGER:
120                      currentRow.addElement(
121                         new Long( rs.getLong( i ) ) );
122                   break;
123                default:
124                   System.out.println( "Type was: " +
125                      rsmd.getColumnTypeName( i ) );
126             }
127
128          return currentRow;
129       }
130
131       public void shutDown()
132       {
133          try {
134             connection.close();
135          }
136          catch ( SQLException sqlex ) {
137             System.err.println( "Unable to disconnect" );
138             sqlex.printStackTrace();
139          }
140       }
141
```

Fig. 18.24 Connecting to a database, querying the database and displaying the results (part 3 of 4).

```
142      public static void main( String args[] )
143      {
144         final TableDisplay app = new TableDisplay();
145
146         app.addWindowListener(
147            new WindowAdapter() {
148               public void windowClosing( WindowEvent e )
149               {
150                  app.shutDown();
151                  System.exit( 0 );
152               }
153            }
154         );
155      }
156   }
```

Authors table from Books			_ □ ×
AuthorID	FirstName	LastName	YearBorn
1	Harvey	Deitel	1946
2	Paul	Deitel	1968
3	Tem	Nieto	1969

Fig. 18.24   Connecting to a database, querying the database and displaying the results (part 4 of 4).

Line 4 imports package **java.sql** which contains classes and interfaces for manipulating relational databases in Java. Line 11 declares a **Connection** reference (package **java.sql**) called **connection**. This will refer to an object that implements interface **Connection**. A **Connection** object manages the connection between the Java program and the database. It also provides support for executing SQL statements to manipulate the database and transaction processing (discussed at the end of this chapter).

The constructor for class **TableDisplay** (line 14) attempts the connection to the database, and, if successful, queries the database and displays the results by calling utility method **getTable** (defined at line 47). Lines 19 through 21

```
String url = "jdbc:odbc:Books";
String username = "anonymous";
String password = "guest";
```

specify the database *URL (Uniform Resource Locator)* that helps the program locate the database (possibly on a network or in the local file system of the computer), the *username* for logging in to the database and the *password* for logging in to the database. The URL specifies the *protocol* for communication (**jdbc**), the *subprotocol* for communication (**odbc**) and the name of the database (**Books**). The subprotocol **odbc** indicates that the program will be using **jdbc** to connect to a *Microsoft ODBC data source* (we show how to set up that data source in Section 18.6.1). ODBC is a technology developed by Microsoft to allow generic access to disparate database systems on the Windows platform (and some UNIX platforms). The Java 2 Software Development Kit (J2SDK) comes with the *JDBC-to-ODBC-bridge database driver* to allow any Java program to access any ODBC data source. The driver is defined by class *JdbcOdbcDriver* in package *sun.jdbc.odbc*.

The class definition for the database driver must be loaded before the program can connect to the database. Line 25

```
Class.forName( "sun.jdbc.odbc.JdbcOdbcDriver" );
```

uses **static** method *forName* of class *Class* (package **java.lang**) to load the class definition for the database driver (this line throws a *java.lang.ClassNotFoundException* if the class cannot be located). Notice that the statement specifies the complete package name and class name—**sun.jdbc.odbc.JdbcOdbcDriver**.

Software Engineering Observation 18.2

Most major database vendors provide their own JDBC database drivers and many third-party vendors provide JDBC drivers as well.

For more information on JDBC drivers and supported databases visit the Sun Microsystems JDBC Web site

```
http://java.sun.com/products/jdbc/
```

Lines 27 and 28

```
connection = DriverManager.getConnection(
    url, username, password );
```

use **static** method *getConnection* of class *DriverManager* (package **java.sql**) to attempt a connection to the database specified by **url**. The **username** and **password** arguments are passed here because we intentionally set up the data source to require the user to log in. Our database is set up with one username—**anonymous**—and one password—**guest**—for demonstration purposes. If the **DriverManager** cannot connect to the database, method **getConnection** throws a *java.sql.SQLException*. If the connection attempt is successful, line 41 calls utility method **getTable** (defined at line 47) to retrieve data from the **Authors** table.

Utility method **getTable** queries the database then calls utility method **displayResultSet** to create a *JTable* (package **javax.swing**) containing the results of the query. Line 49 declares a **Statement** (package **java.sql**) reference that will refer to an object that implements interface **Statement**. This object will submit the query to the database. Line 50 declares a **ResultSet** (package **java.sql**) reference that will refer to an object that implements interface **ResultSet**. When a query is performed on a database, a **ResultSet** object is returned containing the results of the query. The methods of interface **ResultSet** allow the programmer to manipulate the query results.

Line 53 defines the query to perform. In this example, we will select all the records from the **Authors** table.

Line 55

```
statement = connection.createStatement();
```

invokes **Connection** method *createStatement* to obtain an object that implements the **Statement** interface. We can now use **statement** to query the database.

Line 56

```
resultSet = statement.executeQuery( query );
```

performs the query by calling **Statement** method *executeQuery*. This method returns an object that implements **ResultSet** and contains the results of the query. The **ResultSet** is passed to utility method **displayResultSet** (defined at line 65), then the statement is closed on line 58 to indicate that we are done processing the query.

Line 69 of method **displayResultSet**

```
boolean moreRecords = rs.next();
```

positions to the first record in the **ResultSet** with **ResultSet** method *next*. Initially the **ResultSet** is positioned before the first record, so this method must be called before you can access the results. Method **next** returns a **boolean** indicating if it was able to position to the next record. If the method returns **false**, there are no more records to process. If there are records, line 81 defines a **Vector** to store the column names of the columns in the **ResultSet** and line 82 defines a **Vector** to store the rows of data from the **ResultSet**. These **Vector**s are used with the **JTable** constructor to build a **JTable** that displays the data from the **ResultSet**.

Line 86

```
ResultSetMetaData rsmd = rs.getMetaData();
```

obtains the *meta data* for the **ResultSet** and assigns it to a *ResultSetMetaData* (package **java.sql**) reference. The meta data for the **ResultSet** describes the contents of a **ResultSet**. This information can be used to programmatically obtain information about the names and types of the **ResultSet** columns and can help the programmer process a **ResultSet** dynamically when detailed information about the **ResultSet** is not known in advance of the query. We use the **ResultSetMetaData** in lines 88 and 89 to retrieve the names of each column in the **ResultSet**. **ResultSetMetaData** method *getColumnCount* returns the number of columns in the **ResultSet** and **ResultSetMetaData** method *getColumnName* returns the name of the specified column.

Lines 92 through 94

```
do {
   rows.addElement( getNextRow( rs, rsmd ) );
} while ( rs.next() );
```

retrieve each row of the **ResultSet** using utility method **getNextRow** (defined at line 108). Method **getNextRow** returns a **Vector** containing the data for one row of the **ResultSet**. Notice the condition **rs.next()**. This moves the **ResultSet** *cursor* that keeps track of the current record in the **ResultSet** to the next record in the **ResultSet**. Remember that method next returns false when there are no more records in the **ResultSet**. Therefore, the loop will terminate when there are no more records.

After all the rows are converted to **Vector**s, line 97 creates the **JTable** GUI component that displays the records in the **ResultSet**. The constructor we use in this program receives two **Vector**s as arguments. The first argument is a **Vector** of **Vector**s (similar to a double-subscripted array) that contains all the row data. The second argument is a **Vector** containing the column names for each column. The **JTable** constructor uses these **Vector**s to populate the table.

Method **getNextRow** (line 108) receives a **ResultSet** and its corresponding **ResultSetMetaData** as arguments and creates a **Vector** containing one row of data from the **ResultSet**. The **for** structure at line 114 loops through each column of the result set and executes the **switch** structure at line 115 that determines the column's data type. **ResultSetMetaData** method *getColumnType* returns a constant integer from class *Types* (package **java.sql**) indicating the type of the data. The only types of data in our database are strings and long integers. The SQL type for strings is *Types.VAR-CHAR* and the SQL type for long integers is *Types.INTEGER*. Line 117 uses **ResultSet** method *getString* to get the **String** from a column of type **Types.VARCHAR**. Lines 120 and 121 use **ResultSet** method *getLong* to get the long integer from a column of type **Types.INTEGER**.

Method **shutDown** at line 131 closes the connection to the database with **Connection** method **close** (line 134).

18.6.1 Registering Books.mdb as an ODBC Data Source

The preceding example assumes that **Books.mdb** is already registered as an ODBC data source. This section illustrates how to set up an ODBC source on a Microsoft Windows computer. *Note:* The computer must have Microsoft Access installed. To connect to the database, an *ODBC data source* must be registered with the system through the *ODBC Data Sources* option in the Windows **Control Panel**. Double-click this option to display the *ODBC Data Source Administrator* dialog (Fig. 18.25).

This dialog is used to register our *User Data Source Name* (*User DSN*). Make sure that the **User DSN** tab is selected, then click **Add...** to display the *Create new Data Source* dialog (Fig. 18.26). Because we are using a Microsoft Access database, we select *Microsoft Access Driver* and click **Finish**.

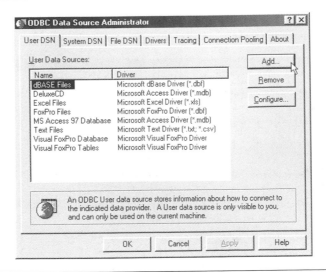

Fig. 18.25   ODBC Data Source Administrator dialog.

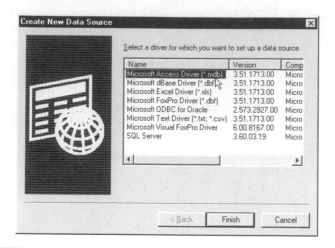

Fig. 18.26   Create New Data Source dialog.

The ***ODBC Microsoft Access 97 Setup*** dialog now appears (Fig. 18.27). We enter the name (e.g., **Books**) that we will use to reference the database with JDBC in the ***Data Source Name*** text field. You can also enter a description. Click the **Select…** button to display the **Select Database** dialog. Use this dialog to locate and select the **Books.mdb** database file on your system (or on the network). When you are done click **OK** to dismiss the **Select Database** dialog and return to the **ODBC Microsoft Access 97 Setup** dialog. Next click the **Advanced…** button to display the **Set Advanced Options** dialog. Type the username "**anonymous**" and the password "**guest**" in the fields at the top of the dialog, then click **OK** to dismiss the dialog. Click **OK** to dismiss the **ODBC Microsoft Access 97 Setup** dialog.

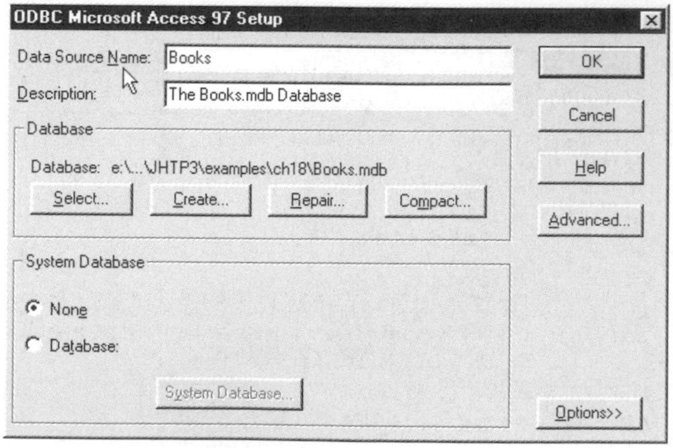

Fig. 18.27   ODBC Microsoft Access 97 Setup dialog.

Notice that the **ODBC Data Source Administrator** dialog now contains the data source **Books** (Fig. 18.28). Clicking **OK** dismisses the dialog. We are now ready to access the ODBC data source through the JDBC-to-ODBC bridge driver. Execute the program of Fig. 18.24 to display the contents of the **Authors** table from the **Books.mdb** database.

18.6.2 Querying the Books.mdb Database

The example of Fig. 18.29 enhances the example of Fig. 18.24 by allowing the user to enter any query into the program. When the user presses the **Submit query** button, method **ac-tionPerformed** (line 58) invokes utility method **getTable** (defined at line 84) to perform the query and display the results. The screen capture illustrates a query that displays each title in the **Titles** table with its corresponding publisher from the **Publishers** table. Try entering your own queries.

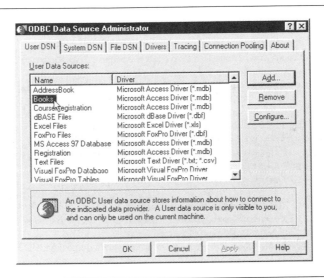

Fig. 18.28   ODBC Data Source Administrator dialog displaying registered drivers.

```
1   // Fig. 18.29: DisplayQueryResults.java
2   // This program displays the ResultSet returned by a
3   // query on the Books database.
4   import java.sql.*;
5   import javax.swing.*;
6   import java.awt.*;
7   import java.awt.event.*;
8   import java.util.*;
9
10  public class DisplayQueryResults extends JFrame {
11      // java.sql types needed for database processing
12      private Connection connection;
13      private Statement statement;
14      private ResultSet resultSet;
```

Fig. 18.29   Submitting queries to the **Books.mdb** database (part 1 of 5).

```
15      private ResultSetMetaData rsMetaData;
16
17      // javax.swing types needed for GUI
18      private JTable table;
19      private JTextArea inputQuery;
20      private JButton submitQuery;
21
22      public DisplayQueryResults()
23      {
24         super( "Enter Query. Click Submit to See Results." );
25
26         // The URL specifying the Books database to which
27         // this program connects using JDBC to connect to a
28         // Microsoft ODBC database.
29         String url = "jdbc:odbc:Books";
30         String username = "anonymous";
31         String password = "guest";
32
33         // Load the driver to allow connection to the database
34         try {
35            Class.forName( "sun.jdbc.odbc.JdbcOdbcDriver" );
36
37            connection = DriverManager.getConnection(
38               url, username, password );
39         }
40         catch ( ClassNotFoundException cnfex ) {
41            System.err.println(
42               "Failed to load JDBC/ODBC driver." );
43            cnfex.printStackTrace();
44            System.exit( 1 );  // terminate program
45         }
46         catch ( SQLException sqlex ) {
47            System.err.println( "Unable to connect" );
48            sqlex.printStackTrace();
49            System.exit( 1 );  // terminate program
50         }
51
52         // If connected to database, set up GUI
53         inputQuery =
54            new JTextArea( "SELECT * FROM Authors", 4, 30 );
55         submitQuery = new JButton( "Submit query" );
56         submitQuery.addActionListener(
57            new ActionListener() {
58               public void actionPerformed( ActionEvent e )
59               {
60                  if ( e.getSource() == submitQuery )
61                     getTable();
62               }
63            }
64         );
65
66         JPanel topPanel = new JPanel();
67         topPanel.setLayout( new BorderLayout() );
```

Fig. 18.29 Submitting queries to the **Books.mdb** database (part 2 of 5).

```
68          topPanel.add( new JScrollPane( inputQuery),
69                     BorderLayout.CENTER );
70          topPanel.add( submitQuery, BorderLayout.SOUTH );
71
72          table = new JTable( 4, 4 );
73
74          Container c = getContentPane();
75          c.setLayout( new BorderLayout() );
76          c.add( topPanel, BorderLayout.NORTH );
77          c.add( table, BorderLayout.CENTER );
78
79          getTable();
80
81          setSize( 500, 500 );
82          show();
83       }
84
85       private void getTable()
86       {
87          try {
88             String query = inputQuery.getText();
89
90             statement = connection.createStatement();
91             resultSet = statement.executeQuery( query );
92             displayResultSet( resultSet );
93          }
94          catch ( SQLException sqlex ) {
95             sqlex.printStackTrace();
96          }
97       }
98
99       private void displayResultSet( ResultSet rs )
100         throws SQLException
101      {
102         // position to first record
103         boolean moreRecords = rs.next();
104
105         // If there are no records, display a message
106         if ( ! moreRecords ) {
107            JOptionPane.showMessageDialog( this,
108               "ResultSet contained no records" );
109            setTitle( "No records to display" );
110            return;
111         }
112
113         Vector columnHeads = new Vector();
114         Vector rows = new Vector();
115
116         try {
117            // get column heads
118            ResultSetMetaData rsmd = rs.getMetaData();
119
```

Fig. 18.29   Submitting queries to the **Books.mdb** database (part 3 of 5).

```
120          for ( int i = 1; i <= rsmd.getColumnCount(); ++i )
121              columnHeads.addElement( rsmd.getColumnName( i ) );
122
123          // get row data
124          do {
125              rows.addElement( getNextRow( rs, rsmd ) );
126          } while ( rs.next() );
127
128          // display table with ResultSet contents
129          table = new JTable( rows, columnHeads );
130          JScrollPane scroller = new JScrollPane( table );
131          Container c = getContentPane();
132          c.remove( 1 );
133          c.add( scroller, BorderLayout.CENTER );
134          c.validate();
135       }
136       catch ( SQLException sqlex ) {
137          sqlex.printStackTrace();
138       }
139    }
140
141    private Vector getNextRow( ResultSet rs,
142                               ResultSetMetaData rsmd )
143       throws SQLException
144    {
145       Vector currentRow = new Vector();
146
147       for ( int i = 1; i <= rsmd.getColumnCount(); ++i )
148          switch( rsmd.getColumnType( i ) ) {
149             case Types.VARCHAR:
150             case Types.LONGVARCHAR:
151                currentRow.addElement( rs.getString( i ) );
152                break;
153             case Types.INTEGER:
154                currentRow.addElement(
155                   new Long( rs.getLong( i ) ) );
156                break;
157             default:
158                System.out.println( "Type was: " +
159                   rsmd.getColumnTypeName( i ) );
160          }
161
162       return currentRow;
163    }
164
165    public void shutDown()
166    {
167       try {
168          connection.close();
169       }
170       catch ( SQLException sqlex ) {
171          System.err.println( "Unable to disconnect" );
```

Fig. 18.29   Submitting queries to the **Books.mdb** database (part 4 of 5).

```
172                sqlex.printStackTrace();
173           }
174       }
175
176       public static void main( String args[] )
177       {
178           final DisplayQueryResults app =
179               new DisplayQueryResults();
180
181           app.addWindowListener(
182               new WindowAdapter() {
183                   public void windowClosing( WindowEvent e )
184                   {
185                       app.shutDown();
186                       System.exit( 0 );
187                   }
188               }
189           );
190       }
191   }
```

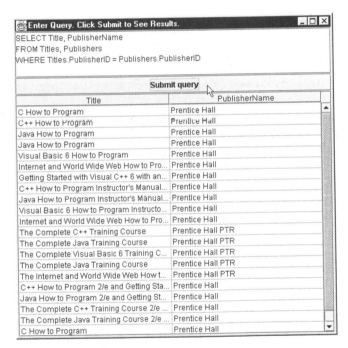

Fig. 18.29 Submitting queries to the **Books.mdb** database (part 5 of 5).

18.7 Reading, Inserting, and Updating a Microsoft Access database

The next example (Fig. 18.30) manipulates a simple, one-table Microsoft Access **Ad-dressBook** database that contains one table (**addresses**) with 11 columns—**ID** (a unique, long integer ID number for each person in the address book), **FirstName**, **Last-Name**, **Address**, **City**, **StateOrProvince**, **PostalCode**, **Country**, **EmailAd-**

dress, **HomePhone** and **FaxNumber**. The fields other than **ID** are all strings. The program provides facilities for inserting new records, updating existing records and searching for records in the database. Once again, we create the database as an ODBC data source and access it in our Java program through the JDBC-to-ODBC bridge database driver.

```
1   // Fig. 18.30: AddressBook.java
2   // Inserting into, updating and searching through a database
3   import java.sql.*;
4   import java.awt.*;
5   import java.awt.event.*;
6   import javax.swing.*;
7
8   public class AddressBook extends JFrame {
9      private ControlPanel controls;
10     private ScrollingPanel scrollArea;
11     private JTextArea output;
12     private String url;
13     private Connection connect;
14     private JScrollPane textpane;
15
16     public AddressBook()
17     {
18        super( "Address Book Database Application" );
19
20        Container c = getContentPane();
21
22        // Start screen layout
23        scrollArea = new ScrollingPanel();
24        output = new JTextArea( 6, 30 );
25        c.setLayout( new BorderLayout() );
26        c.add( new JScrollPane( scrollArea ),
27               BorderLayout.CENTER );
28        textpane = new JScrollPane( output );
29        c.add( textpane, BorderLayout.SOUTH );
30
31        // Set up database connection
32        try {
33           url = "jdbc:odbc:AddressBook";
34
35           Class.forName( "sun.jdbc.odbc.JdbcOdbcDriver" );
36           connect = DriverManager.getConnection( url );
37           output.append( "Connection successful\n" );
38        }
39        catch ( ClassNotFoundException cnfex ) {
40           // process ClassNotFoundExceptions here
41           cnfex.printStackTrace();
42           output.append( "Connection unsuccessful\n" +
43                          cnfex.toString() );
44        }
```

Fig. 18.30 Inserting, finding and updating records (part 1 of 16).

```
45          catch ( SQLException sqlex ) {
46             // process SQLExceptions here
47             sqlex.printStackTrace();
48             output.append( "Connection unsuccessful\n" +
49                             sqlex.toString() );
50          }
51          catch ( Exception ex ) {
52             // process remaining Exceptions here
53             ex.printStackTrace();
54             output.append( ex.toString() );
55          }
56
57          // Complete screen layout
58          controls =
59             new ControlPanel( connect, scrollArea, output);
60          c.add( controls, BorderLayout.NORTH );
61
62          setSize( 500, 500 );
63          show();
64       }
65
66       public static void main( String args[] )
67       {
68          AddressBook app = new AddressBook();
69
70          app.addWindowListener(
71             new WindowAdapter() {
72                public void windowClosing( WindowEvent e )
73                {
74                   System.exit( 0 );
75                }
76             }
77          );
78       }
79    }
```

Fig. 18.30   Inserting, finding and updating records (part 2 of 16).

```
80   // Fig. 18.30: AddRecord.java
81   // Class AddRecord definition
82   import java.awt.*;
83   import java.awt.event.*;
84   import java.sql.*;
85   import javax.swing.*;
86
87   public class AddRecord implements ActionListener {
88      private ScrollingPanel fields;
89      private JTextArea output;
90      private Connection connection;
91
```

Fig. 18.30   Inserting, finding and updating records (part 3 of 16).

```
92    public AddRecord( Connection c, ScrollingPanel f,
93                     JTextArea o )
94    {
95       connection = c;
96       fields = f;
97       output = o;
98    }
99
100   public void actionPerformed( ActionEvent e )
101   {
102      try {
103         Statement statement = connection.createStatement();
104
105         if ( !fields.last.getText().equals( "" ) &&
106              !fields.first.getText().equals( "" ) ) {
107            String query = "INSERT INTO addresses (" +
108               "firstname, lastname, address, city, " +
109               "stateorprovince, postalcode, country, " +
110               "emailaddress, homephone, faxnumber" +
111               ") VALUES ('" +
112               fields.first.getText() + "', '" +
113               fields.last.getText() + "', '" +
114               fields.address.getText() + "', '" +
115               fields.city.getText() + "', '" +
116               fields.state.getText() + "', '" +
117               fields.zip.getText() + "', '" +
118               fields.country.getText() + "', '" +
119               fields.email.getText() + "', '" +
120               fields.home.getText() + "', '" +
121               fields.fax.getText() + "')";
122            output.append( "\nSending query: " +
123                           connection.nativeSQL( query )
124                           + "\n" );
125            int result = statement.executeUpdate( query );
126
127            if ( result == 1 )
128               output.append( "\nInsertion successful\n" );
129            else {
130               output.append( "\nInsertion failed\n" );
131               fields.first.setText( "" );
132               fields.last.setText( "" );
133               fields.address.setText( "" );
134               fields.city.setText( "" );
135               fields.state.setText( "" );
136               fields.zip.setText( "" );
137               fields.country.setText( "" );
138               fields.email.setText( "" );
139               fields.home.setText( "" );
140               fields.fax.setText( "" );
141            }
142         }
```

Fig. 18.30   Inserting, finding and updating records (part 4 of 16).

```
143             else
144                 output.append( "\nEnter at least first and " +
145                                 "last name then press Add\n" );
146
147             statement.close();
148         }
149         catch ( SQLException sqlex ) {
150             sqlex.printStackTrace();
151             output.append( sqlex.toString() );
152         }
153     }
154 }
```

Fig. 18.30　Inserting, finding and updating records (part 5 of 16).

```
155 // Fig. 18.30: FindRecord.java
156 // Class FindRecord defintion
157 import java.awt.*;
158 import java.awt.event.*;
159 import java.sql.*;
160 import javax.swing.*;
161
162 public class FindRecord implements ActionListener {
163     private ScrollingPanel fields;
164     private JTextArea output;
165     private Connection connection;
166
167     public FindRecord( Connection c, ScrollingPanel f,
168                        JTextArea o )
169     {
170         connection = c;
171         fields = f;
172         output = o;
173     }
174
175     public void actionPerformed( ActionEvent e )
176     {
177         try {
178             if ( !fields.last.getText().equals( "" ) ) {
179                 Statement statement =connection.createStatement();
180                 String query = "SELECT * FROM addresses " +
181                                "WHERE lastname = '" +
182                                fields.last.getText() + "'";
183                 output.append( "\nSending query: " +
184                                connection.nativeSQL( query )
185                                + "\n" );
186                 ResultSet rs = statement.executeQuery( query );
187                 display( rs );
188                 output.append( "\nQuery successful\n" );
189                 statement.close();
190             }
```

Fig. 18.30　Inserting, finding and updating records (part 6 of 16).

```
191              else
192                  fields.last.setText(
193                      "Enter last name here then press Find" );
194          }
195          catch ( SQLException sqlex ) {
196              sqlex.printStackTrace();
197              output.append( sqlex.toString() );
198          }
199      }
200
201      // Display results of query. If rs is null
202      public void display( ResultSet rs )
203      {
204          try {
205              rs.next();
206
207              int recordNumber = rs.getInt( 1 );
208
209              if ( recordNumber != 0 ) {
210                  fields.id.setText( String.valueOf( recordNumber));
211                  fields.first.setText( rs.getString( 2 ) );
212                  fields.last.setText( rs.getString( 3 ) );
213                  fields.address.setText( rs.getString( 4 ) );
214                  fields.city.setText( rs.getString( 5 ) );
215                  fields.state.setText( rs.getString( 6 ) );
216                  fields.zip.setText( rs.getString( 7 ) );
217                  fields.country.setText( rs.getString( 8 ) );
218                  fields.email.setText( rs.getString( 9 ) );
219                  fields.home.setText( rs.getString( 10 ) );
220                  fields.fax.setText( rs.getString( 11 ) );
221              }
222              else
223                  output.append( "\nNo record found\n" );
224          }
225          catch ( SQLException sqlex ) {
226              sqlex.printStackTrace();
227              output.append( sqlex.toString() );
228          }
229      }
230  }
```

Fig. 18.30   Inserting, finding and updating records (part 7 of 16).

```
231  // Fig. 18.30: UpdateRecord.java
232  // Class UpdateRecord definition
233  import java.awt.*;
234  import java.awt.event.*;
235  import java.sql.*;
236  import javax.swing.*;
237
238  public class UpdateRecord implements ActionListener {
239      private ScrollingPanel fields;
```

Fig. 18.30   Inserting, finding and updating records (part 8 of 16).

```
240        private JTextArea output;
241        private Connection connection;
242
243        public UpdateRecord( Connection c, ScrollingPanel f,
244                             JTextArea o )
245        {
246           connection = c;
247           fields = f;
248           output = o;
249        }
250
251        public void actionPerformed( ActionEvent e )
252        {
253           try {
254              Statement statement = connection.createStatement();
255
256              if ( ! fields.id.getText().equals( "" ) ) {
257                 String query = "UPDATE addresses SET " +
258                    "firstname='" + fields.first.getText() +
259                    "', lastname='" + fields.last.getText() +
260                    "', address='" + fields.address.getText() +
261                    "', city='" + fields.city.getText() +
262                    "', stateorprovince='" +
263                    fields.state.getText() +
264                    "', postalcode='" + fields.zip.getText() +
265                    "', country='" + fields.country.getText() +
266                    "', emailaddress='" +
267                    fields.email.getText() +
268                    "', homephone='" + fields.home.getText() +
269                    "', faxnumber='" + fields.fax.getText() +
270                    "' WHERE id=" + fields.id.getText();
271                 output.append( "\nSending query: " +
272                    connection.nativeSQL( query ) + "\n" );
273
274                 int result = statement.executeUpdate( query );
275
276                 if ( result == 1 )
277                    output.append( "\nUpdate successful\n" );
278                 else {
279                    output.append( "\nUpdate failed\n" );
280                    fields.first.setText( "" );
281                    fields.last.setText( "" );
282                    fields.address.setText( "" );
283                    fields.city.setText( "" );
284                    fields.state.setText( "" );
285                    fields.zip.setText( "" );
286                    fields.country.setText( "" );
287                    fields.email.setText( "" );
288                    fields.home.setText( "" );
289                    fields.fax.setText( "" );
290                 }
291
```

Fig. 18.30   Inserting, finding and updating records (part 9 of 16).

```
292                     statement.close();
293                 }
294                 else
295                     output.append( "\nYou may only update an " +
296                                     "existing record. Use Find to " +
297                                     "locate the record, then " +
298                                     "modify the information and " +
299                                     "press Update.\n" );
300             }
301         catch ( SQLException sqlex ) {
302             sqlex.printStackTrace();
303             output.append( sqlex.toString() );
304         }
305     }
306 }
```

Fig. 18.30   Inserting, finding and updating records (part 10 of 16).

```
307 // Fig. 18.30: Help.java
308 // Class Help definition
309 import java.awt.*;
310 import java.awt.event.*;
311 import javax.swing.*;
312
313 public class Help implements ActionListener {
314     private JTextArea output;
315
316     public Help( JTextArea o )
317     {
318         output = o;
319     }
320
321     public void actionPerformed( ActionEvent e )
322     {
323         output.append( "\nClick Find to locate a record.\n" +
324                         "Click Add to insert a new record.\n" +
325                         "Click Update to update " +
326                         "the information in a record.\n" +
327                         "Click Clear to empty" +
328                         " the textfields.\n" );
329     }
330 }
```

Fig. 18.30   Inserting, finding and updating records (part 11 of 16).

```
331 // Fig. 18.30: ControlPanel.java
332 // Class ControlPanel definition
333 import java.awt.*;
334 import java.awt.event.*;
335 import java.sql.*;
336 import javax.swing.*;
337
```

Fig. 18.30   Inserting, finding and updating records (part 12 of 16).

```
338  public class ControlPanel extends JPanel {
339     private JButton findName, addName,
340                       updateName, clear, help;
341
342     public ControlPanel( Connection c, ScrollingPanel s,
343                          JTextArea t )
344     {
345        setLayout( new GridLayout( 1, 5 ) );
346
347        findName = new JButton( "Find" );
348        findName.addActionListener( new FindRecord( c, s, t ) );
349        add( findName );
350
351        addName = new JButton( "Add" );
352        addName.addActionListener( new AddRecord( c, s, t ) );
353        add( addName );
354
355        updateName = new JButton( "Update" );
356        updateName.addActionListener(
357           new UpdateRecord( c, s, t ) );
358        add( updateName );
359
360        clear = new JButton( "Clear" );
361        clear.addActionListener( new ClearFields( s ) );
362        add( clear );
363
364        help = new JButton( "Help" );
365        help.addActionListener( new Help( t ) );
366        add( help );
367     }
368  }
```

Fig. 18.30   Inserting, finding and updating records (part 13 of 16).

```
369  // Fig. 18.30: ScrollingPanel.java
370  // Class ScrollingPanel
371  import java.awt.*;
372  import java.awt.event.*;
373  import javax.swing.*;
374
375  public class ScrollingPanel extends JPanel {
376     private JPanel labelPanel, fieldsPanel;
377     private String labels[] =
378                   { "ID number:", "First name:", "Last name:",
379                     "Address:", "City:", "State/Province:",
380                     "PostalCode:", "Country:", "Email:",
381                     "Home phone:", "Fax Number:" };
382     JTextField id, first, last, address,     // package access
383                city, state, zip,
384                country, email, home, fax;
385
```

Fig. 18.30   Inserting, finding and updating records (part 14 of 16).

```
386        public ScrollingPanel()
387        {
388           // Label panel
389           labelPanel = new JPanel();
390           labelPanel.setLayout(
391                           new GridLayout( labels.length, 1 ) );
392
393           ImageIcon ii = new ImageIcon( "images/icon.jpg" );
394
395           for ( int i = 0; i < labels.length; i++ )
396              labelPanel.add( new JLabel( labels[ i ], ii, 0) );
397
398           // TextField panel
399           fieldsPanel = new JPanel();
400           fieldsPanel.setLayout(
401                           new GridLayout( labels.length, 1 ) );
402           id = new JTextField( 20 );
403           id.setEditable( false );
404           fieldsPanel.add( id );
405           first = new JTextField( 20 );
406           fieldsPanel.add( first );
407           last = new JTextField( 20 );
408           fieldsPanel.add( last );
409           address = new JTextField( 20 );
410           fieldsPanel.add( address );
411           city = new JTextField( 20 );
412           fieldsPanel.add( city );
413           state = new JTextField( 20 );
414           fieldsPanel.add( state  );
415           zip = new JTextField( 20 );
416           fieldsPanel.add( zip );
417           country = new JTextField( 20 );
418           fieldsPanel.add( country );
419           email = new JTextField( 20 );
420           fieldsPanel.add( email );
421           home = new JTextField( 20 );
422           fieldsPanel.add( home );
423           fax = new JTextField( 20 );
424           fieldsPanel.add( fax );
425
426           setLayout( new GridLayout( 1, 2 ) );
427           add( labelPanel );
428           add( fieldsPanel );
429        }
430     }
```

Fig. 18.30   Inserting, finding and updating records (part 15 of 16).

```
431   // Fig. 18.30: ClearFields.java
432   // Class ClearFields definition
433   import java.awt.*;
434   import java.awt.event.*;
435
436   public class ClearFields implements ActionListener {
437      private ScrollingPanel fields;
438
439      public ClearFields( ScrollingPanel f )
440      {
441         fields = f;
442      }
443
444      public void actionPerformed( ActionEvent e )
445      {
446         fields.id.setText( "" );
447         fields.first.setText( "" );
448         fields.last.setText( "" );
449         fields.address.setText( "" );
450         fields.city.setText( "" );
451         fields.state.setText( "" );
452         fields.zip.setText( "" );
453         fields.country.setText( "" );
454         fields.email.setText( "" );
455         fields.home.setText( "" );
456         fields.fax.setText( "" );
457      }
458   }
```

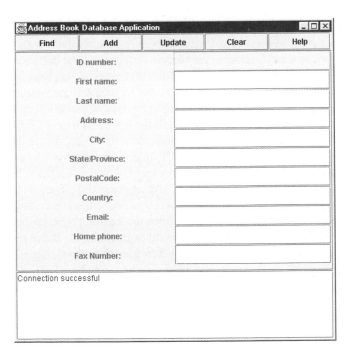

Fig. 18.30 Inserting, finding and updating records (part 16 of 16).

Class **AddressBook** (defined at line 8) uses a **ControlPanel** (defined at line 338) object and a **ScrollingPanel** (defined at line 375) object for the program's GUI. Line 36 establishes the database connection by passing **getConnection** the **String** "**jbdc:odbc:AddressBook**." [*Note:* This assumes that the **AddressBook.mdb** database is registered as an ODBC data source with the User DSN "**AddressBook**." See Section 18.6.1 for information on registering an ODBC data source.] Separate classes are defined to handle events from each of the five buttons in the user interface.

Class **AddRecord** (defined at line 87) adds a new record to the **AddressBook** database in response to the **Add** button in the GUI. **AddRecord**'s constructor (line 92) takes three arguments—a **Connection**, a **ScrollingPanel** and a **JTextArea** which serves as an output area for messages displayed by this program. Line 103 in method **actionPerformed** creates a **Statement** object for manipulating the database. Lines 105 and 106 test that data exist in the first name and last name text fields. If the text fields do not contain data, no record will be added to the database. Lines 107 through 121 build the SQL **INSERT INTO** string that will be used to add a record to the database. The basic format of an **INSERT INTO** SQL statement is

```
INSERT INTO tableName ( columnName1, columnName2, ... )
VALUES ( 'value1', 'value2', ... )
```

where *tableName* is the table in which the data will be inserted. Each column name to be updated is specified in a comma-separated list in parentheses. The value for each column is specified after SQL keyword **VALUES** in another comma-separated list in parentheses. Line 125

```
int result = statement.executeUpdate( query );
```

uses **Statement** method *executeUpdate* to update the database with the new record. The method returns an **int** indicating the success or failure of the update operation which is tested on line 127. If the update is unsuccessful, all the text fields are cleared.

Class **FindRecord** (defined at line 162) searches the **AddressBook** database for a specific record in response to the **Find** button in the GUI. Line 178 tests if the last name text field contains data. If empty, the program sets the last name text field to "**Enter last name here then press Find**". If data does exist in the last name text field, a new **Statement** is created on line 179. The SQL query **String** is created on lines 180 through 182. This query selects only the records that match the last name that was entered in the last name text field. Line 187 calls method **display** and passes it the **ResultSet** returned by the **executeQuery** call. The first record is obtained by calling method **next** on line 205. Line 27 gets the record number from the **ResultSet** object **rs** by calling **getInt**. Line 209 determines if the record number is non-zero. If the record number is non-zero, the text fields are populated with the data from the record. Line 211 displays the first name **String** returned by **ResultSet** method **getString**. The argument **2** refers to the column number (column numbers start from 1) in the record. Similar statements are performed for each text field. When this operation is completed, the GUI displays the first record from the **ResultSet**.

Class **UpdateRecord** (defined at line 238) updates an existing database record. Line 256 tests to see if the **id** for the current record is valid. Lines 257 through 270 create the SQL **UPDATE** query **String query**. A basic **UPDATE** SQL statement has the form

```
UPDATE tableName SET columnName1='value1', columnName2='value2', ...
WHERE criteria
```

where *tableName* is the table to update, the individual columns to update are specified (followed by an equal sign an a new value in single quotes) after the SQL **SET** keyword and the **WHERE** clause determines the record (or records in some cases) to update. Line 274 sends the query to the database by calling method **executeUpdate**.

Class **ClearFields** (defined at line 436) is responsible for clearing the text fields in response to the **Clear** button in the GUI and class **Help** (defined at line 313) displays instructions on how to use the program in the console window on the bottom of the screen.

18.8 Transaction Processing

If the database supports *transaction processing*, changes made to the database can be undone. Java provides transaction processing via methods of interface **Connection**. Method *setAutoCommit* specifies if each individual SQL statement should be performed and committed individually (a **true** argument) or if several SQL statements should be grouped as a transaction (a **false** argument). If the argument to **setAutoCommit** is **false**, the **Statement** that executes the SQL statements must be terminated with a call to **Connection** method *commit* (to commit the changes to the database) or method *rollback* (to return the database to its state before the transaction began). Interface **Connection** also provides method *getAutoCommit* to determine the auto commit state.

Summary

- Database systems provide file-processing capabilities but organize data in a manner to facilitate satisfying sophisticated queries.
- The most popular style of database system on personal computers is the relational database.
- Structured Query Language (SQL) is almost universally used to make relational database queries.
- A database is an integrated collection of data which is centrally controlled.
- A database management system (DBMS) controls the storage and retrieval of data in a database.
- A distributed database is a database that is spread throughout the computer systems of a network.
- A relational database is composed of tables that can be manipulated as a ResultSet objects in Java.
- Any particular row of the table is called a record or a row.
- Each column of the table represents a different field.
- Some users want only certain subsets of the table columns (called projections). Other users wish to combine smaller tables into larger ones to produce more complex tables (called joins).
- A table's primary key uniquely identifies each record in the table. Every record must have a value in the primary key field—Rule of Entity Integrity—and the value must be unique.
- A foreign key is a field in a table for which every entry has a unique value in another table and where the field in the other table is the primary key for that table. The foreign key helps maintain the Rule of Referential Integrity—every value in a foreign key field must appear in another table's primary key field. Foreign keys enable information from multiple tables to be joined together and presented to the user.
- A typical SQL query "selects" information from one or more tables in a database. Such selections are performed by **SELECT** queries. The simplest format of a **SELECT** query is

```
SELECT * FROM TableName
```

where the asterisk (*****) indicates that all fields from *TableName* should be selected and *TableName* specifies the table in the database from which the fields will be selected. To select specific fields from a table, replace the asterisk (*****) with a comma-separated list of the field names to select.

- SQL uses the optional **WHERE** clause to specify the selection criteria for the query. The simplest format of a **SELECT** query with selection criteria is

```
SELECT * FROM TableName WHERE criteria
```

The condition in the **WHERE** clause can contain operators **<**, **>**, **<=**, **>=**, **=**, **<>** and **LIKE**. Operator **LIKE** is used for pattern matching with the wildcard characters asterisk (*****) and question mark (**?**).

- The results of a query can be arranged in ascending or descending order using the optional **ORDER BY** clause. The simplest format of an **ORDER BY** clause is

```
SELECT * FROM TableName ORDER BY field ASC
SELECT * FROM TableName ORDER BY field DESC
```

where **ASC** specifies ascending (lowest to highest) order, **DESC** specifies descending (highest to lowest) order and *field* represents the field that is used for sorting purposes.

- Multiple fields can be used for ordering purposes with an **ORDER BY** clause of the form

```
ORDER BY field1 SortingOrder, field2 SortingOrder, ...
```

where *SortingOrder* is either **ASC** or **DESC**.

- The **WHERE** and **ORDER BY** clauses can be combined in one query.

- An **INNER JOIN** merges records from two tables by testing for matching values in a field that is common to both tables. The simplest format of an **INNER JOIN** clause is

```
SELECT * FROM Table1 INNER JOIN Table2 ON Table1.field = Table2.field
```

The **ON** part of the **INNER JOIN** clause specifies the fields from each table that should be compared to determine which records will be selected.

- The syntax TableName.FieldName is used in a query to distinguish between fields in different tables that have the same name.

- Package **java.sql** contains classes and interfaces for manipulating relational databases in Java.

- Interface **Connection** (package **java.sql**) helps manage the connection between the Java program and the database. It also provides support for executing SQL statements to manipulate the database and transaction processing.

- Connecting to a database requires the database URL (Uniform Resource Locator) that helps the program locate the database (possibly on a network or in the local file system of the computer) and may require a username and password for logging in to the database.

- The database URL specifies the protocol for communication, the subprotocol for communication and the name of the database.

- The subprotocol **odbc** indicates that the program will be using **jdbc** and the JDBC-to-ODBC bridge driver to connect to a Microsoft ODBC data source. ODBC is a technology developed by Microsoft to allow generic access to disparate database systems on the Windows platform.

- The Java 2 Software Development Kit (J2SDK) comes with the JDBC-to-ODBC-bridge database driver to allow any Java program to access any ODBC data source. The driver is defined by class **JdbcOdbcDriver** in package **sun.jdbc.odbc**.

- Method **forName** of class **Class** is used to load the class definition for a database driver. Class **sun.jdbc.odbc.JdbcOdbcDriver** represents the JDBC-to-ODBC bridge driver.

- Method **getConnection** of class **DriverManager** attempts a connection to the database specified by its argument (the database URL). If the **DriverManager** cannot connect to the database, method **getConnection** throws a **java.sql.SQLException**.

- A **Statement** (package **java.sql**) object is used to submit a query to a database.

- When a query is performed on a database, a **ResultSet** (package **java.sql**) object is returned containing the results of the query. The methods of interface **ResultSet** allow the programmer to manipulate the query results.

- **Connection** method **createStatement** obtains a **Statement** object that will be used to manipulate a database.

- **Statement** method **executeQuery** returns an object that implements interface **ResultSet** and contains the results of a query.

- **ResultSet** method **next** positions the cursor to the next record in the **ResultSet**. Initially the **ResultSet** cursor is positioned before the first record, so this method must be called before you can access the results. Method **next** returns a **boolean** value indicating if it was able to position to the next record. If this method returns **false**, there are no more records to process.

- **ResultSet** method **getMetaData** returns the meta data for the **ResultSet** in a **ResultSetMetaData** object. The meta data for the **ResultSet** describes the contents of a **ResultSet**. This information can be used to obtain information about the names and types of the **ResultSet** columns and can help the programmer process a **ResultSet** dynamically when detailed information about the **ResultSet** is not known in advance of the query.

- **ResultSetMetaData** method **getColumnCount** returns the number of columns in the **ResultSet**. **ResultSetMetaData** method **getColumnName** returns the name of the specified column.

- **ResultSetMetaData** method **getColumnType** returns a constant integer from class **Types** (package **java.sql**) indicating the type of the data.

- To connect to an ODBC data source the database must be registered with the system through the **ODBC Data Sources** option in the Windows **Control Panel**.

- The basic format of an **INSERT INTO** SQL statement is

  > **INSERT INTO** *tableName* (*columnName1, columnName2, ...*)
  > **VALUES** (*'value1'*, *'value2'*, ...)

  where *tableName* is the table in which the data will be inserted. Each column name to be updated is specified in a comma-separated list in parentheses. The value for each column is specified after the SQL keyword **VALUES** in another comma-separated list in parentheses.

- **Statement** method **executeUpdate** sends an SQL statement to the database that updates a record or adds a new record. The method returns an **int** indicating the success or failure of the update operation.

- A basic **UPDATE** SQL statement has the form

  > **UPDATE** *tableName* **SET** *columnName1*=*'value1'*, *columnName2*=*'value2'*, ...
  > **WHERE criteria**

  where *tableName* is the table to update, the individual columns to update are specified (followed by an equal sign an a new value in single quotes) after the SQL **SET** keyword and the **WHERE** clause determines a single record to update.

- If the database supports transaction processing—changes made to the database can be undone. Java provides transaction processing via several methods of interface **Connection**.

- Method **setAutoCommit** determines if each individual SQL statement should be performed and committed individually or if several SQL statements should be grouped as a transaction. If the argument to **setAutoCommit** is **false**, the **Statement** used to execute the SQL statements must be terminated with a call to **Connection** method **commit** or method **rollback**. Interface **Connection** also provides method **getAutoCommit** that returns to determine the auto commit state.

Terminology

ANSI (American National Standards Institute)
ASC (ascending order)
asterisk (*****) wildcard character
commit method of interface **Connection**
connect a Java program to a database
Connection interface
createStatement method of **Connection**
criteria clause
current record
data normalization
database
database driver
database file
database management system (DBMS)
database URL
DESC (descending order)
executeQuery method of **Statement**
executeUpdate method of **Statement**
field
field as column of table in relational database
foreign key
forName method of class **Class**
getAutoCommit method of **Connection**
getColumnCount method
getColumnName method
getColumnType method
getConnection method (**DriverManager**)
getMetaData method of **ResultSet**
INNER JOIN ... ON ...
INNER JOIN clause of **SELECT** statement
INSERT INTO SQL statement
java.sql package
jdbc protocol
JDBC-to-ODBC-bridge database driver
join two relational database tables
joined table

JTable class
LIKE operator in a criteria clause
Microsoft Access
next method of interface **ResultSet**
ODBC data source
odbc subprotocol
ORDER BY ... ASC clause
ORDER BY ... DESC clause
primary key field of a record in a table
question mark (**?**) wildcard character
record (row of a table)
record as row of table in relational database
relational database
relational database
ResultSet interface
rollback method of interface **Connection**
row of a table (record)
Rule of Entity Integrity
Rule of Referential Integrity
SELECT ... FROM ... SQL statement
SELECT ... FROM ... WHERE ... ORDER BY ...
setAutoCommit method of **Connection**
SQL (Structured Query Language)
SQLException class
square brackets (**[]**)
Statement interface
sun.jdbc.odbc.JdbcOdbcDriver class
table in a database
transaction processing
Types class
UPDATE SQL statement
URL (Uniform Resource Locator)
view in a relational database
WHERE clause of **SELECT** statement
wildcard characters

Common Programming Errors

18.1   When a field is specified as the primary key field, not providing a value for that field in every record breaks the Rule of Entity Integrity and is an error.

18.2   When a field is specified as the primary key field, providing duplicate values for multiple records is an error.

Good Programming Practice

18.1   By convention, SQL keywords should use all capital letters on systems that are not case sensitive to make the SQL keywords stand out in an SQL query.

Performance Tip

18.1   Using selection criteria improves performance by selecting fewer records from the database.

Portability Tips

18.1   SQL is case sensitive on some database systems.

18.2   Not all database systems support the **LIKE** operator.

Software Engineering Observations

18.1   If a field name contains spaces, it must be enclosed in square brackets (**[ ]**) in the query.

18.2   Most major database vendors provide their own JDBC database drivers and many third-party vendors provide JDBC drivers as well.

Self-Review Exercises

18.1   Fill in the blanks in each of the following:

   a) The most popular database query language is _____.

   b) A table in a database consists of _____ and _____.

   c) Tables are manipulated in Java as _____ objects.

   d) The _____ uniquely identifies each record in a table.

   e) SQL keyword _____ is followed by the selection criteria that specify the records to select in a query.

   f) SQL keyword _____ specifies the order in which records are sorted in a query.

   g) SQL keyword _____ is used to merge data from two or more tables.

   h) A _____ is an integrated collection of data which is centrally controlled.

   i) A _____ is a field in a table for which every entry has a unique value in another table and where the field in the other table is the primary key for that table.

   j) Package _____ contains classes and interfaces for manipulating relational databases in Java.

   k) Interface _____ helps manage the connection between the Java program and the database.

   l) Class _____ represents the JDBC-to-ODBC bridge driver.

   m) A _____ object is used to submit a query to a database.

Answers to Self-Review Exercises

18.1   a) SQL. b) rows, columns. c) **ResultSet**. d) primary key. e) **WHERE**. f) **ORDER BY**. g) **INNER JOIN**. h) database. i) foreign key. j) **java.sql**. k) **Connection**. l) **sun.jdbc.odbc.JdbcOdbcDriver**. m) **Statement**.

Exercises

18.2   Using the techniques shown in this chapter, define a complete query application for the **Books.mdb** database. Provide a series of predefined queries with an appropriate name for each query displayed in a **JComboBox**. Also allow the user to supply their own queries and add them to the **JComboBox**. Provide the following predefined queries:

   a) Select all authors from the **Authors** table.

   b) Select all publishers from the **Publishers** table.

c) Select a specific author and list all books for that author. Include the title, year and ISBN number. Order the information alphabetically by title.

d) Select a specific publisher and list all books published by that publisher. Include the title, year and ISBN number. Order the information alphabetically by title.

e) Provide any other queries you feel are appropriate.

18.3   Modify Exercise 18.2 to define a complete database manipulation application for the **Books.mdb** database. In addition to the querying capabilities, the user should be able to edit existing data and add new data to the database (obeying referential and entity integrity constraints). Allow the user to edit the database in the following ways:

a) Add a new author.

b) Edit the existing information for an author.

c) Add a new title for an author (remember that the book must have an entry in the **AuthorISBN** table). Be sure to specify the publisher of the title.

d) Add a new publisher.

e) Edit the existing information for a publisher.

For each of the preceding database manipulations, design an appropriate GUI to allow the user to perform the data manipulation.

18.4   Microsoft Access comes with several predefined *database wizard templates* (music collection, video collection, wine list, book collection, etc.) that are accessible by selecting **New** from the **File** menu in Microsoft Access and choosing a database from **Database** tab. Create a new database using one of the templates of your choice. Perform exercises 18.2 and 18.3 using the new database and its predefined tables. Provide appropriate queries for the database you choose and allow the user to edit and add data to the database.

18.5   Modify the **Find** capability in Fig. 18.30 to allow the user to scroll through the **ResultSet** in case there is more than one person with the specified last name in the Address Book. Provide an appropriate GUI.

Bibliography

(Bl88)   Blaha, M. R.; W. J. Premerlani; and J. E. Rumbaugh, "Relational Database Design Using an Object-Oriented Methodology," *Communications of the ACM*, Vol. 31, No. 4, April 1988, pp. 414–427.

(Co70)   Codd, E. F., "A Relational Model of Data for Large Shared Data Banks," *Communications of the ACM*, June 1970.

(Co72)   Codd, E. F., "Further Normalization of the Data Base Relational Model," in *Courant Computer Science Symposia*, Vol. 6, *Data Base Systems*. Upper Saddle River, N.J.: Prentice Hall, 1972.

(Co88)   Codd, E. F., "Fatal Flaws in SQL," *Datamation*, Vol. 34, No. 16, August 15, 1988, pp. 45–48.

(De90)   Deitel, H. M., *Operating Systems, Second Edition*. Reading, MA: Addison Wesley Pubishing, 1990.

(Da81)   Date, C. J., *An Introduction to Database Systems*. Reading, MA: Addison Wesley Pubishing, 1981.

(Re88)   Relational Technology, *INGRES Overview*. Alameda, CA: Relational Technology, 1988.

(St81)   Stonebraker, M., "Operating System Support for Database Management," *Communications of the ACM*, Vol. 24, No. 7, July 1981, pp. 412–418.

(Wi88)   Winston, A., "A Distributed Database Primer," *UNIX World*, April 1988, pp. 54–63.

19

Servlets

Objectives

- To be able to write servlets and execute them with the Java Servlet Development Kit (JSDK) WebServer.
- To be able to respond to HTTP **GET** and **POST** requests from an **HttpServlet**.
- To be able to use cookies to store client information during a browsing session.
- To be able to use session tracking from a servlet.
- To be able to read and write files from a servlet.
- To be able to access a database from a servlet.

A fair request should be followed by the deed in silence.
Dante Alighieri

The longest part of the journey is said to be the passing of the gate.
Marcus Terentius Varro

Friends share all things.
Pythagorus

If at first you don't succeed, destroy all evidence that you tried.
Newt Heilscher

If nominated, I will not accept; if elected, I will not serve.
General William T. Sherman

Me want cookie!
The Cookie Monster, Sesame Street

That's the way the cookie crumbles.
Anonymous

Outline

19.1 Introduction

There is much excitement over the Internet and the World Wide Web. The Internet ties the "information world" together. The World Wide Web makes the Internet easy to use and gives it the flair and sizzle of multimedia. Organizations see the Internet and the Web as crucial to their information systems strategies. Java provides a number of built-in networking capabilities that make it easy to develop Internet-based and Web-based applications. Not only can Java specify parallelism through multithreading, but it can enable programs to search the world for information and to collaborate with programs running on other computers internationally, nationally or just within an organization. Java can even enable applets and applications running on the same computer to communicate with one another, subject to security constraints.

Networking is a massive and complex topic. Computer science and computer engineering students will typically take a full-semester, upper-level course in computer networking and continue with further study at the graduate level. Java provides a rich complement of networking capabilities and will likely be used as an implementation vehicle in computer networking courses. In *Java How to Program* we introduce a wide variety of Java networking concepts and capabilities.

Java's networking capabilities are grouped into several packages. The fundamental networking capabilities are defined by classes and interfaces of package **java.net**, through which Java offers *socket-based communications* that enable applications to view networking as streams of data—a program can read from a *socket* or write to a socket as simply as reading from a file or writing to a file. The classes and interfaces of package **java.net** also offer *packet-based communications* that enable individual *packets* of information to be transmitted—commonly used to transmit audio and video over the Internet. In Chapter 21, we show how to create and manipulate sockets and how to communicate with packets of data.

Higher-level views of networking are provided by classes and interfaces in the **java.rmi** packages (five packages) for *Remote Method Invocation (RMI)* and **org.omg** packages (seven packages) for *Common Object Request Broker Architecture (CORBA)* that are part of the Java 2 API. The RMI packages allow Java objects running on separate Java Virtual Machines (normally on separate computers) to communicate via remote method calls. Such method calls appear to be to an object in the same program, but actually have built-in networking (based on the capabilities of package **java.net**) that communicates the method calls to another object on a separate computer. The CORBA packages provide similar functionality to the RMI packages. A key difference between RMI and CORBA is that RMI can only be used between Java objects, whereas CORBA can be used between any two applications that understand CORBA—including applications written in other programming languages. In Chapter 20, we present Java's RMI capabilities. We do not cover CORBA in this text.

Our discussion of networking over the next several chapters focuses on both sides of a *client-server relationship*. The *client* requests that some action be performed and the *server* performs the action and responds to the client. This request-response model of communication is the foundation for the highest-level view of networking in Java—*servlets*. A servlet extends the functionality of a server. The **javax.servlet** package and the **javax.servlet.http** package provide the classes and interfaces to define servlets.

A common implementation of the request-response model is between World Wide Web browsers and World Wide Web servers. When a user selects a Web site to browse through their browser (the client application), a request is sent to the appropriate Web server (the server application). The server normally responds to the client by sending the appropriate HTML Web page.

This chapter begins our networking discussions with *servlets* that enhance the functionality of World Wide Web servers—the most common form of servlet today. Servlet technology today is primarily designed for use with the HTTP protocol of the World Wide Web, but servlets are being developed for other technologies. Servlets are effective for developing Web-based solutions that help provide secure access to a Web site, that interact with databases on behalf of a client, that dynamically generate custom HTML documents to be displayed by browsers and that maintain unique session information for each client.

Many developers feel that servlets are the right solution for database-intensive applications that communicate with so-called *thin clients*—applications that require minimal client-side support. The server is responsible for the database access. Clients connect to the server using standard protocols available on all client platforms. Thus, the logic code can be written once and reside on the server for access by clients.

Our servlet examples will make use of the input/output streams facilities we discussed in Chapter 17 and the JDBC database facilities we discussed in Chapter 18. We placed this chapter after our discussion of JDBC and databases intentionally so that we can build multi-tier client-server applications that access databases. We continue to emphasize that Java is not just a language, but literally a "world" of information technology in which a broad range of technologies have become easily accessible by applications developers, especially enterprise applications developers. Indeed, Java is ready for "prime time."

19.2 Overview of Servlet Technology

In this section we present an overview of Java servlet technology. We discuss at a high level the servlet-related classes, methods and exceptions. The next several sections present live-code examples in which we build multitier client-server systems using servlet and JDBC technology.

The Internet offers many *protocols*. The *HTTP protocol (HyperText Transfer Protocol)* that forms the basis of the World Wide Web uses URLs (*Uniform Resource Locators*, also called *Universal Resource Locators*) to locate data on the Internet. Common URLs represent files or directories and can represent complex tasks such as database lookups and Internet searches. For more information on URL formats visit

```
http://www.ncsa.uiuc.edu/demoweb/url-primer.html
```

For more information on the *HTTP* protocol visit

```
http://www.w3.org/Protocols/HTTP/
```

For general information on a variety of World Wide Web topics visit

```
http://www.w3.org
```

Servlets are the analog on the server side to applets on the client side. Servlets are normally executed as part of a Web server. In fact, servlets have become so popular that they are now supported by most major Web servers, including the Netscape Web servers, Microsoft's *Internet Information Server (IIS)*, the World Wide Web Consortium's Jigsaw Web server and the popular Apache Web server.

The servlets in this chapter demonstrate communication between clients and servers via the HTTP protocol of the World Wide Web. A client sends an HTTP request to the server. The server receives the request and directs it to be processed by appropriate servlets. The servlets do their processing (which often includes interacting with a database), then return their results to the client—normally in the form of HTML documents to display in a browser, but other data formats, such as images and binary data, can be returned.

19.2.1 The Servlet API

Architecturally, all servlets must implement the **Servlet** interface. As with many key applet methods, the methods of interface **Servlet** are invoked automatically (by the server on which the servlet is installed). This interface defines five methods described in Fig. 19.1.

> *Software Engineering Observation 19.1*
>
> *All servlets must implement the **javax.servlet.Servlet** interface.*

The servlet packages define two **abstract** classes that implement the interface **Servlet**—class **GenericServlet** (from the package **javax.servlet**) and class **HttpServlet** (from the package **javax.servlet.http**). These classes provide default implementations of all the **Servlet** methods. Most servlets extend either **GenericServlet** or **HttpServlet** and override some or all of their methods with appropriate customized behaviors.

Method	Description

void init(ServletConfig config)

> This method is automatically called once during a servlet's execution cycle to initialize the servlet. The **ServletConfig** argument is supplied automatically by the server that executes the servlet.

ServletConfig getServletConfig()

> This method returns a reference to an object that implements interface **ServletConfig**. This object provides access to the servlet's configuration information such as initialization parameters and the servlet's **Servlet-Context**, which provides the servlet with access to its environment (i.e., the server in which the servlet is executing).

void service(ServletRequest request, ServletResponse response)

> This is the first method called on every servlet to respond to a client request.

String getServletInfo()

> This method is defined by a servlet programmer to return a **String** containing servlet information such as the servlet's author and version.

void destroy()

> This "cleanup" method is called when a servlet is terminated by the server on which it is executing. This is a good method to use to deallocate a resource used by the servlet (such as an open file or an open database connection).

Fig. 19.1 Methods of interface **Servlet**.

The examples in this chapter all extend class **HttpServlet**, which defines enhanced processing capabilities for servlets that extend the functionality of a Web server. The key method in every servlet is method **service**, which receives both a *ServletRequest* object and a *ServletResponse* object. These objects provide access to input and output streams that allow the servlet to read data from the client and send data to the client. These streams can be either byte-based streams or character-based streams. If problems occur during the execution of a servlet, either **ServletException**s or **IOException**s are thrown to indicate the problem.

19.2.2 HttpServlet Class

Web-based servlets typically extend class **HttpServlet**. Class **HttpServlet** overrides method **service** to distinguish between the typical requests received from a client Web browser. The two most common HTTP *request types* (also known as *request methods*) are *GET* and *POST*. A **GET** request *gets* (or *retrieves*) information from the server. Common uses of **GET** requests are to retrieve an HTML document or an image. A **POST** request posts (or sends) data to the server. Common uses of **POST** requests are to send the server information from an *HTML form* in which the client enters data, to send the server information so it can search the Internet or query a database for the client, to send authentication information to the server, etc.

Class **HttpServlet** defines methods *doGet* and *doPut* to respond to **GET** and **POST** requests from a client, respectively. These methods are called by the **Http-Servlet** class's **service** method, which is called when a request arrives at the server. Method **service** first determines the request type, then calls the appropriate method. Other less common request types are available, but these are beyond the scope of this book. For more information on the HTTP protocol visit the site

http://www.w3.org/Protocols/

Methods of class **HttpServlet** that respond to the other request types are shown in Fig. 19.2 (all receive parameters of type **HttpServletRequest** and **HttpServlet-Response** and return **void**). The methods of Fig. 19.2 are not frequently used.

Methods **doGet** and **doPost** receive as arguments an **HttpServletRequest** object and an **HttpServletResponse** object that enable interaction between the client and the server. The methods of **HttpServletRequest** make it easy to access the data supplied as part of the request. The **HttpServletResponse** methods make it easy to return the servlet's results in HTML format to the Web client. Interfaces **HttpServlet-Request** and **HttpServletResponse** are discussed in the next two sections.

19.2.3 **HttpServletRequest** Interface

Every call to **doGet** or **doPost** for an **HttpServlet** receives an object that implements interface **HttpServletRequest**. The Web server that executes the servlet creates an **HttpServletRequest** object and passes this to the servlet's **service** method (which, in turn, passes it to **doGet** or **doPost**). This object contains the request from the client. A variety of methods are provided to enable the servlet to process the client's request. Some of these methods are from interface *ServletRequest*—the interface that **HttpServletRequest** extends. A few key methods used in this chapter are presented in Fig 19.3.

Method	Description
doDelete	Called in response to an HTTP *DELETE* request. Such a request is normally used to delete a file from the server. This may not be available on some servers because of its inherent security risks.
doOptions	Called in response to an HTTP *OPTIONS* request. This returns information to the client indicating the HTTP options supported by the server.
doPut	Called in response to an HTTP *PUT* request. Such a request is normally used to store a file on the server. This may not be available on some servers because of its inherent security risks.
doTrace	Called in response to an HTTP *TRACE* request. Such a request is normally used for debugging. The implementation of this method automatically returns an HTML document to the client containing the request header information (data sent by the browser as part of the request).

Fig. 19.2 Important methods of class **HttpServlet**.

Method	Description

String getParameter(String name)

Returns the value associated with a parameter sent to the servlet as part of a **GET** or **POST** request. The **name** argument represents the parameter name.

Enumeration getParameterNames()

Returns the names of all the parameters sent to the servlet as part of a **POST** request.

String[] getParameterValues(String name)

Returns an array of **String**s containing the values for a specified servlet parameter.

Cookie[] getCookies()

Returns an array of **Cookie** objects stored on the client by the server. **Cookie**s can be used to uniquely identify clients to the servlet.

HttpSession getSession(boolean create)

Returns an **HttpSession** object associated with the client's current browsing session. An **HttpSession** object can be created by this method (**true** argument) if an **HttpSession** object does not already exist for the client. **HttpSession** objects can be used in similar ways to **Cookie**s for uniquely identifying clients.

Fig. 19.3   Important methods of interface **HttpServletRequest**.

19.2.4 **HttpServletResponse** Interface

Every call to **doGet** or **doPost** for an **HttpServlet** receives an object that implements interface **HttpServletResponse**. The Web server that executes the servlet creates an **HttpServletResponse** object and passes this to the servlet's **service** method (which, in turn, passes it to **doGet** or **doPost**). This object contains the response to the client. A variety of methods are provided to enable the servlet to formulate the response to the client. Some of these methods are from interface *ServletResponse*—the interface that **HttpServletResponse** extends. A few key methods used in this chapter are presented in Fig 19.4.

Method	Description

void addCookie(Cookie cookie)

Used to add a **Cookie** to the header of the response to the client. The **Cookie**'s maximum age and whether the client allows **Cookie**s to be saved determine whether or not **Cookie**s will be stored on the client.

Fig. 19.4   Important methods of **HttpServletResponse** (part 1 of 2).

Method	Description

ServletOutputStream getOutputStream()

Obtains a byte-based output stream that enables binary data to be sent to the client.

PrintWriter getWriter()

Obtains a character-based output stream that enables text data to be sent to the client.

void setContentType(String type)

Specifies the MIME type of the response to the browser. The MIME type helps the browser determine how to display the data (or possibly what other application to execute to process the data). For example, MIME type **"text/html"** indicates that the response is an HTML document, so the browser displays the HTML page.

Fig. 19.4   Important methods of **HttpServletResponse** (part 2 of 2).

19.3 Downloading the Java Servlet Development Kit

Before you can program with servlets, you must download and install the *Java Servlet Development Kit (JSDK)*. You may download the JSDK at no charge from Sun Microsystems at the Web site

http://java.sun.com/products/servlet/index.html

The download is accessible near the bottom of this page. Sun provides download for Windows and UNIX platforms. At the time of this publication, the current version of the JSDK was 2.1.

After downloading the JSDK, install it on your system and carefully read the **README.txt** file supplied in the installation directory. It explains how to set up the JSDK and discusses how to start the *server* that can be used to test servlets if you do not have a Web server that supports servlets. To develop servlets, you also need to copy the **servlet.jar** file containing the JSDK class files from the installation directory to your JDK extensions directory (the directory **c:\jdk1.2.1\jre\lib\ext** on Windows or the directory **~/jdk1.2.1/jre/lib/ext** on UNIX).

The *World Wide Web Consortium (W3C)* is a multinational organization dedicated to developing common protocols for the World Wide Web that "promote its evolution and ensure its interoperability." To that end, W3C provides *Open Source software*—a main benefit of such software is that it is free for anyone to use. W3C provides through their Open Source license a Web server called *Jigsaw* that is written completely in Java and fully supports servlets. Jigsaw and its documentation can be downloaded from

http://www.w3.org/Jigsaw/

For more information on the Open Source license, visit the site

http://www.opensource.org/

19.4 Handling HTTP GET Requests

The primary purpose of an HTTP **GET** request is to retrieve the content of a specified URL—normally the content is an HTML document (i.e., a Web page). The servlet of Fig. 19.5 and the HTML document of Fig. 19.6 demonstrate a servlet that handles HTTP **GET** requests. When the user clicks the **Get Page** button in the HTML document (Fig. 19.6), a **GET** request is sent to the servlet **HTTPGetServlet** (Fig. 19.5). The servlet responds to the request by dynamically generating an HTML document for the client that displays "Welcome to Servlets!" Figure 19.5 shows the **HTTPGetServlet.java** source code. Figure 19.6 shows the HTML document the client loads to access the servlet and shows screen captures of the client's browser window before and after the interaction with the servlet. The HTML document in this example was displayed using Microsoft's Internet Explorer 5 browser; however, the example should work from any browser.

Lines 3 and 4 import the **javax.servlet** and **javax.servlet.http** packages. We use several data types from these packages in the example.

For servlets that handle HTTP **GET** and HTTP **POST** requests, the JSDK provides superclass **HttpServlet** (from package **javax.servlet.http**). This class implements the **javax.servlet.Servlet** interface and adds methods that support HTTP protocol requests. Class **HTTPGetServlet** extends **HttpServlet** (line 7) for this reason.

```
1   // Fig. 19.5: HTTPGetServlet.java
2   // Creating and sending a page to the client
3   import javax.servlet.*;
4   import javax.servlet.http.*;
5   import java.io.*;
6
7   public class HTTPGetServlet extends HttpServlet {
8      public void doGet( HttpServletRequest request,
9                         HttpServletResponse response )
10        throws ServletException, IOException
11     {
12        PrintWriter output;
13
14        response.setContentType( "text/html" );  // content type
15        output = response.getWriter();            // get writer
16
17        // create and send HTML page to client
18        StringBuffer buf = new StringBuffer();
19        buf.append( "<HTML><HEAD><TITLE>\n" );
20        buf.append( "A Simple Servlet Example\n" );
21        buf.append( "</TITLE></HEAD><BODY>\n" );
22        buf.append( "<H1>Welcome to Servlets!</H1>\n" );
23        buf.append( "</BODY></HTML>" );
24        output.println( buf.toString() );
25        output.close();     // close PrintWriter stream
26     }
27  }
```

Fig. 19.5   The **HTTPGetServlet**, which processes an HTTP **GET** request.

Superclass **HTTPServlet** provides method *doGet* to respond to **GET** requests. Its default functionality is to indicate a **BAD_REQUEST** error. Typically this error is indicated in the Internet Explorer with a Web page that states "The page cannot be found" and in Netscape Communicator with a Web page that states "Error: 404"). We override method **doGet** (lines 8 through 26) to provide custom **GET** request processing. Method **doGet** receives two arguments—an object that implements *javax.servlet.http.HttpServletRequest* and an object that implements *javax.servlet.http.HttpServletResponse*. The **HttpServletRequest** object represents the client's request and the **HttpServletResponse** object represents the server's response. If **doGet** is unable to handle a client's request, it throws a *javax.servlet.ServletException*. If **doGet** encounters an error during stream processing (reading from the client or writing to the client), it throws a *java.io.IOException*.

To demonstrate a response to a **GET** request, our servlet creates a small HTML document containing the text "**Welcome to Servlets!**" The text of the HTML document is the response to the client. The response is sent to the client through the **PrintWriter** object that it accessed through the **HTTPServletResponse** object. Line 12 declares **output** as a **PrintWriter**.

Line 14 uses method *setContentType* of the **HTTPServletResponse** object **response** to indicate the content type for the response to the client. This enables the client browser to understand and handle the content. In this example, we specify content type *text/html* to indicate to the browser that the response is an HTML text file. The browser knows that it must read the HTML tags in the HTML file, format the document according to the tags and display the document in the browser window for the user to see.

Line 15 uses method *getWriter* of the **HTTPServletResponse** object **response** to obtain a reference to the **PrintWriter** object that sends the text of the HTML document to the client. [*Note:* If the response is binary data such as an image, method **getOutputStream** is used to obtain a reference to a **ServletOutputStream** object.]

Lines 19 through 23

```
buf.append( "<HTML><HEAD><TITLE>\n" );
buf.append( "A Simple Servlet Example\n" );
buf.append( "</TITLE></HEAD><BODY>\n" );
buf.append( "<H1>Welcome to Servlets!</H1>\n" );
buf.append( "</BODY></HTML>" );
```

create the HTML document by appending strings to **StringBuffer buf**.
Line 24

```
output.println( buf.toString() );
```

sends the response (the contents of the **StringBuffer**) to the client. Line 25 closes the **output PrintWriter** output stream. This flushes the output buffer and sends the information to the client.

The client can only access the servlet if the servlet is running on a server. Web servers that support servlets (such as Sun Microsystems, Inc.'s Java Web Server, the World Wide Web Consortium's Jigsaw Web server or the Apache Group's Apache HTTP server) normally have an installation procedure for servlets. If you intend to execute your servlet as part of a Web server, please refer to your Web server's documentation on how to install a servlet. For our examples, we demonstrate servlets with the JSDK server.

The JSDK comes with the *JSDK WebServer* so you can test your servlets. The JSDK WebServer assumes that the **.class** files for the servlets are *installed* in the subdirectory

```
webpages\WEB-INF\servlets
```

of the JSDK install drectory on Windows or

```
webpages/WEB-INF/servlets
```

on UNIX. To install a servlet, first compile the servlet with **javac** as you normally would any other Java source code file. Next, place the **.class** file containing the compiled servlet class in the **servlets** directory. This installs the servlet on the JSDK WebServer.

In the JSDK install directory are a Windows batch file (**startserver.bat**) and a UNIX shell script (**startserver**) that can be used to start the JSDK WebServer on Windows and UNIX, respectively. [*Note:* The JSDK also provides **stopserver.bat** and **stopserver** to terminate the JSDK WebServer on Windows and UNIX, respectively.] Type the appropriate command for your platform in a command window. When the server starts executing it displays the following command line output:

```
JSDK WebServer Version 2.1
Loaded configuration from file:D:\jsdk2.1/default.cfg
endpoint created: :8080
```

indicating that the JSDK WebServer is waiting for requests on this computer's *port number* 8080. [*Note:* Ports in this case are not physical hardware ports to which you attach cables; rather, they are integers that allow clients to request different services on the same server.] The port number specifies where a server waits for and receives connections from clients—this is frequently called the *handshake point*. When a client connects to a server to request a service, the client must specify the proper port number; otherwise, the client request cannot be processed. Port numbers are positive integers with values up to 65535. Many operating systems reserve port numbers below 1024 for system services (such as email and World Wide Web servers). Generally, these ports should not be specified as connection ports in user programs. In fact, some operating systems require special access privileges to use port numbers below 1024.

With so many ports from which to choose, how does a client know which port to use when requesting a service? You will often hear the term *well-known port number* used when describing popular services on the Internet such as Web servers and email servers. For example, a Web server waits for clients to make requests at port 80 by default. All Web browsers know this number as the well-known port on a Web server where requests for HTML documents are made. So when you type a URL into a Web browser, the browser normally connects to port 80 on the server. Similarly, the JSDK WebServer uses port 8080 as its well-known port number. You can specify a different port for the JSDK WebServer by editing the file **default.cfg** in the JSDK install directory. Change the line

```
server.port=8080
```

to specify the port on which you would like the JSDK WebServer to await requests.

Once the JSDK WebServer is running, you can load the HTML document **HTTPGet-Servlet.html** (Fig. 19.6) into a browser (see the first screen capture).

Line 1 is an HTML multiline comment. HTML comments start with **<!--** and end with **-->**. Line 2 indicates the start of the HTML tags in the document.

Lines 3 through 7 are the header section of the HTML document that starts with tag **<HEAD>** and ends with tag **</HEAD>**. The header section normally includes the title of the document ("**Servlet HTTP Get Example**") as specified between tags **<TITLE>** and **</TITLE>**.

```
1    <!-- Fig. 19.6: HTTPGetServlet.html -->
2    <HTML>
3       <HEAD>
4          <TITLE>
5             Servlet HTTP GET Example
6          </TITLE>
7       </HEAD>
8       <BODY>
9          <FORM
10            ACTION="http://localhost:8080/servlet/HTTPGetServlet"
11            METHOD="GET">
12            <P>Click the button to have the servlet send
13               an HTML document</P>
14            <INPUT TYPE="submit" VALUE="Get HTML Document">
15         </FORM>
16      </BODY>
17   </HTML>
```

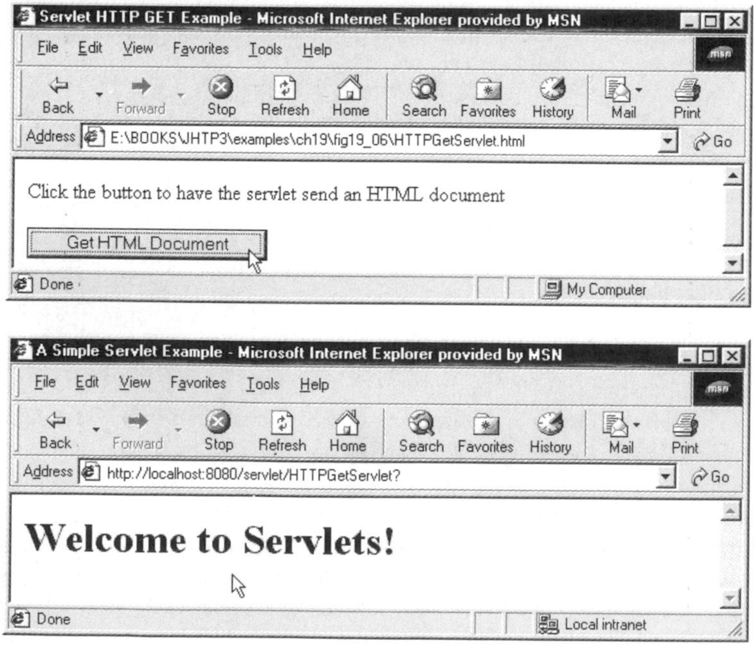

Fig. 19.6   HTML document to issue a **GET** request to **HTTPGetServlet**.

The document's *body* (lines 8 through 16) defines the elements of the Web page that the browser displays to the user. The body appears between tags **<BODY>** and **</BODY>** and contains literal text and tags that help the browser format the Web page.

The important part of the HTML document for this example is the *form* specified at lines 9 through 15 with tags **<FORM>** and **</FORM>**.

```
<FORM
    ACTION="http://localhost:8080/servlet/HTTPGetServlet"
    METHOD="GET">
    <P>Click the button to have the servlet send
        an HTML document</P>
    <INPUT TYPE="submit" VALUE="Get HTML Document">
</FORM>
```

The first three lines indicate that the **ACTION** for this form is

```
"http://localhost:8080/servlet/HTTPGetServlet"
```

and the **METHOD** is **"GET"**. The **ACTION** specifies the server-side *form handler*—in this case, the servlet **HTTPGetServlet**. The **METHOD** is the *request type* that the server uses to decide how to handle the request and possibly causes the browser to attach arguments to the end of the URL specified in the **ACTION**.

Let us take a closer look at the URL for the **ACTION**. The server **localhost** is a well-known server host name on most computers that support TCP/IP-based networking protocols such as HTTP. The server **localhost** refers to your own computer. We often use **localhost** in the book to demonstrate networking programs on one computer so students without a network connection can still learn network programming concepts. In this example, **localhost** indicates that the server on which the servlet is installed is running on the local machine. The server host name is followed by ":**8080**", specifying the port number at which the JSDK WebServer is awaiting requests from clients. Remember that Web browsers assume port 80 by default as the server port at which clients make requests, but the JSDK WebServer awaits client requests at port 8080. If we do not explicitly specify the port number in the URL, the servlet will never receive our request and an error message will be displayed in the browser. Notice that the URL for the **ACTION** contains **/servlet** as the directory in which our servlet resides. Most Web servers have a specific directory in which a servlet is placed to install the servlet on the server. Often this directory is called **servlet** or **servlets**. The JSDK WebServer simulates this by making it appear to the client that servlet **HTTPGetServlet** is in the **servlet** directory on the server. Any servlet that executes through the JSDK WebServer must be accessed in this manner.

Line 14

```
<INPUT TYPE="submit" VALUE="Get HTML Document">
```

indicates the form GUI component to be displayed—an **INPUT** element. The **TYPE** of this element is **"submit"** (normally represented as a button) and the value to display is **"Get HTML Document"** (the label to appear on the button). The default label for a **submit** button is **Submit Query** if no **VALUE** is supplied for the button. When the user presses the **submit** button in a form, the form performs its **ACTION**—the browser connects to the specified server at the specified port number (port 80 if no port is supplied for HTTP protocol) and requests the service (**HTTPGetServlet**). In this example, the browser contacts the JSDK WebServer (i.e., the form handler) specified in the **ACTION** and indicates that the **METHOD** is **GET**. The JSDK WebServer invokes the servlet's **service** method and passes it an **HTTPServletRequest** object that contains the **METHOD** (**GET**) specified by the client and an **HTTPServletResponse** object. The **service** method determines the request type (**GET**) and responds with a call to its **doGet** method that returns the Web page shown in the second screen capture of Fig. 19.6.

In the second screen capture, notice that the **Address** field of the browser contains the URL specified as our **ACTION** in the HTML document. Also notice the "**?**" at the end of the URL. If there are any parameters to pass to the server-side form handler, the "**?**" character separates the URL and the arguments.

You can also see the affect of this servlet by simply typing the URL

```
http://localhost:8080/servlet/HTTPGetServlet
```

as the Web page for the browser to display. The default action for the Web browser is to issue a **GET** request to the server—in this case the **HTTPGetServlet**.

19.5 Handling HTTP POST Requests

An HTTP **POST** request is often used to post data from an HTML form to a server-side form handler that processes the data. For example, when you respond to a Web-based survey a **POST** request normally supplies the information you specify in the HTML form to the Web server.

Browsers often *cache* (save on disk) Web pages so they can quickly reload the pages. There are no changes between the last version stored in the cache and the current version on the Web. This helps speed up your browsing experience by minimizing the amount of data that must be downloaded for you to view a Web page. Browsers typically do not cache the server's response to a **POST** request because the next **POST** may not return the same result. For example, in a survey, many users could visit the same Web page and respond to a question. The survey results could then be displayed for the user. Each new response changes the overall results of the survey.

When you use a Web-based search engine, a **GET** request normally supplies the information you specify in the HTML form to the search engine. The search engine performs the search, then returns the results to you as a Web page. Such pages are often cached in case you perform the same search again. As with **POST** requests, **GET** requests can supply parameters as part of the request to the Web server.

The servlet of Fig. 19.7 stores the results of a survey about favorite pets in a file on the server. When a user responds to the survey, the servlet **HTTPPostServlet** sends an HTML document to the client summarizing the results of the survey to this point. The user selects a radio button on the Web page (Fig. 19.8) indicating their favorite pet and presses **Submit**. The browser sends an HTTP **POST** request to the servlet. The servlet responds by reading the previous survey results from a file on the server, updating the survey results, writing the survey results back to the file on the server and sending a Web page to the client indicating the cumulative results of the survey. For the purpose of this example, we loaded the HTML document in the Netscape Communicator 4.51 browser.

```
1   // Fig. 19.7: HTTPPostServlet.java
2   // A simple survey servlet
3   import javax.servlet.*;
4   import javax.servlet.http.*;
5   import java.text.*;
6   import java.io.*;
7   import java.util.*;
8
9   public class HTTPPostServlet extends HttpServlet {
10      private String animalNames[] =
11         { "dog", "cat", "bird", "snake", "none" };
12
13      public void doPost( HttpServletRequest request,
14                          HttpServletResponse response )
15         throws ServletException, IOException
16      {
17         int animals[] = null, total = 0;
18         File f = new File( "survey.txt" );
19
20         if ( f.exists() ) {
21            // Determine # of survey responses so far
22            try {
23               ObjectInputStream input = new ObjectInputStream(
24                  new FileInputStream( f ) );
25
26               animals = (int []) input.readObject();
27               input.close();    // close stream
28
29               for ( int i = 0; i < animals.length; ++i )
30                  total += animals[ i ];
31            }
32            catch( ClassNotFoundException cnfe ) {
33               cnfe.printStackTrace();
34            }
35         }
36         else
37            animals = new int[ 5 ];
38
39         // read current survey response
40         String value =
41            request.getParameter( "animal" );
42         ++total;    // update total of all responses
43
44         // determine which was selected and update its total
45         for ( int i = 0; i < animalNames.length; ++i )
46            if ( value.equals( animalNames[ i ] ) )
47               ++animals[ i ];
48
49         // write updated totals out to disk
50         ObjectOutputStream output = new ObjectOutputStream(
51            new FileOutputStream( f ) );
52
```

Fig. 19.7   The **HTTPPostServlet** that processes an HTTP **POST** request
(part 1 of 2).

```
53        output.writeObject( animals );
54        output.flush();
55        output.close();
56
57        // Calculate percentages
58        double percentages[] = new double[ animals.length ];
59
60        for ( int i = 0; i < percentages.length; ++i )
61            percentages[ i ] = 100.0 * animals[ i ] / total;
62
63        // send a thank you message to client
64        response.setContentType( "text/html" ); // content type
65
66        PrintWriter responseOutput = response.getWriter();
67        StringBuffer buf = new StringBuffer();
68        buf.append( "<html>\n" );
69        buf.append( "<title>Thank you!</title>\n" );
70        buf.append( "Thank you for participating.\n" );
71        buf.append( "<BR>Results:\n<PRE>" );
72
73        DecimalFormat twoDigits = new DecimalFormat( "#0.00" );
74        for ( int i = 0; i < percentages.length; ++i ) {
75            buf.append( "<BR>" );
76            buf.append( animalNames[ i ] );
77            buf.append( ": " );
78            buf.append( twoDigits.format( percentages[ i ] ) );
79            buf.append( "%  responses: " );
80            buf.append( animals[ i ] );
81            buf.append( "\n" );
82        }
83
84        buf.append( "\n<BR><BR>Total responses: " );
85        buf.append( total );
86        buf.append( "</PRE>\n</html>" );
87
88        responseOutput.println( buf.toString() );
89        responseOutput.close();
90    }
91 }
```

Fig. 19.7   The **HTTPPostServlet** that processes an HTTP **POST** request (part 2 of 2).

As in Fig. 19.5, **HTTPPostServlet** extends **HttpServlet** at line 9 so that each **HTTPPostServlet** is capable of handling HTTP **GET** and **POST** requests. Lines 10 and 11 define **String** array **animalNames** to contain the names of the animals in the survey. These are used to determine the response to the survey and update the counter for the appropriate animal.

Method *doPost* (lines 13 through 90) responds to **POST** requests. Its default functionality is to indicate a **BAD_REQUEST** error. We override this method to provide custom **POST** request processing. Method **doPost** receives the same two arguments as **doGet**—an object that implements **javax.servlet.http.HttpServletRequest** and an object that implements **javax.servlet.http.HttpServletResponse** to represent the client's request and the servlet's response, respectively. Method **doPost** throws a ***javax.servlet.ServletException*** if it is unable to handle a client's request and throws an **IOException** if a problem occurs during stream processing.

Method **doPost** begins by determining if the file **survey.txt** exists on the server. Line 18 defines a **File** object **f** for this purpose. The program does not provide a location for the file. By default, files that are created by a servlet executed with the JSDK Web-Server are stored in the JSDK installation directory (**jsdk2.1**). You can specify the storage location for the file as part of creating the **File** object. At line 20, if the file exists, the contents of that file will be read into the servlet so the survey results can be updated and returned to the current client. If the file does not exist (i.e., the current request is the first survey response), method **doPost** creates the file later in the method.

Integer array **animals** stores the number of responses for each type of animal. If the file containing the previous survey results exists, lines 23 through 30 open an **ObjectInputStream** to read the integer array **animals** and total the number of responses that have been received to this point. When the servlet creates the file and stores the integer array, it uses an **ObjectOutputStream** to write the file.

Lines 40 and 41

```
String value =
        request.getParameter( "animal" );
```

use method **getParameter** of interface **javax.servlet.ServletRequest** to retrieve the survey response **POST**ed by the client. This method receives as its argument the name of the parameter (**"animal"**) as specified in the HTML document of Fig. 19.8 that we will discuss shortly. The method returns a **String** containing the value of the parameter or **null** if the parameter is not found. The HTML file (Fig. 19.8) that uses this servlet as a form handler contains five radio buttons, each of which is named **animal** (lines 11 through 15 of Fig. 19.8). Because only one radio button can be selected, the **String** returned by **getParameter** represents the one radio button selected by the user. The value for each radio button is one of the strings in the **animalNames** array in the servlet. [*Note:* If we were processing a form that could return many values for a particular parameter, method **getParameterValues** would be used here instead to obtain a **String** array containing the values.]

Line 42 increments the **total** to indicate one more survey response. Lines 45 through 47 determine the animal selected by the client and update the appropriate animal's total. Lines 50 through 55 open an **ObjectOutputStream** to store the updated survey results to the file **survey.txt**. This file ensures that even if the servlet is stopped and restarted, the survey results will persist on disk.

Lines 58 through 61 prepare for each animal the percentage of the **total** votes that represent each animal. These results are returned to the user as part of the **HttpServletResponse**. We prepare the response beginning at line 64, where **ServletResponse** method **setContentType** specifies that the content will be the text of an HTML document (**text/html**).

Line 66 uses **ServletResponse** method **getWriter** to obtain a reference to a **PrintWriter** object and assigns it to **responseOutput**. This reference is used to send the response to the client. **StringBuffer buf** (line 67) stores the content of the response as the servlet prepares the HTML. Lines 68 through 86 prepare the content with a series of calls to **StringBuffer** method **append**. Lines 71 and 86 append the HTML tags **<PRE>** and **</PRE>** to specify that the text between them is *preformatted text*. Preformatted text is normally displayed in a fixed-width (also called monospaced) font where all characters have the same width. Several lines also insert the **
** tag to indicate a *break*—the browser should start a new line of text.

Line 88

```
responseOutput.println( buf.toString() );
```

sends the content of **buf** to the client. Line 89 closes the **responseOutput** stream.

Once the servlet is running, you can load the HTML document **HTTPPost-Servlet.html** (Fig. 19.8) into a browser (see the first screen capture).

```
1   <!-- Fig. 19.8: HTTPPostServlet.html -->
2   <HTML>
3      <HEAD>
4         <TITLE>Servlet HTTP Post Example</TITLE>
5      </HEAD>
6
7      <BODY>
8         <FORM METHOD="POST" ACTION=
9            "http://localhost:8080/servlet/HTTPPostServlet">
10           What is your favorite pet?<BR><BR>
11           <INPUT TYPE=radio NAME=animal VALUE=dog>Dog<BR>
12           <INPUT TYPE=radio NAME=animal VALUE=cat>Cat<BR>
13           <INPUT TYPE=radio NAME=animal VALUE=bird>Bird<BR>
14           <INPUT TYPE=radio NAME=animal VALUE=snake>Snake<BR>
15           <INPUT TYPE=radio NAME=animal VALUE=none CHECKED>None
16           <BR><BR><INPUT TYPE=submit VALUE="Submit">
17           <INPUT TYPE=reset>
18        </FORM>
19     </BODY>
20  </HTML>
```

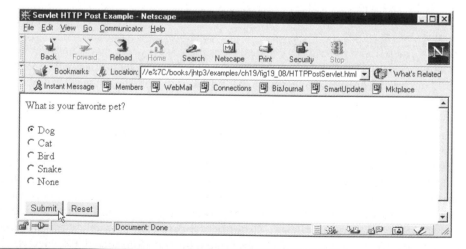

Fig. 19.8   Issuing a **POST** request to **HTTPPostServlet** (part 1 of 2).

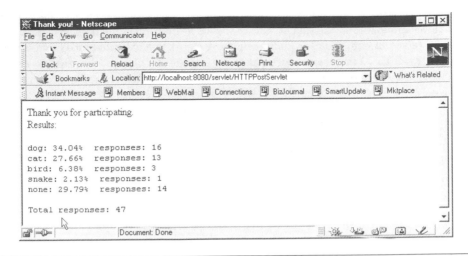

Fig. 19.8   Issuing a **POST** request to **HTTPPostServlet** (part 2 of 2).

The important part of the HTML document for this example is the form specified at lines 8 through 18.

```
<FORM METHOD="POST" ACTION=
   "http://localhost:8080/servlet/HTTPPostServlet">
   What is your favorite pet?<BR><BR>
   <INPUT TYPE=radio NAME=animal VALUE=dog>Dog<BR>
   <INPUT TYPE=radio NAME=animal VALUE=cat>Cat<BR>
   <INPUT TYPE=radio NAME=animal VALUE=bird>Bird<BR>
   <INPUT TYPE=radio NAME=animal VALUE=snake>Snake<BR>
   <INPUT TYPE=radio NAME=animal VALUE=none CHECKED>None
   <BR><BR><INPUT TYPE=submit VALUE="Submit">
   <INPUT TYPE=reset>
</FORM>
```

Line 8 indicates that the **METHOD** for this form **"POST"** and the **ACTION** is

```
"http://localhost:8080/servlet/HTTPGetServlet"
```

The **ACTION** specifies the server-side form handler—**HTTPPostServlet**. The **METH-OD** helps the servlet decide how to handle the request and possibly causes the browser to attach arguments to the end of the URL specified in the **ACTION**.

Lines 11 through 15 specify the radio buttons form components. The **TYPE** of each element is *radio*, the *name* of each is **animal** and the **value** of each is the string to post when the form contents are sent to the servlet (**POST**ed). Providing the same name for each radio button indicates to the browser that these radio buttons are in the same group and only one can be selected at a time. Initially, the radio button defined on line 15 is *CHECKED* (i.e., *selected*). Following the **<INPUT>** tag on each of lines 11 through 15 is the string displayed by the browser to the right of each radio button in the HTML document. Line 16 defines the **submit** button that causes the form's **ACTION** to execute (i.e., post the form data to the servlet). When the user clicks the button, the browser sends a **POST** request to the servlet specified in the **ACTION**. Because the **METHOD** is **POST**, the browser also attaches to the request the **value**s associated with each HTML form component. For the radio button group, the selected radio button's value is attached to the request. The servlet reads the values submitted as part of the request using method **getParameter** of interface **javax.servlet.ServletRequest**. If the user clicks the **Reset** button (defined at line 17 in the HTML documentation), the browser resets the form to its initial state with the option **None** selected.

Notice that as you repeatedly submit votes, the servlet keeps track of all votes tallied so far (even if you terminate the servlet and run it again). You can repeatedly submit votes by pressing **Submit** to submit a vote, pressing the **Back** button in your browser to go back to the survey page, selecting a new animal (or the same animal) and pressing **Submit** again. You can also reload the **HTTPPostServlet.html** file into the browser repeatedly. We do not synchronize access to the file in this example. It is possible that two clients could access the survey at the same time and two (or more) separate server threads may attempt to modify the file at the same time. Two possible ways to fix this problem are to use the thread synchronization techniques discussed in Chapter 15, "Multithreading," or to implement the tagging interface **javax.servlet.SingleThreadModel**. This interface indicates that the implementing servlet should handle only one client request at a time.

19.6 Session Tracking

Many Web sites today provide custom Web pages and/or functionality on a client-by-client basis. For example, some Web sites allow you to customize their home page to suit your needs. An excellent example of this is the *Yahoo!* Web site. If you go to the site

```
http://my.yahoo.com/
```

you can customize how the Yahoo! site appears to you in the future when you revisit the site [*Note:* You need to get a free Yahoo! ID to do this.] The HTTP protocol does not support persistent information that could help a Web server determine that a request is from a particular client. As far as a Web server is concerned, every request could be from the same client or every request could be from a different client.

Another example of a service that is customized on a client-by-client basis is a shopping cart for shopping on the Web. Obviously, the server must distinguish between clients so the company can determine the proper items and charge the proper amount for each client. After all, when we go shopping we do not all buy the same items!

A third purpose of customizing on a client-by-client basis is marketing. Companies often track the pages you visit throughout a site so they can display advertisements that are targeted to your browsing trends. A problem with tracking is that many people consider it to be an invasion of their privacy, an increasingly sensitive issue in our information society.

To help the server distinguish between clients, each client must identify itself to the server. There are a number of popular techniques for distinguishing between clients. For the purpose of this chapter, we introduce two techniques to track clients individually—*cookies* (Section 19.6.1) and *session tracking* (Section 19.6.2).

19.6.1 Cookies

A popular way to customize Web pages is via *cookies*. Cookies can store information on the user's computer for retrieval later in the same browsing session or in future browsing sessions. For example, cookies could be used in a shopping application to indicate the client's preferences. When the servlet receives the client's next communication, the servlet can examine the cookie(s) it sent to the client in a previous communication, identify the client's preferences and immediately display products of interest to the client.

Cookies are small files that are sent by a servlet (or another similar technology) as part of a response to a client. Every HTTP-based interaction between a client and a server includes a *header* that contains information about the request (when the communication is from the client to the server) or information about the response (when the communication is from the server to the client). When an **HttpServlet** receives a request, the header includes information such as the request type (e.g., **GET** or **POST**) and cookies stored on the client machine by the server. When the server formulates its response, the header information includes any cookies the server wants to store on the client computer.

Software Engineering Observation 19.2

Some clients do not allow cookies to be written on them. When a client declines a cookie the client is normally informed that such a refusal may prevent browsing the site.

Depending on the *maximum age* of a cookie, the Web browser either maintains the cookie for the duration of the browsing session (i.e., until the user closes the Web browser) or stores the cookies on the client computer for future use. When the browser makes a request of a server, cookies previously sent to the client by that server are returned to the server (if they have not expired) as part of the request formulated by the browser. Cookies are automatically deleted when they *expire* (i.e., reach their maximum age).

The next example demonstrates cookies. The servlet (Fig. 19.9) handles both **GET** and **POST** requests. The HTML document of Fig. 19.10 contains four radio buttons (**C**, **C++**, **Java** and **Visual Basic 6**) and two buttons **Submit** and **Reset**. When the user presses **Submit**, the servlet is invoked with a **POST** request. The servlet responds by adding a cookie containing the selected language to the response header and sends an HTML page to the client. Each time the user clicks **Submit**, a cookie is sent to the client. This example does not allow duplicate cookies to be written. The HTML document of Fig. 19.11 presents the user with a button they can press to get a book recommendation based on their programming language selection from the previous HTML document. When the user presses the button **Recommend Books**, the servlet in Fig. 19.9 is invoked with a **GET** request. The browser sends any cookies previously received from the servlet back to the servlet. The servlet responds by getting the cookies from the request header and creating an HTML document that recommends a book for each language the user selected from the HTML document of Fig. 19.10. We discuss the servlet followed by the two HTML documents.

Lines 8 and 10 declare **String** arrays that store the programming language names and ISBN numbers for the books that will be recommended, respectively. [*Note:* ISBN is an abbreviation for "International Standard Book Number"—a numbering scheme publishers worldwide use to give each different book title a unique identification number.] Method **doPost** (line 14) is invoked in response to the **POST** request from the HTML document of Fig. 19.10. Line 19 gets the user's **language** selection (the value of the selected radio button on the Web page) with method **getParameter**.

Line 21 passes the **language** value to the **_javax.servlet.http.Cookie_** class constructor in the statement

```
Cookie c = new Cookie( language, getISBN( language ) );
```

```
1   // Fig. 19.9: CookieExample.java
2   // Using cookies.
3   import javax.servlet.*;
4   import javax.servlet.http.*;
5   import java.io.*;
6
7   public class CookieExample extends HttpServlet {
8      private String names[] = { "C", "C++", "Java",
9                                 "Visual Basic 6" };
10     private String isbn[] = {
11        "0-13-226119-7", "0-13-528910-6",
12        "0-13-012507-5", "0-13-528910-6" };
13
14     public void doPost( HttpServletRequest request,
15                         HttpServletResponse response )
16        throws ServletException, IOException
17     {
18        PrintWriter output;
19        String language = request.getParameter( "lang" );
20
21        Cookie c = new Cookie( language, getISBN( language ) );
22        c.setMaxAge( 120 );  // seconds until cookie removed
23        response.addCookie( c );  // must precede getWriter
24
25        response.setContentType( "text/html" );
26        output = response.getWriter();
27
28        // send HTML page to client
29        output.println( "<HTML><HEAD><TITLE>" );
30        output.println( "Cookies" );
31        output.println( "</TITLE></HEAD><BODY>" );
32        output.println( "<P>Welcome to Cookies!<BR>" );
33        output.println( "<P>" );
34        output.println( language );
35        output.println( " is a great language." );
36        output.println( "</BODY></HTML>" );
37
38        output.close();      // close stream
39     }
40
41     public void doGet( HttpServletRequest request,
42                        HttpServletResponse response )
43                        throws ServletException, IOException
44     {
45        PrintWriter output;
46        Cookie cookies[];
47
48        cookies = request.getCookies(); // get client's cookies
49
50        response.setContentType( "text/html" );
51        output = response.getWriter();
52
```

Fig. 19.9   Demonstrating **Cookie**s (part 1 of 2).

```
53            output.println( "<HTML><HEAD><TITLE>" );
54            output.println( "Cookies II" );
55            output.println( "</TITLE></HEAD><BODY>" );
56
57            if ( cookies != null ) {
58                output.println( "<H1>Recommendations</H1>" );
59
60                // get the name of each cookie
61                for ( int i = 0; i < cookies.length; i++ )
62                    output.println(
63                        cookies[ i ].getName() + " How to Program. " +
64                        "ISBN#: " + cookies[ i ].getValue() + "<BR>" );
65            }
66            else {
67                output.println( "<H1>No Recommendations</H1>" );
68                output.println( "You did not select a language or" );
69                output.println( "the cookies have expired." );
70            }
71
72            output.println( "</BODY></HTML>" );
73            output.close();     // close stream
74        }
75
76        private String getISBN( String lang )
77        {
78            for ( int i = 0; i < names.length; ++i )
79                if ( lang.equals( names[ i ] ) )
80                    return isbn[ i ];
81
82            return "";   // no matching string found
83        }
84    }
```

Fig. 19.9   Demonstrating **Cookie**s (part 2 of 2).

The first constructor argument specifies the *cookie name* (the **language**) and the second constructor argument specifies the *cookie value*. The cookie name identifies the cookie and the cookie value is the information associated with the cookie. As the **Cookie**'s value in this example, we use the ISBN number for a book that will be recommended to the user when the servlet receives a **GET** request. Note that the user of a browser can turn off cookies, so this example may not function properly on certain users' computers (no errors are reported if cookies are disabled). A minimum of 20 cookies per Web site and 300 cookies per user are supported by browsers that support cookies. Browsers may limit the cookie size to 4K (4096 bytes). Cookies can be used only by the server that created the cookie.

Line 22

```
c.setMaxAge( 120 );   // seconds until cookie removed
```

sets the maximum age for the cookie. In this example, the cookie exists for 120 seconds (2 minutes). The argument to **setMaxAge** is an integer value. This allows a cookie to have a maximum age of up to 2,147,483,647 (or approximately 24,855 days). We set the maximum age of the **Cookie** in this example emphasize that cookies are automatically deleted when they expire.

Software Engineering Observation 19.3

By default cookies only exist for the current browsing session (until the user closes the browser). To make cookies persist beyond the current session, call **Cookie** *method* **set-MaxAge** *to indicate the number of seconds until the cookie expires.*

Line 23

```
response.addCookie( c );   // must precede getWriter
```

adds the cookie to the client response. Cookies are sent to the client as part of the HTTP header (i.e., information such as requests, the request's status, etc.). The header information is always provided to the client first, so the cookies should be added to the **response** with **addCookie** before any other information.

Software Engineering Observation 19.4

Call method **addCookie** *to add a cookie to the* **HTTPServletResponse** *before writing any other information to the client.*

After the cookie is added, the servlet sends an HTML document to the client (see the second screen capture of Fig. 19.10).

Method **doGet** (line 41) is invoked in response to the **GET** request from the HTML document of Fig. 19.11. The method reads any **Cookie**s that were written to the client in **doPost**. For each **Cookie** written, the servlet recommends a Deitel book on the subject. Up to four books are displayed on the Web page created by the servlet.

Line 48

```
cookies = request.getCookies(); // get client's cookies
```

retrieves the cookies from the client using **HttpServletRequest** method *getCookies*, which returns an array of **Cookie**s. When a **GET** or **POST** operation is performed to invoke the servlet, the cookies associated with that server are automatically sent to the servlet.

If method **getCookies** does not return **null** (i.e., there were no cookies), the **for** structure at line 61 retrieves the name of each **Cookie** using **Cookie** method **getName**, retrieves the value of each **Cookie** (i.e., the ISBN number) using **Cookie** method **getValue** and writes a line to the client indicating the name of a recommended book and the ISBN number for the book.

Figure 19.10 shows the HTML document the user loads to select a language. Lines 7 and 8 specify that the **ACTION** of the form is to **POST** information to the **CookieExample** servlet.

```
1   <!-- Fig. 19.10: SelectLanguage.html -->
2   <HTML>
3   <HEAD>
4      <TITLE>Cookies</TITLE>
5   </HEAD>
```

Fig. 19.10 HTML document that invokes the cookie servlet with a **POST** request and passes the user's language selection as an argument (part 1 of 2).

```
6    <BODY>
7       <FORM ACTION="http://localhost:8080/servlet/CookieExample"
8            METHOD="POST">
9          <STRONG>Select a programming language:<br>
10         </STRONG><BR>
11         <PRE>
12         <INPUT TYPE="radio" NAME="lang" VALUE="C">C<BR>
13         <INPUT TYPE="radio" NAME="lang" VALUE="C++">C++<BR>
14         <INPUT TYPE="radio" NAME="lang" VALUE="Java"
15              CHECKED>Java<BR>
16         <INPUT TYPE="radio" NAME="lang"
17              VALUE="Visual Basic 6">Visual Basic 6
18         </PRE>
19         <INPUT TYPE="submit" VALUE="Submit">
20         <INPUT TYPE="reset"> </P>
21      </FORM>
22   </BODY>
23   </HTML>
```

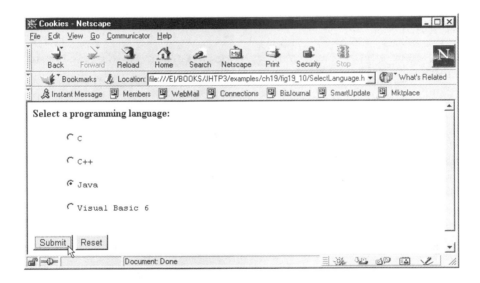

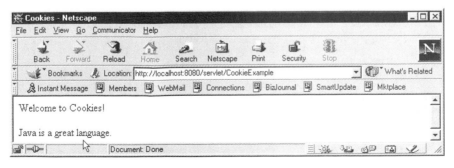

Fig. 19.10 HTML document that invokes the cookie servlet with a **POST** request and passes the user's language selection as an argument (part 2 of 2).

The HTML document in Fig. 19.11 invokes the servlet in response to a button press. Lines 7 and 8 specify that the form's **ACTION** is to **GET** information from the **CookieExample** servlet. Because we set the cookie's maximum age to 2 minutes, you must load this HTML document and press **Recommend Books** within 2 minutes of your interaction with the servlet from the HTML document of Fig. 19.10. Otherwise, the cookie will expire before you can receive a recommendation. Normally, a cookie's lifetime is set to a larger value. Remember, we intentionally set a small value to demonstrate that cookies are automatically deleted when they expire. After receiving your book recommendation, wait 2 minutes to ensure that the cookie expires. Then, go back to the HTML document of Fig. 19.11 and press **Recommend Books** again. The third screen capture in Fig. 19.11 shows the returned HTML document when there are no cookies as part of the request from the client. [*Note:* Not all Web browsers adhere to the expiration date of a cookie.]

```
1   <!-- Fig. 19.11: BookRecommendation.html -->
2   <HTML>
3   <HEAD>
4      <TITLE>Cookies</TITLE>
5   </HEAD>
6   <BODY>
7      <FORM ACTION="http://localhost:8080/servlet/CookieExample"
8          METHOD="GET">
9         Press "Recommend books" for a list of books.
10        <INPUT TYPE=submit VALUE="Recommend books">
11     </FORM>
12  </BODY>
13  </HTML>
```

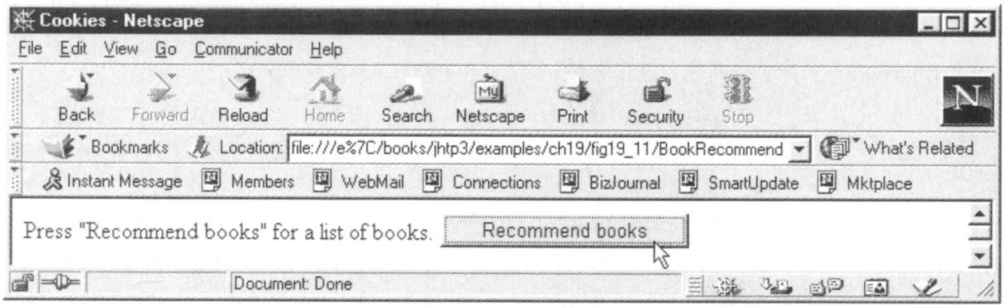

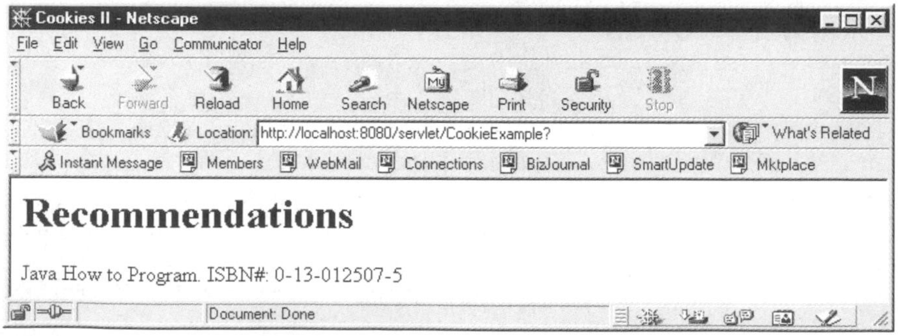

Fig. 19.11 HTML document for a servlet that reads a client's cookies (part 1 of 2).

Fig. 19.11 HTML document for a servlet that reads a client's cookies (part 2 of 2).

Various **Cookie** methods are provided to manipulate the members of a **Cookie**. Some of these methods are listed in Fig. 19.12.

Method	Description
getComment()	Returns a **String** describing the purpose of the cookie (**null** if no comment has been set with **setComment**).
getDomain()	Returns a **String** containing the cookie's domain. This determines which servers can receive the cookie. By default cookies are sent to the server that originally sent the cookie to the client.
getMaxAge()	Returns an **int** representing the maximum age of the cookie in seconds.
getName()	Returns a **String** containing the name of the cookie as set by the constructor.
getPath()	Returns a **String** containing the URL prefix for the cookie. Cookies can be "targeted" to specific URLs that include directories on the Web server. By default a cookie is returned to services operating in the same directory as the service that sent the cookie or a subdirectory of that directory.
getSecure()	Returns a **boolean** value indicating if the cookie should be transmitted using a secure protocol (**true**).
getValue()	Returns a **String** containing the value of the cookie as set with **setValue** or the constructor.
getVersion()	Returns an **int** containing the version of the cookie protocol used to create the cookie. Cookies are currently undergoing standardization. A value of 0 (the default) indicates the original cookie protocol as defined by Netscape. A value of 1 indicates the version currently undergoing standardization.

Fig. 19.12 Important methods of class **Cookie** (part 1 of 2).

Method	Description
setComment(String)	The comment describing the purpose of the cookie that is presented by the browser to the user (some browsers allow the user to accept cookies on a per-cookie basis).
setDomain(String)	This determines which servers can receive the cookie. By default cookies are sent to the server that originally sent the cookie to the client. The domain is specified in the form ".deitel.com", indicating that all servers ending with .deitel.com can receive this cookie.
setMaxAge(int)	Sets the maximum age of the cookie in seconds.
setPath(String)	Sets the "target" URL indicating the directories on the server that lead to the services that can receive this cookie.
setSecure(boolean)	A **true** value indicates that the cookie should only be sent using a secure protocol.
setValue(String)	Sets the value of a cookie.
setVersion(int)	Sets the cookie protocol for this cookie.

Fig. 19.12 Important methods of class **Cookie** (part 2 of 2).

19.6.2 Session Tracking with HttpSession

An alternative approach to cookies is to track a session with the JSDK's interfaces and classes from package **javax.servlet.http** that support session tracking. To demonstrate basic session tracking techniques, we modified the servlet from Fig. 19.9 that demonstrated **Cookie**s to use objects that implement interface **HttpSession** (Fig. 19.13). Once again the servlet handles both **GET** and **POST** requests. The HTML document of Fig. 19.14 contains four radio buttons (i.e., **C**, **C++**, **Java** and **Visual Basic 6**) and two buttons, **Submit** and **Reset**. When the user presses **Submit**, the servlet (Fig. 19.13) is invoked with a **POST** request. The servlet responds by creating a session for the client (or using an existing session for the client) and adds the selected language and an ISBN number for the recommended book to the **HttpSession** object, then sends an HTML page to the client. Each time the user clicks **Submit**, a new language/ISBN pair is added to the **HttpSession** object. If the language was already added to the **HttpSession** object, it is simply replaced with the new pair of values. The HTML document of Fig. 19.15 presents the user with a button they can press to get a book recommendation based on their programming language selection from the previous HTML document. When the user presses the button **Recommend Books**, the servlet in Fig. 19.13 is invoked with a **GET** request. The servlet responds by getting the value names (i.e., the languages) from the **HttpSession** object and creating an HTML document that recommends a book for each language the user selected from the HTML document of Fig. 19.14. We discuss the servlet followed by the two HTML documents.

```
1    // Fig. 19.13: SessionExample.java
2    // Using sessions.
3    import javax.servlet.*;
4    import javax.servlet.http.*;
5    import java.io.*;
6
7    public class SessionExample extends HttpServlet {
8       private final static String names[] =
9          { "C", "C++", "Java", "Visual Basic 6" };
10      private final static String isbn[] = {
11         "0-13-226119-7", "0-13-528910-6",
12         "0-13-012507-5", "0-13-528910-6" };
13
14      public void doPost( HttpServletRequest request,
15                          HttpServletResponse response )
16         throws ServletException, IOException
17      {
18         PrintWriter output;
19         String language = request.getParameter( "lang" );
20
21         // Get the user's session object.
22         // Create a session (true) if one does not exist.
23         HttpSession session = request.getSession( true );
24
25         // add a value for user's choice to session
26         session.putValue( language, getISBN( language ) );
27
28         response.setContentType( "text/html" );
29         output = response.getWriter();
30
31         // send HTML page to client
32         output.println( "<HTML><HEAD><TITLE>" );
33         output.println( "Sessions" );
34         output.println( "</TITLE></HEAD><BODY>" );
35         output.println( "<P>Welcome to Sessions!<BR>" );
36         output.println( "<P>" );
37         output.println( language );
38         output.println( " is a great language." );
39         output.println( "</BODY></HTML>" );
40
41         output.close();     // close stream
42      }
43
44      public void doGet( HttpServletRequest request,
45                         HttpServletResponse response )
46                         throws ServletException, IOException
47      {
48         PrintWriter output;
49
50         // Get the user's session object.
51         // Don't create a session (false) if one does not exist.
52         HttpSession session = request.getSession( false );
53
```

Fig. 19.13 Session tracking example (part 1 of 2).

```
54        // get names of session object's values
55        String valueNames[];
56
57        if ( session != null )
58            valueNames = session.getValueNames();
59        else
60            valueNames = null;
61
62        response.setContentType( "text/html" );
63        output = response.getWriter();
64
65        output.println( "<HTML><HEAD><TITLE>" );
66        output.println( "Sessions II" );
67        output.println( "</TITLE></HEAD><BODY>" );
68
69        if ( valueNames != null && valueNames.length != 0 ) {
70            output.println( "<H1>Recommendations</H1>" );
71
72            // get value for each name in valueNames
73            for ( int i = 0; i < valueNames.length; i++ ) {
74                String value =
75                    (String) session.getValue( valueNames[ i ] );
76
77                output.println(
78                    valueNames[ i ] + " How to Program. " +
79                    "ISBN#: " + value + "<BR>" );
80            }
81        }
82        else {
83            output.println( "<H1>No Recommendations</H1>" );
84            output.println( "You did not select a language or" );
85            output.println( "the session has expired." );
86        }
87
88        output.println( "</BODY></HTML>" );
89        output.close();       // close stream
90    }
91
92    private String getISBN( String lang )
93    {
94        for ( int i = 0; i < names.length; ++i )
95            if ( lang.equals( names[ i ] ) )
96                return isbn[ i ];
97
98        return "";   // no matching string found
99    }
100 }
```

Fig. 19.13 Session tracking example (part 2 of 2).

Lines 8 and 10 declare **String** arrays that store the programming language names and ISBN numbers for the books that will be recommended, respectively. Method **doPost** (line 14) is invoked in response to the **POST** request from the HTML document of Fig.

19.14. Line 19 gets the user's **language** selection (the value of the selected radio button on the Web page) with method **getParameter**.

Line 23

```
HttpSession session = request.getSession( true );
```

obtains the **HttpSession** object for the client with **HttpServletRequest** method *getSession*. If the client already has an **HttpSession** object from a previous request during the client's browsing session, method **getSession** returns that **HttpSession** object. Otherwise, the **true** argument indicates that the servlet should create a unique **HttpSession** object for the client (a **false** argument would cause method **getSession** to return **null** if the **HttpSession** object for the client did not already exist).

Line 26

```
session.putValue( language, getISBN( language ) );
```

puts the language and the corresponding recommended book's ISBN number into the **HttpSession** object.

Software Engineering Observation 19.5

*Name value pairs added to an **HttpSession** object with **putValue** remain available until the client's current browsing session ends or until the session is explicitly invalidated by a call to the **HttpSession** object's **invalidate** method.*

After the values are added to the **HttpSession** object, the servlet sends an HTML document to the client (see the second screen capture of Fig. 19.14).

Method **doGet** (line 44) is invoked in response to the **GET** request from the HTML document of Fig. 19.15. The method obtains the **HttpSession** object for the client, reads the data stored in the object, and for each value stored in the session, recommends a book on the subject. Up to four books are displayed in the Web page created by the servlet.

Line 52

```
HttpSession session = request.getSession( false );
```

retrieves the **HttpSession** object for the client using **HttpServletRequest** method **getSession**. If an **HttpSession** object does not exist for the client, the **false** argument indicates that the servlet should not create one.

If method **getSession** does not return **null** (i.e., there was no **HttpSession** object for the client), line 58

```
valueNames = session.getValueNames();
```

uses **HttpSession** method **getValueNames** to retrieve the value names (i.e., names used as the first argument to **HttpSession** method **putValue**) and assigns the array of **String**s to **valueNames**. Each name is used to retrieve the ISBN of a book from the **HttpSession** object. The **for** structure at lines 73 through 80 uses the statement

```
String value =
    (String) session.getValue( valueNames[ i ] );
```

to get the value associated with each name in **valueNames**. Method **getValue** receives the name and returns an **Object** reference to the corresponding value. The cast operator allows the program to use the returned reference as a **String** reference. Next, a line is written in the response to the client containing the title of the recommended book and that book's ISBN number.

Figure 19.14 shows the HTML document the user loads to select a language. Lines 7 and 8 specify that the **ACTION** of the form is to **POST** information to the **Session-Example** servlet.

```
1    <!-- Fig. 19.14: SelectLanguage.html -->
2    <HTML>
3    <HEAD>
4       <TITLE>Sessions</TITLE>
5    </HEAD>
6    <BODY>
7       <FORM ACTION="http://localhost:8080/servlet/SessionExample"
8            METHOD="POST">
9         <STRONG>Select a programming language:<br>
10        </STRONG><BR>
11        <PRE>
12        <INPUT TYPE="radio" NAME="lang" VALUE="C">C<BR>
13        <INPUT TYPE="radio" NAME="lang" VALUE="C++">C++<BR>
14        <INPUT TYPE="radio" NAME="lang" VALUE="Java"
15            CHECKED>Java<BR>
16        <INPUT TYPE="radio" NAME="lang"
17            VALUE="Visual Basic 6">Visual Basic 6
18        </PRE>
19        <INPUT TYPE="submit" VALUE="Submit">
20        <INPUT TYPE="reset"> </P>
21      </FORM>
22    </BODY>
23    </HTML>
```

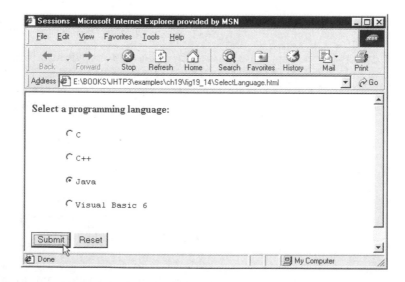

Fig. 19.14   HTML document that invokes the session tracking servlet with a **POST** request and passes the language selection as an argument (part 1 of 2).

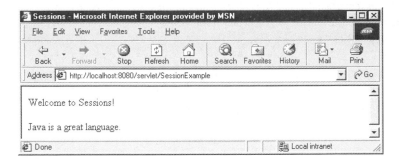

Fig. 19.14   HTML document that invokes the session tracking servlet with a **POST** request and passes the language selection as an argument (part 2 of 2).

The HTML document in Fig. 19.15 invokes the servlet in response to a button press. Lines 7 and 8 specify that the **ACTION** of the form is to **GET** information from the servlet **SessionExample**. The third screen capture in Fig. 19.15 shows the returned HTML document when there is no **HttpSession** object for the client or there are no values stored in the **HttpSession** object.

```
1   <!-- Fig. 19.15: BookRecommendation.html -->
2   <HTML>
3   <HEAD>
4      <TITLE>Sessions</TITLE>
5   </HEAD>
6   <BODY>
7      <FORM ACTION="http://localhost:8080/servlet/SessionExample"
8         METHOD="GET">
9         Press "Recommend books" for a list of books.
10        <INPUT TYPE=submit VALUE="Recommend books">
11     </FORM>
12  </BODY>
13  </HTML>
```

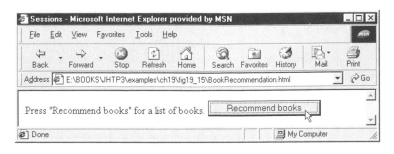

Fig. 19.15   HTML that interacts with the session tracking servlet to read the session information and return book recommendations to the user (part 1 of 2).

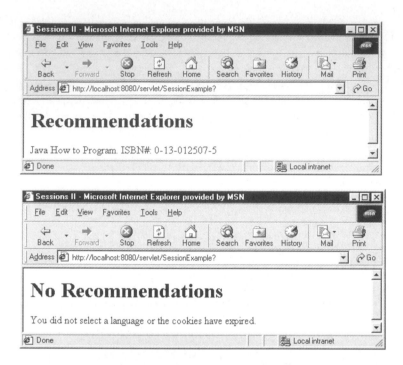

Fig. 19.15   HTML that interacts with the session tracking servlet to read the session information and return book recommendations to the user (part 2 of 2).

19.7 Multitier Applications: Using JDBC from a Servlet

Servlets can communicate with databases via JDBC (Java Database Connectivity). As we discussed in Chapter 18, JDBC provides a uniform way for a Java program to connect with a variety of databases in a general manner without having to deal with the specifics of those database systems.

Many of today's applications are *three-tier distributed applications,* consisting of a *user interface*, *business logic* and *database access*. The user interface in such an application is often created using HTML (as shown in this chapter) or Dynamic HTML. In some cases, Java applets are also used for this tier. HTML is the preferred mechanism for representing the user interface in systems where portability is a concern. Because HTML is supported by all browsers, designing the user interface to be accessed through a Web browser guarantees portability across all platforms that have browsers. Using the networking provided automatically by the browser, the user interface can communicate with the middle-tier business logic. The middle tier can then access the database to manipulate the data. All three tiers may reside on separate computers that are connected to a network.

In multitier architectures, Web servers are increasingly used to build the middle tier. They provide the business logic that manipulates data from databases and that communicates with client Web browsers. Servlets, through JDBC, can interact with popular database systems. Developers do not need to be familiar with the specifics of each database system. Rather, developers use SQL-based queries and the JDBC driver handles the specifics of interacting with each database system.

Figures 19.16 and 19.17 demonstrate a three-tier distributed application that displays the user interface in a browser using HTML. The middle tier is a Java servlet that handles requests from the client browser and provides access to the third tier—a Microsoft Access database (set up as an ODBC data source) accessed via JDBC. The servlet in this example is a guest book servlet that allows the user to register for several different mailing lists. When the servlet receives a **POST** request from the HTML document of Fig. 19.17, it ensures that the required data fields are present, then stores the data in the database and sends a confirmation page to the client.

```java
1   // Fig. 19.16: GuestBookServlet.java
2   // Three-Tier Example
3   import java.io.*;
4   import javax.servlet.*;
5   import javax.servlet.http.*;
6   import java.util.*;
7   import java.sql.*;
8
9   public class GuestBookServlet extends HttpServlet {
10     private Statement statement = null;
11     private Connection connection = null;
12     private String URL = "jdbc:odbc:GuestBook";
13
14     public void init( ServletConfig config )
15        throws ServletException
16     {
17        super.init( config );
18
19        try {
20           Class.forName( "sun.jdbc.odbc.JdbcOdbcDriver" );
21           connection =
22              DriverManager.getConnection( URL, "", "" );
23        }
24        catch ( Exception e ) {
25           e.printStackTrace();
26           connection = null;
27        }
28     }
29
30     public void doPost( HttpServletRequest req,
31                         HttpServletResponse res )
32        throws ServletException, IOException
33     {
34        String email, firstName, lastName, company,
35               snailmailList, cppList, javaList, vbList,
36               iwwwList;
37
38        email = req.getParameter( "Email" );
39        firstName = req.getParameter( "FirstName" );
40        lastName = req.getParameter( "LastName" );
```

Fig. 19.16 GuestBookServlet, which allows client to register for mailing lists (part 1 of 3).

```
41        company = req.getParameter( "Company" );
42        snailmailList = req.getParameter( "mail" );
43        cppList = req.getParameter( "c_cpp" );
44        javaList = req.getParameter( "java" );
45        vbList = req.getParameter( "vb" );
46        iwwwList = req.getParameter( "iwww" );
47
48        PrintWriter output = res.getWriter();
49        res.setContentType( "text/html" );
50
51        if ( email.equals( "" ) ||
52             firstName.equals( "" ) ||
53             lastName.equals( "" ) ) {
54           output.println( "<H3> Please click the back " +
55                           "button and fill in all " +
56                           "fields.</H3>" );
57           output.close();
58           return;
59        }
60
61        /* Note: The GuestBook database actually contains fields
62         * Address1, Address2, City, State and Zip that are not
63         * used in this example. However, the insert into the
64         * database must still account for these fields. */
65        boolean success = insertIntoDB(
66           "'" + email + "','" + firstName + "','" + lastName +
67           "','" + company + "',' ',' ',' ',' ',' ','" +
68           ( snailmailList != null ? "yes" : "no" ) + "','" +
69           ( cppList != null ? "yes" : "no"  ) + "','" +
70           ( javaList != null ? "yes" : "no"  ) + "','" +
71           ( vbList != null ? "yes" : "no"  ) + "','" +
72           ( iwwwList != null ? "yes" : "no"  ) + "'" );
73
74        if ( success )
75           output.print( "<H2>Thank you " + firstName +
76                         " for registering.</H2>" );
77        else
78           output.print( "<H2>An error occurred. " +
79                         "Please try again later.</H2>" );
80
81        output.close();
82     }
83
84     private boolean insertIntoDB( String stringtoinsert )
85     {
86        try {
87           statement = connection.createStatement();
88           statement.execute(
89              "INSERT INTO GuestBook values (" +
90              stringtoinsert + ");" );
91           statement.close();
92        }
```

Fig. 19.16 GuestBookServlet, which allows client to register for mailing lists (part 2 of 3).

```
93          catch ( Exception e ) {
94             System.err.println(
95                "ERROR: Problems with adding new entry" );
96             e.printStackTrace();
97             return false;
98          }
99
100         return true;
101      }
102
103      public void destroy()
104      {
105         try {
106            connection.close();
107         }
108         catch( Exception e ) {
109            System.err.println( "Problem closing the database" );
110         }
111      }
112   }
```

Fig. 19.16 GuestBookServlet, which allows client to register for mailing lists (part 3 of 3).

Class **GuestBookServlet** extends class **HttpServlet** (line 9) so it is capable of responding to **GET** and **POST** requests. Servlets are initialized by overriding method **init** (line 14). Method **init** is called exactly once in a servlet's lifetime and is guaranteed to complete before any client requests are accepted. Method **init** takes a **Servlet-Config** argument and throws a **ServletException**. The argument provides the servlet with information about its *initialization parameters* (i.e., parameters not associated with a request, but passed to the servlet for initializing servlet variables). These parameters can be specified in a file that is normally called **servlets.properties** and resides in the subdirectory **webpages\WEB-INF** in the JSDK install directory (other Web servers may name this file differently and may store it in a directory specific to the Web server). The most common properties that are typically specified are *servletname*.**code** and *servletname*.**initparams**, where *servletname* is any name you want to specify as your servlet's name. This name would be used in the invocation of the servlet from a Web page. For a sample **servlets.properties** file, see the one provided with the JSDK in the subdirectory **webpages\WEB-INF** in the JSDK install directory.

In this example, the servlet's **init** method performs the connection to the Microsoft Access database. The method loads the **JdbcOdbcDriver** at line 20 with

```
Class.forName( "sun.jdbc.odbc.JdbcOdbcDriver" );
```

Lines 21 and 22 attempts to open a connection to the **GuestBook** database. When method **insertIntoDB** (line 84) is called by the servlet, lines 87 through 91

```
statement = connection.createStatement();
statement.execute(
   "INSERT INTO GuestBook values (" +
   stringtoinsert + ");" );
statement.close();
```

create **statement** to perform the next insert into the database, call **statement.execute** to execute an **INSERT INTO** statement (**stringtoinsert** is the **String** passed into **insertIntoDB**) and close the **statement** to ensure that the insert operation is committed to the database.

When a **POST** request is received from the HTML document in Fig. 19.17, method **doPost** (line 30) responds by reading the HTML form field values from the **POST** request, formatting the field values into a **String** for use in an **INSERT INTO** operation on the database and sending the **String** to method **insertIntoDB** (line 84) to perform the insert operation. Each form field's value is retrieved in lines 38 through 46.

The **if** structure at lines 51 through 59 determines if the email, first name or last name parameters are empty **String**s. If so, the servlet response asks the user to return to the HTML form and enter those fields.

Lines 65 through 72 formulate the call to **insertIntoDB**. The method returns a **boolean** value indicating if the insert into the database was successful.

Line 103 defines method **destroy** to ensure that the database connection is closed before the servlet terminates.

Figure 19.17 defines the HTML document that presents the guest book form to the user and **POST**s the information to the servlet of Fig. 19.16.

```
1    <!-- Fig. 19.17: GuestBookForm.html -->
2    <HTML>
3    <HEAD>
4       <TITLE>Deitel Guest Book Form</TITLE>
5    </HEAD>
6
7    <BODY>
8       <H1>Guest Book</H1>
9       <FORM
10         ACTION=http://localhost:8080/servlet/GuestBookServlet
11         METHOD=POST><PRE>
12         * Email address: <INPUT TYPE=text NAME=Email>
13         * First Name:    <INPUT TYPE=text NAME=FirstName>
14         * Last name:     <INPUT TYPE=text NAME=LastName>
15         Company:         <INPUT TYPE=text NAME=Company>
16
17                          * fields are required
18         </PRE>
19
20         <P>Select mailing lists from which you want
21         to receive information<BR>
22         <INPUT TYPE=CHECKBOX NAME=mail VALUE=mail>
23            Snail Mail<BR>
24         <INPUT TYPE=CHECKBOX NAME=c_cpp VALUE=c_cpp>
25            <I>C++ How to Program & C How to Program</I><BR>
26         <INPUT TYPE=CHECKBOX NAME=java VALUE=java>
27            <I>Java How to Program</I><BR>
28         <INPUT TYPE=CHECKBOX NAME=vb VALUE=vb>
29            <I>Visual Basic How to Program</I><BR>
```

Fig. 19.17 HTML that invokes the **GuestBookServlet** (part 1 of 2).

```
30        <INPUT TYPE=CHECKBOX NAME=iwww VALUE=iwww>
31           <I>Internet and World Wide Web How to Program</I><BR>
32        </P>
33        <INPUT TYPE=SUBMIT Value="Submit">
34     </FORM>
35  </BODY>
36  </HTML>
```

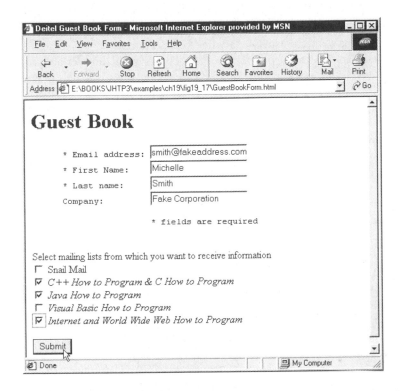

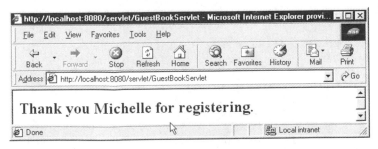

Fig. 19.17   HTML that invokes the **GuestBookServlet** (part 2 of 2).

Lines 9 through 11 specify that the form's **ACTION** is to **POST** information to the **GuestBookServlet**. The screen captures show the form filled with one set of information (the first screen) and the confirmation Web page that was sent back to the client as the response to the **POST** request.

19.8 Electronic Commerce

There is a revolution going on now in electronic commerce. As this book entered production already one-third of stock transactions were being transacted over the Internet by individuals. Companies like *amazon.com*, *barnesandnoble.com* and *borders.com* are handling huge volumes of electronic sales. Servlet technology will help more organizations get into electronic commerce.

There is also an explosion occurring in so-called business-to-business transactions. As Internet transmission becomes more secure, more and more organizations will entrust increasing portions of their business activities to the Internet.

Companies are finding it possible to offer clients with Internet access all kinds of value-added services. Today, people often contact companies over the Internet and enter their own information rather than phoning it in verbally.

Two popular applications that many companies have off-loaded to the Web are shipment tracking and invoice tracking. People want to know where the products they have ordered are. Vendors want to know when they will be paid.

Small businesses are particularly excited about electronic commerce possibilities. By putting up a respectable Web site, they present themselves to the world and can considerably leverage their business activities.

For client-server systems, many developers prefer a full Java solution with applets on the client and servlets on the server.

19.9 Servlet Internet and World Wide Web Resources

This section lists a variety of servlet resources available on the Internet and provides a brief description of each. For other Java Internet resources, see the appendix "Internet and World Wide Web Resources."

http://java.sun.com/products/servlet/index.html
> The servlet page at the *Sun Microsystems, Inc. Java* Web site provides access to the latest servlet information, servlet resources and the *Java Servlet Development Kit (JSDK)*.

http://www.servlets.com
> This is the Web site for the book *Java Servlet Programming* published by O'Reilly. The book provides a variety of resources. This book is an excellent resource for programmers who are learning servlets.

http://www.servletcentral.com
> *Servlet Central* is an online magazine for server-side Java programmers. This includes technical articles and columns, news and "Ask the Experts." Resources include: books, servlet documentation links on the Web, a servlet archive, a list of servlet-enabled applications and servers, and servlet development tools.

http://www.servletsource.com
> *ServletSource.com* is a general servlet resource site containing code, tips, tutorials and links to many other Web sites with information on servlets.

http://www.cookiecentral.com
> A good all-around resource site for cookies.

Summary

- Often, networking is a client-server relationship. The client requests that some action be performed and the server performs the action and responds to the client.

- A common use of the request-response model is between World Wide Web browsers and World Wide Web servers. When a user selects a Web site to browse through a Web browser (the client application), a request is sent to the appropriate Web server (the server application), which normally responds to the client by sending the appropriate HTML Web page.

- A servlet extends the functionality of a server. Most servlets enhance the functionality of World Wide Web servers.

- The Internet offers many protocols, the most common being The HTTP protocol (HyperText Transfer Protocol) that forms the basis of the World Wide Web.

- All servlets must implement the **Servlet** interface.

- As with many key applet methods, the methods of interface **Servlet** are invoked automatically (by the server on which the servlet is installed).

- **Servlet** method **init** takes one **ServletConfig** argument and throws a **ServletException**. The **ServletConfig** argument provides the servlet with information about its initialization parameters (i.e., parameters not associated with a request, but passed to the servlet for initializing servlet variables).

- **Servlet** method **getServletConfig** returns a reference to an object that implements interface **ServletConfig**. This object provides access to the servlet's configuration information such as initialization parameters and the servlet's **ServletContext**.

- The servlet packages define two abstract classes that implement interface **Servlet**—**GenericServlet** and **HttpServlet**. These classes provide default implementations of all methods of interface **Servlet**. Most servlets extend one of these classes and override some or all of their methods with appropriate customized behaviors.

- The key method in every servlet is method **service**, which receives both a **ServletRequest** object and a **ServletResponse** object. These objects provide access to input and output streams that allow the servlet to read data from the client and send data to the client.

- Web-based servlets typically extend class **HttpServlet**. Class **HttpServlet** overrides method **service** to distinguish between the typical requests received from a client Web browser.

- The two most common HTTP request types (also known as request methods) are **GET** and **POST**.

- Class **HttpServlet** defines methods **doGet** and **doPut** to respond to **GET** and **POST** requests from a client, respectively. These methods are called by the **HttpServlet** class's **service** method, which first determines the request type, then calls the appropriate method.

- Methods **doGet** and **doPost** each receive as arguments an **HttpServletRequest** object and an **HttpServletResponse** object that enable interaction between the client and the server. The **HttpServletRequest** object represents the client's request and the **HttpServletResponse** object represents the server's response.

- The method **getParameter** of interface **ServletRequest** retrieves the survey response **POST**ed by the client. The method returns a **String** containing the value of the parameter or **null** if the parameter is not found.

- The method **getParameterNames** of interface **ServletRequest** returns an **Enumeration** of **String** names of all the parameters **POST**ed by the client.

- **HttpServletResponse** method **getOutputStream** obtains a byte-based output stream that enables binary data to be sent to the client.

- **HttpServletResponse** method **getWriter** obtains a character-based output stream that enables text data to be sent to the client.

- **HttpServletResponse** method **setContentType** specifies the MIME type of the response to the browser. The MIME type helps the browser determine how to display the data (or possibly what other application to execute to process the data). For example, type **"text/html"** indicates that the response is an HTML document, so the browser displays the HTML page.

- If **doGet** or **doPut** is unable to handle a client's request, it throws a **javax.servlet.ServletException**. If **doGet** encounters an error during stream processing (reading from the client or writing to the client), it throws a **java.io.IOException**.

- The client can only access a servlet if the servlet is running on a server. The JSDK WebServer can be used to test servlets.

- When a client connects to a server to request a service, the client must specify the proper port number; otherwise, the client request cannot be processed.

- The term well-known port number is used to describe the default port for many Internet services. For example, a Web server waits for clients to make requests at well-known port 80 by default.

- The JSDK WebServer uses port 8080 as its well-known port number.

- An HTML **FORM** allows the client to submit information to the server.

- The **FORM** attribute **ACTION** specifies the server-side form handler, i.e., the program that will handle the request. The **ACTION** is performed when the user submits the form.

- The **FORM** attribute **METHOD** is the request type that the server uses to decide how to handle the request and possibly causes the browser to attach arguments to the end of the **ACTION** URL.

- The server **localhost** is a well-known server name on all computers that support TCP/IP-based networking protocols such as HTTP. The server **localhost** refers to your own computer.

- The HTML tag **INPUT** creates a GUI component for the form. The kind of GUI element is specified with the **TYPE** attribute. Two types are "**submit**" and "**radio**".

- Browsers often cache (save on disk) Web pages so they can quickly reload the pages. However, browsers typically do not cache the server's response to a **POST** request because the next **POST** may not return the same result.

- Many Web sites keep track of individual clients as they browse in order to have specific information about a particular user. This is often done to provide customized content and/or to gather data on browsing habits.

- Two common techniques used to track clients individually are cookies and session tracking.

- Cookies are small files that are sent by a servlet (or another similar technology) as part of the HTTP header and can store information on the user's computer for retrieval later in the same or in future browsing sessions.

- When the browser makes a request of a server, cookies previously sent to the client by that server are returned to the server (if they have not expired) as part of the request formulated by the browser. Cookies are automatically deleted when they expire (i.e., reach their maximum age).

- The method **setMaxAge** of class **Cookie** sets the maximum age for the cookie. The method **getMaxAge** of class **Cookie** returns the maximum age for the cookie.

- The user of a browser can turn off cookies.

- **HttpServletRequest** method **getCookies**, which returns an array of **Cookies**, retrieves the cookies from the client. **HttpServletResponse** method **addCookie** adds a **Cookie** to the header of the response.

- The method **getName** of class **Cookie** returns a **String** containing the name of the cookie as set with **setName** or the constructor.

- The method **getValue** of class **Cookie** returns a **String** containing the name of the cookie as set with **setValue** or the constructor.

- Session Tracking uses **HttpSession** objects.

- The **HttpServletRequest** method **getSession** returns an **HttpSession** objects for the client. Supplying the boolean true as an argument to this function will cause a session to be created if there is not one already.

- The **HttpSession** method **getValue** returns the object that was associated with a particular name using **putValue**.

- The **HttpSession** method **getValueNames** returns a list of names of the values already set.

- Servlets can communicate with databases via JDBC (Java Database Connectivity).

- Many of today's applications are three-tier distributed applications, consisting of a user interface, business logic and database access. The user interface in such an application is often created using HTML or Dynamic HTML. Java applets are also used for this tier.

- In multitier architectures, Web servers are increasingly used to build the middle tier. They provide the business logic that manipulates data from databases and that communicates with client Web browsers.

- Servlets, through JDBC, can interact with popular database systems. Developers do not need to be familiar with the specifics of each database system. Rather, developers use SQL-based queries and the JDBC driver handles the specifics of interacting with each database system.

Terminology

ACTION HTML attribute
addCookie method
BAD_REQUEST error
<BODY> and **</BODY>** html tags
business logic
class **Cookie**
class **GenericServlet**
class **HttpServlet**
client-server relationship
destroy method of **Servlet** interface
doDelete method of **HttpServlet** class
doGet method of **HttpServlet** class
doOptions method of **HttpServlet** class
doPost method of **HttpServlet** class
doPut method of **HttpServlet** class
doTrace method of **HttpServlet** class
Dynamic **HTML**
<FORM> and **</FORM>** html tags
GET request
getComment method of class **Cookie**
getCookies method
getDomain method of class **Cookie**
getMaxAge method of class **Cookie**
getName method of class **Cookie**
getOutputStream method
getParameter method
getParameterNames method
getPath method of class **Cookie**
getSecure method of class **Cookie**
getServletConfig method **Servlet**

getServletInfo method of **Servlet**
getSession method
getValue method of class **Cookie**
getValue method of interface **HttpSession**
getValueNames method of **HttpSession**
getVersion method of class **Cookie**
getWriter method
handshake point
<HEAD> and **</HEAD>** HTML tags
header
HTTP protocol
init method of **Servlet** interface
INPUT HTML tag
interface **HttpServletRequest**
interface **HttpServletResponse**
interface **HttpSession**
java.rmi packages
java.servletname.code argument
java.servletname.initargs argument
javax.servlet package
javax.servlet.http package
JSDK WebServer
localhost
METHOD HTML attribute
org.omg packages
POST request
putValue method of interface **HttpSession**
"radio" **INPUT** type
request-response model
request types / request methods

service method of **Servlet** interface
Servlet interface
servlet.properties file
ServletConfig class
ServletException
servlets
ServletRequest object
ServletResponse object
setComment method of class **Cookie**
setContentType method
setDomain method of class **Cookie**
setMaxAge method of class **Cookie**
setPath method of class **Cookie**

setSecure method of class **Cookie**
setValue method of class **Cookie**
setVersion method of class **Cookie**
socket-based communications
startserver
startserver.bat
"**submit**" **INPUT** type
thin clients
three-tier distributed applications
<TITLE> and **</TITLE>** HTML tags
TYPE HTML attribute
VALUE html attribute
well-known port number

Software Engineering Observations

19.1 All servlets must implement the **javax.servlet.Servlet** interface.
19.2 Some clients do not allow cookies to be written on them. When a client declines a cookie the client is normally informed that such a refusal may prevent browsing the site.
19.3 By default cookies only exist for the current browsing session (until the user closes the browser). To make cookies persist beyond the current session, call **Cookie** method **set-MaxAge** to indicate the number of seconds until the cookie expires.
19.4 Call method **addCookie** to add a cookie to the **HTTPServletResponse** before writing any other information to the client.
19.5 Name value pairs added to an **HttpSession** object with **putValue** remain available until the client's current browsing session ends or until the session is explicitly invalidated by a call to the **HttpSession** object's **invalidate** methods

Self-Review Exercises

19.1 Fill in the blanks in each of the following:
  f) Classes **HttpServlet** and **GenericServlet** implement the _____ interface.
  g) Class **HttpServlet** defines the methods _____ and _____ to respond to **GET** and **POST** requests from a client.
  h) **HttpServletResponse** method _____ obtains a character-based output stream that enables text data to be sent to the client.
  i) Attribute **FORM** _____ specifies the server-side form handler, i.e., the program that will handle the request.
  j) _____ is the well-known server name that refers to your own computer.
  k) **Cookie** method _____ returns a **String** containing the name of the cookie as set with _____ or the constructor.
  l) **HttpServletRequest** method **getSession** returns an _____ object for the client.
19.2 State whether each of the following is *true* or *false*. If *false*, explain why.
  a) **Servlet**s usually are used on the client side of a networking application.
  b) Servlet methods are executed automatically.
  c) The two most common **HTTP** requests are **GET** and **PUT**.
  d) The well-known port number for Web requests is 55.
  e) **Cookie**s never expire.

f) **HttpSession**s expire only when the browsing session ends or when the **invalidate** method is called.

g) The **HttpSession** method **getValue** returns the object associated with a particular name.

Answers to Self-Review Exercises

19.1   a)**Servlet**.b)**doGet,doPost**.c)**getWriter**.d)**ACTION**.e)**localhost**.f)**getName, setName**. g) **HttpSession**.

19.2   a) False. Servlets are usually used on the server side.
   b) True.
   c) False. The two most common **HTTP** requests are **GET** and **POST**.
   d) False. The well-known port number for Web requests is 80.
   e) False. **Cookie**s expire when they reach their maximum age.
   f) True.
   g) True.

Exercises

19.3   Modify the **Cookie** example in of Figs. 19.9 through 19.11 to have the book recommendation list prices for each book. Also, allow the user to select some or all of the recommended books and "order" them.

19.4   Modify the **HttpSession** example in of Fig. 19.13 through 19.15 to have the book recommendation list prices for each book. Also, allow the user to select some or all of the recommended books and "order" them.

19.5   Modify the **GuestBook** example in Figs. 19.16 and 19.17 to implement the fields **Address1**, **Address2**, **City**, **State** and **Zip**. Modify it further to lookup a guest by name or email address and return an HTML page with all of the guest's information.

19.6   Modify the servlet of Fig. 19.7 to synchronize access to the **survey.txt** file using the techniques illustrated in Chapter 15, "Multithreading."

19.7   Modify the servlet of Fig. 19.7 to synchronize access to the **survey.txt** file by having the HTTPPostServlct class implement **javax.servlet.SingleThreadModel**.

19.8   *(Project: Auction Servlet)* Create your own auction servlet. Create a database of several items that are being auctioned. Make a Web page that allows the user to select an item on which to place a bid. When the user places the bid they should be notified if the bid is lower than the previous high bid and asked to submit their bid again. Allow the user to return to the servlet and query it to determine if they won the auction.

19.9   Modify Exercise 19.8 to use session tracking such that when the client connects to the servlet again, the client is automatically sent a web page indicating the status of the bidding on the items for which they have previously bid.

20

Remote Method Invocation (RMI)

Objectives

- To understand the notions of client/server distributed computing.
- To understand the architecture of RMI.
- To understand the notion of stubs.
- To be able to use RMI (Remote Method Invocation) to implement a three-tier client/server distributed application.
- To use a URL stream connection to read an HTML document on a Web server.
- To use **InputStreamReader** and **BufferedReader** to read streams of characters from an **InputStream**.

Dealing with more than one client at a time is the business world's equivalent of bigamy. It's so awkward to tell one client that you're working on someone else's business that you inevitably start lying.
Andrew Frothingham

They also serve who only stand and wait.
John Milton

Rule 1: The client is always right.

Rule 2: If you think the client is wrong, see Rule 1.
Sign seen in shops

I love being a writer. What I can't stand is the paperwork.
Peter De Vries

Outline

20.1 Introduction

In the preceding chapter, we began our presentation of Java's networking and distributed computing capabilities with a discussion of servlets. A client Web browser simply indicates the server to which to connect and the servlet that is to perform some service. The networking that allows the client and server to communicate happens seamlessly through the Internet and World Wide Web.

In this chapter, we continue our discussion of Java's networking and distributed computing capabilities with *Remote Method Invocation (RMI)*. RMI allows Java objects running on the same or separate computers to communicate with one another via *remote method calls*. Such method calls appear the same as those operating on objects in the same program.

RMI is based on a similar earlier technology for procedural programming called *remote procedure calls (RPCs)* developed in the 1980s. RPC allows a procedural program (i.e., a program written in C or another procedural programming language) to call a function residing on another computer as conveniently as if that function where part of the same program running on the same computer. A goal of RPC was to allow programmers to concentrate on the required tasks of an application by calling functions, while making transparent to the programmer the mechanism that allows the application's parts to communicate over a network. RPC performs all the networking and *marshaling of the data* (i.e., packaging of function arguments and return values for transmission over a network). A disadvantage of RPC is that it supports a limited set of simple data types. Therefore, RPC is not suitable for passing and returning Java objects. Another disadvantage of RPC is that it requires the programmer to learn a special *interface definition language (IDL)* to describe the functions that can be invoked remotely.

RMI is Java's implementation of RPC for Java-object-to-Java-object distributed communication. Once a method (or *service*) of a Java object is registered as being remotely accessible, a client can "look up" that service and receive a reference that allows the client to use that service (i.e., call the method). The syntax of the method call is identical to that of a call to a method of another object in the same program. As with RPC, the marshaling of the data is handled by RMI. However, RMI provides for transfer of objects of complex data types via the object serialization mechanism discussed in Chapter 17, "Files and Streams." Class **ObjectOutputStream** converts any **Serializable** object into a stream of bytes that can be transmitted across a network. Class **ObjectInputStream** reconstructs the original object for use in the receiving method. The programmer need not be concerned with the transmission of the data over the network. RMI does not require the programmer to learn an IDL because all the networking code is generated directly from the existing classes in the program. Also, because RMI supports only one language, Java, no language-neutral IDL is required; Java's own interfaces are sufficient.

We present a substantial RMI example and discuss the key concepts of RMI as they are encountered throughout the example. After studying this example, you should have a basic understanding of the RMI model of networking and should be able to begin building Java-to-Java distributed applications.

[*Note:* For Java to non-Java communication you can use Java IDL (introduced in Java 1.2). Java IDL enables applications and applets written in Java to communicate with objects written in any language that supports CORBA (Common Object Request Broker Architecture), anywhere on the World Wide Web. CORBA is beyond the scope of this book.]

20.2 Case Study: Creating a Distributed System with RMI

In the next several sections, we present an RMI example that downloads the *Travelers Forecast* weather information from the National Weather Service Web site:

http://iwin.nws.noaa.gov/iwin/us/traveler.html

[*Note:* As we developed this example, the format of the *Travelers Forecast* Web page changed several times (a common occurrence with today's dynamic Web pages). The information we use in this example depends directly on the format of the *Travelers Forecast* Web page. If you have trouble running this example, please refer to the FAQ page on our Web site **http://www.deitel.com**.]

We store the *Travelers Forecast* information on a server that accepts requests for weather information through remote method calls.

The four major steps in this example include:

1. Define a *remote interface* that describes how the client and the server communicate with one another.

2. Define the server application that implements the remote interface. [Note: By convention, the server implementation class has the same name as the remote interface and ends with **Impl**.]

3. Define the client application that uses a *remote interface reference* to interact with the server implementation of the interface (i.e., an object of the class that implements the remote interface).

4. Compile and execute the server and the client.

20.3 Defining the Remote Interface

The first step in creating a client/server distributed application with RMI is to define the remote interface that describes the *remote methods* which the client will use to interact with the remote server object through RMI. To create a remote interface, define an interface that extends interface **Remote** (package **java.rmi**). Interface **Remote** is a *tagging interface*—it does not declare any methods, and so places no burden on the implementing class. An object of a class that implements interface **Remote** directly or indirectly is a *remote object* and can be accessed—security permitting—from any Java virtual machine that has a connection to the computer on which the remote object executes.

Software Engineering Observation 20.1

Every remote method must be part of an interface that extends **java.rmi.Remote**.

Software Engineering Observation 20.2

An object of a class that implements the **Remote** *interface can be exported as a remote object to make it available to receive remote method calls.*

Interface **TemperatureServer** (Fig. 20.1) is the remote interface in this case study. It describes the method a client will call to interact with the remote object and obtain its services. To create a remote server object, the method described by this interface must be implemented by the server class. Note that a remote interface can declare more than one method.

Interface **TemperatureServer** extends interface **Remote** (package **java.rmi**) on line 5. Any time computers communicate over a network, there is the potential for communication problems. For example, a server computer could malfunction, a network resource could malfunction, etc. If a communication problem occurs during a remote method call, a remote method throws a **RemoteException** (a type of checked exception).

Software Engineering Observation 20.3

Each method in a **Remote** *interface must have a* **throws** *clause indicating the potential for a* **RemoteException**.

20.4 Implementing the Remote Interface

Next, we define the class **TemperatureServerImpl** (Fig. 20.2) that implements the **Remote** interface **TemperatureServer**. The client will interact with an object of class **TemperatureServerImpl** to obtain the actual weather information. Class **TemperatureServerImpl** uses an array of **WeatherInfo** (Fig. 20.3) objects to store the weather data. A copy of this array is sent to a **TemperatureClient** when the client invokes remote method **getWeatherInfo**. The National Weather Service updates the Web page from which we retrieve information twice a day. However, class **TemperatureServerImpl** downloads this information only once when the server is started. The exercises ask you to modify the server to update the data twice a day. [*Note:* **TemperatureServerImpl** is the class that is affected if the National Weather Service changes the format of the *Travelers Forecast* Web page. If you encounter problems with this example, visit the FAQ page at our Web site **http://www.deitel.com**.]

```
1   // Fig. 20.1: TemperatureServer.java
2   // TemperatureServer interface definition
3   import java.rmi.*;
4
5   public interface TemperatureServer extends Remote {
6       public WeatherInfo[] getWeatherInfo()
7           throws RemoteException;
8   }
```

Fig. 20.1   **TemperatureServer** interface.

```
1    // Fig. 20.2: TemperatureServerImpl.java
2    // TemperatureServerImpl definition
3    import java.rmi.*;
4    import java.rmi.server.*;
5    import java.util.*;
6    import java.io.*;
7    import java.net.*;
8
9    public class TemperatureServerImpl extends UnicastRemoteObject
10                                  implements TemperatureServer {
11       private WeatherInfo weatherInformation[];
12
13       public TemperatureServerImpl() throws RemoteException
14       {
15          super();
16          updateWeatherConditions();
17       }
18
19       // get weather information from NWS
20       private void updateWeatherConditions()
21          throws RemoteException
22       {
23          try {
24             System.err.println(
25                "Updating weather information..." );
26
27             // Traveler's Forecast Web Page
28             URL url = new URL(
29                "http://iwin.nws.noaa.gov/iwin/us/traveler.html" );
30
31             BufferedReader in =
32                new BufferedReader(
33                   new InputStreamReader( url.openStream() ) );
34
35             String separator = "</PRE><HR> <BR><PRE>";
36
37             // locate first horizontal line on Web page
38             while ( !in.readLine().startsWith( separator ) )
39                ;      // do nothing
40
41             // s1 is the day format and s2 is the night format
42             String s1 =
43                "CITY            WEA      HI/LO    WEA      HI/LO";
44             String s2 =
45                "CITY            WEA      LO/HI    WEA      LO/HI";
46             String inputLine = "";
47
48             // locate header that begins weather information
49             do {
50                inputLine = in.readLine();
51             } while ( !inputLine.equals( s1 ) &&
52                       !inputLine.equals( s2 ) );
53
```

Fig. 20.2   Class **TemperatureServerImpl** (part 1 of 3).

```
54              Vector cityVector = new Vector();
55
56              inputLine = in.readLine();  // get first city's info
57
58              while ( !inputLine.equals( "" ) ) {
59                 // create WeatherInfo object for city
60                 WeatherInfo w = new WeatherInfo(
61                    inputLine.substring( 0, 16 ),
62                    inputLine.substring( 16, 22 ),
63                    inputLine.substring( 23, 29 ) );
64
65                 cityVector.addElement( w ); // add to Vector
66                 inputLine = in.readLine();  // get next city's info
67              }
68
69              // create array to return to client
70              weatherInformation =
71                 new WeatherInfo[ cityVector.size() ];
72
73              for ( int i = 0; i < weatherInformation.length; i++ )
74                 weatherInformation[ i ] =
75                    ( WeatherInfo ) cityVector.elementAt( i );
76
77              System.err.println( "Finished Processing Data." );
78              in.close();  // close connection to NWS server
79           }
80           catch( java.net.ConnectException ce ) {
81              System.err.println( "Connection failed." );
82              System.exit( 1 );
83           }
84           catch( Exception e ) {
85              e.printStackTrace();
86              System.exit( 1 );
87           }
88        }
89
90        // implementation for TemperatureServer interface method
91        public WeatherInfo[] getWeatherInfo()
92        {
93           return weatherInformation;
94        }
95
96        public static void main( String args[] ) throws Exception
97        {
98           System.err.println(
99              "Initializing server: please wait." );
100
101          // create server object
102          TemperatureServerImpl temp =
103             new TemperatureServerImpl();
104
105          // bind TemperatureServerImpl object to the rmiregistry
106          String serverObjectName = "//localhost/TempServer";
```

Fig. 20.2   Class **TemperatureServerImpl** (part 2 of 3).

```
107         Naming.rebind( serverObjectName, temp );
108         System.err.println(
109            "The Temperature Server is up and running." );
110    }
111  }
```

Fig. 20.2   Class **TemperatureServerImpl** (part 3 of 3).

Class **TemperatureServerImpl** extends class *UnicastRemoteObject* (package **java.rmi.server**) and implements **Remote** interface **Temperature-Server** (lines 9 and 10). Class **UnicastRemoteObject** provides the basic functionality required for all remote objects. In particular, its constructor *exports* the object to make it available to receive remote calls. Exporting the object enables the remote server object to wait for client connections on an anonymous port number (i.e., one chosen by the computer on which the remote object executes). This sets up the object to allow *unicast communication* (point-to-point communication between two objects via method calls) using standard *streams-based socket connections*. In Chapter 21, "Networking," we discuss the details of streams-based socket connections. However, in this chapter, RMI performs these lower-level details. The **TemperatureServerImpl** constructor (line 13) invokes the default constructor for class **UnicastRemoteObject** and calls **private** method **updateWeatherConditions**. Other constructors for class **UnicastRemoteOb-ject** allow the programmer to specify additional information such as an explicit port number where the remote object should receive calls. All **UnicastRemoteObject** constructors throw **RemoteException**s.

Software Engineering Observation 20.4

Because UnicastRemoteObject *throws checked* **RemoteException***s, subclasses of* UnicastRemoteObject *must define constructors that throw* **RemoteException***s.*

Software Engineering Observation 20.5

Class UnicastRemoteObject *provides basic functionality required by remote objects. Classes for remote objects do not need to extend this class if they export the object with* static *method* exportObject *of class* UnicastRemoteObject *to allow the object to receive remote requests.*

Software Engineering Observation 20.6

Class UnicastRemoteObject*'s constructor exports the remote object to make it available for remote method calls at an anonymous port on the server computer.*

Lines 20 through 89 define method **updateWeatherConditions** which reads the weather information from the *Traveler's Forecast* Web page and stores it in an array of **WeatherInfo** objects.

Lines 28 and 29

```
URL url = new URL(
    "http://iwin.nws.noaa.gov/iwin/us/traveler.html" );
```

creates a *URL* object that contains the URL for the *Traveler's Forecast* Web page. The **URL** constructor throws a checked **MalformedURLException** if the URL is an incorrect format (e.g., if the **:** after **http** is missing).

Lines 31 to 33

```
BufferedReader in =
   new BufferedReader(
      new InputStreamReader( url.openStream() ) );
```

attempt to open a connection to the file specified by the **URL**. Method *openStream* of class **URL** opens a network connection to the location represented by **url** using the **http** protocol (HyperText Transfer Protocol). If the network connection is successful an **InputStream** object is returned. Otherwise, **openStream** throws an **IOException**. In this example, we would like to read one line at a time from the file, so the **InputStream** object is passed to the *InputStreamReader* constructor to create a stream object that translates the bytes in the file into Unicode characters. The **InputStreamReader** object is passed to the *BufferedReader* constructor to create a stream object that buffers the characters read and enables reading of one line at a time with **BufferedReader** method **readLine** which returns a **String** when it encounters a newline character or end-of-file. Newline characters are discarded.

When this program reads from the URL, it reads the actual HTML file containing the HTML tags (not just the text you see if you load this Web page in a Web browser). Line 35 defines a sentinel **String**—**"</PRE><HR>
<PRE>"**—that determines the starting point from which we locate the weather information relevant to this program. Line 38 reads line-by-line through the *Traveler's Forecast* HTML file until the sentinel is reached. If you load the *Travelers Forecast* in your Web browser, you can see the second horizontal line that is represented by the **<HR>** tag in the sentinel. We do not use any of the information before this horizontal line in the example, so we skip it.

Lines 42 through 45 define two **String**s that represent the column heads for the weather information. These are used as the sentinel values in the **do/while** loop (lines 49 through 52) which continues reading from the HTML file until it reaches the first line of data we intend to use in this example. The two **String**s represent the column header information for the traveler's forecast. Depending on the time of day, the column headers are either

```
     "CITY              WEA     HI/LO    WEA      HI/LO"
```

after the morning update (normally around 10:30 AM Eastern Standard Time) or

```
     "CITY              WEA     LO/HI    WEA      LO/HI"
```

after the evening update (normally around 10:30 PM Eastern Standard Time).

Lines 54 through 67 read each city's weather information and use it to create a **WeatherInfo** object containing the city's name, temperature and a description of the weather. Line 54 creates a **Vector** (package **java.util**) to store each **WeatherInfo** object after it is created in the **while** loop (line 58). Lines 60 through 63 construct a **WeatherInfo** object for a single city. The first 16 characters of **inputLine** are the city name—**String** method **substring** is used to extract these characters from **inputLine**. The next 6 characters of **inputLine** are the description (i.e., weather forecast). The next 6 characters of **inputLine** are the high and low temperatures. The last two columns of data represent the next day's weather forecast and are not used in this example. Line 65 adds the **WeatherInfo** object to the **Vector** with a call to **addElement**.

The **for** loop at line 73 creates an array of **WeatherInfo** objects to return to the client. The loop assigns each element in the **Vector** to a **WeatherInfo** reference stored in array **weatherInformation**. Because **Vector** method **elementAt** returns **Object** references, each reference must be downcast to a **WeatherInfo** reference.

When the HTML file has been read and parsed, the input stream and network connection are closed with the call **input.close()** (line 78).

Method **getWeatherInfo** (line 91) is the method from interface **Temperature-Server** that must be implemented in the **TemperatureServerImpl**. The method returns a reference to the **WeatherInfo** array. This method is called remotely by a client to obtain the weather information.

Method **main** (lines 96 through 110) starts the **TemperatureServerImpl** remote object that accepts remote method calls from clients and returns weather information to the clients. Lines 102 and 103 create a **TemperatureServerImpl** object. When the constructor executes it exports the object so the object can start listening for client requests. Line 106 defines the *name of the server object* that will be used by clients to attempt their connection. The name is normally of the form

//host:port/remoteObjectName

where *host* represents the computer that is running the *registry for remote objects* (this will also be the computer on which the remote object executes), *port* represents the port number where the registry can be found on the *host* and *remoteObjectName* is the name the client will supply when it attempts to locate the remote object through the registry. The registry for remote objects is managed by the ***rmiregistry*** utility program included with the J2SDK. The default port number for the **rmiregistry** is 1099.

Software Engineering Observation 20.7

*RMI clients assume that they should connect to port 1099 on a server computer when attempting to locate a remote object through the **rmiregistry** (unless specified otherwise with an explicit port number in the URL for the remote object).*

Software Engineering Observation 20.8

*A port number need be specified only if **rmiregistry** is started on a port other than the default port, 1099.*

Remote objects use the *host* and *port* to locate the **rmiregistry** so they can register themselves as remote services. Clients use the *host* and *port* to locate a service. In this program, the remote server object name is

//localhost/TempServer

indicating that the **rmiregistry** is located on the **localhost** (i.e., the same computer) and that the name the client must use to locate the service is **TempServer**. Because the name **localhost** is associated (by convention) with the IP address **127.0.0.1**, the preceding remote server object name is equivalent to

//127.0.0.1/TempServer

Line 107

```
Naming.rebind( serverObjectName, temp );
```

calls **static** method *rebind* of class *Naming* (package **java.rmi**) to bind the remote **TemperatureServerImpl** object **temp** to the **rmiregistry** and gives the remote object the name **//localhost/TempServer**—the name used by the client in our example to reference the remote object on the server. There is also a *bind* method to bind a remote object to the registry. Method **rebind** is normally used instead of **bind** because it guarantees that if the remote object's name was registered previously, the new remote object being registered with that name will replace the object that was registered previously with that name (method **bind** does not replace the previously registered object). This may be important if a new version of a remote server object becomes available.

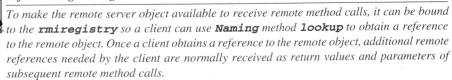

Software Engineering Observation 20.9

To make the remote server object available to receive remote method calls, it can be bound to the **rmiregistry** *so a client can use* **Naming** *method* **lookup** *to obtain a reference to the remote object. Once a client obtains a reference to the remote object, additional remote references needed by the client are normally received as return values and parameters of subsequent remote method calls.*

Class **WeatherInfo** (Fig. 20.3) is used by the **TemperatureServerImpl** to store data retrieved from the National Weather Service Web site. The class stores the city, temperature and descriptions as **String**s. Get methods are provided to access the data.

```
1   // Fig. 20.3: WeatherInfo.java
2   // WeatherInfo class definition
3   import java.rmi.*;
4   import java.io.Serializable;
5
6   public class WeatherInfo implements Serializable {
7      private String cityName;
8      private String temperature;
9      private String description;
10
11     public WeatherInfo( String city, String desc, String temp )
12     {
13        cityName = city;
14        temperature = temp;
15        description = desc;
16     }
17
18     public String getCityName() { return cityName; }
19
20     public String getTemperature() { return temperature; }
21
22     public String getDescription() { return description; }
23  }
```

Fig. 20.3   **WeatherInfo** class definition.

20.5 Define the Client

The next step is to define the client code that will obtain weather information from the **TemperatureServerImpl**. Class **TemperatureClient** defines the client application that calls remote class **TemperatureServerImpl** method **getWeatherInfo** through RMI. Class **TemperatureClient** uses objects of class **WeatherItem** to graphically display the weather information for each city. When **TemperatureClient** executes it makes a remote method call to the temperature server defined in Fig. 20.2.

```
1   // Fig. 20.4: TemperatureClient.java
2   // TemperatureClient definition
3   import java.awt.*;
4   import java.awt.event.*;
5   import javax.swing.*;
6   import java.rmi.*;
7
8   public class TemperatureClient extends JFrame
9   {
10     public TemperatureClient( String ip )
11     {
12        super( "RMI TemperatureClient..." );
13        getRemoteTemp( ip );
14
15        setSize( 625, 567 );
16        setResizable( false );
17        show();
18     }
19
20     // obtain weather information from TemperatureServerImpl
21     // remote object
22     private void getRemoteTemp( String ip )
23     {
24        try {
25           // name of remote server object bound to rmi registry
26           String serverObjectName = "//" + ip + "/TempServer";
27
28           // lookup TemperatureServerImpl remote object
29           // in rmiregistry
30           TemperatureServer mytemp = ( TemperatureServer )
31              Naming.lookup( serverObjectName );
32
33           // get weather information from server
34           WeatherInfo weatherInfo[] = mytemp.getWeatherInfo();
35           WeatherItem w[] =
36              new WeatherItem[ weatherInfo.length ];
37           ImageIcon headerImage =
38              new ImageIcon( "images/header.jpg" );
39
40           JPanel p = new JPanel();
41
```

Fig. 20.4 **TemperatureClient** class definition (part 1 of 2).

```
42          // determine number of rows for the GridLayout;
43          // add 3 to accommodate the two header JLabels
44          // and balance the columns
45          p.setLayout(
46             new GridLayout( ( w.length + 3 ) / 2, 2 ) );
47          p.add( new JLabel( headerImage ) ); // header 1
48          p.add( new JLabel( headerImage ) ); // header 2
49
50          for ( int i = 0; i < w.length; i++ ) {
51             w[ i ] = new WeatherItem( weatherInfo[ i ] );
52             p.add( w[ i ] );
53          }
54
55          getContentPane().add( new JScrollPane( p ),
56                            BorderLayout.CENTER );
57       }
58       catch ( java.rmi.ConnectException ce ) {
59          System.err.println( "Connection to server failed. " +
60             "Server may be temporarily unavailable." );
61       }
62       catch ( Exception e ) {
63          e.printStackTrace();
64          System.exit( 1 );
65       }
66    }
67
68    public static void main( String args[] )
69    {
70       TemperatureClient gt = null;
71
72       // if no sever IP address or host name specified,
73       // use "localhost"; otherwise use specified host
74       if ( args.length == 0 )
75          gt = new TemperatureClient( "localhost" );
76       else
77          gt = new TemperatureClient( args[ 0 ] );
78
79       gt.addWindowListener(
80          new WindowAdapter() {
81             public void windowClosing( WindowEvent e )
82             {
83                System.exit( 0 );
84             }
85          }
86       );
87    }
88 }
```

Fig. 20.4   **TemperatureClient** class definition (part 2 of 2).

The constructor (line 10) passes to method **getRemoteTemp** the IP address (or host name) for the **TemperatureServerImpl**. As we will see shortly, the IP address (or host name) is passed to the application as a command-line argument.

Method **getRemoteTemp** (line 22) creates the client's GUI and makes one remote method call to the **TemperatureServerImpl** server object using RMI. Line 26 defines the **String** that is used to locate the remote object through the **rmiregistry**. The string contains the IP address or host name of the server on which the client will search for the remote object. The client will connect to port 1099 on that server to locate the **rmiregistry**. Lines 30 and 31 call **static** method *lookup* of class **Naming** to obtain a remote reference that enables the client to invoke methods of the remote **TemperatureServerImpl** object. Method **lookup** returns a **Remote** reference to an object that implements remote interface **TemperatureServer**. Because this method returns a **Remote** reference, the returned reference is downcast to **TemperatureServer** and assigned to **mytemp**. The client uses **mytemp** to call the server objects's remote method as if it is a method of another object defined locally in the client application—all the networking that supports the communication between the objects and the transfer of arguments and return values between the objects is supplied by RMI!

Software Engineering Observation 20.10

Method **lookup** *of class* **Naming** *interacts with the* **rmiregistry** *to help the client obtain a reference to a remote object so the client can use the remote object's services.*

Line 34 performs the remote call to **getWeatherInfo** to retrieve an array of **WeatherInfo** objects. It is important to note that RMI returns a copy of the array stored in the **TemperatureServerImpl**. So, returning a reference from a remote method is different from returning a reference from a local method. RMI uses object serialization to send the array of **WeatherInfo** objects to the client. Lines 35 and 36 create an array of **WeatherItem** (defined in Fig. 20.5) references. This array stores **WeatherItem**s that encapsulate the functionality for displaying the weather information for the cities.

Lines 45 and 46 set **JPanel p**'s layout to **GridLayout**. The number of rows is determined by taking the number of components to display, adding three and dividing by two. We add three to account for the two **JLabel** components (lines 47 and 48) that are added to the **JPanel** as column headers and to ensure the proper number of rows in the grid. For example, if there are 33 or 34 cities of information, the number of rows will be 18 (one row for the headers and 17 rows for the weather information). In integer division, the calculations 36 / 2 and 37 / 2 both yield 18 (the number of rows for 33 or 34 cities).

The **for** structure (line 50) creates each **WeatherItem** object that is added to **p**. The **WeatherItem** constructor receives the **WeatherInfo** object for one city. As we will soon see, class **WeatherItem** is a subclass of **JLabel**, therefore **WeatherItem**s can be added to the **GridLayout**.

Method **main** (lines 68 through 87) creates a **TemperatureClient** object and passes its constructor either the **String "localhost"** or an IP address (or host name) that is specified as a command line argument to the application.

Class **WeatherItem** (Fig. 20.5) stores information about each city's weather. Several **static** variables are defined to store the weather images, weather condition strings and weather image names so they are available to all **WeatherItem** objects. Reference **backgroundImage** and array **weatherImages** are both initialized in the *static initializer block* (lines 18 through 26). A **static** initializer block allows complex initialization of a class's **static** variables when the class is loaded. The class extends **JLabel** and overrides method **paintComponent** to display the weather information.

```
1   // Fig. 20.5: WeatherItem.java
2   // WeatherItem definition
3   import java.awt.*;
4   import javax.swing.*;
5
6   public class WeatherItem extends JLabel {
7      private static ImageIcon weatherImages[], backgroundImage;
8      private final static String weatherConditions[] =
9         { "SUNNY", "PTCLDY", "CLOUDY", "MOCLDY", "TSTRMS",
10          "RAIN", "SNOW", "VRYHOT", "FAIR", "RNSNOW",
11          "SHWRS", "WINDY", "NOINFO", "MISG" };
12     private final static String weatherImageNames[] =
13        { "sunny", "pcloudy", "mcloudy", "mcloudy", "rain",
14          "rain", "snow", "vryhot", "fair", "rnsnow",
15          "showers", "windy", "noinfo", "noinfo" };
16
17     // static initializer block to load weather images
18     static {
19        backgroundImage = new ImageIcon( "images/back.jpg" );
20        weatherImages =
21           new ImageIcon[ weatherImageNames.length ];
22
23        for ( int i = 0; i < weatherImageNames.length; ++i )
24           weatherImages[ i ] = new ImageIcon(
25              "images/" + weatherImageNames[ i ] + ".jpg" );
26     }
27
28     // instance variables
29     private ImageIcon weather;
30     private WeatherInfo weatherInfo;
31
32     public WeatherItem( WeatherInfo w )
33     {
34        weather = null;
35        weatherInfo = w;
36
37        // locate image for city's weather condition
38        for ( int i = 0; i < weatherConditions.length; ++i )
39           if ( weatherConditions[ i ].equals(
40              weatherInfo.getDescription().trim() ) ) {
41              weather = weatherImages[ i ];
42              break;
43           }
44
45        // pick the "no info" image if either there is no
46        // weather info or no image for the current
47        // weather condition
48        if ( weather == null ) {
49           weather = weatherImages[ weatherImages.length - 1 ];
50           System.err.println( "No info for: " +
51                               weatherInfo.getDescription() );
52        }
53     }
```

Fig. 20.5   **WeatherItem** class definition (part 1 of 2).

```
54
55       public void paintComponent( Graphics g )
56       {
57           super.paintComponent( g );
58           backgroundImage.paintIcon( this, g, 0, 0 );
59
60           Font f = new Font( "SansSerif", Font.BOLD, 12 );
61           g.setFont( f );
62           g.setColor( Color.white );
63           g.drawString( weatherInfo.getCityName(), 10, 19 );
64           g.drawString( weatherInfo.getTemperature(), 130, 19 );
65
66           weather.paintIcon( this, g, 253, 1 );
67       }
68
69       // make WeatherItem's preferred size the width and height of
70       // the background image
71       public Dimension getPreferredSize()
72       {
73           return new Dimension( backgroundImage.getIconWidth(),
74                                 backgroundImage.getIconHeight() );
75       }
76   }
```

Fig. 20.5   **WeatherItem** class definition (part 2 of 2).

Class **WeatherItem** contains two instance references (lines 29 and 30): **weather** (an **ImageIcon**) and **weatherInfo** (a **WeatherInfo**). Reference **weather** refers to the image that represents the current weather conditions. Reference **weatherInfo** refers to an object that stores the current weather conditions for a city. Class **Weather-Item** uses objects of these reference types to determine and display images that correspond to each city's weather condition.

The constructor (line 32) sets the instance references and determines the appropriate image to display for the weather. For example, if the **WeatherInfo** object's **getDescription** method returns "**SUNNY**," then an image of the sun is assigned to **weather**. This is performed for most descriptions that are given from the National Weather Service. If the **NO INFO** image appears, either the description has not yet been programmed into class **WeatherItem** or no information was available from the National Weather Service. [*Note:* Line 40 uses **String** method **trim** to remove whitespace from the weather description string. The weather condition strings in array **weatherConditions** are not stored as fixed-width strings as they are in the *Traveler's Forecast*. So, method **trim** is called to remove trailing spaces from the strings read from the Web page.]

The images used in this example are available with all the examples from this text on the CD that accompanies the text and as a download from our web site

```
http://www.deitel.com
```

Click the **Downloads** link and download the examples for *Java How to Program, Third Edition.*

20.6 Compile and Execute the Server and the Client

Now that the pieces are in place, we can build and execute our distributed application; this requires several steps. First, the classes must be compiled using **javac**.

Next, the remote server class (**TemperatureServerImpl**) must be compiled using the ***rmic*** *compiler* (one of the utilities supplied with the J2SDK) to produce a *stub class*. An object of the stub class allows the client to invoke the server object's remote methods. The stub object receives each remote method call and passes it to the Java RMI system which performs the networking that allows the client to connect to the server and interact with the remote server object. The command line

```
rmic -v1.2 TemperatureServerImpl
```

generates the file **TemperatureServerImpl_Stub.class**. This class must be available to the client (either locally or via download) to enable remote communication with the server object. Depending on the command line options passed to **rmic**, this may generate several files. In Java 1.1, two classes were produced by **rmic**—a stub class and a *skeleton class*. Java 2 no longer requires the skeleton class. The command line option **-v1.2** indicates that the classes in this example will be used only by Java 2; therefore, only the stub class should be created.

Software Engineering Observation 20.11

*The **rmic** compiler creates a stub class that passes remote method calls from the client to the RMI system which performs the networking that allows the client to connect to the server and use the remote object's methods.*

We can now test our RMI application. The next step is to start the **rmiregistry** so the **TemperatureServerImpl** object can register itself with the registry. This is done from the command window. The command line

```
rmiregistry
```

launches the RMI registry and *binds* it to port 1099 on the machine on which the command is executed. The command line window (Fig. 20.6) will not show any text in response to this command.

Common Programming Error 20.1

*Not starting the **rmiregistry** before attempting to bind the remote object to the registry results in a **java.rmi.ConnectException** indicating a refusal to connect to the registry.*

```
e:\books\jhtp3\examples\ch20>rmiregistry
```

Fig. 20.6   The **rmiregistry** running.

To make the remote server object available to receive remote method calls, it must be bound to the registry. Run the **TemperatureServerImpl** application from the command line as follows:

```
java TemperatureServerImpl
```

The **main** method of class **TemperatureServerImpl** creates an object of class **TemperatureServerImpl**. When the **TemperatureServerImpl** constructor executes, it calls its superclass **UnicastRemoteObject**'s constructor, which exports the remote object. Then, method **main** binds the **TemperatureServerImpl** object to the **rmiregistry** with **Naming** method **rebind**. This allows the **rmiregistry** to provide the host and port number where the remote object is executing to clients looking for this remote object (the RMI system uses this information when performing the network connections). When the **TemperatureServerImpl** is ready to accept remote method calls, the console will display "**The Temperature Server is up and running.**", as shown in Fig. 20.7. The window also shows two lines of text that are displayed when the **TemperatureServerImpl** is downloading and processing the weather information.

Common Programming Error 20.2

*Not starting the server application and binding the remote object to the **rmiregistry** prevents a client from looking up the remote object. This will be indicated to the client via a **java.rmi.ConnectException** refusing connection to the server.*

The **TemperatureClient** program can now be executed to connect with the **TemperatureServerImpl** on the local host with the command

```
java TemperatureClient
```

The resulting window is shown in Fig. 20.8. When the program executes, the **TemperatureClient** connects to the remote server object and displays the current weather information.

If the **TemperatureServerImpl** is running on a different machine from the client, you can specify the IP address or host name of the server computer as a command line argument when executing the client. For example, to access a server computer with IP address 192.168.0.150, enter the command

```
java TemperatureClient 192.168.0.150
```

```
MS JAVA                                                           _ □ ×
e:\books\jhtp3\examples\ch20>java TemperatureServerImpl
Initializing server: please wait.
Updating weather information...
Finished Processing Data.
The Temperature Server is up and running.
```

Fig. 20.7   The **TemperatureServerImpl** remote object executing.

Fig. 20.8   `TemperatureClient` running.

Summary

- RMI allows Java objects running on separate computers (or possibly the same computer) to communicate with one another via remote method calls.

- RMI is based on a similar earlier technology for procedural programming called remote procedure calls (RPC). RPC allows a procedural program to call a function of another computer as conveniently as if that function were part of the same program running on the same computer.

- A goal of RPC was to allow programmers to concentrate on the required tasks of an application by calling functions and make the networking transparent to the programmer. RPC performs all the networking and marshaling of the data.

- A disadvantage of RPC is that it supports a limited set of simple data types.

- Another disadvantage of RPC is that it requires the programmer to learn a special interface definition language (IDL) to describe the functions that can be invoked remotely.

- RMI is Java's implementation of RPC for Java-object-to-Java-object distributed communication. Once a method (or service) of a Java object is registered as being remotely accessible, a client can "look up" that service and receive a reference that allows the client to use that service. As with RPC, marshaling of data is handled by RMI. RMI provides for transfer of objects of complex data types via the object serialization mechanism.

- The first step in creating a client/server distributed application with RMI is to define the remote interface that describes the methods that the client will use to interact with the remote server object through RMI. To create a remote interface, define an interface that extends interface **Remote**.

- Interface **Remote** is a tagging interface.

- Objects of classes that implement interface **Remote** directly or indirectly are remote objects and can be accessed from any Java virtual machine.

- Every method's **throws** clause in a **Remote** interface must indicate the potential for **Remote-Exception**s to occur.

- The second step in creating a remote object is to define a class that implements an interface that extends **Remote**.

- The server class should extend class **UnicastRemoteObject**, which provides the basic functionality required for all remote objects. Class **UnicastRemoteObject**'s constructor exports the object to make it available for remote calls.

- Before registering the remote object with the **rmiregistry**, choose the name of the server object that will be used by clients to attempt their connection. The name is normally of the form

  //*host*:*port*/*remoteObjectName*

  where *host* represents the computer that is running the registry for remote objects, *port* represents the port number where the registry can be found on the host and *remoteObjectName* is the name the client will supply when it attempts to locate the remote object through the registry.

- Remote objects use the *host* and *port* to locate the **rmiregistry** so they can register themselves as remote services. Clients use the host and port to locate a service.

- The default port number to which clients and servers connect for the **rmiregistry** is 1099.

- Method **rebind** of class **Naming** binds the remote object to the **rmiregistry**. There is also a **bind** method to bind a remote object to the registry. Method **rebind** is normally used because it guarantees that if the remote object's name was previously registered, the new remote object being registered with that name will replace the object that was previously registered with that name.

- Method **lookup** of class **Naming** is used by a client to obtain a **Remote** reference to a remote object. Because this method returns a **Remote** reference, the returned reference should be cast to the appropriate **Remote** interface type.

- RMI handles all the networking that supports the communication between clients and remote objects, and the transfer of arguments and return values between the objects.

- The remote server class must be compiled using the **rmic** compiler to produce a stub class. An object of the stub class passes remote method calls to the RMI system which implements the networking that allows the client to connect to the server and interact with the remote server object.

- To start the **rmiregistry**, execute the **rmiregistry** command at the command line.

- To make the remote server object available to receive remote method calls, it can be bound to the **rmiregistry** so a client can use **Naming** method **lookup** to obtain a reference to the remote object.

Terminology

bind method of class **Naming**
BufferedReader class
bind to a port
export an object
host
//*host*:*port*/*remoteObjectName*
interface definition language (IDL)
InputStreamReader class

java.net.ConnectException class
java.rmi package
java.rmi.ConnectException class
java.rmi.server package
"look up" a service
lookup method of class **Naming**
marshalling data
name of the server object

ObjectInputStream class
ObjectOutputStream class
object serialization
point-to-point communication
port
port number
rebind method of class **Naming**
registry for remote objects
RemoteException class
remote interface
Remote interface
remote interface reference
remote method
remote method call
Remote Method Invocation (RMI)

remote objects
remote procedure call (RPC)
RMI
rmic compiler
rmiregistry
RPC
Serializable interface
skeleton class
stream-based socket connection
stub class
tagging interface
unicast communication
UnicastRemoteObject class
URL class

Common Programming Errors

20.1   Not starting the **rmiregistry** before attempting to bind the remote object to the registry results in a **java.rmi.ConnectException** indicating a refusal to connect to the registry.

20.2   Not starting the server application and binding the remote object to the **rmiregistry** prevents a client from looking up the remote object. This will be indicated to the client via a **java.rmi.ConnectException** refusing connection to the server.

Software Engineering Observations

20.1   Every remote method must be part of an interface that extends **java.rmi.Remote**.

20.2   An object of a class that implements the **Remote** interface can be exported as a remote object to make it available to receive remote method calls.

20.3   All methods in a **Remote** interface must have a **throws** clause indicating the potential for a **RemoteException**.

20.4   Because **UnicastRemoteObject** throws checked **RemoteException**s, subclasses of **UnicastRemoteObject** must define constructors that throw **RemoteException**s.

20.5   Class **UnicastRemoteObject** provides basic functionality required by remote objects. Classes for remote objects do not need to extend this class if they export the object with **static** method **exportObject** of class **UnicastRemoteObject** to allow the object to receive remote requests.

20.6   Class **UnicastRemoteObject**'s constructor exports the remote object to make it available for remote method calls at an anonymous port on the server computer.

20.7   A port number need be specified only if **rmiregistry** is started on a port other than the default port, 1099.

20.8   RMI clients assume that they should connect to port 1099 on a server computer when attempting to locate a remote object through the **rmiregistry** (unless specified otherwise with an explicit port number in the URL for the remote object).

20.9   To make the remote server object available to receive remote method calls, it can be bound to the **rmiregistry** so a client can use **Naming** method *lookup* to obtain a reference to the remote object. Once a client obtains a reference to the remote object, additional remote references needed by the client are normally returned by the server's remote methods called by the client.

20.10 Method *lookup* of class **Naming** interacts with the **rmiregistry** to help the client obtain a reference to a remote object so the client can use the remote object's services.

20.11   The **rmic** compiler creates a stub class that passes remote method calls from the client to the RMI system which performs the networking that allows the client to connect to the server and use the remote object's methods.

Self-Review Exercises

20.1   Fill in the blanks in each of the following:

h) The remote server class must be compiled using the _____ to produce a stub class.

i) RMI is based on a similar technology for procedural programming called _____.

j) Method _____ of class **Naming** is used by a client to obtain a remote reference to a remote object.

k) To create a remote interface, define an interface that extends interface _____ from package _____.

l) Method _____ or _____ of class **Naming** can be used to bind a remote object to the **rmiregistry**.

m) The server class normally extends class _____, which provides the basic functionality required for all remote objects.

n) Remote objects use the _____ and _____ to locate the **rmiregistry** so they can register themselves as remote services. Clients use these to locate a service.

o) The default port number for the **rmiregistry** is _____.

p) Interface **Remote** is a _____.

q) _____ allows Java objects running on separate computers (or possibly the same computer) to communicate with one another via remote method calls.

20.2   State whether each of the following is *true* or *false*. If *false*, explain why.

a) Not starting the **rmiregistry** before attempting to bind the remote object to the registry results in a **RuntimeException** refusing connection to the registry.

b) Every remote method must be part of an interface that extends **java.rmi.Remote**.

c) The **stubcompiler** creates a stub class that performs the networking that allows the client to connect to the server and use the remote object's methods.

d) Class **UnicastRemoteObject** provides basic functionality required by remote objects.

e) An object of a class that implements interface **Serializable** can be registered as a remote object and receive a remote method call.

f) All methods in a **Remote** interface must have a **throws** clause indicating the potential for a **RemoteException**.

g) RMI clients assume that they should connect to port 80 on a server computer when attempting to locate a remote object through the **rmiregistry**.

h) Once a remote object is bound to the **rmiregistry** with method **bind** or **rebind** of class **Naming**, the client can look up the remote object with **Naming** method **lookup**.

i) Method **find** of class **Naming** interacts with the **rmiregistry** to help the client obtain a reference to a remote object so the client can use the remote object's services.

Answers to Self-Review Exercises

20.1   a) **rmic** compiler. b) RPC. c) **lookup**. d) **Remote**, **java.rmi**. e) **bind**, **rebind**. f) **UnicastRemoteObject**. g) host, port. h) 1099. i) tagging interface. j) RMI.

20.2   a) False. This results in a **java.rmi.ConnectException**.

b) True.

c) False. The **rmic** compiler creates a stub class.

d) True.

e) False. An object of a class that implements a subinterface of **java.rmi.Remote** can be registered as a remote object and receive remote method calls.

f) True.

g) False. RMI clients assume port 1099 by default. Web browser clients assume port 80.

h) True.

i) False. Method **lookup** interacts with the **rmiregistry** to help the client obtain a reference to a remote object.

Exercises

20.3   The current implementation of class **TemperatureServerImpl** downloads the weather information only once. Modify class **TemperatureServerImpl** to obtain weather information from the National Weather Service twice a day.

20.4   Modify interface **TemperatureServer** to include support for obtaining the current day's forecast and the next day's forecast. Study the *Travelers Forecast* Web page

```
http://iwin.nws.noaa.gov/iwin/us/traveler.html
```

at the NWS Web site for the format of each line of information. Next, modify class **Temperature-ServerImpl** to implement the new features of the interface. Finally, modify class **TemperatureClient** to allow the user to select the weather forecast for either day. Modify the support classes **WeatherInfo** and **WeatherItem** as necessary to support the changes to classes **TemperatureServerImpl** and **TemperatureClient**.

20.5   *(Project: Weather for Your State)* There is a wealth of weather information on the National Weather Service Web site. Study the following Web pages:

```
http://iwin.nws.noaa.gov/
http://iwin.nws.noaa.gov/iwin/textversion/main.html
```

and create a complete weather forecast server for your state. Design your classes for reusability.

20.6   *(Project: Weather for Your State)* Modify the Exercise 20.5 project solution to allow the user to select the weather forecast for any state.

20.7   *(For international readers)* If there is a similar World Wide Web-based weather service in your own country, provide a different **TemperatureServerImpl** implementation with the same remote interface **TemperatureServer** (Fig. 20.1). The server should return weather information for major cities in your country.

20.8   *(Remote Phone Book Server)* Create a remote phone book server that maintains a file of names and phone numbers. Define interface **PhoneBookServer** with the following methods:

```
public PhoneBookEntry[] getPhoneBook()
public void addEntry( PhoneBookEntry entry )
public void modifyEntry( PhoneBookEntry entry )
public void deleteEntry( PhoneBookEntry entry )
```

Class **PhoneBookServerImpl** should implement interface **PhoneBookServer**. Class **PhoneBookEntry** should contain **String** instance variables that represent the first name, last name and phone number for one person. The class should also provide appropriate *set*/*get* methods and perform validation on the phone number format. Remember that class **PhoneBookEntry** must also implement **Serializable** so objects of this class can be serialized by RMI.

Class **PhoneBookClient** should define a user interface that allows the user to scroll through entries, add a new entry, modify an existing entry and delete an existing entry. The client and the server should provide proper error handling (e.g., the client cannot modify an entry that does not exist).

21

Networking

Objectives

- To understand the elements of Java networking with URLs, sockets and datagrams.
- To implement Java networking applications using sockets and datagrams.
- To understand how to implement Java clients and servers that communicate with one another.
- To understand how to implement network-based collaborative applications.
- To be able to write programs that "walk the Web."
- To construct a multithreaded server.

If the presence of electricity can be made visible in any part of a circuit, I see no reason why intelligence may not be transmitted instantaneously by electricity.
Samuel F. B. Morse

Mr. Watson, come here, I want you.
Alexander Graham Bell

What networks of railroads, highways and canals were in another age, the networks of telecommunications, information and computerization … are today.
Bruno Kreisky, Austrian Chancellor

Science may never come up with a better office-communication system than the coffee break.
Earl Wilson

It's currently a problem of access to gigabits through punybaud.
J. C. R. Licklider

Outline

21.1 Introduction

In Chapters 19 and 20, we began our presentation of Java's networking and distributed computing capabilities with discussions of Servlets and Remote Method Invocation—two high-level networking technologies that enable programmers to develop distributed applications in Java. In this chapter, our discussion focuses on several fundamental networking technologies that support Java's Servlet and RMI capabilities and can be used independently to build distributed applications.

We revisit the client/server relationship between World Wide Web browsers and World Wide Web servers to demonstrate an applet that causes the Web browser to load a new Web page. Networking introduces many security risks, so browsers may limit the capabilities of applets. We discuss some of these limitations in Section 21.9.

We demonstrate the Swing GUI component **JEditorPane** and its ability to render an HTML document downloaded from the World Wide Web.

We also introduce Java's *socket-based communications,* which enable applications to view networking as if it were file I/O—a program can read from a *socket* or write to a socket as simply as reading from a file or writing to a file. We show how to create and manipulate sockets.

Java provides *stream sockets* and *datagram sockets.* With *stream sockets* a process establishes a *connection* to another process. While the connection is in place, data flows between the processes in continuous *streams.* Stream sockets are said to provide a *connection-oriented service.* The protocol used for transmission is the popular *TCP (Transmission Control Protocol).*

With *datagram sockets*, individual *packets* of information are transmitted. This is not the right protocol for everyday users because unlike TCP, the protocol used, *UDP*—the *User Datagram Protocol*, is a *connectionless service*, and does not guarantee that packets arrive in any particular order. In fact, packets can be lost, can be duplicated, and can even arrive out of sequence. So with UDP, significant extra programming is required on the user's part to deal with these problems (if the user chooses to do so). Stream sockets and the TCP protocol will be the most desirable for the vast majority of Java programmers.

Performance Tip 21.1

Connectionless services generally offer greater performance but less reliability than connection-oriented services.

Portability Tip 21.1

The TCP protocol and its related set of protocols enable a great variety of heterogeneous computer systems (i.e., computer systems with different processors and different operating systems) to intercommunicate.

Once again, we will see that many of the networking details for the examples in this chapter are handled by the Java classes we use.

21.2 Manipulating URLs

As we mentioned in Chapter 19, the Internet offers many protocols. The **http** protocol (HyperText Transfer Protocol) that forms the basis of the World Wide Web uses URLs (Uniform Resource Locators, also called Universal Resource Locators) to locate data on the Internet. Common URLs represent files or directories and can represent complex tasks such as database lookups and Internet searches. If you know the URL of publicly available HTML files anywhere on the World Wide Web, you can access that data through **http**. Java makes it easy to manipulate URLs. Using a URL as an argument to the ***showDocument*** method of interface ***AppletContext*** causes the browser in which the applet is executing to display the URL. The applet of Fig. 21.1 enables the user to select a Web page from a **JList** and cause the browser to display the corresponding Web page.

This applet takes advantage of applet parameters specified in the HTML document that invokes the applet (see Section 16.8 for more information on applet parameters). The applet reads from the HTML document (**SiteSelector.html** at lines 1 through 10) the choices that will be displayed in the applet's **JList**. Each choice has two parameters in the HTML document—a title to be displayed in the **JList** and a location to pass to the browser so it can switch Web pages. The applet assumes that the name of each title parameter is **title#**, where the value of # starts at **0** and increments by one for each new title. For example, an applet that specifies three titles would have parameters named **title0**, **title1** and **title2**. Each title should have a corresponding location parameter of the form **location#**, where the value of # starts at **0** and increments by one for each new location. The HTML document can specify as many titles and locations as needed. The applet is designed to loop until it cannot locate the next **title#** parameter in sequence.

```
 1    <APPLET CODE= "SiteSelector.class" WIDTH=300 HEIGHT=75>
 2    <PARAM NAME="title0" VALUE="Java Home Page">
 3    <PARAM NAME="location0" VALUE="http://java.sun.com/">
 4    <PARAM NAME="title1" VALUE="Deitel">
 5    <PARAM NAME="location1" VALUE="http://www.deitel.com/">
 6    <PARAM NAME="title2" VALUE="Gamelan">
 7    <PARAM NAME="location2" VALUE="http://www.gamelan.com/">
 8    <PARAM NAME="title3" VALUE="JavaWorld">
 9    <PARAM NAME="location3" VALUE="http://www.javaworld.com/">
10    </APPLET>
```

Fig. 21.1   Loading a document from a URL into a browser (part 1 of 3).

```
11    // Fig. 21.1: SiteSelector.java
12    // This program uses a button to load a document from a URL.
13    import java.net.*;
14    import java.util.*;
15    import javax.swing.*;
16    import javax.swing.event.*;
17    import java.awt.*;
18    import java.applet.AppletContext;
19
20    public class SiteSelector extends JApplet {
21       private Hashtable sites;
22       private Vector siteNames;
23
24       public void init()
25       {
26          sites = new Hashtable();
27          siteNames = new Vector();
28
29          getSitesFromHTMLParameters();
30
31          Container c = getContentPane();
32          c.add( new JLabel( "Choose a site to browse" ),
33                  BorderLayout.NORTH );
34
35          final JList siteChooser = new JList( siteNames );
36          siteChooser.addListSelectionListener(
37             new ListSelectionListener() {
38                public void valueChanged( ListSelectionEvent e )
39                {
40                   Object o = siteChooser.getSelectedValue();
41                   URL newDocument = (URL) sites.get( o );
42                   AppletContext browser = getAppletContext();
43                   browser.showDocument( newDocument );
44                }
45             }
46          );
47          c.add( new JScrollPane( siteChooser ),
48                  BorderLayout.CENTER );
49       }
50
51       private void getSitesFromHTMLParameters()
52       {
53          // look for applet parameters in the HTML document
54          // and add sites to Hashtable
55          String title, location;
56          URL url;
57          int counter = 0;
58
59          while ( true ) {
60             title = getParameter( "title" + counter );
61
62             if ( title != null ) {
63                location = getParameter( "location" + counter );
```

Fig. 21.1   Loading a document from a URL into a browser (part 2 of 3).

```
64
65                          try {
66                             url = new URL( location );
67                             sites.put( title, url );
68                             siteNames.addElement( title );
69                          }
70                          catch ( MalformedURLException e ) {
71                             e.printStackTrace();
72                          }
73                       }
74                       else
75                          break;
76
77                       ++counter;
78                    }
79                 }
80              }
```

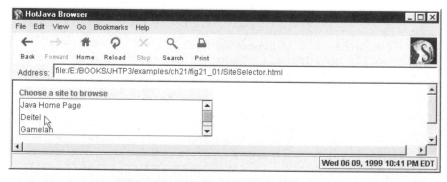

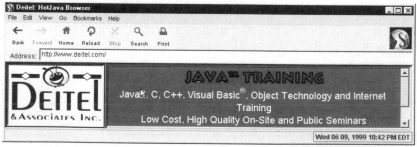

Fig. 21.1   Loading a document from a URL into a browser (part 3 of 3).

Class **SiteSelector** (line 20) uses a *Hashtable* (package *java.util*) to store the World Wide Web site names and URLs. A **Hashtable** is used to store *key/value pairs*. A *key* is used to store and retrieve an associated *value* in the **Hashtable**. In this example, the key is the **String** used in the **JList** to represent the Web site name and the value is a **URL** object that stores the URL of the Web site to display in the browser. Class **Hashtable** provides two methods of importance in this example—*put* and *get*. Method **put** takes two arguments—a key and its associated value—and places the value in the **Hashtable** at a location determined by the key. Method **get** takes one argument—a key—and retrieves the value (as an **Object** reference) associated with the key.

Class **SiteSelector** also contains a **Vector** (package **java.util**) in which the site names are placed so they can be used to initialize the **JList** (one version of the **JList** constructor receives a **Vector** object). A **Vector** is a dynamically resizable array of **Object**s. Class **Vector** provides method *addElement* to add a new element to the end of the **Vector**. Classes **Hashtable** and **Vector** are discussed in detail in Chapter 23.

Lines 26 and 27 in method **init** create the **Hashtable** and **Vector** objects. Line 29 calls our utility method **getSitesFromHTMLParameters** (defined at line 51) to read the HTML parameters from the HTML document that invoked the applet.

In the infinite loop in method **getSitesFromHTMLParameters**, line 60

```
title = getParameter( "title" + counter );
```

uses **Applet** method **getParameter** to obtain a Web site title. If the **title** is not **null**, line 63

```
location = getParameter( "location" + counter );
```

uses **Applet** method **getParameter** to obtain the corresponding location. The **location** is used as the initial value of a new **URL** object (line 66). The **URL** constructor determines if the **String** passed as an argument represents a valid Uniform Resource Locator. If so, the **URL** object is initialized to contain the Uniform Resource Locator; otherwise, a *MalformedURLException* is thrown. Notice that the **URL** constructor must be called in a **try** block. If the **URL** constructor generates a **MalformedURLException**, the call to **printStackTrace** (line 71) causes program to display a stack trace. Then, the program attempts to read the next Web site title. The site for the invalid URL is not added to the **Hashtable** and will not be displayed in the **JList**.

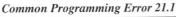
Common Programming Error 21.1

*A **MalformedURLException** is thrown when a **String** that is not in proper URL format is passed to a **URL** constructor.*

If the **URL** is constructed properly, line 67

```
sites.put( title, url );
```

places the **title** and **URL** into the **Hashtable** and line 68

```
siteNames.addElement( title );
```

adds the **title** to the **Vector**. When the call to **getParameter** at line 60 returns **null**, the loop terminates (with the **break** statement at line 75).

When method **getSitesFromHTMLParameters** returns to **init**, the applet's GUI is constructed. Lines 32 and 33 add the **JLabel** "**Choose a site to browse**" to the **NORTH** of the content pane's **BorderLayout**. Lines 36 through 46 register an instance of an anonymous inner class that implements **ListSelectionListener** to handle the **siteChooser**'s events. Lines 47 and 48 add **siteChooser** to the **CENTER** of the content pane's **BorderLayout**.

When the user selects one of the Web sites in **siteChooser**, method **valueChanged** (line 38) is called. Line 40

```
Object o = siteChooser.getSelectedValue();
```

obtains the selected site name from the **JList**. Line 41

```
URL newDocument = (URL) sites.get( o );
```

passes the selected site name (the key) to **Hashtable** method **get**, which locates and returns an **Object** reference to the corresponding **URL** object (the value). The **URL** cast operator converts the reference to a **URL** that can be assigned to reference **newDocument**.
Line 42

```
AppletContext browser = getAppletContext();
```

uses **Applet** method **getAppletContext** to get a reference to an **AppletContext** object that represents the browser in which the applet is executing. Line 43

```
browser.showDocument( newDocument );
```

uses the **AppletContext** reference **browser** to invoke **AppletContext** method *showDocument*, which receives a **URL** object as an argument and passes it to the **AppletContext** (i.e., the browser). The browser displays the World Wide Web resource associated with that **URL**. In this example, all the resources are World Wide Web sites.

For programmers familiar with *HTML frames* (the second screen capture of Fig. 21.1 illustrates a Web site with frames in the Sun HotJava browser), there is a second version of **AppletContext** method **showDocument** that enables an applet to specify the so-called *target frame* in which World Wide Web resource should be displayed. The other version of **showDocument** takes two arguments—a **URL** object specifying the resource to display and a **String** representing the target frame. There are some special target frames that can be used as the second argument. The target frame *_blank* results in a new Web browser window to display the URL. The target frame *_self* specifies that the URL should be displayed in the same frame as the applet (the applet's HTML page is replaced in this case). The target frame *_top* specifies that the browser should remove the current frames in the browser window, then display the URL in the current window. For more information on HTML and frames, see the World Wide Web site

```
http://www.w3.org
```

[*Note:* This applet must be run from a World Wide Web browser such as Netscape's Communicator, Microsoft's Internet Explorer or Sun's HotJava to see the results of displaying another Web page. The **appletviewer** is only capable of executing applets—it ignores all other HTML tags. If the Web sites in the program contained Java applets, only those applets would appear in the **appletviewer** when a Web site is selected. Each applet would execute in a separate **appletviewer** window. Of the three browsers mentioned here, only Sun's HotJava browser currently supports the features of Java 2. You will need to use the Java Plug-in (discussed in Chapter 16) to execute this applet in Netscape's Communicator or Microsoft's Internet Explorer.]

21.3 Reading a File on a Web Server

The application of Fig. 21.2 uses Swing GUI component *JEditorPane* (from package **javax.swing**) to display the contents of a file on a Web server. The user inputs the URL in the **JTextField** at the top of the window and the corresponding document (if it exists) is displayed in the **JEditorPane**. Class **JEditorPane** is able to render both plain text and HTML formatted text, so this application acts as a simple Web browser. The application also demonstrates how to process *HyperlinkEvents* when the user clicks a hyperlink in the HTML document. The screen captures in Fig. 21.2 illustrate that the **JEditorPane** can display both simple text (the first screen) and HTML text (the second screen). The techniques shown in this example can also be used in applets. However, applets are only allowed to read files on the server from which the applet was downloaded.

```java
1   // Fig. 21.2: ReadServerFile.java
2   // This program uses a JEditorPane to display the
3   // contents of a file on a Web server.
4   import java.awt.*;
5   import java.awt.event.*;
6   import java.net.*;
7   import java.io.*;
8   import javax.swing.*;
9   import javax.swing.event.*;
10
11  public class ReadServerFile extends JFrame {
12      private JTextField enter;
13      private JEditorPane contents;
14
15      public ReadServerFile()
16      {
17          super( "Simple Web Browser" );
18
19          Container c = getContentPane();
20
21          enter = new JTextField( "Enter file URL here" );
22          enter.addActionListener(
23              new ActionListener() {
24                  public void actionPerformed( ActionEvent e )
25                  {
26                      getThePage( e.getActionCommand() );
27                  }
28              }
29          );
30          c.add( enter, BorderLayout.NORTH );
31
32          contents = new JEditorPane();
33          contents.setEditable( false );
34          contents.addHyperlinkListener(
35              new HyperlinkListener() {
36                  public void hyperlinkUpdate( HyperlinkEvent e )
37                  {
38                      if ( e.getEventType() ==
39                              HyperlinkEvent.EventType.ACTIVATED )
40                          getThePage( e.getURL().toString() );
41                  }
42              }
43          );
```

Fig. 21.2   Reading a file through a URL connection (part 1 of 3).

```
44              c.add( new JScrollPane( contents ),
45                  BorderLayout.CENTER );
46
47              setSize( 400, 300 );
48              show();
49          }
50
51          private void getThePage( String location )
52          {
53              setCursor( Cursor.getPredefinedCursor(
54                      Cursor.WAIT_CURSOR ) );
55
56              try {
57                  contents.setPage( location );
58                  enter.setText( location );
59              }
60              catch ( IOException io ) {
61                  JOptionPane.showMessageDialog( this,
62                      "Error retrieving specified URL",
63                      "Bad URL",
64                      JOptionPane.ERROR_MESSAGE );
65              }
66
67              setCursor( Cursor.getPredefinedCursor(
68                      Cursor.DEFAULT_CURSOR ) );
69          }
70
71          public static void main( String args[] )
72          {
73              ReadServerFile app = new ReadServerFile();
74
75              app.addWindowListener(
76                  new WindowAdapter() {
77                      public void windowClosing( WindowEvent e )
78                      {
79                          System.exit( 0 );
80                      }
81                  }
82              );
83          }
84      }
```

Fig. 21.2   Reading a file through a URL connection (part 2 of 3).

The application class **ReadServerFile** contains **JTextField enter**, in which the user enters the URL of the file to read and **JEditorPane contents** to display the contents of the file. When the user presses the *Enter* key in the **JTextField**, the **actionPerformed** method (line 24) is called. Line 26

```
getThePage( e.getActionCommand() );
```

uses **ActionEvent** method **getActionCommand** to get the **String** the user typed in the **JTextField** and passes that string to utility method **getThePage** (defined at line 51).

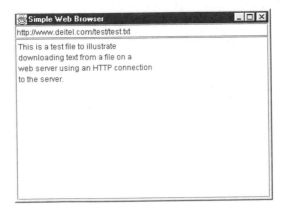

Fig. 21.2   Reading a file through a URL connection (part 3 of 3).

Lines 53 and 54 in method **getThePage**

```
setCursor( Cursor.getPredefinedCursor(
            Cursor.WAIT_CURSOR ) );
```

use method **setCursor** (inherited into class **JFrame** from class **Component**) to change the mouse cursor to the *wait cursor* (an hourglass). If the file being downloaded is large, the wait cursor indicates to the user that the program is performing a task and the user should wait for the task to complete. The **static Cursor** method **getPredefined-Cursor** receives an integer indicating the cursor type (**Cursor.WAIT_CURSOR** in this case). See the API documentation for class **Cursor** for a complete list of cursors.

Line 57

```
contents.setPage( location );
```

uses **JEditorPane** method *setPage* to download the document specified by **location** and display it in the **JEditorPane contents**. If there is an error downloading the document, method **setPage** throws an **IOException** and the **catch** handler at line 60 displays an error message dialog box. If the document is successfully loaded, line 58 displays the current location in the **JTextField enter**.

Lines 67 and 68

```
setCursor( Cursor.getPredefinedCursor(
            Cursor.DEFAULT_CURSOR ) );
```

sets the **Cursor** back to the default **Cursor** (*Cursor.DEFAULT_CURSOR*) to indicate that the document download is complete.

Typically, an HTML document contains *hyperlinks*—text, images or GUI components which, when clicked, provide quick access to another document on the Web. If an HTML document is displayed in a **JEditorPane** and the user clicks a hyperlink, the **JEditorPane** generates a *HyperlinkEvent* (package **javax.swing.event**) and notifies all registered *HyperlinkListeners* (package **javax.swing.event**) of that event. Lines 34 through 43 register a **HyperlinkListener** to handle **HyperlinkEvent**s. When a **HyperlinkEvent** occurs, method **hyperlinkUpdate** (line 36) is called. The **if** condition at lines 38 and 39

```
if ( e.getEventType() ==
     HyperlinkEvent.EventType.ACTIVATED )
```

uses **HyperlinkEvent** method *getEventType* to determine the type of the **HyperlinkEvent**. Class **HyperlinkEvent** contains **public** inner class *EventType* that defines three hyperlink event types *ACTIVATED* (the user clicked a hyperlink to change Web pages), *ENTERED* (the user moved the mouse over a hyperlink) and *EXITED* (the user moved the mouse away from a hyperlink). If a hyperlink was **ACTIVATED**, line 40

```
getThePage( e.getURL().toString() );
```

uses **HyperlinkEvent** method *getURL* to obtain the URL represented by the hyperlink. Method **toString** is called with the returned **URL** reference to convert the URL to a **String** format that can be passed to utility method **getThePage**.

21.4 Establishing a Simple Server (Using Stream Sockets)

Establishing a simple server in Java requires five steps. Step 1 is to create a *ServerSocket* object. A call to the *ServerSocket* constructor such as

```
ServerSocket s = new ServerSocket( port, queueLength );
```

registers an available *port number* and specifies a maximum number of clients that can request connections to the server (i.e., the **queueLength**). If the queue is full, client connections are automatically refused. The preceding statement establishes the port where the server waits for connections from clients (also known as *binding the server to the port*). Each client will ask to connect to the server on this *port*.

Each client connection is managed with a ***Socket*** object. Once the **ServerSocket** is established (Step 2), the server listens indefinitely (or *blocks*) for an attempt by a client to connect. This is accomplished with a call to the **ServerSocket accept** method as in

```
Socket connection = s.accept();
```

which returns a **Socket** object when a connection is established.

Step 3 is to get the **OutputStream** and **InputStream** objects that enable the server to communicate with the client. The server sends information to the client via an **OutputStream** object. The server receives information from the client via an **Input-Stream** object. To obtain the streams, the server invokes method **getOutputStream** on the **Socket** to get a reference to the **OutputStream** associated with the **Socket** and invokes method **getInputStream** on the **Socket** to get a reference to the **Input-Stream** associated with the **Socket**.

The **OutputStream** and **InputStream** objects can be used to send or receive individual bytes or sets of bytes with the **OutputStream** method **write** and the **InputStream** method **read**, respectively. Often it is useful to send or receive values of primitive data types (such as **int** and **double**) or class data types (such as **String** and **Employee**) rather than sending bytes. In this case, we can use the techniques of Chapter 17, "Files and Streams," to *chain* other stream types (such as **ObjectOutputStream** and **ObjectInputStream**) to the **OutputStream** and **InputStream** associated with the **Socket**. For example,

```
ObjectInputStream input =
    new ObjectInputStream( connection.getInputStream() );

ObjectOutputStream output =
    new ObjectOutputStream( connection.getOutputStream() );
```

The beauty of establishing these relationships is that whatever the server writes to the **ObjectOutputStream** is sent via the **OutputStream** and is available at the client's **InputStream** and whatever the client writes to its **OutputStream** (with a corresponding **ObjectOutputStream**) is available via the server's **InputStream**.

Step 4 is the processing phase in which the server and the client communicate via the **InputStream** and **OutputStream** objects. In Step 5, when the transmission is complete, the server closes the connection by invoking the **close** method on the **Socket**.

Software Engineering Observation 21.1

With sockets, network I/O appears to Java programs to be identical to sequential file I/O. Sockets hide much of the complexity of network programming from the programmer.

Software Engineering Observation 21.2

With Java's multithreading, we can easily create multithreaded servers *that can manage many simultaneous connections with many clients; this multithreaded-server architecture is precisely what is used in popular UNIX, Windows NT and OS/2 network servers.*

Software Engineering Observation 21.3

A multithreaded server can be implemented to take the **Socket** *returned by each call to* **accept** *and create a new thread that would manage network I/O across that* **Socket***, or a multithreaded server can be implemented to maintain a pool of threads ready to manage network I/O across the new* **Socket***s as they are created.*

Performance Tip 21.2

*In high-performance systems in which memory is abundant, a multithreaded server can be implemented to create a pool of threads that can be assigned quickly to handle network I/O across each new **Socket** as it is created. Thus, when a connection is received, the server need not incur the overhead of thread creation.*

21.5 Establishing a Simple Client (Using Stream Sockets)

Establishing a simple client in Java requires four steps. In Step 1, we create a **Socket** to connect to the server. The connection to the server is established using a call to the Socket constructor with two arguments—the server's Internet address and the port number—as in

```
Socket connection = new Socket( serverAddress, port );
```

If the connection attempt is successful, this statement returns a **Socket**. A connection attempt that fails throws an instance of a subclass of **IOException**, so many programs simply catch **IOException**.

Common Programming Error 21.2

*An **UnknownHostException** is thrown when a server address indicated by a client cannot be resolved. A **ConnectException** is thrown when an error occurs while attempting to connect to a server.*

In Step 2, **Socket** methods **getInputStream** and **getOutputStream** are used to get references to the **Socket**'s associated **InputStream** and **OutputStream**, respectively. **InputStream** method **read** can be used to input individual bytes or sets of bytes from the server. **OutputStream** method **write** can be used to output individual bytes or sets of bytes to the server. As we mentioned in the preceding section, often it is useful to send or receive values of primitive data types (such as **int** and **double**) or class data types (such as **String** and **Employee**) rather than sending bytes. If the server is sending information in the form of actual data types, the client should receive the information in the same format. Thus, if the server sends values with an **ObjectOutputStream**, the client should read those values with an **ObjectInputStream**.

Step 3 is the processing phase in which the client and the server communicate via the **InputStream** and **OutputStream** objects. In Step 4 when the transmission is complete, the client closes the connection by invoking the **close** method on the **Socket**. When processing information sent by a server, the client must determine when the server is done sending information so the client can call **close** to close the **Socket** connection. For example, the **InputStream** method **read** returns –1 when end-of-stream (also called EOF—end-of-file) is detected. If an **ObjectInputStream** is used to read information from the server, an **EOFException** is generated when the client attempts to read a value from a stream on which end-of-stream is detected.

When the client closes the **Socket**, an **IOException** may be thrown. The **getInputStream** and **getOutputStream** methods may also throw **IOException**s.

21.6 Client/Server Interaction with Stream Socket Connections

The applications of Figs. 21.3 and 21.4 use *stream sockets* to demonstrate a simple *client/server chat application*. The server waits for a client connection attempt. When a client application connects to the server, the server application sends a **String** object indicating that the connection was successful to the client and the client displays the message. Both the client and the server applications contain **JTextField**s, which allow the user to type a message and send it to the other application. When the client or the server sends the **String** "**TERMINATE**", the connection between the client and the server terminates. Then, the server waits for the next client to connect. The definition of class **Server** is given in Fig. 21.3. The definition of class **Client** is given in Fig. 21.4. The screen captures showing the execution between the client and the server are shown as part of Fig. 21.4.

```java
1   // Fig. 21.3: Server.java
2   // Set up a Server that will receive a connection
3   // from a client, send a string to the client,
4   // and close the connection.
5   import java.io.*;
6   import java.net.*;
7   import java.awt.*;
8   import java.awt.event.*;
9   import javax.swing.*;
10
11  public class Server extends JFrame {
12     private JTextField enter;
13     private JTextArea display;
14     ObjectOutputStream output;
15     ObjectInputStream input;
16
17     public Server()
18     {
19        super( "Server" );
20
21        Container c = getContentPane();
22
23        enter = new JTextField();
24        enter.setEnabled( false );
25        enter.addActionListener(
26           new ActionListener() {
27              public void actionPerformed( ActionEvent e )
28              {
29                 sendData( e.getActionCommand() );
30              }
31           }
32        );
33        c.add( enter, BorderLayout.NORTH );
34
35        display = new JTextArea();
36        c.add( new JScrollPane( display ),
37              BorderLayout.CENTER );
38
39        setSize( 300, 150 );
40        show();
41     }
```

Fig. 21.3   Server portion of a client/server stream socket connection (part 1 of 3).

```java
42
43   public void runServer()
44   {
45      ServerSocket server;
46      Socket connection;
47      int counter = 1;
48
49      try {
50         // Step 1: Create a ServerSocket.
51         server = new ServerSocket( 5000, 100 );
52
53         while ( true ) {
54            // Step 2: Wait for a connection.
55            display.setText( "Waiting for connection\n" );
56            connection = server.accept();
57
58            display.append( "Connection " + counter +
59               " received from: " +
60               connection.getInetAddress().getHostName() );
61
62            // Step 3: Get input and output streams.
63            output = new ObjectOutputStream(
64                        connection.getOutputStream() );
65            output.flush();
66            input = new ObjectInputStream(
67                        connection.getInputStream() );
68            display.append( "\nGot I/O streams\n" );
69
70            // Step 4: Process connection.
71            String message =
72               "SERVER>>> Connection successful";
73            output.writeObject( message );
74            output.flush();
75            enter.setEnabled( true );
76
77            do {
78               try {
79                  message = (String) input.readObject();
80                  display.append( "\n" + message );
81                  display.setCaretPosition(
82                     display.getText().length() );
83               }
84               catch ( ClassNotFoundException cnfex ) {
85                  display.append(
86                     "\nUnknown object type received" );
87               }
88            } while ( !message.equals( "CLIENT>>> TERMINATE" ) );
89
90            // Step 5: Close connection.
91            display.append( "\nUser terminated connection" );
92            enter.setEnabled( false );
93            output.close();
94            input.close();
```

Fig. 21.3   Server portion of a client/server stream socket connection (part 2 of 3).

```
95                     connection.close();
96
97                 ++counter;
98             }
99         }
100        catch ( EOFException eof ) {
101            System.out.println( "Client terminated connection" );
102        }
103        catch ( IOException io ) {
104            io.printStackTrace();
105        }
106    }
107
108    private void sendData( String s )
109    {
110        try {
111            output.writeObject( "SERVER>>> " + s );
112            output.flush();
113            display.append( "\nSERVER>>>" + s );
114        }
115        catch ( IOException cnfex ) {
116            display.append(
117                "\nError writing object" );
118        }
119    }
120
121    public static void main( String args[] )
122    {
123        Server app = new Server();
124
125        app.addWindowListener(
126            new WindowAdapter() {
127                public void windowClosing( WindowEvent e )
128                {
129                    System.exit( 0 );
130                }
131            }
132        );
133
134        app.runServer();
135    }
136 }
```

Fig. 21.3   Server portion of a client/server stream socket connection (part 3 of 3).

Class **Server**'s constructor creates the GUI of the application (a **JTextField** and a **JTextArea**). The **Server** object displays its output in a **JTextArea**. When the **main** method (line 121) executes, it creates an instance of class **Server**, registers a **WindowListener** to terminate the program when the user clicks the window's close box and calls method **runServer** (defined at line 43).

Method **runServer** does the work of setting up the server to receive a connection and processing the connection when it is received. The method declares a **Server-Socket** called **server** (line 45) to wait for connections, a **Socket** called **connec-**

tion (line 46) to process the connection from a client and an integer **counter** to keep track of the total number of connections processed.

In the **try** block (line 49), the **ServerSocket** is set up (line 51) to listen for a connection from a client at port **5000**. The second argument to the constructor is the number of connections that can wait in a queue to connect to the server (**100** in this example). If the queue is full when a connection is attempted, the connection is refused.

Software Engineering Observation 21.4

Port numbers can be between 0 and 65535. Many operating systems reserve port numbers below 1024 for system services (such as email and World Wide Web servers). Generally, these ports should not be specified as connection ports in user programs. In fact, some operating systems require special access privileges to use port numbers below 1024.

In the infinite **while** loop (line 53), line 56

```
connection = server.accept();
```

uses **ServerSocket** method **accept** to listen for a connection from a client. This method blocks until a connection is received (i.e., the thread in which **accept** is called stops executing until a connection is received). Once a connection is received, **connection** is assigned a **Socket** object that will be used to manage the connection. Lines 58 through 60 append text to the **JTextArea**, indicating that a connection was received. The expression

```
connection.getInetAddress().getHostName()
```

uses **Socket** method **getInetAddress** to obtain the Internet address of the client computer that connected to this server. This method returns an *InetAddress* reference, which is used in a chained method call to invoke **InetAddress** method **getHostName**, which returns the client computer's host name. For example, if the Internet address of the computer is **127.0.0.1**, the corresponding host name would be **localhost**.

Lines 63 through 67

```
output = new ObjectOutputStream(
             connection.getOutputStream() );
output.flush();
input = new ObjectInputStream(
             connection.getInputStream() );
```

create the **ObjectOutputStream** and **ObjectInputStream** objects that send and receive **Object**s between the server and the client. These objects are connected to the **OutputStream** returned by **Socket** method **getOutputStream** and the **InputStream** returned by **Socket** method **getInputStream**, respectively. Notice the call to **ObjectOutputStream** method **flush** at line 65. This statement causes the **ObjectOutputStream** on the server to send a *stream header* to the corresponding client's **ObjectInputStream**. The stream header contains information such as the version of object serialization being used to send objects. This information is required by the **ObjectInputStream** so it can prepare to receive those objects correctly.

Software Engineering Observation 21.5

When using an ObjectOutputStream and ObjectInputStream to send and receive objects over a network connection, always create the ObjectOutputStream first and flush the stream so the client's ObjectInputStream can prepare to receive the data.

Line 73

```
output.writeObject( message );
```

uses **ObjectOutputStream** method **writeObject** to send the string "**SERVER>>>
Connection successful**" to the client. Line 74 flushes the output stream to ensure
that the object is sent immediately; otherwise, the object may be held in an output buffer
until more information is available to send.

Performance Tip 21.3

*Output buffers are typically used to increase the efficiency of an application by sending larg-
er amounts of data fewer times. The input and output components of a computer are typically
much slower than the memory of the computer.*

The **do/while** structure at lines 77 though 88 loops until the server receives the message "**CLIENT>>> TERMINATE**". Line 79

```
message = (String) input.readObject();
```

uses **ObjectInputStream** method **readObject** to read a **String** from the client.
Line 80 displays the message in the **JTextArea**. Lines 81 and 82 use **JTextComponent** method *setCaretPosition* to position the input cursor in the **JTextArea** after the last character in the **JTextArea**. This allows the **JTextArea** to scroll as text is
appended to it.

When the transmission is complete, the streams and the **Socket** are closed with lines
93 through 95

```
output.close();
input.close();
connection.close();
```

Next, the server awaits the next connection attempt from a client by continuing with line
56 at the beginning of the **while** loop.

When the user of the server application enters a **String** in the **JTextField** and
presses the *Enter* key, method **actionPerformed** (line 27) reads the **String** from the
JTextField and calls utility method **sendData** (defined at line 108). Method **send-
Data** sends the **String** object to the client, flushes the output buffer and appends the
same **String** to the **JTextArea** in the server window.

Notice that the **Server** receives a connection, processes the connection, closes the
connection and waits for the next connection. A more likely scenario would be a **Server**
that receives a connection, sets up that connection to be processed as a separate thread of
execution, then waits for new connections. The separate threads that process existing connections can continue to execute while the **Server** concentrates on new connection
requests.

Like class **Server**, class **Client**'s (Fig. 21.4) constructor creates the GUI of the
application (a **JTextField** and a **JTextArea**). The **Client** object displays its output
in a **JTextArea**. When the **main** method (line 108) executes, it creates an instance of
class **Client**, registers a **WindowListener** to terminate the program when the user
clicks the window's close box and calls method **runClient** (defined at line 43).

```
1   // Fig. 21.4: Client.java
2   // Set up a Client that will read information sent
3   // from a Server and display the information.
4   import java.io.*;
5   import java.net.*;
6   import java.awt.*;
7   import java.awt.event.*;
8   import javax.swing.*;
9
10  public class Client extends JFrame {
11     private JTextField enter;
12     private JTextArea display;
13     ObjectOutputStream output;
14     ObjectInputStream input;
15     String message = "";
16
17     public Client()
18     {
19        super( "Client" );
20
21        Container c = getContentPane();
22
23        enter = new JTextField();
24        enter.setEnabled( false );
25        enter.addActionListener(
26           new ActionListener() {
27              public void actionPerformed( ActionEvent e )
28              {
29                 sendData( e.getActionCommand() );
30              }
31           }
32        );
33        c.add( enter, BorderLayout.NORTH );
34
35        display = new JTextArea();
36        c.add( new JScrollPane( display ),
37              BorderLayout.CENTER );
38
39        setSize( 300, 150 );
40        show();
41     }
42
43     public void runClient()
44     {
45        Socket client;
46
47        try {
48           // Step 1: Create a Socket to make connection.
49           display.setText( "Attempting connection\n" );
50           client = new Socket(
51              InetAddress.getByName( "127.0.0.1" ), 5000 );
52
```

Fig. 21.4   Demonstrating the client portion of a stream socket connection
between a client and a server (part 1 of 4).

```
53              display.append( "Connected to: " +
54                 client.getInetAddress().getHostName() );
55
56              // Step 2: Get the input and output streams.
57              output = new ObjectOutputStream(
58                          client.getOutputStream() );
59              output.flush();
60              input = new ObjectInputStream(
61                          client.getInputStream() );
62              display.append( "\nGot I/O streams\n" );
63
64              // Step 3: Process connection.
65              enter.setEnabled( true );
66
67              do {
68                 try {
69                    message = (String) input.readObject();
70                    display.append( "\n" + message );
71                    display.setCaretPosition(
72                       display.getText().length() );
73                 }
74                 catch ( ClassNotFoundException cnfex ) {
75                    display.append(
76                       "\nUnknown object type received" );
77                 }
78              } while ( !message.equals( "SERVER>>> TERMINATE" ) );
79
80              // Step 4: Close connection.
81              display.append( "Closing connection.\n" );
82              input.close();
83              output.close();
84              client.close();
85           }
86           catch ( EOFException eof ) {
87              System.out.println( "Server terminated connection" );
88           }
89           catch ( IOException e ) {
90              e.printStackTrace();
91           }
92        }
93
94        private void sendData( String s )
95        {
96           try {
97              message = s;
98              output.writeObject( "CLIENT>>> " + s );
99              output.flush();
100             display.append( "\nCLIENT>>>" + s );
101          }
```

Fig. 21.4   Demonstrating the client portion of a stream socket connection between a client and a server (part 2 of 4).

```
102             catch ( IOException cnfex ) {
103                 display.append(
104                     "\nError writing object" );
105             }
106         }
107
108         public static void main( String args[] )
109         {
110             Client app = new Client();
111
112             app.addWindowListener(
113                 new WindowAdapter() {
114                     public void windowClosing( WindowEvent e )
115                     {
116                         System.exit( 0 );
117                     }
118                 }
119             );
120
121             app.runClient();
122         }
123     }
```

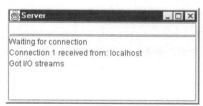
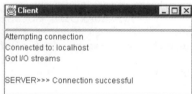

The **Server** and **Client** windows after the **Client** connects to the **Server**

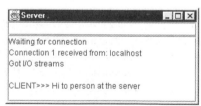
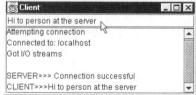

The **Server** and **Client** windows after the **Client** sends a message to the **Server**

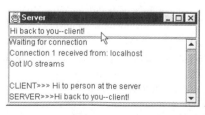

The **Server** and **Client** windows after the **Server** sends a message to the **Client**

Fig. 21.4   Demonstrating the client portion of a stream socket connection between a client and a server (part 3 of 4).

 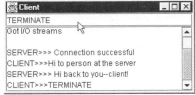

The **Server**
and **Client**
windows after
the **Client**
terminates the
connection

Fig. 21.4   Demonstrating the client portion of a stream socket connection
between a client and a server (part 4 of 4).

Client method **runClient** performs the work necessary to connect to the
Server, to receive data from the **Server** and to send data to the **Server**. The method
declares a **Socket** called **client** (line 45) to establish a connection. The **Client** will
use an **ObjectOutputStream** to send data to the server and an **ObjectInput-
Stream** to receive data from the server. In the **try** block, lines 50 and 51

```
client = new Socket(
    InetAddress.getByName( "127.0.0.1" ), 5000 );
```

create a **Socket** with two arguments to the constructor—the Internet address of the server
computer and the port number (5000) where that computer is awaiting client connections.
The call to **InetAddress** method **getByName** in the first argument returns an **Inet-
Address** object containing the Internet address **127.0.0.1** (i.e., **localhost**). Method **getByName** can receive a **String** containing either the actual Internet address or the
host name of the server. The first argument also could have been written other ways:

```
InetAddress.getByName( "localhost" )
```

or

```
InetAddress.getLocalHost()
```

Also, there are versions of the **Socket** constructor that receive a **String** for the Internet
address or host name. The first argument could have been specified as **"127.0.0.1"** or
"localhost". *[Note: We chose to demonstrate the client/server relationship by connecting between programs executing on the same computer (**localhost**). Normally, this
first argument would be the Internet address of another computer. The **InetAddress** object for another computer can be obtained by specifying the Internet address or host name
of the other computer as the **String** argument to **InetAddress.getByName**.]*

The **Socket** constructor's second argument is the server port number. This number
must match the port number at which the server is waiting for connections (called the *handshake point*). Once the connection is made, a message is displayed in the **JTextArea**
(lines 53 and 54) indicating the name of the server computer to which the client connected.

Lines 57 through 61

```
output = new ObjectOutputStream(
            client.getOutputStream() );
output.flush();
input = new ObjectInputStream(
            client.getInputStream() );
```

create the **ObjectOutputStream** and **ObjectInputStream** objects that are connected to the **OutputStream** and **InputStream** objects associated with **client**.

The **do/while** structure at lines 67 though 78 loops until the client receives the message "**SERVER>>> TERMINATE**". Line 69

```
message = (String) input.readObject();
```

uses **ObjectInputStream** method **readObject** to read a **String** from the server. Line 70 displays the message in the **JTextArea**. Lines 71 and 72 use **JTextComponent** method **setCaretPosition** to position the input cursor in the **JTextArea** after the last character in the **JTextArea**.

When the transmission is complete, the streams and the **Socket** are closed with lines 82 through 84

```
output.close();
input.close();
connection.close();
```

When the user of the client application enters a **String** in the **JTextField** and presses the *Enter* key, method **actionPerformed** (line 27) reads the **String** from the **JTextField** and calls utility method **sendData** (defined at line 94). Method **sendData** sends the **String** object to server client, flushes the output buffer and appends the same **String** to the **JTextArea** in the client window.

21.7 Connectionless Client/Server Interaction with Datagrams

We have been discussing *connection-oriented, streams-based transmission.* Now we consider *connectionless transmission with datagrams.*

Connection-oriented transmission is like the telephone system in which you dial and are given a *connection* to the telephone you wish to communicate with; the connection is maintained for the duration of your phone call, even when you are not talking.

Connectionless transmission with *datagrams* is more like the way mail is carried via the postal service. If a large message will not fit in one envelope, you break it into separate message pieces that you place in separate, sequentially numbered envelopes. Each of the letters is then mailed at once. The letters may arrive in order, out of order or not at all (although the last case is rare, it does happen). The person at the receiving end reassembles the message pieces into sequential order before attempting to make sense of the message. If your message is small enough to fit in one envelope, you do not have to worry about the "out-of-sequence" problem, but it is still possible that your message may not arrive. One difference between datagrams and postal mail is that duplicates of datagrams may arrive on the receiving computer.

The programs of Figs. 21.5 and 21.6 use datagrams to send packets of information between a client application and a server application. In the **Client** application, the user types a message into a **JTextField** on the client application and presses *Enter*. The message is converted into a **byte** array and placed in a datagram packet that is sent to the server. The server receives the packet and displays the information in the packet, then *echoes* the packet back to the client. When the client receives the packet, the client displays the information in the packet. In this example, the **Client** and **Server** classes are implemented similarly.

```
1    // Fig. 21.5: Server.java
2    // Set up a Server that will receive packets from a
3    // client and send packets to a client.
4    import java.io.*;
5    import java.net.*;
6    import java.awt.*;
7    import java.awt.event.*;
8    import javax.swing.*;
9
10   public class Server extends JFrame {
11      private JTextArea display;
12
13      private DatagramPacket sendPacket, receivePacket;
14      private DatagramSocket socket;
15
16      public Server()
17      {
18         super( "Server" );
19
20         display = new JTextArea();
21         getContentPane().add( new JScrollPane( display),
22                          BorderLayout.CENTER );
23         setSize( 400, 300 );
24         show();
25
26         try {
27            socket = new DatagramSocket( 5000 );
28         }
29         catch( SocketException se ) {
30            se.printStackTrace();
31            System.exit( 1 );
32         }
33      }
34
35      public void waitForPackets()
36      {
37         while ( true ) {
38            try {
39               // set up packet
40               byte data[] = new byte[ 100 ];
41               receivePacket =
42                  new DatagramPacket( data, data.length );
43
44               // wait for packet
45               socket.receive( receivePacket );
46
47               // process packet
48               display.append( "\nPacket received:" +
49                  "\nFrom host: " + receivePacket.getAddress() +
50                  "\nHost port: " + receivePacket.getPort() +
51                  "\nLength: " + receivePacket.getLength() +
52                  "\nContaining:\n\t" +
```

Fig. 21.5   Demonstrating the server side of connectionless client/server computing with datagrams (part 1 of 2).

```
53                      new String( receivePacket.getData(), 0,
54                              receivePacket.getLength() ) );
55
56               // echo information from packet back to client
57               display.append( "\n\nEcho data to client..." );
58               sendPacket =
59                  new DatagramPacket( receivePacket.getData(),
60                                      receivePacket.getLength(),
61                                      receivePacket.getAddress(),
62                                      receivePacket.getPort() );
63               socket.send( sendPacket );
64               display.append( "Packet sent\n" );
65               display.setCaretPosition(
66                   display.getText().length() );
67            }
68            catch( IOException io ) {
69               display.append( io.toString() + "\n" );
70               io.printStackTrace();
71            }
72         }
73      }
74
75      public static void main( String args[] )
76      {
77         Server app = new Server();
78
79         app.addWindowListener(
80            new WindowAdapter() {
81               public void windowClosing( WindowEvent e )
82               {
83                  System.exit( 0 );
84               }
85            }
86         );
87
88         app.waitForPackets();
89      }
90  }
```

The **Server** window after the client sends a packet of data

Fig. 21.5   Demonstrating the server side of connectionless client/server computing with datagrams (part 2 of 2).

Class **Server** (Fig. 21.5) defines two **DatagramPacket**s that are used to create the packets to send and receive information and one **DatagramSocket** that is used to send and receive these packets. The constructor for class **Server** (line 16) first creates the graphical user interface where the packets of information will be displayed. Next, the constructor creates the **DatagramSocket** the **try** block. Line 27

```
socket = new DatagramSocket( 5000 );
```

uses the **DatagramSocket** constructor that takes an integer port number argument (**5000**) to bind the server to a port where packets can be received from clients. **Client**s sending packets to this **Server** specify port **5000** in the packets they send. The constructor throws a *SocketException* if it fails to bind the **DatagramSocket** to a port.

Common Programming Error 21.3

Specifying a port that is already in use or specifying an invalid port number when creating a DatagramSocket results in a BindException.

Server method **waitForPackets** (line 35) uses an infinite loop to wait for packets to arrive at the **Server**. First, it creates a **DatagramPacket** (lines 40 through 42) in which a received packet of information can be stored. The **DatagramPacket** constructor for this purpose receives two arguments—a **byte** array in which the data is stored and the length of the **byte** array. Next, line 45

```
socket.receive( receivePacket );
```

waits for a packet to arrive at the **Server**. The *receive* method blocks until a packet arrives then stores the packet in its **DatagramPacket** argument (**receivePacket**). Method **receive** throws an **IOException** if an error occurs receiving a packet.

When a packet arrives, lines 48 through 54 append the packet's contents to **JTextArea display**. **DatagramPacket** method *getAddress* (line 49) returns an **InetAddress** object containing the host name of the computer from which the packet was sent. Method *getPort* (line 50) returns an integer specifying the port number through which the host computer sent the packet. Method *getLength* (line 51) returns an integer representing the number of bytes of data that were sent. Method *getData* (line 53) returns a **byte** array containing the data that was sent. The **byte** array is used to initialize a **String** in our program so the data can be output to the **JTextArea**.

Next, **sendPacket** (the one to be sent back to the client) is instantiated and four arguments are passed to the **DatagramPacket** constructor (lines 58 through 62). The first argument specifies the **byte** array to be sent. The second argument specifies the number of bytes to be sent. The third argument specifies the client computer's Internet address to which the packet will be sent. The fourth argument specifies the port where the client is waiting to receive packets. Line 63

```
socket.send( sendPacket );
```

sends the packet over the network. Method *send* throws an **IOException** if an error occurs sending a packet.

Class **Client** (Fig. 21.6) works similarly to class **Server** except that the **Client** sends packets only when it is told to do so by the user typing a message in a **JTextField** and pressing the *Enter* key in the **JTextField**. When this occurs, method **actionPerformed** (line 69) is invoked, the **String** the user entered in the **JTextField** is converted into a **byte** array (line 76) and the **byte** array is used to create a

DatagramPacket. The **DatagramPacket** is initialized with the **byte** array, the length of the **String** that was entered by the user, the Internet address to which the packet is to be sent (**InetAddress.getLocalHost()** in this example) and the port number at which the **Server** is waiting for packets. Then the packet is sent. Note that the client in this example must know that the server is receiving packets at port 5000; otherwise, the packets will not be received by the server.

```
1   // Fig. 21.6: Client.java
2   // Set up a Client that will send packets to a
3   // server and receive packets from a server.
4   import java.io.*;
5   import java.net.*;
6   import java.awt.*;
7   import java.awt.event.*;
8   import javax.swing.*;
9
10  public class Client extends JFrame implements ActionListener {
11      private JTextField enter;
12      private JTextArea display;
13
14      private DatagramPacket sendPacket, receivePacket;
15      private DatagramSocket socket;
16
17      public Client()
18      {
19          super( "Client" );
20
21          enter = new JTextField( "Type message here" );
22          enter.addActionListener( this );
23          getContentPane().add( enter, BorderLayout.NORTH );
24          display = new JTextArea();
25          getContentPane().add( new JScrollPane( display ),
26                            BorderLayout.CENTER );
27          setSize( 400, 300 );
28          show();
29
30          try {
31              socket = new DatagramSocket();
32          }
33          catch( SocketException se ) {
34              se.printStackTrace();
35              System.exit( 1 );
36          }
37      }
38
```

Fig. 21.6   Demonstrating the client side of connectionless client/server computing with datagrams (part 1 of 3).

```
39        public void waitForPackets()
40        {
41           while ( true ) {
42              try {
43                 // set up packet
44                 byte data[] = new byte[ 100 ];
45                 receivePacket =
46                    new DatagramPacket( data, data.length );
47
48                 // wait for packet
49                 socket.receive( receivePacket );
50
51                 // process packet
52                 display.append( "\nPacket received:" +
53                    "\nFrom host: " + receivePacket.getAddress() +
54                    "\nHost port: " + receivePacket.getPort() +
55                    "\nLength: " + receivePacket.getLength() +
56                    "\nContaining:\n\t" +
57                    new String( receivePacket.getData(), 0,
58                                 receivePacket.getLength() ) );
59                 display.setCaretPosition(
60                    display.getText().length() );
61              }
62              catch( IOException exception ) {
63                 display.append( exception.toString() + "\n" );
64                 exception.printStackTrace();
65              }
66           }
67        }
68
69        public void actionPerformed( ActionEvent e )
70        {
71           try {
72              display.append( "\nSending packet containing: " +
73                              e.getActionCommand() + "\n" );
74
75              String s = e.getActionCommand();
76              byte data[] = s.getBytes();
77
78              sendPacket = new DatagramPacket( data, data.length,
79                 InetAddress.getLocalHost(), 5000 );
80              socket.send( sendPacket );
81              display.append( "Packet sent\n" );
82              display.setCaretPosition(
83                 display.getText().length() );
84
85           }
86           catch ( IOException exception ) {
87              display.append( exception.toString() + "\n" );
88              exception.printStackTrace();
89           }
90        }
```

Fig. 21.6   Demonstrating the client side of connectionless client/server computing
with datagrams (part 2 of 3).

```
91
92      public static void main( String args[] )
93      {
94         Client app = new Client();
95
96         app.addWindowListener(
97            new WindowAdapter() {
98               public void windowClosing( WindowEvent e )
99               {
100                  System.exit( 0 );
101               }
102            }
103         );
104
105         app.waitForPackets();
106      }
107   }
```

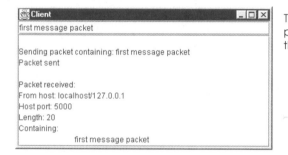

The **Client** window after sending a packet to the server and receiving the packet back from the server

Fig. 21.6   Demonstrating the client side of connectionless client/server computing with datagrams (part 3 of 3).

Notice that the **DatagramSocket** constructor call (line 31) in this application does not specify any arguments. This allows the computer to select the next available port number for the **DatagramSocket**. The client does not need a specific port number because the server receives the client's port number as part of the **DatagramPacket** sent by the client. Thus, the server can send packets back to the same computer and port number from which the server receives a packet of information.

Client method **waitForPackets** (line 39) uses an infinite loop to wait for packets using the statement

```
socket.receive( receivePacket );
```

at line 49, which blocks until a packet is received. Note that this does not prevent the user from sending a packet because the GUI events are handled in a different thread. It only prevents the **while** loop from continuing until a packet arrives at the **Client**.

When a packet arrives, it is stored in **receivePacket** and its contents are displayed in the **JTextArea**. The user can type information into the **Client** window's **JTextField** and press the *Enter* key at any time, even while a packet is being received. The **actionPerformed** method processes the **JTextField** event and sends the packet containing the data in the **JTextField**.

21.8 Client/Server Tic-Tac-Toe Using a Multithreaded Server

In this section, we present our capstone networking example—the popular game Tic-Tac-Toe implemented using client/server techniques with stream sockets. The program consists of a **TicTacToeServer** application (Fig. 21.7) that allows two **TicTacToeClient** applets (Fig. 21.8) to connect to the server and play Tic-Tac-Toe (outputs shown in Fig. 21.9). As each client connection is received by the server, an instance of class **Player** (line 133 of Fig. 21.7) is created to process the client in a separate thread of execution. This enables the clients to play the game independently. The first client to connect is automatically assigned Xs (X makes the first move) and the second client to connect is automatically assigned Os. The server maintains the information about the board so it can determine if a requested move by one of the players is a valid or invalid move. Each **TicTacToeClient** applet maintains its own GUI version of the Tic-Tac-Toe board on which the state of the game is displayed. The clients can only place a mark in an empty square on the board. Class **Square** (line 168 of Fig. 21.8) is used to implement each of the nine squares on the board. Class **TicTacToeServer** and class **Player** are implemented in file **TicTacToeServer.java** (Fig. 21.7). Class **TicTacToeClient** and class **Square** are implemented in file **TicTacToeClient.java** (Fig. 21.8).

```
1   // Fig. 21.7: TicTacToeServer.java
2   // This class maintains a game of Tic-Tac-Toe for two
3   // client applets.
4   import java.awt.*;
5   import java.awt.event.*;
6   import java.net.*;
7   import java.io.*;
8   import javax.swing.*;
9
10  public class TicTacToeServer extends JFrame {
11     private byte board[];
12     private boolean xMove;
13     private JTextArea output;
14     private Player players[];
15     private ServerSocket server;
16     private int currentPlayer;
17
18     public TicTacToeServer()
19     {
20        super( "Tic-Tac-Toe Server" );
21
22        board = new byte[ 9 ];
23        xMove = true;
24        players = new Player[ 2 ];
25        currentPlayer = 0;
26
27        // set up ServerSocket
28        try {
29           server = new ServerSocket( 5000, 2 );
30        }
```

Fig. 21.7   Server side of client/server Tic-Tac-Toe program (part 1 of 6).

```
31              catch( IOException e ) {
32                 e.printStackTrace();
33                 System.exit( 1 );
34              }
35
36           output = new JTextArea();
37           getContentPane().add( output, BorderLayout.CENTER );
38           output.setText( "Server awaiting connections\n" );
39
40           setSize( 300, 300 );
41           show();
42        }
43
44        // wait for two connections so game can be played
45        public void execute()
46        {
47           for ( int i = 0; i < players.length; i++ ) {
48              try {
49                 players[ i ] =
50                    new Player( server.accept(), this, i );
51                 players[ i ].start();
52              }
53              catch( IOException e ) {
54                 e.printStackTrace();
55                 System.exit( 1 );
56              }
57           }
58
59           // Player X is suspended until Player O connects.
60           // Resume player X now.
61           synchronized ( players[ 0 ] ) {
62              players[ 0 ].threadSuspended = false;
63              players[ 0 ].notify();
64           }
65
66        }
67
68        public void display( String s )
69        {
70           output.append( s + "\n" );
71        }
72
73        // Determine if a move is valid.
74        // This method is synchronized because only one move can be
75        // made at a time.
76        public synchronized boolean validMove( int loc,
77                                               int player )
78        {
79           boolean moveDone = false;
80
```

Fig. 21.7   Server side of client/server Tic-Tac-Toe program (part 2 of 6).

```
81          while ( player != currentPlayer ) {
82             try {
83                wait();
84             }
85             catch( InterruptedException e ) {
86                e.printStackTrace();
87             }
88          }
89
90          if ( !isOccupied( loc ) ) {
91             board[ loc ] =
92                (byte) ( currentPlayer == 0 ? 'X' : 'O' );
93             currentPlayer = ( currentPlayer + 1 ) % 2;
94             players[ currentPlayer ].otherPlayerMoved( loc );
95             notify();     // tell waiting player to continue
96             return true;
97          }
98          else
99             return false;
100      }
101
102      public boolean isOccupied( int loc )
103      {
104          if ( board[ loc ] == 'X' || board [ loc ] == 'O' )
105             return true;
106          else
107             return false;
108      }
109
110      public boolean gameOver()
111      {
112          // Place code here to test for a winner of the game
113          return false;
114      }
115
116      public static void main( String args[] )
117      {
118          TicTacToeServer game = new TicTacToeServer();
119
120          game.addWindowListener( new WindowAdapter() {
121             public void windowClosing( WindowEvent e )
122                {
123                   System.exit( 0 );
124                }
125             }
126          );
127
128          game.execute();
129      }
130 }
131
```

Fig. 21.7   Server side of client/server Tic-Tac-Toe program (part 3 of 6).

```
132   // Player class to manage each Player as a thread
133   class Player extends Thread {
134      private Socket connection;
135      private DataInputStream input;
136      private DataOutputStream output;
137      private TicTacToeServer control;
138      private int number;
139      private char mark;
140      protected boolean threadSuspended = true;
141
142      public Player( Socket s, TicTacToeServer t, int num )
143      {
144         mark = ( num == 0 ? 'X' : 'O' );
145
146         connection = s;
147
148         try {
149            input = new DataInputStream(
150                        connection.getInputStream() );
151            output = new DataOutputStream(
152                        connection.getOutputStream() );
153         }
154         catch( IOException e ) {
155            e.printStackTrace();
156            System.exit( 1 );
157         }
158
159         control = t;
160         number = num;
161      }
162
163      public void otherPlayerMoved( int loc )
164      {
165         try {
166            output.writeUTF( "Opponent moved" );
167            output.writeInt( loc );
168         }
169         catch ( IOException e ) { e.printStackTrace(); }
170      }
171
172      public void run()
173      {
174         boolean done = false;
175
176         try {
177            control.display( "Player " +
178               ( number == 0 ? 'X' : 'O' ) + " connected" );
179            output.writeChar( mark );
180            output.writeUTF( "Player " +
181               ( number == 0 ? "X connected\n" :
182                             "O connected, please wait\n" ) );
183
```

Fig. 21.7   Server side of client/server Tic-Tac-Toe program (part 4 of 6).

```
184            // wait for another player to arrive
185            if ( mark == 'X' ) {
186                output.writeUTF( "Waiting for another player" );
187
188                try {
189                    synchronized( this ) {
190                        while ( threadSuspended )
191                            wait();
192                    }
193                }
194                catch ( InterruptedException e ) {
195                    e.printStackTrace();
196                }
197
198                output.writeUTF(
199                    "Other player connected. Your move." );
200            }
201
202            // Play game
203            while ( !done ) {
204                int location = input.readInt();
205
206                if ( control.validMove( location, number ) ) {
207                    control.display( "loc: " + location );
208                    output.writeUTF( "Valid move." );
209                }
210                else
211                    output.writeUTF( "Invalid move, try again" );
212
213                if ( control.gameOver() )
214                    done = true;
215            }
216
217            connection.close();
218        }
219        catch( IOException e ) {
220            e.printStackTrace();
221            System.exit( 1 );
222        }
223    }
224 }
```

Fig. 21.7   Server side of client/server Tic-Tac-Toe program (part 5 of 6).

We begin with a discussion of the server side of the Tic-Tac-Toe game. When the **TicTacToeServer** application is executed, the **main** method (line 116) creates a **Tic-TacToeServer** object called **game**. The constructor (defined at line 18) attempts to set up a **ServerSocket**. If successful, the server window is displayed and the **TicTacToeServer** method **execute** is invoked from **main**. Method **execute** (line 45) loops twice, waiting each time for a connection from a client. When a connection is received, a new **Player** object is created to manage the connection as a separate thread and that object's **start** method is invoked.

Fig. 21.7 Server side of client/server Tic-Tac-Toe program (part 6 of 6).

When the **Player** is created, its constructor (line 142) takes the **Socket** object representing the connection to the client and gets the associated input and output streams. The **Player**'s **run** method (line 172) controls the information that is sent to the client and the information that is received from the client. First, it tells the client that the client's connection has been made, then it passes to the client the character that the client will place on the board when a move is made. Lines 189 through 192 suspend each **Player** thread as it starts executing because neither player is allowed to make a move when it first connects. Player X can only move when player O connects, and player O can only make a move after player X.

At this point the game can be played and the **run** method begins executing its **while** structure (line 203). Each iteration of this **while** structure reads an integer representing the location where the client wants to place a mark and invokes the **TicTacToeServer** method **validMove** to check the move. A message is sent to the client indicating if the move was valid. Locations are maintained as numbers from 0 to 8 (0 through 2 for the first row, 3 through 5 for the second row and 6 through 8 for the third row).

Method **validMove** (line 76 in class **TicTacToeServer**) is a **synchronized** method that allows only one move to be attempted at a time. This prevents both players from modifying the state information of the game simultaneously. If the **Player** attempting to validate a move is not the current player (i.e., the one allowed to make a move), the **Player** is placed in a *wait* state until it is his or her turn to move. If the position for the move being validated is already occupied on the board, **false** is returned. Otherwise, the server places a mark for the player in its local representation of the board, notifies the other **Player** object that a move has been made (so the client can be sent a message), invokes the **notify** method so the waiting **Player** (if there is one) can validate a move and returns **true** to indicate that the move is valid.

When a **TicTacToeClient** (Fig. 21.8) applet begins execution, it creates a **JTextArea** in which messages from the server are displayed and a representation of the board using nine **Square** objects. The applet's **start** method (line 70) opens a connection to the server and gets the associated input and output streams from the **Socket** object. Class **TicTacToeClient** implements the **Runnable** interface so that a separate thread can be used to continually read messages that are sent from the server to the client. After the connection to the server is established, the **Thread** object **outputThread** is created and initialized with the applet, then the thread's **start** method is invoked. The applet's **run** method (line 90) controls the separate thread of execution. The method first reads the mark character (X or O) from the server, then loops continually and reads messages from the server. The messages are passed to the applet's **processMessage** method (line 115) for processing.

If the message received is the string "**Valid move.**", the message "**Valid move, please wait.**" is displayed, the client's mark is set in the current square (the one in which the user clicked) and the square is repainted. If the message received is "**Invalid move, try again**", the message is displayed so the user can click a different square. If the message received is "**Opponent moved**", an integer is read from the server indicating where the opponent moved and a mark is placed in that square of the board. If any other message is received, the message is simply displayed.

```
1   // Fig. 21.8: TicTacToeClient.java
2   // Client for the TicTacToe program
3   import java.awt.*;
4   import java.awt.event.*;
5   import java.net.*;
6   import java.io.*;
7   import javax.swing.*;
8
9   // Client class to let a user play Tic-Tac-Toe with
10  // another user across a network.
11  public class TicTacToeClient extends JApplet
12                                 implements Runnable {
13      private JTextField id;
14      private JTextArea display;
15      private JPanel boardPanel, panel2;
16      private Square board[][], currentSquare;
17      private Socket connection;
18      private DataInputStream input;
19      private DataOutputStream output;
20      private Thread outputThread;
21      private char myMark;
22      private boolean myTurn;
23
24      // Set up user-interface and board
25      public void init()
26      {
27          display = new JTextArea( 4, 30 );
28          display.setEditable( false );
29          getContentPane().add( new JScrollPane( display ),
30                              BorderLayout.SOUTH );
31
32          boardPanel = new JPanel();
33          GridLayout layout = new GridLayout( 3, 3, 0, 0 );
34          boardPanel.setLayout( layout );
35
```

Fig. 21.8   Client side of client/server Tic-Tac-Toe program (part 1 of 5).

```
36            board = new Square[ 3 ][ 3 ];
37
38            // When creating a Square, the location argument to the
39            // constructor is a value from 0 to 8 indicating the
40            // position of the Square on the board. Values 0, 1,
41            // and 2 are the first row, values 3, 4, and 5 are the
42            // second row. Values 6, 7, and 8 are the third row.
43            for ( int row = 0; row < board.length; row++ )
44            {
45               for ( int col = 0;
46                          col < board[ row ].length; col++ ) {
47                  board[ row ][ col ] =
48                     new Square( ' ', row * 3 + col );
49                  board[ row ][ col ].addMouseListener(
50                     new SquareListener(
51                        this, board[ row ][ col ] ) );
52
53                  boardPanel.add( board[ row ][ col ] );
54               }
55            }
56
57            id = new JTextField();
58            id.setEditable( false );
59
60            getContentPane().add( id, BorderLayout.NORTH );
61
62            panel2 = new JPanel();
63            panel2.add( boardPanel, BorderLayout.CENTER );
64            getContentPane().add( panel2, BorderLayout.CENTER );
65         }
66
67      // Make connection to server and get associated streams.
68      // Start separate thread to allow this applet to
69      // continually update its output in text area display.
70      public void start()
71      {
72         try {
73            connection = new Socket(
74               InetAddress.getByName( "127.0.0.1" ), 5000 );
75            input = new DataInputStream(
76                       connection.getInputStream() );
77            output = new DataOutputStream(
78                       connection.getOutputStream() );
79         }
80         catch ( IOException e ) {
81            e.printStackTrace();
82         }
83
84         outputThread = new Thread( this );
85         outputThread.start();
86      }
87
```

Fig. 21.8 Client side of client/server Tic-Tac-Toe program (part 2 of 5).

```
88      // Control thread that allows continuous update of the
89      // text area display.
90      public void run()
91      {
92         // First get player's mark (X or O)
93         try {
94            myMark = input.readChar();
95            id.setText( "You are player \"" + myMark + "\"" );
96            myTurn = ( myMark == 'X' ? true  : false );
97         }
98         catch ( IOException e ) {
99            e.printStackTrace();
100        }
101
102        // Receive messages sent to client
103        while ( true ) {
104           try {
105              String s = input.readUTF();
106              processMessage( s );
107           }
108           catch ( IOException e ) {
109              e.printStackTrace();
110           }
111        }
112     }
113
114     // Process messages sent to client
115     public void processMessage( String s )
116     {
117        if ( s.equals( "Valid move." ) ) {
118           display.append( "Valid move, please wait.\n" );
119           currentSquare.setMark( myMark );
120           currentSquare.repaint();
121        }
122        else if ( s.equals( "Invalid move, try again" ) ) {
123           display.append( s + "\n" );
124           myTurn = true;
125        }
126        else if ( s.equals( "Opponent moved" ) ) {
127           try {
128              int loc = input.readInt();
129
130              board[ loc / 3 ][ loc % 3 ].setMark(
131                    ( myMark == 'X' ? 'O' : 'X' ) );
132              board[ loc / 3 ][ loc % 3 ].repaint();
133
134              display.append(
135                 "Opponent moved. Your turn.\n" );
136              myTurn = true;
137           }
```

Fig. 21.8   Client side of client/server Tic-Tac-Toe program (part 3 of 5).

```
138                catch ( IOException e ) {
139                    e.printStackTrace();
140                }
141            }
142            else
143                display.append( s + "\n" );
144
145            display.setCaretPosition(
146                display.getText().length() );
147        }
148
149        public void sendClickedSquare( int loc )
150        {
151            if ( myTurn )
152                try {
153                    output.writeInt( loc );
154                    myTurn = false;
155                }
156                catch ( IOException ie ) {
157                    ie.printStackTrace();
158                }
159        }
160
161        public void setCurrentSquare( Square s )
162        {
163            currentSquare = s;
164        }
165 }
166
167 // Maintains one square on the board
168 class Square extends JPanel {
169     private char mark;
170     private int location;
171
172     public Square( char m, int loc)
173     {
174         mark = m;
175         location = loc;
176         setSize ( 30, 30 );
177
178         setVisible(true);
179     }
180
181     public Dimension getPreferredSize() {
182         return ( new Dimension( 30, 30 ) );
183     }
184
185     public Dimension getMinimumSize() {
186         return ( getPreferredSize() );
187     }
188
189     public void setMark( char c ) { mark = c; }
```

Fig. 21.8   Client side of client/server Tic-Tac-Toe program (part 4 of 5).

```
190
191      public int getSquareLocation() { return location; }
192
193      public void paintComponent( Graphics g )
194      {
195         super.paintComponent( g );
196         g.drawRect( 0, 0, 29, 29 );
197         g.drawString( String.valueOf( mark ), 11, 20 );
198      }
199   }
200
201   class SquareListener extends MouseAdapter {
202      private TicTacToeClient applet;
203      private Square square;
204
205      public SquareListener( TicTacToeClient t, Square s )
206      {
207         applet = t;
208         square = s;
209      }
210
211      public void mouseReleased( MouseEvent e )
212      {
213         applet.setCurrentSquare( square );
214         applet.sendClickedSquare( square.getSquareLocation() );
215      }
216   }
```

Fig. 21.8   Client side of client/server Tic-Tac-Toe program (part 5 of 5).

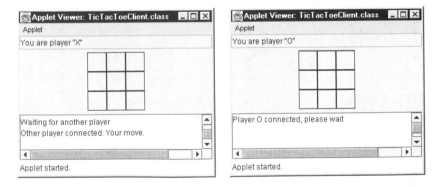

Fig. 21.9   Sample outputs from the client/server Tic-Tac-Toe program (part 1 of 2).

21.9 Security and the Network

As much as we look forward to writing a great variety of powerful network-based applications, our efforts will be crimped because of limitations imposed on Java because of security concerns.

Many Web browsers, such as Netscape Communicator and Microsoft Internet Explorer, by default prohibit Java applets from doing file processing on the machines on which they execute. Think about it. A Java applet is designed to be sent to your browser via an HTML document that could be downloaded from any Web server in the world. Often you will know very little about the sources of Java applets that will execute on your system. To allow these applets free reign with your files could be disastrous.

A more subtle situation occurs with limiting the machines to which executing applets can connect. To build truly collaborative applications, we would ideally like to have our applets communicate with machines almost anywhere. But Web browsers often restrict an applet so that it can only communicate with the machine from which it was originally downloaded.

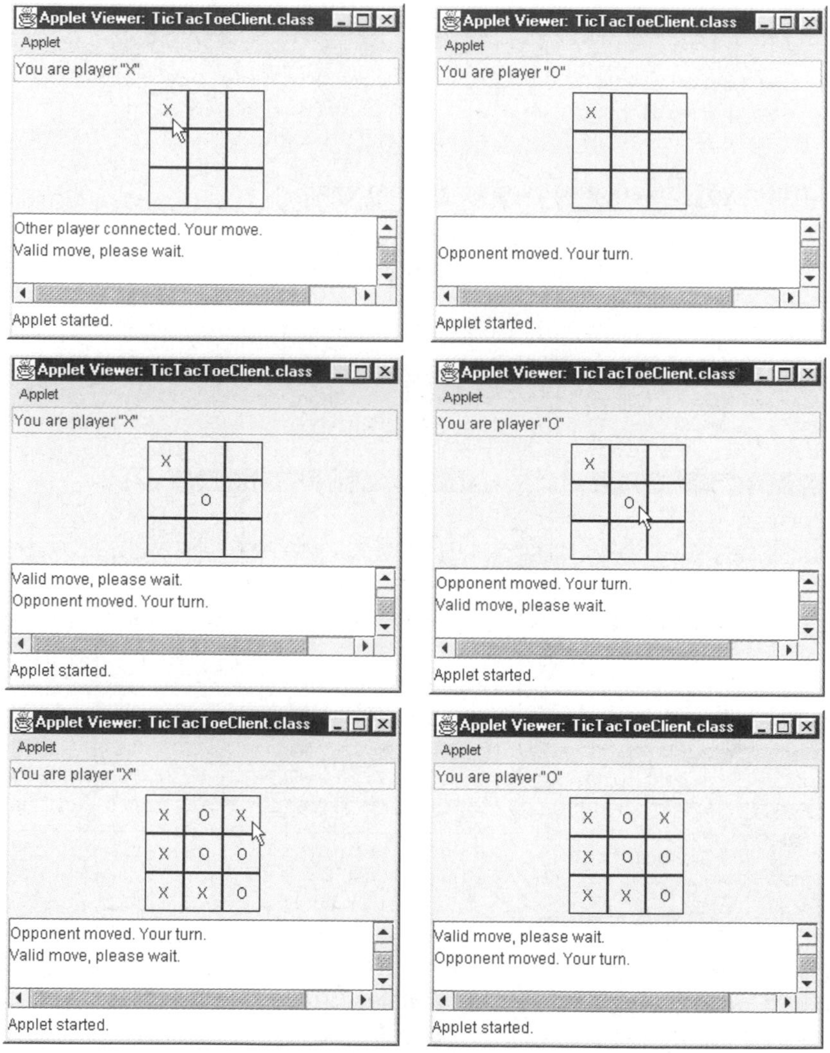

Fig. 21.9   Sample outputs from the client/server Tic-Tac-Toe program (part 2 of 2).

These restrictions may seem too harsh. However, Java Security API now provides capabilities for signed applets that will enable browsers to determine if an applet is downloaded from a *trusted source*. In cases where an applet is trusted, the applet can be given additional access to the computer on which the applet is executing. The features of the Java Security API and additional networking capabilities are discussed in our text *Advanced Java How to Program*.

Summary

- Java provides stream sockets and datagram sockets. With stream sockets a process establishes a connection to another process. While the connection is in place, data flows between the processes in continuous streams. Stream sockets are said to provide a connection-oriented service. The protocol used for transmission is the popular TCP (Transmission Control Protocol).

- With datagram sockets, individual packets of information are transmitted. This is not the right protocol for everyday users because unlike TCP, the protocol used, UDP—the User Datagram Protocol—is a connectionless service, and does not guarantee that packets arrive in any particular way. In fact, packets can be lost, can be duplicated and can even arrive out of sequence. So with UDP, significant extra programming is required on the user's part to deal with these problems (if the user chooses to do so).

- The **http** protocol (HyperText Transfer Protocol) that forms the basis of the World Wide Web uses URLs (Uniform Resource Locators, also called Universal Resource Locators) to locate data on the Internet. Common URLs represent files or directories and can represent complex tasks such as database lookups and Internet searches.

- A **Hashtable** is used to store key/value pairs. A key is used to store and retrieve an associated value in the **Hashtable**. **Hashtable** method **put** takes two arguments—a key and its associated value—and places the value in the **Hashtable** at a location determined by the key. **Hashtable** method **get** takes one argument—a key—and retrieves the value (as an **Object** reference) associated with the key.

- A **Vector** is a dynamically resizable array of **Object**s. **Vector** method **addElement** adds a new element to the end of the **Vector**.

- **Applet** method **getAppletContext** returns a reference to an **AppletContext** object that represents the applet's environment (i.e., the browser in which the applet is executing).

- **AppletContext** method **showDocument** receives a **URL** object as an argument and passes it to the **AppletContext** (i.e., the browser), which displays the World Wide Web resource associated with that **URL**.

- A second version of **AppletContext** method **showDocument** enables an applet to specify the target frame in which Web resource should be displayed. Special target frames include **_blank** (display the URL in a new Web browser window), **_self** (display the URL in the same frame as the applet) and **_top** (the browser should remove the current frames, then display the URL in the current window).

- Method **setCursor** (inherited into class **JFrame** from class **Component**) changes the mouse cursor when the cursor is positioned over a specific GUI component. The **Cursor** constructor receives an integer indicating the cursor type (such as **Cursor.WAIT_CURSOR** or **Cursor.DEFAULT_CURSOR**).

- **JEditorPane** method **setPage** downloads the document specified by its argument and displays it in the **JEditorPane**.

- Typically, an HTML document contains hyperlinks—text, images or GUI components which, when clicked, provide quick access to another document on the Web. If an HTML document is displayed in a **JEditorPane** and the user clicks a hyperlink, the **JEditorPane** generates a **HyperlinkEvent** (package **javax.swing.event**) and notifies all registered **HyperlinkListener**s (package **javax.swing.event**) of that event.

- **HyperlinkEvent** method **getEventType** determines the type of the **HyperlinkEvent**. Class **HyperlinkEvent** contains **public** inner class **EventType**, which defines three hyperlink event types **ACTIVATED** (the user clicked a hyperlink), **ENTERED** (the user moved the mouse over a hyperlink) and **EXITED** (the user moved the mouse away from a hyperlink).

- **HyperlinkEvent** method **getURL** obtains the URL represented by the hyperlink.

- A **ServerSocket** object establishes the port where a server waits for connections from clients. The second argument to the **ServerSocket** constructor specifies the number of clients that can wait for a connection and be processed by the server. If the queue of clients is full, client connections are automatically refused.

- Stream-based connections are managed with **Socket** objects.

- The **ServerSocket** method **accept** waits indefinitely (i.e., blocks) for a connection from a client and returns a **Socket** object when a connection is established.

- The **Socket** method **getOutputStream** gets a reference to the **OutputStream** associated with a **Socket**. The **Socket** method **getInputStream** gets a reference to the **InputStream** associated with the **Socket**.

- When transmission over a **Socket** connection is complete, the server closes the connection by issuing the **close** method on the **Socket**.

- A **Socket** object connects a client to a server by specifying the server name and port number when the **Socket** object is created. A failed connection attempt throws an **IOException**.

- The **InputStream** method **read** returns –1 when end-of-stream is detected.

- An **EOFException** is generated when a **ObjectInputStream** attempts to read a value from a stream on which end-of-stream is detected.

- **InetAddress** method **getByName** returns an **InetAddress** object containing the host name of the computer for which the **String** host name or **String** Internet address is specified as an argument.

- **InetAddress** method **getLocalHost** returns an **InetAddress** object containing the local host name of the computer on which the program is executing.

- The port where a client connects to a server is sometimes called the *handshake point*.

- Connection-oriented transmission is like the telephone system in which you dial and are given a *connection* to the telephone you wish to communicate with; the connection is maintained for the duration of your phone call, even when you are not talking.

- Connectionless transmission with *datagrams* is like the way mail is carried via the postal service. A large message that will not fit in one envelope can be broken into separate message pieces that are placed in separate, sequentially numbered envelopes. Each of the letters is then mailed at once. The letters may arrive in order, out of order or not at all.

- **DatagramPacket**s are used to create the packets to send and receive information. **DatagramSocket**s are used to send and receive **DatagramPacket**s.

- The **DatagramSocket** constructor that takes no arguments sets up a socket for sending packets out over the network on an available port. The **DatagramSocket** constructor that takes an integer port number argument sets up a port for receiving packets from the network.

- If a **DatagramSocket** constructor fails to set up a **DatagramSocket** properly, a **SocketException** is thrown.

- **DatagramSocket** method **receive** waits until a packet arrives, then stores the packet in its argument.
- **DatagramPacket** method **getAddress** returns an **InetAddress** object containing the name of the host from which the packet was sent.
- **DatagramPacket** method **getPort** returns an integer specifying the port number through which the host sent the **DatagramPacket**.
- **DatagramPacket** method **getLength** returns an integer representing the number of bytes of data in a **DatagramPacket**.
- **DatagramPacket** method **getData** returns a byte array containing the data in a **Datagram-Packet**.
- The **DatagramPacket** constructor for a packet to be sent takes four arguments—the **byte** array to be sent, the number of bytes to be sent, the client address to which the packet will be sent and the port number where the client is waiting to receive packets.
- **DatagramSocket** method **send** sends a **DatagramPacket** out over the network.
- If an error occurs when receiving or sending a **DatagramPacket**, an **IOException** is thrown.
- Many Web browsers prohibit Java applets from doing file processing on the machines on which they execute.
- Web browsers often restrict an applet so that it can only communicate with the machine from which it was originally downloaded.

Terminology

accept a connection
accept method of **ServerSocket** class
addElement method of class **Vector**
AppletContext interface
BindException class
bind to a port
client
client connects to a server
client/server relationship
client-side socket
close a connection
close method of class **Socket**
collaborative computing
computer networking
connect to a port
connect to a World Wide Web site
ConnectException class
connection
connection request
connectionless service
connectionless transmission with datagrams
connection-oriented service
Cursor class
Cursor.DEFAULT_CURSOR
Cursor.WAIT_CURSOR
datagram

datagram socket
DatagramPacket class
DatagramSocket class
deny a connection
duplicated packets
get method of class **Hashtable**
getAddress method of **DatagramPacket**
getAppletContext method of class **Applet**
getByName method of **InetAddress**
getData method of class **DatagramPacket**
getEventType method
getInputStream method of class **Socket**
getLength method of **DatagramPacket**
getLocalHost method
getLocalHost method of **InetAddress**
getOutputStream method of class **Socket**
getPort method of class **DatagramPacket**
getPredefinedCursor method of Cursor
getURL method of class **HyperlinkEvent**
handshake point
Hashtable class
heterogeneous computer systems
host
Hyperlink.EventType class
Hyperlink.EventType.ACTIVATED
Hyperlink.EventType.ENTERED

Common Programming Errors

21.1 A **MalformedURLException** is thrown when a **String** that is not in proper URL format is passed to a **URL** constructor.

21.2 An **UnknownHostException** is thrown when a server address indicated by a client cannot be resolved. A **ConnectException** is thrown when an error occurs while attempting to connect to a server.

21.3 Specifying a port that is already in use or specifying an invalid port number when creating a **DatagramSocket** results in a **BindException**.

Performance Tips

21.1 Connectionless services generally offer greater performance but less reliability than connection-oriented services.

21.2 In high-performance systems in which memory is abundant, a multithreaded server can be implemented to create a pool of threads that can be assigned quickly to handle network I/O across each new **Socket** as it is created. Thus, when a connection is received, the server need not incur the overhead of thread creation.

21.3 Output buffers are typically used to increase the efficiency of an application by sending larger amounts of data fewer times. The input and output components of a computer are typically much slower than the memory of the computer.

Portability Tip

21.1   The TCP protocol and its related set of protocols enable a great variety of heterogeneous computer systems (i.e., computer systems with different processors and different operating systems) to intercommunicate.

Software Engineering Observations

21.1   With sockets, network I/O appears to Java programs to be virtually identical to sequential file I/O. Sockets hide much of the complexity of network programming from the programmer.

21.2   With Java's multithreading, we can easily create multithreaded servers that can manage many simultaneous connections with many clients; this multithreaded-server architecture is precisely what is used in popular UNIX, Windows NT and OS/2 network servers.

21.3   A multithreaded server can be implemented to take the **Socket** returned by each call to accept and create a new thread that would manage network I/O across that **Socket**, or a multithreaded server can be implemented to maintain a pool of threads ready to manage network I/O across the new **Socket**s as they are created.

21.4   Many operating systems reserve port numbers below 1024 for system services (such as email and World Wide Web servers). Generally, these ports should not be specified as connection ports in user programs. In fact, some operating systems require special access privileges to use port numbers below 1024.

21.5   When using an **ObjectOutputStream** and **ObjectInputStream** to send and receive objects over a network connection, always create the **ObjectOutputStream** first and flush the stream so the client's **ObjectInputStream** can prepare to receive the data.

Self-Review Exercises

21.1   Fill in the blanks in each of the following:

a) An _____ is thrown when an input/output error occurs when closing a socket.

b) An _____ is thrown when a server address indicated by a client cannot be resolved.

c) If a **DatagramSocket** constructor fails to set up a **DatagramSocket** properly, a is thrown.

d) The **URL** constructor determines if the **String** passed as an argument represents a valid Uniform Resource Locator. If so, the **URL** object is initialized to contain the Uniform Resource Locator; otherwise, a _____ is generated.

e) Many of Java's networking classes are contained in the _____ package.

f) Class _____ is used to create a socket for unreliable datagram transmission.

g) An object of class _____ contains an Internet address.

h) The two types of sockets we discussed in this chapter are _____ sockets and _____ sockets.

i) The acronym URL stands for _____.

j) The key protocol that forms the basis of the World Wide Web is _____.

k) **AppletContext** method _____ receives a URL object as an argument and displays in a browser the World Wide Web resource associated with that URL.

l) **InetAddress** method **getLocalHost** returns an _____ object containing the local host name of the computer on which the program is executing.

21.2   State whether each of the following is *true* or *false*. If *false*, explain why.

a) A **URL** object once created cannot be changed.

b) UDP is a connection-oriented protocol.

c) With stream sockets a process establishes a connection to another process.

d) A server waits at a port for connections from a client.

e) Datagram packet transmission over a network is reliable—packets are guaranteed to arrive in sequence.

f) For security reasons, many Web browsers such as Netscape Communicator allow Java applets to do file processing only on the machines on which they execute.

g) Web browsers often restrict an applet so that it can only communicate with the machine from which it was originally downloaded.

Answers to Self-Review Exercises

21.1   a) **IOException**. b) **UnknownHostException**. c) **SocketException**. d) **MalformedURLException**. e) **java.net**. f) **DatagramSocket**. g) **InetAddress**. h) stream, datagram. i) Uniform Resource Locator. j) **http**. k) **showDocument**. l) **InetAddress**.

21.2   a) true. b) false; UDP is a connectionless protocol and TCP is a connection-oriented protocol. c) true. d) true. e) false; packets could be lost and packets can arrive out of order. f) false; most browsers prevent applets from doing file processing on the client machine. g) true.

Exercises

21.3   Distinguish between connection-oriented network services and connectionless network services.

21.4   How does a client determine the host name of the client computer?

21.5   Under what circumstances would a **SocketException** be thrown?

21.6   How can a client get a line of text from a server?

21.7   Describe how a client applet or application can read a file from a server through a URL connection.

21.8   Describe how a client connects to a server.

21.9   Describe how a server sends data to a client.

21.10   Describe how to prepare a server to receive a streams-based connection request from a single client.

21.11   Describe how to prepare a server to receive connection requests from multiple clients where each client that connects should be processed in parallel with all other connected clients.

21.12   How does a server listen for connections at a port?

21.13   What determines how many connect requests from clients can wait in a queue to connect to a server?

21.14   As described in the text, what reasons might cause a server to refuse a connection request from a client?

21.15   Use a socket connection to allow a client to specify a file name and have the server send the contents of the file or indicate that the file does not exist.

21.16   Modify Exercise 21.15 to allow the client to modify the contents of the file and send the file back to the server for storage. The user can edit the file in a **JTextArea**, then click a *save changes* button to send the file back to the server.

21.17   Modify program of Fig. 21.1 to allow users to add their own sites to the list and remove sites from the list.

21.18   Multithreaded servers are quite popular today, especially because of the increasing use of multiprocessing servers. Modify the simple server application presented in Section 21.6 to be a multithreaded server. Then use several client applications and have each of them connect to the server simultaneously.

21.19   In the text we presented a tic-tac-toe program controlled by a multithreaded server. Develop a checkers program modeled after the tic-tac-toe program. The two users should alternate making moves. Your program should mediate the players' moves, determining whose turn it is and allowing only valid moves. The players themselves will determine when the game is over.

21.20   Develop a chess-playing program modeled after the checkers program in the previous exercises.

21.21   Develop a black jack card game program in which the server application deals cards to each of the client applets. The server should deal additional cards (as per the rules of the game) to each player as requested.

21.22   Develop a poker card game in which the server application deals cards to each of the client applets. The server should deal additional cards (as per the rules of the game) to each player as requested.

21.23   *(Modifications to the Multithreaded Tic-Tac-Toe Program)* The programs of Figs. 21.7 and 21.8 implemented a multithreaded, client/server version of the game Tic-Tac-Toe. Our goal in developing this game was to demonstrate a multithreaded server that could process multiple connections from clients at the same time. The server in the example is really a mediator between the two client applets—it makes sure that each move is valid and that each client moves in the proper order. The server does not determine who won or lost or if there was a draw. Also, there is no capability to allow a new game to be played or to terminate an existing game.

The following is a list of suggested modifications to the multithreaded Tic-Tac-Toe application and applet.

a) Modify the **TicTacToeServer** class to test for a win, loss or draw on each move in the game. Send a message to each client applet that indicates the result of the game when the game is over.

b) Modify the **TicTacToeClient** class to display a button that when clicked allows the client to play another game. The button should only be enabled when a game completes. Note that both class **TicTacToeClient** and class **TicTacToeServer** must be modified to reset the board and all state information. Also, the other **TicTacToeClient** should be notified that a new game is about to begin so its board and state can be reset.

c) Modify the **TicTacToeClient** class to provide a button that allows a client to terminate the program at any time. When the button is clicked, the server and the other client should be notified. The server should then wait for a connection from another client so a new game can begin.

d) Modify the **TicTacToeClient** class and the **TicTacToeServer** class so the winner of a game can choose game piece X or O for the next game. *Remember:* X always goes first.

e) If you would like to be ambitious, allow a client to play against the server while the server waits for a connection from another client.

21.24   *(3-D Multithreaded Tic-Tac-Toe)* Modify the multithreaded, client/server Tic-Tac-Toe program to implement a three-dimensional 4-by-4-by-4 version of the game. Implement the server application to mediate between the two clients. Display the three-dimensional board as four boards containing four rows and four columns each. If you would like to be ambitious, try the following modifications:

a) Draw the board in a three-dimensional manner.

b) Allow the server to test for a win, loss or draw. Beware! There are many possible ways to win on a 4-by-4-by-4 board!

21.25   *(Networked Morse Code)* Modify your solution to Exercise 10.26 to enable two applets to send Morse Code messages to each other through a multithreaded server application. Each applet should allow the user to type normal characters in **JTextArea**s, translate the characters into Morse Code and send the coded message through the server to the other client. When messages are received, they should be decoded and displayed as normal characters and as Morse Code. The applet should have two **JTextArea**s: one for displaying the other client's messages and one for typing.

22

Data Structures

Objectives

- To be able to form linked data structures using references, self-referential classes and recursion.
- To be able to create and manipulate dynamic data structures such as linked lists, queues, stacks and binary trees.
- To understand various important applications of linked data structures.
- To understand how to create reusable data structures with classes, inheritance and composition.

Much that I bound, I could not free;
Much that I freed returned to me.
Lee Wilson Dodd

'Will you walk a little faster?' said a whiting to a snail,
'There's a porpoise close behind us, and he's treading on my tail.'
Lewis Carroll

There is always room at the top.
Daniel Webster

Push on—keep moving.
Thomas Morton

I think that I shall never see
A poem lovely as a tree.
Joyce Kilmer

Outline

22.1 Introduction

We have studied fixed-size *data structures* such as single and double-subscripted arrays. This chapter introduces *dynamic data structures* that grow and shrink at execution time. *Linked lists* are collections of data items "lined up in a row"—insertions and deletions can be made anywhere in a linked list. *Stacks* are important in compilers and operating systems—insertions and deletions are made only at one end of a stack—its *top*. *Queues* represent waiting lines; insertions are made at the back (also referred to as the *tail*) of a queue, and deletions are made from the front (also referred to as the *head*) of a queue. *Binary trees* facilitate high-speed searching and sorting of data, efficient elimination of duplicate data items, representing file system directories and compiling expressions into machine language. These data structures have many other interesting applications.

We will discuss each of the major types of data structures and implement programs that create and manipulate them. We use classes, inheritance and composition to create and package these data structures for reusability and maintainability. In Chapter 23, "Java Utilities Package and Bit Manipulation," and Chapter 24, "Collections," we discuss Java's predefined classes that implement the data structures discussed in this chapter.

The chapter examples are practical programs that you will be able to use in more advanced courses and in industrial applications. The programs are especially heavy on reference manipulation. The exercises include a rich collection of useful applications.

We encourage you to attempt the major project described in the special section entitled "Building Your Own Compiler." You have been using a compiler to translate your Java programs to bytecodes so that you could execute these programs on your computer. In this project, you will actually build your own compiler. It will read a file of statements written in a simple, yet powerful high-level language similar to early versions of the popular language Basic. Your compiler will translate these statements into a file of Simpletron Machine Language (SML) instructions—SML is the language you learned in the Chapter 7 special section, "Building Your Own Computer." Your Simpletron Simulator program will then execute the SML program produced by your compiler! Implementing this project using an object-oriented approach will give you a wonderful opportunity to exercise most of what you have learned in this book. The special section carefully walks you through the specifications of the high-level language, and describes the algorithms you will need to convert each type of high-level language statement into machine language instructions. If you enjoy being challenged, you might attempt the many enhancements to both the compiler and the Simpletron Simulator suggested in the Exercises.

22.2 Self-Referential Classes

A *self-referential class* contains a reference member that refers to a class object of the same class type. For example, the definition

```
class Node {
    private int data;
    private Node next;

    public Node( int d )          { /* constructor body */ }
    public void setData( int d ) { /* method body */ }
    public int getData()          { /* method body */ }
    public void setNext( Node nextNode ) { /* method body */ }
    public Node getNext()         { /* method body */ }
}
```

defines a type, **Node**. This type has two **private** instance variables—integer **data** and **Node** reference **next**. Member **next** references an object of type **Node**—an object of the same type as the one being declared here, hence the term "self-referential class." Member **next** is referred to as a *link* (i.e., **next** can be used to "tie" an object of type **Node** to another object of the same type). Type **Node** also has five methods: a constructor that receives an integer to initialize **data**, a **setData** method to set the value **data**, a **getData** method to return the value of **data**, a **setNext** method to set the value of **next** and a **getNext** method to return the value of member **next**.

Self-referential objects can be linked together to form useful data structures such as lists, queues, stacks and trees. Figure 22.1 illustrates two self-referential objects linked together to form a list. A backslash—representing a **null** reference—is placed in the link member of the second self-referential object to indicate that the link does not refer to another object. The slash is for illustration purposes; it does not correspond to the backslash character in Java. A **null** reference normally indicates the end of a data structure.

Common Programming Error 22.1

*Not setting the link in the last node of a list to **null** is a common logic error.*

22.3 Dynamic Memory Allocation

Creating and maintaining dynamic data structures requires *dynamic memory allocation*—the ability for a program to obtain more memory space at execution time to hold new nodes and to release space no longer needed. As we have already learned, Java programs do not explicitly release dynamically allocated memory. Rather, Java performs automatic garbage collection.

Fig. 22.1   Two self-referential class objects linked together.

The limit for dynamic memory allocation can be as large as the amount of available physical memory in the computer or the amount of available disk space in a virtual-memory system. Often, the limits are much smaller because the computer's available memory must be shared among many users.

Operator **new** is essential to dynamic memory allocation. Operator **new** takes as an operand the type of the object being dynamically allocated and returns a reference to a newly created object of that type. For example, the statement

```
Node nodeToAdd = new Node( 10 );
```

allocates the appropriate amount of memory to store a **Node** and stores a reference to this object in **nodeToAdd**. If no memory is available, **new** throws an **OutOfMemoryError**. The 10 is the **Node** object's data.

The following sections discuss lists, stacks, queues and trees. These data structures are created and maintained with dynamic memory allocation and self-referential classes.

Good Programming Practice 22.1

*When using **new**, test for an **OutOfMemoryError**. Perform appropriate error processing if the requested memory is not allocated.*

22.4 Linked Lists

A *linked list* is a linear collection (i.e., a sequence) of self-referential class objects, called *nodes,* connected by reference *links*—hence, the term "linked" list. A linked list is accessed via a reference to the first node of the list. Each subsequent node is accessed via the link-reference member stored in the previous node. By convention, the link reference in the last node of a list is set to **null** to mark the end of the list. Data are stored in a linked list dynamically—each node is created as necessary. A node can contain data of any type, including objects of other classes. Stacks and queues are also linear data structures, and, as we will see, are constrained versions of linked lists. Trees are nonlinear data structures.

Lists of data can be stored in arrays, but linked lists provide several advantages. A linked list is appropriate when the number of data elements to be represented in the data structure is unpredictable. Linked lists are dynamic, so the length of a list can increase or decrease as necessary. The size of a "conventional" Java array, however, cannot be altered, because the array size is fixed at creation time. "Conventional" arrays can become full. Linked lists become full only when the system has insufficient memory to satisfy dynamic storage allocation requests. The **java.util** package of the Java API contains class **LinkedList** for implementing and manipulating linked lists that grow and shrink during program execution. We will discuss class **LinkedList** in Chapter 24, "Collections."

Performance Tip 22.1

An array can be declared to contain more elements than the number of items expected, but this can waste memory. Linked lists can provide better memory utilization in these situations. Linked lists allow the program to adapt at run time.

Performance Tip 22.2

Insertion into a linked list is fast—only two references have to be modified (after you have located the place to do the insertion). All existing nodes remain at their current locations in memory.

Linked lists can be maintained in sorted order simply by inserting each new element at the proper point in the list (it does, of course, take time to locate the proper insertion point). Existing list elements do not need to be moved.

Performance Tip 22.3

Insertion and deletion in a sorted array can be time consuming—all the elements following the inserted or deleted element must be shifted appropriately.

Performance Tip 22.4

The elements of an array are stored contiguously in memory. This allows immediate access to any array element because the address of any element can be calculated directly based on its offset from the beginning of the array. Linked lists do not afford such immediate access to their elements—an element can be accessed only by traversing the list from the front.

Linked list nodes are normally not stored contiguously in memory. Rather, they are logically contiguous. Figure 22.2 illustrates a linked list with several nodes.

Performance Tip 22.5

Using dynamic memory allocation (instead of arrays) for data structures that grow and shrink at execution time can save memory. Keep in mind, however, that references occupy space, and that dynamic memory allocation incurs the overhead of method calls.

The program of Fig. 22.3 (whose output is shown in Fig. 22.4) uses a **List** class to manipulate a list of miscellaneous object types. The main method of the **ListTest** class creates a list of objects, inserts objects at the beginning of the list using method **insertAtFront**, inserts objects at the end of the list using method **insertAtBack**, deletes objects from the front of the list using method **removeFromFront** and deletes objects from the end of the list using method **removeFromBack**. After each insertion and deletion operation, the **print** method is invoked to display the contents of the list. A detailed discussion of the program follows. If an attempt is made to remove an item from an empty list, an **EmptyListException** (defined on line 143 of Fig. 22.3) is thrown. Exercise 22.20 asks you to implement a recursive method that prints a linked list backwards, and Exercise 22.21 asks you to implement a recursive method that searches a linked list for a particular data item.

The program of Fig. 22.3 consists of three classes—**ListNode List**, and **EmptyListException**. The **List** and **ListNode** classes are placed in package **com.deitel.jhtp3.ch22** for reuse purposes. Encapsulated in each **List** object is a linked list of **ListNode** objects. The **ListNode** class consists of package-access members **data** and **next**. **ListNode** member **data** can refer to any **Object**. **ListNode** member **next** stores a reference to the next **ListNode** object in the linked list.

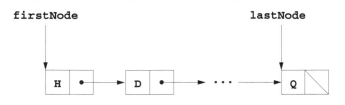

Fig. 22.2   A graphical representation of a linked list.

```java
1   // Fig. 22.3: List.java
2   // Class ListNode and class List definitions
3   package com.deitel.jhtp3.ch22;
4
5   class ListNode {
6      // package access data so class List can access it directly
7      Object data;
8      ListNode next;
9
10     // Constructor: Create a ListNode that refers to Object o.
11     ListNode( Object o ) { this( o, null ); }
12
13     // Constructor: Create a ListNode that refers to Object o and
14     // to the next ListNode in the List.
15     ListNode( Object o, ListNode nextNode )
16     {
17        data = o;           // this node refers to Object o
18        next = nextNode;    // set next to refer to next
19     }
20
21     // Return a reference to the Object in this node
22     Object getObject() { return data; }
23
24     // Return the next node
25     ListNode getNext() { return next; }
26  }
27
28  // Class List definition
29  public class List {
30     private ListNode firstNode;
31     private ListNode lastNode;
32     private String name;  // String like "list" used in printing
33
34     // Constructor: Construct an empty List with s as the name
35     public List( String s )
36     {
37        name = s;
38        firstNode = lastNode = null;
39     }
40
41     // Constructor: Construct an empty List with
42     // "list" as the name
43     public List() { this( "list" ); }
44
45     // Insert an Object at the front of the List
46     // If List is empty, firstNode and lastNode will refer to
47     // the same object. Otherwise, firstNode refers to new node.
48     public synchronized void insertAtFront( Object insertItem )
49     {
50        if ( isEmpty() )
51           firstNode = lastNode = new ListNode( insertItem );
```

Fig. 22.3   Manipulating a linked list (part 1 of 5).

```
52            else
53                firstNode = new ListNode( insertItem, firstNode );
54        }
55
56        // Insert an Object at the end of the List
57        // If List is empty, firstNode and lastNode will refer to
58        // the same Object. Otherwise, lastNode's next instance
59        // variable refers to new node.
60        public synchronized void insertAtBack( Object insertItem )
61        {
62            if ( isEmpty() )
63                firstNode = lastNode = new ListNode( insertItem );
64            else
65                lastNode = lastNode.next = new ListNode( insertItem );
66        }
67
68        // Remove the first node from the List.
69        public synchronized Object removeFromFront()
70                throws EmptyListException
71        {
72            Object removeItem = null;
73
74            if ( isEmpty() )
75                throw new EmptyListException( name );
76
77            removeItem = firstNode.data;   // retrieve the data
78
79            // reset the firstNode and lastNode references
80            if ( firstNode.equals( lastNode ) )
81                firstNode = lastNode = null;
82            else
83                firstNode = firstNode.next;
84
85            return removeItem;
86        }
87
88        // Remove the last node from the List.
89        public synchronized Object removeFromBack()
90                throws EmptyListException
91        {
92            Object removeItem = null;
93
94            if ( isEmpty() )
95                throw new EmptyListException( name );
96
97            removeItem = lastNode.data;   // retrieve the data
98
99            // reset the firstNode and lastNode references
100           if ( firstNode.equals( lastNode ) )
101               firstNode = lastNode = null;
102           else {
103               ListNode current = firstNode;
104
```

Fig. 22.3   Manipulating a linked list (part 2 of 5).

```
105              while ( current.next != lastNode )  // not last node
106                 current = current.next;        // move to next node
107
108              lastNode = current;
109              current.next = null;
110           }
111
112        return removeItem;
113     }
114
115     // Return true if the List is empty
116     public synchronized boolean isEmpty()
117        { return firstNode == null; }
118
119     // Output the List contents
120     public synchronized void print()
121     {
122        if ( isEmpty() ) {
123           System.out.println( "Empty " + name );
124           return;
125        }
126
127        System.out.print( "The " + name + " is: " );
128
129        ListNode current = firstNode;
130
131        while ( current != null ) {
132           System.out.print( current.data.toString() + " " );
133           current = current.next;
134        }
135
136        System.out.println( "\n" );
137     }
138 }
```

Fig. 22.3 Manipulating a linked list (part 3 of 5).

```
139 // Fig. 22.3: EmptyListException.java
140 // Class EmptyListException definition
141 package com.deitel.jhtp3.ch22;
142
143 public class EmptyListException extends RuntimeException {
144    public EmptyListException( String name )
145    {
146       super( "The " + name + " is empty" );
147    }
148 }
```

Fig. 22.3 Manipulating a linked list (part 4 of 5).

```
149  // Fig. 22.3: ListTest.java
150  // Class ListTest
151  import com.deitel.jhtp3.ch22.List;
152  import com.deitel.jhtp3.ch22.EmptyListException;
153
154  public class ListTest {
155     public static void main( String args[] )
156     {
157        List objList = new List();  // create the List container
158
159        // Create objects to store in the List
160        Boolean b = Boolean.TRUE;
161        Character c = new Character( '$' );
162        Integer i = new Integer( 34567 );
163        String s = "hello";
164
165        // Use the List insert methods
166        objList.insertAtFront( b );
167        objList.print();
168        objList.insertAtFront( c );
169        objList.print();
170        objList.insertAtBack( i );
171        objList.print();
172        objList.insertAtBack( s );
173        objList.print();
174
175        // Use the List remove methods
176        Object removedObj;
177
178        try {
179           removedObj = objList.removeFromFront();
180           System.out.println(
181              removedObj.toString() + " removed" );
182           objList.print();
183           removedObj = objList.removeFromFront();
184           System.out.println(
185              removedObj.toString() + " removed" );
186           objList.print();
187           removedObj = objList.removeFromBack();
188           System.out.println(
189              removedObj.toString() + " removed" );
190           objList.print();
191           removedObj = objList.removeFromBack();
192           System.out.println(
193              removedObj.toString() + " removed" );
194           objList.print();
195        }
196        catch ( EmptyListException e ) {
197           System.err.println( "\n" + e.toString() );
198        }
199     }
200  }
```

Fig. 22.3   Manipulating a linked list (part 5 of 5).

```
The list is: true

The list is: $ true

The list is: $ true 34567

The list is: $ true 34567 hello

$ removed
The list is: true 34567 hello

true removed
The list is: 34567 hello

hello removed
The list is: 34567

34567 removed
Empty list
```

Fig. 22.4   Sample output for the program of Fig. 22.3.

The **List** class consists of **private** members **firstNode** (a reference to the first **ListNode** in a **List** object) and **lastNode** (a reference to the last **ListNode** in a **List** object). The default constructor initializes both references to **null**. The primary methods of the **List** class are the **synchronized** methods **insertAtFront**, **insertAtBack**, **removeFromFront** and **removeFromBack**. These methods are declared **synchronized** so **List** objects can be *multithread safe* when used in a multi-threaded program. If one thread is modifying the contents of a **List** object, no other thread is allowed to modify the same **List** object at the same time. Method **isEmpty** is called a *predicate method*—it does not alter the list in any way; rather, it determines if the list is empty (i.e., the reference to the first node of the list is **null**). If the list is empty, **true** is returned; otherwise, **false** is returned. Method **print** displays the list's contents. Both **isEmpty** and **print** are also **synchronized**.

Over the next several pages, we will discuss each of the methods of the **List** class in detail. Method **insertAtFront** (Fig. 22.5 illustrates the operation) places a new node at the front of the list. The method consists of several steps:

1. Call **isEmpty** to determine if the list is empty (line 50).

2. If the list is empty, both **firstNode** and **lastNode** are set to the **ListNode** allocated with **new** and initialized with **insertItem** (line 51). The **ListNode** constructor at line 11 calls the **ListNode** constructor at line 15 to set instance variable **data** to refer to the **insertItem** passed as an argument and sets the **next** reference to **null**.

3. If the list is not empty, the new node is "threaded" (not to be confused with multithreading) into the list by setting **firstNode** to the **ListNode** object that was allocated with **new** and initialized with **insertItem** and **firstNode** (line

53). When the **ListNode** constructor (line 15) executes, it sets instance variable **data** to refer to the **insertItem** passed as an argument and performs the insertion by setting the **next** reference to the **ListNode** passed as an argument.

Figure 22.5 illustrates method **insertAtFront**. Part a) of the figure shows the list and the new node during the **insertAtFront** operation and before the new node has been threaded into the list. The dotted arrows in part b) illustrate step 3 of the **insertAtFront** operation that enables the node containing **12** to become the new list front.

Method **insertAtBack** (Fig. 22.6 illustrates the operation) places a new node at the back of the list. The method consists of several steps:

1. Call **isEmpty** to determine if the list is empty (line 62).

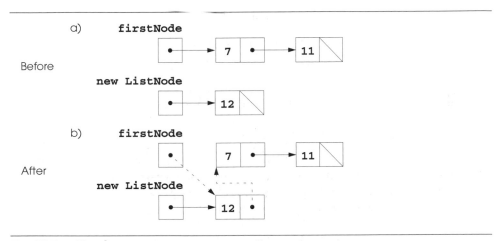

Fig. 22.5   The **insertAtFront** operation.

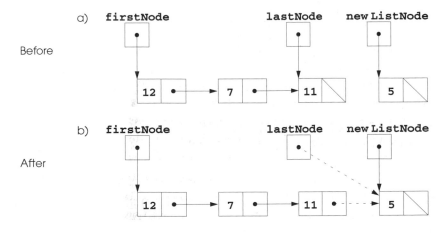

Fig. 22.6   A graphical representation of the **insertAtBack** operation.

2. If the list is empty, both **firstNode** and **lastNode** are set to the **ListNode** allocated with **new** and initialized with **insertItem** (line 63). The **ListNode** constructor at line 11 calls the **ListNode** constructor at line 15 to set instance variable **data** to refer to the **insertItem** passed as an argument and sets the **next** reference to **null**.

3. If the list is not empty, the new node is threaded into the list by setting **LastNode** and **lastNode.next** to the **ListNode** that was allocated with **new** and initialized with **insertItem** (line 65). When the **ListNode** constructor (line 11) executes, it sets instance variable **data** to refer to the **insertItem** passed as an argument and sets the **next** reference to **null**.

Figure 22.6 illustrates an **insertAtBack** operation. Part a) of the figure shows the list and the new node during the **insertAtBack** operation and before the new node has been threaded into the list. The dotted arrows in part b) illustrate the steps of method **insertAtBack** that enable a new node to be added to the end of a list that is not empty.

Method **removeFromFront** (illustrated in Fig. 22.7) removes the front node of the list and returns a reference to the removed data. The method throws an **EmptyListException** (lines 74 and 75) if an attempt is made to remove a node from an empty list. Otherwise, a reference to the removed data is returned. The method consists of several steps:

1. Assign **removeItem** to refer to **firstNode.data** (the data being removed from the list).

2. If the objects to which **firstNode** and **lastNode** refer are equal (line 80) (i.e., the list has only one element prior to the removal attempt), then set **firstNode** and **lastNode** to **null** (line 81) to "dethread" (remove) the node from the list (leaving the list empty).

3. If the list has more than one node prior to removal, then leave **lastNode** as is and simply set **firstNode** to **firstNode.next** (line 83) [i.e., modify **firstNode** to reference what was the second node prior to removal (and now, the new first node].

4. Return the **removeItem** reference.

Figure 22.7 illustrates method **removeFromFront**. Part a) illustrates the list before the removal operation. Part b) shows actual reference manipulations.

Method **removeFromBack** (Fig. 22.8 illustrates the operation) removes the last node of a list and returns a reference to the removed data. The method throws an **EmptyList-Exception** (lines 94 and 95) if an attempt is made to remove a node from an empty list. The method consists of several steps:

1. Assign **removeItem** to refer to **lastNode.data** (the data being removed from the list).

2. If the objects to which **firstNode** and **lastNode** refer are equal (line 100) (i.e., if the list has only one element prior to the removal attempt), then set **firstNode** and **lastNode** to **null** (line 101) to dethread (remove) that node from the list (leaving the list empty).

3. If the list has more than one node prior to removal, then create the **ListNode** reference **current** and initialize it to **firstNode**.

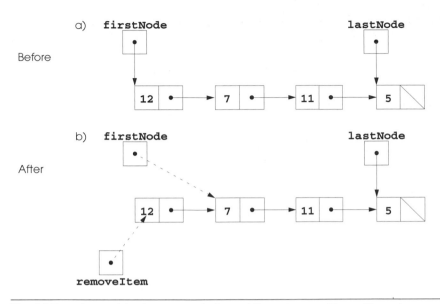

Fig. 22.7   A graphical representation of the **removeFromFront** operation.

4. Now "walk the list" with **current** until it references the node before the last node. This is done with a **while** loop that keeps replacing **current** by **current.next** while **current.next** is not **lastNode**.

5. Copy **current** to **lastNode** to dethread the back node from the list.

6. Set the **current.next** to **null** in the new last node of the list.

7. Return the **removeItem** reference.

Figure 22.8 illustrates method **removeFromBack**. Part a) illustrates the list before the removal operation. Part b) shows the actual reference manipulations.

Method **print** (line 120) first determines if the list is empty. If so, **print** displays **"The list is empty"** and terminates. Otherwise, it prints the data in the list. The method prints a string consisting of the string **"The "**, the **String** object **name** and the string **" is: "**. Then the **ListNode** reference **current** is created and initialized with **firstNode**. While **current** is not **null, current.data.toString()** is printed and **current.next** is assigned to **current**. Note that if the link in the last node of the list is not null, the printing algorithm will erroneously print past the end of the list. The printing algorithm is identical for linked lists, stacks and queues.

22.5 Stacks

A *stack* is a constrained version of a linked list—new nodes can be added to a stack and removed from a stack only at the top. For this reason, a stack is referred to as a *last-in, first-out (LIFO)* data structure. The link member in the bottom (i.e., last) node of the stack is set to null to indicate the bottom of the stack.

Common Programming Error 22.2

*Not setting the link in the bottom node of a stack to **null** is a common logic error.*

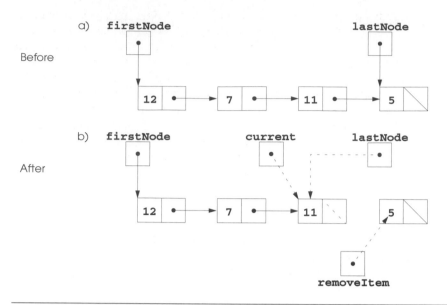

Fig. 22.8   A graphical representation of the **removeFromBack** operation.

The primary methods used to manipulate a stack are *push* and *pop*. Method **push** adds a new node to the top of the stack. Method **pop** removes a node from the top of the stack and returns the **data** object from the popped node.

Stacks have many interesting applications. For example, when a method call is made, the called method must know how to return to its caller, so the return address is pushed onto the *program execution stack*. If a series of method calls occurs, the successive return values are pushed onto the stack in last-in, first-out order so that each method can return to its caller. Stacks support recursive method calls in the same manner as conventional nonrecursive method calls.

The program execution stack contains the space created for local variables on each invocation of a method during a program's execution. When the method returns to its caller, the space for that method's local variables is popped off the stack, and those variables are no longer known to the program.

Stacks are also used by compilers in the process of evaluating arithmetic expressions and generating machine language code to process the expressions. The exercises in this chapter explore several applications of stacks, including using them to develop a complete working compiler. The **java.util** package of the Java API contains class **Stack** for implementing and manipulating stacks that can grow and shrink during program execution. We will discuss class **Stack** in Chapter 23, "Java Utilities Package and Bit Manipulation."

We will take advantage of the close relationship between lists and stacks to implement a stack class primarily by reusing a list class. We use two different forms of reusability. First, we implement the stack class through inheritance of the **List** class. Then we implement an identically performing stack class through composition by including a **List** object as a **private** member of a stack class. The list, stack and queue data structures in this chapter are implemented to store **Object** references to encourage further reusability. Thus, any object type can be stored in a list, stack or queue.

Figure 22.9 (output in Fig. 22.10) creates a stack class through inheritance from class **List** of Fig. 22.3. We want the stack to have methods **push**, **pop**, **isEmpty** and **print**. These are essentially the **insertAtFront**, **removeFromFront**, **isEmpty** and **print** methods of class **List**. Of course, class **List** contains other methods (i.e., **insertAtBack** and **removeFromBack**) that we would rather not make accessible through the public interface to the stack class. It is important to remember that all methods in the public interface of the **List** class are also **public** methods of the derived class **StackInheritance**. We demonstrate another way to build the stack using our **List** class in Fig. 22.11. When we implement the stack's methods, we have each **StackInheritance** method call the appropriate **List** method—method **push** calls **insertAtFront**, method **pop** calls **removeFromFront**, **isEmpty** calls **super.isEmpty** to invoke the base class version and **print** calls **super.print** to invoke the base class version. Note that the methods in class **StackInheritance** are not synchronized. Each of the methods in this class calls a **synchronized** method from class **List**. If two threads call **push** on the same stack object, only one of the threads at a time will be able to call **List** method **insertAtFront**. Class **StackInheritance** is defined as part of package **com.deitel.jhtp3.ch22** for reuse purposes.

```
1   // Fig. 22.9: StackInheritance.java
2   // Derived from class List
3   package com.deitel.jhtp3.ch22;
4
5   public class StackInheritance extends List {
6      public StackInheritance() { super( "stack" ); }
7      public void push( Object o )
8         { insertAtFront( o ); }
9      public Object pop() throws EmptyListException
10        { return removeFromFront(); }
11     public boolean isEmpty() { return super.isEmpty(); }
12     public void print() { super.print(); }
13  }
```

Fig. 22.9   A simple stack program (part 1 of 3).

```
14  // Fig. 22.9: StackInheritanceTest.java
15  // Class StackInheritanceTest
16  import com.deitel.jhtp3.ch22.StackInheritance;
17  import com.deitel.jhtp3.ch22.EmptyListException;
18
19  public class StackInheritanceTest {
20     public static void main( String args[] )
21     {
22        StackInheritance objStack = new StackInheritance();
23
24        // Create objects to store in the stack
25        Boolean b = Boolean.TRUE;
26        Character c = new Character( '$' );
```

Fig. 22.9   A simple stack program (part 2 of 3).

```
27              Integer i = new Integer( 34567 );
28              String s = "hello";
29
30              // Use the push method
31              objStack.push( b );
32              objStack.print();
33              objStack.push( c );
34              objStack.print();
35              objStack.push( i );
36              objStack.print();
37              objStack.push( s );
38              objStack.print();
39
40              // Use the pop method
41              Object removedObj = null;
42
43              try {
44                  while ( true ) {
45                      removedObj = objStack.pop();
46                      System.out.println( removedObj.toString() +
47                                              " popped" );
48                      objStack.print();
49                  }
50              }
51              catch ( EmptyListException e ) {
52                  System.err.println( "\n" + e.toString() );
53              }
54          }
55      }
```

Fig. 22.9   A simple stack program (part 3 of 3).

The **StackInheritance** class is used in **StackInheritanceTest**'s **main** method to instantiate a stack of **Object**s called **objStack**. A **Boolean** object containing **true**, a **Character** object containing **$**, an **Integer** object containing **34567** and a **String** object containing **hello** are pushed onto **objStack** and then popped off **objStack**. The objects are popped from the stack in an infinite **while** loop. When there are no objects left to pop, an **EmptyListException** is thrown and a message is displayed stating that the stack is empty.

Another way to implement a stack class is by reusing a list class through composition. The class in Fig. 22.11 uses a **private** object of the **List** class (line 6) in the definition of class **StackComposition**.

Composition enables us to hide the methods of class **List** that should not be in the interface to our stack by providing public interface methods only to the required **List** methods. This technique of implementing each stack method as a call to a **List** method is called *delegating*—the stack method invoked *delegates* the call to the appropriate **List** method. The **StackCompositionTest** class uses an identical **main** method to the **StackInheritanceTest** class, except an object of class **StackComposition** is instantiated instead. The output is also the same.

```
The stack is: true

The stack is: $ true

The stack is: 34567 $ true

The stack is: hello 34567 $ true

hello popped
The stack is: 34567 $ true

34567 popped
The stack is: $ true

$ popped
The stack is: true

true popped
Empty stack

com.deitel.jhtp3.ch22.EmptyListException:
    The stack is empty
```

Fig. 22.10   Sample output from the program of Fig. 22.9.

```
1   // Fig. 22.11: StackComposition.java
2   // Class StackComposition definition with composed List object
3   package com.deitel.jhtp3.ch22;
4
5   public class StackComposition {
6       private List s;
7
8       public StackComposition() { s = new List( "stack" ); }
9       public void push( Object o )
10          { s.insertAtFront( o ); }
11      public Object pop() throws EmptyListException
12          { return s.removeFromFront(); }
13      public boolean isEmpty() { return s.isEmpty(); }
14      public void print() { s.print(); }
15  }
```

Fig. 22.11   A simple stack class using composition.

22.6 Queues

Another common data structure is the *queue*. A queue is similar to a checkout line in a supermarket—the first person in line is serviced first, and other customers enter the line only at the end and wait to be serviced. Queue nodes are removed only from the *head* of the queue, and are inserted only at the *tail* of the queue. For this reason, a queue is referred to as a *first-in, first-out (FIFO)* data structure. The insert and remove operations are known as **enqueue** and **dequeue**.

Queues have many applications in computer systems. Most computers have only a single processor, so only one user at a time can be serviced. Entries for the other users are placed in a queue. The entry at the front of the queue is the next to receive service. Each entry gradually advances to the front of the queue as users receive service.

Queues are also used to support print spooling. A multiuser environment may have only a single printer. Many users may be generating outputs to be printed. If the printer is busy, other outputs may still be generated. These are "spooled" to disk (much as thread is wound onto a spool) where they wait in a queue until the printer becomes available.

Information packets also wait in queues in computer networks. Each time a packet arrives at a network node, it must be routed to the next node on the network along the path to the packet's final destination. The routing node routes one packet at a time, so additional packets are enqueued until the router can route them.

A file server in a computer network handles file access requests from many clients throughout the network. Servers have a limited capacity to service requests from clients. When that capacity is exceeded, client requests wait in queues.

Figure 22.12 (output in Fig. 22.13) creates a queue class through inheritance from a list class. We want the **QueueInheritance** class to have methods **enqueue**, **dequeue**, **isEmpty**, and **print**. We note that these are essentially the **insertAtBack**, **removeFromFront**, **isEmpty** and **print** methods of class **List**. Class **QueueInheritance** is defined in package **com.deitel.jhtp3.ch22** for reuse purposes.

Common Programming Error 22.3

*Not setting the link in the last node of a queue to **null** is a common logic error.*

Of course, the list class contains other methods (i.e., **insertAtFront** and **removeFromBack**) that we would rather not make accessible through the public interface to the queue class. Remember that all methods in the **public** interface of the **List** class are also **public** methods of the derived class **QueueInheritance**. When we implement the queue's methods, we have each **QueueInheritance** method call the appropriate **List** method—method **enqueue** calls **insertAtBack**, method **dequeue** calls **removeFromFront**, **isEmpty** and **print** calls invoke their base class versions.

```
1   // Fig. 22.12: QueueInheritance.java
2   // Class QueueInheritance definition
3   // Derived from List
4   package com.deitel.jhtp3.ch22;
5
6   public class QueueInheritance extends List {
7      public QueueInheritance() { super( "queue" ); }
8      public void enqueue( Object o )
9         { insertAtBack( o ); }
10     public Object dequeue()
11        throws EmptyListException { return removeFromFront(); }
12     public boolean isEmpty() { return super.isEmpty(); }
13     public void print() { super.print(); }
14  }
```

Fig. 22.12   Processing a queue (part 1 of 2).

```
15   // Fig. 22.12: QueueInheritanceTest.java
16   // Class QueueInheritanceTest
17   import com.deitel.jhtp3.ch22.QueueInheritance;
18   import com.deitel.jhtp3.ch22.EmptyListException;
19
20   public class QueueInheritanceTest {
21      public static void main( String args[] )
22      {
23         QueueInheritance objQueue = new QueueInheritance();
24
25         // Create objects to store in the queue
26         Boolean b = Boolean.TRUE;
27         Character c = new Character( '$' );
28         Integer i = new Integer( 34567 );
29         String s = "hello";
30
31         // Use the enqueue method
32         objQueue.enqueue( b );
33         objQueue.print();
34         objQueue.enqueue( c );
35         objQueue.print();
36         objQueue.enqueue( i );
37         objQueue.print();
38         objQueue.enqueue( s );
39         objQueue.print();
40
41         // Use the dequeue method
42         Object removedObj = null;
43
44         try {
45            while ( true ) {
46               removedObj = objQueue.dequeue();
47               System.out.println( removedObj.toString() +
48                                   " dequeued" );
49               objQueue.print();
50            }
51         }
52         catch ( EmptyListException e ) {
53            System.err.println( "\n" + e.toString() );
54         }
55      }
56   }
```

Fig. 22.12   Processing a queue (part 2 of 2).

```
The queue is: true

The queue is: true $

The queue is: true $ 34567

The queue is: true $ 34567 hello

true dequeued
The queue is: $ 34567 hello

$ dequeued
The queue is: 34567 hello

34567 dequeued
The queue is: hello

hello dequeued
Empty queue

com.deitel.jhtp3.ch22.EmptyListException:
    The queue is empty
```

Fig. 22.13   Sample output from the program in Fig. 22.12.

The **QueueInheritance** class is used in **QueueInheritanceTest**'s **main** method to instantiate a queue of **Object**s called **objQueue**. A **Boolean** object containing **true**, a **Character** object containing **$**, an **Integer** object containing **34567** and a **String** object containing **hello** are enqueued in **objQueue** and then dequeued from **objQueue** in first-in, first-out order. The objects are dequeued from the queue in an infinite **while** loop. When there are no objects left to dequeue, an **EmptyListException** is thrown and a message is displayed stating that the queue is empty.

22.7 Trees

Linked lists, stacks and queues are *linear data structures (i.e., sequences)*. A tree is a nonlinear, two-dimensional data structure with special properties. Tree nodes contain two or more links. This section discusses *binary trees* (Fig. 22.14)—trees whose nodes all contain two links (none, one or both of which may be **null**). The *root node* is the first node in a tree. Each link in the root node refers to a *child*. The *left child* is the first node in the *left subtree,* and the *right child* is the first node in the *right subtree*. The children of a node are called *siblings*. A node with no children is called a *leaf node*. Computer scientists normally draw trees from the root node down—exactly the opposite of the way most trees grow in nature.

Common Programming Error 22.4

*Not setting to **null** the links in leaf nodes of a tree is a common logic error.*

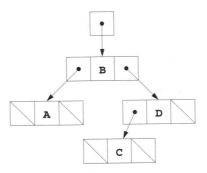

Fig. 22.14   A graphical representation of a binary tree.

In this section, a special binary tree called a *binary search tree* is created. A binary search tree (with no duplicate node values) has the characteristic that the values in any left subtree are less than the value in its parent node, and the values in any right subtree are greater than the value in its parent node. Figure 22.15 illustrates a binary search tree with 12 integer values. Note that the shape of the binary search tree that corresponds to a set of data can vary, depending on the order in which the values are inserted into the tree.

Figure 22.16 (output in Fig. 22.17) creates a binary search tree of integers and traverses it (i.e., walks through all its nodes) three ways—using recursive *inorder, preorder* and *postorder traversals*. The program generates 10 random numbers and inserts each in the tree. Class **Tree** is defined in package **com.deitel.jhtp3.ch22** for reuse purposes.

Let us walk through the binary tree program of Fig. 22.16. Method **main** of class **TreeTest** begins by instantiating an empty **Tree** object and storing it in reference **tree** (line 108). The program randomly generates 10 integers, each of which is inserted in the binary tree through a call to **synchronized** method **insertNode** (line 116). The program then performs preorder, inorder and postorder traversals (these will be explained shortly) of **tree**.

Now, let us walk through the class definitions and methods. We begin with the **TreeNode** class (line 5), which declares as package access data the node's **data** value, and references **left** (to the node's left subtree) and **right** (to the node's right subtree). The constructor (line 12) sets the **data** value to the value supplied as a constructor argument, and sets references **left** and **right** to **null** (thus initializing this node to be a leaf node). Method **insert** is invoked by the **Tree** class **insertNode** method to insert data into a tree that is not empty. This method will be discussed in detail shortly.

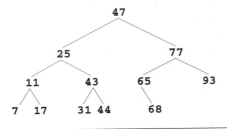

Fig. 22.15   A binary search tree.

```
1   // Fig. 22.16: Tree.java
2   package com.deitel.jhtp3.ch22;
3
4   // Class TreeNode definition
5   class TreeNode {
6      // package access members
7      TreeNode left;    // left node
8      int data;         // data item
9      TreeNode right;   // right node
10
11     // Constructor: initialize data to d and make this a leaf node
12     public TreeNode( int d )
13     {
14        data = d;
15        left = right = null;   // this node has no children
16     }
17
18     // Insert a TreeNode into a Tree that contains nodes.
19     // Ignore duplicate values.
20     public synchronized void insert( int d )
21     {
22        if ( d < data ) {
23           if ( left == null )
24              left = new TreeNode( d );
25           else
26              left.insert( d );
27        }
28        else if ( d > data ) {
29           if ( right == null )
30              right = new TreeNode( d );
31           else
32              right.insert( d );
33        }
34     }
35  }
36
37  // Class Tree definition
38  public class Tree {
39     private TreeNode root;
40
41     // Construct an empty Tree of integers
42     public Tree() { root = null; }
43
44     // Insert a new node in the binary search tree.
45     // If the root node is null, create the root node here.
46     // Otherwise, call the insert method of class TreeNode.
47     public synchronized void insertNode( int d )
48     {
49        if ( root == null )
50           root = new TreeNode( d );
```

Fig. 22.16   Creating and traversing a binary tree (part 1 of 3).

```
51            else
52                root.insert( d );
53        }
54
55        // Preorder Traversal
56        public synchronized void preorderTraversal()
57            { preorderHelper( root ); }
58
59        // Recursive method to perform preorder traversal
60        private void preorderHelper( TreeNode node )
61        {
62            if ( node == null )
63                return;
64
65            System.out.print( node.data + " " );
66            preorderHelper( node.left );
67            preorderHelper( node.right );
68        }
69
70        // Inorder Traversal
71        public synchronized void inorderTraversal()
72            { inorderHelper( root ); }
73
74        // Recursive method to perform inorder traversal
75        private void inorderHelper( TreeNode node )
76        {
77            if ( node == null )
78                return;
79
80            inorderHelper( node.left );
81            System.out.print( node.data + " " );
82            inorderHelper( node.right );
83        }
84
85        // Postorder Traversal
86        public synchronized void postorderTraversal()
87            { postorderHelper( root ); }
88
89        // Recursive method to perform postorder traversal
90        private void postorderHelper( TreeNode node )
91        {
92            if ( node == null )
93                return;
94
95            postorderHelper( node.left );
96            postorderHelper( node.right );
97            System.out.print( node.data + " " );
98        }
99    }
```

Fig. 22.16   Creating and traversing a binary tree (part 2 of 3).

```
100  // Fig. 22.16: TreeTest.java
101  // This program tests the Tree class.
102  import com.deitel.jhtp3.ch22.Tree;
103
104  // Class TreeTest definition
105  public class TreeTest {
106     public static void main( String args[] )
107     {
108        Tree tree = new Tree();
109        int intVal;
110
111        System.out.println( "Inserting the following values: " );
112
113        for ( int i = 1; i <= 10; i++ ) {
114           intVal = ( int ) ( Math.random() * 100 );
115           System.out.print( intVal + " " );
116           tree.insertNode( intVal );
117        }
118
119        System.out.println ( "\n\nPreorder traversal" );
120        tree.preorderTraversal();
121
122        System.out.println ( "\n\nInorder traversal" );
123        tree.inorderTraversal();
124
125        System.out.println ( "\n\nPostorder traversal" );
126        tree.postorderTraversal();
127        System.out.println();
128     }
129  }
```

Fig. 22.16 Creating and traversing a binary tree (part 3 of 3).

```
Inserting the following values:
39 69 94 47 50 72 55 41 97 73

Preorder traversal
39 69 47 41 50 55 94 72 73 97

Inorder traversal
39 41 47 50 55 69 72 73 94 97

Postorder traversal
41 55 50 47 73 72 97 94 69 39
```

Fig. 22.17 Sample output from the program of Fig. 22.16.

Class **Tree** has as **private** data **root**—a reference to the root node of the tree. The class has public methods **insertNode** (insert a new node in the tree) and **preorder-Traversal**, **inorderTraversal** and **postorderTraversal**, each of which walks the tree in the designated manner. Each of these methods calls its own separate recursive utility method to perform the appropriate operations on the internal representation of the tree. The **Tree** constructor initializes **root** to **null** because the tree is initially empty.

The **Tree** class's **synchronized** method **insertNode** (line 47) first determines if the tree is empty. If so, it allocates a new **TreeNode**, initializes the node with the integer being inserted in the tree and assigns the new node to the **root** reference. If the tree is not empty, the **TreeNode** method **insert** is called to recursively insert a node into the tree. *A node can only be inserted as a leaf node in a binary search tree.*

The **TreeNode** method **insert** compares the value to be inserted with the **data** value in the root node. If the insert value is less than the root node data, the program determines if the left subtree is empty (line 23). If so, a new **TreeNode** is allocated and initialized with the integer being inserted and the **left** reference is set to the new node (line 24). Otherwise, **insert** recursively calls itself (line 26) for the left subtree to insert the value in the left subtree. If the insert value is greater than the root node data, the program determines if the right subtree is empty (line 29). If so, a new **TreeNode** is allocated and initialized with the integer being inserted and the **right** reference is set to the new node (line 30). Otherwise, **insert** recursively calls itself (line 32) for the right subtree to insert the value in the right subtree.

Methods **inorderTraversal**, **preorderTraversal** and **postorderTraversal** call helper methods **inorderHelper**, **preorderHelper** and **postorderHelper**, respectively to traverse the tree (Fig. 22.18) and print the node values. The purpose of the helper methods in class **Tree** is to allow the programmer to start a traversal without the need to first obtain a reference to the **root** node, then call the recursive method. Methods **inorderTraversal**, **preorderTraversal** and **postorderTraversal** simply take the **private root** reference and pass it to the appropriate helper method to initiate a traversal.

The steps for an **inorderTraversal** (defined at line 71) are:

1. Traverse the left subtree with a call to **inorderHelper** (defined at line 75).

2. Process the value in the node (i.e., print the node value).

3. Traverse the right subtree with a call to **inorderHelper**.

The value in a node is not processed until the values in its left subtree are processed. The **inorderTraversal** of the tree in Fig. 22.18 is

       6 13 17 27 33 42 48

Note that the **inorderTraversal** of a binary search tree prints the node values in ascending order. The process of creating a binary search tree actually sorts the data—and thus this process is called the *binary tree sort.*

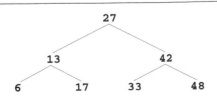

Fig. 22.18   A binary search tree.

The steps for a **preorderTraversal** (defined at line 56) are:

1. Process the value in the node.
2. Traverse the left subtree with a call to **preorderHelper** (defined at line 60).
3. Traverse the right subtree with a call to **preorderHelper**.

The value in each node is processed as the node is visited. After the value in a given node is processed, the values in the left subtree are processed, then the values in the right subtree are processed. The **preorderTraversal** of the tree in Fig. 22.18 is

        27 13 6 17 42 33 48

The steps for a **postorderTraversal** (defined at line 86) are:

1. Traverse the left subtree with a **postorderHelper** (defined at line 90).
2. Traverse the right subtree with a **postorderHelper**.
3. Process the value in the node.

The value in each node is not printed until the values of its children are printed. The **postorderTraversal** of the tree in Fig. 22.18 is

        6 17 13 33 48 42 27

The binary search tree facilitates *duplicate elimination.* As the tree is created, attempts to insert a duplicate value are recognized because a duplicate follows the same "go left" or "go right" decisions on each comparison as the original value did. Thus, the duplicate eventually is compared with a node containing the same value. The duplicate value may simply be discarded at this point.

Searching a binary tree for a value that matches a key value is also fast, especially for *tightly packed* trees. In a tightly packed tree, each level contains about twice as many elements as the previous level. Figure 22.18 is a tightly packed binary tree. So a binary search tree with n elements has a minimum of $\log_2 n$ levels, and thus at most $\log_2 n$ comparisons would have to be made either to find a match or to determine that no match exists. This means, for example, that when searching a (tightly packed) 1000-element binary search tree, approximately 10 comparisons need to be made because $2^{10} > 1000$. When searching a (tightly packed) 1,000,000-element binary search tree, approximately 20 comparisons need to be made because $2^{20} > 1,000,000$.

In the Exercises, algorithms are presented for several other binary tree operations, such as deleting an item from a binary tree, printing a binary tree in a two-dimensional tree format and performing a *level-order traversal of a binary tree*. The level-order traversal of a binary tree visits the nodes of the tree row-by-row starting at the root node level. On each level of the tree, the nodes are visited from left to right. Other binary tree exercises include allowing a binary search tree to contain duplicate values, inserting string values in a binary tree and determining how many levels are contained in a binary tree.

Summary

- Dynamic data structures can grow and shrink at execution time.
- Linked lists are collections of data items "lined up in a row"—insertions and deletions can be made anywhere in a linked list.

- Stacks are important in compilers and operating systems—insertions and deletions are made only at one end of a stack—its top.

- Queues represent waiting lines; insertions are made at the back (also referred to as the tail) of a queue, and deletions are made from the front (also referred to as the head) of a queue.

- Binary trees facilitate high-speed searching and sorting of data, efficient elimination of duplicate data items, representing file system directories and compiling expressions into machine language.

- A self-referential class contains a reference that refers to a class object of the same class type. Self-referential objects can be linked together to form useful data structures such as lists, queues, stacks and trees.

- Creating and maintaining dynamic data structures requires dynamic memory allocation—the ability for a program to obtain more memory space at execution time to hold new nodes and to release space no longer needed.

- The limit for dynamic memory allocation can be as large as the available physical memory in the computer or the amount of available disk space in a virtual-memory system. Often, the limits are much smaller because the computer's available memory must be shared among many users.

- Operator **new** takes as an operand the type of the object being dynamically allocated and returns a reference to a newly created object of that type. If no memory is available, **new** throws an **OutOfMemoryError**. The 10 is the **Node** object's data.

- A linked list is a linear collection (i.e., a sequence) of self-referential class objects, called nodes, connected by reference links.

- A linked list is accessed via a reference to the first node of the list. Each subsequent node is accessed via the link-reference member stored in the previous node.

- By convention, the link reference in the last node of a list is set to **null** to mark the end of the list.

- A node can contain data of any type, including objects of other classes.

- Trees are nonlinear data structures.

- A linked list is appropriate when the number of data elements to be represented in the data structure is unpredictable. Linked lists are dynamic, so the length of a list can increase or decrease as necessary.

- The size of a "conventional" Java array cannot be altered—the array size is fixed at creation time.

- Linked lists become full only when the system has insufficient memory to satisfy dynamic storage allocation requests.

- Linked lists can be maintained in sorted order simply by inserting each new element at the proper point in the list.

- List nodes are normally not stored contiguously in memory. Rather, they are logically contiguous.

- Methods that manipulate the contents of a list should be declared **synchronized** so list objects can be multithread safe when used in a multithreaded program. If one thread is modifying the contents of a list, no other thread is allowed to modify the same list at the same time.

- A stack is a constrained version of a linked list—new nodes can be added to a stack and removed from a stack only at the top. A stack is referred to as a last-in, first-out (LIFO) data structure.

- The link member in the bottom node of a stack is set to null to indicate the bottom of the stack.

- The primary methods used to manipulate a stack are **push** and **pop**. Method **push** adds a new node to the top of the stack. Method **pop** removes a node from the top of the stack and returns the **data** object from the popped node.

- Stacks have many interesting applications. When a method call is made, the called method must know how to return to its caller, so the return address is pushed onto the program execution stack.

If a series of method calls occurs, the successive return values are pushed onto the stack in last-in, first-out order so that each method can return to its caller.

- The program execution stack contains the space created for local variables on each invocation of a method. When the method returns to its caller, the space for that method's local variables is popped off the stack, and those variables are no longer known to the program.

- Stacks are also used by compilers in the process of evaluating arithmetic expressions and generating machine language code to process the expressions.

- The technique of implementing each stack method as a call to a **List** method is called delegating—the stack method invoked delegates the call to the appropriate **List** method.

- A queue is a constrained version of a list.

- A queue is similar to a checkout line in a supermarket—the first person in line is serviced first, and other customers enter the line only at the end and wait to be serviced.

- Queue nodes are removed only from the head of the queue, and are inserted only at the tail of the queue. For this reason, a queue is referred to as a first-in, first-out (FIFO) data structure.

- The insert and remove operations for a queue are known as **enqueue** and **dequeue**.

- Queues have many applications in computer systems. Most computers have only a single processor, so only one user at a time can be serviced. Entries for the other users are placed in a queue. The entry at the front of the queue is the next to receive service. Each entry gradually advances to the front of the queue as users receive service.

- Queues are also used to support print spooling. A multiuser environment may have only a single printer. Many users may be generating outputs to be printed. If the printer is busy, other outputs may still be generated. These are "spooled" to disk (much as thread is wound onto a spool) where they wait in a queue until the printer becomes available.

- Information packets also wait in queues in computer networks. Each time a packet arrives at a network node, it must be routed to the next node on the network along the path to the packet's final destination. The routing node routes one packet at a time, so additional packets are enqueued until the router can route them.

- A file server in a computer network handles file access requests from many clients throughout the network. Servers have a limited capacity to service requests from clients. When that capacity is exceeded, client requests wait in queues.

- A tree is a nonlinear, two-dimensional data structure.

- Tree nodes contain two or more links.

- A binary tree is a tree whose nodes all contain two links. The root node is the first node in a tree.

- Each link in the root node refers to a child. The left child is the first node in the left subtree, and the right child is the first node in the right subtree.

- The children of a node are called siblings. A node with no children is called a leaf node.

- Computer scientists normally draw trees from the root node down.

- A binary search tree (with no duplicate node values) has the characteristic that the values in any left subtree are less than the value in its parent node, and the values in any right subtree are greater than the value in its parent node.

- A node can only be inserted as a leaf node in a binary search tree.

- An inorder traversal of a binary search tree processes the node values in ascending order.

- The process of creating a binary search tree actually sorts the data—and thus this process is called the binary tree sort.

- In a preorder traversal, the value in each node is processed as the node is visited. After the value in a given node is processed, the values in the left subtree are processed, then the values in the right subtree are processed.

- In a postorder traversal, the value in each node is processed after the values of its children.

- The binary search tree facilitates duplicate elimination. As the tree is created, attempts to insert a duplicate value are recognized because a duplicate follows the same "go left" or "go right" decisions on each comparison as the original value did. Thus, the duplicate eventually is compared with a node containing the same value. The duplicate value may simply be discarded at this point.

- Searching a binary tree for a value that matches a key value is also fast, especially for tightly packed trees. In a tightly packed tree, each level contains about twice as many elements as the previous level. So a binary search tree with n elements has a minimum of $\log_2 n$ levels, and thus at most $\log_2 n$ comparisons would have to be made either to find a match or to determine that no match exists. This means, for example, that when searching a (tightly packed) 1000-element binary search tree, approximately 10 comparisons need to be made because $2^{10} > 1000$. When searching a (tightly packed) 1,000,000-element binary search tree, approximately 20 comparisons need to be made because $2^{20} > 1,000,000$.

Terminology

binary search tree	nonlinear data structure
binary tree	**null** reference
binary tree sort	**OutOfMemoryError**
child node	parent node
children	**pop**
delete a node	postorder traversal of a binary tree
delegating	preorder traversal of a binary tree
dequeue	program execution stack
duplicate elimination	**push**
dynamic data structures	queue
enqueue	recursive tree traversal algorithms
FIFO (first-in, first-out)	right child
head of a queue	right subtree
inorder traversal of a binary tree	root node
insert a node	self-referential class
leaf node	stack
left child	subtree
left subtree	tail of a queue
level-order traversal of a binary tree	top of a stack
LIFO (last-in, first-out)	traversal
linear data structure	tree
linked list	visit a node
node	

Common Programming Errors

22.1 Not setting the link in the last node of a list to **null** is a common logic error.

22.2 Not setting the link in the bottom node of a stack to **null** is a common logic error.

22.3 Not setting the link in the last node of a queue to **null** is a common logic error.

22.4 Not setting to **null** the links in leaf nodes of a tree is a common logic error.

Good Programming Practice

22.1   When using **new**, test for an *OutOfMemoryError*. Perform appropriate error processing if the requested memory is not allocated.

Performance Tips

22.1   An array can be declared to contain more elements than the number of items expected, but this can waste memory. Linked lists can provide better memory utilization in these situations. Linked lists allow the program to adapt at run time.

22.2   Insertion into a linked list is fast—only two references have to be modified (after you have located the place to do the insertion). All existing nodes remain at their current locations in memory.

22.3   Insertion and deletion in a sorted array can be time consuming—all the elements following the inserted or deleted element must be shifted appropriately.

22.4   The elements of an array are stored contiguously in memory. This allows immediate access to any array element because the address of any element can be calculated directly based on its offset from the beginning of the array. Linked lists do not afford such immediate access to their elements—an element can be accessed only by traversing the list.

22.5   Using dynamic memory allocation (instead of arrays) for data structures that grow and shrink at execution time can save memory. Keep in mind, however, that references occupy space, and that dynamic memory allocation incurs the overhead of method calls.

Self-Review Exercises

22.1   Fill in the blanks in each of the following:

a)   A self-_____ class is used to form dynamic data structures that can grow and shrink at execution time.

b)   Operator _____ is used to dynamically allocate memory; this operator returns a reference to the allocated memory.

c)   A _____ is a constrained version of a linked list in which nodes can be inserted and deleted only from the start of the list; this data structure returns node values in last-in, first-out order.

d)   A method that does not alter a linked list but simply looks at the list to determine if it is empty is referred to as a _____ method.

e)   A queue is referred to as a _____ data structure because the first nodes inserted are the first nodes removed.

f)   The reference to the next node in a linked list is referred to as a _____.

g)   Automatically reclaiming dynamically allocated memory in Java is called _____.

h)   A _____ is a constrained version of a linked list in which nodes can be inserted only at the end of the list and deleted only from the start of the list.

i)   A _____ is a nonlinear, two-dimensional data structure that contains nodes with two or more links.

j)   A stack is referred to as a _____ data structure because the last node inserted is the first node removed.

k)   The nodes of a _____ tree contain two link members.

l)   The first node of a tree is the _____ node.

m)   Each link in a tree node refers to a _____ or _____ of that node.

n)   A tree node that has no children is called a _____ node.

o)   The four traversal algorithms we mentioned in the text for binary search trees are _____, _____, _____ and _____.

22.2   What are the differences between a linked list and a stack?

22.3   What are the differences between a stack and a queue?

22.4   Perhaps a more appropriate title for this chapter would have been "Reusable Data Structures." Comment on how each of the following entities or concepts contributes to the reusability of data structures:
  a) classes
  b) inheritance
  c) composition

22.5   Manually provide the inorder, preorder and postorder traversals of the binary search tree of Fig. 22.19.

Answers to Self-Review Exercises

22.1   a) referential.   b) **new**.   c) stack.   d) predicate.   e) first-in, first-out (FIFO).   f) link.   g) garbage collection.   h) queue.   i) tree.   j) last-in, first-out (LIFO).   k) binary.   l) root.   m) child or subtree.   n) leaf.   o) inorder, preorder, postorder, level order.

22.2   It is possible to insert a node anywhere in a linked list and remove a node from anywhere in a linked list. Nodes in a stack may only be inserted at the top of the stack and removed from the top of a stack.

22.3   A queue has references to both its head and its tail so that nodes may be inserted at the tail and deleted from the head. A stack has a single reference to the top of the stack where both insertion and deletion of nodes are performed.

22.4   a) Classes allow us to instantiate as many data structure objects of a certain type (i.e., class) as we wish.
  b) Inheritance enables us to reuse code from a superclass in a subclass so that the derived class data structure is also a base-class data structure.
  c) Composition enables us to reuse code by making a class object data structure a member of a composed class; if we make the class object a **private** member of the composed class, then the class object's public methods are not available through the composed object's interface.

22.5   The inorder traversal is

        11 18 19 28 32 40 44 49 69 71 72 83 92 97 99

The preorder traversal is

        49 28 18 11 19 40 32 44 83 71 69 72 97 92 99

The postorder traversal is

        11 19 18 32 44 40 28 669 72 71 92 99 97 83 49

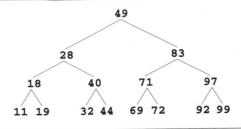

Fig. 22.19   A 15-node binary search tree.

Exercises

22.6   Write a program that concatenates two linked list objects of characters. Class `ListConcat` should include method `concatenate` that takes references to both list objects as arguments and concatenates the second list to the first list.

22.7   Write a program that merges two ordered list objects of integers into a single ordered list object of integers. Method `merge` of class `ListMerge` should receive references to each of the list objects to be merged, and should return a reference to the merged list object.

22.8   Write a program that inserts 25 random integers from 0 to 100 in order into a linked list object. The program should calculate the sum of the elements and the floating-point average of the elements.

22.9   Write a program that creates a linked list object of 10 characters, then creates a second list object containing a copy of the first list, but in reverse order.

22.10   Write a program that inputs a line of text and uses a stack object to print the line reversed.

22.11   Write a program that uses a stack to determine if a string is a palindrome (i.e., the string is spelled identically backward and forward). The program should ignore spaces and punctuation.

22.12   Stacks are used by compilers to help in the process of evaluating expressions and generating machine language code. In this and the next exercise, we investigate how compilers evaluate arithmetic expressions consisting only of constants, operators and parentheses.

Humans generally write expressions like **3 + 4** and **7 / 9** in which the operator (**+** or **/** here) is written between its operands—this is called *infix notation*. Computers "prefer" *postfix notation* in which the operator is written to the right of its two operands. The preceding infix expressions would appear in postfix notation as **3 4 +** and **7 9 /**, respectively.

To evaluate a complex infix expression, a compiler would first convert the expression to postfix notation, and then evaluate the postfix version of the expression. Each of these algorithms requires only a single left-to-right pass of the expression. Each algorithm uses a stack object in support of its operation, and in each algorithm the stack is used for a different purpose.

In this exercise, you will write a Java version of the infix-to-postfix conversion algorithm. In the next exercise, you will write a Java version of the postfix expression evaluation algorithm. In a later exercise, you will discover that code you write in this exercise can help you implement a complete working compiler.

Write class **InfixToPostfixConverter** to convert an ordinary infix arithmetic expression (assume a valid expression is entered) with single-digit integers such as

```
(6 + 2) * 5 - 8 / 4
```

to a postfix expression. The postfix version of the preceding infix expression is (note that no parenthesis are needed)

```
6 2 + 5 * 8 4 / -
```

The program should read the expression into **StringBuffer infix**, and use one of the stack classes implemented in this chapter to help create the postfix expression in **StringBuffer postfix**. The algorithm for creating a postfix expression is as follows:

    a) Push a left parenthesis **' ('** on the stack.
    b) Append a right parenthesis **') '** to the end of **infix**.
    c) While the stack is not empty, read **infix** from left to right and do the following:
            If the current character in **infix** is a digit, append it to **postfix**.
            If the current character in **infix** is a left parenthesis, push it on the stack.

If the current character in **infix** is an operator:

Pop operators (if there are any) at the top of the stack while they have equal or higher precedence than the current operator, and append the popped operators to **postfix**.

Push the current character in **infix** on the stack.

If the current character in **infix** is a right parenthesis:

Pop operators from the top of the stack and append them to **postfix** until a left parenthesis is at the top of the stack.

Pop (and discard) the left parenthesis from the stack.

The following arithmetic operations are allowed in an expression:

+	addition
–	subtraction
*	multiplication
/	division
^	exponentiation
%	modulus

The stack should be maintained with stack nodes that each contain an instance variable and a reference to the next stack node. Some of the methods you may want to provide are:

a) Method **convertToPostfix**, which converts the infix expression to postfix notation.

b) Method **isOperator**, which determines if **c** is an operator.

c) Method **precedence**, which determines if the precedence of **operator1** (from the infix expression) is less than, equal to, or greater than the precedence of **operator2** (from the stack). The method returns **true** if **operator1** has lower precedence than **operator2**. Otherwise, **false** is returned.

d) Method **stackTop** (this should be added to the stack class), which returns the top value of the stack without popping the stack.

22.13 Write class **PostfixEvaluator**, which evaluates a postfix expression (assume it is valid) such as

        6 2 + 5 * 8 4 / -

The program should read a postfix expression consisting of digits and operators into a **StringBuffer**. Using modified versions of the stack methods implemented earlier in this chapter, the program should scan the expression and evaluate it. The algorithm is as follows:

a) Append a right parenthesis (**')'**) to the end of the postfix expression. When the right-parenthesis character is encountered, no further processing is necessary.

b) When the right-parenthesis character has not been encountered, read the expression from left to right.

If the current character is a digit:

Push its integer value on the stack (the integer value of a digit character is its value in the computer's character set minus the value of **'0'** in Unicode).

Otherwise, if the current character is an *operator*:

Pop the two top elements of the stack into variables **x** and **y**.

Calculate **y** *operator* **x**.

Push the result of the calculation onto the stack.

c) When the right parenthesis is encountered in the expression, pop the top value of the stack. This is the result of the postfix expression.

[*Note:* In b) above (based on the sample expression at the beginning of this exercises), if the operator is **'/'**, the top of the stack is **2** and the next element in the stack is **8**, then pop **2** into **x**, pop **8** into **y**, evaluate **8 / 2** and push the result, **4**, back on the stack. This note also applies to operator **'-'**.]
The arithmetic operations allowed in an expression are:

+ addition
– subtraction
* multiplication
/ division
^ exponentiation
% modulus

The stack should be maintained with one of the stack classes introduced in this chapter. You may want to provide the following methods:

    a) Method **evaluatePostfixExpression**, which evaluates the postfix expression.
    b) Method **calculate**, which evaluates the expression **op1 operator op2**.
    c) Method **push**, which pushes a value on the stack.
    d) Method **pop**, which pops a value off the stack.
    e) Method **isEmpty**, which determines if the stack is empty.
    f) Method **printStack**, which prints the stack.

22.14 Modify the postfix evaluator program of Exercise 22.13 so that it can process integer operands larger than 9.

22.15 *(Supermarket Simulation)* Write a program that simulates a checkout line at a supermarket. The line is a queue object. Customers (i.e., customer objects) arrive in random integer intervals of 1 to 4 minutes. Also, each customer is serviced in random integer intervals of 1 to 4 minutes. Obviously, the rates need to be balanced. If the average arrival rate is larger than the average service rate, the queue will grow infinitely. Even with "balanced" rates, randomness can still cause long lines. Run the supermarket simulation for a 12-hour day (720 minutes) using the following algorithm:

    a) Choose a random integer between 1 and 4 to determine the minute at which the first customer arrives.
    b) At the first customer's arrival time:
       Determine customer's service time (random integer from 1 to 4).
       Begin servicing the customer.
       Schedule the arrival time of the next customer (random integer 1 to 4 added to the current time).
    c) For each minute of the day:
          If the next customer arrives:
             Say so.
             Enqueue the customer.
             Schedule the arrival time of the next customer.
          If service was completed for the last customer:
             Say so.
             Dequeue next customer to be serviced.
             Determine customer's service completion time (random integer from 1 to 4 added to the current time).

Now run your simulation for 720 minutes and answer each of the following:

    a) What is the maximum number of customers in the queue at any time?
    b) What is the longest wait any one customer experiences?
    c) What happens if the arrival interval is changed from 1 to 4 minutes to 1 to 3 minutes?

22.16 Modify the program of Fig. 22.15 to allow the binary tree object to contain duplicates.

22.17 Write a program based on the program of Fig. 22.16 that inputs a line of text, tokenizes the sentence into separate words (you may want to use the **StreamTokenizer** class from the **java.io** package), inserts the words in a binary search tree and prints the inorder, preorder and postorder traversals of the tree.

22.18   In this chapter, we saw that duplicate elimination is straightforward when creating a binary search tree. Describe how you would perform duplicate elimination using only a single-subscripted array. Compare the performance of array-based duplicate elimination with the performance of binary-search-tree-based duplicate elimination.

22.19   Write a method **depth** that receives a binary tree and determines how many levels it has.

22.20   (*Recursively Print a List Backwards*) Write a method **printListBackwards** that recursively outputs the items in a linked list object in reverse order. Write a test program that creates a sorted list of integers and prints the list in reverse order.

22.21   (*Recursively Search a List*) Write a method **searchList** that recursively searches a linked list object for a specified value. Method **searchList** should return a reference to the value if it is found; otherwise, null should be returned. Use your method in a test program that creates a list of integers. The program should prompt the user for a value to locate in the list.

22.22   (*Binary Tree Delete*) In this exercise, we discuss deleting items from binary search trees. The deletion algorithm is not as straightforward as the insertion algorithm. There are three cases that are encountered when deleting an item—the item is contained in a leaf node (i.e., it has no children), the item is contained in a node that has one child or the item is contained in a node that has two children.

If the item to be deleted is contained in a leaf node, the node is deleted and the reference in the parent node is set to null.

If the item to be deleted is contained in a node with one child, the reference in the parent node is set to reference the child node and the node containing the data item is deleted. This causes the child node to take the place of the deleted node in the tree.

The last case is the most difficult. When a node with two children is deleted, another node in the tree must take its place. However, the reference in the parent node cannot simply be assigned to reference one of the children of the node to be deleted. In most cases, the resulting binary search tree would not adhere to the following characteristic of binary search trees (with no duplicate values): *The values in any left subtree are less than the value in the parent node, and the values in any right subtree are greater than the value in the parent node.*

Which node is used as a *replacement node* to maintain this characteristic? Either the node containing the largest value in the tree less than the value in the node being deleted, or the node containing the smallest value in the tree greater than the value in the node being deleted. Let us consider the node with the smaller value. In a binary search tree, the largest value less than a parent's value is located in the left subtree of the parent node and is guaranteed to be contained in the rightmost node of the subtree. This node is located by walking down the left subtree to the right until the reference to the right child of the current node is null. We are now referencing the replacement node which is either a leaf node or a node with one child to its left. If the replacement node is a leaf node, the steps to perform the deletion are as follows:

    a) Store the reference to the node to be deleted in a temporary reference variable.
    b) Set the reference in the parent of the node being deleted to reference the replacement node.
    c) Set the reference in the parent of the replacement node to null.
    d) Set the reference to the right subtree in the replacement node to reference the right subtree of the node to be deleted.
    e) Set the reference to the left subtree in the replacement node to reference the left subtree of the node to be deleted.

The deletion steps for a replacement node with a left child are similar to those for a replacement node with no children, but the algorithm also must move the child into the replacement node's position in the tree. If the replacement node is a node with a left child, the steps to perform the deletion are as follows:

a) Store the reference to the node to be deleted in a temporary reference variable.

b) Set the reference in the parent of the node being deleted to reference the replacement node.

c) Set the reference in the parent of the replacement node reference to the left child of the replacement node.

d) Set the reference to the right subtree in the replacement node reference to the right subtree of the node to be deleted.

e) Set the reference to the left subtree in the replacement node to reference the left subtree of the node to be deleted.

Write method **deleteNode**, which takes as its argument the value to be deleted. Method **deleteNode** should locate in the tree the node containing the value to be deleted and use the algorithms discussed here to delete the node. If the value is not found in the tree, the method should print a message that indicates whether or not the value is deleted. Modify the program of Fig. 22.16 to use this method. After deleting an item, call the methods **inorderTraversal**, **preorderTraversal** and **postorderTraversal** to confirm that the delete operation was performed correctly.

22.23 (*Binary Tree Search*) Write method **binaryTreeSearch**, which attempts to locate a specified value in a binary search tree object. The method should take as an argument a search key to be located. If the node containing the search key is found, the method should return a reference to that node; otherwise, the method should return a null reference.

22.24 (*Level-Order Binary Tree Traversal*) The program of Fig. 22.16 illustrated three recursive methods of traversing a binary tree—inorder, preorder, and postorder traversals. This exercise presents the *level-order traversal* of a binary tree, in which the node values are printed level-by-level starting at the root node level. The nodes on each level are printed from left to right. The level-order traversal is not a recursive algorithm. It uses a queue object to control the output of the nodes. The algorithm is as follows:

a) Insert the root node in the queue.

b) While there are nodes left in the queue:

Get the next node in the queue.

Print the node's value.

If the reference to the left child of the node is not null:

Insert the left child node in the queue.

If the reference to the right child of the node is not null:

Insert the right child node in the queue.

Write method **levelOrder** to perform a level-order traversal of a binary tree object. Modify the program of Fig 22.16 to use this method. [*Note:* You will also need to use queue-processing methods of Fig. 22.12 in this program.]

22.25 (*Printing Trees*) Write a recursive method **outputTree** to display a binary tree object on the screen. The method should output the tree row-by-row with the top of the tree at the left of the screen and the bottom of the tree toward the right of the screen. Each row is output vertically. For example, the binary tree illustrated in Fig. 22.19 is output as shown on the top of the next page.

Note that the rightmost leaf node appears at the top of the output in the rightmost column and the root node appears at the left of the output. Each column of output starts five spaces to the right of the preceding column. Method **outputTree** should receive an argument **totalSpaces** representing the number of spaces preceding the value to be output (this variable should start at zero so the root node is output at the left of the screen). The method uses a modified inorder traversal to output the tree—it starts at the rightmost node in the tree and works back to the left. The algorithm is as follows:

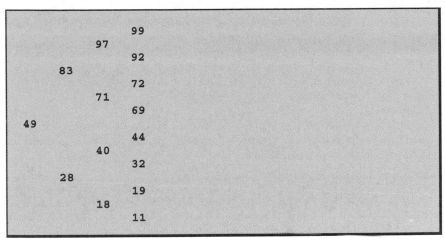

```
                                99
                        97
                                92
                83
                                72
                        71
                                69
        49
                                44
                        40
                                32
                28
                                19
                        18
                                11
```

While the reference to the current node is not null:

    Recursively call **outputTree** with the right subtree of the current node and **totalSpaces** + 5.

    Use a **for** structure to count from 1 to **totalSpaces** and output spaces.

    Output the value in the current node.

    Set the reference to the current node to refer to the left subtree of the current node.

    Increment **totalSpaces** by 5.

Special Section: Building Your Own Compiler

In Exercises 7.42 and 7.43, we introduced Simpletron Machine Language (SML) and you implemented a Simpletron computer simulator to execute programs written in SML. In this section, we build a compiler that converts programs written in a high-level programming language to SML. This section "ties" together the entire programming process. You will write programs in this new high-level language, compile these programs on the compiler you build and run the programs on the simulator you built in Exercise 7.43. You should make every effort to implement your compiler in an object-oriented manner.

22.26 (*The Simple Language*) Before we begin building the compiler, we discuss a simple, yet powerful high-level language similar to early versions of the popular language Basic. We call the language *Simple*. Every Simple *statement* consists of a *line number* and a Simple *instruction*. Line numbers must appear in ascending order. Each instruction begins with one of the following Simple *commands*: **rem**, **input**, **let**, **print**, **goto**, **if/goto** or **end** (see Fig. 22.20). All commands except **end** can be used repeatedly. Simple evaluates only integer expressions using the **+**, **-**, ***** and **/** operators. These operators have the same precedence as in Java. Parentheses can be used to change the order of evaluation of an expression.

    Our Simple compiler recognizes only lowercase letters. All characters in a Simple file should be lowercase (uppercase letters result in a syntax error unless they appear in a **rem** statement, in which case they are ignored). A *variable name* is a single letter. Simple does not allow descriptive variable names, so variables should be explained in remarks to indicate their use in a program. Simple uses only integer variables. Simple does not have variable declarations—merely mentioning a variable name in a program causes the variable to be declared and initialized to zero automatically. The syntax of Simple does not allow string manipulation (reading a string, writing a string, comparing strings, etc.). If a string is encountered in a Simple program (after a command other than **rem**), the compiler generates a syntax error. The first version of our compiler assumes that Simple programs are entered correctly. Exercise 22.29 asks the reader to modify the compiler to perform syntax error checking.

Simple uses the conditional **if/goto** statement and the unconditional **goto** statement to alter the flow of control during program execution. If the condition in the **if/goto** statement is true, control is transferred to a specific line of the program. The following relational and equality operators are valid in an **if/goto** statement: **<, >, <=, >=, ==** or **!=**. The precedence of these operators is the same as in Java.

Let us now consider several programs that demonstrate Simple's features. The first program (Fig. 22.21) reads two integers from the keyboard, stores the values in variables **a** and **b** and computes and prints their sum (stored in variable **c**).

Command	Example statement	Description
rem	50 rem this is a remark	Any text following the command **rem** is for documentation purposes only and is ignored by the compiler.
input	30 input x	Display a question mark to prompt the user to enter an integer. Read that integer from the keyboard and store the integer in **x**.
let	80 let u = 4 * (j - 56)	Assign **u** the value of **4 * (j - 56)**. Note that an arbitrarily complex expression can appear to the right of the equal sign.
print	10 print w	Display the value of **w**.
goto	70 goto 45	Transfer program control to line **45**.
if/goto	35 if i == z goto 80	Compare **i** and **z** for equality and transfer program control to line **80** if the condition is true; otherwise, continue execution with the next statement.
end	99 end	Terminate program execution.

Fig. 22.20 Simple commands.

```
1    10 rem    determine and print the sum of two integers
2    15 rem
3    20 rem    input the two integers
4    30 input a
5    40 input b
6    45 rem
7    50 rem    add integers and store result in c
8    60 let c = a + b
9    65 rem
10   70 rem    print the result
11   80 print c
12   90 rem    terminate program execution
13   99 end
```

Fig. 22.21   Simple program that determines the sum of two integers.

The program of Fig. 22.22 determines and prints the larger of two integers. The integers are input from the keyboard and stored in **s** and **t**. The **if/goto** statement tests the condition **s >= t**. If the condition is true, control is transferred to line **90** and **s** is output; otherwise, **t** is output and control is transferred to the **end** statement in line **99**, where the program terminates.

Simple does not provide a repetition structure (such as Java's **for, while** or **do/while**). However, Simple can simulate each of Java's repetition structures using the **if/goto** and **goto** statements. Figure 22.23 uses a sentinel-controlled loop to calculate the squares of several integers. Each integer is input from the keyboard and stored in variable **j**. If the value entered is the sentinel value **-9999**, control is transferred to line **99**, where the program terminates. Otherwise, **k** is assigned the square of **j, k** is output to the screen and control is passed to line **20**, where the next integer is input.

Using the sample programs of Figs. 22.21, 22.22 and 22.23 as your guide, write a Simple program to accomplish each of the following:

a) Input three integers, determine their average and print the result.

b) Use a sentinel-controlled loop to input 10 integers and compute and print their sum.

c) Use a counter-controlled loop to input 7 integers, some positive and some negative, and compute and print their average.

```
1    10 rem     determine and print the larger of two integers
2    20 input s
3    30 input t
4    32 rem
5    35 rem     test if s >= t
6    40 if s >= t goto 90
7    45 rem
8    50 rem     t is greater than s, so print t
9    60 print t
10   70 goto 99
11   75 rem
12   80 rem     s is greater than or equal to t, so print s
13   90 print s
14   99 end
```

Fig. 22.22 Simple program that finds the larger of two integers.

```
1    10 rem     calculate the squares of several integers
2    20 input j
3    23 rem
4    25 rem     test for sentinel value
5    30 if j == -9999 goto 99
6    33 rem
7    35 rem     calculate square of j and assign result to k
8    40 let k = j * j
9    50 print k
10   53 rem
11   55 rem     loop to get next j
12   60 goto 20
13   99 end
```

Fig. 22.23 Calculate the squares of several integers.

d) Input a series of integers and determine and print the largest. The first integer input indicates how many numbers should be processed.

e) Input 10 integers and print the smallest.

f) Calculate and print the sum of the even integers from 2 to 30.

g) Calculate and print the product of the odd integers from 1 to 9.

22.27 (*Building A Compiler; Prerequisite: Complete Exercises 7.42, 7.43, 22.12, 22.13, and 22.26*) Now that the Simple language has been presented (Exercise 22.26), we discuss how to build a Simple compiler. First, we consider the process by which a Simple program is converted to SML and executed by the Simpletron simulator (see Fig. 22.24). A file containing a Simple program is read by the compiler and converted to SML code. The SML code is output to a file on disk, in which SML instructions appear one per line. The SML file is then loaded into the Simpletron simulator, and the results are sent to a file on disk and to the screen. Note that the Simpletron program developed in Exercise 7.43 took its input from the keyboard. It must be modified to read from a file so it can run the programs produced by our compiler.

The Simple compiler performs two *passes* of the Simple program to convert it to SML. The first pass constructs a *symbol table* (object) in which every *line number* (object), *variable name* (object) and *constant* (object) of the Simple program is stored with its type and corresponding location in the final SML code (the symbol table is discussed in detail below). The first pass also produces the corresponding SML instruction object(s) for each of the Simple statements (object, etc.). If the Simple program contains statements that transfer control to a line later in the program, the first pass results in an SML program containing some "unfinished" instructions. The second pass of the compiler locates and completes the unfinished instructions, and outputs the SML program to a file.

First Pass

The compiler begins by reading one statement of the Simple program into memory. The line must be separated into its individual *tokens* (i.e., "pieces" of a statement) for processing and compilation (the **StreamTokenizer** class from the **java.io** package can be used). Recall that every statement begins with a line number followed by a command. As the compiler breaks a statement into tokens, if the token is a line number, a variable or a constant, it is placed in the symbol table. A line number is placed in the symbol table only if it is the first token in a statement. The **symbolTable** object is an array of **tableEntry** objects representing each symbol in the program. There is no restriction on the number of symbols that can appear in the program. Therefore, the **symbolTable** for a particular program could be large. Make the **symbolTable** a 100-element array for now. You can increase or decrease its size once the program is working.

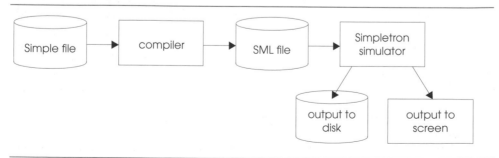

Fig. 22.24   Writing, compiling and executing a Simple language program.

Each **tableEntry** object contains three members. Member **symbol** is an integer containing the Unicode representation of a variable (remember that variable names are single characters), a line number or a constant. Member **type** is one of the following characters indicating the symbol's type: **'C'** for constant, **'L'** for line number or **'V'** for variable. Member **location** contains the Simpletron memory location (**00** to **99**) to which the symbol refers. Simpletron memory is an array of 100 integers in which SML instructions and data are stored. For a line number, the location is the element in the Simpletron memory array at which the SML instructions for the Simple statement begin. For a variable or constant, the location is the element in the Simpletron memory array in which the variable or constant is stored. Variables and constants are allocated from the end of Simpletron's memory backwards. The first variable or constant is stored at location **99**, the next at location **98**, etc.

The symbol table plays an integral part in converting Simple programs to SML. We learned in Chapter 7 that an SML instruction is a four-digit integer comprised of two parts—the *operation code* and the *operand*. The operation code is determined by commands in Simple. For example, the simple command **input** corresponds to SML operation code **10** (read), and the Simple command **print** corresponds to SML operation code **11** (write). The operand is a memory location containing the data on which the operation code performs its task (e.g., operation code **10** reads a value from the keyboard and stores it in the memory location specified by the operand). The compiler searches **symbolTable** to determine the Simpletron memory location for each symbol, so the corresponding location can be used to complete the SML instructions.

The compilation of each Simple statement is based on its command. For example, after the line number in a **rem** statement is inserted in the symbol table, the remainder of the statement is ignored by the compiler because a remark is for documentation purposes only. The **input**, **print**, **goto** and **end** statements correspond to the SML *read*, *write*, *branch* (to a specific location) and *halt* instructions. Statements containing these Simple commands are converted directly to SML (note that a **goto** statement may contain an unresolved reference if the specified line number refers to a statement further into the Simple program file; this is sometimes called a forward reference).

When a **goto** statement is compiled with an unresolved reference, the SML instruction must be *flagged* to indicate that the second pass of the compiler must complete the instruction. The flags are stored in 100-element array **flags** of type **int** in which each element is initialized to **-1**. If the memory location to which a line number in the Simple program refers is not yet known (i.e., it is not in the symbol table), the line number is stored in array **flags** in the element with the same subscript as the incomplete instruction. The operand of the incomplete instruction is set to **00** temporarily. For example, an unconditional branch instruction (making a forward reference) is left as **+4000** until the second pass of the compiler. The second pass of the compiler will be described shortly.

Compilation of **if/goto** and **let** statements is more complicated than other statements— they are the only statements that produce more than one SML instruction. For an **if/goto** statement, the compiler produces code to test the condition and to branch to another line if necessary. The result of the branch could be an unresolved reference. Each of the relational and equality operators can be simulated using SML's *branch zero* and *branch negative* instructions (or possibly a combination of both).

For a **let** statement, the compiler produces code to evaluate an arbitrarily complex arithmetic expression consisting of integer variables and/or constants. Expressions should separate each operand and operator with spaces. Exercises 22.12 and 22.13 presented the infix-to-postfix conversion algorithm and the postfix evaluation algorithm used by compilers to evaluate expressions. Before proceeding with your compiler, you should complete each of these exercises. When a compiler encounters an expression, it converts the expression from infix notation to postfix notation, then evaluates the postfix expression.

How is it that the compiler produces the machine language to evaluate an expression containing variables? The postfix evaluation algorithm contains a "hook" where the compiler can generate SML instructions rather than actually evaluating the expression. To enable this "hook" in the compiler, the postfix evaluation algorithm must be modified to search the symbol table for each symbol it encounters (and possibly insert it), determine the symbol's corresponding memory location and *push the memory location on the stack (instead of the symbol)*. When an operator is encountered in the postfix expression, the two memory locations at the top of the stack are popped and machine language for effecting the operation is produced using the memory locations as operands. The result of each subexpression is stored in a temporary location in memory and pushed back onto the stack so the evaluation of the postfix expression can continue. When postfix evaluation is complete, the memory location containing the result is the only location left on the stack. This is popped and SML instructions are generated to assign the result to the variable at the left of the **let** statement.

Second Pass

The second pass of the compiler performs two tasks: resolve any unresolved references and output the SML code to a file. Resolution of references occurs as follows:

  a) Search the **flags** array for an unresolved reference (i.e., an element with a value other than **-1**).
  b) Locate the object in array **symbolTable** containing the symbol stored in the **flags** array (be sure that the type of the symbol is **'L'** for line number).
  c) Insert the memory location from member **location** into the instruction with the unresolved reference (remember that an instruction containing an unresolved reference has operand **00**).
  d) Repeat steps 1, 2, and 3 until the end of the **flags** array is reached.

After the resolution process is complete, the entire array containing the SML code is output to a disk file with one SML instruction per line. This file can be read by the Simpletron for execution (after the simulator is modified to read its input from a file). Compiling your first Simple program into an SML file and then executing that file should give you a real sense of personal accomplishment.

A Complete Example

The following example illustrates complete conversion of a Simple program to SML as it will be performed by the Simple compiler. Consider a Simple program that inputs an integer and sums the values from 1 to that integer. The program and the SML instructions produced by the first pass of the Simple compiler are illustrated in Fig. 22.25. The symbol table constructed by the first pass is shown in Fig. 22.26.

Simple program	SML location and instruction		Description
`5 rem sum 1 to x`	*none*		**rem** ignored
`10 input x`	00	+1099	read **x** into location **99**
`15 rem check y == x`	*none*		**rem** ignored
`20 if y == x goto 60`	01	+2098	load **y** (**98**) into accumulator
	02	+3199	sub **x** (**99**) from accumulator
	03	+4200	branch zero to unresolved location
`25 rem    increment y`	*none*		**rem** ignored
`30 let y = y + 1`	04	+2098	load **y** into accumulator

Fig. 22.25 SML instructions produced after the compiler's first pass (part 1 of 2).

Simple program	SML location and instruction		Description
	05	+3097	add **1** (**97**) to accumulator
	06	+2196	store in temporary location **96**
	07	+2096	load from temporary location **96**
	08	+2198	store accumulator in **y**
35 rem add y to total	*none*		**rem** ignored
40 let t = t + y	09	+2095	load **t** (**95**) into accumulator
	10	+3098	add **y** to accumulator
	11	+2194	store in temporary location **94**
	12	+2094	load from temporary location **94**
	13	+2195	store accumulator in **t**
45 rem loop y	*none*		**rem** ignored
50 goto 20	14	+4001	branch to location **01**
55 rem output result	*none*		**rem** ignored
60 print t	15	+1195	output **t** to screen
99 end	16	+4300	terminate execution

Fig. 22.25 SML instructions produced after the compiler's first pass (part 2 of 2).

Symbol	Type	Location
5	L	00
10	L	00
'x'	V	99
15	L	01
20	L	01
'y'	V	98
25	L	04
30	L	04
1	C	97
35	L	09
40	L	09
't'	V	95
45	L	14
50	L	14

Fig. 22.26 Symbol table for program of Fig. 22.25 (part 1 of 2).

Symbol	Type	Location
55	L	15
60	L	15
99	L	16

Fig. 22.26 Symbol table for program of Fig. 22.25 (part 2 of 2).

Most Simple statements convert directly to single SML instructions. The exceptions in this program are remarks, the **if/goto** statement in line **20** and the **let** statements. Remarks do not translate into machine language. However, the line number for a remark is placed in the symbol table in case the line number is referenced in a **goto** statement or an **if/goto** statement. Line **20** of the program specifies that if the condition **y == x** is true, program control is transferred to line **60**. Because line **60** appears later in the program, the first pass of the compiler has not as yet placed **60** in the symbol table (statement line numbers are placed in the symbol table only when they appear as the first token in a statement). Therefore, it is not possible at this time to determine the operand of the SML *branch zero* instruction at location **03** in the array of SML instructions. The compiler places **60** in location **03** of the **flags** array to indicate that the second pass completes this instruction.

We must keep track of the next instruction location in the SML array because there is not a one-to-one correspondence between Simple statements and SML instructions. For example, the **if/goto** statement of line **20** compiles into three SML instructions. Each time an instruction is produced, we must increment the *instruction counter* to the next location in the SML array. Note that the size of Simpletron's memory could present a problem for Simple programs with many statements, variables and constants. It is conceivable that the compiler will run out of memory. To test for this case, your program should contain a *data counter* to keep track of the location at which the next variable or constant will be stored in the SML array. If the value of the instruction counter is larger than the value of the data counter, the SML array is full. In this case, the compilation process should terminate and the compiler should print an error message indicating that it ran out of memory during compilation. This serves to emphasize that although the programmer is freed from the burdens of managing memory by the compiler, the compiler itself must carefully determine the placement of instructions and data in memory and must check for such errors as memory being exhausted during the compilation process.

A Step-by-Step View of the Compilation Process

Let us now walk through the compilation process for the Simple program in Fig. 22.25. The compiler reads the first line of the program

```
5 rem sum 1 to x
```

into memory. The first token in the statement (the line number) is determined using the **StreamTokenizer** class (see Chapter 10 for a discussion of Java's string manipulation methods). The token returned by the **StreamTokenizer** is converted to an integer using **static** method **Integer.parseInt()** so the symbol **5** can be located in the symbol table. If the symbol is not found, it is inserted in the symbol table.

Since we are at the beginning of the program and this is the first line, no symbols are in the table yet. So, **5** is inserted into the symbol table as type **L** (line number) and assigned the first location in SML array (**00**). Although this line is a remark, a space in the symbol table is still allocated for the line number (in case it is referenced by a **goto** or an **if/goto**). No SML instruction is generated for a **rem** statement, so the instruction counter is not incremented.

The statement

```
10 input x
```

is tokenized next. The line number **10** is placed in the symbol table as type **L** and assigned the first location in the SML array (**00** because a remark began the program, so the instruction counter is currently **00**). The command **input** indicates that the next token is a variable (only a variable can appear in an **input** statement). Because **input** corresponds directly to an SML operation code, the compiler simply has to determine the location of **x** in the SML array. Symbol **x** is not found in the symbol table. So, it is inserted into the symbol table as the Unicode representation of **x**, given type **V**, and assigned location **99** in the SML array (data storage begins at **99** and is allocated backwards). SML code can now be generated for this statement. Operation code **10** (the SML read operation code) is multiplied by 100, and the location of **x** (as determined in the symbol table) is added to complete the instruction. The instruction is then stored in the SML array at location **00**. The instruction counter is incremented by one because a single SML instruction was produced.

The statement

```
15 rem    check y == x
```

is tokenized next. The symbol table is searched for line number **15** (which is not found). The line number is inserted as type **L** and assigned the next location in the array, **01** (remember that **rem** statements do not produce code, so the instruction counter is not incremented).

The statement

```
20 if y == x goto 60
```

is tokenized next. Line number **20** is inserted in the symbol table and given type **L** with the next location in the SML array **01**. The command **if** indicates that a condition is to be evaluated. The variable **y** is not found in the symbol table, so it is inserted and given the type **V** and the SML location **98**. Next, SML instructions are generated to evaluate the condition. Since there is no direct equivalent in SML for the **if/goto**, it must be simulated by performing a calculation using **x** and **y** and branching based on the result. If **y** is equal to **x**, the result of subtracting **x** from **y** is zero, so the *branch zero* instruction can be used with the result of the calculation to simulate the **if/goto** statement. The first step requires that **y** be loaded (from SML location **98**) into the accumulator. This produces the instruction **01 +2098**. Next, **x** is subtracted from the accumulator. This produces the instruction **02 +3199**. The value in the accumulator may be zero, positive or negative. Since the operator is **==**, we want to *branch zero*. First, the symbol table is searched for the branch location (**60** in this case), which is not found. So, **60** is placed in the **flags** array at location **03**, and the instruction **03 +4200** is generated (we cannot add the branch location because we have not yet assigned a location to line **60** in the SML array). The instruction counter is incremented to **04**.

The compiler proceeds to the statement

```
25 rem    increment y
```

The line number **25** is inserted in the symbol table as type **L** and assigned SML location **04**. The instruction counter is not incremented.

When the statement

```
30 let y = y + 1
```

is tokenized, the line number **30** is inserted in the symbol table as type **L** and assigned SML location **04**. Command **let** indicates that the line is an assignment statement. First, all the symbols on the line are inserted in the symbol table (if they are not already there). The integer **1** is added to the symbol table as type **C** and assigned SML location **97**. Next, the right side of the assignment is converted from infix to postfix notation. Then the postfix expression (**y 1 +**) is evaluated. Symbol **y** is located in the symbol table and its corresponding memory location is pushed onto the stack. Symbol **1** is also located in the symbol table and its corresponding memory location is pushed onto the stack. When the operator **+** is encountered, the postfix evaluator pops the stack into the right operand of the operator and pops the stack again into the left operand of the operator, then produces the SML instructions

```
04  +2098     (load y)
05  +3097     (add 1)
```

The result of the expression is stored in a temporary location in memory (**96**) with instruction

```
06  +2196     (store temporary)
```

and the temporary location is pushed on the stack. Now that the expression has been evaluated, the result must be stored in **y** (i.e., the variable on the left side of **=**). So, the temporary location is loaded into the accumulator and the accumulator is stored in **y** with the instructions

```
07  +2096     (load temporary)
08  +2198     (store y)
```

The reader will immediately notice that SML instructions appear to be redundant. We will discuss this issue shortly.

When the statement

```
35 rem    add y to total
```

is tokenized, line number **35** is inserted in the symbol table as type **L** and assigned location **09**.

The statement

```
40 let t = t + y
```

is similar to line **30**. The variable **t** is inserted in the symbol table as type **V** and assigned SML location **95**. The instructions follow the same logic and format as line **30**, and the instructions **09 +2095**, **10 +3098**, **11 +2194**, **12 +2094** and **13 +2195** are generated. Note that the result of **t + y** is assigned to temporary location **94** before being assigned to **t** (**95**). Once again, the reader will note that the instructions in memory locations **11** and **12** appear to be redundant. Again, we will discuss this shortly.

The statement

```
45 rem    loop y
```

is a remark, so line **45** is added to the symbol table as type **L** and assigned SML location **14**.

The statement

```
50 goto 20
```

transfers control to line **20**. Line number **50** is inserted in the symbol table as type **L** and assigned SML location **14**. The equivalent of **goto** in SML is the *unconditional branch* (**40**) instruction that transfers control to a specific SML location. The compiler searches the symbol table for line **20** and finds that it corresponds to SML location **01**. The operation code (**40**) is multiplied by 100 and location **01** is added to it to produce the instruction **14 +4001**.

The statement

```
55 rem    output result
```

is a remark, so line **55** is inserted in the symbol table as type **L** and assigned SML location **15**.
The statement

     60 print t

is an output statement. Line number **60** is inserted in the symbol table as type **L** and assigned SML location **15**. The equivalent of **print** in SML is operation code **11** (*write*). The location of **t** is determined from the symbol table and added to the result of the operation code multiplied by 100.
The statement

     99 end

is the final line of the program. Line number **99** is stored in the symbol table as type **L** and assigned SML location **16**. The **end** command produces the SML instruction **+4300** (**43** is *halt* in SML) which is written as the final instruction in the SML memory array.

This completes the first pass of the compiler. We now consider the second pass. The **flags** array is searched for values other than **–1**. Location **03** contains **60**, so the compiler knows that instruction **03** is incomplete. The compiler completes the instruction by searching the symbol table for **60**, determining its location, and adding the location to the incomplete instruction. In this case, the search determines that line **60** corresponds to SML location **15**, so the completed instruction **03 +4215** is produced, replacing **03 +4200**. The Simple program has now been compiled successfully.

To build the compiler, you will have to perform each of the following tasks:

a) Modify the Simpletron simulator program you wrote in Exercise 5.43 to take its input from a file specified by the user (see Chapter 17). The simulator should output its results to a disk file in the same format as the screen output. Convert the simulator to be an object-oriented program. In particular, make each part of the hardware an object. Arrange the instruction types into a class hierarchy using inheritance. Then execute the program polymorphically simply by telling each instruction to execute itself with an **executeInstruction** message.

b) Modify the infix-to-postfix evaluation algorithm of Exercise 22.12 to process multidigit integer operands and single-letter variable name operands. (*Hint:* Class **StreamTokenizer** can be used to locate each constant and variable in an expression, and constants can be converted from strings to integers using **Integer** class method **parseInt**.) [*Note:* The data representation of the postfix expression must be altered to support variable names and integer constants.]

c) Modify the postfix evaluation algorithm to process multidigit integer operands and variable name operands. Also, the algorithm should now implement the "hook" discussed above so that SML instructions are produced rather than directly evaluating the expression. (*Hint:* Class **StreamTokenizer** can be used to locate each constant and variable in an expression, and constants can be converted from strings to integers using **Integer** class method **parseInt**.) [*Note:* The data representation of the postfix expression must be altered to support variable names and integer constants.]

d) Build the compiler. Incorporate parts b) and c) for evaluating expressions in **let** statements. Your program should contain a method that performs the first pass of the compiler and a method that performs the second pass of the compiler. Both methods can call other methods to accomplish their tasks. Make your compiler as object oriented as possible.

22.28   (*Optimizing the Simple Compiler*) When a program is compiled and converted into SML, a set of instructions is generated. Certain combinations of instructions often repeat themselves, usually in triplets called *productions*. A production normally consists of three instructions, such as *load*, *add* and *store*. For example, Fig. 22.27 illustrates five of the SML instructions that were produced in the compilation of the program in Fig. 22.25. The first three instructions are the production that adds **1**

to **y**. Note that instructions **06** and **07** store the accumulator value in temporary location **96**, then load the value back into the accumulator so instruction **08** can store the value in location **98**. Often a production is followed by a load instruction for the same location that was just stored. This code can be *optimized* by eliminating the store instruction and the subsequent load instruction that operate on the same memory location, thus enabling the Simpletron to execute the program faster. Figure 22.28 illustrates the optimized SML for the program of Fig. 22.25. Note that there are four fewer instructions in the optimized code—a memory-space savings of 25%.

Modify the compiler to provide an option for optimizing the Simpletron Machine Language code it produces. Manually compare the nonoptimized code with the optimized code, and calculate the percentage reduction.

1	**04**	**+2098**	*(load)*
2	**05**	**+3097**	*(add)*
3	**06**	**+2196**	*(store)*
4	**07**	**+2096**	*(load)*
5	**08**	**+2198**	*(store)*

Fig. 22.27   Unoptimized code from the program of Fig. 22.25.

Simple program	SML location and instruction		Description
5 rem sum 1 to x	*none*		**rem** ignored
10 input x	00	+1099	read **x** into location **99**
15 rem check y == x	*none*		**rem** ignored
20 if y == x goto 60	01	+2098	load **y** (**98**) into accumulator
	02	+3199	sub **x** (**99**) from accumulator
	03	+4211	branch to location **11** if zero
25 rem increment y	*none*		**rem** ignored
30 let y = y + 1	04	+2098	load **y** into accumulator
	05	+3097	add **1** (**97**) to accumulator
	06	+2198	store accumulator in **y** (**98**)
35 rem add y to total	*none*		**rem** ignored
40 let t = t + y	07	+2096	load **t** from location (**96**)
	08	+3098	add **y** (**98**) accumulator
	09	+2196	store accumulator in **t** (**96**)
45 rem loop y	*none*		**rem** ignored
50 goto 20	10	+4001	branch to location **01**
55 rem output result	*none*		**rem** ignored
60 print t	11	+1196	output **t** (**96**) to screen
99 end	12	+4300	terminate execution

Fig. 22.28 Optimized code for the program of Fig. 22.25.

22.29   (*Modifications to the Simple Compiler*) Perform the following modifications to the Simple compiler. Some of these modifications may also require modifications to the Simpletron simulator program written in Exercise 5.43.

    a) Allow the modulus operator (**%**) to be used in **let** statements. Simpletron Machine Language must be modified to include a modulus instruction.

    b) Allow exponentiation in a **let** statement using **^** as the exponentiation operator. Simpletron Machine Language must be modified to include an exponentiation instruction.

    c) Allow the compiler to recognize uppercase and lowercase letters in Simple statements (e.g., **'A'** is equivalent to **'a'**). No modifications to the Simpletron simulator are required.

    d) Allow **input** statements to read values for multiple variables such as **input x, y**. No modifications to the Simpletron simulator are required to perform this enhancement to the Simple compiler.

    e) Allow the compiler to output multiple values using a single **print** statement such as **print a, b, c**. No modifications to the Simpletron simulator are required to perform this enhancement.

    f) Add syntax-checking capabilities to the compiler so error messages are output when syntax errors are encountered in a Simple program. No modifications to the Simpletron simulator are required.

    g) Allow arrays of integers. No modifications to the Simpletron simulator are required to perform this enhancement.

    h) Allow subroutines specified by the Simple commands **gosub** and **return**. Command **gosub** passes program control to a subroutine and command **return** passes control back to the statement after the **gosub**. This is similar to a method call in Java. The same subroutine can be called from many **gosub** commands distributed throughout a program. No modifications to the Simpletron simulator are required.

    i) Allow repetition structures of the form

```
for x = 2 to 10 step 2
    Simple statements
next
```

       This **for** statement loops from **2** to **10** with an increment of **2**. The **next** line marks the end of the body of the **for** line. No modifications to the Simpletron simulator are required.

    j) Allow repetition structures of the form

```
for x = 2 to 10
    Simple statements
next
```

       This **for** statement loops from **2** to **10** with a default increment of **1**. No modifications to the Simpletron simulator are required.

    k) Allow the compiler to process string input and output. This requires the Simpletron simulator to be modified to process and store string values. [*Hint:* Each Simpletron word can be divided into two groups, each holding a two-digit integer. Each two-digit integer represents the Unicode decimal equivalent of a character. Add a machine-language instruction that will print a string beginning at a certain Simpletron memory location. The first half of the word at that location is a count of the number of characters in the string (i.e., the length of the string). Each succeeding half word contains one Unicode character expressed as two decimal digits. The machine language instruction checks the length and prints the string by translating each two-digit number into its equivalent character.]

l)   Allow the compiler to process floating-point values in addition to integers. The Simpletron Simulator must also be modified to process floating-point values.

22.30   (*A Simple Interpreter*) An interpreter is a program that reads a high-level language program statement, determines the operation to be performed by the statement and executes the operation immediately. The high-level language program is not converted into machine language first. Interpreters execute slower than compilers do because each statement encountered in the program being interpreted must first be deciphered at execution time. If statements are contained in a loop, the statements are deciphered each time they are encountered in the loop. Early versions of the Basic programming language were implemented as interpreters. Most Java programs are run interpretively.

Write an interpreter for the Simple language discussed in Exercise 22.26. The program should use the infix-to-postfix converter developed in Exercise 22.12 and the postfix evaluator developed in Exercise 22.13 to evaluate expressions in a **let** statement. The same restrictions placed on the Simple language in Exercise 22.26 should be adhered to in this program. Test the interpreter with the Simple programs written in Exercise 22.26. Compare the results of running these programs in the interpreter with the results of compiling the Simple programs and running them in the Simpletron simulator built in Exercise 7.43.

22.31   (*Insert/Delete Anywhere in a Linked List*) Our linked list class allowed insertions and deletions at only the front and the back of the linked list. These capabilities were convenient for us when we used inheritance or composition to produce a stack class and a queue class with a minimal amount of code simply by reusing the list class. Linked lists are normally more general than those we provided. Modify the linked list class we developed in this chapter to handle insertions and deletions anywhere in the list.

22.32   (*Lists and Queues without Tail References*) Our implementation of a linked list (Fig. 22.3) used both a **firstNode** and a **lastNode**. The **lastNode** was useful for the **insertAtBack** and **removeFromBack** methods of the **List** class. The **insertAtBack** method corresponds to the **enqueue** method of the **Queue** class.

Rewrite the **List** class so that it does not use a **lastNode**. Thus, any operations on the tail of a list must begin searching the list from the front. Does this affect our implementation of the **Queue** class (Fig. 22.12)?

22.33   (*Performance of Binary Tree Sorting and Searching*) One problem with the binary tree sort is that the order in which the data is inserted affects the shape of the tree—for the same collection of data, different orderings can yield binary trees of dramatically different shapes. The performance of the binary tree sorting and searching algorithms is sensitive to the shape of the binary tree. What shape would a binary tree have if its data were inserted in increasing order? in decreasing order? What shape should the tree have to achieve maximal searching performance?

22.34   (*Indexed Lists*) As presented in the text, linked lists must be searched sequentially. For large lists, this can result in poor performance. A common technique for improving list searching performance is to create and maintain an index to the list. An index is a set of references to key places in the list. For example, an application that searches a large list of names could improve performance by creating an index with 26 entries—one for each letter of the alphabet. A search operation for a last name beginning with 'Y' would then first search the index to determine where the 'Y' entries begin, and then "jump into" the list at that point and search linearly until the desired name is found. This would be much faster than searching the linked list from the beginning. Use the **List** class of Fig. 22.3 as the basis of an **IndexedList** class.

Write a program that demonstrates the operation of indexed lists. Be sure to include methods **insertInIndexedList**, **searchIndexedList** and **deleteFromIndexedList**.

Java Utilities Package and Bit Manipulation

Objectives

- To understand containers such as classes **Vector** and **Stack**, and the **Enumeration** interface.
- To be able to create **Hashtable** objects and persistent hash tables called **Properties** objects.
- To understand random number generation with instances of class **Random**.
- To use bit manipulation and **BitSet** objects.

Nothing can have value without being an object of utility.
Karl Marx

I've been in Who's Who, *and I know what's what, but this is the first time I ever made the dictionary.*
Mae West

O! many a shaft at random sent
Finds mark the archer little meant!
Sir Walter Scott

There was the Door to which I found no Key;
There was the Veil through which I might not see.
Edward FitzGerald, *The Rubáiyát of Omar Khayyám*, st. 32

"It's a poor sort of memory that only works backwards," the Queen remarked.
Lewis Carroll [Charles Lutwidge Dodgson]

Not by age but by capacity is wisdom acquired.
Titus Maccius Plautus, *Trinummus*, act II, sc. ii, 1.88

Outline

23.1 Introduction

In this chapter we discuss a variety of utility classes in the **java.util** package. We examine the **Vector** class which enables us to create array-like objects that can grow and shrink dynamically as a program's data storage requirements change. We consider the **Enumeration** interface which we use in conjunction with class **Vector** to allow a program to iterate its way through the elements of a container such as a **Vector**.

We discuss the **Stack** class that offers the conventional stack operations **push** and **pop** along with several others we did not consider in Chapter 22.

We present class **Dictionary** which is an **abstract** class that gives us the framework for storing keyed data in tables and retrieving that data. We explain the theory of "hashing," a technique for rapidly storing and retrieving information from tables, and we demonstrate the construction and manipulation of hash tables with Java's **Hashtable** class. We consider the **Properties** class that enables us to create persistent hash tables, i.e., hash tables that can be written to a file with an output stream and eventually read back into the system on demand from an input stream.

We overview class **Random** that provides a richer collection of random number capabilities than is available with **Math.random**.

We present an extensive discussion of bit manipulation operators and then discuss class **BitSet** that enables the creation of bit-array-like objects for setting and getting individual bits.

Chapter 24, "Collections," introduces a framework for manipulating groups of objects called *collections*. Objects of type **Vector**, **Stack** and **Hashtable** are collections.

23.2 **Vector** Class and **Enumeration** Interface

In most programming languages, including Java, conventional arrays are fixed in size—they cannot grow or shrink in response to an application's changing storage requirements. Java class *Vector* provides the capabilities of array-like data structures that can dynamically resize themselves.

At any time the **Vector** contains a certain number of elements which is less than or equal to its *capacity*. The capacity is the space that has been reserved for the array.

Performance Tip 23.1

*Inserting additional elements into a **Vector** whose current size is less than its capacity is a relatively fast operation.*

If a **Vector** needs to grow, it grows by an increment that you specify or by a default assumed by the system.

Performance Tip 23.2

*It is a relatively slow operation to insert an element into a **Vector** that needs to grow larger to accommodate the new element.*

If you do not specify a capacity increment, the system will automatically double the size of the **Vector** each time additional capacity is needed.

Performance Tip 23.3

*The default capacity increment of doubling the size of the **Vector** may seem wasteful of storage, but it is actually an efficient way for many **Vector**s to grow quickly to be "about the right size." This is much more efficient time-wise than growing the **Vector** each time by only as much space as it takes to hold a single element. But it can waste space.*

Performance Tip 23.4

*If storage is at a premium, use the **trimToSize** method of the **Vector** class to trim a **Vector** to its exact size. This will optimize a **Vector**'s use of storage. But be careful. If an additional element needs to be inserted in the **Vector**, this will be slow because it will force the **Vector** to grow dynamically—trimming leaves no room for growth.*

Vectors are designed to store references to **Object**s. Thus, a reference to an object of any class type can be stored in a **Vector**. If you would like to store values of primitive data types in **Vector**s, you must use the type-wrapper classes (e.g., **Integer**, **Long**, **Float**, etc.) from the **java.lang** package to create objects containing the primitive data type values.

The application of Fig. 23.1 demonstrates class **Vector** and many of its methods. A **JButton** is provided for each of the methods. The user can type a **String** into the provided **JTextField**, then press a button to see what the method does. Messages are displayed in a **JLabel** to indicate the results of each operation.

```
1   // Fig. 23.1: VectorTest.java
2   // Testing the Vector class of the java.util package
3   import java.util.*;
4   import java.awt.*;
5   import java.awt.event.*;
6   import javax.swing.*;
7
8   public class VectorTest extends JFrame {
9
10      public VectorTest()
11      {
12          super( "Vector Example" );
13
```

Fig. 23.1   Demonstrating class **Vector** of package **java.util** (part 1 of 5).

```
14          final JLabel status = new JLabel();
15          Container c = getContentPane();
16          final Vector v = new Vector( 1 );
17
18          c.setLayout( new FlowLayout() );
19
20          c.add( new JLabel( "Enter a string" ) );
21          final JTextField input = new JTextField( 10 );
22          c.add( input );
23
24          JButton addBtn = new JButton( "Add" );
25          addBtn.addActionListener(
26             new ActionListener() {
27                public void actionPerformed( ActionEvent e )
28                {
29                   v.addElement( input.getText() );
30                   status.setText( "Added to end: " +
31                                     input.getText() );
32                   input.setText( "" );
33                }
34             }
35          );
36          c.add( addBtn );        // add the input value
37
38          JButton removeBtn = new JButton( "Remove" );
39          removeBtn.addActionListener(
40             new ActionListener() {
41                public void actionPerformed( ActionEvent e )
42                {
43                   if ( v.removeElement( input.getText() ) )
44                      status.setText( "Removed: " +
45                                        input.getText() );
46                   else
47                      status.setText( input.getText() +
48                                        " not in vector" );
49                }
50             }
51          );
52          c.add( removeBtn );
53
54          JButton firstBtn = new JButton( "First" );
55          firstBtn.addActionListener(
56             new ActionListener() {
57                public void actionPerformed( ActionEvent e )
58                {
59                   try {
60                      status.setText( "First element: " +
61                                        v.firstElement() );
62                   }
```

Fig. 23.1   Demonstrating class **Vector** of package **java.util** (part 2 of 5).

```
63                    catch ( NoSuchElementException exception ) {
64                       status.setText( exception.toString() );
65                    }
66                 }
67              }
68           );
69           c.add( firstBtn );
70
71           JButton lastBtn = new JButton( "Last" );
72           lastBtn.addActionListener(
73              new ActionListener() {
74                 public void actionPerformed( ActionEvent e )
75                 {
76                    try {
77                       status.setText( "Last element: " +
78                                         v.lastElement() );
79                    }
80                    catch ( NoSuchElementException exception ) {
81                       status.setText( exception.toString() );
82                    }
83                 }
84              }
85           );
86           c.add( lastBtn );
87
88           JButton emptyBtn = new JButton( "Is Empty?" );
89           emptyBtn.addActionListener(
90              new ActionListener() {
91                 public void actionPerformed( ActionEvent e )
92                 {
93                    status.setText( v.isEmpty() ?
94                       "Vector is empty" : "Vector is not empty" );
95                 }
96              }
97           );
98           c.add( emptyBtn );
99
100          JButton containsBtn = new JButton( "Contains" );
101          containsBtn.addActionListener(
102             new ActionListener() {
103                public void actionPerformed( ActionEvent e )
104                {
105                   String searchKey = input.getText();
106
107                   if ( v.contains( searchKey ) )
108                      status.setText( "Vector contains " +
109                                        searchKey );
110                   else
111                      status.setText( "Vector does not contain " +
112                                        searchKey );
113                }
114             }
115          );
```

Fig. 23.1   Demonstrating class **Vector** of package **java.util** (part 3 of 5).

```
116            c.add( containsBtn );
117
118            JButton locationBtn = new JButton( "Location" );
119            locationBtn.addActionListener(
120               new ActionListener() {
121                  public void actionPerformed( ActionEvent e )
122                  {
123                     status.setText( "Element is at location " +
124                                     v.indexOf( input.getText() ) );
125                  }
126               }
127            );
128            c.add( locationBtn );
129
130            JButton trimBtn = new JButton( "Trim" );
131            trimBtn.addActionListener(
132               new ActionListener() {
133                  public void actionPerformed( ActionEvent e )
134                  {
135                     v.trimToSize();
136                     status.setText( "Vector trimmed to size" );
137                  }
138               }
139            );
140            c.add( trimBtn );
141
142            JButton statsBtn = new JButton( "Statistics" );
143            statsBtn.addActionListener(
144               new ActionListener() {
145                  public void actionPerformed( ActionEvent e )
146                  {
147                     status.setText( "Size = " + v.size() +
148                        "; capacity = " + v.capacity() );
149                  }
150               }
151            );
152            c.add( statsBtn );
153
154            JButton displayBtn = new JButton( "Display" );
155            displayBtn.addActionListener(
156               new ActionListener() {
157                  public void actionPerformed( ActionEvent e )
158                  {
159                     Enumeration enum = v.elements();
160                     StringBuffer buf = new StringBuffer();
161
162                     while ( enum.hasMoreElements() )
163                        buf.append(
164                           enum.nextElement() ).append( "  " );
165
```

Fig. 23.1   Demonstrating class **Vector** of package **java.util** (part 4 of 5).

```
166                       JOptionPane.showMessageDialog( null,
167                           buf.toString(), "Display",
168                           JOptionPane.PLAIN_MESSAGE );
169                   }
170               }
171           );
172           c.add( displayBtn );
173           c.add( status );
174
175           setSize( 300, 200 );
176           show();
177       }
178
179       public static void main( String args[] )
180       {
181           VectorTest app = new VectorTest();
182
183           app.addWindowListener(
184               new WindowAdapter() {
185                   public void windowClosing( WindowEvent e )
186                   {
187                       System.exit( 0 );
188                   }
189               }
190           );
191       }
192   }
```

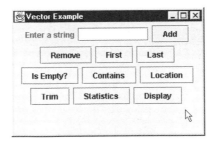

Fig. 23.1   Demonstrating class **Vector** of package **java.util** (part 5 of 5).

The application's constructor creates a **Vector** with the statement (line 16)

```
final Vector v = new Vector( 1 );
```

which creates a **Vector** with an initial capacity of one element. This **Vector** will double
in size each time it needs to grow to accommodate more elements.

Class **Vector** provides three other constructors. The no-argument constructor creates
an empty **Vector** with an *initial capacity* of 10 elements. The constructor that takes two
arguments and creates a **Vector** with an *initial capacity* specified by the first argument
and a *capacity increment* specified by the second argument. Each time this **Vector** needs
to grow, it will add space for the specified number of elements in the capacity increment.
The constructor that takes a **Collection** allows a collection to be manipulated using
Vector methods. In Chapter 24, we discuss **Collection**s.

The statement (line 29)

```
v.addElement( input.getText() );
```

calls **Vector** method *addElement* to add its argument to the end of the **Vector**. The **Vector**'s capacity is increased (if necessary) to accommodate the new element. Class **Vector** also provides method *insertElementAt* to insert an element (the method's first argument) at a specified position (the method's second argument) in the **Vector** and method *setElementAt* to set the element (the method's first argument) at a specific position (the method's second argument) in the **Vector**. Method **insertElementAt** makes room for the new element by shifting elements. Method **setElementAt** replaces the element at the specified position with its argument.

The expression (line 43)

```
v.removeElement( input.getText() )
```

calls **Vector** method *removeElement* to remove the first occurrence of its argument from the **Vector**. The method returns **true** if the element is found in the **Vector**; otherwise, **false** is returned. If the element is removed, all elements after that element in the **Vector** are shifted one position toward the beginning of the **Vector** to fill in the position of the removed element. Class **Vector** also provides method **removeAllElements** to remove every element from the **Vector** and method **removeElementAt** to remove the element at the index specified as an argument.

The expression (line 61)

```
v.firstElement()
```

calls **Vector** method *firstElement* to return a reference to the first element in the **Vector**. This method throws a **NoSuchElementException** if there are no elements currently in the **Vector**.

The expression (line 78)

```
v.lastElement()
```

calls **Vector** method *lastElement* to return a reference to the last element in the **Vector**. This method throws a **NoSuchElementException** if there are no elements currently in the **Vector**.

The expression (line 93)

```
v.isEmpty()
```

calls **Vector** method *isEmpty* to determine if the **Vector** is empty. The method returns **true** if there are no elements in the **Vector**; otherwise, **false** is returned.

The expression (line 107)

```
v.contains( searchKey )
```

calls **Vector** method *contains* to determine if the **Vector** contains the **searchKey** specified as an argument. Method **contains** returns **true** if **searchKey** is in the **Vector**; otherwise, **false** is returned. Method **contains** uses **Object** method **equals** to determine if the **searchKey** is equal to one of the **Vector**'s elements.

The expression (line 124)

```
v.indexOf( input.getText() )
```

calls **Vector** method *indexOf* to get the index of the first location of the argument in the **Vector**. The method returns **–1** if the argument is not found in the **Vector**. There is an overloaded version of this method that takes a second argument specifying the index in the **Vector** where the search should begin.

The statement (line 135)

```
v.trimToSize();
```

calls **Vector** method *trimToSize* to cut the capacity of the **Vector** to the current number of elements in the **Vector** (i.e., the size of the **Vector**).

The expressions (line 147 and 148)

```
v.size()
v.capacity()
```

use **Vector** methods *size* and *capacity* to determine the number of elements currently in the **Vector** and the number of elements that can be stored in the **Vector** without allocating more memory, respectively.

The statement (line 159)

```
Enumeration enum = v.elements();
```

calls **Vector** method *elements* to return a reference to an *Enumeration*. An **Enumeration** provides two methods that allow a program to walk through a set of elements one element at a time. The expression (line 162)

```
enum.hasMoreElements()
```

returns **true** as long as there are more elements in the **Vector**. The expression (line 164)

```
enum.nextElement()
```

returns a reference to the next element in the **Vector**. If there are no more elements, a **NoSuchElementException** is thrown.

For more information on the **Vector** methods, see the Java API documentation.

23.3 Stack Class

In Chapter 22, "Data Structures," we learned how to build fundamental data structures such as linked lists, stacks, queues and trees. In a world of "reuse, reuse, reuse," instead of building data structures as we need them, we will often be able to take advantage of existing data structures classes. In this section, we investigate class *Stack* in the Java utilities package (**java.util**).

We have already discussed class **Vector,** which implements a dynamically resizable array. Class **Stack** extends class **Vector** to implement a stack data structure. Like **Vector**, class **Stack** is designed to store **Object**s; to store primitive data types, you must use the appropriate type-wrapper class (**Boolean**, **Byte**, **Character**, **Short**, **Integer**, **Long**, **Float** or **Double**).

The application of Fig. 23.2 provides a GUI that enables you to test each of the **Stack** methods. The statement (line 17)

```
final Stack s = new Stack();
```

creates an empty **Stack**.

```
1   // Fig. 23.2: StackTest.java
2   // Testing the Stack class of the java.util package
3   import java.util.*;
4   import java.awt.*;
5   import java.awt.event.*;
6   import javax.swing.*;
7
8   public class StackTest extends JFrame {
9
10      public StackTest()
11      {
12          super( "Stacks" );
13
14          Container c = getContentPane();
15
16          final JLabel status = new JLabel();
17          final Stack s = new Stack();
18
19          c.setLayout( new FlowLayout() );
20          c.add( new JLabel( "Enter a string" ) );
21          final JTextField input = new JTextField( 10 );
22          c.add( input );
23
24          JButton pushBtn = new JButton( "Push" );
25          pushBtn.addActionListener(
26              new ActionListener() {
27                  public void actionPerformed( ActionEvent e )
28                  {
29                      status.setText( "Pushed: " +
30                          s.push( input.getText() ) );
31                  }
32              }
33          );
34          c.add( pushBtn );
35
36          JButton popBtn = new JButton( "Pop" );
37          popBtn.addActionListener(
38              new ActionListener() {
39                  public void actionPerformed( ActionEvent e )
40                  {
41                      try {
42                          status.setText( "Popped: " + s.pop() );
43                      }
```

Fig. 23.2   Demonstrating class **Stack** of package **java.util** (part 1 of 3).

```
44                      catch ( EmptyStackException exception ) {
45                         status.setText( exception.toString() );
46                      }
47                   }
48                }
49             );
50             c.add( popBtn );
51
52             JButton peekBtn = new JButton( "Peek" );
53             peekBtn.addActionListener(
54                new ActionListener() {
55                   public void actionPerformed( ActionEvent e )
56                   {
57                      try {
58                         status.setText( "Top: " + s.peek() );
59                      }
60                      catch ( EmptyStackException exception ) {
61                         status.setText( exception.toString() );
62                      }
63                   }
64                }
65             );
66             c.add( peekBtn );
67
68             JButton emptyBtn = new JButton( "Is Empty?" );
69             emptyBtn.addActionListener(
70                new ActionListener() {
71                   public void actionPerformed( ActionEvent e )
72                   {
73                      status.setText( s.empty() ?
74                         "Stack is empty" : "Stack is not empty" );
75                   }
76                }
77             );
78             c.add( emptyBtn );
79
80             JButton searchBtn = new JButton( "Search" );
81             searchBtn.addActionListener(
82                new ActionListener() {
83                   public void actionPerformed( ActionEvent e )
84                   {
85                      String searchKey = input.getText();
86                      int result = s.search( searchKey );
87
88                      if ( result == -1 )
89                         status.setText( searchKey + " not found" );
90                      else
91                         status.setText( searchKey +
92                            " found at element " + result );
93                   }
94                }
95             );
96             c.add( searchBtn );
```

Fig. 23.2   Demonstrating class **Stack** of package **java.util** (part 2 of 3).

```
97
98            JButton displayBtn = new JButton( "Display" );
99            displayBtn.addActionListener(
100              new ActionListener() {
101                 public void actionPerformed( ActionEvent e )
102                 {
103                    Enumeration enum = s.elements();
104                    StringBuffer buf = new StringBuffer();
105
106                    while ( enum.hasMoreElements() )
107                       buf.append(
108                          enum.nextElement() ).append( " " );
109
110                    JOptionPane.showMessageDialog( null,
111                       buf.toString(), "Display",
112                       JOptionPane.PLAIN_MESSAGE );
113                 }
114              }
115           );
116           c.add( displayBtn );
117           c.add( status );
118
119           setSize( 675, 100 );
120           show();
121        }
122
123        public static void main( String args[] )
124        {
125           StackTest app = new StackTest();
126
127           app.addWindowListener(
128              new WindowAdapter() {
129                 public void windowClosing( WindowEvent e )
130                 {
131                    System.exit( 0 );
132                 }
133              }
134           );
135        }
136     }
```

Fig. 23.2   Demonstrating class **Stack** of package **java.util** (part 3 of 3).

The expression (line 30)

```
s.push( input.getText() )
```

calls **Stack** method **push** to add its argument to the top of the stack. The method returns an **Object** reference to its argument.

The expression (line 42)

    s.pop()

calls **Stack** method ***pop*** to remove the top element of the stack. The method returns an **Object** reference to the element that was removed. If there are no elements in the **Stack**, an ***EmptyStackException*** is thrown.

The expression (line 58)

    s.peek()

calls **Stack** method ***peek*** to look at the top element of the stack without removing it. The method returns an **Object** reference to the element.

The expression (line 73)

    s.empty()

calls **Stack** method ***empty*** to determine if the stack is empty. If so, **true** is returned; otherwise, **false** is returned.

The expression (line 86)

    int result = s.search(searchKey);

calls **Stack** method ***search*** to determine if its argument is in the stack. If so, the position of the element in the stack is returned. *The top element is position 1.* If the element is not in the stack, **−1** is returned.

The entire **public** interface of class **Vector** is actually part of class **Stack** because **Stack** inherits from **Vector**. To prove this, our example provides a button to display the contents of the stack. This button invokes method **elements** to get an **Enumeration** of the stack. The **Enumeration** is then used to walk through the stack elements.

Testing and Debugging Tip 23.1

*Because **Stack** inherits from **Vector**, the user may perform operations on **Stack** objects that are ordinarily not allowed on conventional stack data structures. This could corrupt the elements of the **Stack** and destroy the integrity of the **Stack**.*

23.4 Dictionary Class

A ***Dictionary*** maps *keys* to *values*. A key is supplied and the **Dictionary** returns a value. **Dictionary** is an **abstract** class. In particular, it is the superclass of the **Hashtable** class we will discuss shortly. Class **Dictionary** provides the **public** interface methods required to maintain a table of *key/value pairs* where the keys represent the "rows" of the table and the values are "columns" in the table. Each key in the table is unique. The data structure is similar to a dictionary of words and definitions—the word is the *key* that is used to look up the definition (i.e., the *value*).

Method **size** returns the number of occupied slots in the **Dictionary** object. The method ***isEmpty*** returns **true** if the **Dictionary** is empty, **false** otherwise. Method ***keys*** returns an **Enumeration** that iterates through a **Dictionary**'s keys. The method **elements** enumerates the **Dictionary**'s elements. Method ***get*** returns the object that corresponds to a given key value. Method ***put*** puts an object into the table; the object is associated with a given key. Method ***remove*** removes an element corresponding to a given key and returns a reference to it.

23.5 `Hashtable` Class

Object-oriented programming languages make it easy to create new types. When a program creates objects of new or existing types, it then needs to manage those objects efficiently. This includes storing and retrieving objects. Storing and retrieving information with arrays is efficient if some aspect of your data directly matches the key value and if those keys are unique and tightly packed. If you have 100 employees with 9-digit Social Security numbers and you want to store and retrieve employee data by using the Social Security number as a key, it would nominally require an array with 999,999,999 elements, because there are 999,999,999 unique 9-digit numbers. This is impractical for virtually all applications that key on Social Security numbers. But if you could have an array that large, you could get very high performance storing and retrieving employee records by simply using the Social Security number as the array index.

There are a huge variety of applications that have this problem, namely that either the keys are of the wrong type (i.e., not nonnegative integers), or they may be of the right type but sparsely spread over a huge range.

What is needed is a high-speed scheme for converting keys such as Social Security numbers, inventory part numbers, and the like into unique array subscripts. Then, when an application needs to store something, the scheme could rapidly convert the application key into a subscript and the record of information could be stored at that slot in the array. Retrieval is accomplished the same way: Once the application has a key for which it wants to retrieve the data record, the application simply applies the conversion to the key—this produces the array subscript for the data where the array is stored and the data is retrieved.

The scheme we describe here is the basis of a technique called *hashing*. Why the name? Because when we convert a key into an array subscript we literally scramble the bits, forming a kind of "mishmashed" number. The number actually has no real significance beyond its usefulness in storing and retrieving this particular number data record.

A glitch in the scheme occurs when *collisions* occur [i.e., two different keys "hash into" the same cell (or element) in the array]. Since we cannot store two different data records in the same space, we need to find an alternative home for all records beyond the first that hash to a particular array subscript. There are many schemes for doing this. One is to "hash again" (i.e., to reapply the hashing transformation to the key to provide a next candidate cell in the array). The hashing process is designed to be quite random, so the assumption is that with just a few hashes an available cell will be found.

Another scheme uses one hash to locate the first candidate cell. If that cell is occupied, successive cells are searched linearly until an available cell is found. Retrieval works the same way: The key is hashed once, the cell pointed to is checked to see if it contains the desired data. If it does, the search is finished. If it does not, successive cells are searched linearly until the desired data is found.

The most popular solution to hash table collisions is to have each cell of the table be a hash "bucket," typically a linked list of all the key/value pairs that hash to that cell. This is the solution that Java's **`Hashtable`** class (from package **`java.util`**) implements.

One factor that affects the performance of hashing schemes is called the *load factor*. This is the ratio of the number of occupied cells in the hash table to the size of the hash table. The closer this ratio gets to 1.0, the greater the chance of collisions.

Performance Tip 23.5

The load factor in a hash table is a classic example of a space/time trade-off: By increasing the load factor, we get better memory utilization, but the program runs slower due to increased hashing collisions. By decreasing the load factor, we get better program speed because of reduced hashing collisions, but we get poorer memory utilization because a larger portion of the hash table remains empty.

The complexity of programming hash tables properly is too much for most casual programmers. Computer science students study hashing schemes thoroughly in courses called "Data Structures" and/or "Algorithms." Recognizing the value of hashing to most programmers, Java provides class **Hashtable** and some related features to enable programmers to take advantage of hashing without having to worry about the messy details.

Actually, the preceding sentence is profoundly important in our study of object-oriented programming. Classes encapsulate and hide complexity (i.e., implementation details) and offer user-friendly interfaces. Crafting classes to do this properly is one of the most valued skills in the field of object-oriented programming.

The application of Fig. 23.3 provides a GUI that enables you to test many of the **Hashtable** methods. The statement (line 15)

```
final Hashtable table = new Hashtable();
```

creates an empty **Hashtable** with a default capacity of 101 elements and a default load factor of .75. When the number of occupied slots in the **Hashtable** becomes more than the capacity times the load factor, the table will automatically grow larger. Class **Hashtable** also provides a constructor that takes one argument specifying the capacity and a constructor that takes two arguments, specifying the capacity and load factor, respectively.

```
1   // Fig. 23.3: HashtableTest.java
2   // Demonstrates class Hashtable of the java.util package.
3   import java.util.*;
4   import java.awt.*;
5   import java.awt.event.*;
6   import javax.swing.*;
7
8   public class HashtableTest extends JFrame {
9
10      public HashtableTest()
11      {
12          super( "Hashtable Example" );
13
14          final JLabel status = new JLabel();
15          final Hashtable table = new Hashtable();
16          final JTextArea display = new JTextArea( 4, 20 );
17          display.setEditable( false );
18
19          JPanel northPanel = new JPanel();
20          northPanel.setLayout( new BorderLayout() );
21          JPanel northSubPanel = new JPanel();
```

Fig. 23.3   Demonstrating class **Hashtable** (part 1 of 5).

```
22          northSubPanel.add( new JLabel( "First name" ) );
23          final JTextField fName = new JTextField( 8 );
24          northSubPanel.add( fName );
25
26          northSubPanel.add( new JLabel( "Last name (key)" ) );
27          final JTextField lName = new JTextField( 8 );
28          northSubPanel.add( lName );
29          northPanel.add( northSubPanel, BorderLayout.NORTH );
30          northPanel.add( status, BorderLayout.SOUTH );
31
32          JPanel southPanel = new JPanel();
33          southPanel.setLayout( new GridLayout( 2, 5 ) );
34          JButton put = new JButton( "Put" );
35          put.addActionListener(
36             new ActionListener() {
37                public void actionPerformed( ActionEvent e )
38                {
39                   Employee emp = new Employee(
40                      fName.getText(), lName.getText() );
41                   Object val = table.put( lName.getText(), emp );
42
43                   if ( val == null )
44                      status.setText( "Put: " + emp.toString() );
45                   else
46                      status.setText( "Put: " + emp.toString() +
47                         "; Replaced: " + val.toString() );
48                }
49             }
50          );
51          southPanel.add( put );
52
53          JButton get = new JButton( "Get" );
54          get.addActionListener(
55             new ActionListener() {
56                public void actionPerformed( ActionEvent e )
57                {
58                   Object val = table.get( lName.getText() );
59
60                   if ( val != null )
61                      status.setText( "Get: " + val.toString() );
62                   else
63                      status.setText( "Get: " + lName.getText() +
64                                      " not in table" );
65                }
66             }
67          );
68          southPanel.add( get );
69
70          JButton remove = new JButton( "Remove" );
```

Fig. 23.3   Demonstrating class **Hashtable** (part 2 of 5).

```
71            remove.addActionListener(
72               new ActionListener() {
73                  public void actionPerformed( ActionEvent e )
74                  {
75                     Object val = table.remove( lName.getText() );
76
77                     if ( val != null )
78                        status.setText( "Remove: " +
79                                            val.toString() );
80                     else
81                        status.setText( "Remove: " +
82                           lName.getText() + " not in table" );
83                  }
84               }
85            );
86            southPanel.add( remove );
87
88            JButton empty = new JButton( "Empty" );
89            empty.addActionListener(
90               new ActionListener() {
91                  public void actionPerformed( ActionEvent e )
92                  {
93                     status.setText( "Empty: " + table.isEmpty() );
94                  }
95               }
96            );
97            southPanel.add( empty );
98
99            JButton containsKey = new JButton( "Contains key" );
100           containsKey.addActionListener(
101              new ActionListener() {
102                 public void actionPerformed( ActionEvent e )
103                 {
104                    status.setText( "Contains key: " +
105                       table.containsKey( lName.getText() ) );
106                 }
107              }
108           );
109           southPanel.add( containsKey );
110
111           JButton clear = new JButton( "Clear table" );
112           clear.addActionListener(
113              new ActionListener() {
114                 public void actionPerformed( ActionEvent e )
115                 {
116                    table.clear();
117                    status.setText( "Clear: Table is now empty" );
118                 }
119              }
120           );
121           southPanel.add( clear );
122
```

Fig. 23.3   Demonstrating class **Hashtable** (part 3 of 5).

```
123          JButton listElems = new JButton( "List objects" );
124          listElems.addActionListener(
125             new ActionListener() {
126                public void actionPerformed( ActionEvent e )
127                {
128                   StringBuffer buf = new StringBuffer();
129
130                   for ( Enumeration enum = table.elements();
131                         enum.hasMoreElements(); )
132                      buf.append(
133                         enum.nextElement() ).append( '\n' );
134
135                   display.setText( buf.toString() );
136                }
137             }
138          );
139          southPanel.add( listElems );
140
141          JButton listKeys = new JButton( "List keys" );
142          listKeys.addActionListener(
143             new ActionListener() {
144                public void actionPerformed( ActionEvent e )
145                {
146                   StringBuffer buf = new StringBuffer();
147
148                   for ( Enumeration enum = table.keys();
149                         enum.hasMoreElements(); )
150                      buf.append(
151                         enum.nextElement() ).append( '\n' );
152
153                   JOptionPane.showMessageDialog( null,
154                      buf.toString(), "Display",
155                      JOptionPane.PLAIN_MESSAGE );
156                }
157             }
158          );
159          southPanel.add( listKeys );
160          Container c = getContentPane();
161          c.add( northPanel, BorderLayout.NORTH );
162          c.add( new JScrollPane( display ), BorderLayout.CENTER );
163          c.add( southPanel, BorderLayout.SOUTH );
164
165          setSize( 540, 300 );
166          show();
167       }
168
169       public static void main( String args[] )
170       {
171          HashtableTest app = new HashtableTest();
172
```

Fig. 23.3   Demonstrating class **Hashtable** (part 4 of 5).

```
173          app.addWindowListener(
174             new WindowAdapter() {
175                public void windowClosing( WindowEvent e )
176                {
177                   System.exit( 0 );
178                }
179             }
180          );
181       }
182 }
183
184 class Employee {
185    private String first, last;
186
187    public Employee( String fName, String lName )
188    {
189       first = fName;
190       last = lName;
191    }
192
193    public String toString() { return first + " " + last; }
194 }
```

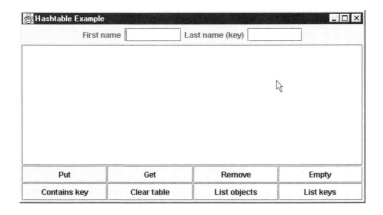

Fig. 23.3   Demonstrating class **Hashtable** (part 5 of 5).

The statement (line 41)

```
Object val = table.put( lName.getText(), emp );
```

calls **Hashtable** method **put** to add a *key* (the first argument) and a *value* (the second argument) into the **Hashtable**. If there was no value in the **Hashtable** for the specified key, **null** is returned. If there was a value in the **Hashtable** for the specified key, the original value in the **Hashtable** is returned; this helps the program manage cases in which it intends to replace the value stored for a given key. If either the key or the value is **null**, a **NullPointerException** is thrown. The value can be located in the **Hashtable** with the statement (line 58)

```
Object val = table.get( lName.getText() );
```

that calls **Hashtable** method *get* to locate the value that is associated with the key specified as an argument. The method returns an **Object** reference to the value if it is located; otherwise, **null** is returned.

The statement (line 75)

```
Object val = table.remove( lName.getText() );
```

calls **Hashtable** method *remove* to remove from the table the value associated with the key specified as an argument. The method returns an **Object** reference to the removed value. If there is no value mapped to the specified key, the method returns **null**.

The expression (line 93)

```
table.isEmpty()
```

returns **true** if the **Hashtable** is empty; **false** otherwise.

The expression (line 105)

```
table.containsKey( lName.getText() )
```

calls **Hashtable** method *containsKey* to determine if the key specified as an argument is in the **Hashtable** (i.e., a value is associated with that key). If so, the method returns **true**; otherwise, **false** is returned. Class **Hashtable** also provides method *contains* to determine if the **Object** specified as its argument is in the **Hashtable**.

The statement (line 116)

```
table.clear();
```

empties the **Hashtable**.

The expression (line 130)

```
table.elements()
```

returns an **Enumeration** of the values in the **Hashtable**.

The expression (line 148)

```
table.keys()
```

returns an **Enumeration** of the keys in the **Hashtable**.

For more information on the **Hashtable** methods, see the Java API documentation.

23.6 Properties Class

A *Properties* object is a persistent **Hashtable** object. By persistent, we mean that the **Hashtable** object can be written to an output stream and directed to a file, then read back in through an input stream. In fact, most objects in Java can now be output and input with Java's object serialization (see Chapter 17, "Files and Streams," for information on classes **ObjectOutputStream** and **ObjectInputStream** of package **java.io**). The **Properties** class extends class **Hashtable**, so the methods we discussed in Fig. 23.3 can be used for **Properties** objects also. The keys and values in a **Properties** object must be of type **String**. Class **Properties** provides some additional methods that are demonstrated in the application of Fig. 23.4.

```
1  // Fig. 23.4: PropertiesTest.java
2  // Demonstrates class Properties of the java.util package.
3  import java.io.*;
4  import java.util.*;
5  import java.awt.*;
6  import java.awt.event.*;
7  import javax.swing.*;
8
9  public class PropertiesTest extends JFrame {
10     private JLabel status;
11     private Properties table;
12     private JTextArea display;
13
14     public PropertiesTest()
15     {
16        super( "Properties Test" );
17
18        table = new Properties();
19        Container c = getContentPane();
20        JPanel northPanel = new JPanel();
21        northPanel.setLayout( new BorderLayout() );
22        JPanel northSubPanel = new JPanel();
23        JPanel southPanel = new JPanel();
24
25        northSubPanel.add( new JLabel( "Property value" ) );
26        final JTextField propVal = new JTextField( 10 );
27        northSubPanel.add( propVal );
28        northPanel.add( northSubPanel, BorderLayout.NORTH );
29
30        northSubPanel.add( new JLabel( "Property name (key)" ) );
31        final JTextField propName = new JTextField( 10 );
32        northSubPanel.add( propName );
33
34        display = new JTextArea( 4, 35 );
35
36        JButton put = new JButton( "Put" );
37        put.addActionListener(
38           new ActionListener() {
39              public void actionPerformed( ActionEvent e )
40              {
41                 Object val = table.put( propName.getText(),
42                                         propVal.getText() );
43
44                 if ( val == null )
45                    showStatus( "Put: " + propName.getText() +
46                                " " + propVal.getText() );
47                 else
48                    showStatus( "Put: " + propName.getText() +
49                       " " + propVal.getText() +
50                       "; Replaced: " + val.toString() );
51
```

Fig. 23.4   Demonstrating class **Properties** (part 1 of 4).

```
52                           listProperties();
53                        }
54                     }
55                  );
56                  southPanel.setLayout( new GridLayout( 1, 5 ) );
57                  southPanel.add( put );
58
59                  JButton clear = new JButton( "Clear" );
60                  clear.addActionListener(
61                     new ActionListener() {
62                        public void actionPerformed( ActionEvent e )
63                        {
64                           table.clear();
65                           showStatus( "Table in memory cleared" );
66                           listProperties();
67                        }
68                     }
69                  );
70                  southPanel.add( clear );
71
72                  JButton getProperty = new JButton( "Get property" );
73                  getProperty.addActionListener(
74                     new ActionListener() {
75                        public void actionPerformed( ActionEvent e )
76                        {
77                           Object val = table.getProperty(
78                              propName.getText() );
79
80                           if ( val != null )
81                              showStatus( "Get property: " +
82                                 propName.getText() + " " +
83                                 val.toString() );
84                           else
85                              showStatus( "Get: " + propName.getText() +
86                                 " not in table" );
87
88                           listProperties();
89                        }
90                     }
91                  );
92                  southPanel.add( getProperty );
93
94                  JButton save = new JButton( "Save" );
95                  save.addActionListener(
96                     new ActionListener() {
97                        public void actionPerformed( ActionEvent e )
98                        {
99                           try {
100                              FileOutputStream output;
101
102                              output = new FileOutputStream( "props.dat" );
103                              table.store( output, "Sample Properties" );
104                              output.close();
```

Fig. 23.4   Demonstrating class **Properties** (part 2 of 4).

```
105                        listProperties();
106                     }
107                     catch( IOException ex ) {
108                        showStatus( ex.toString() );
109                     }
110                  }
111               }
112            );
113            southPanel.add( save );
114
115            JButton load = new JButton( "Load" );
116            load.addActionListener(
117               new ActionListener() {
118                  public void actionPerformed( ActionEvent e )
119                  {
120                     try {
121                        FileInputStream input;
122
123                        input = new FileInputStream( "props.dat" );
124                        table.load( input );
125                        input.close();
126                        listProperties();
127                     }
128                     catch( IOException ex ) {
129                        showStatus( ex.toString() );
130                     }
131                  }
132               }
133            );
134            southPanel.add( load );
135
136            status = new JLabel();
137            northPanel.add( status, BorderLayout.SOUTH );
138
139            c.add( northPanel, BorderLayout.NORTH );
140            c.add( new JScrollPane( display ), BorderLayout.CENTER );
141            c.add( southPanel, BorderLayout.SOUTH );
142
143            setSize( 550, 225 );
144            show();
145         }
146
147         public void listProperties()
148         {
149            StringBuffer buf = new StringBuffer();
150            String pName, pVal;
151
152            Enumeration enum = table.propertyNames();
153
154            while( enum.hasMoreElements() ) {
155               pName = enum.nextElement().toString();
156               pVal = table.getProperty( pName );
157               buf.append( pName ).append( '\t' );
```

Fig. 23.4　Demonstrating class **Properties** (part 3 of 4).

```
158            buf.append( pVal ).append( '\n' );
159         }
160
161      display.setText( buf.toString() );
162   }
163
164   public void showStatus( String s )
165   {
166      status.setText( s );
167   }
168
169   public static void main( String args[] )
170   {
171      PropertiesTest app = new PropertiesTest();
172      app.addWindowListener(
173         new WindowAdapter() {
174            public void windowClosing( WindowEvent e )
175            {
176               System.exit( 0 );
177            }
178         }
179      );
180   }
181 }
```

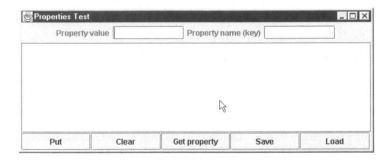

Fig. 23.4   Demonstrating class **Properties** (part 4 of 4).

The statement (line 18)

```
table = new Properties();
```

uses the no-argument constructor to create an empty **Properties** table with no default properties. There is also an overloaded constructor that is passed a reference to a default **Properties** object containing default property values. This version is useful for maintaining a set of default values for use with method **getProperty** later.

The statement (line 77)

```
Object val = table.getProperty(
    propName.getText() );
```

calls **Properties** method *getProperty* to locate the value associated with the specified key. If the key is not found in this **Properties** object, the default **Properties** object (if there is one) is used. The process continues recursively until there are no more default **Properties** objects (remember that every **Properties** object can be initialized with a default **Properties** object), at which point **null** is returned. An overloaded version of this method is provided that takes two arguments, the second of which is the default value to return if **getProperty** cannot locate the key.

The statement (line 103)

```
table.store( output, "Sample Properties" );
```

calls **Properties** method *store* to save the contents of the **Properties** object to the **OutputStream** object specified as the first argument (in this case a **FileOutput-Stream**). The **String** argument is a description of the **Properties** object. Class **Properties** also provides method *list*, which takes a **PrintStream** argument. This method is useful for displaying the set of properties.

Testing and Debugging Tip 23.2

*Use **Properties** method **list** to display the contents of a **Properties** object for debugging purposes.*

The statement (line 124)

```
table.load( input );
```

calls **Properties** method *load* to restore the contents of the **Properties** object from the **InputStream** specified as the first argument (in this case a **FileInputStream**).

The expression (line 152)

```
table.propertyNames()
```

calls **Properties** method *propertyNames* to obtain an **Enumeration** of the property names. The value of each property can be determined using method **getProperty**.

23.7 Random Class

We discussed random number generation in Chapter 6, "Methods," where we used **Math** class method **random**. Java provides extensive additional random number generation capabilities in class *Random*. We briefly walk through the API calls here.

A new random number generator can be created by using

```
Random r = new Random();
```

This form uses the time to seed its random number generator differently each time it is called and thus generates different sequences of random numbers each time.

To create a pseudorandom-number generator with "repeatability," use

```
Random r = new Random( seedValue );
```

Each time this form is used with the same **long seedValue**, the same sequence of random numbers is generated.

Testing and Debugging Tip 23.3

The repeatability of random numbers that occurs when the same seed value is useful for testing and debugging. While a program is under development, use the form **Random(seedValue)** *that produces a repeatable sequence of random numbers. If a bug occurs, fix the bug and test with the same* **seedValue**; *this allows you to reconstruct the exact same sequence of random numbers that caused the bug. Once the bugs have been removed, use the form* **Random()** *that generates a new sequence of random numbers each time the program is run.*

The call

```
r.setSeed( seedValue );
```

resets **r**'s seed value at any time.
The calls

```
r.nextInt()
r.nextLong()
```

generate uniformly distributed random integers. You can use **Math.abs** to take the absolute value of the number produced by **nextInt**, thus giving a number in the range zero through approximately 2 billion. Then use the **%** operator to scale the number. For example, to roll a die from 1 to 6, if you scale with a 6, you will get a number in the range 0 through 5. Then simply shift this value by adding 1 to produce a number in the range 1 through 6. The expression is as follows:

```
Math.abs( r.nextInt() ) % 6 + 1
```

The calls

```
r.nextFloat()
r.nextDouble()
```

generate uniformly distributed values in the range $0.0 <= x < 1.0$.
The call

```
r.nextGaussian()
```

generates a **double** value with a probability density of a *Gaussian* (i.e., "normal") distribution (mean of 0.0 and standard deviation of 1.0).

23.8 Bit Manipulation and the Bitwise Operators

Java provides extensive bit manipulation capabilities for programmers who need to get down to the so-called "bits-and-bytes" level. Operating systems, test equipment software, networking software and many other kinds of software require that the programmer communicate "directly with the hardware." In this and the next section, we discuss Java's bit manipulation capabilities. We introduce Java's bitwise operators and we demonstrate their use in live-code examples.

All data is represented internally by computers as sequences of bits. Each bit can assume the value **0** or the value **1**. On most systems, a sequence of 8 bits forms a byte—

the standard storage unit for a variable of type **byte**. Other data types are stored in larger numbers of bytes. The bitwise operators are used to manipulate the bits of integral operands (i.e., those having type **byte**, **char**, **short**, **int** and **long**).

Note that the bitwise operator discussions in this section show the binary representations of the integer operands. For a detailed explanation of the binary (also called base 2) number system, see Appendix E, "Number Systems."

The bitwise operators are: *bitwise AND (**&**), bitwise inclusive OR (|), bitwise exclusive OR (^), left shift (<<), right shift with sign extension (>>), right shift with zero extension (>>>)* and *complement (~)*. The bitwise AND, bitwise inclusive OR, and bitwise exclusive OR operators compare their two operands bit-by-bit. The bitwise AND operator sets each bit in the result to 1 if the corresponding bit in both operands is 1. The bitwise inclusive OR operator sets each bit in the result to 1 if the corresponding bit in either (or both) operand(s) is 1. The bitwise exclusive OR operator sets each bit in the result to 1 if the corresponding bit in exactly one operand is 1. The left shift operator shifts the bits of its left operand to the left by the number of bits specified in its right operand. The right shift operator with sign extension shifts the bits in its left operand to the right by the number of bits specified in its right operand—if the left operand is negative, **1**s are shifted in from the left; otherwise, **0**s are shifted in from the left. The right shift operator with zero extension shifts the bits in its left operand to the right by the number of bits specified in its right operand—**0**s are shifted in from the left. The bitwise complement operator sets all **0** bits in its operand to **1** in the result and sets all **1** bits to **0** in the result. Detailed discussions of each bitwise operator appear in the following examples. The bitwise operators are summarized in Fig. 23.5.

Operator	Name	Description
&	bitwise AND	The bits in the result are set to **1** if the corresponding bits in the two operands are both **1**.
|	bitwise inclusive OR	The bits in the result are set to **1** if at least one of the corresponding bits in the two operands is **1**.
^	bitwise exclusive OR	The bits in the result are set to **1** if exactly one of the corresponding bits in the two operands is **1**.
<<	left shift	Shifts the bits of the first operand left by the number of bits specified by the second operand; fill from the right with **0** bits.
>>	right shift with sign extension	Shifts the bits of the first operand right by the number of bits specified by the second operand. If the first operand is negative, **1**s are shifted in from the left; otherwise, **0**s are shifted in from the left.
>>>	right shift with zero extension	Shifts the bits of the first operand right by the number of bits specified by the second operand; **0**s are shifted in from the left.
~	one's complement	All **0** bits are set to **1** and all **1** bits are set to **0**.

Fig. 23.5   The bitwise operators .

When using the bitwise operators, it is useful to display values in their binary representation to illustrate the effects of these operators. The application of Fig. 23.6 allows the user to enter an integer into a **JTextField** and press *Enter*. Method **actionPerformed** reads the **String** from the **JTextField**, converts it to an integer and invokes method **getBits** (line 38) to obtain **String** representation of the integer in bits. The result is displayed in the output **JTextField**. The integer is displayed in its binary representation in groups of eight bits each. Method **getBits** uses the bitwise AND operator to combine variable **value** with variable **displayMask**. Often, the bitwise AND operator is used with an operand called a *mask*—an integer value with specific bits set to **1**. Masks are used to hide some bits in a value while selecting other bits. In **getBits**, mask variable **displayMask** is assigned the value **1 << 31** (**10000000 00000000 00000000 00000000**). The left shift operator shifts the value **1** from the low-order (rightmost) bit to the high-order (leftmost) bit in **displayMask**, and fills in **0** bits from the right.

```
1   // Fig. 23.6: PrintBits.java
2   // Printing an unsigned integer in bits
3   import java.awt.*;
4   import java.awt.event.*;
5   import javax.swing.*;
6
7   public class PrintBits extends JFrame {
8
9      public PrintBits()
10     {
11        super( "Printing bit representations for numbers" );
12
13        Container c = getContentPane();
14        c.setLayout( new FlowLayout() );
15        c.add( new JLabel( "Enter an integer " ) );
16        final JTextField output = new JTextField( 33 );
17        JTextField input = new JTextField( 10 );
18        input.addActionListener(
19           new ActionListener() {
20              public void actionPerformed( ActionEvent e )
21              {
22                 int val = Integer.parseInt(
23                    e.getActionCommand() );
24                 output.setText( getBits( val ) );
25              }
26           }
27        );
28        c.add( input );
29
30        c.add( new JLabel( "The integer in bits is" ) );
31        output.setEditable( false );
32        c.add( output );
33
34        setSize( 720, 70 );
```

Fig. 23.6   Displaying the bit representation of an integer (part 1 of 2).

```
35            show();
36        }
37
38        private String getBits( int value )
39        {
40            int displayMask = 1 << 31;
41            StringBuffer buf = new StringBuffer( 35 );
42
43            for ( int c = 1; c <= 32; c++ ) {
44                buf.append(
45                    ( value & displayMask ) == 0 ? '0' : '1' );
46                value <<= 1;
47
48                if ( c % 8 == 0 )
49                    buf.append( ' ' );
50            }
51
52            return buf.toString();
53        }
54
55        public static void main( String args[] )
56        {
57            PrintBits app = new PrintBits();
58            app.addWindowListener(
59                new WindowAdapter() {
60                    public void windowClosing( WindowEvent e )
61                    {
62                        System.exit( 0 );
63                    }
64                }
65            );
66        }
67    }
```

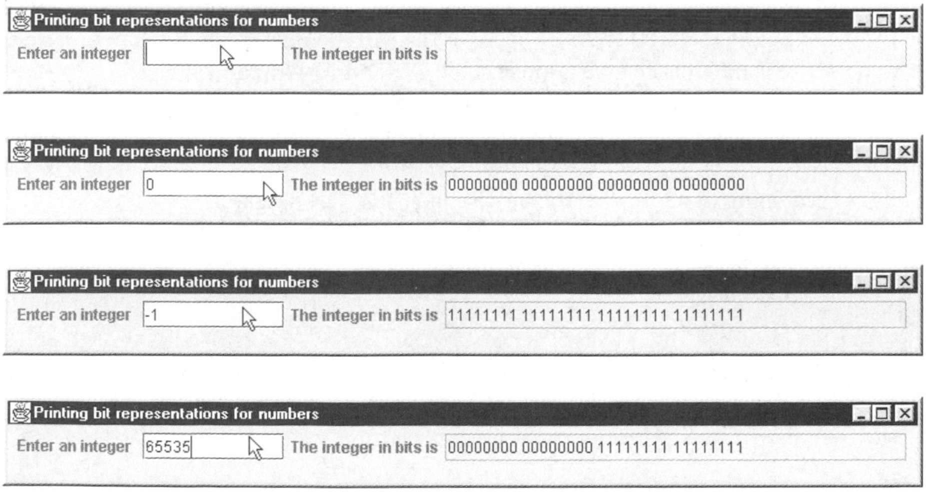

Fig. 23.6   Displaying the bit representation of an integer (part 2 of 2).

The statement (line 44)

```
buf.append(
    ( value & displayMask ) == 0 ? '0' : '1' );
```

determines whether a **1** or a **0** should be appended to **StringBuffer buf** for the current leftmost bit of variable **value**. Assume that **value** contains **4000000000 (11101110 01101011 00101000 00000000)**. When **value** and **displayMask** are combined using **&**, all the bits except the high-order bit in variable **value** are "masked off" (hidden) because any bit "ANDed" with **0** yields **0**. If the leftmost bit is **1**, **value & display-Mask** evaluates to **1**, and **1** is appended—otherwise, **0** is appended. Variable **value** is then left shifted one bit by the expression **value <<= 1** (this is equivalent to **value = value << 1**). These steps are repeated for each bit in variable **value**. At the end of method **getBits**, the **StringBuffer** is converted to a **String** with the statement (line 52)

```
return buf.toString();
```

then returned from the method. Figure 23.7 summarizes the results of combining two bits with the bitwise AND (**&**) operator.

Common Programming Error 23.1

*Using the logical AND operator (**&&**) for the bitwise AND operator (**&**) is a common programming error.*

The program of Fig. 23.8 demonstrates the use of the bitwise AND operator, the bitwise inclusive OR operator, the bitwise exclusive OR operator and the bitwise complement operator. The program uses method **getBits** to get a **String** representation of the integer values. The program allows the user to enter values into **JTextField**s and press *Enter* (for the binary operators, two values must be entered). The user can then press the button representing the operation they would like to test and the result is displayed in both integer and bit representations.

The first output window for Fig. 23.8 shows the results of combining the value **65535** and the value **1** with the bitwise AND operator (**&**). All the bits except the low-order bit in the value **65535** are "masked off" (hidden) by "ANDing" with the value **1**.

The bitwise inclusive OR operator is used to set specific bits to 1 in an operand. The second output window for Fig. 23.8 shows the results of combining the value **15** and the value **241** using the bitwise OR operator—the result is **255**. Figure 23.10 summarizes the results of combining two bits with the bitwise inclusive OR operator.

Bit 1	Bit 2	Bit 1 & Bit 2
0	0	0
1	0	0
0	1	0
1	1	1

Fig. 23.7   Results of combining two bits with the bitwise AND operator (**&**).

```
1   // Fig. 23.8: MiscBitOps.java
2   // Using the bitwise AND, bitwise inclusive OR, bitwise
3   // exclusive OR, and bitwise complement operators.
4   import java.awt.*;
5   import java.awt.event.*;
6   import javax.swing.*;
7
8   public class MiscBitOps extends JFrame {
9      private JTextField input1, input2, bits1, bits2;
10     private int val1, val2;
11
12     public MiscBitOps()
13     {
14        super( "Bitwise operators" );
15
16        JPanel inputPanel = new JPanel();
17        inputPanel.setLayout( new GridLayout( 4, 2 ) );
18
19        inputPanel.add( new JLabel( "Enter 2 ints" ) );
20        inputPanel.add( new JLabel( "" ) );
21
22        inputPanel.add( new JLabel( "Value 1" ) );
23        input1 = new JTextField( 8 );
24        inputPanel.add( input1 );
25
26        inputPanel.add( new JLabel( "Value 2" ) );
27        input2 = new JTextField( 8 );
28        inputPanel.add( input2 );
29
30        inputPanel.add( new JLabel( "Result" ) );
31        final JTextField result = new JTextField( 8 );
32        result.setEditable( false );
33        inputPanel.add( result );
34
35        JPanel bitsPanel = new JPanel();
36        bitsPanel.setLayout( new GridLayout( 4, 1 ) );
37        bitsPanel.add( new JLabel( "Bit representations" ) );
38
39        bits1 = new JTextField( 33 );
40        bits1.setEditable( false );
41        bitsPanel.add( bits1 );
42
43        bits2 = new JTextField( 33 );
44        bits2.setEditable( false );
45        bitsPanel.add( bits2 );
46
47        final JTextField bits3 = new JTextField( 33 );
48        bits3.setEditable( false );
49        bitsPanel.add( bits3 );
50
51        JPanel buttonPanel = new JPanel();
52        JButton and = new JButton( "AND" );
```

Fig. 23.8   Demonstrating the bitwise AND, bitwise inclusive OR, bitwise exclusive
OR and bitwise complement operators (part 1 of 4).

```
53        and.addActionListener(
54           new ActionListener() {
55              public void actionPerformed( ActionEvent e )
56              {
57                 setFields();
58                 result.setText( Integer.toString( val1 &
59                                                    val2 ) );
60                 bits3.setText( getBits( val1 & val2 ) );
61              }
62           }
63        );
64        buttonPanel.add( and );
65
66        JButton inclusiveOr = new JButton( "Inclusive OR" );
67        inclusiveOr.addActionListener(
68           new ActionListener() {
69              public void actionPerformed( ActionEvent e )
70              {
71                 setFields();
72                 result.setText( Integer.toString( val1 |
73                                                    val2 ) );
74                 bits3.setText( getBits( val1 | val2 ) );
75              }
76           }
77        );
78        buttonPanel.add( inclusiveOr );
79
80        JButton exclusiveOr = new JButton( "Exclusive OR" );
81        exclusiveOr.addActionListener(
82           new ActionListener() {
83              public void actionPerformed( ActionEvent e )
84              {
85                 setFields();
86                 result.setText( Integer.toString( val1 ^
87                                                    val2 ) );
88                 bits3.setText( getBits( val1 ^ val2 ) );
89              }
90           }
91        );
92        buttonPanel.add( exclusiveOr );
93
94        JButton complement = new JButton( "Complement" );
95        complement.addActionListener(
96           new ActionListener() {
97              public void actionPerformed( ActionEvent e )
98              {
99                 input2.setText( "" );
100                bits2.setText( "" );
101                int val = Integer.parseInt( input1.getText() );
102                result.setText( Integer.toString( ~val ) );
103                bits1.setText( getBits( val ) );
```

Fig. 23.8   Demonstrating the bitwise AND, bitwise inclusive OR, bitwise exclusive OR and bitwise complement operators (part 2 of 4).

```
104                    bits3.setText( getBits( ~val ) );
105               }
106           }
107       );
108       buttonPanel.add( complement );
109
110       Container c = getContentPane();
111       c.setLayout( new BorderLayout() );
112       c.add( inputPanel, BorderLayout.WEST );
113       c.add( bitsPanel, BorderLayout.EAST );
114       c.add( buttonPanel, BorderLayout.SOUTH );
115
116       setSize( 600, 150 );
117       show();
118   }
119
120   private void setFields()
121   {
122       val1 = Integer.parseInt( input1.getText() );
123       val2 = Integer.parseInt( input2.getText() );
124
125       bits1.setText( getBits( val1 ) );
126       bits2.setText( getBits( val2 ) );
127   }
128
129   private String getBits( int value )
130   {
131       int displayMask = 1 << 31;
132       StringBuffer buf = new StringBuffer( 35 );
133
134       for ( int c = 1; c <= 32; c++ ) {
135          buf.append(
136             ( value & displayMask ) == 0 ? '0' : '1' );
137          value <<= 1;
138
139          if ( c % 8 == 0 )
140             buf.append( ' ' );
141       }
142
143       return buf.toString();
144   }
```

Fig. 23.8   Demonstrating the bitwise AND, bitwise inclusive OR, bitwise exclusive OR and bitwise complement operators (part 3 of 4).

Common Programming Error 23.2

Using the logical OR operator (| |) for the bitwise OR operator (|) is a common programming error.

The bitwise exclusive OR operator (^) sets each bit in the result to 1 if *exactly* one of the corresponding bits in its two operands is 1. The third output of Fig. 23.8 shows the results of combining the value **139** and the value **199** using the exclusive OR operator—the result is **76**. Figure 23.9 summarizes the results of combining two bits with the bitwise exclusive OR operator.

```
145
146    public static void main( String args[] )
147    {
148       MiscBitOps app = new MiscBitOps();
149       app.addWindowListener(
150          new WindowAdapter() {
151             public void windowClosing( WindowEvent e )
152             {
153                System.exit( 0 );
154             }
155          }
156       );
157    }
158  }
```

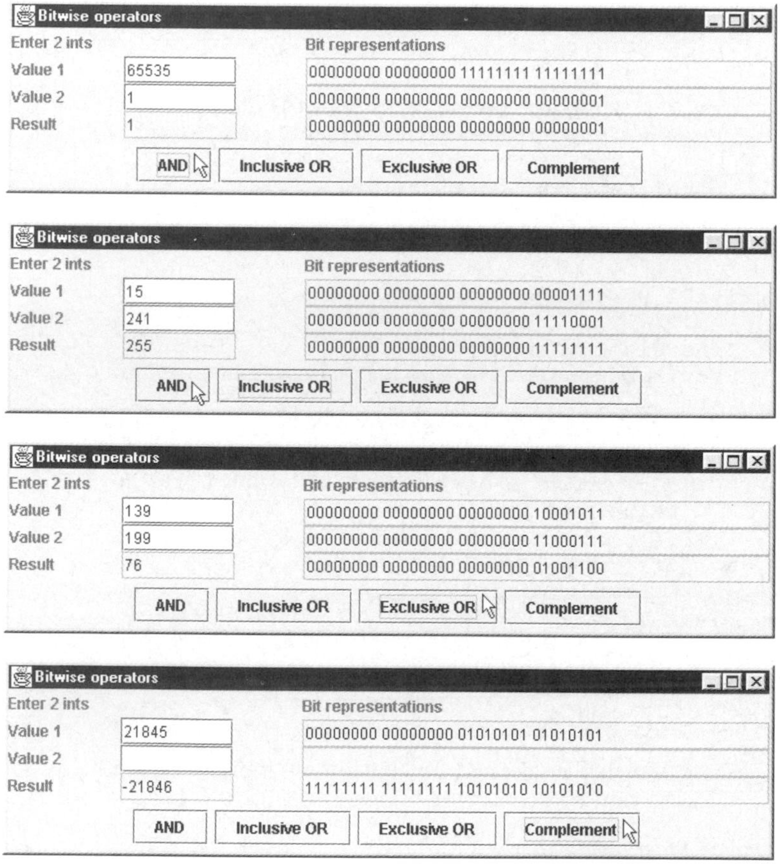

Fig. 23.8   Demonstrating the bitwise AND, bitwise inclusive OR, bitwise exclusive OR and bitwise complement operators (part 4 of 4).

The *bitwise* complement operator (~) sets all **1** bits in its operand to **0** in the result and sets all **0** bits to **1** in the result—otherwise referred to as "taking the *one's complement* of the value." The fourth output window for Fig. 23.8 shows the results of taking the one's complement of the value **21845**. The result is **–21846**.

Bit 1	Bit 2	Bit 1 ^ Bit 2
0	0	0
1	0	1
0	1	1
1	1	0

Fig. 23.9   Results of combining two bits with the bitwise exclusive OR operator (^).

Bit 1	Bit 2	Bit 1 | Bit 2
0	0	0
1	0	1
0	1	1
1	1	1

Fig. 23.10   Results of combining two bits with the bitwise inclusive OR operator (|).

The program of Fig. 23.11 demonstrates the *left shift operator* (**<<**), the *right shift operator with sign extension* (**>>**) and the *right shift operator with zero extension* (**>>>**). Method **getBits** obtains a **String** containing the bit representation of the integer values. The program allows the user to enter an integer in a **JTextField** and press *Enter*. The bit representation of the integer is displayed in a second **JTextField**.

```
1   // Fig. 23.11: BitShift.java
2   // Using the bitwise shift operators.
3   import java.awt.*;
4   import java.awt.event.*;
5   import javax.swing.*;
6
7   public class BitShift extends JFrame {
8
9      public BitShift()
10     {
11        super( "Shifting bits" );
12
13        Container c = getContentPane();
14        c.setLayout( new FlowLayout() );
15        final JTextField bits = new JTextField( 33 );
16        c.add( new JLabel( "Integer to shift " ) );
17
18        final JTextField value = new JTextField( 12 );
```

Fig. 23.11   Demonstrating the bitwise shift operators (part 1 of 4).

```
19        value.addActionListener(
20           new ActionListener() {
21              public void actionPerformed( ActionEvent e )
22              {
23                 int val = Integer.parseInt( value.getText() );
24                 bits.setText( getBits( val ) );
25              }
26           }
27        );
28        c.add( value );
29
30        bits.setEditable( false );
31        c.add( bits );
32
33        JButton left = new JButton( "<<" );
34        left.addActionListener(
35           new ActionListener() {
36              public void actionPerformed( ActionEvent e )
37              {
38                 int val = Integer.parseInt( value.getText() );
39                 val <<= 1;
40                 value.setText( Integer.toString( val ) );
41                 bits.setText( getBits( val ) );
42              }
43           }
44        );
45        c.add( left );
46
47        JButton rightSign = new JButton( ">>" );
48        rightSign.addActionListener(
49           new ActionListener() {
50              public void actionPerformed( ActionEvent e )
51              {
52                 int val = Integer.parseInt( value.getText() );
53                 val >>= 1;
54                 value.setText( Integer.toString( val ) );
55                 bits.setText( getBits( val ) );
56              }
57           }
58        );
59        c.add( rightSign );
60
61        JButton rightZero = new JButton( ">>>" );
62        rightZero.addActionListener(
63           new ActionListener() {
64              public void actionPerformed( ActionEvent e )
65              {
66                 int val = Integer.parseInt( value.getText() );
67                 val >>>= 1;
68                 value.setText( Integer.toString( val ) );
```

Fig. 23.11   Demonstrating the bitwise shift operators (part 2 of 4).

```
69                         bits.setText( getBits( val ) );
70                      }
71                  }
72              );
73          c.add( rightZero );
74
75          setSize( 400, 120 );
76          show();
77      }
78
79      private String getBits( int value )
80      {
81          int displayMask = 1 << 31;
82          StringBuffer buf = new StringBuffer( 35 );
83
84          for ( int c = 1; c <= 32; c++ ) {
85              buf.append(
86                  ( value & displayMask ) == 0 ? '0' : '1' );
87              value <<= 1;
88
89              if ( c % 8 == 0 )
90                  buf.append( ' ' );
91          }
92
93          return buf.toString();
94      }
95
96      public static void main( String args[] )
97      {
98          BitShift app = new BitShift();
99          app.addWindowListener(
100             new WindowAdapter() {
101                 public void windowClosing( WindowEvent e )
102                 {
103                     System.exit( 0 );
104                 }
105             }
106         );
107     }
108 }
```

Fig. 23.11 Demonstrating the bitwise shift operators (part 3 of 4).

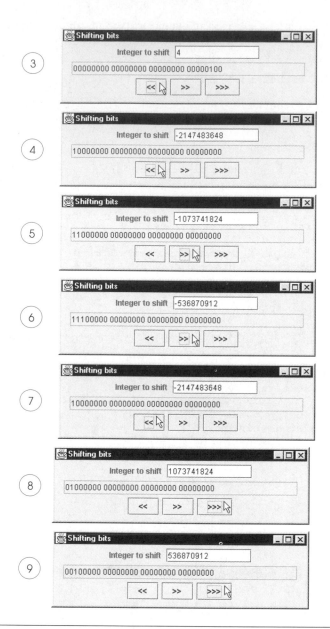

Fig. 23.11   Demonstrating the bitwise shift operators (part 4 of 4).

A button is provided for each shift operator. As the user clicks each button, the bits in the integer shift left or right by one bit. The new integer value and new bit representation are displayed in the **JTextField**s.

The left shift operator (**<<**) shifts the bits of its left operand to the left by the number of bits specified in its right operand. Bits vacated to the right are replaced with **0**s; **1**s shifted off the left are lost. The first four output windows of Fig. 23.11 demonstrate the left shift operator. Starting with the value 1, the left shift button was pressed twice, resulting in the values 2 and 4, respectively. The fourth output window shows the result of **value1** being shifted 31 times. Note that the result is a negative value. That is because a 1 in the high-order bit is used to indicate a negative value in an integer.

The right shift operator with sign extension (**>>**) shifts the bits of its left operand to the right by the number of bits specified in its right operand. Performing a right shift causes the vacated bits at the left to be replaced by **0**s if the number is positive and **1**s if the number is negative. Any **1**s shifted off the right are lost. The fifth and sixth output windows show the results of right shifting (with sign extension) the value in the fourth output window two times.

The right shift operator with zero extension (**>>>**) shifts the bits of its left operand to the right by the number of bits specified in its right operand. Performing a right shift causes the vacated bits at the left to be replaced by **0**s. Any **1**s shifted off the right are lost. The eighth and ninth output windows show the results of right shifting (with zero extension) the value in the seventh output window two times.

Each bitwise operator (except the bitwise complement operator) has a corresponding assignment operator. These *bitwise assignment operators* are shown in Fig. 23.12 and are used in a similar manner to the arithmetic assignment operators introduced in Chapter 4.

23.9 `BitSet` Class

The **BitSet** class makes it easy to create and manipulate *bit sets*. Bit sets are useful for representing a set of **boolean** flags. **BitSet**s are dynamically resizeable. More bits can be added as needed and a **BitSet** object will grow to accommodate the additional bits.

> BitSet b = new BitSet();

creates a *BitSet* which is initially empty.

> BitSet b = new BitSet(size);

creates a **BitSet** with **size** bits.

> b.set(bitNumber);

sets bit **bitNumber** of **BitSet b** "on."

Bitwise assignment operators	
&=	Bitwise AND assignment operator.
|=	Bitwise inclusive OR assignment operator.
^=	Bitwise exclusive OR assignment operator.
<<=	Left shift assignment operator.
>>=	Right shift with sign extension assignment operator.
>>>=	Right shift with zero extension assignment operator.

Fig. 23.12 The bitwise assignment operators.

```
b.clear( bitNumber );
```

sets bit **bitNumber** of **BitSet b** "off."

```
b.get( bitNumber );
```

gets bit **bitNumber** of **BitSet b**. The result is returned as **true** if the bit is on or **false** if the bit is off.

```
b.and( b1 );
```

performs a bit-by-bit logical AND between **BitSet**s **b** and **b1**. The result is stored in **b**. Bitwise logical OR and bitwise logical XOR are performed by

```
b.or( b1 );
b.xor( b2 );
```

The expression

```
b.size()
```

returns the size of **BitSet b**.

The expression

```
b.equals( b1 )
```

compares the two **BitSet**s for equality.

```
b.clone()
```

clones a **BitSet** and returns an **Object** reference to the new **BitSet**.

```
b.toString()
```

converts **BitSet b** to a **String**. This is helpful for debugging.

The expression

```
b.hashCode()
```

provides a hash code useful for storing and retrieving **BitSet** objects in hash tables.

Figure 23.13 revisits the Sieve of Eratosthenes for finding prime numbers we discussed in Exercise 7.27. A **BitSet** is used instead of an array to implement the algorithm. The program displays all the prime numbers from 1 to 1023 in a **JTextArea** and provides a **JTextField** in which the user can type any number from 1 to 1023 to determine if that number is prime (in which case a message is displayed in a **JLabel**).

```
1   // Fig. 23.13: BitSetTest.java
2   // Using a BitSet to demonstrate the Sieve of Eratosthenes.
3   import java.awt.*;
4   import java.awt.event.*;
5   import java.util.*;
6   import javax.swing.*;
7
```

Fig. 23.13   Demonstrating the Sieve of Eratosthenes using a **BitSet** (part 1 of 3).

```
8
9    public class BitSetTest extends JFrame {
10
11       public BitSetTest()
12       {
13          super( "BitSets" );
14
15          final BitSet sieve = new BitSet( 1024 );
16          Container c = getContentPane();
17          final JLabel status = new JLabel();
18          c.add( status, BorderLayout.SOUTH );
19          JPanel inputPanel = new JPanel();
20
21          inputPanel.add( new JLabel( "Enter a value from " +
22                                      "1 to 1023" ) );
23          final JTextField input = new JTextField( 10 );
24          input.addActionListener(
25             new ActionListener() {
26                public void actionPerformed( ActionEvent e )
27                {
28                   int val = Integer.parseInt( input.getText() );
29
30                   if ( sieve.get( val ) )
31                      status.setText( val + " is a prime number" );
32                   else
33                      status.setText( val +
34                                         " is not a prime number" );
35                }
36             }
37          );
38          inputPanel.add( input );
39          c.add( inputPanel, BorderLayout.NORTH );
40
41          JTextArea primes = new JTextArea();
42          ScrollPane p = new ScrollPane();
43          p.add( primes );
44
45          c.add( p, BorderLayout.CENTER );
46
47          // set all bits from 1 to 1023
48          int size = sieve.size();
49
50          for ( int i = 1; i < size; i++ )
51             sieve.set( i );
52
53          // perform Sieve of Eratosthenes
54          int finalBit = ( int ) Math.sqrt( sieve.size() );
55
56          for ( int i = 2; i < finalBit; i++ )
57             if ( sieve.get( i ) )
58                for ( int j = 2 * i; j < size; j += i )
59                   sieve.clear( j );
60
```

Fig. 23.13   Demonstrating the Sieve of Eratosthenes using a **BitSet** (part 2 of 3).

```
61          int counter = 0;
62
63          for ( int i = 1; i < size; i++ )
64             if ( sieve.get( i ) ) {
65                primes.append( String.valueOf( i ) );
66                primes.append( ++counter % 7 == 0 ? "\n" : "\t" );
67             }
68
69          setSize( 300, 250 );
70          show();
71       }
72
73       public static void main( String args[] )
74       {
75          BitSetTest app = new BitSetTest();
76          app.addWindowListener(
77             new WindowAdapter() {
78                public void windowClosing( WindowEvent e )
79                {
80                   System.exit( 0 );
81                }
82             }
83          );
84       }
85    }
```

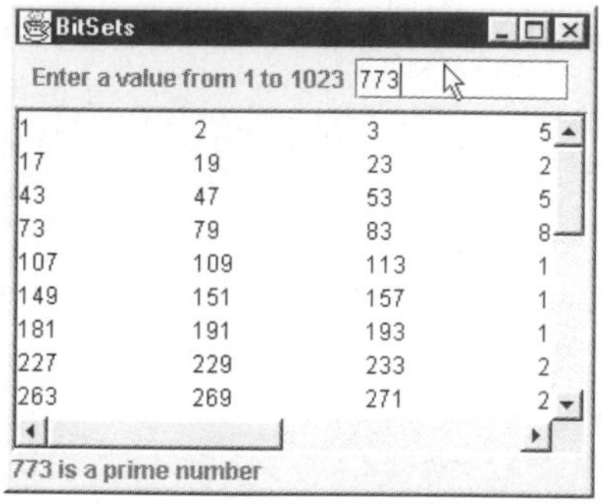

```
BitSets                              _ □ X
Enter a value from 1 to 1023  773   

1              2             3            5
17             19            23           2
43             47            53           5
73             79            83           8
107            109           113          1
149            151           157          1
181            191           193          1
227            229           233          2
263            269           271          2

773 is a prime number
```

Fig. 23.13   Demonstrating the Sieve of Eratosthenes using a **BitSet** (part 3 of 3).

The statement (line 14)

```
final BitSet sieve = new BitSet( 1024 );
```

creates a **BitSet** of 1024 bits. We ignore the bit at position 0 in this program. After all the bits in the **BitSet** are set to on (line 47), the code (line 52)

```
// perform Sieve of Eratosthenes
int finalBit = ( int ) Math.sqrt( sieve.size() );

for ( int i = 2; i < finalBit; i++ )
   if ( sieve.get( i ) )
      for ( int j = 2 * i; j < size; j += i )
         sieve.clear( j );
```

determines all the prime numbers from 1 to 1023. The integer **finalBit** is used to determine when the algorithm is complete. The basic algorithm is that a number is prime if it has no divisors other than 1 and itself. The number 1 is prime. Starting with the number 2, once we know a number is prime, we can eliminate all multiples of that number. The number 2 is only divisible by 1 and itself, so it is prime. Therefore, we can eliminate 4, 6, 8, and so on. The number 3 is divisible by 1 and itself. Therefore, we can eliminate all multiples of 3 (keep in mind that all even numbers have already been eliminated).

Summary

- Class **Vector** provides the capabilities of dynamically resizable arrays. At any time the **Vector** contains a certain number of elements which is less than or equal to its *capacity*. The capacity is the space that has been reserved for the array.

- If a **Vector** needs to grow, it grows by an increment that you specify or by a default assumed by the system. If you do not specify a capacity increment, the system will automatically double the size of the **Vector** each time additional capacity is needed.

- **Vector**s are designed to store references to **Object**s. If you would like to store values of primitive data types in **Vector**s, you must use the type-wrapper classes (**Byte**, **Short**, **Integer**, **Long**, **Float**, **Double**, **Boolean** and **Character**) to create objects containing the primitive data type values.

- Class **Vector** provides three constructors. The no-argument constructor creates an empty **Vector**. The constructor that takes one argument creates a **Vector** with an initial capacity specified by the argument. The constructor that takes two arguments creates a **Vector** with an *initial capacity* specified by the first argument and a *capacity increment* specified by the second argument.

- **Vector** method **addElement** adds its argument to the end of the **Vector**. Method **insertElementAt** inserts an element at the specified position. Method **setElementAt** sets the element at a specific position.

- **Vector** method **removeElement** removes the first occurrence of its argument. Method **removeAllElements** removes every element from the **Vector**. Method **removeElementAt** removes the element at the specified index.

- **Vector** method **firstElement** returns a reference to the first element. Method **lastElement** returns a reference to the last element.

- **Vector** method **isEmpty** determines if the **Vector** is empty. Method **contains** determines if the **Vector** contains the **searchKey** specified as an argument.

- Method **indexOf** gets the index of the first location of its argument. The method returns **-1** if the argument is not found in the **Vector**.

- **Vector** method **trimToSize** cuts the capacity of the **Vector** to the **Vector**'s size. Methods **size** and **capacity** determine the number of elements currently in the **Vector** and the number of elements that can be stored in the **Vector** without allocating more memory, respectively.

- **Vector** method **elements** returns a reference to an **Enumeration** containing the elements of the **Vector**.

- **Enumeration** method **hasMoreElements** determines if there are more elements. Method **nextElement** returns a reference to the next element.

- Class **Stack** extends class **Vector**. **Stack** method **push** adds its argument to the top of the stack. Method **pop** removes the top element of the stack. Method **peek** returns an **Object** reference to the top element of the stack without removing the element. **Stack** method **empty** determines if the stack is empty.

- A **Dictionary** transforms keys to values.

- Hashing is a high-speed scheme for converting keys into unique array subscripts for storage and retrieval of information. The load factor is the ratio of the number of occupied cells in a hash table to the size of the hash table. The closer this ratio gets to 1.0, the greater the chance of collisions.

- The no-argument **Hashtable** constructor creates a **Hashtable** with a default capacity of 101 elements and a default load factor of .75. The **Hashtable** constructor that takes one argument specifies the initial capacity, and the constructor that takes two arguments specifies the initial capacity and load factor, respectively.

- **Hashtable** method **put** adds a *key* and a *value* into a **Hashtable**. Method **get** locates the value associated with the specified key. Method **remove** deletes the value associated with the specified key. Method **isEmpty** determines if the table is empty.

- **Hashtable** method **containsKey** determines if the key specified as an argument is in the **Hashtable** (i.e., a value is associated with that key). Method **contains** determines if the **Object** specified as its argument is in the **Hashtable**. Method **clear** empties the **Hashtable**. Method **elements** obtains an **Enumeration** of the values. Method **keys** obtains an **Enumeration** of the keys.

- A **Properties** object is a persistent **Hashtable** object. Class **Properties** extends **Hashtable**. Keys and values in a **Properties** object must be **String**s.

- The **Properties** no-argument constructor creates an empty **Properties** table with no default properties. There is also an overloaded constructor that is passed a reference to a default **Properties** object containing default property values.

- **Properties** method **getProperty** locates the value of the key specified as an argument. Method **store** saves the contents of the **Properties** object to the **OutputStream** object specified as the first argument. Method **load** restores the contents of the **Properties** object from the **InputStream** object specified as the argument. Method **propertyNames** obtains an **Enumeration** of the property names.

- Java provides extensive random number generation capabilities in class **Random**. Class **Random**'s no-argument constructor uses the time to seed its random number generator differently each time it is called. To create a pseudorandom-number generator with repeatability, use the **Random** constructor that takes a seed argument.

- **Random** method **setSeed** sets the seed. Methods **nextInt** and **nextLong** generate uniformly distributed random integers. Methods **nextFloat** and **nextDouble** generate uniformly distributed values in the range $0.0 <= x < 1.0$.

- The bitwise AND (**&**) operator sets each bit in the result to 1 if the corresponding bit in both operands is 1.

- The bitwise inclusive OR (**|**) operator sets each bit in the result to 1 if the corresponding bit in either (or both) operand(s) is 1.

- The bitwise exclusive OR (**^**) operator sets each bit in the result to 1 if the corresponding bit in exactly one operand is 1.

- The left shift (**<<**) operator shifts the bits of its left operand to the left by the number of bits specified in its right operand.

- The right shift operator with sign extension (**>>**) shifts the bits in its left operand to the right by the number of bits specified in its right operand—if the left operand is negative **1**s are shifted in from the left; otherwise, **0**s are shifted in from the left.

- The right shift operator with zero extension (**>>>**) shifts the bits in its left operand to the right by the number of bits specified in its right operand—**0**s are shifted in from the left.

- The bitwise complement (~) operator sets all **0** bits in its operand to **1** in the result and sets all **1** bits to **0** in the result.
- Each bitwise operator (except complement) has a corresponding assignment operator.
- The no-argument **BitSet** constructor creates an empty **BitSet**. The one-argument **BitSet** constructor creates a **BitSet** with the number of bits specified by its argument.
- **BitSet** method **set** sets the specified bit "on." Method **clear** sets the specified bit "off." Method **get** returns **true** if the bit is on or **false** if the bit is off.
- **BitSet** method **and** performs a bit-by-bit logical AND between **BitSet**s. The result is stored in the **BitSet** that invoked the method. Bitwise logical OR and bitwise logical XOR are performed by methods **or** and **xor**.
- **BitSet** method **size** returns the size of a **BitSet**. Method **clone** copies a **BitSet** and returns a reference to the new **BitSet**. Method **toString** converts a **BitSet** to a **String**.

Terminology

addElement method of class **Vector**
and method of class **BitSet**
ArrayIndexOutOfBoundsException
bit set
BitSet class
bitwise assignment operators
    &= bitwise AND
    ^= bitwise exclusive OR
    |= bitwise inclusive OR
    <<= left shift
    >>= right shift
    >>>= right shift with zero extension
bitwise manipulation operators
    & bitwise AND
    ^ bitwise exclusive OR
    | bitwise inclusive OR
    << left shift
    >> right shift
    >>> right shift with zero extension
    ~ one's complement
capacity increment of a **Vector**
capacity method of class **Vector**
capacity of a **Vector**
clear method of class **Hashtable**
clone method of class **BitSet**
collision in hashing
contains method of class **Vector**
containsKey method of class **Hashtable**
defaults
Dictionary class
dynamically resizable array
elementAt method of class **Vector**
elements method of class **Dictionary**
elements method of class **Vector**

empty method of class **Vector**
EmptyStackException class
enumerate successive elements
Enumeration interface
equals method of class **Object**
firstElement method of class **Vector**
get method of class **Dictionary**
getProperty method of class **Properties**
hashCode method of class **Object**
hashing
Hashtable class
hasMoreElements method (**Enumeration**)
IllegalArgumentException
indexOf method of class **Vector**
initial capacity of a **Vector**
insertElementAt method of class **Vector**
isEmpty method of class **Dictionary**
isEmpty method of class **Vector**
iterate through container elements
iterator operations
java.util package
key in a **Dictionary**
key/value pair
keys method of class **Dictionary**
lastElement method of class **Vector**
last-in-first-out (LIFO) stack
list method of class **Properties**
load method of class **Properties**
load factor in hashing
nextDouble method of class **Random**
nextElement method of **Enumeration**
nextFloat method of class **Random**
nextInt method of class **Random**
nextLong method of class **Random**

Common Programming Errors

23.1   Using the logical AND operator (**&&**) for the bitwise AND operator (**&**) is a common programming error.

23.2   Using the logical OR operator (**| |**) for the bitwise OR operator (**|**) is a common programming error.

Performance Tips

23.1   Inserting additional elements into a **Vector** whose current size is less than its capacity is a relatively fast operation.

23.2   It is a relatively slow operation to insert an element into a **Vector** that needs to grow larger to accommodate the new element.

23.3   The default capacity increment of doubling the size of the **Vector** may seem wasteful of storage, but it is actually an efficient way for many **Vector**s to grow quickly to be "about the right size." This is much more efficient time-wise than growing the Vector each time by only as much space as it takes to hold a single element. But it can waste space.

23.4   If storage is at a premium, use the **trimToSize** method of the **Vector** class to trim a **Vector** to its exact size. This will optimize a **Vector**'s use of storage. But be careful. If an additional element needs to be inserted in the **Vector**, this will be slow because it will force the array to grow dynamically—trimming leaves no room for growth.

23.5   The load factor in a hash table is a classic example of a space/time trade-off: By increasing the load factor, we get better memory utilization, but the program runs slower due to increased hashing collisions. By decreasing the load factor, we get better program speed because of reduced hashing collisions, but we get poorer memory utilization because a larger portion of the hash table remains empty.

Testing and Debugging Tips

23.1   Because **Stack** inherits from **Vector**, the user may perform operations on **Stack** objects that are ordinarily not allowed on conventional stack data structures. This could corrupt the elements of the **Stack** and destroy the integrity of the **Stack**.

23.2   Use **Properties** method **list** to display the contents of a **Properties** object for debugging purposes.

23.3   The repeatability of random numbers that occurs when the same seed value is used is useful for testing and debugging. While a program is under development, use the form **Ran-**

dom(seedValue) that produces a repeatable sequence of random numbers. If a bug occurs, fix the bug and test with the same *seedValue*; this allows you to reconstruct the exact same sequence of random numbers that caused the bug. Once the bugs have been removed, use the form *Random()* that generates a new sequence of random numbers each time the program is run.

Self-Review Exercises

23.1 Fill in the blanks in each of the following:

    a) Java class _____ provides the capabilities of array-like data structures that can dynamically resize themselves.

    b) If you do not specify a capacity increment, the system will automatically _____ the size of the **Vector** each time additional capacity is needed.

    c) If storage is at a premium, use the _____ method of the **Vector** class to trim a **Vector** to its exact size.

23.2 State whether each of the following is *true* or *false*. If *false*, explain why.

    a) Values of primitive data types may be directly stored in a **Vector**.

    b) With hashing, as the load factor increases, the chance of collisions decreases.

23.1 Under what circumstances is an **EmptyStackException** thrown?

23.1 Fill in the blanks in each of the following:

    a) Bits in the result of an expression using operator _____ are set to 1 if the corresponding bits in each operand are set to 1. Otherwise, the bits are set to zero.

    b) Bits in the result of an expression using operator _____ are set to 1 if at least one of the corresponding bits in either operand is set to 1. Otherwise, the bits are set to zero.

    c) Bits in the result of an expression using operator _____ are set to 1 if exactly one of the corresponding bits in either operand is set to 1. Otherwise, the bits are set to zero.

    d) The bitwise AND operator (**&**) is often used to _____ bits, that is, to select certain bits from a bit string while zeroing others.

    e) The _____ operator is used to shift the bits of a value to the left.

    f) The _____ operator is shifts the bits of a value to the right with sign extension, and the _____ operator shifts the bits of a value to the right with zero extension.

Answers to Self-Review Exercises

23.1 a) **Vector**. b) double. c) **trimToSize**.

23.2 a) False; a **Vector** stores only **Object**s. You must use the type-wrapper classes (**Byte, Short, Integer, Long, Float, Double, Boolean** and **Character**) from package **java.lang** to create **Object**s containing the primitive data type values. b) False; as the load factor increases, there are fewer available slots relative to the total number of slots, so the chance of selecting an occupied slot with a hashing operation (i.e., a collision) increases.

23.3 **pop** an empty **Stack** object; **peek** an empty **Stack** object.

23.4 a) bitwise AND (**&**).   b) bitwise inclusive OR (**|**). c) bitwise exclusive OR (**^**).   d) mask. e) left shift operator (**<<**). f) right shift operator with sign extension (**>>**), right shift operator with zero extension (**>>>**).

Exercises

23.2 Define each of the following terms in the context of hashing:

    a) application key.

    b) collision.

    c) hashing transformation.

d) load factor.
e) space/time trade-off.
f) **Hashtable** class.
g) capacity of a **Hashtable**.

23.3   Explain briefly the operation of each of the following methods of class **Vector**:
a) **addElement**.
b) **insertElementAt**.
c) **setElementAt**.
d) **removeElement**.
e) **removeAllElements**.
f) **removeElementAt**.
g) **firstElement**.
h) **lastElement**.
i) **isEmpty**.
j) **contains**.
k) **indexOf**.
l) **trimToSize**.
m) **size**.
n) **capacity**.

23.4   Explain why inserting additional elements into a **Vector** object whose current size is less than its capacity is a relatively fast operation and why inserting additional elements into a **Vector** object whose current size is at capacity is a relatively slow operation.

23.5   In the text we state that the default capacity increment of doubling the size of a **Vector** may seem wasteful of storage, but it is actually an efficient way for **Vector**s to grow quickly to be "about the right size." Explain this statement. Explain the pros and cons of this doubling algorithm. What can a program do when it determines that the doubling is wasting space?

23.6   Explain the use of the **Enumeration** interface with objects of class **Vector**.

23.7   By extending class **Vector**, Java's designers were able to create class **Stack** quickly. What are the negative aspects of this use of inheritance, particularly for class **Stack**?

23.8   Explain briefly the operation of each of the following methods of class **Hashtable**:
a) **put**.
b) **get**.
c) **remove**.
d) **isEmpty**.
e) **containsKey**.
f) **contains**.
g) **clear**.
h) **elements**.
i) **keys**.

23.9   Explain how to use the **Random** class to create pseudorandom numbers with the kind of repeatability we need for debugging.

23.10   Use a **Hashtable** to create a reusable class for choosing one of the 13 predefined colors in class **Color**. The name of the color should be used as keys and the predefined **Color** objects should be used as values. Place this class in a package that can be imported into any Java program. Use your new class in an application that allows the user to select a color and draw a shape in that color.

23.11   Modify your solution to Exercise 13.18—the polymorphic painting program—to store every shape the user draws in a **Vector** of **MyShape** objects. For the purpose of this exercise, create your own **Vector** subclass called **ShapeVector** that manipulates only **MyShape** objects. Provide the following capabilities in your program:

    a) Allow the user of the program to remove any number of shapes from the **Vector** by clicking an **Undo** button.

    b) Allow the user to select any shape on the screen and move it to a new location. This requires the addition of a new method to the **MyShape** hierarchy. The method's first line should be

```
public boolean isInside()
```

       This method should be overridden for each subclass of **MyShape** to determine if the coordinates where the user pressed the mouse button are inside the shape.

    c) Allow the user to select any shape on the screen and change its color.

    d) Allow the user to select any shape on the screen that can be filled or unfilled and change its fill state.

23.12 What does it mean when we state that a **Properties** object is a "persistent" **Hashtable** object? Explain the operation of each of the following methods of the **Properties** class:

    a) **load**.
    b) **store**.
    c) **getProperty**.
    d) **propertyNames**.
    e) **list**.

23.13 Why might you want to use objects of class **BitSet**? Explain the operation of each of the following methods of class **BitSet**:

    a) **set**.
    b) **clear**.
    c) **get**.
    d) **and**.
    e) **or**.
    f) **xor**.
    g) **size**.
    h) **equals**.
    i) **clone**.
    j) **toString**.
    k) **hashCode**.

23.14 Write a program that right shifts an integer variable 4 bits with sign extension and then right shifts the same integer variable 4 bits with zero extension. The program should print the integer in bits before and after each shift operation. Run your program once with a positive integer and run it again with a negative integer.

23.15 Show how shifting an integer left by 1 can be used to simulate multiplication by 2 and how shifting an integer right by 2 can be used to simulate division by 2. Be careful to consider issues related to the sign of an integer.

23.16 Write a program that reverses the order of the bits in an integer value. The program should input the value from the user and call method **reverseBits** to print the bits in reverse order. Print the value in bits both before and after the bits are reversed to confirm that the bits are reversed properly. You might want to implement both a recursive and an iterative solution.

23.17 Modify your solution to Exercise 22.10 to use class **Stack**.

23.18 Modify your solution to Exercise 22.12 to use class **Stack**.

23.19 Modify your solution to Exercise 22.13 to use class **Stack**.

24

Collections

Objectives

- To understand what collections are.
- To understand Java 2's new array capabilities.
- To be able to use collections framework implementations.
- To be able to use collections framework algorithms to manipulate various collections.
- To be able to use the collections framework interfaces to program polymorphically.
- To be able to use iterators to walk through the elements of a collection.
- To understand synchronization wrappers and modifiability wrappers.

I think this is the most extraordinary collection of talent, of human knowledge, that has ever been gathered together at the White House—with the possible exception of when Thomas Jefferson dines alone.
John F. Kennedy

The shapes a bright container can contain!
Theodore Roethke

Journey over all the universe in a map.
Miguel de Cervantes

It is an immutable law in business that words are words, explanations are explanations, promises are promises — but only performance is reality.
Harold S. Green

Outline

24.1 Introduction

In Chapter 22 we discussed how to create and manipulate data structures. The discussion was "low-level" in the sense that we painstakingly created each element of each data structure dynamically with **new** and modified the data structures by directly manipulating their elements and references to their elements. In this chapter we consider the *Java collections framework,* which gives the programmer access to prepackaged data structures as well as algorithms for manipulating those data structures.

With collections, instead of having to create data structures via extensive reference manipulation and dynamic memory allocation (potentially error-prone operations), the programmer simply uses existing data structures without concern for how these data structures are implemented. This is a marvelous example of code reuse. Programmers can code faster and can expect excellent performance, maximizing execution speed and minimizing memory consumption. We will discuss the *interfaces* of the collections framework, the *implementation classes,* the *algorithms* that process them and the *iterators* that "walk" through them.

Some examples of collections are the cards you hold in a card game, your favorite songs stored in your computer and the real estate records in your local registry of deeds (which map book numbers/page numbers to property owners). Java 2 provides an entire collections framework, whereas earlier versions of Java provided just a few collection classes, such as **Hashtable**, **Stack** and **Vector** (see Chapter 23, "Java Utilities Package and Bit Manipulation"), as well as built-in array capabilities. If you know C++, you may be familiar with its collections framework, which is called the *Standard Template*

Library (STL) [see Chapter 20 of *C++ How to Program: Second Edition*, by H. M. Deitel and P. J. Deitel, ©1998, Prentice Hall].

The Java collections framework provides you with ready-to-go reusable componentry; you do not need to write your own collection classes. The collections are standardized so applications can share them easily, without having to be concerned with implementation details. These collections are written for broad reuse. They are tuned for rapid execution as well as efficient use of memory. The collections framework encourages further reusability. As new data structures and algorithms are developed that fit this framework, they will have a large base of programmers familiar with the interfaces and algorithms.

24.2 Overview

A *collection* is a data structure—actually an object—that can hold other objects. The *collection interfaces* define the operations that can be performed on each type of collection. The *collection implementations* implement these operations in particular ways, some more appropriate than others for specific kinds of applications. These are carefully constructed for rapid execution and efficient use of memory. Collections encourage software reuse by providing convenient functionality.

The collections framework provides interfaces that define the operations to be performed generically on various types of collections. Some of the interfaces are **Set**, **List** and **Map**. These interfaces are implemented in various ways within the framework. Programmers may also provide implementations specific to their own requirements.

The collections framework includes a number of other features that minimize the amount of coding programmers need to do to create and manipulate collections.

The classes and interfaces that comprise the collections framework are members of the **java.util** package. In the next section, we begin our discussion with the capabilities that have been added for array manipulation.

24.3 Class **Arrays**

We begin our discussion of the collections framework with class **Arrays**—which provides **static** methods for manipulating arrays. In Chapter 7, our discussion of array manipulation was "low-level" in the sense that we painstakingly wrote code to sort and search arrays. Class **Arrays** provides "high-level" methods—such as **binarySearch** for searching a sorted array, **equals** for comparing arrays, **fill** for placing values into an array and **sort** for sorting an array. These methods are overloaded for primitive-type arrays and **Object** arrays. Figure 24.1 demonstrates the use of these methods.

Line 14

```
Arrays.fill( filledInt, 7 );    // fill with 7s
```

calls method **fill** to populate all ten elements of array **filledInt** with **7**s. Overloaded versions of **fill** allow the programmer to populate a specific range of elements with the same value.

Line 15 sorts array **doubleValues**' elements. Overloaded versions of **sort** allow the programmer to sort a specific range of elements. Method **sort** orders the array's elements in ascending order by default. We discuss how to sort in descending order later in the chapter.

```
1    // Fig. 24.1 : UsingArrays.java
2    // Using Java arrays
3    import java.util.*;
4
5    public class UsingArrays {
6        private int intValues[] = { 1, 2, 3, 4, 5, 6 };
7        private double doubleValues[] = { 8.4, 9.3, 0.2, 7.9, 3.4 };
8        private int filledInt[], intValuesCopy[];
9
10       public UsingArrays()
11       {
12           filledInt = new int[ 10 ];
13           intValuesCopy = new int[ intValues.length ];
14           Arrays.fill( filledInt, 7 );    // fill with 7s
15           Arrays.sort( doubleValues );    // sort doubleValues
16           System.arraycopy( intValues, 0, intValuesCopy,
17                             0, intValues.length );
18       }
19
20       public void printArrays()
21       {
22           System.out.print( "doubleValues: " );
23           for ( int k = 0; k < doubleValues.length; k++ )
24              System.out.print( doubleValues[ k ] + " " );
25
26           System.out.print("\nintValues: " );
27           for ( int k = 0; k < intValues.length; k++ )
28              System.out.print( intValues[ k ] + " " );
29
30           System.out.print("\nfilledInt: " );
31           for ( int k = 0; k < filledInt.length; k++ )
32              System.out.print( filledInt[ k ] + " " );
33
34           System.out.print("\nintValuesCopy: " );
35           for ( int k = 0; k < intValuesCopy.length; k++ )
36              System.out.print( intValuesCopy[ k ] + " " );
37
38           System.out.println();
39       }
40
41       public int searchForInt( int value )
42       {
43           return Arrays.binarySearch( intValues, value );
44       }
45
46       public void printEquality()
47       {
48           boolean b = Arrays.equals( intValues, intValuesCopy );
49
50           System.out.println( "intValues " + ( b ? "==" : "!=" )
51                               + " intValuesCopy" );
52
53           b = Arrays.equals( intValues, filledInt );
```

Fig. 24.1   Using methods of class **Arrays** (part 1 of 2).

```
54          System.out.println( "intValues " + ( b ? "==" : "!=" )
55                             + " filledInt" );
56      }
57
58      public static void main( String args[] )
59      {
60          UsingArrays u = new UsingArrays();
61
62          u.printArrays();
63          u.printEquality();
64
65          int n = u.searchForInt( 5 );
66          System.out.println( ( n >= 0 ? "Found 5 at element " + n :
67                             "5 not found" ) + " in intValues" );
68          n = u.searchForInt( 8763 );
69          System.out.println( ( n >= 0 ? "Found 8763 at element "
70                             + n : "8763 not found" )
71                             + " in intValues" );
72      }
73  }
```

```
doubleValues: 0.2 3.4 7.9 8.4 9.3
intValues: 1 2 3 4 5 6
filledInt: 7 7 7 7 7 7 7 7 7
intValuesCopy: 1 2 3 4 5 6
intValues == intValuesCopy
intValues != filledInt
Found 5 at element 4 in intValues
8763 not found in intValues
```

Fig. 24.1   Using methods of class **Arrays** (part 2 of 2).

Lines 16 and 17

```
System.arraycopy( intValues, 0, intValuesCopy,
                  0, intValues.length );
```

copy array **intValues** into array **intValuesCopy**. The first argument (**intValues**) passed to **System** method *arraycopy* is the array from which elements are copied. The second argument (**0**) is the array (i.e., **intValues**) subscript that specifies the starting point in the range of elements to copy. This value can be any valid array subscript. The third argument (**intValuesCopy**) specifies the array that stores the copy. The fourth argument (**0**) specifies the subscript in the destination array (i.e., **intValuesCopy**) where the first copied element is stored. The last argument (**intValues.length**) specifies the number of source array (i.e., **intValues**) elements to copy.

Line 43 calls method **binarySearch** to perform a binary search on **intValues** using **value** as the key. If **value** is found, **binarySearch** returns the subscript location where **value** was found. If the **int** is not found, **binarySearch** returns a negative value. Method **binarySearch** determines this negative value by first calculating the *insertion point* (i.e., the index where the value was expected to be found) and changing the insertion point's sign to negative. Finally, **binarySearch** subtracts one from the insertion point to obtain the return value. For example in Fig. 24.1, the number **8763** is expected to be found at index 6. This insertion point is changed to –6 and one is subtracted. The value returned is –7. This return value is useful for adding elements to a sorted array.

Common Programming Error 24.1

*Passing an unsorted array to **binarySearch** is a logic error. The value returned by **binarySearch** is undefined.*

Lines 48 and 53 call method **equals** to determine if the elements of two arrays are equivalent. Method **equals** returns **true** if the arrays are equivalent.

One of the most important features of the collection framework is the ability to manipulate the elements of one collection type through a different collection type—regardless of the collection's internal implementation. The **public** set of methods through which collections are manipulated is called a *view*.

Class **Arrays** provides method **asList** for viewing an array as a **List** collection type (a type that encapsulates behavior similar to the linked lists created in Chapter 22, "Data Structures"—we will say more about **List**s later in the chapter). A **List** view allows the programmer to programmatically manipulate the array as if it were a **List** by calling **List** methods. Any modifications made through the **List** view change the array, and any modifications made to the array change the **List** view. Figure 24.2 demonstrates method **asList**.

Line 7 declares a **List** reference called **theList**. Line 11

```
theList = Arrays.asList( values );
```

uses **Arrays** method **asList** to obtain a fixed-size **List** view of array **values**.

Performance Tip 24.1

*Using **Arrays.asList** creates a fixed-size **List** which operates faster than any of the provided **List** implementations.*

Common Programming Error 24.2

*A **List** created with **Arrays.asList** is fixed in size; calling methods **add** or **remove** throws an **UnsupportedOperationException**.*

Line 12

```
theList.set( 1, "green" );
```

uses **List** method *set* to change the contents of **List** element one to **"green"**. Because the array is being viewed through a **List**, **values[1]** is changed from **"white"** to **"green"**. Any changes made to the **List** view are made to the array.

Software Engineering Observation 24.1

*With the collections framework, there are many methods that apply to **List**s and **Collections** that you would like to be able to use for arrays. **Arrays.asList** allows you to pass an array into a **List** or **Collection** parameter.*

On line 18 method *size* is used to get the number of items in the **List**, and on line 19 method *get* is used to retrieve an individual item from the **List**. Notice that the value returned by **size** is equal to the number of elements in array **values** and that the values returned by **get** are equal to the values contained in array **values**.

```
1   // Fig. 24.2 : UsingAsList.java
2   // Using method asList
3   import java.util.*;
4
5   public class UsingAsList {
6      private String values[] = { "red", "white", "blue" };
7      private List theList;
8
9      public UsingAsList()
10     {
11        theList = Arrays.asList( values );    // get List
12        theList.set( 1, "green" );            // change a value
13     }
14
15     public void printElements()
16     {
17        System.out.print( "List elements : " );
18        for ( int k = 0; k < theList.size(); k++ )
19           System.out.print( theList.get( k ) + " " );
20
21        System.out.print( "\nArray elements: " );
22        for ( int k = 0; k < values.length; k++ )
23           System.out.print( values[ k ] + " " );
24
25        System.out.println();
26     }
27
28     public static void main( String args[] )
29     {
30        new UsingAsList().printElements();
31     }
32  }
```

```
List elements : red green blue
Array elements: red green blue
```

Fig. 24.2 Using **static** method **asList**.

24.4 Interface Collection and Class Collections

Interface *Collection* is the root interface in the collections hierarchy from which interfaces **Set** (a collection that does not contain duplicates—discussed in Section 24.7) and **List** are derived. Interface **Collection** contains *bulk operations* (i.e., operations performed on the entire collection) for adding, clearing, comparing and retaining objects (also called *elements*) in the collection. Conversion of a **Collection** to an array is another service provided. Interface **Collection** also provides a method for getting an object that allows a collection's elements to be accessed—called an *Iterator*. **Iterator**s are similar to the **Enumeration**s introduced in Chapter 23. The primary difference between an **Iterator** and an **Enumeration** is that **Iterator**s can remove elements—**Enumeration**s cannot. Interface **Collection** also provides operations for determining a collection's size, a collection's hash code, and whether or not the collection is empty.

Software Engineering Observation 24.2

Collection *is commonly used as a method parameter type to allow polymorphic processing of collections.*

Software Engineering Observation 24.3

Most collection implementations provide a constructor that takes one **Collection** *argument—thereby allowing one collection type to be treated as another collection type.*

Class **Collections** provides **static** methods that manipulate collections polymorphically. These methods implement algorithms for searching, sorting, etc. You will learn more about these algorithms in Section 24.6.

Other **Collections** methods include *wrapper methods* that return new collections. We discuss wrapper methods in Sections 24.9 and 24.10.

24.5 Lists

A **List** is an ordered **Collection** that may contain duplicate elements. A **List** is sometimes called a *sequence*. Like arrays, **List**s are zero based (i.e., the first element's *index* is zero). In addition to the interface inherited from **Collection**, **List** provides methods for manipulating elements using their indices, manipulating a specified range of elements, searching the elements and getting a **ListIterator** to access the elements.

Interface **List** is implemented by classes **ArrayList**, **LinkedList** and **Vector**. Class **ArrayList** is a resizable-array implementation of a **List**. Class **ArrayList**'s behavior, and capabilities are similar to the **Vector** class introduced in Chapter 23. A **LinkedList** is a linked list implementation of a **List**.

Performance Tip 24.2

ArrayList*s behave like un***synchronized Vector***s and therefore execute faster than* **Vector***s because they are not thread-safe.*

Software Engineering Observation 24.4

LinkedList*s can be used to create stacks, queues, trees and deques (double-ended queues).*

Figure 24.3 uses an **ArrayList** to demonstrate some of the **Collection** interface capabilities. The program places **String**s and **Color**s in an **ArrayList** and uses an **Iterator** to remove the **String**s from the **ArrayList** collection.

```
1   // Fig. 24.3 : CollectionTest.java
2   // Using the Collection interface
3   import java.util.*;
4   import java.awt.Color;
5
6   public class CollectionTest {
7      private String colors[] = { "red", "white", "blue" };
8
```

Fig. 24.3   Using an **ArrayList** to demonstrate **Collection** interface features (part 1 of 2).

```
9    public CollectionTest()
10   {
11      ArrayList aList = new ArrayList();
12
13      aList.add( Color.magenta );        // add a color object
14
15      for ( int k = 0; k < colors.length; k++ )
16         aList.add( colors[ k ] );
17
18      aList.add( Color.cyan );           // add a color object
19
20      System.out.println( "\nArrayList: " );
21      for ( int k = 0; k < aList.size(); k++ )
22         System.out.print( aList.get( k ) + " " );
23
24      removeStrings( aList );
25
26      System.out.println( "\n\nArrayList after calling" +
27                          " removeStrings: " );
28      for ( int k = 0; k < aList.size(); k++ )
29         System.out.print( aList.get( k ) + " " );
30   }
31
32   public void removeStrings( Collection c )
33   {
34      Iterator i = c.iterator();      // get iterator
35
36      while ( i.hasNext() ) // loop while collection has items
37
38         if ( i.next() instanceof String )
39            i.remove();                  // remove String object
40   }
41
42   public static void main( String args[] )
43   {
44      new CollectionTest();
45   }
46 }
```

```
ArrayList:
java.awt.Color[r=255,g=0,b=255] red white blue ja-
va.awt.Color[r=0,g=255,b=255]

ArrayList after calling removeStrings:
java.awt.Color[r=255,g=0,b=255] java.awt.Col-
or[r=0,g=255,b=255]
```

Fig. 24.3 Using an **ArrayList** to demonstrate **Collection** interface features (part 2 of 2).

Line 11 creates a reference **aList** to an instance of an **ArrayList**. Lines 13 through 18 populate **aList** with **Color**s and **String**s. Each element of **aList** is then output (lines 20 through 22). Method **get** is called to retrieve individual element values, and method *size* is called to get the number of **ArrayList** elements. Line 24

        removeStrings(aList);

calls programmer-defined method **removeStrings** passing **aList** as an argument. Method **removeStrings** deletes **String**s from a collection and is defined on lines 32 through 40. We will discuss **removeStrings** in more detail momentarily.

Lines 26 through 29 print the elements of **aList** after **removeStrings** has been called. Notice that the output in Fig. 24.3 contains only **Color**s.

Method **removeStrings** declares one **Collection** parameter reference that allows any collection type to be passed as an argument to this method. Each collection element is accessed using an **Iterator**. Line 34

        Iterator i = c.iterator();   // get iterator

calls method *iterator* to get an **Iterator** for **Collection** c. The **while** loop condition (line 36)

        i.hasNext()

calls **Iterator** method *hasNext* to determine if the **Collection** contains another element. Method **hasNext** returns **true** if another element exists and **false** otherwise.

The **if** condition (line 38)

        i.next() instanceof String

tests if the *next* element's **Object** is a **String** using the object comparison operator **instanceof**. If the **Object** is a **String**, **Iterator** method *remove* is called to remove the **String** from the **Collection**.

Figure 24.4 demonstrates operations on **LinkedList**s. The program creates two **LinkedList**s that each contain **String**s. The elements of one **List** are added to the other. All elements are then converted to uppercase before deleting a range of elements.

```
1   // Fig. 24.4 : ListTest.java
2   // Using LinkLists
3   import java.util.*;
4
5   public class ListTest {
6       private String colors[] = { "black", "yellow", "green",
7                                   "blue", "violet", "silver" };
8       private String colors2[] = { "gold", "white", "brown",
9                                    "blue", "gray", "silver" };
10
11      public ListTest()
12      {
13          LinkedList link = new LinkedList();
14          LinkedList link2 = new LinkedList();
```

Fig. 24.4   Using **List**s and **ListIterator**s (part 1 of 3).

```
15
16              for ( int k = 0; k < colors.length; k++ ) {
17                 link.add( colors[ k ] );
18                 link2.add( colors2[ k ] );    // same length as colors
19              }
20
21              link.addAll( link2 );               // concatenate lists
22              link2 = null;                        // release resources
23
24              printList( link );
25              uppercaseStrings( link );
26              printList( link );
27              System.out.print( "\nDeleting elements 4 to 6..." );
28              removeItems( link, 4, 7 );
29              printList( link );
30           }
31
32           public void printList( List listRef )
33           {
34              System.out.println( "\nlist: " );
35              for ( int k = 0; k < listRef.size(); k++ )
36                 System.out.print( listRef.get( k ) + " " );
37
38              System.out.println();
39           }
40
41           public void uppercaseStrings( List listRef2 )
42           {
43              ListIterator listIt = listRef2.listIterator();
44
45              while ( listIt.hasNext() ) {
46                 Object o = listIt.next();          // get item
47
48                 if ( o instanceof String )        // check for String
49                    listIt.set( ( ( String ) o ).toUpperCase() );
50              }
51           }
52
53           public void removeItems( List listRef3, int start, int end )
54           {
55              listRef3.subList( start, end ).clear();   // remove items
56           }
57
58           public static void main( String args[] )
59           {
60              new ListTest();
61           }
62        }
```

Fig. 24.4 Using **List**s and **ListIterator**s (part 2 of 3).

LinkedLists **link** and **link2** are constructed on lines 13 and 14, respectively. The **for** loop (lines 16 to 19) calls method **add** to append elements from arrays **colors** and **colors2** to the end of **link** and **link2**.

```
list:
black yellow green blue violet silver gold white brown
blue gray silver

list:
BLACK YELLOW GREEN BLUE VIOLET SILVER GOLD WHITE BROWN
BLUE GRAY SILVER

Deleting elements 4 to 6...
list:
BLACK YELLOW GREEN BLUE WHITE BROWN BLUE GRAY SILVER
```

Fig. 24.4   Using **List**s and **ListIterator**s (part 3 of 3).

Line 21

```
link.addAll( link2 );
```

calls method **addAll** to append all elements of **link2** to the end of **link**. The elements appended are **link2**'s elements. Line 22 sets **link2** to **null**. Lines 24 through 29 call programmer-defined method **printList** three times to print the **List** and programmer-defined methods **uppercaseStrings** to convert the **String** elements to uppercase and **removeItems** once to remove elements.

Method **printList** (lines 32 through 39) prints the elements of the **List** passed to it. The **for** loop on lines 35 and 36 calls **System.out.print** to display the **List**. Method **size** is called to get the number of elements in the **List**. In the **for** body, method **get** is called to retrieve an object at the specified index.

Method **uppercaseStrings** (lines 41 through 51) changes lowercase **String** elements in the **List** passed to it to uppercase **String**s. Line 43

```
ListIterator listIt = listRef2.listIterator();
```

calls method **listIterator** to get a *bidirectional iterator* (i.e., an iterator that can traverse a **List** backward and forward) for the **List**. In the **while** condition, method **hasNext** is called to determine if the **List** contains another element. Line 46

```
Object o = listIt.next();
```

gets the next **Object** from the **List** and assigns it to **o**. The **if** condition tests **o** for an **instanceof** a **String**. Line 49

```
listIt.set( ( ( String ) o ).toUpperCase() );
```

casts **o** to a **String** and calls method **toUpperCase** to get an uppercase version of the **String**. Method **set** replaces the current **String** that **listIt** refers to with the **String** returned by **toUpperCase**.

Programmer-defined method **removeItems** (lines 53 through 56) removes a range of items from the list. Line 55

```
listRef3.subList( start, end ).clear();
```

calls method *subList* to get a portion of the **List** called a *sublist*. Method **subList** takes two arguments—the beginning index for the sublist and the ending index for the sublist. [Note: the ending index is not part of the sublist range. In this example, we pass **4** for the beginning index and **7** for the ending index to **subList**. The sublist returned is the elements with indices 4 through 6.] Method *clear* is called to remove the sublist elements from the **List**. Any changes made to a sublist are also made to the **List** (i.e., the sublist is a **List** view of its corresponding **List** elements).

Figure 24.5 uses method *toArray* to get an array from a collection (e.g., **LinkedList**). The program adds a series of **String**s to a **LinkedList** and calls method **toArray** to get an array from the **LinkedList**.

```
1   // Fig. 24.5 : UsingToArray.java
2   // Using method toArray
3   import java.util.*;
4
5   public class UsingToArray {
6
7      public UsingToArray()
8      {
9         LinkedList links;
10        String colors[] = { "black", "blue", "yellow" };
11
12        links = new LinkedList( Arrays.asList( colors ) );
13
14        links.addLast( "red" );    // add as last item
15        links.add( "pink" );       // add to the end
16        links.add( 3, "green" );   // add at 3rd index
17        links.addFirst( "cyan" );  // add as first item
18
19        // get the LinkedList elements as an array
20        colors = ( String [] ) links.toArray( new String[ 0 ] );
21
22        System.out.println( "colors: " );
23        for ( int k = 0; k < colors.length; k++ )
24           System.out.println( colors[ k ] );
25     }
26
27     public static void main( String args[] )
28     {
29        new UsingToArray();
30     }
31  }
```

Fig. 24.5   Using method **toArray** (part 1 of 2).

```
colors:
cyan
black
blue
yellow
green
red
pink
```

Fig. 24.5   Using method **toArray** (part 2 of 2).

Line 12

```
links = new LinkedList( Arrays.asList( colors ) );
```

constructs a **LinkedList** containing the elements of **colors** and assigns the **LinkedList** to **links**. Line 14 calls method **addLast** to add **"red"** to the end of **links**. Method **add** is called on lines 15 and 16 to add **"pink"** as the last element and **"green"** as the third element, respectively. Line 17 calls method **addFirst** to add **"cyan"** as the first item in the **LinkedList**. [*Note:* When **"cyan"** is added as the first element, **"green"** becomes the fourth element in the **LinkedList**.]

Line 20

```
colors = ( String [] ) links.toArray( new String[ 0 ] );
```

calls method **toArray** to get a **Color** array from **links**. The array is a copy—modifying the contents of the array does not modify the **LinkedList**. The array passed to method **toArray** is the same data type returned by **toArray**. If the number of elements in the array is greater than the number of elements in the **LinkedList**, the array passed to **toArray** is returned. If the **LinkedList** has more elements than the elements in the array passed to **toArray**, new memory is allocated to store the array created by **toArray**.

 Common Programming Error 24.3

*Passing an array that contains data to **toArray** can create logic errors. If the number of elements in the array is smaller than the number of elements in the **Object** calling **toArray**, new memory is allocated to store the **Object**'s elements—without preserving the array's elements. If the number of elements in the array is greater than the number of elements in the **Object**, the array elements (starting at subscript 0) are overwritten with the **Object**'s elements. Array elements not overwritten retain their values.*

24.6 Algorithms

The collections framework provides a variety of high-performance *algorithms* for manipulating collection elements. These algorithms are implemented as **static** methods. Algorithms **sort**, **binarySearch**, **reverse**, **shuffle**, **fill** and **copy** operate on **List**s. Algorithms **min** and **max** operate on **Collections**.

Algorithm *reverse* reverses the elements of a **List**, *fill* sets every **List** element to refer to a specified **Object** and **copy** copies references from one **List** into another **List**.

Software Engineering Observation 24.5

The collections framework algorithms are polymorphic. Each of these algorithms can operate on objects that offer given interfaces without concern to the underlying implementations.

24.6.1 Algorithm `sort`

Algorithm **sort** sorts the elements of a **List**. The order is determined by the natural order of the elements' type. The **sort** call may specify a second argument of a *Comparator* object that specifies how the ordering is determined. We will say more about **Comparator**s in a moment.

Algorithm **sort** uses a *stable sort* (i.e., one that does not reorder equivalent elements while sorting). The **sort** algorithm is fast. For readers who have studied some complexity theory in data structures or algorithms courses, this sort runs in $n \log(n)$ time. For readers not familiar with complexity theory, rest assured that this is an extremely fast algorithm.

Software Engineering Observation 24.6

The Java API documentation sometimes provides implementation details. For example, **sort** *is implemented as a modified merge sort. Avoid writing code that is dependent on implementation details—because they can change.*

Figure 24.6 uses algorithm **sort** to order the elements of an **ArrayList** into ascending order with the statement (line 17)

```
Collections.sort( theList );
```

The sorted **ArrayList** elements are displayed in the console window with **System.out.println**.

```
1   // Fig. 24.6 : Sort1.java
2   // Using algorithm sort
3   import java.util.*;
4
5   public class Sort1 {
6      private static String suits[] = { "Hearts", "Diamonds",
7                                        "Clubs", "Spades" };
8
9      public void printElements()
10     {
11        ArrayList theList =
12                  new ArrayList( Arrays.asList( suits ) );
13
14        System.out.println( "Unsorted array elements:\n" +
15                            theList );
16
17        Collections.sort( theList );    // sort the List
18
19        System.out.println( "Sorted array elements:\n" +
20                            theList );
21     }
```

Fig. 24.6   Using algorithm **sort** (part 1 of 2).

```
22
23      public static void main( String args[] )
24      {
25         new Sort1().printElements();
26      }
27   }
```

```
Unsorted array elements:
[Hearts, Diamonds, Clubs, Spades]
Sorted array elements:
[Clubs, Diamonds, Hearts, Spades]
```

Fig. 24.6   Using algorithm **sort** (part 2 of 2).

Figure 24.7 sorts the same **String**s used in Fig. 24.6 into descending order. The example introduces the **Comparator** object for sorting a **Collection**'s elements in a different order.

```
1    // Fig. 24.7 : Sort2.java
2    // Using a Comparator object with algorithm sort
3    import java.util.*;
4
5    public class Sort2 {
6       private static String suits[] = { "Hearts", "Diamonds",
7                                         "Clubs", "Spades" };
8
9       public void printElements()
10      {
11         List theList = Arrays.asList( suits );   // get List
12         System.out.println( "Unsorted array elements:\n" +
13                             theList );
14
15         // sort in descending order
16         Collections.sort( theList, Collections.reverseOrder() );
17
18         System.out.println( "Sorted list elements:\n" +
19                             theList );
20      }
21
22      public static void main( String args[] )
23      {
24         new Sort2().printElements();
25      }
26   }
```

```
Unsorted array elements:
[Hearts, Diamonds, Clubs, Spades]
Sorted list elements:
[Spades, Hearts, Diamonds, Clubs]
```

Fig. 24.7   Using a **Comparator** object in **sort**.

Line 16

```
Collections.sort( theList, Collections.reverseOrder() );
```

calls **Collections**' method **sort** to order the **List** view of the array into descending order. Method *reverseOrder* returns a **Comparator** object that represents the collection's reverse order. For sorting a **List** view of a **String** array, the reverse order is a *lexicographical comparison*—the Unicode values that represent each element are compared—in descending order.

24.6.2 Algorithm `shuffle`

Algorithm **shuffle** randomly orders a **List**'s elements. In Chapter 10, we presented a card shuffling and dealing simulation where we used a loop to shuffle a deck of cards. In Fig. 24.8 we use algorithm **shuffle** to shuffle the deck of cards. Much of the code is the same as Fig. 10.21.

The shuffling of the deck is implemented on line 47

```
Collections.shuffle( theList );
```

which calls **Collections** method **shuffle** to shuffle the array through the array's **List** view.

```
1   // Fig. 24.8 : Cards.java
2   // Using algorithm shuffle
3   import java.util.*;
4
5   class Card {
6      private String face;
7      private String suit;
8
9      public Card( String face, String suit )
10     {
11        this.face = face;
12        this.suit = suit;
13     }
14
15     public String getFace() { return face; }
16
17     public String getSuit() { return suit; }
18
19     public String toString()
20     {
21       StringBuffer buf = new StringBuffer( face + " of " + suit );
22
23       buf.setLength( 20 );
24       return ( buf.toString() );
25     }
26  }
27
```

Fig. 24.8   Card shuffling and dealing example (part 1 of 3).

```
28   // class Cards definition
29   public class Cards {
30      private static String suits[] = { "Hearts", "Clubs",
31                                "Diamonds", "Spades" };
32      private static String faces[] = { "Ace", "Deuce", "Three",
33                                "Four", "Five", "Six",
34                                "Seven", "Eight", "Nine",
35                                "Ten", "Jack", "Queen",
36                                "King" };
37      private List theList;
38
39      public Cards()
40      {
41         Card deck[] = new Card[ 52 ];
42
43         for ( int k = 0; k < deck.length; k++ )
44           deck[ k ] = new Card( faces[ k % 13 ], suits[ k / 13 ] );
45
46         theList = Arrays.asList( deck );    // get List
47         Collections.shuffle( theList );     // shuffle deck
48      }
49
50      public void printCards()
51      {
52         int half = theList.size() / 2 - 1;
53
54         for ( int k = 0, k2 = half; k <= half; k++, k2++ )
55            System.out.println( theList.get( k ).toString() +
56                               theList.get( k2 ) );
57      }
58
59      public static void main( String args[] )
60      {
61         new Cards().printCards();
62      }
63   }
```

Fig. 24.8   Card shuffling and dealing example (part 2 of 3).

24.6.3 Algorithms reverse, fill, copy, max and min

Class **Collections** provides algorithms for reversing, filling and copying **List**s. Algorithm **reverse** reverses the order of the elements in a **List** and **fill** overwrites elements in a **List** with a specified value. The **fill** operation is useful for reinitializing a **List**. Algorithm **copy** takes two arguments: a destination **List** and a source **List**. Each source **List** element is copied to the destination **List**. The destination **List** must be at least as long as the source **List**—otherwise, an **IndexOutOfBoundsException** is thrown. If the destination **List** is longer, the elements not overwritten are unchanged.

Each of the algorithms we have seen so far operates on a **List**s. Algorithms **min** and **max** each operate on **Collections**.

King of Diamonds	Ten of Spades
Deuce of Hearts	Five of Spades
King of Clubs	Five of Clubs
Jack of Diamonds	Jack of Spades
King of Spades	Ten of Clubs
Six of Clubs	Three of Clubs
Seven of Clubs	Jack of Clubs
Seven of Hearts	Six of Spades
Eight of Hearts	Six of Diamonds
King of Hearts	Nine of Diamonds
Ace of Hearts	Four of Hearts
Jack of Hearts	Queen of Diamonds
Queen of Clubs	Six of Hearts
Seven of Diamonds	Ace of Spades
Three of Spades	Deuce of Spades
Seven of Spades	Five of Diamonds
Ten of Hearts	Queen of Hearts
Ten of Diamonds	Eight of Clubs
Nine of Spades	Three of Diamonds
Four of Spades	Ace of Clubs
Four of Clubs	Four of Diamonds
Nine of Clubs	Three of Hearts
Eight of Diamonds	Deuce of Diamonds
Deuce of Clubs	Nine of Hearts
Eight of Spades	Five of Hearts
Ten of Spades	Queen of Spades

Fig. 24.8   Card shuffling and dealing example (part 3 of 3).

Algorithm **min** returns the smallest element in a **List**, and algorithm **max** returns the largest element in a **List**. Both of these algorithms can be called with a **Comparator** object as a second argument. Figure 24.9 demonstrates the use of algorithms **reverse**, **fill**, **copy**, **min** and **max**.

```
1   // Fig. 24.9 : Algorithms1.java
2   // Using algorithms reverse, fill, copy, min and max
3   import java.util.*;
4
5   public class Algorithms1 {
6      private String letters[] = { "P", "C", "M" }, lettersCopy[];
7      private List theList, copyList;
8
9      public Algorithms1()
10     {
11        theList = Arrays.asList( letters );     // get List
12        lettersCopy = new String[ 3 ];
13        copyList = Arrays.asList( lettersCopy );
14
```

Fig. 24.9   Using algorithms **reverse**, **fill**, **copy**, **max** and **min** (part 1 of 2).

```
15        System.out.println( "Printing initial statistics: " );
16        printStatistics( theList );
17
18        Collections.reverse( theList );          // reverse order
19        System.out.println( "\nPrinting statistics after " +
20                            "calling reverse: " );
21        printStatistics( theList );
22
23        Collections.copy( copyList, theList );   // copy List
24        System.out.println( "\nPrinting statistics after " +
25                            "copying: " );
26        printStatistics( copyList );
27
28        System.out.println( "\nPrinting statistics after " +
29                            "calling fill: " );
30        Collections.fill( theList, "R" );
31        printStatistics( theList );
32     }
33
34     private void printStatistics( List listRef )
35     {
36        System.out.print( "The list is: " );
37        for ( int k = 0; k < listRef.size(); k++ )
38           System.out.print( listRef.get( k ) + " " );
39
40      System.out.print( "\nMax: " + Collections.max( listRef ) );
41        System.out.println( "  Min: " +
42                            Collections.min( listRef ) );
43     }
44
45     public static void main( String args[] )
46     {
47        new Algorithms1();
48     }
49  }
```

```
Printing initial statistics:
The list is: P C M
Max: P  Min: C

Printing statistics after calling reverse:
The list is: M C P
Max: P  Min: C

Printing statistics after copying:
The list is: M C P
Max: P  Min: C

Printing statistics after calling fill:
The list is: R R R
Max: R  Min: R
```

Fig. 24.9   Using algorithms **reverse**, **fill**, **copy**, **max** and **min** (part 2 of 2).

Line 18

```
Collections.reverse( theList );
```

calls **Collections** method *reverse* to reverse the order of **List theList**. Method **reverse** takes one **List** argument (**theList** is a **List** view of **String** array **letters**). Array **letters** now has its elements in reverse order.

Line 23 copies the elements of **theList** into **copyList** with **Collections** method **copy**. Changes to **copyList** do not change **letters**—this is a separate **List** that is not a **List** view for **letters**. Method **copy** requires two **List** arguments.

Line 30 calls **Collections** method **fill** to place the **String "R"** in each element of **theList**. Because **theList** is a **List** view of **letters**, each element in **letters** is changed to **"R"**. Method **fill** requires a **List** for the first argument and an **Object** for the second argument.

Lines 40 and 42 call **Collection** methods **max** and **min** to find the largest element and the smallest element in **theList**.

24.6.4 Algorithm `binarySearch`

Earlier in the text we studied the high-speed binary search algorithm. This algorithm is built right into the Java collections framework. The **binarySearch** algorithm locates an **Object** in a **List** (i.e., **LinkedList**, **Vector** and **ArrayList**) If the **Object** is found, the index (position relative to 0) of that **Object** is returned. If the **Object** is not found, **binarySearch** returns a negative value. Algorithm **binarySearch** determines this negative value by first calculating the insertion point and changing the insertion point's sign to negative. Finally, **binarySearch** subtracts one from the insertion point to obtain the return value.

Figure 24.10 uses the **binarySearch** algorithm to search for a series of **String**s in an **ArrayList**.

```
1   // Fig. 24.10 : BinarySearchTest.java
2   // Using algorithm binarySearch
3   import java.util.*;
4
5   public class BinarySearchTest {
6      private String colors[] = { "red", "white", "blue",
7                                  "black", "yellow",
8                                  "purple", "tan", "pink" };
9      private ArrayList aList;          // ArrayList reference
10
11     public BinarySearchTest()
12     {
13        aList = new ArrayList( Arrays.asList( colors ) );
14        Collections.sort( aList );    // sort the ArrayList
15        System.out.println( "Sorted ArrayList: " + aList );
16     }
17
```

Fig. 24.10   Using algorithm **binarySearch** (part 1 of 2).

```
18      public void printSearchResults()
19      {
20         printSearchResultsHelper( colors[ 3 ] ); // first item
21         printSearchResultsHelper( colors[ 0 ] ); // middle item
22         printSearchResultsHelper( colors[ 7 ] ); // last item
23         printSearchResultsHelper( "aardvark" );  // below lowest
24         printSearchResultsHelper( "goat" );      // doesnt exist
25         printSearchResultsHelper( "zebra" );     // doesnt exist
26      }
27
28      private void printSearchResultsHelper( String key )
29      {
30         int result = 0;
31
32         System.out.println( "\nSearching for: " + key );
33         result = Collections.binarySearch( aList, key );
34         System.out.println( ( result >= 0 ? "Found at index "
35                            + result
36                            : "Not Found (" + result + ")" ) );
37      }
38
39      public static void main( String args[] )
40      {
41         new BinarySearchTest().printSearchResults();
42      }
43   }
```

```
Sorted ArrayList: black blue pink purple red tan white
yellow
Searching for: black
Found at index 0

Searching for: red
Found at index 4

Searching for: pink
Found at index 2

Searching for: aardvark
Not Found (-1)

Searching for: goat
Not Found (-3)

Searching for: zebra
Not Found (-9)
```

Fig. 24.10   Using algorithm **binarySearch** (part 2 of 2).

Line 14 calls **Collections** method **sort** to sort **List aList** into ascending order. Line 33 calls **Collections** method **binarySearch** to search **aList** for **key**. Method **binarySearch** takes a **List** as the first argument and an **Object** as the second argument. An overloaded version of **binarySearch** takes a **Comparator** object as its third argument.

If the search key is found, method **binarySearch** returns the **List** index of the element containing the search key. When a search key is found in the **List**, the value returned by **binarySearch** is greater than or equal to zero. If the search key is not found, method **binarySearch** returns a negative number.

Software Engineering Observation 24.7

*Java does not guarantee which item will be found first when a **binarySearch** is performed on a **List** containing multiple elements equivalent to the search key.*

24.7 Sets

A *Set* is a **Collection** that contains unique elements (i.e., no duplicate elements). The collections framework contains two **Set** implementations—*HashSet* and *TreeSet*. **HashSet** stores its elements in a hash table and **TreeSet** stores its elements in a tree. Figure 24.11 uses a **HashSet** to remove duplicate **String**s from an **ArrayList**.

```
1   // Fig. 24.11 : SetTest.java
2   // Using a HashSet to remove duplicates
3   import java.util.*;
4
5   public class SetTest {
6      private String colors[] = { "red", "white", "blue",
7                                   "green", "gray", "orange",
8                                   "tan", "white", "cyan",
9                                   "peach", "gray", "orange" };
10
11     public SetTest()
12     {
13        ArrayList aList;
14
15        aList = new ArrayList( Arrays.asList( colors ) );
16        System.out.println( "ArrayList: " + aList );
17        printNonDuplicates( aList );
18     }
19
20     public void printNonDuplicates( Collection c )
21     {
22        HashSet ref = new HashSet( c );    // create a HashSet
23        Iterator i = ref.iterator();       // get iterator
24
25        System.out.println( "\nNonduplicates are: " );
26        while ( i.hasNext() )
27           System.out.print( i.next() + " " );
28
29        System.out.println();
30     }
31
```

Fig. 24.11   Using a **HashSet** to remove duplicates (part 1 of 2).

```
32       public static void main( String args[] )
33       {
34          new SetTest();
35       }
36   }
```

```
ArrayList: [red, white, blue, green, gray, orange, tan,
white, cyan, peach, gray, orange]

Nonduplicates are:
orange cyan green tan white blue peach red gray
```

Fig. 24.11   Using a **HashSet** to remove duplicates (part 2 of 2).

Programmer-defined method **printNonDuplicates** (lines 20 through 30) takes a **Collection** argument. Line 22

```
HashSet ref = new HashSet( c );
```

constructs a **HashSet** from the **Collection** passed to **printNonDuplicates**. The **HashSet** removes any duplicates in the **Collection** when it is constructed. By definition, **HashSet ref** does not contain any duplicates. Line 23 gets an **Iterator** for the **HashSet**. The **while** loop (lines 26 and 27) calls **Iterator** methods **hasNext** and **next** to access the **HashSet** elements.

Interface *SortedSet* extends **Set** and maintains its elements in sorted order (i.e., the elements' natural order or an order specified by a **Comparator**). Class **TreeSet** implements **SortedSet**.

The program of Fig. 24.12 places **String**s into a **TreeSet**. The **String**s are automatically sorted when they are added to the **TreeSet**. *Range-view* methods (i.e., methods that allow a portion of a collection to be viewed) are also demonstrated in this example.

```
1    // Fig. 24.12 : SortedSetTest.java
2    // Using TreeSet and SortedSet
3    import java.util.*;
4
5    public class SortedSetTest {
6       private static String names[] = { "yellow", "green", "black",
7                                         "tan", "grey", "white",
8                                         "orange", "red", "green" };
9
10      public SortedSetTest()
11      {
12         TreeSet m = new TreeSet( Arrays.asList( names ) );
13
14         System.out.println( "set: " );
15         printSet( m );
16
```

Fig. 24.12   Using **SortedSet**s and **TreeSet**s (part 1 of 2).

```
17              // get headSet based upon "orange"
18              System.out.print( "\nheadSet (\"orange\"):   " );
19              printSet( m.headSet( "orange" ) );
20
21              // get tailSet based upon "orange"
22              System.out.print( "tailSet (\"orange\"):   " );
23              printSet( m.tailSet( "orange" ) );
24
25              // get first and last elements
26              System.out.println( "first: " + m.first() );
27              System.out.println( "last : " + m.last() );
28          }
29
30          public void printSet( SortedSet setRef )
31          {
32              Iterator i = setRef.iterator();
33
34              while ( i.hasNext() )
35                  System.out.print( i.next() + " " );
36
37              System.out.println();
38          }
39
40          public static void main( String args[] )
41          {
42              new SortedSetTest();
43          }
44      }
```

```
set:
black green grey orange red tan white yellow

headSet ("orange"):   black green grey
tailSet ("orange"):   orange red tan white yellow
first: black
last : yellow
```

Fig. 24.12 Using **SortedSet**s and **TreeSet**s (part 2 of 2).

Line 12 constructs a **TreeSet** object containing the elements of **names** and assigns a reference to this object to **m**. Line 19

```
        printSet( m.headSet( "orange" ) );
```

calls method *headSet* to get a subset of the **TreeSet** less than **"orange"**. Any changes made to the subset are made to the **TreeSet** (i.e., the subset returned is a view of the **TreeSet**). Line 23 calls method *tailSet* to get a subset greater than or equal to **"orange"**. Like **headSet**, any changes made through the **tailSet** view are made to the **TreeSet**. Lines 26 and 27 call methods *first* and *last* to get the smallest and largest elements, respectively.

Programmer-defined method **printSet** takes a **SortedSet** (e.g., a **TreeSet**) as an argument and prints it. Line 32 gets an **Iterator** for the **Set**. In the **while** loop body, each element of the **SortedSet** is printed.

24.8 Maps

Maps associate keys to values and cannot contain duplicate keys (i.e., each key can map to only one value—this is called *one-to-one mapping*). **Map**s differ from **Set**s in that **Map**s contain keys and values, whereas **Set**s contain only the key. Classes *HashMap* and *TreeMap* implement the **Map** interface. **HashMap**s store elements in **HashTable**s, and **TreeMap**s store elements in trees. Interface *SortedMap* extends **Map** and maintains i s elements in sorted order (i.e., the elements' natural order or an order specified by a **Comparator**). Class **TreeMap** implements **SortedMap**.

Figure 24.13 uses a **HashMap** to count the number of **String**s that begin with a given letter.

```
1   // Fig. 24.13 : MapTest.java
2   // Using a HashMap to store the number of words that
3   // begin with a given letter
4   import java.util.*;
5
6   public class MapTest {
7      private static String names[] = { "one", "two", "three",
8                                         "four", "five", "six",
9                                         "seven", "two", "ten", "four" };
10
11     public MapTest()
12     {
13        HashMap m = new HashMap();
14        Integer i;
15
16        for ( int k = 0; k < names.length; k++ ) {
17           i = ( Integer ) m.get( new Character(
18                                   names[ k ].charAt( 0 ) ) );
19
20           // if key is not in map then give it value one
21           // otherwise increment its value by 1
22           if ( i == null )
23              m.put( new Character( names[ k ].charAt( 0 ) ),
24                     new Integer( 1 ) );
25           else
26              m.put( new Character( names[ k ].charAt( 0 ) ),
27                     new Integer( i.intValue() + 1 ) );
28        }
29
30        System.out.println( "\nnumber of words beginning with "
31                            + "each letter:      " );
32        printMap( m );
33     }
```

Fig. 24.13 Using **HashMap**s and **Map**s (part 1 of 2).

```
34
35      public void printMap( Map mapRef )
36      {
37          System.out.println( mapRef.toString() );
38          System.out.println( "size: " + mapRef.size() );
39          System.out.println( "isEmpty: " + mapRef.isEmpty() );
40      }
41
42      public static void main( String args[] )
43      {
44          new MapTest();
45      }
46  }
```

```
number of words beginning with each letter:
{t=4, s=2, o=1, f=3}
size: 4
isEmpty: false
```

Fig. 24.13   Using **HashMap**s and **Map**s (part 2 of 2).

Line 13 constructs **HashMap m**. The **for** loop of lines 16 through 28 uses **m** to store the number of words in **names** that begin with a given letter. Lines 17 and 18

```
i = ( Integer ) m.get( new Character(
                     names[ k ].charAt( 0 ) ) );
```

call method *get* to retrieve a **Character** (the first letter of a **String** in **names**) from the **HashMap**. If the **HashMap** does not contain a mapping for the **Character**, **get** returns **null**. If the **HashMap** does contain the mapping for the **Character**, its mapping value is returned as an **Object**. The returned value is cast to **Integer** and assigned to **i**.

If **i** is **null**, the **Character** is not in the **HashMap** and lines 23 and 24

```
m.put( new Character( names[ k ].charAt( 0 ) ),
    new Integer( 1 ) );
```

call method *put* to write an **Integer** containing **1** to the **HashMap**. The **Integer** value stored in the **HashMap** is the number of words beginning with that **Character**.

If the **Character** is in the **HashMap**, lines 26 and 27 increment the **Integer** counter by 1 and write the updated counter to the **HashMap**. Because a **HashMap** cannot contain duplicates, the previous **Integer** object is replaced with the new one.

Programmer-defined method **printMap** takes one **Map** argument and prints it using method **toString**. Method *size* and *isEmpty* are called to get the number of values in the **Map** and a **boolean** indicating whether or not the **Map** is empty.

24.9 Synchronization Wrappers

In Chapter 15 we discussed multithreading. The built-in collections are unsynchronized. Concurrent access to a **Collection** by multiple threads could cause indeterminate results or fatal errors. To prevent potential threading problems, *synchronization wrappers* are used around collection classes that might be accessed by multiple threads. A *wrapper class* receives method calls, adds some functionality for thread safety and then delegates the calls to the wrapped class.

The **Collections** API provides a set of **public static** methods for converting collections to synchronized versions. Method headers for the synchronization wrappers are listed in Fig. 24.14.

Performance Tip 24.3

*As a general rule, a **Vector** is faster than the **List** returned from* **Collections.synchronizedList(aList)**, *where **aList** is an **ArrayList**.*

24.10 Unmodifiable Wrappers

The **Collections** API provides a set of **public static** methods for converting collections to unmodifiable versions (called *unmodifiable wrappers*) of those collections. Method headers for these are listed in Fig. 24.15. Unmodifiable wrappers throw **UnsupportedOperationException**s if attempts are made to modify the collection.

Software Engineering Observation 24.8

When creating an unmodifiable wrapper, not holding a reference to the backing collection ensures non-modifiability.

Software Engineering Observation 24.9

You can use an unmodifiable wrapper to create a collection that offers read-only access to others while allowing read-write access to yourself. You do this simply by giving others a reference to the unmodifiable wrapper while you also retain a reference to the wrapped collection itself.

24.11 Abstract Implementations

The collections framework provides various *abstract implementations* (i.e., "bare bones" implementations of collection interfaces from which the programmer can quickly "flesh out" complete customized implementations). These abstract implementations are: a thin **Collection** implementation called an **AbstractCollection**, a thin **List** implementation with random-access backing called an **AbstractList**, a thin **Map** implementation called an **AbstractMap**, a thin **List** implementation with sequential-access backing called an **AbstractSequentialList** and a thin **Set** implementation called an **AbstractSet**.

To write a custom implementation, begin by selecting as a base the abstract implementation class that best meets your needs. Then implement each of the class's **abstract** methods. Then, if your collection is to be modifiable, override any concrete methods that prevent modification.

Summary

- The Java collections framework gives the programmer access to prepackaged data structures as well as algorithms for manipulating those data structures.

- Java 2 provides an entire collections framework, whereas earlier versions of Java provided just a few collection classes like **HashTable** and **Vector**, as well as built-in array capabilities.

---

public static method header

```
Collection synchronizedCollection( Collection c )
List synchronizedList( List aList )
Set synchronizedSet( Set s )
SortedSet synchronizedSortedSet( SortedSet s )
Map synchronizedMap( Map m )
SortedMap synchronizedSortedMap( SortedMap m )
```

Fig. 24.14 Synchronization wrapper methods.

---

public static method header

```
Collection unmodifiableCollection( Collection c )
List unmodifiableList( List aList )
Set unmodifiableSet( Set s )
SortedSet unmodifiableSortedSet( SortedSet s )
Map unmodifiableMap( Map m )
SortedMap unmodifiableSortedMap( SortedMap m )
```

Fig. 24.15 Unmodifiable wrapper methods.

- A collection is a data structure, actually an object that can hold other objects. The collection interfaces define the operations that can be performed on each type of collection.

- The collections framework includes a number of other features that minimize the amount of work programmers need to do to create and manipulate collections. This is an effective implementation of the notion of reuse.

- The classes and interfaces that comprise the collections framework are members of the **java.util** package.

- Class **Arrays** provides **static** methods for manipulating arrays. Class **Arrays** methods include **binarySearch** for searching a sorted array, **equals** for comparing arrays, **fill** for placing items in an array, **sort** for sorting an array and **asList**.

- Class **Arrays** provides method **asList** for getting a "**List** view" of the array. A **List** view allows the programmer to programmatically manipulate the array as if it were a **List**. This allows the programmer to treat an array as a collection. Any modifications made through the **List** view change the array, and any modifications to the array change the **List** view.

- Method **size** gets the number of items in a **List**, and method **get** gets an individual **List** element.

- Interface **Collection** is the root interface in the collections hierarchy from which interfaces **Set** and **List** are derived. Interface **Collection** contains bulk operations for adding, clearing, comparing and retaining objects in the collection.

- Interface **Collection** provides a method **iterator** for getting an **Iterator**.

- Class **Collections** provides **static** methods for manipulating collections. Many of the methods are implementations of polymorphic algorithms for searching, sorting, etc.

- A **List** is an ordered **Collection** that may contain duplicate elements. A **List** is sometimes called a sequence.

- Interface **List** is implemented by classes **ArrayList**, **LinkedList** and **Vector**. Class **ArrayList** is a resizable-array implementation of a **List**. **ArrayList** behavior and capabilities are similar to those of class **Vector**. A **LinkedList** is a linked list implementation of a **List**.

- **Iterator** method **hasNext** determines if a **Collection** contains another element. Method **hasNext** returns **true** if another element exists and **false** otherwise. Method **next** returns the next object in the **Collection** and advances the **Iterator**.

- Method **subList** gets a portion of the **List** called a sublist. Any changes made to a sublist are also made to the **List** (i.e., the sublist is a "list view" of its corresponding **List** elements).

- Method **clear** removes elements from a **List**.

- Method **toArray** returns the contents of a collection as an array.

- Algorithms **sort**, **binarySearch**, **reverse**, **shuffle**, **fill** and **copy** operate on **List**s. Algorithms **min** and **max** operate on **Collection**s. Algorithm **reverse** reverses the elements of a **List**, **fill** sets every **List** element to a specified **Object** and **copy** copies elements from one **List** into another **List**. Algorithm **sort** sorts the elements of a **List**.

- Algorithms **min** and **max** find the smallest item and the largest item in a **Collection**.

- The **Comparator** object provides a means of sorting a **Collection**'s elements in an order other than the **Collection**'s natural order.

- Method **reverseOrder** returns a **Comparator** object that represents the reverse order for a collection.

- Algorithm **shuffle** randomly orders the elements of a **List**.

- Algorithm **binarySearch** locates an **Object** in a **List**.

- A **Set** is a **Collection** that contains no duplicate elements. The collections framework contains two **Set** implementations—**HashSet** and **TreeSet**. **HashSet** stores its elements in a hash table, and **TreeSet** stores its elements in a tree.

- Interface **SortedSet** extends **Set** and maintains its elements in sorted order. Class **TreeSet** implements **SortedSet**.

- Method **headSet** gets a subset of a **TreeSet** less than a specified element. Any changes made to the subset are made to the **TreeSet**. Method **tailSet** gets a subset greater than or equal to a specified element. Any changes made through the **tailSet** view are made to the **TreeSet**.

- **Map**s map keys to values and cannot contain duplicate keys. **Map**s differ from **Set**s in that **Map**s contain both the key and the value, whereas **Set**s contain only the key. Classes **HashMap** and **TreeMap** implement the **Map** interface. **HashMap**s store elements in a **HashTable**, and **TreeMap**s store elements in a tree.

- Interface **SortedMap** extends **Map** and maintains its elements in sorted order. Class **TreeMap** implements **SortedMap**.

- The built-in collections are unsynchronized. Concurrent access to a **Collection** by independent threads could cause indeterminate results. To prevent this, synchronization wrappers are used around classes that might be accessed by multiple threads.

- The **Collections** API provides a set of **public static** methods for converting collections to unmodifiable versions. Unmodifiable wrappers throw **UnsupportedOperationException**s if attempts are made to modify the collection.

- The collections framework provides various abstract implementations (i.e., "bare bones" implementations of collection interfaces from which the programmer can quickly "flesh out" complete customized implementations).

Terminology

AbstractCollection class	iterator
AbstractList class	**Iterator** interface
AbstractMap class	key
AbstractSequentialList class	**LinkedList** class
AbstractSet class	**List** interface
add method	**ListIterator**
addFirst method	map
addLast method	**Map** collection interface
algorithms	mapping keys to values
ArrayList	mappings
Arrays.asList	maps as collections
arrays	**max** algorithm
arrays as collections	**min** algorithm
bidirectional iteration	modifiable collections
binarySearch algorithm	natural ordering
clear method	**next** method
Collection interface	one-to-one mapping
collections	ordered collection
Collections class	ordering
collections framework	queue
collections placed in arrays	**reverse** algorithm
Comparator object	**reverseOrder** method
copy algorithm	sequence
data structures	**Set** interface
delete an element from a collection	**shuffle** algorithm
deque	**size** method
double-ended queue (deque)	**sort** algorithm
duplicate elements	sort a **List**
Enumeration interface	**SortedMap** collection interface
fill algorithm	**SortedSet** collection interface
hasNext method	stable sort
HashMap class	synchronization wrappers
HashSet class	**TreeMap** class
Hashtable class	**TreeSet** class
hash table implementation	unmodifiable collections
implementation classes	view
insert an element in a collection	**Vector** class
interface	view an array as a **List**
isEmpty method	wrapper class

Common Programming Errors

24.1   Passing an unsorted array to **binarySearch** is a logic error. The value returned by **binarySearch** is undefined.

24.2   A **List** created with **Arrays.asList** is fixed in size; calling methods **add** or **remove** throws an **UnsupportedOperationException**.

24.3   Passing an array that contains data to **toArray** can create logic errors. If the number of elements in the array is smaller than the number of elements in the **Object** calling **toArray**, new memory is allocated to store the **Object**'s elements—without preserving the array's elements. If the number of elements in the array is greater than the number of elements in the **Object**, the array elements (starting at subscript 0) are overwritten with the **Object**'s elements. Array elements not overwritten retain their values.

Performance Tips

24.1   Using **Arrays.asList** creates a fixed-size **List** which operates faster than any of the provided **List** implementations.

24.2   **ArrayList**s behave like un**synchronized Vector**s and therefore execute faster than **Vector**s.

24.3   As a general rule, a **Vector** is faster than the **List** returned from **Collections.synchronizedList(aList)**, where **aList** is an **ArrayList**.

Software Engineering Observations

24.1   With the collections framework, there are many methods that apply to **List**s and **Collection**s that you would like to be able to use for arrays. **Arrays.asList** allows you to pass an array into a **List** or **Collection** parameter.

24.2   **Collection** is commonly used as a method parameter type to allow polymorphic processing of collections.

24.3   Most collection implementations provide a constructor that takes one **Collection** argument—thereby allowing one collection type to be treated as another collection type.

24.4   **LinkedList**s can be used to create stacks, queues, trees and deques (double-ended queues).

24.5   The collections framework algorithms are polymorphic. Each of these algorithms can operate on objects that offer given interfaces without concern to the underlying implementations.

24.6   The Java API documentation sometimes provides implementation details. For example, **sort** is implemented as a modified merge sort. Avoid writing code that is dependent on implementation details—because they can change.

24.7   Java does not guarantee which item will be found first when a **binarySearch** is performed on a **List** containing multiple elements equivalent to the search key.

24.8   When creating an unmodifiable wrapper, not holding a reference to the backing collection ensures nonmodifiability.

24.9   You can use an unmodifiable wrapper to create a collection that offers only read-only access to others while allowing read-write access to yourself. You do this simply by giving others a reference to the unmodifiable wrapper while you also retain a reference to the wrapped collection itself.

Self-Review Exercises

24.1   Fill in the blanks in each of the following:
   a) **Object**s in a collection are called _____.
   b) Elements in a **List** can be accessed using the element's _____.
   c) **List**s are sometimes called _____.
   d) You can use a/an _____ to create a collection that offers only read-only access to others while allowing read-write access to yourself.
   e) _____ can be used to create stacks, queues, trees and deques (double-ended queues).

24.2   State whether each of the following is *true* or *false*. If *false*, explain why.
   a) A **Set** can contain duplicates.

b) A **Map** can contain duplicate keys.
c) A **LinkedList** can contain duplicates.
d) **Collections** is an **interface**.
e) **Iterator**s and **Enumeration**s behave differently.

Answers to Self-Review Exercises

24.1 a) elements. b) index. c) sequences. d) unmodifiable wrapper. e) **LinkedList**s.

24.2 a) False. A **Set** cannot contain duplicate values.
b) False. A **Map** cannot contain duplicate keys.
c) True.
d) False. **Collections** is a **class** and **Collection** is an **interface**.
e) True. **Iterator**s can remove elements, **Enumeration**s cannot.

Exercises

24.3 Define each of the following terms:
a) **Collection**
b) **Collections**
c) **Comparator**
d) **List**

24.4 Briefly answer the following questions.
a) What is the primary difference between a **Set** and a **Map**?
b) Can a double-subscripted array be passed to **Arrays** method **asList**? If you answered yes, how would an individual element be accessed?
c) What must you do first before adding a primitive data type (e.g., **double**) to a collection?

24.5 Explain briefly the operation of each of the following **Iterator**-related methods:
a) **iterator**
b) **hasNext**
c) **next**

24.6 State whether each of the following is *true* or *false*. If *false*, explain why.
a) Elements in a **Collection** must be sorted in ascending order before performing a **binarySearch**.
b) Method **first** gets the first element in a **TreeSet**.
c) A **List** created with **Arrays.asList** is resizable.
d) Class **Arrays** provides static method **sort** for sorting array elements.

24.7 Rewrite method **printList** of Fig. 24.4 to use a **ListIterator**.

24.8 Rewrite lines 13 through 19 in Fig. 24.4 to be more concise by using the **asList** method and the **LinkedList** constructor that takes a **Collection** argument.

24.9 Write a program that reads in a series of first names and stores them in a **LinkedList**. Do not store duplicate names. Allow the user to search for a first name.

24.10 Modify the program of Fig. 24.13 to count the number of occurrences for all letters (e.g., 5 occurrences of "o" in the example). Display the results.

24.11 Write a program that determines and prints the number of duplicate words in a sentence. Treat uppercase and lowercase letters the same. Ignore punctuation.

24.12 Rewrite your solution to Exercise 22.8 to use a **LinkedList** collection.

24.13 Rewrite your solution to Exercise 22.9 to use a **LinkedList** collection.

24.14 Write a program that takes a whole number input from a user and determines if it is prime. If the number is prime, add it to a **JTextArea**. If the number is not prime, display the prime factors for the number in a **JLabel**. Remember that a prime number's factors are only 1 and the prime number itself. Every number that is not prime has a unique prime factorization. For example, consider the number 54. The factors of 54 are 2, 3, 3 and 3. When the values are multiplied together, the result is 54. For the number 54, the prime factors output should be 2 and 3. Use **Set**s as part of your solution.

24.15 Rewrite your solution to Exercise 22.21 to use a **LinkedList**.

24.16 Write a program that tokenizes (using class **StreamTokenizer**) a line of text input by the user and places each token in a tree. Print the sorted tree elements.

25

JavaBeans

Objectives

- To understand JavaBeans and how they facilitate component-oriented software construction.
- To overview the JavaBeans Development Kit.
- To use the **BeanBox** test container to modify bean properties and link beans through events.
- To wrap class definitions as JAR files for use as JavaBeans and stand-alone applications.
- To define JavaBean properties and events.

Mirrors should reflect a little before throwing back images.
Jean Cocteau

Television is like the invention of indoor plumbing. It didn't change people's habits. It just kept them inside the house.
Alfred Hitchcock

And this is good old Boston,
The home of the bean and the cod,
Where the Lowells talk only to Cabots,
And the Cabots talk only to God.
Toast at Holy Cross alumni dinner, 1910

A writer is like a bean plant—
he has his little day and then gets stringy.
E. B. White

The power of the visible is the invisible.
Marianne Moore

Language is the archives of history.
Ralph Waldo Emerson

Outline

25.1   Introduction

In this chapter, we present Java's reusable software component model—*JavaBeans*. Java-Beans (often called *beans)* allow developers to reap the benefits of rapid application development in Java by assembling predefined software components to create powerful applications and applets. *Graphical programming and design environments* (often called *builder tools*) that support beans provide programmers with tremendous flexibility by allowing programmers to reuse and integrate existing disparate components that in many cases were never intended to be used together. These components can be linked together to create applets, applications or even new beans for reuse by others.

JavaBeans and other component-based technologies have led to a new type of programmer—the *component assembler*—who uses well-defined components to create more robust functionality. Component assemblers do not need to know the implementation details of a component. Rather, they need to know the services provided by a component so they can have other components interact with it. Component assemblers are often more concerned with the design of the graphical user interface of an application or with the functionality that the application provides to a user.

As an example of the bean concept (we frequently say "bean" when we should more precisely say "JavaBean"), assume a component assembler has an animation bean that has methods to **startAnimation** and **stopAnimation**. The component assembler may want to provide two buttons—one that will start the animation and one that will stop the animation (an example you will see later in this chapter). With beans, we can simply "hook up" a button to the animation's **startAnimation** method and "hook up" a button to the animation's **stopAnimation** method such that when a button is pressed, the appropriate method of the animation bean is called. The builder tool does all the work of associating the button press event with the appropriate method to call on the animation bean. All the programmer needs to do is tell the builder tool which two components to hook up.

The benefit of beans in this example is that the animation bean and the button beans do not need to know about each other before they are assembled in a builder tool. Someone else can be responsible for defining the concept of a button in a reusable manner (as is done with the **javax.swing** components). A button is not specific to our example. Rather, it is a component used in many applications and applets. When the user of a program presses a button, they expect an action specific to that program to occur (some buttons such as an **OK** button typically have the same meaning in all programs). But the basic concept of a button—how it is displayed, how it works and how it notifies other components that it was pressed—is the same in every application (although we typically customize its label). The component assembler's job is not to create the concept of a button, but rather to use the pre-existing button component to provide functionality to the user of the program.

Component assemblers can make beans communicate through the beans' well-defined services (i.e., methods), typically without writing any code (the code is often generated by the builder tool and sometimes even hidden from the programmer—depending on the tool). Indeed, a component assembler can often create complex applications literally by connecting the dots.

We will show you how to use existing beans and how to create your own basic beans. After studying this chapter, you will have a foundation in JavaBeans programming that will enable you to rapidly develop applications and applets using the more advanced features of integrated development environments that support beans. You will also have a solid foundation for further study of JavaBeans.

For more information, visit the Sun Microsystems Web site for JavaBeans:

http://java.sun.com/beans/

This site provides a complete set of resources for learning and using JavaBeans.

25.2 BeanBox Overview

This section introduces the **BeanBox**—a utility from the *JavaBeans Development Kit (BDK)* that can be downloaded at no charge from the Sun Microsystems Web site

http://java.sun.com/beans/software/index.html

At the time of this publication, the most recent version of the BDK was BDK 1.1 from April, 1999. There are several versions of the download available, including the Windows version, the Solaris version and a version that can be used on any platform that supports J2SDK 1.2. If you are using this book, you should already have J2SDK 1.2 (or higher). The site also provides access to the previous version of the BDK for use with JDK 1.1 (the previous version of Sun's Java implementation). [*Note:* At the time of this publication, there was a minor bug in the install program for the Windows version of the BDK. The BDK will not execute correctly from its default install directory (**C:\Program Files\BDK1.1**). When executing the install program, simply remove "**Program Files**" from the default install location (or choose any directory path that does not include space characters) and the BDK will execute properly.]

The **BeanBox** is a *test container* for your JavaBeans. It is designed to allow programmers to preview how a bean they created will be displayed and manipulated in a *builder tool*. However, it is not meant to be used as a robust development tool. This section presents an overview of the **BeanBox** features and several of the demonstration beans supplied with the **BeanBox**.

Testing and Debugging Tip 25.1

The **BeanBox** *can be used to test and debug JavaBeans.*

 Software Engineering Observation 25.1

The **BeanBox** *is not a builder tool. Rather, the* **BeanBox** *allows programmers to preview how a bean will be displayed and used by a builder tool.*

Once the BDK is installed, you can execute the **BeanBox** by locating the **BDK1.1** *directory* where you installed the JavaBeans Development Kit. In that directory is the **beanbox** *subdirectory*. Another important subdirectory is **doc**, where you will find the on-line HTML help files for the **BeanBox** (use file **beanbox.html** to get started). The help files discuss in depth all the features of the **BeanBox**.

The **beanbox** directory contains start-up files for both Windows (**run.bat**) and Solaris (**run.sh**). To run the **BeanBox**, execute the proper file for your operating system—on Windows, double-click **run.bat** in Windows Explorer; on Solaris, execute the shell script **run.sh** from your command shell. [*Note:* If you are not using one of these operating systems, you will have to run the **BeanBox** as you would normally execute a Java application on your platform.]

This section uses screen captures from a Windows environment. Figure 25.1 shows the four **BeanBox** windows—**ToolBox**, **BeanBox**, **Properties** and **Method Tracer**—that appear when the application is started.

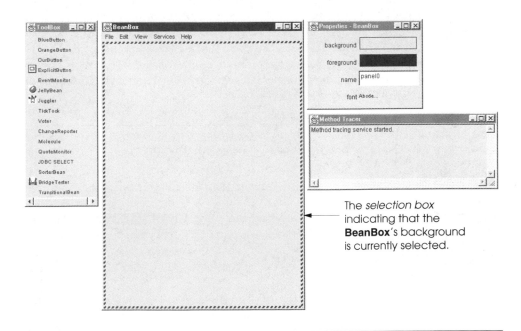

Fig. 25.1   The **ToolBox**, **BeanBox**, **Properties** and **Method Tracer** windows of the **BeanBox**.

The **ToolBox** window contains 16 demonstration JavaBeans you can use to learn the **BeanBox** and the basics of programming with JavaBeans. These can also be used to interact with any new beans you are testing. The **BeanBox** window is used to test a bean. The **Properties** window allows the programmer to customize the currently selected bean. Builder tools often refer to the **Properties** window (or their version of this window) as the *property sheet*. The **Method Tracer** window displays simple debugging messages and helps trace method calls (we do not discuss this window in this book).

Initially, the background of the **BeanBox** window is *selected* as indicated with the dashed *selection box* around the background of the window in Fig. 25.1. The background of the **BeanBox** window is actually an object of class `java.awt.Panel`. The currently selected bean's properties that can be manipulated by the programmer are displayed in the **Properties** window. For the background panel of the **BeanBox** window, the properties we can configure are the *background*, *foreground*, *name* and *font*.

Click the rectangle to the right of property *background* in the **Properties** window to customize the background color of the **BeanBox** background panel. This displays the *ColorEditor property editor* (Fig. 25.2). A property editor allows the programmer to customize a property's value.

Select **yellow** as the background color. Notice that the background color of the **BeanBox** window changes to yellow immediately. Click **Done** in **ColorEditor** window to dismiss the **ColorEditor** dialog.

Next, we will place a JavaBean in the **BeanBox** window. In the **ToolBox** window, click the `ExplicitButton` bean. Your mouse cursor should change to a crosshair cursor. Position the mouse cursor at the position on the **BeanBox** window where you want the center of your bean to be located and click the mouse to place the bean. Figure 25.3 shows the **BeanBox** window with the new `ExplicitButton` bean selected and the **Properties** window containing the `ExplicitButton`'s properties. If you click the button, it will appear to function just as a `JButton` functioned earlier in the book.

The **Properties** window *exposes the properties of the bean*. The bean's exposed properties can be changed at design time in a development environment to customize the bean for use in a specific program.

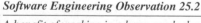

Software Engineering Observation 25.2

A benefit of working in a bean-ready development environment is that the environment visually presents the properties of the bean to the programmer for easy modification and customization of the bean at design time.

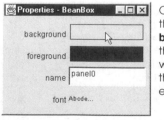
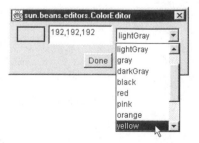

Click the rectangle to the right of the **background** property in the **Properties** window (left) to open the **ColorEditor** property editor (right).

Fig. 25.2   Changing the **background** property for the **BeanBox**.

In the **Properties** window, one of the changeable properties is the **Explicit-Button**'s *label*. Because we will use this button to start an animation, we would like to change its **label** property to "**Start the Animation**" instead of the current value "**press**." Click in the text field to the right of the **label** property and change the text on the button to "**Start the Animation**." Press the *Enter* key when you are done. Notice that the label on the button changes and the button automatically resizes itself to fit the new label, which is wider than the original label. Figure 25.4 shows the button and its new label.

Next we would like to move the button. If the button is not selected (i.e., the selection box does not appear around the button), click the button to select it. [*Note:* If clicking a bean in the **BeanBox** window does not select it, you may need to click just outside the bean's boundary to select it.] Position the mouse cursor over the top, bottom, left or right edges of the selection box for the button. The *move cursor* should appear as shown in Fig. 25.5.

Fig. 25.3   The **BeanBox** window with the **ExplicitButton** bean selected.

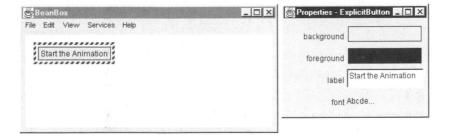

Fig. 25.4   The **ExplicitButton** with its new label.

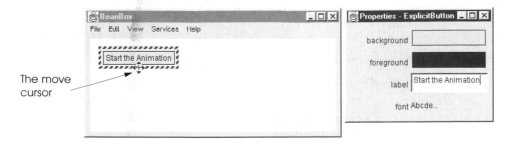

Fig. 25.5   The move cursor.

Hold your mouse button down and drag the button to the right side of the **BeanBox** window. The window should appear as in Fig. 25.6. Notice that as you drag the button, a red rectangle indicating the boundaries of the button follows the mouse cursor. This provides you with visual feedback that helps you move or resize a bean.

Next we would like to resize the button. If the button is not currently selected (i.e., the selection box does not appear around the button), click the button to select it. Position the mouse cursor over the upper-left, upper-right, lower-left or lower-right corner of the selection box for the button. The *resize cursor* should appear as shown in Fig. 25.7.

Hold your mouse button down and drag the corner of the selection box to make the button taller. The window should appear as in Fig. 25.8. Notice that as you drag the mouse, a red rectangle indicating the new boundaries of the button follows the mouse cursor. This provides visual feedback that helps you resize the button accurately.

Next, add another button to the **BeanBox**. This button will be used to stop the animation. Repeat the preceding steps to create another **ExplicitButton** with the label "**Stop the Animation**." Figure 25.9 shows the **BeanBox** window with both buttons.

Next, we will add an animation bean to the **BeanBox**, customize the bean and set up the button events that will enable us to start and stop the animation. In the **ToolBox**, select the **Juggler** bean and add it to the **BeanBox** window. The **BeanBox** window and the properties for the **Juggler** bean are shown in Fig. 25.10.

Notice that the **Juggler** animation begins immediately once the **Juggler** bean is *dropped* onto the **BeanBox** window (i.e., once you click in the **BeanBox** to place the bean).

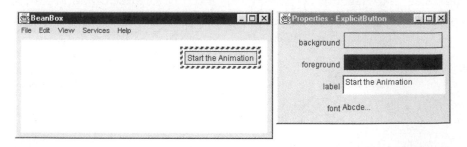

Fig. 25.6   The **ExplicitButton** after moving.

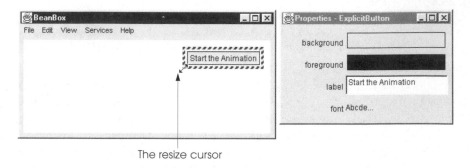

Fig. 25.7   The resize cursor.

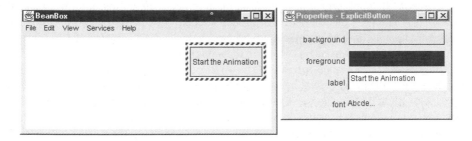

Fig. 25.8   The **ExplicitButton** after resizing.

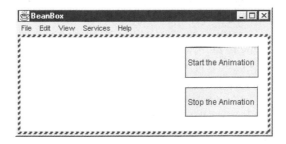

Fig. 25.9   The **BeanBox** window with two **ExplicitButton** beans.

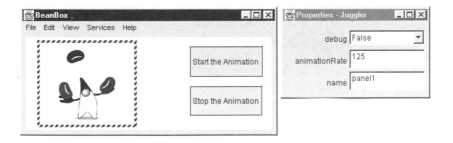

Fig. 25.10   The **BeanBox** window with the new **Juggler** bean.

Software Engineering Observation 25.3

A benefit of working in a bean-ready development environment is that the beans typically execute live in the development environment. This allows you to view and test the functionality of your program immediately in the design environment rather than using the standard edit, compile and execute programming cycle.

Also, notice that the **Properties** window is now displaying properties for the **Juggler**. One of the properties we can configure for the **Juggler** is its *animationRate*. The **animationRate** is actually the sleep time for the thread that displays the images in the animation (the default sleep time is 125 milliseconds). Decreasing the **animationRate** increases the animation speed. Increasing the **animationRate** decreases the animation speed. Try changing the **animationRate** property. Remember to press the *Enter* key after changing the value in the text field to set the new **animationRate**.

Next we will "hook up" the events from the buttons to the animation to start and stop the animation. Because the animation is already executing, we begin with the stop button.

The *Edit* menu in the **BeanBox** window provides access to the events supported by a bean that is an *event source* (i.e, any bean that can notify a *listener* that an event occurred using the standard event-handling model shown throughout this book). In fact, Swing GUI components are all beans. Select the "**Stop the Animation**" button, then click the **Edit** menu and position the mouse over the *Events* menu item. A submenu appears (Fig. 25.11) containing menu items for each type of event supported by the currently selected bean. The two supported events are **button push**—when a user presses the button—and **bound property change**—notifying a listener when a property value changes (we discuss bound properties in detail in Section 25.8). Position the mouse over the **button push** menu item. A submenu appears containing method **actionPerformed**. As you know from GUI event handling, **actionPerformed** is the method invoked on an **ActionListener** object when an **ActionEvent** (such as a button push) occurs. The menu item names displayed for each event type in the **Edit** menu's **Events** menu item can be customized for each bean (we show how to do this in Section 25.9).

Click the **actionPerformed** menu item to indicate that you would like to specify what happens when the button is pressed (i.e., stop the animation). As you move the mouse around the **BeanBox** window after selecting the event, you will see a red line following the mouse. This *target selector line* (Fig. 25.12) helps us specify the *target of the event*—the object on which we intend to call a method when the button is pushed. We like to call this *connect-the-dots programming*—the dots are the beans and the target selector line helps us connect the dots.

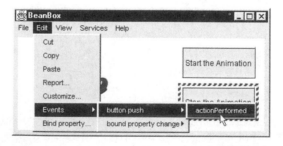

Fig. 25.11   Selecting the button-push event for an **ExplicitButton**.

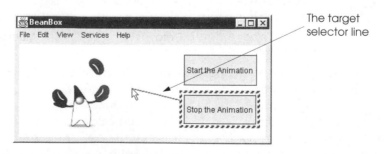

Fig. 25.12   The target selector line.

Position the mouse over the **Juggler** and click to specify the **Juggler** as the target of the event. This displays the ***EventTargetDialog*** *window* listing the **public** methods that can be called on the target (Fig. 25.13). From this list you can select the target's method that will be called when the user clicks the **Stop the Animation** button.

The **Juggler** provides two methods of importance to us in this example—method ***startJuggling*** starts the animation and method ***stopJuggling*** stops the animation. Select **stopJuggling** from the list, then press the **OK** button to complete the *event hookup*. The **EventTargetDialog** displays the message "Generating and compiling adapter class" to indicate that the **BeanBox** is writing a new class definition (called the *hookup class* or the *event adapter class*). One object of this new class is automatically created and registered as the **ActionListener** for the **Stop the Animation** button. At this point you can click the **Stop the Animation** button to stop the animation. When the event occurs, the **actionPerformed** method of the hookup class calls method **stopJuggling** on the target **Juggler**. Figure 25.14 illustrates the interaction.

Repeat the process of hooking up a button-push event for the **Start the Animation** button. In the **EventTargetDialog** window, select method **startJuggling** as the target method to call when the button is pressed. At this point you can click **Start the Animation** to start the animation.

Fig. 25.13   The **EventTargetDialog** window displays the list of methods that can be called on the target of an event.

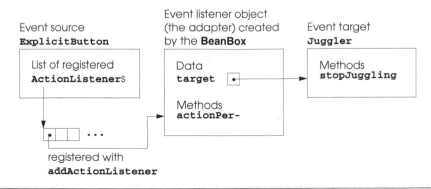

Fig. 25.14   The interaction between the **ExplicitButton** and the **Juggler**.

The **BeanBox** provides several ways to save your design including: saving the design to be reloaded into the **BeanBox** later (the **File** menu's *Save... menu item*) and saving the design as a Java applet (the **File** menu's *MakeApplet... menu item*). There is a third option—*SerializeComponent...*—that can be used to help create a new JavaBean. For more information on this option, refer to the on-line documentation for the **BeanBox** (found in the **doc** directory where you installed the BDK).

To save the design so it can be reloaded into the **BeanBox** at a later time, select the **File** menu's **Save...** menu item. This displays the *Save BeanBox File dialog box* in Fig. 25.15. This option uses object serialization to save the beans in the design. We named our file **OurJuggler.ser** (we are using the *.ser extension* to indicate that the design is a serialized file). There is no file naming requirement for this option, so you can name the file any way you like. By default your file will be saved in the **beanbox** directory in the BDK directory structure. If you want to save the file in another location, use the dialog to change the directory before clicking the **Save** button to save the design.

To see that your file was saved correctly, select the **File** menu's *Clear menu item* to empty the **BeanBox**. Next, select the **File** menu's *Load... menu item* to display the *Load saved BeanBox* dialog (Fig. 25.16). Select the file you saved previously (**OurJuggler.ser**), then click the **Open** button to reload the design. Notice that the animation begins automatically when the design is reloaded. This is because the **Juggler** bean is actually an applet. When an applet bean is reloaded, it begins execution with its **start** method (just as an applet does when it is reloaded into a Web browser). The **Juggler**'s **start** method creates a new thread to restart the animation.

To save your design as an applet, select the *MakeApplet... menu item* from the **File** menu. This displays the *Make an Applet* dialog in Fig. 25.17. The default name of the applet class is **MyApplet**, but you can customize the name by clicking the *Choose JAR File... button* to display the *Choose JAR File* dialog in Fig. 25.18. When the **BeanBox** creates an applet from your design, it stores the **.class** files in a *Java Archive File (JAR file)*. JavaBeans are stored in JAR files (we discuss JAR files later in this chapter). When you choose a different name for the JAR file, the name of the applet class is changed accordingly. Name the JAR file **OurJuggler.jar** by typing the name in the **File name** field.

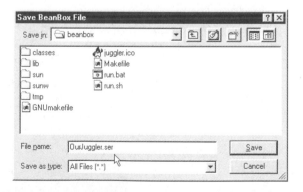

Fig. 25.15   The **Save BeanBox File** dialog.

You can also change the directory in which the JAR file will be stored in this dialog. After choosing the file name and directory, click **Save** to return to the **Make an Applet** dialog in Fig. 25.19. By default our applet will be stored in the directory.

```
BDK\beanbox\tmp\myApplet
```

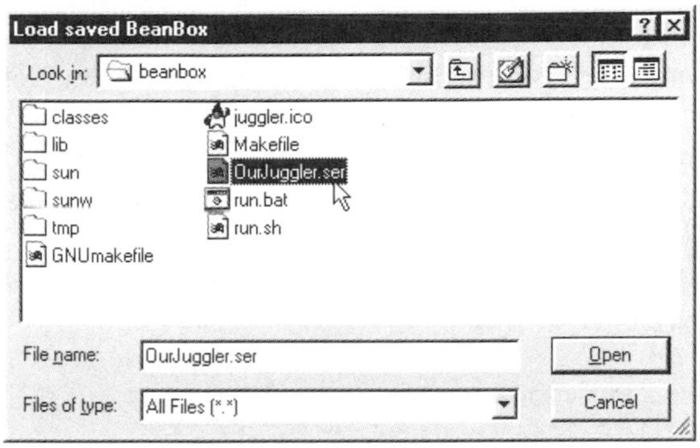

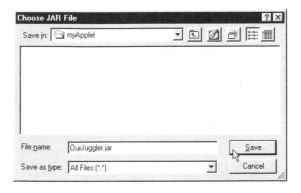

Fig. 25.16   The **Load saved BeanBox** dialog.

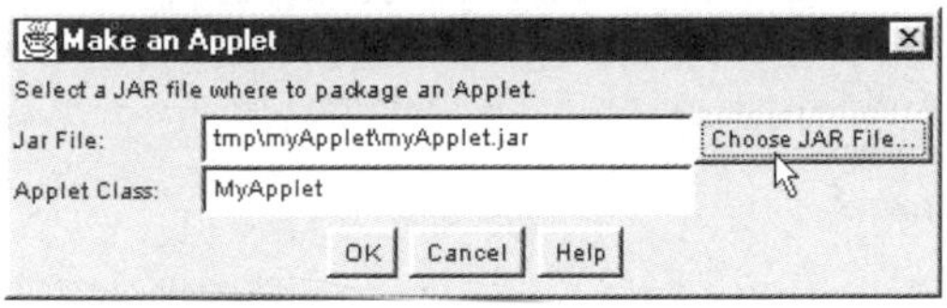

Fig. 25.17   The **Make an Applet** dialog.

Fig. 25.18   The **Choose JAR File** dialog.

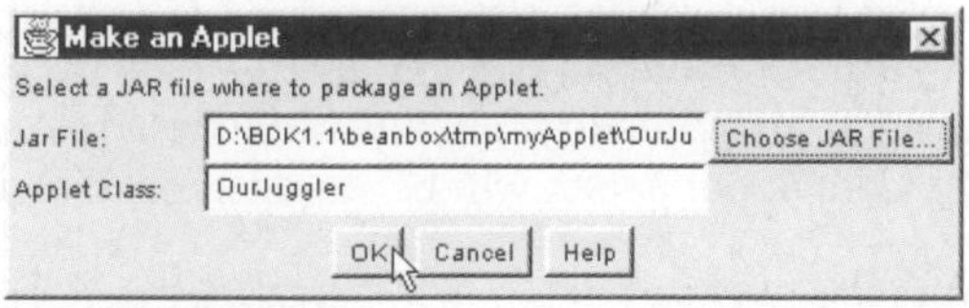

Make an Applet

Select a JAR file where to package an Applet.

Jar File: D:\BDK1.1\beanbox\tmp\myApplet\OurJu   [Choose JAR File...]

Applet Class: OurJuggler

[OK]   [Cancel]   [Help]

Fig. 25.19   The **Make an Applet** dialog after changing the default file name.

To run the applet in the **appletviewer**, go to the command line and switch to the directory where you saved the applet. If you named the file as specified previously, there will be a file called **OurJuggler.html** that you can load into the **appletviewer**. The loaded applet is shown in Fig. 25.20. Notice that the applet does not have the yellow background of the **BeanBox**. This is because the **BeanBox** container to which we attach components is not saved as part of the applet. The applet already is a container and is capable of holding the beans that are part of the applet.

Inspect the source code for the applet's HTML file generated by the **BeanBox** (Fig. 25.21). Notice lines 12 through 15

```
archive="./OurJuggler.jar,./support.jar
   ,./juggler.jar
   ,./buttons.jar
"
```

This is the ***archive*** *property* of the **<applet>** tag. It specifies a comma-separated list of JAR files containing the code that is used to execute this applet. Each JAR file for a bean we used is listed in addition to **OurJuggler.jar**, which contains the code for class **OurJuggler**. Also notice line 16

```
code="OurJuggler"
```

which specifies the name of the applet class that will begin the execution of our applet.

If you would like to view the source code for the applet that was written by the **BeanBox**, the directory **OurJuggler_files** where the applet was saved contains all the source code generated by the **BeanBox**.

Fig. 25.20   The **OurJuggler** applet running in **appletviewer**.

```
1   <html>
2   <head>
3   <title>Test page for OurJuggler as an APPLET</Title>
4   </head>
5   <body>
6   <h1>Test for OurJuggler as an APPLET</h1>
7   This is an example of the use of the generated
8   OurJuggler applet.  Notice the Applet tag requires several
9   archives, one per JAR used in building the Applet
10  <p>
11  <applet
12      archive="./OurJuggler.jar,./support.jar
13          ,./juggler.jar
14          ,./buttons.jar
15      "
16      code="OurJuggler"
17      width=382
18      height=150
19  >
20  Trouble instantiating applet OurJuggler!!
21  </applet>
```

Fig. 25.21   The **OurJuggler.html** file generated by the **BeanBox**.

25.3 Preparing a Class to Be a JavaBean

The following example and next several sections present an animation of a Deitel & Associates, Inc. logo (**LogoAnimator**) as seen in Chapter 16. Previously, the animation was demonstrated as a stand-alone application running in a **JFrame**. In this section, we demonstrate the **LogoAnimator** as a stand-alone application and as a bean for use in the **BeanBox**. The program code in Fig. 25.22 and the four screen captures demonstrate the bean running as a stand-alone application. Our **LogoAnimator** class is a subclass of **JPanel**, so it has properties and events inherited from class **JPanel**. When a **LogoAnimator** bean is loaded into the **BeanBox**, we can take advantage of some of these predefined properties and events, such as the background color and mouse events. This section also demonstrates interactions between **BeanBox** demonstration beans and our **LogoAnimator** bean.

```
1   // Fig. 25.22: LogoAnimator.java
2   // Animation bean
3   package jhtp3beans;
4
5   import java.awt.*;
6   import java.awt.event.*;
7   import java.io.*;
8   import java.net.*;
9   import javax.swing.*;
10
```

Fig. 25.22   The **LogoAnimator** as a stand-alone application (part 1 of 3).

```
11    public class LogoAnimator extends JPanel
12          implements ActionListener, Serializable {
13       protected ImageIcon images[];
14       protected int totalImages = 30,
15                     currentImage = 0,
16                     animationDelay = 50; // 50 millisecond delay
17       protected Timer animationTimer;
18
19       public LogoAnimator()
20       {
21          setSize( getPreferredSize() );
22
23          images = new ImageIcon[ totalImages ];
24
25          URL url;
26
27          for ( int i = 0; i < images.length; ++i ) {
28             url = getClass().getResource(
29                     "deitel" + i + ".gif" );
30             images[ i ] = new ImageIcon( url );
31          }
32
33          startAnimation();
34       }
35
36       public void paintComponent( Graphics g )
37       {
38          super.paintComponent( g );
39
40          if ( images[ currentImage ].getImageLoadStatus() ==
41               MediaTracker.COMPLETE ) {
42             g.setColor( getBackground() );
43             g.drawRect(
44                0, 0, getSize().width, getSize().height );
45             images[ currentImage ].paintIcon( this, g, 0, 0 );
46             currentImage = ( currentImage + 1 ) % totalImages;
47          }
48       }
49
50       public void actionPerformed( ActionEvent e )
51       {
52          repaint();
53       }
54
55       public void startAnimation()
56       {
57          if ( animationTimer == null ) {
58             currentImage = 0;
59             animationTimer = new Timer( animationDelay, this );
60             animationTimer.start();
61          }
```

Fig. 25.22   The **LogoAnimator** as a stand-alone application (part 2 of 3).

```
62              else  // continue from last image displayed
63                 if ( ! animationTimer.isRunning() )
64                     animationTimer.restart();
65          }
66
67          public void stopAnimation()
68          {
69              animationTimer.stop();
70          }
71
72          public Dimension getMinimumSize()
73          {
74              return getPreferredSize();
75          }
76
77          public Dimension getPreferredSize()
78          {
79              return new Dimension( 160, 80 );
80          }
81
82          public static void main( String args[] )
83          {
84              LogoAnimator anim = new LogoAnimator();
85
86              JFrame app = new JFrame( "Animator test" );
87              app.getContentPane().add( anim, BorderLayout.CENTER );
88
89              app.addWindowListener(
90                 new WindowAdapter() {
91                     public void windowClosing( WindowEvent e )
92                     {
93                         System.exit( 0 );
94                     }
95                 }
96              );
97
98              app.setSize( anim.getPreferredSize().width + 10,
99                           anim.getPreferredSize().height + 30 );
100             app.show();
101         }
102 }
```

Fig. 25.22   The **LogoAnimator** as a stand-alone application (part 3 of 3).

There are two minor modifications to this program that will enable us to use the class as a JavaBean. First, notice that we added a **package** statement (line 3) to the file for the **LogoAnimator** class. Normally, classes that represent a bean are first placed into a package. Remember that you must compile your packaged classes using the **-d** option with the Java compiler as in

```
javac -d . LogoAnimator.java
```

As shown above, the "**.**" represents the directory in which the **jhtp3beans** package should be placed ("**.**" represents the current directory, which we used here for simplicity). After the class is compiled, we can wrap the class into a JavaBean stored as a *Java Archive File (JAR file)* that ends with the **.jar** *extension*. A single JAR file can contain many Java-Beans. JAR files are created with the **jar** *utility* that comes with the JDK. We discuss creating the JAR file in the next section.

The second modification is on line 12, where the class specifies that it implements the **Serializable** interface to support *persistence*—saving a bean object in its current state for future use. Objects of our **LogoAnimator** class can be serialized with **ObjectOutputStream**s and **ObjectInputStream**s (shown in Chapter 17, "Files and Streams"). Implementing interface **Serializable** allows programmers using a builder tool to save their customized bean by *serializing the bean* to a file.

Software Engineering Observation 25.4

JavaBeans should all implement the **Serializable** *interface to support persistence.*

Other than these minor modifications to the **LogoAnimator** shown here to make the animation serializable, the code is the same as the animation shown in Chapter 16. The next section discusses creating a JavaBean from the **LogoAnimator**. The following section discusses using the JavaBean in the **BeanBox**.

25.4 Creating a JavaBean: Java Archive Files and the jar Utility

To use a class as a JavaBean, it must first be placed in a Java Archive file (JAR file). Before we can create the JAR file, we first create a text file called **manifest.tmp**. The *manifest file* (as it is called) is used by the **jar** utility to describe the contents of the JAR file. This is important for integrated development environments that support JavaBeans. When a JAR file containing a JavaBean (or a set of JavaBeans) is loaded into an IDE, the IDE looks at the *manifest file* to determine which of the classes in the JAR represent JavaBeans. These classes are made available to the programmer in a visual manner as you saw in the **Bean-Box** overview earlier in this chapter. The **jar** Java archive utility uses **manifest.tmp** to create a file called **MANIFEST.MF** that is included in the **META-INF** *directory* of the JAR file. All JavaBean-aware development environments know to look for the **MANI-FEST.MF** file in the **META-INF** directory of the JAR file. Also, the Java interpreter can execute an application directly from a JAR file if the manifest file indicates which class in the JAR contains **main**. The **manifest.tmp** file for the **LogoAnimator** is shown in Fig. 25.23.

Software Engineering Observation 25.5

You must define a manifest file that describes the contents of a JAR file if you intend to either use the bean in a bean-aware integrated development environment or if you intend to execute an application directly from a JAR file.

```
1   Main-Class: jhtp3beans.LogoAnimator
2
3   Name: jhtp3beans/LogoAnimator.class
4   Java-Bean: True
```

Fig. 25.23   The **manifest.tmp** file for the **LogoAnimator** bean.

In this particular manifest file, we included line 1, which specifies that the **jhtp3beans.LogoAnimator** class is the class that contains method **main** to run the bean as an application. When a **main** application class is stored in a JavaBean, the application can be executed directly from the bean by using the Java interpreter with the **-jar** command-line option as follows:

> **java -jar LogoAnimator.jar**

The interpreter will automatically look at the manifest file for the class specified with the **Main-Class:** *manifest file property* and begin execution with the **main** method of that class. The application can also be executed from the JAR file that does not contain a manifest with the command

> **java -cp LogoAnimator.jar jhtp3beans.LogoAnimator**

where **-cp** indicates the *class path* (i.e., the JAR file in which the interpreter should search for classes). The **-cp** option is followed by the JAR file containing the application class. The last command line argument is the explicit class name (including the package name) for the application class.

With Java 2, many platforms automatically issue the preceding command when the user runs the Java application as they would any other application on that platform. For example, in Microsoft Windows, the user can execute a Java application from a JAR file by double-clicking the JAR file name in Windows Explorer.

Line 3 of the manifest file specifies the **Name:** of the file containing the bean class (including the **.class** file name extension) using its package and class name. Notice that the dots (**.**) typically used in a package name are replaced with forward slashes (**/**) for the **Name:** in the manifest file. Line 4 specifies that the class named on line 3 is, in fact, a Java-Bean (**Java-Bean: True**). It is possible to have in a JAR file classes that are not Java-Beans. Such classes are typically used to support the JavaBeans in the archive. For example, a linked-list bean might have a supporting linked-list-node class whose objects are used to represent each node in the list. Each class listed in the manifest file should be separated from all other classes by a blank line. If the class is a bean it's **Name:** line should be immediately followed by its **Java-Bean:** line.

Software Engineering Observation 25.6

*In the manifest file, a bean's name is specified with the **Name:** property followed by the complete package name and class name of the bean. The dots (**.**) normally used to separate package names and class names are replaced with forward slashes (**/**) in this line of the manifest file.*

Software Engineering Observation 25.7

*If a specific class represents a bean, the line following the **Name:** property for that class must specify **Java-Bean: True**. Otherwise, IDEs will not recognize the class as a bean.*

Software Engineering Observation 25.8

If a class containing main is included in a JAR file, that class can be used by the interpreter to execute the application directly from the JAR file by specifying the **Main-Class:** *property on a line by itself at the beginning of the manifest file. The full package name and class name of the class should be specified with the usual dot (.) separating the package names and class name.*

Common Programming Error 25.1

Not specifying a manifest file or specifying a manifest file with incorrect syntax when creating a JAR file is an error. Builder tools will not recognize the beans in the JAR file.

Next, we create the JAR file for the **LogoAnimator** bean. This is accomplished with the **jar** utility at the command line (such as the MS-DOS prompt or UNIX shell). The command

```
jar cfm LogoAnimator.jar manifest.tmp jhtp3beans\*.*
```

creates the JAR file. [*Note:* This command uses **** as the directory separator from the MS-DOS prompt. UNIX would use **/** as the directory separator.] In the preceding command, **jar** is the Java archive utility used to create JAR files. Next are the options for the **jar** utility—**cfm**. The letter **c** indicates that we are creating a JAR file. The letter **f** indicates that the next argument in the command line (**LogoAnimator.jar**) is the name of the JAR file to create. The letter **m** indicates that the next argument in the command line is the **manifest.tmp** file that is used by **jar** to create the file **MANIFEST.MF** in directory **META-INF** of the JAR. Following the options, JAR file name and **manifest.tmp** file are the actual files that will be included in the JAR file. We specified **jhtp3beans*.***, indicating that all the files in the **jhtp3beans** directory should be included in the JAR file. The **jhtp3beans** package directory contains the **.class** files for the **LogoAnimator** and its supporting classes as well as the images used in the animation. [*Note:* You can include selected files by specifying the path and file name for each individual file.] It is important that the directory structure in the JAR file match the directory structure used in the **manifest.tmp** file. Therefore, we executed the **jar** command from the directory in which **jhtp3beans** is located.

To confirm that the files were archived directly, you can issue the command

```
jar tvf LogoAnimator.jar
```

which produces the listing in Fig. 25.24. In the preceding command, the options for the **jar** utility are **tvf**. The letter **t** indicates that the table of contents for the JAR should be listed. The letter **v** indicates that the output should be verbose (the verbose output includes the file size in bytes and the date and time each file was created in addition to the directory structure and file name). The letter **f** specifies that the next argument on the command line is the JAR file to use.

Try executing the **LogoAnimator** application with the command

```
java -jar LogoAnimator.jar
```

You will see that the animation appears in its own window on your screen.

```
   0 Sun Mar 14 11:36:16 EST 1999 META-INF/
 163 Sun Mar 14 11:36:16 EST 1999 META-INF/MANIFEST.MF
4727 Thu Feb 15 00:37:04 EST 1996 jhtp3beans/deitel0.gif
4858 Thu Feb 15 00:39:32 EST 1996 jhtp3beans/deitel1.gif
4374 Thu Feb 15 00:55:46 EST 1996 jhtp3beans/deitel10.gif
4634 Thu Feb 15 00:56:52 EST 1996 jhtp3beans/deitel11.gif
4852 Thu Feb 15 00:58:00 EST 1996 jhtp3beans/deitel12.gif
4877 Thu Feb 15 00:59:10 EST 1996 jhtp3beans/deitel13.gif
4926 Thu Feb 15 01:00:20 EST 1996 jhtp3beans/deitel14.gif
4765 Thu Feb 15 01:01:32 EST 1996 jhtp3beans/deitel15.gif
4886 Thu Feb 15 01:05:16 EST 1996 jhtp3beans/deitel16.gif
4873 Thu Feb 15 01:06:12 EST 1996 jhtp3beans/deitel17.gif
4739 Thu Feb 15 01:07:18 EST 1996 jhtp3beans/deitel18.gif
4566 Thu Feb 15 01:08:24 EST 1996 jhtp3beans/deitel19.gif
4819 Thu Feb 15 00:41:06 EST 1996 jhtp3beans/deitel2.gif
4313 Thu Feb 15 01:09:48 EST 1996 jhtp3beans/deitel20.gif
3910 Thu Feb 15 01:10:46 EST 1996 jhtp3beans/deitel21.gif
3076 Thu Feb 15 01:12:02 EST 1996 jhtp3beans/deitel22.gif
3408 Thu Feb 15 01:13:16 EST 1996 jhtp3beans/deitel23.gif
4039 Thu Feb 15 01:14:06 EST 1996 jhtp3beans/deitel24.gif
4393 Thu Feb 15 01:15:02 EST 1996 jhtp3beans/deitel25.gif
4626 Thu Feb 15 01:16:06 EST 1996 jhtp3beans/deitel26.gif
4852 Thu Feb 15 01:17:18 EST 1996 jhtp3beans/deitel27.gif
4929 Thu Feb 15 01:18:18 EST 1996 jhtp3beans/deitel28.gif
4914 Thu Feb 15 01:19:16 EST 1996 jhtp3beans/deitel29.gif
4769 Thu Feb 15 00:42:52 EST 1996 jhtp3beans/deitel3.gif
4617 Thu Feb 15 00:43:54 EST 1996 jhtp3beans/deitel4.gif
4335 Thu Feb 15 00:47:14 EST 1996 jhtp3beans/deitel5.gif
3967 Thu Feb 15 00:49:40 EST 1996 jhtp3beans/deitel6.gif
3200 Thu Feb 15 00:50:58 EST 1996 jhtp3beans/deitel7.gif
3393 Thu Feb 15 00:52:32 EST 1996 jhtp3beans/deitel8.gif
4006 Thu Feb 15 00:53:48 EST 1996 jhtp3beans/deitel9.gif
 420 Sun Mar 14 11:36:16 EST 1999 jhtp3beans/LogoAnima-
tor$1.class
3338 Sun Mar 14 11:36:16 EST 1999 jhtp3beans/LogoAnima-
tor.class
```

Fig. 25.24   The contents of **LogoAnimator.jar**.

25.5 Adding Beans to the BeanBox

Now that the **LogoAnimator** is wrapped in a JAR file as a JavaBean, we can use the new bean in the **BeanBox**. There are two ways to load the bean into the **BeanBox**—place the JAR file in the **BDK1.1\jars** directory or use the **BeanBox File** menu's **LoadJar...** option to locate the JAR file on your system and load it into the **BeanBox**'s **ToolBox**. If you place the JAR file in the **BDK1.1\jars** directory, it will be automatically loaded into the **ToolBox** when the **BeanBox** is executed. Figure 25.25 shows the **File** menu's **Load-Jar...** option, the **Load beans from JAR File** dialog and the **ToolBox** with **Logo-Animator** loaded.

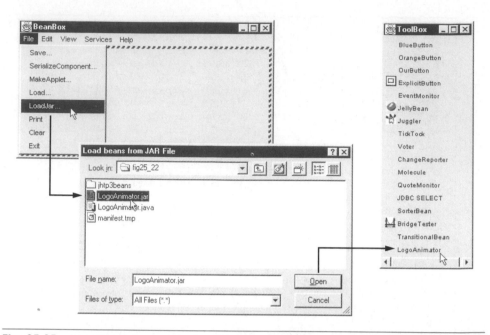

Fig. 25.25   Loading a bean into the **BeanBox**'s **Toolbox**.

To add a **LogoAnimator** to the **BeanBox** design area, click the **LogoAnimator** bean in the **ToolBox**, move the crosshair cursor over the **BeanBox** design area and click where you want the center of the **LogoAnimator** to appear. As soon as you click, the **BeanBox** creates an object of type **LogoAnimator** that immediately begins loading and displaying the images of the animation. Notice that the **Properties** window now contains the properties of the **LogoAnimator**. Figure 25.26 shows the **BeanBox** design area with the **LogoAnimator** and the **Properties** window with the **LogoAnimator** properties.

Notice that the **Properties** window shows several **LogoAnimator** properties. These properties were all inherited from class **JPanel**. In the example of Section 25.7, we will add our own property to control the speed of the animation. Our **LogoAnimator** bean can already be configured even though we did not create our own properties yet. Because we used transparent GIF images in the animation, you can choose the **background** color for the animation. Simply click the rectangle to the right of the **background** property in the **Properties** window. This displays the **BeanBox**'s **ColorEditor** property editor. Here you can choose a new background color for the animation. Figure 25.27 shows the **ColorEditor** property editor and the **LogoAnimator** in the **BeanBox** design area with its new background color.

25.6 Connecting Beans with Events in the BeanBox

Recall that our **LogoAnimator** bean provides methods **stopAnimation** and **start-Animation** that allow the animation to be stopped and restarted. We will now connect two buttons to the **LogoAnimator**—**Stop** and **Start**. As we saw earlier in the chapter, the **BeanBox** comes with several buttons. We will attach two **ExplicitButton**s to the **LogoAnimator**.

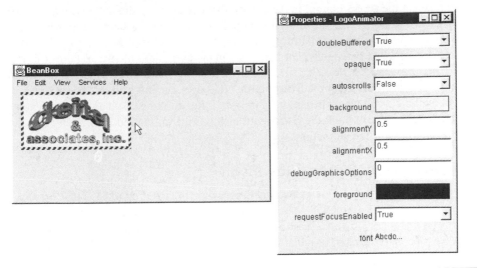

Fig. 25.26   The **LogoAnimator** on the **BeanBox** design area.

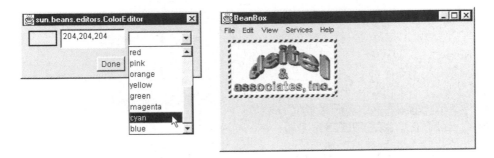

Fig. 25.27   Changing the background color of the **LogoAnimator**.

Place two **ExplicitButton**s on the **BeanBox** design area. Change the label on one **ExplicitButton** to **Start** and the other to **Stop**. Figure 25.28 shows the **BeanBox** with the **LogoAnimator** and two **ExplicitButton**s.

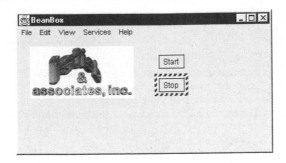

Fig. 25.28   Two **ExplicitButton**s to start and stop the animation.

Next, select the **Stop** button. In the **BeanBox Edit** menu, select the **button-push** event as shown in Fig. 25.29. Position the mouse pointer over the **LogoAnimator** and click to display the **EventTargetDialog** window. Next, we select the method on the target (i.e., the **LogoAnimator**) that will be called when the user clicks the **Stop** button. Scroll down to **stopAnimation**, select it, then press the **OK** button to complete the event hookup. Repeat the process for the **Start** button and select method **startAnimation** as the target method to call when the button is pressed. After hooking up the two button events to the **LogoAnimator**, click the **Stop** button to see the animation stop, then click the **Start** button to restart the animation.

25.7 Adding Properties to a JavaBean

In this section, we demonstrate adding an **animationDelay** property to our **LogoAnimator** to control the animation's speed. For this purpose, we extend class **LogoAnimator** to create class **LogoAnimator2**. The new code for our property is defined by method **setAnimationDelay** (line 12) and method **getAnimationDelay** (line 18) in Fig. 25.30.

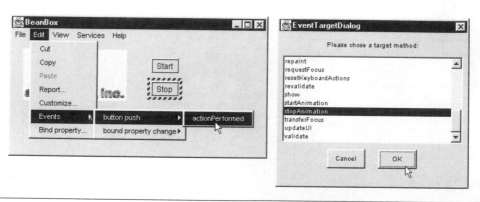

Fig. 25.29   Setting up the button-push event for the **Stop** button.

```
1   // Fig. 25.30: LogoAnimator2.java
2   // Animation bean with animationDelay property
3   package jhtp3beans;
4
5   import java.awt.*;
6   import java.awt.event.*;
7   import javax.swing.*;
8
9   public class LogoAnimator2 extends LogoAnimator {
10      // the following two methods are
11      // for the animationDelay property
12      public void setAnimationDelay( int value )
13      {
14          animationDelay = value;
```

Fig. 25.30   **LogoAnimator2** with property **animationDelay** (part 1 of 2).

```
15              animationTimer.setDelay( animationDelay );
16          }
17
18          public int getAnimationDelay()
19          {
20              return animationTimer.getDelay();
21          }
22
23          public static void main( String args[] )
24          {
25              LogoAnimator2 anim = new LogoAnimator2();
26
27              JFrame app = new JFrame( "Animator test" );
28              app.getContentPane().add( anim, BorderLayout.CENTER );
29
30              app.addWindowListener(
31                  new WindowAdapter() {
32                      public void windowClosing( WindowEvent e )
33                      {
34                          System.exit( 0 );
35                      }
36                  }
37              );
38
39              app.setSize( anim.getPreferredSize().width + 10,
40                          anim.getPreferredSize().height + 30 );
41              app.show();
42          }
43      }
```

Fig. 25.30 **LogoAnimator2** with property **animationDelay** (part 2 of 2).

To create the **animationDelay** property, we defined the **setAnimationDelay**
and **getAnimationDelay** methods. A *read/write* property of a bean is defined as a *set/
get* method pair of the following form:

> **public void set***PropertyName***(** *DataType* **value)**
> **public** *DataType* **get***PropertyName***()**

These methods are often referred to as a "property *set* method" and "property *get* method,"
respectively.

Software Engineering Observation 25.9

A JavaBean read/write property is defined by a set/get *method pair in which the* set *method
returns* **void** *and takes one argument, and the* get *method returns the same type as the corresponding* set *method's argument and takes no arguments. It is also possible to have read-
only properties (defined with only a* get *method) and write-only properties (defined with only
a* set *method).*

Software Engineering Observation 25.10

For a property with the name **propertyName***, the corresponding* set/get *method pair
would be* **setPropertyName/getPropertyName** *by default. Note that the first letter
of* **propertyName** *is capitalized in the* set/get *method names.*

If the property is a **boolean** data type, the *set/get* method pair is normally defined as

```
public void setPropertyName( boolean value )
public boolean isPropertyName()
```

where the *get* method name begins with the word **is** rather than **get**.

When a builder tool examines a bean, it inspects the methods of the bean for pairs of *set/get* methods that can represent properties (some builder tools also expose read-only and write-only properties). This is a process known as *introspection*. If an appropriate *set/get* method pair is found during the introspection process, the builder tool exposes that pair of methods as a property in the bean. In the first **LogoAnimator**, the pair of methods

```
public void setBackground( Color c )
public Color getBackground()
```

that were inherited from class **JPanel** allowed the **BeanBox** to expose the **background** property in the **Properties** window for customization. Notice that the naming convention for the *set/get* method pair uses a capital first letter for the property name, but the exposed property in the property sheet is shown with a lowercase first letter.

 Software Engineering Observation 25.11

> *When a builder tool examines a bean, if it locates a* set/get *method pair that matches the JavaBeans property pattern, it exposes that pair of methods as a property in the bean.*

Remember that you must wrap the **LogoAnimator2** class as a JavaBean to load it into the **BeanBox** or a builder tool. First compile the class

```
javac -d . LogoAnimator2.java
```

This places the package directory **jhtp3beans** in the current ("**.**") directory. Next, package the class into a JAR file

```
jar cfm LogoAnimator2.jar manifest.tmp jhtp3beans\*.*
```

The manifest file for this example is shown in Fig. 25.31. Line 1 specifies the name of the class file (**jhtp3beans\LogoAnimator2.class**) that represents the bean. Line 2 specifies that the class named in line 1 is a JavaBean. Line 3 specifies that **jhtp3beans.LogoAnimator2** is also the **Main-Class** for this application (when it is executed as an application).

In Fig. 25.32, we show a **LogoAnimator2** bean in the **BeanBox** with the **Properties** window. Notice that the **animationDelay** property is now exposed in the **Properties** window. Try changing the value of the property to see its effect on the speed of the animation (you must press enter after changing the value to effect the change). Smaller values cause the animation to spin faster, and larger values cause the animation to spin slower. Try typing 1000 to see one frame of the animation per second.

```
1   Main-Class: jhtp3beans.LogoAnimator2
2
3   Name: jhtp3beans/LogoAnimator2.class
4   Java-Bean: True
```

Fig. 25.31   The manifest file for the **LogoAnimator2** bean.

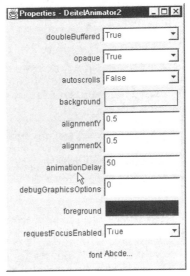

Fig. 25.32   The **LogoAnimator2** bean with property **animationDelay** exposed in the property sheet.

25.8 Creating a JavaBean with a Bound Property

A *bound property* causes the object that owns the property to notify other objects when there is a change in the bound property's value. This is accomplished using standard event-handling features demonstrated earlier in the text—all registered ***PropertyChange-Listener****s* are notified when the property's value changes. To support this feature, the ***java.beans*** *package* provides interface **PropertyChangeListener** so listeners can be set up to receive notification of the property change, class ***PropertyChange-Event*** to provide information to a **PropertyChangeListener** about the change in the property's value and class ***PropertyChangeSupport*** to provide the listener registration and notification services (i.e., maintaining the list of listeners and notifying them when an event occurs). Each type is discussed in the context of its use in Fig. 25.33.

Software Engineering Observation 25.12

A bound property causes the object that owns the property to notify other objects that there has been a change in the value of a property.

The next example presents our own new GUI component (**SliderFieldPanel**) that extends **JPanel** and includes one object of type **JSlider** and one object of type **JTextField**. When the **JSlider** value changes, our new GUI component automatically updates the **JTextField** with the new value. Also, when a new value is entered in the **JTextField** and the user presses the *Enter* key, the **JSlider** is automatically repositioned to the appropriate location. Our purpose in defining this new component is to eventually link one of these to the **LogoAnimator2** animation to control the speed of the animation. When the **SliderFieldPanel** value changes, we want the animation speed to change. Figure 25.33 presents the code for class **SliderFieldPanel** and shows a screen capture of our new component's appearance in the **BeanBox**.

```
1   // Fig. 25.33: SliderFieldPanel.java
2   // A subclass of JPanel containing a JSlider and a JTextField
3   package jhtp3beans;
4
5   import javax.swing.*;
6   import javax.swing.event.*;
7   import java.io.*;
8   import java.awt.*;
9   import java.awt.event.*;
10  import java.beans.*;
11
12  public class SliderFieldPanel extends JPanel
13                                      implements Serializable {
14     private JSlider slider;
15     private JTextField field;
16     private Box boxContainer;
17     private int currentValue;
18
19     // object to support bound property changes
20     private PropertyChangeSupport changeSupport;
21
22     public SliderFieldPanel()
23     {
24        // create PropertyChangeSupport for bound properties
25        changeSupport = new PropertyChangeSupport( this );
26
27        slider =
28           new JSlider( SwingConstants.HORIZONTAL, 1, 100, 1 );
29        field = new JTextField(
30                   String.valueOf( slider.getValue() ), 5 );
31
32        boxContainer = new Box( BoxLayout.X_AXIS );
33        boxContainer.add( slider );
34        boxContainer.add( Box.createHorizontalStrut( 5 ) );
35        boxContainer.add( field );
36
37        setLayout( new BorderLayout() );
38        add( boxContainer );
39
40        slider.addChangeListener(
41           new ChangeListener() {
42              public void stateChanged( ChangeEvent e )
43              {
44                 setCurrentValue( slider.getValue() );
45              }
46           }
47        );
48
```

Fig. 25.33   Class **SliderFieldPanel** definition (part 1 of 3).

```
49          field.addActionListener(
50             new ActionListener() {
51                public void actionPerformed( ActionEvent e )
52                {
53                   setCurrentValue(
54                      Integer.parseInt( field.getText() ) );
55                }
56             }
57          );
58       }
59
60       // methods for adding and removing PropertyChangeListeners
61       public void addPropertyChangeListener(
62          PropertyChangeListener listener )
63       {
64          changeSupport.addPropertyChangeListener( listener );
65       }
66
67       public void removePropertyChangeListener(
68          PropertyChangeListener listener )
69       {
70          changeSupport.removePropertyChangeListener( listener );
71       }
72
73       // property minimumValue
74       public void setMinimumValue( int min )
75       {
76          slider.setMinimum( min );
77
78          if ( slider.getValue() < slider.getMinimum() ) {
79             slider.setValue( slider.getMinimum() );
80             field.setText( String.valueOf( slider.getValue() ) );
81          }
82       }
83
84       public int getMinimumValue()
85       {
86          return slider.getMinimum();
87       }
88
89       // property maximumValue
90       public void setMaximumValue( int max )
91       {
92          slider.setMaximum( max );
93
94          if ( slider.getValue() > slider.getMaximum() ) {
95             slider.setValue( slider.getMaximum() );
96             field.setText( String.valueOf( slider.getValue() ) );
97          }
98       }
99
```

Fig. 25.33   Class **SliderFieldPanel** definition (part 2 of 3).

```
100     public int getMaximumValue()
101     {
102         return slider.getMaximum();
103     }
104
105     // property currentValue
106     public void setCurrentValue( int current )
107     {
108         int oldValue = currentValue;
109         currentValue = current;
110         slider.setValue( currentValue );
111         field.setText( String.valueOf( currentValue ) );
112         changeSupport.firePropertyChange(
113             "currentValue", new Integer( oldValue ),
114             new Integer( currentValue ) );
115     }
116
117     public int getCurrentValue()
118     {
119         return slider.getValue();
120     }
121
122     // property fieldWidth
123     public void setFieldWidth( int cols )
124     {
125         field.setColumns( cols );
126         boxContainer.validate();
127     }
128
129     public int getFieldWidth()
130     {
131         return field.getColumns();
132     }
133
134     public Dimension getMinimumSize()
135     {
136         return boxContainer.getMinimumSize();
137     }
138
139     public Dimension getPreferredSize()
140     {
141         return boxContainer.getPreferredSize();
142     }
143 }
```

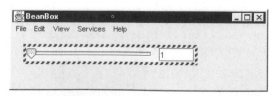

Fig. 25.33   Class **SliderFieldPanel** definition (part 3 of 3).

Class **SliderFieldPanel** begins by specifying it will be part of the **jhtp3beans** package (line 3). The class is a subclass of **JPanel**, so we can add a **JSlider** and a **JTextField** to it. Objects of class **SliderFieldPanel** can then be added to other containers.

The declarations of lines 14 through 20 specify instance variables of type **JSlider** (**slider**) and **JTextField** (**field**) that represent the subcomponents the user will use to set the value of the **SliderFieldPanel**, a **Box** (**boxContainer**) that will manage the layout of objects of our class, an **int** (**currentValue**) that stores the current value of the **SliderFieldPanel** and a **PropertyChangeSupport** (**changeSupport**) that will provide the listener registration and notification services.

In the constructor, line 25

```
changeSupport = new PropertyChangeSupport( this );
```

creates the **PropertyChangeSupport** object. The argument **this** specifies that an object of this class (**SliderFieldPanel**) is the source of the **PropertyChange-Event**. Lines 40 through 47 of the constructor register the **ChangeListener** for **slider**. When **slider**'s value changes, line 44 calls **setCurrentValue** to update **field** and notify registered **PropertyChangeListener**s of the change in value. Similarly, lines 49 through 57 register the **ActionListener** for **field**. When **field**'s value changes, lines 53 and 54 call **setCurrentValue** to update **slider** and notify registered **PropertyChangeListeners** of the change in value.

To support registration of listeners for changes to our **SliderFieldPanel**'s bound property, we define methods **addPropertyChangeListener** (lines 61–65) and **removePropertyChangeListener** (lines 67–71). Each of these methods calls the corresponding method in the **PropertyChangeSupport** object **changeSupport**. This object will provide the event notification services when the property value changes.

> ***Software Engineering Observation 25.13***
>
> *To define an event for a bean, you must supply a listener interface and an event class, and the bean must define methods that allow adding and removing of listeners. For bound property events, the listener interface and the event class are already defined (**PropertyChangeListener** and **PropertyChangeEvent**, respectively). A bean that supports bound property events must define method **addPropertyChangeListener** and method **removePropertyChangeListener** to provide listener registration services.*

Class **SliderFieldPanel** provides several properties. Property **minimumValue** is defined by method **setMinimumValue** (line 74) and method **getMinimumValue** (line 84). Property **maximumValue** is defined by method **setMaximumValue** (line 90) and method **getMaximumValue** (line 100). Property **fieldWidth** is defined by method **setFieldWidth** (line 123) and method **getFieldWidth** (line 129). Methods **getMinimumSize** (line 134) and **getPreferredSize** (line 139) are defined to return the minimum size and preferred size of the **Box** object **boxContainer** that manages the layout of the **JSlider** and **JTextField**.

> ***Software Engineering Observation 25.14***
>
> *If a bean will appear as part of a user interface, the bean should define method **getPreferredSize**, which takes no arguments and returns a **Dimension** object containing the preferred width and height of the bean. This helps the layout manager size the bean.*

Methods **setCurrentValue** (line 106) and **getCurrentValue** (line 117) define the *bound property* **currentValue**. When the bound property changes, the registered **PropertyChangeListener**s must be notified of the change. The JavaBeans specification requires that each bound property listener be presented with the old and new property values when notified of the change (the values can be **null** if they are not needed). For this reason, line 108 saves the previous value of the property. Line 109 sets the new value of the property. Lines 110 and 111 ensure that the **JSlider** and **JText-Field** show the appropriate new values. Lines 112 through 114 invoke the **Property-ChangeSupport** object's **firePropertyChange** method to notify each registered **PropertyChangeListener**. The first argument is a **String** containing the property name that changed—**currentValue**. The second argument is the old value of the property. The third argument is the new value of the property.

Software Engineering Observation 25.15

*PropertyChangeListeners are notified of a property change event with both the old and the new value of the property. If these values are not needed, they can be **null**.*

Software Engineering Observation 25.16

*Class **PropertyChangeSupport** is provided as a convenience to implement the listener registration and notification support for property change events.*

Remember that you must wrap the **SliderFieldPanel** class as a JavaBean to load it into the **BeanBox** or a builder tool. First compile the class

```
javac -d . SliderFieldPanel.java
```

This places the package directory **jhtp3beans** in the current (".") directory. Next, archive the class in a JAR file

```
jar cfm SliderFieldPanel.jar manifest.tmp jhtp3beans\*.*
```

The manifest file for this example is shown in Fig. 25.34. Line 1 specifies the name of the class file (**jhtp3beans\SliderFieldPanel.class**) that represents the bean. Line 2 specifies that the class named in line 1 is a JavaBean. There is no **Main-Class:** line in this file because the **SliderFieldPanel** is not an application.

To demonstrate the functionality of the bound property, place a **SliderField-Panel** bean and a **Juggler** bean on the **BeanBox**. Select the **SliderFieldPanel** bean, set its **maximumValue** property to 1000 and set its **currentValue** to 125 (the default animation speed for the **Juggler**). Next, select the **Bind property...** menu item from the **Edit** menu. The **PropertyNameDialog** in Fig. 25.35 appears.

Locate the name of the bound property (**currentValue**), select it and click **OK**. A red target selector line appears leading from your **SliderFieldPanel**. Connect this line to the **Juggler** and click the mouse. The dialog in Fig. 25.36 appears.

```
1   Name: jhtp3beans/SliderFieldPanel.class
2   Java-Bean: True
```

Fig. 25.34   Manifest file for the **SliderFieldPanel** JavaBean.

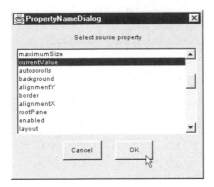

Fig. 25.35   Selecting the bound property from the **PropertyNameDialog**.

Fig. 25.36   Selecting the target property from the **PropertyNameDialog**.

The **PropertyNameDialog** shows only the target properties that have the same data type as the bound property. Select the **Juggler**'s **animationRate** property (the only one displayed) and click OK. The **animationRate** property is now bound to the **SliderFieldPanel**'s **currentValue** property. Figure 25.37 shows the **Slider-FieldPanel** and the **Juggler** in the **BeanBox**.

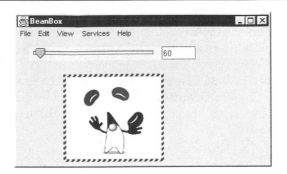

Fig. 25.37   The **BeanBox** window with the **SliderFieldPanel** and Juggler beans.

Try adjusting the slider to see the animation speed change. Move the slider left to see the speed of the animation increase and move the slider right to see the animation speed decrease. Also, try typing a new value in the text field and pressing *Enter* to change the animation speed.

25.9 Specifying the `BeanInfo` Class for a JavaBean

As mentioned previously, Java's introspection mechanism can be used by a builder tool to automatically expose a JavaBean's properties, methods and events if the programmer follows the proper JavaBean *design patterns* (such as the special naming conventions discussed for *set/get* method pairs that define a property of a bean). Builder tools use the classes and interfaces of package *java.lang.reflect* to perform introspection services. For JavaBeans that do not follow the JavaBean design patterns or for JavaBeans in which the programmer wants to customize the exposed set of properties, methods and events, the programmer can supply a class that implements interface *BeanInfo* (package *java.beans*). The *BeanInfo* class describes to the builder tool how to present the features of the bean to the programmer.

Software Engineering Observation 25.17

A JavaBean's properties, methods and events can be exposed automatically by a builder tool if the programmer follows the proper JavaBean design patterns.

Software Engineering Observation 25.18

*Every **BeanInfo** class must implement interface **BeanInfo**. This interface describes the methods used by a builder tool to determine the features of a bean described by that bean's **BeanInfo** class.*

Software Engineering Observation 25.19

*A **BeanInfo** class can be used to describe a JavaBean to a builder tool so the tool can present the features of the bean to a programmer. This is useful for JavaBeans that do not follow the JavaBean design patterns or for JavaBeans in which the programmer wants to customize the exposed set of properties, methods and events.*

In the last example, you may have noticed when you selected the **SliderField-Panel** bean in the **BeanBox** that 14 different properties were exposed and 10 categories of events (see the **BeanBox Edit** menu's **Events** menu item) were exposed. For this bean, we only want the programmer to see properties **fieldWidth**, **currentValue**, **minimumValue** and **maximumValue** (the other properties were inherited from class **JPanel** and are not truly relevant to our bean). Also, the only event we want the programmer to use for our component is the bound property event.

Figure 25.38 presents class **SliderFieldPanelBeanInfo** to customize the properties and events exposed in the **BeanBox** (or any other builder tool) for our **Slider-FieldPanel** bean. The screen captures in Fig. 25.38 show the exposed features of the **SliderFieldPanel** JavaBean.

Software Engineering Observation 25.20

*By default, the **BeanInfo** class has the same name as the bean and end with **BeanInfo**.*

Software Engineering Observation 25.21

*By default, the **BeanInfo** class is included in the same JAR file as the **SliderField-Panel** JavaBean. When the bean is loaded, the **BeanBox** (or builder tool) determines if the JAR file contains a **BeanInfo** class for a bean. If a **BeanInfo** class is found, it is used to determine the exposed features of the bean. Otherwise, standard introspection is used to determine the exposed features of the bean.*

Software Engineering Observation 25.22

*By default, the **BeanInfo** class is placed in the same **package** as the bean it describes.*

```
1   // Fig. 25.38: SliderFieldPanelBeanInfo.java
2   // The BeanInfo class for SliderFieldPanel
3   package jhtp3beans;
4
5   import java.beans.*;
6
7   public class SliderFieldPanelBeanInfo extends SimpleBeanInfo {
8      public final static Class beanClass =
9         SliderFieldPanel.class;
10
11     public PropertyDescriptor[] getPropertyDescriptors()
12     {
13        try {
14           PropertyDescriptor fieldWidth =
15              new PropertyDescriptor( "fieldWidth", beanClass );
16           PropertyDescriptor currentValue =
17              new PropertyDescriptor(
18                 "currentValue", beanClass );
19           PropertyDescriptor maximumValue =
20              new PropertyDescriptor(
21                 "maximumValue", beanClass );
22           PropertyDescriptor minimumValue =
23             new PropertyDescriptor( "minimumValue", beanClass );
24
25           // ensure PropertyChangeEvent occurs for this property
26           currentValue.setBound( true );
27
28           PropertyDescriptor descriptors[] = { fieldWidth,
29              currentValue, maximumValue, minimumValue };
30
31           return descriptors;
32        }
33        catch ( IntrospectionException ie ) {
34           throw new RuntimeException( ie.toString() );
35        }
36     }
37
```

Fig. 25.38   Demonstrating class **SliderFieldPanelBeanInfo** in the **BeanBox** (part 1 of 2).

```
38      // the index for the currentValue property
39      public int getDefaultPropertyIndex()
40      {
41          return 1;
42      }
43
44      public EventSetDescriptor[] getEventSetDescriptors() {
45          try {
46              EventSetDescriptor changed =
47                  new EventSetDescriptor( beanClass,
48                  "propertyChange",
49                  java.beans.PropertyChangeListener.class,
50                  "propertyChange");
51
52              changed.setDisplayName(
53                  "SliderFieldPanel value changed" );
54
55              EventSetDescriptor[] descriptors = { changed };
56
57              return descriptors;
58          }
59          catch (IntrospectionException e) {
60              throw new RuntimeException(e.toString());
61          }
62      }
63  }
```

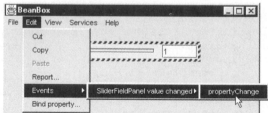

Fig. 25.38 Demonstrating class **SliderFieldPanelBeanInfo** in the BeanBox (part 2 of 2).

Every **BeanInfo** class must implement interface **BeanInfo**. This interface describes the methods used by a builder tool to determine the exposed features of the bean described by its corresponding **BeanInfo** class. As a convenience, the **java.beans** package includes class *SimpleBeanInfo*, which provides a default implementation of every method in interface **BeanInfo**. The programmer can extend this class and selectively override its methods to implement a proper **BeanInfo** class. Class **Slider-FieldPanelBeanInfo** extends class **SimpleBeanInfo** (line 7).

Software Engineering Observation 25.23

*Class **SimpleBeanInfo** provides a default implementation of every method in interface **BeanInfo**. The programmer can selectively override methods of this class to implement a proper **BeanInfo** class.*

In this example, we override **BeanInfo** methods *getPropertyDescriptors*, *getDefaultPropertyIndex* and *getEventSetDescriptors*.

Lines 8 and 9

```
public final static Class beanClass =
    SliderFieldPanel.class;
```

define a reference (**beanClass**) to a *Class* object. Class **Class** (defined in package **java.lang**) enables a program to refer to a class definition (and provides many other interesting features as well). Class **Class** is used by the introspection mechanism to refer to the class that will be searched for the features described in the **BeanInfo** class. Lines 8 and 9 cause the **SliderFieldPanel.class** file to be loaded into memory. The reference is declared **final** because it should not be modified in the class definition. The reference is declared **static** because only one instance of the **Class** is needed.

Lines 11 through 36 override method **getPropertyDescriptors** to return an array of *PropertyDescriptor* objects. Each **PropertyDescriptor** indicates a specific property that should be exposed by a builder tool. There are several ways to construct a **PropertyDescriptor**. In this example, each of the **PropertyDescriptor** constructor calls has the form

```
new PropertyDescriptor( "propertyName", beanClass );
```

where *propertyName* is a **String** that specifies the name of a property defined by the pair of methods **set***PropertyName* and **get***PropertyName*. Note that the *propertyName* **String** should begin with a lowercase letter and the corresponding property methods begin the property name with an uppercase first letter. We defined **PropertyDescriptor**s for **fieldWidth**, **currentValue**, **minimumValue** and **maximumValue**.

Software Engineering Observation 25.24

If the set/get *methods for a property do not use the JavaBeans naming convention for properties, there are two other* ***PropertyDescriptor*** *constructors in which the actual method names are passed. This allows the builder tools to use nonstandard property methods to expose a property for manipulation by the programmer at design time. This is particularly useful in retrofitting a class as a JavaBean when that class was not originally designed and implemented using JavaBeans design patterns.*

Line 26

```
currentValue.setBound( true );
```

specifies that property **currentValue** is a bound property. Some builder tools visually treat bound property events separately from other events. For example, the **BeanBox** has **Edit** menu item **Bind property...** to allow the programmer to hook up a bound property event. Note that the **BeanBox** also provides an entry for the bound property event in the **Edit** menu's **Events** menu item.

Lines 28 and 29 create the **PropertyDescriptor** array that is returned by the method at line 31. Note the exception handler for *IntrospectionException*s. If a **PropertyDescriptor** constructor is unable to confirm the property in the corresponding **Class** object that represents the class definition, the constructor throws an **IntrospectionException**. Because the **BeanInfo** class and its methods are actually used by the builder tool at design time (i.e., during the development of the program in the IDE), the **RuntimeException** thrown in the **catch** handler would normally be caught by the builder tool.

Lines 39 through 42 define method ***getDefaultPropertyIndex*** to return the value 1, indicating that the property at position 1 in the **PropertyDescriptor** array returned from **getPropertyDescriptors** is the *default property* for developers to customize in a builder tool. Typically, the default property is automatically selected when you click on a bean. In this example, property **currentValue** is the default property.

Lines 44 through 62 override method ***getEventSetDescriptors*** to return an array of ***EventSetDescriptor*** objects that describes to a builder tool the events supported by this bean. Lines 46 through 50

```
EventSetDescriptor changed =
    new EventSetDescriptor( beanClass,
    "propertyChange",
    java.beans.PropertyChangeListener.class,
    "propertyChange" );
```

define an **EventSetDescriptor** object for the **PropertyChangeEvent** associated with the bound property **currentValue**. The four arguments to the constructor describe the event that should be exposed by the builder tool. The first argument is the **Class** object (**beanClass**) representing the *event source* (the bean that generates the event). The second argument is a **String** representing the *event set* name (e.g., the **mouse** event set includes **mousePressed**, **mouseClicked**, **mouseReleased**, **mouseEntered** and **mouseExited**). In this example, the event set name is ***propertyChange***.

Software Engineering Observation 25.25

*When using the standard JavaBeans design patterns, the event set name is part of all the data type names and method names used to process the event. For example, the types and methods for the **propertyChange** event set are: **PropertyChangeListener** (the interface an object must implement to be notified of an event in this event set), **PropertyChange-Event** (the type passed to a listener method for an event in this event set), **addProperty-ChangeListener** (the method called to add a listener for an event in this event set), **removePropertyChangeListener** (the method called to remove a listener for an event in this event set) and **firePropertyChange** (the method called to notify listeners when an event in this event set occurs—this method is only named this way by convention).*

The third argument is the **Class** object representing the event listener interface implemented by listeners for this event. This argument is specified with

```
java.beans.PropertyChangeListener.class
```

which loads the "**.class**" file and automatically creates an anonymous object of type **Class**. Finally, the last argument is a **String** representing the name of the listener method to call (**propertyChange**) when this event occurs.

Software Engineering Observation 25.26

EventSetDescriptor *can be constructed with other arguments to expose events that do not follow the standard JavaBeans design patterns.*

A benefit of an **EventSetDescriptor** is customizing the name for the event set for display in the builder tool. Lines 52 and 53

```
changed.setDisplayName(
    "SliderFieldPanel value changed" );
```

call method ***setDisplayName*** on the **EventSetDescriptor** to indicate that its displayed name should be "**SliderFieldPanel value changed**" (see the screen capture in Fig. 25.38).

![Good Programming Practice icon] **Good Programming Practice 25.1**

Customizing the event set name displayed by a builder tool can make the purpose of that event set more understandable to the programmer using the bean.

Lines 55 and 57 create the **EventSetDescriptor** array and return it, respectively. Note the exception handler for **IntrospectionException**s at line 59. If an **EventSetDescriptor** constructor is unable to confirm the event in the corresponding **Class** object that represents the class definition, the constructor **throws** an **IntrospectionException**.

25.10 JavaBeans World Wide Web Resources

If you have access to the Internet and the World Wide Web, there are a large number of JavaBean resources available to you. The best place to start is at the source—the Sun Microsystems, Inc. Java Web site **http://java.sun.com**.

http://java.sun.com/beans/
This is the *JavaBeans Home Page* at the Sun Microsystems, Inc. Web site. Here, you can download the *Beans Development Kit (BDK)* and other bean-related software. Other features of the site include: JavaBeans documentation and specifications, a frequently asked questions list, an overview of Integrated Development Environments that support JavaBeans development, training and support, upcoming JavaBeans events, a searchable directory of JavaBeans components, a support area for marketing your JavaBeans, and a variety of on-line resources for communicating with other programmers regarding JavaBeans.

http://java.sun.com/beans/spec.html
Visit this site to download the JavaBeans specification.

http://java.sun.com/beans/tools.html
Visit this site for information about JavaBeans-enabled development tools.

http://java.sun.com/beans/directory/
Visit this site for a searchable directory of available beans.

http://java.sun.com/products/hotjava/bean/index.html
Download an evaluation version of the *HotJava HTML Component*. This JavaBean allows developers to provide HTML rendering capabilities in any Java application. The bean supports HTTP 1.1 protocol, HTML 3.2 and many standard features of Web browsers.

Summary

- The **BeanBox** is a test container for your JavaBeans.
- Once you have installed the JavaBeans Development Kit, you can execute the **BeanBox** by locating the **BDK1.1** directory where you installed the JavaBeans Development Kit. The subdirectory **beanbox** directory contains start-up files for both Windows (**run.bat**) and Solaris (**run.sh**).
- The **doc** directory contains the on-line HTML help files for the **BeanBox** (use file **beanbox.html** to get started). The help files discuss in depth all the features of the **BeanBox**.
- The four windows of the **BeanBox** are **ToolBox**, **BeanBox**, **Properties** and **Method Tracer**.

- A property editor allows the programmer to customize a property's value.

- When selecting a bean from the **ToolBox**, your mouse cursor should change to a crosshair cursor. Position the mouse cursor at the location on the **BeanBox** window where you want the center of your bean to be located and click the mouse to place the bean.

- To customize a bean, select the bean by clicking it with the mouse. If clicking a bean in the **BeanBox** window does not select it, you may need to click just outside the bean's boundary to select it. The properties of the currently selected bean are displayed in the **Properties** window.

- The **BeanBox** window **Edit** menu's **Events** menu item provides access to the events supported by a bean that is an event source (i.e, any bean that can notify a listener that an event occurred).

- As you move the mouse around the **BeanBox** window after selecting an event, you will see a red target selector line following the mouse. This is used to specify the *target* of the event. Click the target object to display the **EventTargetDialog** window listing the **public** methods that can be called on the target.

- The **BeanBox** provides the ability to save a design to be reloaded into the **BeanBox** later (the **File** menu's **Save...** menu item) or save a design as a Java applet (the **File** menu's **MakeApplet...** menu item).

- The **archive** property of the applet tag specifies a comma-separated list of JAR files containing the code that is used to execute the applet.

- Classes that represent a bean are placed in a package using the **-d** option with the Java compiler.

- JavaBeans should all implement the **Serializable** interface so they can be saved from a builder tool after being customized by the programmer.

- To use a class as a JavaBean, it must first be placed in a JAR file. A text file called **manifest.tmp** is used by the **jar** utility to describe the contents of the JAR file. The **jar** utility uses the file **manifest.tmp** to create a file called **MANIFEST.MF** that is included in the **META-INF** directory of the archive file.

- When a JAR file containing a JavaBean (or set of JavaBeans) is loaded into an IDE, the IDE looks at the manifest to determine which of the classes in the JAR represent JavaBeans. These classes are made available for use by the programmer in a visual manner.

- When an application class containing **main** is stored in a JAR, the application can be executed directly from the JAR using the Java interpreter with the **-jar** command-line option as follows:

```
java -jar LogoAnimator.jar
```

  The interpreter looks at the manifest file in a JAR for the class specified as the **Main-Class** to begin execution with its **main** method.

- With Java 1.2 (the Java 2 platform), many platforms assume that a JAR file contains an application and attempt to execute it.

- The command

```
jar cfm JARFileName.jar manifest.tmp files
```

  creates the JAR file. In the preceding command, **jar** is the Java archive utility used to create JAR files. Next are the options for the **jar** utility—**cfm**. The letter **c** indicates that we are creating a JAR file. The letter **f** indicates that the next argument is the name of the JAR file. The letter **m** indicates that the next argument is the **manifest.tmp** file that will be used by **jar** to create **MANIFEST.MF** in the **META-INF** directory of the JAR. Following the options, JAR file name and **manifest.tmp** file are the actual *files* to include in the JAR file.

- The directory structure in the JAR file must match the directory structure used in the **manifest.tmp** file. Both should match the package structure.

- There are two ways to load the bean into the **BeanBox**—place the JAR file in the **BDK1.1\jars** directory or use the **File** menu's **LoadJar...** option to locate the JAR file on your system and load it into the **BeanBox**'s **ToolBox**. If you place the JAR file in the **BDK1.1\jars** directory, it will automatically be loaded into the **ToolBox** when the **BeanBox** is executed.

- A read-write property of a bean is defined as a pair of *set/get* methods of the following form:

      public void set *PropertyName* **(** *DataType* **value)**
      public *DataType* **get** *PropertyName* **()**

  If the property is **boolean** data type, the *set/get* method pair is normally defined as

      public void set *PropertyName* **(boolean value)**
      public boolean is *PropertyName* **()**

  When a builder tool examines a bean, if it locates a *set/get* method pair with the preceding formats, the builder tool exposes that pair of methods as a property in the bean.

- A bound property causes the object that owns the property to notify other objects that there has been a change in the value of that property. All registered **PropertyChangeListener**s are automatically notified when the property's value changes. The **java.beans** package provides interface **PropertyChangeListener** to create listeners that can receive notification of the property change, class **PropertyChangeEvent** to provide information to a **Property-ChangeListener** about the change in the property's value and class **PropertyChange-Support** to provide the listener registration and notification services.

- To support registration of listeners for changes to a bound property, a bean must provide methods **addPropertyChangeListener** and **removePropertyChangeListener**. Each of these methods typically calls the corresponding method in a **PropertyChangeSupport** object that provides the event notification services when the property value changes.

- When a bound property changes, the registered **PropertyChangeListener**s must be notified of the change. Each listener is presented with old and new property values when notified of the change. The **PropertyChangeSupport** object's **firePropertyChange** method notifies each registered **PropertyChangeListener**.

- When a bean provides bound properties, there will be a **Bind property...** menu item in the **Bean-Box**'s **Edit** menu. Select the **Bind property...** menu item from the **Edit** menu to display the **PropertyNameDialog**. Select the bound property. Connect the red target selector line to the target of the property change event to select the method to call.

- Using introspection, a JavaBean's properties, methods and events can be exposed automatically by a builder tool if the programmer follows the proper JavaBean design patterns. For JavaBeans that do not follow the JavaBean design patters or for JavaBeans in which the programmer wants to customize the exposed set of properties, methods and events, the programmer can supply a **BeanInfo** class that describes to the builder tool how to present the features of the bean.

- Every **BeanInfo** class must implement the **BeanInfo** interface that describes the methods used by a builder tool to determine the features of a bean. Class **SimpleBeanInfo** provides a default implementation of each method in the **BeanInfo** interface. The programmer can extend this class and selectively override methods of this class to implement a proper **BeanInfo** class.

- Override method **getPropertyDescriptors** to return an array of **PropertyDescriptor** objects in which **PropertyDescriptor** indicates a property a builder tool should expose.

- If the *set/get* methods for a property do not use the JavaBeans naming convention for properties, there are two other **PropertyDescriptor** constructors in which the actual method names are passed. This allows the builder tools to use nonstandard property methods to expose a property for manipulation by the programmer at design time.

- Override method **getEventSetDescriptors** to return an array of **EventSetDescriptor** objects that describe to a builder tool the events supported by a bean.

- **EventSetDescriptor**s can be constructed with different arguments to expose events that do not follow the standard JavaBeans design patterns.

Terminology

adapter class
adding events to a bean
adding properties to a bean
addPropertyChangeListener method
applet tag archive property
BDK directory
BDK\jars directory
BDK (JavaBeans Development Kit)
bean
BeanBox
beanbox subdirectory of **BDK** directory
BeanBox window of the **BeanBox**
BeanInfo interface
bound property of a bean
builder tool
Choose JAR File dialog box
ColorEditor property editor of the **BeanBox**
connecting beans
"connect the dots" programming
creating a JAR file
customize a JavaBean
deserialize an object
design pattern
dropping a bean on the **BeanBox**
Edit menu **Events** menu item
event
event adapter class
event hookup
event listener
event set
EventSetDescriptor class
event source
event target
EventTargetDialog dialog box
execute an application from a JavaBean
ExplicitButton BeanBox demo bean
exposing the events of a bean
exposing the properties of a bean
File menu **Clear** menu item
File menu **Load...** menu item
File menu **MakeApplet...** menu item
File menu **Save...** menu item
File menu **SerializeComponent...** menu item
firePropertyChange method
getDefaultPropertyIndex method
getEventSetDescriptors method
get method
getPropertyDescriptors method
hook up an event
hookup class
introspection
IntrospectionException class
.jar (Java archive) file extension

jar (Java Archive File) utility
Java Archive File (JAR File)
java -jar (execute an application from a bean)
java.beans package
java.beans.BeanInfo interface
java.beans.EventSetDescriptor class
java.beans.IntrospectionException
java.beans.PropertyChangeEvent
java.beans.PropertyChangeListener
java.beans.PropertyChangeSupport
java.beans.PropertyDescriptor class
java.beans.SimpleBeanInfo class
java.io.ObjectInputStream class
java.io.ObjectOutputStream class
java.io.Serializable interface
JavaBean
JavaBeans Development Kit (BDK)
java.lang.reflect package
Juggler BeanBox demo bean
Load saved BeanBox dialog box
Make an Applet dialog box
manifest file
META-INF directory of a JAR file
move cursor
ObjectInputStream class
ObjectOutputStream class
object serialization
persistence
Properties window of the **BeanBox**
property
PropertyChangeEvent class
PropertyChangeListener interface
PropertyChangeSupport class
PropertyDescriptor class
property *get* method
PropertyNameDialog dialog box
property *set* method
property sheet
removePropertyChangeListener method
resize cursor
Save BeanBox File dialog box
selection box
.ser (serialized file) extension
Serializable interface
serializing a bean
set method
SimpleBeanInfo class
target of an event
target selector line
ToolBox window of the **BeanBox**
transient classes and fields (not serialized)
viewing the contents of a JAR file

Common Programming Error

25.1   Not specifying a manifest file or specifying a manifest file with incorrect syntax when creating a JAR file is an error. Builder tools will not recognize the beans in the JAR file.

Good Programming Practice

25.1   Customizing the event set name displayed by a builder tool can make the purpose of that event set more understandable to the programmer using the bean.

Software Engineering Observations

25.1   The **BeanBox** is not a builder tool. Rather, the **BeanBox** allows programmers to preview how a bean will be displayed and used by a builder tool.

25.2   A benefit of working in a bean-ready development environment is that the environment visually presents the properties of the bean to the programmer for easy modification and customization of the bean at design time.

25.3   A benefit of working in a bean-ready development environment is that the beans typically execute live in the development environment. This allows you to view and test the functionality of your program immediately in the design environment rather than using the standard edit, compile and execute programming cycle.

25.4   JavaBeans should all implement the **Serializable** interface to support persistence.

25.5   You must define a manifest file that describes the contents of a JAR file if you intend to either use the bean in a bean-aware integrated development environment or if you intend to execute an application directly from a JAR file.

25.6   In the manifest file, a bean's name is specified with the **Name:** property followed by the complete package name and class name of the bean. The dots (**.**) normally used to separate package names and class names are replaced with forward slashes (**/**) in this line of the manifest file.

25.7   If a specific class represents a bean, the line following the Name: property for that class must specify **Java-Bean: True**. Otherwise, IDEs will not recognize the class as a bean.

25.8   If a class containing main is included in a JAR file, that class can be used by the interpreter to execute the application directly from the JAR file by specifying the **Main-Class:** property on a line by itself at the beginning of the manifest file. The full package name and class name of the class should be specified with the usual dot (**.**) separating the package names and class name.

25.9   A JavaBean read/write property is defined by a *set*/*get* method pair in which the *set* method returns **void** and takes one argument, and the *get* method returns the same type as the corresponding *set* method's argument and takes no arguments. It is also possible to have read-only properties (defined with only a *get* method) and write-only properties (defined with only a *set* method).

25.10   For a property with the name **propertyName**, the corresponding *set*/*get* method pair would be **setPropertyName**/**getPropertyName** by default. Note that the first letter of **propertyName** is capitalized in the *set*/*get* method names.

25.11   When a builder tool examines a bean, if it locates a *set*/*get* method pair that matches the JavaBeans property pattern, it exposes that pair of methods as a property in the bean.

25.12   A bound property causes the object that owns the property to notify other objects that there has been a change in the value of a property.

25.13   To define an event for a bean, you must supply a listener interface and an event class, and the bean must define methods that allow adding and removing of listeners. For bound property events, the listener interface and the event class are already defined (**PropertyChange-Listener** and **PropertyChangeEvent**, respectively). A bean that supports bound property events must define method **addPropertyChangeListener** and method **removePropertyChangeListener** to provide listener registration services.

25.14 If a bean will appear as part of a user interface, the bean should define method **getPreferredSize**, which takes no arguments and returns a **Dimension** object containing the preferred width and height of the bean. This helps the layout manager size the bean.

25.15 **PropertyChangeListener**s are notified of a property change event with both the old and the new value of the property. If these values are not needed, they can be **null**.

25.16 Class **PropertyChangeSupport** is provided as a convenience to implement the listener registration and notification support for property change events.

25.17 A JavaBean's properties, methods and events can be exposed automatically by a builder tool if the programmer follows the proper JavaBean design patterns.

25.18 Every **BeanInfo** class must implement interface **BeanInfo**. This interface describes the methods used by a builder tool to determine the features of a bean described by that bean's **BeanInfo** class.

25.19 A **BeanInfo** class can be used to describe a JavaBean to a builder tool so the tool can present the features of the bean to a programmer. This is useful for JavaBeans that do not follow the JavaBean design patterns or for JavaBeans in which the programmer wants to customize the exposed set of properties, methods and events.

25.20 By default, the **BeanInfo** class has the same name as the bean and end with **BeanInfo**.

25.21 By default, the **BeanInfo** class is included in the same JAR file as the **SliderFieldPanel** JavaBean. When the bean is loaded, the **BeanBox** (or builder tool) determines if the JAR file contains a **BeanInfo** class for a bean. If a **BeanInfo** class is found, it is used to determine the exposed features of the bean. Otherwise, standard introspection is used to determine the exposed features of the bean.

25.22 By default, the **BeanInfo** class is placed in the same **package** as the bean it describes.

25.23 Class **SimpleBeanInfo** provides a default implementation of every method in interface **BeanInfo**. The programmer can selectively override methods of this class to implement a proper **BeanInfo** class.

25.24 If the *set/get* methods for a property do not use the JavaBeans naming convention for properties, there are two other **PropertyDescriptor** constructors in which the actual method names are passed. This allows the builder tools to use nonstandard property methods to expose a property for manipulation by the programmer at design time. This is particularly useful in retrofitting a class as a JavaBean when that class was not originally designed and implemented using JavaBeans design patterns.

25.25 When using the standard JavaBeans design patterns, the event set name is part of all the data type names and method names used to process the event. For example, the types and methods for the **propertyChange** event set are: **PropertyChangeListener** (the interface an object must implement to be notified of an event in this event set), **PropertyChangeEvent** (the type passed to a listener method for an event in this event set), **addPropertyChangeListener** (the method called to add a listener for an event in this event set), **removePropertyChangeListener** (the method called to remove a listener for an event in this event set) and **firePropertyChange** (the method called to notify listeners when an event in this event set occurs—this method is only named this way by convention).

25.26 **EventSetDescriptor**s can be constructed with other arguments to expose events that do not follow the standard JavaBeans design patterns.

Testing and Debugging Tip

25.1 The **BeanBox** can be used to test and debug JavaBeans.

Self-Review Exercises

25.1   Fill in the blanks in each of the following:
   a) The four windows of the **BeanBox** are _____, _____, _____ and _____.
   b) A _____ allows the programmer to customize a property's value.
   c) The **BeanBox** window **Edit** menu's _____ menu item provides access to the events supported by a bean that is an event source.
   d) The _____ is used to specify the target of an event.
   e) The _____ property of the **<applet>** tag specifies a comma-separated list of JAR files containing the code that is used to execute the applet.
   f) JavaBeans should all implement the _____ interface so they can be saved from a builder tool after being customized by the programmer.
   g) All registered _____ are automatically notified when a bound property's value changes.
   h) When a bean provides bound properties, there will be a _____ menu item in the **BeanBox**'s **Edit** menu.
   i) A builder tool uses _____ to expose a JavaBean's properties, methods and events.
   j) For JavaBeans that do not follow the JavaBean design pattern or for JavaBeans in which the programmer wants to customize the exposed set of properties, methods and events, the programmer can supply a _____ class that describes to the builder tool how to present the features of the bean.
   k) A _____ object describes a property that a builder tool should expose.
   l) A _____ object describes an event that a builder tool should expose.

Answers to Self-Review Exercises

25.1   a) **Toolbox**, **BeanBox**, **Properties**, **Method Tracer**. b) property editor. c) **Events**. d) target selector line. e) **archive**. f) **Serializable**. g) **PropertyChangeListener**s. h) **Bind property...**. i) introspection. j) **BeanInfo**. k) **PropertyDescriptor**. l) **EventSetDescriptor**.

Exercises

25.2   Try each of the demonstration JavaBeans supplied with the **BeanBox**. The documentation that comes with the BDK provides overviews of the demonstration beans. While using each bean, try the following:
   a) Inspect the properties of each bean and try modifying them.
   b) Inspect the events supported by each bean and try using those events to hook various demonstration beans together.

25.3   Using the **SliderFieldPanel** as a foundation, create your own **ColorSelector** GUI component that contains three instances of our **SliderFieldPanel** bean. Each should have values in the range 0 to 255 for the red, green and blue parts of a color. The programmer using your bean should be able configure the default color when their application executes. Make **color** a bound property such that other objects can be notified when the color changes. Test your bean in the **BeanBox** by changing the background color of the **BeanBox** when a new color is selected. To specify the **BeanBox** as the target of an event, simply aim the target selector line at the background of the **BeanBox** window and click.

25.4   Modify Exercise 25.3 to provide a mechanism for viewing the selected color. For this purpose add a **JPanel** object to the bean. Test your bean in the **BeanBox** by changing the background color of the **BeanBox** when a new color is selected.

25.5   Create a **BeanInfo** class for the **LogoAnimator2** bean that exposes only the **background** and **animationDelay** properties. Test your bean in the **BeanBox**.

25.6   Using the graphics techniques discussed in Chapter 11, implement your own subclass of **JPanel** that supports drawing of a variety of shapes. The user should be able to select which shape to draw, then use the mouse to draw the shape. All shapes should be maintained as objects in a hierarchy of shape types. You can use either of the hierarchies described in Exercises 9.28 and 9.29, or you can use the predefined classes of the Java2D API as discussed in Chapter 11. Store all the shape objects in a **Vector**. Wrap your class as a JavaBean and test it in the **BeanBox**.

25.7   Modify your solution to Exercise 25.6 to allow the user to select the color and fill characteristics of the shape. Wrap your class as a JavaBean and test it in the **BeanBox**.

25.8   Add a **saveShapes** method and a **loadShapes** method to the JavaBean in Exercise 25.7. Method **saveShapes** should store a **Vector** of objects to a file on disk, and method **loadShapes** should load a **Vector** of objects from a file on disk. Both methods should take no arguments—the **Vector** should be part of the bean. The file should be manipulated with the object serialization techniques discussed in Chapter 17. When method **saveShapes** is called, display a **JFileChooser** dialog that allows the user to select a file in which to save the **Vector**'s contents, then write the **Vector** into the file. When method **loadShapes** is called, display a **JFileChooser** dialog that allows the user to select a file from which to read the **Vector**'s contents, then load the **Vector**. Wrap your class as a JavaBean and test it in the **BeanBox**. Hook up a button to your bean such that when the button is pressed, method **saveShapes** is called. Hook up a second button to your bean such that when the button is pressed, method **loadShapes** is called.

Appendix A
Java Demos

A.11 Introduction

[*Note:* This appendix was written by Abbey Deitel of Deitel & Associates, Inc., and Paul Brandano, a Junior at Boston College and a participant in the Deitel & Associates, Inc. College Internship Program.]

Our contribution to this textbook is as World Wide Web surfers. In this appendix, we list some of the best Java demos we found on the Web.

We began our journey at `http://www.gamelan.com`. This site is an incredible Java resource and has some of the best Java demos including a huge compilation of games written in Java. The code ranges from basic to complex. Many of the authors of these games and other resources have provided source code. We hope you enjoy surfing these sites as much as we did.

May we ask a favor? We will be keeping this appendix up to date on the Deitel Web site

> `http://www.deitel.com`

Please send us your favorite sites that you want to share with others. We will post your suggestions promptly. Please send us email at

> `deitel@deitel.com`

A.12 The Sites

`http://www.developer.com/directories/pages/dir.java.html`
   Visit the *Developer.com* Web site at `http://www.developer.com` for a wide variety of information on Java and Internet-related topics. The Java directory page contains links to thousands of Java applets and other Java resources.

`http://www.gamelan.com`
   Developer.com includes another Web site that has been a wonderful Java resource since the early days of Java—*Gamelan*. The Gamelan site calls itself the "Official Directory for Java." This site originally was a large Java repository where individuals traded ideas on Java and examples of Java programming. One of its early

benefits was the volume of Java source code that was available to the many people learning Java. It is now an all-around Java resource with Java references, free Java downloads, areas where you can ask questions to Java experts, discussion groups on Java, a glossary of Java-related terminology, upcoming Java-related events, directories for specialized industry topics and hundreds of other Java resources.

http://www.jars.com

Another Developer.com Web site is *JARS*—originally called the *Java Applet Rating Service*. The JARS site calls itself the "#1 Java Review Service." This site originally was a large Java repository for applets. Its benefit was that it rated every applet registered at the site as top 1%, top 5% and top 25%, so you could immediately view the best applets on the Web. Early in the development of the Java language, having your applet rated here was a great way to demonstrate your Java programming abilities. JARS is now another all-around resource for Java programmers. Many of the resources for this site, Gamelan and Developer.com, are now shared as these sites are all owned by EarthWeb.

http://www.geocities.com/SiliconValley/Haven/4274/on-line/pyrs.htm

Pyramids is a simple puzzle game written in Java.

http://hprbg1.informatik.tu-muenchen.de/gnatzm/Web-Billiard.html

Web Billiard is an Internet pool game written in Java, complete with animation and audio.

http://www.glom.net/blitz/game/index.html

The Blitz game was written using Java. It runs on Windows, Unix, and in some cases runs on the Macintosh as well.

http://www.fouda.de/html/index1.htm

The Bumpy Lens 3D graphic allows you to move a magnifying glass over an image. The affect is cool, but it takes a while to download.

http://members.xoom.com/javacliu/

This page has several Java demos, including a few which have won awards. You can view live demos of each program and check out the documentation.

http://student.twi.tudelft.nl/~tw636365/index.html

The JVO Java site has some cool Java applets and tutorials so you can learn how to create the applets yourself.

http://www.demicron.se/gallery/index.html?photoalbum

The PhotoAlbum II has some of the coolest effects we have found on the web. The effects include liquid, folding the image into a paper airplane and a few other fun effects.

http://www.blaupunkt.de/simulations/svdef_en.html

The *Sevilla RDM 168* is a simulation, built with Java, of a car Radio and CD player. You can tune into a variety of on-line radio stations or CDs, adjust the volume, clock settings and more.

http://www.frontiernet.net/~imaging/play_a_piano.html

Play A Piano is a Java applet that allows you to play the piano or watch the sound waves and listen as the piano plays itself.

http://www.lamatek.com/lamasoft/Panoramic/test.html

Panoramania is a Java applet that has a panoramic, smooth-scrolling image. You can pause the scroll, reverse the direction and zoom in or out on the image.

http://www.java4fun.com

Java4fun has an extensive listing of games written in Java. The source code is provided for several games.

http://www.gamesdomain.co.uk/GamesArena/goldmine/
  Goldmine. This is a fun game using simple animation.

http://www.tdb.uu.se/~karl/java/tube/
  Tube. This game is similar to the Pacman game we all played in the 1980's.

http://www.tdb.uu.se/~karl/java/noids/
  Urbanoids. This is a fun game with animation, audio and cool graphics. Source code is provided.

http://www.tdb.uu.se/~karl/java/warp15/
  Warp 1.5. This animated game has great graphics and includes audio.

http://www.tdb.uu.se/~karl/java/3dblox/
  The Iceblox game. This is a fun game that uses a little animation.

http://www.javagamepark.com/
  If you are looking for games, the *Java Game Park* site has loads of them. All of the games are written in Java. The source code is provided in some cases.

http://teamball.sdsu.edu/~boyns/java/
  This site has a few fun and interesting games written in Java. A few more *Teamball* demos follow.

http://teamball.sdsu.edu/~boyns/java/centipedo/
  Centipedo is similar to the Centipede video game. The source code is provided.

http://teamball.sdsu.edu/~boyns/java/crazycounter/
  The Crazy Counter is a page access counter which counts the number of hits on a page. The source code is provided so that you may install the Crazy Counter on your web page.

http://teamball.sdsu.edu/~boyns/java/logo/
  Animated SDSU Logo. View the source code provided here and learn how to create animated Java applets.

http://teamball.sdsu.edu/~boyns/java/mc/
  Missile Commando is another video game with sound effects. The source code is provided.

http://www.cruzio.com/~sabweb/arcade/index.html
  Sab's Game Arcade is another source for Java video games. Source code is provided for many of the games. Don't miss the SabBowl bowling game.

http://www.sover.net/~manx/hyprcube.html
  Stereoscopic Animated Hypercube. If you happen to possess the old red and blue 3D glasses, check this site out. The programmer was able to create a 3D image using Java. It isn't really a complicated image, just some cubes, however the idea that you can create images that will jump off your screen is a great concept!

http://www.npac.syr.edu/projects/vishuman/VisibleHuman.html
  This site was once featured by Gamelan and has won various awards. You can look at different cross sections of the human body. The Java source code is provided.

http://www-groups.dcs.st-and.ac.uk/~history/Java/
  Famous Curves Applet Index. Provides graphs of complex curves. Allows the user to alter the parameters to the equations that calculate the curves. Source code is available.

Appendix B
Java Resources

B.13 Introduction

[*Note:* This appendix was written by Abbey Deitel of Deitel & Associates, Inc., and Paul Brandano, a Junior at Boston College and a participant in the Deitel & Associates, Inc. College Internship Program.]

    There is a bounty of Java information on the World Wide Web. Many people are experimenting with Java and sharing their thoughts, discoveries, ideas and source code with each other via the Internet. If you would like to recommend other sites, please send us email at

        deitel@deitel.com

and we will put links to the sites you suggest on our Web site

        http://www.deitel.com.

B.14 Resources

http://java.sun.com
> The *Sun Microsystems, Inc. Java Web site* is an essential stop when searching the web for Java information. Go to this site to download the Java 2 Software Development Kit. This site is also a complete resource with news, information, on-line support, code samples and more.

http://www.developer.com/directories/pages/dir.java.html
> Visit the *Developer.com* Web site at **http://www.developer.com** for a wide variety of information on Java and Internet-related topics. The Java directory page contains links to thousands of Java applets and other Java resources.

http://www.gamelan.com
> Developer.com includes another Web site that has been a wonderful Java resource since the early days of Java—*Gamelan*. The Gamelan site calls itself the "Official Directory for Java." This site originally was a large Java repository where individuals traded ideas on Java and examples of Java programming. One of its early benefits was the volume of Java source code that was available to the many people

learning Java. It is now an all-around Java resource with Java references, free Java downloads, areas where you can ask questions to Java experts, discussion groups on Java, a glossary of Java-related terminology, upcoming Java-related events, directories for specialized industry topics and hundreds of other Java resources.

http://www.jars.com

Another Developer.com Web site is *JARS*—originally called the *Java Applet Rating Service*. The JARS site calls itself the "#1 Java Review Service." This site originally was a large Java repository for applets. Its benefit was that it rated every applet registered at the site as top 1%, top 5% and top 25%, so you could immediately view the best applets on the Web. Early in the development of the Java language, having your applet rated here was a great way to demonstrate your Java programming abilities. JARS is now another all-around resource for Java programmers. Many of the resources for this site, Gamelan and Developer.com, are now shared as these sites are both owned by EarthWeb.

http://java.sun.com/jdc/

On the Sun Microsystems Java Web site, visit the *Java Developer Connection*. This free site has close to one million members. The site includes technical support, discussion forums, on-line training courses, technical articles, resources, announcements of new Java features, early access to new Java technologies, and links to other important Java Web sites. Even though the site is free, you must register to use it.

http://www.taxon.demon.nl/JW/javawoman.html

The *Java Woman* web site has one of the most extensive list of Java related links we have found on the web. You will find lists of links for Java books, Integrated Development Environments, FAQs, examples, documentation, tutorials, tools and advanced topics.

http://www.nikos.com/javatoys/

The *Java Toys* web site includes links to the latest Java news, Java User Groups (JUGs), FAQs, tools, Java-related mailing lists, books and white papers.

http://www.java-zone.com/

The Development Exchange Java Zone site includes Java discussion groups, and "ask the Java Pro" section and some recent Java news.

http://www.acme.com/java/

This page has an animated Java applet with the source code provided. This site is an excellent resource for information on Java. The page provides software, notes and a list of hyperlinks to other resources. Under "software" you will find some animated applets, utility classes and applications.

http://www.sunsite.unc.edu/javafaq

This site provides the latest Java news. It also has some helpful Java resources including the following: the Java FAQ List, a tutorial called Brewing Java, Java User Groups, Java Links, the Java Book List, Java Trade Shows, Java Training and Exercises.

http://www.progsource.com

The *Programmers Source* is a great resource for information on many programming languages, including Java. You will find lists of development tools, tutorials, newsgroups, FAQs, employment opportunities and links to other Java resources.

http://www.teamjava.com

Team Java assists Java consultants in search of contracts and helps to promote Java. They have also listed some resourceful sites. A few of the sites are included in this list of resources.

`http://dir.yahoo.com/Computers_and_Internet/Programming_Languages/`
`Java/`

> *Yahoo*, a popular World Wide Web search engine, provides a complete Java resource. You can initiate a search using key words or explore the categories listed at the site including games, contests, events, tutorials and documentation, mailing lists, security and more.

`http://www.ibm.com/developer/java/`

> The *IBM Developers Java Technology Zone* site lists the latest news, tools, code, case studies and events related to IBM and Java.

B.15 Products

`http://java.sun.com/products/`

> Download the Java 2 SDK and other Java products from the *Sun Microsystems Java Products page*.

`http://www.netbeans.com/`

> The *NetBeans* IDE is a customizable, platform independent, visual programming development environment.

`http://www.borland.com/jbuilder/`

> The *Borland JBuilder* IDE home page has news, product information and customer support.

`http://www.towerj.com`

> At this site you will find information on how to enhance the performance of server-side Java applications along with free evaluation copies of native Java compilers.

`http://cafe.symantec.com/`

> Visit the *Symantec* site for information on their *Visual Café Integrated Development Environment*.

`http://www.software.ibm.com/ad/vajava/`

> Download or read more about the IBM Visual Age for Java development environment.

`http://www.metrowerks.com/`

> The *Metrowerks CodeWarrior* IDE supports a few programming languages, including Java.

B.16 FAQs

`http://www.taxon.demon.nl/JW/javawoman.html`

> The *Java Woman* web site has one of the most extensive list of Java related links we have found on the web. You will find lists of links for Java books, Integrated Development Environments, FAQs, examples, documentation, tutorials, tools and advanced topics.

`http://java.sun.com/products/jdk/rmi/faq.html`

> This site is the *Sun RMI and Object Serialization FAQ*.

`http://java.sun.com/products/jdbc/faq.html`

> This is the *Sun JDBC FAQ*.

`http://www.nikos.com/javatoys/`

> The *Java Toys* web site includes links to the latest Java news, Java User Groups (JUGs), FAQs, tools, Java-related mailing lists, books and white papers.

`http://www.java-zone.com/`

> The *Development Exchange Java Zone* site includes Java discussion groups, and "ask the Java Pro" section and some recent Java news.

`http://www.sunsite.unc.edu/javafaq`

This site provides the latest Java news. It also has some helpful Java resources including the following: the Java FAQ List, a tutorial called Brewing Java, Java User Groups, Java Links, the Java Book List, Java Trade Shows, Java Training and Exercises.

`http://www.progsource.com`

The *Programmers Source* is a great resource for information on many programming languages, including Java. You will find lists of development tools, tutorials, newsgroups, FAQs, employment opportunities and links to other Java resources.

B.17 Tutorials

`http://java.sun.com/docs/books/tutorial/`

The *Java Tutorial Site* has a number of tutorials, including sections on JavaBeans, JDBC, RMI, Servlets, Collections and Java Native Interface.

`http://www.taxon.demon.nl/JW/javawoman.html`

The *Java Woman* web site has one of the most extensive list of Java related links we have found on the web. You will find lists of links for Java books, Integrated Development Environments, FAQs, examples, documentation, tutorials, tools and advanced topics.

`http://www.sunsite.unc.edu/javafaq`

This site provides the latest Java news. It also has some helpful Java resources including the following: the Java FAQ List, a tutorial called Brewing Java, Java User Groups, Java Links, the Java Book List, Java Trade Shows, Java Training and Exercises.

`http://www.progsource.com`

The *Programmers Source* is a great resource for information on many programming languages, including Java. You will find lists of development tools, tutorials, newsgroups, FAQs, employment opportunities and links to other Java resources.

B.18 Magazines

`http://www.javaworld.com`

The *JavaWorld* on-line magazine is an excellent resource for current Java information. You will find news clips, conference information and links to Java-related web sites.

`http://www.sys-con.com/java/`

Catch up with the latest Java news at the *Java Developer's Journal* site. This magazine is one of the premier resources for Java news.

`http://www.javareport.com/`

The *Java Report* is a great resource for Java Developers. You will find the latest industry news, sample code, event listings, products and jobs.

`http://www.Sun.COM/sunworldonline/`

SunWorld is the on-line magazine "for the Sun community." You will find some news and information related to Java.

`http://www.intelligence.com/java/default.asp`

Intelligence.com is a great resource for Java news and information. You will find a collection of the latest articles, book reviews, interviews and case studies from various trade publications.

B.19 Java Applets

http://java.sun.com

If you have access to the Internet and the World Wide Web, there are a large number of Java applet resources available to you. The best place to start is at the source—the Sun Microsystems, Inc. Java Web site. In the upper-left corner of the Web page is an Applets hyperlink that takes you to the Sun Applets Web page.

http://java.sun.com/applets/index.html

This page contains a variety of Java applet resources, including free applets you can use on your own World Wide Web site, the demonstration applets from the J2SDK and a variety of other applets (many of which can be downloaded and used on your own computer). There is also a section entitled "Applets at Work" where you can read about uses of applets in industry.

http://java.sun.com/jdc/

On the Sun Microsystems Java Web site, visit the *Java Developer Connection*. This free site has close to one million members. The site includes technical support, discussion forums, on-line training courses, technical articles, resources, announcements of new Java features, early access to new Java technologies, and links to other important Java Web sites. Even though the site is free, you must register to use it.

http://www.developer.com/directories/pages/dir.java.html

Visit the *Developer.com* Web site at http://www.developer.com for a wide variety of information on Java and Internet-related topics. The Java directory page contains links to thousands of Java applets and other Java resources.

http://www.gamelan.com

Developer.com includes another Web site that has been a wonderful Java resource since the early days of Java—*Gamelan*. The Gamelan site calls itself the "Official Directory for Java." This site originally was a large Java repository where individuals traded ideas on Java and examples of Java programming. One of its early benefits was the volume of Java source code that was available to the many people learning Java. It is now an all-around Java resource with Java references, free Java downloads, areas where you can ask questions to Java experts, discussion groups on Java, a glossary of Java-related terminology, upcoming Java-related events, directories for specialized industry topics and hundreds of other Java resources.

http://www.jars.com

Another Developer.com Web site is *JARS*—originally called the *Java Applet Rating Service*. The JARS site calls itself the "#1 Java Review Service." This site originally was a large Java repository for applets. Its benefit was that it rated every applet registered at the site as top 1%, top 5% and top 25%, so you could immediately view the best applets on the Web. Early in the development of the Java language, having your applet rated here was a great way to demonstrate your Java programming abilities. JARS is now another all-around resource for Java programmers. Many of the resources for this site, Gamelan and Developer.com, are now shared as these sites are both owned by EarthWeb.

B.20 Multimedia

http://java.sun.com/products/java-media/jmf/

The *Java Media Framework home page* on the Java Web site. Here you can download the latest Sun implementation of the JMF. The site also contains the documentation for the JMF.

http://java.sun.com/products/java-media/jmf/forDevelopers/playerapi/packages.html

The on-line site for the **javax.media** API descriptions. These can also be downloaded from the JMF home page.

`http://www.nasa.gov/gallery/index.html`

The *NASA multimedia gallery* contains a wide variety of images, audio clips and video clips that you can download and use to test your Java multimedia programs.

`http://sunsite.sut.ac.jp/multimed/`

The *Sunsite Japan Multimedia Collection* also provides a wide variety of images, audio clips and video clips that you can download for educational purposes.

`http://www.anbg.gov.au/anbg/index.html`

The *Australian National Botanic Gardens* Web site provides links to sounds of many animals. Try the Common Birds link.

`http://java.sun.com/products/java-media/jmf/forDevelopers/`
`playerguide/index.html`

This site provides an HTML-based on-line guide to the Java Media Player.

B.21 Servlets

`http://java.sun.com/products/servlet/index.html`

The servlet page at the Sun Microsystems, Inc. Java Web site provides access to the latest servlet information, servlet resources and the Java Servlet Development Kit (JSDK).

`http://www.servlets.com`

This is the Web site for the book *Java Servlet Programming* published by O'Reilly. The book provides a variety of resources. This book is an excellent resource for programmers who are learning servlets.

`http://www.servletcentral.com`

Servlet Central is an online magazine for server-side Java programmers. This includes technical articles and columns, news and "Ask the Experts." Resources include: books, servlet documentation links on the Web, a servlet archive, a list of servlet-enabled applications and servers and servlet development tools.

`http://www.servletsource.com`

ServletSource.com is a general servlet resource site containing code, tips, tutorials and links to many other Web sites with information on servlets.

`http://www.cookiecentral.com`

A good all-around resource site for cookies.

`http://www.purpletech.com/java/servlet-faq/`

The *Purple Servlet FAQ* is a great resource with dozens of links to tutorials, other servlet FAQs, mailing lists and newsgroups, articles, web servers, whitepapers and Java e-mail resources.

`http://www.servletforum.com/`

Servletforum.com is an on-line newsgroup dedicated to Java Servlets. Post your own questions or check out the archived list of previously asked questions.

`http://www.enhydra.org/`

Enhydra is an open source Java/XML application server and development environment available for free download.

`http://www.locomotive.org/locolink/disp?home`

The *Locomotive Project* is an open source, servlet-compatible, web application server available for free download.

`http://www.servlet.com/srvpages/srvdev.html`

The *Servlet, Inc. Servlet Developer's Forum* has links to numerous web resources, examples, products that use servlets and server-enabled web servers.

B.22 JavaBeans

`http://java.sun.com/beans/`

This is the *JavaBeans Home Page* at the Sun Microsystems, Inc. Web site. Here, you can download the Beans Development Kit (BDK) and other bean-related software. Other features of the site include: JavaBeans documentation and specifications, a FAQ, an overview of Integrated Development Environments that support JavaBeans development, training and support, upcoming JavaBeans events, a searchable directory of JavaBeans components, a support area for marketing your JavaBeans, and a variety of on-line resources for communicating with other programmers regarding JavaBeans.

`http://java.sun.com/beans/spec.html`

Visit this site to download the JavaBeans specification.

`http://java.sun.com/beans/tools.html`

Visit this site for information about JavaBeans-enabled development tools.

`http://java.sun.com/beans/directory/`

Visit this site for a searchable directory of available beans.

`http://java.sun.com/products/hotjava/bean/index.html`

Download an evaluation version of the *HotJava HTML Component*. This JavaBean allows developers to provide HTML rendering capabilities in any Java application. The bean supports HTTP 1.1 protocol, HTML 3.2 and many standard features of Web browsers.

B.23 Java CORBA

`http://www.omg.org/`

The *Object Management Group* web site is an excellent resource for CORBA information. You will find tutorials, newsgroups, a reading room with books and magazines, links and news.

`http://www.iona.com/`

IONA Technologies is a CORBA ORB vendor. Learn more about their pure-Java ORB, Orbix-Web, and OrbixHome, a "fully-integrated development, assembly and deployment environment for CORBA and Enterprise JavaBeans."

`http://www.corba.org`

The *CORBA homepage* has a list of success stories from companies committed to CORBA and links to their web sites.

B.24 Newsgroups

`news:comp.lamg.java`
`news:comp.lang.java.advocacy`
`news:comp.lang.java.announce`
`news:comp.lang.java.beans`
`news:comp.lang.java.corba`
`news:comp.lang.java.databases`
`news:comp.lang.java.gui`
`news:comp.lang.java.help`
`news:comp.lang.java.machine`
`news:comp.lang.java.programmer`
`news:comp.lang.java.softwaretools`
`news:cz.comp.lang.java`

```
news:fj.comp.lang.java
news:news.admin.lang.java
news:news.admin.lang.java.advocacy
news:news.admin.lang.java.corba
news:news.admin.lang.java.databases
news:news.admin.lang.java.machine
news:news.admin.lang.java.security
news:news.groups.lang.java.announce
news:news.groups.lang.java.beans
news:news.groups.lang.java.programmer
news:news.groups.lang.java.security
```

Appendix C
Operator Precedence Chart

Operators are shown in decreasing order of precedence from top to bottom.

Operator	Type	Associativity
( ) [ ] .	parentheses array subscript member selection	left to right
++ – –	unary postincrement unary postdecrement	right to left
++ – – + – ! ~ (*type*)	unary preincrement unary predecrement unary plus unary minus unary logical negation unary bitwise complement unary cast	right to left
* / %	multiplication division modulus	left to right
+ –	addition subtraction	left to right
<< >> >>>	bitwise left shift bitwise right shift with sign extension bitwise right shift with zero extension	left to right

Fig. C.39 Operator precedence chart (part 1 of 2).

Operator	Type	Associativity
`<`	relational less than	left to right
`<=`	relational less than or equal to	
`>`	relational greater than	
`>=`	relational greater than or equal to	
`instanceof`	type comparison	
`==`	relational is equal to	left to right
`!=`	relational is not equal to	
`&`	bitwise AND	left to right
`^`	bitwise exclusive OR	left to right
	boolean logical exclusive OR	
`|`	bitwise inclusive OR	left to right
	boolean logical inclusive OR	
`&&`	logical AND	left to right
`||`	logical OR	left to right
`?:`	ternary conditional	right to left
`=`	assignment	right to left
`+=`	addition assignment	
`-=`	subtraction assignment	
`*=`	multiplication assignment	
`/=`	division assignment	
`%=`	modulus assignment	
`&=`	bitwise AND assignment	
`^=`	bitwise exclusive OR assignment	
`|=`	bitwise inclusive OR assignment	
`<<=`	bitwise left shift assignment	
`>>=`	bitwise right shift with sign extension assignment	
`>>>=`	bitwise right shift with zero extension assignment	

Fig. C.39 Operator precedence chart (part 2 of 2).

Appendix D
ASCII Character Set

	0	1	2	3	4	5	6	7	8	9
0	nul	soh	stx	etx	eot	enq	ack	bel	bs	ht
1	nl	vt	ff	cr	so	si	dle	dc1	dc2	dc3
2	dc4	nak	syn	etb	can	em	sub	esc	fs	gs
3	rs	us	sp	!	"	#	$	%	&	'
4	(	)	*	+	,	-	.	/	0	1
5	2	3	4	5	6	7	8	9	:	;
6	<	=	>	?	@	A	B	C	D	E
7	F	G	H	I	J	K	L	M	N	O
8	P	Q	R	S	T	U	V	W	X	Y
9	Z	[	\	]	^	_	'	a	b	c
10	d	e	f	g	h	i	j	k	l	m
11	n	o	p	q	r	s	t	u	v	w
12	x	y	z	{			}	~	del		

The digits at the left of the table are the left digits of the decimal equivalent (0-127) of the character code, and the digits at the top of the table are the right digits of the character code. For example, the character code for 'F' is 70, and the character code for '&' is 38.

Note: Most users of this book are interested in the ASCII character set used to represent English characters on many computers. The ASCII character set is a subset of the Unicode character set used by Java to represent characters from most of the world's languages. For more information on the Unicode character set, visit the World Wide Web site

`http://unicode.org`

Appendix E

Number Systems

Objectives

- To understand basic number systems concepts such as base, positional value, and symbol value.
- To understand how to work with numbers represented in the binary, octal, and hexadecimal number systems
- To be able to abbreviate binary numbers as octal numbers or hexadecimal numbers.
- To be able to convert octal numbers and hexadecimal numbers to binary numbers.
- To be able to covert back and forth between decimal numbers and their binary, octal, and hexadecimal equivalents.
- To understand binary arithmetic, and how negative binary numbers are represented using two's complement notation.

Here are only numbers ratified.
William Shakespeare

Nature has some sort of arithmetic-geometrical coordinate system, because nature has all kinds of models. What we experience of nature is in models, and all of nature's models are so beautiful.

It struck me that nature's system must be a real beauty, because in chemistry we find that the associations are always in beautiful whole numbers—there are no fractions.
Richard Buckminster Fuller

Outline

E.25 Introduction

In this appendix, we introduce the key number systems that Java programmers use, especially when they are working on software projects that require close interaction with "machine-level" hardware. Projects like this include operating systems, computer networking software, compilers, database systems, and applications requiring high performance.

When we write an integer such as 227 or -63 in a Java program, the number is assumed to be in the *decimal (base 10) number system*. The *digits* in the decimal number system are 0, 1, 2, 3, 4, 5, 6, 7, 8, and 9. The lowest digit is 0 and the highest digit is 9—one less than the *base* of 10. Internally, computers use the *binary (base 2) number system*. The binary number system has only two digits, namely 0 and 1. Its lowest digit is 0 and its highest digit is 1—one less than the base of 2.

As we will see, binary numbers tend to be much longer than their decimal equivalents. Programmers who work in assembly languages and in high-level languages like Java that enable programmers to reach down to the "machine level," find it cumbersome to work with binary numbers. So two other number systems the *octal number system (base 8)* and the *hexadecimal number system (base 16)*—are popular primarily because they make it convenient to abbreviate binary numbers.

In the octal number system, the digits range from 0 to 7. Because both the binary number system and the octal number system have fewer digits than the decimal number system, their digits are the same as the corresponding digits in decimal.

The hexadecimal number system poses a problem because it requires sixteen digits—a lowest digit of 0 and a highest digit with a value equivalent to decimal 15 (one less than the base of 16). By convention, we use the letters A through F to represent the hexadecimal digits corresponding to decimal values 10 through 15. Thus in hexadecimal we can have numbers like 876 consisting solely of decimal-like digits, numbers like 8A55F consisting of digits and letters, and numbers like FFE consisting solely of letters. Occasionally, a hexadecimal number spells a common word such as FACE or FEED—this can appear strange to programmers accustomed to working with numbers.

Each of these number systems uses *positional notation*—each position in which a digit is written has a different *positional value*. For example, in the decimal number 937 (the 9, the 3, and the 7 are referred to as *symbol values*), we say that the 7 is written in the *ones position*, the 3 is written in the *tens position*, and the 9 is written in the *hundreds position*. Notice that each of these positions is a power of the base (base 10), and that these powers begin at 0 and increase by 1 as we move left in the number (Fig. E.3).

Binary digit	Octal digit	Decimal digit	Hexadecimal digit
0	0	0	0
1	1	1	1
	2	2	2
	3	3	3
	4	4	4
	5	5	5
	6	6	6
	7	7	7
		8	8
		9	9
			A (decimal value of 10)
			B (decimal value of 11)
			C (decimal value of 12)
			D (decimal value of 13)
			E (decimal value of 14)
			F (decimal value of 15)

Fig. E.40   Digits of the binary, octal, decimal and hexadecimal number systems.

Attribute	Binary	Octal	Decimal	Hexadecimal
Base	2	8	10	16
Lowest digit	0	0	0	0
Highest digit	1	7	9	**F**

Fig. E.41   Comparison of the binary, octal, decimal and hexadecimal number systems.

Positional values in the decimal number system			
Decimal digit	9	3	7
Position name	Hundreds	Tens	Ones
Positional value	100	10	1
Positional value as a power of the base (10)	10^2	10^1	10^0

Fig. E.42   Positional values in the decimal number system.

For longer decimal numbers, the next positions to the left would be the *thousands position* (10 to the 3rd power), the *ten-thousands position* (10 to the 4th power), the *hundred-thousands position* (10 to the 5th power), the *millions position* (10 to the 6th power), the *ten-millions position* (10 to the 7th power), and so on.

In the binary number 101, we say that the rightmost 1 is written in the *ones position*, the 0 is written in the *twos position*, and the leftmost 1 is written in the *fours position*. Notice that each of these positions is a power of the base (base 2), and that these powers begin at 0 and increase by 1 as we move left in the number (Fig E.4).

For longer binary numbers, the next positions to the left would be the *eights position* (2 to the 3rd power), the *sixteens position* (2 to the 4th power), the *thirty-twos position* (2 to the 5th power), the *sixty-fours position* (2 to the 6th power), and so on.

In the octal number 425, we say that the 5 is written in the *ones position*, the 2 is written in the *eights position*, and the 4 is written in the *sixty-fours position*. Notice that each of these positions is a power of the base (base 8), and that these powers begin at 0 and increase by 1 as we move left in the number (Fig. E.5).

For longer octal numbers, the next positions to the left would be the *five-hundred-and-twelves position* (8 to the 3rd power), the *four-thousand-and-ninety-sixes position* (8 to the 4th power), the *thirty-two-thousand-seven-hundred-and-sixty eights position* (8 to the 5th power), and so on.

In the hexadecimal number 3DA, we say that the A is written in the *ones position*, the D is written in the *sixteens position*, and the 3 is written in the *two-hundred-and-fifty-sixes position*. Notice that each of these positions is a power of the base (base 16), and that these powers begin at 0 and increase by 1 as we move left in the number (Fig. E.6).

Positional values in the binary number system			
Binary digit	1	0	1
Position name	Fours	Twos	Ones
Positional value	4	2	1
Positional value as a power of the base (2)	2^2	2^1	2^0

Fig. E.43   Positional values in the binary number system.

Positional values in the octal number system			
Decimal digit	4	2	5
Position name	Sixty-fours	Eights	Ones
Positional value	64	8	1
Positional value as a power of the base (8)	8^2	8^1	8^0

Fig. E.44   Positional values in the octal number system.

Positional values in the hexadecimal number system			
Decimal digit	**3**	**D**	**A**
Position name	Two-hundred-and-fifty-sixes	Sixteens	Ones
Positional value	**256**	**16**	**1**
Positional value as a power of the base (16)	16^2	16^1	16^0

Fig. E.45   Positional values in the hexadecimal number system.

For longer hexadecimal numbers, the next positions to the left would be the *four-thousand-and-ninety-sixes position* (16 to the 3rd power), the *sixty-five-thousand-five-hundred-and-thirty-six position* (16 to the 4th power), and so on.

E.26 Abbreviating Binary Numbers as Octal Numbers and Hexadecimal Numbers

The main use for octal and hexadecimal numbers in computing is for abbreviating lengthy binary representations. Figure E.7 highlights the fact that lengthy binary numbers can be expressed concisely in number systems with higher bases than the binary number system.

Decimal number	Binary representation	Octal representation	Hexadecimal representation
0	0	0	0
1	1	1	1
2	10	2	2
3	11	3	3
4	100	4	4
5	101	5	5
6	110	6	6
7	111	7	7
8	1000	10	8
9	1001	11	9
10	1010	12	A
11	1011	13	B
12	1100	14	C
13	1101	15	D
14	1110	16	E
15	1111	17	F
16	10000	20	10

Fig. E.46   Decimal, binary, octal, and hexadecimal equivalents.

A particularly important relationship that both the octal number system and the hexadecimal number system have to the binary system is that the bases of octal and hexadecimal (8 and 16 respectively) are powers of the base of the binary number system (base 2). Consider the following 12-digit binary number and its octal and hexadecimal equivalents. See if you can determine how this relationship makes it convenient to abbreviate binary numbers in octal or hexadecimal. The answer follows the numbers.

Binary Number	Octal equivalent	Hexadecimal equivalent
100011010001	**4321**	**8D1**

To see how the binary number converts easily to octal, simply break the 12-digit binary number into groups of three consecutive bits each, and write those groups over the corresponding digits of the octal number as follows

```
100     011     010     001
4       3       2       1
```

Notice that the octal digit you have written under each group of thee bits corresponds precisely to the octal equivalent of that 3-digit binary number as shown in Fig. E.7.

The same kind of relationship may be observed in converting numbers from binary to hexadecimal. In particular, break the 12-digit binary number into groups of four consecutive bits each and write those groups over the corresponding digits of the hexadecimal number as follows

```
1000     1101     0001
8        D        1
```

Notice that the hexadecimal digit you wrote under each group of four bits corresponds precisely to the hexadecimal equivalent of that 4-digit binary number as shown in Fig. E.7.

E.27 Converting Octal Numbers and Hexadecimal Numbers to Binary Numbers

In the previous section, we saw how to convert binary numbers to their octal and hexadecimal equivalents by forming groups of binary digits and simply rewriting these groups as their equivalent octal digit values or hexadecimal digit values. This process may be used in reverse to produce the binary equivalent of a given octal or hexadecimal number.

For example, the octal number 653 is converted to binary simply by writing the 6 as its 3-digit binary equivalent 110, the 5 as its 3-digit binary equivalent 101, and the 3 as its 3-digit binary equivalent 011 to form the 9-digit binary number 110101011.

The hexadecimal number FAD5 is converted to binary simply by writing the F as its 4-digit binary equivalent 1111, the A as its 4-digit binary equivalent 1010, the D as its 4-digit binary equivalent 1101, and the 5 as its 4-digit binary equivalent 0101 to form the 16-digit 1111101011010101.

E.28 Converting from Binary, Octal, or Hexadecimal to Decimal

Because we are accustomed to working in decimal, it is often convenient to convert a binary, octal, or hexadecimal number to decimal to get a sense of what the number is "really" worth. Our diagrams in Section E.1 express the positional values in decimal. To convert a number to decimal from another base, multiply the decimal equivalent of each digit by its positional value, and sum these products. For example, the binary number 110101 is converted to decimal 53 as shown in Fig. E.8.

To convert octal 7614 to decimal 3980, we use the same technique, this time using appropriate octal positional values as shown in Fig. E.9.

To convert hexadecimal AD3B to decimal 44347, we use the same technique, this time using appropriate hexadecimal positional values as shown in Fig. E.10.

E.29 Converting from Decimal to Binary, Octal, or Hexadecimal

The conversions of the previous section follow naturally from the positional notation conventions. Converting from decimal to binary, octal, or hexadecimal also follows these conventions.

Suppose we wish to convert decimal 57 to binary. We begin by writing the positional values of the columns right to left until we reach a column whose positional value is greater than the decimal number. We do not need that column, so we discard it. Thus, we first write:

Converting a binary number to decimal					
Positional values:	32	16	8	4	2	1
Symbol values:	1	1	0	1	0	1
Products:	1*32=32	1*16=16	0*8=0	1*4=4	0*2=0	1*1=1
Sum:	= 32 + 16 + 0 + 4 + 0 + 1 = 53					

Fig. E.47 Converting a binary number to decimal.

Converting an octal number to decimal			
Positional values:	512	64	8	1
Symbol values:	7	6	1	4
Products	7*512=3584	6*64=384	1*8=8	4*1=4
Sum:	= 3584 + 384 + 8 + 4 = 3980			

Fig. E.48 Converting an octal number to decimal.

Converting a hexadecimal number to decimal			
Positional values:	4096	256	16	1
Symbol values:	A	D	3	B
Products	A*4096=40960	D*256=3328	3*16=48	B*1=11
Sum:	= 40960 + 3328 + 48 + 11 = 44347			

Fig. E.49 Converting a hexadecimal number to decimal.

Positional values: **64   32   16   8   4   2   1**

Then we discard the column with positional value 64 leaving:

Positional values: **32   16   8   4   2   1**

Next we work from the leftmost column to the right. We divide 32 into 57 and observe that there is one 32 in 57 with a remainder of 25, so we write 1 in the 32 column. We divide 16 into 25 and observe that there is one 16 in 25 with a remainder of 9 and write 1 in the 16 column. We divide 8 into 9 and observe that there is one 8 in 9 with a remainder of 1. The next two columns each produce quotients of zero when their positional values are divided into 1 so we write 0s in the 4 and 2 columns. Finally, 1 into 1 is 1 so we write 1 in the 1 column. This yields:

Positional values:	**32**	**16**	**8**	**4**	**2**	**1**
Symbol values:	**1**	**1**	**1**	**0**	**0**	**1**

and thus decimal 57 is equivalent to binary 111001.

To convert decimal 103 to octal, we begin by writing the positional values of the columns until we reach a column whose positional value is greater than the decimal number. We do not need that column, so we discard it. Thus, we first write:

Positional values: **512 64   8   1**

Then we discard the column with positional value 512, yielding:

Positional values: **64   8   1**

Next we work from the leftmost column to the right. We divide 64 into 103 and observe that there is one 64 in 103 with a remainder of 39, so we write 1 in the 64 column. We divide 8 into 39 and observe that there are four 8s in 39 with a remainder of 7 and write 4 in the 8 column. Finally, we divide 1 into 7 and observe that there are seven 1s in 7 with no remainder so we write 7 in the 1 column. This yields:

Positional values:	**64**	**8**	**1**
Symbol values:	**1**	**4**	**7**

and thus decimal 103 is equivalent to octal 147.

To convert decimal 375 to hexadecimal, we begin by writing the positional values of the columns until we reach a column whose positional value is greater than the decimal number. We do not need that column, so we discard it. Thus, we first write

Positional values: **4096 256   16   1**

Then we discard the column with positional value 4096, yielding:

Positional values: **256 16   1**

Next we work from the leftmost column to the right. We divide 256 into 375 and observe that there is one 256 in 375 with a remainder of 119, so we write 1 in the 256 column. We divide 16 into 119 and observe that there are seven 16s in 119 with a remainder of 7 and write 7 in the 16 column. Finally, we divide 1 into 7 and observe that there are seven 1s in 7 with no remainder so we write 7 in the 1 column. This yields:

```
Positional values:        256  16   1
Symbol values:             1    7   7
```

and thus decimal 375 is equivalent to hexadecimal 177.

E.30 Negative Binary Numbers: Two's Complement Notation

The discussion in this appendix has been focussed on positive numbers. In this section, we explain how computers represent negative numbers using *two's complement notation*. First we explain how the two's complement of a binary number is formed, and then we show why it represents the negative value of the given binary number.

Consider a machine with 32-bit integers. Suppose

```
int value = 13;
```

The 32-bit representation of **value** is

```
00000000 00000000 00000000 00001101
```

To form the negative of **value** we first form its *one's complement* by applying Java's bit-wise complement operator (~):

```
onesComplementOfValue = ~value;
```

Internally, **~value** is now **value** with each of its bits reversed—ones become zeros and zeros become ones as follows:

```
value:
00000000 00000000 00000000 00001101
```

```
~value  (i.e., value's ones complement):
11111111 11111111 11111111 11110010
```

To form the two's complement of **value** we simply add one to **value**'s one's complement. Thus

```
Two's complement of value:
11111111 11111111 11111111 11110011
```

Now if this is in fact equal to -13, we should be able to add it to binary 13 and obtain a result of 0. Let us try this:

```
  00000000 00000000 00000000 00001101
 +11111111 11111111 11111111 11110011
 -----------------------------------
  00000000 00000000 00000000 00000000
```

The carry bit coming out of the leftmost column is discarded and we indeed get zero as a result. If we add the one's complement of a number to the number, the result would be all 1s. The key to getting a result of all zeros is that the twos complement is 1 more than the one's complement. The addition of 1 causes each column to add to 0 with a carry of 1. The carry keeps moving leftward until it is discarded from the leftmost bit, and hence the resulting number is all zeros.

Computers actually perform a subtraction such as

```
x = a - value;
```

by adding the two's complement of **value** to **a** as follows:

```
x = a + (~value + 1);
```

Suppose **a** is 27 and **value** is 13 as before. If the two's complement of **value** is actually the negative of **value**, then adding the two's complement of value to a should produce the result 14. Let us try this:

```
a  (i.e., 27)         00000000 00000000 00000000 00011011
+(~value + 1)        +11111111 11111111 11111111 11110011
                     ------------------------------------
                      00000000 00000000 00000000 00001110
```

which is indeed equal to 14.

Summary

- When we write an integer such as 19 or 227 or -63 in a Java program, the number is automatically assumed to be in the decimal (base 10) number system. The digits in the decimal number system are 0, 1, 2, 3, 4, 5, 6, 7, 8, and 9. The lowest digit is 0 and the highest digit is 9—one less than the base of 10.

- Internally, computers use the binary (base 2) number system. The binary number system has only two digits, namely 0 and 1. Its lowest digit is 0 and its highest digit is 1—one less than the base of 2.

- The octal number system (base 8) and the hexadecimal number system (base 16) are popular primarily because they make it convenient to abbreviate binary numbers.

- The digits of the octal number system range from 0 to 7.

- The hexadecimal number system poses a problem because it requires sixteen digits—a lowest digit of 0 and a highest digit with a value equivalent to decimal 15 (one less than the base of 16). By convention, we use the letters A through F to represent the hexadecimal digits corresponding to decimal values 10 through 15.

- Each number system uses positional notation—each position in which a digit is written has a different positional value.

- A particularly important relationship that both the octal number system and the hexadecimal number system have to the binary system is that the bases of octal and hexadecimal (8 and 16 respectively) are powers of the base of the binary number system (base 2).

- To convert an octal number to a binary number, simply replace each octal digit with its three-digit binary equivalent.

- To convert a hexadecimal number to a binary number, simply replace each hexadecimal digit with its four-digit binary equivalent.

- Because we are accustomed to working in decimal, it is convenient to convert a binary, octal or hexadecimal number to decimal to get a sense of the number's "real" worth.

- To convert a number to decimal from another base, multiply the decimal equivalent of each digit by its positional value, and sum these products.

- Computers represent negative numbers using two's complement notation.

- To form the negative of a value in binary, first form its one's complement by applying Java's bitwise complement operator (~). This reverses the bits of the value. To form the two's complement of a value, simply add one to the value's one's complement.

Terminology

base	digit
base 2 number system	hexadecimal number system
base 8 number system	negative value
base 10 number system	octal number system
base 16 number system	one's complement notation
binary number system	positional notation
bitwise complement operator (~)	positional value
conversions	symbol value
decimal number system	two's complement notation

Self-Review Exercises

E.1   The bases of the decimal, binary, octal, and hexadecimal number systems are _____, _____, _____, and _____ respectively.

E.2   In general, the decimal, octal, and hexadecimal representations of a given binary number contain (more/fewer) digits than the binary number contains.

E.3   (True/False) A popular reason for using the decimal number system is that it forms a convenient notation for abbreviating binary numbers simply by substituting one decimal digit per group of four binary bits.

E.4   The (octal / hexadecimal / decimal) representation of a large binary value is the most concise (of the given alternatives).

E.5   (True/False) The highest digit in any base is one more than the base.

E.6   (True/False) The lowest digit in any base is one less than the base.

E.7   The positional value of the rightmost digit of any number in either binary, octal, decimal, or hexadecimal is always _____.

E.8   The positional value of the digit to the left of the rightmost digit of any number in binary, octal, decimal, or hexadecimal is always equal to _____.

E.9   Fill in the missing values in this chart of positional values for the rightmost four positions in each of the indicated number systems:

decimal	**1000**	**100**	**10**	**1**
hexadecimal	...	**256**	...	...
binary	...	...	...	...
octal	**512**	...	**8**	...

E.10 Convert binary **110101011000** to octal and to hexadecimal.

E.11 Convert hexadecimal **FACE** to binary.

E.12 Convert octal **7316** to binary.

E.13 Convert hexadecimal **4FEC** to octal. (Hint: First convert 4FEC to binary then convert that binary number to octal.)

E.14 Convert binary **1101110** to decimal.

E.15 Convert octal **317** to decimal.

E.16 Convert hexadecimal **EFD4** to decimal.

E.17 Convert decimal **177** to binary, to octal, and to hexadecimal.

E.18 Show the binary representation of decimal **417**. Then show the one's complement of **417**, and the two's complement of **417**.

E.19   What is the result when the one's complement of a number is added to itself?

Self-Review Answers

E.1   **10, 2, 8, 16**.

E.2   Fewer.

E.3   False.

E.4   Hexadecimal.

E.5   False. The highest digit in any base is one less than the base.

E.6   False. The lowest digit in any base is zero.

E.7   **1** (the base raised to the zero power).

E.8   The base of the number system.

E.9   Fill in the missing values in this chart of positional values for the rightmost four positions in each of the indicated number systems:

decimal		**1000**	**100**	**10**	**1**
hexadecimal	**4096**	**256**	**16**		**1**
binary		**8**	**4**	**2**	**1**
octal		**512**	**64**	**8**	**1**

E.10   Octal **6530**; Hexadecimal **D58**.

E.11   Binary **1111 1010 1100 1110**.

E.12   Binary **111 011 001 110**.

E.13   Binary **0 100 111 111 101 100; Octal 47754**.

E.14   Decimal **2+4+8+32+64=110**.

E.15   Decimal **7+1*8+3*64=7+8+192=207**.

E.16   Decimal **4+13*16+15*256+14*4096=61396**.

E.17   Decimal **177**
to binary:

```
256 128 64 32 16 8 4 2 1
128 64 32 16 8 4 2 1
(1*128)+(0*64)+(1*32)+(1*16)+(0*8)+(0*4)+(0*2)+(1*1)
10110001
```

to octal:

```
512 64 8 1
64 8 1
(2*64)+(6*8)+(1*1)
261
```

to hexadecimal:

```
256 16 1
16 1
(11*16)+(1*1)
(B*16)+(1*1)
B1
```

E.18   Binary:

```
512 256 128 64 32 16 8 4 2 1
256 128 64 32 16 8 4 2 1
(1*256)+(1*128)+(0*64)+(1*32)+(0*16)+(0*8)+(0*4)+(0*2)+
(1*1)
110100001
```

One's complement: **001011110**
Two's complement: **001011111**
Check: Original binary number + its two's complement

```
110100001
001011111
---------
000000000
```

E.19   Zero.

Exercises

E.20   Some people argue that many of our calculations would be easier in the base **12** number system because **12** is divisible by so many more numbers than **10** (for base **10**). What is the lowest digit in base **12**? What might the highest symbol for the digit in base **12** be? What are the positional values of the rightmost four positions of any number in the base **12** number system?

E.21   How is the highest symbol value in the number systems we discussed related to the positional value of the first digit to the left of the rightmost digit of any number in these number systems?

E.22   Complete the following chart of positional values for the rightmost four positions in each of the indicated number systems:

	1000	100	10	1
decimal	**1000**	**100**	**10**	**1**
base 6	. . .	. . .	**6**	. . .
base 13	. . .	**169**	. . .	. . .
base 3	**27**	. . .	. . .	. . .

E.23   Convert binary **100101111010** to octal and to hexadecimal.

E.24   Convert hexadecimal **3A7D** to binary.

E.25   Convert hexadecimal **765F** to octal. (Hint: First convert **765F** to binary, then convert that binary number to octal.)

E.26   Convert binary **1011110** to decimal.

E.27   Convert octal **426** to decimal.

E.28   Convert hexadecimal **FFFF** to decimal.

E.29   Convert decimal **299** to binary, to octal, and to hexadecimal.

E.30   Show the binary representation of decimal **779**. Then show the one's complement of **779**, and the two's complement of **779**.

E.31   What is the result when the two's complement of a number is added to itself?

E.32   Show the two's complement of integer value **-1** on a machine with 32-bit integers.

Appendix F
Object-Oriented Elevator Simulator

Objectives

- To introduce the elements of object orientation in parallel with the early text discussion. This will enable students to begin working on their term projects from the beginning of their introductory computer science and computer engineering courses.
- To introduce students to the elements of the object-oriented design process.
- To enable students to pursue an object-oriented design of a reasonably substantial application.
- To implement a substantial term project using Java's more advanced features including graphics, graphical user interfaces, exception handling, multithreading, and multimedia including audios, images and animation.
- To suggest a number of challenging modifications to the project for the more advanced students.

F.1 Introduction

In this appendix, you will perform the various steps of an object-oriented design (OOD). You will implement an elevator simulator using the techniques of object-oriented programming (OOP). For now, this assignment may seem a bit complex. Please do not be concerned. You will attempt only a small portion of the problem at a time. The elevator simulator is a large project suitable for a term project. It is also suitable as a group project.

We begin with an introduction to object orientation. We will see that object orientation is a natural way of thinking about the world and of writing computer programs.

We start by introducing some of the key terminology of object orientation. Look around you in the real world. Everywhere you look you see them—*objects*! People, watches, tricycles, computers, satellites, roller coasters, pipes, cards, footballs, cats and the like. Humans think in terms of objects. We have the marvelous ability of *abstraction* that enables us to view screen images as objects such as flowers, trees, helicopters, and clouds rather than individual dots of color (i.e., pixels). We can, if we wish, think in terms of beaches instead of grains of sand, forests rather than trees, and houses rather than bricks.

We might be inclined to divide objects into two categories—animate objects and inanimate objects. Animate objects are "alive" in some sense. They move around and do things. Inanimate objects, like rocks, seem not to do much at all. They just kind of "sit around." All these objects, however, do have some things in common. They all have *attributes* like size, shape, color, mass, and the like. And they all exhibit various *behaviors*, e.g., a ball rolls, bounces, inflates, and deflates; a baby sleeps, cries, crawls, walks, drools, and blinks; a car accelerates, brakes and turns, etc.

Humans learn about objects by studying their attributes and observing their behaviors. Different objects can have many of the same attributes and exhibit similar behaviors. Comparisons can be made, for example, between babies and adults, and between humans and chimpanzees. Cars, trucks, little red wagons and roller skates have much in common.

Object oriented programming (OOP) models real-world objects with software counterparts. It takes advantage of *class* relationships where objects of a certain class—such as a class of vehicles—have the same characteristics. It takes advantage of *inheritance* relationships where newly created classes of objects are derived by inheriting characteristics of existing classes, yet contain unique characteristics of their own. Objects of class **Convertible** have the characteristics of class automobile, but the roof goes up and down.

Object-oriented programming gives us a more natural and intuitive way to view the programming process, namely by *modeling* real-world objects, their attributes, and their behaviors. OOP also models communication between objects. Just as people send messages to one another (e.g., a person standing on a corner and signaling a taxicab driver for a ride), objects also communicate via messages.

OOP *encapsulates* (or "wraps") data (attributes) and methods (behavior) into units called *objects*; the data and methods of an object are intimately tied together. Objects have the property of *information hiding*. This means that although objects may know how to communicate with one another across well-defined interfaces, objects normally are not allowed to know how other objects are implemented—implementation details are hidden within the objects themselves. Surely it is possible to drive a car effectively without knowing the intricate details of how engines, alternators, batteries, transmissions and exhaust systems work internally. We will see why information hiding is so crucial to good software engineering.

In C and other procedural programming languages, programming tends to be *action-oriented*, whereas in Java, programming is object-oriented. In C, the unit of programming is the *function*. In Java the unit of programming is the *class* from which objects are eventually *instantiated* (i.e., created).

C programmers concentrate on writing functions. Groups of actions that perform some common task are formed into functions, and functions are grouped to form programs. Data is certainly important in C, but the view is that data exists primarily in support of the actions that programs perform. The *verbs* in a system specification help the C programmer determine the set of functions that work together to implement the system.

Java programmers concentrate on creating their own *user-defined types* called classes. Each class contains data as well as the set of methods that manipulate the data. The data components of a class are called *instance variables*. Just as an instance of a built-in type such as **int** is called a *variable*, an instance of a user-defined type (i.e., a class) is called an *object*. The programmer uses built-in types as the building blocks for constructing user-defined types. The focus of attention in Java is on objects rather than methods. The *nouns* in a system specification help the Java programmer determine the set of classes from which objects will be created that will work together to implement a system.

F.2 Problem Statement

A company intends to build a two-story office building and equip it with the "latest" in elevator technology. The company wants you to develop a Java applet that simulates the operation of the elevator to determine if it will meet their needs.

The elevator, which has a capacity of one person, is designed to conserve energy, so it only moves when necessary. The elevator starts the day waiting with its doors closed on the building's first floor. The elevator, of course, alternates directions—first up, then down.

Your simulator has a simple graphical user interface—an applet with a single **New Person** push button. When the button is clicked, the simulator creates a "new" person and places that person on a floor (i.e., floor one or floor two). The arrival floor of the person is randomly determined. The person then presses the floor's call button. The person's destination floor is never equal to the floor on which that person is created.

If the first person of the day arrives on floor one, the person can immediately get on the elevator (after pressing the call button, and waiting for the floor doors and the elevator doors to open, of course!). If the first person arrives at floor two, the elevator should proceed to floor two and "pick up" the person. For simplicity, in this version of the simulation, the elevator moves between the floors in zero time. This will be made more realistic in future versions of your elevator applet.

The elevator's arrival at a floor is signaled by turning on a light on that floor above the doors and by ringing the floor bell. The floor button and the elevator button are reset, the elevator's doors open, the floor's doors open, and the passenger gets out of the elevator. If a passenger is waiting on that floor the passenger boards the elevator and presses a destination button. If the elevator needs to begin moving, it determines in which direction it should go (a simple decision on a two-story elevator!), and begins moving to the other floor. For simplicity, assume that all the events that happen once the elevator reaches a floor and until the floor's doors are closed, take zero time. The elevator always knows its current floor and its destination floor.

Due to the fact that all events in this version of the simulation take zero time, only one person can be in the simulation at a time. The simulator should process each person completely before the next person arrives in the simulation. In other words, when a person is created, that person should press the call button, be picked up by the elevator, be moved to the opposite floor and should exit the elevator before the next person walks onto a floor to wait for the elevator.

F.3 Elevator Laboratory Assignment 1

(Prerequisites: Chapters 2–4)

In this and the next few assignments, you will perform the separate steps of an object-oriented design. The first step is to identify the classes in the problem. You will eventually describe these classes in a formal way and implement them. For this assignment, you should do the following:

1. Identify the classes in the simulation problem. The problem statement specifies many class objects working together to simulate the elevator and its interactions with the passenger, the floors, the bell, etc. Locate the *nouns* from the problem statement; with high likelihood, these represent most of the classes necessary to implement the elevator simulation.

2. For each class identified, write one brief, precisely worded paragraph that captures the facts about that class from the problem statement.

Notes

1. This is a good team exercise. Ideally you should work in a group of two to four people. You and your teammates will reinforce one another's efforts, challenge and refine each other's design and implementation approaches.

2. Your group should compete with other groups in your class to develop the "best" design and implementation.

3. In Chapter 6, "Methods", we discuss how to use random number generation. You will learn how to use the **static Math** class method **random** to randomly select the floor onto which a person walks when the "New Person" button is pushed by the simulator user.

4. We have made a number of simplifying assumptions. You may choose to supply additional details.

5. Because the real world is so object oriented, it will be quite natural for you to pursue this project even though you probably have not formally studied object-orientation.

6. Do not worry about perfection. System design is not a perfect and complete process, so you should pursue this project on a best-efforts basis.

7. Java is fun. Java inspires creativity. Go beyond the basic description presented here, by adding your own enhancements to the elevator simulator. If you would like to share your simulators with us, please email them to us at **deitel@deitel.com**.

F.4 Elevator Laboratory Assignment 2

(Prerequisite: Chapter 6)

In the previous assignment, we began the first phase of an object-oriented design for our elevator simulator, namely identifying the classes needed to implement the simulator. As a starting point, you were encouraged to list the nouns in the problem statement. In doing so, you discovered that some of the classes in your simulator were the elevator itself, people, floors, the building, various buttons and so on.

Classes have attributes and behaviors. Attributes are represented in Java programs by data. Behaviors are represented by methods. In this assignment we concentrate on determining the attributes of the classes needed to implement the elevator simulator. In the next assignment we will concentrate on behaviors. In Assignment 4, we will concentrate on the interactions between the objects in the elevator simulator.

Let us discuss attributes of real-world objects before we begin the assignment. A person's attributes include height and weight. A TV's attributes include channel setting, volume setting, picture size (measured diagonally in inches), brand, etc. A car's attributes include current speedometer and odometer readings. A house's attributes include style ("colonial," "ranch," etc.), number of rooms, square footage, and lot size. A computer's attributes include manufacturer (Apple, Compaq, IBM, Sun, etc.), type of screen (monochrome or color), main memory size (in megabytes), hard disk size (in megabytes or gigabytes), etc.

1. To get the process started, type into a word processor or editor program the text of the problem statement for the elevator simulation presented in *Elevator Laboratory Assignment 1*.

2. Extract all the *facts* from the problem. Eliminate all irrelevant text and place each fact on a separate line of your text file (there are several dozen facts in the problem statement). Here is a portion of what your fact file might look like:

   two-story office building
   elevator
   person
   floor doors
   elevator doors
   directions-up and down
   floor is occupied
   person in elevator
   person on floor
   person's destination floor
   person gets on elevator
   elevator closes its doors

3. Group all your facts by class. This will help confirm that you properly identified the classes in *Assignment 1*. Use an outline form in which the classes are listed at the left margin of the page and the facts related to each class are listed below that class and indented one tab. Some facts mention only one class while other facts mention several classes. Each fact should initially be listed under every class the fact mentions. Note that some facts like "directions-up and down" do not explicitly mention a class but should nevertheless be grouped with a class (in this case

the direction is clearly the direction in which the elevator is moving). This outline file will be used in this assignment and in the next several assignments.

4. Now separate the facts for each class into two groups. Label the first group *Attributes* and the second group *Other Facts*. For now, actions (behaviors) should be grouped under *Other Facts*. As you place an action under *Other Facts* consider creating an additional entry under Attributes if appropriate. For example, the fact "elevator closes its doors" is an action that for now is grouped under *Other Facts*, but it indicates that an attribute of "doors" is that they are either open or shut. The fact "floor is occupied" is an attribute of the floor, more specifically, floor is either occupied (by one person—the stated capacity of each floor) or unoccupied at any time. Some attributes of the elevator are: whether it is "moving" or "stopped," whether it does or does not have a passenger, and if it is moving—whether it is moving "up" or "down." An attribute of the floor button is whether it is "on" or "off." An attribute of a person is the person's destination floor. And so on.

Notes

1. Begin by listing the class attributes that are explicitly mentioned in the problem statement. Then list attributes that are implied by the problem statement.

2. Add appropriate attributes as it becomes apparent that they are needed.

3. System design is not a perfect process; simply do the best you can for now. Be prepared to modify your design as you proceed with this exercise in subsequent sections.

4. An object of a class (actually, a reference to an object of a class) can be an attribute of another class. This is called *composition*. For example, there are references to button objects for floor one and floor two inside class elevator—the person presses one of these buttons to select a destination floor. For the purposes of this exercise, treat all the objects as peers—do not allow composition (we will do this later).

5. In Chapter 6, you learned about random number generation. When you eventually implement the elevator simulator, the statement

```
int arrivalFloor = ( int ) ( 1 + Math.random() * 2 );
```

can be used to randomly choose the floor (1 or 2) where a person is "created."

Notes

1. You may consider using packages in your solution.

F.5 Elevator Laboratory Assignment 3

(Prerequisite: Chapter 8)

In the previous two assignments, we performed the first two phases of an object-oriented design for our elevator simulator, namely identifying the classes needed to implement the simulator and identifying the attributes of those classes. In this assignment we concentrate on determining the behaviors of the classes needed to implement the elevator simulator. In the next section, we concentrate on the interactions between the classes.

Let us consider the behaviors of some real-world objects. A radio's behaviors include having its station set and having its volume set. A car's behaviors include accelerating (by pressing the gas pedal), decelerating (by pressing the brake pedal) and setting the direction (by turning the wheel).

Objects do not ordinarily perform their behaviors spontaneously. Rather, a specific behavior is normally invoked when a method call is sent to the object, requesting that the object perform that specific behavior.

1. Continue working with the facts file you created in *Assignment 2*. You had separated the facts relating to each class into two groups—*Attributes* and *Other Facts*.

2. For each object, add a third group called *Behaviors*. Place in this group every behavior of a class that can be invoked by telling an object of that class to do something, i.e., by sending a method call to the object. For example, a button can be pressed (by a person), so list **pressCallButton** as a behavior of the **Button** class. The class's attributes (such as whether a **Button** object is "on" or "off") are instance variables of the **Button** class. A class's methods typically manipulate the class's instance variables (such as **pressCallButton** changing one of class **Button**'s attributes to "on"). Methods often send method calls to objects of other classes (such as a **Button** object sending a **callElevator** method call to summon the **Elevator** object). Assume that the elevator has "thermal" buttons that become illuminated when someone presses them. When the elevator arrives at a floor, the elevator will want to send a **resetCallButton** method call to turn the button's light off. The elevator may want to determine if a particular button has been pressed, so we can provide another behavior called **isOn** that simply examines a button and returns **true** or **false** to indicate that the button is currently "on" or "off." You will probably want the elevator's doors to respond to method calls **openDoors** and **closeDoors**. And so on.

3. For each behavior you assign to an object, provide a brief description of what the behavior does. List any attribute changes the behavior causes, and list any method calls the behavior sends to other objects.

Notes

1. References to class **Button** do not refer to **java.awt.Button**.

F.6 Elevator Laboratory Assignment 4

(Prerequisite: Chapter 8)

This is the last of the initial design assignments before you begin writing the code for your elevator simulator. In this section we concentrate on the interactions between class objects. This section will help you "tie it all together." You will probably make some additions to the list of classes, their attributes and their behaviors that you developed in the previous assignments.

We have learned that objects do not ordinarily do things spontaneously. Rather, the objects respond to stimuli in the form of method calls.

Let us consider several of the interactions among the classes in the elevator simulation. The problem statement says, "Person presses the floor's "call button." The "subject" of that clause is person and the object is button. This is an example of an interaction between objects. The person object sends a method call i.e., **pressCallButton**, to the button object. In the last assignment, we made **pressCallButton** a method of the **Button** class.

At this point, under *Other Facts* for each of the classes in your simulation, about all you should have left are interactions between classes. Consider a statement like

"person waits for elevator doors to open"

In the last assignment, we listed two behaviors of the elevator's doors, namely **openDoors** and **closeDoors**. Now we want to determine which classes *send* these method calls. This is not *explicitly* stated in the preceding quoted phrase. So we think about this a bit and we realize that the elevator itself sends these messages to the doors. These interactions between classes are *implicit* in the problem statement and are more difficult to recognize than *explicit* interactions.

Continue refining the *Other Facts* sections for each class in your elevator simulator. These sections should now contain mostly interactions among classes. View each of these interactions as

1. a *sending class*

2. sending a particular method call

3. to a particular receiving class.

Under each class, add the section *Method Calls Sent to Other Classes* and list the remaining interactions between classes, i.e., under the **Person** class, include the entry

Person sends **pressCallButton** *method call to the* **Button**

For the **Button** class under *Method Calls Sent to Other Classes,* place the message

Button sends **callElevator** *message to* **Elevator**

From the perspective of the sending class, a method call sent to another class is a *collaboration*. From the perspective of the receiving class, a method call invokes a behavior.

As you make these entries, you may add attributes and behaviors to your classes. This is perfectly natural. As you complete this assignment, you will have a reasonably complete listing of the classes you will need to implement your elevator simulator. For each class, you will have a reasonably complete listing of that class's attributes and behaviors, and the method calls that class sends to other classes.

F.7 Elevator Laboratory Assignment 5

(Prerequisite: Chapter 8)
In the previous assignments, we introduced the fundamentals of object orientation and walked you through a basic, object-oriented design for your elevator simulator. At this point, you are ready (and probably eager!) to begin programming your simulator.

1. For each of the classes you identified in the previous assignments, write an appropriate class definition. Each class definition should be written in a separate file with the **.java** extension.

2. Write a driver applet that tests each of these classes and attempts to run the complete elevator simulation. *CAUTION:* You will probably need to complete the next assignment before you will be able to create a reasonable working version of your simulator, so be patient and implement only those portions of the elevator

simulator that you can with the knowledge you have gained so far. In the next assignment, we will discuss composition, i.e., creating classes that contain references to objects of other classes as instance variables; this technique might help you represent the button objects inside the elevator as members of the elevator, for example.

3. For the first version of your simulator, design only a simple, text-oriented output that displays a message for each significant event that occurs. Your messages might include strings such as: "Person 1 arrives on Floor 1," "Person 1 presses Call Button on Floor 1," "Elevator moved to Floor 1," etc. We suggest that you capitalize the words that represent objects in your simulation. Note also that you may choose to defer this portion of the lab assignment until you have read the next assignment.

F.8 Elevator Laboratory Assignment 6

(Prerequisite: Chapter 8)

In the last assignment you began programming your elevator simulator. In this assignment we discuss composition, a capability that allows you to create classes that have as members references to objects. Composition enables you to create a building class that contains references to the elevator and to the floors, and, in turn, create an elevator class that contains references to buttons.

1. Each time a person enters the simulator, you should use **new** to create a **Person** object to represent that person. Note that **new** will be used with a constructor call that will initialize the object properly.

2. List the composition relationships among the classes you have implemented for your elevator simulator. Modify the class definitions you created in the last assignment to reflect these composition relationships.

3. Complete the implementation of a working simulator program. We will suggest enhancements and refine the problem statement in the next assignment.

Notes

1. For simplicity, you may choose to treat the floor doors and the elevator doors as one unit.

F.9 Elevator Laboratory Assignment 7

(Prerequisites: Chapters 11–13)

At this point you should have version 1 of your elevator simulator working. Over the next several assignments, we will make the elevator simulator more realistic by having the elevator take time to move between the floors, by allowing more than one person in the simulation at once, by using graphical representations of the elevator and the other objects, by animating the motion of the elevator and the people, and the like. This assignment will focus on enhancing the elevator's graphical user interface. Figure F.1 shows the basic GUI design for this assignment (Note: The floor control boards and the elevator control board are to be implemented in Assignment 8).

1. Create another push button and add it to the applet. Name one button **Floor 1** and the other button **Floor 2**. These buttons will be used to create a new person who

wants to board the elevator specifically on that floor. This does not require any additional GUI changes other than adding the new button.

2. Create a new class called **FloorCanvas** that extends the **JPanel** class. The **FloorCanvas** class **paintComponent** method should draw a single line representing the floor. A **FloorCanvas** object should be created for each floor.

3. Create a new class called **ElevatorCanvas** that extends the **JPanel** class. The **ElevatorCanvas** class **paintComponent** method should draw a solid rectangle representing the elevator.

4. Create a new class called **ClockTimer** that extends the **JPanel** class. The **ClockTimer** class **paintComponent** method should draw a circle representing a clock. The clock should have a line inside it representing a "hand."

Notes

1. Try to place the components using the layout shown in Fig. F.1.

2. At this point, do not worry about "tying in" the GUI to what is occurring in the code. We will discuss how to do this in subsequent assignments.

3. When this assignment is completed, your elevator should work the same as before, except the GUI should display the components created above.

F.10 Elevator Laboratory Assignment 8

(Prerequisites: Chapters 11–13)

This assignment builds on the GUI you developed in Assignment 7. In this assignment, you will add to the GUI and begin graphically representing the events occurring in your simulation.

1. Create a new class called **ElevatorBoard** that extends the **JPanel** class. The **ElevatorBoard** class **paintComponent** method should draw a rectangle containing two circles. Each circle represents a button inside the elevator.

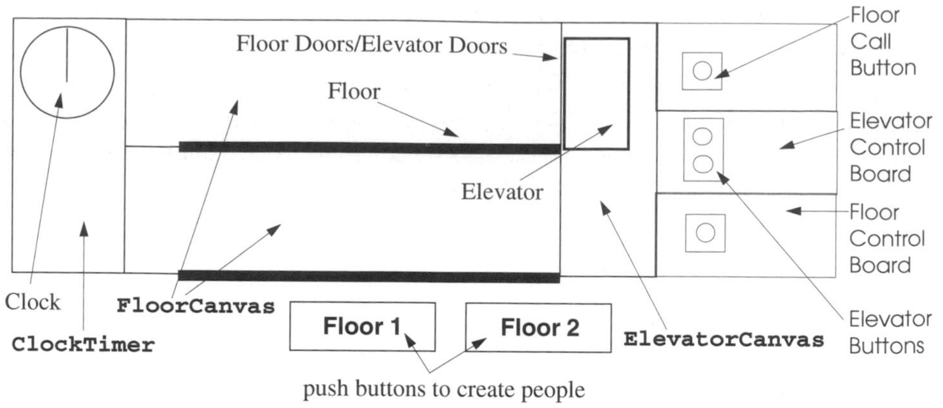

Fig. F.50   Graphical representation of the elevator simulator GUI.

2. Create a new class called **FloorControlBoard** that extends the **JPanel** class. The **FloorControlBoard** class **paintComponent** method should draw a rectangle containing a circle. The circle represents the floor call button. Two **FloorControlBoard** objects should be instantiated.

3. Write the code that shows the visual interactions between the text output and the buttons. In other words, when a button is pressed in the simulation the appropriate button should "light up." For example, if a person presses a call button on floor one, then the **FloorControlBoard JPanel** should paint the circle representing the button yellow.

Notes

1. You may wish to defer Part 3 until Assignment 10, which will provide for a smoother interaction.

2. Part 3 also corresponds to the elevator buttons.

F.11 Elevator Laboratory Assignment 9

(Prerequisite: Chapter 15)

This assignment covers the steps necessary to provide interaction between the GUI and events generated by your simulator. The interaction in many cases will be done with multithreading.

1. Modify your simulator to allow multiple people to be in the building at once. Remember there can be a maximum of one person in the elevator and one person on each floor at the same time; thus there can be 0, 1, 2, or 3 people active in your simulator at once. When the a push button is clicked, a new person should enter

the simulation (assuming that the target floor is not already occupied). Each person should be represented as a thread.

2. Modify the elevator to be a thread. The elevator should continuously monitor the call button actions of each floor.

3. Modify the clock to be a thread. The elevator should take one cycle of the clock (i.e., allow the hand to move one complete 360 degree rotation) to move between floors. The clock is only applicable to the elevator. Provide a text output to indicate when the clock has completed one cycle.

Notes

1. The elevator is now "smarter;" it "knows" when to move.

2. Parts 2 and 3 may need to be done simultaneously.

3. Your program should still print information to the console. This will help you confirm that your elevator is behaving properly.

4. The elevator does not have to move graphically between the floors in this assignment. We ask you to animate the movement of the elevator in the next assignment.

5. The clock hand does not have to move. We ask you to animate the movement of the clock hand in the next assignment.

F.12 Elevator Laboratory Assignment 10

(Prerequisite: Chapter 15)

This assignment covers the steps necessary to provide animation for your simulator.

1. Modify the simulator to animate the clock. When the elevator begins moving between floors, the clock hand should also begin moving. When the clock hand reaches its original position, the elevator should arrive at the next floor.

2. Modify the elevator to move graphically between floors. When the clock hand begins moving, the "box" representing the elevator should begin moving between floors. The elevator should stop on the next floor when the clock hand completes one rotation.

3. Modify your simulator to animate the opening and closing of the floor doors and the elevator doors.

Notes

1. The floor doors and elevator doors open or close on each floor in unison so only one line is necessary for this representation.

2. The doors are best done as part of the floor **JPanel**.

3. If you have not done so, the floor buttons and the elevator buttons should turn on and turn off when pressed and reset.

F.13 Elevator Laboratory Assignment 11

(Prerequisite: Chapter 16)

This assignment covers the steps necessary to provide additional animation as well some audio for your simulator. Figure F.2 shows the placement of animation objects in the GUI.

1. Modify the simulator to display a person walking onto the floor. Use a GIF file for the animation. The same GIF file should also be displayed to show the person leaving the floor.

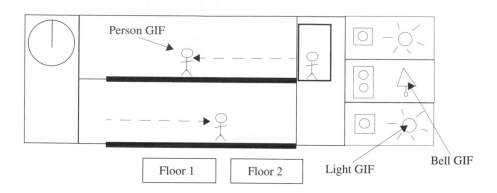

Fig. F.2   Graphical representation of the elevator simulator GUI.

2. Modify the simulator to show a passenger riding inside the elevator. The same GIF file used in Part 1 above should be used.

3. Add a GIF image to the **FloorControlBoard** to represent the floor light. The GIF image should appear "lighted" when the elevator reaches a floor and should then turn off.

4. Add a GIF image to the **ElevatorBoard** that represents a bell. The bell should always be displayed and should not do anything graphically. Add audio that announces the arrival of the elevator. You may consider using the **Toolkit** method **beep** for this purpose.

5. Add audio to play a "clicking" sound when a button is pressed.

6. Add audio to play a "stepping" sound when someone walks on a floor.

7. Add audio to play "soft" elevator music when the elevator moves between floors (hard rock is OK, too!).

Notes

1. If possible, you should use transparent GIF images. Most graphics programs allow you to save GIF images as transparent.

2. You will probably need two GIF images to represent a floor light. One image in which the floor light is on and one image in which the floor light is off.

3. You may want to give the user the option of "isolating" a particular sound such as the bell ringing. Too many sounds playing at once could be unpleasant. This is perhaps best done as a separate frame with the appropriate check boxes for the dif-

ferent sounds. Keep in mind that hardware limitations may only allow you to play a certain number of sounds.

4. Due to the nature of multithreading, the animation of the floor lights may be inconsistent.

5. You may suffer a decrease in the performance due to the number of threads running.

6. A person should graphically be allowed to exit a floor at the same time another person is arriving on that same floor. A floor should be considered to be unoccupied if the only person on the floor is exiting.

7. You should enforce the only one occupant per floor rule by disabling the create person (**Floor 1** or **Floor 2**) button when a floor is occupied.

8. This is the Assignment where you will take advantage of the fact that a person executes as a separate thread of execution.

F.14 Elevator Laboratory Assignment 12

(Prerequisite: Chapter 14)
This assignment enhances the animation of the previous assignment.

1. Use a variety of GIF images to represent people in the simulation.

Notes

1. Search for public domain images and audio files on the Internet; you may want to use several of these in your elevator simulator.

2. To make the simulator more realistic, the GIF file used to represent a person can be randomly selected.

F.15 Design Review Questions

1. How might you decide if the elevator is able to handle the anticipated traffic volume?

2. Why is it more complicated to implement a three-story (or higher) building?

3. Once we have created one elevator object, it is easy to create as many as we want. What problems do you foresee in having several elevators, each of which may pick up and discharge passengers at every floor in the building?

4. For simplicity, we have given our elevator and each of the floors a capacity of one person. What problems do you foresee in being able to increase these capacities?

F.16 Recommended Modifications

1. (Prerequisite: Chapter 22) Modify the simulator to allow a maximum of three people to "queue up" on each floor. Each floor should implement a **Queue** class object.

2. (Prerequisite: Chapter 16) Use a series of GIF images to show a person "walking" across the floor (i.e., with the person's legs moving and the person's arms swinging).

3. Change the number of floors in the simulation from 2 floors to 3 or more.

4. After completing the previous modification, add one or more elevators to the simulator.

5. After completing the previous two modifications, modify the floor ranges each elevator covers. One elevator should be an "express" elevator, which goes from floor one to the top floor without stopping on any floor in between.

6. Increase the capacity of each floor to six or more people. Also increase the capacity of the elevator to three or more people.

7. (Prerequisite: Chapter 23) Use a **Vector** to store the **People** object in your simulation.

8. (Prerequisite: Chapter 21) Modify the elevator simulator to incorporate client-server capabilities, such that when the user clicks on either create person button the simulator connects to the "person server" and requests information about the person (i.e., person number and the necessary GIF images).

9. (Prerequisite: Chapter 17) Modify the simulator to write, at regular intervals (such as every minute), "vital statistics" to a file. The statistics should include the total number of people in the building, the number of people waiting on each floor, the number of people in the elevator, etc.

10. Modify the simulator to graphically include a set of stairs. Each person created has a 10% chance of taking the stairs in preference to the elevator.

11. Modify the elevator to guarantee that each person in the simulation at any given time is unique. In other words, if a person is being drawn on either floor or in the elevator; that same person should not enter the simulation. You must of course have a sufficient number of images to support this. You may consider using features of the collections framework introduced in Chapter 24.

12. Simplify your threading by using the **Timer** class introduced in Chapter 16.

Appendix G
Creating HTML Documentation with `javadoc`

Objectives
- To introduce the **`javadoc`** J2SDK tool.
- To introduce documentation comments.
- To understand **`javadoc`** tags.
- To be able to generate HTML API documentation with **`javadoc`**.
- To understand **`javadoc`** generated documentation files.

Oh I get by with a little help from my friends.
John Lennon and Paul McCartney

I feel
The link of nature draw me.
John Milton

I think I shall never see
A poem lovely as a tree.
Joyce Kilmer

There is only one religion, though there are a hundred versions of it.
George Bernard Shaw

What I like in a good author is not what he says, but what he whispers.
Logan Pearsall Smith

I shall return.
Douglas MacArthur

Outline

G.1 Introduction

In this appendix, we provide an introduction to *javadoc* for creating HTML files that document Java code. This is the tool used by Sun to create the Java API documentation (Fig. G.1). We discuss the special Java comments and tags required by **javadoc** to create documentation based on your source code and how to execute the **javadoc** tool.

links to packages are displayed in this frame

the selected Web page is displayed in this frame

links to classes and interfaces are displayed in this frame. Interfaces are italicized

Fig. G.1   Java API documentation.

For detailed information on **javadoc**, visit the **javadoc** home page at

`http://java.sun.com/products/jdk/javadoc/index.html`

G.2 Documentation Comments

Before HTML files can be generated with the **javadoc** tool, programmers must insert special comments—called *documentation comments*—into their source files. Documentation comments are the only comments recognized by **javadoc**. Documentation comments begin with **/**** and end with ***/**. An example of a simple documentation comment is

`/** Sorts integer array using MySort algorithm */`

Like other comments, documentation comments are not translated into bytecodes. Because **javadoc** is used to create HTML files, documentation comments can contain HTML tags. For example, the documentation comment

`/** Sorts integer array using <B>MySort</B> algorithm */`

which contains the HTML bold tags **<B>** and **</B>** is valid. In the generated HTML files, **MySort** will appear in bold. As we will see, **javadoc** *tags* can be inserted into the documentation comments to help **javadoc** document your source code. These tags—which begin with an **@** symbol—are not HTML tags.

G.3 Documenting Java Source Code

In this section, we document a modified version of the **Time3** class from Fig. 8.5 using documentation comments. In the text that follows the example, we thoroughly discuss each of the **javadoc** tags used in the documentation comments. We discuss how to use the **javadoc** tool to generate HTML documentation from this file in Section G.4.

```
1   // Fig. G.2 Time3.java
2   // Time3 class definition
3   package com.deitel.jhtp3.appenG;    // place Time3 in a package
4   import java.text.DecimalFormat;     // used for number formatting
5
6   /**
7    * This class maintains the time in 24-hour format.
8    * @see java.lang.Object
9    * @author Deitel & Associates, Inc.
10   */
11  public class Time3 extends Object {
12
13      private int hour;      // 0 - 23
14      private int minute;    // 0 - 59
15      private int second;    // 0 - 59
16
```

Fig. G.2   A Java source code file containing documentation comments (part 1 of 4).

```
17        /**
18         *   Time3 default constructor initializes each
19         *   instance variable to zero. This ensures that Time3
20         *   object starts in a consistent state.
21         *   @throws Exception in the case of an invalid time
22         */
23        public Time3() throws Exception
24           { setTime( 0, 0, 0 ); }
25
26        /**
27         *   Time3 constructor
28         *   @param hour the hour
29         *   @throws Exception In the case of an invalid time
30         */
31        public Time3( int h ) throws Exception
32           { setTime( h, 0, 0 ); }
33
34        /**
35         *   Time3 constructor
36         *   @param hour the hour
37         *   @param minute the minute
38         *   @throws Exception In the case of an invalid time
39         */
40        public Time3( int h, int m ) throws Exception
41           { setTime( h, m, 0 ); }
42
43        /**
44         *   Time3 constructor
45         *   @param hour the hour
46         *   @param minute the minute
47         *   @param second the second
48         *   @throws Exception In the case of an invalid time
49         */
50        public Time3( int h, int m, int s ) throws Exception
51           { setTime( h, m, s ); }
52
53        /**
54         *   Time3 constructor
55         *   @param time A Time3 object with which to initialize
56         *   @throws Exception In the case of an invalid time
57         */
58        public Time3( Time3 time ) throws Exception
59        {
60           setTime( time.getHour(),
61                    time.getMinute(),
62                    time.getSecond() );
63        }
64
```

Fig. G.2   A Java source code file containing documentation comments
(part 2 of 4).

```
65      /**
66       *   Set a new time value using universal time. Perform
67       *   validity checks on the data. Set invalid values to zero.
68       *   @param h the hour
69       *   @param m the minute
70       *   @param s the second
71       *   @see com.deitel.jhtp3.appenG.Time3#setHour
72       *   @see Time3#setMinute
73       *   @see #setSecond
74       *   @throws Exception In the case of an invalid time
75       */
76      public void setTime( int h, int m, int s ) throws Exception
77      {
78         setHour( h );     // set the hour
79         setMinute( m );   // set the minute
80         setSecond( s );   // set the second
81      }
82
83      /**
84       *   Sets the hour.
85       *   @param h the hour
86       *   @throws Exception In the case of an invalid time
87       */
88      public void setHour( int h ) throws Exception
89      {
90         if ( h >= 0 && h < 24 )
91            hour = h;
92         else
93            throw( new Exception() );
94      }
95
96      /**
97       *   Sets the minute.
98       *   @param m the minute
99       *   @throws Exception In the case of an invalid time
100      */
101     public void setMinute( int m ) throws Exception
102     {
103        if ( m >= 0 && m < 60 )
104           minute = m;
105        else
106           throw( new Exception() );
107     }
108
109     /**
110      *   Sets the second.
111      *   @param s the second.
112      *   @throws Exception In the case of an invalid time
113      */
114     public void setSecond( int s ) throws Exception
115     {
116        if ( s >= 0 && s < 60 )
```

Fig. G.2   A Java source code file containing documentation comments (part 3 of 4).

```
117              second = s;
118          else
119              throw( new Exception() );
120      }
121
122      /**
123       *  Gets the hour.
124       *  @return an <code>integer</code> specifying the hour.
125       */
126      public int getHour() { return hour; }
127
128      /**
129       *  Gets the minute.
130       *  @return an <code>integer</code> specifying the minute.
131       */
132      public int getMinute() { return minute; }
133
134      /**
135       *  Gets the second.
136       *  @return an <code>integer</code> specifying the second.
137       */
138      public int getSecond() { return second; }
139
140      /** Convert to String in universal-time format
141       *  @return a <code>String</code> representation
142       *  of the time universal-time format
143       */
144      public String toUniversalString()
145      {
146          DecimalFormat twoDigits = new DecimalFormat( "00" );
147
148          return twoDigits.format( getHour() ) + ":" +
149                 twoDigits.format( getMinute() ) + ":" +
150                 twoDigits.format( getSecond() );
151      }
152
153      /** Convert to String in standard-time format
154       *  @return a <code>String</code> representation
155       *  of the time in standard-time format
156       */
157      public String toString()
158      {
159          DecimalFormat twoDigits = new DecimalFormat( "00" );
160
161          return ( ( getHour() == 12 || getHour() == 0 ) ?
162              12 : getHour() % 12 ) + ":" +
163              twoDigits.format( getMinute() ) + ":" +
164              twoDigits.format( getSecond() ) +
165              ( getHour() < 12 ? " AM" : " PM" );
166      }
167  }
```

Fig. G.2   A Java source code file containing documentation comments
(part 4 of 4).

Documentation comments are placed on the line before a class definition, an interface definition, a constructor, a method and a field (i.e., an instance variable or a reference). The first documentation comment (line 6 through 10)

```
/**
 * This class maintains the time in 24-hour format.
 * @see java.lang.Object
 * @author Deitel & Associates, Inc.
 */
```

introduces class **Time3**. The line

```
 * This class maintains the time in 24-hour format.
```

is a description of class **Time3** provided by the programmer. The description can contain as many lines as necessary to provide a description of the class to any programmer who may use it. Tags **@see** and **@author** are used to specify a *See Also:* note and an *Author:* note, respectively in the HTML documentation (Fig. G.3). The **See Also:** note specifies other related classes that may be of interest to a programmer using this class. The **@author** tag specifies the author of the class. More than one **@author** tag can be used to document multiple authors. Note that the asterisks (*****) on each line between **/**** and ***/** are not required. This is a convention used by programmers to align descriptions and **javadoc** tags. When parsing a documentation comment, **javadoc** discards all whitespace characters up to the first non-whitespace character in each line. If the first non-whitespace character encountered is an asterisk, it is also discarded.]

Notice that this documentation comment immediately precedes the class definition—any code placed between the documentation comment and the class definition causes **javadoc** to ignore the documentation comment. This is also true of other code structures (e.g., constructors, methods, instance variables, etc.).

Common Programming Error G.1

*Placing an **import** statement between the class comment and the class declaration is a logic error. This causes the class comment to be ignored by **javadoc**.*

Software Engineering Observation G.1

*Defining several fields in one comma-separated statement with a single comment above that statement, will result in **javadoc** using that comment for all of the fields.*

The documentation comment on lines 26 through 30

```
/**
 *   Time3 constructor
 *   @param hour the hour
 *   @throws Exception In the case of an invalid time
 */
```

describes the **Time3** constructor. Tag **@param** describes a parameter to the method. Parameters appear in the HTML document in a **Parameters:** note (Fig. G.4) that is followed by a list of all parameters specified with the **@param** tag. For this constructor, the parameter's name is **hour** and its description is "**the hour**." Tag **@param** can be used only with methods and constructors.

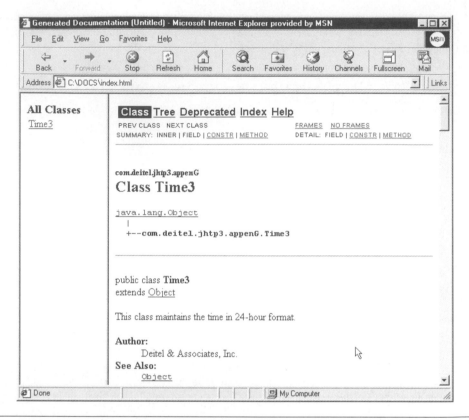

Fig. G.3   HTML documentation for class **Time3**.

The tag **@throws** specifies the exceptions thrown by this method. Like **@param** tags, **@throws** tags are only used with methods and constructors. One **@throws** should be supplied for each type of exception thrown by the method.

Software Engineering Observation G.2

*To produce proper **javadoc** documentation, you must declare every instance variable on a separate line.*

Documentation comments can contain multiple **@param** and **@see** tags. The documentation comment at lines 65 through 75

```
/**
 *  Set a new time value using universal time. Perform
 *  validity checks on the data. Set invalid values to zero.
 *  @param h the hour
 *  @param m the minute
 *  @param s the second
 *  @see com.deitel.jhtp3.appenG.Time3#setHour
 *  @see Time3#setMinute
 *  @see #setSecond
 *  @throws Exception In the case of an invalid time
 */
```

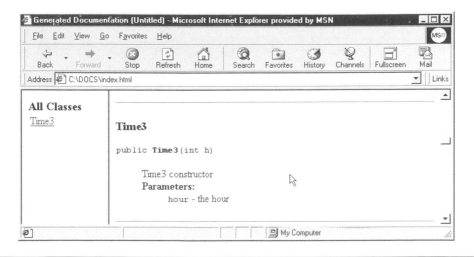

Fig. G.4   The **Parameters:** note generated by **javadoc**.

describes method **setTime**. The HTML generated for this method is shown in Fig. G.5. Three **@param** tags describe the method's parameters. This results in one **Parameters:** note which lists the three parameters. Methods **setHour**, **setMinute** and **setSecond** are tagged with **@see** to create hyperlinks to their descriptions in the HTML document. A **#** character is used instead of a dot when tagging a method or a field. This creates a link to the name that follows the **#** character. We demonstrate three different ways (i.e., the fully qualified name, class name qualification and no qualification) to tag methods using **@see** on lines 71 through 73. If the fully qualified name is not given (lines 72 and 73), **javadoc** looks for the specified method or field in the following order: current class, superclasses, package and imported files.]

The only other tag used in this file is **@return** which specifies a **Returns:** note in the HTML documentation (Fig. G.6). The comment at lines 122 through 125

```
/**
 *   Gets the hour.
 *   @return an <code>integer</code> specifying the hour.
 */
```

documents method **getHour**. Tag **@return** describes a method's return type to help the programmer understand how to use the return value of the method. By **javadoc** convention, programmers typeset source code (i.e., keywords, identifiers, expressions, etc.) with the HTML tags **<code>** and **</code>**.

Good Programming Practice G.1

*Changing source code fonts in **javadoc** tags helps code names stand out from the rest of the description.*

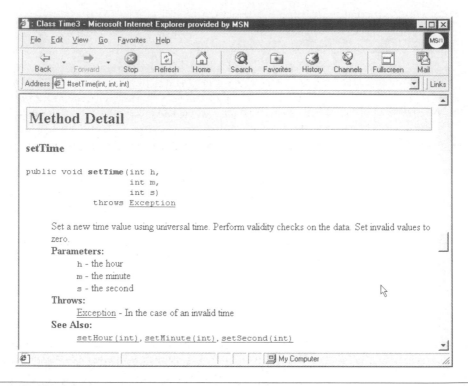

Fig. G.5   HTML documentation for method **setTime**.

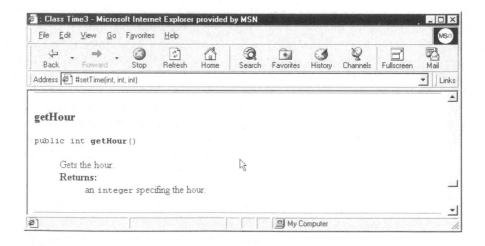

Fig. G.6   HTML documentation for **getHour**.

In addition to the tags presented in this example, **javadoc** recognizes six other tags which are briefly summarized in Fig. G.7.

javadoc tag	Description
@deprecated	Adds a **Deprecated** note. These are notes to programmers indicating that they should not use the specified features of the class. **Deprecated** notes normally appear when a class has been enhanced with new and improved features, but older features are maintained for backwards compatibility.
{@link}	This allows the programmer to insert an explicit hyperlink to another HTML document.
@since	Adds a **Since** note. These notes are used for new versions of a class to indicate when a feature was first introduced. For example, the Java API documentation uses this to indicate features that were introduced in Java 1.0, Java 1.1 and Java 2.
@version	Adds a **Version** note. These notes help maintain version number of the software containing the class or method.

Fig. G.7   Some other common **javadoc** tags.

G.4 javadoc

In this section, we discuss how to execute the **javadoc** tool on a Java source file to create HTML documentation for the class in the file. Like other tools, **javadoc** is executed from the command line. The general form of the **javadoc** command is

> **javadoc** *options packages sources @files*

where *options* is a list of command line options, *packages* is a list of packages the user would like to document, *sources* is a list of java source files to document and *@files* is a text file containing the names of *packages* and/or *source files* to send to the **javadoc** utility. [*Note:* All items are separated by spaces and *@files* is one word.] Figure G.8 shows a DOS window containing the **javadoc** command we typed to generate the HTML documentation.

In Fig. G.8, the **-d** argument specifies the directory (e.g., **c:\docs**) where the HTML files will be stored on disk. We use the **-link** option so that our documentation links to Sun's documentation (installed on our **E:** drive). This creates a hyperlink between our documentation and Sun's documentation (see Fig. G.5 where Java class **Exception** from package **java.lang** is hyperlinked). Without the **-link** argument, **Exception** appears as text in the HTML document—not a hyperlink. The **-author** argument instructs **javadoc** to process the **@author** tag (it ignores this tag by default).

G.5 Files Produced by javadoc

In the last section, we executed the **javadoc** tool on the **Time3.java** file. When **javadoc** executes, it displays the name of each HTML file it creates (see Fig. G.8). From the source file, **javadoc** created an HTML document for the class named **Time3.html**. If the source file contained multiple classes or interfaces, a separate HTML document is created for each class. Because class **Time3** belongs to a package, the page is created in the directory **C:\docs\com\deitel\jhtp3\appenG** (on Win32 platforms). The **c:\docs** directory was specified with the **-d** command line option of **javadoc**, and the remaining directories were created based on the **package** statement.

Another file that **javadoc** creates is *index.html* the starting HTML page in the documentation. To view the documentation you generate with **javadoc**, load **index.html** into your web browser. In Fig. G.9, the right frame contains the page **index.html** and the left frame contains the page *allclasses-frame.html* which contains links to the source code's classes. [*Note:* Because our example does not contain multiple packages, there is no frame listing the packages. Normally this frame would appear above the left frame (containing "All Classes") as in Fig. G.1.]

The *navigation bar* (at the top of the right frame in Fig. G.9) indicates which HTML page is currently loaded by highlighting the page's link (e.g., the **Class** link in Fig. G.9).

Clicking the **Tree** link (Fig. G.10) displays a class hierarchy for all the classes displayed in the left frame. In our example, we documented only class **Time3**—which extends **Object**. Clicking the **Deprecated** link loads **deprecated-list.html** into the right frame. This page contains a list of all deprecated names. Because we did not use the **@deprecated** tag in this example, this page does not contain any information. Clicking the **Index** link loads the *index-all.html* page which contains an alphabetical list of all classes, interfaces, methods and fields.

Figure G.11 shows class **Time3**'s **index-all.html** page loaded into a Web browser.Clicking the **Help** link loads *helpdoc.html* (Fig. G.12). This is a help file for navigating the documentation. A default help file is provided, however the programmer can specify other help files.

Among the other files generated by **javadoc** are *serialized-form.html* which documents **Serializable** and **Externalizable** classes and *package-list.txt* which is used by the **-link** command-line argument and is not actually part of the documentation.

```
f:\>javadoc Time3.java -d c:\docs -link e:\jdk1.2.1\docs\api -author
Loading source file Time3.java...
Constructing Javadoc information...
Building tree for all the packages and classes...
Building index for all the packages and classes...
Generating c:\docs\overview-tree.html...
Generating c:\docs\index-all.html...
Generating c:\docs\deprecated-list.html...
Building index for all classes...
Generating c:\docs\allclasses-frame.html...
Generating c:\docs\index.html...
Generating c:\docs\packages.html...
Generating c:\docs\com\deitel\jhtp3\appenG/Time3.html...
Generating c:\docs\serialized-form.html...
Generating c:\docs\package-list...
Generating c:\docs\help-doc.html...
Generating c:\docs\stylesheet.css...

f:\>_
```

Fig. G.8   Using the **javadoc** tool.

frames   highlighted link   navigation bar

Fig. G.9   Class **Time3**'s **index.html**.

Terminology

allclasses-frame.html	**@version** tag
@author **javadoc** tag	**-d** argument
-author argument	**Exception** note
Class item in the navigator bar	**Help**
@deprecated tag	**helpdoc.html**
deprecated-list.html	index-all.html
documentation comment	**index.html**
@exception tag	**javadoc**
@link tag	**-link** argument
@param tag	**name-frame.html**
@see tag	**Overrides:** note
@serial tag	**Parameters:** note
@serialData tag	**Returns:** note
@since tag	**See Also:** note
@return tag	**serialized-form.html**
@throws tag	**Tree** link

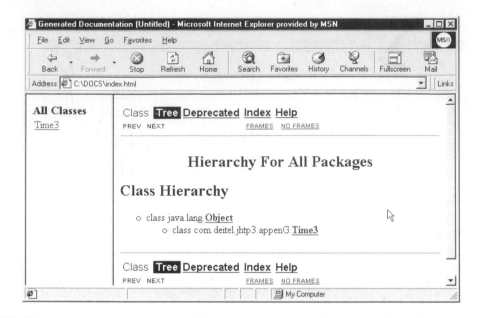

Fig. G.10 Tree page.

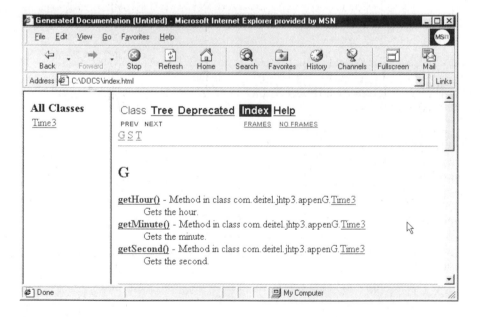

Fig. G.11 Index page.

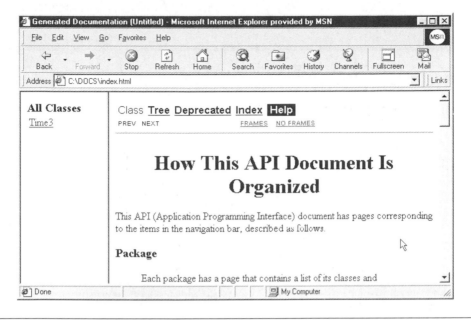

Fig. G.12 Index page.

Common Programming Error

G.1   Placing an **import** statement between the class comment and the class declaration is a logic error. This causes the class comment to be ignored by **javadoc**.

Good Programming Practice

G.1   Changing source code fonts in **javadoc** tags helps code names stand out from the rest of the description.

Software Engineering Observation

G.1   Defining several fields in one comma-separated statement with a single comment above that statement, will result in **javadoc** using that comment for all of the fields.

G.2   To produce proper **javadoc** documentation, you must declare every instance variable on a separate line.

Appendix H
Enterprise JavaBeans (EJB) Web Resources

H.1 Introduction

[*Note:* This appendix was written by Abbey Deitel, Chief Operating Officer of Deitel & Associates, Inc., and Paul Brandano, a Junior at Boston College and a participant in the Deitel & Associates, Inc. College Internship Program.]

Just as this book was due to enter publication we attended the JavaOne tradeshow in San Francisco. The excitement over Enterprise JavaBeans (EJB) was evident. But we did not have time to do the kind of chapter-length, live-code treatment our readers expect of us. So, we searched the Web for EJB resources including tutorials, specifications, demos, magazines, products, FAQs and the like. These are listed here to help you get a head start on this important new Java-based technology from Sun Microsystems.

If you would like to recommend other sites, please send us email at

deitel@deitel.com

and we will put links to the sites you suggest on our Web site

http://www.deitel.com.

H.2 Tutorials

http://java.sun.com/products/ejb/
>
> This Web site is THE place to begin your Enterprise JavaBeans education. Sun Microsystems has developed this comprehensive Web site as a way of showcasing this new and exciting technology. The site offers news articles, customer success stories, enterprise momentum information, feedback, information on the Java 2 platform, an EJB directory, case studies, FAQ and EJB specifications.

http://ejbhome.iona.com/
>
> A group of Enterprise JavaBeans developers have organized this Web site and dedicated a large portion of it to Enterprise JavaBeans. The offer a free in-depth tutorial on EJB's called the Order Tutorial.

`http://www.execpc.com/~gopalan/`

The web cornucopia has a detailed presentation on Enterprise JavaBeans The presentation is a total of 48 slides on the web. The author also offers a multitude of development links.

`http://developer.netscape.com/viewsource/`
`index_frame.html?content=fields_beans.html`

Netscape has written their summary of this new exciting technology. The article explains what Enterprise JavaBeans are and how they can be used. The article includes examples of the Netscape uses of EJBs and as well as a comparison of Enterprise JavaBeans versus JavaBeans

`http://www.redbooks.ibm.com/SG245192/redpage.htm`

This document discusses IBM's use of Enterprise JavaBeans with the AS/400 system. This is a comprehensive look at EJB technology. The chapters that are present on the Web site include: *An Introduction to Enterprise JavaBeans, Developing Enterprise JavaBeans, Introduction to BEA Weblogic Application Server, an overview of the Order Entry Application, EJB Application Development Scenario, Building Java Applications with Enterprise JavaBeans, Enterprise JavaBeans Deployment and a chapter on AS/400 Unique Considerations.* The chapters are available in PDF format.

H.3 Demos

`http://www.oracle.com/java/`

Oracle Corporation has recently included Enterprise JavaBeans in its Oracle8I software. This will allow users to write programs and deploy them across other oracle platforms.

`http://java.sun.com/products/ejb/ottawa.html`

The University of Ottawa Heart Institute wanted to improve the management of patients care by improving their computer systems. If they could build a secure Internet based customer management system they could greatly reduce costs and improve customer service. It would mean coordinating information across multiple platforms. See how they used Enterprise JavaBeans to achieve their goals

`http://java.sun.com/products/ejb/genscope.html`

Enterprise JavaBeans have recently been used to solve difficult management problems efficiently. PE Genscope recently used Enterprise JavaBeans to develop a system that could analyze gene expression patterns. This Sun Microsystems Web site describes the PE Genscope success story.

`http://www.weblogic.com/docs/classdocs/API_ejbdesign.html`

BEA Weblogic has compiled a tutorial on how to design a BEA Weblogic EJB application. Although this is a specific example from one vendor, it will give you a good idea of the technology and how it is used. The tutorial/demo is broken up into discussions on Entity Beans and Session Beans.

H.4 Resources

`http://careers.computerworld.com/home/features.nsf/all/`
`981026ejblinks`

ComputerWorld Magazine offers a few articles on EJB. ComputerWorld keeps all EJB information up to date. This particular site offers links to a number of EJB related sites and articles.

`http://www.developer.com`

At the time of publication Developer.com was in the process of building a dedicated link to Enterprise JavaBeans technology. Developer.com is an excellent source of information for computer developers.

http://www.dnai.com/~cityjava/sfjughom.htm
> The world's largest independent Java forum is open for EJB discussion at this web city. CityJava is the San Francisco based Java Users Group (JUG). You can view transcripts that include questions and concerns of industry professionals who want the scoop on Enterprise Java Beans and other Java topics.

http://home.earthlink.net/~richkatz/
> This site is jam-packed with upper level Java topics including EJB.

http://www.gamelan.com/
> Like Developer.com, this Web site is included in the Earthweb family of sites. This site differs from developer.com in that its focus is on the Java language. As Enterprise JavaBeans gains further notice in the global Java community this site should become an active forum for EJB information. The site includes articles, an "ask-the-experts" forum, as well as demos and code examples.

http://www.javabeans-zone.com/
> JavaBeans zone, part of DevX.com, is dedicated to JavaBeans and Enterprise JavaBeans. It includes articles, discussion groups, and important Java links. The DevX.com main Web site is another source of valuable development information.

http://www.openmaster.com/ejb/doc/roles.html
> Openmaster offers EJB development tools. This particular page offers a description of the product, its uses, and the process in which it works. The chapters outlined on the site describe the function of each part of the EJB development process.

http://www.technetcast.com/tnc_981023.html
> At the time of publication this Web site was still in the early stages of its development. It was however focused on Enterprise JavaBeans and may be a site to look for reference materials.

H.5 Developers

http://www.javalobby.org/
> The Java Lobby site is a world class resource for developer information. You can find the latest news, products and services, as well as carry on communications with other developers by posting stories, questions, concerns etc. With over 38,000 members, Javalobby offers developers a great forum for Enterprise JavaBeans questions and discussions.

http://www.java-pro.com/
> This site is an excellent resource of information for Java Developers. This site is divided into separate, searchable zones for each topic. Java-Pro also has product reviews, magazine links, conference information, an "ask-the-Pros" section, a large source code database, discussion groups, reference resources and more! This site is definitely worth a look

H.6 Specifications

http://java.sun.com/products/ejb/docs.html
> Sun Microsystems Enterprise JavaBeans specifications are available in PDF and PostScript formats on this site. PDF files can be viewed with the Adobe Acrobat Reader software, which is available free for download from the adobe Web site: **http://www.adobe.com**

H.7 Frequently Asked Questions

`http://java.sun.com/products/ejb/faq.html`

Find answers to your Enterprise JavaBeans questions on the EJB home page.

H.8 Magazines

`http://java.tqn.com/library/weekly/aa061498.htm`

Java.tqn.com offers information on various Java related topics. It offers a collection of articles about EJB.

`http://www.infoworld.com/`

InfoWorld is a key Web site for finding the hottest news in Information Technology. A complete listing of breaking news, interviews, columns, forums, research tools, career search features and a testing area make this site a key stop for anyone interested in Enterprise JavaBeans. A total of eight email newsletters are available. These newsletters cover a wide variety of topics and are free on the InfoWorld Web site.

`http://www.intelligence.com/java/default.asp`

Intelligenc.com is Java news at its best. This site is a collection of articles covering the newest and hottest Java topics, product reviews, corporate profiles, personal profiles and interviews of Java celebrities, conference information, links to other development topics and much more.

`http://www.javadevelopersjournal.com/java/index2.html`

This online magazine offers its readers the most up-to-date information on Enterprise JavaBeans, and other Java topics. Java Developers Journal describes itself as the "World's Leading Java Resource". It offers its users access to recent articles, source code, a Java forum, job search, a developer store and a discount on the printed version of Java Developers Journal.

`http://www.javareport.com/`

This online version of Java Report is another excellent resource for Java information. This Web site highlights the latest in Java products, services, events, source code and Java-related jobs. Java Report is available in both print and digital form.

`http://www.javaworld.com/`

JavaWorld is a great resource for the latest Java news and information. They offer a collection of EJB articles.

`http://www.slip.net/~scaruffi/computer/sun3.html`

This is an impressive collection of articles about Enterprise JavaBeans complied by a professor from Italy.

`http://www.ncworldmag.com/`

Network Centric World Magazine Online (NCWorld) is another source of in-depth articles on EJB.

`http://www.techweb.com`

Techweb is an online magazine that offers the latest in high tech news. It periodically offers information regarding Enterprise Java Beans.

`http://www.zdnet.com/`

Zdnet is a great place to search for current information on Enterprise JavaBeans. Their powerful search engine is a great way to find general information on EJB and other high tech issues.

Appendix I
JINI Web Resources

I.6 Introduction

[*Note:* This appendix was written by Abbey Deitel of Deitel & Associates, Inc., and Paul Brandano, a Junior at Boston College and a participant in the Deitel & Associates, Inc. College Internship Program.]

Jini technology—based on Java—enables various kinds of digital devices to be easily and quickly connected into networks. The connected devices share services on the network. Sun's goal was to make using networks of devices as easy as using your phone. Jini will be used with consumer electronic devices like palmtop computers, TVs, digital cameras and cell phones. Just as this book was due to enter publication we attended the JavaOne tradeshow in San Francisco. The excitement over Jini was evident. But we did not have time to do the kind of chapter-length, live-code treatment our readers expect of us. So, we have searched the Web for Jini resources including tutorials, specifications, demos, magazines, products, FAQs and the like. These are listed here to help you get a head start on this important new Java-based technology from Sun Microsystems.

If you would like to recommend other sites, please send us email at

`deitel@deitel.com`

and we will put links to the sites you suggest on our Web site

`http://www.deitel.com`

I.7 Tutorials

`http://www.sun.com/JINI/`

Sun's award winning Jini technology is showcased here. Product information, press releases, source code, awards, and product specs can all be found at this Web site. If you are interested in learning about Jini technology this is a great place to start.

http://www.jini.org/homepage.html

Go to *Jini.org* to become a member of the Jini Technology Developers Community. You can join in on a Jini discussion, exchange source code, read up on current issues in Jini technology and become a pioneer in this new language.

http://www.jinivision.com/

This is an excellent Jini site where you can catch up on the latest industry news, download software, choose from five different Listserv newsletter options, submit an article on Jini or check the selection of links.

I.8 Resources

http://www.w3com.com/paulcho/javalinux/jini.shtml

This site offers high quality links too Web sites offering important information about JINI Technology. These links include a JINI FAQ, the JINI Home page, and links to specific articles featuring JINI. The page is frequently updated and offers headline news on JINI issues.

http://www.sun.com/JINI/community/

The Sun JINI Community is a meeting place for JINI developers and companies interested in utilizing this exciting technology.

http://developer.java.sun.com/developer/products/jini/product.offerings.html

In order to begin developing in JINI you need to get the development software first. Download Sun Microsystems' JINI development software at this Web site.

http://www.sun.com/jini/news/index.html

Sun Microsystems offers a collection of recent articles about their award winning technology.

http://wwwswest2.sun.com/jini/news/artcliprev.html

At this sun resource you will find articles audio clips, and reviews of Jini connection technology.

http://www.sun.com/jini/subscribe.html

Sign on here to become a member of Sun Microsystems Jini mailing list.

http://www.gamelan.com/

Gamelan is good source of current articles and information on Jini.

http://www.artima.com/jini/index.html

Artima is a great online resource for Java and Jini developers. The "Jini Corner" of the site offers a FAQ, discussion forum, recommended readings, links, and a chat room.

http://www.devdaily.com/Dir/Java/Articles_and_Tutorials/Jini/

This site offers quality links including tutorials, demos, specifications and general information Web sites.

http://javaboutique.internet.com/jini/

Java Boutique offers users the chance to learn the newest information on JINI by offering a Jini Watch section of their Web site. The Jini Watch features recent Jini news, a chat room and links to top Jini sites.

http://www.webtools.com/weekend/jini.html

Webtools has recently built a Jini dedicated Web site. Get up-to-date news and a brief explanation of Jini technology.

http://dir.yahoo.com/Computers_and_Internet/Communications_and_Networking/Protocols/Jini/

Yahoo links you to a number of Jini Web sites.

I.9 Demos

`http://www.sun.com/JINI/demos/;$sessionid$XZAWOVIAAMHSXAMUVFZE3NQ`
> This site features a few amazing Jini demos from Sun Microsystems. Demos include audio/video presentations.

`http://www.enete.com/download/#_nuggets_`
> Noel's nuggets are pieces of code that will help you get started. These pieces have been compiled from all over the Web and offer examples of Jini development techniques.

`http://www.artima.com/javaseminars/modules/Jini/index.html`
> This lecture hand-out includes code examples and explanations of runtime structure and Java-Spaces.

I.10 Specifications

`http://www.sun.com/jini/specs/jini1_1spec.html;$session-id$XZAWOVIAAMHSXAMUVFZE3NQ`
> Check out the Jini specifications on this site. There is also a link to sign up for the Jini mailing list.

I.11 FAQs

`http://www.sun.com/jini/faqs/index.html`
> Find the answers to your Jini questions at the Sun Microsystems FAQ site.

`http://www.artima.com/jini/faq.html`
> *Artima* has an extensive Jini FAQ.

I.12 Magazines

`http://www.javaworld.com/`
> This online magazine is a great source of current Jini information. This site is updated daily.

`http://www.intelligence.com/`
> Intelligence.com an online source of information on a wide variety of topics. Check out their collection of Jini articles.

`http://www.infoworld.com`
> *Infoworld* is an online magazine with top stories across the high tech industry.

`www.internetweek.com`
> *Internetweek* is an online publication that delivers technical news. This is a good place to search for new JINI information

`http://www.zdnet.com/`
> Search *Zdnet* for the most recent Jini news and information.

Bibliography

Sun Microsystems Resources

(Bl99)   Block, J., "Tutorial: Collections", `http://java.sun.com/docs/books/tutorial/collections/index.html`, 1999

(Fi99)   Fisher, M., "The JDBC Tutorial and Reference: Second Edition Chapter 3 Excerpt" `http://developer.java.sun.com/developer/Books/JDBCTutorial/index.html`, 1999

(Go96)   Gosling, J., and McGilton, H., "The Java Language Environment: a White Paper", `http://java.sun.com/docs/white/langenv/`, 1996

(Kl99)   Kluyt, O., "JavaBeans: Unlocking the BeanContext API," `http://developer.java.sun.com/developer/technicalArticles/Beans/BeanContext/index.html`

(Me99f)   Meloan, M.D. "The Science Of Java Sound" `http://developer.java.sun.com/developer/technicalArticles/Media/JavaSoundAPI/index.html`

(Pa99)   Papageorge, J., "Getting Started with JDBC" `http://developer.java.sun.com/developer/technicalArticles/Interviews/StartJDBC/index.html`, 1999

(Sn99   Sundsted, T., "XML and JAVA Tackle Entries Application Integration" `http://developer.java.sun.com/developer/technicalArticles/Networking/XMLAndJava/index.html`, 1999

(Su99b)   Sun Microsystems, "JavaBeans Specifications and Tutorials", `http://java.sun.com/beans/docs/spec.html`

(Su99c)   Sun Microsystems, "Enterprise JavaBeans Specifications and Tutorials", `http://java.sun.com/products/ejb/newspec.html`

(Su99d)   Sun Microsystems, "Java 2D API Specifications and Tutorials", `http://java.sun.com/products/java-media/2D/forDevelopers/2Dapi/index.html`

(Su99e)   Sun Microsystems, "RMI Specifications and Tutorials", `http://java.sun.com/products/jdk/1.2/docs/guide/rmi/`

(Su99f)   Sun Microsystems, "Java Servlets API Specifications and Tutorials", `http://ja-va.sun.com/products/servlet/index.html`, 1999

(Su99g)   Sun Microsystems, "Java Foundation Classes: White Paper", `http://ja-va.sun.com/marketing/collateral/foundation_classes.html`, 1999

(Su99h)   Sun Microsystems, "The Collections Framework Overview", `http://ja-va.sun.com/products/jdk/1.2/docs/guide/collections/over-view.html`, 1999

(Su99i)   Sun Microsystems, "Java Database Connectivity", `http://java.sun.com/mar-keting/collateral/jdbc_ds.html`

(Su99j)   Sun Microsystems, "Getting Started with Swing", `http://java.sun.com/docs/books/tutorial/uiswing/start/index.html`

(Su99k)   Sun Microsystems "Swing Features and Concepts" `http://java.sun.com/docs/books/tutorial/uiswing/overview/index.html`

(Su99l)   Sun Microsystems "Using Swing Components" `http://java.sun.com/docs/books/tutorial/uiswing/components/index.html`

(Su99m)   Sun Microsystems "Converting to swing" `http://java.sun.com/docs/books/tutorial/uiswing/converting/index.html`

(Su99n)   Sun Microsystems "Laying Out Components within a Container" `http://ja-va.sun.com/docs/books/tutorial/uiswing/layout/index.html`

(Ta99)   Tallman, G., "Java 3D: for Developers and End Users," `http://sun.com/desktop/java3d/collateral/presentation/;$session-id$2VWKVVYABDCPVAMUVFZE5YQ`, 1999

(Zu99)   Zucowski, J., "Mastering Java 2 Chapter 16: Transferring Data" `http://develop-er.java.sun.com/developer/Books/MasteringJava/Ch16/index.ht-ml`, 1999

(Zu99a)   Zucowski, J., "Mastering Java 2 Chapter 17: Java Collections" `http://develop-er.java.sun.com/developer/Books/MasteringJava/Ch17/index.ht-ml`, 1999

Other Resources

(An97)   Anath, P., "Delivering JDBC-Based Applications," *Java Developer's Journal*, May 1997, pp 42-44.

(Ar99)   Arruza, B., "Digital Neural network Control using JINI: Delay the conversion of your hard-ware control libraries," *Java Developer's Journal,* May 1999, pp. 38-40

(Ba99)   Barnebee, J., "Java NT Services: Migrating you Java Server from Unix to an NT Boot-Time Environment," *Java Developer's Journal,* February 1999, pp. 54-56

(Be98)   Bell, D. and Parr, M., *Java for Students Second Edition,* London, UK: Prentice Hall Europe, 1999

(Bg98)   Berg, C.J., *Advanced Java Development for Enterprise Applications,* Upper Saddle River, NJ: Prentice Hall, 1998

(Bh97)   Berg, D. and Fritzinger, J.S., *Advanced Techniques for Java Developers,* New York, NY: John Wiley & Sons, Inc. 1997

(Bo99) Brogden, B., *Exam Cram: Java 2 Exam 310-025*, Scottsdale, AZ: The Coriolis Group, 1999

(Br99) Brown, K.; Craig, G; Hester, G.; and Jakab, P., "Using Server-Side Java Successfully, *Java Developer's Journal,* June 1999, pp. 51-60

(By99) Bryson, T., "Exploring the Java 3D API," *Performance Computing,* April 1999, pp. 28-34

(Ca98) Callahan, T., "So You Want a Standalone Database for Java," *Java Developer's Journal,* December 1998, pp. 28-36

(Cl99) Catalano, C., "Java Applets", *ComputerWorld,* May 3, 1999, p. 72

(Cm99) Campione, M.; Walrath, K.; Huml, A.; and the Tutorial Team, *The Java Tutorial Continued: The Rest of the JDK*, Reading, MA: Addison-Wesley, 1999

(Cn99) Coad, P.; Mayfeild, M.;and Kern, J., *Java Design: Building Better Apps and Applets: Second Edition,* Upper Saddle River, NJ: Yourdon Press, 1999

(Co99) Coffee, P., "Java, Thin Clients Give Video Provider Tele-'Vision'," *PC Week,* April 12, 1999, p. 55

(Cr99) Crawford, J. M., "Native Territory', *Java Report,* March 1999, pp. 65-71

(Da98) Darby, C., "Developing 3-Tier Database Applications with Java Servlets," *Java Developer's Journal,* February 1998, pp. 16-28

(De99) Detlefs, D., "Concurrent Coffee," *Performace Computing*, July 1999, pp.25-29

(Do98) Downing, T. B., *Java RMI: Remote Method Invocation,* Foster City, CA: IDG Books Worldwide, Inc., 1999

(En97) Englander, R., *Developing Java Beans,* Sabastopol, CA: O'Reilly & Associates, Inc., 1997

(Fa98) Farley, J., *Java Distributed Computing,* Sebastopol CA: O'Reilly & Associates, Inc., 1998

(Fl96) Flynn, J., and B. Clarke, "The World Wakes up to Java!" *Computer Technology Review,* 1996, pp. 33–37.

(Fl97) Flanagan, D., *Java Examples: In a Nutshell,* Sebastopol, CA: O'Reilly & Associates, Inc., 1997

(Ge99) George, J., "Java - Into Its Fourth Year," *Java Developer's Journal,* February 1999, p. 66

(Gi98) Gilbert, S., and McCarty, B., *Object-Oriented Design in Java,* Corte Madera, CA: Waite Group Press, 1998

(Go99) Gollub, R., "Corba vs Servlets: What to Use Where," *Java Developer's Journal,* March 1999, pp. 16-18

(Gn99) Gonsalves, A., "Jini Not Just a Dream," *PC Week*, January 18, 1999, p. 6

(Ha99) Haggar, P., "Effective Exception Handling in Java," *Java Report,* April 1999, pp. 55- 64

(Hb99) Halfhill, T. R. "How to Soup up Java: Part 1," *Byte Magazine*, May 1998, pp. 60-80

(Hc99) Haverlock, K. "Object Serialization, Java, and C++," *Dr. Dobb's Journal*, August 1998, pp. 32-34

(He98) Harrison, G., "Browsing the JDBC API," *Java Developer's Journal,* April 1998, pp. 44 -52

(Hl99) Heller, P., and Roberts, S., *Java 2 Developers Handbook,* Alameda, CA: Sybex, Inc., 1999

(Hm99) Hemrajani, A., "Programming with I/O Streams: Part 3," *Java Developer's Journal,* February 1999,pp. 18-22

(Hn98)   Hilerio, I., "URLClassLoader: The Network is the Hard Drive," *Java Developer's Journal,* January 1998, pp. 46-51

(Ho96)   Hof, R. D., and J. Verity, "Scott McNealy's Rising Sun," Cover Story, *Business Week,* January 22, 1996, pp. 66–73.

(Ho97)   Hobbs, A., "Serialized Database Connectivity," *Java Developer's Journal,* March 1997, pp. 52-54

(Hr98)   C. S. Horstmann and Cornell, G., *Core Java: Volume II-Advanced Features,* SunSoft Press, Upper Saddle River, NJ: Prentice Hall, 1998.

(Hr99)   C. S. Horstmann and Cornell, G., *Core Java 2 Volume I: Fundamentals,* SunSoft Press, Upper Saddle River, NJ: Prentice Hall, 1999.

(Ht99)   Hunt J., "The Collection API," *Java Report,* April 1999, pp. 17-32

(Hu98)   Hunter, J., "What's New with Servlets," *Javaworld,* March 26, 1998, online

(Hu98a)   Hunter, J., and Kadel, R., "Everywhere You Look: Enterprise Server-Side Java", *Javaworld,* March 27, 1998, online

(Hu98b)   Hunter, J. and Crawford, W. *Java Servlet Programming,* Sabastopol, CA: O'Reilly & Associates, Inc., 1998

(Kr99)   Krumel, A., "Revolutionary RMI: Dynamic class loading and behavior objects," *Javaworld,* December 1999, online

(La97)   Lai, S. L., and Lim, J. H, "Web Database Publishing," *Java Developer's Journal,* July 1997, pp. 20-27

(Le98)   Lemay, L., and C. L. Perkins, *Teach Yourself Java 1.2 in 21 Days,* Indianapolis, IN: Sams.net Publishing, 1998.

(Lu99)   Lauinger, T., "Object-Oriented Software Development in Java," *Java Report,* February 1999, pp. 59-61

(Ja98)   Jaworski, J., *Java 1.2 Unleashed,* Indianapolis, IN: Sams.net Publishing, 1998

(Ma98)   Malarvannan, M., "A Multithreaded Server in Java", *Web Techniques,* October 1998, pp. 47-51

(Mb99)   Maruyama, H.; Tamura, K.; and Uramoto Naohiko, *XML and JAVA: Developing Web Applications,* Reading, MA: Addison-Wesley Publishing Company, Inc., 1999

(Mo97)   Morrison, M., *Presenting JavaBeans,* Indianapolis, IN: Sams.net Publishing, 1997

(Ni98)   Nickerson, D., *Netscape Javabeans Developers Guide,* Research Triangle Park, NC: Ventana Communications Group, 1998

(Oa96)   Oaks, S., "How Do I Create My Own UI Component?" *Java Report,* March/April 1996, pp. 64, 63.

(Oa96a)   Oaks, S., "Two Techniques for Handling Events," *Java Report,* July/August, 1996. p. 80.

(Oa97)   Oaks, S. and H. Wong, *Java Threads,* Sebastopol, CA: O'Reilly & Associates, Inc., 1997.

(Ob99)   O'Brien, L., "Servlet Solutons," *Java Pro,* July 1999, pp.62-67

(Or99)   Oracle's SQLJ Dev Team, "Oracle Extends Support for Standards Based SQLJ," *Java Developer's Journal,* February 1999, pp. 44-46

(Os99)   Orenstein, D., "CORBA Vendors Forge Closer Links to Java,' *ComputerWorld,* p. 14

(Pr97)   Pratik P. and Moss, K. *Java Database Programming with JDBC: Second Edition,* Scotts-
           dale, AZ: The Coriolis Group, 1997

(Ri98)   RineHart, M., *Java Database Development,* Berkeley, CA: Osborn/McGraw-Hill, 1998

(Ro99)   Rodrigues, L., "On JavaBeans Customization", *Java Developer's Journal,* May 1999, pp.-
           21

(Sa97)   Sagar, A., "Servlets & Friends" *Java Developer's Journal,* January 1997, pp. 27-35

(Se97)   Seshadri, G., "Distributed Java Computing Using RMI," *Java Report,* November 1997, pp.
           39-46

(Sd97)   Sridharan, P., *Advanced Java Networking,* Upper Saddle River, NJ: Prentice Hall, 1997.

(Ta99)   Tan, E. M., "Java-The Software Design," *Java Developer's Journal,* January 1999, pp. 58-
           59

(Ty97)   Taylor, A., *JDBC Developer's Resource,* Informix Press, Saddle River, NJ: Prentice Hall,
           1998

(Ve98)   Venners, B., *Inside the Java Virtual Machine,* New York, NY: McGraw-Hill, 1998

(Vo98)   Vogel, A., and Duddy, K., *Java Programming with CORBA: Second Edition,* New York,
           NY: Wiley Computer Publishing, 1998

(Wa98)   Walsh, A., and Fronckowiak, J., *Java Bible,* Foster City, CA; IDG Books Worldwide, Inc.
           1998

(We99)   Westra, J., "EJB Home: Enterprise JavaBeans," *Java Developer's Journal,* June 1999, pp.
           74-80

(Wi98)   Williams,A., "Born to Serve," *Web Techniques,* August 1998, pp.30-34

(Wi99)   Williams, A., "JINI: The Universal Network?," *Web Techniques,* March 1999, pp. 55-60

(Wl98)   Williamson, A., "The Data Series: JDBC," *Java Developer's Journal,* April 1998, pp. 64-
           66

(Wu97)   Wutka, M., et. al., *Hacking Java,* Indianapolis, IN: Que Corporation, 1997.

Index

License Agreement and Limited Warranty

READ THE FOLLOWING TERMS AND CONDITIONS CAREFULLY BEFORE OPENING THIS SOFTWARE PACKAGE. THIS LEGAL DOCUMENT IS AN AGREEMENT BETWEEN YOU AND PRENTICE-HALL, INC. (THE "COMPANY"). BY OPENING THIS SEALED SOFTWARE PACKAGE, YOU ARE AGREEING TO BE BOUND BY THESE TERMS AND CONDITIONS. IF YOU DO NOT AGREE WITH THESE TERMS AND CONDITIONS, DO NOT OPEN THE SOFTWARE PACKAGE. PROMPTLY RETURN THE UNOPENED SOFTWARE PACKAGE AND ALL ACCOMPANYING ITEMS TO THE PLACE YOU OBTAINED THEM FOR A FULL REFUND OF ANY SUMS YOU HAVE PAID.

1. GRANT OF LICENSE: In consideration of your purchase of this book, and your agreement to abide by the terms and conditions of this Agreement, the Company grants to you a nonexclusive right to use and display the copy of the enclosed software program (hereinafter the "SOFTWARE") on a single computer (i.e., with a single CPU) at a single location so long as you comply with the terms of this Agreement. The Company reserves all rights not expressly granted to you under this Agreement.

2. OWNERSHIP OF SOFTWARE: You own only the magnetic or physical media (the enclosed media) on which the SOFTWARE is recorded or fixed, but the Company and the software developers retain all the rights, title, and ownership to the SOFTWARE recorded on the original media copy(ies) and all subsequent copies of the SOFTWARE, regardless of the form or media on which the original or other copies may exist. This license is not a sale of the original SOFTWARE or any copy to you.

3. COPY RESTRICTIONS: This SOFTWARE and the accompanying printed materials and user manual (the "Documentation") are the subject of copyright. The individual programs on the media are copyrighted by the authors of each program. Some of the programs on the media include separate licensing agreements. If you intend to use one of these programs, you must read and follow its accompanying license agreement. You may not copy the Documentation or the SOFTWARE, except that you may make a single copy of the SOFTWARE for backup or archival purposes only. You may be held legally responsible for any copying or copyright infringement which is caused or encouraged by your failure to abide by the terms of this restriction.

4. USE RESTRICTIONS: You may not network the SOFTWARE or otherwise use it on more than one computer or computer terminal at the same time. You may physically transfer the SOFTWARE from one computer to another provided that the SOFTWARE is used on only one computer at a time. You may not distribute copies of the SOFTWARE or Documentation to others. You may not reverse engineer, disassemble, decompile, modify, adapt, translate, or create derivative works based on the SOFTWARE or the Documentation without the prior written consent of the Company.

5. TRANSFER RESTRICTIONS: The enclosed SOFTWARE is licensed only to you and may not be transferred to any one else without the prior written consent of the Company. Any unauthorized transfer of the SOFTWARE shall result in the immediate termination of this Agreement.

6. TERMINATION: This license is effective until terminated. This license will terminate automatically without notice from the Company and become null and void if

you fail to comply with any provisions or limitations of this license. Upon termination, you shall destroy the Documentation and all copies of the SOFTWARE. All provisions of this Agreement as to warranties, limitation of liability, remedies or damages, and our ownership rights shall survive termination.

7.   MISCELLANEOUS: This Agreement shall be construed in accordance with the laws of the United States of America and the State of New York and shall benefit the Company, its affiliates, and assignees.

8.   LIMITED WARRANTY AND DISCLAIMER OF WARRANTY: The Company warrants that the SOFTWARE, when properly used in accordance with the Documentation, will operate in substantial conformity with the description of the SOFTWARE set forth in the Documentation. The Company does not warrant that the SOFTWARE will meet your requirements or that the operation of the SOFTWARE will be uninterrupted or error-free. The Company warrants that the media on which the SOFTWARE is delivered shall be free from defects in materials and workmanship under normal use for a period of thirty (30) days from the date of your purchase. Your only remedy and the Company's only obligation under these limited warranties is, at the Company's option, return of the warranted item for a refund of any amounts paid by you or replacement of the item. Any replacement of SOFTWARE or media under the warranties shall not extend the original warranty period. The limited warranty set forth above shall not apply to any SOFTWARE which the Company determines in good faith has been subject to misuse, neglect, improper installation, repair, alteration, or damage by you. EXCEPT FOR THE EXPRESSED WARRANTIES SET FORTH ABOVE, THE COMPANY DISCLAIMS ALL WARRANTIES, EXPRESS OR IMPLIED, INCLUDING WITHOUT LIMITATION, THE IMPLIED WARRANTIES OF MERCHANTABILITY AND FITNESS FOR A PARTICULAR PURPOSE. EXCEPT FOR THE EXPRESS WARRANTY SET FORTH ABOVE, THE COMPANY DOES NOT WARRANT, GUARANTEE, OR MAKE ANY REPRESENTATION REGARDING THE USE OR THE RESULTS OF THE USE OF THE SOFTWARE IN TERMS OF ITS CORRECTNESS, ACCURACY, RELIABILITY, CURRENTNESS, OR OTHERWISE.

IN NO EVENT, SHALL THE COMPANY OR ITS EMPLOYEES, AGENTS, SUPPLIERS, OR CONTRACTORS BE LIABLE FOR ANY INCIDENTAL, INDIRECT, SPECIAL, OR CONSEQUENTIAL DAMAGES ARISING OUT OF OR IN CONNECTION WITH THE LICENSE GRANTED UNDER THIS AGREEMENT, OR FOR LOSS OF USE, LOSS OF DATA, LOSS OF INCOME OR PROFIT, OR OTHER LOSSES, SUSTAINED AS A RESULT OF INJURY TO ANY PERSON, OR LOSS OF OR DAMAGE TO PROPERTY, OR CLAIMS OF THIRD PARTIES, EVEN IF THE COMPANY OR AN AUTHORIZED REPRESENTATIVE OF THE COMPANY HAS BEEN ADVISED OF THE POSSIBILITY OF SUCH DAMAGES. IN NO EVENT SHALL LIABILITY OF THE COMPANY FOR DAMAGES WITH RESPECT TO THE SOFTWARE EXCEED THE AMOUNTS ACTUALLY PAID BY YOU, IF ANY, FOR THE SOFTWARE.

SOME JURISDICTIONS DO NOT ALLOW THE LIMITATION OF IMPLIED WARRANTIES OR LIABILITY FOR INCIDENTAL, INDIRECT, SPECIAL, OR

CONSEQUENTIAL DAMAGES, SO THE ABOVE LIMITATIONS MAY NOT ALWAYS APPLY. THE WARRANTIES IN THIS AGREEMENT GIVE YOU SPECIFIC LEGAL RIGHTS AND YOU MAY ALSO HAVE OTHER RIGHTS WHICH VARY IN ACCORDANCE WITH LOCAL LAW.
ACKNOWLEDGMENT

YOU ACKNOWLEDGE THAT YOU HAVE READ THIS AGREEMENT, UNDERSTAND IT, AND AGREE TO BE BOUND BY ITS TERMS AND CONDITIONS. YOU ALSO AGREE THAT THIS AGREEMENT IS THE COMPLETE AND EXCLUSIVE STATEMENT OF THE AGREEMENT BETWEEN YOU AND THE COMPANY AND SUPERSEDES ALL PROPOSALS OR PRIOR AGREEMENTS, ORAL, OR WRITTEN, AND ANY OTHER COMMUNICATIONS BETWEEN YOU AND THE COMPANY OR ANY REPRESENTATIVE OF THE COMPANY RELATING TO THE SUBJECT MATTER OF THIS AGREEMENT.

Should you have any questions concerning this Agreement or if you wish to contact the Company for any reason, please contact in writing at the address below.

Robin Short
Prentice Hall PTR
One Lake Street
Upper Saddle River, New Jersey 07458

Borland® JBuilder™3 University Edition Authorized Book Publisher License Statement and Limited Warranty for Inprise Products

IMPORTANT – READ CAREFULLY

This license statement and limited warranty constitutes a legal agreement ("License Agreement") for the software product ("Software") identified above (including any software, media, and accompanying on-line or printed documentation supplied by Inprise) between you (either as an individual or a single entity), the Book Publisher from whom you received the Software ("Publisher"), and Inprise International, Inc. ("Inprise").

BY INSTALLING, COPYING, OR OTHERWISE USING THE SOFTWARE, YOU AGREE TO BE BOUND BY ALL OF THE TERMS AND CONDITIONS OF THE LICENSE AGREEMENT. If you are the original purchaser of the Software and you do not agree with the terms and conditions of the License Agreement, promptly return the unused Software to the place from which you obtained it for a full refund.

Upon your acceptance of the terms and conditions of the License Agreement, Inprise grants you the right to use the Software solely for educational purposes, in the manner provided below. No rights are granted for deploying or distributing applications created with the Software.

This Software is owned by Inprise or its suppliers and is protected by copyright law and international copyright treaty. Therefore, you must treat this Software like any other copyrighted material (e.g., a book), except that you may either make one copy of the Software solely for backup or archival purposes or transfer the Software to a single hard disk provided you keep the original solely for backup or archival purposes.

You may transfer the Software and documentation on a permanent basis provided you retain no copies and the recipient agrees to the terms of the License Agreement. Except as provided in the License Agreement, you may not transfer, rent, lease, lend, copy, modify, translate, sublicense, time-share or electronically transmit or receive the Software, media or documentation. You acknowledge that the Software in source code form remains a confidential trade secret of Inprise and/or its suppliers and therefore you agree not to modify the Software or attempt to reverse engineer, decompile, or disassemble the Software, except and only to the extent that such activity is expressly permitted by applicable law notwithstanding this limitation.

Though Inprise does not offer technical support for the Software, we welcome your feedback.

This Software is subject to U.S. Commerce Department export restrictions, and is intended for use in the country into which Inprise sold it (or in the EEC, if sold into the EEC).

LIMITED WARRANTY

The Publisher warrants that the Software media will be free from defects in materials and workmanship for a period of ninety (90) days from the date of receipt. Any implied warranties on the Software are limited to ninety (90) days. Some states/jurisdictions do not allow limitations on duration of an implied warranty, so the above limitation may not apply to you.

The Publisher's, Inprise's, and the Publisher's or Inprise's suppliers' entire liability and your exclusive remedy shall be, at the Publisher's or Inprise's option, either (a) return of the price paid, or (b) repair or replacement of the Software that does not meet the Limited Warranty and which is returned to the Publisher with a copy of your receipt. This Limited Warranty is void if failure of the Software has resulted from accident, abuse, or misapplication. Any replacement Software will be warranted for the remainder of the original warranty period or thirty (30) days, whichever is longer. **Outside**

the United States, neither these remedies nor any product support services offered are available without proof of purchase from an authorized non-U.S. source.

TO THE MAXIMUM EXTENT PERMITTED BY APPLICABLE LAW, THE PUBLISHER, INPRISE, AND THE PUBLISHER'S OR INPRISE'S SUPPLIERS DISCLAIM ALL OTHER WARRANTIES AND CONDITIONS, EITHER EXPRESS OR IMPLIED, INCLUDING, BUT NOT LIMITED TO, IMPLIED WARRANTIES OF MERCHANTABILITY, FITNESS FOR A PARTICULAR PURPOSE, TITLE, AND NON-INFRINGEMENT, WITH REGARD TO THE SOFTWARE, AND THE PROVISION OF OR FAILURE TO PROVIDE SUPPORT SERVICES. THIS LIMITED WARRANTY GIVES YOU SPECIFIC LEGAL RIGHTS. YOU MAY HAVE OTHERS, WHICH VARY FROM STATE/JURISDICTION TO STATE/JURISDICTION.

LIMITATION OF LIABILITY

TO THE MAXIMUM EXTENT PERMITTED BY APPLICABLE LAW, IN NO EVENT SHALL THE PUBLISHER, INPRISE, OR THE PUBLISHER'S OR INPRISE'S SUPPLIERS BE LIABLE FOR ANY SPECIAL, INCIDENTAL, INDIRECT, OR CONSEQUENTIAL DAMAGES WHATSOEVER (INCLUDING, WITHOUT LIMITATION, DAMAGES FOR LOSS OF BUSINESS PROFITS, BUSINESS INTERRUPTION, LOSS OF BUSINESS INFORMATION, OR ANY OTHER PECUNIARY LOSS) ARISING OUT OF THE USE OF OR INABILITY TO USE THE SOFTWARE PRODUCT OR THE PROVISION OF OR FAILURE TO PROVIDE SUPPORT SERVICES, EVEN IF INPRISE HAS BEEN ADVISED OF THE POSSIBILITY OF SUCH DAMAGES. IN ANY CASE, INPRISE'S ENTIRE LIABILITY UNDER ANY PROVISION OF THIS LICENSE AGREEMENT SHALL BE LIMITED TO THE GREATER OF THE AMOUNT ACTUALLY PAID BY YOU FOR THE SOFTWARE PRODUCT OR U.S. $25; PROVIDED, HOWEVER, IF YOU HAVE ENTERED INTO A INPRISE SUPPORT SERVICES AGREEMENT, INPRISE'S ENTIRE LIABILITY REGARDING SUPPORT SERVICES SHALL BE GOVERNED BY THE TERMS OF THAT AGREEMENT. BECAUSE SOME STATES AND JURISDICTIONS DO NOT ALLOW THE EXCLUSION OR LIMITATION OF LIABILITY, THE ABOVE LIMITATION MAY NOT APPLY TO YOU.

HIGH RISK ACTIVITIES

The Software is not fault-tolerant and is not designed, manufactured or intended for use or resale as on-line control equipment in hazardous environments requiring fail-safe performance, such as in the operation of nuclear facilities, aircraft navigation or communication systems, air traffic control, direct life support machines, or weapons systems, in which the failure of the Software could lead directly to death, personal injury, or severe physical or environmental damage ("High Risk Activities"). The Publisher, Inprise, and their suppliers specifically disclaim any express or implied warranty of fitness for High Risk Activities.

U.S. GOVERNMENT RESTRICTED RIGHTS

The Software and documentation are provided with RESTRICTED RIGHTS. Use, duplication, or disclosure by the Government is subject to restrictions as set forth in subparagraphs (c)(1)(ii) of the Rights in Technical Data and Computer Software clause at DFARS 252.227-7013 or subparagraphs (c)(1) and (2) of the Commercial Computer Software-Restricted Rights at 48 CFR 52.227-19, as applicable.

GENERAL PROVISIONS

This License Agreement may only be modified in writing signed by you and an authorized officer of Inprise. If any provision of this License Agreement is found void or unenforceable, the remainder will remain valid and enforceable according to its terms. If any remedy provided is determined to have failed for its essential purpose, all limitations of liability and exclusions of damages set forth in the Limited Warranty shall remain in effect.

This License Agreement shall be construed, interpreted and governed by the laws of the State of California, U.S.A. This License Agreement gives you specific legal rights; you may have others which vary from state to state and from country to country. Inprise reserves all rights not specifically granted in this License Agreement.

Sun Microsystems, Inc.
Binary Code License Agreement

READ THE TERMS OF THIS AGREEMENT AND ANY PROVIDED SUPPLEMENTAL
LICENSE TERMS (COLLECTIVELY "AGREEMENT") CAREFULLY BEFORE OPENING THE
SOFTWARE MEDIA PACKAGE. BY OPENING THE SOFTWARE MEDIA PACKAGE, YOU
AGREE TO THE TERMS OF THIS AGREEMENT. IF YOU ARE ACCESSING THE SOFTWARE
ELECTRONICALLY, INDICATE YOUR ACCEPTANCE OF THESE TERMS BY SELECTING
THE "ACCEPT" BUTTON AT THE END OF THIS AGREEMENT. IF YOU DO NOT AGREE TO
ALL THESE TERMS, PROMPTLY RETURN THE UNUSED SOFTWARE TO YOUR PLACE OF
PURCHASE FOR A REFUND OR, IF THE SOFTWARE IS ACCESSED ELECTRONICALLY,
SELECT THE "DECLINE" BUTTON AT THE END OF THIS AGREEMENT.

1. LICENSE TO USE. Sun grants you a non-exclusive and non-transferable license for the internal
use only of the accompanying software and documentation and any error corrections provided by
Sun (collectively "Software"), by the number of users and the class of computer hardware for which
the corresponding fee has been paid.

2. RESTRICTIONS Software is confidential and copyrighted. Title to Software and all associated
intellectual property rights is retained by Sun and/or its licensors. Except as specifically authorized
in any Supplemental License Terms, you may not make copies of Software, other than a single copy
of Software for archival purposes. Unless enforcement is prohibited by applicable law, you may not
modify, decompile, reverse engineer Software. Software is not designed or licensed for use in on-
line control of aircraft, air traffic, aircraft navigation or aircraft communications; or in the design,
construction, operation or maintenance of any nuclear facility. You warrant that you will not use
Software for these purposes. No right, title or interest in or to any trademark, service mark, logo or
trade name of Sun or its licensors is granted under this Agreement.

3. LIMITED WARRANTY. Sun warrants to you that for a period of ninety (90) days from the date
of purchase, as evidenced by a copy of the receipt, the media on which Software is furnished (if any)
will be free of defects in materials and workmanship under normal use. Except for the foregoing,
Software is provided "AS IS". Your exclusive remedy and Sun's entire liability under this limited
warranty will be at Sun's option to replace Software media or refund the fee paid for Software.

4. DISCLAIMER OF WARRANTY. UNLESS SPECIFIED IN THIS AGREEMENT, ALL
EXPRESS OR IMPLIED CONDITIONS, REPRESENTATIONS AND WARRANTIES, INCLUD-
ING ANY IMPLIED WARRANTY OF MERCHANTABILITY, FITNESS FOR A PARTICULAR
PURPOSE, OR NON-INFRINGEMENT, ARE DISCLAIMED, EXCEPT TO THE EXTENT THAT
THESE DISCLAIMERS ARE HELD TO BE LEGALLY INVALID.

5. LIMITATION OF LIABILITY. TO THE EXTENT NOT PROHIBITED BY LAW, IN NO
EVENT WILL SUN OR ITS LICENSORS BE LIABLE FOR ANY LOST REVENUE, PROFIT
OR DATA, OR FOR SPECIAL, INDIRECT, CONSEQUENTIAL, INCIDENTAL OR PUNITIVE
DAMAGES, HOWEVER CAUSED REGARDLESS OF THE THEORY OF LIABILITY, ARISING
OUT OF OR RELATED TO THE USE OF OR INABILITY TO USE SOFTWARE, EVEN IF SUN
HAS BEEN ADVISED OF THE POSSIBILITY OF SUCH DAMAGES. In no event will Sun's lia-
bility to you, whether in contract, tort (including negligence), or otherwise, exceed the amount paid
by you for Software under this Agreement. The foregoing limitations will apply even if the above
stated warranty fails of its essential purpose.

6. Termination. This Agreement is effective until terminated. You may terminate this Agreement at
any time by destroying all copies of Software. This Agreement will terminate immediately without

notice from Sun if you fail to comply with any provision of this Agreement. Upon Termination, you must destroy all copies of Software.

7. Export Regulations. All Software and technical data delivered under this Agreement are subject to US export control laws and may be subject to export or import regulations in other countries. You agree to comply strictly with all such laws and regulations and acknowledge that you have the responsibility to obtain such licenses to export, re-export, or import as may be required after delivery to you.

8. U.S. Government Restricted Rights. Use, duplication, or disclosure by the U.S. Government is subject to restrictions set forth in this Agreement and as provided in DFARS 227.7202-1 (a) and 227.7202-3(a) (1995), DFARS 252.227-7013 (c)(1)(ii)(Oct 1988), FAR 12.212 (a) (1995), FAR 52.227-19 (June 1987), or FAR 52.227-14(ALT III) (June 1987), as applicable.

9. Governing Law. Any action related to this Agreement will be governed by California law and controlling U.S. federal law. No choice of law rules of any jurisdiction will apply.

10. Severability. If any provision of this Agreement is held to be unenforceable, This Agreement will remain in effect with the provision omitted, unless omission would frustrate the intent of the parties, in which case this Agreement will immediately terminate.

11. Integration. This Agreement is the entire agreement between you and Sun relating to its subject matter. It supersedes all prior or contemporaneous oral or written communications, proposals, representations and warranties and prevails over any conflicting or additional terms of any quote, order, acknowledgment, or other communication between the parties relating to its subject matter during the term of this Agreement. No modification of this Agreement will be binding, unless in writing and signed by an authorized representative of each party.

For inquiries please contact: Sun Microsystems, Inc. 901 San Antonio Road, Palo Alto, California 94303

Java™ 2 SDK, Standard Edition, Version 1.2.2
Supplemental License Terms

These supplemental terms ("Supplement") add to the terms of the Binary Code License Agreement ("Agreement"). Capitalized terms not defined herein shall have the same meanings ascribed to them in the Agreement. The Supplement terms shall supersede any inconsistent or conflicting terms in the Agreement.

1. Limited License Grant. Sun grants to you a non-exclusive, non-transferable limited license to use the Software without fee for evaluation of the Software and for development of Java™ applets and applications provided that you: (i) may not re-distribute the Software in whole or in part, either separately or included with a product. (ii) may not create, or authorize your licensees to create additional classes, interfaces, or supplicates that are contained in the "java" or "sun" packages or similar as specified by Sun in any class file naming convention; and (iii) agree to the extent Programs are developed which utilize the Windows 95/98 style graphical user interface or components contained therein, such applets or applications may only be developed to run on a Windows 95/98 or Windows NT platform. Refer to the Java 2 Runtime Environment Version 1.2.2 binary code license (http://java.sun.com/products/jdk/1.2/jre/LICENSE) for the availability of runtime code which may be distributed with Java applets and applications.

2. Java Platform Interface. In the event that Licensee creates an additional API(s) which: (i) extends the functionality of a Java Environment; and, (ii) is exposed to third party software developers for the purpose of developing additional software which invokes such additional API, Licensee must promptly publish broadly an accurate specification for such API for free use by all developers.

3. Trademarks and Logos. This Agreement does not authorize Licensee to use any Sun name, trademark or logo. Licensee acknowledges as between it and Sun that Sun owns the Java trademark and all Java-related trademarks, logos and icons including the Coffee Cup and Duke ("Java Marks") and agrees to comply with the Java Trademark Guidelines at http://java.sun.com/trademarks.html.

4. High Risk Activities. Notwithstanding Section 2, with respect to high risk activities, the following language shall apply: the Software is not designed or intended for use in on-line control of aircraft, air traffic, aircraft navigation or aircraft communications; or in the design, construction, operation or maintenance of any nuclear facility. Sun disclaims any express or implied warranty of fitness for such uses.

5. Source Code. Software may contain source code that is provided solely for reference purposes pursuant to the terms of this Agreement.

NetBeans™ DeveloperX2 2.1
Binary Code License Agreement

PLEASE READ THIS DOCUMENT CAREFULLY. BY DOWNLOADING THE SOFTWARE, YOU ARE AGREEING TO BECOME BOUND BY THE TERMS OF THIS AGREEMENT. IF YOU DO NOT AGREE TO THE TERMS OF THE AGREEMENT, PLEASE DO NOT DOWN-LOAD THE SOFTWARE.

This is a legal Agreement between you and NetBeans, Inc. ("NetBeans"). This Agreement states the terms and conditions upon which NetBeans offers to license the software together with all related documentation and accompanying items including, but not limited to, the executable programs, drivers, libraries and data files associated with such programs (collectively, the "Software").

1.   LICENSE. NetBeans grants to you ("Licensee") a nonexclusive, nontransferable, worldwide, royalty-free license to use this version of the Software for non-commercial and educational purposes.

2.   COPYRIGHT. The Software is owned by NetBeans and is protected by United States copyright laws and international treaty provisions. You may not remove the copyright notice from any copy of the Software or any copy of the written materials, if any, accompanying the Software.

3.   ONE ARCHIVAL COPY. You may make one (1) archival copy of the machine-readable portion of the Software for backup purposes only in support of your use of the Software on a single computer, provided that you reproduce on the copy all copyright and other proprietary rights notices included on the originals of the Software.

4.   TRANSFER OF LICENSE. You may not transfer your license of the Software to a third party.

5.   DECOMPILING, DISASSEMBLING, OR REVERSE ENGINEERING. You acknowledge that the Software contains trade secrets and other proprietary information of NetBeans and its licensors. Except to the extent expressly permitted by this Agreement or by the laws of the jurisdiction where you are located, you may not decompile, disassemble or otherwise reverse engineer the Software, or engage in any other activities to obtain underlying information that is not visible to the user in connection with normal use of the Software. In particular, you agree not for any purpose to transmit the Software or display the Software's object code on any computer screen or to make any hard copy memory dumps of the Software's object code. If you believe you require information related to the interoperability of the Software with other programs, you shall not decompile or disassemble the Software to obtain such information, and you agree to request such information from NetBeans. Upon receiving such a request, NetBeans shall determine whether you require such information for a legitimate purpose and, if so, NetBeans will provide such information to you within a reasonable time and on reasonable conditions. In any event, you will notify NetBeans of any information derived from reverse engineering or such other activities, and the results thereof will constitute the confidential information of NetBeans that may be used only in connection with the Software.

6.   TERMINATION. The license granted to you is effective until terminated. You may terminate it at any time by destroying the Software (including any portions or copies thereof) currently in your possession or control. The license will also terminate automatically without any notice from Net-Beans if you fail to comply with any term or condition of this Agreement. You agree upon any such termination to destroy the Software (including any portions or copies thereof). Upon termination, NetBeans may also enforce any and all rights provided by law. The provisions of this Agreement that protect the proprietary rights of NetBeans will continue in force after termination.

7.   NO WARRANTY. ANY USE BY YOU OF THE SOFTWARE IS AT YOUR OWN RISK. THE SOFTWARE IS PROVIDED FOR USE "AS IS" WITHOUT WARRANTY OF ANY KIND.

TO THE MAXIMUM EXTENT PERMITTED BY LAW, NetBeans DISCLAIMS ALL WARRAN-
TIES OF ANY KIND, EITHER EXPRESS OR IMPLIED, INCLUDING, WITHOUT LIMITA-
TION, IMPLIED WARRANTIES OR CONDITIONS OF MERCHANTABILITY AND FITNESS
FOR A PARTICULAR PURPOSE.

NetBeans does not warrant that the functions contained in the Software will meet your requirements
or that the operation of the Software will be uninterrupted or error-free. Any representation, other
than the warranties set forth in this Agreement, will not bind NetBeans. You assume full responsibility for the selection of the Software to achieve your intended results, and for the downloading, use
and results obtained from the Software. You also assume the entire risk as it applies to the quality
and performance of the Software.

This warranty gives you specific legal rights, and you may also have other rights which vary from
country/state to country/state. Some countries/ states do not allow the exclusion of implied warranties, so the above exclusion may not apply to you.

8.   NO LIABILITY FOR DAMAGES, INCLUDING WITHOUT LIMITATION CONSEQUEN-
TIAL DAMAGES.

In no event shall NetBeans or its Licensors be liable for any damages whatsoever (including, without
limitation, incidental, direct, indirect, special or consequential damages, damages for loss of business profits, business interruption, loss of business information, or other pecuniary loss) arising out
of the use or inability to use this Software, even if NetBeans or its Licensors have been advised of
the possibility of such damages. Because some states/ countries do not allow the exclusion or limitation of liability for consequential or incidental damages, the above limitation may not apply to you.

9.   INDEMNIFICATION BY YOU. If you distribute the Software in violation of this Agreement,
you hereby indemnify, hold harmless and defend NetBeans from and against any and all claims or
lawsuits, including attorney's fees and costs that arise, result from or are connected with the use or
distribution of the Software in violation of this Agreement.

10. GENERAL. This Agreement is binding on you as well as your employees, employers, contractors and agents, and on any successors and assignees. Neither the Software nor any information
derived therefrom may be exported except in accordance with the laws of the U.S. or other applicable provisions. This Agreement is governed by the laws of the Czech Republic. This Agreement is
the entire Agreement between you and NetBeans and you agree that NetBeans will not have any liability for any untrue statement or representation made by its agents or anyone else (whether inno-
cently or negligently) upon which you relied upon entering this Agreement, unless such untrue
statement or representation was made fraudulently. This Agreement supersedes any other under-
standings or agreements, including, but not limited to, advertising, with respect to the Software.

If any provision of this Agreement is deemed invalid or unenforceable by any country or government
agency having jurisdiction, that particular provision will be deemed modified to the extent necessary
to make the provision valid and enforceable, and the remaining provisions will remain in full force
and effect.

For questions concerning this Agreement, please contact NetBeans at info@netbeans.com

The DEITEL & DEITEL Suite of Products...

C++
How to
Program
Second Edition

©1998, 1130 pp Paper,
0-13-528910-6

The world's best-selling
introductory/intermediate
C++ text, this book
focuses on the principles of good software engineering with C++, and stresses program clarity and teaching by example. Revised and updated to cover the latest enhancements to ANSI/ISO C++ and the Standard
Template Library (STL), this second edition places a
strong emphasis on pedagogy. It uses the Deitels'
signature "live-code" approach, presenting every C++
object-oriented programming concept in the context
of a complete, working C++ program followed by a
screen capture showing the program's output.
Includes a rich collection of exercises and valuable
insights into common programming errors, as well as
software engineering observations, portability tips,
and debugging hints.

C How to
Program
Second Edition

©1994, 926 pp Paper,
0-13-226119-7

Among the pedagogical
devices featured in
this best-selling
introductory C text are
a thorough use of the
structured programming methodology, complete
programs and sample outputs to demonstrate key C
concepts, objectives and an outline at the beginning
of every chapter, and a substantial collection of
self-review exercises and answers. *C How to Program*
takes the Deitels' "live-code" approach featuring
hundreds of complete working ANSI/ISO C programs
with thousands of lines of code. The result is a
rigorous treatment of both theory and practice,
including helpful sections on good programming
practices, performance tips, and software engineering
observations, portability tips, and common programming errors.

Internet and
World Wide
Web How to
Program
BOOK / CD-ROM

©2000, 1100 pp,
Paper bound w/CD-ROM,
0-13-015879-8

The World Wide Web is exploding, and with it the
deployment of a new breed of multi-tiered,
Web-based applications. This innovative new book
in the Deitels' *How to Program Series* presents
traditional introductory programming concepts using
the new scripting and markup languages of the Web.
Now you can teach programming fundamentals
"wrapped in the metaphor of the Web." Employing
the Deitels' signature "live-code" approach, the book
covers markup langauges (HTML, Dynamic HTML),
client-side scripting (Javascript), and server-side
scripting (VBscript, Active Server Pages). Advanced
topics include XML and developing e-commerce
applications. Updates are regularly posted to
www.deitel.com and the book includes a CD-
ROM with software tools, source code, and live links.

Getting
Started
with
Microsoft
Visual C++™ 6
with an
Introduction
to MFC

©2000, 200 pages, 0-13-016147-0

This exciting new book, developed in cooperation with
Microsoft, is intended to be a companion to the
ANSI/ISO standard C++ best-selling book, *C++ How
to Program, Second Edition*. Learn how to use
Microsoft's Visual Studio 6 integrated development
environment (IDE) and Visual C++ 6 to create
Windows programs using the Microsoft Foundation
Classes (MFC). The book includes 17 "live-code"
Visual C++/MFC programs with screen captures;
dozens of tips; recommended practices and cautions;
and exercises accompanying every chapter. Includes
coverage of Win32 and console applications; online
documentation and Web resources; GUI controls;
dialog boxes; graphics; message handling; the
resource definition language; and the debugger.

These complete packages include books and interactive multimedia CD-ROMs, and are perfect for anyone interested in learning Java, C++, Visual Basic, and Internet/World Wide Web programming. They are exceptional and affordable resources for college students and professionals learning programming for the first time, or reinforcing their knowledge.

The Complete Internet and World Wide Web Programming Training Course

BOXED SET

©2000, Boxed book and software, 0-13-085611-8

Includes the book *Internet and World Wide Web How To Program*, and a fully interactive browser-based *Multimedia Cyber Classroom* CD-ROM that features:

- Hundreds of programs that can be run inside the student's browser
- Over 8 hours of audio explaining key Internet programming concepts
- Hundreds of exercises—many solved
- Monitor your progress with an integrated course completion and assessment summary feature
- Full text searching, hyperlinking and more
- Hundreds of tips, terms and hints.
- Master Client and Server Side Programming, including JavaScript, VBScript, ActiveX, ASP, SQL, XML, database, and more!

Runs on Windows 95, 98, and NT 4.0 or higher

The Complete C++ Training Course
Second Edition

BOXED SET

©1998, Boxed book and software, 0-13-916305-0

The *Complete C++ Training Course* features the complete, best-selling introductory book *C++ How to Program, Second Edition* and a fully-interactive *Multimedia Cyber Classroom* CD-ROM that features:

- Hundreds of working programs that students can run with a mouse click
- Over 8 hours of audio walkthroughs of key C++ concepts
- More than 1000 exercises
- Solutions are provided for approximately half the exercises, including many of the projects
- Thousands of hyperlinked index entries with full-text searching
- Helpful hints, marked with icons, that help teach good practices

Runs on Solaris 2.5 or higher and Windows 95, 98, and NT 4.0 or higher

License Agreement and Limited Warranty

Software System Requirements

Borland® Jbuilder™ 3, University Edition

Minimum system requirements:
- Intel Pentium 90MHz or higher
- Microsoft Windows 95 or Windows NT
- 24 Mb (32 Mb recommended) RAM
- 50 Mb hard disk space
- CD-ROM drive

Java™ 2 SDK, Standard Edition, v 1.2.1

The Java 2 SDK software is available on three platforms:
- Win32 Version for Windows 95, Windows 98 and Windows NT 4.0 on Intel hardware. A 486/DX or faster processor. 32 megabytes RAM minimum, 48 megabytes RAM recommended.
- Solaris/SPARC Version. Only Solaris versions 2.5.1, 2.6 and 7 (also known as 2.7) are supported. 32 megabytes RAM minimum, 48 megabytes RAM recommended.
- Solaris/Intel Version. Only Solaris versions 2.5.1, 2.6 and 7 (also known as 2.7) are supported. A 486/DX or faster processor. 32 megabytes RAM minimum, 48 megabytes RAM recommended.

On all systems you should have 65 megabytes of free disk space before attempting to install the Java 2 SDK software. If you also install the separate documentation download bundle, you need an additional 90 megabytes of free disk space.

Solaris users will want to check the list of recommended and required patches <http://java.sun.com/products/jdk/1.2/install-solaris-patches.html> on the Java Software web site.

It is strongly recommended that Solaris 2.6 users load the SUNWilof package for optional Latin-1 fonts. This package is in the "Entire Distribution" Cluster, available on the Solaris software installation CD-ROM. SUNWilof contains English Monotype TrueType fonts specified in the font properties files. Without this package, fonts will default to the LucidaSans font for off-screen text and to Type1 font for text in components.

NetBeans™ DeveloperX2 2.1

X86 platforms:

Minimum configuration: Windows 95/98/NT/Linux:Pentium 133, 48 MB RAM

Recommended configuration: Windows 95/98/NT/Linux: pentium 200, 96 MB RAM

Linux users will generally require more RAM than Win platforms due to the memory intensive requirements of JVM's on this platform.

Sparc:

Minimum configuration: SparcStation 5, 170MHz, 96 MB RAM

Recommended configuration: UltraSPARC 5, 270MHz, 128 MB RAM

Macintosh:

Minimum configuration: PowerPC 90MHz, 64 MB RAM

Recommended configuration: PowerPC 200MHz, 96 MB RAM